ELEMENTS *of* SONATA THEORY

ELEMENTS *of* SONATA THEORY

Norms, Types, and Deformations in the
Late-Eighteenth-Century Sonata

James Hepokoski
Warren Darcy

OXFORD
UNIVERSITY PRESS

OXFORD

UNIVERSITY PRESS

Oxford University Press, Inc., publishes works that further
Oxford University's objective of excellence
in research, scholarship, and education.

Oxford   New York

Auckland   Cape Town   Dar es Salaam   Hong Kong   Karachi
Kuala Lumpur   Madrid   Melbourne   Mexico City   Nairobi
New Delhi   Shanghai   Taipei   Toronto

With offices in

Argentina   Austria   Brazil   Chile   Czech Republic   France   Greece
Guatemala   Hungary   Italy   Japan   Poland   Portugal   Singapore
South Korea   Switzerland   Thailand   Turkey   Ukraine   Vietnam

Copyright © 2006 by Oxford University Press, Inc.
First published as an Oxford University Press paperback, 2011

Published by Oxford University Press, Inc.
198 Madison Avenue, New York, New York 10016

www.oup.com

Oxford is a registered trademark of Oxford University Press

Library of Congress Cataloging-in-Publication Data
Hepokoski, James A. (James Arnold), 1946–
Elements of sonata theory: norms, types, and deformations in the
late-eighteenth-century sonata / James Hepokoski, Warren Darcy.
p. cm.
Includes bibliographical references and index
ISBN-13: 978-0-19-977391-6
1. Sonata form.   2. Instrumental music—18th century—Analysis, appreciation.
I. Darcy, Warren.   II. Title
MT62.H46 2006
784.18'3'09033—dc22   2005006674

Printed in the United States of America
on acid-free paper

Preface

This book offers a fresh approach to one of the most familiar topics in the field of music: the study of sonata-form movements and the larger workings of multimovement sonatas, symphonies, and chamber music of the "early classical" and "classical" period. While remaining in dialogue with the several current approaches to this subject, it provides something different, and from time to time it challenges established views of the sonata. Both of the authors have been leading classes and seminars in this method over the past decade at Yale University, Oberlin College Conservatory, and the University of Minnesota. Large portions of *Elements of Sonata Theory*, both in earlier incarnations and in this much-expanded one, have been required reading in these courses.

From one perspective the *Elements* is a research report, the product of our analyses of hundreds of individual movements by Haydn, Mozart, Beethoven, and many surrounding composers of the time (as well as later composers). In our work we have been looking for patterns within sonata-composition, for shared gestures, for ranges of options, for a sense of the typical. Our intention was to devise an explanation of how varying degrees of the normative can be altered, stretched, or occasionally overridden altogether to produce an individualized "deformation." To be sure, the theoretical discussions of eighteenth- and early- nineteenth-century writers are relevant (Koch, Galeazzi, Reicha, and others), and these insights are integrated into the book. Our preference, though, was to let the composers themselves teach us how sonatas work. Our method of understanding sonatas ("Sonata Theory") strikes a balance between inductively inferred norms and the unpredictability that one finds in these pieces.

Late-eighteenth-century sonatas are most productively heard within the context of a broad, flexible background-knowledge of what had come to be more or less standard compositional options at each point in the sonata. Any individual work within a genre (such as sonata form) interacts with the listener's (or composer's) expectations. Our book provides a detailed map of those expectations at that point in history. Not surprisingly, this turns out to be a complex matter. How can we know whether Haydn's choice here or Mozart's there was to be heard as normative, as strikingly unusual, or as something in between? And how can a composer's early choices influence the range of continuation-options down the road? Understanding any compositionally selected gesture requires an awareness of the backdrop of typical choices against which it was written and within whose world of norms the piece was to be grasped in the first place. The *Elements* seeks to fill in many details of that backdrop. This perspective has the advantage of permitting one to pass beyond the confines of the acoustic surface alone (what one literally hears, what is actually notated) in order to notice, for instance, which normative things might be absent. It could be that such absences—generically expected events that the composer might keep from happening within an individual work—should be understood as essential constituents of the piece's meaning.

This book divides into two large parts. In the first of these, chapters 1–15, we lay out the basics of the essential system, working section by section, zone by zone, through the most often encountered type of sonata form ("Type 3," with an exposition, development, and recapitulation), and considering also the differing implications within minor-mode sonata form and the multimovement sonata as a whole. In several of our analytical seminars earlier versions of chapters 1–15 alone served as the text. The discussions found in the second part, chapters 16–22, are more complex and extended, especially from chapter 17 onward. These chapters provide elaborately detailed studies of the other sonata formats of the period (Types 1, 2, 4, and 5). The increased intensity of these chapters is no accident. Confronting these differing formats at all—the "sonata without development" (Type 1), the "binary" sonata (Type 2, without a full recapitulation), the sonata-rondo (Type 4), and concerto first-movement form (Type 5)—throws one directly into the midst of ongoing debates and passionately held, sharply diverging views. Given the existing state of the discussion, we were obliged to present these thorny issues with an enhanced rigor, constructing step-by-step solutions to these often misconstrued matters and providing evidence and justification for our decisions along the way. Nowhere is this situation more evident than in the case of the first movements of Mozart's concertos. This Type 5 structure is the most difficult of the sonata types, and it is a topic concerning which even the most rudimentary features of terminology and sonata-form perception have been ardently contested over the past century. Covering this problem adequately required four extended chapters (19–22)—virtually a separate monograph on the Mozartian Type 5 sonata, though one that is entirely dependent on one's grasp of the book's first eighteen chapters.

In addition to furnishing a new mode of analysis for the late-eighteenth-century instrumental repertory, the *Elements* also provides a foundation for considering works from the decades to come—late Beethoven, Schubert, Weber, Mendelssohn, Schumann, Liszt, Brahms, Bruckner, Strauss, Mahler, the "nationalist composers," and so on. As we point out from time to time, most of these sonata norms remained in place as regulative ideas throughout the nineteenth century, even as the whole sonata-form genre, with its various options, was continuously updated, altered, and further personalized with unforeseen accretions, startling innovations, and more radical deformations. (The "three-key expositions" sometimes found in Schubert and Brahms, for example—though surfacing in some earlier composers as well—seem to have been encouraged by the eighteenth-century expositional strategy of the "trimodular block" and its "apparent double medial caesuras." Similarly, the "de-energizing transition" and occasional suppression of the medial caesura in, say, Schumann or Brahms, surely emerged from the precedents of the "blocked medial caesura" coupled with "expanded caesura-fill" in Haydn and Mozart.)

What follows is a blend of musicological and music-theoretical thinking. What at first may seem to be a work of music theory turns out in the end to be a set of reflections on what sonata form is and how it can be understood to mean anything at all. In its drive to get to the bottom of things, Sonata Theory is informed by a not-always-tacit dialogue with current philosophy and literary criticism. While the book does not flaunt its intersections with certain strands of thought of the past decades—genre theory, phenomenology-oriented hermeneutics, reader (listener)-generated artistic texts, the slippage and dispersion of meanings once supposed to be unitary, and so on—the importance to us of those modes of thinking should be evident to most readers. (The more generalized axioms grounding our conceptual system and modes of inquiry are laid out in appendix 1 at the end of the book.) There are no tacit social agendas to our research of which we are aware, except that of seeking to understand what sonatas are and how they work. Still, Sonata Theory does have an interpretational, self-reflective, or philosophical tilt to it, an urge to explore a more fundamental questioning of this music's methods and purposes. We are committed to understanding musical practice not only as a self-contained technical language but also as a metaphor for human action or communication. We hope that our work will illuminate other perspectives and will open the investigation of sonata form and its diversified meanings to questions of serious concern to a new, younger generation of musicians and scholars.

The musical examples in this book were created by Marcus Lofthouse, a recent graduate of the Oberlin Conservatory of Music, using Sibelius 3. Passages for solo piano are reproduced in full; string quartet excerpts are presented on two staves, but nothing has been omitted. Most orchestral passages are presented in two-stave reductions that eliminate some octave doublings but retain the melody and bass lines, accompaniment, and any inner voices or counterpoint, all in their original registers. Space limitations necessitated reducing most concerto passages to two staves, one for the soloist (usually piano), the other for the orchestral accompaniment. The solo passages are presented as completely as possible, eliminating only a few low doublings as well as those measures where the piano functions as a thoroughbass instrument. The orchestral passages required a bit more in the way of compromise, but the one-staff reductions do show all the essentials of the textures. The examples were checked against the most authoritative editions available. Although fidelity to the score is balanced by practical considerations of legibility, our aim has been to make these examples as complete, as faithful to the original, and as helpful as possible. The figures and tables in the various chapters were reproduced by Zachariah Victor, using Adobe Illustrator 10.

In referring to individual works in the text we normally use the full versions of the most widely known, easily recognizable titles and numberings (and even nicknames), even when those designations might be more popular—or customary—than scholarly. (Additionally, when we do not explicitly flag a key as "minor," we mean that it is major: "in D" means "in D major.") As all scholars of the period are aware, Mozart's "Symphony No. 39 in E-flat, K. 543" is not at all his thirty-ninth composed symphony—nor did the composer think of it in that way—although for a very long time it has been commonly referred to as that in standard discussions and shows no sign of even beginning to shake off this now "historically fixed" number. And merely to refer to the work, *de haut en bas*, as the Symphony in E-flat [Major] or only as K. 543, without any other identifying reference, could either oblige some readers to scurry off to Köchel-number lists or discourage them from trying to remember which piece this actually is. These issues are particularly noticeable in references to Mozart's piano concertos, which in the literature are often referred to only by Köchel number, sometimes accompanied by the key ("K. 488" alone or "Piano Concerto in A, K. 488," as opposed to our preferred—though not literally correct—"Piano Concerto No. 23 in A, K. 488"). We recognize the historical inaccuracies embedded in "No. 39" and "No. 23," but our intention, because we cite so many references to so many individual works, has been to simplify things for the reader. For similar reasons, within the text proper our references to Köchel numbers are only to the familiar, "traditional" numbers, thereby avoiding the clutter and pedantic flavor of the double-descriptions that append the revised K. numbers as well, when such numbers exist. Thus instead of the scholarly precise "Piano Concerto in C, K. 415/387*b*" we prefer the more reader-friendly (albeit "incorrect" or not fully up-to-date with regard to the catalogue) "Piano Concerto No. 13 in C, K. 415." (No reader could possibly be confused by the absence of the much less familiar "updated number.") Not all of the K. numbers have these issues associated with them, but when they do, the dual number is provided in the index. Related issues and choices were made in citing the works of Haydn, Beethoven, Schubert, and others.

Any book of this scope is inevitably indebted to the many colleagues and students—too numerous to mention individually—with whom, along the way, we have shared information, proposed new ideas, developed concepts, and worked through analyses. We are grateful for all of these conversations and critiques, which have helped to shape our own thinking over the years. Apart from its use in academic classes and seminars, much of the first half of this book was "officially launched" at a workshop of the Mannes Institute for Advanced Studies in Music Theory (Institute on Musical Form) on June 24–27, 2004. This workshop was ably led by Daniel Harrison, and we thank him for doing so. We are also pleased to acknowledge the assistance and encouragement of Oxford University Press from the book's initial inception back in the mid- and late-1990s onward. We are grateful to Maribeth Payne, then music editor at Oxford, and to the group of anonymous reviewers that read and commented on an early version of this text around seven years ago. And we are indebted to the team at Oxford, Kimberley Robinson, Eve Bachrach, Robert Milks, Norman Hirschy, and others, who have been crucial in guiding this book through the production process and into print. Still additional thanks are due to Thomas Hepokoski, who helped to sustain this project to the end in important ways. Finally, we thank our immediate families—and especially our wives, Barbara and Marsha—for having the willingness, love, and patience to persevere through the seemingly endless sessions of our research, writing, and revisions. There may be, finally, light at the end of the tunnel.

Contents

SEVEN

The Secondary Theme (S) and Essential Expositional Closure (EEC): Initial Considerations 117

EIGHT

S-Complications: EEC Deferral and Apparent Double Medial Caesuras (TMB)   150

NINE

The Closing Zone (C)   180

SIXTEEN

Sonata Types and the Type 1 Sonata   343

SEVENTEEN

The Type 2 Sonata   353

TWENTY-TWO

The Type 5 Sonata: Mozart's Concertos (Development and Recapitulation: From Solo 2 through Ritornello 4)   563

Appendix 1. Some Grounding Principles of Sonata Theory   603

Appendix 2. Terminology: "Rotation" and "Deformation"   611

Terms and Abbreviations

PAC = perfect authentic cadence (a phrase-concluding formula featuring V-I root-position bass motion; the upper voice ends on scale-degree $\hat{1}$ above the tonic chord)

IAC = imperfect authentic cadence (similar to PAC, but the upper voice ends on scale-degree $\hat{3}$ or $\hat{5}$ above the tonic chord)

HC = half-cadence (a cadence ending on an active V chord; this dominant chord will also end a phrase)

DC = deceptive cadence (V-vi, or V followed by any non-tonic chord containing $\hat{1}$, where an authentic cadence is expected)

V_T = a V that is tonicized; the dominant sounded as a key (as in second themes of major-mode expositions)

V_A = a V that is an active chord, not a key; the A stands for "active," and it indicates that the dominant is being sounded but not tonicized; instead, it implies a resolution to the existing or implied tonic.

C = closing zone (within an exposition, musical material following the EEC. Its internal modules are designated as C^1, C^2, etc.; in this case the superscript integers should be advanced only after a PAC.)

CF = caesura-fill (connective material, of variable length, bridging a caesura—either a medial caesura or a final caesura—to the next thematic module)

$C^{\text{pre-EEC}}$ = A "C"-like theme that occurs before the EEC proper within a continuous exposition. (Within a two-part exposition, such a theme is designated as S^C.)

CRI = coda-rhetoric interpolation (coda-like material interpolated shortly before the close of the recapitulatory rotation, which then resumes to complete the recapitulation proper)

DE = display episode (in a Type 5 sonata [concerto movement] the solo-virtuosic closing portion, ending with an emphatic trill cadence, of S1 and S3—the solo exposition and solo recapitulation. The location of the display episode is usually included in the label, as in S1:\DE. See S1:\.)

EEC = essential expositional closure (within an exposition, usually the first satisfactory PAC that occurs within S and that proceeds onward to differing material. An immediate repetition of the melody or cadence—or certain other procedures, outlined in chapter 8—can defer this point to the next PAC.)

ESC = essential structural closure (within a recapitulation, usually the first satisfactory PAC that occurs within S and that proceeds onward to differing material. Like the EEC, the ESC can also be deferred through certain procedures to the next PAC. The ESC is normally the recapitulation's parallel point to the exposition's EEC, although exceptions do exist.)

FS = *Fortspinnung* modules (usually in the continuous-exposition context of TR⇒FS)

MC = medial caesura (within an exposition, I:HC MC represents a medial caesura built around the dominant of the original tonic; V:HC MC represents an MC built around V/V; etc. The presence of an MC identifies the exposition-type as two-part—the most common type—and leads directly to an S theme. In nearly all cases, if there is no MC, there is no S. Cf. the alternative, TR⇒FS.)

MMS = multimodular S (an S that tracks through two or more different, often contrasting ideas—$S^{1.1}$, $S^{1.2}$, and so on—before driving to its first satisfactory PAC with a cadential module. The numbers after the decimal point—the "decimal designators"—provide a method of labeling and identifying these separate modules. A *trimodular S* is particularly common: see TMS.)

P = primary-theme zone (whose individual modules may be described as $P^{1.1}$, $P^{1.2}$, etc. A module that precedes or sets up what is taken to be the "P-theme proper" may be designated as P^0 or $P^{1.0}$.)

PMC = postmedial caesura (any emphatic MC-effect that occurs in an exposition *after* the first MC; a "second" MC-production, sounded several measures past an initial, fully successful MC.)

P^{rf} = the specialized P-theme within a Type 4 sonata—sonata-rondo—that also functions as a recurring, refrain theme with "rondo character," often also displaying a characteristic refrain-theme structure.

R1 = the initial ritornello (Ritornello 1 or opening tutti) at the opening of a Type 5 sonata (concerto movement). Similarly, R2, R3, and R4 stand for the second, third, and fourth ritornellos (or tuttis), each of which also has a specialized function and role to play within a Type 5 sonata.

R1:\ = prefix indicating material within R1 of a Type 5 sonata (concerto movement). (Thus R1:\P, R1:\S, and R1:\EEC represent the modules functioning as the primary theme, the secondary theme, and the rhetorical EEC within the opening tutti of a Type 5 sonata.)

RT = retransition (a connective passage of preparation, usually leading to the onset of a new rotation, that is, to the repeat of the exposition, to the onset of the recapitulation, or to the beginning of the coda)

S = secondary-theme zone (follows an MC. This is built from precadential, pre-EEC thematic modules. Differing musical ideas within it, when they exist, are designated with superscripts as $S^{1.1}$, $S^{1.2}$, and so on. [See MMS and TMS.] A module that precedes or sets up the S-theme proper may be designated as S^0 or $S^{1.0}$. Not to be confused with S1.)

S1 = the first solo section, Solo 1, of a Type 5 sonata (concerto movement), typically marked by the first entrance of the soloist following the orchestral R1 and ending with a trill cadence precipitating the onset of the second ritornello or tutti, R2. S1 is also the "solo exposition," even though, as discussed in Chapters 19 and 21, this is normally extended into a "larger exposition"—rotationally defined—with the addition of the immediately subsequent R2. Similarly, within concerto movements S2 and S3 stand for the second and third solo section. S2 is usually the developmental space of the Type 5 sonata. S3 (or sometimes R3⇒S3) is normally the "solo recapitulation," also extendable into the "larger recapitulation" with the addition of R4 (chapter 22). (Notice that in the concerto-space designation, S1, the numeral is not superscripted. When it is, as in S^1, S^2, and so on, it refers not to Solo 1 but to a portion of secondary-theme space. In concerto movements the two may appear in the same description, as with $S1:\backslash S^{1.2}$, or "the second module of S-space within Solo 1 of a Type 5 sonata." See S.)

S1:\ = prefix indicating material within the S1 zone of a Type 5 sonata. (Thus S1:\P, S1:\S, and S1:\EEC represent the modules functioning as the primary theme, the secondary theme, and the EEC within the Solo 1 space of a Type 5 sonata. See S1.)

S^C = a theme within S-space (and thus before any clear articulation of an EEC) that, for any number of reasons, seems to take on the features and style more characteristic of a closing theme (C). Cf. $C^{pre\text{-}EEC}$.

TI = tutti interjection (in a Type 5 sonata, any brief, interrupting tutti impulse within what is otherwise a solo section, such as S1, S2, or S3. The first of these to appear, $S1:\backslash TI^1$, shortly into Solo 1, is often formulaic and stylized, as noted in chapter 21.)

TMB = trimodular block (an especially emphatic type of multimodular structure in an exposition or recapitulation, always associated with the phenomenon of *apparent double medial caesuras*. Individual modules may be designated as TM^1, TM^2, and TM^3. Of these, TM^1 and TM^3 are usually "thematic." TM^1

follows the first apparent MC, TM^2 often reinvigorates the TR-style [often TM^1 merges into TM^2, $TM^1 \Rightarrow TM^2$] and helps to set up the second apparent MC, and TM^3 follows that second MC-effect. A TMB leads, at its end, to the EEC. Either TM^1 or TM^3 may give the impression of being the "real" S depending on the individual circumstances. Cf. TMS.)

TMS = trimodular S (a common type of MMS with three S-modules. Within the sonata narrative the first proves "unable" to produce a PAC; the second often thematizes the threat or difficulty; the third is a decisive cadential module. It differs from the TMB in its lack of apparent double medial caesuras: there is no second "apparent" MC after the second S module.)

TR = transition (following P, the energy-gaining modules driving toward the medial caesura)

TR⇒FS = the broad middle section of a continuous exposition that begins as a transition (TR) but at a crucial "point of conversion" midway through is often better described as *Fortspinnung* (FS) or, in other cases, a chain of thematic modules. Either procedure avoids producing a clear MC and the resultant two-part exposition. The ⇒ ("becomes" or "merges into") represents the conceptual point of conversion.

About the Authors

James Hepokoski, professor of music at Yale University, specializes in formal structure and hermeneutic issues in sonata-form-based repertories, ca. 1750–1920. He is the author of four books and numerous articles in a variety of areas, including Italian opera (Verdi), early-modernist composers (Sibelius, Strauss, Elgar), American and Germanic music-historical methodologies, and current literary-critical/cultural approaches to music. He was a co-editor of the journal *19th-Century Music* from 1992 to 2006.

Warren Darcy is professor of music theory and former director of the Division of Music Theory at the Oberlin College Conservatory. He has lectured and published widely on Wagnerian opera, and his book *Wagner's "Das Rheingold"* (Oxford, 1993) won the Society for Music Theory's 1995 Wallace Berry Award. He has also published on the music of Bruckner and Mahler and is currently engaged in a large-scale study of rotational form in Mahler's symphonies.

ELEMENTS *of*
SONATA THEORY

CHAPTER ONE

Contexts

Differing Approaches to Sonata Form

There is no consensus regarding the manner in which sonata form in the decades around 1800 is to be grasped. On the contrary, analysts are confronted with a clutch of diverse approaches with differing emphases, interests, and terminologies. This is contested terrain, particularly since the structure is basic to how we conceptualize the Austro-Germanic art-music enterprise stemming from Haydn, Mozart, Beethoven, and Schubert. Our contribution, Sonata Theory, provides a *via media* among these approaches, remaining open to the positive insights that each has to offer and for the most part remaining methodologically compatible with them all. At the same time we propose new, genre-based perspectives, along with useful ways of formulating analytical questions and moving on to productive hermeneutic endeavors—interpretations of meaning.

Situating oneself within a conflicted field is a risky, fallible enterprise, in part because one is obliged reductively to characterize the work of others—and those others nearly always object (often rightly so) to such characterizations. And yet it may be helpful to sketch out some rough descriptions of viable approaches to the subject of sonata form, if only to suggest an impression

of the larger playing field. In influential English-language scholarship today one might recognize four general trends: two broad musicological lines and two broad music-theory lines. To be sure, the categories overlap—they are anything but airtight—and within each there are differences and varied accents in the way the general method is formulated. Still, musicology and music theory have often pursued distinct paths, generating different questions and answers.

The two broad musicological approaches, sometimes intersecting, are: (1) the style of eclectic analytical writing favored by Donald Francis Tovey and carried on (and varied) by such differing writers as Joseph Kerman and Charles Rosen and (2) the more strictly "historical-evidentiary-empirical" concerns of such diverse figures as William S. Newman, Jan LaRue, Eugene K. Wolf, Leonard G. Ratner, and their successors. The two broad music-theoretical approaches are: (3) Schenkerian and post-Schenkerian methodologies and (4) lines of analysis emphasizing motivic growth from small musical cells, as well as the identification of phrase-shapes and the patterns of larger sectional blocks—a style of analysis associated with Arnold Schoenberg, Rudolph Réti, and Hans Keller, and including the work of Erwin Ratz and, most recently, William E.

Caplin.[1] At the risk of oversimplification (and with apologies to those unmentioned), we might characterize the interests of these four categories by citing an example of an important text within each.

1. Our first-category illustration is Charles Rosen's *Sonata Forms* (1980, rev. 1988).[2] Drawing on the analytical and prose style of Tovey and grounded in a vast knowledge of the repertory, Rosen's *magnum opus* stressed the variety of procedures that one can encounter in the "texture" or "process" that we now call sonata form. (Hence his plural, "forms," echoing Tovey.)[3] Rather than elaborating an intricate background plan for the form, Rosen preferred to demonstrate how difficult—or futile—it is to provide a set of detailed expectations regarding it because of the unique things that occur in individual pieces by composers of genius. As a matter of principle Rosen shunned the idea of a "general practice" for the construction of sonatas—except for a few tonal requirements and common textural choices—although there were clearly better and more masterly solutions to the general set of problems at hand.[4] This somewhat intuitive approach, acute and invariably musical, also emphasized the concept of tonal "polarization" (usually tonic and dominant) in expositions and famously regarded the expositional shift to a non-tonic key as an "opposition[al]" move, a "large-scale dissonance" ("structural dissonance" or "dissonant

section") that needs to be resolved in the recapitulation.[5] A central feature of Rosen's writing (as well as that of Tovey and Kerman) was the description of individual compositional styles and preferences, along with the pronouncement of cleanly-divided aesthetic judgments of the works at hand—strong praise for the masterworks contrasted with tart dismissals of works deemed not to make the grade.

2. The second category is best represented by Leonard G. Ratner's *Classic Music* (1980).[6] Somewhat parallel to the scholarly-inventory work of William S. Newman and Jan LaRue, Ratner sought to reconstruct the concept of the eighteenth-century style from the point of view of the eighteenth century itself. The book was to be

> a full-scale explication of the stylistic premises of classic music, a guide to the principles according to which this music was composed. . . . The exposition of 18th-century musical rhetoric is found in theoretical and critical treatises. . . . [These writings] point to what was current *then*, illuminating our present view of the music. Coordinated with analysis of the music itself, the data gleaned from these writings make it possible to determine the basic criteria of expression, rhetoric, structure, performance, and style that govern classic music. . . . This book allows the student to approach the music and musical precepts of the 18th century in much the same way a listener of that time would have done.[7]

---

1. But even these broad categories are too limiting. Intermixed throughout them all are the various traditions passed on in the *Formenlehre*, the academic textbooks of form, which seem to have a separate reception-life of their own. In addition, other influential European perspectives that sometimes escape from or provide alternative havens within the above four categories have also proven provocative for current work—one thinks, for example, of the work of Jens Peter Larsen and Carl Dahlhaus. Moreover, in recent years differing scholars have begun to seek new ways to blend together formerly differing methodologies.

2. Rosen, *Sonata Forms*, rev. ed. (New York: Norton, 1988 [first ed. 1980]).

3. Donald Francis Tovey, "Sonata Forms," originally two different entries for the 11th (1911) and 14th (1929) eds., the latter of which is reprinted in Tovey, *Musical Articles from the Encyclopaedia Britannica* (London: Oxford

University Press, 1944) [reissued in 1956 under the title *The Forms of Music*], pp. 208–32.

4. Rosen, *Sonata Forms*, rev. ed., pp. 4–7. Cf. the differing impression conveyed in W. Dean Sutcliffe's review, in *Music & Letters* 79 (1998), 601–4, of Rosen's modest revision of his earlier work *The Classical Style: Haydn, Mozart, Beethoven*, exp. ed. (New York: Norton, 1997 [orig. ed., 1971]). This review, in part, calls attention to the earlier book's apparent "emphasis on the normative aspects of the style . . . stereotypes and formulas"—concerns that raise a host of questions in these more skeptical times and ones that Rosen himself had sought to clarify in the later *Sonata Forms*.

5. Rosen, *Sonata Forms*, rev. ed., pp. 98–99, 229, 287. See also Rosen, *The Classical Style*, exp. ed., p. 33.

6. Ratner, *Classic Music: Expression, Form, and Style* (New York: Schirmer, 1980).

7. Ratner, Preface to *Classic Music*, pp. xiv–xvi.

Not surprisingly, Ratner paid close attention to the early theorists' descriptions of what came to be called (c. 1824–1845) "sonata form." The Newman-LaRue-Ratner projects (however they might differ in other respects) were ones of data-gathering and recovery. One of their features was to urge analysts to sideline nineteenth- or twentieth-century views of sonata form in order to gain a more period-conscious conception of the form.[8] (In this regard these interests are not without parallel to the performance-practice movement and its quest for "authenticity.") To varying degrees scholars within this circle seek to describe sonata form (and other forms) from the perspective of late-eighteenth-century theorists—favoring their terminology and concerns and being cautious about going beyond them.[9] Writers influenced by this point of view call upon the authority of late-eighteenth-century or early nineteenth-century writers on the form (such as the important statements of Heinrich Christoph Koch, Francesco Galeazzi, Augustus Kollmann, and Anton Reicha). Several of them have also tended to view harmony (modulations, key-areas visited, and so on) as the primary feature of sonata form in the years from roughly 1750 to 1820—giving it the upper hand over thematic arrangement. In the mid-twentieth century Ratner famously contested the earlier, thematic view of the sonata, which he regarded as discredited, an anachronistic, nineteenth-century (mis-)understanding of the form as it had been originally grasped in Beethovenian and pre-Beethovenian decades.[10] Some writers influenced by Ratner's work are also concerned with identifying his-

torically defensible musical "topics" (standardized musical gestures or types within phrases) and eighteenth-century conceptions of "rhetoric" in this repertory.

3. Moving to the music-theory side of things, the touchstone of the third category is Heinrich Schenker's *Der freie Satz* (1935, translated as *Free Composition*).[11] For many music theorists interested in sonata form, no text is more central than this one. Opposed to traditional ways of discussing musical structure, Schenker was convinced that he had discovered a new theory of form, "a new concept, one inherent in the works of the great masters; indeed, it is the very secret and source of their being: the concept of organic coherence."[12] This theory was to be grounded not in phrase- or section-repetitions or in thematic manipulation but rather in linear-contrapuntal views of the sonata as the unfolding of a "fundamental structure" (*Ursatz*) by means of more elaborate middleground and foreground structures. Middlegrounds and foregrounds are understood as florid "diminutions" of more simple, elemental background gestures elaborated over the course of an entire movement. The method is highly sensitive to contrapuntal, linear voice-leading, long-range prolongations or descents of important individual pitches, and the like. Here sonata form is understood as divided into two parts (exposition-development ‖ recapitulation) with a crucial harmonic "interruption" (‖) at the end of the development and a subsequent rebeginning at the onset of the recapitulation, which restates and finally completes the fundamental structure interrupted at the end of the first part.[13]

---

8. See, e.g., Eugene K. Wolf, "Sonata Form," in *The New Harvard Dictionary of Music,* ed. Don Michael Randel (Cambridge, Mass.: Harvard University Press, 1986), pp. 764–67. This essay outlines the rhetorical-tonal structure at hand and provides a historical overview of the origins and transformations of the form.

9. In other respects Ratner-related styles of analysis seem to be musicological variants of the well-established sector of music theory, "history of music theory." A more purely music-theoretical analogue is Joel Lester, *Compositional Theory in the Eighteenth-Century* (Cambridge, Mass.: Harvard University Press, 1992).

10. The *locus classicus* of this position is Ratner, "Harmonic Aspects of Classic Form," *Journal of the American Musicological Society* 11 (1949), 159–68.

11. Schenker, *Free Composition* (German original, *Der freie Satz,* 1935), trans. and ed. (with additional commentary) Ernst Oster (New York: Longman, 1979). Especially relevant is part 3, ch. 5 ("Form"), pp. 128–145. "Section 3," on "Sonata Form" (including Oster's famous footnote), is found on pp. 133–41.

12. Schenker, *Free Composition,* p. xxi.

13. Also to be noted in terms of Schenkerian and post-Schenkerian analysis is the summary of sonata form in Allen Cadwallader and David Gagné, *Analysis of Tonal Music: A Schenkerian Approach* (New York: Oxford University Press, 1998), esp. ch. 11, "Sonata Principle," pp. 303–59. Similarly, one should mention William Rothstein, *Phrase Rhythm in Tonal Music* (New York: Schirmer, 1989), particularly ch. 4, "Phrase Rhythm

4. Our example of the fourth category is William E. Caplin's *Classical Form* (1998).[14] Its opening paragraph proclaimed the need for "a new theory of classical form," one that avoids "ill-defined concepts and ambiguous terminology derived from theories that have long fallen into disrepute." Following the work of Schoenberg and Ratz,[15] Caplin viewed form as a *grouping structure*, and he set out to identify and classify the "formal functions" of smaller thematic/formal units. In practice, this entailed close attention to the structures and subparts of three fundamental theme types: the *sentence* (consisting, for Caplin, of presentation, continuation, and cadential functions; or basic idea [usually repeated, perhaps with variation] + fragmentation + cadence); the *period* (antecedent + consequent); and the *small ternary* (A−B−A'). Much attention was also given to the anatomy of numerous "*hybrids*" that mix aspects of the more standard theme types (as defined by the author). As the musical parts are assembled, they can take on "framing functions," "interthematic functions," "harmonic functions," "initiating functions," "continuation functions," and so on, often at more large-scale levels. One aim of analysis is to be able to recognize the theme types (and hybrids) and to place them into a larger functional system of interrelated parts. In the end, what was provided was an elaborate taxonomy of different kinds of phrase-and-section juxtapositions.

The War against the Textbooks

One prominent feature of the study of sonata form in recent decades—very much in the wake of Tovey's similar assertions[16]—has been the repeated declaration that the "textbook" view of sonata form is inadequate to deal with the actual musical structures at hand. At best, such a scheme represents a conformist trap that master-composers avoid falling into. In addition, the implication has sometimes been that to undertake any such "textbook" description of norms, however nuanced or sophisticated, is a mistaken enterprise. It is not difficult to find conventionalized avowals on these matters. Here is a strong version of the credo from Claudio Spies, excerpted from an essay in a book of *Brahms Studies* (1991):

> There is nothing new about "forms" with whose aid pieces of music are easily and lazily categorized or typified, tagged, pigeon-holed, and conveniently stored away without further—or even prior—hearing, and without further thought. We were all initiated into the non-mysterious stolidities of "form," particularly the most fictitious one of all, "Sonata Form." Nor is there, I hasten to add, anything new in the notion that such "forms"—and especially "Sonata Form"—*are* fictions to whose specifications and proclaimed norms very few pieces of music worth any further thought actually conform in any appreciable way. . . . It is almost as if Brahms had decided to compose [the *Tragic Overture*] as a potent rebuttal of notions propounded by the tenets of *Formenlehre*, although [it] is by no means unique among his works in this respect.

The same point, put more gently—and after an admirably detailed study of Brahms—may be found from James Webster in the same volume:

> From examples like these it is clear that norms of formal procedure, whether the bad old textbook

---

and Form: Some Preliminaries," pp. 102−20. This is an analytically sophisticated discussion of forms in general (including sonata form) and, in part, it seeks to blend some of the concerns of Schenkerians with the more musicological (and often emphatically non-Schenkerian) studies by Rosen, Ratner, and others.

14. Caplin, *Classical Form: A Theory of Formal Functions for the Instrumental Music of Haydn, Mozart, and Beethoven* (New York: Oxford University Press, 1998).

15. Schoenberg, *Fundamentals of Musical Composition*, ed. Gerald Strang and Leonard Stein (London: Faber & Faber, 1967); Ratz, *Einführung in die musikalische For-*

menlehre: Über Formprinzipien in den Inventionen und Fugen J. S. Bachs und ihre Bedeutung für die Kompositionstechnik Beethovens, 3rd ed., enl. (Vienna: Universal, 1973 [1st ed., 1951]).

16. See, e.g., Donald Francis Tovey, "Some Aspects of Beethoven's Art Forms" and "Musical Form and Matter," in *The Main Stream of Music and Other Essays* (Oxford: Oxford University Press, 1949), pp. 272−73, 160−62; and Tovey, "Sonata Forms," pp. 210−12 ("There are no rules whatever for the number or distribution of themes in sonata form").

models or the numerical averages developed earlier in this paper, can never satisfactorily account for the reality of individual compositions. In fact, when Brahms's technique seems most paradoxical—as in the timeless, themeless, tonic retransition we have just analysed—the artistic result is often the most poetic.[17]

Remarks along these lines could hardly be more familiar. Even earlier, by midcentury, it had become a scholarly point of honor to declare war on the textbooks and, for some (again, in varying degrees), on the often-wooden limitations of classifying schemes in general. Whether uttered in stronger or gentler versions, such declarations advanced unswervingly orthodox late-twentieth-century convictions, and they were caught up in the traditional philosophical dilemma of universals and particulars. For the most part—again, much as Tovey had done—they took partisan positions on behalf of the particulars, or at least on behalf of the ultimate noncapturability of the great masters. Apart from assessing this neonominalist argument on its own terms, it would also be valuable to investigate the modernist assumptions that made such views possible: the mystification of genius; the belief in the compulsion of the true artist to escape from confining, externally applied rules or systems; the precept that what we most revere in music must not only be beyond the grasp of academic minds and rational classification but must always be declared to be so; and so on.

Studying and teaching musicology and music theory in the 1960s, 1970s, and 1980s, the authors of this book absorbed such views into the marrow of their bones. We also agreed—and we continue to agree—that prior textbooks had invited a too rigid understanding of sonata form. So far as the gravamen of the charge goes, the literal point is correct and has the added benefit of bringing caution to any new analytical inquiry. Still, the problem of determining the role of convention within this "classical" repertory

was more complex than the reflex denunciations suggested. The reiterated conviction that there was no single plan for sonata form in the later eighteenth century, true enough in its narrow, literal sense, rises to the level of an error when it is naively taken either to dismiss the presence of substantially more complex systems of standard practices or to discourage inquiry into those practices. Is there a more effective way of examining conventional musical gestures (or calling forth that which *was* conventional within individualized musical gestures) without producing ideas that were reductive, stiff, mechanical, prescriptive? Is an aesthetically sensitive openness to the study of convention within composition possible?

The most strongly formulated arguments against generalized principles of sonata practice concealed a substantial weakness: in their intensity they tempted one to overstate the degree to which such classifications were ever intended to be equivalent to scientific laws. Within the humanities norms, generic options, and more-or-less standard procedures are not laws at all. And since they are not, there was no need to suppose that the existence of numerous exceptions or deviations invalidated the norm. Perhaps the many deviations were purposeful dialogues with the background norm. But this would mean, paradoxically, that the deviations helped to reinforce the socially shared norm that was being temporarily overridden. (Otherwise how could they be perceived as deviations at all?) But what is meant by a norm? And how could one come to an understanding of what such norms might have been? We began to seek a way out of the dilemma. The most profitable guidelines for our solution lay within the domains of current genre theory and hermeneutics.

Given the flexibility found in the large-scale architecture of later-eighteenth-century composition, the main descriptive problem was the difficulty of positing convincing categories of typical procedures. As scholars of eighteenth-

---

17. Spies, "'Form' and the *Tragic Overture*: An Adjuration," and James Webster, "The General and the Particular in Brahms's Later Sonata Forms," in *Brahms Studies:* *Analytical and Historical Perspectives*, ed. George S. Bozarth (Oxford: Clarendon, 1990), pp. 391 (Spies) and 75 (Webster).

century music perennially point out, surprising occurrences and variants abound—all the more so when one's investigation takes a panoramic view, extending beyond Haydn, Mozart, and early Beethoven to include the works of less-explored composers. It is for this reason that attempts to describe normative sonata procedures tend to bog down in trying to account for a host of seemingly unusual cases (of which there is an especially abundant supply in Haydn's *œuvre*).

So much is evident, but the only alternative to throwing up one's hands in the face of such diversity (rallying around the cry, "Anything can happen!," which is obviously untrue) was to find a reasonable middle ground between confiningly rigid schemata and the claim of a near-total freedom. It was necessary to retrieve a workable hermeneutic space between the reductive textbook models of the nineteenth and early twentieth centuries and the unhelpful (though still fashionable) "lowest-common-denominator" harmonic models, whose claims to adequacy have been challenged on both historical and conceptual grounds in an important essay from 1991 by Mark Evan Bonds.[18] In that essay Bonds distinguished between "conformational" and "generative" concepts of sonata form, traced the fortunes of these concepts historically, and submitted the mid-twentieth-century ascendancy of the generative models to a critique. Among his conclusions:

> Few analyses [today] openly acknowledge the extent to which composers worked within the context of formal conventions. . . . But it would be ludicrous to argue that sonata form was not at least in part an *a priori* schema available to the composer. . . . Sonata form, for Haydn, was in fact a point of departure, a mold, albeit a flex-

ible one. . . . What is needed, then, is a general theory of form that can account for conventional patterns and at the same time do justice to the immense diversity that exists within the framework of these patterns.[19]

Thus the challenge: to articulate the implied pattern-types that appear in some of the clearest or most notable exemplars and to do this with as much detail and specificity as the material encourages. These heuristic norms need not be considered as literally existing "things." Rather, they may be understood as what Dahlhaus, following Max Weber, regarded as ideal types or what we prefer to consider as regulative guides for interpretation. Moreover, these norms would have to be defined neither by unusual cases nor by expressive deformations of more standard choices. Rather, they would derive from the standard choices themselves, insofar as the frequency of those choices (not their inevitability) permit one, inductively, to infer a background set of guidelines shared by composers and a community of listeners at a given historical time and place. As we constructed these models, then, we were concerned to identify types or tendencies that (in retrospect) were influential generic participants in the eventual crystallization or early reification phase of the sonata in the mid-eighteenth century, when the preferred options became both clearer and somewhat more consistent.[20] The result was the system that we call Sonata Theory.

Our intention is not to lay down binding laws or invariant rules concerning either the parts of a sonata or the sonata as a whole. Instead, we are trying to sketch the outlines of a complex set of common options or generic defaults. It is not that any attempt to recover standard pat-

---

18. Bonds," The Paradox of Musical Form," ch. 1 of *Wordless Rhetoric: Musical Form and the Metaphor of the Oration* (Cambridge, Mass.: Harvard University Press, 1991), pp. 13–52.
19. Bonds, "The Paradox of Musical Form," p. 29.
20. E.g., as articulated in Wolf, "Sonata Form," *The New Harvard Dictionary of Music*, p. 766: "By about 1765, however, full sonata form [i.e., with full recapitulation]—though never the rigid textbook variety—was rapidly becoming the norm in fast movements and many slow movements of symphonies and

related genres, works for chamber ensemble, and solo and accompanied sonatas in all but a few major centers." Similar observations regarding the increasing normativity of certain kinds of sonata procedures—especially those identified with the Viennese Classicism of Haydn, Mozart, and early Beethoven in the period circa 1770–1800—may be found in the writings of virtually every author who has investigated such things. See, e.g., the many similar remarks in Charles Rosen, *Sonata Forms*, rev. ed., pp. 145, 153, 156–58, 161, and 286–87.

terns is a flawed enterprise; rather, it is that prior attempts have been inadequately conceived. We offer Sonata Theory as a heuristic construct that can help the task of analysis and hermeneutics. At any point, the method outlined here can be expanded or modified through criticism, correction, or nuance. Indeed, we invite this. The proposed construct is intended only as a beginning, as a work-in-progress—not as a fixed set of finalized dicta. As an assemblage of separate subparts, each of which should be subjected to constant testing and refinement, the utility of Sonata Theory as a whole does not rest on the unexceptionable validity of any correctible subpart.

Sonata Theory: Introductory Remarks

What follows lays the groundwork of a method of approaching analytically any sonata-form movement from the period of Haydn, Mozart, and Beethoven. A central premise of this method is the conviction that we must seek to understand the backdrop of normative procedures within the different zones or action-spaces of the late-eighteenth-century sonata. Much of this book sketches out key technical features of those norms as we currently understand them.

At any given point in the construction of a sonata form, a composer was faced with an array of common types of continuation-choices established by the limits of "expected" architecture found in (and generalized from) numerous generic precedents. (To produce a keyboard-sonata or symphonic movement was to place one's individual achievement into a dialogue with a community-shared pool of preexisting works, probably including some well-known ones, that formed the new work's context of understanding.) This is not to say that any skilled composer soberly pondered these choices, one by one, in the act of composing. Surely the most common decisions were made efficiently, expertly, and tacitly on the basis of norms that had been internalized (rendered automatic) through experience and familiarity with the style. Still, even before a sonata form was begun, a composer might, consciously or not, confront an array of initial questions acting as a filter for all that fol-lowed: symphony movement? overture? sonata? chamber music? how long or "grand" a movement? how complex? how "original"? how "intense" or "challenging" to listeners? what is the expected audience? for connoisseurs or amateurs (*Kenner* or *Liebhaber*)? how "unusual" in its internal language and manner of presentation? in competition with whom? whom am I trying to impress? for what occasion? and so on.

Once these gateways had been determined and work begun in earnest—the task of creating an engaging musical pathway through pre-established, generically obligatory stations—the composer faced practical issues of musical continuation from one idea to its successor. (A succeeding phrase, even an utterly contrasting phrase, would typically be heard as "reacting to" what had been established up to that point—moving outward to another branch of the musical ramification.) A sonata form required that certain audible goals be successively articulated and secured, even though the individual details of each sonata journey could differ remarkably. A composer's choices involved not only varying senses of the propriety of "what sorts of things could reasonably be expected next" within the style but also how delectable surprises, even varying degrees of seeming transgressions, might be folded into the expanding network of ideas. Within each compositional zone (action-space) or subsection these "internalized" features included such things as generically appropriate types of themes and textures; reasonable lengths of individual passages (which depended on the anticipated length and complexity of the whole composition); dynamics; degrees of anticipated contrast; standard "topics" or thematic formulas; properly placed cadences and/or cadential delay or frustration; the handling of major- and minor-mode coloration; boundaries of taste; and the limits of eccentricity.

The options available from compositional zone to zone existed conceptually within the knowledgeable musical community as something on the order of tasteful generic advice—enabling and constraining guidelines (not inviolable rules) within the "sonata-game"—given by a shared knowledge of precedents. Moreover, the available guidelines for each moment (primary theme, transition, medial caesura, secondary theme, and so on) were not accessible in an arbitrary, non-weighted fashion. Some choices were virtually obligatory; others less so, sometimes in discernible degrees. (For novice-composers, one might wittily fantasize—provided that the image is not taken too literally—something on the order of an aggressively complex "wizard" help feature within a late-eighteenth-century musical computer application, prompting the still-puzzled apprentice with a welter of numerous, successive dialog boxes of general information, tips, pre-selected weighted options, and strong, generically normative suggestions as the act of composition proceeded. What would have been urged here were such things as thematic-modular shape, style, effect, and format appropriate to the relevant action-space moment—not literal content, the burden of which was still placed on the composer.)

Within the late-eighteenth-century style some of the options were much more frequently chosen: To suggest the strength and pre-established hierarchical ordering of these options we call the more normative procedures *first- and second-level defaults* within the various zones.[21] Most simply put, composers selected (or adapted) first-level options more frequently than second-level ones, and so on. (Writers of minor-mode sonatas, for instance, more often modulated to the major mediant, III, in the exposition, than to the minor dominant, v—a less common option.) As we use it, however, the term *default* connotes more than a merely preferred option for otherwise detached consideration. First-level defaults were almost reflexive choices—the things that most composers might do as a matter of course, the first option that would normally occur to them. More than that: not to activate a first-level-default option (for example, to provide an expositional move to v instead of to III) would require a more fully conscious decision—the striving for an effect different from that provided by the usual choice. An additional

implication is that not to choose the first-level default would in most cases lead one to consider what the second-level default was—the next most obvious choice. If that, too, were rejected, then one was next invited to consider the third-level default (if it existed), and so on. Or perhaps at some point in this process a composer might decide to do something unusual by rejecting all of the default choices altogether, in pursuit of a *deformation* of that compositional moment.

As might be imagined, the whole system was highly complex, typically involving at any compositional point more than two default levels of options. This is why it requires so much time—and space—to reconstruct the background system. But it is only through an understanding of what the main options were that we can come to grips with the implications of a composer's choices from moment to moment.

In confronting any individual composition we seek to determine which gestures in it were normative within the style, which were elaborate, elegant, or strained treatments of the culturally available norms, and which were not normative at all. Sonata Theory starts from the premise that an individual composition is a musical utterance that is set (by the composer) into a dialogue with implied norms. This is an understanding of formal procedures as *dynamic, dialogic*. Our conception of the sonata as an instance of *dialogic form* is not accurately described as seeking to reinstate a bluntly "conformational" view of that structure (in Bonds's original sense of that category). Viewed more subtly, it is not the obligation of a sonata to "conform" to a fixed background pattern, which then, in turn, might be construed as an "ideal" or "well formed" shape from which deviations might be regarded as compositional errors or aesthetically undesirable distortions. Rather, the composer generates a sonata—which we regard as a *process*, a linear series of compositional choices—to enter into a dialogue with an intricate web of interrelated norms as an ongoing action in time. The acoustic surface of any sonata form (what we literally hear) sets forth

---

21. At some level the literal, computer-definition concept of *default*—an assumption prebuilt into the large-scale automatic (but alterable) decisions of a software program at the moment of its initialization—is not fully congruent with our free adaptation of it here (in the sense of ongoing, strongly weighted advice, standard choices, and normatively arrayed options). As mentioned earlier, the metaphorical implication, if applicable at all, is to be worn loosely.

the sonic traces of this individualized, processual dialogue, one that, from the standpoint of reception, it is the task of the analyst to reinvigorate. The backdrop of norms against which a sonata or any of its successive zones is placed into dialogue is no monodimensional, reified "thing." On the contrary, that backdrop comprises complex sets (or constellations) of flexible action-options, devised to facilitate the dialogue. Understanding form as dialogue also helps us to realize that in some cases standard procedures may be locally overridden for certain expressive effects. These effects differ from composition to composition: each needs to be interpreted individually. The more piece-specific one's readings can be along these lines, the better. In any analysis merely to assert that something is done "for expressive reasons" or "for reasons of variety" is obviously inadequate.

Background norms and standard options are classifiable into common and less common selections at different times and different places. Within an individual composition, a markedly exceptional procedure here or there is just that—exceptional. We call such an occurrence a generic deformation: a stretching or distortion of a norm beyond its understood limits; a pointed overriding of a standard option. The term "deformation," in this specific context, is a narrow-definitional, technical one, grounded in precedents in literary theory and other research areas. In its strictly limited, analytical usage within Sonata Theory, "deformation" carries no negative charge, no negative assessment. On the contrary, such deformations are typically engaging, aesthetically positive occurrences that contribute to the appeal and interest of a piece. As we use the term, it signifies only a purposely strained or non-normative realization of a musical action-space, a surprising or innovative departure from the constellation of habitual practices, an imaginative teasing or thwarting, sometimes playful,

of expectations, presumably in order to generate an enhanced or astonishing poetic effect.[22]

Deformations—unusual or strongly characterized, *ad hoc* moments—are common within the works of many different late-eighteenth-century composers. Indeed, they are rampant in Haydn, who delighted in producing surprising effects. Such occurrences, in dialogue with a norm, should not be regarded as redefining that norm unless the composer continued to employ that idiosyncratic feature in other works (thus customizing the norm for his own use) or unless later composers picked up the deformation as one of their more or less standard options. When this later occurrence happens, the original exception is no longer to be regarded as a deformation *per se* but becomes one of the lower-level defaults within the Sonata-Theory system. What was a deformation in Beethoven could become a lower-level default in Schumann, Liszt, or Wagner—part of a larger network of nineteenth-century sonata-deformation families.

The essence of Sonata Theory lies in uncovering and interpreting the dialogue of an individual piece with the background set of norms. This style of analysis considers every aspect of the individual work: themes, harmonic and contrapuntal motion, large- and small-scale shapes, textures, dynamics, instrumentation, tempos, repeat conventions, and so on. The main requirement for the application of the method is to grasp the controlled flexibility of the implicit underlying system of conventions. Elaborating that system is the goal of the *Elements*.

At every turn, our aim has been to focus on the most basic features of the sonata and never to forget why we perform and listen to this music in the first place. To overlook fundamental things leads one's analyses astray or renders them sterile, bookish, or irrelevant. The best analytical system is the one that seeks to reawaken or

---

22. It would be a mistake, therefore, to read into this technical usage any residual connotations of the evaluatively negative, such as the "*de*formed" (in its more typical meaning), the "*dis*figured," the "*mis*shapen," the "abnormal," the "*poorly* formed," or the "ugly." Those are not our connotations, and within the framework of Sonata Theory terminology we distance ourselves from them as strongly as we can. The central thing is to be able to grasp the intended nuance of the technical term

"deformation"—to be able to perceive in it a genre-enabled, *positive* sense of strain, a deliberately manufactured tension set apart in this aesthetic-analytical, "artificial" context from any implication of criticism or (much less) censure. These connotational points are revisited and amplified in the "Deformation" section of appendix 2, which also offers further reflections on the concepts of *dialogic form* and sonata-form action-spaces.

re-energize the latent drama, power, wit, and wonder within individual compositions. Whenever an analytical system diverts attention from the impact of the music as real experience—or, even more, when it fails to heighten our own experience of the music—then that analytical system is in need of correction. We hope that Sonata Theory, in its practical application, will lead beyond the academic explanations and interpretations of the self-enclosed work into a larger reflection on the changing meanings of this music within society.

In part, we do this by redirecting analytical attention to those portions of the sonata that have been taken for granted or passed over in relative silence in most preceding discussions. These include the composer's treatment of *caesuras* (medial and final), the textural drive toward important *cadences* (including especially the moments of what we call *essential expositional closure [EEC]* and *essential structural closure [ESC]*), the *rotational* aspect of the sonata movement as a whole (its tendency to cycle repeatedly through large, thematically differentiated blocks), and many other considerations. Although this was by no means clear to us when we began this project, one result of our work has been to defamiliarize the sonatas of Haydn, Mozart, and Beethoven—permitting us to hear them in what we have found to be more rewarding ways. To some extent, we discovered early on that we often had to overcome our own patterns of habituation in analysis and understanding "in order [to adapt the words of Viktor Shklovsky] to return sensation to our limbs, in order to make us feel objects, to make a stone feel stony."[23] The idiosyncratic concerns—even the idiosyncratic terms—of Sonata Theory can help in this regard.

For the authors, one of the most challenging burdens in devising Sonata Theory has been to remain willing to submit all components of cur-

rently "orthodox wisdom" regarding sonatas to radical questioning—comfortable trenches of thought that had long been part of our own reflexive modes of approaching this music. From the beginning we sought to listen carefully to this repertory, trying to remain open to what it seemed to want to tell us on its own terms, insofar as we could apprehend those terms in our own, very different times. Before long we came to understand that everything that we had considered to be established about sonata-analysis had to be rethought. If only for this reason, we realize how curious Sonata Theory might at first appear, especially to scholars habituated within other modes of analysis and accustomed to other kinds of theoretical questions. The value of any analytical system, however, lies in the robustness of its interpretive power. It is that interpretive adequacy that we have been seeking. Whenever existing terminology was adequate, we have retained it; whenever it was misleading or connotatively unhelpful, we have decided to change it; whenever it lacked a term for a crucial concept, we have been obliged to devise a new one.

Readers might initially find that the basic concerns of Sonata Theory are learned relatively quickly—like the moves of chess. These concerns may seem simple precisely because they are simple. At all points in the analysis of a sonata, we have tried to emphasize the most essential features and dramatized musical goals. Beyond the elementary principles of Sonata Theory, though, lies an elaborate network of possibility, nuance, flexibility, sophistication, and detail that takes patience to master. As with chess, again, one may learn the moves rapidly, but to play the game at a fully proficient level is more difficult. Notwithstanding its many postulates and axioms, Sonata Theory is no mechanical system. Rather, in proper application it is an art that requires training, musical sensi-

---

23. Shklovsky, *Theory of Prose* [from second edition, 1929], transl. Benjamin Sher (Elmwood Park, Ill.: Dalkey Archive Press, 1990), p. 6. In order to accomplish these things, declared the Russian Formalist Shklovksy, "[we have] been given the tool of art. . . . By 'enstranging' objects and complicating form, the device

of art makes perception long and 'laborious'. . . . *Art is a means of experiencing the process of creativity. The artifact itself is quite unimportant.*" Sher defends his translation, "enstranging" (as opposed to the more traditional choices, "defamiliarizing" and "estranging"), on p. xix.

tivity, and much experience with the repertory in question.

At the heart of the theory is the recognition and interpretation of *expressive/dramatic trajectories toward generically obligatory cadences*. For the present, we might only register the degree to which this concern resonates with Heinrich Schenker's much-quoted description of musical motion and dramatized process in *Free Composition* (*Der freie Satz*, 1935):

The *goal* and the course to the goal are primary. Content comes afterward: without a goal there can be no content.

In the art of music, as in life, motion toward the goal encounters obstacles, reverses, disappointments, and involves great distances, detours, expansions, interpolations, and, in short, retardations of all kinds. Therein lies the source of all artistic delaying, from which the creative mind can derive content that is ever new.[24]

---

24. Schenker, *Free Composition*, p. 5.

CHAPTER TWO

~~~~~~~~~

Sonata Form as a Whole
Foundational Considerations

Sonata form is the most important large structure of individual movements from the "common-practice" tonal era. It sets forth and resolves its musical discourse within a large-scale binary format. The term "sonata form" was almost surely unknown to Haydn, Mozart, early Beethoven, and their contemporaries: it seems to have surfaced only in the 1820s and 1830s. In the late-eighteenth and early-nineteenth century this structure would have been grasped primarily as the customary design of first movements within sonatas, chamber music, and symphonies, although it was by no means confined only to first movements (nor only to rapid-tempo movements). The varying descriptions from contemporary theorists were more convoluted. There the form was variously described as: "the first

allegro of the symphony [or sonata]", disposed in "two sections" [*zwey Theile*] and three "main periods" [*Hauptperioden*] (Koch 1793); within "larger pieces of music" a "well-conducted melody [!] . . . divided into two parts, either connected, or separated in the middle by a repeat sign" (Galeazzi 1796); "an elaborate movement [or] a long movement . . . generally divided into *two sections*" (Kollmann 1799); "grand binary form" [*grande coupe binaire*] (Reicha 1826); and so on.[1] Still, "sonata form" (*Sonatenform*) seems to have been a familiar term by the mid-1820s, at least in A. B. Marx's *Berliner allgemeine musikalische Zeitung* circle, where it referred both to the multimovement cycle as a whole and, occasionally, to the form of an individual movement.[2] It was only in 1838 and 1845, though, in technical

---

1. Heinrich Christoph Koch, *Versuch einer Anleitung zur Composition* (Leipzig: Adam Friedrich Böhme, 1793; rpt., Hildesheim: Georg Olms, 1969), pp. 304–5 (from section 101), trans. Nancy Kovaleff Baker in Koch, *Introductory Essay on Composition: The Mechanical Rules of Melody, Sections 3 and 4* (New Haven, Conn.: Yale University Press, 1983), p. 199; Francesco Galeazzi, *Elementi teorico-pratici di musica*, vol. 2 (Rome: Puccinelli, 1796), the relevant extracts of which were excerpted and translated in Bathia Churgin, "Francesco Galeazzi's Description (1796) of Sonata Form," *Journal of the American Musicological Society* 21 (1968), 181–99 (above quotations from pp. 189–90); A. F. C. Kollmann, *An Essay*

on Practical Musical Composition (London, 1799; rpt. New York: Da Capo Press, 1973), p. 4 [ch. 1, section 10]; Anton Reicha, *Traité de haute composition musicale* (Paris, 1826), discussed, e.g., in Ian Bent and William Drabkin, *Analysis* (New York: Norton, 1987), pp. 18–20, and especially Peter A. Hoyt, "The Concept of *développement* in the Early Nineteenth Century," in *Music Theory in the Age of Romanticism*, ed. Ian Bent (Cambridge: Cambridge University Press, 1996), pp. 141–62.
2. In the journal's first year of publication (1824) the term 'sonata form' appeared in both senses. The first, apparently initially the more common, was a description of the entire multimovement cycle (used by Marx,

discussions of the form's particulars, that Marx put the stamp of approval on the term "Sonaten-form" with regard to the individual-movement structure.[3] Throughout this book we use that term as a familiar quick-reference, even as we realize that that designation was not current in the eighteenth century.

Sonata form is neither a set of "textbook" rules nor a fixed scheme. Rather, it is a constellation of normative and optional procedures that are flexible in their realization—a field of enabling and constraining guidelines applied in the production and interpretation of a familiar compositional shape. Existing at any given moment, synchronically, as a mappable constellation (although displaying variants from one location to another, from one composer to another), the genre was subjected to ongoing diachronic transformation in history, changing via incremental nuances from decade to decade. Haydn's conception of what was customary within sonata form in 1770 differed somewhat from Beethoven's conception in 1805. However such models might be said to have differed, they also shared certain crucial, genre-defining features that make them all recognizable as sonata form. Here we are dealing primarily with the model that crystallized during the second half of the eighteenth century and that reached a peak in the mature works of Haydn and Mozart and the early works of Beethoven.

What we now call sonata form was developed as a response to aspects of the world view of the Enlightenment and the concomitantly emerging modernism. Considered generally, it could be understood as an abstract metaphor for disciplined, balanced action in the world, a generalized action involving differing types of idealized mid- and late-eighteenth-century personalities. (Its potential for "extramusical" connotations and analogues is discussed in the final section of chapter 11, "Narrative Implications: The Sonata as Metaphor for Human Action.") Sonata form emphasized short-range topical flexibility, grace, and forward-driving dynamism combined—in both the short and long range—with balance, symmetry, closure, and the rational resolution of tensions. By the mid-eighteenth century it had become obligatory for the first movement of a standard multimovement instrumental work; it had also become a common, if optional, choice for the slow movement and the finale. Slow movements and finales sometimes also displayed different adaptations of the form. Although the guidelines in most of this book were written predominantly with first and last movements and single-movement overtures in mind (all energetic "Allegro movements"), they are also applicable, occasionally with some modifications, to slow movements.

From the compositional point of view sonata form was an ordered system of generically available options permitting the spanning of ever larger expanses of time. A sonata-form project was a feat of engineering, like the construction of a bridge "thrown out" into space. In the eighteenth-century style this temporal span was to be built from rather simple materials: trim, elementary musical modules whose brevity and small-scale balances seemed best suited to short-winded compositions. In the hands of most composers, constructing a sonata-form movement was a task of *modular assembly*: the forging of a succession of short, section-specific

Heinrich Joseph Birnbach, and others), a usage that persisted throughout much of the nineteenth century, especially in German-speaking regions. The other use of "Sonatenform" referred to the structure of an individual movement. It first appeared in a casual, unexplained way—as if it were already a common label—in Marx's 1824 essay on the E-minor second movement (Prestissimo) of Beethoven's Piano Sonata in E, op. 109 ("Es bildet mit dem letzen Satze die eigentliche Sonate und ist auch in der Sonaten-Form hingeworfen," *BamZ*, I, 1824, 37b) and in Carl Loewe's discussion of the first movement of Beethoven's Cello Sonata, op. 102 no.1 ("Hart und rauh, im männlichen Zorne, beginnt ein kurzes Allegro (A-moll) in der Sonatenform," *BamZ*, 1824, 410b). See the discussion of terminology and quotation of sources in the entry by Hans-Joachim Hinrichsen, "Sonatenform, Sonatenhauptsatzform" [1996], in Hans Heinrich Eggebrecht, ed., *Handwörterbuch der musikalischen Terminologie* (Stuttgart: Steiner, n.d.), pp. 1–7. 3. A. B. Marx, *Die Lehre von der musikalischen Komposition, praktisch-theoretisch*, vols. 2 and 3, 1st eds. (Leipzig, 1838 and 1845), 2:482, 497; 3:195; cited in Hinrichsen, "Sonatenform, Sonatenhauptsatzform" [1996], pp. 6–7. See also Marx, *Musical Form in the Age of Beethoven: Selected Writings on Theory and Method*, ed. and trans. Scott Burnham (Cambridge: Cambridge University Press, 1997).

musical units (spaces of action) linked together into an ongoing linear chain—pressing down and connecting one appropriately stylized musical tile after another.[4] One of the challenges facing the mid- and late-eighteenth-century composer was to use a seemingly unassuming, *galant* language, grounded in structural punctuation and periodicity, to produce ever more spectacular spans for occasions of enhanced dignity, prestige, or social importance. Ever-larger, thematically differentiated binary structures (sonata forms, often with built-in repetitions of individual sections), eventual accretions to the structure (slow introductions and longer codas), and multimovement conventions all had their roles to play in this process of generic enlargement. And ultimately they led to the grandly monumental, personalized structures of Haydn, Mozart, and Beethoven.

The most typical sonata forms (what we call Type 3 sonatas) articulate an overall rounded binary structure. The two parts of this larger structure are, in modern terminology: (1) the exposition and (2) the development and recapitulation. As will be elaborated at the end of this chapter, both parts may be marked for repeat, or the composer may eliminate the repeat of part 2 or, under some circumstances, both repeats. Notwithstanding its binary origins, the normative, Type 3 sonata consists of three musical action-spaces (again, the exposition, development, and recapitulation), laid out in a large A‖BA' format. Hence the common observation that the form consists of an originally binary structure often arrayed in a ternary plan. Each of the three spaces is usually subjected to thematic and textural differentiation. Each is marked by several successive themes and textures, all of which are normally recognizable as generically appro-

priate for their specified location. These three spaces can be viewed as expansions of the three phases of the continuous rounded binary form (the rounded binary structure in which the first part ends in a secondary key). We shall take up these spaces individually. (In figure 2.1 we have provided two diagrams of Sonata Theory's conception of the most common type of sonata form: 2.1a refers to the exposition; 2.1b to the whole sonata-form movement.)

Exposition

As with all of the action-spaces the exposition is assigned a double-task, one harmonic and the other thematic-textural ("rhetorical"). Its *harmonic* task is to propose the initial tonic and then, following any number of normative (and dramatized) textural paths, to move to and cadence in a secondary key. In major-mode sonatas—the most common in the eighteenth century—this was the key of the dominant (which may be indicated as V_T, meaning "a V that is tonicized"), thereby generating tonal tension. In minor-mode sonatas this was usually the key of the major mediant (III), although a less-often-selected choice (second-level default) was the minor dominant (v). The differing psychological and structural world of minor-mode sonatas is dealt with in chapter 14. Here, for the most part, we shall focus on major-mode practice.

The exposition's *rhetorical* task, no less important, is to provide a referential arrangement or layout of specialized themes and textures against which the events of the two subsequent spaces—development and recapitulation—are to be measured and understood. We refer to this layout as *Rotation 1* or the *expositional rotation*.[5]

---

4. To be sure—and particularly in the hands of the master composers of the period—certain passages within individual sonata forms may from time to time give the impression of a broader continuity of internal ramification. This is especially the case with the startlingly original musical language of Haydn, who, even within a generally modular and "sectionalized" concept of formal practice, often favored passages of ongoing *Fortspinnung* (a moment-to-moment "spinning-out" of modular growth and elaboration). For brief characterizations of Haydn's often-"vitalistic" compositional style, see ch.

11, subsection "Recompositions, Reorderings, Interpolations" (especially n. 2 and the text to which it refers), and ch. 18, subsection "Haydn's Treatments of Type 4 Finales" (especially n. 49 and related text).

5. Sonata-form structures are centrally concerned with the formal principle that we call *rotational form* or the *rotational process*: two or more (varied) cyclings—*rotations*—through a modular pattern or succession laid down at the outset of the structure. Appendix 2 provides a broader introduction to this principle, which pervades the discussion of sonata form in this book.

a. Exposition only: the Essential Expositional Trajectory (to the EEC)

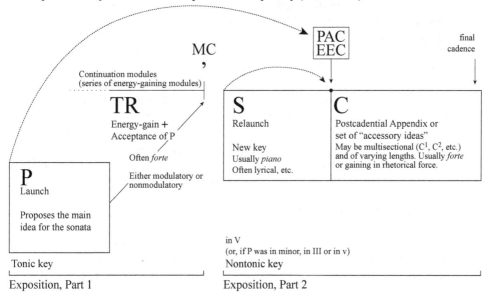

b. The entire structure: the Essential Sonata Trajectory (to the ESC)

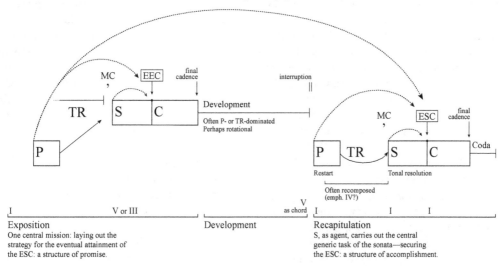

FIGURE 2.1   The Generic Layout of Sonata Form

Because the exposition's succession of events serves, especially in its second half, to predict the plan and purpose of the entire third space—the recapitulation, which finally resolves the work—its layout may be understood as articulating a *structure of promise* (indicating how it proposes that "things work out" in the recapitulatory rotation-to-come). Because the arrangement of rhetorical modules in Rotation 1 provides the ordered set of events that articulates the uniqueness and specific personality of that piece, it should be kept in mind when assessing all of the later events in the movement.

Within the expositional rotation the tonal and rhetorical tasks unfold simultaneously, intertwined with each other in mutually reinforcing ways. The exposition begins with a *primary theme* or *primary idea* (P) in the tonic that sets the emotional tone of the whole work. The most common layout for the remainder of the exposition continues with an energy-gaining zone of transition (TR) that leads to a mid-expositional break or medial caesura (MC). This is typically followed by the onset of a specialized, secondary-theme zone (S) in the new key. The generically essential tonal purpose of the exposition is to drive to and produce a secure perfect authentic cadence (PAC) in the new key (notated as V:PAC in major-mode sonatas, III:PAC or v:PAC in minor-mode ones). We refer to the first satisfactory PAC within the secondary key that goes on to differing material as the point of *essential expositional closure* (the EEC): this is one of the central concepts of Sonata Theory and one that is dealt with at length in other chapters.[6] Producing the EEC is the generically assigned task of the S-idea(s). The large dotted-line arrow in figure 2.1a suggests a broadly vectored trajectory from the start of the exposition to the EEC; the smaller dotted-line arrow below it suggests a subordinate trajectory from the beginning of S to its own point of PAC-closure at the EEC. In performing or listening to any sonata-form exposition one should sense the broad drive of these generic vectors. Whenever one hears the onset of S-space within any exposition, one should listen with an alert sense of anticipation for any subsequent PAC—how it might be approached, secured, delayed, thwarted, or deferred. One should experience any sonata form with a strongly "directed" preparatory set, pressing forward conceptually and anticipating genre-defining events-to-come.

Following the EEC one or more additional cadences (PACs) may follow within the *closing zone* or *closing space* (C). (Not all expositions contain C-modules; it is possible for the S-concluding EEC to be delayed until the end of the exposition, in which case there is no closing zone.) Whether or not C-modules are present, the final cadence of the exposition will generally be a perfect authentic cadence in the secondary key (again, V:PAC, III:PAC, or v:PAC). This final cadence might not occur directly at the double bar. Frequently the final cadence is followed by a C-module that prolongs the newly reinforced tonality by means of a pedal-point or some other device. Additionally, the final cadence is sometimes followed by a reactivation of V in preparation for a repeat of the entire exposition: if so, this reactivating passage is the *retransition* (RT).

Development

This action-space renders the established tonal tension more fluid and complex. While the exposition had split its tonal assertions into two broad blocks or contrasting planes (I and V in major-mode sonatas), the development typically initiates more active, restless, or frequent tonal shifts—a sense of comparative tonal instability. Here one gets the impression of a series of changing, coloristic moods or tonal adventures,

---

6. For the moment, we might emphasize that the first *satisfactory* PAC in the new key is often but not always the *first* PAC in that key. A first PAC, for instance, might be followed by a thematic repetition of all or part of the S-idea that we have just heard—which would automatically defer the EEC to the next satisfactory PAC further ahead. Additionally, there are other ways of deferring the sense of a clear EEC (ch. 8). The clearest way of suggesting all of this in brief is to define the EEC as the first new-key PAC that *proceeds onward to differing or contrasting material*—or, of course, that closes the exposition itself, if there are no closing modules that follow that PAC.

often led (in major-mode works) through the submediant key, vi, or other minor-mode keys with shadowed, melancholy, or anxious connotations. Any authentic-cadence attainment in a non-tonic key is to be understood as an important developmental event—a cadential ratification of an attained tonal station. (A vi: PAC is especially common in major-mode sonatas.) Ultimately, the standard development culminates on an active dominant (V_A, meaning "a V that is an active chord, not a key"). At this point the dominant from the end of the (major-mode) exposition is usually recaptured, detonicized, and reactivated.

This last point needs underscoring. In the development the final cadence is usually a half-cadence in the tonic (I:HC), although a cadence in a related minor key, normally followed by a brief reactivation of V, is also a possibility. In addition, a I:HC is frequently followed by a prolongation of dominant harmony, a "dominant-lock" or "dominant preparation." The typical I:HC conclusion of the development—just before the onset of the recapitulation—brings us to a harmonic *interruption*. (This crucial interruption is a defining feature of the Schenkerian conception of sonata form.) The V_A at the end of the development is not resolved to the I that usually begins the recapitulation. Rather, the phrase—and the development section as a whole—is normally "interrupted" on V_A (notwithstanding any foregrounded or local, connective "fill" that might bridge the end of the development to the recapitulation), and the next cycle of events is newly launched with the opening of the recapitulation. True, this more fundamental interruption on the dominant may sometimes be masked on the foreground with an *apparent* V–I cadence (with the I triggering the recapitulation). But the more fundamental or background concept is that of harmonic interruption on V_A. (Those unfamiliar with the Schenkerian, linear-contrapuntal view of things might notice that this interruption divides the entire sonata form at the end of the development. This contrasts with the eighteenth-century "binary" division of sonata form at the end of the exposition.)

In terms of their *rhetorical* strategies, developments may or may not be fully or partially *rotational* (that is, guided in large part by the ordered thematic pattern established in the exposition). Developments often refer back to (or take up as topics) one or more of the ideas from the exposition, most commonly selected, as it happens, from Rotation 1's first half (P and TR). More often than not, the modules taken up and worked through in the development are presented in the order that they had originally appeared in the exposition (even though several expositional modules are normally left out entirely). Thus the modular succession encountered in the development—not only the expositional events referred to, but also the possibility of an episode or largely new theme—is never to be considered arbitrary. On the contrary, even within this more unpredictable, developmental texture the thematic choice and arrangement is of paramount importance and derives its significance through a comparison with what had happened in the exposition. The development is variable in length, although in the period 1760–90 one would normally expect it to occupy a smaller space than that established by the exposition. Longer, more elaborate developments in the 1780s, 1790s, and later decades are monumentalized statements that invite special attention.

Recapitulation

This action-space resolves the tonal tension originally generated in the exposition by rebeginning on the tonic (with the initial theme in the most common Sonata Types, 1, 3, 4, and 5) and usually by restating all of the non-tonic modules from part 2 of the exposition (S and C material) in the tonic key. For this reason—its largely referential retracing of the rhetorical materials laid out in the exposition (Rotation 1)—we also call the recapitulation the *recapitulatory rotation*. (Exceptions and reorderings of thematic material may be found in some sonatas.) Because of its function in bringing tonal closure to the entire form, we refer to the S/C complex in the recapitulation as the *tonal resolution*. Its shape and manner of unfolding had been established by the exposition's structure of promise. Correspondingly, we consider the recapitulation to articulate a *structure of accomplishment*. Minor-mode sonatas that had sounded S and C in the major mediant (III) in the exposition have the additional option of sounding them in either the major or minor mode in the recapitulation.

The recapitulation's S, launching the tonal resolution following a recapitulatory MC, leads to the production of a satisfactory I:PAC that goes on to differing, non-S material. This is the moment of *essential structural closure* (the ESC), most often a point parallel to the exposition's EEC. The ESC represents the tonal goal of the entire sonata form, the tonal and cadential point toward which the trajectory of the whole movement had been driving: this is suggested by the longest dotted-line arrow in figure 2–1b. From the perspective of Sonata Theory, it is only here where the movement's tonic is fully called forth, stabilized as a reality as opposed to a mere potential. As in the exposition, C-material will follow, now in the tonic. The recapitulation's final cadence is generally a I:PAC (or, in minor, sometimes a i:PAC), although this too may be followed by a prolongation of tonic harmony or by a transition leading either back to a repeat (of the entire development and recapitulation) or forward into the coda.

A coda (outside of sonata space) may or may not follow the recapitulation. More information about codas, along with a discussion of the other optional or parageneric feature of some sonatas, the introduction, may be found in chapter 13.

Repetition Schemes

Within eighteenth-century sonatas and symphonies one may find both parts repeated (‖:

exposition :‖: development–recapitulation :‖). This is the most formal and earliest norm. Many late-century first movements, especially those after about 1760, repeat only the first part (the exposition), although in works prior to 1790 one need not be surprised to see the second part also repeated. After that date, repeating the second part is an uncommon gesture that invites analytical interpretation. It is also possible to find both parts unrepeated. This occurs in lighter works, in some midcentury symphonies (some Stamitz symphonies from the 1750s; some early Mozart symphonies; and so on) and in some slow movements (especially those in the format of the less expansive, Type 1 sonata, lacking a development). The nonrepeated exposition is also a generic feature of the overture or *sinfonia*. (In other words, expositional repeats will not appear in either operatic or concert overtures; this is also true of the overture's mid-nineteenth-century offspring, the symphonic poem).[7] In this aspect the lighter overture is to be distinguished generically from the more formal first movement of a sonata or grand symphony, which at least had available the common option of expositional repetition. Nonrepeated expositions within first movements do sometimes occur in more broadly scaled and ambitious works after 1780, but when they do—as in Mozart's Symphony No. 35 in D, K. 385, "Haffner,"[8] or in Beethoven's Violin Sonata in C Minor, op. 30 no. 2, his Piano Sonata in F Minor, op. 57, "Appassionata," and his String Quartet in F, op. 59 no. 1—they are exceptional and need to be considered as consciously expressive choices.[9]

One curious (and rare) possibility is that of literally writing out an expositional repeat,

7. Thus the rule. Exceptions are extremely rare and disconcertingly puzzling, such as the repeat of the exposition in young Mozart's Overture to *Apollo et Hyacinthus*, K. 38 (1767), labeled as the "Prologus/Intrada" to the opera. This piece is a Type 2 sonata (Chapter 17) whose first rotation (exposition) is provided with a repeat sign. Much later, the odd "expositional" (?) written-out and slightly varied repetition in Berlioz's Overture, *Le carnaval romain* is also curious, suggesting that the form of this unusual piece is more purely rotational (or perhaps instrumental-strophic with *fortissimo* refrain) than a sonata per se, although it is also manifestly in dialogue with certain sonata norms.
8. Other examples within Mozart's major works include the first movements of his Symphonies Nos. 31 in D, K. 297, "Paris," and 34 in C, K. 338, along with

those of the Serenades in D, K. 320, "Posthorn," and in E-flat, K. 375. Such examples—perhaps related to earlier or existing concepts of repeat-convention options in overture-symphonies, in smaller-scale symphonies, or in some serenades—require individual attention. Within the larger symphony it may be that during the 1770s (though not, it seems, in the 1780s) Mozart was exploring the possibility of the omission of the expositional repeat as a lower-level default.
9. The solution of Beethoven's op. 59 no. 1/i, which initially suggests an expositional repeat only to abort it almost immediately in favor of development, is anticipated in the first movements of Mozart's Serenade in E-flat for Eight Winds, K. 375, and Haydn's Piano Sonata in D, Hob. XVI:51.

normally including variants the second time around. This occurred most famously in C. P. E. Bach's unusual set of six keyboard *Sonaten mit veränderten Reprisen,* H. 136–39, 126, 140 (W. 50/1–6, Sonatas with Varied Repetitions), composed in 1758–59 and published in Berlin the following year. In Haydn's works the procedure surfaces only (and wisely, in Tovey's view) in a few "purely lyric slow movements," such as the Adagios of the Quartet in C, op. 33 no. 3, "Bird," and the Symphony No. 102 in B-flat.[10] (Both slow movements are in F major; in the quartet the Adagio is the third movement; in the symphony it is the second.)

What are the purposes of large-scale repeats within sonata form? Central to the concept of the grand sonata or symphony is a system of schematic repeat-conventions, balances, symmetries and proportions that call attention to and help to define the genre. The emphatically architectural construction calls attention to the genre's ordered formality—and in the case of the grand symphony, also to its grandeur and public splendor. Repeats were an important feature of a sumptuous, high-prestige display of grand architecture, one to which large-scale repetitions were essential —especially that of the expositional repeat in the first movement. The stylized form thus celebrated the "Enlightenment" (or "modern") culture that makes such an impressive, moving, or powerful art possible. One of the structure's implications would have been that this culture had devised a rational, balanced means to shape and contain the fluid, raw, elemental power of music. By extension, the process probably also represented the controlling or harnessing of those impulsive, instinctive, libidinal, or "uncivilized" elements within ourselves.

Control, balance, generic identification, and formal architectural splendor: these would appear to be the central reasons why literal repetition played such a prominent role in the style.

Consequently, repeat signs should not be taken for granted, passed over lightly in analysis, or omitted in performance. Repeat signs are never insignificant.[11] Block-repetitions are an integral component of the style, and composers can work with this defining convention in a variety of ways. When previously obligatory (or exceptionally strong first-level default) expositional repeats began gradually to disappear—especially in the early nineteenth century, with certain works of Beethoven (op. 30 no. 2, op. 57, op. 59 no. 1, and so on, and later with Mendelssohn, Schumann, and others)—the genre itself was undergoing a major rethinking.[12] The familiar, current views—Schenkerian and otherwise—that propose that some repeats are structurally insignificant while others are more important (because of the unfolding of certain structural tones or other significant events, perhaps under a first-ending sign) miss the larger point of repeat signs as generic identifiers.[13] Even when the structural-tone aspects might be convincing (but, perhaps paradoxically, only as local details), the gist of these claims seems to be based on later-nineteenth-century premises, which came to look on all unaltered repetition as an aesthetic error. Such a conviction also came to affect performance in the omission of repeats or in the insistence on an altered interpretation in the repeat. It may be, though, that saying the same thing twice was what the composer had in mind.

It is easy to object to our general argument here. One could strive to minimize the impor-

---

10. Tovey, "Sonata Forms," *Musical Articles*, p. 214: "Haydn saw that the only place for C. P. E. Bach's device was in purely lyric slow movements. Even there he never had the patience to plod and pose (as C. P. E. Bach did to the bitter end) through a repetition [recapitulation] of both parts. When his second part comes to recapitulate the second group it combines both versions."
11. For the quintessential statement of that which the present argument opposes, see Douglass M. Green, *Form in Tonal Music: An Introduction to Analysis*, 2nd ed. (New York: Holt, Rinehart, and Winston, 1979), p. 82: "HISTORICAL NOTE [*sic:*] Ordinarily the repetition of a part is of little significance in formal analysis."

12. Curiously, in 1826 Reicha suggested—in passing and without explanation (*Traité de haute composition musicale*, p. 300)—that finales may lack an explicit repeat: "When the first part is not repeated, as in overtures and finales..." ("Quand la première partie n'a pas de reprise, comme dans les ouvertures ou dans les finales ..."). It may be that Reicha had sonata-rondos, Type 4 sonatas, in mind (ch. 18).
13. Cf., e.g., Jonathan Dunsby, "The Formal Repeat," *Journal of the Royal Musical Association* 112/2 (1987), 196–207.

tance of the usual repetition schemes by an appeal to history: deriving them step-by-step from the earlier binary forms, then asserting that the persistent lingering of the repeat conventions into the 1780–1820 period of the grand symphony was an outdated survival, vestigial, unnecessary to the perception of the genre. The larger question, though, is why the convention remained available into the later phases of 1780–1820 period and beyond (particularly after Beethoven's occasional removals of the expositional repeat had occurred). The expositional repeat must have persisted, however sporadically, because it was not merely vestigial. It continued to be genre-defining, a sign of special grandeur and formality—with an ear attuned also to the grand tradition and historical lineage that had led to the mid- and later-nineteenth-century sonata and symphony.

Of the two standard large-scale repeats, the second, longer one (development-recapitulation) was the one more vulnerable to suppression. This second repetition was increasingly reduced to the status of an easily discardable option in the 1780–1800 period.[14] In some cases, concerns of absolute length or a sense of redundancy in closing particularly dramatic sonatas twice might have overridden the genre-defining principle of long-range architectural repetition and balance, at least with regard to this development–recapitulation section. Perhaps the logic of the situation suggested that the obligatory repeat of section 1 alone (the expositional repeat) was to be viewed as sufficient as a genre definer.

However we decide this matter, we should note three things. First, the issue of notationally indicating a repeat of section 2 was still part of the historical concept of "grand binary" form (within a symphonic first movement) around 1800, even when that repeat was notationally elided. Its conceptual presence remained there, counterpointed against the given, simpler structure. It persisted as historical-generic memory, even when it was not made physically present on the acoustic surface of the music. Second, any retention of the second repeat toward the end of the eighteenth century should be regarded as expressively significant, especially since its strongest composers—Haydn and Mozart—were apparently coming to believe that repeat 2 was not as obligatory as that of repeat 1. When the repeat was called for, it must have been placed there for a reason, as in the slow movement and finale of Mozart's Symphony No. 41 in C, K. 551 ("Jupiter"), where formal processes and monumentalized grandeur are principal topics throughout the whole work. Third, given a nineteenth-century work lacking an indication of that second block-repetition, any reworked referencing back to this increasingly atavistic repeat 2 within a longer, discursive coda, as in the first movement of Beethoven's Symphony No. 3 in E-flat, op. 55, "Eroica," should be viewed as such, not as an innovative addition or accretion to a previously postulated, differing symphonic practice.

---

14. See, e.g, Michael Broyles, "Organic Form and the Binary Repeat," *The Musical Quarterly* 66 (1980), 339–60.

CHAPTER THREE

The Medial Caesura and the Two-Part Exposition

An exposition has both a tonal and a rhetorical function. Its basic tonal plot—moving from an initial tonic to a secondary key, then securing that new key with one or more cadences—constitutes the exposition's *tonal form*. This tonal form, generally the same in all sonatas, is worked out in different sonatas in individualized ways, according to localized rhetorical plots. Tonal form is to be distinguished from *rhetorical form*, which includes personalized factors of design and *ad hoc* expression: modular and textural layout, selection and arrangement of musical topics, varieties of structural punctuation, and so on. The compositional ordering of these processes produces a distinct, singular musical shape. This layout serves as the *referential rotation* (or *expositional rotation*) that also guides our understanding of the ordering of modular events in the subsequent action-spaces of the sonata—development, recapitulation, and coda. An exposition may be disposed in either of two rhetorical formats: the *two-part exposition* (containing a medial caesura) or the *continuous exposition* (lacking a successfully articulated medial caesura). In this chapter we are concerned with the former.

The Two-Part Exposition

This is the format most frequently employed by most composers of the second half of the eighteenth century. Hence when one confronts any sonata form from this period, the most reasonable initial expectation would be that one is about to encounter a two-part exposition. (As will be seen in chapter 4, a continuous exposition often plays upon, then overrides, this expectation.) The cardinal feature identifying this exposition type is the presence of a sufficiently deployed medial caesura and (often contrasting) second theme.

Part 1 comprises the establishment of the tonic and the energized drive to the medial caesura. It contains two action-spaces, the *primary-theme zone (P)* and the *transitional zone (TR)*, and culminates in the *medial caesura (MC)*, which we indicate by an apostrophe ('). Part 2 comprises the post-MC material and lasts until the end of the exposition. This section is concerned with the cadential affirmation of the new key (V in major-key sonatas, III or v in minor-key ones). Part 2 subdivides into the *secondary-theme zone (S)*—which normally concludes with the sounding of the first satisfactory perfect authentic cadence (PAC) in the new key that proceeds onward to differing material, the event that we

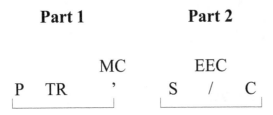

FIGURE 3.1   The Two-Part Exposition

call the moment of *essential expositional closure* (EEC), indicated here by a slash (/)—and the *closing zone (C)*. The two-part exposition may be represented as in figure 3.1.

When beginning the analysis of any exposition, we recommend that the first task be to locate and identify the treatment of the MC—to determine, first, if one exists at all and, if so, to investigate what kind it is, where it falls within the exposition, what complications might surround it, and whether the moment identified actually leads to an acceptable secondary theme (S). The second task should be to examine the strategy surrounding the EEC. Productive analyses often start in the middle of the exposition and work outward to the beginning and the end.

The Medial Caesura (MC): Definitions and Overview

The *medial caesura* is the brief, rhetorically reinforced break or gap that serves to divide an exposition into two parts, tonic and dominant (or tonic and mediant in most minor-key sonatas).[1] (A touchstone occurrence of this familiar break may be consulted in example 3.1 below: the first movement of Mozart's Piano Sonata in D, K.

284, occupying all of m. 21, with the literal gap on beat 4.) In rapid-tempo compositions a medial caesura is usually built around a strong half cadence that has been rhythmically, harmonically, or texturally reinforced. The half cadence proper—the moment of cadential arrival on an active dominant—often occurs before the MC itself. Very commonly, this active V (V_A) is then prolonged, kept alive, for several more measures as an actual or implied dominant pedal-point, a *dominant-lock*, driving aggressively toward the MC articulation. Thus while the moment of the MC proper—the articulation of the gap—is frequently not literally identical with the moment of the half-cadence arrival (the HC, which could have happened several bars earlier), the larger drive to and execution of most MCs are nonetheless "built around" a half-cadence effect or "dominant-arrival effect" in either the tonic or the dominant key.[2]

Viewed broadly, the entire process from the half-cadence arrival proper through the literal execution of the terminal MC-break, which might occur several measures further ahead, expresses a purposefully activated and prolonged half-cadence effect. In referring to medial caesuras as often being "built around" half cadences, we of course distinguish between the point of initial half-cadence arrival and the MC moment itself, in those cases where these two events differ. Nevertheless we also use the shorthand symbols I:HC MC (a medial caesura that often terminates the sustaining of an active V in the tonic) or V:HC MC (one that often terminates the sustaining of an active V in the dominant) to suggest this whole complex of musical activity, one in which the literal MC moment is to be interpreted referentially to any preceding moment of half-cadence arrival.

1. Much of what follows is adapted and updated from Hepokoski and Darcy, "The Medial Caesura and Its Role in the Eighteenth-Century Sonata Exposition," *Music Theory Spectrum* 19 (1997), 115–54. Some of the adaptations seek to clarify and make more precise issues raised regarding that article by William E. Caplin in "The Classical Cadence: Conceptions and Misconceptions," *Journal of the American Musicological Society* 57 (2004), 51–117. While we do adopt some of Caplin's cadential terminology—identifying a moment of "ca-

dential arrival," for instance—our view of the activity surrounding the MC-event differs from his in several respects, as will emerge.

2. Defining precisely what consitutes a half cadence is no easy matter. For one version of the concept of dominant arrival, as opposed to a half cadence proper, see Caplin, *Classical Form*, pp. 79–81. Cf. nn. 6, 11, and 14 below, on the claim that the dominant-lock is best regarded as "postcadential."

The medial caesura has two functions: it marks the end of the first part of the exposition (hence our adjective "medial"), and it is simultaneously the highlighted gesture that makes available the second part. The MC is the device that forcibly opens up S-space and defines the exposition type. Somewhat whimsically, it may be thought of as metaphorically analogous to the moment of the opening of elevator doors onto a higher floor—making S-space possible or opening to the second part of the exposition. The medial caesura provides a firmly established platform from which the secondary theme, launching part 2, may emerge. In order for the MC to do its job most effectively within rapid-tempo compositions, energy must be applied. This energy is furnished by TR, the transitional zone. As a rule of thumb, once TR has begun, the *forte* energy should be kept constant or on the increase all the way to the medial caesura proper. Any flagging of energy or vigor within TR—any *diminuendo* or faltering drop to *piano*—is countergeneric and constitutes an event that invites interpretation. It may suggest the production of something unusual: a medial caesura deformation or the presence of a troubled expressive problem being unfolded in the musical narrative.

The Medial Caesura: Harmonic Defaults

As indicated above, the MC is most commonly the final gesture—the "break" or "gap" at the end—of a more complex musical passage constructed around and often sustaining a half cadence (HC) or dominant arrival, in either the tonic key (I:HC) or the dominant key (V:HC). As will become clearer as we proceed, I:HC MCs are generally more appropriate for shorter, lighter pieces. On the other hand, V:HC MCs tend to be more frequent within ambitious works of moderate length and larger, especially toward the end of the eighteenth century. As such—and even though one can come across

exceptions to the proposed idea—encountering either the one MC or the other can be a signal both of the level of complexity at hand and of the probable proportions of what is to follow. A I:HC MC helps to predict a work on a relatively modest scale; a V:HC MC—suggesting a more harmonically complex option—proposes an exposition with "grander" proportions. (Such considerations are related to the concept of the "deployment sequence of medial caesura options," discussed separately below: a composer sometimes seems to pass up a I:HC MC possibility in order to pursue a V:HC MC down the road.)

The later eighteenth century saw a general increase in the expansiveness and ambition of individual movements. As a result, in most major-mode cases the MC is constructed around a half cadence or active-dominant arrival in the dominant key: the familiar V:HC option. Because of this statistical frequency, we refer to it as a *first-level default* for this expositional moment when we are dealing with works of at least moderate length.[3] (For more unassuming pieces, on the other hand, one might argue that the I:HC MC could be the first-level default or "most obvious" choice.) In the case of the V:HC MC the transition will have modulated from the original tonic to the dominant. In many transitions the preparation for the major-mode S (in V) is accomplished through a darkened or stressful pathway in the parallel minor of that new-tonic-to-come. In such situations, therefore, the TR-drive to the V:HC MC is produced with a concomitant shift to the minor mode. This means that the moment of the MC is locally sounded as the terminal gesture of a prolonged half-cadence-effect in the minor dominant, *v:HC*, whereupon S follows, more brightly, in the major mode. (A particularly charged instance of this dramatic *chiaroscuro* may be found in the first movement of Beethoven's Symphony No. 2 in D, op. 36, with mm. 61–71 delivered aggressively on A minor [MC at m. 71] and S emerging in A major at m. 73, after

---

3. An array of statistical evidence regarding the frequency of what we call V:HC and I:HC medial caesuras in Haydn, Mozart, and others has been compiled in Robert S. Winter, "The Bifocal Close and the Evo-

lution of the Viennese Classical Style," *Journal of the American Musicological Society* 42 (1989), 275–337. (We, however, do not find the term "bifocal close" for the I:HC MC to be helpful.)

two bars of major-inflected caesura-fill.) Such occurrences participate in a dialogue with the normative, major-mode MC expectation. The v:HC MC option is a commonly elected negative overlay onto the conceptual first-level default, V:HC. We still have a first-level default MC, but one subjected to the additional surface feature of temporary minor-mode mixture—a momentary "lights-out" feature. (Chapter 14 considers the expressive implications of such a mixture.)

Additionally, within the first-level default in either major-mode or minor-mode expositions one occasionally finds a seventh included in the V chord at the MC point. This seventh is best regarded as a passing tone. In the first movement of Haydn's Symphony No. 100 in G ("Military"), for example, the structural V/V, the half cadence proper, is articulated at the downbeat of m. 62, after which it is prolonged. During this prolongation the seventh is added (entering first in mm. 64–65, though most prominently in mm. 69–73), suggesting a V^{8-7} figure. The seventh ($\hat{4}$ of the new key) resolves to an inner-voice $\hat{3}$ at the onset of S (m. 75). This addition of the seventh during the drive to the MC proper is not uncommon but is normally limited to the first-level default (V:HC MC). If the seventh were added to the dominant of a second-level default (I:HC), the tendency of the resultant V^7 to resolve to the tonic would preclude the requisite tonal shift to the key of the dominant. Nevertheless, this can occur at the MC point of the initial tutti rotation of a Type 5 sonata (concerto movement), where a modulation is not required, as in Mozart's Piano Concerto No. 21 in C, K. 467, mm. 20–26.

On rare occasions one encounters the substitution of an inversion for the V or V^7 chord at the MC point. Regardless of whether the dominant has previously appeared in root position, this situation should be understood as a *medial-caesura deformation*, which might well impact on the subsequent S. In Beethoven's C-minor *Coriolan* Overture a strenuous TR manages to lock onto V^6 of E-flat (here entering as E-flat minor) in m. 46. (Obviously, this cannot be construed as a half cadence proper.) After four measures of convulsive upheavals around that chord, a V^6/iii MC-effect occurs in m. 50. Two bars of de-scending caesura-fill in the first violins lead to the E-flat-major start of S in m. 52. In this case the rhetorical effect produced is that of the half-cadence MC—the passage is clearly in dialogue with that norm—but the music is dramatically staged as being "unable" to produce the more normative HC at this point. Somewhat similarly, in Mozart's C-major Overture to *La clemenza di Tito*, K. 621, a suddenly introduced V^6_5/V (m. 28) seems to startle the music into nothing less than a fermata-stop (m. 29) that serves as the exaggerated GP-gap of a $^{\text{I}}V^6_5$/V MC deformation. S begins in G major in m. 30.

At least in works of substantial length the second most common major-mode option, the *second-level default*, is to build an MC around a half cadence or dominant arrival in the original tonic, a *I:HC*. (As mentioned above, in shorter works, a case might be made that the I:HC MC is somewhat more appropriate: it might be regarded as a first-level default in certain situations. For the present, the discussion is framed around works with grander proportions.) In this second-level default, I:HC, the transition will not have modulated: it will have begun and ended in the tonic, and it will be up to the ensuing S-space to establish the new key, usually by beginning directly in it. Because second-level MC choices are not infrequent, TR-space cannot be defined in terms of modulation. Once again, first- and second-level MC defaults are not expressively equivalent. The first, V:HC MC, is a more decisive gesture: it announces the intention to open part 2 more solidly, with its new key already in hand. The second, I:HC, is weaker, usually occurs early on, predicts a briefer or less ambitious sonata, and sometimes purposefully generates problems in what follows.

The minor-mode, derivative analogues to the above are III:HC or v:HC as strong first-level defaults, depending on the key to which one is modulating (moving to the minor dominant occurs much less frequently), and i:HC as the second-level default. While examples of the former are frequent—an MC built around a half cadence in the new key is the most common choice—examples of the latter are relatively rare. The reason why is obvious. While major-mode statements of the I:HC MC (second-level default) may easily become the tonic chord of the new key (V) and the S-to-come, this is not the case in minor-mode works. In other words, i:HC MC (say, a G-major chord sounded as an active V in C minor) is obliged to yield at once—as a *quasi non sequitur*—to the tonic of the mediant major with the onset of S (the key of E-flat in a C-minor exposition, whose appearance also produces a cross-relation between the original dominant chord's B natural and the new tonic's B flat). When this does occur, the effect can be striking: a sudden pull out of the ominous tonic minor into the brighter, more "hopeful" mediant major.[4] The touchstone examples may be found in the Prestissimo finale of Beethoven's Piano Sonata in C Minor, op. 10 no. 1 (i:HC MC at m. 16, stalled with a quizzical fermata, followed directly by the forthright S in E-flat at m. 17) and in both the opening ritornello and solo exposition of Mozart's Piano Concerto No. 20 in D Minor, K. 466 (a literal i:HC at m. 28, proceeding into a dominant-lock and i:HC MC at m. 32 and a sudden shift to F major, III, for the opening of the ritornello's secondary-theme space at m. 33; see also the solo exposition, with its i:HC MC at m. 114). From time to time the production of a i:HC MC can be presented as a compositional problem that needs immediate emendation. In the first movement of Beethoven's Quartet in C Minor, op. 18 no. 4, a i:HC MC-effect in m. 25 leads not to S proper but to a classic situation of "medial caesura declined" and the initiation of one type of trimodular block (TMB)—both of which strategies are discussed separately below. Decades later, Mendelssohn would provide the B-minor *Hebrides* Overture with a i:HC MC (m. 43; notice also the earlier i:HC MC-

effect in m. 39, which is returned to and recaptured in m. 43) and assign the modulation to III to the "poetic" caesura-fill bridging the MC to the onset of the *cantabile* S in D major (m. 47).

Most sonata forms display either a first- or second-level default MC, one built around a half cadence that may or may not have been prolonged by means of a dominant-lock. Much less frequently, one may find an MC-function produced by a perfect authentic cadence in the new key (PAC). In major-mode sonatas this *third-level default* is V:PAC MC, which occurs, for instance, in the first movement of Mozart's Quartets in D, K. 155, m. 28; in E-flat, K. 428, m. 40; and in B-flat, K. 589, m. 45. This procedure is also found with some frequency in earlier and briefer works. (The V:PAC MC in the first movement of Haydn's Symphony No. 10 in D, m. 23—one of several examples in early Haydn—could hardly be clearer.) The minor-mode-sonata analogue is normally III:PAC, as in (though with subsequent complications) the first movement of Mozart's Quartet in D Minor, K. 421, m. 24 (see example 4.3 and the accompanying discussion in chapter 4). Alternatively, in works that shift to the minor dominant key, one might find a v:PAC MC.[5]

PAC MCs are stronger tonal and rhetorical gestures than are HC MCs. Because they are heard as signs of closure, not of expectancy, and because they sound the same perfect authentic cadence that will define the EEC concluding the secondary theme, they present problems of understanding. From time to time they emerge after a composer has already dallied with the V:HC option—perhaps already producing an HC arrival in that key, or very nearly so. When this happens, it is as though the music at first

---

4. In effect the juxtaposition is produced by a chromatic 5–6 shift, in which both the third and the fifth of the active V (the G-major chord within a C-minor exposition) are altered. Recent neo-Riemannian theory might also describe this as a PL shift: a simultaneous application of a color-shift to the parallel (P) mode (a G-major chord, V of C minor, thus inflects to G minor) followed by a "leading-tone exchange" or *Leittonwechsel* (L) (the resultant G-minor sonority inflects its fifth, D, to E-flat, thus producing an E-flat chord). This familiar juxtaposition is discussed in somewhat more detail in ch. 10 in conjunction with the final active-dominant

chord of the recapitulation, where the more typical V_A sonority is sometimes replaced by V/vi (V of A minor within a C-major movement, for example, giving way almost immediately to the C-major recapitulation).
5. An extremely rare—and clearly deformational—alternative is found in Beethoven's D-minor Largo e mesto slow movement of the Piano Sonata in D, op. 10 no. 3, which features a VII:PAC MC (a PAC on V of III, C major, in m. 17)—as if seeking to "close" early, albeit in the "wrong" major mode. The S and C that follow are in A minor (v).

"decides" to drive toward the normative V:HC MC, only suddenly to "change its mind," abandoning the normative implications of the dominant-lock (if that lock had indeed been initiated), and pushing instead, impulsively, toward the stronger PAC in the new key. Thus a V:PAC MC is sometimes produced in a context that has suggested, then overridden, a more normative half-cadence-effect MC option.[6] (In K. 155/i, for instance, the half cadence and dominant-lock, V:HC, occurs at m. 20. The lock proper sustains the V_A through mm. 20–23 but is abandoned at m. 24 in order to plunge into the emphatic V:PAC MC at m. 28. The subsequent S theme, m. 29, as it happens, appears to register its surprise by beginning off-tonic, on the supertonic chord.) In some of these instances V:PAC MCs are elaborate, more decisive versions of caesura-fill of the $\hat{5} - \hat{1}$ -descent type, and distinguishing between the two can be difficult or very much a matter of individual interpretation. (This last feature is discussed in more detail below, in the discussion of caesura-fill.)

Such observations lead to larger speculations: the very concept of a V:PAC MC is potentially problematic. What leads us to think that what we call a V:PAC MC is not the EEC? (Such an early EEC would define that exposition as continuous, not as two-part, since there would have been no prior MC.) One might reason that if the generic goal of an exposition is to produce a satisfactory PAC in the secondary key, any such V:PAC-effect at this point might initially lead us to suspect that that aim has been achieved. One soon learns that it is part of the expressive character of a local V:PAC MC to threaten to preempt the sense of tonal closure that we associate with the EEC—the V:PAC that must be re-produced down the road at the end of S. But how certain can we be that such a V:PAC should not be taken for the EEC? This decision is a crucial one. It concerns the structural importance of that first V:PAC at what might well be the MC: is it a secondary, local effect (perhaps describable as the strongest possible "tonicization" of V of I at the MC point)? Or is it to be taken as a decisive structural event within the genre—nothing less than the EEC? Or can there even be other options for interpretation?

Deciding this matter in individual cases depends on three factors, each of which involves matters of interpretation and experience. The first is the question of how far into the exposition the V:PAC is sounded. Once we have proceeded past about 65 or 70 percent through—in other words, once we have experienced a proportionally overlong transition—V:PACs become less convincing as MCs, since a medial caesura normally occurs earlier in the exposition. The later the V:PAC is produced, the more likely it will be taken as the EEC. (Put another way, normally the only way that a composer can have a V:PAC serve as an MC is to expand the proportions of what follows to the point where it can be regarded as a convincing part 2: S and C. For this reason the V:PAC MC option typically suggests an exposition and subsequent sonata of notable proportions.) The second factor concerns how the V:PAC was prepared and produced (idiosyncrasies in the preceding TR). The third is the character of the module that follows. If it is a clear, contrasting theme, is it S-like or

---

6. In response to one case of this as illustrated in our article, "The Medial Caesura," pp. 129–30 (Beethoven, Piano Trio in G, op. 1 no. 2, first movement, mm. 98–99), Caplin ("The Classical Cadence," pp. 108–12) insisted that the PAC-effect at m. 99, while displaying "cadential *content*" (the two-chord combination V^7–I), could not be considered a PAC proper because it lacked "cadential *function*," at least according to his "highly constrained" (p. 56), much-restricted definition of that function. In Caplin's view, once an HC-arrival has been attained in TR, all that follows in the dominant-lock must *ipso facto* be considered "postcadential" and by that definition incapable of producing a PAC at its end. That argument, however, fails to consider the possibility that a dominant-lock might be abandoned *en route*—in other words, that it might be staged as "changing its mind"—in order to proceed to a PAC. Such a procedure would "unfreeze" the locked dominant (still an active dominant, a V_A, after all) and treat it as more of a "normal" V_A that can proceed onward toward resolution. In any event, we agree that Beethoven's op. 1 no. 2/i provides a problematic case along these lines, since the lurch to the V:PAC happens so rapidly and so closely resembles caesura-fill of the $\hat{5} - \hat{1}$ -descent type. The following example mentioned in the text, Mozart's K. 155/i, provides a clearer illustration of the process. Some of these issues are revisited in n. 14. Cf. also n. 2 and nn. 11 and 14.

C-like? Deciding this is not always easy. This general situation arises with some frequency in Haydn, who had a fondness for planting a decisive V:PAC in the 55–70 percent range of the exposition.[7] Alternatively, what follows the first V:PAC might be less of a "theme" than one or more short modules that recapture or restate that mid-expositional cadence. When that occurs, we are dealing with what we regard as the second type of continuous exposition, a possibility dealt with in chapter 4.

The even rarer option, a I:PAC MC, may be considered a *fourth-level default*. In eighteenth-century works a I:PAC or IAC-substitute (imperfect authentic cadence) leading to an obvious S in the new key may occasionally be found in light, small-scale works, in some telescoped or abbreviated expositions, and in some slow movements. Generally the PAC or IAC closes off a brief, straightforward P, and the resulting impression is that of omitting the TR-zone altogether. Because of the effective ellipsis of TR, the I:PAC or IAC at the end of P is asked to do double duty as the rhetorical MC. This occurs in the first movement of Mozart's Symphony "No. 7" in D, K. 45, m. 16 (I:IAC MC, with S in V at m. 17) and his String Quartet in A, K. 169, m. 11 (I:PAC MC, with S in V at m. 12).

In larger, more ambitious pieces the extremely infrequent I:PAC or IAC MC can carry a different implication. Here, following P, one enters what seems rhetorically to begin as a normative TR. That TR, however, proves unable (or unwilling) to produce any of the three more standard MC defaults: V:HC, I:HC, or V:PAC. In some expositions it may "try" to produce one of those—or to initiate a motion in one of those directions—before being drawn back to the original tonic. In other cases it may simply bask in an ultra-stable tonic without any gesture toward a typical MC. In either situation one confronts a "failed" (or gesturally weak?

or obstinate?) TR that, still in the grip of the grounding tonal principle of the P-zone, dwells on an unusually static tonic. This emphasis, in turn, demands analytical and hermeneutic interpretation.

The classic example occurs in the first movement of Mozart's String Quintet in G Minor, K. 516. In this extraordinary exposition the negative pull of G minor is apparently so strong that TR (beginning in m. 9 as a TR of the dissolving-consequent type) finds itself unable to escape its control. The result is one of the bleakest MCs in the repertory, the i:PAC at m. 29. The preceding, *forte* i:PAC at m. 24, Neapolitan-enhanced (m. 23) and brusquely closing the door on the fatalistic G minor, foreshadows this MC-effect. What intervenes in mm. 25–29 is a "timid," failed attempt to wrest free of the clutches of G minor through a momentary glance at VI. Being drawn back once again to G minor and to the i:PAC in mm. 27–29 is chilling—a second confirmation of the countergeneric inability to escape from the gravitational negativity of the tonic. The S that follows in m. 30 (the rhetorical signals make it clear that this is S) begins in the same, inescapable G minor and finally manages to hoist itself up to the proper mediant major in mm. 36–37 (although further damage to S is also apparent in subsequent measures).

It may also happen that a longer stretch of caesura-fill, branching out from the tonic authentic cadence at the end of TR, is called upon to accomplish the modulation to the new key. This is uncommon in eighteenth-century works but turns up occasionally in works in the nineteenth century, as in the first movement of Schubert's Symphony No. 8 in B Minor, "Unfinished," D. 759, first movement—i:IAC MC at m. 38 (perhaps interpretable as a i:PAC), with a modulatory caesura-fill leading to an S-space in G major that begins in m. 42.[8]

---

7. Haydn often gives us an emphatic V:PAC at a point where it is difficult to decide what its intended function might be: EEC? MC? witty or purposefully "difficult" gesture? Is its very point to place us in an ambiguous interpretive position? Or might it be the articulation of a different (third?) type of exposition altogether—perhaps one customized by Haydn for individual use or perhaps one known to him from more local traditions?

(Similar situations crop up also in midcentury sonatas of less well-known composers) However one regards it, this V:PAC option (not too far past the midpoint of the exposition) is one of the important features of Haydn's conception of sonata form.

8. Related instances would include modulatory CF passages following a purposefully "wrong-key" MC, such as that in first movement of Schubert's Piano Sonata

The Medial Caesura: Common Characteristics

Within Allegro compositions (first movements and finales, most overtures) the medial caesura is often the final moment of articulation following one or more measures of preparation on a prolonged structural dominant (dramatically sustaining the earlier arrival of a I:HC or V:HC). A common sequence of events is: (1) the initial stages of TR, by and large consistently gaining in energy; (2) the attaining of the structural dominant by means of a half-cadence arrival (usually either a V:HC or a I:HC—or the minor-mode-sonata equivalents), which is frequently then locked onto as a literal or implied pedal-point (*structural-dominant lock*); (3) the prolongation of this still-active V (V_A) and the rhetorical drive to the medial caesura—a drive that sustains or even increases the energy accumulated thus far; (4) the articulation of the MC proper, the terminal gesture of the entire process. Example 3.1 shows the opening of the first movement of Mozart's Piano Sonata in D, K. 284: TR begins in m. 9; the half-cadence arrival and the dominant-lock (I:HC), holding fast onto that V_A, occur in m. 17; the second-level default MC (I:HC MC—the concluding gesture of a prolonged half-cadence process) is articulated in m. 21; S ensues in m. 22.

Not all Allegro compositions articulate all four of these events. It is possible—for a less rhetorical effect—to sound the MC at the moment of the arrival of the half cadence, thus omitting the structural-dominant lock altogether. This would be an instance of a nonelaborate, straightforward articulation of the MC. Generally considered—and if not overridden by other evidence—if TR produces a notable HC that is immediately followed by an "acceptable" new theme in the proper subordinate key, that HC may be interpreted as a medial caesura. (Put another way, the situation is staged as if the apparent S-theme has "understood" that HC to have been one.) An example may be found in the first movement of Mozart's Piano Sonata in C, K. 309, in which TR begins in m. 21 and the structural dominant is reached only with the arrival of the V:HC MC in m. 32. In addition, many slow movements—generally lyrical movements—omit the dominant-lock. The MC-effect in these gentler movements is often produced by a mere half cadence without much additional rhetorical emphasis. (The situation in the C-major Andante movement of Mozart's Piano Sonata in G, K. 283, is typical: V:HC MC in m. 8.) It may be that any prolonged dominant-lock in slow movements was intended as an unusually strong or expansive gesture.

Normally, however, in Allegro movements, in order to function as a normative medial caesura, the *forte* half-cadence arrival within TR must be additionally reinforced. The whole process often proceeds as follows:

1. The structural dominant (the half-cadence arrival, which typically precedes the MC, sometimes by several measures) is often approached through a chromatically altered predominant harmony that contains $\sharp\hat{4}$. (This scale-step is reckoned in the key within which the half cadence is to be sounded. In the case of directed motion into a V:HC, $\hat{4}$ of the new key would be $\sharp\hat{1}$ of the original tonic.) This altered predominant is frequently an applied chord (V/V, V^7/V, vii°/V, or vii°^{7}/V in root position or inversion) or an augmented sixth chord.[9] The chromatic line $\hat{4}-\sharp\hat{4}-\hat{5}$ or $\hat{3}-\sharp\hat{4}-\hat{5}$ often appears in one

in C, D. 279. Here we have an unequivocal arrival on the "wrong dominant," iii:HC (V of E minor!) at m. 37, which V_A is immediately frozen as a dominant-lock ending with a iii:HC MC, mm. 37–41. Four bars of expanded fill, mm. 41–44, accomplish the modulation to the generically proper key, G major (V), in which S then begins, m. 45.

9. According to Allen Cadwallader and David Gagné, *Analysis of Tonal Music: A Schenkerian Approach* (New York: Oxford University Press, 1998), p. 409, n. 23 (referring to a situation in the first movement of Beethoven's Piano Sonata in G, op. 49 no. 2, discussed on pp. 311–29), when the half cadence arrival is preceded by its own applied dominant (V of V, V^6 of V, and so on), "we might refer to this goal as a *tonicized half cadence*." While accurate, this terminology might be potentially confusing. This surely means only that an unequivocal half cadence is locally supported by its own dominant. One continues to experience that dominant arrival as an active V, as V_A, not as a tonic (V_T), particularly in "lighter" cases of a mere $\hat{4}-\sharp\hat{4}-\hat{5}$ or $\hat{3}-\sharp\hat{4}-\hat{5}$ motion in one of the outer voices—where any sense of "tonicization" in the normal sense of the word is virtually nonexistent. Thus there can be no claim that anything like a "full" tonicization of that V_A has occurred: the arrival on V is still a half cadence, not a concretized

of the outer voices ($\hat{4}-\sharp\hat{4}-\hat{5}$ as the bass-line approach to V_A is especially characteristic); if an augmented sixth chord is employed, the typical bass line is $\flat\hat{6}-\hat{5}$ and the $\sharp\hat{4}-\hat{5}$ move occurs in the upper voice.[10] The texture at this moment is vigorous, highly active; the dynamics, usually a strong *forte*, will persist or even gain in intensity in the subsequent drive to the medial caesura.

As mentioned earlier, within major-mode sonatas it is not uncommon to encounter inter-mixtures with the minor mode, perhaps even a shift to the minor mode—usually that of the new key—in the vicinity of this half-cadence arrival or dominant-lock point, although, if this occurs at all, it may also take place earlier or later in TR, perhaps even persisting through the MC itself. An appearance of the negative minor mode participates in the generic expectation of the intensification process, either enhancing it or engaging in some other kind of dialogue with it. The mixture with minor may suggest the introduction of uncertainty, doubt, or peril into the narrative thread—or (as sometimes in Beethoven) the onset of a grim struggle in the production of the MC and S. Following such a modal shift, the ensuing *major-mode* S emerges with a sense of brightness and relief.

2. Once attained, the structural dominant is frequently prolonged, perhaps by neighbor motion, as part of the drive to the MC proper (*dominant-lock*). This may involve alternating V with a neighboring $^{6}_{4}$, producing $^{\hat{5}-\hat{6}-\hat{5}}_{\hat{3}-\hat{4}-\hat{3}}$ neighbor motion. Sometimes the neighboring $^{6}_{4}$ is supported by $\hat{1}$ in the bass, creating an apparent V–I–V alternation. The larger point, though, is that the V_A of the half-cadence arrival is vigorously seized onto, frozen in place, kept alive by means of a specialized pedal-point effect that announces that TR is ending with a continued push toward the MC. The sense of an "HC-moment" is not released and left behind as a mere past event—as happens with most other kinds of HC phrase endings—but rather is held onto, brandished as an achievement, sustained as a continuing function with a specific role to play at this point in the form.[11]

3. The normative, unflagging drive in the space between the locking onto the structural dominant and the actual articulation of the MC is of paramount importance. Any attenuation of dynamics here should be viewed as countergeneric, or perhaps—especially by the later eighteenth century—as a less common, second-level default that calls attention to itself and challenges the prevailing norm of energy-gain. Depending on the circumstances a dynamic collapse in this space might represent the staging of a momentary crisis of confidence in one's decision to enter S-space. The S that follows the dynamically underprepared MC might

---

tonicization of that V. The difficulties of interpretation increase, however, as the sense of that "tonicization" becomes increasingly intense with differing strengths of applied dominants to the V_A. (It is possible to imagine a continuum of differing applied-chord strengths, for instance, that ultimately lead one to cases that appear to articulate a V:PAC as the MC.)

10. For a stronger sense of rhetorical emphasis it is possible to approach the structural dominant—or half-cadence arrival—more than once in fairly rapid succession. Thus once the structural dominant is sounded, it can be immediately re-sounded through energetic reiterations of the half cadence. The music can go through the cadence several times, reapproaching and rearticulating it, helping to produce the rhetorical drive toward the MC proper. The touchstone example occurs in the first movement of Beethoven's Piano Sonata in F Minor, op. 2 no. 1, where the predominant $\hat{4}-\sharp\hat{4}-\hat{5}$ bass motion preceding the half-cadence arrival is first stated in mm. 15–16, then restated twice more, mm. 17–18, 19–20. (M. 20 is the MC proper, but, unusually, it also initiates a dominant-lock and the onset of an S^0 (or $S^{1.0}$)

theme, over that V. Such S-theme beginnings are discussed in ch. 7.

11. Thus our view differs from that of Caplin ("The Classical Cadence," passim, but see especially pp. 89–91, 98–100, 108–12), who, as mentioned above (n. 6), regards this dominant-lock as "postcadential" in function. We find it preferable to think of this stretch of music not so much as existing "after" the half-cadence arrival (which in a literal sense, it does) as keeping that arrival alive, refusing to let it go, animatedly spreading its sense of being still active over several more measures. Put another way, the dominant-lock may be considered a special prolongational technique that extends and "holds in place" the HC-arrival effect for a specific rhetorical purpose. See also n. 14. Caplin's English-language term for such harmonic locks is "standing on the dominant," a translation of Erwin Ratz's "stehen auf der Dominante," which had appeared in the latter's *Einführung in die musikalische Formenlehre* (3rd ed., enl., 1973). (See Caplin, "The Classical Cadence," especially p. 90, n. 101; and Caplin, *Classical Form*, pp. 16 ("postcadential standing on the dominant"), 75, 77–78, 144–45.)

EXAMPLE 3.1   Mozart, Piano Sonata in D, K. 284, i, mm. 1–24

Example 3.1 (*continued*)

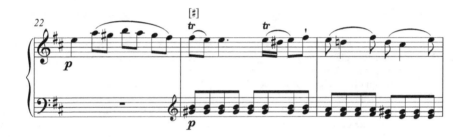

compensate for this enervation (as is suggested also at the end of no. 6).

4. At the point of the MC proper—the whole passage's terminal gesture—one often hears several *forte* hammer-blows (three is the most common number; two are also not infrequent) that ostentatiously reiterate the final dominant chord.[12] The hammer-blow effect is a common means of simultaneously bringing the energy-gain of TR to a terminal peak and beginning to discharge that tension for the subsequent drop to S (see nos. 5 and 6). The first hammer blow typically falls on a strong beat, normally on a strongly accented measure of hypermeter. The triple-hammer-blow effect may be disguised or embellished through inner subdivision of the relevant beats. (See also the similar variant in example 3.1, m. 21.) Particularly characteristic is the disposition of the hammer blows—when they are present—in such a way that the second (or second and third) is sounded an octave below the first. Within melodic phrase endings Koch referred to this formulaic octave-drop gesture (on weak beats or measures) both as a type of *Nachschlag* (a "striking afterward"—although clearly all second and third hammer blows are also a kind of *Nachschlag* regardless of octave disposition) and as a "Cäsur" that has been provided with an "Ueberhang" (an "overhanging") or "einen weiblichen Ausgang" ("a feminine ending").[13] Ascending octave leaps—presumably more energetic and expectant than descending ones—are also possible as part of this *Nachschlag* figure.

5. At the point of the MC one frequently encounters a general pause (GP), or rest, in all voices. This is one of the hallmarks of an unequivocal MC (the word "caesura" means a pause or a break in the texture), and it signals the precise arrival of the medial caesura. The silence of the caesura-gap is a watershed

moment relinquishing the preceding drive and energy-gain: it articulates and represents *energy-loss,* thus initiating, usually, the subsequent drop to *piano* for S. From the vantage-point of TR the point is that a higher level of activity and energy has been now attained: the gears have shifted, and we are now prepared to enter the next stage of the exposition. In the normative mid- or late-eighteenth-century style this GP-gap typically lasts for only a beat or two (a "quick breath")—perhaps for a bar, but rarely longer. Moreover, it is certainly possible—even normative—to fill this brief gap with sound, perhaps a held note or simple scalar connective figure in one voice: we call this common procedure *caesura-fill.* This is discussed in a separate section below.

When S begins with an upbeat, that upbeat might occupy the implied GP-gap. In other words, the MC will be sounded normatively, but at the precise moment that one would expect a gap of silence, the upbeat for S ensues, dovetailed into the GP-gap. Example 3.2 provides an illustration, the TR and MC of the first movement of Mozart, Piano Sonata in D, K. 311. Following a half-cadence arrival and dominant-lock in m. 13 (introduced via a normative $\hat{4} - \sharp\hat{4} - \hat{5}$ motion in the bass), the I:HC MC occurs normatively in m. 16 (with implied hammer blows on beats 1, 2, and 3). Instead of encountering a rest (GP-gap) on the fourth beat of m. 16, we find that S begins (*piano*) with an upbeat to m. 17.

Toward the later decades of the eighteenth century (and even more so in the nineteenth) composers began to explore the effects of widening that caesura gap—opening it to a span of three, four, or more bars—and filling it with connective caesura-fill (representing energy-loss) that might serve a variety of expressive purposes. At first this widening may have

12. Within the mid- and late-eighteenth-century style the triple-hammer-blow gestures (and variants thereof) are formulaic markers of important points of structural articulation. When they are present in the exposition, they are most likely to occur as indicators of one or more of three crucial spots: the exposition's beginning; the point of the MC; the conclusion of the exposition. Needless to say, they often also appear in the same spots in the recapitulation: hence midcentury and even late-

century pieces often end with references to the triple hammer blows.
13. Koch, *Versuch einer Anleitung zur Composition,* part 2, p. 394 (within subsection 95 and subsequent subsections, which deal with the central concept of the caesura). See also Koch, *Introductory Essay on Composition,* trans. Nancy Kovaleff Baker, pp. 23–24 (the translation used here).

Example 3.2   Mozart, Piano Sonata in D, K. 311, i, mm. 7–18

been considered a deformation (a purposeful, significant distortion or overriding of the norm), but it soon became a common option (though still an expressive one) within the style.

6. Immediately following the MC proper (after the implied or actual GP-gap), one expects to find the launching of a characteristic secondary theme (S)—which may exemplify any of a number of types. (See chapter 7.) One of the most common types features a sudden change of texture after the MC-point, usually combined with a precipitous drop from an energetic *forte* to *piano* and the unfolding of a melody articulating the second expositional key. This abrupt dynamic/textural change suggests the immediate emergence of a normative rhetorical candidate for S-status (the onset of the second part of the exposition), an emergence that confirms the MC-status of the preceding HC. Particularly in large-scale compositions, this criterion is crucial: the change of texture and/or dynamics functions as a standard gesture that accepts and ratifies the preceding caesura as the MC. Refusing to initiate any of the characteristic opening types of an S-theme at this moment may signal that the preceding, proposed MC is being declined by subsequent events.

But to this general norm of the *piano* S, probably the most standard option, one should add a word of caution. Although it cannot be maintained that the beginning of an S-theme can never be articulated at a *forte* dynamic level—bustling or energetic S-ideas are especially common in midcentury orchestral works—in the context of the later eighteenth century such suddenly blurted or surging S-themes are almost invariably reactive to some earlier complication in the TR zone (especially to a complication in the MC, one type of which is suggested in no. 3 above). To be sure, the unusual, *forte* S may be found to great effect here and there in Mozart and Beethoven, but it seems to have been of special interest to the mature, ever-inventive Haydn, in whose works the S-ness of the *forte* theme, when it occurs, is usually identifiable through its monothematic incipit, recalling P. (It is encountered in several of the "London" Symphonies, with locally clever implications, as in the first movement of Symphony No. 99 in E flat, m. 48.)

As another illustration of these principles, the V:HC medial caesura in the first movement of Haydn's Symphony No. 104 (example 3.3) is reinforced by conditions 1 (approach to the dominant through V_5^6/V, with $\hat{4}-\sharp\hat{4}-\hat{5}$ in the bass, mm. 56–57), 2 (prolongation of V_A by $\hat{5}-\hat{6}-\hat{5}/\hat{3}-\hat{4}-\hat{3}$ neighbor motion, mm. 57–62) fortified by a constant energy-gain up to the MC, 3 (unflagging energy-drive to the MC), 4 (three hammer-blows, mm. 63–64), 5 (general pause, m. 64), and 6 (change of texture and emergence of the new key, m. 65). The III:HC medial caesura in the first movement of Mozart's Symphony No. 40 in G minor, K. 550 (example 3.4) is also bolstered by these six features. Here the dominant (the half-cadence arrival) is approached through V^7/V (mm. 34–37), the neighboring $\frac{6}{4}$ motion is expanded to include vii^{o7}/V over a dominant pedal, and there are only two hammer blows (m. 42, including the characteristic octave drop). Because these two medial caesuras are reinforced by the same conditions, they may be heard as roughly equivalent in strength.

Similarly, one might recall the I:HC (second-level-default) medial caesura in the first movement of Beethoven's Symphony No. 1 in C, op. 21, m. 52. Here we find the GP gap, m. 52 (two quarter rests); the triple hammer blows leading up to it, mm. 51–52; the preparatory (pre-MC) $\hat{4}-\sharp\hat{4}-\hat{5}$ motion (in the tonic) in the bass, mm. 44–45; the alternation of V with a neighboring $\frac{6}{4}$, mm. 45–51 (here also anticipating the hammer blows); the drop to piano dynamics for S at m. 53. Even though we are confronting a second-level-default MC (one that marks the endpoint of a nonmodulating TR), this MC may also be considered a paradigm: it is normative in just about every way imaginable.

The Deployment Sequence of Medial Caesura Options

Another issue surrounding the identification of a medial caesura is its temporal (proportional) appropriateness—its precise placement within an exposition. This is complicated by the fact that an MC (including the possibility of a third-level default, V:PAC in major-mode works)

EXAMPLE 3.3 Haydn, Symphony No. 104 in D, i, mm. 54–66

could occur anywhere from about 15 to 70 percent of the way through an exposition. To be sure, this is a broad expanse of expositional space, even though most cases fall before the halfway point. Our research suggests that the deployment of the I:HC MC is flexible, occurring typically within the 15–45 percent range. Noteworthy here is the early availability of the I:HC MC. Beyond the 45 percent point—and especially in grand-scale works, such as symphonies, often earlier than this—the I:HC MC seems to have been considered either eclipsed or increasingly and rapidly left behind as a practical option. This reinforces our earlier observation that the I:HC MC was appropriate for shorter works, and indeed for more modest works it may be a more commonly selected option than the V:HC MC.

We have proposed, however, that for most analysts the conceptual reference is likely to be more ambitious in moderate- to large-scale movements, within which it is more accurate to regard the I:HC MC as the second-level default (after the V:HC MC). This results in the seemingly paradoxical situation in which the second-level default I:HC MC (which only means the one less commonly selected) is the first temporally available MC-deployment option. Some expositions even take up this norm of temporal MC availability as part of their compositional strategy. An exposition, for example, might make an early feint toward the I:HC option (by seeming to move toward or even onto the relevant structural dominant) only to renounce it or pass it by in order to produce a later V:HC or V:PAC MC. In this situation, when a I:HC is actually articulated *en route* as a seeming point-of-arrival and a dominant-lock begun on that V$_A$—as though it were charging normatively toward an imminent I:HC MC—such an attained lock would have to be shaken off (or "unfrozen") with a decisive plunge into further harmonic activity that now leads the music toward a modulation and a quite different

Example 3.4 Mozart, Symphony No. 40 in G Minor, K. 550, i, mm. 28–47

MC option. A classic instance may be found in the first movement of Mozart's Quartet in B-flat, K. 172. Standard $\hat{4}-\sharp\hat{4}-\hat{5}$ motion in the bass (on the last beat of m. 17) leads to what at first seems to be an "attempt" to sound a I:HC structural-dominant-lock in mm. 18–22 (albeit one decorated through oscillations with its own V_3^6 in mm. 19 and 21). A set of largely parallel, descending $^6_3$ chords, enhanced with 7–6 suspensions, shakes loose of this dominant in mm. 23–25 and moves the music instead toward an abruptly produced V:HC MC in m. 26.[14] This witty effect, found also in many of Haydn's "Paris" and "London" Symphonies, can be that of demonstrating the compositional options that the composer is choosing *not* to deploy ("No! We *won't* use this I:HC MC option! Let's select something else instead! Onward!").

The normally available range for the more common, first-level-default V:HC MC overlaps broadly with that of the I:HC MC but in general occurs slightly later. When selected, the V:HC MC option is typically placed from about 25 to 50 percent (more rarely, 60 percent) of the way through the exposition.[15] Again, this suggests that the choice of either a V:HC MC or a I:HC MC also served to predict the proportions of the remainder of the exposition and hence of the remainder of the work. I:HC MCs promise

more compact works; V:HC MCs usually lead us to expect broader structures. The third-level default V:PAC MC is located in the 50–70 percent (very rarely, 75 percent) range. This is the last available deployment option, and, as mentioned earlier, it is sometimes encountered as a recovery from the staging of a failed attempt at producing a V:HC MC. Any strong caesura falling outside these boundaries is either an exceptional MC (in which case a cogent argument on its behalf would have to be offered) or, more often, no MC at all.

The precise percentage numbers admit of exceptions. More important than exact figures is the overarching principle of the normative deployment sequence of potential structural dominants and/or MCs. The initially available I:HC possibility soon overlaps with and eventually gives way to the V:HC option. If the V:HC option is not selected, the last chance to produce a two-part exposition resides with an appropriately placed V:PAC MC. Any relatively late V:PAC MC brings with it structural complications and potential ambiguities: Is it an MC or is it better regarded as the EEC?

The deployment sequence for major-mode sonatas may be represented diagrammatically (and roughly) as in figure 3.2. In summary, the important points to observe are: (1) the second-

---

14. In K. 172/i the emphatically sentential character of mm. 18–26—with the move away from the V_A of I only in the sentence's continuation—also contributes to this effect. Observing that mm. 18–26 are structured as a sentence, however, once again addresses the issue of Caplin's description of such post-HC dominant-locks as merely postcadential. (See the preceding remarks in nn. 6 and 11.) In K. 172/i such an assertion can lead one into contradictions, because, by Caplin's definitions, the presentation of a sentence is essentially precadential. In other words, by this logic what is claimed to start out postcadentially here—the initial dominant-lock—must also be regarded as simultaneously functioning precadentially as a sentence presentation, although in the case of K. 172/i one might observe this only in retrospect. Our mode of approaching such questions is to remain flexible, to realize that generically "predicted" behavior can and often does "change its mind" *en route* within this most mercurial of musical styles. One could even imagine other instances in which a dominant-lock that remains "locked" could be structured as a sentence—once again inviting the precadential-postcadential contradiction within Caplin's system.

15. From time to time Haydn's drive for unpredictable or non-normative originality produces extraordinary exceptions to this principle. What appears to be the V:HC MC in the first movement of Symphony No. 82 in C ("Bear"), for instance, occurs in m. 69, 68 percent of the way through the exposition. In part this occurs as a result of Haydn's earlier prolonged dalliance with the I:HC option. Jens Peter Larsen, "Sonata Form Problems," *Handel, Haydn, and the Viennese Classical Style* [orig. publ. as "Sonatenform-Probleme," in *Festschrift Friedrich Blume zum 70 Geburtstag*, ed. Anna Amalie Abert and Wilhelm Pfannkuch (Kassel: Barenreiter, 1963)], trans. Ulrich Krämer (Ann Arbor: UMI, 1988), p. 274, takes the following *piano* theme, m. 70, to be an archetypal example of the opening of the third part of a "three-part division of the exposition" (what we call a continuous exposition—the exposition-format discussed in ch. 4). In this case we disagree. Based both on the peculiar rhetorical narrative produced in TR and on the acceptably S-like rhetoric of the *piano* theme at m. 70, anticipated in the preceding drive to the MC, we believe it preferable to understand that theme as an extraordinarily late S.

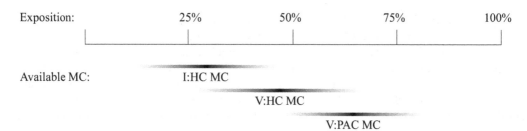

FIGURE 3.2   The Deployment Sequence of Medial-Caesura Options in Major-Mode Expositions

level default MC (I:HC) in terms of statistical occurrence is the first temporally available MC in the standard deployment sequence; (2) the first-level default MC (V:HC, the most common option in works of larger proportions) is the second temporally available MC in the standard deployment sequence; (3) the third-level default MC is the last temporally available MC in the standard deployment sequence.

As a general principle, each MC option is normally accessible only one time during an exposition. This may be considered the nonredundancy feature of medial caesura practice. To use a metaphorical illustration, it is as if at the outset the composer is given only one token for each of the potential MCs, and once that token has been spent (deployed) or has expired temporally, it is no longer on hand for later expositional reuse. Once one has declined a I:HC MC, gestured mildly at that MC (as if considering it) and passed it over, or extended TR beyond its normal deployment space, then the I:HC is no longer available as an MC. At that point one shifts to the next option, the V:HC. If the V:HC is declined or passed by (or fails to stick), then, in most cases, the only option remaining is the V:PAC MC, which, if placed late in the exposition, can cause difficulties by its being taken for a premature EEC. Haydn, in particular, delighted in the deployment sequence and its potential for witty and expressive implication. The main exceptions to the nonredundancy feature of MC options occur—infrequently—either in a backing-up and recapturing of an already planted medial caesura (in effect moving back in compositional time to revisit an earlier moment and recompose its continuation) or, with something of the same effect, in certain unusual

dispositions of the trimodular block strategy (TMB), an apparent-double-medial-caesura effect within expositions that is discussed further in chapter 8.

Caesura-Fill (CF)

The literal presence of the general-pause gap (the brief rest in all voices before the onset of S) is the most normative option at the medial-caesura point, especially in the mid- and late-eighteenth century. Almost as common, however, is the technique of implying that gap but filling it in with a brief sonic link in one voice (or, sometimes, in more than one). One function of this link is to articulate with sound the most important expressive obligation of this moment: the representation of the *energy-loss* that bridges the vigorous end of TR (MC) to what is frequently the low-intensity beginning of S (part 2).

We refer to this filling-in of the generically implied silence—plugging the MC gap—as *caesura-fill (CF)*. Caesura-fill is part of neither TR nor S: it represents the sonic articulation of the gap separating the two zones. It should not be confused with another possibility, mentioned above: filling the caesura-gap with the upbeat to S. Haydn, Mozart, Beethoven, and other composers sometimes treated caesura-fill in inventive and expressive ways. At times the nature of this CF can help to determine the character of what follows. When the implied GP-gap is brief (a beat or two, the mid-eighteenth-century norm), the presence of caesura-fill presents no problem of identification. The fill-music consists, usually, of a single held voice, as in the first movement of Haydn's Symphony No. 100 in G, "Military," slightly expanded to two bars in mm. 73–74, or a perfunctory linear descent in a single voice from $\hat{5}$ to $\hat{1}$ (or, perhaps, from $\hat{5}$ to $\hat{3}$) in the new key (see the discussion below, "caesura-fill of the $\hat{5}-\hat{1}$ type"), as in the finale of Mozart's Piano Sonata in B-flat, K. 281, m. 27.

But the issue can become more complicated. In some situations the GP-gap is pulled apart, expanded to two, three, four, or more measures, and filled with more crafted material. Creating this wider caesura-gap, a space of nonmotion or relative stasis between the more active TR and S, may reflect a particularly elegant shaping of the caesura-moment (similar to the exquisite crafting of a corner of a prized eighteenth-century table); it may suggest the need for a larger space of energy-loss after a particularly vigorous TR; it may suggest a moment of wit, surprise, or strain within otherwise normatively constructed surroundings; it may even, in rare cases (particularly from Schubert onward), be called upon to accomplish a modulation to the generically proper new key following a deformationally "wrong-key" or other problematic sounding of the MC.[16] Whatever its intended effect, widening the customarily short caesura-gap requires that something more composed will have to fill it—some sort of connective leading us across the blank from the MC point proper to the onset of S. We refer to this as *expanded caesura-fill*. Again, conceptually it belongs to neither TR nor S, although motivically it may look backward or forward to the one or the other.

Expanded caesura-fill provides an opportunity for careful compositional fashioning, elegant or special effects, wit, or an exquisitely poised attenuation of previously gained energy combined with a psychological preparation for the S-to-come. Because the underlying, implied GP-gap represents energy-loss, expanded CF will normally feature a *diminuendo* preparing the onset of S. Any persistence of a *forte* dynamic throughout an expanded CF—perhaps with a

sudden collapse to *piano* at the end—would be an overriding of the norm calling for special interpretation (as in the "juggernaut" type discussed below). The same would be true of any countergeneric *crescendo* within a passage of expanded caesura-fill.

Certain kinds of expanded caesura-fill were used often enough—or were used in such well-known pieces—that they became recognizable, generic options for later composers. One, already mentioned above, was caesura-fill of the $\hat{5}-\hat{1}$-descent type ($\hat{5}-\hat{1}$ linear fill). This can follow a V:HC MC, which always has $\hat{5}$ of the new key in the bass and may also have that $\hat{5}$ in the highest voice. Here the task of the two, three, or more measures of caesura-fill is to guide the ear, either in the upper or the lower register, from the $\hat{5}$ at the MC moment to the $\hat{1}$ that begins S. In other words, this kind of caesura-fill (which can be either of normal or expanded length) leads from the V:HC down to the tonic pitch of the newly established V, as though the fill's task were to lay down the tonic platform on which S will make its appearance.

At times the $\hat{5}-\hat{1}$ descent might suggest something cadential: it will seem that the V:HC is being led to an authentic cadence in the dominant. In most instances such an event is better considered a secondary, linear move that directs our attention from the harmonic interruption on V (the medial caesura) to the restart on the new tonic that follows. Nevertheless, strong occurrences can give the impression of rejecting the originally sounded V:HC MC by converting it decisively into a V:PAC ("Not there . . . but *here!*") An illustration occurs in the first movement of Mozart's Sonata for Two Pianos in D, K. 448/375a, Example 3.5. Here one finds a V:HC MC-effect at m. 25; what follows is an extended passage of caesura-fill that expands beyond generic norms of appropriate length and leads to its own V:PAC in m. 33. That V:PAC serves as the "real" MC, and S begins, in A major, in m. 34.[17]

---

16. See n. 8 and its related text for two examples from Schubert.
17. For additional examples—from the opening movements of Beethoven's first two piano trios, op. 1 nos. 1 and 2—see our discussion in "The Medial Caesura,"

pp. 128–29. Cf. also the remarks concerning the Piano Trio No. 1 in G, op. 1 no. 2, in n. 6 above (in part a reply to terminological criticism of our analysis by William E. Caplin).

EXAMPLE 3.5   Mozart, Sonata for Two Pianos in D, K. 448/375*a*, i,
mm. 23–35

EXAMPLE 3.5 *(continued)*

Such examples suggest, as already mentioned in our discussion on third-level default MCs, that expanded caesura-fill $\hat{5}-\hat{1}$ motion may have been a conceptual source of one type of the third-level default V:PAC medial caesura. One should also note that, especially from time to time in Mozart's hands, one comes across even more extended examples, situations that one might wish to set apart and designate as extraordinarily expanded caesura-fill, in which the CF persists for a longer period of time and can even display a marked thematic character as it "floats," almost airborne, through the normative caesura gap, eventually to terminate with a V:PAC, sometimes leading to S proper and sometimes not (moving instead directly into closing material). Three prominent examples in Mozart—seemingly interrelated among themselves—are: a prominent, deliciously extended passage of CF from the solo exposition of the first movement of the Sinfonia Concertante in E-flat, K. 364, mm. 106–25; the curiously prolonged CF in the first movement of Mozart's Symphony in D, K. 385, "Haffner," mm. 48–58 (though with a V:IAC, not a V: PAC, in m. 58);[18] and the similar passage of CF in the opening ritornello of the first movement of Piano Concerto No. 13 in C, K. 415, mm. 24–36 (which in this case, displaces any normative second theme and proceeds directly into what we regard as ritornello-closing material at m. 36).[19]

It also seems likely that this type of expanded fill—when carried out at considerable length (perhaps over a dozen measures) and when marked by a persistent, gentle, *decrescendo* yielding to the S that follows—is the source of the mid- and later-nineteenth-century procedure that we call the *de-energizing transition*. Assuming that in its sheer extent one might also hear such expanded CF as seeking to be understood

as part of TR (as opposed to the norm, existing merely in the gap after it), this produces the effect of a broader TR that toward its end, counter to the eighteenth-century norm, seems to lose energy, not to gain it. We find this "Romantic," prolonged, gentle approach to S, for example, in the first movements of Schumann's Symphony No. 4 and Brahms's Symphonies No. 2 and 3. Apparently, in fully developed instances of the de-energizing TR, the MC could be obscured or perhaps not even articulated at all (at least in any clear way). For this reason its historical roots also lie in eighteenth-century "blocked-caesura" effects, discussed separately below.

Related to linear descents of the $\hat{5}-\hat{1}$ type would be any instances of caesura-fill linear *ascent*, typically in the upper voice, from $\hat{5}$ to $\hat{8}$ or even to the $\hat{3}$ above that. One such occurrence within a much-expanded CF may be found in the initial orchestral ritornello of the first movement of Mozart's Piano Concerto No. 24 in C Minor, K. 491. Here the rhetorical i:HC MC is sounded in m. 34, complete with *Nachschlag* and GP-gap, albeit one filled in with still-pulsating horns on the dominant. The much-expanded, ascending fill picks up on the horns' dominant pitch and ascends, mostly chromatically, from G_4 to $E\flat_5$ in the oboe, then the flute, in mm. 35–44. (The fill's onset after the GP-gap is also unusual—suggesting a dialogue with what we call the S^0 or $S^{1.0}$ principle.) Once attained, the $E\flat_5$ in m. 44 launches the tutti rotation's S-space. While this effect does not appear in the subsequent solo exposition, it does surface again in the recapitulation, mm. 435–44 (though minus the original horn prompting).

A second option for expanded treatment may be called *caesura-fill of the "juggernaut" type*. In this procedure the motivic drive and rhetorical energy of the preceding TR are so great that they spill over the MC proper, invading

---

18. The "Haffner" example introduces further complications. The V:IAC at m. 58 seems to launch a standard "C-theme" type—the *forte* P-based C (ch. 9)—but in fact, retrospectively, this is apparently an instance of that type of theme "invading" what is otherwise the apparent vacuum of S-space, perhaps wittily "baited" into this through the preceding expanded CF. In this astonishingly non-normative exposition—one of Mozart's most deformational, on which our own opinions

have fluctuated several times—we currently place the EEC at m. 74, with "new" C-material at m. 75. Differing readings of mm. 59–94, however, are certainly possible.

19. Cf. also the opening ritornello of the Flute Concerto in G, K. 313, mm. 15–23, 70–79. See additionally the discussion of this procedure in ch. 20, n. 28, and surrounding text.

the expanded MC-gap with continued *forte* energy, momentarily refusing to lose energy in the normative, generic way. Often the juggernaut, *forte* effect will last all the way up to S, where it will either collapse back to *piano* or be suddenly hushed for the S-theme proper.

One clear instance occurs in Mozart's Symphony No. 39 in E-flat, K. 543, first movement. Here one encounters a clear V:HC MC with octave-drop *Nachschlag* in m. 90. Mozart suggests in this case, however, that the MC-articulation is insufficient to stop the juggernaut, triple-time momentum. Directly with the sounding of the MC there ensues an expanded caesura-fill, featuring $\hat{5}-\hat{4}-\hat{3}-\hat{2}-\hat{1}$ linear motion in the strings, presumably still *forte* (mm. 91–97), that arrives on the new tonic B-flat (*sfp*), with the effect both of a pseudocadence and, perhaps, of a finally-exhausted gasp (m. 97). The ensuing S (apparently with its "metrical head" spinning from the effects of what has preceded it) begins at m. 98, *piano*, in the key of the dominant. An earlier (and simpler) case of such high nerves at the MC point may be consulted in Mozart's Serenade in D, K. 204, first movement, mm. 27–28 (I:HC MC at m. 27), leading finally to a sudden drop to piano for S in m. 29. A later example may be found in Beethoven's Symphony No. 2 in D, op. 36, first movement, mm. 71–72, which is also, as it happens, an illustration of CF of the $\hat{5}-\hat{1}$-descent type.

Medial Caesura Declined

Not infrequently, one finds early on an MC-effect (usually a I:HC) that does not lead to a satisfactory S-theme. The impression is that of offering a potential MC but brusquely declining to accept it as such, preferring instead to remain within pre-MC space and defer the real MC (of which only first- and third-level defaults are now available, according to the principle of non-redundancy within the deployment sequence) until later. This rejection of an MC offer is what we call *medial caesura declined*; the MC-effect it-self is referred to as a *proposed MC*.[20] Medial caesura declined is a strong gesture, an emphatic device used for expressions of willfulness, caprice, self-assertion, a sudden change of mind ("No!"), and so on. Occasionally—though by no means invariably—medial-caesura-declined effects will also be in dialogue with one type of trimodular block (TMB) strategy. (The two procedures may be profitably considered alongside one another. Our discussion of the TMB occurs in chapter 8.)

The subsequent music may decline an apparent MC in a number of ways. One is by returning to the P theme, still in the tonic, as if rebeginning. Although this situation is in dialogue with the principle of medial caesura declined (since the reinforced I:HC could have been used by the composer as an MC), it is a very mild instance of it. Normally this sort of thing occurs early within a composition, and the I:HC quasi-MC effect articulates the concluding moments of what we call a *grand antecedent*—a lengthy, multimodular antecedent idea that constitutes the first extended limb of P. A grand antecedent, sometimes ending with quasi-MC rhetorical emphasis, will usually be followed by the onset of a *grand consequent* (including the return to the initial P in the tonic), although one that usually soon dissolves into more recognizable TR-activity. (Our discussion of this common procedure, including the citation of examples—such as the opening of Mozart's Symphony No. 40 in G Minor, K. 550—will be deferred until chapter 5.)

A second way to decline a I:HC MC is by remaining in the tonic key, even though a new theme is sounded. Following the proposed I:HC MC, the music refuses to modulate, staying in the original tonic key and providing new material. In such cases the medial-caesura-declined status of the gesture is much clearer. The *locus classicus* occurs in the finale of Beethoven's Second Symphony. (Although this movement is a Type 4 sonata—a sonata-rondo—its expositional principles are those of unmixed sonata form.) Here one finds an early I:HC caesura at

---

20. A more thorough treatment of MC-declined, including closer analyses of examples and a more thorough discussion of what constitutes a satisfactory S, may be found in our essay "The Medial Caesura," pp. 138–45.

m. 25, one bearing many of the formulaic features of a typical MC. Certainly a standard S-theme could emerge at this point, although it would be early within the exposition to do so. And indeed, the new idea that follows (m. 26, *piano* and lyrical, emerging in cellos and basses) exhibits normative S-behavior in all respects save one: it is solidly anchored in the tonic key. After several broad tonic-dominant oscillations (perhaps suggesting the tonal process of a fugal exposition based upon a modulatory subject), it moves toward V/V (m. 44), whereupon a new thematic module reinvigorates TR-activity and presses toward a V:HC caesura finally articulated at m. 50. Two bars of caesura-fill lead to a new lyrical theme in the key of the dominant (m. 52, unmistakably S proper).[21]

A third way that an MC may be declined is by suddenly veering off into an unexpected or foreign key. This produces a tonal *non sequitur*, often suggesting a foreign, flat-side key or chord (♭III, ♭VI, and so on). Moreover, the subsequent music does not proceed efficiently to a PAC in the proper key. (If it does—a rare event in the eighteenth-century style—it might be better interpreted as an S-deformation, one that begins with an off-tonic disturbance, perhaps as the onset of an auxiliary cadence). Although the passage may begin lyrically, it usually moves rapidly into transitional or *Fortspinnung* texture, as if to demonstrate its non-S-status and reinforce its impact as a rejection of the proposed MC. After several measures this reinvigorated TR will produce the real MC—usually a V:HC MC, the next MC selection available within the normative deployment sequence.

The tonal unexpectedness of this type of declined medial caesura suggests an impulsive "No!" to the preceding caesura. Its effect differs according to its circumstances and manner of articulation (lyrical/nonlyrical; loud/soft). It might suggest a willful, *forte* assertion of personality or eccentricity; a dogged determination not

to succumb to a weak caesura; or, conversely, a momentary failure of nerve and tragic slippage onto the wrong key or into a zone of shadowy escape. Generally considered, it suggests either a decisive rejection of the offer to open S-space or a seeming (if temporary) inability to do so.

Paradigmatic examples of this procedure may be found in two Beethovenian first movements. The first occurs in the String Quartet in C Minor, op. 18 no. 4. Here the second-level default i:HC MC-effect is at m. 25; the effect of declining it happens at m. 26 through a shift to a new module, *non sequitur*, on the key of A-flat, VI of C minor—though beginning on the pitch of E♭—reinforced with a *fp* dynamic shock and a sequential seeking of a preferable III:HC MC. That MC is finally sounded in m. 33. A second, even clearer instance may be seen in his Violin Sonata No. 5 ("Spring") in F, op. 24. A I:HC MC-effect is unambiguously proposed in m. 25. This is emphatically declined by a sudden shift to a *fortissimo* scalar unfolding of V^7–I in A♭ (♭III in the key of F, ♭VI in the key of the coming C major) in mm. 26–28. As a result more TR ensues—something of a "corrective" TR by this point—and the "real" V:HC MC is laid down in m. 37.

A fourth, rarer option for MC declined occurs after a first-level default MC (V:HC or, in minor, III:HC or v:HC) when the new key is accepted but the music refuses to drop to *piano* and initiate a proper S-theme, thus reinvigorating TR-texture. Because the new key is accepted—and because *forte* S-themes are anything but unthinkable within the style—this situation is difficult to insist upon with any certainty. The analytical discomfort lies in our resistance to considering the new-key material to function as a proper S-theme—perhaps interpreting its vigor and TR-like *Fortspinnung* bluster and/or alarm as some kind of "No!" gesture. One should be cautious in asserting this type of MC-declined situation: one might, for ex-

---

21. The same rhetorical events in the recapitulation can strike us differently. Since tonic-*grounding*, not modulation, is the reigning principle there, the "new-tonic-theme" of the exposition, originally part of a thematized TR (m. 26), could be heard in the recapitulation as more legitimately S-like (m. 210), perhaps the on-

set of a recapitulatory trimodular block (with double MCs at mm. 209 and 234). This illustrates the potential of a recapitulation to reconceive—and often smooth over—structural difficulties planted within the exposition.

ample, be confronting either a normatively *forte* S or an S-deformation (in this case, a deformation of normative dynamics and texture), not a declining of the MC. In weighing a decision one might consider such things as the persistence or nonpersistence of TR-motives after the supposed MC.

We have argued elsewhere that a reasonable case for an MC declined might be made along these lines in the initial movement of Mozart's Symphony No. 20 in D, K. 133 (proposed V: HC MC in m. 34). More difficult—and more ambiguous—is the situation that occurs in the initial movement of Mozart's String Quartet in C, K. 465, "Dissonance," following the potential V:HC MC in m. 55. However we decide to interpret this remarkable passage (mm. 56–71), Mozart must have intended his best listeners to hear it as unusual. Our current preference is to hear it as an S-deformation (and hence not an example of MC declined), although we could imagine other interpretations.[22]

Deformation: The Blocked Medial Caesura

Occasionally one comes across MC-effects that are distortions or significant reworkings of normative practice: the MC-effect is in some way altered but yet made present conceptually in one way or another. One of the most common of these deformations—and the one most far-reaching in its historical consequences—is the *blocked medial caesura*. In these cases the energetic TR proceeds normatively and perhaps even provides a clear structural-dominant lock on the way to what would appear to promise to be a standard MC gesture. Shortly before the expected articulation of the MC chord, however, the *forte* music seems to run into a dynamic blockage (like the hitting of a wall) perhaps on a predominant chord or perhaps with the arrival of a cadential $^6_4$. Thus the drive to the normal MC completion is prematurely shattered in mid-phrase. At this point the dynamics will be suddenly reduced to *piano* (suggesting, perhaps

a caesura-fill texture), and a bridge-like arc of music is cast forth to connect the blocked MC (the predominant or $^6_4$ chord) to the S-theme proper. In other words, the MC-dynamic-effect is present (a sudden drop to *piano*), but that effect occurs prematurely, as though the energetic TR had been kept from its normative MC goal-chord.

The expressive impact of the whole is similar to that of observing a projectile cast forth and sailing in the empty space of air in order to land gracefully at its destination. The impression provided is that a normative CF-bridge cannot be built over the empty caesura-gap. Because the normative MC was not permitted to occur, one cannot properly anchor the CF on this side of the gap. Lacking this anchor, something else will have to be shot forth over the abyss, something that will land on the S-side of the chasm. The blocked-MC-effect usually results in an extended CF-like passage that ends with a gentle V:PAC elided or flush-juxtaposed with the onset of S.

Classic examples are found in the first movements of Haydn, Symphony No. 83 in G Minor ("Hen," new-key cadential $^6_4$ block at m. 41, III: PAC at m. 45); Mozart, Symphony No. 36 in C, K. 425 ("Linz," new-key ii[6]-chord block at m. 62, V:PAC at m. 71); and Mozart, Symphony No. 38 in D, K. 504 ("Prague," new-key vi-chord block at m. 95, exquisitely dovetailed V:PAC and launch of S at m. 97). Similarly instructive is Mozart's D-major Overture to *Idomeneo*, K. 366. Here, following the onset of TR at m. 23, a blocked MC occurs in m. 41 on a cadential $^6_4$ of the new key, A major. A de-energizing fill (mm. 41–45), begun in the first and second violins, thickens into a full-blown V:PAC at m. 45. At this cadence the mode shifts to an ominous A minor for the onset of a complex S. (See chapter 7 on minor-mode beginnings of S-themes.) A related, more deformational example occurs in the second movement (scherzo section) of Beethoven's Symphony No. 9 in D Minor, op. 125. Here the blocked-MC effect occurs on V of the new key (V/VII!) at

---

22. Both pieces are discussed in Hepokoski and Darcy, "The Medial Caesura," pp. 143–45.

m. 77—the effect of blockage comes from its sense of rash prematurity and incompleteness—and the subsequent VII:PAC (C major) is reached in m. 93, elided with the *fortissimo* S.

Exceptional in the decades around 1800, the blocked-MC effect would have telling repercussions in the nineteenth century. In confronting a work from the mid-1800s one should be less surprised to encounter a blocked (or even suppressed) MC, followed (or replaced) by a broadly expansive *de-energizing transition* with reduced dynamics or sounded in *diminuendo*, non-normative by earlier, eighteenth-century standards. In most cases a de-energizing transition falls to a PAC in the new key, thus unlocking the secondary-theme zone. (See also the mention of the de-energizing TR above, in the discussion of caesura-fill of the $\hat{5}$—$\hat{1}$ -descent type—which cited as examples the initial movements of Schumann's Symphony No. 4 and Brahms's Symphonies Nos. 2 and 3.)

Troubleshooting MC Identifications

Normally, there are two classes of problems that one might encounter: (1) identifying the moment of the MC seems possible, but what follows does not seem to be a convincing S; or (2) the identification of S seems clear—even unequivocal—but what precedes it does not seem to be a normative medial caesura.

In Situation 1—seeming MC but problematic S—one should consider four possibilities. First, one may be confronting a situation of medial caesura declined, as discussed above. Second, one might have misidentified the MC point. Is there a preferable, more effective MC point either earlier or later? One should be cautious about identifying any relatively early I:PAC (or IAC) as an MC: this is more likely to be the end of a lengthy P. When this seems not to be the case, one might recall that problematic I:HC MC situations may be intertwined with trimodular-block (TMB) issues (See also the discussion of the extremely rare fourth-level default MCs above.) Similarly, a late V:PAC within the exposition may be the EEC. Third, the problem with the subsequent S might be only apparent. Is it an S governed by

the new dominant key but one that happens to begin off-tonic (or off the tonic chord)? Is that S (beginning off-tonic) soon redirected onto the proper key? If so, then the initially proposed location of the MC was probably correct, and it is the discussion of the ensuing S that will have to be clarified and nuanced.

Fourth, the piece at this point might be introducing an S-deformation: an unusual, non-normative treatment of S. In this case the MC status of what precedes it remains secure. But before one comes to this conclusion, it is best to be certain that there are no better choices in the exposition for the MC and the S. One such S-deformation may be found in the E-major Largo of Beethoven's Piano Concerto No. 3 in C Minor, op. 37. A TR beginning in m. 25 leads to a clear V:HC MC in m. 34. Although we expect a normative S-theme to ensue, Beethoven provides only a brief, much-foreshortened cadential module, mm. 35–37, with V:PAC (EEC) at m. 37, effectively ending the exposition. Referring to mm. 35–37 merely as S seems counterintuitive: the extraordinary expansiveness of P and TR is brought here to an abrupt, disproportionate close. And yet, with the sounding of the MC, this is not a continuous exposition. One solution is to propose that mm. 35–37 are to be understood as an S-deformation—a jettisoning of any normative S in favor, still within S-space, of a brief cadential module.

In Situation 2—clear S but problematic MC (whose difficulties might be either harmonic or rhetorical, or both)—one should consider four possibilities. First, is there literally no conceivable MC at all, or is there a half cadence present that happens not to have been reinforced normatively? In other words, does the potentially "acceptable" S (perhaps starting off thematically as a sentence or period) at least follow a half cadence within TR? If so, as already mentioned, one could conclude that although the HC MC-effect is weak, S is nevertheless presented as though it were accepting that HC-arrival as a workable MC.

Second, if this is not the case, it would be wise to rethink one's analysis: perhaps one's identification of S is mistaken? Is there a better choice? Might we be dealing with a continuous exposition (one that lacks a medial caesura and an S)? This possibility is especially enticing if the composer is Haydn. One should remember that thematic events can happen within the broad center-section of a continuous exposition (chapter 4), especially around the point of the cadential module. It may be inappropriate to identify that moment as S merely because it momentarily "sounds thematic." One should do so only if the rhetoric of the presumed S-theme is compelling and normatively S-like in unmistakable ways, as suggested in the fourth possibility below.

Third, if what precedes the S is marked *diminuendo*, or with a dynamic lower than *mf*, one might be looking at a situation of expanded caesura-fill. This is even more likely if the preceding music ends with a V:PAC at the point that S begins. One should look for a clearer MC (usually V:HC) a few bars earlier, paying attention to the moment when *tutti* orchestration or a forte dynamic suddenly drops away. (In mid-nineteenth-century pieces—Schumann, Brahms, and so on—one might also be dealing with the special case of the de-energizing TR, as discussed above in connection with the blocked MC.)

Fourth, one might be confronting a genuinely unusual situation, an overriding of the norm—a medial caesura deformation. Once we have declared in favor of this solution, we should be prepared to propose an explanation for why the composer chose this option. Which expressive purposes seem to have been intended with this unusual treatment? How does the MC-deformation play into the narrative purposes of this exposition? Unequivocal S themes lacking a preceding MC are very rare. For this reason the burden of proof falls on one's conviction regarding the unmistakable S-signals of the proposed S-theme. In Haydn this situation is sometimes made more recognizable by the quirks of his own compositional practice. Here it is normative (albeit not invariable) to find that the S-theme is based on P. At times Haydn led his TR and MC-point into witty difficulties that had to be bailed out by the appearance of the normative S, even though that S was not fully released by a successful MC. Still, lacking a proper MC, such expositions thematize ambi-

guities and conceptual discomforts, which are sometimes played out cleverly in what follows in the rest of the structure.

The initial movement of Haydn's Piano Sonata in E-flat, Hob. XVI:52, is a textbook illustration of the uncertainties involved with these sorts of issues. Merely to label the sturdy, dominant-key reappearance in m. 17 of the head-motive of P as "S" would be reductive without a sufficient accompanying explanation. Here one also finds some obvious but incompletely carried out TR signals. These include a dominant lock in the parallel minor of the new key, v:HC, at m. 14, although much of TR is rendered indecisive by countergeneric soft dynamics and, ultimately, a *diminuendo* in m. 16. In the face of significant dynamic decay, one might argue that the *forte* P-based S seeks to save the day by striding forth unprepared onto the stage, blurting out its first-level-default S-theme. If so, then S-space is declared by *fiat* in that measure. This in turn leads to complications down the road: is the early V:PAC in m. 27, for example, the EEC? And if so, how does one account for the re-emergence of a *forte*, P-based module at m. 33? In this movement, "preprepared" generic themes seem wittily to enter in the wrong (non-normative) places. Surely the work is about these ambiguities, which should be folded into any analytical discussion of the movement. The point of any analysis is not to smooth over difficulties but rather to bring forth the tensions and dilemmas presented by the piece at hand.

Similarly problematic MC deformations also occur from time to time in Beethoven. In the first movement of the String Trio in C Minor, op. 9 no. 3, the triple hammer blows of the presumed I:HC MC seem so vigorous that in the third hammer blow (m. 20) the upper voices are chromatically knocked out of their usual places. The result is that the last MC-chord shifts to a dominant chord of A♭ (V$^6_5$/VI—an "impermissible" or non-normative MC chord), in which key, then, S is obliged to commence before correcting itself to E-flat major a few bars later. Or one might recall the witty finale of the Symphony No. 8 in F, op. 93. Here TR (beginning in m. 29) gets stuck—like an eccentrically ramshackle, mechanical contraption with out-of-control gears, levers, pulleys, and puffing pipes—and cannot accomplish the articulation of the MC. The requisite sonata-gears shift nonetheless, and the contrasting S breaks in unmistakably in m. 48, although at first in A-flat major (♭III), the "wrong key." One more swelling gear-shift, mm. 56–59, smooths out the S-process into the correct key, C major. (More wit follows: the S-theme proves unable to produce an EEC.) Another example of a seemingly "obvious" S-theme that is unprepared by a medial caesura may be found in the first movement of Schubert's Piano Sonata in A Minor, D. 845. Here TR (m. 26) leads smoothly, in an unbroken string, to what turns out to be treated as a motivically related S in III at m. 40: notice its much-varied (and soon problematized) repeti-

tion as a thematic block, for instance, beginning in m. 51.[23]

Sometimes MC ambiguities are combined with fourth-level default (I:PAC or I: IAC MC) effects. This situation suggests a permeation of the first half of the exposition by a tonic reluctant or unable to relinquish its grasp. In Beethoven's Symphony No. 6 in F, op. 68, "Pastoral," first movement, it seems clear that S begins (initially over the dominant) at m. 67. But where is the preceding MC? Is it the I:IAC-effect (!) in m. 53, with the intervening measures serving as an expanded caesura-fill—one that initiates (but does not yet complete) the modulation to V? Are there other options?

---

23. In D. 845/i it is also relevant that this "unprepared S" proves incapable of sustaining itself all the way to the EEC at m. 77. Instead, "S" breaks down *in extremis* at mm. 59–63, whereupon it is the negative, *C-minor* intrusion of the P-idea at m. 64 that carries this zone to the EEC—a sinister "lights-out" effect seeping into the emptiness of the void thus produced. (For a discus-

sion of the reappearance of P-ideas in such S-contexts, see ch. 7.) Notice also that with the sounding of the EEC the "S-idea" returns in *C major* (m. 77), muttered out *pianissimo* as a "lost" or "failed" idea in what is best regarded C-space—the unusual procedure of "C as S-aftermath" mentioned in ch. 9.

CHAPTER FOUR

The Continuous Exposition

While noted in passing, the continuous exposition has been only cursorily
treated in the scholarly literature, and it is often overlooked in practical analysis. Apparently
the first scholar to identify this format was Jens
Peter Larsen, who in 1963 called it the "three-
part division of the exposition" (*Dreiteilung . . .
der Exposition*). Although this label, sometimes
slightly adapted ("three-part organization," and
so on), turns up in subsequent literature, especially on Haydn, the designation can be misleading, because it refers to the surface features
of only one variant of the continuous exposition, of which we have identified two subtypes,
and because in individual analyses some writers
have placed the boundaries of the three parts in

questionable places (at least from the standpoint
of Sonata Theory).[1] Additionally, as will be observed, not all continuous expositions—even of
the general subtype noted by Larsen—display
"three parts."

The continuous exposition is identified by
its lack of a clearly articulated medial caesura
followed by a successfully launched secondary
theme. Instead of providing a TR that leads to
a medial caesura and thence to an S, as with
the two-part exposition, the continuous exposition, especially in Haydn's works, usually
fills up most of the expositional space with the
relentlessly ongoing, expansive spinning-out
(*Fortspinnung*) of an initial idea or its immediate
consequences.[2] Whatever the character of the

---

1. Larsen, "Sonata Form Problems," pp. 269–79. (In
the original German, "Sonatenform Probleme," "*Dreiteilung*" is found on p. 226). Cf., e.g., Michelle Fillion,
"Sonata Exposition Procedures in Haydn's Keyboard
Sonatas," *Haydn Studies. Proceedings of the International
Haydn Congress, Washington, D.C., 1975*, ed. Jens Peter Larsen, Howard Serwer, and James Webster (New
York: Norton, 1981), pp. 475–81. Charles Rosen also
wrote of Haydn's occasional "three-part organization"
in *Sonata Forms*, rev. ed., pp. 100–4, and provided an
example with the Symphony No. 44 ("Trauer"), first
movement. Our analysis of that movement differs from
Rosen's.
2. See A. Peter Brown, *Joseph Haydn's Keyboard Music*
(Bloomington: Indiana University Press, 1986), p. 295

("a totally different exposition structure" for Haydn's
Sonata in C minor, Hob. XVI: 20/1, in which "there
is now an expansive transition that . . . dominates the
entire exposition"); James Webster, *Haydn's "Farewell"
Symphony and the Idea of Classical Style* (Cambridge:
Cambridge University Press, 1991), p. 166 ("one of
Haydn's special features of form: the so-called 'three-
part' exposition. This centers around a long, unstable
Entwicklungspartie or 'expansion section' in the middle,
preceded by a short first group in the tonic and followed
by a short, contrasting, *piano* theme and codetta in the
dominant"). See also Webster, p. 326, for another example of an "expansion section" (in Symphony No. 99,
first movement).

central texture of the exposition—either that of *Fortspinnung* proper or that of something more overtly thematically based—one should suspect the presence of a continuous exposition if one cannot locate a convincing medial caesura dividing the exposition into two parts. As a result, when one is dealing with a continuous exposition, one should not try to determine where the secondary theme (S) is located: there is none, since that concept pertains only to the two-part exposition. Seeking to determine where the secondary theme is within a continuous exposition makes invalid assumptions about expected thematic treatment. *If there is no medial caesura, there is no secondary theme.*

The continuous exposition is encountered frequently in works of the second third of the eighteenth century and in several of the works of Haydn, who employed it throughout his career. A few examples of the many continuous expositions in Haydn include the first movements of his Symphonies No. 13, No. 44 ("Trauer"), 45 ("Farewell"), 88, 96 ("Miracle"), 97, and 103 ("Drumroll"), as well as the finale of the String Quartet in B Minor, op. 33 no. 1 and the first movement of the Quartet in E-flat, op. 33 no. 2 ("Joke"). Continuous expositions are less common in the later Mozart and in early Beethoven, although they do exist.

Continuous Exposition Subtype 1 (*"Expansion-Section" Subtype*)

This is the more familiar subtype alluded to in the literature on Haydn. Following a P-idea, the composer enters TR and continues to spin it out in a succession of thematic or sequential modules for most of the rest of the exposition, never pausing for the MC breath and the subsequent launch of S (even though some of the modules might impress us in passing as thematic). TR-rhetoric proceeds considerably past the last possible point where one would expect to find an MC and subsequent S (given the pro-

portions or scale of the exposition). In 1963 Larsen dubbed the large center portion of such an exposition the *Entwicklungspartie*. In its initial translation this was rendered as the "elaboration section." More commonly, it has been referred to in English as the *expansion section*.[3]

The presence of a continuous exposition involves issues of musical perception, interpretation, and reinterpretation. When first confronting an eighteenth- or early-nineteenth-century exposition, our most reasonable expectation would be that we are about to experience the far more common type, the two-part exposition with an MC and a subsequent S. When we are presented instead with a continuous exposition of the expansion-section subtype, there is usually a moment of psychological conversion (provided that we are aware of our interpretive options)—a personal understanding at some mid-expositional point that the more standard, two-part form is not going to be realized. This expectation may have been shared by the competent listener in the decades surrounding 1800. Haydn, in particular, often made the process of conversion from one exposition type to the other into a central feature of his pieces with continuous expositions. Demonstrating this process rhetorically is often what Haydn's expositions are about. The mechanism through which this conversion is suggested cannot be investigated without understanding the norms surrounding medial caesuras, for in most cases of the continuous exposition potential MCs are first suggested, then abandoned.

As we move through most later-eighteenth-century continuous expositions, what we at first suppose is an ongoing TR (on its way to an MC) continues past the last possible S-point, or what we designate as the *point of conversion*. (This may also be described as a brief zone or process of conversion.) Sensing that TR has passed beyond this conceptual point forces our reassessment of what is occurring generically. We come to realize that we are dealing instead with an expansion section. This section may now be grounded

---

3. "Elaboration section" appears in Ulrich Krämer's translation of Larsen. "Expansion section"—or slight variants thereof—appears in Fillion, Brown, and Webster: see nn. 1–2.

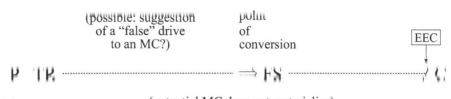

(potential MC does not materialize)

FIGURE 4.1 The Continuous Exposition (Expansion-Section Subtype)

in a succession of *Fortspinnung* modules *(FS)*, an moment-to-moment "spinning-out" of motives (most common in Haydn), or it may be a succession of differing, melodically profiled modular links, more a thematic chain than *Fortspinnung* proper (as sometimes in Mozart). To avoid undue complication in our symbols, we will refer to both procedures as FS. However it might be disposed, this caesura-free succession typically occupies the large center portion of the exposition (perhaps its middle 60–80 percent), now understood as a continuous, not a two-part, exposition. We schematize our experience of this large, central section as *TR⇒FS*, in which the symbol ⇒ stands for the word "becomes."[4] What begins (we think) as TR — it may even provide indications that a predicted MC is in preparation — shifts conceptually to the FS modules (or, alternatively, to the unbroken thematic chain) characteristic of the continuous exposition (an FS that will drive, without an S, toward the EEC). Thus the symbol of "becomes," ⇒, also represents the process of conversion. All of this may be represented as in figure 4.1.

At the basis of this understanding is the assumption that a listener adequate to the demands of the piece actually can experience such a process of conversion. Sensing it depends both on an experience with the style — having a large inventory of normative exemplars at hand — and on grasping the proportions that a composer seems to promise at or near a piece's outset. One function of the opening ideas of each exposition is to predict the rhetorical scale that will follow.

Some sonatas are brief, while others, with larger P and TR zones, are monumentalized.

Once we have attained the ability to project the proportion-to-come, there occurs a point during the course of the TR where we begin to expect a locking onto a structural dominant and a subsequent drive to a medial caesura. TR⇒FS can pass through the zone of conversion in a number of ways. We may imagine the manifold possibilities as arranged on a continuum representing the various degrees to which we sense that a potential MC has been suggested. For heuristic purposes we might identify three situations within this sliding scale (each case pushes the sense of an MC toward a clearer articulation): (1) the TR⇒FS can move past the last possible S-point with no caesura signals whatever; (2) it can reach and perhaps prolong the structural dominant — even initiate a clear, generic drive to the MC — but fail to crystallize a medial caesura; or (3) it can actually articulate a seeming (or potential) MC and perhaps even enter a process of caesura-fill but then both decline to furnish an immediate, subsequent S and refuse to drive toward a more acceptable MC in the ensuing bars. This last case is sometimes difficult to distinguish from extreme examples of the second. It belongs generally to the category of *medial caesura declined*, but the psychology of its production is perhaps best understood in its relation to the first two cases. What is needed at this point is a closer look at each possibility.[5]

1. FS may move past the S-point without our noticing it. In other words, we eventually come

---

4. We have adopted this symbol for "becomes" from Caplin, *Classical Form*, p. 47, where ⇒ also "denotes a retrospective reinterpretation of formal function."

5. Closer discussions, with printed musical examples, are found in Hepokoski and Darcy, "The Medial Caesura," pp. 133–38.

to realize that we are beyond any conceivable S-point. By all reasonable standards, it is now too late for an S-theme, although we did not register our having passed by its potential moment: we heard neither a medial caesura nor any compelling generic signals of an approach to one. To be sure, such pure instances of the continuous exposition are rare among celebrated works of the later-eighteenth-century composers—the *Presto* finale of Haydn's Quartet in B Minor, op. 33 no. 1 is a *locus classicus*: TR⟹FS extends from m. 13 to the III:PAC EEC at m. 51, followed by C-material in mm. 52–63. Another is the first-movement exposition of his Symphony No. 13 in D—notable also because the TR⟹FS portion of the exposition (m. 14 beat 3 to m. 34) pushes all the way to its end: in other words, this exposition lacks a C-zone altogether. This is a case, therefore, where the third of Larsen's supposed "three parts" does not exist. Still another, much later, is the exposition of the finale of his Piano Trio in C, Hob:XV: 27. Here the relentlessly churning TR⟹FS (mm. 43–81, with C occupying mm. 81–93) follows its conceptual opposite, a square-cut, rounded-binary P, mm. 1–43 (a characteristic finale theme of "rondo character," even though what follows is not a sonata-rondo: see chapter 18). This type of continuous exposition also appears in pieces from the earlier part of the century. Elementary examples may be found in some of the Sammartini symphonies from around the early 1740s and in several of the first movements of C. P. E. Bach's keyboard sonatas from the same time, such as the "Prussian" (1740–43) and "Württemberg" (1742–44) Sonatas.[6]

2. The composer may create the expectation of an imminent MC only to veer away from it for more Fortspinnung or other elaboration. How close we get to the implied caesura-point varies from case to case. The MC-point proper, of course, results from the laying-down of the structural dominant, the harmony that could potentially articulate a I:HC, V:HC, or III:HC medial caesura. The structural dominant may be touched lightly and immediately rejected (as if hot) with a new burst of *Fortspinnung* that overrides (or writes over) the normal tendency of the exposition to divide into two parts at this mid-expositional point. In other cases one might produce a half-cadence dominant arrival, lock onto the structural dominant to prolong the still-active V, and perhaps even furnish some additional signals to suggest the production of an MC—the music begins to "fall into" pre-MC behavior—only to draw away from it before that MC turns into a reality.

An example of the latter situation is provided in the first movement of Haydn's String Quartet in E-flat, op. 33 no. 2 ("Joke," example 4.1). Here TR sets out in the tonic in m. 13 and moves almost immediately to the dominant arrival, V/V on the third beat of m. 14. This newly locked structural dominant now underpins a generic drive to what we presume will be a standard V:HC MC, a drive beginning in earnest with the reiterated figures in m. 15. The reiterations and hypermetrical implications clearly suggest the production of a normative medial caesura in m. 19. It would be easy to imagine a differing m. 19 that consists (assuming the most generic of choices) of three hammer-blow

---

6. In the first movement of Sammartini's Symphony "No. 3" in D Major (J-C 15, before c. 1742) the first half of the binary (proto-sonata) structure may be construed as: P (mm. 1–8); a short-winded FS (mm. 9–19) that never suggests anything caesura-like but does lead to the EEC (V:PAC) at m. 19; a brief, cadential close (C, mm. 20–28). The score is available in *The Symphonies of G.B. Sammartini.: Vol. 1: The Early Symphonies*, ed. Bathia Churgin (Cambridge, Mass.: Harvard University Press, 1968), 76–77. "No. 3" is renumbered as "No 14" in Newell Jenkins and Bathia Churgin, eds., *Thematic Catalogue of the Works of Giovanni Battista Sammartini: Orchestral and Vocal Music* (Cambridge, Mass.: Harvard University Press, 1976), p. 54.

In C. P. E. Bach one often finds a similar format: an initial P-gesture; a modulatory TR⟹FS (typically sequential—and rarely very long) that proceeds to a PAC (the EEC); and a (brief) "appendix" theme (C) at the end to solidify the new key. Because C. P. E. Bach's textures often feature breaks and discontinuities, the caesura situation is sometimes difficult to assess. For a general discussion of C. P. E. Bach and the frequent inappropriateness of the concept of the "second theme," see David Schulenberg, *The Instrumental Music of Carl Philipp Emanuel Bach* (Ann Arbor: UMI Research Press, 1984), e.g., pp. 100–105; and William S. Newman, *The Sonata in the Classic Era*, 2nd ed., pp. 420–21.

F-major chords (V of B-flat), followed by a rest, a drop to *piano*, and (since this is Haydn) a monothematic S theme — or perhaps a contrasting one — beginning with the upbeat to m. 20. But instead, at the last moment, in m. 19, Haydn slips out of the caesura-loop by sustaining the first violin and cello, unsettling the prolonged V:A dominant (thus inaugurating a new harmonic progression at the precise moment when we had expected everything to stop) and gliding forward into a reinvigorated melodic figure in the outer voices. This new figure (grounded in much that has preceded it) is immediately imitated in the second violin, and then, in m. 20, in the viola. In short, a renewed thematic idea emerges and pushes through the expected MC-moment ("writes over it"), canceling the local MC implications with a new burst of *Fortspinnung*. Mm. 19–20 represent the point (or zone) of conversion, the point at which a two-part exposition is renounced, and the *Fortspinnung* continues by merging smoothly into a cadential module beginning on the new tonic in m. 21 and expanding outward until the EEC is attained on the third beat of m. 28. The exposition itself ends four bars later, in m. 32. The weak V:PAC-effect at m. 21 should not be considered the EEC: m. 21 is a direct and relatively uninterrupted continuation of the figuration of the preceding bars. This PAC is probably better understood not as concluding anything (it lacks a truly cadential function) but as marking the tonic-chord onset of a thematically profiled cadential module, a common feature of the conclusion of Haydn's expansion sections.

As a whole, this passage from op. 33 no. 2 illustrates the procedure that we call the *bait-and-switch tactic*: Haydn baits us into anticipating an imminent medial caesura, the hallmark of the two-part exposition, then swerves away from the caesura-point and switches to a continuous exposition of the expansion-section subtype — all for the sake, one supposes, of high generic play and the splendid exhilaration found in sophisticated musical humor.

3. *In extreme cases of the bait-and-switch tactic we find the MC fully articulated before the plug is pulled on the two-part exposition.* Such situations involve undermining the caesura-fill that follows the MC, thus refusing to permit the caesura-fill to rest or anchor itself with an S-theme on its other side. Instead, the fill is reinvigorated into an expanded *Fortspinnung* or "thematic" modular chain that takes on a life of its own. In such a situation the decisive change in the character and function of the caesura-fill cancels the effect of the preceding MC. It represents a change of mind after the fact.

Such a situation occurs in the first movement of Haydn's Symphony No. 96 in D ("Miracle," example 4.2). Setting aside the delicious complications that bring us to the V:HC MC point (including a typically Haydnesque attempt to reopen the I:HC MC possibility in mm. 48–51, aborted in m. 52, perhaps because the I:HC option had already been used up earlier in m. 31), we may note that mm. 54–55 drive to the new structural dominant, V/V, which is attained in m. 56. This leads to the manufacture of a nearly immediate V:HC MC with upward *Nachschlag* on the first beat of m. 57, followed at once by an eighth rest. (As a result of the earlier complications, this is an exceptionally late first-level-default MC, occurring, as we eventually learn, some 61 percent of the way through the exposition, if we consider the expositional space as continuing through m. 83.) The upbeat to m. 58 in the strings, with its characteristic energy-loss drop to *piano*, begins a recognizable expanded caesura-fill in octaves. Its upward motion, however, is non-normative, gaining rather than losing registral energy. Consequently, the caesura-fill is made to overshoot its tonic-pitch goal in m. 60, then to draw itself up questioningly on $\hat{4}$ of A major (m. 61), and finally to abandon the "fill" function altogether with the incongruous intercutting of a *sforzando* G^7–C progression (momentarily calling our attention to ♮III of the anticipated A major) in mm. 62–63. The top voice in the strings of this C-major chord (m. 63) recaptures the E_5 of the MC *Nachschlag* (m. 57), whereupon a descending fifth progression (from $\hat{5}$ in m. 63 through $\hat{4}$–$\hat{3}$–$\hat{2}$ in mm. 64–65 to $\hat{1}$ in m. 71) leads to a V:PAC in m. 71. The cadential $^6_4$ of m. 67 recovers the dominant of A major, now understood as having been prolonged from m. 56. The V:PAC of m. 71 is no "late" medial caesura. Appearing some 82 percent of the way through the exposition and eliding with a clearly "codetta-like" C theme,

EXAMPLE 4.1 Haydn, String Quartet in E-flat, op. 33 no. 2, i, mm. 13–28

EXAMPLE 4.1 *(continued)*

EXAMPLE 4.2   Haydn: Symphony No. 96 in D ("Miracle"), i,
mm. 54–71

it serves unambiguously as the EEC. Here the "witty" zone of conversion from a two-part to a continuous exposition is best heard as occurring in mm. 61–63: what began as caesura-fill is converted into a structural linear descent. Notwithstanding the pointed MC in m. 57, by m. 63 the potential two-part exposition has been discarded.

The *bait-and-switch retrospective cancellation* could be applied even further into the exposition. It would even be possible to initiate an S theme (following an MC and caesura-fill, thus declaring on behalf of a two-part exposition), then to abort that theme decisively and to back up the music to reanimate the motives that had characterized the pre-MC TR, as if recapturing or reawakening the possibilities that had existed before the MC.

Such bait-and-switch procedures as we find in op. 33 no. 2, Symphony No. 96, and many other works are typical of Haydn's continuous expositions, most of which are grounded in gestures toward two-part expositions that are abandoned to pursue other structural paths. What differs from case to case are the unfailingly engaging details and the degree toward which the jettisoned two-part proclivities remain perceptible through the continuous musical surface. Haydn's inventiveness along these lines never ceases to astonish. The general psychology at work—seeming to promise one thing but delivering another—is at the core of his imagination as a master composer.

Once past the point of conversion, the TR⇒FS may spin out further, sometimes at considerable length. Often its constituent modules can be rather thematic and even be sounded entirely in the second key area (usually V). Still, none of these modules should be considered to be S, since there has been no medial caesura.[7] In the simpler types of continuous exposition the extended TR⇒FS will finally arrive at a cadential module that leads to a PAC that should be regarded as the EEC. This first PAC/EEC is subject to the usual possibilities for being reopened via thematic or cadential repetition, and so on, as discussed in chapter 8. It may or may not be followed by a brief closing idea or set of closing ideas.

A more complicated option, sometimes also found in Haydn, was to move past the point of conversion (thus making the music behave as though it had renounced an MC proper, thereby declaring the exposition to be continuous, not two-part), but then—seemingly "too late"—to lead that already lengthy TR⇒FS to a pause on a dominant-oriented chord (V or V[7]) or even to a more vigorous half-cadence effect (!). In other words, the ongoing TR⇒FS modular chain, which in most cases proceeds onward to a PAC, is in this case stopped short on some sort of active-dominant-oriented gap or pause that appears to function as an attempt at to produce a *restored caesura* (or *compensatory caesura*).[8] Moreover this late-MC effect is typically followed by a decisively new module or theme—a "change of idea." If that idea can be heard as an arguably convincing, if "late," S, then, as perhaps in the first movement of Symphony No. 97 (m. 76), the earlier TR⇒FS impression will have been *reconverted* at the last possible moment back to a two-part structure. The once-"lost" MC will have been found once again, possibly in a much-debilitated condition, as in mm. 73–75 of the

---

7. As mentioned in ch. 3, the only exception to this—subject to interpretation in individual cases—would be a situation in which, once TR has been decisively initiated, a thematically profiled module (an "S-like" module) in the new key sprouts forth (in an otherwise continuous texture) directly following a light V:HC, as though that HC were being "understood" by the thematic module to be a mild, nonreinforced MC. For an example, see the V:HC in m. 37 of the finale of Mozart's Violin Concerto No. 4 in D, K. 218. What follows (upbeat to m. 38) is a sentential module in the dominant that may be construed as opening secondary-theme space.

8. What is being "restored" here, of course, need not be literally an earlier, abandoned MC or near-MC proper, although that does sometimes occur, but rather the concept of the two-part exposition, which is defined by the presence of that caesura (whose possibility or effectiveness had been abandoned in an earlier passage). On some connotations of "compensatory" in this context, see n. 12.

same work.[9] Such analytical decisions involve assessments of tone and rhetoric that might differ from one person to another.

On the other hand, if the new idea after the MC-effect is *not* likely to be accepted by the listener as a viable S (as other interpreters of Symphony No. 97, m. 76, might contend), but rather seems more to employ characteristic C-rhetoric (for Haydn, relaxed, folklike, popular, codetta-like, and so on), this would mean that a C-like theme has appeared even though C-space has not yet been opened normatively with the attaining of the EEC. In this case the restored caesura-effect will have failed (doubtless because of its "too-late" placement), since it is not followed by convincing S-material. Interpreting such a situation in this way depends on perceiving two things. First, one should be convinced of the non-normative "lateness" of the restored HC MC-gesture. (We must have already concluded that a more sustained *Fortspinnung*—or chain of thematic modules—was underway.) Second, the theme that follows the MC effect must be, within Haydn's normative practice, more "C-like" than it is S-like. Some of the examples that Larsen cited of Haydn's "three-part division of the exposition" may fall into this category—perhaps the first movement of the Piano Sonata in C Minor, Hob. XVI:20, for instance (with the restored caesura effect best placed at m. 31 and the sentential, C-rhetoric idea in mm. 32–37).[10]

This rather rare situation presents conceptual and terminological problems that are not easily resolved. Notwithstanding such a theme's "C rhetoric," there has been no EEC—which by definition is the only way of releasing the music into C-space. We designate this new idea within continuous expositions as $C^{\text{pre-EEC}}$.[11] This admittedly awkward label indicates the ambiguity of the zone. By this point, normative expositional functions have been thoroughly upset. As a result, contrary to the definition of C-space, the $C^{\text{pre-EEC}}$ itself must remedy the situation (however "inadvertently" in terms of its own "C-rhetoric consciousness") by accomplishing the EEC, its first satisfactory PAC that moves onward to differing material. The C-rhetoric-generated EEC might or might not be followed by additional modules that are now more normatively to be regarded as in what is finally a fully opened C-space. The result of such high play is best regarded as a special, Haydnesque variant of the expansion-section subtype of

---

9. In Symphony No. 97/i the not-fully-stabilized dominant-lock effect starting in m. 68 also contributes to the (deformational) caesura impression at mm. 73–75. See also the related discussions in ch. 3, nn. 7 and 15 and the textual contexts to which they refer.

10. The case regarding Hob. XVI:20/i, however, is anything but clear. The exposition of the first movement of this C-minor sonata is problematic in a number of respects. It unfolds more as a moment-to-moment *process* than as a clear illustration of any schematic form. Even so, it is in the explication of just such situations that the flexibility of Sonata Theory—more an art or a mode of dialogical, hermeneutic practice than a mechanistic "system" of labeling—shows its utility. Following a straightfoward, periodic P (mm. 1–8), TR begins at m. 9, arriving with the III:HC at the downbeat of m. 19 into the suggestion of a light III:HC MC. Instead of acting directly upon that potential MC, the immediately ensuing caesura-fill expands outward (mm. 19–26), in the process seeming to "lose" the earlier MC-effect, or perhaps seeking in vain to stabilize the whole passage into a convincing MC event. The pause with fermata at m. 26, with its pronounced ninth, C_6, held wide-eyed over the sustained dominant seventh of E-flat major, is a musical question mark: "What next?" Instead of taking the "V^9" fermata-chord (!) as an MC-effect, the music reignites with a decisive cadential module in E-flat (second half of m. 26, beginning on the typical I^6 of an expanded cadential progression), as if clearly abandoning the idea of any secondary theme and deciding instead to conclude the larger zone of *Fortspinnung* (now finally understood as TR⇒FS) with an efficient, unmistakable cadential idea ("Punkt!"). But this predicted cadence, too, fails to materialize. *En route* to the expected cadence the harmonic motion stalls on a dominant-lock, mm. 29–31, culminating in m. 31 with the generic ("MC-like") gap on beat 4—albeit on V^7 of E-flat. With the TR⇒FS zone still unclosed, a completely new codetta-like, sentential theme with C-rhetoric emerges at m. 32 and is finally able to produce the needed III: PAC (the EEC) at m. 37.

11. In ch. 9 we designate the equivalent situation within a two-part exposition as S^C. This could involve, for instance, the staging of a "breakdown" of S proper, followed by the subsequent articulation of a theme with "C-character," even though no EEC has yet been attained.

the continuous exposition, one in which the "C-like" theme can also be understood as the concluding module of a broad TR⇒FS space that had attempted, late in the game, to produce a restored-caesura effect.[12]

Continuous Exposition Subtype 2: Early PAC in the New Key Followed by (Varied) Reiterations of the Cadence

In the second continuous-exposition subtype an early structural perfect authentic cadence (PAC) in the second key area (typically occurring around 50 to 70 percent of the way through the exposition) is followed not by a genuine secondary theme but by multiple, perhaps varied or expanded restatements of the immediately preceding cadential module. In some instances the "restatement" aspect is obvious; in other, more varied cases this may be less evident. In most cases, though, a defining hallmark of this circumstance is, following the first PAC, the presence of an unusually brief succeeding module — one that is too brief to be considered a satisfactory S and one whose main function, in such close proximity to the just-heard PAC, is to confirm that cadence with another one. Such cadential reiterations continue throughout much (sometimes all) of the remainder of the exposition. The result is a differing sort of mid-expositional expansion section, one that keeps *reopening* seemingly closed authentic cadences through varied modular repetitions (see figure 4.2).

One function of the cadential repetitions is to extend expositional space to a point at which an acceptable EEC may be sounded. In other words, if the first V:PAC is not to be used as an MC (third-level default), then the next option would be to have it function as the EEC. But in these situations, we are to suppose that this is too early in the exposition to sound an EEC. Thus more expositional space must be crafted — by means of repetition and/or expansions of

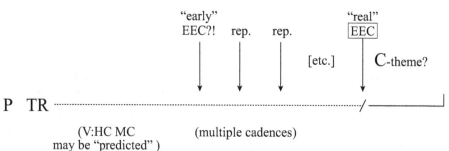

("premature" PAC/EEC-effects, each reopened by cadential repetition)

Figure 4.2   The Continuous Exposition (Subtype with Early PAC and Cadential Reiterations)

---

12. In this case the listener seems invited to conclude that the "too-late" MC-effect tries to compensate for its earlier absence, as if pretending (or hoping?) that the normative MC option were still legitimately open. But once the MC-restoration effect has been sounded—long past the point where it normatively belongs—the S-option that such a gesture invites is shown to be futile. A "genuine" S is no longer available, since that option had been cast overboard by earlier, extended FS activity, which has now tracked us "too far" into the exposition for any convincing S. And yet the nature of any caesura-effect is to prepare the onset of another theme, major section, or zone. The only thematic possibility that remains at this relatively late expositional point is therefore the "C-rhetoric" option, which does arrive "on schedule," even though it has not been properly prepared by a preceding EEC. The witty effect is that of C stepping onto the stage, blissfully "unaware" of any past difficulties ("All right! Here I am!") — as if it had been looking only at its "expositional pocket-watch" and waiting for its pre-assigned moment of arrival, the one allotted to it through an earlier generic agreement.

the cadence in question—until a sufficiently convincing, proportionally apt EEC-moment is attained. Nonetheless, the obsessive cadential repetitions themselves soon take on their own self-propelling, reiterative momentum and sometimes have to be stopped through the application of outside compositional force.

For the analyst the initial indications that this procedure is being employed involve the coordinated appearance of four factors at the potential MC and S-point. The first is an early and emphatic PAC in the new key. (Initially one might suppose this to be a third-level default MC, to be followed by an S.) The second—as mentioned above, one of the most important clues—is that the subsequent, potential S-module is unusually brief (often four measures or fewer): a concise, single phrase only, and one whose aims are emphatically cadential, leading at once to its own PAC in the new key. The third is that, upon examination, this cadential module may suggest a recapturing or restating of the preceding cadence, perhaps through a reference (however veiled) to the module that produced the preceding PAC. The fourth is that the cadential module (which is being assessed as a potential S) is often subjected to immediate repetition—one that may be literal, made briefer, or, conversely, decorated through considerable expansion. When all of these factors are in play (especially 1, 2, and 4), one should normally conclude that this is a continuous exposition (subtype 2) rather than a two-part exposition. At this point one realizes that the exposition has no second theme and no medial caesura—only a new-key PAC with (varied) cadential reiterations.

This procedure underpins the psychology of the first movement of Mozart's String Quartet in B-flat, K. 458 ("Hunt"). Within TR mm. 42ff provide a characteristic half cadence and structural-dominant lock (V:HC), the apparent beginning of a drive toward a V:HC MC. The possibility of that MC erodes away with motivic repetition (and the *piano* dynamic, refusing to energize), and the music gives the impression of changing its mind, unfreezing the dominant-lock, and plunging (mostly *forte*) toward an early V:PAC in m. 54. What follows is not S (and the V:PAC is consequently no third-level default MC), because the music consists entirely of varied repetitions of the cadence that we have just heard. This produces multiple, quasi-stuttering PACs in mm. 60, 66, and 69—each overriding its predecessor as an MC or EEC candidate— before the cadential-repetition process breaks down with the three successive diminished-seventh chords in mm. 71–73. The EEC follows in m. 77, and the subsequent C begins in m. 78.

A similar procedure may be found in the first movement of Haydn's Symphony No. 88 in G, in which the cadential repetitions of the early V:PAC in m. 61 (approximately 54 percent of the way through the exposition) are wittily overextended into a prolonged series of multiple, chattering reappearances—a recurring cadence-idea that one cannot shake off. The first movement of Beethoven's Symphony No. 7 in A, op. 92, also plays on the memory of this continuous-exposition subtype, although in this case the first cadential repetition is extremely brief (mm. 130–34) and what begins as its immediate restatement (m. 134) is deformationally expanded, bringing us through an unexpected set of harmonic adventures before driving again to an authentic cadence in m. 164. Regardless of the subtype encountered, attempts to analyze continuous expositions as if they were two-part expositions (by undertaking a fruitless search for a second theme) can lead only to a misunderstanding of their internal processes.

The second subtype also affords the opportunity for creating delicious ambiguities between the two-part and continuous expositions. One of the most artful may be found in the first movement of Mozart's Quartet in D Minor, K. 421 (example 4.3). On the face of it, this would seem to be a clear two-part exposition, with a III:PAC MC on the third beat of m. 24 (after an initial dominant-lock feint in mm. 18–20) and a modestly contrasting, sentential S beginning in F major at m. 25. (We had mentioned this as a possible example of the third-level default MC in chapter 3.) A closer examination, though, notices that the proposed S begins with an uncommonly short S-module (four bars) that moves efficiently to another III:PAC on

EXAMPLE 4.3   Mozart, String Quartet in D Minor, K. 421, i, mm. 14–28

EXAMPLE 4.3 *(continued)*

the third beat of m. 28—reclosing that cadence "too soon" for any normative S. Moreover, the bass-line of that S-module is merely a cadential formula—that of the "expanded cadential progression" leading off from I⁶ in m. 25—and over its four bars it essentially expands the bass line of the cadence of the presumed MC (m. 24, beats 1–3, also a motion from I⁶).

From this perspective our supposed S may be understood as an expanded reiteration of the preceding III:PAC—in other words, as the initial defining gesture of a continuous exposition, subtype 2. The decorated reiteration of this four-bar cadential module in mm. 29–32 reinforces this view, and what follows may be heard as compressed reiterations of the same PAC—thus continuing to defer the real EEC further down the road. (Opinions may differ about which of these PACs serves as that EEC.) Is this, then, nothing but a continuous exposition, subtype 2—foreshadowing that of the "Hunt" Quartet to come? Merely to claim this also seems unsatisfactory, since the S-character of the first-violin theme in mm. 25–28 (varied in mm. 29–32) also seems strong. We have here a ravishingly clever ambiguity. It is as if in mm. 25–29 the upper voice wishes to proceed with S (and a two-part exposition) while the lower voice wishes to reiterate the preceding cadence. This is a brilliantly crafted moment of structure, a passage of the highest subtlety, poised between the two exposition types—and partaking of both.

Difficult Cases: Incipient or Not-Fully-Realized Medial Caesuras

We have already suggested some possibilities for MC deformation, including first-level-default MC-effects on chordal inversions and the blocked-MC effect. In addition, somewhat common in early sonatas (from the 1740s, 1750s, and 1760s) is the expositional situation of an apparently continuous exposition that "almost" produces an MC and second theme that "almost" manages to divide the structure into a two-part exposition. (In some instances, for example, this might signal the presence of a light HC-effect but no unequivocally convincing "S" identifier in the next module). In such cases feeling obliged to decide unequivocally in favor of the one or the other seems counter-intuitive, Procrustean. (One thinks of cell division—mitosis: in metaphase and anaphase the two cells have begun to divide but have not fully succeeded in doing so.) In such cases it can be difficult to decide whether we should consider the "new module" (?) in the middle to be an S or not, since that "almost viable" S-possibility may not be a fully characteristic S or may not be prepared by all aspects of the rhetoric commonly associated with the MC—especially the clear MC-gap, one of the principal signals of an MC. In such cases—and with all similar problems of ambiguity within Sonata Theory—one should not force a decision into one rigid binary category or the other. This is precisely the kind of inflexible categorization that we seek to discourage. Instead, one explicates what is actually there. Toward this end the more normative categories of Sonata Theory (two-part and continuous expositions, medial-caesura characteristics, and so on) help to provide the vocabulary to describe the nuances of the situation in question. By no means does every case have to be slotted bluntly into either the one category or the other.[13]

---

13. Such situations turn up with some frequency in C. P. E. Bach's early keyboard sonatas—the "Prussian" sonatas and others. One also finds them in early symphonic practice. They are not uncommon, for instance, in the Allegro movements of Georg Christoph Wagenseil's symphonies in and around the 1750s. In general, Wagenseil favored the continuous exposition (subtype 1), but some of the rapid-tempo movements seem to "want" to divide into two parts. In the first movement of the Symphony in E, WV 393, a TR leads eventually to a dominant lock (V/V) at m. 25—thus seeming to promise an immanent V:HC MC. But the music never stops to articulate that MC, even though a new thematic module takes off, with an energetic *forte*, in m. 35. Was m. 34 in some way an implied MC? The evidence for one is weak: the MC was never articulated as such, and the *Trommelbass* figure keeps moving through TR and into the new idea at m. 35. Here we are probably confronting a continuous exposition that has almost subdivided into a two-part format.

CHAPTER FIVE

The Primary Theme (P)

The primary theme (P) is the idea that begins the sonata process.[1] From this point the large-scale trajectories toward the EEC and ESC begin to take flight. With the initial impulse of P, we have taken the first step that will trigger sequentially the other sonata stages; we have entered into a generic contract to carry out the trajectory to the ESC—and sometimes beyond. This *Hauptgedanke* (principal idea) may take on a number of expressive roles: that of the emotional stance or referential character around which the subsequent sonata will be built; that of the structural decision to act decisively (launching the sonata with determination); or, especially in minor-mode works, that of establishing the prevailing situation of the sonata-drama.

At the same time P establishes its rhetorical function as the initiator of rotations. Its first appearance signals the beginning of the expositional rotation, the referential layout that serves as the rule for interpretation of much that follows. Once the exposition is completed, a decisive, prepared return to P or a recognizable variant thereof may indicate the onset of a new conceptual rotation, which may be either full or partial (references to P only, or to P and TR only). This is self-evidently the case with the recapitulatory rotation, which normally recycles all or most of the expositional materials. It may also be the case in developments and codas, although local circumstances and implications differ from piece to piece.

P may be launched in various ways. Many characteristic topics (patterned styles) are appropriate for P-theme *Hauptgedanken*, and P-ideas frequently visit a volatile succession of contrasting topics as they proceed. As Ratner has noted, P-themes within symphonies were often styled as marches, befitting their roles as opening pieces of eighteenth-century concerts. But many other selections were also common. Ratner's list of standard topics for what he called "key area I" includes: hunt, polonaise, passepied, singing style, *alla breve*, brilliant style, and *contredanse*.[2]

---

1. Here and elsewhere, what we for convenience—and in part out of tradition—refer to as a "theme" indicates only the leading musical idea (usually the initial idea or initial-idea complex) of an expositional zone. "Theme" should not be understood exclusively to connote a melody, much less a self-contained and closed one. Many P-zones (and TR-, S-, and C-zones) begin with characteristic textures rather than melodies in the narrow sense of the term.

2. Ratner, *Classic Music*, pp. 222–23, which also include examples of the topics mentioned. Ratner also includes "recitative obligé" (Beethoven, Quartet in F Minor, op. 95) and "waltz" (for the opening of the *Eroica!*).

One formulaic device to initiate a P-zone is that of a triple-hammer-blow—three bold chords, as if to awaken sonata-space with a vigorous gesture—usually followed by a contrasting topic of differing material. (As discussed in chapter 3, triple-blows are also characteristic MC markers. They are additionally often used as concluding signs of expositions and recapitulations. In other words the gesture can serve as an indicator of the major points of articulation within sonata-space.) Within P these chords are sometimes largely preparatory, P^0 or $P^{1.0}$ modules, which are discussed below. The three chords may articulate the tonic alone, they may outline a I–V–I gesture (perhaps with an activating $\hat{1} - \hat{2} - \hat{3}$ in the upper voice, as in the opening of Haydn's Quartet in G, op. 76 no. 1), perhaps merely with $\hat{8} - \hat{7} - \hat{8}$, and so on), or they may be sounded in some other configuration. Other conventional possibilities for openings—sometimes intermixed with other topics—called on fanfare-like gestures (sturdy outlines of triads) or the sounding of a musical idea *all'unisono* (in unison) or in octaves.[3]

The P-theme may begin aggressively, at a strong dynamic level. This is the *strong-launch option*, and, as mentioned above, it often features chordal or fanfare-like gestures, flashy *coups d'archet*, dotted rhythms, octave drops or leaps, triadic articulations, an emphatic, *forte* theme, a bold, P^0 or $P^{1.0}$ motto, or something similar. Sometimes an initial *forte* basic idea is riddled with back-and-forth interpolated *piano* responses—hesitant, gentler, contrasting, or questioning replies, as in J. C. Bach, much of Mozart, and so on. The strong-launch option is particularly appropriate in large-scale, public, or ambitious works that lack a slow introduction.

Alternatively, the sonata might set forth with the *weak-launch option*—beginning *piano*, either with an unassuming, lyrical melody (first movements of Mozart, Symphony No. 29 in A, K. 201; Piano Sonata in B-flat, K. 333) or with

the onset of some sort of bustling *crescendo* effect. The weak-launch option may stand on its own (K. 201), but, as has been widely remarked, the sounding of a *piano* theme is especially attractive after a slow introduction—something that the mature Haydn used to great effect.[4] The weak-launch, lyrical-theme opening invites a TR of the *forte* affirmation or restatement type (chapter 6), a common strategy in Allegro movements in symphonies (Mozart, K. 201; standard practice in many of later Haydn's symphonies).

From time to time one also encounters the seemingly paradoxical use of closing formulas to begin a piece, although in some cases the two-chord cadential idea, as a kind of preface, is most strictly classified as preceding P-space proper. This general idea was apparently a fairly widely recognized procedure in the eighteenth century. Such an obvious displacement of typical function must have had witty or other clever resonances that were especially appealing to connoisseurs. The archetypal cadential formula, typically reduced to its most essential progression of dominant (or dominant seventh) to tonic, was wrenched free of its normative function—that of concluding a larger phrase or zone—in order to serve, incongruously, as a compact initiating gesture.

As might be expected, the technique is characteristic of Haydn, one strand of whose *Witz* featured modular dislocations—ideas in "wrong places"—and surprises of different kinds. One obvious example is the purposely banal V^7–I (an apparent PAC-effect) at the Vivace assai opening of his Quartet in G, op. 33 no. 5, mm. 1–2 (example 5.1). To be sure, the issue of whether such an isolated two-chord gesture may still be considered a "cadence" proper, strictly considered, has been raised recently, but *au fond* the dispute about such matters is idle and rests on an adamantly tenacious adherence to overly exclusionary definitions.[5] There can

---

3. For a discussion of the latter see Wolfgang Gratzer, "Mozart, oder? Der Unisono-Beginn in Streichquartetten der Wiener Klassik: Fragment zu einer Poetik des musikalischen Anfangs," *Mozart-Jahrbuch 1991* [1991 Salzburg Conference Report] (Kassel: Bärenreiter, 1992), pp. 641–49.

4. As mentioned also, e.g., in Rosen, *Sonata Forms*, rev. ed., p. 243.

5. The argument *contra* the term "cadence" in such situations—and several others besides—has been made by Caplin, "The Classical Cadence," especially pp. 83–85 (dealing with the famous, only partially parallel case at

EXAMPLE 5.1   Haydn, String Quartet in G, op. 33 no. 5, i, mm. 1–10

be little doubt that—"cadence" or not—Haydn expected his listeners to understand the opening here as a witty "closing formula" that has been transferred to the apparently "wrong" spot of the piece. As the movement proceeds Haydn resituates that cadence formula in a more proper location—both at the end of the initial thematic phrase, mm. 9–10, for example, and at the end of the movement, where it is made to assume its most natural function.[6] A more exaggerated version of this cadential-ending-as-beginning may be found in the Quartet in C, op. 74 no. 1, mm. 1–2 (sounded virtually outside of any tempo or pulse, the dominant seventh is provided with a fermata, with a second fermata separating the tonic chord from P-proper, the

---

the opening of the trio in the third movement of Mozart's Symphony No. 41 in C, K. 551). In Caplin's view such a two-chord succession may have "cadential content" but not a "cadential function," because "it cannot be construed to end a formal unit," which is a *sine qua non* in Caplin's definitional apparatus. (No chordal succession rises to the level of the term "cadence" unless it displays both cadential content and phrase-ending function.) Needless to say, most cadences do indeed serve as the "last event" of a "larger formal unit" or "phrase" of a handful of measures (pp. 57–58) that often display a tonic–predominant–dominant-tonic motion. But what is true of most cadences within this style need not be elevated into a rigid criterion to apply to all of them. Within the flexible sonata style, it is possible that in special adaptations and under special, quasi-formulaic circumstances, some emphatically staged, two-chord progressions might be heard as invocations of the "cadence" proper and hence, *pari passu*, might be reasonably regarded as "cadences" (which in this case, perhaps more precisely, could mean "cadence-alluding formulas"). "Cadential" openings to such works as Haydn's

op. 33 no. 5 would be one such situation—for hearing this moment as a separate, cadential displacement (as an isolated two-chord cadential formula presented starkly as a "bare fact," shorn of its normative functional role of larger-phrase closure) is the precise point of this initial gesture. (The situation in the K. 551/iii trio, we agree, is more problematic.) Another instance—similarly disallowed as "cadences" by Caplin (pp. 90–95)—would be the succession of emphatic V–I chords (often without preceding tonic and predominant chords) sometimes found at the ends of expositions. We suspect that most listeners intuitively hear such chords as recrafted, emphatic reiterations of the final portion (the "cadence" element proper) of a more complete cadential progression heard just before them. To strip them of legitimate cadential status (in favor only of the "postcadential" role of "codettas") is counter-intuitive. See also the discussion in ch. 9.

6. In the case of op. 33 no. 5 the opening two bars combine features of the "brief in-tempo introduction" and the P^0 or $P^{1.0}$ concepts (discussed separately below in the subsection on "P^0 and $P^{1.0}$ modules/themes").

Allegro moderato, in m. 3), while that of the Quartet in D, op. 50 no. 6, mm. 1–4, is slightly more thematically elaborate. Unusual variants and expansions of the technique abound: recall, for instance, the (post-introduction) P-theme of the first movement of the Symphony No. 94 in G, "Surprise." Similar effects, filtered through different musical sensibilities, can be found here and there in Mozart and Beethoven.

When a slow introduction precedes the faster P-theme, one normally expects to find a clear separation between them—a fermata or some other unmistakable conclusion to the introduction. This renders the onset of P independent and distinct. In intensely dramatic orchestral works from the 1790s and thereafter, however, we occasionally come across either a "run-on" introduction without a clear pause or an introduction ending with an *accelerando* or other cumulative effect that gains energy and merges directly with P and that may also cross over the new tempo marking in the process.[7] In the latter case P springs forth from the wind-up accumulation of the introduction instead of initiating its own spark of momentum, and the expositional rotation can begin several measures into the Allegro tempo. One instance had occurred in Cherubini's Overture to *Les deux journées* (1800), but the procedure is most familiar from some of Beethoven's orchestral works: the first movement of the Symphony No. 4 in B-flat, op. 60 (wind-up beginning in m. 35; Allegro vivace in place at m. 39; exposition proper, P, at m. 43 with expositional repetition marked at m. 45); the *Leonore* Overture No. 1, op. 138 (wind-up beginning in m. 37, which A. B. Marx believed in 1859 to be the gathering of Leonora's courage and steely resolve, *der Entschluss zu ihrer That*;[8] Allegro con brio in place, m. 42; exposition, P, at m. 58); and the *Egmont* Overture, op. 84 (Allegro in place, m. 25, itself initiating the wind-up; P proper shot forth at m. 29). These early examples are among the sources for the later-nineteenth-century generative introductions—to the first movements, for example,

of Schumann's Symphony No. 4 in D Minor, Franck's later symphony in the same key, or Mahler's Symphony No. 1 in D—even though those introductions might not exemplify all the features of the source-models.

P-theme characteristics also vary according to the prescribed performing forces of the work. Certain kinds of P-themes are characteristic of keyboard sonatas; others of chamber music; others of orchestral pieces. In 1979, for example, László Somfai submitted Haydn's keyboard sonatas to an extensive stylistic survey. Haydn's first-movement opening ideas, he found, displayed a wide variety of shapes and topical styles, changing throughout his career. At least in this repertory P often begins with a strongly emphasized dotted-rhythm idea. This idea may be immediately contrasted with a *cantabile* theme (Sonatas in D and E-flat, Hob. XVI:19 and 45); the dotted-rhythm itself may be carried out *in extenso* ("monochrome" rhythm) or subjected to characteristic keyboard embellishments (Sonatas in B-flat, C, F, C, and B-flat, Hob. XVI:18, 21, 23, 35, and 41); it may be in the French Overture style, implicitly subject to overdotting (Sonata in D: Hob. XVI:14); or it may be more complex, march-like, or wide-ranging in compass (Sonata in E-flat, Hob. XVI:52).

In Somfai's view, sometimes Haydn's keyboard P-theme, especially in minor-mode sonatas (C Minor, Hob. XVI:20), is more "abstract" (less purely keyboard-oriented), closed, and of an "instrumental character." Other movements begin with a "striking instrumental effect" manifestly idiomatic for the keyboard: an initial rolled, broken, or asserted single chord propelling the sonata into action (two sonatas in E major, Hob: XVI: 13 and 22; Sonata in F, Hob. XVI:29); or "bare-bones" staccato themes that Somfai judged to be reminiscent of Scarlatti (C major, Hob. XVI:50). Most of Haydn's opening movements were in duple time (4/4 or 2/4). Those in 3/4 that "are not stylized or accelerated minuets are relatively rare" (Sonata in D and two sonatas in E-flat, Hob. XVI:24, 28,

---

7. The adjective "run-on" in this context comes from James Webster, *Haydn's "Farewell" Symphony and the Idea of Classical Style*, pp. 162–65.

8. Adolph Bernhard Marx, *Ludwig van Beethoven: Leben und Schaffen* (Berlin: Janke, 1859), 1:337.

and 49). Somfai also assessed P-themes in terms of symmetry and asymmetry: "The asymmetric model is earlier and richer in variants. Perhaps it is more characteristic of Haydn; at least it occurs somewhat more frequently."[9]

Structure

The structural type that the composer selects for P is no neutral choice: it is an important factor in the personality and drama of each individual work. P may be shaped as a simple period, a sentence, a single phrase, or a more complex structure. For the sake of convenience in describing these formats, we use, though sometimes in adapted ways, most of the terminology advocated in Caplin's *Classical Form* for the structure of periods, sentences (including the terms "presentation" "continuation," and "continuation⇒cadential"), and their hybrids.[10] In general, sentences are more active, more restless, more forward-driving than periods, which tend to be more static and symmetrical. P might also be unfolded as a multimodular succession comprising several ideas. (See the section on "Thematic-Modular Designations.")

Some P-ideas display the characteristics of periods and sentences at different structural levels. We might, for example, come across a period whose antecedent (and whose consequent as well, if the period is stated completely) is articulated as a smaller-scale sentence (a sentential antecedent). The unusually broad, antecedent-like phrase (mm. 26–39) that opens the first-movement exposition of Mozart's Symphony No. 39 in E-flat, K. 543, can serve as an illustration (example 5.2). Here the large antecedent is structured as a compound sentence ending with a half cadence: the presentation (mm. 26–29; 30–33) is followed by a continuation module (mm. 34–39). In this case the antecedent is followed by a sentential consequent (mm. 40–54), whose I:PAC is elided with the onset of an independent, *forte* transition. In other instances the parallel consequent may dissolve into TR rhetoric before attaining its expected cadence:

---

9. László Somfai, *The Keyboard Sonatas of Joseph Haydn: Instruments and Performance Practice, Genres and Styles* [orig. in Hungarian, 1979], trans. Somfai in collaboration with Charlotte Greenspan (Chicago: University of Chicago Press, 1995). This data, and other information not mentioned above, may be found in ch. 15, "The Primary Theme," pp. 237–61 ("monochrome," pp. 243–44; "abstract" and "instrumental character," p. 247; "striking instrumental effect" and "idiomatic," pp. 251–52; "bare bones" and Scarlatti, pp. 253–54; "are not stylized or accelerated minuets," p. 254; "The asymmetric model," p. 241).

10. N. 14 below suggests one way in which our view of a sentence is more flexible that that of Caplin. (We also find the concept of "hybrids" to be problematic, although for the sake of convenience we have provisionally employed that term in this book.) Still another difference between our descriptions is in our diverging conceptions of what constitutes a "phrase." We regard the normative "phrase" as a more or less complete musical thought involving motion to a cadence. The presence of a cadence at its end—except, perhaps, in deformational or other rare and extraordinary instances (which do sometimes occur)—is central to our preferred view of the term. Caplin's definition is cast in a way that does not require a cadence. In his system the word "phrase" is "a functionally neutral term of grouping structure [that] refers, in general, to a discrete group approximately four measures in length" (*Classical Form*, p. 260, n. 5); a phrase is "minimally, a four-measure unit, often, but not necessarily, containing two ideas" (p. 256; cf. p. 263, nn. 4, 11). What Caplin calls a phrase we would often call a subphrase or module—although "module" is intended to be a flexible term covering any of a number of small building-blocks within a work, ranging from each of Caplin's two smaller ideas, to any slightly larger unit without strong inner contrasts, to, at times, a consistent "phrase" itself.

The differing understandings of the term "phrase" (with or without the necessity of a cadence) are rooted in differing analytical traditions that we need not explicate here. We might note only that the varying conceptions of the phrase invite differently nuanced understandings of larger musical motion. One of the clearest advocates of the necessity of the terminal cadence is William Rothstein, as in his book *Phrase Rhythm in Tonal Music* (New York: Schirmer Books, 1989), p. 5: "A phrase should be understood as, among other things, a directed motion in time from one tonal entity to another; these entities may be harmonies, melodic tones (in any voice or voices), or some combination of the two. *If there is no tonal motion, there is no phrase.*" Oversimplifying the matter considerably (to confine ourselves for practical purposes only to discussions carried on in the past fifteen years), we may acknowledge a Caplin-Rothstein split regarding this matter—one in which our preferences lie with Rothstein. See Darcy, rev. of Caplin, *Classical Form*, in *Music Theory Spectrum* 22 (2000), 122–25.

EXAMPLE 5.2   Mozart, Symphony No. 39 in E-flat, K. 543, i, mm. 26–57
(melodic line only)

in this case we consider the TR to begin with the consequent (chapter 6).

Another complex structure (a rarer one) is that of a rounded binary form: ABA', with a harmonic interruption at the end of the B section. (The A section may itself be structured as a period, sentence, or hybrid.) The presence of such an elaborate shape can produce not only a breadth or vastness to the P–idea, but also an uncommon roundedness or completeness for it. In some cases, it may happen that the onset of the last limb (the A' reprise) soon dissolves into transitional material (TR of the dissolving-final-element type; we regard TR as beginning directly with that A', even before the moment of literal dissolution). This occurs in the massive opening F-minor paragraphs of Cherubini's Overture to *Médée* (initial A ending with a half cadence, m. 20), in the first movement of Schubert's Quintet in C, D. 956 (B in m. 26, A' in m. 33), and in a few other pieces. For hermeneutic purposes it is sometimes helpful to notice that the ABA' structure, when more vocal, lyrical, or *cantabile* in character, might have been in-

tended to suggest an untexted song. Quite often such a song implies an "absent" text of around eight poetic lines in length. (A typical scheme is 2 + 2 + 2 + 2 lines, perhaps responding more comfortably to the schema, aa'ba''.) We identify such a *cantabile* "song without words" as a lyric binary, a subset of the binary form proper.

When these more complex forms are closed (when their final modules are brought to a perfect authentic cadence), one might even find local repeat signs within the theme. Repeat signs within an opening melody are more often signals of a rondo theme and hence predictive of either a pure rondo or a Type 4 sonata (sonata-rondo). Still, things are not always so clear. In the sparkling finale of Mozart's String Quintet in D, K. 593, one finds a standard sonata form (a Type 3 sonata) in which P is a rounded binary theme with local, interior repeats. The editors of the relevant volume of the *Neue Mozart Ausgabe* misconstrued this and introduced without comment a nonexistent, additional repeat sign after P proper (at m. 37), thus providing directions for an impossible, hopelessly misconstrued form, one whose expositional repeat returns only to TR.[11] The nineteenth-century Mozart edition had provided the correct repeats. A similar interior-repeat situation, thankfully without the editorial error, may be found in the Allegro vivace finale of Schubert's Symphony No. 5 in B-flat, and in several other works. On rare occasions one might find rounded-binary P themes within Type 3 finales in which the internal repeats, instead of being notated with repeat signs, are fully written-out, with perhaps only minor variants, if any. Examples occur in the last movements of Haydn's Symphonies No. 76 in E-flat and No. 77 in B-flat and of Mozart's Symphony No. 40 in G Minor, K. 550. (Repeat signs within sonata-rondo P themes are considered in chapter 18.)

Thematic/Modular Designations: Numberings

We have already established our letter-designations for the four potential zones (action-spaces) of a standard expositional layout, or first rotation: P (primary); TR (transition); S (secondary); C (closing). For many purposes it is sufficient to indicate these zones without reference to any of their inner subdivisions, in which case the letters alone are appropriate. It sometimes happens, though, that one wishes to single out individual modules or small subsections within these spaces. In order to indicate constituent elements within P-, TR-, S-, and C-space we use exponential numbers—superscripted numerals—such as P^1, C^2, and so on. These numbers are assigned according to certain principles.

Our first principle is that in none of the zones do we notch a superscript integer upward from 1 to 2, from 2 to 3, and so on, unless a perfect authentic cadence has been sounded in a key appropriate to that musical space. This is advisable because so much of Sonata Theory is concerned with the attainment or nonattainment of cadences. Music designated as P^1 will move

on to P^2 only after the first PAC has been attained. (Obviously, if what follows merely reiterates or slightly varies the music leading into the cadence, that would be a full or partial repetition of P^1, not a P^2 module in its own right. The same is true of modules within TR, S, or C.) Any P-module labeled P^3 should have been preceded by two differing thematic spans, each ending in a PAC. Thus the integer 1 means: "belonging to the first perfect-authentic-cadential span" or "preceding the first PAC." The integer 2 means: "belonging to the second perfect-authentic-cadential span" or "following the first PAC." Note that within P it is possible to have no PACs at all (tonal underdetermination of P): the music can dissolve away (via a TR) from that potential before an authentic cadence is reached. In that case the mere letter P can suffice to designate pre-TR space; or, if it is useful to subdivide the modules of the P-span further, one could designate it as P^1 with some added indicator of the modules' locations or functions, perhaps by means of the decimal designators described below. Yet another possibility, in each of the zones, is a preliminary or otherwise preparatory "zero-module" (P^0 or $P^{1.0}$, for example). This is a more complex issue treated separately further below.

Many P-zones (and other zones) are multimodular: they consist of smaller, sometimes contrasting units that we might want to single out for any number of purposes. We may be interested in parsing the theme itself. We may wish to suggest a functional or hermeneutic role for one or more of the P-modules. Or we may simply wish to be able to refer to that isolated module later in the piece—perhaps only one or two modules of P are actually used in the development. How might P or P^1 be subdivided? If P is a period, one might wish to designate its two parts as P^{ant} and P^{cons}. A complementary labeling plan could be used for the sentence. Or one might wish to adapt some of Caplin's terminology from *Classical Form*, "basic idea" (b.i.),

11. See this measure of K. 593/iv in Mozart, *Neue Ausgabe sämtliche Werk*, Serie VIII, Werkgruppe 19, Abteilung I: Streichquintette, ed. Ernst Hess and Ernst Fritz Schmid (Kassel: Bärenreiter, 1967), p. 134. A photograph of the relevant page of Mozart's autograph score (the second manuscript page of the finale)—with no indication of a repeat at this point—may be consulted in Ernst Hess, "Die 'Varianten' im Finale des Streichquentettes KV 593," *Mozart-Jahrbuch* 1960/61 (Salzburg, 1961), pp. 68–77, facing p. 77.

"contrasting idea" (c.i.), and other descriptions, as part of one's superscript designation of the modules. We advise flexibility along these lines. One should use the subdesignations that seem most appropriate to the analytical concerns brought to bear on the themes themselves.

In general, we refer to modules within a perfect-authentic-cadential span by means of decimal designators: 1.1, 1.2, 1.3, and so on. Such designators can furnish much information at a glance. $P^{1.2}$, for example, may be explicated as "within the first perfect-authentic-cadential span of the P-zone (prior to the first sounding of a I:PAC, if it exists at all), the module that follows the immediately opening idea." $P^{2.1}$ means: "still in P-space, the next P-module after the first PAC." It should be underscored that the practice of decimal designators is no rigid system but merely a conceptual tool to be used by the individual analyst as he or she sees fit. Most flexibly understood, the numerals following the decimal need imply no more than that they tally modules that we wish to notice for one reason or another. Often, however, they will correspond to certain thematic features of the period or sentence, including "basic ideas," "contrasting ideas," the beginning of the continuation of a sentence, and so on. (Whenever possible, we prefer to identify the beginning of the continuation of a sentence with a 1.2 designation, with the presentation modules being labeled as 1.1. But even here, given the details of individual cases, absolute consistency must sometimes be sacrificed.) Differing analysts and analytical purposes might arrive at differing decimal designations—which is generally fine. In most cases, however, the predecimal integers, registering perfect authentic cadences, should remain constant from one analysis to another.

Exceptions in Thematic Numberings

As indicated above, within the P zone and in all other zones it is normally only when one moves past a perfect authentic cadence onto differing material still in that zone that the integer 1 gives way to 2, 2 to 3, and so on. There are two exceptions to this principle. One concerns the convention of labeling the constituent parts of a trimodular block (the TMB, associated

with apparent double medial caesuras) in the middle of an exposition. Here the convention is to identify the differing modules as TM^1, TM^2, and TM^3, even though in most cases the whole TMB covers only a single cadential span (see chapter 8). The other exception concerns the special case of "zero-modules" (especially P^0, S^0, and C^0), a topic dealt with directly below. Proceeding from a zero-module to the ensuing "1" theme implies nothing with regard to the existence or nonexistence of a PAC between the two modules.

"Zero-Modules": General Considerations

It is not uncommon for individual zones—especially P and S—to begin with music that, even while opening that zone, seems preparatory to a more decisive (or more fully launched) module that follows. This aspect can take on different realizations, some of which are "thematic," some of which are not. One might find: an introductory vamp or accompaniment figure; an initial group of "set-apart," emphatic chords; a quasi-fanfare motto, sometimes *all'unisono*, that "clears the way" and then proceeds onward to contrasting material; an obvious anacrusis module or other preliminary module; a thematic module that has not yet fully stabilized over a root position tonic (especially within the S-zone); and the like. A zero designation—P^0, S^0, and (the rarer) C^0—indicates the results of an interpretive decision that proposes either that the module at hand displays an overt preparatory function (often in the sense of "get ready!") or that the initial module conveys the sense of something "destabilized" or not yet fully moored to tonic root-support. If the analyst decides that such an introductory module is not as fully separate from what follows to merit the "zero" label per se, a lighter alternative is the use of a 1.0 label: $P^{1.0}$, $S^{1.0}$, $C^{1.0}$, the next module of which, still more decisive, would be understood as 1.1. At issue here are only degrees of strength and analytical nuance: often either the "zero" or the 1.0 label will be workable. In either case, the zero-module will lead directly into something more secured and normative for that zone. Zero-modules rarely last longer than a few bars (although a few broader exceptions do exist) before calling forth, moving into, merging into, or otherwise precipitating the relevant P^1, S^1, or C^1. In highly exceptional cases, one might confront a situation in which the "zero" passage is itself multimodular. Within the P-zone, for example, this could suggest a $P^{0.1}$, $P^{0.2}$ sequence of numberings before P^1 is reached.

Zero-modules are not musical ideas that stand outside of the zone proper. A P^0- or $P^{1.0}$-module launches the P-zone and therefore belongs to P-space (and hence to expositional space); an S^0- or $S^{1.0}$ module launches the S-zone; on those rare occasions when it can be found, a C^0- or $C^{1.0}$-module launches the C-zone. In most cases (though not all) the zero-module will not be separated from its "integer-one" successor by a PAC. Nonetheless—as an exception to the general principle of numbering—one notches up any P^0 number from zero to one at this point, in large part to indicate that the preparatory or "not fully opened" character of the music has now taken on a more decisive and normative aspect.

The zero concept covers a wide range of preparatory or otherwise quasi-"tentative" initiating functions within these zones. Since the zero concept indicates a function, not a thematic or modular type, zero-modules can differ widely from each other in character and format. Some standard types of P^0 modules are not characteristic of S^0 modules, and vice versa. One should not expect the ones to "sound like" the others. Apart from these generalized remarks intending to introduce the zero concept broadly, one should consult the separate discussions of P^0- or $P^{1.0}$-modules (below), S^0- and $S^{1.0}$-modules (chapter 7), and C^0- and $C^{1.0}$-modules (chapter 9) in order to deal with specific instances and typical cases.

Tonal Under- and Overdetermination

As elsewhere in sonata-space, cadence attainment or nonattainment within P is a crucial aspect of its character. One structural function of P is to set forth an unambiguous tonic that will nevertheless be attained as a fuller, more stabilized reality at the point of the ESC. While P-themes are rarely if ever tonally ambiguous,

it is also true that according to the generic contract in force this P-key is under obligation to be lost or abandoned (for the keys of S / C; for the keys of the modulatory development) before being reattained more securely in the recapitulation. The tonic key at the opening exists as a proposition to be undermined (or unfolded) on the way to reaching a higher level of closure. To be sure, the vigorous postulating of a diatonic collection within P leaves no doubt with regard to the local tonic being asserted. Nevertheless, grasping the still-provisional nature of the tonic at P is central to the hermeneutic aspect of Sonata Theory. It is an essential component of its understanding of the *raison d'être* of the trajectory of the sonata as a whole toward the ESC. (See chapter 11 for the concept of tonic presence.)

On this understanding, it becomes important to notice whether P is tonally open or closed before it proceeds into TR. Open, closed, and multiply closed P-themes cannot be regarded as expressively neutral choices. Obviously, a P that is brought to a single I:PAC (or IAC) has fully declared its tonic and stabilized it, at least locally, with a cadence. Here the tonic proposition is fully carried out and may be considered adequately determined (or, more simply, normal). It often happens that the I:PAC moment is elided with TR—frequently a *forte* or aggressive TR, as occurs in Mozart's Symphony No. 39 in E-flat, K. 543, m. 54 (example 5.2). In such cases P is articulated as a completed, locally centered entity before embarking on the process of destabilization.

In other situations P proper never attains a I:PAC at all: it is destabilized with TR material before reaching its own tonic closure. This is the case in many instances of TRs of the "dissolving" type: TRs that begin as a closing element of the P-idea (a consequent, a sentence-continuation, a concluding final A' element, and so on) but that redirect the expected thematic closure into TR-*Fortspinnung* or other recognizable devices. Such P-themes should be regarded as tonally *underdetermined*: their tonics are clearly understood but not secured with an authentic cadence. Celebrated examples include the large-antecedent openings (with dissolving-consequent TRs) of Beethoven's Piano Sonatas in C, op. 53, "Waldstein," and in F Minor, op. 57, "Appassionata."

Of particular interest are instances of the other extreme: P-zones that consist of multiple modules, several of which end with a I:PAC or IAC. In such cases the tonic is locally *overdetermined*, and the subsequent tonic-phrases after the initial PAC can take on a number of different characters. In the most typical instances the varied modules of the overdetermined P are sounded at a relatively quiet dynamic. When there is a sudden *forte* or tutti-affirmation outburst elided with the downbeat of a I:PAC, it is usually preferable, on rhetorical grounds, to regard that as the onset of a TR (which itself might be overdetermined with regard to initial-tonic cadences, as discussed in chapter 6). Above all, what is clear is that the multiple I:PACs within P produce an effect of local redundancy. In turn this suggests an unusually powerful tonic field at the outset of P, one from which the narrative subject is either obstinately unwilling or (tragically?) unable to depart. Or it may be that for purposes that will become clear as the sonata proceeds it will have proven important to lay down an unusually forceful local tonic at the beginning. All such situations invite a hermeneutic interpretation. (For more on the terms "under-" and "overdetermination" see chapter 11, n. 32.)

Within Allegro compositions perhaps the most common trope of P-overdetermination involves the suggestion of a temporizing, smug, or static reluctance to get the sonata moving off the initial tonic. This holding all-too-fast to the tonic-spot is typically corrected with a strong, *forte* TR-jolt that suddenly shifts the overdetermined tonic onto a different tonal plane—as an impatient *non sequitur* ("Enough! Let's get on with it!")—and instantly redirects the indecisive stasis into linear, forward motion. The most well-known case occurs in the first movement of Mozart's Piano Sonata in F, K. 332 (example 5.3). Following a soon-cloying succession of self-satisfied tonic PACs (mm. 12, 20, 21, and 22), the TR-jolt is provided with the locally D-minor (vi) *Sturm und Drang* outburst at m. 23. (Compare this with the Allegro assai finale of the same sonata, which in several ways recomposes and rethinks the structural details

of the first movement: tonic PACs at mm. 14, 22, 32, followed by a prolonged tonic pedal; sudden shift onto vi in m. 36.) Closely related examples in Mozart may be found in the openings of Piano Concerto No. 14 in E-flat, K. 449 (quasi-*Sturm-und-Drang* TR-displacement in vi in m. 17 following redundant cadences) and the Quartet in D, "Hoffmeister," K. 499 (urgent TR-shift on vi in m. 23). It recurs also in the solo exposition of the first movement of Piano Concerto No. 15 in B-flat, K. 450 (sudden shift to vi, G minor, in mm. 86–87, the beginning of that exposition's TR). The same procedure is also locatable in Haydn, as in the opening of the Quartets in D, op. 20 no. 4 (aggressive move onto vi in m. 31), and in B-flat, op. 50 no. 1 (explosive augmented-triad TR-ignition in m. 28). On the other hand, while Haydn's Quartet in B-flat, op. 64 no. 3, overdetermines the tonic at the outset through a non-sequitur P^2 interpolation (mm. 8–17), the onset of TR (m. 18) comes as less of a shock, more of an efficient returning-to-business.

Another important trope of I:PAC overdetermination occurs more frequently in lyrical slow movements. The second movements to Beethoven's Piano Concerto No. 3, op. 37, and his Symphony No. 6, "Pastoral," op. 68, furnish the paradigmatic illustrations. In both cases P first unfolds as a lyrical theme closed off with a structural I:PAC: in op. 37 we encounter an expansive multimodular theme that ends decisively with the tonic cadence at m. 17; in op. 68, the *Szene am Bach*, we find two circular statements of a sentential phrase, each concluding with a I:PAC, in mm. 7 and 13. And in both we find that once the essential structure of P has been attained, we are released into a specially highlighted, postcadential, codetta-like phrase or *Nachsatz* of uncommon satisfaction (in the concerto mm. 17–21 with cadential reiterations, mm. 22–24; in the symphony—shown in example 5.4—mm. 14–15, 16–17, with bobbing reiterations of the tonic, mm. 17–18; in op. 68 the phrase also resurfaces in differing contexts throughout the movement).

Such luminous P-codetta moments cry out for an interpretation beyond facile labeling. They are particularly suitable, as here, for conveying moments of heightened reverence or

EXAMPLE 5.3   Mozart, Piano Sonata in F, K. 332, i, mm. 1–26

EXAMPLE 5.4 Beethoven, Symphony No. 6 in F, op. 68 ("Pastoral"), ii, mm. 13–18

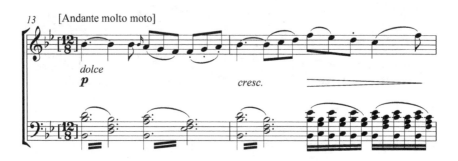

grateful contemplation. Indeed, the impression can be that, having completed P's essential structure with a clear, final PAC, the composer opens a free or extra space of valediction, thanks, benediction, or prayer—confirming the initial tonic and resettling definitively on it (perhaps even being folded and refolded into a tonic sonority over a tonic pedal) before moving on to the next zone of the larger structure. In turn this can strike us as a space of formally unnecessary, surplus blessedness set forth in a sonorous zone freed from the structural constraint of having to conclude the thematic form. That form proper is already finished, and one is ready to reap the rewards of accomplishment in an extra zone of special reverence, a benediction-suffix. (The glowing, backwards-reflective effect would not be lost on later nineteenth-century composers, where it emerges also in compositions that are not sonatas: the slow movements of Mendelssohn's Violin Concerto [mm. 40–44, then, elided again, 44–48] and Mahler's Symphony No. 6 [mm. 10–20]; Brahms's *Schicksalslied*, mm. 23–29.) In the minor mode, however, such a P-codetta can suggest quite the opposite: a frozen, "additional" zone of inescapable grief, as in the F-sharp-minor Andante movement of Mozart's Piano Concerto in A, K. 488, mm. 12–20.

Some Special P-Types

P as Grand Antecedent

This P-type consists of a lengthy, often multimodular antecedent phrase (one that contains several subphrases or thematic modules linked together, producing a larger-than-normal antecedent) that ends at the point of the I:HC with grand, rhetorical flourishes, sometimes even MC-like flourishes. Its very length and breadth suggests a striving for monumental proportions. Not infrequently, the grand antecedent is itself constructed as a sentence (sentential grand antecedent).

Consider the grand-antecedent P-themes

launching the first movements of Mozart's Symphonies No. 40 in G Minor, K. 550 (example 5.5; see also example 3.4), and No. 41 in C, K. 551 ("Jupiter"). Both are unfolded as sentences; both highlight and emphasize rhetorically their HC arrivals. In K. 550 the dominant is reached in m. 16 and expanded grandly for four bars. In K. 551 the dominant is reached in m. 19 and elaborated for 4 mm. up to a fermata (!) HC close in m. 23. Both symphonies then begin a parallel grand consequent that soon dissolves into TR rhetoric. (In both we consider TR to begin with the consequent; the TR is that of the "dissolving-consequent" type.) The rhetorically enhanced HC arrivals of these particular antecedents may "sound like" a potential (if "too early") MC, even though in neither piece have any clear signs of TR activity been launched in the grand antecedent. Once any (parallel) grand consequent begins, however, one realizes that any MC potential for this moment, however slight, is being passed over.

A more challenging example—a large, multimodular grand antecedent that is *not* constructed as a sentence—is the P-theme of the finale of Beethoven's Symphony No. 5 in C Minor. This consists of a chain of four modules: $P^{1.1}$, the triumphant, march-based head-motive, mm. 1–4; $P^{1.2}$, the ascending scalar idea, mm. 5–12; $P^{1.3}$, the drive to the dominant, mm. 13–18 (landing on the structural V [dominant lock] at m. 18); $P^{1.4}$, the prolongation of the dominant, mm. 18–22. Four bars of extravagantly dramatic, scalar caesura-fill (though not *medial* caesura-fill) ensue, mm. 22–26. This leads not to a dissolving parallel consequent (we do not return to the triumphant, march-based P-theme) but to a new idea that aggressively launches TR (m. 26). Considered according to Caplin's phrase-hybrid classifications, what is implied is not a grand period but a structure that might be identified as a grand hybrid. (Hybrid 1 in this classification consists of antecedent + continuation, essentially what occurs in grander format here.[12] M. 26 thus launches a TR of the dissolving-continuation type.)

The effect of a grand antecedent can occasion-

---

12. Caplin, *Classical Form*, pp. 59–60.

EXAMPLE 5.5 Mozart, Symphony No. 40 in G Minor, K. 550, i, mm. 1–30

EXAMPLE 5.5 (*continued*)

ally include even more striking complications. Sometimes one encounters more obviously generic TR activity (standard *forte* gestures, often at the downbeat of a I:PAC, which one would normally take as a TR-launch) *before* the I:HC quasi-MC effect. When this occurs—as in the first movement of Haydn's Symphonies No. 96 in D, "Miracle," and No. 101 in D, "Clock," along with the finale of Mozart's Symphony No. 41 in C, K. 551, "Jupiter"—the impression given is that of a TR-space decisively entered following a clearly delimited P, then aborted through a surprising or witty change of mind. We refer to the section from the beginning of the exposition through these brief, aborted TR textures ("false" TRs before the I:HC caesura effect, then the I:HC proper) as a complex grand antecedent.

The additional adjective indicates that the "antecedent-effect" may comprise more than one phrase (more than one interior cadence, which would not be the case with an antecedent proper) and that, as a result, the TR-effect before the I:HC had been more convincing or elaborate than in a normative grand antecedent (which is by definition an expanded single phrase). What follows the I:HC MC-effect is usually to be regarded as the real TR, which can take the character of any of various TR types. The MC moment at the end of a complex grand antecedent is conceptually close to that of a I:HC MC-declined situation. Can one distinguish between them? Assuming that the distinction promises to have hermeneutic value (if not, the distinction is not worth bothering with), it may pivot on our personal assessment of the strength of the intervening TR-effect. If the TR-effect before the I:HC MC-effect is more elaborate even than that found in a complex grand antecedent—such as the one in Haydn's "Clock" Symphony—it may be better to regard the situation as one of medial caesura declined. Obviously, one should not frame a major hermeneutic point around any such presumed distinction in what is self-evidently an analytically ambiguous situation.

Mozartian "Loops": A Specialized Variant of the Sentence

One commonly encountered type of Mozartian theme begins with a short module (two to six measures)—usually closing with a cadential progression—that is either elided or flush-juxtaposed with a repetition of itself before moving forward into differing material. One touchstone instance occurs at the opening (P-theme) of the Piano Sonata in C, K. 279 (example 5.6). Mm. 1–3 articulate a compact progression ending with a I:PAC in m. 3, simultaneously setting off a repetition of the same three bars, mm. 3–5. The impression given is that of circular repetition, a "loop" of self-replication that could continue indefinitely unless something intervenes to break the pattern. That "breakout" occurs at m. 5, at the moment of the theme's second PAC. Here the music breaks free of its initial circularity and shoots forth with a differing idea in a more clearly linear vector. A slightly more expanded example may be found in the P-theme of the first movement of Piano Concerto No. 9 in E-flat, K. 271 (example 5.7). Mm. 1–4 comprise a characteristically brief, Mozartian double-idea: an opening, annunciatory, triadic gesture *all'unisono* (mm. 1–2) followed by a responding melodic module that ends with a cadential progression and PAC at m. 4. This four-bar idea is then elided with a literal repetition of itself (mm. 4–7). In this case the exit from the circular repetition is handled with a more relaxed smoothness. Instead of beginning at once with a directly elided contrasting idea on the downbeat (the more common procedure), as happens in K. 279/i, m. 5, the "elision" at m. 7 proceeds more in the manner of a flush-juxtaposition. In K. 271/i much of m. 7 also serves as a space separating the two ideas, a graceful slide into a new, lyrical module, whose downbeat proper occurs in m. 8.

While the psychology of circular, self-repetitive loops is the primary expressive factor in play here, from a secondary but still important perspective the format of such themes, considered as wholes, is also in dialogue with the structural principle of the sentence: a presentation module appears twice in the manner of a potentially continuous loop and releases it-

EXAMPLE 5.6 Mozart, Piano Sonata in C, K. 279, i, mm. 1–20

EXAMPLE 5.6   (*continued*)

EXAMPLE 5.7   Mozart, Piano Concerto No. 9 in E-flat, K. 271, i,
mm. 1–14

self into a broader, forward-moving continuation.[13] (In this case, one typically encounters a contrasting sentence-continuation—an important, often overlooked type—rather than one that displays the more commonly encountered fragmentation of material from the presentation, increase in the rate of harmonic activity, and so on.)[14] We consider such structures to be specialized stylizations of the sentence, "sentences of the loop type." This thematic strategy always consists of two sections: the initial loops themselves and the "breakout," an escape from the loop-pattern and the onset of a drive toward a differing goal. When an initial, circular idea is quite brief—two or three measures—and does not display significant contrasting material within itself, we call it a *simple loop*. This would be the situation in K. 279/i. In the case of K. 271/i, however, the loop more clearly consists of two differing modules. Each of these presentation modules may be described, using Caplin's terminology, as a compound basic idea (c.b.i.): a basic idea (b.i.) followed by an emphatically contrasting idea (c.i.). Accordingly, one may call this a *compound* or *binary loop*, a modular type frequently found in Mozart's works, in both P and S themes.

One way in which the loop-variant of the compound sentence typically differs from the more normative type is the unmistakable cadence (PAC) at the end of each loop (K. 279/i, mm. 3 and 5; K. 271/i, mm. 4 and 7). In other words, the loop typically traces through an efficient cadential progression, tonic–predominant–dominant–tonic, which is then immediately recycled with a literal or only slightly varied repetition. In the most local sense this would appear to contradict the general principle that the presentation portion of a sentence (or compound sentence) does not end with a cadence. Here the crucial observation is that although the two cadences are obvious enough—perfectly recognizable as enacting the final elements of cadential-progression formulas—both within their larger sentential format and within their own context of appearing at the ends of reiterated loops, they are incapable of serving as structural goals that conclude the broader musical idea. Their local cadences are subsumed under their larger presentational function, that of opening a larger sentential idea.

We may also approach this observation from a slightly different angle, one that will also be resonant with fundamental principles of EEC

---

13. Not all initially repeated ideas ending with a cadence are to be understood as loops that function as the presentation of a larger sentence. As mentioned above, presentation-loops are normally brief, from two to six measures in length. Additionally, they do not typically display the standard 4 + 4 formats (or variants thereof) characteristic of the classical period, sentence, or hybrid. In other words, absent other, *ad hoc* evidence one should not consider as a presentation-loop any theme in which the repeated idea is formatted as a normative period, sentence, or hybrid. If this is the case, that theme is better regarded as a standard P-idea subjected to immediate repetition—which is also a fairly common procedure. For examples of 4 + 4 P-themes that are immediately repeated and that we do *not* classify as presentation-loops, see the opening of Mozart's Violin Sonata in A, K. 305 (mm. 1–4, 5–8, restated in mm. 9–12, 13–16—a repeated "hybrid 3" theme, compound basic idea + continuation) and the onset of the exposition in the first movement of Haydn's Symphony No. 102 in B-flat (mm. 23–26, 27–30, restated with different orchestration and dynamics, mm. 31–34, 35–38—a repeated parallel period).
14. In the broadest sense (cf. n. 10), we understand the sentence as a modular shape that is best defined *gestur-*

ally (or anapestically) as an initial double- (or triple-) impulse that proceeds to "take off" into a longer or more conclusive idea: two preliminary bounces on the diving-board, followed by a third that precipitates the actual dive. While many, perhaps even most, sentence presentations are tonic-prolongational, not all of them are: we do not regard tonic prolongation itself as a necessary feature of a presentation. Additionally, the continuations can be of highly variable length and can either continue to work with material from the presentation or can proceed, in varying degrees, with an entirely new idea that springs forth as a distinct contrast to the two presentational "bounces." For two familiar examples of utterly contrasting continuations following otherwise model presentations, see the openings of the first movements of Mozart's *Eine Kleine Nachtmusik*, K. 525, and Beethoven's Piano Sonata in F, op. 10 no. 2. Similar examples abound in this repertory—as well as in the music of the ensuing decades of the nineteenth century. (For us, Caplin's discussion of "continuation function" within a sentence, e.g., *Classical Form*, p. 41, remains too narrow, too restrictively defined, by concerning itself primarily with only one type of typical continuation, albeit an important one, within sentences of normative length.)

deferral in chapters 7 and 8. A standard technique of reopening the local apparent-closure of any PAC is by immediate repetition. Under this conception, the repetition of the initial loop reopens or "undoes" the seeming finality of that PAC and proceeds to its own PAC further down the line. Similarly, the breakout-continuation also undoes the second PAC by declaring itself to function, within this specific, readily recognizable paradigm, as the continuation of a larger-scale sentence. This continuation function is capable of undoing the full-closure effectiveness of any immediately preceding PAC, since it indicates that we are to understand the earlier loops as only the first portion of a larger sentence, which is the real governing format at this point. Notwithstanding the two obvious PACs, the positionality of those cadences within the larger sentential-thematic structure, along with their subordination to the circular loops within which they are generated, weakens the usual sense of a PAC as a sign of emphatic structural closure and renders them incapable of functioning as normative structural cadences. These perfect authentic cadences, in short, cannot "end" the theme in question.[15] They serve only as specialized openers to the larger theme, the sentence, within which they are embedded.[16]

As a consequence, it is clarifying not to regard such breakouts as we find in m. 5 of K. 279/i and m. 7 of K. 271/i as P^2 modules (following a structural, conclusive PAC) but rather as $P^{1.2}$ modules—presuming here the convention whereby the continuation of the sentence should normally be indicated by the 1.2 decimal designator.[17] The breakout itself is often constructed as a sentence: it can proceed as a sentential continuation. In K. 279/i, mm. 5–6 provide a musical pattern that is imaginatively varied and intensified in mm. 7–8: taken together, these may be understood as a new presentation, with the corresponding continuation⇒cadential portion ($P^{1.3}$) beginning at m. 9 and finally arriving at the desired structural I:PAC on the third beat of m. 12. (The remainder of this example will be discussed in chapter 6.) In K. 271/i, the "new sentence" breaking free from the loops also begins with its own presentational modules, here still in a *piano* dynamic, in mm. 8–9 and 10–11. In this case it is only with the "new sentence's" continuation, m. 12, that the dynamic shifts suddenly to *forte*.

If the "$P^{1.2}$" breakout-idea leads to its own I:PAC (as in K. 279/i, m. 12, beat 3), then its status within P-space is normally secure, absent any other factors that might lead us to think otherwise. Another option, though, would not lead the breakout-continuation to that PAC but drive it instead to a half-cadence arrival and subsequent MC. In these cases the breakout is simultaneously the onset of the transition. The $P^{1.2}$ continuation will have been merged with TR, producing a "P⇒TR merger," a special case often encountered with sentential P-themes (as outlined in chapter 6). (More literally, this may be represented as $P^{1.2}$⇒TR.) This is the situation in K. 271/i, where what begins as a $P^{1.2}$ breakout (m. 7), though initially in a *piano* dynamic, leads to a *forte*-driven half-cadence and dominant-lock (in effect) in m. 14. A I:HC

---

15. We agree with Caplin's more recent discussion of this issue ("The Classical Cadence," p. 86)—which also cited K. 279/i as an example. Here Caplin also invoked the utility of "hierarchical perspective. For it is sometimes valid to speak of cadential content having an actual cadential function at one level of structure while also recognizing that this same content loses its function at a higher level of structure. In these cases, it might be useful to invoke the notion of *limited cadential scope* to account for the effect of such cadences."

16. One consequence of this within S-themes that begin with loops is that no compound loop, ending with a PAC, should be considered to be capable of producing the EEC. (The classic instance is found in the loops that begin the secondary theme of Piano Concerto No. 21 in C, K. 467, e.g., in the opening ritornello, the two loops

of mm. 28–32 and 32–36: see example 8.5 and its surrounding discussion.) Thus the general principle: notwithstanding any local PAC that it might contain, no module that participates in a loop of normative size can provide a cadence strong enough to be taken to mark the end of a major structural unit. The "looped theme" should always be considered as proceeding forward into the breakout-continuation, however contrasting that continuation might be.

17. Following this convention, however, can lead to some complexities when dealing with a compound loop (b.i. + c.i.) in which one wishes to identify each smaller module with a separate label. One solution is to label b.i. and c.i. as $P^{1.1a}$ and $P^{1.1b}$ (K. 271, mm. 1–2 and 3–4, with upbeat).

MC will follow in m. 24. In other instances the moment of the ("$P^{1.2}$") breakout may itself begin with a sudden *forte* or at least an aggressive plunge forward, even more clearly suggesting at this point the effective onset of TR.

There are many examples of similarly looped themes in Mozart, and when dealing with that composer the analyst is well advised to be on the lookout for them, particularly in order to be able to interpret the presentational PACs appropriately. Other examples of pieces that open with this technique include the Quartet in B-flat, K. 172 (mm. 3–6, 7–10, following an initial set of separate, P^0 hammerstrokes on the tonic);[18] Symphony No. 28 in C, K. 200 (another classic instance, like K. 271/i, of the compound loop, mm. 1–7, 7–13, with a *forte* breakout at m. 13);[19] and Symphony No. 30 in D, K. 202 (three separate, flush-juxtaposed loops—a triple-loop, each repetition of which is slightly varied, mm. 1–4, 5–8, 9–12, with an elided *forte* breakout at m. 12).[20]

P^0- and $P^{1.0}$-Modules/Themes

In some Allegro movements one gets the impression that the "real" P-theme ($P^{1.1}$) begins two, three, four, or more bars into the piece, and that this theme is preceded by a brief, different Allegro idea, perhaps an opening flourish or other initializing gesture, that in some way prepares us for it (typically in the sense of "get ready!" or "attention!"). We identify such a preparatory gesture as either a P^0- or a $P^{1.0}$-module, depending on one's assessment of its conceptual separability from $P^{1.1}$—a P^0 idea being somewhat more hypothetically "dispensable" than a $P^{1.0}$ idea. In making such a distinction, one might try to imagine whether it would have been possible for the composer to have suppressed that

opening module completely. Could the movement just as easily have begun with the existing $P^{1.1}$? If so, or if that possibility at least seems reasonable to consider, then the designation P^0 may be taken to imply that judgment. On the other hand, if it seems that $P^{1.1}$ is set into motion or otherwise "reacts" in a more dependent way to the initial impulse—if one cannot really imagine the piece starting with that $P^{1.1}$ gesture—then the label $P^{1.0}$ is more appropriate, suggesting its function as a more "necessary" preparation for the particular $P^{1.1}$ that follows it. The distinction between P^0- and $P^{1.0}$-modules is by no means absolute. Each label represents a broad span of modular types on a continuum of possibilities, shading into each other. In many cases it seems pointless to haggle in favor of the one designator over the other. (At some level one would assume that every P^0 conditions the nature of what follows it.) P^0-modules need not be (and are normally not) separated from $P^{1.1}$ modules by a PAC. (See the discussions above of "zero-modules" and "exceptions in thematic numberings.")

Before identifying some common zero-types within P, we should stress that not all prefatory Allegro gestures should be regarded as P^0- or $P^{1.0}$-modules. Sometimes this initial gesture is merely a *brief, in-tempo introduction*, not a zero-module proper. This would be the case with the opening chords of Beethoven's *Eroica* Symphony. Its generic forebears, the hammer-blow openings of many mid-eighteenth-century works, also usually fall into this category. But when this initial gesture, with its undeniably introductory feel, is included in any immediate restatement of the P-theme, or when it is included in the repeat of the exposition and perhaps also begins the recapitulation—as in the quadruple-hammer-blow P^0 in mm. 1–2 of the

---

18. The loops of K. 172/i are also notable in employing the circular $\hat{8}-\flat\hat{7}-\hat{6}-\natural\hat{7}-\hat{8}$ motion discussed as a P-theme option later in this chapter.

19. In K. 200/i each loop ends not with a PAC proper but rather with an obvious substitute, a $\hat{5}-\hat{4}-\hat{3}-\hat{2}-\hat{1}$ descent in the upper voice, mm. 3–7, 9–13.

20. Other examples include the opening of Symphony "No. 1" in E-flat, K. 16, and what appears to be its much more sophisticated recomposition at the beginning of Piano Concerto No. 22 in E-flat, K. 482. The

initial-loop strategy may also be subjected to deformation. The opening of Piano Sonata in C, K. 309, invokes the paradigm only to block the normative completion (!) of the second compound loop at mm. 13–14. Mozart then bursts impulsively through the staged blockage by suddenly grasping onto a workable breakout-continuation, *forte*, at m. 15. Once the paradigm is grasped, one might regard the opening of the Overture to Mozart's *Le nozze di Figaro*, for instance, as a much-expanded variant of the compound-loop technique.

first movement of Mozart's Quartet in B-flat, K. 172—then it seems grouped as part of the launching idea of the sonata proper. The musical context tells us that it is conceptualized as part of the P-theme complex.

Qualifications like these lead inevitably to situations that are open to interpretation. In practice, such distinctions are not always so unequivocally made. It is not uncommon to find examples where an initial gesture hovers somewhere between an introduction and a P^0 theme. In Haydn's String Quartet in G, op. 33 no. 5, for example (example 5.1), one might initially suppose that the opening V^7–I of mm. 1–2 constitutes a brief, in-tempo introduction: because mm. 1–2 are not included in the expositional repeat, they seem introductory. On the other hand, those measures are soon folded into expositional space proper in mm. 9–10, suggesting their after-the-fact conceptual incorporation into P. They also reappear in mm. 182–83 to launch the recapitulatory rotation. Thus mm. 1–2 blend aspects of P^0 into what seems most intuitively to be a brief, in-tempo introduction. A similar situation crops up in the opening three hammer-blows of the Quartet in G, op. 76 no. 1. On the face of it, these would appear to constitute a brief, in-tempo introduction, but a mild, P^0 function of the gesture is underscored when the three-chord rhythm resurfaces in the lower parts near the opening of the development, mm. 89–90 (cello), mm. 93–94 (viola)—neatly linked, as it happens, with the three-chord gesture that closes the exposition.

There are different types of P^0- and $P^{1.0}$-modules. Among them:

Accompanimental Figuration (Rhythmic Stream). In these cases one first hears a measure or two of accompaniment—as with the accompaniment to a song (without words)—on top of which the theme proper is soon overlaid. The accompaniment or rhythmic stream is almost always best regarded as $P^{1.0}$. The opening bar of Mozart's Symphony No. 40 in G minor (Example 5.5) can be considered a brief $P^{1.0}$ of the accompanimental type. A similar opening is provided in the celebrated F-major Andante of his Piano Concerto in C, K. 467. A slightly more extended $P^{1.0}$ along these lines may be recognized

in the first movement of Schubert's Quartet No. 13 in A Minor, D. 804: two bars of a twisting "background" pattern are soon overlaid with the theme proper, $P^{1.1}$, in m. 3. By this time in the nineteenth century—and certainly in subsequent decades—the accompanimental opening became more common (for example, at the beginning of Mendelssohn's Violin Concerto in E Minor and many other pieces).

The Anacrusis-Module. Occasionally a composed-out initial gesture is elided with the onset of $P^{1.1}$, functioning as a large upbeat to it. The touchstone illustration of this type of $P^{1.0}$ (or perhaps P^0) occurs in the opening movement of Schubert's Symphony No. 5 in B-flat, D. 485. Here one encounters a *pianissimo* $P^{1.0}$, mm. 1–4, of considerable psychological subtlety. $P^{1.0}$ serves as a gracefully expanded anacrusis, as if providing a corridor transporting us from our own worlds into that of the symphony proper. $P^{1.0}$ is included in the expositional repeat, and while it does not begin the recapitulation, the preceding development is essentially a large-scale expansion of it. In other words, the development marks the onset of a large second rotation that persists until the end of the recapitulation. A related example may be consulted in the D-major Adagio non troppo movement of the Flute Concerto in G, K. 313 (a Type 5 sonata movement): one and a half bars of solemn "entry" or "invocation" (P^0 or $P^{1.0}$) precede the onset of the actual P^1 theme (m. 2, beat 3). That "invocation" reappears to begin the solo exposition (m. 10) and the recapitulation (m. 38).

The Motto, Emblem, or Head-Motive. This is common in minor-mode works, where we often find—as a normal generic option—an abrupt, peremptory initial stamp, a negative head motive, played *forte*, usually in octaves, before the "real" theme ($P^{1.1}$) starts to flow forward. The opening of Haydn's Symphony No. 44 in E Minor ("Trauer") is typical (Example 5.8): the P^0 peremptory stamp (perhaps also construable as $P^{1.0}$) occurs, *forte*, in mm. 1–4; $P^{1.1}$ ensues, *piano*, in m. 5. Here P^0 reappears in m. 13 and—probably the central criterion—is included in the expositional repeat. Similarly, at the beginning of Haydn, Symphony No. 95 in C Minor: P^0

EXAMPLE 5.8 Haydn, Symphony No. 44 in E Minor ("Trauer"), i,
mm. 1–20

unisons, *forte*, mm. 1–2; $P^{1.1}$ proper, *piano*, with the upbeat to m. 4. In a much more compressed manner the opening of Beethoven's Quartet in E Minor, op. 59 no. 2, also participates in this logic (notice that the opening two hammerblows are recaptured in the exposition's first ending), as does that of his Symphony No. 5 in C Minor, op. 67. In the latter case $P^{1.0}$ is much less conceptually separated from $P^{1.1}$: $P^{1.0}$, *forte*, mm. 1–5; $P^{1.1}$, *piano*, begins with the upbeat to m. 7. (It may be that peremptory, *forte* octave openings to minor-key works in general—certainly a commonly encountered feature—may be related to the P^0 concept. Or, of course, vice versa.) Much later in the century, Brahms would open his Symphony No. 3 with a latter-day variant of the $P^{1.0}$-motto or emblem—in this case also a kind of emblematic anacrusis—swelling dynamically into an explosive $P^{1.1}$.

Another example from Mozart illustrates an instance in which $P^{1.0}$ seems closely linked conceptually with an otherwise sharply contrasting $P^{1.1}$: the opening gestures of his Violin Concerto No. 4 in D, K. 218 (example 5.9). Here the initial flourish leads to a contrasting, *piano*-dynamic $P^{1.1}$ theme with the upbeat to m. 5: one could hardly imagine the concerto beginning with the music of mm. 5ff. It is also typical of such $P^{1.1}$ themes that they are structured as sentence presentations. In the Violin Concerto the opening four bars sound a stiff, march-like fanfare in octaves. The contrasting module, m. 5 (abandoning the *all'unisono* texture), is non-elided to the fanfare, although it is linked to it by a sustained D♮ in the horns and doubled by the violas, which also articulate a *Trommelbass* reiteration of that pitch. Mm. 5–12 are obviously sentential (mm. 5–6 and 7–8, a $P^{1.1}$ presentation; mm. 8 (beat 3)–12, $P^{1.2}$ continuation—beginning with a bass recalling the fanfare—and cadence). The first movement of the Sonata for Two Solo Pianos in D, K. 448/375*a*, is also a member of this strategy-set.

At times a P^0 theme may be developed considerably beyond the brief formulaic flourish. It can be more extended and assertive, only to withdraw for the onset of what probably comes to be regarded as P^1 proper. The openings of Schubert's last two string quartets provide paradigms: in both instances P^0 suggests the presence of a calamitous situation to be confronted. In the Quartet No. 14 in D Minor, D. 810 ("Death and the Maiden"), mm. 1–14 burst forth at their outset, then recede into *pianissimo* and before long into stasis (fermata on V, m. 14), as if parting the curtain for the main-theme proper, P^1, beginning in m. 15. Schubert made use of a structurally similar procedure in the Quartet No. 15 in G, D. 887. Here the modally tormented initial declaration—like a tragic or defiant initial stamp, a bold illuminated initial—flares up at once, urgently seizes the listener, then recedes (mm. 11–14, again with fermata) to make way for the second launch, or the start of the "real" *Hauptsatz* in G major, P^1, *pianissimo* in m. 15. Perhaps in both cases Schubert may have had in mind the opening of Beethoven's C-minor *Coriolan* Overture, which had also begun with an analogous set of P^0 outbursts before P^1 proper gets underway: P^0, *fortissimo*, mm. 1–14 (a musical battering-ram, breaking down the barriers to sonata-action); P^1 begins, *pianissimo*, at m. 15. Here there is no repeat sign to guide us in distinguishing this from a brief, in-tempo introduction. The rhetorical recapitulation, though (beginning famously in the key of the subdominant), announces its presence with the P^0 theme.

Double Introductory Gestures. Is it possible to imagine a situation in which the "real" P theme is preceded by not one but *two* introductory gestures? This is extremely rare, but it does happen. The classic example occurs at the opening of Schubert's Symphony No. 8 in B Minor ("Unfinished"). In this case the best choices for labels are P^0 for the opening "motto" and $P^{1.0}$ for the subsequent rhythmic stream. Thus we have P^0 in the cellos and basses, mm. 1–8, followed by $P^{1.0}$ with the subsequent rhythmic-stream accompaniment in the strings, mm. 9–12. (Here it is useful to recall that that prepa-

---

21. On the opening of K. 172/i, see also n. 16. The "loops" referred to in that note start with the upbeat to m. 3, after the quadruple-stroke P^0 idea in mm. 1–2.

The recapitulation also begins with this P^0-module, mm. 72–73.

EXAMPLE 5.9 Mozart, Violin Concerto No. 4 in D, K. 218, i, mm. 1–12

ratory rhythmic streams are almost always best labeled with 1.0 designations.) P^1 is the theme proper, sounded by the oboe and clarinet at m. 13.[22] In cases where the second of these preparatory modules does not seem adequately labeled as $P^{1.0}$, one could designate the two modules as $P^{0.1}$ and $P^{0.2}$.

The "Circular" $\hat{8}-\flat\hat{7}-\hat{6}-\natural\hat{7}-\hat{8}$ Pattern in P-Space

One common modular formula in this style involves the circular rotation of an $\hat{8}-\flat\hat{7}-\hat{6}-\natural\hat{7}-\hat{8}$ melodic pattern against a literal or implied tonic pedal. In E-flat major, for example, this would be the pattern $e\flat-d\flat-c-d\natural-e\flat$ produced either in one of the upper voices or in the bass against a persistent or persistently implied $E\flat$. The module is typically used to ground a tonic not through a normative cadence but by a melodic-harmonic motion revolving around it, also expressible harmonically as: $I-V^7/IV$ $-IV_4^6-vii^{o6}$ (or $V^{[7]}$)$-I$ (or, when the pattern is in the bass, $I-V_2^4/IV-IV^6-V^6$ or V_3^6 [or vii^{o7}?]$-I$). In all instances in which it appears it functions recursively, as a static, circular orbit around a fixed tonic—a cycling "out-of-focus" to the opposite pole, the subdominant chord, and an oscillation through the dominant back to the tonic. The manifest stasis of the pattern stands in contrast with the more normative linear motion of the various zones of the sonata. Consequently, its most natural sites of operation within expositions would be in areas of tonic-affirmation following the attainment of a structural cadence—namely, in C-space (following the EEC as a codetta) and as a P-codetta following a "concluding" I:PAC. These two

common usages are dealt with elsewhere: the C-appearances in chapter 9 and the P-codetta appearances (often part of a strategy of dissolution at the outset of TR) in chapter 6.

Most curious, however, are the numerous instances in the repertory where this seemingly closing or affirmational circumscribing of a tonic is used to *open* a composition.[23] In such instances the first significant chordal changes will be an applied dominant to IV, then a move to an inversion of IV itself—an apparent early tilt in the subdominant direction. And yet this is less a structural tip toward the subdominant proper than the beginning of a wheeling process of recursion around the tonic, as part of an initiatory effect of static grounding: beginning with stasis and affirmation.[24] The central thing is the decision to begin P not with a decisive linear thrust forward, as is more normative, but with one or two orbiting circles—a ceremonial *circumambulatio*—before finally allowing the linear vector of the composition to shoot forward "progressively." (Compare this technique, for example, to that of Mozartian "loops," a quite different production of an initial circular effect, discussed earlier.) Savoring the single- or double-cycle of stasis before proceeding onward is central to any expressive or hermeneutic understanding of the P theme. Examples abound in the repertory (often, but not always, in E-flat major), as in the first movements of: Mozart, Piano Quartet in E-flat, K. 493 (a touchstone example, mm. 1–5; this is also an example of a $P^{1.0}$ theme—and a prominent member of the opening-strategy set mentioned in the discussion of $P^{1.0}$ themes above); Haydn, Piano Sonata in E-Flat, Hob. XVI:52 (another touchstone, mm. 1–2); Beethoven, Piano Trio in E flat, op. 1 no.

---

22. For a related—yet different—double-gesture situation, see the opening of the E-flat-major Adagio (third movement) of the Serenade for Thirteen Winds in B-flat, K. 361. Here m. 1, outlining a solemn tonic-chord stretch *all'unisono*, constitutes a brief, in-tempo introduction. This is a one-time event that does not reappear at the point of recapitulation (nor is the exposition repeated). Mm. 2–3, on the other hand, lay down a rhythmic-stream accompaniment ($P^{1.0}$) that precedes the P^1-theme proper in the oboe, m. 4. One measure of this rhythmic-stream figuration also returns at the beginning of the recapitulation, m. 27.

23. Perhaps not surprisingly, the $\hat{8}-\flat\hat{7}-\hat{6}-\natural\hat{7}-\hat{8}$ pat-

tern seems much less common at the beginnings of S-themes (where it would suggest locally an immediate shift back to the tonic—or at least a strong looking-back at what had just been relinquished). One example of such a usage, however, occurs in very early Mozart: the first movement of the Violin Sonata in B-flat, K. 8, mm. 15–18.

24. The effect of beginning in this manner is not limited to sonata-form compositions. See, e.g., the opening of the Sarabande from Bach's Partita No. 1 in B-flat (mm. 1–4), a pattern that also appears over a more mobile bass in the Sarabande from the French Suite No. 4 in E-flat (mm. 1–5). Cf. n. 25.

1; Beethoven, Quartet in E-flat, K. 74, "Harp"; and many other works, several of which have been recently noted in this regard.[25]

Mozart's Piano Sonata in F, K. 332 (example 5.3), opens with a particularly graceful employment of the $\hat{8}-\flat\hat{7}-\hat{6}-\natural\hat{7}-\hat{8}$ pattern. Here the initial circular stasis, mm. 1–5, contributes to the general sense of nonmotion within P, its overlong lingering around the tonic: this is the P-area discussed earlier as an example of tonic overdetermination. Perhaps even more sophisticated variants of the technique may be found in the principal theme of Piano Concerto No. 17 in G, K. 453, first movement, and at the opening of the exposition in the initial movement of Symphony No. 38 in D, "Prague," K. 504. Once the $\hat{8}-\flat\hat{7}-\hat{6}-\natural\hat{7}-\hat{8}$ model of P-ignition is firmly in mind—along with its generic and hermeneutic implications—we may additionally recognize the much-noted bass motion at the onset of Beethoven's *Eroica* Symphony, $e\flat-d-c\sharp-d-e\flat$ (mm. 1–11), as a deformational variant. Here the contour and general effect of the pattern are retained, but the compression of the formula into semitones produces the famous $c\sharp$ with its harmonic and textural distortions, reverberating through the remainder of the movement.

P^{gen} and P^{tel} Themes

Almost all P-themes (and certainly all eighteenth-century themes) place their chief thematic burdens at their openings. Themes are usually identified and remembered by their incisive beginnings. These themes may be called *expository themes* and they generally follow the pattern, memorable head-idea + continuation to cadence. But the opening gesture of the first movement of Beethoven's Symphony No. 9 in D Minor, op. 125, does not follow this format. Instead, it grows from silence (*creatio ex nihilo*) and finally announces the theme proper only at its end. In other words, this theme is end-accented. The whole P-zone is a process of growth and intensification (*Steigerung*) toward the production of this thematic goal or *telos* (the goal toward which a process strives). This is a *teleological theme* (one that forms itself toward a goal at its end), not an expository theme. Again: In its most basic form, a teleological theme features two components: a generative *crescendo* that leads inexorably toward an emphatically uttered thematic/tonal goal (*telos*). We distinguish these two components with the labels P^{gen} and P^{tel}. The labels are useful in Beethoven's Ninth Symphony and in many (most) of the Bruckner symphonies. P^{tel} may either be a theme clearly implied by the generative crescendo (the *creatio ex nihilo* type) or it may be a new theme altogether (the double-theme type).[26]

---

25. See, e.g., Mark Anson-Cartwright, "Chromatic Features of E♭-Major Works of the Classical Period," *Music Theory Spectrum* 22 (2000), 177–204 (especially pp. 180 and appendices 1–3, pp. 197–200), with useful citations to previous studies along these lines, including Henry Burnett and Shaugn O'Donnell, "Linear Ordering of the Chromatic Aggregate in Classical Symphonic Music," *Music Theory Spectrum* 18 (1996), pp. 22–50, especially p. 49.

26. The concepts are developed further in Darcy, "Bruckner's Sonata Deformations," in *Bruckner Studies*, ed. Timothy L. Jackson and Paul Hawkshaw (Cambridge: Cambridge University Press, 1997), pp. 256–77.

CHAPTER SIX

The Transition (TR)

Here we are concerned with the zone that brings the initial idea, P, to the moment of relaunch at S (assuming a two-part exposition). The standard designation for this music, *transition* (or *bridge*), is problematic, at times misleading. It can be particularly deceptive within analytical contexts that assume as a first principle that tonal considerations trump all others, thus suggesting that the term means a transition or bridge from one *key* to another. This view inappropriately sidelines such other factors as texture, dynamics, thematic ordering, and rhetoric. As will emerge later in this chapter, TR-zones are characterized mostly by dispositional location within a system of generic expectation (where they occur in the exposition; their functional drive to the MC) and by texture (energy-gain). It is mistaken to define a transition primarily in terms of an expectation of modulation. Some transitions do not modulate at all—for example, those leading to a I:HC MC.

The problem of terminology and definitions does not stop there. In a two-part exposition TR will end with a medial caesura (MC). But where does P conclude and TR begin? This is not always an easy question to answer, and it is probably a question that an eighteenth-century composer either would not have recognized or would not have considered significant. It may be that the (nineteenth-century) concept of a separately understood "transition-zone" (A. B. Marx's *Uebergang*)[1] was not part of the conception of the eighteenth-century composer. Rather, it is more likely that Haydn, Mozart, Beethoven, and their contemporaries thought instead of an initial idea (P) followed by a series of continuation modules,[2] the upshot of which was to provide the energy-gain needed to produce an effective MC (or, in a continuous exposition, to drive past the point of conversion toward the EEC). Another of A. B. Marx's descriptions of this zone, *Der Fortgang zum Seitensatz* (the continuation or advance toward the secondary theme), conveys the fundamental idea more accurately.[3]

What we today call the transition was probably nothing more than the convention of following an initial idea with an appropriate, inten-

---

1. E.g., A. B. Marx, *Die Lehre von der musikalischen Komposition, praktisch theoretisch*, 4th ed. (Leipzig: Breitkopf und Härtel, 1868), 3:224, 276.
2. In this and similar contexts "continuation" is used in its general sense, not in the technical sense specific

to the analysis of musical sentences (which can contain presentation, continuation, and cadential modules).
3. Marx, *Die Lehre*, 3:267–81; occasionally, more explicitly an "advance forward," e.g., *Die Fortschreitung zum Seitensatz* on 3:277.

sifying move forward—a set of phased modular continuations that accepted the preceding P-idea as the basis for a sonata and brought the music into the next generic zone of the sonata process. Because the term "transition" spawns analytical pseudo-problems that are merely terminological, not musically substantive, we have from time to time been tempted to abandon it altogether—to substitute for it something like *post-P continuation modules.*[4] For the present we have concluded that the word "transition" is too ingrained into the current analytical tradition to dispense with. But we do treat it with caution—and skeptically.

In sum, the term "transition" should not be understood to imply an obligatory modulation, even though the S that follows will be in a new key. TR may modulate or it may not. What the term TR should imply might be described differently for Allegro compositions (especially orchestral works) and slow movements. In the former, TR suggests the post-P expectation of a normative, rhetorical energy-gain, a passage of rhythmic verve and increased harmonic action, driving toward and finally accomplishing the MC. In orchestral Allegro compositions, the onset of TR (especially following a relatively soft P-theme) is frequently marked with a strong tutti entrance: the *tutti affirmation* or *forte affirmation* of the theme. Slow movements, on the other hand, often continue their head-motive P with lyrical, (quasi-) thematic, connective material that is not intensifying in a way analogous to normative transition procedure in Allegro movements. Here TR (post-P continuation) modules are recognizable through their participation in a number of TR structural conventions, most of which are described below, and through their functional articulation of an MC (perhaps a mere half cadence) at their conclusions—followed, of course, by a recognizable S-theme in the new key.

In the analysis of TR-zones one should first get an overall view of the drama of its trajectory to the MC. What musical adventures are the TR-modules put through? Is TR unusually long? brief? Is it motivically related to P, as an energetic extension of its idea? Does it antici-

pate S? Does it predict one type of MC possibility (usually that built around the I:HC) only to abandon it and drive toward the next one in the deployment sequence? How is its overall trajectory of energy-gain managed? Are there any dynamic drops within the general pattern of intensification? If so, for which expressive purposes? If TR modulates, where and how does the modulation takes place (common chord? chromatic inflection? enharmonic reinterpretation? sudden shift?). Is TR a single phrase or a succession of phrases or modules? Through which common devices is the structural dominant gained and the MC prepared? How strong is the medial caesura? Is there caesura fill? Why?

When Does a Transition Begin?

Certain kinds of TR rhetoric (again, particularly in compositions in Allegro tempo or faster) are readily recognizable as transitional in texture. These include: motivic *Fortspinnung*, sequential activity, accumulative rhetorical energy, a drive toward a structural dominant, and perhaps a concern for modulation. Once this sort of rhetoric is underway, there is never any doubt about being in a TR-zone. The problematic issue, rather, is: when may we consider TR to have begun? Much of the remainder of this chapter will be concerned with strategies of initiating and continuing the post-P extension modules. How TRs end has already been dealt with at length in chapters 3 and 4.

Determining the beginning-point of TR-zones is probably a modern analytical preoccupation, not an eighteenth-century one. As such, in difficult cases, one should remain flexible in suggesting a solution to the problem of TR-beginnings—realizing that in most formally underdetermined or ambiguous situations, this attaching of a label does not usually claim a telling analytical point. On the other hand, the field of TR-designation is not thrown open for free interpretation. More frequently the musical passages in question are not structurally ambiguous. Most passages present clear signals of

---

4. Cf. n. 2.

standard extension types, and we should be prepared to recognize them.

What we elect to designate as the onset of the TR-zone may or may not begin with a change of texture or theme from P. Some TRs begin in a clearly demarcated way that indicates at once that a new zone has been entered (*non-merged transitions*). In these cases the boundaries of TR are unmistakably laid out. Other types of TR (such as those that begin as consequents that soon dissolve into more characteristic TR-rhetoric) do not announce their new-zone status at the outset but begin only as extensions of P-activity (*merged transitions*). In the case of merged transitions the initial bars of TR may not seem "transitional" at all, but instead of completing their thematic idea with a cadence they dissolve mid-phrase into transitional procedures.

In general, we discourage the practice of conferring TR-status in the middle of an ongoing phrase, even though the texture and musical process begin to alter at that moment. Such an *ad hoc* labeling, though registering an intuitive perception that we share, encourages one to overlook the passage's participation in a set of standard methods of composing TR, methods that we outline below. Therefore, whenever possible we prefer to identify the onsets of TR-zones with the beginnings of phrases. Once we perceive the appearance of clear TR-activity (mid-phrase), we return to the opening of the phrase, however thematically contoured it might be, and assign the TR-label to that spot. Unless we are dealing with a compressed P⇒TR merger (typically a sentence with a dissolving continuation, as in the opening movement of Mozart's Piano Sonata in C, K. 545, discussed below as one of the "dissolving" TR types), our strong tendency is to regard P as ending with a cadence (authentic or half) and TR as beginning a new phrase (which may or may not be elided with P's cadence). This means that many TRs begin as a P-restatement or as a consequent to P's antecedent: they begin with some sort of reiteration of the opening of P (sometimes referred to by other writers as the counterstatement) but then turn mid-phrase into more typical transitional behavior. In these instances we consider TR, as a structural concept, to have been launched at the thematic opening of the phrase.

Common Transition Strategies: The Independent and Developmental Types

The Independent (Separately Thematized) Transition

Eighteenth- and early-nineteenth-century composers developed a number of transitional strategies (strategies of modular continuation). One of the most common involved the building of TR upon a new theme (the "transition theme") or a marked change of musical topic, rhythmic motion, and/or figure. An independent transition, often ignited by P's PAC in the tonic key, may begin either by continuing in the tonic (Mozart, Piano Sonata in F, K. 280, first movement, m. 13, elided with I:PAC [example 6.1]; Piano Sonata in G, K. 283, first movement, m. 17; Piano Sonata in C, K. 309, first movement, m. 21—following the cadence of $P^{1.2}$—and finale, m. 20 (within a Type 4 sonata, here labeled "Rondeau"), or by plunging at once into a new tonal area, often the submediant following a tonally overdetermined P-space, as discussed in chapter 5 (Mozart, Piano Sonata in F, K. 332, first movement, m. 23, and finale, m. 36; Quartet in D, K. 499, first movement, anacrusis to m. 24). In the symphonic genre the onset of an independent transition is often marked by a tutti affirmation (or *forte* affirmation), typically elided with the PAC that ends P, as in the first movements of Mozart, Symphonies No. 36 in C, "Linz", K. 425, m. 42, and No. 39 in E-flat, K. 543, m. 54, and Haydn, Symphonies No. 100 in G, "Military," m. 39, No. 103 in E-flat, "Drumroll," m. 48, and No. 104 in D, "London," m. 32. In orchestral pieces the first solid *forte* following a generally *piano* P-theme is often a generic signal for the onset of TR. (But see the caveats in the separate section below.)

The Developmental Transition

It may happen that a TR that one interpreter might call independent might strike others as elaborative of certain motives contained in P, as though TR were reworking some of the ideas or figures just sounded in P. The independent transition shades by degrees into a developmental transition, and along this continuum differ-

EXAMPLE 6.1   Mozart, Piano Sonata in F, K. 280, i, mm. 1–26

EXAMPLE 6.1 *(continued)*

ent analysts might come to differing conclusions. (What qualifies as a genuinely new idea?) In many cases making the distinction is of little importance—a matter of which aspect of the transition one wishes to emphasize, its seeming newness of tone and verve or its relatedness to certain features of past material. The *forte*-affirmation TR of the first movement of Haydn's Symphony No. 102 in B-flat, m. 38, might impress one listener as a brilliant, more or less independent statement, while another might perceive its rolling cascades of eighth notes as a developmental working-out of a characteristic figure from P. Both views are defensible. In other instances the sense of an impulsive developmental continuation of P is paramount—as if the music is eager to "get on with it." The onset of TR may elide with the PAC cadence ending P proper. A touchstone example may be found in the finale of Mozart's Symphony No. 40 in G Minor, K. 550, m. 32.

In confronting this TR type certain complications can arise. Consider the first movement of Beethoven's Sonata in C Minor, op. 13, "Pathétique" (example 6.2). After the Grave introduction P begins (m. 11) with an agitated nine-bar phrase that cadences i:PAC (m. 19). This elides with an almost identical phrase-repetition whose cadence is altered to i:HC (m. 27). The active dominant is prolonged though various neighboring chords, during which the music "marks time" by stating and repeating a new four-bar eighth-note idea. Up to this point, it is possible to construe mm. 11–circa 35 as the aa'b portion of a potential rounded-binary format (aa'ba'')—an expectation that will not be realized. Alternatively, had Beethoven filled out the last half of m. 35 with a rest, he could have created the impression of a grand antecedent, awaiting a parallel grand consequent. (And this consequent could have dissolved into a transition, as happens in the finale of the Sonata in C-sharp Minor, op. 27 no. 2 and the first movement of the Sonata in C, op. 53, "Waldstein.") Instead, m. 35 re-energizes the music (after its dominant-harmony stasis) and begins a sequential development of P-material, during which the bass rises chromatically from G to B-flat. This process hoists the i:HC up two notches, transforming it into a III:HC (m. 43), which is

EXAMPLE 6.2   Beethoven, Piano Sonata in C Minor, op. 13 ("Pathétique"), i, mm. 11–55

EXAMPLE 6.2   (*continued*)

EXAMPLE 6.2   *(continued)*

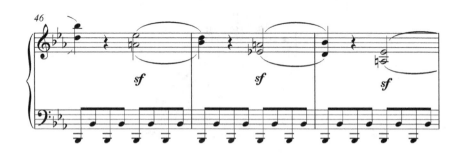

then extended via a dominant-lock into the medial caesura (m. 49). After a touch of caesura-fill, S begins in m. 51. In sum, the re-entrance of P-material at m. 35 does not sound like a re-beginning. Rather, the music bypasses the expected rebeginning in favor of impulsive motivic development and harmonic action. Here both the *agitato* character and the manic overriding of more common TR-generic norms contribute to the expressive character of the music—its sense of impatience, forward press, and dogged struggle to escape the minor mode. In this case it leads to an S that appears in the mediant minor, destabilized by a dominant pedal, in the manner of an S⁰ theme. This suggests that S is "injured" or subjected to a deformation, perhaps as a result of the impetuosity of the transition. See also the discussion of this piece—and of the principles of minor-mode sonatas in general—in chapters 7 and 14.

Common Transition Strategies: The "Dissolving" Types

Another frequently encountered strategy is to begin a thematic restatement, complement, or reprise that before long branches off into self-evident TR-elaboration. What is "dissolved" along the way is the expectation of normative thematic completion, which could have been fulfilled by attaining the cadence predicted by the model begun in P.[5] These transition types may be subdivided according to the immediate structural impression or function provided by the opening of TR.

The Dissolving Restatement

When P closes I:PAC, TR may begin as a repetition or restatement of P, although it soon transforms into transitional activity. Examples include the first movements of Mozart, Piano Sonata in B-flat, K. 333, m. 11, and his Quartet in G, K. 387, m. 11. The restatement has the effect of reopening the closure provided by the I:PAC. The opening of the P-theme is restated, but it now takes a different path, one that leads away from symmetry and the tonic closure of P. The first movement of the Piano Sonata in A Minor, K. 310, m. 9, is also in dialogue with this TR type, although the elision of the restatement with the expected i:PAC (suppressing the expected tonic pitch in the upper voice) also serves locally to suggest a destabilizing of full closure at this moment. The symphonic genre usually marks the beginning of a dissolving-restatement transition in Allegro compositions with the generic tutti *(or forte)* affirmation, suggesting that the full orchestra enthusiastically accepts the proposed theme as the basis for a sonata, at the same time boosting the music's energy in preparation for the drive to the medial caesura.

The tutti affirmation is a powerful generic signal within symphonies and overtures. In most cases the listener should be aware at once that the music has entered the TR-zone. Even though the presence of this exuberant outburst can be a definer of TR-space that overrides other potential interpretations, its TR-authority is not absolute. Complications with and exceptions to the tutti-affirmation principle are considered as part of a separate section later in this chapter, "Premature or Delayed Tutti Affirmations."

The Dissolving Consequent

If P closes I:HC, in the manner of an antecedent (or, more commonly, grand antecedent), TR may begin as a parallel consequent that is diverted before long into transitional processes. In Allegro compositions this would be more appropriate in works that begin with larger, multimodular, or grand antecedents, since shorter ones run the risk of precipitating the work into TR too rapidly.[6] Examples following grand an-

---

5. Cf., e.g., the similar concept in Marx, *Die Lehre*, e.g., 3:259–61, *Die Periode mit aufgelöstem Nachsatz*. Marx's illustration, as it happens, is the opening of Beethoven's Piano Sonata in F Minor, op. 2 no. 1. Later in this chapter we consider op. 2 no. 1 to illustrate instead the dissolving hybrid—adapting here the terminology of William E. Caplin.

6. One might also recall that the more extended P-theme cases that we call *complex* grand antecedents (ch. 5) produce a "false" TR-effect (usually beginning with a local I:PAC) before the onset of the grand consequent. From certain perspectives, this might be considered a "TR⁰"-effect—since it leads directly into TR¹·¹, the dissolving consequent.

tecedents abound in the literature, including the first movements of Mozart's Symphonies No. 40 in G Minor, K. 550, m. 21 (Example 5.5), and No. 41 in C Major, "Jupiter," K. 551, m. 24; and Beethoven, Piano Sonatas in C major, op. 53, "Waldstein," m. 14, and F Minor, op. 57, "Appassionata," m. 17. Slow movements with modest proportions—at least in principle—permit the application of the dissolving-consequent TR to smaller, more normative antecedent phrases, although even here the period is more typically completed before TR proper (of a different type) is launched.

As with the TR of the dissolving-restatement type, the dissolving consequent has the character of a second launch—one that pushes the music toward the medial caesura. In this case there is no sense of reopening previous harmonic closure. On the contrary, TR first suggests that it will attempt to close the harmonic situation left open by P but soon abandons this effort. Thus the hermeneutic implications of the dissolving restatement and the dissolving consequent are different. In the first an idea has been brought to authentic-cadence completion; in the second the P-idea veers away (or decays away) from that PAC-completion in order to pursue different expositional aims, and P proper is thereby tonally underdetermined.

Period with Dissolving-Consequent Restatement (or Sentence with Dissolving-Continuation Restatement)

It sometimes happens that a complete period or sentence is sounded only to have the beginning of its second portion—consequent or continuation—resounded (as if a full restatement is to be expected) but then subjected to dissolution. Following the logic of the above TR types, we consider TR to begin with the onset of the undermined restatement. For example, in Beethoven's Piano Sonata in G, op. 49 no. 2, P is structured as a larger-scale sentence with a presentation of 4 + 4 bars and a continuation-conclusion of four bars (mm. 9–12) ending in I:PAC. Because the size of the second portion of a sentence often balances (or even extends) that of the presentation, the cadence in m. 12 may strike us as premature—and indeed,

the upper voice moves through this cadence and begins to repeat the continuation module, as if preparing to deliver a more satisfactory I:PAC four bars later. M. 14, however, introduces $\sharp\hat{4}$ in the bass, and leads to a I:HC in m. 15, followed by a dominant-lock—thus submitting the previous cadence to a deformation and leading to self-evident TR-procedures, with a I:HC MC at the downbeat of m. 20. In this example P and TR have again been merged through what we might call the "dissolving consequent-restatement," which in this case involves the deformational repetition of the entire final portion of a sentence. TR proper thus begins with the anacrusis to m. 13.

The Dissolving P-Codetta: Reiterated Cadences (Dissolving Cadential Reinforcement)

When P concludes with a I:PAC, it may be followed by repeated cadential units (often two of them) designed to reinforce that cadence. Thus our initial impression is that of a P-codetta. At times it is best to regard it as that—as an emphatically concluding portion of P-space, part of the P-landing-strip, so to speak. This seems unequivocally the case when the P-codetta is bluntly separated off from what follows by a full break, producing an unmistakable sense of closure ("Punkt!") and a clear shift into the subsequent TR-zone. Here there is no TR-dissolution, and P is merely supplied with a self-closing codetta of cadential reiterations. Such is the case in the finale of Mozart's Piano Sonata in C, K. 330, in which, following the I:PAC of an unproblematically periodic P[1], we are given two loops of repeated tonic cadences (mm. 16–20) concluding with the archetypally Mozartian closure-figure $\hat{8}-\hat{5}-\hat{1}$ in octaves (m. 20)—nailing the door shut on P-space. TR follows in m. 21.

But related analytical situations are rarely so easily decided. It may happen that the (usually) two looped cadences are not so clearly set off by a full break from what follows. It may be that the second reinforcing unit leads more directly into a differing module that turns transitional in function, often advancing rather quickly to the medial caesura (frequently I:HC). In this case the effect is that of undoing the I:PAC reiterations and transforming them into the half cadence that marks the medial caesura. Moreover, it is clear that the doubleness of the cadential reiterations is in dialogue with the presentation modules of a sentence, one whose continuation is represented by the music that follows the two looped cadences. In turn this can suggest that we have a sentential TR that begins with a tonic-reiterative, cadential presentation. In this sense the TR-"sentence" (if that is the impression obtained) is perceived as beginning with the onset of the cadential reiterations. Here one should note the double-function of the repeated cadences: on the one hand, they first strike us as P-codetta; on the other hand, we come to understand that they were actually the beginning of a TR—possibly a sentential TR. Such a TR is a subset of the "dissolving" transition types. What starts out as one thing is converted *en route* into something else that is self-evidently more transitional in procedure.

Obviously, the pivotal factor in a decision here (P-codetta or TR?) is our judgment concerning the presence or absence of that potential full break after the cadential reiterations. When the full break seems absent or when what follows is clearly reactive to or continuative of the cadential figures, then we may speak properly of a TR of the dissolving cadential reinforcement type. This procedure occurs with some frequency in the first movements of Mozart's piano sonatas. One exemplary model is that in the Piano Sonata in C, K. 330 (example 6.3). Here P is structured as a sentence (aa', mm. 1–2, 3–4; continuation, mm. 5–8, varied repetition of the continuation, mm. 9–12) ending with a I:PAC in m. 12. Following a bar of fill we hear two varied reiterations of the preceding cadence, mm. 13–14, 15–16. M. 16 provides no full break. On the contrary, it is elided immediately with contrasting material launching a drive to the I:HC MC in m. 18. We consider TR proper to begin at m. 13. Three sixteenth notes of caesura-fill (CF) lead into the onset of the compound-sentence S, m. 19. Another, more extravagant example of this type of TR occurs in the opening movement of Beethoven's Quartet in C Minor, op. 18 no. 4, m. 13.

The Dissolving P-Codetta: Tonic Prolongation via the "Circular" $\hat{8}-\flat\hat{7}-\hat{6}-\natural\hat{7}-\hat{8}$ Model

This procedure operates on a logic parallel with the cadential P-codetta discussion directly above. In this case, though, we are not given overt cadential reiterations of P's I:PAC. Instead, the now-attained tonic is held fast with a pedal point, usually in the bass, while a twice-repeated holding-pattern figure cycles above it in one or more upper voices. This creates the impression of an "in-and-out-of-focus" stasis circling around the fixed tonic, a shift into a gratified circular recursion—even a modest celebration—following the linear progress into P's I:PAC. This may be accomplished with any of several simple harmonic patterns, including tonic-dominant oscillations.

Of particular interest is the prolongation of the cadential stasis by locking onto a tonic pedal above which is rotated an $\hat{8}-\flat\hat{7}-\hat{6}-\natural\hat{7}-\hat{8}$ melodic motion in one of the upper voices—usually outlining the chordal pattern, $I-V^7/IV-IV_4^6-vii^{o6}$ (or $V^{[7]}$)$-I$. (More rarely, the $\hat{8}-\flat\hat{7}-\hat{6}-\natural\hat{7}-\hat{8}$ model may be transferred to the bass.) The $\hat{8}-\flat\hat{7}-\hat{6}-\natural\hat{7}-\hat{8}$ module is a stock contrapuntal pattern within the style. Its most natural function is the grounding of cadences with a static motion of circular rotation around an attained tonic. The linear motion of the preceding phrase(s) convert here into a recursive, circular stasis. For this reason the figure is especially appropriate for postcadential closing ideas (post-EEC C-space) and, as here, in what amount to P-codettas. (Occasionally, the static figure is used with notable effect to launch P-space: See the discussion in chapter 5.) Typically the figure makes two full cycles through the $\hat{8}-\flat\hat{7}-\hat{6}-\natural\hat{7}-\hat{8}$ pattern.

Within the context of the potential P-codetta the figure's tonic pedal and circular recursion give it a character that suggests immediate cadential reinforcement, a keeping-open of P-space. (This is so even if the pattern introduces a more or less new figuration into the piece. In this sense it can also partake thematically in the strategy of the independent transition, discussed below.) As was the case with cadential reiterations, if the $\hat{8}-\flat\hat{7}-\hat{6}-\natural\hat{7}-\hat{8}$ pattern is not merged directly with a continuative or reactive subsequent

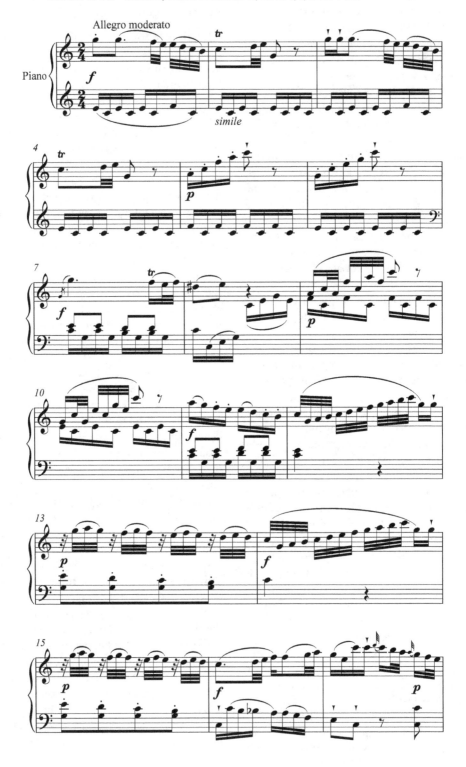

EXAMPLE 6.3 Mozart, Piano Sonata in C, K. 330, i, mm. 1–20

Example 6.3   *(continued)*

module—if it is clearly separated off from what follows by some sort of full break—then it gives the impression of belonging wholly to P-space. This type of P-codetta may be found in the first movements of Mozart's Quartet in B-flat, K. 589, mm. 12–20 (with a full-break GP-gap in m. 20 and TR proper beginning in m. 21, albeit one that preserves a motivic figure from what precedes it); and Beethoven's Quartet in D, op. 18 no. 3, mm. 27–35. Another example at least beginning with the $\hat{8}-\flat\hat{7}-\hat{6}-\natural\hat{7}-\hat{8}$ pattern, here producing a tonally overdetermined P followed by the characteristic TR-jolt to the submediant, occurs in the first movement of Haydn, Piano Sonata in E-flat, Hob. XVI:25 (P-codetta, m. 8; TR, second half of m. 12).

It may also happen that the two $\hat{8}-\flat\hat{7}-\hat{6}-\natural\hat{7}-\hat{8}$ "codetta"-cycles are followed without such a break into a contrasting module of continuation. Again, as with cadential reiterations, what originally seemed marked as P-codetta begins to take on the presentation function of a TR-sentence. At the same time, the circular loops divert almost immediately into more recognizable TR-processes and their once-again linear implication. Following the argument outlined above, in these cases we again consider TR to have begun with the onset of the first cycle of the pattern.

One comes across this issue in several of Mozart's piano sonatas. The first movement of the Sonata in C, K. 279 (see chapter 5, example 5.6) provides an illustration. In the preceding chapter we have already discussed this P, mm. 1–12, as a touchstone example of the Mozartian "loop" variant of the classical sentence. Beginning with the cadence on the third beat of m. 12 (the elided onset of TR) are two cycles of the

$\hat{8}-\flat\hat{7}-\hat{6}-\natural\hat{7}-\hat{8}$ pattern ($C_5-B\flat_4-A_4-B\natural_4-C_5$), which ground the C-tonic statically, then push into linear motion on the third beat of m. 14, now driving toward the I:HC MC in m. 16. (Example 5.6 also shows the opening of an extremely unusual S, a sentence that begins off-tonic, m. 17, with a bar-by-bar circle-of-fifth descent through the presentation into a tonic continuation.)

Similar examples of the dissolving $\hat{8}-\flat\hat{7}-\hat{6}-\natural\hat{7}-\hat{8}$ pattern may be found in the first movement of Mozart's Sonata in D, K. 284 (shown in example 3.1, TR at m. 9, beginning with two loops of the pattern, literally in mm. 9–10, implicit in mm. 11–12) and the finale of the Sonata in G, K. 283 (TR at m. 24, two loops, mm. 24–28, mm. 28–32). Some related passages include the first movement of the Sonata in B-flat, K. 281 (m. 8, initiating two soundings of a I–IV$^6_4$–I motion, but one clearly related to the pattern); the finale of the Sonata in F, K. 280 (beginning in m. 17, TR is literally an independent sentence, yet it begins with two presentation modules over the familiar tonic pedal); and the slow movement of the Sonata in B-flat, K. 333—whose initial harmonic swaying is restricted to tonic and dominant.

Sentence with Dissolving Continuation Module

In this case the sonata begins in the manner of a sentence, generally some sort of a a′ b format. P is restricted to the normative presentation modules only, a a′, sometimes a mere four bars (2 + 2), while it is the continuation (b) that ramifies into TR-activity—rhythmic verve and accelerated harmonic action that drives toward the medial caesura. TR is considered as beginning with b (transition of the dissolving-continuation type). Before dealing with the *locus classicus*, the opening of Mozart's *sonate facile*, the Piano Sonata in C, K. 545, it may be useful to consider one larger issue.

We have insisted that in nearly every case we understand TR to begin with the onset of a new phrase. If we remain consistent with our definition of a phrase—a stretch of music ending in a cadence—this TR-situation is the exception. This is because, by accepted definition, a sentence's presentation is so harmonically weak (perhaps only oscillations between I and V) that it is not considered normatively to end with a cadence. (True, oscillations to I or V might strike us as protocadential—almost there—but the fact remains that they are not normally regarded as producing a "cadence" proper.) Thus by our preferred definition of a phrase, a standard-length sentence is usually a single phrase from presentation through continuation and cadence.[7] Since it is the continuation that dissolves here, in this case TR does not begin with the onset of a phrase. On the other hand, there is always a clear separation of thematic modules as one moves from presentation to (dissolving) continuation. One might at least claim that TR begins with a new module.

One paradigmatic instance is found at the opening of the A-major slow movement of the Quartet in D, K. 155 (shown in chapter 17, example 17.4a). Another occurs at the opening of Mozart's Quartet in G, K. 156 (mm. 1–18, ending I:HC, S at m. 19). More familiar is his Piano Sonata in C, K. 545, first movement (example 6.4): Here the opening appears structured as a single phrase (as strictly defined), mm. 1–12,

that leads toward a half cadence (m. 11) and a well-articulated I:HC medial caesura at its end. There can be no doubt that what follows it is S (an $S^{1.0}$ vamp in m. 13, the onset of a sentential S-proper in m. 14). The opening four measures suggest a normative sentence presentation, aa' (mm. 1–2, 3–4) with the characteristic harmonic oscillations around the tonic. The four bars do not end with a cadence. (This is also the case in the other examples cited above, K. 155/ii and K. 156/i.) Instead they prolong the tonic with neighboring motions in the bass. Therefore they do not constitute a phrase—only a module (or a complementary pair of two-bar modules). The sentence's continuation module begins in mm. 5–8 (b, with its typical sequential treatment of a shorter structural unit). Mm. 9–12 constitute the conclusion of the sentence with the cadential module (essentially ii^6–V in the tonic key). But mm. 9–12 also take on the transitional features of a typical drive to a medial caesura, including a dominant lock at m. 11 and a triple-hammer-blow gesture I:HC MC at m. 12. The continuation portion of P overlaps with TR, and P and TR thus merge (P⇒TR).

The Dissolving Hybrid

In Caplin's *Classical Form* the classifications of common phrase types are not limited to periods and sentences. Also included are four types of "hybrids" between the two, a set of categories that, in order to avoid further complications, we adopt within our own discussions here.[8] According to that method, an antecedent, for example, may be followed not by a parallel consequent but by a nonparallel phrase more typi-

---

7. The most obvious exception to this involves the loop-variant of the sentence, in which the initial loops typically end with local I:PACs, thereby qualifying as phrases. In other words, a sentence designed in this loop-format will typically consist of three phrases: the first and second loops and the continuation, which will itself end with a cadence. See the discussion of Mozartian "loops" in ch. 5. Other types of large-scale sentences may also provide exceptions to this general principle of the noncadential quality of the presentation.

8. Cf. ch. 5, nn. 10 and 14. From a larger perspective, though, it is not self-evident why the sentence and the parallel period alone should be taken to be exclusively

fundamental, with the result that any of the common deviations away from those models (weakened cadential-effects or mere dominant arrivals, nonparallel "second halves," and the like) should be understood as "hybrids" between the two. We would prefer to posit more flexible, but still normative, phrase-models with which any individual exemplar is understood to be in dialogue, at times even deformationally. Under such a conception, an apparent deviation from the norm does not produce an example of a new, "hybrid" category but rather an individualized realization—for particular expressive purposes—understood to interact conceptually with the most relevant background model.

EXAMPLE 6.4 Mozart, Piano Sonata in C, K. 545, i, mm. 1–17

EXAMPLE 6.4   *(continued)*

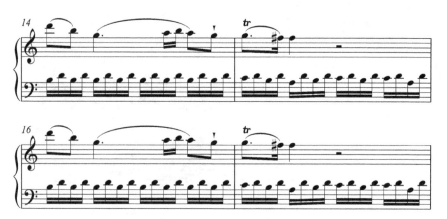

cal of the continuation of a sentence. This *antecedent + continuation* combination is Hybrid 1 of Caplin's four.[9] Pursuing the logic of the above paragraphs, it stands to reason that such hybrids, too, may also dissolve into TR-procedures. In the case of Hybrid 1 this would suggest the pattern *antecedent + dissolving continuation*. Examples of it may be found in the Andante movement of Mozart's Symphony No. 35 in D, K. 385, "Haffner" (antecedent ending I:IAC, mm. 1–4; TR of the dissolving continuation type, mm. 5–16, reaching a dominant lock in m. 12 and a I:HC MC in m. 16); and at the opening of Beethoven's Piano Sonata in F Minor, op. 2 no. 1 (sentential antecedent ending i:HC, mm. 1–8; dissolving-continuation TR, mm. 9–20, leading to a III:HC MC, m. 20, followed by an unusual S⁰-like module retaining the dominant in the bass, m. 21ff; the entire exposition of this much-cited piece is decidedly non-normative).[10] Such dissolving hybrids are not confined to Caplin's first type, although with the basic principle now self-evident we shall forego further elaboration here.

Larger, Rounded Structure (ABA', aa'ba") with Dissolving Reprise

Yet another strategy is to structure P as a broader, more amply rounded structure whose final ele-

ment—normally some sort of mini-reprise—is subjected to TR-dissolution. This might be, for instance, an ABA' form cast into a standard rounded-binary format, almost invariably suggesting a large-scale "occupation" of P-space. In this case A might be a single phrase, it might be two phrases subdivisible into an antecedent-consequent pair, aa', or it might be disposed in a sentence format, while B + A' articulate the second part of the binary, with the usual harmonic interruption at the end of B. The dissolving TR would therefore begin with A'.

One example is provided by the implicitly rounded-binary opening of the first movement of Mozart's Quartet in B-flat, K. 458, "Hunt" (example 6.5). Here A is provided by the antecedent-consequent pair, mm. 1–4, 5–8. The sentential B stretches from m. 9 to m. 26, with dominant lock at m. 20 and harmonic interruption at m. 26—a moment somewhat similar to a I:HC MC. Yet if we recognize the formal genre to which this broader P appeals as a whole, we will not mistake it for one. Here the onset of the reprise in the tonic, m. 27—along with the general character of B as it has proceeded—informs us that we are to understand P as implying instead a large, tuneful rounded-binary block, as if P were promised to be a large, inset dance or song squarely claiming a large and tonally static expanse of P-space. With the reprise A', though

---

9. Caplin, *Classical Form*, pp. 59–61.

10. Cf. n. 5.

EXAMPLE 6.5   Mozart, String Quartet in B-flat, K. 458 ("Hunt"), i,
mm. 1–33

EXAMPLE 6.5 (*continued*)

(m. 27), the block-like "tune" begins to dissolve into transitional behavior (not all of which is shown in the example). TR thus begins at m. 27. (See also the discussion of this movement as an illustration of a Type 2 continuous exposition, chapter 4.) The same general logic governs the openings of Mozart's Quartet in D minor, K. 421, with the onset of the dissolution occurring earlier (with the outburst in m. 14) and Beethoven's Symphony No. 3 in E-flat, "Eroica", where the dissolving reprise, TR, begins with the *fortissimo* restatement in m. 37—leading to an abruptly precipitous plunge into the V: HC MC, m. 45, and subsequent *dolce* S⁰ theme (m. 46), with an early S¹ at m. 57.

As mentioned in chapter 5, these large primary zones may sometimes strike us as untexted songs, as songs without words, often construable in the familiar format aa'ba'', with at least an implicit two lines of text for each letter. If we wish for hermeneutic purposes to suggest that the music may be understood as carrying such a lyrical allusion—as a personalized song, instrumentalized operatic extract, or the like, which is subsequently interrupted by or bursts into full-fledged sonata-practice—we might wish to identify it not merely as a rounded binary form (which would certainly be accurate) but as a subset thereof, which could be called a *lyric binary*, a term now associated with operatic song.[11] This is arguably the case with the opening of Mozart's D-minor Quartet, K. 421, to which Momigny, around 1803–6, even set words in an early analysis of the piece.[12] Other large rounded binaries with dissolving reprises,

however, have no such vocal implication at all: Cherubini's Overture to *Médée*, or the first movement of Schubert's Quintet in C Major. The term "lyric binary" has no relevance to such works.

Special Minor-Mode and Other Mixed Cases

The selection of a minor mode as a tonic key can serve as a license for unusual procedures. Additionally, minor-mode works confront options that are less frequent or virtually nonexistent in major-mode sonatas. In minor-mode expositions the move to the key of the mediant major frequently occurs rather early, almost in a premature or precipitous manner. This leap into the mediant may occur at the beginning of TR, as seems to happen in the initial movement of Mozart's Symphony No. 25 in G Minor, K. 183, first movement, although one may construe the evidence in more than one way. Here—at least on this line of interpretation—TR plays itself out entirely in III, B-flat major. It is triggered as a startling, *forte non sequitur* in m. 29, where it bursts forth as a re-energizing module (perhaps also in dialogue with the principle of MC declined) reacting to the preceding enervation, which had petered out on V/i.[13] Sometimes a shift to III may occur—or begin to occur—at the end of P, as in the first movement of Haydn, Symphonies No. 44 in E Minor, "Trauer"—shown in example 5.8, modulating directly into TR, which begins at m. 20, and No. 95 in C Minor, whose TR *forte* begins in m. 16. In each of these cases TR begins in III and

---

11. The term (also identified as "lyric form") and the social connotations of the structure (as "natural" or nonartificial song) are considered in Hepokoski, "*Ottocento* Opera as Cultural Drama: Generic Mixtures in *Il trovatore*," in *Verdi's Middle Period 1849–1859: Source Studies, Analysis, and Performance Practice*, ed. Martin Chusid (Chicago: University of Chicago Press, 1997), pp. 147–96. (See especially pp. 157–60.)

12. Jérôme-Joseph de Momigny, *Cours complet d'harmonie et de composition*, 3 vols. (Paris: Momigny, 1803–6), 3:109–56. See the discussion and transcription in Albert Palm, "Mozarts Streichquartett D-moll, KV 421, in der Interpretation Momignys," *Mozart-Jahrbuch 1962/63* (Salzburg, Zentralinstitut für Mozartforschung der Internationalen Stiftung Mozarteum, 1964), pp. 256–79.

13. Another interpretation might suggest the onset here of TM¹ within a trimodular block (TMB): the double MC-effects occur at mm. 27–28 (i:HC) and 58 (iii: HC). In order to sustain this interpretation one would interpret the material prior to m. 28 as already initiating a deformational, enervated (and collapsing) TR of the dissolving consequent type (mm. 13–28). A precedent for this type of TMB—at least with i:HC and III:HC MCs and a forte TM¹ (though with no prior enervation) that sets up a more normative, *piano* S at TM³ may be found in Johann Vanhal's Symphony in D Minor [d1], finale (dated c. 1768–71). (Mozart's Symphony, K. 183, dates from 1773.)

moves eventually to the medial caesura.[14] If one is considering these TR-passages under the old paradigm (which had misleadingly suggested that modulation must be a hallmark of the TR), one might at first question whether the term "transitional zone" applies here, since these TRs are tonally stable in III. In the paradigm presented by Sonata Theory, however, modulation is an optional aspect of TR-activity, an option not selected in some transitional zones.

Sometimes the leap into the mediant will occur not at the beginning of TR but shortly thereafter. In the first movement of Mozart's Symphony No. 40 in G Minor, K. 550 (example 5.5), P is a single long phrase (a grand antecedent structured as a sentence—also discussed in chapter 5 under P-types) that ends in a forceful half cadence in the tonic. TR begins in m. 21 as a dissolving consequent; the modulation to III, however, occurs quickly (within the presentation section of the smaller-scale sentence). At this point, m. 28, the orchestra delivers the generic tutti outburst on a new thematic idea, functioning also as a differing continuation to the sentence's altered presentation modules. The effect is that of jettisoning the dissolving-consequent TR in favor of an independent, tonally stable TR; although in retrospect we may label these two parts as TR[1.1] (P-based) and TR[1.2], such taxonomic labeling fails to explain the details of the situation. As so often within Sonata Theory, the point is not merely to affix a label onto a passage of music (to force a decision in difficult circumstances) but to call forth the tensions and ambiguities at hand, ones presumably composed into the music.

A somewhat similar situation occurs in the first movement of Mozart's Piano Sonata in C Minor, K. 457. Here TR begins in m. 19 as an elided dissolving restatement that modulates quickly to the mediant. As in the G-minor Symphony, K. 550, the initial type of TR is abandoned, this time in favor of an independent, tonally stable TR of the lyrical variety: a new thematic idea now enters in the key of the

mediant (m. 23). The new theme brings new complications: while unprepared by any normative MC, it bears distinctly S-rhetoric—as if one potential idea for S had been sprung too soon, within what is probably best regarded as TR-space. The whole passage is problematic and involves an unanticipated swerve into expositional deformations—expressive distortions away from standard procedures. M. 23 may also be understood as a mildly problematic TM[1] within one type of TMB, the mid-expositional trimodular block, discussed later in this book. (In this reading, the more satisfactory S—TM[3]—would occur at m. 36, following the III:HC MC in m. 34.)

The preceding suggests that some transitions fall into more than one category. In some situations the effect is that of beginning one type of transition, then abandoning it for a different type. Although we have illustrated this with minor-mode pieces, the effect is by no means confined to minor. In some of these pieces it makes sense to speak of two TR-attempts, the first of which (for whatever reason) is composed to "go wrong" and must be aborted. One should not be surprised to observe that a single "successful" TR employs several techniques. In the first movement of Mozart's Quartet in A, K. 464, for example, the restatement of P at m. 17 (following a I:PAC in m. 16) begins *forte* in the parallel minor and soon moves into a "learned"—hence developmental—four-part stretto. Here the abrupt change of mode and dynamics immediately suggests that this is no mere restatement. Nevertheless, the feeling of rebeginning is undeniably present (if deformationally). After proceeding in a four-part stretto, it moves on to a new musette-like strain on the key of C major (m. 25, mediant of A minor—as if suggesting, while still within TR, a soon-aborted "S"-thought that might have been possible—an ephemeral shaft of light—had the A *minor* actually been the tonic) before driving towards the medial caesura on V of E minor (m. 36). Rather than suggesting that this expo-

---

14. From a Schenkerian perspective, the precipitous entry of III might represent the unfolded upper third of the tonic triad rather than the arrival of the mediant scale-step; thus the beginning of TR is still governed by the tonic scale-step. In this case the duty of TR is to move from the mediant *chord* to the mediant *scale step*, which arrives only with the entrance of S.

sition abandons one type of transition in favor of another, it seems more appropriate to realize that a single transition may pass through several phases in its drive to the medial caesura, and that each phase employs a different technique. This transition is best considered as combining aspects of two common TR types, thus furnishing a developmental adaptation of the "dissolving-restatement" type. We could thus speak of a mixed transition.

Premature or Delayed Tutti Affirmations

We often consider the tutti affirmation to be a strong generic signal that TR has begun. This is because it coincides with the implication of the group's enthusiastic acceptance of an earlier, *piano* idea that had been proposed more modestly. In most cases the successional effect invites a dialogic understanding, perhaps something like, "I propose this idea," followed by a vigorous "Agreed! On with it!" At times it is this feature alone, in otherwise underdetermined situations, that tips the balance in an analytical decision regarding the onset of TR. But nuances are everything, and this observation needs to be counterbalanced with caveats not to regard all tutti affirmations as automatically signaling the beginning of TR and conversely not to suppose that all, or most, TRs begin with a *forte* outburst. In the first place, the tutti-affirmation convention is particularly suited to Allegro-tempo orchestral works and is less frequently encountered (though by no means altogether absent) in chamber works and sonatas. Moreover, even within orchestral compositions a sudden *forte* vigor is not an inevitable marker of the onset of TR. Some affirmations may be understood as arriving prematurely, within P-space; others, strikingly late, as a second or third module in TR-space.

The most common situation in which one might find an early tutti affirmation toward the end of P-space is that when the *forte* completes and brings to a cadence an otherwise incomplete structure of P. One classic instance is a vigorous, *forte* consequent to a piano antecedent. Especially within rapid-fire finales this procedure suggests a rash, rough-and-tumble intervention

from the full-orchestral "group"—a sign, perhaps, of impatience, as though it cannot wait (more normatively) until the conclusion of P to announce its eagerness to get into the sonata game and spur the music onward. Such an effect may be found in the finales of Mozart's Symphonies No. 35 in D, K. 385, "Haffner" (mm. 1–8, *piano*; mm. 9–20, *forte*, eliding with TR at m. 20), and No. 39 in E-flat, K. 543 (mm. 1–8, *piano*; mm. 9–16, *forte*, eliding with TR at m. 16). In these cases TR begins (and continues, *forte*) with the elided PAC that concludes P. Had the consequent phrase not been brought to a I:PAC—had it dissolved into *Fortspinnung*—we would have judged TR to have begun with the beginning of the *forte* consequent (TR of the dissolving-consequent type).

The opposite case occurs when TR begins *piano* and soon thereafter shifts suddenly into a *forte* dynamic. Here the effect is often that of a double-stage (or multistage) TR. One familiar type involves minor-mode pieces whose dissolving consequent (TR) begins *piano* but soon lurches into a strong *forte*, often in the mediant, as discussed above in the first movement of Mozart's Symphony No. 40 in G Minor. In such instances the fact of the onset of the dissolving consequent, even in the *piano* dynamic, urges us to understand that moment as the onset of a multistage or mixed TR, the next stage of which is the characteristic *forte* affirmation. From another perspective this may be described as the beginning of a balanced response that is subverted, either because its modal consequences (remaining in the minor mode) are too grim or possibly because the delayed burst of energy intentionally suggests the effect of a change of mind or strategy.

Another type of alteration of the *forte* affirmation takes place in what might be considered the reversal of the *piano-forte* (P-TR) convention. This reversal-effect, not uncommon in Haydn's orchestral works, occurs when a blustery, *forte* P theme persists all the way up to its cadence. Thus the *forte* is already aggressively in place, and perhaps in compensation TR begins *piano*, as if in an attempt to quiet things down. Before long the previously prevailing *forte* returns—usually suddenly—producing the incidental effect of a delayed *forte* affirmation as the second module within TR. The *locus classicus* occurs at the opening of Haydn's Symphony No. 45 in F-sharp Minor, "Farewell" (P, Allegro assai, implicitly *forte*, mm. 1–16; TR of the dissolving restatement type, *piano*, beginning in m. 17; the *forte* returns, insisting locally on a jump into the major-mode III, at m. 21; what follows is a continuous exposition). On the other hand, the beginning of Haydn's Symphony No. 82 in C, "Bear," may be understood as combining the principle of the largely noisy and boisterous P (mm. 1–20) with the dissolving consequent that begins—here wittily—*piano* (m. 21).

Other Problematic TR-Issues

Tutti-Affirmation Full Restatements: One or More I:PACs within TR

Sometimes the *tutti* restatement will retrack P all the way to its concluding PAC before dissolving into more recognizable TR-activity. This happens in the first movement of Haydn's Symphony No. 99 in E-flat (mm. 19–26, *piano*, concluding I:PAC, followed by a one-bar link to a *forte* restatement, mm. 27–34). Such cases present complications in affixing the at times artificial TR-label. One might well suppose that the first, tutti restatement serves as the second part of an extended (and tonally overdetermined) P, one with multiple authentic cadences. Alternatively, one might argue that the tutti affirmation is itself a sufficiently strong, generic TR signal. In this case we would understand TR as beginning with an emphatic repetition of P, including its cadence. This decision, however, is often a matter of individual interpretation and can vary according to the local circumstances. In Haydn's Symphony No. 99 the I:PAC in m. 34 elides directly with the still-*forte*, rambunctious music that follows, suggesting that it is continuing an ongoing affirmation. At the opening of Mozart's Piano Concerto in F, K. 459, however, the *forte* P-restatement in Ritornello 1 (mm. 9–16) comes to a full stop, nonelided with what is apparently the *piano* beginning of the TR that in this case follows (m. 17).

Another such situation involves a *forte* affirmation that is not a repetition of P and that

nonetheless leads to one or more tonic PACs down the road. There can be no question that the initial tonic is being overdetermined by multiple PACs: this is the more important fact that carries greater implications for hermeneutics. But at which point should one consider TR to have begun? After much wrestling with this pseudo-issue—creating exceptions to any general principle here generates vexing tangles of logic—we have concluded that in most cases, when confronted with this situation, it is cleanest to consider TR as beginning with the first *forte* affirmation (after a complete and substantial P) regardless of how many tonic PACs might follow thereafter.

This suggests an interpretation whereby TR is understood to begin with the decision to reaffirm or overdetermine the tonic key (as opposed to housing all of the overdetermination within P-space). In turn, we are invited to read the essential events in larger interpretive terms: perhaps as a reluctance to leave the tonic; or as the presence of an unusually strong, solidified tonal force-field from which one has difficulty escaping; or as the urge to reinforce the opening into an absolutely rock-solid tonic launch; or as the effect of *reculer pour mieux sauter*; and so on. In the first movement of Mozart, Symphony No. 39 in E-flat, P, a broad *piano* period, stretches from m. 26 to the I:PAC in m. 54 (see example 5.2). This is elided with a *forte* affirmation based on a new idea (independent TR), and this first TR-section drives to another, emphatic I:PAC—a cadence forcefully clubbed into solidity—at m. 71. This in turn elides with the still-*forte* TR^2 (the exponent now indicating that it succeeds a PAC within the same zone), with its cascading scales obviously alluding to the introduction, and TR^2 comes to provide the drive to the new V:HC dominant lock at m. 83 and V:HC MC at m. 90 (followed by the classical example of juggernaut caesura-fill, mm. 91–97).

TR Rhetoric Lacking? The Modulating Consequent

Some sonata movements conceived on a small scale—some first movements of "early" symphonies or sonatas and some lighter slow movements—employ a two-part exposition in which part 1 comprises only a modulating period (without any characteristic TR-rhetoric). In these instances a major-mode antecedent phrase cadences I:HC and is followed by a simple, parallel consequent phrase that tonicizes the dominant scale-step and cadences V:PAC (without obvious MC rhetoric). This V:PAC then functions as the medial caesura (third-level default) and is followed by S and C in the dominant. This format (modulating period + S) sometimes surfaces in less fully elaborated movements, such as those found in Clementi sonatinas: it appears, for example, in the first movements of op. 36 nos. 1, 2, 4, and 5.[15] At times one might question whether such unassuming structures rise to the level of being sonata forms at all—rather than remaining content to be regarded only as rounded binary structures. This can be a close (possibly meaningless) call, but much of it hinges on our sense of an MC and the presentation of a genuine S-theme.

A more well-known instance occurs in the B-flat Adagio movement of Mozart's Piano Sonata in F, K. 332. Mm. 1–4 provide a sentential antecedent ending I:HC. The consequent begins in m. 5 with a chilling shift to B-flat minor (the lights-out effect), and that phrase continues melodically and modulates to a v:PAC conclusion, with Picardy third (locally F major) in m. 8. Two beats of fill lead directly to S in F major, mm. 9–19 (EEC). In no sense do we experience a dissolving consequent here, since no textural dissolution has taken place. Rather, one encounters an ominous, modulating consequent that comes to take on, mostly in retrospect, the function of a TR insofar as it sets up what eventually functions as the MC (the Picardy F-major chord in m. 8, followed by CF). For such small-scale sonata-form movements we suggest that this situation be considered an underdeveloped, fully lyrical case of P⇒TR merger, in which the second phrase functions simultaneously both as the consequent of P and as TR.

When the consequent phrase does not lead to a V:PAC, the situation can become even cloudier. This brings us to further problems of classification, discussed in the next section.

TR Rhetoric Lacking? Multiple Phrases Ending HC Eventually Lead to S

This occurs, for example, in some of the sonata-form slow movements of J. C. Bach's symphonies, such as the B-flat-major slow movement of the Symphony in E-flat, op. 3 no. 3. (In some cases, again, these movements might alternatively be considered simply as rounded-binary structures, not as fully developed sonata forms per se.) We may find, for example, three phrases, each ending HC and leading to some sort of GP-gap (perhaps mildly filled) before we arrive at what appears to be S-proper in V. The first HC is usually I:HC (a simple antecedent). The next phrase may be either parallel or contrasting with the first—as though it were forming a consequent—but once again lead to an HC (either I:HC or attaining V:HC): thus what we have is either a repeated antecedent or a "false consequent" that remains open at the end—followed by yet another lyrical phrase. (The third phrase is more likely to reach V:HC—as in J. C. Bach's op. 3 no. 3—but it need not.) Eventually, one of these HCs is taken for the MC and S proper ensues. In most cases all of the phrases after the first (or after its repetition) can be understood as P⇒TR mergers; alternatively, the final phrase may retrospectively be understood to have served as a lyrical TR-module.

In such circumstances it is difficult to be certain at first glance where S-proper begins (especially if it, too, begins with an antecedent phrase). The implied layout of the movement can sometimes be clarified by examining the recapitulation to see what happens after the return of the first P-phrase (which usually returns literally, or nearly so, up to its HC). It sometimes happens in J. C. Bach, for instance, that some of

---

15. In op. 36 nos. 1 and 2 each phrase of the modulating period is a mere four bars in length. In nos. 4 and 5, however, these lengths are doubled. Moreover, both antecedent and consequent appear to contain two phrases, creating a double period design. Consequently,

it is easier to hear TR as a separate entity and less tempting to hear it as merged with P. Thus it begins to approach the "dissolving consequent" type that also terminates V:PAC.

the pre-S phrases are replaced by new material, which encourages us to think of that material as a recomposed TR. What we choose to consider as S (and C, when it exists) will usually be re-stated intact.

TR Rhetoric Lacking? P Ends with I:PAC or I:IAC and S Follows Directly

In this variant of the above two possibilities, P cadences I:PAC or I:IAC. What one finds is: *nonmodulating period (or sentence) + S*. There are conceptual problems with this category. If the function of an MC (here, implied at the end of the period?) is forcibly to open up S-space, how can this task be accomplished by a PAC (or IAC) in the tonic key—especially if what precedes it has not displayed any characteristic TR-rhetorical signs? We have dealt with re-lated matters concerning this infrequently en-countered I:PAC MC situation earlier, where we labeled it a (rare) fourth-level default op-tion for the MC—something that should not be invoked casually in any analysis. The essential problem in the cases immediately at hand is that TR rhetoric is lacking altogether and hence that the I:PAC will be heard merely as closing off P (especially if it is the only PAC or IAC in P), not as an opening-up of S-space. This would imply either that S will begin in the new key or that S will begin in the tonic key and itself modulate to the new key, thus appropriating the function normally accorded the TR.

In actuality, the situation occurs infrequently and is mostly confined to brief or small-scale movements. One instance would seem to be Clementi's Sonatina in C, op. 36 no. 3. Here P is structured as a period with a double con-sequent phrase (4 + 4 + 4 bars). The first con-sequent cadences weakly on I:IAC (m. 8), fol-lowed by a varied restatement that drives toward a strong I:PAC. S follows at once in the key of the dominant. Note, however, that the I:PAC in m. 12 displays the triple-hammer-blow ges-ture and general pause typical of an MC, and m. 12 is preceded by a harmonic and dynamic intensification. Thus it is at least conceivable

that mm. 9–12 contain a transitional zone of the consequent-restatement type—but instead of dissolving, this restatement drives toward the I:PAC that, for better or worse, will have to serve as the MC. This interpretation seems to be reinforced by the fact that in the recapitu-lation the consequent-restatement is expanded and leads this time to a I:HC MC, thus replac-ing a clear MC-deformation with a more nor-mative MC. (A similar situation—though one with an abrupt one-bar link jammed mischie-vously between the I:PAC and the subsequent S—may be found at the opening of Mozart's String Quartet in F, K. 158: I:PAC at m. 10; S at m. 12.)

TR as Energy-Loss?

As pointed out at the beginning of this chapter, the most normative characteristic of TR within Allegro compositions is energy-gain driving to-ward an MC. On infrequent occasions, though, one might come across a TR that is counterge-neric or weakened, that expresses a sense either of energy-loss *en route*—perhaps even after an initial *forte* burst at its opening—or of at least an inability to generate the expected level of inten-sity characteristic of most TRs. One possibility, particularly in the middle and later decades of the nineteenth century (Schumann, Brahms), is what we call the *de-energizing transition*. In chap-ter 3 we suggested that its late-eighteenth-cen-tury origins lie in the techniques of expanded caesura-fill of the $\hat{5}-\hat{1}$-descent type and in the "blocked medial caesura." In other cases, TR seems unable to summon up the will to con-tinue to produce the normative energy-gain all the way to the end—a situation with provoca-tive hermeneutic implications. This situation, suggesting that normative TR-processes are be-ing partially suppressed or stifled, crops up from time to time in Schubert, as in the first move-ment of his Violin Sonata in A Minor, D. 385 (TR starts *forte* at m. 15, recedes back to *piano* at m. 19, and proceeds with further *descrescendi* to the III:PAC MC at m. 23).

CHAPTER SEVEN

The Secondary Theme (S) and Essential Expositional Closure (EEC)

Initial Considerations

Its cue having been sounded, the secondary theme (S) strides onto the stage through the doorway opened by the medial caesura. If there is no MC, there is no S. If there is no medial caesura, we are confronting not a two-part exposition but a continuous exposition for which the concept of S is inappropriate.[1] In a two-part exposition S usually begins no later than 50 percent or 60 percent of the way through the exposition, although more often it begins earlier. Responding to the medial caesura, the secondary theme launches the second phase of the two-part exposition; part 2 extends from this point until the exposition's final cadence. (In the recapitulation the music of part 2 will also be called the *tonal resolution*.) Part 2 may be occupied completely by S or, more commonly, it may subdivide into a secondary-theme and closing-theme zone (S / C). The demarcation between the two zones is the point of *essential expositional closure* (EEC). This is the most important generic and tonal goal of the exposition, the moment when S attains a satisfactory perfect authentic cadence in the new key and gives way

to differing material. S-space lasts until it has produced this expected PAC. All else that follows is normally to be regarded as C.

Because of its role within the larger structure S is the most privileged zone of the expositional rotation, just as any references to S-materials within later rotations are similarly to be flagged for heightened attention. To S alone is assigned the task of laying down the planks of musical space that lead directly to the EEC (and that are expected to accomplish the corresponding ESC in the recapitulation). What happens in S makes a sonata a sonata. Far from being passive or pejoratively "secondary" (in the sense of "lesser"), S takes on the role of the agent in achieving the sonata's most defining tonal moments. S may be regarded as an additional facet of the social or personal self initially projected in P and TR, a preplanned phase in the sequence of events that will carry out the sonata as a whole. There is no reason to suppose that in the late-eighteenth-century sonata S is to be conceived generically as a polar opposite to P.[2] "Opposition" and "polarity" are unhelpful words in this context.

---

1. Any exception to this principle—a self-evident S that is not prepared by a clear MC (and that must be judged as an S for other compelling reasons)—should be regarded as both highly unusual and deformational. Such rare cases, found, for instance, in the finale of Beethoven's Eighth Symphony, are considered in ch. 8.

2. We note here Somfai's observation in *The Keyboard Sonatas of Joseph Haydn*, pp. 266–67 (an observation specifically tailored to Haydn's customary practice): "In the last third of the eighteenth century, however, a contrasting second subject was certainly neither a requisite nor an ideal. Koch suggests that the . . . *cantabler Satz* [S]

However turbulent it may seem *en route*, a sonata operates more like a cleverly coordinated relay from one anticipated station to the next.

Since it is the task of S to bring about a PAC in the new key, its sounding triggers the expectation that we are on the approach to that crucial cadence. Our listening strategies can reflect this. To hear S-material, here and in later rotations, is to alert oneself to what that thematic zone exists to do. The onset of S is a signal that we are being urged to listen with a keen readiness for the cadence-to-come—the PAC that will be the next obligatory generic station in the sonata's process of realization. Once S begins, we track its progress or lack of it along a forward vector toward the EEC, sharing psychologically in its trajectory toward closure. Along with S, we, too, should be on the lookout for the EEC lying ahead of us, and we ought to register a sense of satisfaction once that PAC in the new key is attained.

S serves additionally as both a proposal and a prediction for the manner in which the ESC is likely to be effected in the recapitulation. While it is true that the basic function of part 2 is to ground or stabilize the new key of the dominant, it is also the case that the exposition's part 2 (S / C) is fashioned to articulate a rhetorical and tonal structure of promise that, when transposed in the recapitulation, will bring the trajectory of the entire sonata to a successful, resolved conclusion. Even as our immediate expositional anticipations are satisfied with the EEC that brings S-space to a close, the larger effect of the whole is to establish a higher-level set of anticipations for the remainder of the sonata. In the recapitulation—still far down the road—the exposition's structure of promise is destined to become a structure of accomplishment.

Historical Discussions of P- and S-Space

Eighteenth- and early-nineteenth-century theorists invariably collapsed what we currently call the exposition of sonata form into only its two-part format. They persistently ignored the continuous-exposition format, which was less frequently selected as a compositional option. Many of these theorists noted the often-differing characters of the first and second themes (P and S). The convention of two themes, for instance, was alluded to by Riepel in 1755 and Vogler in 1778. The themes were described more colorfully by Koch in 1793 (in which the first theme is *ein erweiterter, oder mit mehr melodischen Theilen verbindener, und etwas rauschender Satz* ["a somewhat noisy/boisterous theme, expanded or bound together in several melodic parts"] and the second, in the dominant, is *ein cantabler Satz* ["a cantabile theme"]), by Galeazzi in 1796 (in which the second theme is the *passo caratteristico* ["the characteristic passage"]), and by Kollmann in 1799.

The two-part format was also the exposition type outlined in Reicha's famous 1824–26 diagram of *la grande coupe binaire* ("the grand binary design," whose *exposition des idées* included a *première idée mère* and a *seconde idée mère*). After Reicha it was most notably elaborated by Birnbach in his 1827 outline of what he called the *Hauptform* ("principal form,' including an initial *Thema* followed by *der zweite Gedanke* ['the second thought"] or *das zweite Thema*—the first use of the specific term "second theme"), Gathy in 1835 (*Hauptgedanke* and *Nebengedanke*), Czerny in circa 1837–49 ("first subject" and "middle subject"), Marx in 1837–47 (*Hauptsatz* and *Seitensatz*—which became the standard Germanic terms for the two themes), and others.[3] In some of his sketches from around 1800

... should not be in utter contrast to the primary theme but should rather present a specific variation reminiscent of it. In 1777, Carl Ludwig Junker stated [in his *Tonkunst* (Bern, 1777)], 'Each secondary subject [*Nebenthemata*] is a consequence of the original ruling passion of the work and so is related to it. Otherwise the whole piece will be incoherent, and the fundamental emotion will remain hidden.'" See also the remarks on the eighteenth-century concepts of contrast and "antithesis" (then understood more in a classically rhetorical sense than a

proto-Hegelian one) as elaborated in Fred Ritzel, *Die Entwicklung der 'Sonatenform' im musiktheoretischen Schrifttum des 18. and 19. Jahrhunderts* (Wiesbaden, Breitkopf & Härtel, 1968), p. 102–5. E.g. (p. 105): "Kontrast bleibt für die formalen Konstellationen sekundär, aber nicht wesentliches Element eines dialektischen Formprozesses."

3. Early descriptions of the sonata are documented in many sources. See, e.g., Fred Ritzel, *Die Entwicklung der 'Sonatenform' im musiktheoretischen Schrifttum des 18. and 19.*

(the op. 18 quartets, the violin sonatas from op. 30, the piano sonatas from p. 31), Beethoven seems to have referred to the S-theme with the abbreviation, "m.g." William Drabkin has suggested that this (foreshadowing the terminology of Czerny?) may have been an abbreviation for *Mittel-Gedanke*, an observation that seems increasingly likely as further evidence from the later works comes to light.[4]

Tonal Choices for S

As indicated in chapters 2 and 3, minor-mode sonatas usually move to the major mediant (III) for S and C. Considerably less frequently, S and C are deployed in the minor dominant (v), with much more negative implications. (Chapter 14 discusses the role of the minor mode in eighteenth-century practice and also glances at some alternative choices for the key of S—such as VI—explored in the nineteenth century.) In major-mode sonatas before 1800 moving to the dominant key (V) for S was the only standard choice. From time to time one might find the beginning of S in the dominant minor (as in Mozart's Overture to *Idomeneo*), and this option is treated in a separate section below. Similarly, a major-mode S (in V) might contain unstable local inflections of the dominant minor or be subjected to a restatement in the dominant minor. These are significant gestures within the individualized narrative at hand, and they demand hermeneutic attention.

Around 1800 Beethoven began to investigate the deformation of moving to III for part 2, not

Jahrhunderts; Birgitte Moyer, "Concepts of Musical Form in the Nineteenth Century with Special Reference to A.B. Marx and Sonata Form," Diss. Stanford, 1969; William S. Newman, *The Sonata in the Classic Era: The Second Volume of A History of the Sonata Idea*, 2nd ed. (New York: Norton, 1972), pp. 19–42; Leonard G. Ratner, *Classic Music: Expression, Form, and Style* (New York: Schirmer, 1980), pp. 217–47; Ian Bent, *Analysis* (New York: Norton, 1987), pp. 12–32; Hans-Joachim Hinrichsen, "Sonatenform, Sonatenhauptsatzform" [1996], in Hans Heinrich Eggebrecht, ed., *Handwörterbuch der musikalischen Terminologie* (Stuttgart: Steiner, n.d.), pp. 1–7. The above refer to virtually all of these figures. More specifically: For Koch, see the *Versuch einer Anleitung zur Composition*, vol. 3, sections 100–3 ("Von der Sinfonie"), 141, and 147 (1793; rpt. Hildesheim: Georg Olms, 1969), p. 301–11, 363–66, 381–86 ; in this case the thematic descriptions are taken from sections 141 and 147, pp. 364, 385; translations of much of Koch are available in Koch, *Introductory Essay on Composition: The Mechanical Rules of Melody, Sections 3 and 4*, trans. Nancy Kovaleff Baker (New Haven, Conn.: Yale University Press, 1983). For Galeazzi, see Bathia Churgin, "Francesco Galeazzi's Description (1796) of Sonata Form," *Journal of the American Musicological Society* 21 (1968), 181–99. For Kollmann, see his *An Essay on Practical Musical Composition* [1799], (rpt New York: Da Capo, 1973), excerpted also in *Music in the Western World: A History in Documents*, ed. Piero Weiss and Richard Taruskin (New York: Schirmer, 1984), pp. 316–19 and Ratner, *Classic Music*, p. 219. For Reicha see Bent, *Analysis*, pp. 18–20 and especially Peter A. Hoyt, "The Concept of *développement* in the Early Nineteenth Century," in *Music Theory in the Age of Romanticism*, ed. Ian Bent (Cambridge: Cambridge University Press, 1996), pp. 141–62. For Birnbach and Gathy, see Moyer, "Concepts of Musical Form," pp. 56–57, and Bent, *Analysis*,

p. 25. For Czerny and Marx, see Moyer, "Concepts of Musical Form," pp. 65 and 69–125.
4. William Drabkin, "Beethoven's Understanding of 'Sonata Form': The Evidence of the Sketchbooks," in *Beethoven's Compositional Process*, ed. William Kinderman (Lincoln: University of Nebraska Press, 1991), pp. 14–19 ("m.g." on p. 18). Further evidence from the sketches for a "secondary theme," "similar to [a] second subject," marked "m.g." is found in the Benedictus of the *Missa Solemnis*, as noted in William Kinderman, *Artaria 195: Beethoven's Sketchbook for the Missa solemnis and the Piano Sonata in E Major, Opus 109* (Urbana and Chicago: University of Illinois Press, 2003), vol. 1, Commentary, pp. 109–10, which refers to the "m.g." detail in the sketch itself, p. 93 (in vol. 2, Facsimile, and vol. 3, Transcription). In a personal communication to the authors (November 22, 2004), Kinderman additionally noted that "m.g." or "Mittelgedanke" also "appears in Beethoven's sketches for his unfinished Piano Trio in F minor from 1816 in the Scheide Sketchbook at Princeton, where the 'second subject' in D-flat major is so labeled." In the same message Kinderman noted that Beethoven's terminology also included "m.s." for "Mittelsatz," meaning "a large internal section, often though not always corresponding to our 'development section,'" and cited evidence of the "m.s" indication from several works, including the second movement of the Piano Sonata in E, op. 109 (also discussed in the *Artaria 195* volumes). Beethoven's term for exposition was normally "'erster [or '1ter'] Theil," while he referred to the remainder of the movement, from the development onward, as "2ter Theil." Following the publication of the *Artaria 195* facsimile, we now know that Beethoven continued to use this terminology in his later period. We thank William Kinderman for drawing this to our attention.

to V, within major-mode sonata-based structures. This might have been suggested by analogy to the role of the mediant in minor-mode sonatas. Examples may be found in the first movements of his Piano Sonatas in G, op. 31 no. 1 (S first in B major, m. 66, then repeated in B minor, m. 74, which key persists for the rest of the exposition) and in C, op. 53 ("Waldstein," S in E major), in the *Leonore* Overtures Nos. 2 and 3 (P in C major; S and C in E major), and in the finale of the Piano Trio in E-flat, op. 70 no. 2 (S and C in G major).[5] Moving to III was not the only alternative that Beethoven explored around this time. In the first movement of the String Quintet in C, op. 29, he deployed the secondary theme in VI. Here the S-theme begins in a bright A major, VI (mm. 41–51), but soon decays to A minor, vi (m. 52, with an immediate, transient "escape attempt" toward F major in mm. 54–56), for the remainder of the exposition. A similar procedure may be observed in the first movement of the Triple Concerto in C, op. 56, whose solo exposition moves to A major, then, eventually, to A minor, while the first movement of the Piano Trio in B-flat, op. 97, "Archduke," deploys its S- and C-ideas entirely in G major. Schubert was another who experimented with other expositional possibilities. By the mid-nineteenth century the move to V, the key of generic tradition, remained a first-level default for expositions, but other tonal choices were also acceptable (especially various shades of mediants and submediants) as lower-level defaults for idiosyncratic structural implications—among which the unwillingness or staged "inability" to move to the traditionally normative V was by no means the least telling.

Also conceivable around 1800, although still rare, were "tonally migratory" S-themes that begin in one key and move into another to produce the EEC. Beethoven's C-minor *Coriolan* Overture, op. 62, is the touchstone here:

its S-theme moves sequentially from the "noble" E-flat major, through F minor, and into G minor for the EEC and C-idea. (See the chapter 14 discussion of this piece in the context of i–III–v motions in minor-mode expositions.) Tonally migratory S-areas are also found in the first movements of a few concertos of the period (chapters 20 and 21). Such practices can produce what have sometimes been regarded as three-stage expositions, in which, in effect, part-2 space was divided into two tonal regions. In some cases, these provide deformational complications associated with apparent double medial caesuras (the trimodular-block effect, or TMB), to be discussed in chapter 8.

Essential Expositional Closure: The First-PAC Rule

One central feature of Sonata Theory is its emphasis, after the onset of the secondary theme, on the attainment of the first satisfactory perfect authentic cadence that proceeds onward to differing material. This is the moment that we term *essential expositional closure* ("the EEC"). It is toward the accomplishing of this PAC, marking the end of S-space, that we understand all of the preceding music to have been aiming. This issue of "the first PAC" is a complex matter, and we do not wish to minimize its difficulties. (We shall revisit it again below in "Some Schenkerian Implications" and at some length in chapter 8 in our consideration of EEC deferrals—specific situations in which it is a later PAC that effects the EEC.) At stake is the issue of when S may be considered to have ended or, conversely, when the closing ideas (C) may be said to have begun. There are two general approaches to the question. These two approaches—the larger versus the more restricted understanding of S (or the brief versus the broader concept of C)—may be

---

5. An important predecessor here is what may regarded as the (deformational) exposition of the slow movement of Beethoven's Piano Sonata in C, op. 2 no. 3 (E major moving, after a modal collapse to E minor, to G major). This movement undertakes a dialogue with certain sonata principles and expectations. It has both an expositional and a recapitulatory rotation—suggesting the presence of a Type 3 sonata—although the whole is problematized by the persistence of TR-figuration through the end of the exposition, which also flows through most of the developmental space. To understand this movement as a "special rondo form," as does Tovey, is inadequate. See Tovey, *A Companion to Beethoven's Pianoforte Sonatas* (London, 1931), pp. 27–29. Cf. William E. Caplin's "large ternary form" solution in *Classical Form*, pp. 216, 282, nn. 40 and 41.

represented by the positions of William E. Caplin and William Rothstein. We favor Rothstein's conclusions for reasons that emerge below.

Caplin's view, in *Classical Form* (1998), was to restrict the concept of closing music to nonthematic materials only. Consequently he preferred the term "closing section" to "closing theme" (which term he assessed as confusing, for example as found in Charles Rosen's *Sonata Forms*), and he distinguished it as a "group of codettas" from the genuine "themes" of the "subordinate-theme group." On this interpretation "a closing section usually contains several different codettas," often shortening in overall length. In another description he defined the closing section as "a postcadential intrathematic function following a perfect authentic cadence. It consists of a group of codettas, often featuring fragmentation and a recessive dynamic." The perfect authentic cadence in question here is the final PAC of the "subordinate-theme group," which may display several successive PACs disposed in "multiple subordinate themes": "each one of these themes ends with a perfect authentic cadence in the subordinate key." Thus Caplin decided on behalf of the larger view of S, an additive S-grouping principle that construed S-space as potentially occupied by a succession of themes that each end with a PAC. This subordinate-theme group "almost always demands a postcadential passage [of codettas] either to dissipate the accumulated energy or, sometimes, to sustain that energy even further beyond the actual moment of cadential closure."[6]

In short, Caplin interpreted the end of S-space to occur when the "themes" stop and the "codettas" begin, with their characteristically "postcadential function" and their "general sense of compression of musical material." With few exceptions closing sections would encompass only the final bars of most expositions. They would comprise only those reinforcing sections that are clearly not graspable as "themes" in Ca-

plin's sense, and many S-theme "groups" would extend far beyond their first PACs. While this reasoning is internally consistent, it appears to have been decided by *fiat*, perhaps also partly in resonance with mid-twentieth-century analytical assumptions: there is not much by way of an appeal to earlier historical evidence to support the claim. Caplin recognized, though only in passing, that Rothstein had come to a different conclusion, but he presented no counterargument to shore up his own position.[7]

In claiming priority for the "first strongly articulated perfect cadence in the goal key"—at the time (1989) a striking claim—Rothstein had elaborated the central problem at a more fundamental level and had stood on firmer historical ground:

> There may be some question [once the second group has begun] as to which of two or three cadences is *the* closing cadence. Normally, it is the first perfect cadence in the key of the second group. . . . The cadences that come later may be considered reinforcements of the closing cadence; their purpose is often to satisfy some element of closure left incomplete in the closing cadence itself. Elements of closure, beyond the harmonic cadence, may involve the register of the bass or melody, the presence or absence of some important melodic tone, . . . the presence or absence of a subdominant-type harmony in the cadential progression, or any of a number of other factors.[8]

In support of this view Rothstein had also written:

> Actually, the subdivisions of the second group have been better described by older theorists such as Koch and Reicha than by most of their successors. Following cadence structure as usual, both of these theorists distinguish sharply between any passages *preceding* the first perfect cadence in the goal key of the exposition and any passages *following* that cadence. The former they consider part of the main body of the exposition, the latter not. . . .

---

6. Caplin, *Classical Form*, pp. 121–22.
7. Caplin, *Classical Form*, pp. 122, 273 n. 82 ("frequently identifies"). In an earlier article, "The 'Expanded Cadential Progression': A Category for the Analysis of Classical Form," *Journal of Musicological Research* 7 (1987), 215–57, Caplin had argued that the sec-

ondary-theme group lasted through an expanded cadential progression (ECP)—basically the articulation of a I^6–predominant–V^{6-5}_{4-3}–I progression spread out over a broader space of four or more bars. Cf. n. 15.
8. Rothstein, *Phrase Rhythm in Tonal Music*, p. 116.

Following the reasoning of these older theorists, we will term as closing theme, or in some cases codetta, only the suffix or suffixes to the exposition—that is, only those portions of the second group following the first strongly articulated perfect cadence in the goal key. . . .

Emphasis on the first perfect cadence in the second group as the critical point in its form corresponds closely to the ideas of Koch and Reicha. It also conforms to the usual analytical practice of Schenker.[9]

Here Rothstein's appeal to Koch probably refers to the latter's remark in the *Versuch* of 1793 concerning the role of cadences, or "formal phrase-endings" in the latter portion of the exposition: "[In the first period (exposition) of a symphony] following the cadence a clarifying period [*ein erklärender Periode*] is often appended that continues and closes in the same key in which the preceding one had also closed. Thus it is nothing else than an appendix [*Anhang*] to the first period and both united may quite properly be considered a single main period."[10] Similar conclusions might be drawn from an even earlier description by Georg Joseph Vogler in 1778 in his periodical *Betrachtungen der Mannheimer Tonschule*. In the process of pointing out what he called the five *Perioden* (sections) of the "first part" (exposition) of the first movement of an

F-major keyboard sonata by Franz Mezger, Vogler wrote that the fourth section (our S) continued "until finally . . . a formal cadence in C appears," a cadence that "receives its confirmation [*Bestätigung*] by the following cadential section [*schlussfallmäsigen Periode*]" (our C).[11]

Such lines of argument strike us as persuasive, and we should add a few additional remarks regarding our similar prioritizing of the first PAC in our concept of essential expositional closure. What is meant by "essential"? Within smaller, earlier-eighteenth-century binary structures, the most notable ancestors of sonata-form movements, the first part, when modulatory, had driven to a single PAC close—in major-mode pieces, a close in the dominant. This cadence represented the essential generic task of the first section—the single thing that part 1 needed to accomplish. At times, as with some of Domenico Scarlatti's sonatas, the first section contained *two* cadences near the end: the generically obligatory one and an extra one completing a brief, additional passage of codetta-like reinforcement, an added passage of new-key stabilization that Ralph Kirkpatrick wittily compared to the effect of the coasting on a "landing strip" once an airplane has touched down.[12]

As the binary structure expanded and was

---

9. Rothstein, *Phrase Rhythm*, pp. 116–17. In a footnote Rothstein adds that Schenker's analysis of the *Eroica* does *not* take the first PAC as the end of S: as such it is exceptional. (On the other hand, we do accept that first V:PAC here, m. 83, as the EEC. In part our differing interpretation brings up issues that we deal with below in "Some Schenkerian Implications"; in addition, we interpret what follows immediately, mm. 84ff, as a rare instance of a C⁰ theme, discussed in ch. 9.)
10. English version as in *Introductory Essay*, trans. Nancy Kovaleff Baker, p. 199. In Koch, *Versuch*, vol. 3, section 101, p. 305, the original reads: "Oft ist zwar nach der Cadenz desselben noch ein erklärender Periode angehängt, der aber in ebenderselben Tonart fortmodulirt und schließt, in welcher der vorher gehende auch geschlossen hatte; daher können wir ihn für nichts anders, als blos für einen Anhang des ersten Perioden erklären, und können gar füglich beyde vereinigt als einen einzigen Hauptperioden betrachten." Baker's translation of a "formal phrase-ending" is Koch's "förmlichen Absatz" (p. 306).
11. Quoted in Jane R. Stevens, "Theme, Harmony, and Texture in Classic-Romantic Descriptions of Concerto

First-Movement Form," *Journal of the American Musicological Society* 27 (1974), 32, from which we have adapted the above translation. Stevens also provides the relevant original German text in the context of a broader discussion of Vogler. Along the same lines, in 1796 Galeazzi maintained that the *passo caratteristico* (our S) ends with its "final cadence" (following, perhaps, a thematic repetition) after which one may "elegantly add a new period, called a Coda [our C, of variable length], which is an addition or prolongation of the cadence." Galeazzi's "Coda" appears to be more than a mere "codetta," especially since he goes on to suggest that it may refer back to (or at least lead back into) the original expositional ideas (perhaps suggesting our P-based C): "it serves very well to link the ideas which end the first part with those which have begun it, or with those with which the second part begins." See Churgin, "Francesco Galeazzi's Description (1796) of Sonata Form," p. 194, from which we have adapted the translation.
12. Kirkpatrick, *Domenico Scarlatti* (Princeton, N.J.: Princeton University Press, 1953), p. 255. Kirkpatrick used the apt simile to refer to the "reiterated cadences" following the "final resolution into the closing tonal-

transformed through thematic differentiation and specialization, the central feature of the generically essential PAC must surely have been retained—the idea of that first necessary, "touch-down" cadence before any "landing strip" of additional ideas. (The tonally generic point of an exposition, after all, is to secure the new key in part 2.) PACs in the second key of an exposition are never to be taken lightly. Moreover, the first of these PACs produces the sense that at least the minimal generic-harmonic requirements of the form have been satisfied. If only for this reason, the first satisfactory (non-repeated or otherwise overridden) perfect authentic cadence within an exposition's part 2 is conceptually privileged. Generically it represents the attainment, however rudimentary, of the *essential exposition*—the accomplishment of the one thing that all expositions are expected to do. Thus this PAC has a dual function. On the one hand, viewed more locally, it closes the thematic materials of the S-zone. On the other hand, viewed from the point of view of the function of the S-zone as a whole within the broader structure, it marks the successful arrival and cadential securing of the secondary key, the accomplishment of a guided trajectory that had been generically "in mind" from the first moments of the piece. (See figure 2.1a.)

In considering this issue, it is also significant to observe that there is no generic requirement for a major-mode exposition to have more than one V:PAC, although many in fact do. Therein lies the difficulty. The obvious complication is that instead of producing merely one or two V:PACs (as in the earlier binary structure), the typical exposition might have sounded four, five, six, or more, depending on aspects of thematic restatement, concatenation of diverse thematic modules, and so on. Moreover, it was possible, even common, for these later V:PACs to bring an even more emphatic closure (both dynamic and textural) to thematic phrases. Which of these was now to be considered the generically "essential" cadence? There is no denying

that with this multiplication of cadences, the generic question of "essential closure" (when does S end?) opened itself to ambiguity and the potential for differing interpretations. And as we have mentioned, analysts today disagree with regard to this matter.

A close study of the music itself repeatedly suggests that the first satisfactory V:PAC that goes on to different material remained a generically significant moment. It was normally the end of the essential exposition, to which different kinds of (as Reicha put it) "accessory ideas" (our C-zone) could be added to produce any number of effects. To be sure, the first-PAC rule is more of a guideline than a "rule": it is anything but inflexible. Composers devised a number of strategies to override that implication—in other words, to demonstrate that the first PAC was being reopened—and to defer the EEC to the next PAC by means of immediate thematic repetition or variation, the continuation of an accompaniment figure, the later placement of a nonelided cadence, and the like. A few examples will be provided in this chapter, and the topic of EEC deferral will be dealt with in more detail in chapter 8.

In short, we have learned that evidence found in the music itself regularly reaffirms our principle of the EEC. Our analytical encounter with "new" pieces seems continually to reinforce these conclusions—and only very rarely to challenge them (although this may be clearer only as our discussion proceeds in subsequent chapters). This reinforcing happens, for example, when a clear shift to certain readily identifiable C-types is made following the EEC-point: with the EEC nailed down, the music is liberated into a freer closing-space or "appendix" (Koch's *Anhang*) of "accessory ideas." One eventually comes to realize that certain types of C^1-theme (the onset of C) became normative. These C^1-identifiers (especially the *forte* P-based C^1) can help to support the general proposition about the role of the first PAC (or if deferred, its later counterpart), even as they can help in making judg-

---

ity" in the "second half" of the binary structure. Since Kirkpatrick did not specifically focus on the attainment of cadences, this passage is a bit obscure, but it appears that he was referring to the additional [quasi-C-space] cadences following what we would call, even within

this binary form, the ESC. Malcolm Boyd, *Domenico Scarlatti: Master of Music* (New York: Schirmer, 1986), p. 168, also quoted the phrase by Kirkpatrick and applied it to the "codetta . . . reinforcing the closing tonality of the section."

ments about the location of the EEC in difficult cases. All of these things need to be considered in assessing the possibility of EEC deferrals past the first PAC in the new key. But the bulk of the evidence overwhelmingly bolsters our general conclusion. Both historically and generically, the essential exposition—by no means the complete exposition—should be considered as normally extended to that first satisfactory PAC proceeding onward to differing material. That PAC is given a special priority.

As a word of caution, we should underscore this one more time: the EEC need not be—and often is not—the strongest cadence within the exposition. Stronger cadences—more emphatic expanded-cadential-progression cadences (I^6–predominant–V^{6-5}_{4-3}–I),[13] trill-cadences, and so on—often occur as reinforcement-work in C-space. One should not determine an EEC on the basis of what one imagines an EEC should "feel" like in terms of force or unassailably conclusive implication. Nor should one assume that we are making grand claims regarding either the completeness or the degree of the closure implied by the EEC. Its "closure" may not in fact be absolute or "fully satisfying" from the perspective of the larger proportions or other telling factors within the exposition as a whole. This first PAC closing the essential exposition is primarily an attainment of an important generic requirement—nothing more and nothing less. It may be composed, however, in such a way as virtually to demand the "accessory ideas" of a more decisive C-zone, which can certainly include broadly thematic and energy-gaining modules. Our main point remains. With the first satisfactory PAC the exposition has now accomplished what it set out essentially to do: to cadence decisively in the second key, thus setting up and forecasting the parallel point of *essential structural closure* (ESC) in the recapitulation.

Proportions of S- and C-Space

As indicated above, part 2 is normally subdivided into S- and C-space, with the EEC marking the point of division separating the one from the other (S / C). There is no way of predicting what proportion of part 2 will be occupied by S or C. Sometimes an expanded S blocks out the possibility of any C; sometimes C is merely a brief codetta to S; sometimes C is more elaborate, unfolded with two, three, or more thematic or cadential modules, filling up more part-2-space than had S. (Figure 7.1 provides a visual suggestion of some possibilities.) The only caveat—albeit an important one—is that there seems to be a contextually informed limit below which S-space would reasonably be considered too brief to provide a sufficient sense of closure to the freshly launched zone. (This situation this is discussed in chapter 8.) Developing a feel for the manifold ways in which part-2-space may be rhetorically subdivided (each bearing its own expressive/proportional implications) is an important step toward understanding sonatas as a whole.

Structure

S may be articulated in an abundance of differing shapes: period, repeated period, sentence, hybrid phrase, and so on. Sometimes one finds chains of these characteristic shapes (as in the multimodular S) linked either by subverted or evaded cadences—thus avoiding the crucial PAC—or by some sort of cadence- or phrase-repetition or recapturing of pre-existing S-material, both of which techniques defer the EEC to the next PAC down the road. As with P-themes one often finds nested hierarchies of structure within S. A composer might construct the antecedent and consequent phrases of a parallel-period S as sentences. Or an S may begin by seeming to announce itself as a period only to have its consequent undermined, requiring the conversion of the whole into a larger sentence. This happens when the antecedent and "unsuccessful" consequent—or the antecedent submitted only to a repetition—are reinterpreted as the characteristic a + a' of a larger sentence's presentation section. The next module, often a contrasting one, will begin the b portion, or continuation, of this broader sentence.

---

13. See n. 7.

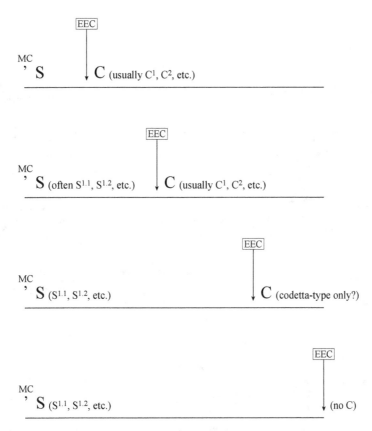

FIGURE 7.1   Varying Placements of the EEC within Part 2 of the Exposition

A good example of multiple structural hierarchies occurs with the secondary theme of Beethoven's Symphony No. 1 in C, first movement (example 7.1). Here S begins with what we first might suppose will be an antecedent (mm. 53–60—itself sentential) and a consequent. The expected consequent, however, fails to close with a PAC (m. 68), and the music pushes onward (m. 69), as if in a struggle to shake loose the generically required cadence. With m. 69 (and in retrospect) one converts the earlier view of mm. 53–60 and 61–68 into that of two broad presentation modules, a + a', of a larger sentence (in this case, each ending with a half cadence), while mm. 69ff mark the onset of the sentence's

b-portion, the continuation. A V:PAC is finally declared—as if with finality—at m. 77, and we immediately assume that it will serve as the EEC. Yet this assumption, too, is instantly undermined. Instead of moving directly into C, S-material is retained with a sardonic, *pianissimo*, after-the-fact back-reference to the opening of S. In effect, this is an unanticipated extra zone, a darkened interpolation dropping simultaneously into the minor dominant, just as the bottom of the earlier V:PAC seems to drop out as one starts to plunge flatward, down the circle of fifths, before the V:PAC is reinstated, and with it the EEC proper, at m. 88.[14] A generically standard P-based C[1]-theme follows.

14. The definition of the EEC as the first *satisfactory* V:PAC means both that the material producing the cadence is not immediately recycled in a repetition and that characteristic S-melodic-material is also relin-

quished with a shift into differing ideas. In this case the typical P-based C[1] that follows (m. 88) confirms this interpretation. Chapter 8 considers EEC deferrals more generally.

EXAMPLE 7.1   Beethoven, Symphony No. 1 in C, op. 21, i, mm. 53–90

EXAMPLE 7.1 (*continued*)

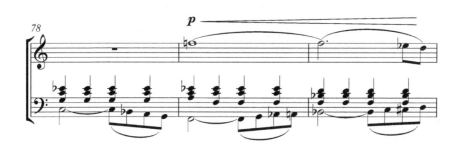

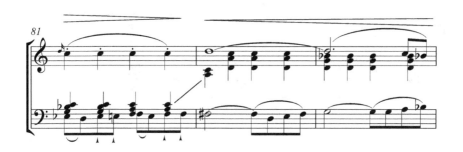

EXAMPLE 7.1 (continued)

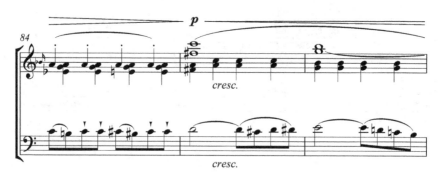

A particularly common strategy is to launch S as a simple parallel period, sentence, or other brief, closed structure—thus bringing it to an efficient PAC (often with the effect of its having arrived "too soon")—and then to submit it to a florid, expanded repetition, thereby undoing the EEC-effect of the first PAC. This strategy converts what might be expected to be a mere repetition into a billowing fantasy on the S-idea, moving decoratively or expansively toward the "real" EEC or perhaps toward merely another PAC that may itself be reopened in one way or another. An expressive feature of this technique is that of comparing the simpler, square-cut model of the first thematic statement—something easily retained in the memory as a symmetrical, fixed block—with the unconstrained, flowing freedom of its varied restatement. The result can be a quasi-theatrical demonstration of the art of composition, of the imagination's fantasy-like reinterpretation of a simple idea, or of the breathtaking disclosure of the otherwise hidden potential of the earlier, more generically quadratic module.

This technique of cleverly enhanced restatement—theme and expanded variant—is especially characteristic of Mozart. Consider the S-theme of the Symphony No. 34 in C, K. 338, first movement, mm. 41–48, 49–64 (example 7.2). Here the initial eight-bar phrase is structured as a compound basic idea plus a continuation (Caplin's Hybrid 3), and it produces a V:PAC at m. 48—given the proportions of the movement a rather "early" point to have articulated the EEC. In any event, its varied repetition reopens the V:PAC, thus deferring the EEC-issue to the subsequent V:PAC. Here Mozart kept the compound basic idea intact but expanded the Lombard-rhythm continuation, thereby creating a heightened expectation for the cadence-to-come, and added a new, "synthesizing" cadential module (mm. 59–64) to bring about the EEC in m. 64. Parallel or similar examples abound in the repertory; they are characteristic of the style. In some cases the initial PAC of the first, simple statement of S—so easily attained there—is lost or endangered in the repetition. Recovering it becomes no easy matter, and there are a variety of strategies that can be used to bring the S-zone to the EEC.

All of this works to prolong the S-zone considerably—to extend S over a broader expanse of time.

Regardless of its phrase-structure, one thing is *de rigueur*: S must be harmonically and tonally stable. If not—if S is tonally unstable, or if it is undergirded with a dominant pedal or some other tension-producing device—then one is dealing with the deformation of a generic norm. In addition, over its entire course S will usually accomplish a clear, traceable *linear descent*, $\hat{5} - \hat{4} - \hat{3} - \hat{2} - \hat{1}$, in the new key. S will normally last until the completion of this first linear fifth-descent. Ideally, in order to be fully "satisfactory," each of these scale degrees should receive harmonic support from the bass, and in fact they often do, although sometimes in ways that are not immediately obvious to those inexperienced in Schenkerian analysis. Although the full descent is clearly the ideal, or the first-level default, in practice one or more scale degrees are sometimes omitted or exist only as implied in the linear descent that most immediately precedes the PAC. In some instances—notwithstanding the presence of the PAC and its function as the EEC—this might be interpreted as resulting in a somewhat weakened EEC. This situation suggests that there is additional reinforcement-work that needs to be accomplished within C.

Clearly, the $\hat{2}$ and $\hat{1}$ should coincide with the first satisfactory PAC: the $\hat{2}$ will be supported by a root-position dominant chord, and the $\hat{1}$ by a root-position tonic. In addition, the preceding $\hat{3}$ is also usually supported by a dominant in the bass (the cadential $\frac{6}{4}$ chord). If the PAC is to be articulated with maximum harmonic strength and closure—which is not always the case (numerous variants and complex contrapuntal treatments are possible)—$\hat{5}$ can be supported by a I^6 chord and $\hat{4}$ by a predominant harmony. This linear fifth progression or *Zug* (as Schenker termed it) is extremely important—and also complex in its implications and exceptions. In confronting any S-theme, one should try to isolate the crucial pitches of this $\hat{5} - \hat{4} - \hat{3} - \hat{2} - \hat{1}$ descent. In minor-mode sonatas the linear descent within S (usually in III) is often produced as $\hat{3} - \hat{2} - \hat{1}$, although $(\hat{5} - \hat{4}) - \hat{3} - \hat{2} - \hat{1}$ is also a possibility.

EXAMPLE 7.2   Mozart, Symphony No. 34 in C, K. 338, i, mm. 41–64

EXAMPLE 7.2   (*continued*)

Theme Types within Allegro Movements

As indicated earlier, when an entire cadential sequence from the I⁶ onward — very common within this repertory — is spread out emphatically over four or more bars, we have what Caplin called an *expanded cadential progression* (ECP).[15] This is a strong sign of closure, a stock formula upon which composers could ring many changes. From the perspective of Sonata Theory, composers will sometimes postpone a full articulation of the ECP until the C-zone. In other words, once again, in these cases the first PAC will not be the strongest PAC within the exposition — only the first satisfactory one. The EEC cadence may well be less strongly articulated than one or more of the cadences within C-space: indeed, this is not uncommonly the case.

Many S-themes will not begin directly with 5̂ in the upper voice: in these situations there must be an *initial ascent* up to that 5̂. These ascents can be vividly dramatized — sometimes turned into considerable struggles, as often in Beethoven. Similarly, the descent downward to 1̂ can be problematized (sometimes frustratingly), and one frequently sees the last-moment undermining of the implied PAC as a highly characteristic strategy of prolonging S-space. The implicit drama involved in producing the first satisfactory linear fifth-descent in the new key (a task of central importance to the sonata as a whole) is often the whole point of S — its implied difficulty in fulfilling its mission, the production of the EEC. One should be attentive to the adventures of S on its way to the EEC. Some of these issues are rejoined at the end of this chapter in the subsection, "Some Schenkerian Implications."

Although both *piano* and *forte* S-themes are options within the late-eighteenth- and early-nineteenth-century style, the former is the more common choice. S is usually introduced as a reduction of sonic forces, a drop to a *piano* dynamic after the preceding TR, which had maintained or gained intensity through the MC. So much seems obvious to those familiar with the style, and yet the observation can prove misleading, particularly when understood through the lenses of later nineteenth- and twentieth-century transformations of the sonata. It is by no means the case that eighteenth-century S-themes are predominantly lyrical and *cantabile*, although many of them are. The temptation to apply reductive, sentimentalized, or gender-ideological nineteenth-century descriptions of S-themes to late-eighteenth-century sonatas — *Gesangsthema*, "feminine" theme, and so on — leads to unwarranted conclusions within both analysis and hermeneutics. What we actually find in the music is a wide variety of thematic types. Additionally, individual S-spaces are anything but consistent in character. They often contain much inner surprise, wit, change, and contrast: sudden outbursts of *forte*, quick drops back to *piano*, unforeseen changes of mode, unprepared interruptions, concluding *forte* drives toward the cadence, and the like. No single adjective or thumbnail characterization does justice to such a wide range of volatile possibilities. Nervous energy and rapid changes of strategy are as much at home within S-space as is the gentler *dolce* theme.

15. See n. 7 and Caplin's discussion of the ECP within his later *Classical Form*, defined in the glossary, p. 255, as "an expansion of the cadential progression to the extent of supporting a complete phrase (of at least four measures) or group of phrases." On Caplin's use of the term "phrase" see ch. 5 above, n. 10.

We regard the common drop to *piano* for the beginning of S as a first-level default. Continuing to bluster forward by maintaining an energetic *forte* on the other side of the MC is a considerably less common, second-level default. The notable preference for the former, the *piano* S, suggests that the usual function for this moment is that of relaunch—a second start midway through the exposition. The *piano* convention may have been devised as a means of setting this relaunch into high relief. Within the *piano* convention certain types of thematic modules, at least at the opening of S, were more appropriate than others. Such a view accounts for the several characteristic types of S-incipits. While no eighteenth-century theorist gave the slightest thought to inventorying all of the possibilities, several of them noticed the *piano* convention (which was anything but an ironclad rule) and sought to give abbreviated descriptions of some of the effects within it that they remembered. It would be naïve to regard Koch's descriptions from 1793, for instance, as limiting the range of possibilities or as generally adequate as covering concepts for all eighteenth-century S-themes (most famously, *cantabler Satz* and *einem mehr singbaren, und gemeiniglich mit verminderter Stärke des Tons vorzutragenden Satze* [literally, "a more singable idea, one usually to be performed with a diminished strength of sound"])[16] Perhaps the most engaging eighteenth-century description was that of Galeazzi in 1796, who cited S as a new theme (*una nuova idea*) of sharply defined character, a "characteristic passage or intermediate passage" (*Il Passo Caratteristico, o Passo di mezzo*) introduced "for the sake of greater beauty" (*per maggior vaghezza*). He went on to insist that the relevant music be "gentle, expressive, and tender in almost all kinds of compositions" (*deve questo esser dolce, espressivo, e tenero quasi in ogni genere di composizione*).[17]

The evidence found in the music supports these generalizations in only a limited way. More important is the suppleness of change and surprise within S-space, its potential for agile changes of character *en route*. What seems clear, though, is this: in terms of its rhetorical character and motivic/thematic derivation the S-zone normally participates in a generic system of melodic S-conventions, many of which are in sharp contrast with each other. More helpful than trying to assert what S is like "in general" is being aware of some of the most recognizable options within this constellation of conventional options. These options are best understood as only heuristic categories, and because they sometimes overlap they are not to be regarded as airtight. They include but are not limited to the following.

The Bustling, *Staccato*, Energetically *Galant*, or Jauntily Self-Confident S

This is a familiar eighteenth-century S type marked not so much by a *cantabile* character as by light, strutting steps, much motivic repetition, perhaps a leaning toward a musical eccentricity, and a strong forward momentum. Sometimes high-alert, nervous quirks animate the effervescent figuration—frisky, clipped, or Lombard rhythms, *Schleifer*-like decorative slides, and the like. Occasionally such "stylized" themes begin with a *forte* impulse; more typically, they begin *piano* but may contain a few edgy outbursts of *forte*. In virtually all cases the expressive effect is that of the opening's high energy continuing into the exposition's part 2, a retained sizzle of excitation now only barely constrained under *piano* wraps and eager to erupt again into *forte*. This theme type is especially typical of briskly animated, midcentury *galant* works, but one also finds it as a frequently selected option in later decades.

A good example of this familiar S-theme type is provided in the first movement of Haydn's Symphony No. 83 in G Minor ("Hen"—this theme doubtless contributed to the symphony's nickname), mm. 46–59.[18] (Example 7.3a presents the initial statement of S only, omitting its slightly rescored repetition.) Another *locus clas-*

---

16. Koch, *Versuch*, vol. 3, pp. 306, 364, 385. See n. 3.

17. Churgin, "Francesco Galeazzi's Description (1796) of Sonata Form," p. 193. See n. 3.

18. The S-theme of the "Hen" follows a touchstone real-ization—not shown in example 7.3a—of the "blocked medial caesura" (see ch. 3), ending with a decline of energy into a III:PAC at the downbeat of m. 45.

EXAMPLE 7.3a   Haydn, Symphony No. 83 in G Minor ("Hen"), i, mm. 46–52

sicus of this theme type may be found in Mozart's Overture to *The Marriage of Figaro*, mm. 59–107. (Example 7.3b shows the first module of this lengthy, multimodular theme.) Other touchstone examples include the S-themes of the first movements of Mozart's Symphonies No. 22 in C, K. 162 (mm. 32–48), No. 25 in G Minor, K. 183 (mm. 59–74, also an example of a *piano* S-theme repeated *forte*), and No. 34 in C, K. 338 (see the earlier example 7.2, especially from m. 44 onward).

The Lyrically "Singing" or Gracefully *Cantabile* S

This is the S type long assumed to have been standard for sonatas in the decades around 1800—singing melody, *piano*, over accompanimental bass—and it is doubtless the type alluded to briefly in Koch (*cantabler Satz*) and Galeazzi (*dolce, espressivo, o tenero*). It is also the type that would flower into the characteristically expansive, maximally contrasting *Gesangsthema* of many nineteenth-century works. Because our seeming familiarity with this category is so ingrained—and often so lacking in nuances—it is helpful to remind ourselves not only of the many other types of S but also of

the variety found within this type itself. This "contrasting" S may be distinguished from the "bustling" type cited above by its broader lyrical lines, its tendency toward legato or slurred articulation, its flow and continuity of texture (instead of being broken up by frequent rests or abrupt changes of topic), and its general sense of contentment with its *piano* dynamic (as opposed to giving the impression of being eager to burst out of this containment). The difficulty is that *cantabile* S types shade by degrees back into the bustling types and vice versa. Many themes fall between the two heuristic categories.

The S-theme of the finale of Mozart's Symphony No. 40 in G Minor shows some of the complexities potentially in play. (Its initial statement, mm. 71–85, is shown in example 7.4.) At first glance it would seem to be an archetypal illustration of the *cantabile* type, and yet it simultaneously suggests some intersections with the preceding type as well as displaying a few curiosities in itself. Following a *forte* TR and III:HC MC (m. 70), S begins with a drop to *piano* at m. 71 and proceeds as an asymmetrical (8 + 7) period with varied and compressed consequent (mm. 79–85). On the one hand, the legato textures throughout are characteristic, giving the impression of an easy flow through S-space, and

EXAMPLE 7.3b Mozart, Overture to *The Marriage of Figaro*, K. 492, mm. 59–67

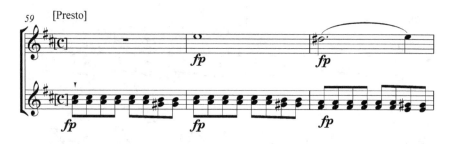

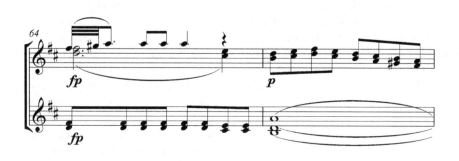

EXAMPLE 7.4   Mozart, Symphony No. 40 in G Minor, K. 550, iv, mm. 71–85

the *piano* dynamic is generally constant throughout the passage. On the other hand, although the theme probably has a predominantly *cantabile* basis, it also suggests features of the bustling type. The Allegro assai tempo and the residual retention of the *Trommelbass* impulses from TR in the descending bass (mm. 71–74, 79–80) continue a sense of nervous tension and forward press from the preceding music. The compression of the consequent (a sign of impatience?) may also contribute to this "mixed" effect. In addition, the extra push of the *mfp* up to $\hat{8}$ in m. 73 (the onset of an "if only" sigh?), fortified by two preparatory appoggiaturas on $\hat{5}$ (m. 72) before the leap and echoed with the fleet, iambic steps of mm. 75–76, also suggest an underlying dialogue with an all-propelling higher energy, more characteristic of the bustling type. The III:PAC in m. 85 would serve as the EEC were the entire period not subjected to a varied repeat (mm. 87–101), which defers the EEC to m. 101. A standard P-based C[1] follows in m. 102. (Compare, for example, the well-known S-theme of the first movement of *Eine kleine Nachtmusik*, K. 525, mm. 28–35, a clearer parallel period, 4 + 4, with EEC at m. 35. While

clearly content with its *piano* dynamic, the cat-like tread of its predominant light staccatos suggests less a lyrical *dolce* theme than a tender and elegant *passo caratteristico*.)

The P-Based S

In this type the incipit (at least) of the S theme is either identical to or an easily recognizable variant of the P theme. At least in their openings P and S are often sonorously congruent: if the one had been sounded *piano*, so is the other—although exceptions do occur. The main thing is that the onset of S is a recapturing or re-sounding of the initial idea. The P-based S gives an altered emphasis to the idea of a two-part exposition. Both parts set out from the same basic idea, even though what follows them will be different. Consequently, this type of sonata suggests that the "narrative subject" (the central musical character or idea of the "drama," stated by P) is still in evidence and is now ready to undertake the second phase of the exposition, S and the production of the EEC. Should the broader S / C space continue, however spottily, to refer here and there to ordered material in P-TR, as if touching upon certain stations of fleeting reference, one might suggest that the expositional rotation as a whole is being conceived as two subrotations, or two varied cycles through similar materials. In such cases the second subrotation (starting with S) would be presented as a varied recasting of the first.

Unlike his contemporaries Haydn appears to have adopted the P-based S as a first-level default (part of his individualized customization of sonata practice), although contrasting S-themes are also found in his works.[19] The P-based S produces what has sometimes been called the "monothematic" exposition (or sonata), although in most cases this is a misnomer: following the EEC, Haydn normally presents an altogether new theme for the C-zone. As always in Haydn there are exceptions, and from time to time one finds the same motive or incipit launching P, S, *and* C, as in the first movement of the String Quartet in C, op. 74 no. 1. Such a dogged retention of opening material may be referred to as the "emphatically monothematic" exposition. Occasionally one finds the P-based S in Mozart (finale of the Symphony No. 39 in E-flat, K. 543—which "emphatically" extends the principle to the C theme; first movements of the Piano Sonata in B-flat, K. 570 and the String Quintet in D, K. 593), although Mozart selected this option considerably less frequently than he did that of the contrasting S. See also the additional considerations below, "P- and TR-material in S-zones."

S as "Contrasting Derivation" from P

This type of theme is related to all of the previously mentioned types: contrasting and P-based. Sometimes the materials for the "contrasting" S can be understood as being motivically related to P. This is what the musicologist Arnold Schmitz early in the twentieth century called the principle of "contrasting derivation" for S. Schmitz viewed this as a central feature of Beethoven's

music in general: one different-sounding theme is motivically derivable from what has preceded it. In the 1970s and 1980s Carl Dahlhaus revived the concept and argued that it was one of the keys to understanding Beethoven.[20] When this occurs, it is clear that P's potential for "thought" has grown into the contrasting S: though contrasting, S is a response to P or an outgrowth of ongoing motivic elaboration. It is by no means limited to the music of Beethoven, of course. A classic instance may be found in the similar intervallic content and general contour of the opening of S (mm. 23–24) in the first movement of Mozart's Piano Sonata in B-flat, K. 333, with that of the P-theme (mm. 1–2). Such subtle resemblances continue as S proceeds, inviting an interpretation of the whole exposition as subrotational.

The *Forte* S

This is a lower-level default than the *piano* S. As such, it is usually to be interpreted as an overriding of expectation, the surprising, threatening, or desperate refusal to drop back to *piano* to launch part 2. By late in the eighteenth century the *forte* S seems to have been an even less frequently selected option, although it certainly remained as a possibility, especially when reacting to a weakened or deformationally "flawed" TR and/or MC. In earlier instances the *forte* S seems to be an overflow of the principle grounding the energetic, bustling S into the *forte* dynamic (the brimming-over of sheer exhilaration beyond the MC, continuing with no dynamic letup). In other pieces it suggests the relentless persistence of a *Sturm und Drang* texture refusing to give way to the more generic *piano* S. It was particularly useful in short-breathed, modest-scale works (such as some of the briskly vigorous early symphonies of Mozart).

In still other cases the *forte* S could take on a broader, even rougher character, with the implication of having sternly overridden (or

---

19. Cf. Somfai on "the 'varied primary theme' as secondary subject'" in *The Keyboard Sonatas of Joseph Haydn*, pp. 270–74.

20. Schmitz, *Beethoven's 'Zwei Prinzipe'* (Berlin and Bonn, 1927). Cf. Dahlhaus, *Nineteenth-Century Music*, trans. J. Bradford Robinson (Berkeley: University of California Press, 1989), p. 84; and *Ludwig van Beethoven: Approaches to His Music*, trans. Mary Whittall (Oxford: Clarendon Press, 1991), pp. 38, 51–52, 96, and elsewhere.

erased) the hope for a more normative, gentle S. These passages usually suggest the onset of an S-deformation. Such is the situation in the D-major Andante of Mozart's Quartet in A, K. 169. Following a disturbingly unusual *piano* and minor-mode TR (mm. 1–15 are built as a sentence with dissolving continuation), a minor-mode i:HC MC (m. 15), and an ominous bar of silence (m. 16), S bursts out in an anxiety-wracked *forte* in the "wrong" key, F major (reacting to the preceding, local D minor), m. 17. The initial distress-module is sequenced on G minor (m. 21) and A minor (m. 25) before leading to a minor-mode v:PAC (!) in m. 34, which should probably be understood as an EEC accomplished under high strain. Subsequent C-modules restore the major dominant.

As this example suggests, S-themes that begin *forte* often compensate for MCs that are unusually weak. This can occur when TR and the MC are submitted to a dynamic deformation—when they are articulated quietly (*piano*) or when a *diminuendo* has been applied to the drive to the preceding MC. In general, if S begins with a strong dynamic—particularly *forte*—one should look for signs of decay, enervation, or faltering in the preceding TR and MC (loss of nerve, inability to sustain a *forte*, reduction of dynamics, alteration of mode, and so on.) In these cases, as suggested also in chapter 3, the *forte* S takes on a compensatory role in response to generic problems composed earlier into the piece. In the first movement of Mozart's Piano Sonata in F, K. 280 (example 7.5), the preceding MC in m. 26 has been submitted to a *piano* dynamic. S, m. 27, is then blurted out with a measure of *forte* only to be hushed back to three bars of *piano* normativity, mm. 28–30, whereupon the dynamic process is repeated—blurt and hush. (Compare this with the witty elaborations of the same idea in the recapitulation.) S proceeds as a compound sentence, with the contrasting continuation beginning in m. 35 and eventually producing the EEC at m. 43. Fourteen bars of closing material round out the exposition.

S as Virtuosic Figuration

In some early keyboard sonatas S is occasionally elaborated with rapid, idiomatic figuration (broken chords, sixteenth- or thirty-second-note figures, lightning-fast scalar or other passagework) rather than any sort of self-evidently lyrical theme. In his study of Haydn's keyboard sonatas Somfai mentioned these as "contrasting themes built on arpeggios."[21] Whatever the figuration-type, the result is that S takes on the character of a florid display of idiosyncratic technique, sometimes additionally at an indicated or implied *forte* dynamic. A good example occurs in the first movement of the Sonata in F, Hob. XVI:23. In response to a V:HC MC in m. 20 S takes off in C major, m. 21, with a volley of thirty-second-note figuration, much of it scalar. A related example may be found in the first movement of the Sonata in E-flat, Hob. XVI:25, with V:HC MC at m. 14 and an energetically figurational, *forte* S launched in B-flat at m. 15.

The "Learned-Style" or Fugal/Imitative S

This is an infrequently selected S type reserved for special effects. Here the composer begins S-space by plunging into the added energy and earnest resolve of fugal entries, which then usually turn out to be short-lived as S proceeds toward its cadence. Quite unlike that of the *cantabile* S, the impression is that of following the MC with a continuation of fidgety vibrancy, compositional self-display, or sparkling, expressive zest. At times these qualities suggest the character of the energetic S. (They may even be combined with it—or with the *forte* S.) Added to it, however, is the self-conscious, "learned-style" texture, in part a memory of a now-eclipsed practice (in some contexts also an age-old sign of compositional practice itself), revived under the aegis of the lighter and fleeter *galant* style. There are a few illustrations of it in Mozart, some of them extremely celebrated. They include: the second movement (Allegro) of the String Quar-

---

21. Somfai, *The Keyboard Sonatas of Joseph Haydn*, pp. 267–69.

EXAMPLE 7.5   Mozart, Piano Sonata in F, K. 280, i, mm. 22–43

tet in G, K. 80 (mm. 16ff, here merged with the idea of the *forte* S); the finale of the String Quartet in G, K. 387 (upbeat to mm. 52ff, again urgent, *forte*); and the finale of the String Quintet in D, K. 593 (mm. 54, beat 2ff, a five-voice set of fugal entrances proceeding from top to bottom, perhaps more playful than earnest, here also with a drop to *piano*). Clear allusions to the practice are also found in the finale of Mozart's Symphony No. 31 in D ("Paris"), K. 297 (mm. 45ff), and in the first movement of the Clarinet Concerto in A, K. 622 (mm. 25ff, an imitative stretto within Ritornello 1).

The Multimodular S (MMS): Lengthy S-Themes (or S-Modular Groups)

It often happens that S does not proceed to an efficient PAC (EEC) at all, blossoming instead into a bouquet of differing S-ideas (each an S-module), none of which, except the last (the cadential module), articulates a PAC. Sometimes the cadential completion of S is consistently undermined for a long span of time. The composer can stage S as frustrated in its pursuit of a decisive EEC, obliging it to pass through differing thematic and expressive modules, as if seeking the right one to produce the EEC. This produces a chain-like, multimodular S (MMS) that can change topics, styles, or theme types from link to link. If we wish to distinguish among the S-modules, all of which are normally sounded before the first satisfactory PAC in the new key (for that is embedded in the definition of S), we may employ the decimal designators explained in chapter 5: $S^{1.1}$, $S^{1.2}$, $S^{1.3}$, and so on. (An S^2 theme would be rare, since the designation implies a new or differing S-module that persists, contrary to the definition of S, beyond that first PAC. This could happen only in cases of EEC deferral, a topic considered in chapter 8. A cogent argument needs to be constructed in defense of each case.)

It may also be that the first module of S arrives purposely weakened or flawed in the sense that it cannot (or chooses not to) produce the PAC/EEC. Obviously, such a situation does not betray a compositional defect or a problem that the composer is experiencing personally. Rather, such unsettling modules play intended roles in the musical narrative that the composer is unfolding. S may give the impression, for example, of arriving too early in the exposition—perhaps entering hastily after a too-early MC or a I:HC MC that is unsatisfactory in one way or another. In such a situation the first S-module needs to be rescued by later S-material.

The MMS strategy is readily found in Haydn, Mozart, and Beethoven, and the expressive aims in play can differ from composer to composer and from piece to piece. In Beethoven, where strenuous striving within the S-zone is common, the strategy can suggest that accomplishing the requirement of the EEC can be a monumental or nearly impossible task. In one common Beethoven scenario S begins more or less unproblematically but then runs into difficulties, represented by an ominous, murky, or threatening central module (often with a diminished-seventh coloration), and finally breaks through to a decisive cadential module that "heroically" claims the EEC. The first movement of the Fifth Symphony is paradigmatic. Following the emphatic hornsignal articulation of the MC in mm. 59–62 (which deformationally combines features of MC and caesura-fill), a *dolce* S sets forth in m. 63, passes through a middle section of considerable uneasiness (mm. 83–c. 93), from out of which it pulls itself, in a grand crescendo of growing will, into a decisive module of heroic confidence (mm. 94–101). The moment of the EEC (m. 110) is celebrated with a P-based C (mm. 111–22), here transforming the original, fatalistic motive into a victory shout of temporary overcoming.

When S themes unfold in three modules, as with the S-zone in the first movement of Beethoven's Fifth Symphony, we sometimes speak of a trimodular S (TMS). The MMS- or TMS-effect can be produced in varying gradations of strength, clarity, and expansiveness. Sometimes the separate modules are distinct, easily distinguishable; sometimes the first module dissolves or decays almost imperceptibly into the second; and so on. In all cases they produce the adventures through which the S-zone tracks on its way to the attainment of the EEC. (One should not confuse the TMS with the trimodular-block effect, TMB, which is signaled by the presence of apparent double medial caesuras. A special S-complication, the TMB is dealt with in chapter 8.)

P- or TR-Material in the Interior of S-Zones

The most common location in which one finds P-material in S-zones is at their openings. This is the normative P-based S, and as already mentioned it is especially characteristic of Haydn. Consider, however, those sonatas that do not feature a P-based S. At least as a first-level default, when S (more precisely, $S^{1.1}$) has declared itself to be something other than P-based, it simultaneously agrees that obvious P-material is not likely to play a major structural role in S. (One exception: it may happen that a common phrase, counterpoint, or accompanimental figure binds together both the P and S themes, as in the famous bass figure, mm. 65–66ff., in the first movement of Beethoven's Fifth Symphony.) Another way of considering this: If S begins with a new theme, this generally signals that the return of the P-idea is being reserved as a possibility for the onset of C, although that possibility need not be acted upon.

Still, things are not always so clear. From time to time one encounters a contrasting (not P-based) S-zone whose apparently normative drive toward an EEC is thwarted, blocked, evaded, or otherwise attenuated, only to lead to an obviously P-based module—a surprising change of course that extends the S-zone beyond its expected end-point. This intervening P-based module, then, ultimately brings S into the EEC. The effect of this P-based $S^{1.2}$ (or $S^{1.3}$, $S^{1.4}$) varies from work to work, but it typically suggests a fresh burst of compositional energy and the onset of an extension or new phase of S. In Haydn it can signify a change of plans, seeming to decide late into the game to fold in a reference to his own first-level-default S-choice, the P-based-S (as if having it both

ways, the contrasting S followed by the non-contrasting S).

This happens in the first movement of Haydn's String Quartet in G, op. 33 no. 5. The V:HC MC occurs in m. 48 (followed by a fermata!), and $S^{1.1}$ begins, *dolce*, in D major, in m. 49. The sentence structure appears headed for an unambiguous PAC (EEC) in m. 65, but at the crucial "tonic-chord" moment the upper voice replaces the expected scale-degree $\hat{1}$ with $\hat{3}$. (Although the point may be arguable, we shall assume here that this does not represent an implied PAC with elided C-theme beginning on $\hat{3}$: Haydn's shift from the leading-tone, $\hat{7}$, to $\hat{3}$ seems staged as a surprise, *sforzando*, with the upper voice veering away from the PAC implication.) At the downbeat of m. 65 the motive that had grounded the P-theme proper bursts in, apparently claiming its due. This P-based $S^{1.2}$ (or $S^{1.3}$, depending on how one had labeled the preceding sentence) launches an extension that eventually produces the EEC at m. 89.[22]

Equally significant are those passages in which S proceeds in such a way as to suggest that it is either delaying the EEC or having difficulty in bringing it about. Into this situation P-material—especially its incipit—can intervene to take control of the drive to the PAC. This can be interpreted in a number of ways. S may simply "drift" back into a recollection of P, at which point the discourse gains in point and focus, vectoring more clearly toward the EEC. In other cases P breaks in as a genuine intervention. In still other cases it may appear that P-material is called upon at the end of S to effect the EEC in a recovery operation. When any of this happens, one might also get the impression that the P-based material seemingly "reserved" as a potential for C^1 is summoned to appear prematurely (in the space originally set aside for S-material proper) to direct the push to the EEC.

A *locus classicus* of this procedure occurs in the first movement of Mozart's Quartet in A,

---

22. That all of this is to be understood within S-space is bolstered by additional musical evidence. The first violin in mm. 78–82 recaptures the melodic descent of mm. 61–64, with some chromatic alterations, and although it now does resolve $\hat{7}-\hat{1}$, this time it is the *bass* that overrides the expected PAC (m. 83) by leap-

ing to the third of the chord instead of the root. (Notice also the back-reference to the abandoned $S^{1.1}$ in the first violin, mm. 83–84.) A final, freer recapturing of the melodic descent in mm. 86–89 finally does provide scale degree $\hat{1}$ in both outer voices, thus effecting the EEC at m. 89.

K. 464. S begins with a new theme, a brief period at m. 37. A varied repetition ensues at m. 45, but that restatement, expanded and spun out at length, postpones the EEC remarkably and finally accomplishes it (m. 83) with a similarly expanded variant of P (mm. 69–83). Further examples may be found in the first movements of Mozart's Quartet in B-flat, K. 589 (m. 61, a blurted intervention) and Beethoven's Piano Sonata in C Minor, op. 10 no. 1 (m. 86). The initial movement of Beethoven's Piano Sonata in D, op. 10 no. 3 (at m. 67, following an unexpected lapse in S in m. 66) provides a generally similar situation. One of the most dramatic illustrations occurs in the S-zone of the first movement of Beethoven's Symphony No. 2 in D, op. 36, in which S seems literally to break down before being rescued by P-based, "premature" C-material (mm. 103ff, with the EEC finally secured at m. 112,[23] followed by the P-based C[1], now in its "proper" place). An ominous, psychologically negative example may be found in the opening movement of Schubert's Piano Sonata in A Minor, D. 845. After the complete breakdown of the "new," C-major S-theme, intrusive, P-based material slithers into the emptiness in C minor (m. 64, *pianissimo*) and accomplishes the EEC on its own sinister terms at m. 77. This is elided directly with a C-major closing passage of "C as S-aftermath," mm. 77–90, interlaced with disturbing interruptions from the dominating P-head-motive.

It may also happen that a motive from a later part of P (not its opening) makes a passing appearance in the middle of S, apparently as a kind of ongoing reference—or that various motives from P, including related accompanimental ideas, keep rearing their heads within sectors of S, as, subtly, in the first movement of Mozart's String Quintet in G Minor, K. 516. Sometimes the "interior" P-figure changes the expressive track of S-space and moves on its own toward the EEC, as in the first movement of Mozart's Quartet in D, K. 575 (mm. 49–50, a fill-figure taken from P, mm. 7–8).

Somewhat related to the unexpected appearance of P toward the middle or end of S is the appearance of TR-material at that point—TR-based motives or themes that spur the music onward to the EEC. Here the situation can be similar to that discussed above: a lengthy S may be presented as problematic or dilatory in its motion toward the EEC, and a part of TR is called upon to complete that trajectory. An example may be found in the first movement of Beethoven, Piano Sonata in C, op. 2 no. 3 (TR intervention, m. 61—taken from mm. 13ff—with EEC at m. 77).

Minor-Mode Modules within S

Sometimes the first S-module within a major-mode work makes its appearance in the *minor* dominant (v) with the implication of tragedy, malevolence, a sudden expressive reversal, or an unexpected complication within the musical plot. This happens in Mozart's D-major Overture to *Idomeneo* (S begins in A minor, upbeat to m. 46, in the aftermath of a paradigmatic blocked MC), in the finale of Mozart's Piano Sonata in F, K. 332 (m. 50; S begins in C minor), and in the first movements of Beethoven's Piano Sonata in C, op. 2 no. 3 (m. 27; S begins in G minor) and Quartet in A, op. 18 no. 5 (m. 25: S begins, somewhat "demonically," in E minor). In virtually all cases the minor-mode effect is corrected later in the exposition, often within S-space itself, as in the F-major Adagio movement of Haydn's Symphony No. 102 in B-flat, with S in C minor, m. 9, brightening to C major only in m. 13 in preparation for the C-major EEC at m. 14. (The effect is replicated, mm. 25–30, in the non-normative, varied repeat of the exposition.)

This procedure may have been rather common in the middle of the eighteenth century. In *Sonata Forms* Charles Rosen singled it out as the first of "three [sonata-form] stereotypes of the 1750s and 1760 that were [later] to disappear."[24] The claim on behalf of its disappearance is exag-

---

23. The cadence at m. 112 may appear to be an imperfect authentic cadence, with the third appearing above in the flute. More likely, the third is a cover tone, and the essential structural cadence, outlined in the strings

and most of the winds, is a PAC. Nonetheless, the presence of the third in the flute does weaken, though not nullify, the EEC-effect.

24. Rosen, *Sonata Forms* (Rev. ed.), pp. 153–54.

gerated, but it is certain that the effect was well known among the contemporaries of young Haydn and young Mozart: it existed as a normative expressive option within their conceptions of S themes. Whether or not its frequency diminished toward the end of the century, it was used by Haydn, Mozart, and Beethoven to produce telling effects.

Related to this are major-mode S themes that turn minor ("lights out") with their repetition, on the way, that is, to the EEC. This is a technique sometimes adopted by Mozart, as in the first movement of the Symphony No. 38 in D, K. 504, "Prague" (S-collapse to A minor, m. 105; restoration of A major, m. 112). Also related are minor-mode intrusions midway into normally major-mode S-space (Beethoven, Quartet in B-flat, op. 18 no. 6, first movement, S at m. 45, decaying into minor by m. 49, regaining the major at m. 62) and the technique of turning an S-theme minor with the onset not of an S-repetition but of a new thematic module within an MMS. For the larger implications of all such minor-mode matters, see chapter 14.

S^0 and $S^{1.0}$ Themes

Each of the zones of an exposition—especially P, S, and C—may begin with a preparatory module that sets up or otherwise precedes what strikes one as the "real" initial theme of the zone. For such initiatory moments we have devised the zero superscript (either 0 or 1.0, the former for stronger effects, modules that seem more clearly separable from what follows) whose general principle was discussed in chapter 5.[25] The lightest type of $S^{1.0}$-effect occurs when an accompanimental figure, vamp, or rhythmic stream is laid down in advance of the S-theme proper. Illustrations may be found the first movements of Mozart's Piano Sonatas in C, K. 309, mm. 33–34 (also in dialogue with the norm of caesura-fill of the $\hat{5}-\hat{1}$ type, even though it follows an MC-gap; S proper ensues in m. 35) and again in C, K. 545, m. 13 (S proper at m. 14); and in

the first movement of his Symphony No. 31 in D, K. 297, "Paris," m. 52 (S proper at m. 53).

Other types of S^0- or $S^{1.0}$-options are more complicated. Following an MC, it sometimes happens that a thematic S-module sets out over a prolonged dominant in the new key. This dominant typically lasts for several measures, then shifts to the tonic for the sounding of a different idea (or thematic module) that seems to be more securely grounded within S space. Unless it is sustained for an unusually long time, we normally designate such an S-holding-pattern over the dominant as $S^{1.0}$. Quite often the brief holding-pattern appears twice, thus taking on the role of a sentence presentation. It is almost always succeeded by a new S-module beginning over the tonic—very commonly the continuation of an ongoing sentence. In general, the $S^{1.0}$ strategy sets up the more decisive arrival of the subsequent new idea: it is a way of staging its entrance. Even though they are preparatory ideas, S^0 and $S^{1.0}$ modules usually participate in the standard range of S-types. They normally feature a drop to *piano* and display "thematic" S-features (perhaps energetic, perhaps lyrical). As themes they do launch S-space and yet seem also to prepare the way for the arrival of something different that is more stable. Because the dominant prolongation usually lasts for several bars, S^0- and $S^{1.0}$-ideas may be distinguished from S themes that happen to begin on a short-lived V chord within the new key.

The immediate effect of an S^0 or $S^{1.0}$ module depends also on the type of medial caesura that precedes it. Such a module can appear in two different contexts, each of which carries different connotations. It is to these that we now turn.

S^0 or $S^{1.0}$ Following a V:HC Medial Caesura (or III:HC in Minor-Mode Sonatas)

Here the dominant underpinning the S^0 or $S^{1.0}$ theme retains the MC's active dominant, which continues to ring through the succeeding music as momentarily fixed or immobile.

---

25. Here we might emphasize once again that the labels S^0 and $S^{1.0}$ are for the most part interchangeable. The only distinction between them lies in one's assessment of how "independent" the relevant thematic module might be. The 1.0 label suggests a closer interconnectedness with the material that follows.

Consequently this type of zero-module functions locally as a prolongation of the caesura-dominant itself, that is, much like caesura-fill of the $\hat{5}-\hat{1}$ type. The distinction between the two — expanded caesura-fill and a genuine S^0 or $S^{1.0}$ module — can be difficult to make, and perhaps in some cases we should not make it at all. It may be that this kind of zero-theme is a thematically emphatic subset of that type of caesura-fill. The impression given by this context is that the caesura-gap has been held open: the gears have been pulled apart, awaiting re-engagement with $S^{1.1}$ proper.

A *locus classicus* of a more prolonged, S^0 theme occurs in the first movement of Beethoven's *Eroica* Symphony (example 7.6). The *forte*-dynamic V:HC MC is reached with an almost disturbing abruptness at m. 45. A new, "questing" theme, *piano*, is sounded over the dominant of B-flat major with the upbeat to m. 46. This dominant in the bass is prolonged for several measures — with thematic material above — until the moment of its decisive tonic resolution at m. 57, which then launches a new theme, S proper: the gears re-engage. Mm. 46–57 constitute S^0. Notice that, especially toward the end (mm. 55–57), they behave much like a thematic caesura-fill of the $\hat{5}-\hat{1}$ type. M. 57 begins $S^{1.1}$, now grounded on the tonic: this is one of the few themes of the symphony that Beethoven kept more or less invariant in his multiple continuity drafts, and it is also a theme alluded to and probably confirmed as S in the coda, m. 673.[26] (Compare this also with the first movement of Beethoven's Ninth Symphony, with an S^0 or $S^{1.0}$ theme — a briefer idea — that emerges in m. 74 after a stifled, somewhat deformational MC-attempt. $S^{1.1}$ follows in m. 80 over the new tonic, B-flat.)

In minor-mode sonatas the equivalent would be an S^0 or $S^{1.0}$ theme that begins (over the dominant) following a III:HC MC. This would include such extraordinary examples as that found in the first movement of Beethoven's Piano Sonata in C Minor, op. 13. (See also the discussion in the previous chapter, along with example 6.2.) Here the presumed "S" theme occurs at considerable length, tonicizing E-flat minor (!), over a prolonged dominant (albeit one that is shifted about in the middle of the theme), mm. 51–88. After several measures this is released to E-flat major (m. 89), and a new theme is produced over the tonic at the point of an evaded PAC (the upper voice momentarily drops out). The lengthy E-flat-minor theme (over V) is an unusually extended S^0 — perhaps suggesting that, absent the immediate presence of the generically expected E-flat major, the initial S-idea is wary of declaring itself as a fully confident or successful theme. The release into E-flat major, then (m. 89), launches what must be regarded as S^1, even though its opportunity for thematic singularity has long since been ceded to S^0. Such a claim may be easy to misinterpret. We are not suggesting that the secondary theme begins with the E-flat major idea in m. 89: this is indefensible. We do acknowledge that the S-theme begins on E-flat minor in measure 51 but observe that in its manner of deployment this theme is more closely related to the concept of S^0. S^0 themes belong emphatically to S-space.[27]

It may occasionally happen that a prolonged-dominant opening to S-space — an S^0 or $S^{1.0}$ identifier — does not so much shift decisively to a clear, differing S^1 module beginning on the new tonic as merge fluidly into more forward-directed music, as if the zero principle comes

26. On the drafts, see Lewis Lockwood, "*Eroica* Perspectives: Strategy and Design in the First Movement," *Beethoven: Studies in the Creative Process* (Cambridge, Mass.: Harvard University Press, 1992), pp. 118–33. "One feature [of the continuity drafts] is particularly striking. The passage that I am calling 'Unit C' in the exposition . . . is [apart from the very opening] . . . the only one that is present in essentially fixed form in all these drafts. . . . It maintains basically the same contour that it is to have in the final version, undergoing some refinement in rhythmic continuation and in its registral position, but remaining fundamentally a fixed element

in the web of transformations. Around it are shaped thematic units that have much further to go before they reach their final linear and harmonic form" (p. 131). It is also instructive to compare the *Eroica* S^0 example with the nearly parallel situation — also in E-flat major — that occurs in the Quartet from Mozart's *Idomeneo*, "Andrò ramingo e solo."

27. The S-theme of op. 13 no. 1/i is also revisited in ch. 14, in the context of a larger discussion about tonal and modal choices within S-zones in minor-mode sonata forms.

EXAMPLE 7.6 Beethoven, Symphony No. 3 in E-flat, op. 55 ("Eroica"), i, mm. 43–60

to lose its grip *en route*. Such a smoother shift into more normative S-activity—$S^{1.0}$ merging into $S^{1.1}$—may be observed in the initial movement of Beethoven's Piano Sonata in F Minor, op. 2 no. 1. A-flat-major S-space sets forth in m. 21 over what seems to be an MC-dominant "frozen" or locked into place. The dominant "thaws" into mobile chordal activity in mm. 25–26, eventually driving to the EEC at m. 41.

S^0 or $S^{1.0}$ Following a I:HC Medial Caesura in Major-Mode Sonatas

Here the contextual situation is different. In this case the V underpinning the S^0 or $S^{1.0}$ (in the new key) and the V articulated at the end of the MC are different pitches. $\hat{5}$ of the original key (say, the pitch G in a C-major sonata, the root of the I:HC MC) leaps suddenly to $\hat{5}$ of the new key (in this case the pitch D in the newly produced G major) as a pedal point underpinning S or, less often, as a dominant chord in its own right. As a result there can be no sense of prolonging the MC dominant and with it the caesura-gap. Instead, one gets the impression of a lurch to the V of the new key—as if one were peremptorily correcting an unsatisfactory MC (that is, as if one would have preferred the V:HC, first-level-default option). The $S^{1.0}$ theme, often *piano*, will then be held over the dominant for a few measures—perhaps as the apparent presentation of a sentence—before the gears re-engage and a new theme, $S^{1.1}$, takes off, beginning its drive toward the EEC. As is the case with all types of S^0 and $S^{1.0}$, the secondary-theme zone proper begins with the zero-module, not with $S^{1.1}$. A perfect example occurs in the first movement of Mozart's Symphony No. 33 in B-flat, K. 319. The I:HC MC is sounded in m. 54. Mm. 55–62 comprise eight lazily drifting bars over V of F, all functioning as a broad anacrusis to the new theme at m. 63 (over an F tonic). M. 55 is best heard as S^0; m. 63 as $S^{1.1}$. Another clear example, probably more likely to be labeled $S^{1.0}$: the first movement of Mozart, Symphony "No. 5" in B-flat, K. 22, m. 19.

Other S^0 and $S^{1.0}$ Types

Related varieties of S^0 theme (in major-mode sonatas after a V:HC MC) are encountered when S begins as a set of either off-tonic sequences or looping, rotary chord successions that finally settle onto the tonic—and a new thematic module—several measures later. The former occurs in Mozart's (E-flat-major) Overture to *The Magic Flute*. After a structural-dominant lock within TR (m. 53, including a mixture with B-flat minor, a common strategy of tension at this point of a TR), one encounters a V:HC MC in m. 57, bridged with caesura-fill. In m. 58 the fill sprouts into a genuine theme, at a *piano* dynamic, that suggests that S-space (and the normative release into B-flat *major*) must have been entered. But the opening chord of this theme is V_5^6/ii of B-flat major, and this initiates a sequence built largely on the descending circle of fifths that floats downward and eventually serves as the broad anacrusis to a new theme on the B-flat tonic at m. 64. "On hold" from m. 58 through m. 63 (S^0—similar to an extension of caesura-fill), the forward course of the exposition relaunches at m. 64: the gears re-engage (S^1).

A complementary S^0 type is provided in Mendelssohn's E-major Overture to *A Midsummer Night's Dream*, with its impression of spinning wheels at the opening of S-space. Here S^0 begins clearly enough on the B-major tonic, but the initial effect is rotary, non-progressive. Two four-bar cycles of an S^0 module (mm. 130–4, 134–8) lead to a finally forward-directed S^1 at m. 139. Lurking in the background here might also be the normative gestures of standard sentence structure.

Additional Issues within S-Space

Gendered S-Themes? (Masculine/Feminine)

It was only around 1845 with A. B. Marx's *Die Lehre von der musikalischen Komposition*—in a fleeting metaphor whose imagery apparently spread like wildfire in the mid- and later nineteenth century—that the P- and S-themes were characterized as masculine and feminine. In this instance Marx, in a characteristically mid-nineteenth-century move, was underscoring the tendency for S to serve as a contrast to P. S was "the [idea] created afterward [*Nachgeschaffne*], serving as a contrast, dependent on and determined by the former—consequently, and according to its nature necessarily, the milder [idea], one more supple [*schmiegsam*] than emphatically shaped, as if it were [*gleichsam*] the feminine to that preceding masculine."[28] Marx did not intend the metaphor so concretely as to pursue it in his own analyses. On the contrary, at times he came to completely different, *ad hoc* conclusions. In 1859 and subsequent years, for instance, he interpreted all of Beethoven's Overture, *Leonore 1*, as a representation of "Leonora's gentle image" (*Leonorens mildes Bild . . . das Alles geht so menschlich, so deutsch* [!] *und weiblich her*), in which P strides forth "with an easy feminine step" [*leichten weiblichen Schritts*], while in the mightier, Florestan-dominated *Leonore 2* and *3* he conversely believed that Leonora *qua* character was nowhere to be found. There he understood S as "Florestan's lament [from the dungeon]" (*tritt wiederum die Klage Florestans*), even while problematizing the theme as estranged from the spirit of what precedes it, nonorganic, a citation from the aria-melody introduction and not a proper [*eigentlicher*] *Seitensatz*.[29]

Today one should be cautious in bringing the masculine-feminine stereotype uncritically to works before 1825 or so.[30] At best the concept is deeply problematic when applied to the early nineteenth century and even more so when transferred back to the eighteenth. Nobody could doubt that initial S-themes of the contrasting type could bring a new topic into view—a change of emotion, sometimes from a vigorous or march-like P to a more sentimental, perhaps even amorous S. Such occurrences may or may not have some gendered implications, but the evidence uncovered along these lines so far is scanty or virtually nonexistent. Deciding this matter seems not to have been a significant preoccupation of eighteenth-century commentators on the music.

It seems likely that the "feminine-S-theme" claim is based on an absorption of a few late-nineteenth or early-twentieth-century assertions combined with an underconsidered view of how S-zones actually work within eighteenth-century sonatas. The *dolce* S is by no means the only S type available: many other styles—energetically bustling, *forte*, fugal—resist or even contradict the sentimentalized nineteenth-century stereotype. Moreover, Haydn's S-themes often begin by restating certain features of P, with real thematic contrast reserved for the C-theme. Recall also that within Sonata Theory, S is construed as the active agent driving toward and securing the EEC—often heroically, as in Beethoven—which role does not square with the common "passive-partner," "domestic," or "inspirational" stereotype that Marx and later commentators on the form seem to have had in mind.

Nor are these the only sticking points in the gender-argument, should it be pushed back into the decades around 1800. Late-eighteenth-century S-zones are anything but consistent in character or topic. It is not uncommon for S to house three or more contrasting modules ($S^{1.1}$, $S^{1.2}$, $S^{1.3}$, and so on), the last of which is decisively cadential. Are all of these to be collapsed under the simple adjective "feminine"? And what about the many varieties of C? Is it all of part 2 that is supposedly gendered as feminine—on the grounds, perhaps, of some proposed ideology of subordination regarding its key?—or is it only S (or part of S—only its opening?) and not the normally emphatic, sometimes vehement C (which, as it happens, often recaptures the P-idea)?

---

28. Marx, *Die Lehre von der musikalischen Komposition*, 2nd ed., vol. 3 (Leipzig, 1845), p. 221. Cf. the translation in Marx, *Musical Form in the Age of Beethoven: Selected Writings on Theory and Material*, ed. and trans. Scott Burnham (Cambridge: Cambridge University Press, 1997), p. 133.

29. Marx, *Ludwig van Beethoven, Leben und Schaffen*, 1st ed. (Berlin: Otto Janke, 1859), I, 335, 338 (*das Alles*), 337 (*leichten weiblichen Schritts*); 3rd ed. (Berlin: Janke, 1875), I, 352 (*die Klage Florestans*), 353–54 ("organic" issues with this S).

30. The Marx issue has been treated in the scholarly literature of the 1990s. See James Hepokoski, "Masculine/Feminine," *The Musical Times* 135 (August 1994), 494–99, and Scott Burnham, "A.B. Marx and the Gendering of Sonata Form," in *Music Theory in the Age of Romanticism*, ed. Ian Bent (Cambridge: Cambridge University Press, 1996), pp. 163–86.

Yet in the nineteenth century, undeniably feminine secondary themes did exist—juxtaposed with masculine first themes. The first explicitly feminine S-theme within an influential, widely admired composition—a gendering that is certain because of the piece's program—appears to be the "Agathe" theme from Weber's Overture to *Der Freischütz* (1821), although claims have been made since the mid-nineteenth century that the S-theme of Beethoven's *Coriolan* Overture represents feminine beseeching (the contemporary evidence for this is anything but clear), and (perhaps) that an image of Clärchen is implicit in part of the S-theme of the *Egmont* Overture.[31] Even if one were to concede these dubious cases, no general stereotype was in place in the initial decades of the nineteenth century. What does one make, for example, of the programmatically feminine *first* theme of the first-movement "sonata form" of Berlioz's *Symphonie fantastique* (1830)?

Instead, the concept seems to emerge more clearly and consistently in certain strands of later nineteenth-century gender representation. The idea of a masculine P (stormy, threatened, troubled) counterposed to a feminine (or otherwise eroticized or idealized) S did inform certain kinds of expositions from about 1840 onward. These pieces not only tended to set S into maximal relief to P but also generally conceived the exposition's parts 1 and 2 as separate blocks, each of which often displayed a relatively consistent, sometimes even monolithic character. One of the earliest examples was Wagner's programmatic Overture to *The Flying Dutchman* (first version, 1841), with its antithetical representations of the Dutchman and Senta. This nineteenth-century expositional format, emphasizing maximal contrast and alterity between parts 1 and 2, may be considered the "Dutch-man type" of exposition, and it was frequently adapted by later composers.[32] But there is no reason to suppose that its implications should be retrojected into earlier decades.

Some Schenkerian Implications

At this point, it may be instructive to compare the S-paradigms outlined here with the broader, Schenkerian view of sonata form (see example 7.7a and 7.7b). As is well known, Schenker was convinced that sonata form grew out of the interruption principle, whereby (for example) an *Ursatz* of the $\frac{\hat{3}\text{-}\hat{2}\text{-}\hat{1}}{I\text{-}V\text{-}I}$ variety, spanning an entire sonata-form movement, attains the specific middleground form $\frac{\hat{3}\text{-}\hat{2}}{I\text{-}V} \parallel \frac{\hat{3}\text{-}\hat{2}\text{-}\hat{1}}{I\text{-}V\text{-}I}$. In Schenker's view the first branch of the interruption structure is completed in the exposition, and its concluding $\frac{\hat{2}}{V}$ is prolonged by the development; the recapitulation rebegins on $\hat{3}$ and progresses this time to $\hat{1}$. In the exposition $\frac{\hat{2}}{V}$ is reached at the beginning of our part 2, and is prolonged by motion into an inner voice—that is, by the linear fifth-progression (*Zug*) $\frac{\hat{5}\text{-}\hat{4}\text{-}\hat{3}\text{-}\hat{2}\text{-}\hat{1}}{I}$ in the key of the dominant. (This fifth-progression thus occurs at the second level of the middleground.) During the second part of the recapitulation the transposition of this fifth progression to the tonic effects the ultimate closure of the interruption structure.[33]

Obviously, within an exposition the first satisfactory PAC in the key of the dominant is often identical with the first satisfactory termination of the middleground fifth progression in the exposition's part 2. It might be reasonable, therefore, to claim that this EEC, this "first satisfactory PAC in the key of the dominant" (the V:PAC that terminates S), is equivalent to the $\frac{\hat{2}\text{-}\hat{1}}{V\text{-}I}$ PAC terminating the *Zug* that prolongs $\frac{\hat{2}}{V}$ at the second level of the middleground. (We shall henceforth refer to this *Zug*-terminating PAC as

---

31. See, e.g., Lawrence Kramer, "The Strange Case of Beethoven's *Coriolan*: Romantic Aesthetics, Modern Subjectivity, and the Cult of Shakespeare," *The Musical Quarterly* 79 (1995), 265–80, which argues on behalf of the feminine-gendering of the S theme of *Coriolan* (which seems to have begun with Wagner). Tovey (*Essays in Musical Analysis*) mentions the Clärchen possibility. The *Coriolan* issue is brought up again in ch. 14.

32. The "Dutchman" exposition is discussed as a nineteenth-century type in Hepokoski, "Masculine-Feminine," and idem, "Beethoven Reception: The Symphonic Tradition," in *The Cambridge History of Nineteenth-Century Music*, ed. Jim Samson (Cambridge: Cambridge University Press, 2002), pp. 448–50.

33. The scenario is basically the same if a $\hat{5}$-line *Ursatz* is involved: the exposition moves $\frac{\hat{5}\text{-}\hat{4}\text{-}\hat{3}\text{-}\hat{2}}{I}$, and $\frac{\hat{2}}{V}$ is prolonged by the fifth-progression (which now attains the status of a true "*Ursatz* parallelism").

EXAMPLE 7.7a   Schenkerian Views of Sonata Form: Major mode

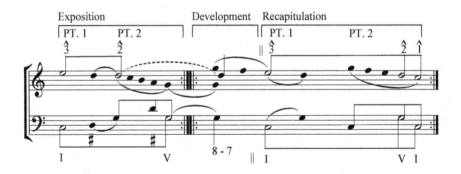

EXAMPLE 7.7b   Schenkerian Views of Sonata Form: Minor mode

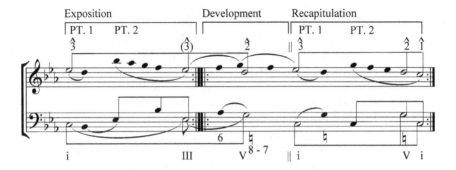

the "ZPAC"—indicating the "real" PAC that produces full closure completing the linear fifth progression.)

But to claim that the EEC invariably (or even usually) is identical to the ZPAC—the real closure of the exposition—immediately raises complex and controversial issues. A glance at example 7.7a reveals the basic conceptual problem. The voice-leading graph shows only one fifth-progression—and consequently only one V:PAC—during the prolongation of $\hat{2}\over V$ in part 2 of the exposition. As we know, however, part 2 generally contains many PACs. The main question is: what is the relationship of the first PAC (the EEC) to this "real" ZPAC? Are they always identical? Sometimes identical? Rarely identical? And why do we single out the first of these PACs as the EEC? Why not the last PAC or the strongest PAC?[34]

Schenker himself would have found this question pointless. In his view an exposition contains several fifth-progressions, and a more detailed graph would show all of these. A deep middleground graph such as example 7.7a collapses them all into a single *Zug*. But to designate the first of these fifth-progressions as S and the rest as C would have seemed to Schenker a reversion to the bad old ways of thematic/motivic analysis. In *Free Composition* he wrote:

> Moreover, the number of linear progressions is not limited. There may be two fifth-progressions, as in [the first movement of Beethoven's Sonata op. 14, no. 2 in G] or, as in Beethoven's Third Symphony, no less than four linear progressions, from $f^2(\hat{3})$ as the $\hat{2}$. To designate the last of these progressions as "closing theme" <in the Third Symphony, mm. 109–44> would seem to be beside the point.[35]

---

34. The strongest V:PAC may indeed be either the first or the last PAC in part 2, but this is not invariably the case.

35. Heinrich Schenker, *Free Composition*, trans. and ed. Ernst Oster (New York: Longman, 1970), p. 136.

This suggests that at the broadest level of understanding all the fifth-progressions (and consequently all the PACs) that occur during the second part of an exposition represent a single conceptual event—namely, the fifth-progression that composes out $\hat{2}\atop V$. In other words, one might well argue that each PAC that we encounter after the MC in some way represents and articulates the ZPAC. Such a decision, although correct from the broadest perspectives, bypasses certain features of rhetorical articulation and theme type that we consider important to the narrative psychology of expositions. Consequently, many analysts will still find it useful to try to determine which of the fifth progressions is the most decisive for the expositional structure: which is the "real" ZPAC, to which the others are subordinated (as descents into an inner voice)?

Nevertheless, in their analyses of the multiple fifth progressions within part 2 of an exposition, Schenkerians may well differ on which is the decisive one. Many will gravitate toward the strongest. For example, analysts might single out an emphatic cadence that features an expanded cadential progression (ECP), a trill on $\hat{2}$, or a return to obligatory register. Or some might simply choose the final PAC. Others might often gravitate toward the first—perhaps in agreement with William Rothstein's cogent, historical argument, which we have already outlined above (in this chapter). Rothstein's reasons for singling out the first PAC in the key of the dominant are persuasive to us, although they might not convince everyone. (And again, one should not regard this principle rigidly. It is wise to leave room for exceptional cases, deformations, and the like.) Other analysts may wish to use different criteria to identify the ZPAC/closing-cadence/EEC.

Ultimately, determining which fifth progression within part 2 is the real ZPAC is a matter of analytical interpretation, depending on the way in which the listener chooses to grasp the presented music. It is not something that can be found (or proven) objectively in the music itself. Insisting on this or that fifth progression as the "obvious" ZPAC usually does little more than reinforce the preconceptions of the analyst. Consequently, Sonata Theory remains resolutely agnostic on the (virtually metaphysical) question of which of the multiple fifth progressions in part 2 best represents the ZPAC. From the standpoint of the theory this need not be predetermined by a general principle. Indeed, it may not need to be decided at all. We agree with Schenker's implication that all of the fifth progressions represent, broadly construed, the same thing. Sonata Theory is compatible with those who hold differing views on this topic.

Where does this leave the concept of the EEC—the first satisfactory PAC (and often the first satisfactory linear fifth descent) in the new key of part 2? We are convinced that historically and conceptually it should be singled out for special attention and that it has a crucial role to play within the exposition, for reasons outlined above. Most significantly—and quite apart from its tonal/cadential importance—the EEC provides the rhetorical signal that S-space has been terminated and that C-space has now been opened for suffixes, appendices, or "accessory ideas." The EEC marks a moment of crucial importance in the rhetorical psychology of the exposition. We claim much on behalf of the EEC, but we stop short of the absolute claim that it must in all cases be identical with the "real" ZPAC.

CHAPTER EIGHT

S-Complications

EEC Deferral and Apparent Double Medial Caesuras (TMB)

The preceding chapter made the case that S-space (the secondary theme) is normally to be considered as ending with the first perfect authentic cadence (PAC) in the new key that moves onward to differing material, with all that follows within the exposition being consigned to closing-space (C, potentially a set of "accessory ideas"). At the same time we suggested that the first-PAC guideline, while a strong first-level default, is not inviolable. It is obvious—as illustrated in chapter 7—that it would be counterintuitive to consider thematic or immediate cadential repetition after the first PAC to launch C-space. Instead, the effect of such a repetition was that of undoing the closure provided by the preceding cadence in order to resituate it a few measures later with the next PAC. Metaphorically, such a situation is like that of closing a door behind one (the first PAC), then reopening it and walking through it a second time (with the second "door-closing" PAC serving as the EEC). The question of whether in doing so one, in effect, "goes back in time" or "turns back the sonata clock" to re-experience the same thing in perhaps a different way (and yet with the awareness that one has done it before) is a phenomenological issue with many ramifications. To pursue it would suggest that compositional time, or the impression of an elastic and manipulable time elaborated aes-thetically in the processes of the work's unfolding, can exist in a provocative interplay with neutral, nonrepeatable, and external clock time, which keeps ticking onward regardless of what happens inside a composition.

Becoming aware of the structural potential of EEC deferral gives rise to a host of questions. Notwithstanding the clarity of any textbook definition of a perfect authentic cadence, when examining the concreteness of individual situations, it is not always clear what is to count as a satisfactory or sufficient PAC (one capable of declaring the EEC unequivocally). An authentic-cadential effect (the suggestion of a V–I conclusion of a phrase) can be produced in a variety of strengths, ranging from definitive to "probably" to "almost" to "probably not." Composers sometimes problematize this cadential moment within S-space. As a result one occasionally finds oneself debating the closure-effectiveness of the apparent first PAC, while also considering a number of other features surrounding it. Can a sudden collapse to *piano* at the arrival of the tonic weaken or undercut the EEC-effect of a PAC? What about an unexpected shift from major to the tonic minor at this point: might that in some instances contribute to the sense of an EEC deferral? What if the treble or bass does not sound $\hat{8}$ or $\hat{1}$ precisely on the downbeat—even though it might be implied—but only a moment or two later? Especially in orchestral works or accompanied sonatas, at the moment of the cadence which lines furnish the structural voices?

Even if we assume the presence of a clear PAC, not all potential instances of EEC deferral are as unambiguous as that of mere S-repetition. Other procedures can reopen the first PAC and transfer the EEC to a later cadential moment. Some of these procedures are immediately persuasive and obvious. Others are less so, by degrees, with the EEC-decision relying eventually on experience and personal judgment. The most interpretive rely on a combination of individually "weak" bits of suggestive evidence within the exposition: while no single circumstance may be sufficient to override the force of the first PAC, the combination of all of them together might tilt a decision in favor of EEC deferral. Such issues arise frequently in middle- and late-Mozart, who had a keen interest in sophisticated methods of suggesting a co-ordinated S-push beyond the first PAC. This is especially true of his piano concertos, although it is by no means limited to them.

That said, one should not get the impression that first PACs are readily and easily overridden. One of our concerns in approaching this topic is that readers could misunderstand it as a justification for a more casual approach to the closure-effect of the first PAC. As a strong first-level default, one normally considers the first satisfactory PAC that goes on to new material to be the EEC unless there is clear and compelling evidence to suggest otherwise. Merely to notice a characteristic, *cantabile*, or *dolce* theme following this cadence is not a sufficient reason to consider the EEC to have been deferred. Nor does the mere presence of a stronger PAC down the road (which happens often) cast doubt on the EEC-effect of the first PAC. Nor should one postpone one's placement of the EEC while waiting for a theme that "sounds" more like what one imagines a C-theme to be. (One possible exception, the presence of a *forte* P-based C—not always by itself confirmatory of the preceding PAC as the "real" EEC—is considered in chapter 9.)

This analytical decision is not a matter of instinct but one that pulls together evidence that the composer has laid out within the exposition. The risk of considering EEC deferral too superficially is that one will be tempted to invoke it too loosely. Even though at certain levels of expertise analysts may come to differing conclusions about the EEC location within certain problematic pieces, one should realize that in ambiguous situations the nod should be given to the first-PAC guideline. Above all, one should not consider deferring the EEC for no clear hermeneutic purpose. Unless the deferral can be understood to mean something within the ongoing logic of the piece, there is no purpose in claiming it to exist.

Retrospective Reopenings of the First PAC with Following Material

Repetition of the Immediately Preceding S-Melody or Its Concluding Portion

As indicated above and in chapter 7, one could not consider S to be completed if either it or its cadential material is immediately restated. The PAC that ends the first statement of S proposes an EEC: by repeating the melody or a portion thereof, the composer reopens the PAC and shifts the EEC forward to the next PAC. As also mentioned in the preceding chapter, in the second statement of S it may happen that the melody is not brought to the same cadence, that the earlier model is varied through expansion or other modifications. This can result in a breathtakingly long delay of the EEC, sometimes suggesting that the EEC might be in danger of being lost altogether.

Persistence of S-Material Past the First PAC

In order for a PAC to "stick" as an EEC, S-material must normally be relinquished at the moment of the cadence, moving on to a differing thematic idea. The main exception to this occurs in the emphatically monothematic exposition, in which P, S, and C are all based on the same material. But when *contrasting* S-ideas persist past the first PAC, the implication is that the impulses that generated or sustained S are not yet finished, even though neither the S-theme nor its cadence is literally repeated. One should be cautious in applying this principle of deferral: the retention of S-based material should be clear and beyond dispute. (Obviously, in some sense any theme can be related to any other.)

The material in question can be either a thematic idea or a characteristic accompaniment figure that passes "unaffected" through the cadence. One example of a motivic or thematic retention of S-ideas past the first PAC has already been provided in the preceding chapter, from the first movement of Beethoven's Symphony No. 1 (example 7.1). Another occurs in the first movement of Mozart's "Prague" Symphony (example 8.1). S begins as a parallel period, mm. 97–104/105–12 (in which the consequent collapses into the minor mode), ending with the first V:PAC in m. 112. There follows a new theme (restoration of the major mode) in m. 112, while overlapping S-based material sets forth again in the bassoons: this proceeds to a second V:PAC in m. 121. The initial period, mm. 97–112, has been conceptually converted to the presentation phase of a larger sentence, whose continuation phase (best labeled as post-cadential, S^2) begins with the first PAC in m. 112. Without the explicit S-retention in the bassoons m. 112 would have been considered to be C. (In this case, illustrative of Mozart's capacity for astonishing combinations of deferral techniques, the second PAC in m. 121 is itself undone by another, TR-based S-appendix, retrospectively understood as S^3 [!], and the EEC is delayed to m.129. Here the central factor is that the V:PAC at m. 129 is nonelided with its subsequent P-based C^1 theme, m. 130—a characteristic C-theme identifier. This differing mode of EEC deferral—later cadences not elided with subsequent material—is discussed in a separate section below.)

A possible example of the retained-accompanimental-figure situation may be found in the first movement of Beethoven's "Waldstein" Sonata (example 8.2). S begins in III at m. 35—a brief parallel period ending with a III:PAC in m. 42. A varied repetition (featuring triplet figuration) ensues in m. 43, arriving at a second PAC at m. 50—clearly a candidate for the EEC. What follows, however, is a long excursus (potentially an S^2, not all of which is shown in the example). Beginning in m. 50 and elided with the PAC, it grows directly out of S's triplet figuration. It builds dramatically and at considerable length, driving toward the articulation of an expanded cadential progression, which seems to complete itself only with the trill cadence at m. 74. (With its preceding drop to *piano* in m. 68—which requires a *crescendo* recovery—and the evaporation of the literal dominant from the bass, this PAC at m. 74 is still problematic.) We regard the "Waldstein" as a difficult case to evaluate in the absence of additional, supporting evidence, such as a later P-based C theme. For the present we have decided to regard m. 74, the later cadence, as the EEC.

Revitalization of a Portion of S- (or FS-) Material after Starting a New Module

Much more infrequently it is possible to encounter a situation in which a cadential figure seems to conclude S (or perhaps TR⇒FS, the center-section of a continuous exposition), whereupon a new phrase begins—which we initially assume to mark the onset of C—only to fall a few measures later into a perhaps slightly varied repetition of the music that had led to the earlier, presumed-EEC cadence. Its effect can be that of a seeming C-module setting forth, then changing its mind and driving to its cadence with recovered S- (or FS-) material. The amount of music restated may vary, but it should be enough to be recognized as an obvious quotation or near-quotation, not merely another cadence (because, from some perspectives, all PACs are formulaically similar).

This situation may be understood in two ways, and good arguments exist on each side. It may be that the composer was suggesting that the closing module (C^1) was seeking a complementary rhyming-cadence with S for rhetorical emphasis, in which case one might consider the EEC not to have been deferred and the post-PAC module's C-status to remain secure. Although individual cases must be assessed on their own terms, this seems to us less likely than the alternative, namely that what had set out as a C-module relinquishes this status after a few bars, tucking itself back into S-space (or TR⇒FS-space in a continuous exposition) by

EXAMPLE 8.1   Mozart, Symphony No. 38 in D, K. 504 ("Prague"), i,
mm. 97–133

EXAMPLE 8.1 (continued)

Example 8.1 *(continued)*

EXAMPLE 8.2   Beethoven, Piano Sonata in C, op. 53 ("Waldstein"), i, mm. 35–53

EXAMPLE 8.2   (*continued*)

revivifying the concluding module or characteristic cadence of the original S.

Our inclination to treat the latter option more favorably is grounded as follows. We regard the EEC-attaining material to be of paramount importance in an exposition. Returning to it to produce a parallel cadence would seem, again, to be a way of turning back the sonata clock to highlight the closure-producing aspect of that idea, thereby effectively placing the intervening "new" material into a conceptual space preceding this re-encountered EEC and thereby folding it back into S-space. While retaining some flexibility in the decision, in most cases this recapturing of the EEC-formula shortly after a presumed EEC should be taken as undoing the earlier EEC-effect and deferring the "real" EEC to the cadential conclusion of its restatement. In a two-part exposition such an S-module should be labeled as S^2 (or $S^{2.1}$), since one new-key PAC has already been sounded that leads to differing material.

One example of this procedure may be observed in the first movement of Mozart's Violin Sonata in D, K. 306. Following a I:HC MC in m. 25, S begins sententially in m. 26 and proceeds through extended multimodular phases to a first V:PAC in m. 52 — an energy-approached cadential event that, when it happens, seems clearly to function as the EEC. A new theme follows in m. 52 that we initially understand to be C^1 — a sudden drop to a *piano* dynamic and

galant elegance. Such an understanding seems unproblematic, at least for the moment, particularly when this "C^1" is closed primly with its own V:PAC in m. 57, and the entire phrase is repeated in mm. 57–62. With the V:PAC in m. 62, however (the third V:PAC in the exposition so far), the music elides with an explicit, slightly varied recovery of the concluding five bars from S, mm. 48–52) that had articulated what we had thought was the EEC. In other words, within what we had supposed to be C-space, the EEC-producing measures of the end of S return emphatically to produce a nearly identical drive to the cadence (mm. 62–68 = mm. 48–52). Indeed, that cadence is now reinforced, since the original mm. 50 and 51 are cycled through twice (mm. 64–65, 66–67) to provide an even stronger wind-up to the V:PAC at m. 68. Such an explicit return to "pre-EEC" music stages an unusually aggressive re-entry into that event — a backing-up into an S-space that we had thought was left far behind. In turn, this suggests that what we had imagined to be "C^1" (the seemingly post-EEC music of mm. 52–57, 57–62) is being reconceptualized as an event within a broader S-space that is now forcefully asserted to persist all the way to the V:PAC at m. 68. What seemed self-evidently to be "C^1" is now reformulated as "S^2" (an attempt "prematurely" to enter a normative closing-space, now reconstrued as a politely *galant* "epilogue" or complementary appendix to S^1). The EEC-effect at m.

52 proves to have been only provisional. The "real" EEC occurs with its second articulation at m. 68—which in this case is nothing less than the fourth V:PAC in this exposition. Seven bars of "real" closing-space conclude the exposition, mm. 68–74: mm. 68–72, in particular, give the impression of being a recomposition of "S²," an elegant *Nachsatz* now reassembled and properly placed for a second, finally "successful" attempt to function as C—which had been its original intention.

Other examples that we have located occur in the music of the less-often analyzed composers of the later eighteenth century. In the second movement—following a slow first movement—of Dittersdorf's Symphony No. 1 in C Major on Ovid's *Metamorphoses* (ca. 1781), "The Four Ages of the World" (in this case the silver age), a I:HC MC in m. 16 leads to a clear S in the dominant in m. 17 that cadences unequivocally, and *forte*, at m. 34 with a V:PAC. This must be interpreted as a proposed EEC. It leads, though, to a nonelided new theme, *piano*, at m. 35. Because of its character we may initially wonder whether this postcadential module is somehow a "real" or "second" S after the fact (?) or whether it is best regarded as a *dolce* C-module following the EEC. Complicating our assessment, this square-cut, sentential theme also leads to a V:PAC in m. 42 and is subjected to an immediate repetition—much in the manner of a C-theme—only this time, at m. 50, it evades its expected cadence and reverts to the *forte* cadential module of the earlier S idea (m. 31) in order to produce a parallel V:PAC in m. 53 (= m. 34), a cadence repeated in mm. 53–56 to conclude the exposition with a much-deferred EEC. It may be that Dittersdorf was playing on

the ambiguity and S-character of the ostensible "C" theme, mm. 35ff, only to clarify and rescue the situation late in the game by recapturing the cadential module of the originally proposed EEC, thereby folding the ambiguous new material into S-space. The whole exposition rests on the witty interplay of predicted zone-proportions and seemingly puzzling thematic characters.[1]

Analytical issues among the *Kleinmeister* can surface in provocative ways in Haydn, Mozart, and Beethoven. Sometimes the recaptured portion of S is not an extended cadential module but a smaller cadential figure, a manner of cadencing that keeps recurring to conclude new ideas as a *refrain cadence*. A paradigmatic instance may be found in the first movement of Mozart's Piano Concerto No. 11 in F, K. 413. In the opening tutti the I:HC MC launches a chain of differing thematic modules, three of which close with the same or slightly varied I:PAC-figure: mm. 40–41, 44–45, and 52–53 (anticipated in mm. 50–51). We take this as an indication that the returns to the stock cadence-pattern override the proposed EEC-effects of the earlier PACs—one of several complementary such techniques in Mozart's piano concertos. Hence these refrain cadences expand ritornello-S-space beyond the first PAC. (For some implications of the concepts of S and the EEC within opening, normally tonic-centered ritornellos in concertos, see chapter 20.) It is only when the figure is relinquished (after m. 53, the EEC within the ritornello) that we move onward to a brief, *piano* C-space. Within the much-recomposed solo exposition the ritornello's S-closing cadence-figure is recaptured yet once again very late in the proceedings, mm.

---

1. Somewhat similar is the first movement of a work from around fifteen years earlier, Johann Vanhal's Symphony in F (F3; composed before 1771). Here we encounter a continuous exposition with TR elaboration occurring in mm. 12–35, concluding with a strong V:PAC, *forte*, at m. 35. An immediate drop to *piano* and a contrasting, characteristic idea occur at this point. Locally we might interpret this as either a delayed S (following a V:PAC MC!) or the onset of C. After a mere four bars of this pseudo-S [?] or C [?] material the music leaps back vigorously, in a sudden *forte*, mm. 39–41, into the earlier cadential-drive figures from mm. 21–23 and

30–32 and produces another, roughly parallel V:PAC in m. 48 (followed by four codetta-bars of C). Since the first V:PAC occurs in m. 35 of a fifty-one-bar exposition (some 69 percent of the way through the exposition), this exposition is best regarded as a variant of the second type of continuous exposition, that with an early V:PAC followed by repeated cadences (albeit in this case combined with a feint toward a "real" S-idea, soon aborted as having been deployed too late). In any event, the EEC-effect of the first V:PAC is retrospectively deferred some fourteen bars until the second one.

171–72 (compare mm. 151–52, 154–55), here within the concluding second tutti (!), suggesting the expansion of conceptual S-space proper through this cadence (and here, non-normatively, well past the standard trill cadence in mm. 163–64).

Related situations and unusual revisitings of seeming S-material—which complicate analyses of several of Mozart's later works, such as the first movement of the "Jupiter" Symphony—must be decided on an individual basis. One should never confront these situations with the aim of mechanically applying a rule or simple formula. On the contrary, the delight and depth of such pieces depend in large measure on the almost ungraspable multiplicity of their deformational connotations, on their power to imply several things simultaneously, on the complexity of their dialogues with the norms of a simpler, more trouble-free sonata practice. Savoring the analytical problem is more to the point than solving it.

Production of an Additional MC-Effect or Nonelided Cadence Shortly into Presumed C-Space

This is a complicated issue, one that involves the hypothesis of what might be called the principle of normative compression within C. It was a strong first-level default within C to elide the modules one with another, with C^2 beginning immediately with the articulation of the PAC that ends C^1, and so on. This seems especially to have been the case toward the beginning of C-space. A common variant or individual case of this nonelision procedure would be to begin the anacrusis portion of a later C-module in such a way that is flush-juxtaposed with its predecessor. In this case the upbeat of C^2, for example, would take off on the next beat of the measure after the PAC of C^1. (This occurs in Mozart's Piano Sonata in B-flat, K. 333, first movement, m. 50. The first PAC ending C^1 occurs on the downbeat, and the sixteenth-note figure initiating C^2 begins with an upbeat that starts on the second half of beat one of the same measure.) The point is that no significant "empty gap" is produced, particularly in the earlier stages of the C-zone. The generic default is to avoid the ap-

pearance of a substantial GP gap between initial C modules.

We distinguish between earlier and later C modules since one occasionally comes across an "afterthought" codetta module, nonelided to what precedes it, at the end of C-space (hence, at the end of an exposition). A classic instance occurs with the final two measures of the exposition of Mozart's Piano Sonata in D, K. 311, first movement. Given the course of this exposition, it is unreasonable to suppose that S-space is being pushed all the way up to this moment. Surely the point of that final module is its afterthought status—an unexpected (and non sequitur) appendix to what had sounded like the decisive end of C-space. Therefore it may be that any production of a significant GP gap within the *earlier* portions of C (almost always bridged over with caesura fill) might have been intended as a signal that S is being extended beyond the first otherwise-satisfactory PAC. This would be especially appropriate to the earlier phases of C, when C's reaffirming and codification function has perhaps not yet been fully realized. This would be the production of either a seemingly "unnecessary" (or extra) HC *postmedial caesura* (PMC) or a nonelided PAC caesura-effect within what we might otherwise assume to be the early stages of C. We shall consider each of these in turn.

In the first situation one encounters an HC PMC-effect within what is initially taken to be C-space. We regard such an additional MC-effect after a proposed EEC as reopening S-space and deferring the EEC to the next PAC after the HC PMC. Thus the *PMC axiom*: No HC medial-caesura-effect may occur within C-space, particularly if C has not yet produced its own first PAC. Or conversely: an HC PMC encountered shortly after the initial EEC-candidate reopens the proposed EEC (thus extending S-space) and defers it to the next PAC.

The classic example occurs in the first movement of Mozart's Piano Sonata in F, K. 332 (example 8.3). Here S^1, a problem-free compound period (mm. 41–48, 49–56), concludes with a V:PAC in m. 56 that one would normally judge to constitute the EEC, notwithstanding the collapse of mode to minor two bars later. Consequently we first assume that an elided C^1 starts

EXAMPLE 8.3   Mozart, Piano Sonata in F, K. 332, i, mm. 41–86

160

EXAMPLE 8.3   (continued)

in m. 56. But shortly thereafter (mm. 66–70, by now fully decayed into the minor mode, with dominant-lock in m. 67) we encounter the preparation for and execution of *another* V:HC [P]MC (m. 70, more precisely, v:HC). The effect is as if Mozart were backing up the temporal flow of the music to revisit this already once-deployed MC possibility. At this point we revise our earlier assessment, realizing that the PMC indicates that S-space has been held open—in which case the EEC-effect of the earlier PAC is overridden, and m. 56 is no longer considered as C[1] but as S[2.1].

As now expected, the v:HC PMC in m. 70 —with a caesura-fill continuing the thirds, but now leading satisfyingly out of the clouds into major-mode sunshine—prepares for yet another theme in m. 71. Fully restoring the major, this theme—at first all noble grace—may now be understood as S[2.2]. (It is not labeled as S[3] because no new PAC has been sounded). This span (S[2.2], mm. 71–81; S[2.3], mm. 82–86) has at least three features that suggest a synthesis of much of what had preceded it. It begins on the subdominant chord of C major, thus fleetingly recalling the sonority of the opening tonic. Its minuet-rhythmic figures (especially mm. 71–72, 73–74) plane out certain rhythmic moments of S[1] (mm. 43–44). And its jagged, offbeat continuation in mm. 82–85 refer back to mm. 56–65, the heart of S[2.1]. The new and definitive EEC is placed at m. 86, and eight bars of exhilarated closing material conclude the exposition. In retrospect, we might now think back to S[2.1] and understand the quick treble-drop away from $\hat{8}$ in m. 56, the subsequent syncopations of anxiety, and the chill to C minor in m. 58 to have betrayed, for whatever reason, an insecurity with the first-proposed EEC that led to its dismantling and reconstruction on other terms. (One might add more generally that the presence of apparent double medial caesuras—albeit here an MC and a PMC—suggests a conceptual relationship to the more normative trimodular-block procedure, TMB, discussed later in this chapter.)

The second situation occurs when a first V:PAC has been articulated and has been elided or flush-juxtaposed with a new, contrasting module. Normally we would take that new idea to be the onset of C-space. But in these cases

that new module quickly produces a strong PAC, followed by a notable GP-gap, perhaps inlaid with caesura fill, before the next C-module begins. Moreover, what follows again begins something new—perhaps more characteristically C-like—after this pronounced rhetorical breath. While prepared to admit the occasional exception, we usually consider a nonelision, or gap, that occurs a few bars after a proposed EEC as an indicator that S-space may have been extended to this point. Thus the nonelision axiom: Normally, no first PAC (or repetition of the first PAC) that occurs shortly after the supposed EEC may produce a pronounced caesura-like gap—a gap of, say, virtually a full measure—on its way to a subsequent, notably contrasting module. If it does, then that nonelided PAC claims for itself the right of functioning as the EEC, thus trumping the apparent EEC-claim of the preceding PAC, and the module should be considered as S[2], an S-appendix or S-codetta. At times the composer will reinforce this interpretation by beginning the "new" C (after the gap) with characteristic C[1]-material, such as the decisive or *forte* P-based C, a lighter, rustic or "folklike" theme, or a postcadential theme sounded over a tonic pedal. Obviously, reinforced interpretations, buttressed with additional evidence, are stronger than nonreinforced ones. When we first hear them, such S-appendices—and they are rare—can strike us as being much like "codetta-type" C themes (see chapter 9).

The first movement of Mozart's "Prague" Symphony presents us with a surprising succession of EEC-deferral techniques, some of which have already been discussed (example 8.1). Following a first deferral of the potential EEC to the PAC in m. 121, the question becomes: is that V:PAC ending S[2] permitted to function as the EEC, ending S? What follows is a direct elision to the next module—whose initial melodic pitch, $\hat{3}$, covers the more fundamental PAC at m. 121—and a throwback to a contrapuntal pre-S idea from m. 55, and it proceeds to a V: PAC at m. 129. At first one might take m. 121 for the EEC and the onset of C. The cadential close of this module, however, m. 129, leads to a significant punctuation gap, not elided with the subsequent module beginning at m. 130 and charged with a forward-driving, juggernaut caesura fill. The nonelision gap in m. 129 suggests that mm. 121–29 should be considered S³, a refrain-like S-appendix functioning as a celebratory, contrapuntal peroration. Moreover—and this additional evidence is confirmatory—the module at m. 130 triumphantly seizes upon a *forte* variant of P¹, a common strategy for the onset of C. With all the evidence finally in hand the EEC is now understood as having been deferred to m. 129. (As it happens, the "spring-loaded" extending of zone-space is characteristic not only of the S-zone but of this entire movement.) Finally, it might be added that the literal PAC that connects S² to the appendix S³ is suppressed, perhaps as a corrective measure, in the recapitulation, m. 270 (omission of the tonic bass).

Another instructive example occurs in the first movement of Mozart's Symphony No. 40 in G minor (example 8.4). S¹ is a brief sequential period, repeated (undoing the PAC at m. 51), with expansion, leading to a potential EEC PAC at m. 66. This is elided with a new module (first taken for C?), marked by a powerful initial syncopation and leading to a decisive scalar descent and PAC at m. 72. (Moreover, the syncopation is a faithful inversion of the chromatic descent within S, as if the syncopation were trying to undo the earlier "sigh-moment" in S. Thus the argument could also be made that the syncopated module is still concerned with material from S.) A new accompaniment pattern begins at m. 72, but the nonelided theme proper begins in m. 73—a return to P¹ material. (Again, the P-based C is a common C¹ strategy.) Under such circumstances we consider mm. 66–72 to be S², an S appendix (making the S-zone broader and more emphatic); m. 73 is the onset of a normative C. This not only squares with but also provides a principle for articulating one's intuitive understanding of this passage. The same effect is replicated in G minor in the recapitulation, mm. 227–60. (Compare the similar situation in Mozart's Symphony No. 39 in E-flat, K. 543, finale; the two structurally parallel moments are obviously related.)

The slow movement of Beethoven's First Symphony provides a clear instance of the nonelided axiom in which the subsequent C is not P-based. Briefly, the S-appendix (S², at first presumed to be C), a codetta-like figure, repeated (mm. 42–46, 46–53), concludes with a nonelided V:PAC at m. 53. C proper begins over a dominant pedal in m. 54.

A word of caution: it is not the case that all nonelided PACs within C-space automatically shift the EEC to that new point. Circumstances differ within individual pieces, and one must factor other, surrounding elements into one's evaluation. Obviously one seeks to avoid contextually counterintuitive decisions. In the finale of Mozart's String Quartet in G, K. 387, a largely fugal-contrapuntal S (mm. 52–91) sounds a decisive V:PAC at m. 91. This is followed by a nonelided contrasting, *buffa*-style C¹ at m. 92, which leads to another V:PAC in m. 99. The mischievous C¹ is subjected to a varied repeat (mm. 100–7), whereupon another nonelided, sparklingly new *buffa* theme (C²) is appended at m. 108. Notwithstanding their nonelision, the two *buffa* ideas are not only related in character but are also set off as a pair from the preceding, learned-style S. In addition, the rapid pace (Molto Allegro) and breathless, scrambling internal motion link the two C-themes together, and the whole C-complex had been separated from S-space by an earlier nonelided V:PAC. Here is a case where a nonelided cadence should be allowed into C-space: the EEC is not deferred and occurs in m. 91. (The dizzyingly multiple combinations of potential deferral techniques found in the finale of the Quartet in C, K. 465 are not so easily decided: notice the impish, cadential recurrences of S-material in supposedly C-space in mm. 109–17 and 126ff.)

Problems with a Potential First PAC: Ineffective or Weakened Cadences

The First PAC Arrives "Too Early"; The Implied S-Zone Is Contextually Too Underdeveloped; Thematic "Loops"

One normally expects an S-theme to display a minimally satisfactory proportion to the expanse of P and TR that has preceded it (even though the succeeding C-space will also contribute to this sense). This is a matter of feel

EXAMPLE 8.4   Mozart: Symphony No. 40 in G Minor, K. 550, i,
mm. 44–74

[Molto allegro]

EXAMPLE 8.4 *(continued)*

and balance not to be captured by a simple rule, but if one is dealing in generally broad proportions within an ambitious work, an S consisting of only a short, perfunctory phrase or "naïve," problem-free period can give the impression of a letdown or unexpectedly facile articulation of a proposed EEC. To be sure, an S-theme may be brief—and it certainly might be a single period—but given the proportions of any individual piece, there seems to be a conceptual threshold short of which it cannot satisfactorily effect expositional closure. One cannot specify this length in absolute numbers of measures. Obviously within an Allegro movement a PAC in the first or second measures—or probably in the third and fourth—would be an example of a premature PAC that could not serve as the EEC. But within a small-scale, midcentury work or briefer sonata what may happily suffice as a satisfactory S might seem out of place, disproportionately simple or abbreviated within a larger-scale work. Tempo and metrical-notational choice are also relevant factors.

When a composer does provide a notably brief S leading to an early PAC, one common strategy is to repeat (and perhaps vary) the theme, in part to defer the EEC-moment to a more proportionally acceptable position. This is one of several motivations that could be implicated in EEC deferral through thematic repetition. More problematic are brief phrases or periods leading to a quickly secured PAC that are not followed by such a repetition. Sometimes the early PAC concludes the "presentation" portion (aa') of a longer sentence. But this proposition should be viewed with caution: the presentation of a sentence of normal thematic length, while occasionally almost cadential, does not end with what we would usually consider to have risen to the level of a full-fledged cadence. When the presentation is more extended, as in a longer or compound sentence, a cadence at its end becomes more conceivable. Nevertheless, if a PAC or seeming PAC is construed as "obviously" the conclusion of a sentence-presentation, that PAC should not be taken as structural in terms of the broader theme. The general principle, in other words, is that no PAC at the end of the presentation of a sentence—even though such a cadence occurs only rarely—should ever be taken as the EEC.

The classic instances of sentence-presentational PACs—to be overridden and deferred until later in the theme—occur in themes that begin as "looped" phrases, relatively brief ideas that cycle back immediately into self-repetition. (This Mozartian subtype of the sentence was considered more generally in chapter 5. See especially n. 16 in that chapter, which introduces the EEC complications in such S-themes.) Such S-themes are uncommon in S-space, but they can occur there. A particularly instructive illustration—on several counts—is provided by the opening ritornello's S in the first movement of Mozart's Piano Concerto No. 21 in C, K. 467 (example 8.5). This S (still in the tonic C major, of course, since this occurs in the concerto's initial tutti) begins with two statements of a compound (or binary) five-bar loop, mm. 28–32 and 32–36. Now in this particular passage, unlike most other loop-theme situations, it may well be that one should not consider each loop—essentially built from a tonic-dominant-tonic oscillation—to have produced a full, bona-fide "cadence" at its end (since the module does not display a full cadential progression, including a predominant), but in this case a mild PAC-"effect" is at least suggested at those ends. (Put another way, one can imagine that "effect" being interpreted by some listeners—rightly or wrongly—as a PAC.) As is typical, the first loop elides into its repetition (m. 32), and the second loop elides directly into a continuation (m. 36). In sum, cadence or not, what we have is a looped presentation connected directly with (in this case) a contrasting continuation. Moreover, the continuation—most unusually—picks up the P-theme *idée fixe* from the piece's opening, clearly beginning a new idea. In such a situation as this there are manifold temptations to consider the EEC to occur at m. 36. And yet it does not. It is deferred past m. 36—which in any case might not fully attain the level of a PAC proper—well into the P-based continuation and beyond. (We revisit this theme in chapter 20 and place the EEC, after several extraordinary deferrals, at m. 64.)

Any "early" PAC concluding a simple phrase or period is not usually in itself a sufficiently determinative reason automatically to regard the proposed EEC as inadequate. Once again, many

EXAMPLE 8.5   Mozart, Piano Concerto No. 21 in C, K. 467, i, mm. 28–39

S-spaces are filled with single periods alone, and we are not suggesting that a mere period is inadequate to the demands of S-space. Context is everything, but when one comes across a suspiciously early PAC—and this is not uncommon in Mozart, particularly in the piano concertos—one should also be on the lookout for any supporting signs of cadential attenuation or EEC deferral. When they are to be found they might include sudden drops of dynamic, mode changes, or the immediate recovery of a characteristic accompaniment figure below an apparently new theme. This last aspect is relevant in the first movement of Mozart's Piano Concerto No. 9 in E-flat, K. 271 (example 8.6), where S¹ within the initial tutti rotation is a brief, guileless period concluding with a PAC, mm. 26–33. Is m. 33 the effective ritornello-EEC? Perhaps not. True, what follows, mm. 34–41, provides a new, nonelided thematic sentence, but its accompanimental pattern by and large retains that of S¹, giving the impression that

mm. 34–41 may be heard as an S², a welcome, balancing complement or symmetrical reply to the brief S¹. Additionally, the onset of a vigorous, completely different *forte* module at m. 41, fully plausible as an onset of C-space (though not in itself determinative of the "correct" EEC-placement) bolsters this interpretation. In such difficult cases we are reminded that any analysis—even a simple labeling—is an act of hermeneutics, not an uncovering of an objectively planted "fact" within the music. We are dealing with readings, with interpretations, not with objectively verifiable "truth claims." As a result, differing analysts might come up with different interpretations of underdetermined musical situations.

Substitution of an Imperfect Authentic Cadence (IAC) for the More Usual PAC

Although rare, it is possible for an EEC to be more weakly secured by an IAC. Before one

EXAMPLE 8.6   Mozart, Piano Concerto No. 9 in E-flat, K. 271, i,
mm. 26–42

[Allegro]

EXAMPLE 8.6 *(continued)*

comes to this decision, the rhetorical signals surrounding this EEC-moment—particularly regarding the status of C—should be overwhelming (sufficiently overwhelming to overpower the EEC-concept, among the strongest of conventions). This appears to be the case in Beethoven's Symphony No. 2 in D, op. 36, first movement, m. 112, in which $\hat{3}$ appears in a nonmelodic voice in the flute at the EEC. These cases require interpretive subtlety. Frequently the effect is that of a PAC in the literal or implied structural voices with a mere cover tone in one of the decorative upper voices—as probably occurs at the EEC-moment in the first movement of Beethoven's Quartet in E-flat, op. 74, "Harp," m. 70. Thus it may be that despite the surface appearance of an IAC the clear sense of a structural-voice PAC carries the day. Alternatively, the composer may have purposely weakened the EEC through the IAC-effect in order to cast more of a burden on the subsequent C-space. This pseudo-IAC situation should not be confused with cases in which the EEC-event elides with a C theme entering in another voice. When that elided C theme begins on $\hat{3}$ or $\hat{5}$, the moment of the EEC/PAC will not have $\hat{1}$ as the highest-sounding voice. Obviously, the implied PAC is not undermined by these circumstances. One must not rely on only a mechanical vertical reckoning above the bass to determine whether or not we have a PAC.

The Evaded PAC

A drive to an anticipated cadence may be undermined or evaded at the last moment. The term "evaded cadence" appears in Caplin's recent *Classical Form* to refer usually to the unexpected motion of a cadential dominant chord to a I⁶ (instead of the normatively cadential I) and the beginning of a new cadential progression, sometimes built around the aptly named "one more time technique," in which "the composer repeats [immediately] previously heard ideas and leads them again to a potential cadence. . . . The composer backs the music up, so to speak, in order for the listener to hear the impending cadential arrival one more time."[2] From the standpoint of Sonata Theory, of course, such an evasion through a drop to the I⁶ chord would never be considered even a proposal for an EEC, since the requisite PAC is still nowhere in view.

We also use the term "evaded cadence" for another situation, one that more closely approaches that of the perfect authentic cadence. This set of circumstances occurs when one structural voice drops out at the tonic-moment of the otherwise normative PAC, creating a momentary blank or absence on the downbeat of the measure in either the treble or the bass. Typically, the abandoned voice will rebegin immediately with new and lively figuration, perhaps relaunching on an off-beat. Such evaded cadences are especially typical of Mozart. As a general guideline (while

2. William E. Caplin, *Classical Form*, pp. 101–7 (quotation from p. 103). As Caplin noted, the colloquial term "one more time technique" was coined by Janet Schmalfeldt. Caplin also used the term "evaded cadence" to refer to other possibilities that we house under the concept of the attenuated cadence (p. 103).

admitting the possibility of an occasional exception), we do not consider these evaded cadences to serve as the EEC. Normally, the S-zone is renewed into another phrase that will continue the drive to the EEC. Two examples from first movements by Mozart: the Piano Sonata in B-flat, K. 281 (evaded PACs within S at mm. 30, 34; EEC delayed until the next PAC at m. 38); and the Piano Sonata in A Minor, K. 310 (the upper voice drops out and resumes in a higher register, m. 35; the EEC is evaded again, with bass dropping out, at m. 40, postponing the EEC until the next PAC at m. 45).

The Attenuated PAC

A PAC can have a weak or attenuated effect —something that instantly problematizes the strength of its potential EEC-status—in more than one way. This may happen, for example, when a *forte* cadential module (concluding S) drives toward the expected cadence but sounds it with a sudden drop to *piano* at the precise tonic-moment of the PAC, as if signaling a last-minute hesitation or failure of nerve. Absent other motivic or thematic evidence, we have tended to consider such attenuated PACs as EECs, albeit ones requiring reinforcement in the C-zone. Each case differs according to the severity of the attenuation and the nature of the surrounding material. At times the issue cannot be decided with a strong degree of confidence. But producing this ambiguity must have been the composer's point at that moment. We should suppose that it plays into the dramatized musical narrative being laid out in the exposition.

Another possibility of PAC-attenuation occurs when at the PAC the mode unexpectedly switches from major to minor—obviously a dramatic signal that something has gone wrong at this crucial moment. What ought to have been a point of self-assurance and attainment is plunged into anxiety and signs of the negative (the "lights-out" effect). To be sure, the expositional "attainment" still exists in a mechanical, literal sense—a PAC has been produced in the new key—but it is simultaneously undermined by doubt, undercutting the generic expectation of major-mode success. Does this mean that the PAC in question is no longer a satisfactory PAC,

even though it proceeds onward to differing material (our criterion for the determining of the EEC)? In some cases it might, although the claim is more persuasive when buttressed with additional evidence. In the first movement of Haydn's Symphony No. 46 in B, S^1 in F-sharp major (mm. 22–36), drifting comfortably toward its cadence in a mild *piano*, shifts suddenly to F-sharp minor and erupts into a jolting *forte* at the first PAC, m. 36 (as if confronted with a body blow, a sudden or desperate "No!"). In this case Haydn clarifies that this was an ineffective PAC a few measures later, when the S^2 idea recovers the original S-cadential module (m. 52 = m. 31) and leads to a less problematic PAC/EEC in due course.

Additional possibilities of PAC-attenuation occur when one encounters a radical register-shift in one or more voices at the tonic-moment, when the linear fifth-descent within S is not fully present prior to the PAC, or when the linear descent occurs in an inappropriate register (too high or too low). These are invariably difficult matters to evaluate, and they often invite a consideration of the techniques and principles of Schenkerian analysis. When potentially structural PACs are problematized or attenuated in one way or another, opinions may differ on the resulting implications for EEC-placement. Within the argument appeals will have to be made to additional material surrounding that PAC. Of particular relevance are matters of motivic or thematic retention or the generic thematic signals provided in the immediately following (presumed) C-space. Do clear C-identifiers, such as the P-based C, seem to announce the onset of closing-space? The musical context of the PAC considered along with the severity of the attenuation can help to decide the situation at hand. In some cases it may be that any simple decision one way or the other is inappropriate. Rather, the point of an adequate analysis might be to explicate the ambiguity.

Apparent Double Medial Caesuras: The Trimodular Block (TMB)

Although the more normative two-part exposition is marked by a single medial caesura somewhere in the center, it is not uncommon to encounter the setup and execution of a second, additional medial caesura before the EEC. This can occur in a variety of contexts, but the invariable impression is that of apparent double medial caesuras, and, concomitantly, the effect of two separate launches of new themes (pre-EEC themes) following those MCs. Depending on the circumstances at hand, the second new theme can seem to be something of a second S. The first new theme, following the first MC, will prove "unable" to move to the EEC and will instead be converted into the preparation for a new MC, possibly including the establishment of a dominant-lock and other features of MC-preparation.[3]

In these situations we find at least three elements: the first new theme after the first caesura; its dissolution and the setting up of the second caesura; and the onset of a differing S-theme, starting its own, renewed journey toward the EEC. We also refer to this characteristic three-phase pattern, with apparent medial caesuras before the first and third elements, as a *trimodular block (TMB)*. The presence of a TMB, a strategy for enriching and extending mid-expositional space, complicates the matter of determining the extent of the associated, potential S-zone. The two MCs in question are usually different, and they almost always follow the deployment sequence of MC options. By far the most common pattern is: I:HC / V:HC. Also possible, though much less frequent are: I:HC / V:PAC; V:HC / V:PAC; and the repetitive option, V:HC / V:HC. Alterations of these patterns are also available as deformations.

Not only is the double-MC-effect a fairly common phenomenon, but it is also of considerable historical and structural importance. In the decades around 1800 one finds it occasionally in Haydn but perhaps with greater frequency in Mozart and Beethoven. It is to be found in all types of compositions—sonatas, quartets, symphonies, and concertos. It took on an especially vital role in many of the solo expositions of Mozart's piano concertos (that is, in the Type 5 sonata), typically expanding and varying the layout of the preceding tutti rotation, which had usually been supplied with only one MC. (The details are laid out in chapter 21.) It is also the foremost expositional strategy that led to some of Schubert's much-noted three-stage (sometimes three-key) expositions (or "double second groups").

The issue of double MCs (and the resulting TMB) is a complicated, sometimes elusive topic, and we have also dealt with it elsewhere.[4] Because on closer consideration the double-MC pattern can occur with differing S and/or TR implications, it can be desirable in some analytical situations either to replace the perhaps-expected $S^{1.1}$, $S^{1.2}$, $S^{1.3}$ numbers with TM^1, TM^2, and TM^3 or to use both in conjunction. The exponential numbers of the TM-modules do not refer to PACs accomplished. For the sake of simplicity (in an already sufficiently entangled topic) this exception to our general rule seems advisable. When TM^3 does not proceed efficiently to the EEC, we might find a need to subdivide it, however, into $TM^{3.1}$, $TM^{3.2}$, and so on. In nearly all cases, TM^3 is self-evidently a different theme from TM^1. Only on very rare occasions are the themes based on the same idea.[5]

One may distinguish among differing types of double-MC-effects. The simplest TMB type occurs entirely within an unequivocal S-space, so that TM^1 is unproblematically equivalent to

---

3. The phenomenon of seemingly "double second themes" in Stamitz was mentioned by Eugene K. Wolf, *The Symphonies of Johann Stamitz: A Study in the Formation of the Classic Style* (Utrecht: Bohn, Scheltema & Holkema, 1981), e.g., pp. 151, 199, and 272. Cf. pp. 327–28 ("false [transition] sections"). Wolf described the post-S^1 TR-texture as a "secondary transition." On p. 200 he mentioned that "this design [including a new, *forte* transition that leads to a second S theme] also appears with some frequency in Viennese symphonies (e.g., by Wagenseil and Dittersdorf)."

4. Hepokoski and Darcy, "The Medial Caesura," pp. 145–50.

5. For an example in which TM^3 returns to the leading idea of TM^1, see the first movement of Haydn's Piano Sonata in C, Hob: XVI/50, mm. 20 and 30. In this case, both TM^1 and TM^3 are also P-based ideas, and the second MC is deformational, with the full clarity of the MC-effect not completely attained.

$S^{1.1}$. This type of TMB might be regarded as a variant of the multimodular or trimodular S, one in which an additional MC-effect and "second" S have been planted somewhere in the middle. (As a rule of thumb: If the double-MC-effect is not present, we are not dealing with a TMB.) This type of TMB begins with an initial caesura (usually a I:HC) that could serve as an MC, followed by a TM^1 that appears with acceptable S-rhetoric, characteristic, lyrical, or *cantabile*, in the expected new key. In this situation TM^1 accepts the proposed MC and launches S-space, although it might also strike us as weak or flawed in some way (minor-mode? thematically problematic? too eager to accept a premature or insufficient MC? drifting back to the original tonic?).

In any event, TM^1 proves in some way unsatisfactory, unable to secure the EEC. As a result that theme is jettisoned, normally by dissolving into what may be regarded as TM^2, the setting-up of another caesura, sometimes preceded by a move back to characteristically transitional (TR) texture. Sometimes one cannot distinguish any extended TM^2 module by texture and content alone. In other words, we might have a $TM^1 \Rightarrow TM^2$ merger, with the TM^2 aspect marked only by the articulation of the new MC at its end. Since we are considering what preceded TM^1 to have been the "real" MC opening up S-space, this second caesura, normally a V:HC, may be considered one type of postmedial caesura (PMC). Nonetheless, the larger effect produced up to this point is that of apparent double medial caesuras. The second caesura (the PMC) occurs in the middle of the already launched S-zone.

The second MC is sometimes articulated more weakly than the first, giving the impression that the "strong" MC energy had already been spent in the preparation for TM^1. Whatever its rhetorical strength—or lack thereof—its function is to restart S or to prepare for a more "successful" S-theme. In this type of TMB that new S is TM^3, which emerges with characteristic S-rhetoric and represents a "second chance" for S. Although it may encounter adventures along the way—and although TM^3 might prove multimodular in its unfolding—this stretch of S-space will produce no further MC effects and will eventually manage to attain the PAC/EEC. Any number of C-modules may then follow.

Considered as a whole, the TMB situation conveys the impression of a flawed or unsatisfactory first S-idea, TM^1 ("No! This theme won't do! This isn't the one we had hoped for!"), followed by some sort of TR-texture-based corrective action, TM^2, and a "better" S idea, TM^3. A good example of this type of TMB occurs in the first movement of Beethoven's Piano Sonata in C, op. 2 no. 3 (example 8.7). Here we find a I:HC medial caesura, with GP gap, in m. 26. What follows is an enormous TMB (with expanded third module) that stretches from m. 27 to the EEC in m. 77. TM^1, or the first S-idea, begins at m. 27 in an expressively "flawed" G minor, the dominant key having unexpectedly collapsed into minor ("lights out") at this point. This "flaw," it seems, will have to be expunged through the TMB strategy. Beginning in the dominant minor, the troubled TM^1 either cannot or chooses not to sustain its G minor, the mark of its imperfection. It begins to modulate sequentially, rising by fifths to a restatement on D minor (m. 33) to new material on A minor (m. 39). M. 39, starting the TM^2-phase, reinvigorates a more characteristic TR-texture and leads to a clear postmedial caesura, V:HC, at m. 45, followed by two bars of caesura fill. TM^3 responds to this second MC in m. 47—a new, *cantabile* theme, now in the radiantly sunlit G major. After reinvoking TR-based material along the way (m. 61) the EEC is strenuously attained only with the V:PAC at m. 77 (not shown in the example).

The above represents only the simplest type of TMB, the case in which the S^1-effect of the first module is clear. But other factors can enter into this apparent double-MC situation. The most obvious complication ensues when TM^1 is not a satisfactory S-candidate. TM^1 may strike us as unacceptable for any number of reasons, and we are then obliged to conclude that S-space has not been genuinely opened by the first apparent MC (which must thus be regarded as a "false MC"). Obviously, if the first MC is a legitimately permissible medial caesura (usually I:HC) and if it does not open S-space, it must in some sense have been a declined offer. In this respect the more complex instances of the

EXAMPLE 8.7   Beethoven: Piano Sonata in C, op. 2 no. 3, i, mm. 23–56

EXAMPLE 8.7 *(continued)*

EXAMPLE 8.7   (*continued*)

TMB are closely related to (sometimes almost indistinguishable from) the situation of MC declined. (In general, to label such an event as MC declined rather than as TM¹ is to make the assessment that most listeners, in any event, would not — or should not — attribute any significant degree of "S-ness" to that module. To label it TM¹ at least admits that possibility.)

In all of these cases one might suppose that the "real" S-function is consequently shifted over to TM³, following the "real" MC. And it is here where the concept of "S" itself might be challenged as inadequate to the situation at hand. Any projecting of such a label as S¹·¹ or S¹·² onto portions of a TMB — and especially onto this more problematic type — insists on interpreting a more complex expositional phenomenon (the TMB) by means of the conceptual categories of a simpler one (the two-part exposition with nonproblematic S). For this reason any mapping of the S-concept onto a TMB tends to be reductive, even though it might seem to be locally clarifying in certain kinds of discussions. A deeper consideration might produce the conclusion that while TM³ might not be said literally to "be" S¹ (since S-situations, those for which the S-concept was devised in the first place, are normally simpler), it is at least in dialogue with the more straightforward S-principle.

What kinds of evidence would suggest that a given TM¹ does not open S-space adequately? It may be that we find disruptions around the site of the first caesura or that the supposedly

first MC was non-normative or subjected to a substantial deformation. In fact, there may be no unequivocal MC effect at all preceding TM¹, which "bites" too early on a falsely offered caesura-lure or other moment of articulation. In such instances the "first MC" is only apparent. It can exist only as a mild glimmer of possibility, if that, which the succeeding module abruptly, and inappropriately, chooses to use as a launching pad for an S-like theme (that turns out to be TM¹). This happens in the first movement of Beethoven's Piano Sonatas in F, op. 10 no. 2 (premature and "wrong-key" MC-effect, V/iii, in m. 18; TM¹ in C major, m. 19 [as if triggered too early]; TM², m. 30; V:HC MC, m. 36, followed by fill; TM³ [more the "real" S], m. 38; EEC, m. 55).

Another example would be the much-discussed G-minor "new theme" in the solo exposition of Mozart's Piano Concerto No. 21 in C, K. 467, m. 109, which seems to leap into the piece impatiently before the first MC-effect (built around a I:HC) is permitted to complete its normative set of hammerblow reiterations. The "bar-too-early" entrance, coupled with the solo's octaves and urgent *forte* dynamics, underscores the desperately interventionist quality of this idea ("Stop!"). While disrupting the drive to the MC, this G-minor theme does appear (unlike the "too-early" TM¹ of Beethoven's op. 10 no. 2) at a mid-expositional location that could easily support the emergence of a secondary theme, and in several of Mozart's other concertos the TM[1] that appears here clearly does serve as an initial S. Thus from one perspective the theme might strike some as a "real" TM[1]-as-S after an MC-deformation; from another its premature intervention and sense of alarm might disbar it from true S-status. However we decide the matter (including the possibility of letting the ambiguity persist), we soon notice that the second MC-effect, v:HC, occurs at m. 124; the fill deliciously unfreezes the minor mode into major, mm. 124–28; and TM[3], another new module—not the one that had been proposed in the tutti rotation, m. 28—shines forth in G major at m. 128.

One might also come across an adequate first MC followed by tonal or thematic problems within TM[1]. Can TM[1] really function as S[1.1] if it emerges with recognizably thematic S-rhetoric but is sounded in the wrong key, either in the tonic or in an "incorrect" new key, thus seeming to decline the proposed MC? The paradigmatic example of the former occurs in the (sonata-rondo or Type 4) finale of Beethoven's Symphony No. 2, while the latter is exemplified in the first movement of Beethoven's Quartet in C Minor, op. 18 no. 4. Both have already been discussed under the rubric of medial caesura declined in chapter 3. In this sense certain cases of MC declined can also be understood as instances of the trimodular block. In the case of the symphony, the recapitulation does not make the potential S-ness of TM[1] an issue; there TM[1], whose tonic-key status is no longer a problem, seems to open S-space (m. 210), which then proceeds as a normative trimodular block.

Still another complication within the double-MC situation is the selection of a lower-level default option for the MCs in question. Again,

most normatively, in a major-key work the two MCs are I:HC / V:HC. When the second caesura is a V:PAC, though, the danger is that it can seem to effect an early EEC. The issues at hand here are similar to those surrounding a late, third-level default MC, already discussed in chapter 3. What makes us think that this V:PAC is a second *caesura* and not the EEC? We may conclude this only if we are convinced that the first caesura was, for whatever reason, not the "real" MC and that, as a result, TM[1] did not define itself clearly as existing within S-space. This may be the preferred understanding of what happens in the highly problematic first movement of Beethoven's Piano Sonata in D, op. 10 no. 3, although with its multiple deformations the evidence at hand could be read in more than one way. Here we encounter what may be heard as a premature and "wrong-key" MC-effect, V/vi, in m. 22, stopped in its tracks by a fermata (and thus producing a handy "gap"). What may be TM[1], m. 23, starts off on B minor, apparently "misinterpreting" the situation or perhaps following the lead of the "wrong" MC. The music proceeds at length (though without any separately demarcated TM[2]) to produce a strong V:PAC at the trill cadence onto m. 53. Provided that we understand what follows in m. 54 as S—which has been the normative understanding of this passage—then we must interpret m. 53 as a third-level default V:PAC MC. The EEC itself is not reached until m. 93.[6]

Equally provocative are the infrequent situations in major-mode works in which *both* of the apparent MCs are similar V:HCs. On the face of it, this would appear to be an exception to the normative deployment sequence of MCs, which would suggest that once a V:HC has been

---

6. An alternative interpretation—perhaps more deformational in implication, but certainly accommodating the facts—would construe the exposition as being in dialogue with the second type of continuous exposition: early V:PAC with reiterated cadences deferring the EEC onward. On this reading, the B-minor theme at m. 23 could be understood as a thematized TR, its lyrical rhetoric set off prematurely by the deceptive fermata-gap in m. 22. What follows the V:PAC in mm. 54–60—the fact of a trill cadence at m. 53 is important (an attempt at full closure?)—could be heard not as S but as mere cadential reinforcement, here shattered into stutter-

ing fragments. Normally such a reinforcement within a continuous exposition would restate more literally the preceding cadential modules. This, however, does not happen. Nonetheless, the asymmetry and brevity of the post-PAC phrase (a mere seven bars) might not seem to qualify for full S-status. The repetition immediately collapses into minor for a decayed restatement (m. 61), then breaks off (mm. 65–66). What follows (mm. 67ff) could be construed as a P-based recovery operation, finally regaining the lost perfect authentic cadence at m. 93, which, even in the type-2 continuous-exposition reading, would be considered the EEC.

laid down that option has been spent, leaving only the V:PAC option remaining. Since the V:HC, instead, is sounded *twice*, it may be that the composer was suggesting a backing-up of sonata-time in order to revisit and correct an earlier moment that had gone astray with the first-proposed S-idea. Such an interpretation is bolstered if the music recaptures an earlier, pre-first-MC idea (as if returning to the source of error to provide a second try), but this literal return to preceding material is apparently not a *sine qua non*. Examples of the double V:HC MC occur in the first movements of Haydn's Sonata in E-flat, Hob. XVI:25 (first V:HC MC—quite weak—in m. 14; TM^1, m. 15; TM^2, m. 18; second, stronger V:HC MC, m. 21; TM^3, m. 22, a now-"successful" variant of TM^1) and his Quartet in B-flat, op. 64 no. 3 (first MC, m. 32; S-like TM^1, m. 33; TM^2, m. 37 [?]; second V:HC, m. 42, with expanded $\hat{5}-\hat{1}$ caesura fill over V, in part suggesting references to the earlier pre-MC music; TM^3, m. 48).

Finally, apparent double MCs may be used to trigger the second two keys of a three-key exposition. While this would be used to remarkable effect by Schubert, one perhaps-influential precedent may be found in Cherubini's E-major Overture to *Les deux journées* (1800), a work that was well known in the immediately subsequent decades. In this case the two MCs are i:HC (m. 59) and V:HC (ca. m. 91, converting itself via fill to a V:PAC MC effect in m. 93). What is curious here is that TM^1 (m. 66) and the first modules of TM^3 (m. 94) are the *same theme*, sounded the first time "unsuccessfully" in G major (♮III, a "relative-major" response to the modally "decayed" i:HC MC, which leads to an expanded, modulating connecting-fill, mm. 59–65) and the second time in the "correct" B major.[7] Thus within a broader E-major context the exposition as a whole arpeggiates the minor triad, E–G–B, with three differing major keys. The recapitulation is complementary, visiting E, C, and E.

Deformation: Failed Expositions

No Secured EEC within the Exposition

The purpose of S within the exposition is to reach and stabilize a perfect authentic cadence in the new key. In eighteenth-century sonatas this aim is almost invariably accomplished: the new key is fastened down with a PAC/EEC and often reinforced with a closing zone. The generic model inherited from the earlier eighteenth century is overwhelming in its consistency and purpose: S exists to drive to a secured PAC. Were that PAC/EEC left unaccomplished—as a fully intended expressive strategy on the part of the composer—the exposition would be an illustration of frustration, nonattainment, or failure. Such a situation is countergeneric. Most failed expositions, then, are nonclosed expositions. S is either kept from articulating a PAC at all (there is no proposed EEC-effect at any point) or attains a PAC that is immediately overridden, perhaps through thematic repetition, and subsequently lost or permanently undermined, thus failing to produce a satisfactory EEC.

The implications of a failed exposition are not merely local but may affect the entire sonata. The normative exposition's rhetorical plan leading to the EEC serves as a predictor of things to come. It functions as a strategy of promise laying out the anticipated path of the eventual recapitulation in the latter's pursuit of the ESC, which is the *telos* of the sonata as a whole, the goal toward which the sonata-trajectory aims. Failure to attain the EEC within the exposition suggests that the entire sonata is threatened with nonclosure in the recapitulation (sonata failure). To undermine S's *raison d'être* in this way suggests that something has gone amiss, that the whole point of undertaking a sonata (as a metaphor for human action) has proven futile.

For the most part this was unthinkable within eighteenth-century sonatas. It occurs only rarely, as in the eccentric first movement of Haydn's Quartet in G Minor, op. 20 no. 3. This exposition is a paragon of distraction and disorder in which an extravagantly multimodular S in

---

7. On the issue of the (rare) thematic identity of TM^1 and TM^3, see n. 5.

B-flat, beginning in m. 27, finds itself unable to reach any III:PAC until m. 87. This cadence, though, is overridden by local repetition, instantly undoing any proposed EEC-effect, and immediately thereafter runs aground by converting the only remaining module into a modulatory retransition that remains stranded on a chordal emblem of baffled perplexity, vii°$\frac{4}{3}$ of the original G minor (m. 94). An altered ending in the recapitulatory rotation manages to produce a corrective, understated ESC toward the end of the movement, m. 251.

Failed expositions convey extreme expressive situations. With Beethoven's heightened dramatization of sonata processes and sonata options (heroic struggles against tyranny, threat, convention, and so on) we occasionally find strenuous S-zones that prove unable to find their way to a PAC capable of securing the EEC. The touchstone example occurs in the C-major finale of his Fifth Symphony, but there are other instances as well: the finales of the Second (a Type 4 sonata or sonata-rondo) and the Eighth Symphonies; perhaps also the Overture to *Fidelio* (whose evidence could provoke differing readings).

Metaphorically, such a failed exposition can be understood in a number of related ways. It could represent the intentional telling of a tale of failure within the exposition, implying a narrative situation of alarm and inadequacy. In such situations the expositional repeat can suggest an attempt to try again, although the second attempt, locked into the pre-established pattern, is also doomed to failure. Or it could indicate metaphorically the strain and difficulty of the "action" that the sonata is intended to represent. Or it could represent the last-minute elusiveness of the goal of satisfaction at the end of the exposition — a PAC within easy reach that slips away like a phantom.

After Beethoven, the failed exposition (as well as a failed recapitulation or sonata failure through a nonresolving recapitulation) becomes a more standard deformational option (a familiar sonata deformation). Typically, once the parallel, failed recapitulation has been completed,

the burden of tonal resolution is then placed on the coda. Structural closure is shifted beyond the action of sonata-space into a not-sonata zone of contingency beyond and external to the standard narrative action/process of the sonata proper. In every sonata in which a failed exposition or failed recapitulation appears — well through the entire nineteenth and early twentieth centuries — it remains a powerful effect. Among other things it can imply a critique of the inadequacy of the older, Enlightenment solutions in more complex, modern times.

Failed Exposition: EEC-Substitute in the Wrong Key

Related to failed expositions that lack an EEC are those that veer into an unusual or "inconceivable" key and use that tonal level as a stand-in for the proper key, sometimes explicitly represented as lost. Consider the B-flat slow movement of Mozart's Piano Concerto No. 14 in E-flat, K. 449. After an initial orchestral tutti lays out the rhetorical materials in the tonic (mm. 1–22), the expanded solo exposition begins in m. 23.[8] Following a V:HC MC in m. 40, S begins in the dominant key, F major (m. 41), but before it can produce a PAC in that key it undergoes a series of harmonic upheavals, shot through with minor-mode alarm, leading ultimately to the final expositional PAC (substitute-EEC) in A-flat major (♭VII!, m. 52, elided with the onset of the developmental rotation). From an expressive standpoint the exposition has failed in its original intention. S had set out with confidence in the generically obligatory V, F major, but with the incursion of unforeseen anxieties has now utterly lost its sense of security and centeredness — slipping off the rails onto the "wrong key," A-flat, understood locally as a port of mediant, major-mode "escape" from the modally decayed dominant, F minor. In this generically "impossible" key, ♭VII, a site of loss, the marooned narrative subject is now obliged to seek whatever consolation it can find, to articulate in a desolately strange location a major-mode EEC-gesture once planned for the proper

---

8. In this instance the piano entry also seems locally like a TR of the dissolving-restatement type. Note, however, that mm. 15–22 of the initial tutti come back as C in the recapitulation, mm. 112–19.

key. This expositional problem is reinterpreted, and corrected, in the recapitulation: the ESC is sounded in the tonic B-flat in m. 112.

A similar occurrence is found in the E-major slow movement of Beethoven's Piano Trio in G, op. 1 no. 2. Here S starts out in the normative B major, m. 26, but this key, as in the Mozart concerto example, is subjected to internal slippage and crisis. No PAC in B major occurs, and the exposition ends with a PAC in the "wrong key," G major (♮III!), in m. 39. In this case these expositional problems produce an even more dire nonresolving recapitulation later in the piece, one of the earliest in the repertory.[9]

These examples involve situations in which S begins normatively, in the proper new key, then—without any kind of postmedial-caesura-effect—loses that new key permanently by wandering away from it or shifting elsewhere. Thus they differ from the double-MC versions of the "three-key exposition," which has been illustrated further above with Cherubini's Overture to *Les deux journées*. The expressive effect of the present type of S-deformation is that of "S gone astray." In all cases the subsequent recapitulation is deeply problematized. Sometimes the recapitulation corrects the expositional de-

cay and produces a successful ESC in the tonic key. In other pieces the recapitulation's S succumbs to the same tonal problem and produces a nonresolving recapitulation.

Finally, these "failed" situations are to be distinguished from other types of modulatory S-themes that manage to inhabit generically acceptable keys. Beethoven's C-minor *Coriolan* Overture, op. 62, launches its S in the usual III, E-flat (m. 52), then modulates sequentially through iv, F minor (m. 64), on the way to v, G minor (m. 72), in which key the EEC finally occurs in m. 102, followed by several bars of closing material in G minor. The fundamental arpeggiation here is i–III–v, and III (E-flat) and v are the first- and second-level default keys for minor-mode expositions. These are by no means "wrong keys," and the exposition in that basic sense has not failed. Processed through a different interpretive filter, however—one that calls attention to S's "tragic" inability to sustain the major-mode III, which slips away into the negative, minor-mode v—the exposition, dashing the protagonist's hopes for a major-mode conclusion later on, can be said to have failed modally.

---

9. The issues of this section are dealt with at greater length in Hepokoski, "Back and Forth from *Egmont*: Beethoven, Mozart, and the Nonresolving Recapitulation," *19th-Century Music* 25 (2001), 127–54.

CHAPTER NINE

The Closing Zone (C)

Upon securing the EEC, the music can enter a *closing zone* (C) of variable length. By definition C is postcadential (post-EEC). Normally we cannot consider anything to be C until S has attained the EEC. As mentioned in chapter 7, writers in the late-eighteenth and early-nineteenth centuries described it as an appendix (*Anhang*, H. C. Koch) or set of accessory ideas (*idées accessoires*, Anton Reicha) of variable length to what we are calling the essential exposition. As an expandable series of "extras," the closing zone spans the space from the EEC to the exposition's final cadence (which may or may not lead to a retransition module, RT). This complex of C-ideas reaffirms and reinforces the new key.

C can differ in length and in character from one exposition to another. As historically early expositions (the first parts of larger binary structures) were subjected to expansion in the mid-eighteenth century, the aim of generating thematic abundance and differentiation often produced a multistaged exposition characterized by a chain-like succession of differing modules. This was particularly the case in part 2, the S / C portion after the MC. The potential for the significant multiplication of thematic modules in part 2, only one of which produces the EEC, led to the possibility of a long zone of closing thematic activity ("accessory ideas") extending past the generically obligatory EEC. One factor involved in the length of C-space must have been a sense that the length of the exposition's part 2 should be kept in some sort of rough balance with that of part 1. If the EEC occurred relatively early, a broader stretch of C became desirable to provide an impression of part-2 proportional adequacy.

Once the C-zone developed the possibility of becoming more extended, it could turn into an extensive tableau of postcadential material. (In this context "postcadential" means that it occurs after the first satisfactory PAC in the secondary key that goes on to new material—in other words, that the C-zone, by definition, exists in post-EEC-space, setting forth only after that generically obligatory cadence has been secured. Obviously, considered locally, C-space can contain phrases that end with unmistakable cadences.) It could present a new, separate argument or turn of events, in this way declaring itself to exist as a legitimate space in its own right. We refer to such a C-tableau as a discursive C or as discursive C-space—an action-zone that has a new theme or set of thematic modules to add to the ongoing exposition. A discursive C-space is more elaborate in its hermeneutic implications than a mere, cadentially reinforcing C-space—a brief codetta or a series of stock cadence formulas. These two possibilities stand at the two ends of a continuum for the articulation of C.[1]

Different kinds of things can happen in the closing zone: opening decisively onto new themes; recalling P-material or, less often, TR-material; articulating repeated, closing cadences in codetta fashion; and so on. C-ideas often end with stronger cadences than had been articulated at the EEC. Additionally, the C-zone is frequently multimodular. It may contain more than one closing idea: C^1, C^2, and so on; decimal designations—$C^{1.1}$, $C^{1.2}$—are also available if needed. (As with the other zones, the pre-decimal numerals are to be notched upward only with the attainment of a PAC and the arrival of a different closing module.) Mozart was fond of presenting three or four such ideas—a blossoming of new events within a grandly discursive C-space—sometimes repeating one or more of them, often with expansions. This is also an area where brilliant passagework may occur.

It seems to have been a general principle (or strong first-level default) that the differing modules of C-space, especially the opening two or three modules, should display either elided or flush-juxtaposed cadences. We normally expect to find no pronounced nonelided cadence producing substantial gaps or breaks (say, of virtually an entire measure's length) between the initial C-modules. Similarly, HC MC-effects (PMCs) are out of place in the C-zone. When these procedures do occur within what we initially interpret as C-space, they may undo the prior, presumed EEC, deferring it to a point after the gap or new HC MC-effect. This situation has been discussed in chapter 8 as one type of EEC deferral. The main exception to this principle is the addition of a brief "afterthought"-tag at the conclusion of C-space, a topic revisited later in this chapter.

The "Non-S-ness" of C

Within the mid- and late-eighteenth-century hierarchy of norms, especially as codified in Haydn, Mozart, and early Beethoven, one principle regarding C seems generally consistent. When the preceding S had been deployed as a contrast to P (when it was not a P-based S within a "monothematic" exposition), then the subsequent C is unlikely to contain significant material from the S-zone, especially at its outset. In particular, the characteristic or lyrical S^1-material (the head-motive of S) seems to have been regarded as not available for the beginning of C—and, at least as a first-level default, from the body of C as well. Thus C will customarily contain material that provides an immediate contrast with the preceding S (especially with S^1)—material that seems to "go on to different things." This makes sense: if S-material were restated toward the beginning of C, one would conclude that the preceding PAC was being reopened by the persistence of S. As a general principle S is not finished until its thematic material is relinquished.

Although the "non-S-ness" of C-space seems to have been a strong norm in the decades around 1800, it was not an inflexible rule. Rather, it was a default that could occasionally be overridden for special cross- or back-references—the effect of connecting certain interior portions of C to S. One comes across scattered exceptions here and there: S-references—perhaps more subtle than overt—embedded somewhere in the midst of C-space, as if an S-idea (not necessarily its head-motive) had somehow invaded C-consciousness. To be recognizable as such this invasion would occur after S-material has already been abandoned for a different C-idea, and, complementarily, it would normally give way to still-differing music on the way to the cadence. (If it did not it could suggest a reflowering of S-space, as described in chapter 8.) In brief, one should be prepared to encounter infrequent overridings of the broad, first-level-default norm of the non-S-ness of C. It is to these that we now turn.

---

1. As indicated in ch. 7, this concept of C differs from those that would restrict closing material to codettas or short modules only.

Exceptions

The main exception occurs in emphatically monothematic expositions, ones in which each of the main thematic zones, P, S, and C, begins with similar material, even though each may have a different character and go on to different continuations (see chapter 7). The effect is like that of an illuminated initial used to set off each of the zones, or like that of an economical (or witty) returning to a generating idea that has different sets of consequences. This technique can appear in varied strengths and certainties. S and C could both be derived in obvious ways from P, even when their onsets are not identical. Regardless of the literalness of its application, this "emphatic" procedure is only one option within "monothematic" expositions. It may also happen that when P and S begin similarly, C will contrast with them both.

A differing kind of exception occurs in both the first and last movements of Mozart's Piano Sonata in G, K. 283. In the first movement S begins in m. 23 with a syncopated theme in the upper voice and proceeds as a large sentence that produces the EEC at m. 43. A differing, flush-juxtaposed and TR-based C-theme begins in that measure, but two bars later, in mm. 45–46, one hears a reference to the syncopations (though not the literal theme) from the beginning of S. The reference is soon overtaken by new cadential material, and the referential module is immediately subjected to a varied repetition. In the finale the EEC, m. 73, is succeeded by a new C-theme in the next measure. The C-cadential material beginning in m. 89, however, is an inverted version of that of S, mm. 65ff. Such relationships of the interior of C with S are infrequent, and here they are doubtless part of the character of K. 283 as a whole.

One can also envision the possibility of *linkage-technique exceptions*, although here the evidence is often capable of being read in differing ways. How should one interpret a situation in which the apparent C-theme grows directly out of the cadential material that produces the EEC? This would exemplify the practice of linkage technique (*Knüpftechnik*), according to which a new phrase springs out of the material that had concluded its predecessor. In this case that material would include neither S's head motive (or main idea) nor the beginning of any of its inner modules. Notwithstanding the linkage some sense of contrast could still remain. Something like this may occur at the moment of what could be taken as the EEC in the first movement of Beethoven's Symphony No. 4 in B-flat, op. 60. Deciding the matter within this exposition is difficult, and interpretations can legitimately differ. Here one strong candidate for the EEC, although attenuated with an unexpected drop to *piano*, occurs in m. 141. What follows is a set of imitative entries launched in the clarinet, based on the cadential-progression figure implied or very nearly stated in increasing diminution in the bass of the preceding few bars (4 mm. + 2 mm., mm. 135–38, 139–40). If we choose to regard m. 141 as launching C, it would emerge as the final stage of diminution. Alternatively, on the basis of the persistence of this figure through the cadence—something commonly associated with linkage technique—we might regard this passage as a further extension of S and adduce the attenuated PAC as supporting evidence for EEC deferral.

C as S-Aftermath

On rare occasions one might find that the concluding idea of a multimodular closing space returns, *piano*, to the idea initially understood as S[1], an ebbing back-reference or quiet summary, as if reflecting on the entire post-MC trajectory. In such cases it seems counterintuitive to extend S-space through this backward-glance. The classic instance occurs in the first movement of Schubert's String Quintet in C, D. 956. Following a i:HC MC-effect (m. 58) and modulatory fill, the E-flat theme likely to be taken as S[1] (m. 60, although it will turn out to bear the uncertainties of a typical TM[1], notwithstanding the absence of any subsequent second-MC-effect) extends through several differing modules to the V:PAC EEC in m. 138. A contrasting, march-like C follows, but it yields at the end to remembrance-echoes of that now-distant "S[1]," fading away over a G-tonic pedal (mm. 146–53).

In the Schubert Quintet the S-recalls followed a differing C-module. It can happen, however—again, rarely—that this aftermath-diminuendo of S-material can occur directly after the EEC, juxtaposed with S-space and unmediated by any prior contrasting C-theme. On the basis of the few examples uncovered, the general pattern of this exception appears to involve the following elements: 1) the presence of a multimodular S (for example, $S^{1.1}$, $S^{1.2}$, $S^{1.3}$), the last element of which is an energetic, hefty drive to cadence; 2) an emphatic EEC—unmistakably articulated, *forte*; and 3) an immediate drop to *piano* after the EEC, followed by a (nonelided) quiet recycling of a characteristic theme or motive from S. At this point the $S^{1.1}$ or $S^{1.2}$ idea is treated cadentially, not melodically. Apparently the aftermath of S may either bring the exposition to a quiet close or give way to a final burst of *forte*, cadential C-modules.

The earliest anticipation—or perhaps realization—of this possibility of which we are presently aware occurs in the first movement of Beethoven's Piano Trio in E-flat, op. 1 no. 1 (ca. 1793). The unmistakable, assertive EEC occurs in m. 80. It is followed by a sudden drop to *piano* and the slightly varied resumption of a quasi-cadential, four-note rhythmic motive (at first sounded over a tonic pedal) that had been a characteristic feature of $S^{1.2}$ (cf. mm. 65–72). This moment may strike one as a continuing reverberation of S-ideas past the EEC, and it eventually breaks out of this self-reflection into bolder cadential material at m. 91. A similar, perhaps even simpler situation is observable in the opening movement, Andante, of Beethoven's small-scale Piano Sonata in G Minor, op. 49 no. 1 (1795/98). The EEC occurs in m. 29, with aftermath echoes of S^1 ebbing away (probably as C) in mm. 30–33.

The most famous example is found in the first movement of Schubert's Symphony No. 8 in B Minor, "Unfinished." Here the starkly alternative, though deeply melancholy S-theme (in G, VI, m. 44, preceded by two bars of $S^{1.0}$) collapses utterly as it is about to secure the expected EEC: the breaking-off at the last cadential moment in m. 62, a bar of grim nothingness followed by a *forzando*, shuddering minor-subdominant chord in m. 63, could not be more negative in its implications. It then proceeds as the "victimized" remainder of a multimodular S that, with much strain, pieces together the shards of a shattered S^1 to secure the EEC in m. 93. Immediately upon sounding the strong VI:PAC, however, the "failed" head-motive of S^1 returns again (!), as a kind of thematic backwater still flowing within C-space. This is striking, and it does not correspond with any of the usual overrides of S-PACs on the way to the EEC. The return to S^1 seems postcadential, thus functioning as an expositional deformation. It is either an unusual, deformational C (which would have to be explicated hermeneutically) or a special S-aftermath for which there appear to be no eighteenth-century generic categories.

Later in the nineteenth century and even into the twentieth this S-aftermath as C occasionally resurfaces. It may be found, for instance, in the first movement of Mahler's Symphony No. 6 in A Minor (mm. 115ff, more clearly C as S-aftermath, somewhat similar to the circumstances in Schubert's "Unfinished"). To all of this, though, a word of caution should be added. Whenever S-modules reverberate, however varied, throughout much or most of C, the fundamental question will always be: are we in C-space at all? It may be that such an apparent C (following a decisive, apparent EEC, and assuming that it is not a clear case of S-aftermath) is better understood as a special-function S-appendix, a varied repetition of moments of S-space in order to produce a particular expressive effect. Composing C as an altered recasting of S may be no normally available default at all: it may be a deformation. In all instances in which it seems to occur, that supposed C-space would be ambiguous, taking on both S-retention and quasi-C functions. As a consequence the precise moment of the EEC would also be ambiguous.

C-Theme Types

C-themes participate in a generic system of closing gestures. Although the following list is by no means intended to be exhaustive, we have found it helpful to identify six typical strategies for closing-zone modules. Each has a different expressive function. Themes of dissimilar types may be linked with each other, producing a string of C-themes, but codetta-materials (the first category listed below) are almost always used only to end the C-block. Normally, a codetta-module would not give way to a subsequent C-theme of another type, although exceptions can occur (as with the "afterthought" *piano* tag, the last type mentioned here). Similarly, both the P-based C and the less-common crescendo-type are commonly used to begin the C-block. The heuristic types identified below are neither absolute nor mutually exclusive. "Close calls" are not infrequent, and the C-theme types sometimes shade into one another. The point is not to insist that every C-theme be pigeonholed into only one of these categories but rather to be able to explicate the connotations and related generic precedents of each C-idea as it appears.

Codetta-Module[s]

Not a theme in the customary sense of the term, a codetta typically consists of cadential material and rhetorical flourishes, such as short-winded, repeated cadences (usually PACs, or at least emphatic reiterations of the V−I progression signifying a more final closure),[2] tonic pedals, or the "rotary" $\hat{8}-\flat\hat{7}-\hat{6}-\natural\hat{7}-\hat{8}$ module (see chapters 5 and 6), any of which may be elaborated in a series of reiterations producing, as Caplin has noted, "a general sense of compression of musical material."[3] This reiterated, aftershock cadential activity, in Allegro compositions nearly always sounded in a declarative *forte* or *fortissimo*, is generally to be regarded as a signal of final closure to a broad zone—in this case to the closing zone and, on a broader structural level, to the whole exposition. Its rhetoric is eas-

ily recognizable and is a standard feature of the sonata style at this time.

In briefer works from the mid-eighteenth century it was common for closing zones to restrict themselves to the post-EEC "landing-strip" of codetta-cadential reinforcement. C-zones that contain only codetta figures are also common in expositions whose EEC is postponed at length, leaving only a small amount of proportional room for closing material. (See figure 7.1.) Codettas may also appear as the final elements of a series of C-modules of different types, as a rhetorical conclusion to the whole set. Notably rarer is the case where a codetta-module abandons its typically "ending" role and is succeeded by a different, more thematic C-module. When this occurs, and it is simultaneously certain that we are within C-space, the impression given is that of the original plans for a conclusion being subjected to a sudden or whimsical change of mind. More typically, if the EEC leads to a codetta-idea that does not close the exposition (or pour into another codetta) but leads instead to a decidedly new C that continues at some length, then one might wish to consider whether it is best construed as an unusual codetta to S, an S-appendix. Individual cases vary in their implications, but this would be an enticing reading if the subsequent C-idea were nonelided, *forte*, and/or P-based. This uncommon mode of EEC deferral is discussed in chapter 8.

The P-Based C

The P-based C (especially C[1]) was one of the foremost options within expositions that also featured a contrasting S. If S[1] presented an idea dif-

---

2. In "The Classical Cadence," pp. 91−93, Caplin insisted that simple V−I reiterations at the end of an exposition were not to be regarded as cadences proper but rather as *postcadential* codettas. This is because the two-chord cadential formula was not part of the larger "cadential function" of a broader progression, usually that of tonic−predominant−dominant−tonic. (Put another way, the final "cadence" that fits this definition has already occurred.) While our differences with this viewpoint are largely definitional, we regard it as counterintuitive to deny the cadential-reiterative aspect of such final modules within an exposition. Such two-chord reiterations are there to provide an even

more emphatic closure—cadential closure, albeit of a different kind—both to the closing zone and, more broadly, to the exposition as a whole. To deny them any cadential status is to underestimate their role within the larger sonata exposition. See also n. 3 and ch. 5, n. 5.
3. Caplin, *Classical Form*, p. 122. See nn. 1 and 2 above. Caplin's separate definition of "codetta" in the glossary is also serviceable: "A postcadential function following a perfect authentic cadence and ranging in length from a single chord to a four-measure phrase. It is supported by a tonic prolongational (occasionally a cadential) progression" (p. 253).

ferent from P, this simultaneously made attractive the option of recovering P-based material within closing space for a rounding effect—as though P-material were being held in reserve as a strong option for C. This expositional rounding has two additional benefits: it can show how the initial condition or "problem" of P has been energized or otherwise transformed by the attainment of the EEC; and it helps to prepare for the return of P at the expositional repeat. While the P-based-C option is by no means invariably selected, the awareness that it may well appear is a central aspect of the psychology of contrasting-S-space, especially in Mozart's and Beethoven's expositions. (Emphatically monothematic expositions would also deploy P-based material for C^1, but when P and S begin similarly, C^1 can also present an altogether new theme, thus taking on the role of contrast in a C-epilogue to the thematically consistent essential exposition.)

Within Allegro compositions one should distinguish between two possibilities: the common, *forte* P-based C, normally encountered at the beginning of C-space after a contrasting S; and the less frequent, *piano* type, sometimes found at the end of a multimodular C. As suggested above, the first option is frequently encountered in Mozart and Beethoven. The frequency of its appearance at the onset of C is one of the strongest arguments on behalf of our concept of the EEC. While no procedure is inevitable, time and again the EEC marks the spot at which the activity of rounding and P-recovery may begin; or conversely, the P-based C^1 may with gratifying consistency be understood as a sign that the essential exposition has just been completed—that the EEC has just occurred. Consequently, especially when sounded decisively or *forte*, the P-based C can be a telling identifier of the onset of the C-zone, one that might then lead to one or more different types of successive modules, including a final codetta. In ambiguous EEC situations or situations of possible EEC deferral the existence of a decisive P-based-C can serve as compelling additional evidence of the beginning of the "extras" or postcadential "accessory ideas" of the closing zone (as shown in the illustrations from Beethoven's First Symphony, example 7.1 above, and Mozart's "Prague" Symphony, example

8.1). While the *forte* P-based C will usually be immediately preceded by what we should take to be an EEC, this principle cannot be regarded as absolute. Each situation will provide a different set of local circumstances. Whatever additional evidence is present must also be factored into our interpretations.

What is described here is the most commonly encountered role of a P-based C-module. A rarer alternative is the retrospective P-based C-module. This option sounds a P-based idea near or at the end of C-space, and that idea is characteristically sounded *piano* (or at least quietly), giving the impression of an ebbing recollection or memory of how the exposition had begun. Unlike the more typical, energetic function of the P-based C, this alternative usage may be more appropriate for expositions that end softly or more reflectively, not a commonly chosen option in the eighteenth century. Sounding remembrance-echoes of P at the end of C also serves a conceptual or literal retransition function, preparing for the repeat of the exposition. One paradigm of the procedure occurs at the end of the exposition of the first movement of Mozart's Quartet in C, K. 465, "Dissonance," mm. 91ff. (Here the *forte* S had burst forth at m. 56; the EEC had been sounded with the trill cadence at m. 71; a "new-theme" C^1 had begun with the gavotte-inflected upbeat to m. 72; the P-based C^2 dissolves into retransition around m. 99. This passage is shown in example 9.2 toward the end of this chapter, where it is discussed in connection with the concept of retransition.) The concluding expositional idea of the first movement of Mozart's Clarinet Quintet in A, K. 581, mm. 75–79, provides another example (contrasting S at m. 42 with early, overridden V:PAC at m. 49; EEC, with trill cadence, at m. 65; "new-theme" C^1—also gavotte-like, as it happens—at m. 66), as does the first movement of Beethoven's String Quintet in C, op. 29, mm. 75–93, although it also includes a crescendo at its end. (Compare these with some of the C-as-S-aftermath examples, cited earlier.)

The TR-Based C

A closing-zone return to TR material, either restated literally or varied, and especially sounded *forte* or *fortissimo*, was less common than the P-based C, but it was available as a normative possibility. The TR material alluded to need not be TR¹·¹. Particularly if TR material continues to the end of C, the result is that the exposition's part 2 rhymes with the end of part 1. Examples include the first movements of Mozart's Symphony No. 39 in E-flat, K. 543 (beginning at m. 119, the EEC, C eventually presents a varied version of TR material from mm. 83–90, most clearly evident in the concluding bars, mm. 135–42), and Beethoven's Piano Sonata in A, op. 2 no. 2 (following the EEC at m. 92, C brings back TR material from mm. 32ff). Later on, in the nineteenth century, another illustration is found in Mendelssohn's Overture to *A Midsummer Night's Dream* (1826), mm. 223–50 (the "hunt" and "Theseus" themes, at first in reversed order, from the *forte*-affirmation TR, beginning with mm. 62–78).

New Theme as C

At least as common as the P-based C was the strategy of appending one or more new thematic ideas after the EEC, either at the beginning of or further into C-space. When C has a strongly independent melodic profile, it usually signals the presence of a discursive C-space or tableau, springing to new life with its own (or only marginally derived) thematic material on the other side of the EEC, with the implication that this action-space is doing something beyond mere, efficient cadential affirmation. Such a larger C is appropriate after a relatively early EEC, permitting the closing zone to function as an expandable, complementary space to fill out the remaining time to permit part 2 (S / C) to achieve an acceptable proportional balance with part 1 (P TR). When S-space had contrasted with P—and when any of the zones are multimodular (when S and/or C contain more than one "new theme")—the impression can be that of a breathtaking plenitude within the exposition, an endless supply of brilliant ideas overtaking each other. This was an effect that Mozart, especially, used to great advantage.

The topical or expressive character of such a theme may vary widely. A new-theme C¹ may sound like another characteristic or lyrical theme with "S-rhetoric." This is a strategy of expansion, announcing the beginning of a discursive C-zone. One should not conclude that S is still continuing past the first PAC merely because this theme "sounds like an S." A new C¹ may also—perhaps more typically—be a more *vigorous* theme, driving toward the first of the string of concluding cadences (and perhaps from that point to a codetta-type C-theme). In each case the C-material must be interpreted in light of what has preceded it. Characteristically, it introduces new expressive complications (a sudden darkening? a new exuberance?) or tries to resolve still-lingering problems from the exposition's S. It may also take on salutary reinforcement work after an attenuated or not fully satisfactory EEC. Or it might suggest a zone of liberation or celebration, a new theme freed from the rigors of the essential exposition, as when Haydn provides a new theme after a monothematic essential exposition.

Crescendo-Module as Onset of C

Sometimes a composer will announce the launching of C with an energy-gaining crescendo, beginning with a bustling *piano* and building up to and finally discharging onto a *forte*, one either marking the peak of the crescendo-module itself or beginning a new module. (Since such crescendos are new thematic modules, they could be considered a subset of the new-theme type.) This is the virtually invariable practice in Rossini overtures. Rossini, in fact, is even more predictable than this: he usually provides either a quasi-mechanical, threefold repetition of the crescendo module—each repetition louder than its predecessor—or a two-stage single crescendo with one brief, repetitive module soon giving way to a second.[4]

Not surprisingly, there are a few eighteenth-century precedents. The onset of C is marked with a crescendo-module in the first movements of Mozart's Symphonies Nos. 32 in G, K. 318

---

4. Philip Gossett, "The Overtures of Rossini," *19th-Century Music* 3 (1979), 3–31.

(EEC and onset of C m. 49), and No. 34 in C, K. 338 (EEC and onset of C, m. 64). Curiously, in K. 338 the crescendo is omitted in the recapitulation. A brief, repeated crescendo-theme also initiates the C-zone of both the initial tutti (mm. 39–47) and the solo exposition (mm. 153–58, subsequently repeated and expanded into something quite different) of the first movement of his Piano Concerto No. 27 in B-flat, K. 595.[5] Quite apart from its "new-theme" impression, there would also seem to be a link between such crescendo-modules and the characteristic "Mannheim crescendo" (which was neither devised in Mannheim nor unique to that court) that was often heard in P or TR zones in the mid-eighteenth century. It may be that the C-crescendo represented something of a displacement of its normative expositional position, or it may simply be a second-level-default position for it.

Concluding C-Module as *Piano* Afterthought

From time to time Mozart gives the impression of concluding an exposition with strong, formally generic cadential or codetta modules—an extroverted *forte* conclusion sometimes even marked by generic hammerblows—only to append a brief, nonelided *piano* tag as a final remark. The usual implication is that of such an abundant overflow of musical ideas that the composer cannot resist offering one more, even after the apparent end of the exposition—in major a delectable sweetmeat set squarely on the tongue or a radiant blessing conferred on the "completed" proceedings; in minor a quiet and solitary acknowledgment of fate. We have already mentioned the concluding two bars of the first-movement exposition of the Piano Sonata in D, K. 311 as an example, and there are many other instances of it throughout his oeuvre. It

may be especially familiar within his concerto first movements, whose initial-tutti rotations sometimes end with just such a tag (possibly terminated with a concluding, *forte* cadence), subsequently held in reserve to provide an irresistible final word at the end of the whole movement.[6] Examples may be recalled in the first movements of the Piano Concertos No. 20 in D Minor, K. 466 (mm. 71–77), 23 in A, K. 488 (mm. 63–66), 25 in C, K. 503 (mm. 82–90), and 27 in B-flat, K. 595 (mm. 77–80).[7]

C^0 Themes

"Zero-theme" designations within the various zones are used to describe introductory or preparatory modules that give the impression of preceding the normative or "real" first theme of that expositional space. While P^0- ($P^{1.0}$-) and S^0-($S^{1.0}$-) themes are quite commonly encountered, C^0- or $C^{1.0}$- themes are extremely rare. Even the concept seems strained: an EEC would have to give way not to a normative C-module but to some sort of dead space or merely preparatory material moving toward yet another, more characteristic launch a few bars further ahead. On the face of it, this would appear to be unlikely.

And yet there is at least one famous example in the first movement of Beethoven's *Eroica* Symphony, mm. 83–108, although within that symphony's reception history that expositional moment has often been mistakenly taken for a "second theme." As already discussed in chapter 7, the second theme proper had begun remarkably early: following an abrupt V:HC MC in m. 45—perhaps suggesting an impatient eagerness for heroic action—we are given an S^0 (upbeat to m. 46) and an S^1 (m. 57), eventually moving to a decisive, *fortissimo* EEC in m. 83. Example 9.1

5. Measure numbers for K. 595 refer to the version with the restored seven bars toward the end of the initial tutti, as in the *Neue Mozart Ausgabe* (*Neue Ausgabe sämtlicher Werke*), Serie 5, Werkgruppe 15, vol. 8, ed. Wolfgang Rehm (Kassel: Bärenreiter, 1960), pp. 97–98, discussed on pp. xxiv–xxv.

6. Compare the discussion in the much-noted model for Mozartian concerto first-movement procedures as outlined in Daniel N. Leeson and Robert D. Levin, "On the Authenticity of K.Anh C.14.01 (279b), a Sym-

phonia Concertante for Four Winds and Orchestra," *Mozart-Jahrbuch* (1976–77), pp. 70–96. Cf. also David Grayson, *Mozart: Piano Concertos No. 20 in D Minor, K. 466, and No. 21 in C Major, K. 467* (Cambridge: Cambridge University Press, 1999), pp. 19–30. This model is also outlined in ch. 20 below. (Chs. 19–22 also discuss in some detail our alternative model for Mozart's concerto practice.)

7. See n. 4.

EXAMPLE 9.1   (continued)

shows the muscular, plunging-octaves approach to the EEC (as if conquering it by driving it into the ground) and the immediately succeeding music. Following this, the first thing to notice is the instant withdrawal into a hushed, *piano* dynamic and the utter change of texture (the very things, of course, that had suggested its contrasting S-ness to commentators). But this module does not proceed to a perfect authentic cadence. On the contrary, by m. 99 it locks onto a dominant and begins a crescendo-build to a new, *forte* module at m. 109, an idea that draws on the procedures of the standard, *forte* P-based C (or at least a C that alludes to the heroic triads that had characterized P).

At this point one needs to reason through the evidence, reconsidering all the options. So recognizably C-like and conclusive in character, m. 109 could by no stretch of the imagination be considered as the beginning of a "real" S. (Nor does it fit the normative conception of the concluding, cadential module of a multimodular S. Clearly something different is beginning here, a C^1.) If that is the case, then the *piano* passage that begins in m. 84 could not be S either, since it leads to no V:PAC before C^1: S ideas do not merely prepare for and serve as grand anacruses for C ideas. None of this need be a problem unless we insist on trying to turn m. 84 into the exposition's secondary theme (or perhaps, alternatively, into a PAC-triggered TM^3). But there is no reason to do this, since the piece's musical processes up to this point have already provided for an MC, an S-space, and a forceful EEC. If m. 109 is best heard as a "heroic" realization of a typical C^1 launch, then what are we to make of its long-upbeat preparation, mm. 84–108? Under these circumstances our preferred decision

is to regard it as C^0, an unusual, perhaps unique deformation.

This interpretation also plays into larger hermeneutic issues. If this sonata form (as suggested by the "Eroica" subtitle) is metaphorically representational of the hero's battlefield—that onto which the narrative subject is drawn into combat—here that hero drops away from normative sonata-action, rests after the conquest (the EEC), withdraws from battle into the shadows, and prepares for the next onslaught (C-space), which within a few bars is greeted with renewed vigor. In a sense mm. 84ff represent a withdrawal after victory, just as their radical transformation into the much-discussed, minor-mode new theme in the development (m. 284) suggests a withdrawal in defeat.[8]

S^C Themes: Apparent C-Zones in the Absence of an EEC

Particularly in sonatas after 1800 S may break down without producing a PAC. This inability is sometimes followed by a decisive, contrasting, potentially "C-like" theme. In such instances the question inevitably arises as to whether the nineteenth-century C, as a by-now reified, separable thematic concept, was capable of forging ahead on its own in the absence of an EEC. On the one hand, this contradicts the definition of C as postcadential (post-EEC): at least within the eighteenth-century norm nothing should exist conceptually as C until the EEC has been secured. On the other hand, one can imagine situations, especially after 1800, in which a composer might have intended to portray just such an S-breakdown. While S fails in its mis-

---

8. Much in the first movement of the *Eroica* has been misunderstood. In part the development of the first movement cannot be properly construed without a clear sense of its expansive dialogue with rotational principles. Within this context m. 284 is most profitably heard as a minor-mode, anti-C^0 referent (this is preferable to hearing it most essentially as a reworking of P), even as the immediately preceding E-minor cadence referred back negatively, and with enormous strain, to the EEC-principle following a vast battle-excursus fugato on S^0. Compare the bass pizzicatos in mm. 285ff with

those in C^0, mm. 86–87, 90–91; compare the contour of the $\hat{5}-\hat{1}$ oboe descent, mm. 287–88, with that in the first violin, mm. 90–91, immediately restated in the winds; and so on. Part of the case for connecting these two ideas (although the former is referred to as the exposition's second theme) has also been made by Robert P. Morgan, "Coda as Culmination: The First Movement of the 'Eroica' Symphony," in *Music Theory and the Exploration of the Past*, ed. Christopher Hatch and David W. Bernstein (Chicago: University of Chicago Press, 1993, pp. 357–76 [esp. p. 369]).

sion, C is left waiting for its "scheduled" turn to appear, and in fact, following the demands of unstoppable clock-time, it does so at the expected moment regardless of S's lapse. The curious thing about such themes is that they seem to bestride both the S- and C-concepts. They are emphatically precadential, pre-EEC (the essence of S-space), and yet, in part because of the block-like layout of the exposition, one suspects that they are simultaneously implying the onset of what "should" be a C-idea.

An early, perhaps defining instance occurs in the first movement of Beethoven's Piano Sonata in F Minor, op. 57, "Appassionata" (discussed in chapter 14). Later examples may be found in the first movements of Brahms's Symphonies Nos. 1 and 3 and in several movements by Bruckner and Mahler. Additionally, in several of these cases a major-mode S breaks down and is overtaken by a parallel-minor-mode drive to cadence. Here one might cautiously entertain the option of defying the definition of C as postcadential and considering the breakdown of S to be an EEC-deformation. Such a deformation would portray a manifest collapse of S before attaining the EEC. Under this interpretive option (relying on the principle that even strong generic norms can be overridden for extreme effects) the S-breakdown would be followed by a precadential (pre-EEC!), rhetorical C that now has to take on the EEC-burden of S. The hermeneutic implications of this situation are obvious. This interpretive option requires stressing the hazy notion of "C rhetoric" in what technically remains S-space.

In order to describe such a situation we have devised the label S^c, which is intended to suggest the presence of a theme literally in precadential, S-space that in other respects sounds as though it is more characteristically a closing theme. Thus S^c means "an S-theme, literally pre-EEC, in the style of a preplanned C-theme." Its equivalent in a continuous exposition (which contains no S) is $C^{pre-EEC}$ (chapter 4). In any event, making a clean, reductive decision about labels and terminology is less important than explicating the crisis or ambiguity created by the breakdown of S.

The Retransition

A retransition (RT) is a passage that prepares for and generally leads to the return of the primary theme (P) in the tonic key. It does this by destabilizing the key in which it begins, then driving toward an active and frequently prolonged dominant. The most natural home of the retransition may be at the end of the developmental space, where it sets up the onset of the recapitulation (in a Type 3, 4, or 5 sonata). But it can also occur at the end of the exposition, where its local function depends on the type of sonata at hand. In a Type 1 sonata (with neither a development nor an expositional repeat) it can prepare for the immediate recapitulation. In a Type 2 ("binary") or Type 3 ("textbook") sonata it can look forward to the repeat of the exposition. In a Type 4 sonata (sonata-rondo), it leads to the second statement of P. (In a Type 4 sonata it can also occur at the end of the recapitulatory space, where it usually readies us for the final return of P.)

EXAMPLE 9.2a   Mozart, String Quartet in C, K. 465 ("Dissonance"), i, mm. 23–26

EXAMPLE 9.2b *(continued)*

When a retransition occurs at the end of the exposition, it may follow the final closing module as an easily separable idea, often P-based, or it may begin as a closing module (or its repetition) and dissolve into retransitional activity (C⇒RT). In general, C extends through its last literal authentic cadence or cadence-reiteration (V–I motion, even if sounded over a pedal). When a new module veers away from authentic-cadential implication and toward a new dominant setup for the return of the tonic, the beginning of that module is considered the start of RT, regardless of the material on which it is based. As with TR, one should not consider RT as beginning in the middle of a phrase or self-standing concluding module.

The end of the exposition of the first movement of Mozart's String Quartet in C, K. 465, shown in example 9.2b, illustrates the basic idea. Here a strong C-module deep into C-space cadences V:PAC at m. 91, which is also marked with a sharp drop to *piano*. At this point Mozart introduced P-based material—the classic *piano* P-based C—in a cadentially reinforcing module that completes its first rhetorical span at m. 99. Mm. 91–99 thus extend C-space: we find tonic-dominant oscillations, first over a *Trommelbass* G-tonic pedal (mm. 91–94), then followed by a short-winded cadential-fadeout ef-

fect supported by triadic motion in the bass in mm. 95–99. At m. 99 we cross a divide. The cadence-reinforcement stops—there is a sense that we have reached the cadential end of a C-module—and even while the P-based material continues, the fadeout now shifts to its reverse, a texture of dynamic and harmonic accumulation. M. 99 thus provides the sense of beginning a new module, a new thought. The melodic idea is shifted to the bass and begins to rise sequentially. M. 100 makes the crescendo explicit, and in m. 102 the introduction of F♯ ($♮\hat{7}$ in the key of the dominant, $\hat{4}$ in the tonic) converts the G-major tonic into an active dominant and prepares for the repeat of the exposition. Two bars of *piano* fill, mm. 105–6, are appended to provide a graceful link back to the opening of the exposition. RT is best assessed as beginning in m. 99. Had the downbeat of m. 99 not given us the sense of a cadentially reinforcing close to the earlier module, we would have considered the RT to have begun in m. 91. The example also demonstrates the occasional relatedness of the *piano* P-based-C concept to that of one type of RT.

In a Type 4 sonata it is not uncommon for a retransition to usurp the place of a closing zone. In the finale of Mozart's Sonata in B-flat, K. 333, the EEC (V:PAC) occurs at m. 36 and is elided with a retransition that reactivates the dominant before the listener has much chance to construe it as a closing section. At the end of the recapitulatory rotation this same passage occurs elided with the ESC (m. 163) and is greatly extended. This expansion may be motivated by the fact that the retransition now begins in the tonic and requires more energy to pull away from it and lead to the active dominant. In this case that dominant takes the form of a cadential $^6_4$ chord that heralds an extended cadenza, a passage that stops sonata-time until the long-awaited return of P proper at m. 199.

CHAPTER TEN

The Development (Developmental Space)

The familiar term "development" can be misleading, since for today's English speakers it can imply an omnipresent working-out of expositional material within that space of the sonata. Although this is the most characteristic procedure, many development sections present "new" material in individual sections, and a few fill that zone almost entirely with contrasting material. (Considering it primarily in harmonic terms, Ratner suggested the synonym "X section" for this musical space.)[1] The word *développement* was introduced into the discourse by Anton Reicha in 1814 in the *Traité de mélodie* and, again, in 1826 in the *Traité de haute composition musicale*, which referred to the *première section de la seconde partie . . . développement principal en modulant sans cesse.* Reicha's meaning was not what we might initially suppose it to have been. He considered everything after the *exposition des idées,* including what we call the recapitulation, to have been their "development." Reicha intermixed concepts taken from classical rhetoric and French dramatic theory in such a way that *développement* was analogous to the process of plot-"unfoldings," to the close discussion of an idea, or to the setting-in of *l'intrigue* or *le noeud* (knot), leading eventually to its *dénouement* (untying).[2]

For German speakers this zone is the *Durchführung,* etymologically "a leading-through." This was originally a term used to describe fugal or polyphonic processes or other intense motivic or thematic treatment (*motivische oder thematische Arbeit*), and in the nineteenth century it came to describe "developmental" activity within differing portions of sonatas and scherzos as well. Along with such similar terms as *Ausführung, Durcharbeitung,* and the like, it seemed an apt description of what usually happened at the "second part" or "middle part" of a sonata—that is, it could feature exposition-based "*Durchführung* periods," as Ernst Friedrich Richter put it in 1852. Increasingly, particularly from the 1860s onward, it referred to the whole section (as in the writings of Arrey von Dommer, 1862, "*Mittelsatz oder Durchführung*"). But *Durchführung* came to be widely accepted as the standard way to refer to the second sonata-part

---

1. Ratner, *Classic Music,* p. 225, "the development, or X section." Cf. pp. 209, 213 (the X section at the opening of the B-portion of small two-reprise forms—AABB—"whose function is to open the way to the final confirmation of the tonic in reprise II").

2. Peter A. Hoyt, "The Concept of *développement* in the Early Nineteenth Century," in Ian Bent, ed., *Music Theory in the Age of Romanticism* (Cambridge: Cambridge University Press, 1996), pp. 141–62.

only in the work of Hugo Leichtentritt (1911): *Exposition–Durchführung–Reprise.*[3]

Neither of the ingrained terms, development and *Durchführung*, are likely to disappear from current analytical discourse, nor do we suggest that they should. Still, when underscoring the idea that not all portions of developments are necessarily "developmental" of expositional ideas (they may feature episodic passages or other events), we sometimes refer to the *developmental space*, signifying that portion of the sonata where a "traditional" [textbook] development would be placed, were that texture to be present at all. The term developmental space does not imply the inescapable presence of thematic back-reference and fragmentation, motivic manipulation, sequencing, and other commonly accepted developmental techniques.

Developmental spaces may be brief or much expanded. Within Type 3 sonatas a typical mid-century development (the "first part of the second section" of a large binary form) was normally a modest affair, perhaps under half the length of the exposition. As sonatas, quartets, symphonies, and concertos grew in their ambitions in the later eighteenth century, the size of their developments began to expand. The amount of space allotted to a development may be taken as an indication of the intended seriousness of purpose, depth of thought, or connoisseur appeal of these works. In the last decades of the eighteenth century developments commonly extended anywhere from about 25 percent to 75 percent of the length of the preceding expositional rotation. In mature Mozart and Haydn we can find more extended developments, occasionally matching the breadth of the exposition itself. And as is well known, Beethoven was capable of writing even longer, more monumental developments, sometimes (as in the first movement of the "Eroica" symphony) exceeding the amount of space allotted to the exposition. This hyperexpansion of the development, along with the resulting size of

the piece as a whole, should be taken as a compositional claim of increased thought-content and prestige.

Longer developments usually displayed a variety of differing, now-familiar developmental strategies: frequent modulation; complete or fragmented references to motivic or thematic material from the exposition, typically shifted through different harmonic and major-minor colors; occasionally interpolated episodes or "new themes"; blocks of sequences; *Sturm-und-Drang* textures; large-scale intensification-drives; surprises and interruptions; fugato or other contrapuntal treatment; the "false-recapitulation" effect; and several others. Some of these will be taken up as individual topics later in this chapter.

Tonal Layout

The Development as a Whole

In more ambitiously realized works, especially from the later eighteenth century onward, the development usually moves through various tonal areas, often by means of sequences or other leveraged shifts. In all cases tonal motion is creatively interrelated with the selection and ordering of thematic material, which is anything but haphazard. It is not uncommon for the original tonic to be visited early on, as nearly all of the theorists around 1800 not only remarked but specified, but in general the development is characterized by a restless, modulatory plan that stakes out one or more nontonic local goals. Although the plan is never random, by the later eighteenth century it was usually tailored to the individual piece. Some keys are merely alluded to, passed through fluidly; others are secured with a cadence and thereby articulated as momentarily "fixed in place," more structurally highlighted.

Analyzing a development's harmonic plan

---

3. See, e.g., Siegfried Schmalzriedt, "Durchführen, Durchführung" [1979], in Hans Heinrich Eggebrecht, ed., *Handwörterbuch der musikalischen Terminologie* (Stuttgart: Steiner, c. 1972ff), pp. 1–16 (here, pp. 9–10). The books cited are: Ernst Friedrich Richter, *Die Grundzüge der musikalischen Formen und ihre Analyse* (Leipzig: Georg Wigand, 1852), pp. 43–44; Arrey von Dommer, *Elemente der Musik* (1862), p. 289; Hugo Leichtentritt, *Musikalische Formenlehre* (1911), p. 128.

includes such things as tracking the bass and upper-voice motion, observing the logic behind the sequential levels visited, noting the tonicizations and modulations and the degrees of strength with which they are suggested, registering the expressive implications of major- and minor-mode transformations of earlier themes, and so on. One should be especially attentive to clearly articulated PACs, IACs, or HCs, along with any developmental MC- or other caesura-effects, especially if preceded by dominant-locks. Similarly, one expects to find individual stretches of common sequential patterns: circle-of-fifth descents and ascents, tonal motion by seconds and thirds, and the like. One should also be sensitive to a shift from one strategy (perhaps a descending circle of fifths) to another (such as sequential rises by whole steps via a chromatic bass line), and also to the tightening or foreshortening impression given by any increases in harmonic rhythm or rate of chord-change.

It was always typical for the developments of major-mode pieces to shift toward more "dramatic" minor-mode regions as an expressive contrast. The submediant, vi, was a common goal, frequently marked with a vi:PAC. In midcentury works this was sometimes the only tonal goal of "the first part of the second section." Developments by J. C. Bach, early Mozart, and many others often drove efficiently toward it, then concentrated on preparing for the recapitulation.[4] Less often the mediant (iii) was selected instead of the submediant. By the time of later Mozart and Haydn — not to mention Beethoven — the tonal plans of these developments grew more complex, the options more varied, the treatment of the standard move to vi or iii more flexible, more inventive. Developments came to have multiple nontonic goals, and the earlier, often single-minded motion toward vi could be displaced altogether. Ambitious development sections grew in length, resulting in a central, much-varied action-tableau setting forth a succession of harmonic and rhetorical adventures.

Following a motion or series of motions to different tonal planes, the development's last task is to prepare for the dramatized return of the tonic (*retransition*), usually by deploying an active dominant (locking onto the structural dominant, almost always V_A of the tonic-to-come) and proceeding forward with it, often gaining energy in the process. In Schenkerian terms the V_A ending the development is then normally subjected to a harmonic interruption and the piece rebegins its governing linear-tonal motion with the onset of the recapitulation. In Type 3, 4, and 5 sonatas what usually follows is a full recapitulatory rotation, beginning with P in the tonic. In the Type 2 sonata what follows is normally S in the tonic. (The Type 1 sonata has no developmental space.)

The retransitional procedures just described — dominant-lock, energy-gain, and so on — can recall those that precede the MC in expositions. Indeed, what is usually produced at the end of the development is a prominent HC caesura (although we reserve the term medial caesura for the center of the layout first provided in the exposition), sometimes followed by caesura-fill bridging the way to the subsequent relaunch of the tonic. Thus apart from their similar local functions there can be important parallels between the expositional MC and the caesura that typically occurs at the end of the development. One may go further: when a development is laid out, as so many are, as a half-rotation (based only on materials from P or P + TR: see the discussion of developmental rotations below), the end-of-development caesura in some respects "stands for" the earlier MC. The end-of-development caesura, of course — unlike the exposition's MC — does not usually lead one to expect S (unless a Type 2 sonata is in play). On the contrary, it can convey a sense of blockage, the impression that one cannot get beyond the MC-point into S (which

---

4. Ratner, *Classic Music*, pp. 225–26, referred to the principal "target" of these earlier developments, normally vi, as the "point of furthest remove" from the original tonic. In his view the development at first continued the process of motion away from the tonic that had been initiated in the exposition, a centrifugal motion, until it reached this goal of "furthest remove." At this point one encounters "a *change of harmonic intention*" — a harmonic divide — and all flows back toward the eventual recovery of the tonic, in a centripetal motion.

in turn requires one to start over again, with P, and execute a full recapitulatory rotation).

Notwithstanding the development's typical modulatory behavior, moving here and there on the local level, it is helpful to stand back from it and consider its larger tonal purpose in relation to the end of the exposition. When a major-mode exposition ends, as it usually does, with a tonicized dominant (V_T), the entire development may be heard as a prolongation of this V, regrasping it and activating it as a chord (V_A) at the end. The development as a whole at first unsettles the exposition's dominant key (usually in a set of related modulations) and eventually recrystallizes it at the end as a dominant chord. Normally the intervening keys are to be interpreted in relation to this process of prolongation. A move to vi can be understood as a tonicization of the upper neighbor of the prolonged V; early tonics in the development may be construed as only "apparent tonics," expressing IV of V or V of IV; and so on. The same reasoning would be operative for minor-mode works whose expositions ended in the dominant minor (v). Most, however, end in the mediant major (III). In this case the V_A at the end of the development completes a large-scale i–III–V bass arpeggiation that began with the onset of the exposition.

Substitutes for V_A at the End of the Development (Lower-Level Defaults)

Leaving behind an active V of the tonic in order to proceed to the recapitulatory relaunch was not the only way to negotiate the development-recapitulation seam. One sometimes finds a replacement of the structural-dominant lock (dominant preparation) on V_A at the close of a development with a seemingly "wrong" dominant, most typically V/vi (for instance, an E-major dominant chord, V of A minor, preceding a C-major recapitulation). The effect is that of predicting a recapitulation that will begin on the submediant ("relative minor") but that is actually followed by one that begins in the proper tonic, I. Expressively, this is like being

plucked from relative darkness (the implication of impending minor) to the renewed brightness of the major mode with the onset of the recapitulation.

This juxtaposition between different phrases (V/vi [interrupted]–I) already had a long history by the later eighteenth century. It had occurred, for example, when the minor-mode middle section of a *da capo* aria pauses on an HC fermata, V/vi, to return to the major-mode opening or occasionally when a second (slow) movement gives way to the third in an early eighteenth-century concerto. Bach's Brandenburg Concerto No. 3 in G provides a familiar example of the latter: the slow movement ends on a B-major chord, V of E minor, and the last movement begins directly in G major. Almost any large-scale connecting-point in which an interrupted dominant was to be succeeded by something new was susceptible to this "surprising" chordal juxtaposition. This could include i:HC MCs in minor-mode sonatas that burst into III for S. It could even be used—though most unusually—as a means of passage from a symphony's slow introduction to the Allegro sonata form proper, as in the first movement of Haydn's Symphony No. 103 in E-flat, "Drumroll." Here the introduction ends somberly on V of C minor (V/vi), and the sonata form proper takes off in E-flat major.

Our present concern is the juncture-point —the seam—where the development gives way to the recapitulation. Here too the juxtaposition, V/vi–I, had a long history of occasional use (second-level-default use, as an alternative to V_A). Since Charles Rosen has dealt with this topic at some length and provided numerous examples in *Sonata Forms*, we shall not repeat that discussion here, except to note that he understood this situation to be a variant of the standard developmental motion toward vi, which stereotype, in his view, had become something of a cliché by around 1800.[5]

The issue has also been discussed from a Schenkerian viewpoint by David Beach, who—expanding on observations by both Schenker and Ernst Oster—regarded the move-

---

5. Rosen, *Sonata Forms*, rev. ed., ch. 10, "Development," pp. 263, 267–70 et seq.

ment back to I through V/vi to exemplify a downward arpeggiation from the dominant secured at the end of the exposition: V–III (as V/vi)–I.[6] From a different perspective, recent neo-Riemannian or transformational theory might be attracted by the V/vi–I shift as one use—intersecting also with other, more traditionally functional understandings—of the "PL" operation (a double-transformation of a major triad: (1) major sonority into the parallel minor plus (2) a concomitant 5–6 shift, or *Leittonwechsel*, reinforced by root-support in the bass) or, within the terminology of Cohn's hexatonic cycles, of the shift between "next-adjacencies" (or "modally matched harmonies") with "two pc [pitch-class] displacements."[7]

The juxtaposition of V/vi and I, a phrase-ending followed by a phrase-beginning, could occur in either a mediated or an unmediated way. When it is unmediated, V/vi will be followed directly by the new phrase on I, with no additional chordal activity between the two sonorities. Examples may be found in the finale of Haydn's Symphony No. 103 in E-flat, "Drum-roll" (mm. 263–64, within a Type 4 sonata); and in the first movement of Beethoven's Violin Sonata in F, op. 24, "Spring" (the development ends with a prolonged V of D minor, mm. 116–23, and the recapitulation begins directly in F major at m. 124). When it is mediated one finds a passage of chordal fill separating the two poles, V/vi and I. The fill bridges the "wrong dominant" with a brief channel of harmonic slippage that usually touches fleetingly upon some version of the "correct dominant," V_A,

at its close. (In cases where the "correct V" is sounded as V^4_3 of I, that is, with $\hat{2}$ of the movement's tonic as its lowest voice, the bass motion from V/vi to the I that normally begins the recapitulation will be $\hat{3} - \hat{2} - \hat{1}$.) In these cases the seam between the development and the recapitulation is often negotiated in a three-stage pattern: (1) a "wrong-dominant"-lock (typically V/vi, but as will be mentioned below, V/iii is also common); (2) a concomitant caesura-effect at the end of this lock; (3) a composed-out corridor of caesura-fill, often brief but sometimes extending for several measures, that eventually leads, through some form of the dominant, to the tonic key and the onset of the recapitulation

The mediated move from V/vi to I may be exemplified in the first movement of Mozart's Piano Sonata in F, K. 280 (example 10.1). Here the central portion of the development treats the S-theme through chords outlining a descending circle of fifths: D minor (m. 67), G minor (m. 69), C major (m. 71), and F major (m. 73, only an apparent tonic in this sequential context). Mm. 75–77 provide a neighbor-note cycling in the bass around V of D minor (V/vi)—augmented sixth, passing $^6_4$, and vii^{o7} of V/vi—before a dominant-lock on V/vi is reached at m. 78 and extended into a caesura-effect at m. 80 (curiously, lacking its upper voice on the downbeat). Strictly considered, the "wrong-dominant" caesura is the last structural moment of the development. The implicit caesura-gap (mm. 80–82) is filled with three bars of chromatic slippage, in this case a relatively brief pas-

6. Heinrich Schenker, *Free Composition (Der freie Satz)*, trans. and ed. Ernst Oster (New York: Longman, 1979), p. 69 (referring to fig. 69 in the volume of examples). Beach, "Schenker's Theories: A Pedagogical View," in Beach, ed. *Aspects of Schenkerian Theory*, pp. 31–32; "A Recurring Pattern in Mozart's Music," *Journal of Music Theory* 27 (1983), 1–29; "Schubert's Experiments with Sonata Form: Formal-Tonal Design versus Underlying Structure," *Music Theory Spectrum* 15 (1993), 6. Beach's reading of Mozart's Piano Sonata in F, K. 332, first movement, has been challenged by David Gagné, "The Compositional Use of Register in Three Piano Sonatas by Mozart," in *Trends in Schenkerian Research*, ed. Allen Cadwallader (New York: Schirmer, 1990), pp. 29–30, 38 n. 13.

7. See, e.g., Richard Cohn, "Maximally Smooth Cycles, Hexatonic Systems, and the Analysis of Late-Romantic Triadic Progressions," *Music Analysis* 15 (1996), 9–40; Cohn, "As Wonderful as Star Clusters: Instruments for Gazing at Tonality in Schubert," *19th-Century Music* 22 (1999), 213–32; the issue of *Journal of Music Theory* devoted to neo-Riemannian theory, 42 (Fall 1998); Brian Hyer (who, following Lewin, helped to stabilize the letter-codes L, P, and R), "Tonal Intuitions in *Tristan und Isolde*," Ph.D. diss. Yale University, 1989, and Hyer, "Reimag(in)ing Riemann," *Journal of Music Theory* 39 (1995), 101–38. The term "modally matched" stems from Daniel Harrison, *Harmonic Function in Chromatic Music: A Renewed Dualist Theory and an Account of Its Precedents* (Chicago: University of Chicago Press, 1994), e.g., p. 52.

EXAMPLE 10.1   Mozart, Piano Sonata in F, K. 280, i, mm. 67–86

[Allegro assai]

sage moving smoothly through the characteristic V_3^4 of I in m. 82, which tips the music into F major for the recapitulation at m. 83.

Comparable illustrative passages—of many possible—may be consulted in the first movements of other piano sonatas of Mozart, such as that of K. 332 in F (lock onto V of D minor, mm. 123–28, with shift to the minor dominant in mm. 127–28 before being adjusted further to V_3^4 and V^7 of F, mm. 129–32; recapitulation in F, m. 133) and K. 547a (with a longer, more composed-out span of mediation between V of D minor and the recapitulation in m. 119); and, additionally, in that of Beethoven's Symphony No. 1 in C, op. 21 (V/vi lock at m. 160–72; wind-tilt in octaves brightening to C major and the recapitulation, mm. 174–78). More extravagant is the expanded fill found at the end of the development in the first movement of Mozart's Piano Sonata in B-flat, K. 333/i (example 10.2). This features what amounts to a "wrong-dominant"-lock onto V/vi at m. 81, interrupted with a caesura-effect at m. 86, and a prolonged, elaborately composed-out passage of modulatory fill, touching affectively also on the tonic minor, from the upbeat of m. 87 through m. 94. In the case of K. 333/i a passage of fill that is obviously relatable to the other instances mentioned above is extended and given a motivic interest (thematic and tonal "reintegration" after a minor-mode assault) to the point where it seems to take on a renewed role of retransition on its own. (Compare example 10.2 with the similar occurrence in Piano Concerto No. 19 in F, K. 459, example 22.4. Such illustrations are easily multiplied.)[8] Once the grounding pattern is recognized, we may perceive instances of its further adaptation or deformation. Some of these are brought up in chapter 12.

As suggested above, the issues at hand are similar to those encountered with develop-

ments whose structural processes proper conclude not on V/vi but on V/iii, the dominant of the mediant. Both shifts (V/vi to I and V/iii to I) are mediant-related juxtapositions, and both V/vi and V/iii contain the leading-tone of the movement's tonic. (In transformational-theory terms, however, V/iii to I involves a more radical shift, since there are no common tones between the two chords.) Here the succession, V/iii–I, is more likely to be mediated with a passage of chordal fill (the last part of the three-stage pattern mentioned above) for obvious reasons: the latter triad may also be heard as the former merely hoisted up a half-step. That fill, at the end, touches on the generically expected V_A at the end of the development.[9] One instructive example occurs in the first movement of Mozart's Symphony No. 35 in D, K. 385, "Haffner" (Example 10.3). Here the "wrong-dominant"-lock on V/iii is produced in mm. 111–16. This V/iii is interrupted with a caesura-effect at m. 116, and the remaining bars before the recapitulation are taken up with an expanded passage of fill moving down the circle of fifths (f♯, C♯⁷, F♯⁷, B⁷, E⁷, A⁷, mm. 117–28) and finally emptying out (not cadencing) on the D-major octaves in m. 129 that launch the recapitulation. Additional examples can be found in the finale of Mozart's C-major "Jupiter" Symphony, mm. 210–24, with a miraculously brightening or clarifying effect (compare also the first movement, where within the development the "false-recapitulation effect" in F, m. 161, is preceded by several bars of V of A minor that drift only at the end to the "proper" dominant); and in the first and last movements of Beethoven's Symphony No. 2 in D (first movement, aggressive lock onto a prolongation of V of F-sharp minor, mm. 198–214; sudden shift to V of D, m. 215; recapitulation in D, m. 216; finale, effective lock onto V of F-sharp minor,

8. Other Mozartian examples are mentioned in David Rosen, "'Unexpectedness' and 'Inevitability' in Mozart's Piano Concertos," *Mozart's Piano Concertos: Text, Context, Interpretation*, ed. Neal Zaslaw (Ann Arbor: University of Michigan Press, 1996), pp. 261–84. Rosen speculated that the procedure may be more prevalent in flat keys, although the claim was controversially disputed by Charles Rosen in the review of the entire

Zaslaw volume published in *Journal of the American Musicological Society* 51 (1998), 373–84.

9. This motion from V/iii to V can be considered a chromatic 5–6 shift—an alteration that also avoids the parallels that would be created in a direct V/iii–I progression. The 5–6 shift is clearest if the dominant occurs in V^6 position but is only slightly obscured if it is in root position V or V^7 position.

EXAMPLE 10.2   Mozart, Piano Sonata in B-flat, K. 332, i, mm. 81–97

EXAMPLE 10.2 *(continued)*

mm. 157–81; quiet shift to V⁶₅ of D, m. 183; recapitulation in D, m. 185, with the P-theme beginning on V⁷).

Somewhat analogous situations at the development-recapitulation seam are provided when the development ends with the conventional vi:PAC (instead of the active dominant, V/vi) and proceeds with little or no significant mediation into the recapitulation. This procedure occurs with some frequency in earlier, midcentury works. It can seem more elementary, cruder, than the normal practice, since it cuts out the need for bridging the submediant PAC to the tonic with an extended passage of retransition. In part it may also recall the effect of *da capo* arias whose center-section ends with full closure on a perfect authentic cadence in the "relative minor." Whatever its historical memory, what is produced is the direct or nearly direct move from closure on vi to a rebeginning on I (connected, at most, by a one-bar link, perhaps gesturing at the "proper" dominant en route)—essentially the "R" operation (to the "relative" major) in terms of transformational theory. This may be found in some of the first movements of Mozart's earliest violin sonatas (in B-flat, K. 8, mm. 46–47; in G, K. 9, mm. 59–60; in F, K. 13, mm. 64–65), and in a scattering of other works. A more sophisticated example of a virtually unmediated case of vi–I juxtaposition at the seam occurs in the

first movement of Haydn's Quartet in B-flat, op. 64 no. 3 (vi:PAC, m. 120, followed by several bars of "grounded" G minor and texture dissolution to the two common tones, B♭ and D; recapitulation in B-flat, m. 126). An example of a brief, two-bar mediation-fill between vi:PAC and a rebeginning on I may be found in the first movement of Mozart's Quartet in F, K. 168, mm. 61–62.

Also possible are developments that end by tonicizing the minor-mode mediant with a iii:PAC, then proceed to the tonic recapitulation by inflecting the fifth of iii up a half-step (the familiar 5–6 shift) to produce the tonic, thus bypassing a strong dominant, although a brief passage of fill might allude *en passant* to the otherwise "missing" dominant. The juxtaposition at the seam is that of iii–I, transformation theory's "L" operation (*Leittonwechsel*)—a process that is also understandable, like the V/vi–I entrance into the recapitulation, as part of a broad V–iii–I downward arpeggiation, reckoned from the end of the exposition. A virtually pure example (though mediated by a brief V⁴₃) may be found in the first movement of Haydn's Quartet in C, op. 33 no. 3, "Bird," mm. 108–11; another occurs in the first movement of his Quartet in C, op. 76 no. 3, mm. 65–79, in which the seeming mediation, here by V⁶, is actually the upbeat to P itself. A more elaborately mediated instance of iii–I occurs in the finale of Mozart's Symphony

EXAMPLE 10.3   Mozart, Symphony No. 35 in D, K. 385 ("Haffner"), i, mm. 111–33

EXAMPLE 10.3 (*continued*)

No. 39 in E-flat, K. 543, mm. 139–53, recalling complementary events in the first movement, mm. 179–84 (V/vi, interruption, mediation, I).

Rhetorical/Thematic Layout: Developmental Rotations

By the mid- and late-nineteenth century it had become common among theorists to imply that thematic choice and patterning within the development followed no guideline whatever. In part this may be the result of one strand of a theoretical tradition that chose to see in the development a creative and culminating "free fantasy," something exempted from the constraints of normative formal architecture (Gathy, Marx and his insistence on "motion" as the guiding developmental element, Dommer, Leichtentritt).[10] Since developments could be found that took up differing parts of the exposition, it was easy to conclude that it was futile or misguided to look for normative background configurations within which individualized developments might have been in dialogue. Descriptions similar to Schoenberg's became the standard view: "The thematic material [of the 'elaboration' or development, which is 'essentially a *contrasting middle section*'] may be drawn from the themes of the exposition in any order."[11]

While in a flat, wooden sense, such statements are correct, they conceal two embedded implications that can block one from further reflection on the significance of postexposi-

tional thematic selection. The first is that if developments do not follow a "rule," no thematic ordering-choice should be regarded as more common than any other—something that is not the case. (Realizing that it is not suggests that recurring patterns can be arranged as hierarchies of defaults.) The second, following on the first, is the potential to encourage the erroneous view that since many different things can happen in a development, thematic choice is arbitrary. But if it is arbitrary, then the composer's decision whether to "develop" P-, TR-, S-, or C-modules means nothing: themes become connotatively neutral, exchangeable carriers for some more fundamental process. Such implications played into the hands of some powerful twentieth-century reframings of the sonata genre—those minimizing the role of themes in order to emphasize linear-harmonic concerns, for example (Schenker), or grounding tonal patterns (Tovey, Ratner, to some extent Rosen).

Our view seeks to understand both tonality and thematic choice as interrelated and mutually vital to the development. Developments based on P and TR are far more common than those based on S and C—and of the latter two, appearances of C are more frequent than those of S. While S does appear in many developments and even dominates some, it may be that its relative infrequency is related to its cadentially "sensitive" role in the exposition. To allude to S might be to call up connotations of its seeking the proper tonal "track" on the way to the ESC (something that can normally happen only in a recapitulation). A tonic appearance of

---

10. See the discussion in Schmalzriedt, "Durchführen, Durchführung," pp. 12–13.

11. Arnold Schoenberg, *Fundamentals of Musical Com-*

position, ed. Gerald Strang and Leonard Stein (London: Faber and Faber, 1967), p. 206.

any S-module, however fleeting—something that almost never happens—would be doubly suggestive along these lines.

The choice and arrangement of thematic references in the development are to be heard against the referential layout provided in the exposition. Developmental treatments of previously heard themes both recall their original roles in the expositional layout and anticipate their future roles in that of the recapitulation. Since P- and TR-ideas are those that set forth vigorously into the relevant rotation and since they are "inert" in the sense that by definition they cannot bring about the eventual ESC, they are particularly suited to dominate developments. Similarly, C-material may also be more "available" for developmental treatment since it exists to confirm the EEC and ESC, not to produce them.

Most—though not all—developments were guided by the principle of presenting their thematic material in such a way as to suggest that its ordering corresponded to that of the exposition. This brings us to a theory of developmental rotations, a topic that invites careful nuances and a step-by-step examination of related issues and possibilities.

Developmental Rotations:
First Principles

Because there are so many exceptions and individual treatments, it has always been difficult to generalize about developments. Nevertheless, anyone charting the patterns of modular selection in works from the mid-eighteenth century onward—well into the nineteenth century (and beyond)—will be struck by the frequency with which the modules that are taken up in the development appear in the same order as that in which they had been presented in the exposition. This is generally the case even if one idea is developed for a long (or short) span before moving to something else: the length of time that any idea in the succession is dwelt upon is unpredictable. P is usually elaborated upon first, and the music may then move forward—though often the cycle may not proceed any further at all—perhaps to TR and thence to a selection from the exposition's part 2: either C-material

alone (the most common choice) or something from S preceding the possibility of C-material.

The first step in understanding developments as rotational is to be aware that individual modules from the exposition may be and usually are left out. By no means does every one have to reappear. The crucial thing is that the order of presentation be roughly the same. And even here one might encourage flexibility and imagination. Two touchstone examples of partial selection—in these cases, P and C—may be found in the first movements of Mozart's Piano Sonata in C, K. 309, and *Eine kleine Nachtmusik*, K. 525. We consider both developments to be fully rotational (that is, containing, in order, both pre-MC and post-MC references). In the sonata the development is grounded in two ideas from the exposition: P is treated at some length, mm. 59–82, shattering (mm. 79–82) into an emphatic cadence on vi, A minor; it is followed by a brief, *patetica* A-minor reaction of C, mm. 82–86. Two "false-starts" of P (first on A, then on B, as part of an unfolded V^7 of C) serve as a retransition to the recapitulatory rotation proper at m. 94. (These are shown in example 12.1.) In the G-major *Eine kleine Nachtmusik* the proportion of P and C material is reversed, though not the order. The opening P-flourishes launch the development in the dominant at m. 56, quickly inflect to V/vi and empty out onto a deceptive resolution to IV (C major) at m. 60. The remainder of the development, brief as it is, is preoccupied with C^1-material, mm. 60–75.

It would be easy to multiply such examples by the hundreds. There are of course exceptions to and complications of this tendency to retain expositional order, and they will be addressed in due course. Nevertheless, at least as an initial observation we may say that the evidence overwhelmingly confirms this rotational tendency to be a strong first-level default within a development, even if not all of the elements necessary to define a full rotation are acoustically present. It is the most normal thing to occur and the most normal thing to expect. Sonatas that feature complete and explicit rotations in their developments are tri-rotational, with exposition, development, and recapitulation each presenting their materials in the same order, though with differences. Should a discursive coda follow that is also grounded in the rotational principle—as in the opening movement of Beethoven's Piano Sonata in F Minor, op. 57, "Appassionata"—the result would be a quadri-rotational sonata.

Although this phenomenon has been noticed by earlier commentators, usually within the contexts of individual works, its implications have not been much investigated.[12] It matters greatly whether it is P-, S-, or C-material that is singled out for treatment; whether P is left out altogether; whether new episodes are interpolated and where. Not all developments are literally rotational. As always, it is a matter of defaults and preferred choices. Where the concept overstrains credulity, we are prepared to acknowledge nonrotational developments.

While none of the eighteenth- or early-nineteenth-century theorists explicitly laid out the rotational principle, their discussions of first-movement form made room for that possibility. Several of the theorists acknowledged the frequency of beginning the "first part of the second section" with P, often in V, and passing on to other ideas, although each of them typically made ample allowances for new themes or other alternative choices—such as beginning with C or with a new episode, noted by Koch in 1793 ("another main melodic idea" may "occasionally" begin this section) and even more explicitly by Galeazzi in 1796 (who heartily recommended these substitutions, mistakenly insisting that the idea of beginning the development with some version of P on the dominant was "in disuse . . . since it does not introduce any variety in compositions").[13] Any adequate theory of developmental rotations needs to take note of the frequency of the rotational or half-rotational patterns found in the majority of developments but is also obliged to include an interpretation of what happens when these patterns are discarded or overridden—as with

Galeazzi's recommended C- or episodic-openings to this section. This brings us to the matter of the differing ways in which developments may begin.

The Onset of the Development; P-Material as the Norm; Fifth-Descents

As noted by virtually all of the theorists and as is readily confirmed by observation, by far the most common thing to do was to begin the development with a restatement of the opening of the P-theme, usually in the same key (V) in which the exposition had just ended. Recalling that one function of P was that of initiating rotations, the frequency of this gesture suggests the background presence of a rotational norm for development sections. Whenever the P-in-V first-level-default option is not selected—which is also quite common—we should take note of it, especially since under certain conditions it might imply that the stronger convention is being "written over" by something else. The conclusion of the expositional cycle (perhaps its second cycle, if there was an expositional repeat) gives way again to the opening of another potential rotation of materials. The remainder of the development may or may not track through the rest of the pattern.

The initial sounding of P in V often gives way almost immediately to a second sounding of P a fifth lower, that is, on I (the tonic). This exemplifies a common strategy to begin the development with a descending circle of fifths on P: {P, P . . .}. The appearance of P in the tonic here should not be misconstrued to suggest anything "reprise-" or "recapitulation-"like. Much ink has been spilled on this matter (dubious claims about a "premature reprise" and so on, especially if articulated with P-material),[14] and it is susceptible to confusion. Instead, the ap-

---

12. Cf. Ratner, *Classic Music*, p. 228, which identifies one common type of development as "a modified review of exposition material," with references to the first movements of Mozart's Quintet in C Major, K. 515 and Beethoven's Quartet in C Minor, op. 18 no. 4; and Caplin, *Classical Form*, p. 139, who also cites in this regard Wallace Berry, *Form in Music*, 2nd ed. (Englewood Cliffs, N.J.: Prentice Hall, 1976), pp. 166–69; and Hugo

Leichtentritt, *Musical Form* (Cambridge, Mass.: Harvard University Press, 1951), pp. 134–38.

13. Koch, *Versuch*, III, pp. 307–8 (section 102); *Introductory Essay*, trans. Baker, p. 200. Churgin, "Francesco Galeazzi's Description (1796) of Sonata Form," *Journal of the American Musicological Society* 21 (1968), 194–95.

14. The premature-reprise theory—much-debated and now discredited—was presented in Oliver Strunk,

parent tonic is only a way-station on the road elsewhere, sometimes to another notch on the descending circle of fifths, to the area of IV, before setting forth into other harmonic regions. In other words, developments often (though not always) begin with a set of sequences moving down the circle of fifths before proceeding to other modulatory patterns. This observation opens the door to a multitude of related issues.

The first concerns the central point that the early visiting of the tonic, far from suggesting a recapitulatory baiting, was a standard expectation, though never a demand, toward the openings of developments, whether or not it was articulated with P-ideas. Koch (1793) makes this clear: "The first and most usual construction of the first period of the second section begins in the key of the fifth with the [P] theme, occasionally also with another main melodic idea. . . . After that it either modulates back into the main key by means of another melodic idea, and from this to the minor key of the sixth [etc.] . . . or it may not first return to the main key."[15] In addition, as has been shown by Peter A. Hoyt, the move back to the tonic was mentioned or exemplified in musical illustrations by most of the theorists of the time, from Georg Simon Löhlein (*Clavier-Schule*, 1765, fourth ed., 1782: after stating P-material in the dominant, "one then ordinarily proceeds . . . back to the tonic"), to Johann Gottlieb Portmann, to Francesco Galeazzi, to Anton Reicha.[16]

In short, early appearances of the tonic in the development normally carried few or no recapitulatory implications. This is especially the case if the tonic appears as part of a downward sequence of fifths or if it has not been preceded by significant modulatory excursions elsewhere or prepared by a strong dominant-lock. (If a P-grounded tonic appearance is pushed significantly later into the development, after P-

material or its substitutes have been abandoned in the rotation, it could strike one quite differently. This will be taken up below, under the issue of the "false-recapitulation effect.")

The second point concerns the norm of descending fifths through the tonic and often beyond at the beginnings of developments. Once the procedure of fifth-descents became typical, it could be subjected to alterations and adaptations by starting the descents a notch or two higher or lower. One way of understanding this is to imagine a chain of fifths arrayed around a central tonic: two fifths above, one fifth above, the tonic, one fifth below, and so on. These stations along the interval cycle may be given numbers that designate their relation to the tonic. In C major, for example, tonal levels reckoned by fifths could be cited as: +3 (A major/minor), +2 (D), +1 (G, the dominant and key of the exposition's close), 0 (C), −1 (F, the subdominant), −2 (B-flat), −3 (E-flat). Normally, a development might move {+1, 0, −1} along the circle of fifths before proceeding to other motion.

To provide an initial startling or sharp-side surprise, a composer could begin the development by unexpectedly ratcheting-up to a higher fifth, perhaps producing a {+3, +2, +1, 0, −1, −2} descent, as in the first movement of Beethoven's Symphony No. 1 in C, op. 21 (example 10.4). After the exposition closes in G and makes a retransitional feint back toward C (mm. 106–9, suggesting a fifth-descent), the music abruptly lurches to the A-major level (+3, as if to say "No!" to the C major, "We're not going back!"), where we find the expected P-material, and the developmental rotation, launched by an A[6] chord at m. 110. This moves by sequence to D[6] (+2, m. 114), to a G[6] (+1, m. 118), to C minor (0, m. 122, tonic "lights-out"), and to F minor (−1, m. 126), and even to a B-flat chord

---

"Haydn's Divertimenti for Baryton, Viola, and Bass," *The Musical Quarterly* 18 (1932), 216–51; rpt. Strunk, *Essays on Music in the Western World* (New York: Norton, 1974), pp. 126–70. Cf. Eugene K. Wolf, *The Symphonies of Johann Stamitz*, pp. 152–53; Mark Evan Bonds, "Haydn's False Recapitulations and the Perception of Sonata Form in the Eighteenth Century," Diss. Harvard University, 1988, pp. 220–24 et seq.; and Charles

Rosen, *Sonata Forms*, rev. ed., pp. 155–61, 223, 238, 267, 276, and 280.

15. Koch, *Introductory Essay*, trans. Baker, p. 200.

16. Peter A. Hoyt, "Haydn's 'False Recapitulations,' Late Eighteenth-Century Theory, and Modern Paradigms of Sonata Form," paper delivered at Yale University, March 30, 2001. We are grateful to Professor Hoyt for sharing this typescript with us.

EXAMPLE 10.4   Beethoven, Symphony No. 1 in C, op. 21, i, mm. 104–44

[Allegro con brio]

EXAMPLE 10.4 (continued)

EXAMPLE 10.4 *(continued)*

(−2, m. 130, effectively a dominant-lock moving toward an eventual MC-effect in m. 142) and a new section beginning on E-flat major (−3, m. 144). Here Beethoven takes a standard opening strategy and submits it to exaggeration to fill most of the first portion of the development.

Similarly, when we find that a development begins with an immediate return to the tonic—seeming to reinstate a tonic-return that had been earlier associated with the expositional repeat—what is doubtless implied is the suppression of the normative +1 (dominant) level (which might be "prematurely" tucked into the second ending or even earlier) in order to begin directly with the 0-level. This occurs in the first movements of Beethoven's Piano Sonata in G, op. 31 no. 1, and his Symphony No. 2 in D, op. 36. In the symphony the developmental space

emerges out of the exposition's second ending (with A major, +1, being converted into an RT-like V_A) to begin the development proper with P on D minor (0-level, m. 138—the tonic return here being substantially colored by the lights-out effect). In turn, D minor gives way to an extraordinary string of fifth-descents—a slippage downward desperately seeking a foothold to stop the sinking, all articulating P-material: G minor (−1, m. 146), C minor (−2, m. 148), F major (−3, m. 150), B-flat major (−4, m. 152), an E dyad (−5, m. 154), and so on, with the chords now changing every bar. In cases where the exposition had not been repeated—as in the first movements of Mozart's Wind Serenade in E-flat, K. 375, Haydn's Piano Sonata in D, Hob. XVI:51, and Beethoven's Quartet in F, op. 59 no. 1—the local impression can be that of an expositional repeat begun, then aborted.[17]

---

17. In finales from the decades immediately around 1800 (for which the Type 4 sonata was a real option),

one might also ascertain that what is being confronted is not a "sonata-rondo." For first movements and over-

While the initial tonal gesture of the development was not invariably associated with allusions to the fifth-chain, it often was, and master composers found creative ways to manipulate the implied rapid changes of bright-to-dark tonal colors. Should a development juxtapose the major-mode end of the exposition with a quick shift into an even-deeper subdominant direction, the effect can be somber indeed—the plunging into an abyss. In the first movement of Mozart's Quartet in D Minor, K. 421 (example 10.5), the exposition's F-major end (III, −3) sinks through its lower fifth (−4, merely a B♭$^6_4$ chord in the second ending, m. 41) to launch the development still another fifth lower, with P-material on E-flat major (−5, m. 42—the Neapolitan of the tonic, D minor). This chilling effect is rendered even more unnerving by the onset of a stepwise, flatward descent of the bass (suggesting another lower-fifth, A-flat minor, −6, m. 44), the shift to an ominously hushed *piano* dynamic in m. 45, and the bleak deep-shadow of the *pianissimo* V$^6_4$ of A minor in m. 46.

Once again, not all developments begin with fifth-descents. Our concern here is only to call attention to this typical procedure and to remind ourselves of the importance of the relationship of the initial developmental key with that of the end of the exposition. Whenever the development begins with a key different from that which ended the exposition, a first-level default option is being bypassed. As listeners we are encouraged to inquire into what the intended effect might be. This is also the case with developments that begin with other than P-material, a topic to which we now turn.

Episodic Openings: "Writing Over"

A P-based opening invites the understanding that a new rotation is underway. This is rein-forced if the development proceeds into TR or, in some developments, into part-2 material (C, less often S), in this latter case producing a full rotation. What are we to make of developments that begin with essentially new material, not with a self-evident restatement of any preceding theme? (Although such episodes may be motivically related to earlier themes, one should not overplay this hand. Within a style grounded in scales, triads, and neighbor-note relations, it is usually an easy matter to "derive" one theme from another.)

Episodic openings are met with fairly frequently—it may be a second-level default option—and it was also a practice recommended by Galeazzi in 1796. An episode suggests a changing of the subject, a reluctance or unwillingness to do the more standard thing. It could also suggest, as often in Mozart, the sudden flowering of a new theme, the exuberant overflow of a thematically abundant master.[18] Or as Tovey put it in 1929, "Such an episode, which is generally placed at the beginning, by no means always indicates a lighter style and texture. It may be a relief from unusually concentrated figure-work in the exposition."[19] Episodes may also occur further into the development—a topic taken up in a separate section below.

When such an episode opens a developmental space, it is important to examine what happens in the remainder of it. If what follows upholds the rotational convention—if what follows brings back selections of expositional material in its original order (perhaps returning to P or TR, perhaps proceeding directly to S- or C-ideas)—then two possibilities exist and may even overlap. The initial episode may be either an interpolation wedged into the work before the onset of the developmental rotation proper or a substitution for the more standard P[1]. In the former, less frequent case we would expect the episode to be followed by a more or less norma-

---

tures in all periods, the Type 4 format (sonata-rondo) was never an option and should not be entertained as a possibility—even in repertories as late as Brahms and Mahler. Since the Type 4 option declined rapidly in the nineteenth century, even within finales, one should normally suppose that mid- and late-nineteenth-century finales—as in Brahms—are in dialogue with Type 1 or Type 3 variants, not with Type 4s.

18. Cf. Caplin in n. 12.
19. Donald Francis Tovey, "Sonata Forms," written for the fourteenth edition of the *Encyclopaedia Britannica* (1929), rpt. in *Musical Articles from the Encyclopaedia Britannica* (London: Oxford University Press, 1944), p. 215; reissued (1956) under the title *The Forms of Music*.

EXAMPLE 10.5 Mozart, String Quartet in D Minor, K. 421, i,
mm. 39–47

tive P^1 module, as if the rotation proper finally starts after a delay. In the latter, more frequent case we say that the episode *writes over* P^1 or a developmental variant thereof. P^1 thus is present only conceptually, as a tacit substratum of implication below the acoustic surface. Accordingly, the developmental rotation begins directly with the episode, even though the characteristic rotation-initiator, P^1 or some other early element, is not literally sounded at that point. It may also happen that the replacement music (the agent of writing over) displays motivic or other topical or rhetorical connections to that which it displaces, as if salient features of the silenced P were pressing into the fabric of what takes its place at the beginning of the development.

Such a procedure of writing over is not uncommon. In the first movement of Mozart's Quartet in B-flat, K. 458, "Hunt," the developmental space begins with a buoyant, triadic theme not sounded in the exposition (mm. 91–106), an episode that is stabilized on an F major prolonged from the end of the exposition. With its cadence the mode shifts to minor and a second section of the development begins (mm. 106–34), one based on reiterations of rhythmic material from the second half of the exposition (mm. 42–70, itself marked by reiterations), and a brief retransition follows to prepare the recapitulation in m. 138. Instead of the usual rotational pattern {P + later material} we find {episode + later material}, suggesting that the episode has written over the expected P. In this case the preceding exposition had staged the difficulty of producing a "proper" second theme, stalling and stuttering at the expected MC point and finally converting into the second type of continuous exposition. (The exposition of K. 458/i is discussed in chapter 4.) The episode could be understood as "lost" S-rhetoric claiming its due, or providing needed "relief" in Tovey's sense, by writing over the more normative treatment of P at the beginning of the development.

Something similar occurs in the famously expanded A-flat episode that opens the development of the finale of Beethoven's Piano Sonata in F Minor, op. 2 no. 1. This episode, *sempre piano e dolce*, could hardly contrast more with the turbulent exposition, which has had barely

a moment to catch a breath and has grimly bypassed the mediant-major to end in a fatalistic dominant-minor. Here, too, we could imagine the surfacing of a stable, "lost" S (even in III) reminding us of what could have been (mm. 59–109), before it careens into P-material that has been all-too-long held in abeyance or written over into temporary but impatient silence. Here the pattern is {episode + P}, which suggests an episodic interpolation into developmental space, followed by a "half-rotational" process (P or P and TR only, as outlined in a separate section below) that before long brings us to the recapitulation.

The potential for one theme writing over a space normatively occupied by another is a central aspect of Sonata Theory. This approach attends not only to what happens acoustically in a piece—what we hear—but also to the things that we expect to happen that do not occur or that are kept from sounding. An individual piece exists primarily in dialogue with a complex array of norms and expectations. When an expectation is not realized, it may be blanked-out by something else, but in its absence it remains conceptually present. What writes over an expectation has a dual mode of existence. It exists as sound in its own right, and it exists as a replacement for something that is not happening, a something whose absence must be related to the substitute's presence. That which writes over has an interest in keeping that which is written over from being realized in acoustic sound; at the least it must be construed as having locally more pressing claims. What is absent is likely to be as important to the expressive content of the piece as what is present. It deserves to be equally noted and threaded into an interpretation of the work's meaning.

Obviously, some of what other commentators have viewed as a largely arbitrary process not susceptible to hermeneutics (Schoenberg's selection of themes "in any order") we would interpret as instances of writing over within a developmental-rotational norm. Such a claim is more defensible in situations where additional nonepisodic developmental material emerges to demonstrate an underlying basis in the rotational principle. If what succeeds the episode continues to confound a rotational understanding of the zone, then we are probably confronting a lower-level-default development—one that has abandoned any references to the more normative rotational conventions. Whether such a nonrotational development as a whole writes over the concept of a rotational one is a provocative issue that we shall not take up here.

C-Based Openings

It sometimes happens that a development begins with C material—an option endorsed by Galeazzi in 1796. We consider this a third-level default. In most cases what begins the development is not C^1 but reverberations of ideas from the end of C. These may last for only a brief span—almost as something of a transitional link, as in the first movement of Mozart's Symphony No. 39 in E-flat, K. 543, mm. 143–46, in this instance on the way to S-material, m. 147, and thence to more C-adaptations; or they may invade and occupy the entire development, as in the initial movements of Mozart's Piano Sonata in C, K. 545, and Beethoven's Piano Sonata in F, op. 10 no. 2, as well as in Beethoven's *Coriolan* Overture, op. 62.

When such C-openings do occur, they imply the presence of a strong "final" idea that captures and arrests our attention, one whose forcible gestures, still echoing, override the more standard appearance of P at this point. The psychology of each example is individual, and there may also be other reasons that the composer avoids the more normative sounding of P. If initial C-material eventually gives way to a succession of post-$P^{1.1}$-themes that would otherwise be considered rotational, C writes over P. In that case we confront a curious overlapping of rotational implications. On the one hand, the conceptual developmental rotation begins at the be-

ginning of the development, since the "absent" P may be understood as normatively launching that space. (Were P replaced merely by an episode, for example, we would still consider the developmental rotation to have begun.) On the other hand, the dogged persistence of the exposition's last-C suggests an extension of the ideas of the expositional rotation into developmental space. Thus at the moment of the development's C-launch we experience the presence of two conceptual rotations—the "normal" developmental one and the one produced by the trespassing of C-cadential material onto a space not its own, an encroachment beyond its customary borders. It is also possible to interpret developments that continue to be dominated by this material to have been entirely written over with the C-obsession. On the acoustic surface such a procedure would displace the sense of rotationality in the development, covering the entire span with a rhetorical extension of the end of the expositional rotation.

While C-launched developments normally center around the module heard at or near the close of the exposition, it may happen, though less frequently, that the *beginning* of C (C^1) becomes the object of concern. One celebrated instance seems to occur in the first movement of Haydn's Symphony No. 100 in G, "Military." But here we must be precise. The development actually begins with two unexpected bars of silence (mm. 125–26), surely standing for the absence of P, which has missed its cue. As if to relieve the discomfort and fill the empty space, the "popular-style" C^1 (which may alternatively be regarded as S^C)[20] re-enters in m. 127 on B-flat ($\flat$III, more immediately $\flat$VI of the preceding D) as pacifyingly bland, almost neutral material—an effect like being placed "on hold" today. However one interprets the situation, the

---

20. In this exposition an independent TR begins at m. 39 and produces a V:HC MC in m. 73, followed by two bars of CF. A P-based S begins at m. 75 and soon drives vigorously toward what promises to be the EEC at m. 93. Precisely on this downbeat, however, the PAC is subjected to strong attenuation: the upper voice drops out (evaded cadence) and the dynamics drop to *piano*. With all this evidence one might suspect EEC-deferral, but the theme that follows, m. 95, preceded by two full bars of preliminary accompaniment, seems as much

like a characteristically late-Haydnesque, "popular" C-theme as one can imagine. If one allows thematic character and the two bars of separational $C^{1.0}$ to be decisive, this theme will be considered C^1, preceded by an EEC-deformation; if the PAC-attenuation becomes primary, it will be considered S^C. Notice the almost perfectly parallel case in the first movement of Symphony No. 99 in E-flat, m. 71; and cf. that of Symphony No. 103 in E-flat, "Drumroll" (with a continuous exposition), m. 80.

silence at the development's opening provokes all that follows. It seems likely that C^1's first developmental appearance is triggered by those two bars of "nothing": in the exposition that theme had been preceded by two bars of $C^{1.0}$ accompanimental background (mm. 93–94, replicated also in mm. 127–28). Before long, of course (this being Haydn), C^1 sprouts into its own developmental elaborations (mm. 133ff) and comes to spread its tendrils to cover almost all of the development (mm. 125–201). The only exception occurs squarely in the middle, at m. 170, where, prompted by a pseudo-replication of the hammer-blows that had ended the exposition (mm. 168–69, now sounded on V/vi in the manner of an MC), the long-absent P-head-motive, which had also doubled as S, peeks in to inquire if it is too late (mm. 170–77, inscribing a falling-fifth motion that even touches on G major, I, in m. 177).[21] It is, apparently, and the remainder of the development reverts back to treatments of C^1 (S^C).

S-Based Openings

It may also happen that a development begins with the S-theme. This is less common than the above options, but it does occur. The reason for its infrequency has already been suggested: because of S's critical role in producing the EEC and ESC—the central generic demands of a sonata—it tends to be treated with more caution than the other, more "inert" modules. Additionally, S's characteristic, bustling, *dolce*, or lyrical tone might have been considered less dramatic, particularly to begin a development.

S-ideas are not often used as interpolations or substitutions at the outset of a developmental space that is otherwise fully or partially rotational. One exception is found in the first movement of Mozart's Quartet in A, K. 169, where a cadential figure from S ($S^{1.3}$, mm. 30–34) is inverted to begin the development (mm. 37–57)

before proceeding onward to P-material (mm. 58–72). Because the S-module selected is the concluding, cadential one (shoring up an evaded cadence at m. 30), the psychology here is akin to that of C-based developmental openings. Whatever its resonances with other patterns the result arrays the development in an {S, P} or {$S^{1.3}$, P} pattern. While one may understand $S^{1.3}$ as an interpolation—probably the best interpretation—taken at face value it gives the superficial impression of producing a reversal of the normative rotational expectation. In general, though, we are skeptical of pursuing the idea that a rotation, a forward-cycling principle, can arbitrarily reverse its course, like a clock-hand suddenly beginning to move backward. A similar situation occurs in the slow movement of Beethoven's Quartet in F, op. 59 no. 1.

Surely the most famous exception occurs in the first movement of Beethoven's *Eroica* Symphony. Perhaps for tacitly programmatic reasons the S^0 "questing" idea from mm. 45 (upbeat to m. 46, discussed in chapter 7) is used to launch the development proper at m. 166 (upbeat to m. 167), following a brief passage of aftermath-linkage from the end of the exposition. S^0 material will dominate much of the first portion of the development, but it first gives way to modulatory P-ideas (m. 178, soon thereafter with C-ideas as counterpoint!) and an MC-effect (V/IV, m. 220) before resuming (m. 221). While S^1 is missing, the remainder of the development, after m. 284 (upbeat to m. 285), is C^0- and C^1-referential (C^0 had been sounded in mm. 84–108). In sum, after the first S^0 statement (mm. 167–78) the development is rotational in implication.[22] Thus the S^0 opening is best regarded as an interpolation, perhaps with the implicit idea of "quest" or seeking the next battle brewing somewhere in the conceptual background, an engagement joined only with the arrival of P-material in m. 178.

From time to time S will dominate the entire

---

21. Alternatively, one could read m. 170 as an allusion to the P-based S, not to P itself. (Who could know?) If the reference at m. 170 is to P rather than to S, however, Haydn may be using the falling-fifths motion to allude subtly to the falling-fifth motion that, P-based, often begins developments.

22. The traditional view is that shared by Ratner, *Classic Music*, p. 228, which characterizes the development of the first movement of the *Eroica* as "[expositional] material freely rearranged."

development or will lead only to C, in which case P and TR will have been suppressed. These sometimes problematic situations are considered below, under "Half-Rotations: S–C?" In most instances part-2 or S-dominated developments can suggest a preoccupation with certain features or problems of S.

Developmental Rotation Types

Half-Rotations: P–TR

As has been mentioned, a fully rotational development opens with a reference to pre-MC material, modules from P and/or TR, followed by a treatment of post-MC material, moments from S and/or C. Here the presence of individual "representatives" from the first and second halves of the expositional materials implies that a full rotational cycle is being tracked through, even though several significant modules fail to appear. By no means, however, is a fully rotational development the only option. On the contrary, one of the most common strategies for the development is to base it on materials from only part 1 of the exposition, P and/or TR, presented in order. The development proceeds only so far with the rotation before it terminates to begin the recapitulation with a restart on P (in a Type 3, 4, or 5 sonata). These are obviously half-rotations, which we also refer to as *incomplete* or *blocked rotations*. Reflecting on their incompleteness is invariably a proper subject for hermeneutic interpretation. As discussed earlier ("Tonal Layout: The Development as a Whole"), the structural-dominant lock on V_A and the harmonic interruption at the end of a half-rotational development are the equivalents of the drive to and the accomplishment of the expositional MC. Examples are readily multiplied: the first movements of Mozart's Piano Sonata in C, K. 279; Quartet in C, "Dissonance," K. 465; Symphony No. 28 in C, K.200; Symphony No. 29 in A, K. 201; Symphony No. 35 in D, "Haffner," K. 385; Beethoven's Piano Sonata in A, op. 2 no. 2; Piano Sonata in G, op. 31 no. 1; and many others.

In minor-mode sonatas there are additional implications associated with this procedure. The first movements of Mozart's Symphony No. 40 in G Minor, K. 550, Beethoven's Piano Sonata in C Minor, op. 13, "Pathétique," and Symphony No. 5 in C Minor, op. 67, are paradigmatic. Expositions in minor usually move to major III for part 2, thereby creating a binary disparity between the minor-mode part 1 and the major-mode part 2. (Chapter 14 considers the larger expressive impact of this.) The subsequent presence of a stormy, blocked rotation in the developments—P and/or TR materials only—signifies that the development is dominated by the negative or fatalistic minor-mode materials of the exposition. Try as it might, the developmental space cannot burst through the MC point to include the equivalent of the major-mode S and C zones of the exposition. Such developments can become powerful representations of tension, of frustration, of hopes dashed.

Half-Rotations: S–C?

What are we to make of developments—such as that in the finale of Beethoven's Fifth Symphony—that do not refer to part 1 of the exposition, that are S- and/or C-dominated? On the one hand, these might be considered instances of nonrotational developments, since the hallmark of a rotational motion would be the re-beginning on or around P. This is certainly an acceptable view. On the other hand, there might be a rotational implication here. Such a development, for instance, might be understood as backing-up and recapturing the expositional rotation's part 2, which may have been problematic in some way. If so, then the putative half-rotation grounded in S keeps alive certain features of the expositional rotation in developmental space. Alternatively, we might imagine that within the development all of the more normative part-1 materials have been subjected to an ellipsis and missed out altogether. Under this interpretation the S or S–C half-rotation would unfold as a separate rotation in its own right. All of these things remain open questions. Whatever our preference, the sheer presence of a dominating S is the central thing. As proposed above, S is a specially privileged zone, one that has an important burden placed on it throughout the sonata.

Double Rotations

It may happen that a development is subdivisible into two cycles, each treating, in order, materials from the exposition's part 1 and part 2. The selected materials may be either the same or different, but they will be treated differently in the two developmental cycles. Sometimes the effect is that of a development beginning to wind down, then getting new life through the onset of yet another ("extra") rotation, as in the first movement of Beethoven's String Quartet in F, op. 59 no. 1 (first cycle, mm. 103–84, starting out as a feint toward an aborted expositional repeat [development proper at m. 112]; second cycle, beginning with a fugato, mm. 184–242; an unusual retransition follows, and the recapitulation proper begins at m. 254).

Another example of a double rotation occurs in the first movement of Mozart's Quartet in G, K. 387. Cycle 1, mm. 56–89, treats P- and C-materials, closing bleakly on an ominous vi:PAC. As if refusing to accept the minor-mode cadence, cycle 2, much briefer, mm. 90–100, reopens the discourse by returning to and making a different selection from P (cf. m. 3), touching on a fragment of S (m. 93; cf. m. 29 but also m. 2, the latter from P-space), and ending with the C-cadence-material that had also ended the first cycle, now brought to a V:PAC—an extremely uncommon occurrence within any development. As it happens, cycle 2's V:PAC, mm. 99–100, virtually replicates the end of the exposition, in a sense becoming identical with it. One again gets the impression of moving back the sonata clock, as if seeking to erase the already articulated presence of the development—the representation of a developmental discourse that extinguishes itself. A seven-bar RT leads to the recapitulation.

Because of the length produced, a double-rotational development is appropriate in extended or particularly ambitious compositions. It is possible, however, to find two briefer cycles, producing a highly efficient double rotation. This occurs in the opening movement of Haydn's Quartet in C, op. 33 no. 3, "Bird" (mm. 60–88, P and C; mm. 88–108, P and S).

Double or Triple Half-Rotations

One might imagine a situation in which one finds a double-cycle of P–TR–(MC). This suggests the presence of a double half-rotation—of a blocked rotation proceeding only so far, then rebeginning a second time. On the other hand, particularly if an MC-effect is also present, it might imply that the second cycle of the P–TR complex is writing over the expected S-space (or, more precisely, part-2 space) of a full rotation. The situation comes up in such works as the first movement of Beethoven's Symphony No. 1 in C Major, op. 21, whose opening was shown in example 10.4. Mm. 110–42 provide a perfect illustration of a rotational procedure passing through P, TR, new-dominant-lock (m. 130, V/♭III), and MC (m. 142, V/♭III). What one would expect, following two bars of caesura-fill, would be an allusion to S. But instead the development brings back P in E-flat, m. 144, suggesting the onset of another rotation. Still, the evidence here may be read in more than one way. Since the exposition's C was P-based, one could also construe m. 144 as an allusion to C, thus continuing the single rotation. (The P-based material shows affinities with both P and C.) In any event, S is omitted altogether—in itself not surprising—and the second "half-rotation," if that is our interpretation, proceeds, overwhelmingly P-based, through the end of the development.

More rare are the few instances of *triple* half-rotations (or subrotations) within the development: three cycles through a pattern that, normally, does not rise to the level of a full rotation. Examples may be found in the first movement of Mozart's Piano Concerto No. 20 in D Minor, K. 466, and in the B-flat slow movement of Beethoven's Symphony No. 6 in F, op. 68, "Pastoral."

Episodic Interpolations or Substitutes in the Center of the Developmental Space

If we are confronted with the developmental rhetorical (thematic) pattern {P, episode, TR, C} or, even more clearly, {P¹·¹, episode, P¹·², C}, it is difficult not to conclude that an episode has been wedged into an otherwise normative full-rotational development. Here it may be that the rotation has been momentarily stilled and that it resumes after that episode has concluded or dissolved back into it through common merging procedures. The central point would be to notice that the expositional elements that are there are present rotationally, in their originally presented order.

On the other hand, if we find such an ordering as {P, episode, S}, it is reasonable to suppose that the "special-character" episode has written over the expected rotational element (here TR), as a substitution for it. The episodic situations can become more (or less) complex depending on the rhetorical layout of the individual development. In a {P, episode} development, for instance—one that begins with the P-theme but goes on to developmental textures based on relatively new material before entering the retransition—one may be confronting a half-rotational development whose TR portion has been written over by a new episodic turn of events. This happens in the first movement of Mozart's Piano Sonata in B-flat, K. 333, with its *Sturm und Drang* episode beginning in m. 71.

Tonic-Centered Episodes

One would normally expect an episode to occupy one or more nontonic keys. Episodes that dwell largely in the tonic are rare, although the occasional example does turn up. One such case may be found in the first movement of Beethoven's Violin Sonata No. 4 in A Minor, op. 23. The development proceeds half-rotationally (P–TR), mm. 72–135, ending with a V_A lock and fermata-pause on the structural dominant (m. 135). At this point one presumes that the recapitulation will ensue. But instead a new, initially *piano* tarantella-idea springs forth, at first in the tonic key, A minor (as if usurping the recapitulation-P-theme's key), then shifts to D minor, and B-flat major (now with added crescendo) before returning to a brief V of A minor at m. 161. The recapitulation proper begins, more or less normally, in m. 164. Here the episode seems to be an interpolation at the expected "recapitulation point"—something willfully added (and bracketed off as an interpolation) at a moment where one has been led to anticipate something else. Although there was no requirement or expectation to do so, Beethoven sometimes brought back such expanded episodes in the coda, as happens here, in part because his longer codas contain passages that review events of the development.

The issue of tonic keys within developments has already been treated above and will return in the section below on the false-recapitulation effect. Visiting the tonic in the developmental space remained an available option for all relatively "inert" thematic material—that is, for all material except S, whose role and expectations elsewhere in EEC and ESC production discouraged any tonic-centered appearance of it—especially with the sense of a "new launch" within a rotation—in the developmental space (unless it was initiating the tonal resolution of a Type 2 sonata). Thus even while they are rare, tonic-centered episodes do not transgress a particularly strong norm, although all returns to the tonic after the exposition are significant and deserve to be addressed individually. The developmental space of Mozart's Overture to *Die Entführung aus dem Serail*, K. 384, is entirely occupied by the minor-mode of the tonic: see the discussion below on "slow-movement" episodes. And several decades later, the ever-surprising Berlioz, with his aesthetics of the *imprévu*, would fill the development of the *Corsair* Overture with an astonishingly long, harmonically static, tonic-key version of the lyrical theme from the introduction.

Introductory Material in Developments

It does not happen often in eighteenth-century music that material from the slow introduction returns within the developmental space. When it does, it gives the impression of rebeginning a rotation not from the expositional point but from a point preceding the onset of P. The rotational principle will have been expanded in such a way as to include {introduction + exposition} within its conceptual framework.

This is why references to and fragmentary returns of slow introductions can occur as abrupt interpolations at the beginnings of developments, such as in Mozart's Overture to *Die Zauberflöte* and in the first movement of

Beethoven's Sonata in C Minor, op. 13, "Pathétique." In the case of the *Flute* the gateway portals of the Adagio return, m. 97, to provide a solemn entry into the largely P-based development proper and are not heard again for the rest of the piece. In the case of the "Pathétique" the tragic C-minor, *grave* incipit is the unshakable condition that provides a prelaunch (m. 133) to the half-rotational development and to the coda (m. 295), though not to the recapitulation. In these instances while the large-rotational concept {introduction + exposition} governs the initial two rotations, there seems to be an understanding that it can be discarded at the recapitulation. A slightly different arrangement may be found in the opening movement of Beethoven's early Piano Sonata in F Minor, WoO 47 no. 2, first movement (from ca. 1783), in which the introduction returns only to provide an entry into the recapitulation. The same procedure—slow introduction before the recapitulation—may be found in a few piano sonatas of Clementi, such as the single movement of the Piano Sonata in C, op. 22 no. 3 (1788); and the second movement of the Sonata in B Minor, op. 40 no. 2 (1802).[23] Other types of returns are considered in chapter 13.

Particularly inventive is the idea of concluding a development by merging into a renotated version of the slow introduction—something not always clearly visible to the eye but readily recognizable to the ear. This suggests that a large rotation, including introduction, is being overlapped with the conclusion of the development, binding together the developmental and recapitulatory spaces. An early example may be found in the first movement of Mozart's Serenade in D major, K. 320, "Posthorn" (1779). At the end of the development the opening Adagio returns, slightly recomposed, without tempo change: Mozart notates this "unusual feature," as Neal Zaslaw put it, "by doubling the note values so that a semibreve in allegro equals a crotchet in adagio."[24] Much the same situation occurs in Schubert's Symphony No. 1 in D, D. 82 (1813).

Eventually the idea arose of basing the entire developmental space on the material from the slow introduction or P^0 parallel. This can produce a Type 3 sonata that is fundamentally double-rotational, with two grand cycles of its {introduction or P^0 + exposition} pattern; the second cycle, of course, encompasses the development and recapitulation. Such a strategy was especially attractive to Schubert. The development of the first movement of Symphony No. 5 in B-flat, D. 485, grows entirely out of the exposition's $P^{1.0}$ figure. Similarly, that of Symphony No. 8 in B Minor, "Unfinished," D. 759, is based upon the preceding exposition's P^0 idea. In both cases development and recapitulation are conceived together as a single large rotation. The basic idea would reappear later in the nineteenth century, in Berlioz, for instance, as suggested in the previous section, but also in the sonata structures of Bruckner.[25]

"Slow-Movement" Episodes within Allegro-Tempo Movements (or Slow Movement as Development)

One sometimes comes across a development in a first movement or in an overture that contains a significant amount of contrasting, slow-movement music, as if a space or gap, a comparatively static center, had been opened up in the otherwise Allegro movement (which will resume its activity at or near the recapitulation point). The *locus classicus* occurs in Mozart's C-major, *presto* Overture to *Die Entführung aus dem Serail*, K. 384, whose developmental space, mm. 119–32, is completely occupied by a C-minor (tonic-minor) slow movement, in this case a mi-

23. Cf. Leon Plantinga, *Clementi: His Life and Music* (London: Oxford University Press, 1977), pp. 129, 181. The first movement of the Sonata in G Minor, op. 34 no. 2, provides a similar example, but in this case the movement is more structurally complicated, featuring something on the order of a "double recapitulation" that merges features of a Type 2 and a Type 3 sonata. Cf. also Plantinga, pp. 170–73.

24. Zaslaw, *Mozart's Symphonies: Context, Performance Practice, Reception* (Oxford: Oxford University Press, 1989), p. 357. Also curious is that the movement lacks an expositional repeat.

25. Darcy, "Bruckner's Sonata Deformations," *Bruckner Studies*, ed. Timothy L. Jackson and Paul Hawkshaw (Cambridge: Cambridge University Press, 1997), pp. 256–77.

nor-mode variant of the first aria in the opera-to-come, Belmonte's "Hier soll ich dich denn sehen, Konstanze." The pattern produced is: exposition — slow movement — recapitulation. (Mozart also first conceived the Overture to *Le nozze di Figaro* along these general lines, then changed his mind and deleted the slow middle section, thereby producing a Type 1 sonata.) A generally similar example, though with brief passages leading in and out of the central slow episode, occurs in Beethoven's *Leonore* Overture No. 1, op. 138.

Other works, such as the first movement of Haydn's Symphony No. 45 in F-sharp Minor ("Farewell"), the finale of Haydn's Symphony No. 67 in F, and the *whole* of Mozart's Symphony No. 32 in G, K. 318, interpolate slow movements or extended slow passages within the development, and a brief, slow episode is also featured in the center of Weber's *Euryanthe* Overture. The plan of Mozart's Symphony No. 32 is especially instructive. The three-movement symphony as a whole is a Type 2 sonata (the "binary" type of sonata with a tonal reprise beginning with S). A "normal," in-tempo development, much of it P-based, stretches from m. 70 to m. 109, pausing on V_A and followed by a fermata. At this point a full recapitulation could follow. Instead we find a G-major (tonic) Andante episode unfolded at length that eventually jump-starts back into the rapid Tempo I and rejoins the referential rotation only midway through to create a "third movement" that also contains the tonal resolution of a Type 2 sonata. (From another perspective, the Andante could be heard as a substitution for P in the recapitulation.)

To place such slow-movement interpolations into a historical context, one needs to be aware of the mid-eighteenth-century tradition of what Jan LaRue has called the *da capo overture* or *da capo symphony* (sometimes also called a *reprise overture*).[26] In this not-uncommon mid-century subgenre, a three-movement *overture symphony* (or *sinfonia*, usually a light, brief work, fast–slow–fast) had its "normal" final movement (often a minuet earlier in the century) replaced by a full or partial reprise of the first movement. The model apparently goes back at least to such works as Reinhard Keiser's Overture to *Croesus* (1730) and Leonardo Leo's Overture to *L'Olimpiade* (1737).[27] In early examples the initial, fast movement sometimes contained a full rounded-binary structure ("sonata") with reprise — only the final part of which was redundantly alluded to in the final (third) movement. Variants, however, were certainly possible.

This procedure must have seemed an archaism in the "serious music" emerging in Austro-Germanic regions around 1800, and yet it would be reconceptualized and take on a new life and significance in future decades. The eighteenth-century procedure of interpolating a slow-movement episode within a developmental space is the most likely source for nineteenth-century "double-function" sonatas (or "multimovement works in a single movement"), as famously in Liszt's Piano Sonata in B Minor, several of his symphonic poems, the tone poems of Richard Strauss, the early works of Schoenberg, and so on.

The "False-Recapitulation Effect"

One much-discussed possibility within developments is that of the so-called false recapitulation. This is the "deceptive" sounding of what

---

26. The concept, though not the term, is included in the substantial revision of the *New Grove* entry, Jan LaRue and Eugene K. Wolf, "Symphony. I 18th Century," *The New Grove Dictionary of Music and Musicians*, 2nd ed. 24:815: "In a further variant [of 'exposition-recapitulation' form], a slow movement may be inserted between the two sections. . . . The latter procedure is, in turn, one version of a da capo or related cycle in which some or all of the first movement returns after the slow movement. Such designs are found in opera overtures throughout the period and occur from time to time in concert symphonies." Cf. the similar terms in Rudolf von Tobel, *Die Formenwelt der klassischen Instrumentalmusik* (Bern and Leipzig: Paul Haupt, 1935), pp. 50–52. For "reprise overture" see the extended discussion in Stephen Carey Fisher, "Haydn's Overtures and Their Adaptations as Concert Orchestral Works," Diss. University of Pennsylvania, 1985 (Section, "The Reprise Overture," pp. 40–41, 57–66).

27. See the discussion in Helmut Hell, *Die Neapolitanische Opernsinfonie in der ersten Hälfte des 18. Jahrhunderts* (Tutzing: Schneider, 1971), esp. pp. 242–43.

might at first be mistakenly taken for the on-set of the recapitulation, the relaunching of the P-idea in a manner more or less parallel with that heard in the exposition: "a seemingly mis-leading statement of the main theme in the tonic as if the return were at hand," as James Webster described it with reference to Haydn, "followed by further development and, eventually, the true return (Haydn, String Quartet op. 17 no. 1, bars 62, 76)."[28] Other often-cited examples—which are open to challenge and capable of other in-terpretations—include Haydn's Symphonies No. 41 in C, first movement (m. 97); No. 48 in C, "Maria Theresia," finale (m. 79); No. 55 in E-flat, first movement (m. 97); and No. 91 in E-flat, first movement (m. 146). Setting up and articulating a tonic-P somewhere in the first third of the development (the location proves to be crucial), then aborting it for further, more extended development, seems to have been a Haydn quirk in the years around 1770. Rather than being considered a standard option within sonatas in general it might be more accurate to view it in these terms. (Mozart's occasional off-tonic adaptations of it will be considered in due course.)

The problems swirling around this topic are numerous and vexing. Writers have elaborated differing criteria for what constitutes a genuine false recapitulation. Bonds, for example—who wrote a 1988 doctoral dissertation on the topic, one that classifies different kinds of recapitu-lation effects—considered only P-statements in the tonic to qualify as false recapitulations, since he regarded only those as capable of sat-isfying the "criterion" of "the connotation of surprise on the part of the listener."[29] Rosen's *Sonata Forms* had been slightly more inclusive: "If a reprise is not in the tonic (or the subdom-inant), it fools only the uneducated."[30] In the *New Grove* article on "Sonata Forms"—and its revision—Webster wrote that "in [Haydn's] later years, the false recapitulation may appear in a foreign key (Haydn, Symphony no. 102 [first movement], bar 185)," and the same view was held by Caplin.[31] Complicating the mat-ter further, Peter A. Hoyt has recently argued that the false recapitulation is for the most part a spurious concept peculiar only to "modern," ahistoric concepts of sonata form.[32]

Beyond the mere definition of what is to count as a false recapitulation—assuming for the moment that it does designate a phenom-enon worth noting as such—Bonds also as-sembled other observations about it. After a painstaking inventory of hundreds of pieces, he reported that "Haydn . . . appears to have been virtually alone in his use of the [tonic] false re-capitulation. An unsystematic review of works by his contemporaries reveals no other com-posers who employed the technique. . . . The technique was clearly not widespread." (Recall again that Bonds did not regard the occasional false-recapitulation effect on the subdominant, as sometimes in Mozart, to meet his criterion.) The idea was a preoccupation of Haydn during the so-called *Sturm und Drang* years of 1768–74: it is found primarily in "the late 1760s and early 1770s." Although "Haydn occasionally reverts to the false recapitulation in a few later works . . . on the whole, false recapitulations in the later years are comparatively rare." In addition, "false recapitulations appear only in sympho-nies and string quartets, traditionally the most intellectually demanding categories of instru-mental music." And he noted the consistency of "the restriction of the false recapitulation to fast movements—first movements and finales."[33] Bonds's list of genuine false recapitulations ex-tends only to seventeen movements by Haydn:

28. Webster, "Sonata Form," *The New Grove Dictionary of Music and Musicians*, 2nd ed., ed. Stanley Sadie (Lon-don: Macmillan, 2001), 23:693.

29. Bonds, "Haydn's False Recapitulations and the Per-ception of Sonata Form in the Eighteenth Century," p. 229.

30. Charles Rosen, *Sonata Forms*, rev. ed., p. 282.

31. James Webster, "Sonata Form," 23:693; William L. Caplin, *Classical Form*, pp. 159, 277 nn. 58 and 59. See

also the summary in Elaine Sisman, *Mozart: The "Jupi-ter" Symphony*, pp. 50–52.

32. Hoyt, "Haydn's 'False Recapitulations,' Late Eigh-teenth-Century Theory, and Modern Paradigms of So-nata Form." Much of the subsequent discussion is di-rectly indebted to Hoyt's analysis and examples.

33. Bonds, "Haydn's False Recapitulations," pp. 343, 321, 342, 317, 320.

twelve within symphonies, five within quartets.[34]

The Continuum of Haydn's "False-Recapitulation Effect"

At stake in all of this is the question of surprise, the degree to which Haydn intended the listener to be misled with such a tonic-P-statement. As emphasized earlier, it was common to begin a development with brief, parallel statements of P-material {P, P}, the first in the dominant, the second in the tonic. The familiar principle of descending fifths could be expanded or altered by beginning higher {V/vi, vi, ii, V, I; or +4, +3, +2, +1, 0} or lower {I, IV; or 0, −1}. In addition, the first P could be written over with other material. In all cases, the early appearance of a tonic-P was not to be mistaken for a deceptive recapitulation. Even though the technique has been erroneously and unfortunately labeled as a "premature reprise," there is nothing recapitulatory about it.[35] It is standard practice. Claims on behalf of Haydn's presumed tonic-key false recapitulations, which usually occur in the first third of the development, must distinguish them from the otherwise unremarkable "premature-reprise" effect. In most cases this is not easy to do.

It is on these grounds that Hoyt, contending with most existing views of the false recapitulation, launches his counterargument. Hoyt insists that any such developmental, generally early return to the tonic (he calls it the "medial return") was normative within eighteenth-century and early nineteenth-century sonatas, as several theorists of the time noted. He then asks us to imagine that Haydn, around 1768–74, became interested in subjecting such unremarkable early developmental tonics (sounding P) to a playful variation. This variation consisted of altering their surroundings: preparing the tonic-P by different harmonies, leading to it

with substitutional, non-P material, preceding it with a fermata or other break of articulation, expanding the material that precedes the tonic-P, and so on. None of these things, he argues, jeopardize the normative "medial return" status of the tonic-P, and he provides several examples to buttress his point. Hoyt's claim, then, is that for the most part the false recapitulation is a concept that the eighteenth century would not have recognized as such. What seems notable to us — what we tend to regard as a baiting of our recapitulatory expectations — might not have struck pre-1800 listeners as anything but a clever adaptation of business as usual.

There is much to commend this argument. And even though when defended too ardently it courts overstatement, it alters at a stroke the way that the "false-recapitulation effect" is to be investigated. The heart of its logic is that it is unwise or impossible to determine precisely at what point a blithely normative tonic-P, either preceded by non-P material or differing harmonies, or pushed incrementally later and later into developmental space, turns into something that is more unusual, something intended to deceive its listeners into construing it as the start of a recapitulation. Questions of this sort surround all of the standard instances of Haydn's false-recapitulation effects. And yet in the most difficult cases it is counterintuitive to suggest that at least *some* sort of intended wit or deception was not involved in the tonic-return of P, even though that explanation alone does not suffice to explain all of the implications at hand. The situation becomes even more challenging when one considers "off-tonic" false-recapitulation effects, as famously in Mozart's D-major Overture to *Don Giovanni*, K. 527 (m. 141, P in G, IV) and the first movements of Mozart's Symphony No. 41, K. 551, "Jupiter" (m. 161, P in F, IV) and Haydn's Symphony No. 102 in B-flat (m. 185, P in C, II), to all of which we shall return.

---

34. Bonds, "Haydn's False Recapitulations," p. 316. These are: Symphonies No. 11/ii; 36/iv; 22/ii; 38/iv; 48/iv; 41/i; 43/i; 42/i; 46/i; 55/i; 71/i; 91/i; and Quartets op. 17/1/i; op. 20/4/i; op. 50/1/iv; op. 54/3/iv; op. 77/1/i. False recapitulations are distinguished from "precursory recapitulations" (the "premature reprise"

effect early in the development, not a recapitulation at all) and "disjunct recapitulations" (the "premature reprise" effect coupled with the later onset of the recapitulation with a later part of P, as if the elements of P had been split apart by a developmental interpolation).

35. See n. 14.

How can we navigate through this dilemma? The first thing to acknowledge is the hermeneutic weakness of the term "false recapitulation." It is a mere label, claiming nothing more than the registering of a momentary personal deception. By itself it explains nothing about the piece. Instead, it is one of a collection of handy terms more often used to short-circuit analytical thought, as if identifying a developmental moment as a false recapitulation provides a sufficient explanation of that event and licenses us to move on to something else. Instead, sensing the potentially false-recapitulation flavor of an individual spot—whether or not we later revise our estimation (as may often happen)—should draw our attention to that moment as a site of compositional and hermeneutic complication. In turn that should open the passage up to question, not close it down. Why is this effect placed here? How might it play into existing or future rotational implications? Which passage, exactly, is being alluded to? How might this affect the recapitulation-to-come?

The next order of business is to discard the idea that we need to declare whether any given developmental tonic-appearance of P is or is not a false recapitulation. This is not a matter to decide as a binary opposition, in which the only permissible answers are yes or no. The reality is that we may confront a potential false-recapitulation effect in varying strengths, along a continuum—and to which different individuals, with different awarenesses of the historical background, can have different reactions. At the weak end of the scale is the normative "premature reprise" {P in V, P in I}, which should have no recapitulatory implication. At the strong end of the scale, at least hypothetically, would be absolutely unequivocal, mid- or late-developmental "deceptions." Haydn's tonic-P effects usually fall somewhere in the weak-to-middle range of this scale.

The question may be reframed thus: assuming that the simplest situation, that of the "premature reprise" {P in V, P in I}, has no false-recapitulation character, what kinds of additive factors does Haydn use that might be understood as providing an increased degree of the false-recapitulation effect? Seven questions may be asked of any such possible effect.

1. How far into the development is it? If it occurs only within the first third of the development—as is generally the case with Haydn—then it can only be, at best, a weak instance of the false-recapitulation effect. Still, if the tonic-P is pushed considerably past the first phrase (that is, if tonic-P is preceded by more material than is expected), the effect will be strengthened.

2. Is the initial phrase of the development, which normatively articulates the dominant as the first element of a {V, I} descent to the tonic, replaced by some other harmonic motion? If so, the effect might be strengthened. A mere backing-up of the circle of fifths to provide the descent downward from a higher position {+3, +2, +1, 0} would not provide a significant enhancement in the false-recapitulation direction, since the convention of descending fifths would be preserved. Haydn frequently, however, replaces the initial dominant with a phrase that lingers on or moves to V/vi (+ 4 in the circle-of-fifths cycle) (more rarely, V/iii, +5), then leads directly into a *nonelided* tonic-P. This means that the tonic-P is not prepared by its own "proper" dominant and emerges out of the substitutional V/vi →I motion. This progression might have a slightly stronger false-recapitulation effect when used in combination with other factors (although, as mentioned earlier, the "real" recapitulation may also begin with this substitute for V_A).

3. Does either a fermata or a brief passage of linear fill (one or two bars) separate the V/vi (or V/iii) from the ensuing tonic-P? The act of pause or separation sets off P as a more emphatic rebeginning, possibly inviting more of a dialogue with false-recapitulation characteristics.

4. Is the tonic-P, on the other hand, set up by its "proper" dominant (V_A of I), perhaps even locking onto it a few bars in advance and/or separated from the tonic-P by a break or passage of fill? If so, this more typically prerecapitulatory behavior would enhance the effect, even in relatively early portions of the development.

5. Is the harmonic motion prior to the P-tonic more complex than either a mere dominant or a brief motion to V/vi? The more harmonic complexity encountered before the tonic-P, the further we move down the continuum into a more pronounced false-recapitulation effect.

6. Is melodic material other than P heard before the tonic-P? If not, then the piece has little of the false-recapitulation effect, remaining more likely to be heard as a variant of the simplest kind of "premature reprise" {P, P}. If on the other hand we hear not-P at the outset of the development, there are sliding degrees of implication. The weakest would be a mere pre-P retention of material that closes the exposition (a standard interpolation or writing-over effect). The next strongest would be the substitution of an episode or new material. Even stronger would be the sounding of S-ideas, since this would begin to challenge the notion of developmental rotation. The strongest would probably be the decision to begin with P, then to leave it behind — proceeding past P in the developmental rotation — then to return to it for the sounding of tonic-P. Here the impression is that a full rotation, however compressed, has been passed through and that a new one is starting.

7. How literal is the tonic-P-reference? Is it really a reference to P^1, or is it a variant — or possibly a reference to the TR-restatement of P? Obviously, the more identical, the more potential for the false-recapitulation effect.

By these lights, the mere combination of a relatively brief, initial V/vi on P-material coupled with a fermata or short linear link to a tonic statement of P would produce a weak false-recapitulation effect, although one stronger than that of a mere "premature reprise." This would include the first movements of Haydn's Symphonies No. 42 in D, No. 43 in E-flat, No. 46 in B, and the finale of the Quartet in E, op. 54 no. 3. Somewhat stronger would be the same harmonic motion through V/vi but the replacement of initial P-material with reverberating ideas from the exposition's close, as in the first movement of Symphony No. 71 — and in this case the pre-tonic-P material extends for a full twenty-one measures, including a prominent V/vi dominant lock and appended two-bar link. Perhaps similar in strength might be the first movement of the Quartet in D, op. 20 no. 4, whose pre-tonic-P strategy extends P-material over eighteen bars on two sequential planes,

V/ii and V/iii, followed by a three-bar link to the tonic-P.

Moving beyond these relatively standard combinations can produce a more robust false-recapitulation effect, while also remaining in dialogue with the norm of an early tonic-P in the development. The finale of the Quartet in B-flat, op. 50 no. 1, the first movement of Symphony No. 41 in C, and the finale of Symphony No. 48 in C all precede the tonic-P with its own dominant — sometimes with an elaborate setup — rather than V/vi. Moreover, the Quartet interpolates TR material before P (this is a Type 3 sonata, but it has the notion of rondo-returns on its mind); Symphony No. 41 alludes to S-material at some length, and its reference to P in the tonic seems only to be to the TR-version of it; and Symphony No. 48 seems to allude to TR⇒FS material (linear chromatic motion) before returning to P in the tonic.

Even stronger would be a lengthier passage of pre-tonic-P music with more complex thematic or harmonic elements. The two most suggestive cases occur in the first movements of Symphonies Nos. 55 and 91, both in E-flat. No. 55 is Rosen's touchstone case for the false recapitulation, and it features an initial statement of P in more than one key, then a digression away from P — an important complicating feature — and a subsequent return to it in the tonic.[36] In addition, the whole of the harmonically clever pre-tonic-P music extends for some thirty measures — thus tonic-P surfaces some 36 percent of the way into the development (very late to be considered a mere postponement) — and may include an additional, if fleeting, "premature-reprise" effect early on. No. 91 also features a long stretch of pre-tonic-P music: some twenty-six bars of it, perhaps about 37 percent of the development, although the recapitulation moment is anything but fully clear. In addition, the thematic pattern of this music is {C, P [wrong key], C, P [proper key]}, suggesting the possibility of having moved through a full or nearly full rotation before lighting upon a brief allusion to P in the tonic, albeit without strong harmonic preparation.

---

36. Rosen, *Sonata Forms*, rev. ed., pp. 276–80.

Haydn's false-recapitulation effects, especially in the years around 1770, are predominantly in dialogue with the convention of an early tonic statement of P, as Hoyt argues. From this perspective they are not to be regarded as "false recapitulations" *tout court*. On the other hand, in varying degrees of transformation, Haydn also plays secondarily with this convention in ways that are also mildly in dialogue with certain kinds of recapitulatory treatments. We thus have a mixed situation in differing degrees of strength, with only the strongest instances—Symphonies No. 55 and 91—beginning to approach the traditional view of a false recapitulation.

The Off-Tonic False-Recapitulation Effect

Although nearly all of Haydn's false-recapitulation effects occurred in the tonic, it was also theoretically possible to reproduce something of that effect at a nontonic pitch level. The most obvious choice here would be the subdominant, since it was at least conceivable that a recapitulation could begin on IV instead of on I. (See chapter 12 on the subdominant recapitulation.) In a rare, early instance Haydn presented an early-P in IV that seems to have something of this effect. This occurred in the finale of Symphony No. 50 in C (1773): the subdominant-P on F (m. 88) sounds much like a recapturing of the piece's opening; it occurs twenty-one measures into the development; it is preceded by other treatments of P-material, as is normative; and its immediately preceding dominant is a seven-bar lock on V/ii (V of vi of F). In the context of the pieces mentioned in the above section, this would appear to be yet another adaptation, in this case a subdominant variant.

Here it is the recognizable setup for and similarity of P-in-IV to the opening that makes all the difference. Obviously, new rotations of P—or new statements of P—can begin at various points in a development, and very few of them would be considered candidates for the false-recapitulation effect. Our examples of the category of double-rotations earlier in this chapter, for instance (the first movements of Mozart's Quartet in G, K. 387, and Beethoven's Quartet in F, op. 59 no. 1), would clearly not

qualify, since the P-elements launching their second rotations do not replicate the character of P either at the beginning of the exposition or at the beginning of a P-based TR.

Particularly interesting, though, are Mozart's relatively few adaptations of the false-recapitulation effect, the most notable cases of which also appear in the subdominant. One is the Overture to *Don Giovanni*, in which the first part of the development extends some twenty measures, from m. 121 to m. 140. The twenty-bar span—probably an acceptable length for a development within an overture (recall that *Figaro* had had none)—is based on the exposition's TM^3. (The exposition, setting out from the tonic D major, had been marked by apparent double MCs: I:HC, m. 55, followed by a vigorous TM^1 in the dominant, though perhaps not a fully acceptable S; and V:HC, m. 76, followed by TM^3 in the dominant, more likely to be heard as the "real" S; the EEC had occurred at m. 99, leading to twenty-two bars of closing material.) A circle-of-fifths motion on TM^3 leads us, mm. 133–41, through chords on B, E, A, and D, all to be heard as local dominants, finally landing in m. 141 on the G-level, IV, for the return of P in the subdominant, m. 141.

From the standpoint of proportion and rotation, the subdominant P-return in the Overture to *Don Giovanni* arrives at a sufficient point—beginning a new rotation—to suggest the possibility of a recapitulation, and its temporary similarity to the exposition's opening only underscores this. On the other hand, given the proportion of the remainder of the development, some fifty more bars, the P-in-IV effect occurs relatively early on, only around 29 percent of the way through, although we learn this only in retrospect. Perhaps most important, the subdominant's dominant (D, mm. 139–40) is not really interrupted in the usual manner of the V_A at the end of a development—it merely falls another notch onto G—and the circle-of-fifths motion preceding the return of P remains characteristic of early developmental strategies (along the circle-of-fifth chain from B to G, +3, +2, +1, 0, −1). Again, we have a mixed case, one aspect tilting toward the adaptation of conventional procedures, especially via the descending fifths, another aspect moving mildly, though anything but conclusively, in the direction of the false-recapitulation effect. Mozart was probably playing on this ambiguity.

A second famous instance—and a more complicated one—occurs in the first movement of the Symphony No. 41 in C, K. 551, "Jupiter." Here not only does the "false" P-in-IV (m. 161) occur at a later point in the development (in m. 41 of a sixty-nine-bar development, thus about 60 percent of the way through), but the preparation for the mid-developmental P-return in IV is made more explicit than had been the case with *Don Giovanni*. The initial portion of the development, mm. 121–60—even broader in span than that of *Don Giovanni*—is preoccupied with a *buffa*-tune that had been unexpectedly interpolated toward the end of the exposition (an extract, as it happens, from the separately composed arietta, "Un bacio di mano," K. 541). This first-development empties out onto a dominant-lock, V of A minor, mm. 153–7, which Elaine Sisman accurately described as a "false retransition."[37] The V/a (V/iii of F) is then mediated through intervening chords, mm. 157–60, to a supposed P-return in F (IV), though only *piano*, at m. 161.

All of this may have been intended to produce a false-recapitulation effect—or at least to make one wonder significantly about that possibility—even though, upon further examination, the P-return is actually the return of the dissolving consequent that had begun TR back in m. 24, and even though the reprise-effect soon merges back into development. To be sure, one could argue that the extended "Bacio di mano" development had written over the antecedent of P within a developmental half-rotation (and somewhere in the deep background of this development such a conception might be lurking), but the more obvious local effect is that of momentary deception, at least provoking

one to consider whether this might not be, in fact, the onset of the recapitulatory rotation.

Finally, we might mention the unusual and instructive case provided by late Haydn in the first movement of the Symphony No. 102 in B-flat. Here the development stretches from m. 111 to m. 226—an extraordinarily long span, more than two dozen bars longer than the eighty-eight-bar exposition. Mm. 111–84 provide a development dominated by materials from the latter portions of the exposition, now treated at considerable length and contrapuntal rigor, although early on one also hears a sounding of P on IV (m. 117). In short, the development is fully rotational up through m. 184. In addition, its length is adequate up to this point; and it ends with a V_A lock (here, V of C minor, V/ii, mm. 181–83) and stops dead with an expectant fermata, m. 184. All the conventional signals—except for the proper key—are in place for a normative recapitulation. Although the key is "wrong," the recapitulatory rotation certainly seems to begin in C major (II) at m. 185 (with the flute carrying the P-melody; cf. the flute at m. 31) before being stopped in its tracks with a *fortissimo* outburst at m. 192 ("No!"), which leads to more development and a preparation for the seemingly "real" recapitulation at m. 227. The off-tonic false-recapitulation effect on II, calculated in retrospect, occurs late in the game, about 65 percent of the way through, though at the moment of its sounding it is perfectly placed for the arrival of a normal recapitulation.

One last curious feature of this case is worth mentioning. The recapitulation proper, at m. 227, begins with the equivalent of the second statement of P in the exposition (mm. 31–38), moving directly into TR. The exposition, however, had begun with a non-normative double-statement of P (mm. 23–30; 31–38, *forte* and *piano*). In some respects the *piano*, flute-led

37. Sisman, *Mozart: The "Jupiter" Symphony*, p. 52. "Thus, what is critical here is that a recapitulation is *expected*, not that the listener is momentarily misled when it appears. . . . What is false here—what misleads the listener—is really the retransition, since there is palpably no recapitulation." This is because the "off-tonic statement of the main theme [P] . . . *immediately* announces itself as suspiciously unlike what a real reca-

pitulation would be." Sisman considers the Overture to *Don Giovanni*, which lacks this false retransition, as a "reprise-interlude" (p. 51), another type of off-tonic appearance of the main theme within developments. In this case there is only a "little preparation" for "a reasonably complete thematic statement . . . that in scoring resembles the opening."

false-recapitulation effect at m. 185 may stand for the first of these P-statements, with dynamics and orchestration reversed, while the "real" recapitulation at m. 227 may stand for the second. This suggests an alternative interpretation, namely that m. 185 initiated an off-tonic recapitulatory rotation (see chapter 12), one locally aborted by an emphatic interruption and readjusted preparation for the proper tonic recapitulation, which then takes off with the P-restatement, now *forte*. Thus late or very late false-recapitulation effects might also be in dialogue with the concept of off-tonic launches to the recapitulatory rotation.

The main feature of a false-recapitulation effect, in whatever degree of persuasiveness it might be experienced, involves the invitation to assume inaccurately that the recapitulatory rotation has begun or at least may be beginning. Through any number of immediate or subsequent signals, however, that music soon "changes its mind"—revokes that implication—and goes on to some other characteristic feature of developmental activity. In terms of the sonata "narrative" at hand, the implication may be revoked for any number of reasons: tonal, textural, proportional, witty, and so on. Each case represents a strong articulation within the development section, and one needs to ask why the composer would have wished to put it there.

Interpreting Developments: Models for Analysis

Sonata Theory does not suggest a single best way to analyze development sections, although the issue of developmental rotations and dialogues with the rotational principle is its most characteristic contribution in this area. Rather than restrict ourselves to only this point, we emphasize the diversity of developments and the need to approach each one individually. What is required is an imaginative, flexible approach to these matters. We encourage interactions between the various available differing methods of development analysis. Each method may be considered a single "lens" (or hermeneutic genre) through which one could interpret what happens in a development. A deeper un-derstanding of any given development emerges when one is open to several different analytical systems, or when many of them are used together. Hence our preference for an interactive approach, within which attention to certain kinds of techniques or observations might seem more appropriate in one development, others in others.

Topical Dramas: The Ordering of Established Rhetorical "Topics"

Styles of analysis stemming from the work of Leonard G. Ratner (including recent work by Wye J. Allanbrook, Kofi Agawu, Elaine Sisman, and others) emphasize the identifying and labeling of musical "topics," styles," and characteristic "rhetorical" figures within melodic textures and musical material. These include noting such things as various dance topics, "singing" style, learned style, hunt and march (including funeral march) topics, *Sturm und Drang*, and so on. Assuming that the musical materials of the exposition can be helpfully identified in this way, it may be that the ordered arrangement of topical/rhetorical modules in the development produce an implied topical drama or narrative trajectory as one module proceeds to the next (or responds to what has preceded it). One should be aware of the implicit or metaphorical (poetic/programmatic) readings that such a dramatic ordering makes possible—especially when this developmental ordering is placed in juxtaposition with the implications of that of the exposition.

Sequence-Blocks: The Ratz-Caplin Model

One of the most common developmental procedures consists of the deployment of model-sequence patterns—sequence-blocks—often based on thematic material from the exposition. Several sequence-blocks, based on differently sized models, may appear in succession or be interspersed with other material. Typically dramatized as a central part of the developmental action, these procedures are sometimes led into with preparatory material. Such sequence-blocks take on a variety of expressive purposes depending both on the nature of the materials selected and on the particular disposition of those materials within the development. The tonal levels visited, the expansion and eventual fragmentation of the blocks, and so on, are central aspects of the whole process.

The importance of such sequences was central to the mid-twentieth-century attempt by Erwin Ratz to devise a fundamental three-part *Grundschema* or background plan supposedly guiding many or most developments of this period—a kind of conceptual master plan behind individualized developmental logic.[38] The Ratz model, first offered in 1951, has recently been revived, adapted, and expanded by Caplin in 1998.[39] Each proposed: (1) an *introductory section* of various types (for Caplin, this is the *pre-core*, which may exemplify a variety of procedures); (2) a central *core* (the term is from Ratz's *Kern der Durchführung*) involving primarily sequence blocks and their eventual liquidation or fragmentation, eventually arriving onto an active V (Caplin's "core" is specific with regard to the size of the "relatively large model" for these sequences, a "relatively long unit, normally four to eight measures");[40] and (3) a *retransition* leading the development to the recapitulation, normally through a pedal point on the dominant.

This is not the place to enter into a technical review of this concept. The Ratz-Caplin models call attention to the presence of the commonly encountered initial introduction (sometimes a link from the preceding exposition), some sense of an onset onto a dramatized central action or set of actions, and the developmental exit from those actions. While the model works well enough with a handful of straightforward development sections around 1800 (such as that of the first movement of Beethoven, Piano Sonata in F Minor, op. 2 no. 1)—developments that doubtless generated the scheme in the first place—other developments are more resistant to interpretation by means of this scheme. We realize that their claims are not absolute: Caplin, in particular, insists that not all developments follow the specifics of the three-part organization: the all-important "core" with its "relatively large model" preceded by a section

of "pre-core" is merely "the phrase-structural technique most characteristic of a development" and "many classical development sections are not organized in the ways just described."[41] In our experience, though, to use Caplin's primary classifications for developments, not to mention his numerous subclassifications and exceptions—pseudocore, transition-like pre-core, incomplete thematic unit, and the like—tangles one in a web of classificatory labeling without any larger explanatory purpose. (Is this model long enough to initiate a real "core"? Which of the many types of "pre-core" might that one be? Is it a "pre-core" at all? and so on.) In practice the Caplin model also seems indifferent to the interpretation of the ordered selection of thematic materials (and their implications) within the development—to issues of rotation, substitution, and so on. We concluded that the system was underdeveloped and overly reliant on only one typical aspect of developmental procedure, sequence-blocks.

Sonata Theory: Overview of Typical Pathways for the Developmental Space

While no standard pathway through a development can be devised in advance, normative developments generally have available to them four available zones, not all of which need be deployed in any given work. Should there also be a rotational or half-rotational plan governing the development (as happens often, in our view), that plan is typically unfolded over the second and third zones. Very briefly, the four zones may be characterized as follows.

The first is a short, optional *link* from the preceding retransition (RT) or from the last module of C. This link often seems to precede our sense of "the development proper," which would begin with the second zone, if present, or with the third, if the second is lacking. The second is the *entry or preparation zone*. This is usually a preparation, often in an anticipatory, *piano* dynamic, for the central-action-to-come. It may be either quite short or quite long, and it

---

38. Erwin Ratz, *Einführung in die musikalische Formlehre*, 1st ed. (Vienna, 1951), e.g., p. 32.
39. Caplin, *Classical Form*, pp. 139–59.
40. Caplin, *Classical Form*, pp. 141, 142.
41. Caplin, *Classical Form*, pp. 141, 155.

may be structured in various ways. It is often P-based, as is especially appropriate at the beginnings of developments, but other options, with different expressive purposes, are also possible. Sometimes the preparatory effect of this passage is very marked. If it is not, the issue of its presence need not be forced.

The third zone comprises *the central action* or *set of actions*. It may be expanded at considerable length, and it may unfold in one, two, three, or more "events" or "parts" (subsections). It characteristically involves such moods as surging restlessness; moves to minor; *Sturm und Drang* outbursts; quieter, reactive moments; special-effect episodes; and so on. One should determine how the different subsections are interrelated into a broader narrative trajectory. The central action may push toward one or more crisis points: if so, on which theme(s) are they based? how might they play into the musical narrative being "told" here? which prior theme is given the strongest emphasis? why? In addition, one should look for tonal patterns and differently managed levels of tonal and textural tension: In general, the ascending fifth and ascending $5-6$ patterns are used to generate tension, while the descending fifth and descending $5-6$ patterns are used to lower or to release tension.

One common option for the central action (or subsections thereof) is the deployment of one or more sequence-blocks, tracking through various dramatic changes. Any number of different dramatizations are possible. The size of the model is variable, but it should be noticed in all instances. Larger models contribute to a greater sense of space and breadth. Two or more sequence-blocks may follow one another directly, usually as constituents of a larger dramatic action, perhaps a broad intensification (*Steigerung*). Another alternative is to encounter multiple sequence-blocks that are separated from one another—each preceded by a new "preparation" and ending with some sort of decisive effect. These effects might include: fragmentation; compression, liquidation; drive to a caesura or a locally structural-dominant lock; and so on. What is placed between the various sequence blocks differs from case to case. The result (as sometimes in Beethoven) can be a dramatic panorama of separate actions or dramatic interactions: ebbs and flows; clashes and retreats.

Other actions besides sequences may play significant roles in the central action-space of the development. These include: fugato (or fugato dissolving into other types of developmental activity); other passages launched or otherwise marked by intense or strenuous contrapuntal activity or imitation; a new theme or episode (which might substitute for or write over an otherwise normative rotational element); other types of intensification (*Steigerung*) effects; manipulations of a false-recapitulation effect; and so on. The conclusion of the central action (as well as of some of its individual parts) typically includes techniques of fragmentation and liquidation of the ideas that have been unfolded. One should look for the signs of any such winding-down or "breakup" of the elements of the central action. The central action sometimes merges directly into the final zone:

The fourth zone is that of the *exit* or *retransition*. This typically involves the music surrounding the preparation for and/or execution of a structural-dominant lock, usually V_A of the principal tonic. This may be treated in any number of dramatized ways. In terms of rotational implication, the developmental rotation often gives way here to a foreshadowing of the imminent recapitulatory rotation: anticipations of P, and the like.

CHAPTER ELEVEN

The Recapitulation (Recapitulatory Space; Recapitulatory Rotation)

What Qualifies as a Recapitulation?

Both historically and within Sonata Theory the term recapitulation (German, *Reprise*) suggests a postdevelopmental recycling of all or most of the expositional materials, beginning again with the module that had launched the exposition.[1] (In Type 1 sonata forms, which lack a development, the recapitulatory cycle begins after the exposition.) Normally, the initiatory P^1 module of the recapitulation replicates the exposition's opening key, mood, and sound. This reinforces the idea of a new start after the harmonic interruption typically found at the end of a development. In some compositions variants were introduced into the P^1-module. This happens, for instance, in Mozart's Overture to *The Magic Flute*, m. 144 — the return to the tonic E-flat and P^1 — where the original fugato texture is

largely abandoned and the theme is recast and destabilized. In addition, Beethoven, in some compositions, such as the opening movement of the First Symphony, was attracted to the idea of sounding what had been a *piano* P-theme in a rough, vigorous *forte*, thus producing a more muscular or dynamically charged recapitulatory launch (m. 178).

Whatever its local variants (or, in the case of the constantly original Haydn, however protean its compositional recastings), the recapitulation provides another complete rotation through the action-zone layout initially set forth in the exposition (P TR ' S / C). We refer to this restatement of the layout as the *recapitulatory rotation*. Its expanse begins with the layout's first module (P^1) and continues until the last one has been sounded. Anything following this is rhetorical *coda-space*. All of this is usually self-evident and

---

1. A full (or nearly full) revisiting of the expositional modules seems to have been part of the structural concept from the start. Other terms used for this portion of the sonata have included: *ripresa or replica* (Galeazzi, 1796, who alone among the early theorists also mentioned the alternative, Type 2 sonata option); *répétition exacte de la première Reprise* or *deuxième partie de la seconde reprise* (Momigny, 1806); *Wiederkehr* (E. T. A. Hoffmann, 1807); *seconde section de la seconde partie* (Reicha, 1826 — echoing the standard "neutral" designation of this section at least from Koch onward); *Wiederholung*

(Gathy, 1835); *die Wiederkehr des Hauptsatzes und alles Weitere* and *die Reprise* (Marx, 1842, 1848); *Repetition* (Lobe, 1844 — "because it repeats the entire first part or at least most of it, and for the most part in the same order"); *[die] Wiederholung des ersten Theiles* (Richter, 1852); and *die Wiederkehr der Themen* (Riemann, 1889). See the review of the terminology in Siegfried Schmalzriedt, "Reprise/ripresa (nach 1600)," in Eggebrecht, ed., *Handwörterbuch der musikalischen Terminologie*, pp. 8–11.

unproblematic in Type 1, 3, 4, and 5 sonatas, in which the modular formats of expositions and recapitulations are kept roughly parallel, albeit with the obligatory adjustments to accomplish the tonal resolution in the recapitulation's second half. The designation *recapitulatory space* is especially appropriate when dealing with non-normative complete rotations whose outer boundaries do not coincide with the customary (tonic) expectations of more standard recapitulations.

On the other hand, if we confront what we at first presume is a recapitulation that begins significantly after the P^1-module (and especially after the first TR-module), thereby producing a space that seems to omit the early portions of the rotation, we should not label that space as a recapitulation at all. In most cases one is examining a variant of or intermixture with the Type 2 sonata, for which the term recapitulation is misleading, and within which the initial part of the operative rotation has been occurring within the developmental space. A "recapitulation" cannot begin with a $TR^{1.2}$ or S-module. To assume that one can leads to such erroneous concepts as "partial," "incomplete," or "reversed" ("mirror") recapitulations, which are definitional contradictions to be avoided. (This point is pursued more fully in chapter 17, "The Type 2 Sonata.") A genuinely truncated recapitulation, described at the end of this chapter, would be one that begins with P^1 but is cut off before the rotation has been completed, perhaps even before part 2 (S / C) has been entered. Recapitulations that begin with the $TR^{1.1}$-module (often a *forte*-affirmation TR of the dissolving-restatement or dissolving-consequent type, giving the impression of having elided the *piano* P-space altogether or telescoped P and TR into a single statement) present an assortment of analytical issues that varies from case to case. Along with deformational or nontonic onsets of recapitulatory spaces—exceptional procedures—they will be considered in chapter 12.

ESC: Tonic Presence and the Precipitation of the Tonic as a Crystallized Reality

The recapitulation delivers the *telos* of the entire sonata—the point of *essential structural clo-sure (ESC)*, the goal toward which the entire sonata-trajectory has been aimed. This is normally the first satisfactory I:PAC within the recapitulation's part 2 that proceeds onward to differing material, or, in the case of a continuous-recapitulation format, at the conclusion of the broad TR⇒FS zone. In most cases the ESC will be the point parallel to the exposition's EEC: the exposition's structure of promise (presented there in the dominant) finds here its goal and resting-point (in the tonic). It may happen, albeit infrequently, that the EEC and ESC are articulated with different modules. This can occur when the module that had produced the apparent-EEC in the exposition is recomposed away from a cadence in the recapitulation. One goal of analysis is to uncover the problem to which the ESC-alteration in the recapitulation provides a solution. (Upon closer reflection, for example, it may be that the exposition's apparent EEC could be reinterpreted as having been conceptually overridden by a sophisticated application of EEC-deferral—although this is not invariably the case.)

The attaining of the ESC is the most significant event within the sonata. Here the tonal expectations of the generically essential sonata action are satisfied, although they may be stabilized further by any reinforcement that the following C-space provides. It is here that the presence of the tonic becomes finally secured as real rather than provisional. (The provisionality of the tonic within the exposition's P-zone—a tonic soon to be abandoned for other keys—has been discussed in the "Tonal Under- and Overdetermination" section of chapter 5.) Only at the ESC is the tonic key attained as a stable reality. The broad trajectory of the sonata may be understood as an act of tonic-realization, a process of tonic-securing. (The hermeneutic ramifications of this issue of tonic presence are discussed at the end of this chapter, under "The Larger Role of the Recapitulation within the Sonata.") With the onset of the recapitulation, and especially with the onset of S, the crucial agent of generic realization, we are driving toward the "moment of truth" within the composition. Recapitulations sometimes show signs of eagerness to arrive at the ESC, jettisoning baggage along the way, perhaps by omission of inert material (thematic repetitions or individual thematic modules regarded now as discardable), by altered dynamics, by telescoped P-areas, and the like, as in the first movement of Mozart's Symphony No. 34 in C, K. 338, in which the recapitulation opens with only the first four bars of P (mm. 158–61)—as if merely to mark the beginning of the rotation—before plunging into a recomposed recapitulatory TR.

Recompositions, Reorderings, Interpolations

In a recapitulation, particularly within a Type 1, 3, or 4 sonata, the rhetorical materials of the exposition normally return in order. This constitutes another rotation of the expositional materials, although modifications here and there (especially of P and TR) are common. In most cases, once past part 1 (P, the recapitulatory TR, and the MC), S and C are brought back more or less intact—now in the tonic—giving the impression of a largely literal restatement of part 2 on a transposed pitch level. The release of S within the recapitulation is usually accompanied by the security of tracking quasi-automatically toward the ultimate goal of the sonata, the ESC: the goal is squarely in view; the motion toward it is inevitable and certain.

The main exceptions to these generalizations are to be found in the works of Haydn. While Haydn's recapitulations almost always retain an underlying, readily traceable principle of rotation, their local details of are often substantially recomposed, with a penchant for remaining doggedly original all the way to the end. This principle of through-composition also resonates with eighteenth-century scientific conceptions of vitalism, according to which individual living particles are understood to grow spontaneously and continuously. Metaphorically, Haydn may be suggesting, at times wittily, that the task of the composer facing such self-willed vitalistic

(musical) particles is to trim and shape their innate tendency toward unstoppable growth and self-mutation, to make certain that their compulsively generative sproutings (*Fortspinnungen*) do not lead the work into blind alleys or counter-generic directions. Apart from Haydn, this practice is exceedingly rare, although it is characteristic of the Haydnesque temperament, seeking constant surprise, invention, and originality.[2] Sometimes Haydn will begin each recapitulatory zone with enough of an incipit to recall the corresponding zone of the exposition (as if marking the arrival of a station), then significantly rework the material of that zone. This might also suggest something of a *synecdochic strategy*, in which a telling part of a theme (its opening) is made to stand for a recapturing of the whole of it. Haydn is exceptional in this practice. One should not draw general conclusions about eighteenth-century recapitulations from his idiosyncratic works.

From time to time one comes across a recapitulation that reorders some of its modules. This occasionally happens in Stamitz symphonies, with a curiously arbitrary, *ars-combinatoria*-like effect (the combining and recombining of largely generic modules, seemingly to demonstrate that they work equally well in different orderings).[3] One can find more telling examples of it in Mozart, as in the F-major slow movement of the Piano Sonata in C, K. 279 (the original TR, especially mm. 7–9, does not appear in the parallel spot in the recapitulation but does recur to open C-space, mm. 69–72, interpolated before C^1 proper, mm. 72–74), and the first movement of the Piano Sonata in D, K. 576 (C^1 makes a surprising appearance, in a self-satisfied *dolce*, to open S-space, m. 122, but before long, perhaps realizing that it is in the wrong place, it runs aground on a V^6 of vi, m. 137; S-proper follows, *forte*, in m. 138 [beginning on vi—a recovery operation]; the ESC is sounded in m. 155, and C^2—the only

2. It would remain similarly rare in the nineteenth century—until, in fact, Gustav Mahler reinstated the practice of substantially reconceived recapitulations in his symphonies. Cf. also the description of Haydn's "vitalistic" style in ch. 18.
3. Eugene K. Wolf noticed "[Stamitz's] growing tendency [throughout his career] in both partial and full

recapitulations to reorder the various segments of the exposition when they recur in the recapitulation." The magnitude of this reordering "may range from small displacements that do not essentially modify the progress of the exposition . . . to [a] thorough scrambling of the segments." Wolf, *The Symphonies of Johann Stamitz*, p. 155.

C-module remaining—follows immediately thereafter). A related variant involves the suppression of an earlier inert module only to have it turn up, like a lost coin, toward the end of the movement. In the finale of Mozart's Piano Sonata in F, K. 332, P³, mm. 22–32, and P⁴, mm. 32–35, both of which had first emerged as the final elements of an extravagantly tonally overdetermined P-space, are omitted from the parallel spot of the recapitulation. Instead, they are shifted to function as what may be regarded as the coda, mm. 232–45, although, under a different interpretation, they could also be construed as a non-normative extension of C-space, that is, as part of the recapitulation proper.

Not surprisingly, recapitulatory reorderings may also be found in Haydn, since, as mentioned above, his recapitulations are always unpredictable. An amusing instance occurs in the much-reordered recapitulation of the "allemande" finale of the Piano Trio in E-flat, Hob. XV:29. The movement is a rapid, triple-time German dance, whose giddy whirling sweeps up and rearranges several of the modules in its recapitulatory path. One also encounters the reordering in certain pieces in the nineteenth century. In the recapitulation of Mendelssohn's Overture to *A Midsummer Night's Dream* the TR-music from the exposition—originally preceding S¹—is relocated to follow a much later thematic module, Sᶜ (the representation of the character of Bottom and the other rude mechanicals). When such a reordering occurs, analytical and hermeneutic complications nearly always ensue, and the ESC may not be located at a rhetorical point that is parallel to the EEC.

If the modular reorderings involve only the recapitulation's part 2 (S and C), one should bear in mind that while expositional C-modules might be interpolated into the recapitulation's now-broader swath of S-space—before the ESC (as in K. 576, mentioned above)—the reverse is much more unlikely: expositional S-modules may not be casually transferred into the recapitulation's C-space, placed into a post-ESC position, without inviting a reconfiguration of the boundaries of secondary-theme space. This is because the sonata's S-zone, its most generically active (least inert) space, is determined by its modules in the exposition: whatever had appeared in S there will normally define itself and its surroundings as occurring within S in the recapitulation, even if a preceding I:PAC has led us to believe that the ESC has already been achieved. Put another way, the surfacing of an original S-module (as defined by the exposition) *after* a supposed ESC suggests the activation of an ESC deferral. S-space, thought to be closed, is now being sprung open to embrace the errant S-module that has appeared later than expected (and, of course, to embrace all that that has preceded it—normally modules that had originally been presented in C-space). The next satisfactory I:PAC after this "misplaced" S-module is then considered to be the real ESC. This is an interpretive situation that comes up with some frequency in the first movements of Mozart's piano concertos, in which modular rearrangements and interpolations are important features. In the case of concertos (Type 5 sonatas) the S-defining referential rotation is provided by the tonic-centered initial tutti (ritornello), as discussed in chapters 19–22.

Although the very notion of such things seems counterintuitive, it is also possible, primarily in earlier composers around midcentury, to encounter surprising interpolations into recapitulatory space, which to today's listeners can produce a willful or disconcertingly capricious impression: an unexpected detour away from the "clean path" of the rotation. Examples may be found in Wagenseil's symphonies from around the 1750s—especially the insertion of a sometimes-lengthy minor-mode ("lights-out") episode immediately before or after the presumed-ESC moment. A classic illustration occurs in the first movement of his Symphony in B-flat, WV 438 (Kucaba B♭²). Two modules of S (S¹·¹, S¹·²) lead, as expected, to a I:PAC, which we at first presume to be the ESC (m. 103). Immediately thereafter, a previously-unheard episode on B-flat minor appears (mm. 103–19)—submitting the I:PAC to a stark and sudden minor-mode deflation—and it leads to a new lock on V of the tonic (m. 111) and new MC-effect (PMC, m. 119), followed by a repetition of S¹·² in B-flat major (m. 120). The upshot of all this is to effect an ESC deferral "after the fact"—in large part triggered by the minor-mode face-slap—and the real ESC is achieved only in m. 129. Similar effects may be found in the first movements of the Symphony in G, WV 413 (Kucaba G²) and the Symphony in D, WV 374 (Kucaba D¹⁰).[4]

The Recapitulatory TR

It was common for a composer to modify the recapitulatory P and/or TR zones. The TR, in particular, was a passage that invited recomposition. Alterations were all the more apt if the exposition's TR had been a modulatory transition, that is, if it had driven toward a V:HC MC (or III:HC MC or v:HC MC in a minor-mode sonata). That same modulatory move was not to be made in the recapitulation's TR. Since S was now to emerge in the tonic, the MC end-point of TR would have to be a I:HC instead, down a fifth from that of the exposition. This observation alone (rather than any more abstract idea of large-scale tonal balance or compensation) is surely the most compelling reason why many recapitulations moved toward the subdominant in their P or TR zones. The basic strategy was recognized in the late eighteenth century by Koch: "[In the 'last period' of the movement (what we call now the recapitulation)] the most prominent phrases are now compressed, as it were, during which the melody usually shifts to the key of the fourth, but, without making a[n authentic] cadence in it, soon again returns to the main key."[5]

The decisiveness of this harmonic point was contested by Rosen in *Sonata Forms*, who declared it a "mistake to identify the appearance of the subdominant" area at this point "with the necessary alteration of harmony to transform an exposition that goes from tonic to dominant into a recapitulation that remains in the tonic." In Rosen's view, the tilt toward IV (or other flat-side region) could occasionally be a mere and momentary feint—accomplished early on—that did not function as the crucial tonal shift that made the tonic arrival of the subsequent S inevitable.[6]

Rosen's case was overstated and asserted in the abstract, overlooking the contextual situatedness of individual pieces within the history of the genre. His example of a "developmental" and structurally nonfunctional flat-side tilt is drawn from the first movement of Beethoven's "Waldstein" Sonata (mm. 167–74), but this is to take a snapshot from the late and much-developed stage in the history of the "classical" sonata—and from a famously deformational structure composed in the high-middle period of a composer obsessed with conceptually "difficult" modifications of standard sonata practice. The "Waldstein" is an illustration of an intellectualist or highly sophisticated deviation from the norm—or at best of a lower-level default—not of the norm itself. Nonetheless it is true, particularly in the more monumental or complex works of the masters from 1780 onward, that not all shifts to IV in the P or TR zones serve as the "quick fix" that brings one automatically to the desired pitch level for S. Some shifts to IV give the impression of existing largely for their own sake, and it is these that Rosen was noticing. And it is these for which some sort of historically aware hypothesis should be suggested.

In our view the phenomenon is almost certainly to be linked with the normative functional shift to IV alluded to by Koch and found in countless mid- and late-century examples. Briefly put, there had arisen an obligation to recompose parts of P–TR—part 1 of the recapitulation—in order to accommodate this generically necessary function. Over time, this doubtless contributed to the general sense that the recapitulation's part 1 was more vulnerable to recomposition—it was less stable or fixed in its modules—than was part 2 (S–C). This recomposition could begin either in the (perhaps varied) P-zone, or P could be presented more or less intact, and the music could be more significantly altered in the TR zone alone. Within the historical state of the genre, the recapitulatory P–TR had acquired a tendency to move toward IV. That was simply "what one

---

4. Our thanks to Jeffrey Tucker for calling this to our attention in a seminar paper on Wagenseil written at Yale in 1999.

5. Koch, *Introductory Essay on Composition*, trans. Baker, p. 201.

6. Rosen, *Sonata Forms*, rev. ed., p. 289.

often did" at this point for reasons that over the decades had served manifestly functional purposes. Given a zone or pair of zones with this generic propensity, it does not take much imagination to suppose that master composers could seize upon that tropism as an opportunity to generate "false" or "surplus" flat-side-leaning passages—decorative or expressive patches—that might prove functionally superfluous with respect to the preparation of the needed MC further down the road.

The issue emerges with particular vividness in the following common compositional situation. If the exposition had contained a I:HC MC any recapitulatory shift toward the subdominant in the P–TR zones—along with any general obligation toward recomposition—was technically unnecessary. Since the recapitulation was also to drive to a I:HC MC, there was no need to alter anything in part 1. (In fact, one sometimes comes across this simple, merely mechanical solution, as in the first movement of Mozart's Quartet in E-flat, K. 160, whose recapitulatory P–TR displays only one or two almost negligible figurational variants.) Interestingly enough, however, master composers frequently did "unnecessarily" recompose portions of part 1 in these situations. And sometimes these recompositions included a generic feint toward the subdominant, as if nodding toward the practice that was obligatory in the more common MC situations, in which the exposition had contained a V:HC MC. Two generic factors are in play in this "superfluous" recomposition: (1) the reference to the more common first-level-default MC situation; (2) the prevailing sense (because of no. 1) that P–TR zones, "in their nature," were less stable than the subsequent thematic modules of the rotation. Beyond these two factors lie the important considerations of art and elegance: the carefully crafted turn of phrase; the surprising, additional detail; the delicious variant—all the more salient for being generically superfluous.

In short, the P–TR music was often subjected to reinterpretation in the recapitulation,

and that reinterpretation often involved a tonal drop (or set of drops) in the subdominant direction. Composers could manage this rethinking in a variety of ways: they could address the problem either simply, with the alteration of a mere bar or two; or they could take the opportunity for a substantial reshaping of the entire section (especially TR). The recapitulation transition (Nicholas Marston's term, which we prefer to alter to *recapitulatory transition*)[7] was the freest available spot for compositional craft and modification within a recapitulation that, for the most part (though usually not in Haydn), was founded upon much literal repetition of the rotational layout.

How this TR-issue is addressed varies from work to work. In some cases TR is shortened, probably with the expressive intention of hastening toward the essential generic moment, S and the ESC. On the other hand—especially in large-scale or ambitious works—the composer might recompose and expand TR (or P–TR) through enhanced *Fortspinnung*, sequential activity, or other "developmental" textures. For this reason some writers have referred to the entire section of recomposed material in part 1 as the "secondary development section." This was Rosen's suggestion of a *raison d'être* for the general subdominant-side tilt of P–TR. The purpose of the secondary development, wrote Rosen, is "to lower harmonic tension without sacrificing interest; it introduces an allusion to the subdominant or to the related "flat" keys. . . . This introduction of the subdominant area . . . serves to make the return of the tonic more decisive. It is the restoration of harmonic equilibrium as well as the need for variation that gives the Secondary Development its function.[8]

The term "secondary development" is unfortunate, since both adjective and noun are imported from other parts of the sonata. Some of the currency of the term may stem from the late-romantic/modernist cachet of the concept of "development" in general. On this view "development" anywhere in a sonata is a good thing—as opposed to supposedly thoughtless

---

7. See, e.g., the discussion in Nicholas Marston, "The Recapitulation Transition in Mozart's Music," *Mozart-Jahrbuch 1991* (Kassel: Bärenreiter, 1992), 793–809.

8. Rosen, *Sonata Forms*, rev. ed., pp. 289–90.

literal repetition. The term "secondary development" is not connotationally neutral. Rosen's account of the rationale behind the move toward IV at this point also seems weak. In what way, precisely, does the desire to "lower harmonic tension" in itself "make the return of the tonic more decisive"? What constitutes decisiveness in this repertory? Why is this decisiveness a good thing? Are S-zones that are *not* preceded by dips into the subdominant *ipso facto* less decisive, less imaginative, or less satisfactory? What does it mean to "restore harmonic equilibrium" by means of a section that is not normally marked by a IV:PAC? On what grounds can we make these claims?[9] Moreover, appeals to the supposed "need for variation" are among the least cogent groundings for any compositional change: they cover everything and explain nothing. Whatever their aims, in pushing forward an easy answer, their result is to discourage hermeneutic reflection, not to promote it. The more precise term *recapitulatory transition* strikes us as superior in every respect. One need only observe that in some cases the recapitulatory TR is given an intense, expanded treatment on its way to the MC. The hermeneutic obligation is to explain why.

Altered MC Treatments in the Recapitulation; "Wrong-Key" Starts for S

Typically, the handling of the MC in the recapitulation parallels that of the exposition (see "The Crux"), although this is by no means inevitable. One consequence of the recomposition of TR is that the treatment of the conceptual apparatus surrounding the expositional medial-caesura moment can be reconceived in the recapitulation. What had been a half-cadence MC in the exposition, for instance, might be changed to a PAC MC. This would produce both a more decisive seizing of the S-space-to-come and a more emphatic division of the recapitulation into two distinct parts. (The reverse, I:PAC MC changed to a I:HC MC, occurs much less frequently. A small-scale example may be found in the first movement of Clementi's Sonatina in C, op. 36 no. 3.) The MC alteration to a I:PAC crops up, for instance, in the works of J. C. Bach. In the first movement of his Symphony in C, op. 3 no. 2, what is first sounded as a V:HC MC (m. 35) returns in the recapitulation, at the end of a recomposed TR, as a decisive, strongly articulated I:PAC (m. 121). It is succeeded by material (mm. 122–33) that had unequivocally been S in the exposition (mm. 36–47). The S-status of this block remains unchanged under such a modification: these modules are defined as S permanently by the referential layout provided in the exposition. One should not be tempted to take any "new" I:PAC MC for the ESC (which in this case is accomplished in m. 133). Similar occurrences may be found in several other works, including the first movements of J. C. Bach's Symphony in D, op. 3 no. 1 (perhaps a variant of a Type 2 sonata) and his Keyboard Sonata in D, op. 5 no. 2.

---

9. In a more recent essay ("Schubert's Inflections of Classical Form," *The Cambridge Companion to Schubert*, ed. Christopher H. Gibbs [Cambridge: Cambridge University Press, 1997], p. 87) Rosen revisited some of these issues: "The reappearance of material in the recapitulation is essentially one of equivalence in Classical form, intended to balance the expository form and to resolve it. That is why a glance at the subdominant traditionally balances some of the tonic-dominant presentation in late eighteenth-century theory and practice, and why Beethoven invariably balances a mediant in the exposition with a submediant in the recapitulation (Opp. 31 No. 1; 53; 127 [*sic*]; 130 [*sic*], 132 [*sic*]) or the submediant with the flatted submediant (Op. 106)." Notwithstanding their authoritative tone, these are puzzling remarks, in part due to incorrectly cited examples. Additionally, the relationship between the submediant and *flatted* submediant in two different portions of a so-nata movement—as in Beethoven's "Hammerklavier" Sonata in B-flat, op. 106/i (G-major S in the exposition; slippage of P–TR [!] to G-flat in the recapitulation, while S reappears in the tonic)—is anything but self-evident and quite unlike the presumably-claimed fifth-relationship of mediant and submediant in parallel passages. How is this either a "balance" or a "resolution"? Rosen also claims the same "balance" (or restoration of "disequilibrium") between the A-flat major (♭VI) of S in the exposition of the first movement of Schubert's four-hand "Grand Duo" in C major, D. 812, with its highly unusual C-*minor* appearance in the recapitulation, "as if the [expositional] A flat had implied a change of mode as well as tonal center." Cf. Rosen's similar remarks on "mediants" in *The Romantic Generation* (Cambridge, Mass.: Harvard University Press, 1995), p. 244. Cf. the section of this chapter, "Altered MC Treatments in the Recapitulation." See also n. 19.

On rare occasions one might encounter, as a deformation, the leading of a rhetorically parallel recapitulatory MC to a tonally incorrect pitch-level, with curious consequences for the beginning of S. One famous example is found in the first movement of Beethoven's Piano Sonata in C Minor, op. 10 no. 1. The exposition's tonally conventional III:HC MC occurs in m. 48, followed by eight bars of a gradually "settling" caesura-fill and the launch of S in E-flat at m. 56. In the recapitulation one expects a i:HC (or I:HC) MC to set up the necessary tonal resolution. As if shying away from the fatalistic C-minor closure-to-come, however, Beethoven plants instead a IV:HC MC in m. 207, and S begins blithely and irresponsibly in F major in m. 215. This staged attempt at escapism—whistling in the dark—cannot last. The generically illicit F major is brutally extinguished into F minor at m. 229, and the S-theme is rebegun in C minor in m. 233, now with a *forte* vengeance and contextually heightened negativity, struggling in resistance all the way to the ESC at m. 271.

Situations such as one finds in op. 10 no. 1/i may be considered *false starts* for the S-theme. These are cases in which for any number of reasons (usually involving MC-treatment as well) the recapitulatory S is first sounded in the "wrong key" and at least for a few bars proceeds as if all were well. Shortly into the theme, though, the "wrong-key" trajectory is aborted, and the music "backs up" to restart S in the proper, tonic key. Thus the recapitulatory S begins twice, first in the wrong key, then in the right one. (The alternative, found in the first movement of Beethoven's "Waldstein" Sonata, would be to correct the generically improper tonality en route, without backing up.) Related examples in Beethoven may be found in the finale of Symphony No. 1 in C, op. 21 (where a recapitulatory IV:HC MC in m. 190 is followed by the F-major onset of S [IV] in m. 192, steered back to the tonic in mm. 198–99, with an immediate backup to a tonally proper restatement of the second presentational module at m. 200

[= m. 196, corrected]); and in the first movements of Piano Sonata in G, op. 31 no. 1 (in which the exposition had moved to the mediant; the recapitulatory false start, following the "wrong" MC, is in E major, m. 218; the second start is in the tonic G, m. 234), Quartet in F Minor, op. 95, "Serioso" (in which the exposition had moved to the submediant, D-flat, for S [m. 24, also interpretable as TM¹] and seeks to do the same thing [!] in the recapitulation, m. 89, with a restart in the tonic, now F major, at m. 93), and Quartet in B-flat, op. 130 (the two recapitulatory starts for S occur in D-flat, m. 162 [or perhaps m. 160, conflating $S^{1.0}$ and caesura-fill], and B-flat, m. 174 [with the parallel interpretive option at m. 172]).

The most notable reconceptions of the recapitulatory MC moment occur when the exposition type is changed. This happens either when a two-part exposition (with MC) is turned into a continuous recapitulation by a suppression or overriding of the caesura-effect or when a continuous exposition is turned into a two-part recapitulation by the addition of an MC lacking in the original layout. A related situation would be the turning of an originally double-medial-caesura situation (an exposition with a trimodular block) into a more normative single-MC recapitulation, thus smoothing out the expositional problematics normally associated with double MCs. These changes are somewhat rare, but from time to time they do occur. In all cases we presume that the alteration is central to the compositional argumentation of the movement as a whole. In the master composers we accept as axiomatic the idea that such altered recapitulations cannot be arbitrary or meaningless. Instead, the recapitulation should be construed as a planned response—the devising of a new strategy—to generic-structural issues (such as errant themes or problematic caesuras or cadences) that had cropped up in the exposition, with the aim of moving the recapitulation in the direction of an enhanced normativity, improvement, or clarification.[10]

Such modifications are common in (but

---

10. These points are pursued further in Hepokoski, "Beyond the Sonata Principle," *Journal of the American Musicological Society* 55 (2002), 91–154 (especially pp. 118–30, concerning the first movement of Haydn's Quartet in B-flat, op. 64 no. 3).

not limited to) the works of Haydn, who was committed to the idea of significant rethinkings of themes and processes in his recapitulations. In the first movement of his Symphony No. 6 in D, "Le matin," the expositional TR proceeds to a normative second-level-default I:HC MC in m. 20. The S that follows in m. 21 is marked at its outset by, if anything, the absence of a theme—a witty effect, perhaps suggesting that a preassigned theme had missed its cue and failed to enter. The S-zone snaps into action only with a sudden *forte* in m. 27 ($S^{1.2}$), driving toward the EEC in m. 35. After a fully rotational development the recapitulatory rotation begins in m. 85 (with an anticipatory announcement of P's first two bars, rebegun in m. 87). This time, apparently steering clear of the "absent" S, the somewhat telescoped recapitulation merges from the first bars of the recapitulatory TR (mm. 94–100) into the middle of the *forte*, $S^{1.2}$ material (c. m. 101 = m. 30). This converts the expositional two-part structure, with MC, into a continuous recapitulation, without MC, redesigned to bypass the $S^{1.1}$ "vacancy."

In Haydn the ploys of each movement are *ad hoc*, unpredictable in advance. Another example of turning a two-part exposition into a continuous recapitulation may be found in the first movement of his Quartet in C, op. 33 no. 3, "Bird." The exposition provides a clear I:HC MC in m. 26, followed by a bar of S^0 (m. 27), then S^1 proper (m. 28). The recapitulation produces no MC whatever, proceeding continuously—and with some omission of the earlier S-material—to articulate the ESC in m. 138. Still another illustration is provided in the first movement of the Quartet in E-flat, op. 50 no. 3. Here, following a two-part exposition (albeit one with a strikingly attenuated, "dominant-arrival" MC at m. 17, on a V^6_5 chord in the key of V), one finds an unusual variant of a Type 2 sonata with a surprisingly early "crux" point (mm. 88 = m. 5; this is preceded by a "redundant," false-crux on IV in m. 82; because this is a Type 2 sonata the specific term "recapitulation" or "false reprise" at either of these points is misleading). What follows proceeds as a continuous rotation, suppressing the MC-deformation that had occurred in the exposition.

The Crux

Correspondence Measures and the Crux

Many recapitulations begin by restating all or most of the exposition's P-materials. Even in instances in which there are alterations shortly into the P-zone, it usually happens that the initial moments of the recapitulation correspond bar-for-bar with those of the exposition (or, less frequently, with those of a literal restatement of P in the exposition). The recapitulation's opening measures are normally mappable onto those of the exposition with no difficulty. If a recapitulation, for instance, begins in m. 73, we might find that m. 73 = m. 1; m. 74 = m. 2; m. 75 = m. 3; and so on. We refer to such bar-for-bar restatements in the recapitulation—in whatever zone they might occur—as *correspondence measures*. One task in the analysis of any recapitulation is to determine which bars are correspondence measures and which have been recomposed.

In most cases after several bars of these correspondence measures—toward the end of P, at the beginning of TR, or even midway through TR—the composer will usually have the music "slip off track," depart from the pattern provided in the exposition. At this point the music will be recomposed on the way to the MC and the S-theme. This deviation from the expositional pattern is an important moment within the early stages of the recapitulation. (As discussed above, the most common generic purpose of this recomposition, often subdominant-inflected, is to resituate the remainder of the music at the proper recapitulatory tonal level that will permit a tonic reprise of part 2—and hence a satisfactory attaining of the ESC.) At some point within this recomposition the composer will once again "settle back on track," usually toward the end of the recapitulatory TR, or perhaps directly at the MC and the onset of S, and begin to write correspondence measures that replicate (even quasi-mechanically, or perhaps with small variants) the pattern established in the exposition—usually at a different tonal level, one that will permit a resolution of part 2 in the tonic key.

This moment of rejoining the events of the expositional pattern after once having departed from them—entering into the larger set of correspondence measures—is the moment of the *crux*, at which point writing the remainder of the recapitulation can become, by and large, a simple matter of transposition.[11] In major-mode sonatas, when the music at the crux is compared with the parallel music of the exposition, it will appear either transposed a fifth lower (or a fourth higher) or at the same pitch level. The transposition (or nontransposition) principle will almost always be conditional on the type of medial caesura that had been deployed in the exposition. If it had been a V:HC MC, the crux will normally be transposed at the level of a fifth. (This is because the recapitulatory TR is now driving toward a I:HC MC; or, if the crux occurs directly at S, that theme, beginning the tonal resolution, will be stated in the tonic, not in the dominant.) Correspondingly, if the exposition's medial caesura had been a I:HC MC, the crux will normally be rejoined at the original pitch level. When this happens, however, the music that directly follows the MC—namely, S (originally heard in V)—will have to be wrenched down a fifth from the level of the exposition, in order that it might now appear in the tonic key. In other words, crux-points at the original pitch level normally require an additional tonal shift immediately after the MC. This produces another kind of crux—a transposed one—directly at the S point, even though the rhetorical correspondence measures had begun several bars earlier.

It is also possible to produce a more explicit double-crux effect. This occurs when a composition locks onto the original expositional track following a passage of substantial recomposition—producing a clear sense of several correspondence measures—then slides off track again to regain yet another crux further down the road. From time to time—especially in compositions in which the expositional medial caesura had been a V:HC MC—the first crux (perhaps a "false crux," since it is soon abandoned) will occur at the original pitch level, while the second (a "true crux") enters the correspondence measures at the proper level, transposed a fifth away from the parallel portion of the exposition. Other types of double-crux effects are also possible.

We refer to any recompositions or modifications before the crux as *precrux alterations*. Because they often involve the mechanics associated with the generically necessary shift of pitch levels, one expects to find pre-crux alterations as standard practice. Once the crux is attained, the composer, beyond the matter of simple transposition, need not alter anything further in the broad rhetorical lines of the music. This is often the case in the works of Mozart and Beethoven, whose S- and C-zones are frequently stated intact or with only small, if telling, variants. A central decision here—a modest exception to the above claim—concerns the often-ignored matter of the recapitulatory register of the melodic line. Will S and C be brought back consistently a fourth higher than the exposition? a fifth lower? or will we hear—generally the

---

11. The term "crux" is adapted from Ralph Kirkpatrick *Domenico Scarlatti*, (Princeton, N.J.: Princeton University Press, 1953), pp. 253–61, who coined it to refer to the similar point within keyboard sonatas of Domenico Scarlatti. Our usage differs slightly from Kirkpatrick's, since his "crux" refers not merely to the onset of correspondence measures within the second portion of part 2 of a Scarlatti sonata but also to the parallel moment in part 1. "The meeting point in each half of the thematic material which is stated in parallel fashion at the ends of both halves with the establishment of the closing tonality is what I have called a *Crux*. (See [Sonata] I, measures 28 and 78; and XLII, measures 30 and 106. . . . In either half of a sonata the Crux occurs just as the closing tonality is being made clear" (Kirkpatrick, p. 255). To avoid misunderstanding, it should be noted that Kirkpatrick's Crux did not imply the necessity of a moment of high articulation within either half: "The Crux may be marked by a clean break (XIV) or it may be concealed by continuous rhythmic movement (IV)" (p. 256). Thus for Kirkpatrick the crux designates two moments within the sonata, one in each half. We use the term only for the parallel moment in the second half (in a sonata, the recapitulation), although we typically indicate its expositional correspondence measure in parentheses, as in "the crux, m. 80 (= m. 25)." This slight adjustment of Kirkpatrick's definition might also have been suggested in Malcolm Boyd, *Domenico Scarlatti: Master of Music* (New York: Schirmer, 1986), p. 168, who wrote of "the point [in part 2] where the parallelism begins (what Kirkpatrick called the 'Crux')."

more common option in the mature Mozart—a carefully considered shifting back and forth between the two? In each case the decision carries potentially significant connotations regarding registral tension. As Esther Cavett-Dunsby put it in an essay on this topic, "The silence of theorists on the subject of recapitulatory register may lead us to believe that it is one of those variables of sonata form which cannot be codified; one of those topics best discussed informally between teacher and student."[12]

With the exception of making local modifications of scoring or figuration to accommodate the altered higher or lower register of part 2, the fact remains that once the crux is joined, the main, measure-to-measure course of the music need not be recomposed. Precisely because they are generically unnecessary, any substantial changes made in the expositional pattern after the crux are of great interest. These might include omitted repetitions, shortened or slightly recast themes, added bars, and the like. (In Haydn's recomposed recapitulations these procedures are often omnipresent, although there is nonetheless usually a clear crux-point.) We refer to such things as *postcrux alterations*. Unlike precrux alterations, they are ruled neither by necessity nor by adherence to a generic norm. Postcrux alterations are self-conscious decisions on the part of the composer, overriding the "easy" mere transposition. Each one invites a hermeneutic explication. Why were such changes made in S and/or C? What relation might they have, if any, to the register or thematic contours of the material of P and TR? What role do any of these changes play in the attainment and preservation of the ESC?

Correspondence Measures and Referential Measures

The term "correspondence measures" identifies those recapitulatory bars that are more or less identical (with only small variants) to those in the exposition. It sometimes happens, though, that significantly recomposed measures might also be relatable on a one-to-one basis with prototypes in the exposition, a situation in which each bar of the otherwise parallel stretches of music has been reconceived (a situation, for example, in which m. 95 = m. 24 varied; m. 96 = m. 25 varied; and so on.) This is especially characteristic of Haydn, where applying the strict concept of correspondence measures, implying a virtually literal restatement, often seems inappropriate. We refer to recapitulatory measures that are compositionally freer than are correspondence measures and yet retain their bar-for-bar mapping capability onto the exposition as *referential measures*. To label such passages as referential measures is to stress one's acknowledgment of their differences from their models; to label them as correspondence measures is to call attention to their similarities. Obviously there are also intermediate cases falling between these purely heuristic categories. As always, the selection of a descriptive term serves as a mere aid to a clearer hermeneutic reading of the music at hand.

The terminological distinction between referential and correspondence measures can be helpful to describe situations when a brief module or two of correspondence measures gives way to a passage of referential measures, or vice-versa: the sense of measure-for-measure retracking remains, although the degree of literal restatement can vary. One recapitulatory strategy of Haydn—once the initial correspondence measures of P^1 have been left behind for the pre-crux alteration of a recomposed $P^{1.2}$ or TR (or TR$\Rightarrow$FS)—is to begin to write significantly varied referential measures that, over a dozen or more bars, come ever closer to becoming correspondence measures, eventually merging into them. In other words, there emerges a moment where a one-to-one relation with expositional measures becomes apparent, even though each recapitulatory measure is different from its model, and this might initiate a process of bringing the subsequent bars increasingly into line with a literal restatement of the expositional measures. Even the moment of

12. Esther Cavett-Dunsby, "Mozart's 'Haydn' Quartets: Composing Up and Down without Rules," *Journal of the Royal Musical Association* 113 (1988), 57–80.

entry into these referential measures might be unclear: at what point does a variant-measure seem clearly to allude to a model-measure in the exposition? Free composition might gradually integrate itself into a pattern of referential measures and thence, eventually, into clearer correspondence measures.

A *locus classicus* occurs in the finale of Haydn's Quartet in B Minor, op. 33 no. 1, in which both the exposition and the recapitulation are continuous, not two-part. The recapitulation begins at m. 110 with nine bars of correspondence measures (mm. 110–18 = mm. 1–9). Precrux alterations take over abruptly at m. 119 to provide a different, urgent continuation of P. With the onset of TR the music snaps back to another set of correspondence measures (mm. 137–48 = mm. 13–24) and thence to another round of precrux alterations, mm. 149–54. By m. 155 Haydn has entered a stretch of (now transposed) referential measures: m. 155 = m. 31; m. 156 = m. 32; and so on. As they proceed, these measures become increasingly like their expositional models: m. 166 is much like m. 42, m. 167 seems even more clearly to be a correspondence measure with m. 43, and by this point the track of correspondence measures proceeds all the way to the ESC (m. 175, parallel with the EEC, m. 51) and beyond (C[1], mm. 176–83 = mm. 52–59, slightly varied). (A passage of *coda-rhetoric interpolation* follows, mm. 184–89, splitting C[1] from C[2], and C[2], consisting mostly of correspondence measures, concludes the movement, mm. 190–94.) In such cases it can be difficult to determine where the crux occurs, and the precision of the term, eminently serviceable when correspondence measures are involved, breaks down. Is the first referential measure (around m. 155) the crux? Or is it the first clear correspondence measure, several bars further onward (around m. 166 or 167)? In such cases explicating the terminological problem is more useful than deciding one way or the other.

The "Sonata Principle": A Problematic Concept

What Needs to Be Resolved in the Recapitulation?

One of the most commonly invoked concepts within much English-language sonata-analysis of the past several decades has been what Edward T. Cone, in 1968, called the "sonata principle." Steering clear of the discredited idea of "form as a pattern"—the notorious textbook reductions of sonata form—Cone famously sought to articulate a "unifying principle behind [sonata form]." This was "not to be found in its bithematicism, or its developmental aspect, or its binary or ternary (take your choice!) structure." Instead the sonata principle

> requires that important statements made in a key other than the tonic must either be re-stated in the tonic, or brought into a closer relation with the tonic, before the movement ends. Expressed thus, the principle covers many aspects of formal treatment. It applies, most obviously, to the role of the "second subject" in exposition and recapitulation. But it also explains why Beethoven takes such pains in the coda of the first movement of the *Eroica* to re-introduce the theme of the development, and in such a way as to modulate directly to the tonic.[13]

Much was claimed here, and what was claimed was rapidly adopted, albeit in a variety of subvariants (since Cone's formulation was overstated), by other influential musical commentators on the "classical" repertory. The ramifications of this seemingly innocuous principle have been manifold and enormously complicated. Since a more sustained critique of the problems associated with this principle has appeared elsewhere, we shall content ourselves here with laying out a few issues and summarizing a handful of conclusions.[14]

On the one hand, and within certain limitations, the claim represents something self-evident: statements outside the tonic in the ex-

---

13. Cone, *Musical Form and Musical Performance* (New York: Norton, 1968), pp. 76–77.

14. Hepokoski, "Beyond the Sonata Principle."

position (normally in S and C) are most often restated in the tonic in the recapitulation. The well-known remarks of Charles Rosen in *Sonata Forms* provide a generally accurate account of one's expectations:

> *All the material played in the dominant* [in the exposition] *is consequently conceived as dissonant, i.e., requiring resolution by a later transposition to the tonic. . . .* What must reappear in the recapitulation . . . is the second group, at least any part of it that has an individual and characteristic aspect, and that does not already have its analogue in the first group. . . . A theme that has been played only at the dominant is a structural dissonance, unresolved until it has been transposed to the tonic.[15]

At first glance all of this, coupled with the general thrust of Cone's remarks, seems unimpeachable, and of course it covers all normative situations. Still, it is possible to be more precise, if only by ruling out situations that are not properly covered under this guideline. Conceptual errors arise, for instance, when the self-evident proposition is extended beyond the confines of the proper spaces of the expositional and recapitulatory rotations. First—to correct an unfortunate claim of Cone (for example, with respect to the *Eroica*)—no nontonic feature of any development (such as a new theme or central episode, even within a Type 4 sonata) is under any obligation to be resolved in the tonic later in the movement (even though it might be recalled retrospectively in the tonic in the coda). Freestanding, nonresolved developmental episodes abound in the repertory. Whatever the sonata principle might be, it should never be invoked with regard to material that first appears in the development (or central episode of a sonata-rondo).

Second, no off-tonic material from part 1 of a two-part exposition (this would normally occur, if at all, in TR) need reappear in the tonic in the recapitulation. It may be sounded in the tonic or it may not, but whether or not it does has nothing to do with any presumed generic norm or requirement. Off-tonic pre-MC material is inert with regard to any need for tonic reappearance later on. This is because pre-MC modules are uninvolved with the generic requirement of EEC/ESC production. The sonata principle should not be called upon as an expectation for any pre-MC module (or for the equivalent portion of a continuous exposition).

Third, the sonata principle is most properly applied to S and C only (as Rosen stated), which by a strong norm almost always appear together, *en bloc*, in the recapitulation. Still, difficult cases and deformations do occur in the repertory—compositions in whose recapitulations the S and C areas do not behave as expected (as in the initial movement of Mozart's Symphony No. 34 in C, K. 338, whose first C-module in the exposition, mm. 64–74, never reappears anywhere else in the movement; or in several of Haydn's recomposed recapitulations, which sometimes omit or replace earlier S-modules, as in the opening movement of the Quartet in C, op. 33 no. 3, "Bird"). But even here we can make distinctions. Because of S's role in driving toward the EEC and ESC (S is active, not inert), the obligation for tonal resolution applies most strongly here—and to the later modules of S more than to the earlier modules. By definition C is postcadential, a set of *idées accessoires*, a surplus extending past the generic cadential requirement. As a result the convention of resolution, while still usually relevant to C, is less stringent than one expects it to be within S.

Fourth, in order to be considered normative, resolutions of S and C should occur within sonata-space—that is, they should occur before the end of the recapitulatory rotation (which concludes with the final module of C, as laid out in the exposition) and not be deferred to a postsonata coda. This, too, corrects an assertion of Cone, who merely required an originally off-tonic theme to reappear in the tonic (or to be brought into a rapprochement with it) before the movement ends. This takes us beyond recapitulatory space into the coda, and in fact all of Cone's examples are drawn from coda statements. But if this principle is accepted, then the sonata principle extends beyond so-

---

15. Rosen, *Sonata Forms*, rev. ed., pp. 25, 287 ("What must appear").

nata-space, and the corollary is that it will not matter whether a module is resolved in the recapitulation or in the coda (or elsewhere). Such things become matters of indifference, since the sonata principle is satisfied. Rosen had claimed as much in *The Classical Style*:

> It is the classical sense for large areas of stability . . . that establishes what might seem to be the one fixed rule of sonata recapitulation: material originally exposed in the dominant must be represented in the tonic fairly completely, even if rewritten and reordered, and only material exposed in the tonic may be omitted. This is, of course, not a rule at all but a sensitivity to tonal relationships. . . .
>
> Material presented outside the tonic must have created, in the eighteenth century, a feeling of instability which demanded to be resolved. When the tonic was reaffirmed in the second half of the piece, the material already presented in the tonic could be, and often was, drastically cut,[16] but the rest of the exposition cried out for resolution in the tonic [that is, normally in the recapitulation].

He then proceeded to discuss some exceptions in Haydn, from the quartets, op. 64 no. 3, "in which one of the second subjects appears nowhere in the recapitulation"; op. 50 no. 6; and op. 77 no. 1.

> These are the rare cases in the Haydn quartets of material exposed in the dominant and missing from the recapitulation, and at each point we have seen that some form of tonic recapitulation has been provided [in the development]. . . . [Here a footnote reads:] I use "recapitulation" here to mean everything that follows the final reintroduction of the tonic, including what is generally called a coda, if there is one.[17]

Such an argument implies that there is no useful hermeneutic distinction to be made between themes that are resolved (generically) in the recapitulatory space (sealed off with the last C-module) and those whose resolutions are either anticipated prematurely in the "wrong place," the developmental space, or deferred to

coda space. Everything becomes standard practice, collapsed into the catch-all notion of "some form" of a broadly expandable "tonic recapitulation." These claims short-circuit serious thought about compositional anomalies. What is unusual about a composition is breezily normalized, and the discussion about the structure's significance is over almost before it begins (because resolutions in the "wrong place" are not taken to have a significance other than that of affirming some version of Cone's sonata principle, however it might be reformulated). Opposed to this style of overaccomodating analytical thinking, we reject any normalizing principle that explains away an obviously nonconforming situation. Since a piece's essence resides in its individualized dialogue with socially established norms, any deviation from those norms—especially recapitulatory deviations—are of the utmost interest. They need to be highlighted and problematized, not swept away with a slogan.

This brings us to a final point. In those rare instances when the issue comes up, omitted S-modules in the recapitulation may or may not have been presented in (or fleetingly on) the tonic in the preceding development. *Pace* Rosen, this issue is unpredictable. The first movement of Haydn's "Bird" Quartet, op. 33 no. 3, for instance, does not not provide a developmental tonic appearance of its missing recapitulatory S-modules, while the quartet movements cited by Rosen do. What does seem to be the case is that if the development has already sounded P or TR modules (or an episode) and then gives way to a new tonic-$S^{1.1}$ module (in other words, if the tonic-$S^{1.1}$ appears mid-development as a component of a rotation) and if that tonic $S^{1.1}$ module is not merely an interior way-station in a set of sequences based on S, then the normal implication would be that the music has entered the tonal resolution of a Type 2 sonata (chapter 17). Once that false tonal resolution is abandoned in favor of more development, then it would seem usually to be the case, as a first-level default, that the S-modules that had been stated in the tonic are no longer available for use in the (Type 3) recapitulation. Present-

---

16. Rosen may be referring here to what we call a Type 2 sonata, discussed in ch. 17.

17. Rosen, *The Classical Style*, pp. 72–74.

ing tonic-S-modules in the development can be a way of extinguishing those modules from further tonic use. This suggests that in normative practice S-modules may appear only once in the tonic throughout the entire composition. One presumes that liquidating S-modules in this manner plays into the strategy of the piece as a whole, within which the "real" recapitulation might emerge as a simplification of problematic structural issues that had surfaced in the exposition.

The Fallacies of "Closer Relation" and a "Resolving" Fifth-Transposition

Cone's original remark was not only overextended with regard to the material that it sought to cover, but it also maintained that tonic resolution per se was not strictly necessary for the sonata principle to have been sustained. All that was needed is that the off-tonic material be brought "into a closer relation with the tonic, before the movement ends." This is indefensible. In the first place it is unclear what a "closer relation with the tonic" might mean. What relation, for example, could be closer than a statement in the dominant (which is what one finds in the exposition)? Cone's example (from the Type 4 finale of Beethoven's *Pathétique* sonata, op. 13) neither clarifies nor delimits the concept, and any number of off-tonic statements of a theme might be seized upon as evidence of this "closer relation." Once again, Cone's formulation encourages solutions that are too facile for the analytical problem at hand. Rather than finding excuses for non-normative events we should savor their exceptionality.

It may be Cone's concept of "closer relation" that occasionally prompts analysts to regard a nontonic theme or passage to have been somehow resolved if it reappears in the recapitulation or coda at a nontonic pitch level, but one a fifth below its original statement in the exposition. This issue sometimes crops up in minor-key sonatas (as in Beethoven's *Egmont* Overture, where the recapitulatory S–C block is sounded entirely in the submediant), but most normally it

emerges in late-eighteenth or early-nineteenth-century major-mode works that replace the conventional V in the exposition's S–C block (or in the first part of a TMB, as sometimes in Schubert's "three-key expositions") with another key, not uncommonly some version of III. Here the reasoning appeals to analogy: if the norm is that an expositional dominant-key theme is to be resolved down a fifth into the tonic in the recapitulation, then a theme originally in, say, III, is supposed to be understood as equivalently resolved, or at least sufficiently "balanced" on the "subdominant side," if it appears a fifth lower, in this case, in VI. One understands the argument on behalf of balance, of course. Without question, in such situations that complementary balance exists and is an important feature of the recapitulation. Nevertheless, nonresolution is nonresolution. And surely this is the whole point of the theme in question: its persistent "alienation" from the tonic, its inability to carry out the culturally grounded norm and, usually, the movement's subsequent interest in repairing (or covering up) the tonal distress in some later passage.[18]

Nonresolving Recapitulations: S Does Not Attain the ESC

Recapitulations with an S That Fails

Much of the pertinent background regarding this "crisis" situation has been treated in chapter 8, under "Deformation: Failed Expositions." Since the main generic requirement of a recapitulation is to secure the ESC with a satisfactory I:PAC at the end of S, any recapitulation that falls short of this obligation, leaving the rhetorical recapitulation tonally or cadentially open, is problematic. Such a "failed" recapitulation is a strong expressive gesture—a deformation—and the expected cadence, and tonal closure for the piece, is deferred beyond sonata-space into a coda. In all instances the interpretive point is that the processes of the sonata have proven insufficient to meet the generic de-

---

18. Cf. n. 9.

mands imposed at the outset of the exposition. A generic contract to produce a sonata had been proposed and accepted, but the actual workings of the piece were staged as unable to carry it out successfully. The hermeneutic burden of the analyst is to explore the inner logic of this inadequacy. Merely to claim that all turns out well because a resolution is eventually secured in the coda is to miss the point. It is more compelling to suggest that the closure in the coda only reflects on what did not happen in the preceding sonata—at times a disillusioned lamenting of the absence of closure in the proper structural space; at times an "external," after-the-fact corrective in a necessarily appended, often discursive surplus-space; at times a desperate attempt to recover from a difficult situation through bluff and bravado.

Assuming that the referential rotation is presented more or less in full, one may distinguish among three types of nonresolving recapitulations. In the first, part 2 (S/C) appears in the tonic, but (like the exposition) cannot attain a satisfactory PAC. (There was no EEC in the exposition, and, correspondingly, there is no ESC in the recapitulation.) The *locus classicus* is the finale of Beethoven's Symphony No. 5 in C Minor, op. 67, in which cadential closure is deferred to the coda. The inability of both exposition and recapitulation to attain their generic goals is the most important structural aspect of this movement. More broadly, the trajectory of the entire symphony has been striving to attain a stable C major (a C:PAC that may be regarded as "real," not merely provisional or vulnerable to subsequent undermining), and the deferral of this event past the sonata-space of the finale's recapitulation plays into the sustained drama of the whole and provides the *raison d'être* of this unusually expansive and exhaustive coda. Additional examples may be found in the finales of Beethoven's Symphony No. 2 in D, op. 36, and No. 8 in F, op. 93, as well as that of his Quartet in C, op. 59 no. 3. The procedure would also turn up in works composed later in the nineteenth century.

A second type of nonresolution occurs when the recapitulation's part 2 begins in the proper (tonic) key with the hope of accomplishing the ESC but loses that key by drifting or being wrenched away from it. This is a powerful deformation of the norm, a misfiring of expected sonata procedures: the ESC, of course, must occur in the tonic. One early instance of this deformational procedure occurs in the E-major slow movement of Beethoven's Piano Trio in G major, Op. 1 no. 2 (composed in 1793–94). In both the exposition and the recapitulation S begins properly—in the conventional key—but veers away from closure in that key. In the exposition S (m. 26) decays away from the normal B major to a closing cadence in G (♮III!, m. 40—notice also that this is the tonic of the outer movements); in the recapitulation S begins in the proper E major (m. 67), but soon veers to C major and thence to a closing PAC in a desolate A minor (iv!, m. 82). What may be understood as a lengthy, discursive coda reviews the bleakness and ultimately settles the movement back onto E major—although it is alternatively possible to interpret this "coda" as a newly appended C-space, provided that one is willing to entertain the non-normative possibility of a rhetorical incongruity with the exposition (within which this presumed "C" had not been permitted to unfold). Under either interpretation we have at least a nonresolving S, the crucial element in the production of the ESC. If what follows is interpreted under the category of a coda (as opposed to a "new" C), then we also have a fully nonresolving recapitulation.[19]

Within such a movement one finds two ESC-effects. The first one, within sonata-space proper (ending S), is a "substitute" or "false" ESC, providing the illusion of closure in the wrong key with an otherwise correctly placed PAC. The real ESC, bringing tonal closure to the whole movement, is articulated on the other side of sonata-space (or at least past the completion of S), normally in a coda. While the first type of nonresolving recapitulation mentioned above did not violate the orthodox conception of the

---

19. These problems and related others are dealt with at greater length in Hepokoski, "Back and Forth from *Egmont*: Beethoven, Mozart, and the Nonresolving Recapitulation," *19th-Century Music* 25 (2001), 127–54, certain points of which the present section provides a summary.

sonata principle, this second type clearly does: the S-block is never resolved in the tonic key.

This is also true of the third type of nonresolving recapitulation, which is found when part 2 appears completely, from its outset, in the wrong key and never recovers. The paradigm is Beethoven's F-minor *Egmont* Overture. Here the exposition is structured normatively: S and C emerge in III, A-flat major (with an unproblematic EEC, III:PAC, in m. 104). The rhetorical recapitulation is parallel to that of the exposition, but its S and C are sounded in VI, D-flat major (the substitute-ESC in D-flat happens in m. 247). A brief coda-extension (mm. 259–86), perhaps implying a reference to the execution of Egmont, descends to an open V of F minor, and a "utopian" coda—probably suggesting a sudden shift to future time after Egmont's execution—provides the "Victory Symphony" coda proper (mm. 287–347) that resolves to F major and provides PAC-closure in that key.[20] A somewhat related example may be found in the C-minor Andante espressivo middle movement ("Abwesenheit," "L'Absence") of Beethoven's Piano Sonata in E-flat, op. 81a, "Les Adieux"—whose expositional structure Tovey identified as "dealing with a series of short themes in *rotation* [emphasis added], recapitulating them in another group of keys."[21] In the exposition, S (m. 15) is sounded in G major (major V!), while in the deformational recapitulatory rotation (setting out in F minor [!], m. 21 [= m. 5]), S returns, fruitlessly (doubtless for programmatic reasons), in F major (IV, m. 31). The onset of a third rotation, m. 37, recycles the music back to a murky "V⁹" and vii°⁷ of C minor

in a brief, P-based transition to the E-flat-major finale. After *Egmont* and the slow movement of "Les Adieux," this type of nonresolving recapitulation became a recognizable sonata-deformation option (in Glinka's Overture to *Ruslan and Lyudmila*; in Tchaikovsky's *Romeo and Juliet*; in the first movements of Brahms's Symphony No. 3 in F, op. 90, Saint-Saëns's Symphony No. 3 in C Minor, op. 78, and Mahler's Symphony No. 6 in A minor; and in several other pieces).

Truncated Recapitulations: Suppression of the S–C Block

The most obvious violation of the supposed sonata principle—and indeed, of the most basic generic norms of ESC-attainment, the mainspring of a sonata—occurs in those few works where the recapitulation is aborted shortly after P or P–TR in the recapitulation, proceeding, usually, into a brief coda. In such extraordinary pieces the recapitulation is kept from entering part 2. It never proceeds beyond its inert portion—that portion generically powerless to produce the ESC, namely P and TR. The sonata thus falls short of its generic mission to provide the requisite tonal resolution with the only action-space, S, that is capable of providing it. The implications of such structures appear to be affected in part by the tempo and movement-type within which they occur. Rapid-tempo examples may carry stronger connotations than slow-tempo ones.

Within Allegro compositions these compositions are extreme deformations, registering some catastrophe or act of violence that has be-

---

20. Something similar happens, although in the major mode and with some additional complications, in the finale of Beethoven's Piano Trio in E-flat, op. 70 no. 2. Here the exposition moves from I to III (G major), and the recapitulation retraces this material in a move from I to VI (C major). In this case, though, near the presumed C-major "end" of the recapitulatory rotation (m. 294 = m. 101), the music is unsettled (mm. 295–301) to "back up" and regrasp the latter stages of TR at the proper E-flat-major pitch level (m. 302 = m. 242 = m. 49) and thereby "correct" the second half of the recapitulation by sounding it again (with variants), now in the proper tonic key. The effect is that of a double-recapitulation of the second half of the rotation, the first off-tonic, the

second in the tonic. (See also the related section at the end of ch. 12, "Double-Recapitulation Effects.")
21. Tovey, *A Companion to Beethoven's Pianoforte Sonatas*, p. 195. Tovey's intuited circularity of such structures ("in rotation") intersects, of course, with our more elaborated concept of rotational structure in general. Cf. Tovey's subsequent remarks on this movement: "This form, musically very simple, admirably solves the problem of expressing the sorrow of absence without inflicting its tedium on the listener. The cycle of thoughts, at first wistful, then yielding to a mood of affectionate reminiscence [etc.] . . . this cycle must recur for ever unless miracles happen."

fallen the structure as a whole. Perhaps not surprisingly, the two paradigmatic examples occur in dramatic overtures: that of Mozart to *Idomeneo*, K. 366, and Beethoven's *Leonore No. 2*. In the Mozart—a classic instance of sonata deformation—the expositional TR (m. 23, starting off in the tonic, D) leads to a blocked MC-effect (cadential $\frac{6}{4}$ of V) in m. 41 followed by the characteristic *piano* descent to a V:PAC in m. 45. The precise moment of cadence is marked with a simultaneous, and ominous, shift to A minor (v). This marks the onset of TM^1 (= S), m. 46, with TM^2 (inflecting momentarily to A minor's III, C major, m. 55, as if seeking a major-mode escape-hatch away from A minor), leading to a second apparent MC (V:HC, apparently a corrective for the earlier blocked MC), m. 63. In turn this sets up the launch of a *forte* TM^3 (m. 64, perhaps with the character of an S^C), which brings about the EEC (m. 81) and the end of the exposition. Following a brief, half-rotational developmental space (based on P, mm. 82–93), the recapitulation begins in m. 93 with a normative stretch of correspondence measures. The recapitulatory TR (m. 115) continues this pattern for several bars until, dropping a fifth, it is sprung forth into an extension at m. 127. From this point onward the music is subjected to decay and eventually to an unspooling of the tension normatively found in TR-zones. Without having left TR the music drops to a dominant-lock on A (m. 137, now V of D minor)—shot through with convulsive *forte* shudders—and thence to a tonic pedal on D (m. 146). But this is almost instantly transformed from a tonic sonor-

ity into V of G minor, as though the principle of descending fifths is now not to be stopped. The piece ends with a iv:HC MC-effect deployed in an enervated augmentation. In sum, the sonata process is shattered with shock-waves that ripple through and extend the recapitulatory TR. In every way the aborted recapitulation marks this as a "failed" sonata. By the end even its tonic has been transformed into a preparatory dominant.

In Beethoven's C-major Overture, *Leonore No. 2*, an obviously representational work (concerned with the liberation of the imprisoned Florestan, the topic itself a metaphor for political emancipation), the originally major-mode P-theme bursts forth *fortissimo* and virtually unprepared in *C minor* (m. 348). This sudden, compulsive onset of an apparent recapitulatory rotation must have been intended to convey a sense of the utmost calamity, of plans gone horribly wrong.[22] And indeed, with the fate-sealing i:PAC only a few bars later (m. 382) the modally altered "recapitulation" seems to self-destruct at once, as if unexpectedly arrested by a counter-revolutionary ambush. Projecting a destroyed recapitulatory process, this dramatic situation is "saved" only by the famous entrance of the trumpet-call, here on E-flat, announcing the arrival of aid from outside of sonata-space. Neither S proper nor C is reached in this extraordinarily brief and strenuous recapitulation attempt.[23] All C-major PAC-resolutions are postponed until what is probably best regarded as coda-space. This "difficult" work, which is capable of supporting more than one reading of

---

22. In the *Leonore No. 3* revision the C-minor passage—the moment of the catastrophic plunge into an attempted recapitulation in *Leonore No. 2*—is alluded to with P-material in C minor beginning in m. 252. There it is absorbed more clearly into the developmental space, even while suggesting ominously the possibility of a C-minor recapitulation-to-come. That potential C-minor recapitulation is forestalled with the entry of the trumpet fanfare, now placed into the development and rewritten on the pitch-level of B-flat major (m. 272).

23. We have written the phrase "S proper," because the recapitulatory situation is somewhat more complex than that described above. One might maintain, for example, that a varied version of the exposition's S (E major, mm. 156ff) does return, varied, in the C-major Adagio

interpolation, mm. 426–32—a passage that, in effect, stands for a recovery of S in the tonic, even though that S-variant immediately proves unable to secure a PAC (ESC). But the exposition's m. 156 S is itself a variant of Florestan's theme from the Adagio introduction (mm. 10–16, A-flat major, quoting from his aria, "In des Lebens Frühlingstagen"). In the m. 426 Adagio what recurs is the introduction-version of this melody, not the S-version proper. Thus one could argue that m. 426 cycles one back to the original "problem" of the overture's introduction (Florestan's imprisonment) rather than recapturing and tonally stabilizing S itself. Both interpretations are viable, and the expressive power of the tonic-key m. 426 moment resides in its multiple connotations.

its structure, is also an early example of a deformation type that we call an *anti-recapitulation*, a category that encompasses recapitulations that instead of affirming the rotationally generic presentation of thematic materials seem to undermine them at every step. These materials might return as alarming distortions or themes under uncommon strains or tensions, as themes that are subjected to liquidation before completion, and so on, as though there were an underlying negative current fighting the recapitulation and ultimately destroying its efficacy.

Allegro movements with truncated recapitulations seem to be extremely rare and reserved for special effects of high distress. Also rare, but perhaps somewhat more common (if sometimes also *Angst*-ridden), are slow-movement omissions of the S and C zones. There are several examples of these in the repertory. These include the slow movements of Haydn's Quartets in G and D, op. 33 nos. 5 and 6;[24] of Mozart's Piano Concerto No. 23 in A, K. 488; of Mozart's Quartet in D, K. 575; and of Beethoven's Piano Concerto No. 1 in C, op. 15, and his Septet in E-flat, op. 20. They seem to occur most often in combination with Type 1 sonatas (those with no development), so that the resulting shape is typically something like: {P TR ' S / C} {P . . .} {coda}. Sonata-space comes to an end with the concluding cadence of part-1 material (sometimes expanded), and the coda may or may not contain veiled (compensatory?) references to the "lost" recapitulatory themes.[25] Because this pattern crops up more than two or three times, it may be best to consider it an alternative structure, albeit one that from our perspective today seems odd, even countergeneric, with its restriction of the recapitulation only to its inert portions. It is therefore probably not a deformation but something of a low-level default option for slow-movement structure.[26]

However we regard it, the impression in each case is that of an incomplete or aborted recapitulatory rotation, one kept from entering into part 2 and any normative attaining of the ESC. Another, perhaps incidental (?) effect of these movements is that of a sonata exposition that converts into what may be roughly described as an ABA' shape, in which B is somehow understood as being represented by the exposition's part 2, even though this is not usually how B-sections are prepared within a large ternary form. In this respect the resulting structure might be grasped as a hybrid between a Type 1 sonata and an ABA' form. Nonetheless, a crucial feature of these movements is that they begin with normative sonata expositions, which suggests that the sonata is the preponderant category in this hybrid. At best, these are problematic structures, and they merit the closest attention. Later, related situations within Type 3 sonatas (with development)—probably written with a knowledge of these Type 1 models—may be found in the second movements of Brahms's Symphonies No. 2 in D, op. 73 (although $S^{1.1}$ is omitted altogether, a variant of $S^{1.2}$, first presented in m. 45, does return in m. 92, but only as a sign of structural wreckage), and No. 3, op. 90 (with $S^{1.1}$ and $S^{1.2}$ omitted, moving directly to the hauntingly hollow "searchlights" of $S^{1.3}$, initially heard in m. 57 and reappearing in m. 116; $S^{1.1}$, from m. 41, will reappear only in the finale).[27]

---

24. In op. 33 no. 5/ii, not a pure example of this procedure, a brief reference to a measure of S (the EEC-producing m. 25, with EEC at m. 26) is briefly recaptured just before the EEC (m. 50, with ESC at m. 51).

25. In particular, Mozart's Quartet, K. 575/ii, seems to allude both to P- and S-fragments in its coda, mm. 62–73.

26. In "Are Mozart's Concertos 'Dramatic'? Concerto Ritornellos versus Aria Introductions in the 1780s," *Mozart's Piano Concertos: Text, Context, Interpretation*, ed. Neal Zaslaw (Ann Arbor: University of Michigan Press, 1996), pp. 129-30, James Webster mentioned that this structure "is precisely one of Mozart's most common aria forms, especially for heartfelt utterances in a slow or moderate tempo." As examples he cited Don Ottavio's

"Il mio tesoro" (*Don Giovanni*) and Ferrando's "Un aura amorosa" (*Così fan tutte*). Of these two, the latter is the clearer illustration. The former, "Il mio tesoro," does not exemplify this structure, since it unfolds essentially as a (double-rotational) Type 1 sonata with a recomposed TR/S space, an interpretation bolstered by the double-cycling through the text. Cf. Webster, "The Analysis of Mozart's Arias," *Mozart Studies*, ed. Cliff Eisen (New York: Oxford University Press, 1991), pp. 121–22.

27. Cf. Elaine Sisman's discussion, from a different perspective, of "Brahms's Slow Movements: Reinventing the 'Closed' Forms," in *Brahms Studies: Analytical and Historical Perspectives*, ed. George S. Bozarth (Oxford: Clarendon, 1990), pp. 79–104.

*The Larger Role of the Recapitulation
within the Sonata*

Tonal Potential, Tonic Presence

Much of the analytical and hermeneutic style of Sonata Theory is grounded upon its registering of the details of a piece's drive to complete an ordered set of cadential goals. The sense of drama within eighteenth-century sonata practice is ingrained in the genre's striving to articulate cadences in a spotlighted, quasi-theatrical, or narrative way. One way of understanding a sonata is to interpret it as a dramatized musical activity that by means of fluctuations of energy seeks to pass through an ordered set of rhetorical and tonal gateways—cadential stations that must be visited on the way to the ESC and thence to the end of the piece. A composition is the representation of a multi-staged strategy—engineered by the composer in dialogue with generic norms—by which the work's ESC can be planned for, set up, and, in most cases, attained (and then, hopefully, held onto).

At the heart of this conception is the postulate that a merely local diatonicism is not sufficient to anchor a tonality. Provisionality becomes reality—a confirmed tonic presence—only when ratified with a cadence, serving in the manner of an "official seal." This postulate operates on both small and large structural levels. Within a phrase, everything that occurs before the cadence defines itself not as a secured tonality *per se* but as tonal potential.[28] To begin a phrase "in E-flat major" is only to ground the opening in the E-flat diatonic scale. This is done either to propose E-flat as a tonic for the phrase or to set out from that diatonic scale in order to move elsewhere. We learn which is the case by observing the cadence at the phrase's end. The E-flat major at the phrase's beginning is not yet fully present. To be sure, it has an unequivocal

diatonic presence: loosely we might say (and often do) that the phrase begins "in E-flat major." But a stricter use of language can lead to more productive hermeneutic conclusions. Hence we arrive at a cardinal axiom of Sonata Theory: Because an initial diatonic presence in a phrase can dissolve, swerve away, or modulate, its "key" exists as a proposition, as something potentially impermanent, mutable, not thoroughly secured. The key does not yet exist for that phrase as a fully actualized reality, however conceptually saturated it may be with promise. A phrase's secured tonic presence comes into being only at the moment of its cadence.

Phrases (along with all larger tonal structures) are end-accented, fluid motions or dramatized trajectories of energy toward cadences. As one phrase is linked to another, a complete composition will emerge from a linear succession of such phrases or cadential spans. Each phrase has its own telos, its own cadential goal. Within the genres that comprise the multimovement-sonata style—and according to the norms implicit within each genre—phrases in combination set up a (generically predetermined) higher-level hierarchy of less and more important cadences. The most structurally important cadence in a sonata is the ESC (completing the essential sonata trajectory)—the generic goal toward which an entire sonata form strives.

What is true of the phrase is also true of the larger structures built up as a concatenation of phrases. At the highest single-movement level, a sonata is a striving toward the realization of tonic presence throughout the course of an extended, conceptually complete structural block, itself built through the linear assembly of smaller blocks. Neither the larger nor the smaller blocks are static: both are more properly regarded as processes characterized by vectored, inner motion ("action-zone blocks of musical motion"—see the section "Connotations of 'Deformation'" in appendix 2). The tonic is solidified and stabi-

---

28. We understand a phrase—as opposed to a module (which may or may not be coextensive with a phrase)—as a more or less complete musical thought involving tonal motion towards a cadence. We find it helpful, for the sake of clarity and consistency within one's own discourse, to regard the normative require-

ment of conclusion with a cadence as crucial. See our outline of differing points of view regarding this matter in ch. 5, n. 10. When cadences are delayed over broad stretches of musical space, it is sometimes preferable—for the sake of clarity—to use the term *cadential span* rather than phrase.

lized only at or very near the end, at the point of the I:PAC that completes the generically obligatory musical process toward which the block had been driving—in this case, the ESC.[29] This reflects an end-accented, goal-oriented view of the form, harnessed to a process of an emerging tonic presence, made "real" only with the attainment of the ESC. Most of the drama of any composition is made possible through an interaction of the generic foreknowledge of the musical goal toward which such compositions (or passages) strive with the particulars of the path that an individualized work takes toward that goal. Whether small- or large-scale, any structure passes through a series of conceptual phases, the analytical interpretation of which is to be governed by the background expectations or tacit knowledge of the normative behavior of the genre within which that structure operates.

While it is self-evidently true that an exposition's P-theme declares the tonic of the work, within P that tonic exists primarily to propose a key to be achieved—crystallized into a real tonal presence—through the process of the larger structure. The tonic asserted by P is only a provisional indication of the tonal goal to be realized much later on. (Again, see the section of chapter 5, "Tonal Under- and Overdetermination.") To provide a dramatic example: it is central to the understanding of the entire symphony to realize that the celebrated inbreaking of C major at the opening of the finale of Beethoven's Fifth Symphony by no means "solves" the extravagantly dramatized minor-major conflict that courses through this work. This triumphant brass arrival and declaration of C major at this point marks only the emergence of the full possibility of a C-major victory down the road, one that will have to be achieved—earned—by a successful sonata process.[30] In the Fifth Symphony C minor is not decisively overturned by C major until the moment of essential structural closure (the ESC) toward the end of the finale—the first satisfactory I:PAC after the onset of S in the recapitulation. As it happens, Beethoven submitted the whole finale-process to the highest of dramas. As mentioned earlier, we have both a strenuously failed exposition (no EEC) and a nonresolving recapitulation (no ESC in the recapitulatory space). This delays closure past the recapitulation—past sonata-space—and into the coda. And even there, securing the ESC "outside the sonata proper" proves no easy task.

Narrative Implications: The Sonata as Metaphor for Human Action

A sonata is a linear journey of tonal realization, onto which might be mapped any number of concrete metaphors of human experience. Since a central component of the sonata genre is its built-in teleological drive—pushing forward to accomplish a generically predetermined goal—the sonata invites an interpretation as a musically narrative genre. A sonata dramatizes a purely musical plot that has a beginning (P, the place from where it sets out with a specific tonal-rhetorical aim in mind), a middle (including a set of diverse musical adventures), and a generic conclusion of resolution and confirmation (the ESC and subsequent music).[31] It is in the

---

29. Such a view is resonant also with Schenkerian conceptions of form, in which an initial instability is either posited or created, an instability that is expanded in "free composition" and is eventually brought to rest with the completion of the *Ursatz*. From the perspective of Sonata Theory the I:PAC marking the point of essential (generically obligatory) structural closure may or may not be understood as identical to the completion of the linear descent of the *Urlinie*—or at least of the governing melodic line of the passage in question. This determination may legitimately differ from analyst to analyst. See the concluding discussion in ch. 7, "Some Schenkerian Implications."

30. While steering clear of any claim for a literal-minded program for the work (it is possible to understand the piece in purely musical terms), one might suggest that one quasi-militaristic metaphor at hand—especially with the added trombones and piccolo at this moment (not to mention the C major)—might well be the eleventh-hour arrival of the reinforcements needed to win the battle-to-come. Again, we concede that Beethoven might not have specifically intended such an image, and our point is not to insist upon it but only to point out that the metaphor is conceptually parallel to the effect of the opening of the finale and its subsequent unfolding.

31. One might similarly claim, for instance, that to follow the details of a Schenkerian foreground or middleground graph is to attend to aspects of a purely musical plot, one that is generically expected to lead to a characteristic, foreordained denouement.

nature of the sonata to set up a quest narrative. In addition to being required to display (or at least refer to) the interior, multitextured norms of sonata practice, a sonata must realize those norms coherently, in such a way as to move toward and secure the ESC and generic closure. This is a narrative that may be understood in exclusively musical terms. In interpreting it, the present-day analyst need not appeal to nonmusical motivations. Still, the music of the period was widely perceived as having a human basis, whether in the emotions, in the intellect, in other schemes of representation or implication, or in various combinations of these.

A sonata is a metaphorical representation of a perfect human action. It is a narrative "action" because it drives through a vectored sequence of energized events toward a clearly determined, graspable goal, the ESC. It is "perfect" because (unless artificially blocked from achieving the goal) it typically accomplishes the task elegantly, proportionally, and completely. It is "human" primarily within eighteenth-century European conceptions of humanness. By "representation" we do not refer to the presence of unequivocal, concrete imagery or extramusical stories. Instead, the sense of representation in sonatas is for the most part suggestive, inlaid (as part of the sonata "game") into their chains of dramatic, linear modules, into their calculated impression of pulling insistently for attention at our sleeves, as if at some deeper level each of them must somehow also be "about" processes

that are fundamental to Western European experience.

The skeptic or the arch-positivist might dismiss such matters as not provable, and in fact they are not. But a facile close-down of the question of broader meaning and implication can seem premature, arbitrary, a decisionistic retreat from an adequately trenchant intellectual engagement with this repertory. Some of the most productive responses to the problem of instrumental music's representational ambiguity are available through heuristic analogy and metaphor. Such approaches are hermeneutic. They are concerned with suggesting reasonable parallels, analogues, and similes within our experience, not with insisting that the single best reading has finally been uncovered within the music ("we now *know* that this Haydn sonata—or this single passage within it—signifies *this* [and *only* this]"). These metaphorical analogues are set into motion only through the active participation and individualized interests of the close listener.

In the absence of verbal clues or instructions, the specifics of any extramusical implication (the applicability of any set of visual or literary images) are *underdetermined*. By this term, in this context, we mean that in nontexted music the evidence at hand is usually not sufficiently clarified to permit a definitive or unambiguous reading in terms of "intended" (or latent) personal, social, or political imagery.[32] The structural shape of any given sonata can respond to

---

32. The terms "underdetermination" and "overdetermination" are loaded words in hermeneutic contexts, and it might be well to mention a few things about our use of them in this book. In ch. 5 we used these terms in an exclusively technical sense, referring to the absence of an attainment of a I:PAC within an exposition's P-zone ("underdetermination" of the tonic) or, by contrast, to the multiple statements of a I:PAC within that zone ("overdetermination" of the tonic). In the present context "underdetermination" addresses different matters: issues of metaphorical meaning and implication; grappling with potentially ambiguous connotations of implicit musical representation and homologous extramusical analogues. Those familiar with literary theory might wonder whether the seemingly opposite term, "overdetermination," might not be the more relevant one in this situation. Stemming from Freud's theory of dreams and adapted famously in the twentieth cen-

tury by such literary critics as I. A. Richards, Simon O. Lesser, Louis Althusser, Wolfgang Iser, and Jean Baudrillard, the multiple literary-critical uses of "overdetermination" point toward the issue of textual *ambiguity*; toward the consequent possibility of the same literary text being interpreted differently by differing reading communities; toward Iser's explication of textual indeterminacy; and toward Althusser's structuralist-marxist insistence that superstructural phenomena (such as literature) have multiple determinative causes (relative autonomy) extending beyond the economic base. To adopt those senses in the more problematic contexts of musical signification (for example, to suggest that the only "vaguely suggested" images or topical associations potentially conjured up by instrumental music are "*over*determined" rather than "*under*determined"), however, strikes us as counterintuitive and probably misleading for most readers in our discipline.

any number of extramusical parallels that listeners might wish to interweave into it, provided that that narrative is governed by the same expressive shape as the music in all of its details. Metaphorical analogues should not be brief catch-phrases or broad generalizations: they should be more thoroughly developed, capable of being elaborated, phrase-by-phrase, throughout all of the action-zones of the sonata.

Since the sonata, *qua* sonata, was capable of dramatizing a set of actions in a general, metaphorical way, composers have from time to time specified or suggested which kinds of narrative or conceptual implications would be appropriate to map onto the music. On the one hand, this could be loosely implied through the well-known "thesaurus of *characteristic figures*" described by Ratner in his discussion of musical topics: conventions of sound and texture that associate styles of certain musical modules with established activities (hunt, march, dance) or standard moods (pastoral, regal, brilliant, *Sturm und Drang*)—all of which could be coupled with the use of time-honored classical figures of argumentation and rhetoric (exordia, antitheses, perorations, repetitions, interruptions, and so on).[33] On the other hand, this could also be done by means of appended paratexts—supplementary indications that instruct the listener how to begin to frame a metaphorical understanding of the otherwise nontexted music. These could include literary titles that conjured up familiar narratives, images, or topical types (Haydn's nicknamed symphonies, Dittersdorf's Symphonies based on Ovid's *Metamorphoses*,

Beethoven's *Egmont* Overture, the *Eroica* and *Pastoral* Symphonies); verbal commentaries or performance indications within the score; composer's explanatory comments made to acquaintances either in correspondence or personally, *a voce*; intertextual allusions to works with verbal texts; and so on.[34]

When such paratexts have not been provided—and given the inherent underdetermination of nontexted music with regard to any implied external referent—one should be cautious in insisting upon the primacy of only one hermeneutic metaphor (or analogue in human experience) to the musical processes that one is encountering in any given piece. Different readings or hermeneutic interpretations of what happens in these works with regard to broader psychological, cultural, or social implications are more than possible. Indeed, they are to be encouraged. The language and concerns of Sonata Theory lead to larger interpretive readings, situations in which technical analysis and an artfully nuanced hermeneutics become different aspects of the same process. We encourage an intellectually and analytically responsible boldness in this regard, an interpretive flair that startles pieces awake as historical and cultural statements. Musical passages need not directly represent a specific experience (that is, they need not be regarded as a sonic image of that experience alone) to be structurally similar to that experience. Submitting a work to a responsible reading is not the same thing as uncovering an objective fact. And laying out a metaphorical analogue in human experience is not the same

---

33. Ratner, *Classic Music*, pp. 9–29 (topics), 91–107 (rhetorical figures). Ratner's topical categories are by now familiar. One category of topic encompassed what he called "types": These included the metric, rhythmic, and thematic impulses behind numerous dance types (minuet, passepied, sarabande, allemande, polonaise, bourée, *contredanse*, gavotte, gigue, siciliano) and various kinds of marches. Another category included different "styles": military and hunt music; fanfares; "the singing style" (aria style, lyrical melody over simple accompaniment) or, if in quick tempo, "singing allegro"; the brilliant style (rapid passagework, sometimes quasi-mechanical, suggesting "clockwork"); French overture, including the initial, unison *coups d'archet*; musette and pastorale; Turkish music; *Sturm und Drang*; sensibility

and *Empfindsamkeit* (intimate, sentimental, personal styles, often confessional in tone, with sighs, etc.); strict and learned styles (fugal/imitative; often ecclesiastical, strict, or traditional in tone—the *stile legato* or *bound* style, sometimes proceeding in the *alla breve* style, in whole- and half-notes; there also existed a freer, more flexible *galant* version); *alla zoppa* ("limping") syncopations; and fantasia, including the possibility of *ombra* (evocation of the supernatural with a turn to minor and other musical effects). Ratner also made provisions for various types of "pictorialisms" and "word-painting."
34. See Richard Will, *The Characteristic Symphony in the Age of Haydn and Beethoven* (Cambridge: Cambridge University Press, 2002).

thing as insisting upon a naively programmatic basis for the music. The most convincing hermeneutic metaphors would be those that are historically sensitive, analytically sophisticated, closely congruent with every moment of the music (thereby avoiding a flat, interpretive reductionism), and grounded in research into the period in question.

Finally, the presence of any sonata deformation whose implications extend over the generic structure of the whole piece would seem *ipso facto* to call into question the legitimacy of the sonata strategy to provide a solution to the compositional or expressive problem at hand. This is especially true of those deformations that articulate a sonata that "fails" to accomplish its generic mission (sonatas with nonresolving recapitulations, minor-mode sonatas whose major-mode, emancipatory ESC's are overturned in the coda, and the like). Extreme formal deformation can suggest an undermining of confidence in the form itself. The demonstration of "sonata failure" became an increasingly attractive option in the hands of nineteenth-century composers who, for one reason or another, wished to suggest the inadequacy of the Enlightenment-grounded solutions provided by generic sonata practice. Deformation of form became identical with deformation of expressive content. Such options could be employed in either programmatic or "absolute" composition.

CHAPTER TWELVE

Non-Normative Openings of the Recapitulatory Rotation

Alternatives and Deformations

The preceding chapter considered the recapitulation as a whole and dealt with uncommon situations that may arise in that rotation's middle and later portions: nonresolving recapitulations (suppressing the ESC within sonata-space) and the even more unusual truncated recapitulations (omitting part 2, S/C). Here we are concerned with potentially problematic beginnings of recapitulatory rotations. These include such practices as seeming to start the recapitulation several measures into the P-zone or initiating the rotation in the parallel mode or a nontonic key. Cropping up not only in the mid- and late-century *Kleinmeister* but also occasionally in Haydn, Mozart, and Beethoven (and later composers), these issues have been challenging for theorists of sonata form, and different descriptions and explanations have been provided for them. From the perspective of Sonata Theory these challenges are faced by looking for the recapitulation not in some abstract sense (which in some prior interpretive systems has been equated with identifying the moment of the return of the tonic)

but for the onset of the recapitulatory rotation. At what point does a $P^{1.1}$ appear that begins the last sonata-space rotation? More precisely, and considered apart from normative expectations of tonic return, at what point, following a separate developmental space in a Type 3, 4, or 5 sonata, does a reintroduction of $P^{1.1}$ launch a series of successive modules—replicating the order of the referential (expositional) rotation—that track, as they proceed, toward the sonata's tonal resolution, the production of the ESC?[1]

In the most common situations the recapitulatory rotation starts with a tonic rebeginning ($P^{1.1}$), typically replicating the opening of the exposition. When this happens the return of the tonic key coincides with the relaunch of the rotation and a set of correspondence measures, and the recapitulation is complementary and parallel to the exposition in nearly every way. But this is not always the case. Any strong norm, firmly concretized within generic expectation, provides an opportunity for composers to experiment with alternatives. The convention remains as background information in listeners'

---

1. The postdevelopmental clause is present here to exclude the second (and final) rotations of Type 2 sonatas (ch. 17) from being considered recapitulatory rotations proper. In these cases the second rotations normally begin the developmental space, which would make the application of the term confusing. Additionally, in a Type 1 sonata, which lacks a development (ch. 16), the recapitulation directly succeeds the exposition and is usually nonproblematic.

minds—the expectant knowledge of what usually happens to define the separate moments in the form—while they are invited to savor the local tinkerings, veilings, or clever ploys actually provided by the composer.

Even though we usually come across these modifications within Type 3 sonata practice—the most commonly encountered type of sonata—some of them are also in dialogue with Type 2 conventions or at least in line with the style of rotational thinking that underpins the Type 2 sonata. Readers who are uncertain about Type 2 principles might wish to consult portions of chapter 17 before proceeding further.

Recapitulations That Appear to Begin after $P^{1.1}$

Since the strongest identifier of the beginning of a rotation is the sounding of its opening module, $P^{1.1}$ (see the opening of chapter 5, noting P's function as the initiator of rotations), any suggestion that a recapitulatory rotation begins with a post-$P^{1.1}$ module—perhaps with the exposition's second or third modules—is at least problematic and possibly an inadequate account of the situation at hand. Is this a rotation that genuinely omits $P^{1.1}$ in order to begin with $P^{1.2}$, P^2, or TR^1? If so, to what end? Or is the $P^{1.2}$, P^2, or TR^1 itself part of an ongoing rotation that had begun earlier with $P^{1.1}$, perhaps off-tonic, within the developmental space? When the latter is the case, we would most likely be confronting either an instance of a Type 2 sonata or an *ad hoc* intermixture of Type 2 and Type 3 principles. The first-presumed moment of recapitulation might instead be a point of *crux*, the onset of a stretch of correspondence measures. Such structures can be clarified only by keeping in mind the theory of rotations.

The "Disjunct" Recapitulation?

In a 1988 study of Haydn's recapitulatory procedures Mark Evan Bonds identified a phenom-

enon that he called a "disjunct" recapitulation. This occurs, he argued, when a tonic P^1 or $P^{1.1}$ module appears a few bars into the development (as it often does, as part of the usual fifth-descent pattern found at this point), proceeds onward to more characteristic development, and is succeeded by an apparent tonic recapitulation launched with $P^{1.2}$ or P^2 (or, more generally, with the module that would be next in line after $P^{1.1}$). The impression given is that the presumed recapitulation may avoid sounding $P^{1.1}$ in part because it had already been presented in the tonic near the beginning of the development. The early-developmental tonic-$P^{1.1}$ and recapitulatory $P^{1.2}$ (or P^1 and P^2, if P^1 had ended with a cadence) are thus separated by a digression into a modulatory development. In Bonds's description, "the material presented with the initial reiteration of the tonic shortly after the double bar is omitted at the moment of true recapitulation. . . . The recapitulation of thematic material, then, is disarticulated—or, more simply—disjunct." The accompanying illustration was drawn from the first movement of Haydn's Quartet in E-flat, op. 1 no. 2, and Bonds also provided a list of several other examples from Haydn's works before 1773, including the first movements of Symphonies Nos. 18, 19, 36, 37, 65, and 72.[2]

What are we to make of such situations? First, one should recognize that Bonds's discussion was intertwined with his own definitions of "true" and "false" recapitulations, "precursory" recapitulations, and the like, claims that have been subsequently disputed (see chapter 10). To confront these matters using those terms—including "disjunct recapitulation"—is already to cede conceptual territory that need not be relinquished. Second, much of the issue revolves around one's view of the status of the tonic-$P^{1.1}$ early in the developmental space. Since such a tonic-sounding of that module was conventional, there is nothing recapitulatory in its appearance there. One should not be tempted (and for the most part Bonds was not) to conclude

---

2. Bonds, "Haydn's False Recapitulations and the Perception of Sonata Form in the Eighteenth Century," p. 225. The list appears on p. 307.

that any kind of recapitulation—either "true" or "false"—had been implied at that early point.

Third, one's understanding of this situation should depend on the development that separates $P^{1.1}$ and $P^{1.2}$ (or P^1 and P^2). It may be, for instance, that the intervening material is $P^{1.1}$-based. In this case the structure of the rotation is preserved, and the tonic-$P^{1.2}$ proceeds as the next available rotational element, set up and highlighted as correspondence measures. Under these circumstances a broad, single rotation can be traced from the early-developmental tonic-$P^{1.1}$ to the correspondence-measures $P^{1.2}$ and beyond. (This is equally the case if the second element in question is not $P^{1.2}$ but P^2 or even TR^1.) Assuming that the development is sufficient in length, the whole movement in this situation is best understood as a *Type 2 sonata with early crux*. One should add, though, that if two other conditions are additionally present—1) a nonrepeated exposition and 2) the immediate succeeding of the end of the exposition with a tonic-$P^{1.1}$ (and not with an off-tonic passage or a preceding $P^{1.1}$ in the dominant or other key)—then one is dealing with an *expanded Type 1 sonata* (chapter 16), and the recapitulation proper will be considered to have begun with the postexpositional tonic $P^{1.1}$.

On the other hand, it may also happen that the music separating the "developmental" $P^{1.1}$ and the "recapitulatory" $P^{1.2}$ is not $P^{1.1}$ based. This situation would be operative if the intervening material goes on to continue its own rotation or half-rotation—that is, if the development proceeds conceptually past the $P^{1.2}$ rotational element to present later ideas (TR, S, or C)—then returns to tonic-$P^{1.2}$ to rebegin another cycle. (Obviously, the presence of developmental episodes would bring up further complications.) Moreover, this tonic-$P^{1.2}$ must reintroduce P-material into the piece as a genuine restart: it would not be immediately preceded by any off-tonic references to $P^{1.1}$ (which could identify an off-tonic recapitulatory opening). This is a different set of circumstances, implying that the recapitulatory rotation does

in fact begin with an ellipsis of its normatively opening bars. Does this suggest any kind of correspondence between $P^{1.2}$ and the "disjunct" tonic-$P^{1.1}$ earlier in the development? Probably not. There is no rule motivating such a seemingly compensatory move. One should not be surprised to encounter tonic-$P^{1.2}$ recapitulatory openings without the earlier appearance of a developmental tonic-$P^{1.1}$. As we reason through individual cases, we should also bear in mind that P- and TR-zones are always generically inert. Because they never produce the EEC or ESC, their modules may be altered, rearranged, or suppressed without damage to the overall structure. What is unusual in these cases is the suppression of the first module, normally the marker of a new rotational launch.

Non-"Disjunct" Recapitulations That Appear to Begin with Tonic-$P^{1.2}$, P^2, or TR

These situations are similar to those described above, except that the development provides no preceding "literal" tonic-$P^{1.1}$ statement. There is no sense that a melodically intact tonic-P-zone (or P–TR zone) has been separated by a digressive, intervening developmental texture.[3] Once again, the same principles apply in coming to an analytical assessment of the overall structure. If the entire development section had at least been based on $P^{1.1}$ (albeit with no tonic statement of that module), then the larger rotational course has been preserved from the exposition onward, and the form is in dialogue with the Type 2 sonata, with correspondence measures beginning with the pseudo-recapitulatory $P^{1.2}$, P^2 or TR. Alternatively, if the development had proceeded rotationally further than the module that seems to begin a recapitulation, then there is no Type 2 allusion, and the recapitulation-effect is genuine: one simply has to confront a reprise that suppresses its opening module.

But situations are not always this simple. Episodes within developments can cloud the matter, as can differing degrees of emphasis on the tonic-return to $P^{1.2}$, P^2 or TR. In the Type 2

---

3. If the development had begun with a "literal" but off-tonic $P^{1.1}$ statement, we would be confronting a Type 2 sonata with early crux.

variant, when such returns are strongly pre-pared—with a solid dominant-lock sustained for several measures, for example, fully in the manner of a dominant preparation for the re-turn of a normative recapitulation—it can seem counterintuitive merely to refer to what follows only as correspondence measures. There often is something expressively "recapitulatory" about such moments, and we might be justified in sug-gesting the possibility of intermixtures between the Type 2 and Type 3 principles: a Type 2 so-nata articulating itself in the manner of a Type 3, for instance; or a Type 3 sonata that suggests a hybridity with Type 2 logic. So long as the situation is not passed over as insignificant, in-dividual discussions and interpretations of its structural meaning may differ.

Of special interest are cases where the reca-pitulation seems to begin with a tonic-TR, as in the first movement of Schubert's Quartet in D Minor, D. 810, "Death and the Maiden" (m. 198).[4] Such issues are further complicated when, as in the above instance, the expositional TR had been P-based: the presumed recapitulation's TR will also sound like a return of P (in this case, P^0). This invites an interpretation based on a telescoping theory, according to which one supposes that the composer's goal was to avoid the redundancy of double-stated P-modules in the recapitulation, even though that had not been considered a problem in the exposition. On this theory the P-based TR, launching the recapitulation, serves double-duty, standing for both P and TR. This is cogent reasoning, but it is uncertain whether composers around 1800 would have shared the later-nineteenth- and twentieth-century (high-modernist) aversion to repetition. For that reason one might be sus-picious of that explanation. (The same line of argument has difficulty in coping with architec-tonic repeat-schemes in general.) Still, the idea that a shortened or telescoped recapitulation can suggest an eagerness to rush toward the central moment, the ESC (as suggested in chapter 11) might be both relevant and viable.

On the other hand, in such cases one should notice whether, for instance, the preceding de-velopment might have been based entirely on P (which is not the case in D. 810/i). If this develop-mental extended-P is taken as rotationally preced-ing the P-based TR with which the supposed re-capitulation begins, then the development and that "recapitulation" together articulate a broad rota-tion in the manner of a Type 2 sonata. This is the situation in the sonata-deformational "scherzo" section of the tonic-key second movement of Beethoven's Symphony No. 9 in D Minor, op. 125. Here, following a P-based development, the *fortissimo*, P-based TR careens headlong in a newly restored D minor (with pseudo-"recapitulatory" effect) at m. 272 (= m. 57). From this perspec-tive the "recapitulation" is better understood as an emphatically underscored tonic-crux midway through the ongoing rotation—another situa-tion of rhetorical and tonal incongruence. And yet when there is also an intense preparation for the return of this TR, it may seem unsatisfac-tory to deflate this event into nothing more than a crux. Such structures have aspects of both Type 2 and Type 3 sonatas. They may be provocatively suspended between Type 2 and Type 3 princi-ples—a conceptual hybrid. Analysts should not feel compelled to decide between these alterna-tives as if they were mutually exclusive binary op-positions, since the suspension itself, deepening the structural implications and strengthening the tightness of the movement, might well be the piece's larger point.

Rhetorical Recapitulations Beginning in the Parallel Mode

Within otherwise major-mode sonatas one occa-sionally finds recapitulations that are ushered in with grim, minor-mode variants of P, a "lights-out" effect that can produce a starkly negative effect. While expressively deformational this procedure typically creates no ambiguities re-garding the point of onset of the recapitulation.[5]

4. Another example may be found in the finale of Haydn's Piano Trio in E-flat, Hob. XV:29 (m. 179). In the Haydn Trio, however, this situation is the initial component of a more general reordering of recapitula-

tory modules. See also the reference to this movement in ch. 11.

5. Ethan Haimo, *Haydn's Symphonic Forms: Essays in Compositional Logic* (Oxford: Clarendon, 1995), p. 31

The strategy was noted as a recapitulatory exception by Tobel in 1935, who cited a number of examples, including the G-major Andante of Haydn's Symphony No. 1 in D, the first movement of Haydn's Symphony No. 24 in D, and the finale of Schubert's Sonata in C for Piano Four Hands, D. 812, "Grand Duo."[6] Several decades later Bonds listed six "parallel-mode recapitulations [in Haydn] before 1768," including the two compositions cited by Tobel and the first movement of the Piano Sonata in C, Hob. XVI:3.[7] According to Rosen, who treated the topic only with condescension, this is a "dramatic mid-century stereotype . . . of Neapolitan origin. Johann Schobert, who worked in Paris in the 1760s, used this effect in his Piano Trio in F major and in the finale of the Piano Quartet in E♭ major, op. 7. . . . This is certainly a trick that loses its effectiveness with repetition."[8] Effective or not, an instance in Mozart may be found in the finale of the Serenade in D, K. 185. The exposition's P, mm. 12–27, is a major-mode period, with both limbs sounded in a rollicking D major. In the recapitulation the period returns, but the antecedent is now in D minor (mm. 112–19) and the consequent restores D major (mm. 120–27). (Most unusually, this finale had been preceded by an Adagio introduction in D major, which included a few shadowy intermixtures with D minor.) In chapter 11 we also considered Beethoven's Overture *Leonore 2* to include a reference to this procedure, one that resulted in a drastic truncation of the reprise, a type of anti-recapitulation.

One of the most extreme illustrations of this modal deformation occurs in Spohr's C-major Overture to *Faust* (1813/1818). This is an unusual sonata deformation in which the normative Allegro vivace exposition is complemented with a minor-mode recasting of all of its essential themes in the recapitulation, which alters the governing mode throughout to C minor, a procedure reflected in the "new" three-flat key signature. The recapitulation presents a tragic or fallen version of the exposition: both P and S/C (along with the ESC) are minorized. In between the two rotations lies a developmental space in a separate, slower tempo, Largo e grave, ushered in by a "Halt!" fanfare and proceeding largely as a ponderous *fugato*. (This middle section recalls the option of slow-movement episodes within Allegro-tempo movements, discussed in chapter 10.) Not surprisingly, the motivation here was programmatic. Spohr appended a note to the overture, explaining that the exposition was intended to represent "Faust's sensual life and the riot of debauchery"; in the slow center-section "he at last pulls himself together and seriously attempts to renounce the evil of his ways; and in the fugato there is a suggestion of good resolutions being formed. It is not long, however, before he is again the prey of new and stronger sensual temptations (tempo primo [the recapitulation]) and, blinded by the deceptive power of the Evil One, he abandons himself more completely than ever to the most uncontrolled desires."[9]

(including n. 27), took a different view, proposing (with regard to the slow movement of Haydn's Symphony No. 1) that in a return of P "in the parallel minor, the sense of return is at least partially compromised and the sense of arrival is not totally satisfactory. . . . [Only with the conversion into the tonic major] is the sense of return secure." Since we prioritize the arrival of the recapitulatory *rotation* rather than the tonic in its original mode, we disagree with this interpretation, which winds up regarding a parallel-mode return of P as "a kind of false reprise." (It might be added that the movement that gave rise to these remarks is also problematic, as Haimo pointed out, because the apparent recapitulation begins with the minorized equivalent of m. 5 of the exposition.)

6. Rudolf von Tobel, *Die Formenwelt der klassischen Instrumentalmusik*, pp. 175–77. Tobel also cited instances in which an originally minor-mode P returns in major, as famously in the first movement of Beethoven's Symphony No. 9 in D Minor, op. 125. For a caveat about the second movement of Haydn's Symphony No. 1, see n. 5.

7. Bonds, "Haydn's False Recapitulations and the Perception of Sonata Form in the Eighteenth Century," p. 241.

8. Rosen, *Sonata Forms*, rev. ed., p. 155, which also cited Mozart's Violin Sonata in G, K. 9, as an example, but this was not a good illustration: while there is a G-minor statement of P in developmental space, the actual recapitulation is sounded in G major at m. 60.

9. Clive Brown, *Louis Spohr: A Critical Biography* (Cambridge: Cambridge University Press, 1984), p. 78.

Rhetorical Recapitulations Beginning in a Nontonic Key

From time to time one comes across what appears to be a Type 3 sonata whose rhetorical recapitulation begins in a nontonic key. This is signaled by the start of an off-tonic recapitulatory rotation after a separate section of development: a nontonic P-idea (often featuring correspondence measures with the opening of the exposition) that before long leads, as expected, into TR material that produces a tonic-key medial caesura and is followed by the tonal resolution provided by S and C. When it occurs, the nontonic beginning of the rotation is usually sounded in IV—less often in vi, V, or some other key—before the tonic is regained at some later point, usually not too much further into the music. Here the normative Type 3 principle of the "double return" is subjected to a deformation. The rebeginning of the P-theme and the reinstating of the tonic are again incongruent. They do not happen simultaneously.

False Starts

When confronting appearances of an off-tonic P in the vicinity of the development-recapitulation seam, one should distinguish among three possibilities. The first encompasses mid- or late-developmental statements that might be initially considered under the problematic rubric of the false recapitulation (discussed in chapter 10). Whatever the difficulties involved with this concept, the implication is that the off-tonic P-statement will be reabsorbed into an ongoing developmental texture continuing at some length. The second includes differing methods of producing a string of off-tonic false starts to the recapitulatory rotation, which eventually takes off at the proper tonic level. The third is the off-tonic beginning to the recapitulatory rotation proper.

In the classic false-start situation the developmental space proper comes to its end with a dominant-key preparation, though often on the "wrong key." At this point P strides forth, as if beginning a recapitulation, but on the wrong pitch level. This leads to one or more immediate restarts, as if P were trying to shake off the effects of the "bad start" and seek its way back to the tonic. Unlike the possible false-recapitulation situation, we do not plunge back into development, although a move toward reinvigorating a brief, separate retransitional link might be present. The overall effect is that of a multiple statement of the P-incipit on different levels—P ("No"), P ("No"), P ("Yes!")—a stuttering reopening of the new rotation, or what Bonds, in his discussion of this phenomenon, called a "kind of 'groping' for the 'proper' key of the principal theme."[10] Additionally, the set of false starts often seems to articulate a strategy of retransition, a way of mediating between two clearly delineated blocks, the development and the recapitulation. In these cases—absent other indications to the contrary—we consider the recapitulation proper to begin with the tonic statement of the theme. The preceding false starts also belong to the recapitulatory rotation, of course, but as tentative and aborted gestures they are reabsorbed and converted into the new beginning of the rotation at the proper tonic-pitch level.

We may cite two paradigmatic instances in Mozart. In the first, from the opening movement of the Piano Sonata in C, K. 309 (example 12.1), the recapitulation proper (m. 94)

EXAMPLE 12.1a   Mozart, Piano Sonata in C, K. 309, i, mm. 1–2

---

10. Bonds, "Haydn's False Recapitulations," p. 259.

EXAMPLE 12.1b   Mozart, Piano Sonata in C, K. 309, i, mm. 82–97

EXAMPLE 12.2a   Mozart, String Quartet in C, K. 465 ("Dissonance"), iv, mm. 1–4

on C is preceded by two false starts of the $P^{1.1}$-idea—two successive hoists. The first begins on A-natural (A minor, m. 86, triggered by a strong vi:PAC concluding a rotational development); the second on B (m. 90, outlining a V^7 of C). In the second, from the Allegro molto finale of his Quartet in C, K. 465 (example 12.2), the development proper ends with a strong caesura on V/III (m. 180, V of E, the "wrong key"). This is followed by three false-start, anticipatory statements of $P^{1.1}$: on E major (mm. 182–84, aborted); on E minor (mm. 186–88, as if questioning, then aborted again); beginning again on E minor, dissolving to a new retransition and a setup on the correct key, V of C (mm. 190–98). The recapitulation itself begins in C major at m. 200, now fully corrected and prepared.

Related cases in Haydn may be found in the first movements of his Quartet in E-flat, op. 33 no. 2 (false start on vi in m. 59; tonic recapitulation in m. 63) and his Symphony No. 43 in E-flat, "Mercury" (false starts on IV and ii, mm. 152 and 157; tonic recapitulation in m. 162). One of the most moving series of false

starts in the repertory is to be found in the first movement of Schubert's Piano Sonata in B-flat, D. 960, where the gentle P-idea vacillates achingly (mm. 188–215) between an unutterably despondent D minor and a seemingly distant B-flat major before being able to pull itself together sufficiently to decide for the latter and the full burden of the recapitulation proper (m. 216).

Recapitulatory Rotations That Begin in IV

A subdominant recapitulation is one that begins its recapitulatory rotation and initial set of correspondence measures with the sounding of $P^{1.1}$ in IV. Subdominant recapitulations typically occur within Type 3 sonatas with rhetorically full and normative P-zones. This may seem self-evident, but dubious assertions have been made that subdominant inflections of later modules are also instances of this practice.[11] Normally, one should not consider the sounding of any later module in IV (even $P^{1.2}$) to be the onset of a subdominant recapitulation. Such a situation is almost always better interpreted as a Type 2 so-

---

11. One of the most remarkable of these is that found in John Irving, *Mozart's Piano Sonatas: Contexts, Sources, Style* (Cambridge: Cambridge University Press, 1997), p. 102, which proposes that a subdominant appearance of an *interior* module of S (we number it $S^{2.2}$) within the developmental space of the opening movement of the Sonata in D, K. 311—m. 58, or the upbeat to m. 59—launches the "Reprise" and thus is "akin" to the practice of what we call the Type 2 sonata, now merged with the possibility of a subdominant recapitulation (as suggested in the related p. 190, n.10). That module's ap-

pearance in IV, however, clearly belongs to developmental space. Confirming this assessment, $S^{2.2}$, first heard with the upbeat to m. 29, reappears within the later tonal resolution—and in the proper tonic key—starting with the upbeat to m. 92. Irving's explanation would have it appear twice, in two different keys, in the "reprise." K. 311/i is the most structurally problematic of Mozart's piano-sonata movements—seemingly a Type 3 sonata that converts midstream (m. 79 with S^1) into a Type 2—and its puzzling structure has led more than one analyst to grasp at straws. See ch. 17.

EXAMPLE 12.2b   Mozart, String Quartet in C, K. 465 ("Dissonance"), iv,
mm. 178–204

nata with early crux, as in the often-cited finale of Mozart's Quartet in G, K. 387, with an emphatically prepared and launched $P^{1.2}$ crux in IV at m. 175 (more clearly, m. 176 = m. 18). In this case $P^{1.2}$ continues the ongoing rotation with correspondence measures: the preceding development, of course, had been based on $P^{1.1}$. The highly dramatized return of $P^{1.2}$ in IV, however, does suggest the secondary infiltration of some aspects of Type 3 logic into the movement.

For most writers today the touchstone cases —setting aside the perhaps misconstrued K. 387/iv—are the first movement of Mozart's Piano Sonata in C, K. 545 (with recapitulation beginning in F major), Beethoven's *Coriolan* Overture, op. 62 (C minor, with recapitulation beginning in F minor), and the first movement of Schubert's Symphony No. 5 in B-flat, D. 485 (with "recapitulation" beginning in E-flat—but see our qualification of this assessment later in this section).[12] Additional examples in Schubert—who was much attracted to this option, particularly between the years 1814 and 1819—may be found in the first movements of the Symphony No. 2 in B-flat, D. 125, the Piano Sonatas in A Minor, D. 537, and B Major, D. 575, and the Piano Quintet in A, D. 667, "Trout."[13]

Although infrequent, recapitulations starting on IV turn up consistently enough in the eighteenth century that we consider it a lower-level default option within the genre, not a deformation. Composers who exercised this option were drawing on several precedents. George R. Hill and A. Peter Brown have suggested that the procedure is characteristically Viennese. According to Brown "an eighteenth-century Viennese connoisseur could interpret this device as a bifocal recapitulation in the subdominant, known from chamber and symphonic works by such composers as Christoph Sonnleithner and [Florian] Gassmann."[14] Adding to our perspective, Bonds informs us that "unlike many of his contemporaries [including Dittersdorf, Gassmann, Stamitz, and D'Ordonez] . . . Haydn was never particularly drawn to this procedure. He experimented with it only occasionally, and even then only on a very limited scale. There is no counterpart in his entire output, for example, to the extended subdominant thematic return in Mozart's Sonata in C Major, K. 545."[15]

Charles Rosen noted the presence of the subdominant return in the first movement of an early (1757, non-Viennese) keyboard sonata (No. 4) of Giovanni Marco (Placido) Rutini and proceeded to disparage it in high-moralistic terms: the Rutini work contains a "full recapitulation of the exposition beginning on the subdominant, a form that was to become a lazy mannerism only after 1800." Rosen's distaste for the practice surfaced elsewhere in his *Sonata Forms*, sometimes taking on a tone of shuddering censure: "There even arose a kind of degenerate recapitulation, which began not in the tonic but in the subdominant, and which made possible a literal reprise of the exposition, transposed down a fifth." "For a massive recapitulation starting at IV, see Hummel's Piano Trio in E♭ major, op. 96, sometimes also labeled op. 93." "The opening of a recapitulation in IV is also used more frequently by Schubert than by any other composer."[16] And so on.

Some of C. P. E. Bach's symphonies (which

---

12. Cf. also the odd tonal structure of the C-minor second movement of Beethoven's Piano Sonata in E-flat, op. 81a, "Les adieux," already discussed in ch. 11. This is a rare example of a Type 1 sonata (thus containing no development) whose recapitulatory rotation begins in iv, F minor (m. 21 = m. 5), a tonal situation made possible by the diminished-seventh sonority launching the recapitulatory rotation in m. 21.

13. The dating claims are to be found in Martin Chusid, "Schubert's Chamber Music: Before and after Beethoven," *The Cambridge Companion to Schubert*, ed. Christopher H. Gibbs (Cambridge: Cambridge University Press, 1997), p. 186. On this basis Chusid preferred a dating earlier than 1823 or 1825 for the A Major

"Trout" Quintet, D. 667. See also the discussion and listing in Tobel, *Die Formenwelt der klassischen Instrumentalmusik*, pp. 170–75.

14. Brown, *Joseph Haydn's Keyboard Music: Sources and Style*, pp. 352–53. See also George R. Hill, "The Concert Symphonies of Florian Leopold Gassmann," Ph.D. Diss., New York University, 1975, pp. 161–96. The Hill- and LaRue-grounded term "bifocal recapitulation" is avoided by Sonata Theory.

15. Bonds, "Haydn's False Recapitulations," pp. 244–46.

16. Rosen, *Sonata Forms*, rev. ed., pp. 144 ("full recapitulation"), 288 ("There even arose"), 289 n. 4 ("For a massive"), and 360 ("The opening").

foreground bizarre effects) contain subdominant entries into the section best regarded as the recapitulatory rotation. (Normative "developments," "recapitulations," and "codas" are sometimes submitted to substantial thematic and tonal deformations in these movements, whose large-scale shapes are rendered coherent chiefly by a readily perceptible adherence to the rotational principle.) Examples occur in four of the first movements of the six "Hamburg" symphonies, Wq 182 (H. 657–62, 1773): No. 1 in G (recapitulatory rotation proper—amidst many other rotational complications—beginning in C, m. 59); No. 3 in C major (recapitulatory rotation starting on F, m. 69); No. 5 in B minor (recapitulatory rotation beginning in E minor, m. 35, after four false-start effects along the ascending circle of fifths, C, G, D minor, and A minor, mm. 33–34); and No. 6 in E (recapitulatory rotation starting in A, m. 53).[17] The subdominant recapitulation also surfaced in several of the piano sonatas of Muzio Clementi from 1780 onward. These include the first movements of op. 5 no. 3 in E-flat, op. 10 no. 3 in B-flat, and op. 13 no. 4 in B-flat, along with the finales of op. 10 no. 2 in D and op. 13 no. 5 in F (revised to include a recapitulation in IV in the ca. 1810 version!).[18]

Within major-mode works there is a self-evident logic behind the choice of a subdominant recapitulation. Since the exposition had moved from I to V (modulating up a fifth), one could always produce a perfectly parallel recapitulation, by-for-bar, that moves from IV to I (again modulating up a fifth), thereby producing the necessary tonal resolution for the S and C zones. This is precisely the solution, for example, found in the first movement of Clementi's Sonata in B-flat, op. 10 no. 3 (whose recapitulation Plantinga described as "proceed[ing] to the end as an exact transposition of the exposition") and in several of Schubert's works.[19] And yet this easier transpositional route was not always taken. Mozart, for instance, did not provide any such slavishly parallel recapitulation in the first movement of K. 545. There the recapitulation contains an interpolated four bars (mm. 50–53) that, at least theoretically, with small modifications, could have been omitted).[20]

More likely, this penchant for the subdomi-

---

17. Especially since these first movements combine an oddity of syntax with the lack of the guidepost of an expositional repeat, their overall plans are easily misconstrued. Usually the return of the P idea marks the onset of a new rotation—development, recapitulation, and coda—although the manner of approaching this P (not to mention issues concerning key patterns and EEC attainment) can be extremely unorthodox. In the first movement of Symphony No. 3, for instance, the main divisions are as follows: exposition, mm. 1–51; developmental space (half-rotational), mm. 51–68; recapitulatory rotation (beginning with P in IV), mm. 69–124; coda (incipient rotation, beginning with P in the tonic), mm. 124–28 [broken off]. As in Haydn's Symphony No. 6/i (mentioned in Ch. 11) the $S^{1.1}$ idea is no theme, registering only a space of thematic absence (mm. 24–27). An $S^{1.4}$ module brings about the EEC at m. 43; the C-theme is found in mm. 44–51. The recapitulatory precrux alterations occur at m. 76; the crux at m. 80 (= m. 11); another eccentrically "wrong" entrance of $S^{1.1}$ (and still on the dominant!) at m. 93; a tonal correction with added postcrux alterations in $S^{1.3}$, mm. 105–8; the ESC at m. 116.

18. Leon Plantinga, *Clementi: His Life and Music* (London: Oxford University Press, 1977), pp. 75–78, 90, and 220.

19. Plantinga, *Clementi*, p. 90. Cf. John L. Snyder, "Schenker and the First Movement of Mozart's Sonata, K. 455: An Uninterrupted Sonata-Form Movement?" *Theory and Practice* 16 (1991), 64: "Schubert on several occasions begins the recapitulation of a major-key sonata-form movement in the subdominant—but always with a preparation and in all cases the transition actually modulates, so that the recapitulation is in fact a transposition of the exposition, measure for measure."

20. Snyder, on the other hand ("Schenker and the First Movement of Mozart's Sonata, K. 545," 57), insisted (mistakenly, in our view) that Mozart's recomposition of the TR (or bridge) was "stylistically imperative": "In the exposition, Mozart had not established the dominant key prior to the appearance of the second subject; that is, the bridge leads to a half cadence *on* the dominant, not *in* the dominant. In a 'normal' sonata-form movement, the tonic is re-established prior to the return of the first subject by a dominant preparation. Since that has not happened here, it becomes stylistically imperative that the tonic be firmly established before the restatement of the second subject, so that there will be no doubt about the resolution of the 'structural dissonance' the second subject represents. A simple transposition of the bridge from the exposition would have failed this task; the extension of the bridge passage is therefore structurally necessary." But there is no "necessity" in such matters. Other compositions with recapitulations beginning in IV, such as the first movement of Clementi's B-flat Piano Sonata, op. 10 no. 3, mentioned above—and

nant could have arisen as an extension of the more common principle of moving toward the subdominant in recapitulations shortly after the initial re-sounding of P in the tonic. As discussed in chapter 11, the subdominant-shift of $P^{1.2}$, P^2, or TR material before the medial caesura is characteristic of recapitulations in general, doubtless because the fleeting tonicization of IV in TR facilitates the impression of a "modulation" up a fifth (corresponding to that of the exposition) that will bring the music back to I. If the IV-convention were to be pushed back further toward the beginning of the rotation—to the point of coinciding with it—one would have produced a recapitulation that began on the subdominant.

This line of reasoning leads one into complications. Consider, for example, the normal structure of the second rotation of a Type 2 sonata (chapter 17). Here the initial, nontonic P-material billows out into a broader development (usually based on P^1, $P^{1.2}$, P^2, or TR) and proceeds eventually to rejoin the expositional track at a point of crux shortly around or before the medial caesura. When the expositional MC had been articulated as a V:HC, that crux is likely to be sounded a fifth lower, in order to produce the desired recapitulatory I:HC MC. For this reason recurrences of correspondence measures a fifth below the expositional model are common occurrences in Type 2 sonatas. In most cases originally dominant-key ideas will be reappearing in the tonic. Now let us suppose that the composer decides to slide that point of transposed-crux further back toward the beginning of the rotation. Once the composer has moved the transposed-crux back into originally tonic material, that material will appear in the subdominant in the recapitulation. (As mentioned earlier, Mozart provides a convenient example in the Type 2 finale of the G-major String Quartet, K. 387. Here the subdominant crux, m. 175, is pushed back to the $P^{1.2}$ point, the correspondence-mea-

sure equivalent of m. 17 of the exposition.) As we continue to inch the transposed-crux point, now tracking in IV, toward the beginning of the rotation—and finally attain it—it would seem that what we have produced is a Type 2 sonata with an unusually advanced crux-point. Or has the sonata-type itself changed? If so, at exactly which point? Is it preferable to insist that when the initial bar of the rotation is touched (or bar 2? bar 3? bar 4?), our conceptual assessment of the structure should change to encourage instead the perception of a Type 3 sonata with subdominant recapitulation?

There can be no denying that there are shadows of Type 2 logic lurking behind aspects of the Type 3 sonata with subdominant recapitulation. Still, one of the essential features of the Type 2 sonata, an expanded development after an off-tonic treatment of P^1, is missing here (although, to be sure, the TR may be "developmentally" recomposed). More to the point, within this Type 3 variant the P-incipit-launch in IV is always preceded by material previously interpreted as development. In other words, were we to insist on interpreting the form primarily through Type 2 expectations, we would have an "extra" or redundant developmental space to account for—a separate development in its own right—which may or may not have begun with a tonic or nontonic sounding of P. From this perspective the subdominant-recapitulation-effect provides at best an extremely awkward variant of a Type 2 sonata.

Thus the Type 3 based interpretation has the upper hand in this potential blending of Type 2 and Type 3 principles. In virtually all cases the two most obviously complete rotations (exposition and recapitulation) are separated by developmental activity. But even having observed this, things are not always so clear. The capacity of the subdominant variant of Type 3 to enter into a dialogue with both types can at times be made a topic of the overall structure of the

---

several works of Schubert as well—do not follow any such "imperative." Moreover, Snyder's premise about [longer passages of?] dominant preparation preceding recapitulations—very much in line with Schenkerian principles of harmonic interruption on the tonic's V—is based entirely on *normative* Type 1, 3, 4, and 5 sonatas.

It overlooks the Type 2 option, in which that dominant preparation did not normally occur. Finally, Snyder's discussion of what we would call a I:HC MC is irrelevant to the matter at hand: such MC's could be—and were—treated in a variety of ways in recapitulations.

piece. This can happen when for one reason or another the material of the developmental space is selected in such a way as to suggest that it belongs conceptually to either the expositional or the recapitulatory rotation. In such cases the analytical task is not to decide whether a given structure "is" exclusively a Type 2 or a Type 3 sonata-variant. Rather, the aim would be to explore the compositional interaction between the two principles and to notice how those differing principles are brought into productive tension within the work at hand.

In the first movement of Mozart's Piano Sonata in C, K. 545, for example, the development section (mm. 29–41) is devoted to an elaboration of the exposition's brief C idea (sounded in mm. 26–28 after the EEC in m. 26). One point of the retention of C-material may be to suggest the persistent echoing presence of the final element of Rotation 1—as if Rotation 1 were still "in the air," even in the developmental space. On this interpretation the onset of the subdominant recapitulation (m. 42) could be understood as the beginning of Rotation 2 of a double-rotational sonata that had included no self-standing, independently rotational (or episodic) developmental space. Such a view would bolster the Type 2 aspect of these Type 3 variants. This observation would be generally applicable for all Type 3s with subdominant recapitulations that also featured preceding developmental spaces (or expanded retransitional links) based on the concluding element(s) of the exposition's C-theme.[21]

The first movement of Schubert's Symphony No. 5 in B-flat, D. 485, addresses the issue in an even more provocative manner. The exposition's P^1 theme (m. 5) is preceded by a clas-

sic instance of a $P^{1.0}$ (mm. 1–4). The apparent recapitulation begins in IV with the P^1 theme. But the preceding development had been a vast expansion of the $P^{1.0}$ idea. Thus the entire structure gives the impression of a large double-rotation (exposition + development-recapitulation), with the crux pushed back to the P^1 point—a moment that, because of the presence of $P^{1.0}$, does not correspond with the beginning of the exposition proper. Notwithstanding its ternary impression, this movement unfolds much like a Type 2 sonata with an early crux.

Finally, one might mention the clever adaptation of the subdominant recapitulation in the finale of Beethoven's Quartet in E-flat, op. 127. In the exposition P stretches out as the first two portions of a broad-spanning ternary plan, ABA'. Following an initial $P^{1.0}$ invocation, P^1 (A) is a closed parallel period, mm. 5–12, 13–20. P^2 (B) is a briefer, thematically contrasting parallel period in the tonic (mm. 21–24, 25–28), immediately subjected to a varied repetition (mm. 29–36). The P^1 reprise (m. 37) seeks to close the ternary scheme with a I:PAC but is unable to accomplish the task. Thus the expositional P^1 comes to be understood as a TR of the dissolving-reprise type, barely touches on any MC at all (multiple interpretations are possible), and launches directly into what has usually been regarded as a blurted, *forte* S in m. 55.

The seeming recapitulation on IV, beginning in A-flat in m. 145, provides us with P^1 and P^2 complete (A–B of the ternary structure) in that key, only undermining the expected cadence of P^2 in m. 176 and thereafter modulating away from A-flat. What one expects at this point is an imminent reprise of P^1, probably returning

---

21. Here one might recall that a retransitional link based on the last module of C connects the two rotations of the Type 2 sonata in the finale of Mozart's Quartet in G major, K. 387. Quite apart from these rotational matters, John Snyder, noticing the lack of the Schenker-required harmonic interruption on V of I before the "recapitulation" in IV in K. 545, has suggested a differing solution, although one that we cannot endorse ("Schenker and the First Movement of Mozart's Sonata, K. 545," 64, 69): "My thesis is to consider the restatement of the principal theme at measure 42 as part of the *development*. It is useful in this regard to remember that sonata form is ancestrally a *binary* form, and that the distinction between the 'development' and the

'recapitulation' was not solidified until the nineteenth century [*sic!*]. In this case, therefore the *Kopfton* [$\hat{5}$] will be recovered with the restatement of the second theme material, in the tonic, beginning at m. 59. . . . The 'subdominant-key recapitulation'—long recognized as an oddity—turns out not to be the recapitulation at all, but merely a statement of the primary material in that key, in the course of the development." To be sure, Snyder may be correct about the *Kopfton* issue, but this line of reasoning, overlooking the rotational principle entirely (and operating from an at best hazy awareness of how "binary" or Type 2 sonatas characteristically unfold in the eighteenth century), runs aground from the perspective of Sonata Theory.

as a recapitulatory TR. In fact, that P[1]—presumably the final limb of the A–B–A melodic structure—recurs in the tonic, E-flat (m. 187, sometimes regarded in the literature as the "true" recapitulation). But instead of providing only a brief concluding reference to the main theme, Beethoven now "backed up" the music to furnish once again not only the full P[1] period (as if correcting the earlier A-flat recapitulation by retracing its steps, albeit with variants) but also a full restatement of P[2] (mm. 203–10, 211–18)—which then merges directly into "S" in E-flat (m. 219). The whole procedure beginning at m. 145 has a false-start flavor (a recapitulation begun "wrong" and set right by rebeginning again), but it is carried on too long to be a genuine false start, and it is also true that the ternary plan of the P-theme, suggesting possibilities for the manipulation of the P-reprise (or TR, mm. 187–218 of the recapitulation), plays a prominent role in the formal conception. Kinderman is probably correct in regarding m. 145 as an example of a subdominant recapitulation; Kerman's earlier suggestion that m. 145 begins "the most obstinate 'false reprise' in the whole classic repertory" is less satisfactory.[22]

Recapitulatory Rotations That Begin in vi, VI, or ♭VI

Very rarely, composers began a concluding Type 3 recapitulatory rotation in a key other than the tonic or the subdominant.[23] When this was the case, the alternative key most often chosen seems to have been that of the submediant, usually with the sense of momentarily locking onto a set of P[1.1] correspondence measures—the usual signal of relaunch. The tonic is soon regained, and the rotation stabilized, three, four, five or more measures into the rotation, perhaps even with its second thematic module. (The rotation is not rebegun in the tonic from the P[1.1] point. If it is, the brief, preceding submediant P[1.1] would be a false start, and the recapitulation proper would begin with the tonic statement. We have already cited the opening movement of Haydn's Quartet in E-flat, op. 33 no. 2, as an example of this.) The correction from nontonic to tonic necessitates the altering or addition of one or more measures shortly into the rotation. Such nontonic recapitulatory openings imply an expressive strain at the beginning of the rotation, as though the tonic-track is still something to be achieved.

Hill has pointed to some instances of this submediant opening in the Viennese concert symphonies of Florian Leopold Gassmann: "In a number of first movements that seem clearly to be in sonata form he begins the recapitulation in the subdominant or submediant (relative minor), achieving a firm return to the tonic only with the reappearance of the second theme."[24] When instances occur in the master composers, the result has sometimes been confusion with regard to where the recapitulation begins. One familiar solution is to suppose that the recapit-

22. William Kinderman, *Beethoven* (Berkeley: University of California Press, 1995), pp. 291–92; Joseph Kerman, *The Beethoven Quartets* (New York: Norton, 1966), pp. 236–37. Note also that both exposition and recapitulation become more stressful as they proceed. No EEC is produced in the exposition; no ESC in the recapitulation. Thus this movement features a nonresolving recapitulation, and the elusive goal of tonal closure is provided only late in the coda, probably with the I:PAC at m. 289—and even then it barely seems to stay put.

23. On the surface there might appear to be certain ritornello-like influences at work here. So far as we are aware, however, no such link between the two principles (sonata and ritornello)—occasionally claimed in casual analysis—has been rigorously demonstrated. On the basis of the evidence available thus far, we are skeptical about any invocation of ritornello (or concerto) principles in Type 1, 2, 3, or 4 sonata forms.

24. George R. Hill, ed., "Introduction," *Florian Leopold Gassmann, 1729–1774: Seven Symphonies*, in *The Symphony 1720–1840*, ed. Barry S. Brook, Series B, vol. 10 (New York: Garland, 1981), p. xix. Cited as examples were the Symphony in B-flat (Hill Thematic Index No. 15), E (No. 63), and C (86). The last of these (from 1769), with a recapitulatory rotation clearly beginning in A minor, m. 59, may be consulted in Hill's edition of seven Gassmann symphonies. The Symphony in C, H86, appears on pp. 225–53. Cf. Hill's similar remarks in the *New Grove Dictionary of Music and Musicians*, 2nd ed., 9:565 (originally found as well in the 1st ed.): "in a first movement, the recapitulation often occurs in the subdominant or relative minor."); and Hill, "The Concert Symphonies of Florian Leopold Gassmann" (n. 14 above).

EXAMPLE 12.3a   Haydn, String Quartet in B-flat, op. 50 no. 1, i, mm. 1–7

ulation starts only when the tonic is regained, even if that occurs mid-phrase, thereby creating a purposeful ambiguity around this important structural seam. However appealing such a claim might be in combating the "textbook" or schematic view of sonata form, it ignores the rotational status of the moment and almost invariably misses the main point. An instructive instance occurs in the first movement of Haydn's Quartet in B-flat, op. 50 no. 1. Example 12.3a shows the opening of P at the beginning of the exposition: two bars of tonic B-flat in the cello followed by the famous "concluding"-formula gesture in mm. 3–6 and a launch of triplets in m. 7. The development is fully rotational and toward its end produces an unexpectedly strong PAC in vi (G minor) at m. 103 (example 12.3b). The gestures of the opening of P follow at once (mm. 103–4 = mm. 1–2), for two measures, at least, implying a rotational restart on vi. This merely implied submediant launch proves unstable. It gives way at once to corrective modulatory shifts, leading P-material through the $^6_3$–$^5_3$ variant of a descending-fifth progression (mm. 105–9), before tracking into the tonic B-

flat at m. 109. As a whole the modulatory mm. 103–9 represent an expansion of mm. 1–4. The twisting mm. 105–8 all flower from m. 3, to which they are apparently seeking a clearer tonal correspondence. Metaphorically, the progress of the music is stalled at a red light. The suggestion of an impending move forward is attained in m. 108, "almost" a correspondence measure with m. 3, and the green light to proceed is provided m. 109, which even more clearly corresponds with m. 4. Mm. 110–15, with small variants, correspond to mm. 5–10. (Precrux alterations, including an enormous ellipsis, soon follow.)

Some English-language descriptions of this music have been predicated on the urge to identify the point of the supposed recapitulation—usually a moment of strong articulation—only with the arrival of the tonic. Thus Janet M. Levy and W. Dean Sutcliffe, in separate studies, pointed to the "ambiguity" and "freedom" of this recapitulation, which is attained only "at a 'mid-way point' of the original theme, at about bar 110."[25] Along the same lines, Charles Rosen insisted that "the recapitulation [in op. 50 no. 1/i] enters [in m. 108]

25. Janet M. Levy, "Gesture, Form, and Syntax in Haydn's Music," in *Haydn Studies: Proceedings of the In-* *ternational Haydn Conference, Washington, D.C.*, 1975, ed. Jens Peter Larsen, Howard Serwer, and James Webster

EXAMPLE 12.3b Haydn, String Quartet in B-flat, op. 50 no. 1, i, mm.
100–12

EXAMPLE 12.3b　*(continued)*

"without warning in the middle of a phrase . . . so that the precise moment of the return to the tonic is almost unnoticed."[26] But is Haydn's musical point really one of understatement and a sly, mid-phrase settling into a recapitulation? This seems unlikely. An exclusive reliance on tonality alone to determine recapitulatory onsets can lead to conclusions that are counterintuitive and countergeneric.

From the perspective of Sonata Theory what is happening here seems clear. On rare occasions one finds a development that ends with a vi:PAC closely juxtaposed with the normative beginning of the recapitulation on I—the "R" operation in terms of transformational theory. A few instances were mentioned in chapter 10 (in the section, "Substitutes for V_A at the End of the Development"): one was the first movement of another quartet by Haydn, op. 64 no. 3. The present, historically prior case, op. 50 no. 1, is similar, except that the opening bars of P themselves—corresponding to mm. 1–4 in the expositional model—take on the task of modulating from vi to I, thus dovetailing a retransitional function with the beginning of the recapitulatory rotation. By the time that the tonic is reached the rotation is already underway. The initiating gesture started in m. 103, which is where we must consider the recapitulatory rotation (or, less precisely, the recapitulation) to have begun. All this, recall, is in response to a particularly aggressive concluding half of the development, and the sheer force with which

the vi:PAC is secured in m. 103 appears to leave the recapitulatory onset of P bludgeoned onto an ominous, minor-mode vi, somewhat dizzily seeking its way back home.

One would normally expect off-tonic recapitulations starting on vi to begin in minor, but Beethoven provided an engaging variant in the first movement of his Piano Sonata in F, op. 10 no. 2.[27] The sonata's *plein-air*, birdsong-bright expositional opening is shown in example 12.4a. The development, shot through with largely minor-mode tonal allusions, frames a stormy central episode (mm. 77–94) with C^2-based figuration (mm. 67–76, 95–113). M. 107 touches briefly on F minor—the tonic minor (example 12.4b)—but by m. 112 the subsequent descending bass slides past the possibility of retaining and further preparing this tonic, eventually touching bottom instead on a dominant-lock, $V_{4=3}^{6=5}$ of D minor in mm. 113–17. The development concludes with V/vi, one of the familiar substitutes for the much more common interrupted V of I. One local implication, following the turbulent and minor-mode-saturated development, is that the piece's original F major (the sign of the positive) has decayed to one of its negative alter-images, D minor. The fermata in m. 117 stands for the dilemma of continuation: are we obliged to begin in D minor (as implied) or can the seemingly lost F major be plucked out of the ashes (the generically customary solution)?

In the face of these alternatives Beethoven

(New York: Norton, 1981), pp. 355–62. Levy's discussion is commented upon in W. Dean Sutcliffe, *Haydn: String Quartets, op. 50* (Cambridge: Cambridge University Press, 1992), p. 70.

26. Rosen, *The Classical Style*, rev. ed., p. 124.

27. For a subtle dialogue with the minor-mode submediant recapitulatory entry in Beethoven, see the Presto finale of the Violin Sonata in A Minor, op. 47, "Kreutzer."

EXAMPLE 12.4a   Beethoven, Piano Sonata in F, op. 10 no. 2, i, mm. 1–12

staged a tonal surprise by splicing a two-sharp signature into m. 117 and beginning the recapitulatory rotation in D major, the major submediant in m. 118. Many implications are folded into this choice. The signature change seeks to transform the notational and conceptual sense of the tonic altogether. What is produced is a double-brightness. Not only does the music shift from the dominant of a minor-mode key into a major key but also, from a generic perspective, the key selected is not the more conventional F major (I) but an "escapist" D major (VI), a sharp-grounded key three notches higher on the ascending circle of fifths—and also, in this case, the parallel major of the implied minor key. This is a false-front mask, a wide-eyed denial of the V/vi problem and the aftershocks of the minor-mode agitation of most of the preceding development.

The recapitulatory rotation proceeds for several bars in this naively radiant D (mm. 118–29, P[1.1] + the more lyrical P[1.2]), as if nothing were in the slightest out of the ordinary. Following a PAC on D major (m. 129), the ground-currents of the "real" tonic start to assert themselves. A measure of pause—another question mark of continuation—brings us to a distorted and expanded restart of P[1] (mm. 131–36), soon pulling the P-idea back to the proper F major (m. 133). The escapism of the D-major signature is extinguished in m. 136, and the music proceeds with a corrected, presumably chastened P[1.2] (mm. 137ff). The whole passage also suggests resonances with the false-start technique (particularly in the "backing-up" recovery-effect at mm. 137–44, restating P[1.2] in the version first provided in mm. 5–12), but in this case the recapitulation is not literally rebegun with P[1.1] tonic-key correspondence measures to mm. 1–4. Here it is preferable to conclude that

EXAMPLE 12.4b   Beethoven, Piano Sonata in F, op. 10 no. 2, i, mm. 107–44

EXAMPLE 12.4b (continued)

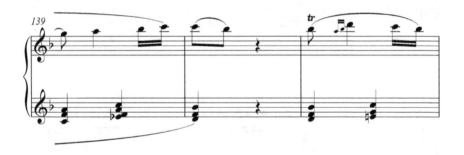

the recapitulation itself begins in VI, m. 118, and self-corrects *en route*.[28]

An apparently later variant of the submediant recapitulation is one in which the recapitulatory rotation is launched on ♭VI before adjusting itself into the tonic. A classic example occurs in the B-flat major second movement, Allegretto vivace e sempre scherzando, of Beethoven's Quartet in F, op. 59 no. 1. In this deformational scherzo-sonata — nightmarishly distorted in tone and structure — the rotation in question begins on G-flat in m. 239. (Mm. 239–53, which include ascending-fifth shifts through D-flat and A-flat at mm. 246 and 253, are largely referential to the material first stated in mm. 1–16.) The tonic B-flat major is reattained only with the arrival of $P^{1.2}$ at m. 259 (= m. 23).

Recapitulatory Rotations That Begin in V

From time to time one encounters a recapitulatory rotation that begins in the dominant, a tonality usually associated with S and C in the exposition. In its simplest manifestations a dominant recapitulation can be a variant of the Type 1 sonata (lacking repeat signs and a development) in which the recapitulatory P begins directly in and continues at length in V, not in I. (Such a variant is counterdefinitional to our view of the normative Type 1 sonata, which we regard as identifying itself with a *tonic* return to P directly after a nonrepeated exposition. See chapter 16.) This produces a bi-rotational scheme in which a two-part exposition moves from I to V and the immediately succeeding recapitulation reverses this course, moving from V (for P) to I (for S and C), and in which there is no significant developmental expansion within the recapitulatory rotation. (If there were — for instance, if $P^{1.2}$ or TR^1 were enlarged into a development — we would classify it as a Type 2 sonata.) Early instances of the structure are provided by a few late-eighteenth-century opera overtures, such as that to Gluck's *Alceste* and some of the operas of Salieri.[29] The young Schubert, a pupil of Salieri, occasionally made use of this variant, as in the first and last movements of his Quartet "No. 6" in D, D. 74 (in the first movement the recapitulation outlines a V–IV–I plan!), and in the tonally unusual finale of the Piano Sonata in A Minor, D. 537 (whose exposition moves i–IV–V, complemented in the immediate recapitulation by v–VII–I). Doubtless related to this way of thinking is the finale of his Piano Quintet in A, D. 667, "Trout," in which the exposition moves from I to IV (!) and a literally transposed recapitulation follows directly, V to I.[30]

When a development section is present — as in a Type 3 sonata — the situation becomes more complex. In the first place, the normative, tonic opening of the recapitulatory rotation is preceded by a substantial dominant prolongation, often a structural-dominant lock leading to the characteristic harmonic interruption before the onset of the recapitulation. To begin that rotation on (or in) the dominant is to superimpose musical procedures that are normally kept separate. The recapitulatory P^1 (or $P^{1.1}$) is called

28. The wrong-key start to the recapitulatory P in the op. 10 no. 2 may be intended to recall the wrong-key onset of the recapitulatory S (on F major, IV) in the first movement of the C-minor sonata, op. 10 no. 1. Both moments suggest an effect of escapism and generic irresponsibility. The pairing of the two works in this respect may be complemented by the first movement of the D-major sonata, op. 10 no. 3, featuring a tonally errant TM^1 in both the exposition (m. 23) and the recapitulation (m. 205). (See the discussion of op. 10 no. 3 in ch. 11.)

29. Tobel, *Die Formenwelt*, p. 177, mentioned *Alceste* as "an early example" of *die dominantische Reprise* before moving on to Beethoven and Schubert. Martin Chusid, "Schubert's Chamber Music: before and after

Beethoven," pp. 175–76, noted Schubert's indebtedness to Salieri and Cherubini in the forms of some of his early works and identified Gluck and Salieri as overture composers who sometimes omit the development and follow the exposition with "recapitulations [that] do not [always] begin in the tonic key." By way of an explanation Chusid cited "the older bipartite sonata form" as "the form . . . of a majority of opera overtures of the time" and "a most important [principle] for Schubert," but his account does not distinguish between what we would call the normative Type 1 sonata, this Type 1 sonata variant, and a Type 2 sonata.

30. Cf. the similar situation in the finale of Schubert's Quartet in B-flat, D. 36, also noted in Rosen, *Sonata Forms*, rev. ed., p. 359.

upon to appear simultaneously with tonal residues of its own dominant preparation.

To be sure, it occasionally happens that otherwise tonic-key recapitulations are ushered in above dominant pedal-points, as famously in the first movement of Beethoven's Piano Sonata in F Minor, op. 57, "Appassionata" (mm. 134ff). In these cases the normal point of harmonic interruption on V at the end of the development is kept audibly open into recapitulatory space. Consequently, the fresh rebeginning sets forth in tandem with a sometimes-suspenseful prolongation of what "in better circumstances" it would have left behind. As is the case with the type of S^0 or $S^{1.0}$ themes that unfold over dominant pedals, the altered P-passage has a double-function: the retention of the last element of an earlier preparatory situation coupled with the beginning of something new.

The same psychology is pushed further when the P-idea is not merely a tonic module over a dominant pedal but a theme beginning in (or on) the dominant key itself. Here again we find the splaying of two ideas normally kept separate — dominant preparation and thematic return — only in a more extreme format. Because such situations are exceptional to normative practice, we consider them to be recapitulatory deformations. The dominant onsets of these recapitulatory rotations fold into themselves aspects of unfinished tonal business from the developmental space. The recapitulatory rotation does indeed begin, although it does so prematurely, without the usual, fuller harmonic preparation. It sometimes happens that a brief patch of *Fortspinnung* is applied after P^1 in order to bring the ongoing rotation back onto the tonic track. Were this fleetingly renewed developmental texture to be succeeded by a return to a tonic P^1 (and thus a new rotational beginning), the dominant-key P should be considered within the general category of the false-recapitulation effect — along with all the conceptual problems that come with that category (chapter 10). But since it empties out instead on a tonic $P^{1.2}$, P^2, or TR, thereby continuing the rotation, it is preferable to construe the whole as a recapitulatory rotation that begins on V.

These considerations can open compositions to interpretational ambiguities, in which a given structure or event appears to be in dialogue with several different generic possibilities, poised tantalizingly among them. Haydn, in particular, enjoyed teasing out and dwelling within these ambiguities. The first movement, Vivace assai, of his Quartet in D, op. 33 no. 6, provides a challenging case that proves instructive. The expositional layout may be schematized as follows: P^1 (mm. 1–4); varied repetition of P^1 (mm. 5–8); P^2 (mm. 9–18); nonmodulatory TR (mm. 19–26), leading to light, first MC-effect (I:HC, m. 26); TM^1 (m. 27–31), merging into TM^2 (mm. 31–34) and leading to a second apparent MC (V:HC, m. 34); TM^3 (mm. 35–43, with a V:PAC in m. 43, probably not to be taken as the EEC); S-space extension based on TM^3 figures (mm. 44–49) with EEC at m. 49; RT (mm. 50–58).

At this point Haydn provides us with a brief, P^1-based development (mm. 59–70), starting on F major and running aground with a fermata-held E-major chord, V of A minor. The fermata on a strongly implicative dominant can suggest the end of a development section, although in this instance the development seems to have closed down too early. What follows is a near-literal statement of the first P^1 on A major (that is, on V, mm. 71–74, corresponding to mm. 1–4) — replicating the initial texture of the exposition — followed by three interpolated bars (prematurely introducing P^2) that shift back to the tonic for the varied repetition of P^1 in I, mm. 78–81 (corresponding to mm. 5–8) and the first three bars of the subsequent P^2, mm. 82–84 (corresponding to mm. 9–11). Notwithstanding the interpolated mm. 75–77, this is an impressive stretch of correspondence measures, and following the twelve bars of development and strong fermata one might wonder whether something recapitulatory might be underway. And yet one must be cautious. We also recall (chapter 10, on varying degrees of the false-recapitulation effect) that early-developmental dominant and tonic statements of P^1 are normative within the style and are usually not recapitulatory at all — even though this one had been preceded by twelve bars of tonally shifting development and a fermata. We are thus situated between two possibilities, perhaps tilting — so far — more toward the latter. Any further interpretation will depend on the musical continuation. Will it proceed in the manner of an ordered rotation?

In fact, it does. The rotation begun with correspondence measures in V at m. 71 proceeds in rigorous order — with some developmental expansions — all the way to the coda. Having heard the two versions of P^1 and the onset of P^2 (and having recovered the D-major tonic), Haydn now provides a *Fortspinnung* (developmental) expansion of P^2, touching on the Neapolitan E-flat (mm. 86–90), moving through a series of shifting tonal levels (mm. 90–99), and finally locking back onto correspondence measures with a first crux (mm. 100–4 = 14–18, the end of P^2). As expected, TR arrives next (mm. 105–8 = 19–22), followed by more recomposed material, designed to iron out the first apparent MC, TM^1, and TM^2 (mm. 109–25). The "real" MC is now altered to a I:PAC (m. 125), and the original TM^3 and its extension follow (mm. 126–44 — now reinterpreted as S). The beginning of this S marks the moment of a second crux and set of correspondence measures, with mm. 138–42 expanding the original single bar, m. 47, to provide the ESC at m. 144. An RT and first ending follow. Everything from m. 71 onward has been strictly rotational, with individual modules of the rotation developmentally expanded here and there.

From a resolutely rotational perspective this is an instance of a recapitulatory rotation that begins on V and shortly thereafter modulates to I and includes some internal *Fortspinnung* jags, perhaps to compensate (as impulses of development still lingering in the air?) for the unusually brief development and premature entrance of P^1. Yet there is no denying that in mm. 71–81 Haydn was also playing on the tradition of presenting P in the dominant and in the tonic early on in a development. In part this implication is made possible by the double-sounding of P^1 — tonic-tonic in the exposition, mm. 1–4 and 5–8, but dominant-tonic in mm. 71–74 and 78–81. In mm. 71–81 Haydn conflates two categories: Type 3 developmental and re-

capitulatory practice. It is imprudent to make a decision on behalf of only one of them, a decision that would overlook the purposeful ambiguity of the compositional situation. Further, if the most obviously developmental bars, mm. 59–70, were not there at all, we would be looking at an example of a Type 2 sonata with early crux. Thus Haydn provided his audience with a witty work cleverly suspended in the force fields of at least three formal categories without declaring definitively on behalf of any of them. The structure is in dialogue with more than one hermeneutic structural type, caught in a web of differing interpretive possibilities.

Simpler, more schematic examples of recapitulatory rotations that begin in V following a development may be found in the first movements of Clementi's Piano Sonata in F Minor, op. 13 no. 6, and Schubert's Symphony No. 4 in C Minor, D. 417.[31] Both composers were attracted to unorthodox, sometimes flagrantly transgressive, tonal layouts in their sonata forms, and in this case the structures of the two pieces are (coincidentally?) similar. In the Clementi movement one finds a C-minor recapitulatory onset, m. 70, with a subsequent S beginning fleetingly in the "wrong key," III — A-flat, m. 84 (the same key in which it had appeared in the exposition) — before falling into the fatalistic F minor. Schubert's symphony-movement has a more unusual key-plan for the exposition: its S is produced entirely in VI, A-flat (two closed statements and an expanded continuation, mm. 67–76, 76–85, 85–130, the whole forming an extremely large sentence). The recapitulation begins in v, G minor, m. 177 (the P-idea seems also to allude to the opening of Beethoven's Quartet in C minor, op. 18 no. 4), and the initial two statements of S (mm. 214–23, 223–32) are sounded, each with a closing PAC, in VI, E-flat. Only with S's expanded continuation, mm. 232–68, is the tonic, C minor, regained to produce the proper ESC. The thematic segments of the broader S — the initial statements — are never sounded in the tonic. Because of this they signify a tonal alienation of this portion of S,

---

31. Another example may be found in the first movement of Schubert's Quartet "No. 4" in C, D. 46.

demonstrating that certain features of post-MC space are forever nonassimilable into the tonic. They remain irrecoverably alienated from tonal resolution. Tonal alienation of this sort may be found in many of Schubert's pieces.

Surely the most celebrated instance of a recapitulatory rotation beginning in the dominant occurs in Beethoven's C-major Overture, *Leonore No. 3*. Following the trumpet-call breakthrough-interpolation into the development (m. 272—thus forestalling the calamitous C-minor recapitulation predicted), the development resettles onto what is clearly to be taken for the generic re-entry dominant lock to the recapitulation (m. 318)—only here on the wrong dominant, V of V (with D in the bass), not V of I. This leads to a G-major, emphatically thematic statement of a variant of P^1 in the flute (mm. 330ff) that, despite its obviously TR-based melodic continuation (mm. 334–38), must have been intended to provide the rhetorical impression of a recapitulation.[32] Still, occurring in V, it is generically in the wrong key, which may help to explain its "inability" to recover the exact melodic contour of the original P-idea. (In other words, its provisional status is highlighted through its more evident congruence with the TR version of the melody.) Over the course of the next several bars the flute melody, in dialogue with the bassoon, seeks a PAC in G major, but at the last moment (m. 352) that cadence is undermined and proceeds instead to an extended crescendo and decisive return to V^7 of the generally proper key, C major (mm. 371–77). This crescendo corresponds gesturally to that located in the later stages of P in the exposition (mm. 49–68)—the sense of a newly begun rotation is continuing—and as in the exposition, it discharges its energy, *sempre ff*, onto an emphatic TR of the tutti affirmation type, now in C major (m. 378; cf. m. 69, the exposition's onset of

TR). In *Leonore No. 3*, the tonic, C major, is regained only at the TR point, m. 378. And this is where most commentators, sometimes with ingenious arguments, have placed the point of recapitulation.[33]

The situation is more complex than is usually acknowledged. Merely to locate the recapitulation at the C-major passage in m. 378—tonally the obvious place—overlooks the earlier (varied) beginning of the recapitulatory rotation, itself prepared by its own structural dominant lock. The earlier passage has been marginalized both because it is sounded in the dominant, not in the tonic, and because of its TR-version references. Here again is a situation where it is useful to distinguish between the onset of a rhetorical recapitulation or recapitulatory rotation (beginning in G in m. 330) and the later, emphatic return to the tonic (beginning with TR in C in m. 378). In this case Beethoven was doubtless expanding the idea of recapitulations that begin over the dominant to suggest that in this programmatic overture the sheer process of reattaining the tonic in the recapitulation—on the way to the ESC—is going to be an uncommonly arduous enterprise.

A similar situation, perhaps modeled on *Leonore No. 3*, occurs in the first movement of Berlioz's *Symphonie fantastique* (C major). Generalizing about such an unusual composition is a perilous procedure, but one productive way to consider this piece is to examine its rotational structure, a guiding thread through the purposely garish deformations. After a repeated exposition and a substantial stretch of development one comes across a much-noted complete statement of the P-theme—the *idée fixe*—in V, G major (m. 239). This G-major full statement marks the beginning of another, varied rotation of expositional materials (with alterations and expansions), and this rotation will lead mid-

---

32. This was also the view of Tobel, *Die Formenwelt*, p. 177, who designated this moment as an example of the group of "dominant reprises."

33. As in Tovey's famous analysis, reprinted in *Symphonies and Other Orchestral Works* (Oxford: Oxford University Press, 1989), p. 138: "We are now beginning to learn a lesson in proportion. . . . [Because of his compressions of *Leonora No. 2*, Beethoven] has thus left

room to grow; and so he continues his development at leisure, with a sunshiny passage in which the flute and bassoon give in G major the substance of the tutti that followed the first subject. . . . This is the sublime and unexpected use of the dominant to which I referred in connexion with the development of *Leonora No. 2*. . . . [The] fortissimo in the tonic . . . does duty for the recapitulation of the first subject."

course to C major and the tonal resolution of the rotational layout. From this perspective we might consider the G-major *idée fixe* as beginning a bizarre rhetorical recapitulation in the dominant. The final, riotous appearance of the *idée fixe* in C major (m. 410) belongs more properly to coda-space than to recapitulatory space, as has sometimes been claimed. Overlooking the rotational aspects of the composition has led commentators (beginning with Schumann) to consider the movement to be most fundamentally arrayed as a symmetrical arch.

Recapitulatory Rotations That Begin in Other Keys

Although nontonic recapitulatory launches happen most often in IV, VI, or V, it is possible to come across more deformational, *ad hoc* nontonic choices. One of the strangest may be found in the first movement of Clementi's Piano Sonata in F, op. 13 no. 5: prompted by some tonal veerings in the development, its recapitulation begins in E-flat, ♭VII, m. 63, and P is articulated fully in that key, even cadencing in it, m. 70, before returning to F major.

Only slightly less odd are recapitulations that begin in ♭III. These are rare, but examples may be found in two of the most well-known pieces in the repertory: the F-major slow movement of Mozart's Piano Concerto in C, K. 467; and finale of Schubert's Symphony No. 9 in C, "The Great," D. 944. In the Mozart, after an initial orchestral tutti in F (mm. 1–22 with an appended bar of fill), the "expanded" exposition proper, with soloist, begins in m. 23. A new TR follows, m. 35, leading to a very light V:HC MC-effect in m. 44 with a sustained dominant-lock replicating material from the initial tutti (minor giving way to major at the end) for the next five bars—although the exposition could also be understood as continuous. The EEC in C major occurs at m. 55, and it is succeeded by a brief development closing on a languidly melancholy V of F minor, mm. 71. As if turning away from the negative implications of the minor tonic, the music "escapes" in a bar of linkage to III of F minor, A-flat major (♭III of F major). It is in that dream-like key that the recapitulation begins, m. 73. Once the presentation modules

(only) of P float past, minor-inflected, modulatory adjustments in mm. 79–82 bring us back to the "reality" of the tonic and achingly familiar correspondence measures, at first mistily in minor, then clarifying into the major at m. 88. After a provisional ESC in m. 93 the suppressed continuation of P (= mm. 30–35) returns in mm. 94–99 with the flavor of a benediction for the whole movement.

In the Schubert "Great C-Major" finale the development ends with a long, 84-bar dominant pedal, V of I, beginning in m. 515. The first portion of this dominant-lock implies C major, mm. 515–52, with a brief intermixture of C minor in mm. 531–37. Before long this expectant passage darkens to V of C minor more permanently (mm. 553ff) and the texture thins out to a single G♮ in octaves (especially by mm. 576–82), with continued anticipations of P jutting upward in the strings. A passing F♮ in the bassoons and trombones (mm. 583–90) resolves downward in the succeeding bars and alters the sonority to bare, throbbing G/E♭ dyad in mm. 591–98. We are still hearing an incomplete V of C minor, but the lone dyad is tonally ambiguous ($\hat{5}$ and $\hat{3}$ of C minor or $\hat{3}$ and $\hat{1}$ of E-flat major?) and in its insistence seems to be tipping in the direction of a potential E-flat major. At m. 599 the full orchestra picks up the implication and begins the recapitulation vigorously in E-flat, ♭III of the tonic C. Here Schubert was probably recalling one alternative treatment of the development-recapitulation seam, the move from V/vi to I, and reinterpreted it unconventionally as V/i leaping away to ♭III, producing a remarkable color-shift by pivoting on the common tones G and E♭.

Double-Recapitulation Effects?

One of the strangest, and rarest, deformations occurs when something that starts out, postdevelopmentally, as an apparently recapitulatory rotation fails to accomplish its tonal mission and is succeeded by what amounts to a fully recomposed—and now more successful—"second recapitulation," rebeginning with P and proceeding all the way to S and C. Here the rotational aspect underlying sonata form takes precedence over normative tonal expectations, although it is also possible that any such second-recapitulation effect might allude generically to the possibility of a second visiting of a recapitulation in the once-standard full repetition of the development and recapitulation.

One prototype for this oddity occurs in the first movement of Clementi's Piano Sonata in G Minor, op. 34 no. 2 (1795). There are many curious features in this movement, one of which is the varied, major-mode return of the opening Largo at the end of the development, mm. 126–35. (See also the section of chapter 10, "Introductory Material in Developments.") What one initially presumes is the recapitulation begins in IV, C minor, in m. 143. $S^{1.0}$ follows in m. 162, but in the "wrong key," VI, E-flat major, and proceeds to stay there to sound the first portions (only) of a multimodular S. Since this supposed recapitulation is in the process of misfiring, Clementi sets things right by dissolving the "flawed" rotation, mm. 183–94 and giving us a corrected version (the "real" re-

capitulation?), with a more clearly identifiable restart of P (m. 195) and the remaining later portion (only) of S (m. 228 = m. 63), now both in the proper tonic, G minor. The broad expanse of the original S-material is split between the two recapitulatory rotations, the "wrong" one and the "right" one.[34]

The oddity of the Clementi piece would perhaps not be worth remarking upon were a related strategy not employed—famously—in one of Beethoven's late quartets, the first movement of the A-minor Quartet, op. 132. Here too we find what amounts to a tonally "wrong" recapitulatory rotation (mm. 121–94, beginning in E minor, v, and moving to C major, III) followed by a notably varied, "right" one (mm. 195–264) in the tonic.[35] Needless to say, the complications surrounding this composition are profound—though not unique, since certain aspects of its procedures are foreshadowed in some of his earlier works.[36]

---

34. Plantinga, *Clementi*, p. 173.

35. The description here is similar to that in Rosen, *Sonata Forms*, rev. ed., p. 355. The accompanying footnote, however, citing movements in Haydn's Symphonies Nos. 75 and 89, is questionable. What Rosen was noticing in those cases were engaging adaptations of two common procedures in Haydn sonata forms: rotational developments and recomposed recapitulations. For other discussions of the double-recapitulation effect in op. 132/i and additional bibliography see Kerman, *The Beethoven Quartets*, pp. 247–50; Robin Wallace, "Background and Expression in the First Movement of Beethoven's op. 132," *The Journal of Musicology*, 7 (1989), 3–20; and Michael Steinberg, "The Late Quartets," in *The Beethoven Quartet Companion*, ed. Robert Winter and Robert Martin (Berkeley: University of California Press, 1994), p. 268. Cf. Kinderman, *Beethoven*, p. 292: "The first movement of the A minor Quartet op. 132 . . . contains a recapitulation in the dominant, as does the Credo of the *Missa Solemnis*."

36. Op. 132/i should not be considered apart from the perhaps-related precedent of the wittily (and wildly) "mechanistic" finale to Symphony No. 8 in F, op. 93. Here the development, mm. 91–161 (itself beginning with P in the tonic after a nonrepeated exposition, recalling the procedure in the Quartet in F, op. 59 no. 1),

leads to a first recapitulation, mm. 162–266 (notice the false start in m. 152), in which P and S are brought back in the proper, tonic key (S begins in D-flat, then adjusts itself to F), although no ESC is attained, paralleling the exposition's lack of an EEC. This first nonresolving recapitulation immediately recycles back to a substantially recomposed revisiting of the entire development-recapitulation complex (a composed-out substitute for the once-conventional repetition of the complex), mm. 267–355 (with a different false start in m. 346) and 356–437. In the "second recapitulation" S is contained fully within the tonic, but once again the ESC is elusive, and F-major closure is obtained only in the coda, which begins in m. 439. Overlooking the obvious, Tovey's much-repeated claim (*Symphonies and Other Orchestral Works*, p. 82) that mm. 267ff constitute "a coda that is nearly as long as the whole body of the movement," is indefensible. One much more compressed precedent for the Eighth's written-out and recomposed development and recapitulation is the discursive "coda"—its compression makes it easier to defend as a coda—to the Symphony No. 3 in E-flat, op. 55, "Eroica," mentioned in this regard at the end of ch. 5 and in ch. 13. Cf. also the related precedent in the finale of the Piano Trio in E-flat, op. 70 no. 2 (two trackings through the recapitulatory S and C), discussed in ch. 11, n. 20.

☙❦❧

CHAPTER THIRTEEN

Parageneric Spaces

Coda and Introduction

By sonata-space we mean that space articulated by the generic sonata form proper: normal treatments of the exposition, developmental space, and recapitulatory rotation. Some sonata movements also feature parageneric spaces (or not-sonata-space), everything else in the movement that may set up, momentarily step outside of, or otherwise alter or frame the presentation of the sonata form. In such movements the most frequently encountered parageneric spaces are *accretions* that in the second half of the eighteenth century came to be increasingly attractive options as add-ons to the basic structure. The most common are codas and introductions—the subjects of this chapter. Other, historically later parageneric spaces include interpolations within the movement that withdraw from the sonata-action, such as some recurrences of a slow introduction (which recurrences, however, might well be implicated in larger rotational structures that stretch over both sonata and not-sonata-space.)

The Coda

Definitions, Traditional Views

Codas may be conceptualized either rhetorically (with regard to their positional relation to the preceding thematic layout) or tonally (with regard only to keys and tonal-contrapuntal "background" resolutions, disregarding the thematic parallels of the recapitulation with the expositional *Anlage*).[1] Sonata Theory favors the rhetorical approach for its definition of a coda. As a rule of thumb the coda begins once the recapitulation has reached the point at which the exposition's closing materials, normally including a final cadence, have been revisited in full.

In analytical work one should identify the referential or correspondence measures in the recapitulation that recapture the way in which the exposition had ended. In most cases once we are past the point where the last expositional measure has been retraced in the reca-

---

1. Esther Cavett-Dunsby, for instance ("Mozart's Codas," *Music Analysis* 7 (1988), 31–51), sought to distinguish between the "formal" and "structural" coda. The formal coda begins "after double barlines and repeat marks towards the end of the movement" (p. 32). The structural coda is defined in explicitly Schenkerian terms, "with reference to the background structure of

the movement [what follows after 'the arrival of the Î'], rather than to its surface form. . . . Schenker's concept of the 'structural coda' (as I shall call it) is a foil to the more familiar notion of the 'formal coda.' As a rule, structural and formal codas in Mozart's sonata forms do not coincide" (p. 34).

pitulation—assuming an otherwise straightforward situation—we have moved into a coda. Its specific treatment may be marked by localized idiosyncrasies. It might happen that as the recapitulation comes to its expected close one finds a last-instant deviation from a strict correspondence with the end of the exposition: a shying-away from the anticipated final cadence or some other alteration or expansion of it. This recomposed recapitulatory conclusion might even pause on an unexpected chord—a dominant, a diminished seventh, an applied dominant, or some other harmonic turn—or it might merge into a transitional passage preparing for the coda proper. One might also find smoothing or blurring features peculiar to the area surrounding the introduction of coda material.[2] One's analytical apparatus should be flexible enough to handle these variants with ease.

The situation may be complicated by the presence of repeat signs. When a repetition of the development and recapitulation is called for, as Rosen noted, a coda could either be included within the repeat signs of the second part of the sonata or it could be appended after that repetition.[3] In other words, reckoning from the beginning of the recapitulation, one might find { . . . P TR ' S / C :‖ coda ‖}, { . . . P TR' S / C coda :‖}, or something like { . . . P TR ' S / C¹ C²—coda-like material—C³ ‖}. This third possibility may or may not lead to a repeat sign after the last C-module returns. To distinguish this last procedure from a coda proper we call it *coda-rhetoric interpolation* (CRI): it will be treated in a separate section below. Finally, one can distinguish all of these options from another common practice of the time, the expansion of a final or penultimate C-module by several bars in such a way as to suggest a wrap-up or coda-effect. Such a C-module expansion with coda-effect (or with CRI-effect) is an interior broadening of an existing phrase, not a separate phrase (or

brief, postphrase module) in its own right.

The coda is a parageneric space that stands outside the sonata form. It is what Schoenberg famously—perhaps wryly—called "an extrinsic addition. The assumption that it serves to establish the tonality is hardly justified; it could scarcely compensate for failure to establish the tonality in the previous sections. In fact, it would be difficult to give any other reason for the addition of a coda than that the composer wants to say something more."[4] Although its length may vary, shorter codas were the norm before longer ones began to appear. Sometimes codas are little more than emphatic, tonic-prolongational tags of one, two, three, or four measures, following the conclusion of the recapitulation's last phrase. In *Classical Form* Caplin, on the basis of formal function, regards such a brief tag as a codetta rather than a coda, reserving the latter term for a longer, "relatively large unit."[5] Our preference is to use the term "codetta" to refer only to a final subsection housed within a larger formal zone, such as S- or C-space. (One variety of C, for example, is the "codetta type.") Under this definition a codetta could not stand alone beyond sonata-space (beyond the recapitulation's articulation of the measure corresponding to the last bar of the exposition). In most cases our tendency is to regard this separate section, short or long, as a coda.

Insisting on hairsplitting terminological distinctions is rarely relevant to the larger tasks of analytical hermeneutics. We see room for flexibility here. We admit the possibility, and at times even the desirability, of interpreting certain instances of a brief "extra" bar or two as being a mere "coda-effect" broadening of the final chord of the concluding recapitulatory measure. This might be the more appealing option when those bars articulate only the tonic chord and are not set off from the normatively final recapitulatory bar by a rest or other break. We

2. A similar point was made in Caplin, *Classical Form*, p. 181.

3. Rosen, *Sonata Forms*, rev. ed., p. 297.

4. Schoenberg, *Fundamentals of Musical Composition*, p. 185. Schoenberg's dismissal of a tonally compensatory coda is incorrect in the case of such sonata deformations as the nonresolving recapitulation (as in, for instance,

Beethoven's *Egmont* Overture): see Hepokoski, "Back and Forth from *Egmont*." The argument of the coda existing "after-the-end" is also pursued in Caplin, *Classical Form*, pp. 179–91—which also began by quoting Schoenberg (as, indeed, did Cavett-Dunsby, "Mozart's Codas," p. 32).

5. Caplin, *Classical Music*, p. 179.

also agree that many short codas have a codetta-function to the entire movement—or to the recapitulation proper.

The more elaborate the coda, the higher a composition's claim to an enhanced prestige, to a heightened "weight and seriousness."[6] In the later-eighteenth and early-nineteenth centuries the coda normally accomplished the standard functions of grounding further the secured territory of the tonic and ending the movement with an appropriate rhetorical flourish. Since the full presence of the tonic key had been precipitated or "made real" only at the moment of the ESC (as discussed in the concluding portions of chapter 11), the coda may also be understood as confirming the reality of the fully secured tonic—celebrating it or basking in it—that it had taken the exertion of the sonata process to accomplish. This interpretation seems particularly apt in longer, more discursive codas. Codas respond to the preceding kinetic thrust of the sonata. As Ratner put it, one of the coda's purposes is to provide "a stronger effect of closure . . . to arrest the momentum generated throughout the movement,"[7] even though some composers, in particularly "grand" compositions, occasionally treated the coda as an extended postsonata space in its own right.

Codas could be treated freely because of their separateness from sonata conventions. The implications of this can be provocative. The mere existence of a coda—especially one of greater length—can provide a challenge to the preceding sonata, as though the normative bringing of sonata-space to completion at the end of the recapitulation were being arraigned as insufficient to the expressive task at hand. In a passage most applicable to extended codas, Rosen noted that "the appearance of a coda always disturbs the binary symmetry of a sonata form. . . . One might say that the coda is a sign of dissatisfaction with the form, a declaration in each individual case that the symmetry is inadequate to the demands of the material, that the simple parallelism has become constraining."[8] This observation poses larger interpretive questions. In what respect would the preceding sonata be considered "inadequate" were it to have been presented without a substantial coda? Why is the coda responding to it at such length?

Thematic-Rhetorical Material in Codas: Rotational Implications

Rhetorically, there were two standard eighteenth-century options. The composer could provide a coda that completes the movement briefly, and *forte*, with generic concluding modules (Ratner: "a few emphatic chords or cadential gestures").[9] Or the composer could begin the coda with a restatement of the primary theme (P) or an obvious adaptation thereof.[10] So common is this practice that the reintroduction of P-material at the end of the recapitulation (proposing a sense of rebeginning, not a mere P-based C) is a strong sign that the coda has begun. With the exception of the final "rondo-theme" appearance of P in a Type 4 sonata, any P following tonally resolved S- and C-zones signifies the onset of a coda.

Codas that begin with P-based music suggest the onset of another rotation of the referential materials. This final return-to-P may correspond with the earlier move from the end of the

6. Rosen, *Sonata Forms*, rev. ed., p. 298, suggesting also that it was in Haydn's Quartets, op. 9, that codas were initially attached to significant sonata-form structures. Rosen, pp. 304–5, notes additionally the added "dignity" given to a composition by means of a coda as well as the responsiveness of the coda to the content that had preceded it in the sonata proper. Ratner, *Classic Music*, p. 231, made essentially the same point about the coda, citing also Koch's 1802 definition of it as "a more complete closing section, following the second reprise of an allegro," along with Reicha's 1813 comparison of a broad coda—as in some of Beethoven's music—as "an oratorical peroration."

7. Ratner, *Classic Music*, p. 230.
8. Rosen, *Sonata Forms*, rev. ed., p. 297.
9. Ratner, *Classic Music*, p. 230. Again, cf. Caplin's differing terminology cited in n. 5.
10. The P-launched coda was also mentioned, particularly with reference to Haydn and Clementi, as the most common procedure in Rosen, *Sonata Forms*, rev. ed., p. 311. Kerman suggested some caveats about the return-to-P procedure in Mozart (see n. 11), although such returns do occur here and there in the works of that composer (for example, in several of the earlier symphonies).

exposition into the development, which often begins with P-based gestures. Complementarily, if the development had begun instead with new or episodic material—sometimes either as a substitute for the more normal P or an interpolation before the treatment of the P-theme proper—the coda might start with a reference to that idea, not to P. The recycling back to an idea from the opening of the development retains the underlying impulses of rotation, potential repeat schemes, and the like.[11] The coda can often be understood as an incomplete coda-rotation, based only on P or a proxy for it. In most cases the rotation is soon stopped short with generically cadential (or other) modules that call an end to the rotational cycling. Longer, more discursive codas may have more elaborate rotational implications.

Needless to say—to consider other thematic options—one should take note of any coda that begins with (or emphasizes) non-P material or of any coda that introduces new themes or textures. When such things occur, we should inquire why they are as they are and what effect they have on the whole. One might also keep in mind Kerman's delicious phrase regarding one characteristic type of later-Mozart coda: "It is as though after having left the party Mozart has a final remark to make *sur l'escalier*—a grieving remark or a wary one, a witticism, a compliment, or a retort."[12]

Discursive Codas

Although there are a handful of celebrated exceptions, a coda in Mozart or Haydn is usually a brief or relatively modest affair. On the other hand, Beethoven often expanded his codas vastly and treated their materials with considerable complexity, although we agree with both Ratner and Kerman that it is inappropriate to consider such lengthy codas as "second" or "terminal developments" (the latter being the term proposed, it seems, by Vincent d'Indy).[13]

When a coda is lengthy, we refer to it as a *discursive coda*. This term conveys the sense that it unfolds a separate, often multisectional discourse beyond sonata space. While one's first instincts might be to point toward discursive codas in some of Beethoven's stormy Allegro compositions, we should recall that he was also attracted, especially in the 1790s (as Plantinga pointed out), to appending lengthy extensions to slow movements. One finds them in the Piano Trios op. 1 no. 1/ii and op. 1 no. 2/ii, in the Piano Sonatas op. 2 no. 1/ii, op. 2 no. 3/ii, op. 7/ii, and op. 10 no. 1/ii; in the Piano Concertos No. 1, op. 15/ii, and No. 2, op. 19; and in several other compositions.[14] A discursive coda is a separate tableau, a surplus-conclusion after the main event. Especially in Beethoven, it may momentarily "lose" the tonic secured at the ESC by slipping into nontonic keys before regaining the tonic near the end. It is always of central interest to come to terms with why this type of coda was added at all.

While some longer codas are largely P-based (representing only an incomplete rotation), one occasionally finds cases in which they give the impression of producing another full rotation through the materials: P and S or P and C. Classic instances occur in the first movements of Beethoven's Piano Sonatas in C, op. 53, "Waldstein" (the coda begins with P on ♭II, m. 249; S appears in the tonic, m. 284) and in F minor, op. 57, "Appassionata" (the coda begins with P in m. 204, soon shifting away from the tonic; S appears on VI at m. 211). Since both sonata movements also feature rotational developments (in the "Waldstein" it is S² that appears there,

---

11. Cf. Kerman, "Notes on Beethoven's Codas," *Beethoven Studies 3*, ed. Alan Tyson (Cambridge: Cambridge University Press, 1982), pp. 142, 146: "Mozart often works without a coda. . . . When he does have a coda it is short and carefully kept subsidiary to the rest of the movement. And it is likely to echo the beginning of the development section. . . . What is quite rare in Mozart is a coda containing a strong return of the movement's first theme. He sometimes makes reference to the first theme in the cadential phrases, of course [our

P-based C-theme], but the effect of this is quite different from that of a full-scale return." Cf. n. 10.
12. Kerman, "Notes on Beethoven's Codas," p. 143.
13. Kerman, "Notes on Beethoven's Codas," pp. 151–52, which also provides the reasoning behind the objection; Ratner, *Classic Music*, p. 231, "not secondary developments . . . but extended areas of arrival."
14. Leon Plantinga, *Beethoven's Concertos: History, Style, Performance* (New York: Norton, 1999), pp. 106–7.

not S[1]), both are examples of quadri-rotational movements. The "Waldstein" movement is additionally rounded off with a further recycling of P—as if beginning a fifth rotation—at the end of its coda (m. 295), while at the comparable place the "Appassionata" refers first to S (m. 240) and then, at the very end, to P (m. 257). Although Kerman did not discuss this issue in these terms, he did mention that Beethoven's codas often begin with P-material (more so than do Mozart's), that they are sometimes inflected at first into "one of the subdominant-area keys (subdominant, supertonic, flattened supertonic, even flattened submediant) before bringing it round to the tonic," and that they also often contain a "distant recollection" of the S-theme later on—a brief statement in which "the feeling is of a distant, nostalgic memory rather than of a firm restatement of reinterpretation."[15]

Another Beethovenian possibility is to employ a discursive coda to give the impression of a recomposed or telescoped repeat of the development and recapitulation. Something along these lines might lie behind aspects of the rotational coda types mentioned above, but the clearest paradigm is provided by the huge coda to the first movement of Beethoven's *Eroica* Symphony. One of the central points of this movement was to provide, in its early nineteenth-century context (presumably using the later Haydn symphonies as a standard of normative monumentality), a sense of hypermonumentality, a heightened sublimity of effort and expanse. (Its chief predecessors in this regard were the first movement

of Mozart's "Prague" Symphony and virtually all of his "Jupiter" Symphony.) In the opening movement of the *Eroica* Beethoven took on this challenge while renouncing the grand extension automatically provided by the increasingly obsolete option of a literal repetition of the development and recapitulation. In compensation he crafted a discursive coda that reviewed, in order, some of the central events of the development and recapitulation. Presumably it is also for this reason that the first part of the coda is modulatory, invoking developmental procedures, while the second part, referring to the recapitulation, is grounded on the E-flat tonic.[16]

Once the fundamental conception is grasped, the ordering of the *Eroica* coda's thematic details fall readily into place. (Some other, climactic functions of this coda are noted in the next section of this chapter.) Following a brief, P-based link with its famous chordal descents (mm. 551–63) some of the varied thematic references in the coda may be mapped, with some flexibility (and adjusting for a sense of a properly "coda flavor"), as: mm. 564ff = 178ff (P-based); 582ff = 285ff (the famous "new theme" from the development, whose reappearance here has provoked much discussion);[17] 603ff = 338ff (dominant preparation; rebuilding for the recapitulation); 631ff = 398ff (P, recapitulation); 673ff = 460ff (bolstering the case that Beethoven had indeed conceptualized this theme as S[1.1], as mentioned also in chapter 7).[18] Similarly instructive instances—with their own variants of the idea—occur in the finales of Beethoven's

---

15. Kerman, "Notes on Beethoven's Codas," pp. 154–55.
16. The essential details of the *Eroica* coda are also summarized, more expansively, in Hepokoski, "Beyond the Sonata Principle," p. 111. A similar observation, though in a different interpretive context, was provided by Robert P. Morgan, "Coda as Culmination: The First Movement of the 'Eroica' Symphony," in *Music Theory and the Exploration of the Past*, ed. Christopher Hatch and David W. Bernstein (Chicago: University of Chicago Press, 1993), p. 371.
17. The "new theme's" coda-tracking through F minor (m. 582), then E-flat minor (m. 590, the tonic minor), is probably less a reaction to an imperative from any presumed "sonata principle," as Edward T. Cone claimed in 1967–68, than it is a back-reference to the development's touching on the tonic E-flat major at m. 316, followed by a quick collapse into E-flat minor (m.

320) and a re-sounding of this "new theme" in that key at m. 323, that is, prior to the formal reactivation of the structural V at m. 338. For Cone's remark, see *Musical Form and Musical Performance*, p. 77.
18. Cf. Theodor W. Adorno, *Beethoven: The Philosophy of the Music*, ed. Rolf Tiedemann, trans. Edmund Jephcott (Stanford: Stanford University Press, 1998), p. 104: "At the very end of the first movement [of the *Eroica*] the original—then interrupted—idea of the second subject group reappears as the last thematic event in the movement (apart from the chord syncopations). It is, as it were, redeemed, vindicated. Cf. Schoenberg's notion of the obligation once contracted.—Moreover, this theme already contains the kernel of the motif—the repeated crotchets—of the consequent [*sic*] phrase which will follow it in the exposition, after the dramatic interruption."

Symphony No. 8 in F, op. 93, and the String Quartet in B-flat, op. 130 (in which the "recapitulatory" portion of the discursive coda is left incomplete). The larger idea behind all of these was recognized by Ratner: a longer coda could begin with "a harmonic digression (optional)," "a firm return to the tonic, generally with the opening theme," and "a set of emphatic cadential gestures. . . . These events review those of part II in compressed form—development, recapitulation, and closure."[19]

When confronted with a multisectional, discursive coda, one often finds that its longer, main section itself ends with a shorter "coda," a passage with the effect of a traditional coda proper or a separate *coda to the coda*. (In some instances this might be reduced to a *codetta to the coda*.) In turn this suggests that the bulk of the discursive tableau may also be understood as an interpolated block wedged between the end of the recapitulatory rotation and its own "coda." Sometimes introduced by a passageway or bridge from the end of the recapitulation, a discursive coda typically subdivides into two main portions: (1) an extended tableau, perhaps multisectional, capable of serving a variety of purposes; and at the end (2) a briefer coda to the coda, wrapping up the movement—something that may be P-based, suggesting the onset of a new incomplete rotation of materials (as in a more standard coda).

The general effect is by no means limited to Beethoven and later composers. Mozart's Overture to *The Marriage of Figaro* is a Type 1 sonata with a discursive coda beginning in m. 236—a "new," P-related crescendo-module leading cumulatively at mm. 250ff to a recapturing of an expositional TR-passage (cf. mm. 43ff), "lost" or omitted in the recapitulation. (As such, this discursive coda takes on a compensatory function, one of the several types mentioned in the section below.) A "codetta-like" coda-to-the-coda effect—one last extension to the preceding excursus—occurs with the final grounding of the tonic in mm. 284–94. The famous coda to the finale of the "Jupiter" Symphony provides

another example of a grandly discursive coda with a final, appended codetta- or coda-like tag at its end.

A "theatrical" discursive-coda effect was produced in Cherubini's Overture to *Les deux journées* (1800): at the end of a rather lengthy, perorational coda (at an Allegro tempo) the last eighteen measures, a P-based "tag," charge forward with a sudden increase in tempo, "sérrés le mouvement" (or Presto in some later editions). Beethoven called upon a similar effect more than once—it would become a standard trope of concluding excitement later in the century—perhaps most famously in the determined tightening of the pulse found in the *sempre più allegro* and Presto conclusion to the finale's coda in the Fifth Symphony. The further possibility of writing all or most of the discursive coda in an increased, more frenetic tempo was additionally explored by Beethoven in other compositions: in some of his middle- and late-quartet movements, for instance, and in several of the overtures: *Leonore 2* and *3*, *Egmont*, and *Fidelio*.

Characteristic Functions of the Discursive Coda

The many potential roles of larger codas have been remarked upon by several scholars. In his 1982 study of Beethoven's codas Joseph Kerman observed that many of them, especially in works after 1800, gave the impression of a removal of difficulties or obstacles set up earlier in the movement—that such concluding sections could serve the larger structural and expressive purposes of "'normalisation,' 'resolution,' 'expansion,' 'release,' 'completion,' and 'fulfilment,'" diverse descriptions containable under the general concept of "thematic 'completion.'"[20] Especially in Beethoven's hands, the coda could become the capstone or *telos* of the entire movement, "providing an emotional resolution, or rather an apotheosis," as Kerman had written elsewhere about the coda to the first movement of the *Eroica*, "so different in spirit and form from the symmetrical resolutions of

---

19. Ratner, *Classic Music*, p. 230.

20. Kerman, "Notes on Beethoven's Codas," pp. 149, 151.

Haydn and Mozart."[21] (Mozart, of course, had provided a few stunning precedents in his later works, most notably in the "Jupiter" finale .)[22] Robert P. Morgan has similarly noted, particularly with reference to the *Eroica* coda, the phenomenon of "coda as culmination," in this case manifesting itself as the goal of a long-range "textural crescendo," a "dynamically evolving process," a culminating, tutti realization of registral, textural, and dynamic space.[23] Focusing on Beethoven's deployment of the "heroic-style coda," Scott Burnham agreed with such views, proposing that in the *Eroica* coda "the [P-based] melodic repetitions at the end . . . [suggest] the possibility of endless repetitions, endless affirmation. . . . Thus the final melodic utterance of the opening theme has thematic stability but not thematic closure—again, what an appropriate way to signal an apotheosis."[24]

Another clear instance of the apotheosis type of coda occurs in the *Egmont* Overture, op. 84, to which Beethoven additionally shifted the burden of tonal resolution, following an unorthodox, nonresolving recapitulation.[25] Perhaps an even more idiosyncratic situation emerges in such pieces as Weber's "Jubilee" Overture (*Jubel-Ouvertüre*, 1818), a sonata form rising in its coda to the *fortissimo* statement, Andante, of a new, but pre-existing and communally shared melody, in this case, "God Save the King." (Brahms produced much the same effect decades later in his *Academic Festival* Overture [1880], which ends with a peroration on "Gaudeamus Igitur.") Such examples suggest that the sonata process that precedes this type of coda is not to be taken as a fully self-sufficient action (as most sonata forms normally were throughout the eighteenth century) but rather as a preliminary exertion that must be undertaken before what happens in the coda is able to emerge as a fully ripened possibility. This treats the preceding sonata as a Wittgensteinian ladder

cast aside once it is scaled and its utilitarian purpose of ascending used up—a generative matrix without which the crowning *Klang* of the coda-apotheosis would have been unattainable.

Still another type of discursive coda sometimes (though infrequently) found in a Type 3 sonata form incorporates a written-out cadenza, suggesting a local intermixture with some of the solo-display features of the Type 5 sonata. Other aspects of the Type 5 sonata, however—most notably its reliance on ritornello pillars—are not relevant to the other portions of such movements. In its most emphatic realizations, the "coda-cadenza" can even include a $^6_4$ platform, some interior tempo changes, and a trill-cadence exit into a separate, additional coda-space. The *locus classicus* occurs after the recapitulation of the first movement of Beethoven's Cello Sonata in F, op. 5 no. 1. Related examples, better classified as instances of coda-rhetoric interpolation (CRI or CRI-effect), may be consulted in the first movement of his Piano Sonata in C, op. 2 no. 3—discussed in more detail below—and in the birdsong cadenza in the second movement of the *Pastoral* Symphony.[26]

Each discursive coda has its own role to play in the larger argument of the movement. Each needs to be studied individually and flexibly. Caplin has outlined a number of categories of "compensatory functions" for such codas. His listing includes: "recollection of main-theme ideas" (our incomplete coda-rotation); "restoration of deleted material from the recapitulation" (as we have suggested occurs in Mozart's Overture to *The Marriage of Figaro*, restoring a TR-idea missing from the recapitulation—although within the style such a restoration was by no means obligatory or even expected); "reference to the development section" (such an event may have rotational or repeat-scheme implications); "shaping a new dynamic curve" (either apotheoses and climaxes, as in Beethoven's *Eroica*

---

21. Kerman, "Theme and Variations" [rev. of Charles Rosen, *Sonata Forms*]," *The New York Review of Books*, 23 October 1980, 52. Cited in Morgan, "Coda as Culmination: The First Movement of the 'Eroica' Symphony," p. 359.

22. Cf. Rosen's remark, "I presume that [Mozart] is the inventor of the contrapuntal coda" (*Sonata Forms*, rev. ed., p. 314).

23. Morgan, "Coda as Culmination: The First Movement of the 'Eroica' Symphony," pp. 357–76.

24. Burnham, *Beethoven Hero* (Princeton, N.J.: Princeton University Press, 1995), p. 19. On the "heroic-style coda" see also pp. 53–60.

25. Hepokoski, "Back and Forth from *Egmont*." Cf. n. 4.

26. See also the discussion in Kerman, "Notes on Beethoven's Codas," pp. 154–55.

Symphony and *Egmont* Overture, or dissolutions, as in the *Coriolan* Overture); and "realization of unrealized implications" (reminding one of Kerman's "thematic completion" or "fulfillment"; Caplin's examples are Beethoven's *Coriolan*, once again, and the slow movements of Mozart's Symphony No. 39 and Beethoven's Piano Sonata, op. 10 no. 1).[27]

Expanded C-Space and Coda-Rhetoric Interpolation (CRI)

As suggested above, a coda is normally considered to have begun once the rhetorical pattern of the exposition has been retraced (in the tonic) to its end in the recapitulation. If there are three C-modules ending the pattern, one would expect the recurrence of all three C-modules before the coda proper begins. In this case we would find {C¹ C² C³ || coda}, in which || represents the point at which the recapitulation has attained the point parallel to the end of the exposition.

Occasionally, though, a composer would interpolate a passage of coda-rhetoric material (strong closing cadences, perhaps a return to the normative P, and so on) before all of the final recapitulatory modules have been sounded. (The new expansion would normally occur in C-space, although not all expositions and recapitulations contain that zone. When the exposition and recapitulation feature an EEC and ESC occurring at or very near their ends, the expansion could be applied to the later stages of S, Sᶜ, or TR⇒FS.) This produced a concluding pattern on the order of {C¹ C² — expansion via coda-like material — C³ |}, which reserves the final C-module, or sometimes the final two C-modules, for the close of the work, thus producing a concluding musical "rhyme" with the end of the exposition. We refer to this procedure as a *coda-rhetoric interpolation* (CRI). This terminology steers clear of two misconceptions. The first would consider the coda to begin after C², thus ignoring the sonata-space, non–coda status of C³, returned to as a set of correspondence measures with the exposition. The second would construe the CRI only as a functionally neutral

expansion of C, which would overlook the relationship of the interpolation with the kind of music commonly found in codas.

What initially seems to be a straightforward concept turns out to be more intricate once one examines it carefully. Since Sonata Theory does not encourage the view that major functional zones can begin mid-phrase, it is more precise to distinguish between CRI proper and a mid-phrase CRI-effect. The former implies the conclusion of a preceding phrase with a cadence and the beginning of a new one (CRI), perhaps elided or flush-juxtaposed with it. (The P-based CRI is the most common option: rebeginning P with a new phrase.) But sometimes the coda-like expansion is not separated off or "enclosed" as a separate phrase between two cadences. Instead, it appears as an interior expansion of a pre-existing module, as though that module had been inflated in the middle to incorporate coda-like rhetoric. In these instances we have a C-module expansion with CRI-effect (or S-, Sᶜ-, or TR⇒FS-module with CRI effect, when those situations apply). One typical pattern might be something like {C¹ — C² with coda-effect expansions — C³ || coda}, although, of course, the number of C-modules present varies from piece to piece.

An additional complication is that not all C-module expansions invariably produce a CRI-effect. The modular expansion may also occur with other implications, sometimes that of preparing for a CRI proper. This could produce a pattern like {C¹ — C², expanded — CRI as new phrase, usually P-based — C³}. Obviously, the degree of CRI-effect in such a C² expansion (in this case) could vary from piece to piece, and different analysts might come up with modestly divergent readings of the evidence. A composer could deploy the CRI-effect in any number of clever and inventive ways, and one should be prepared (especially with the constantly astonishing Haydn) to confront each instance on its own terms.

There are several examples of the CRI in the literature. One paradigmatic case occurs at the end of the first movement of Mozart's Symphony No. 40 in G Minor, K. 550 (Examples

---

27. Caplin, *Classical Form*, pp. 186–91.

13.1a and b). Assuming that the last phrase of the repetition of C^2 (m. 279 = the exposition's m. 91) has been expanded in such a way as to lead into it, the CRI proper is sounded with the *piano*-dynamic P-material in mm. 287–93 (with an exquisitely dovetailed anacrusis beginning in m. 286). As an elided conclusion, C^3 subsequently bursts forth, *forte*, to complete the recapitulation, mm. 293–97 (= the exposition's final mm. 95–99). A brusque, two-bar extension is appended at the very end (mm. 298–99): three pitiless tonic chords, perhaps construable as a small coda proper.[28]

Another instance is found in the first movement of Beethoven's Piano Sonata in C, op. 2 no. 3. Here the recapitulatory C^1 is found in mm. 212–17 with suppressed cadence. Instead of cadencing, the still-active C-module plunges suddenly into a lengthy extension beginning on A flat ($\flat$VI, m. 218) and moving onto a $^6_4$ with fermata (m. 232, beginning) that releases an interior cadenza and a V^7 (m. 232, end) whose effective resolution occurs on the downbeat of m. 233. Strictly considered, mm. 218–33, not a self-contained phrase (no phrase had concluded before it began), are best regarded as a rhetorical expansion of C^1, but their purpose is to set up an unmistakable CRI. This occurs with the elided onset of the next phrase, mm. 233–52 — featuring a telltale return to P^1 — elided again, at the end, with the as-yet-unsounded recapitulatory C^2, which now surfaces to conclude the movement in mm. 252–57.[29]

A classic example of C-module expansion with CRI-effect — in the absence of a CRI proper — occurs in the first movement of Mozart's Symphony No. 39 (examples 13.2a and b). In the midst of the usual round of correspondence measures the ESC occurs at m. 276, and the tonic restatement of C^1 follows, mm. 276–92. In the exposition the concluding C^2 had been articulated as a straightforward eight-bar sentence, mm. 135–42. In the recapitula-

tion we find that the last bar of the sentence's presentation module (m. 295 = 138) veers from its model and launches a formal interior expansion with a strong "coda" flavor. The equivalent of m. 139 is regained around eight bars later, in m. 304, and the C^2 phrase ends with more or less strict correspondence measures with the exposition, mm. 304–7 (= 139–42). The final chord is expanded for two more measures (mm. 308–9), which may be regarded either as a tiny, appended coda or as an example of final-C-module terminal expansion (with coda- or codetta-effect). Something similar occurs in the finale of Mozart's Symphony No. 40, where the interior expansion occurs within the repetition of the C^1 module (mm. 286–301), while the movement itself ends with a more literal transposition of C^2, mm. 301–8.

C-module CRI-effect issues can be handled in varied ways. The situation near the end of the finale of Haydn's Quartet in B Minor, op. 33 no. 1, is fairly straightforward: the P-based CRI occurs in mm. 184–89, and it leads to a varied restatement of C^2, mm. 190–94, which ends the movement. More challenging and diverse are the examples found in the first movements of Mozart's String Quintet in C, K. 515 (featuring an aborted drive to a I:PAC, mm. 320–21, followed by an unsettling, "added" infiltration of the C^2 module [and later, fragments of S] occupying a full thirty-two bars before the correspondence-measure rearticulation of C^2 proper and few concluding bars, mm. 353–68), Haydn's Symphony No. 103 in E-flat, "Drumroll" (strictly considered, a complex S^C-module expansion that includes a return of the introductory Adagio), and Haydn's String Quartet in B-flat, op. 76 no. 4, "Sunrise" (in which the strong, P-based CRI-effect — harmonically, not a separate phrase, despite the preceding fermata — is launched over a subdominant chord, m. 175).

Finally, one potentially problematic issue

---

28. Kerman, "Notes on Beethoven's Codas," p. 143, mentions "the characteristic *calando* effect" (as in the finale of the Piano Concerto No. 24 in C Minor, K. 491) or "a pathetic *calando* followed by some sort of *furioso* conclusion" (as here) of some of Mozart's codas as being an effect that Beethoven sought to replicate in

some of his own works (as in the first movement of the "Pathétique" sonata, op. 13, etc.).

29. Kerman, "Notes on Beethoven's Codas," p. 147, alludes to this procedure (without our terminology) in Beethoven's op. 2 no. 3 and understands it as characteristically Haydnesque.

EXAMPLE 13.1a   Mozart, Symphony No. 40 in G Minor, K. 550, i, mm. 88–100

EXAMPLE 13.1b   Mozart, Symphony No. 40 in G Minor, K. 550, i, mm. 276–99

EXAMPLE 13.1b   *(continued)*

arises when the CRI in question is both P-based and occurs within a movement that is in dialogue with the Type 2 ("binary") sonata—that type in which a full recapitulation beginning with P is not provided. (Chapter 17 lays out the argument more fully.) The error is in imagining the P-based CRI to represent a recapitulatory gesture, one that produces some sort of "mirror form" or "reversed recapitulation." Such claims, for example, have been repeatedly made about the first movement of Mozart's Piano Sonata in D, K. 311—a deformational piece whose complications are not easily summarized in a few sentences. For the present, we might say only that we regard the return of the incipit (only) of P in m. 99 to be a passage of coda-rhetoric interpolation lasting until m. 109, when it is elided with the onset of C^1. In this case the CRI is wedged between S-space—with the ESC at m. 99—and the beginning of C-space. A comparable situation occurs in the related first movement of the Sonata for Violin and Piano in D, K. 306.

The Introduction

From time to time a piece or movement begins with material that precedes the sonata form. This may consist of a brief cadential formula or even only one, two, or three chords (perhaps the formulaic triple-hammer-blow) that, in contrast to more explicit P^0 or P$^{1.0}$ material, are genuinely prefatory. Such a *brief, in-tempo introduction* serves as an initial spur for the entire movement, a gateway emblem or illuminated initial. It is normally not involved either in the expositional repeat (often the repeat sign is placed after the introduction, before the P-theme) or in the launching of the recapitulatory rotation. There are several examples of this kind of opening material in Haydn's quartets (op. 71 no. 3/i [a single chord], op. 74 no. 1/i, op. 76 no. 1/i, and so on), although some of them are "slowed" or provided with other delays through one or more fermatas. Doubtless the opening two measures of Beethoven's *Eroica* Symphony recalls a tradition of brief, in-tempo introductions. (See the discussion in chapter 5 concerning possible intermixtures of this kind of introduction with the P^0 or P$^{1.0}$ idea.)

Also characteristic are more extensive introductions, which usually provide a prolonged sense of anticipation and formal preparation for a rapid-tempo sonata-to-come. The present section will focus on these longer introductions. The longer and more complex an introduction, the more importance is being claimed for the piece as a whole. (This does not mean that pieces

EXAMPLE 13.2a   Mozart, Symphony No. 39 in E-flat, K. 543, i, mm.
132–42

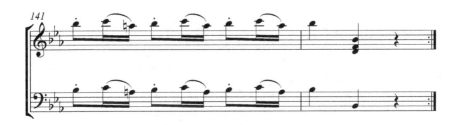

EXAMPLE 13.2b   Mozart, Symphony No. 39 in E-flat, K. 543, i, mm. 289–309

EXAMPLE 13.2b   (*continued*)

without introductions are *ipso facto* less serious. It means only that a sizable introduction more overtly thematizes the claim of the formality of the occasion and the seriousness of the composition.) Almost invariably such broader introductions are in a slow tempo and end with an expectant pause, usually on the dominant, thus setting up the trip-lever effect ("Go!") that sets the subsequent sonata form into motion.

Slow Introductions and Genre or Movement Types

Slow introductions are not equally available to all Allegro movements. Since they typically connote a heightened sense of dignity or grandeur, they were most appropriate in such "public" statements as symphonic first movements, overtures, and some festive serenades (Mozart's Serenade in D, K. 320, "Posthorn"). One mid-eighteenth-century pioneer in the production of orchestral slow introductions was Leopold Hofmann. The current *New Grove Dictionary* reports that "among Hofmann's most important and original contributions to the symphony [c. 1760] was the adoption of a slow introduction to the opening movement, anticipating Haydn."[30] Within Haydn's symphonic output—and even though a few earlier examples may be found—they began to occur more frequently in a spate of symphonies between 1773 and 1775 (chronologically, 50, 54, 57, 60, 53); they continued a few years later with Symphonies Nos. 71, 73, and 75; and the practice seems to have been even more consolidated in the six "Paris" symphonies (1785–86), three of which (84, 85, 86) have slow introductions. By the period of the twelve "London" symphonies—at the time the touchstones of grand, monumental symphonies—these introductions were normative in Haydn (except in the sole minor-mode symphony of the set, No. 95 in C minor). Mozart also had his role to play, writing substantial slow introductions for the first movements of the Symphony No. 36 in C, K. 425, "Linz" (1783), No. 38 in D, K. 504, "Prague" (1786), and No. 39 in E-flat, K. 543 (1788), for

---

30. Hermine Nicolussi-Prohászka and Allan Badley, "Leopold Hofmann," in *The New Grove Dictionary of Music and Musicians*, 2nd ed., 11: 605. This sentence does not appear in the preceding edition of the *New Grove*, in which the Hofmann article was written by Nicolussi-Prohászka alone. Cf. Jan LaRue's summary, in his review of Charles Rosen, *Sonata Forms* (1st ed., 1980), *Journal of the American Musicological Society* 34 (1981), 562: "About 1760 [the Austrian] Leopold Hofmann experimented repeatedly with what became the final design of the symphony (slow introduction plus sonata-allegro; andante; minuet/scherzo plus trio; substantial finale) somewhat earlier than Haydn's occasional pioneering efforts in this framework."

the Overtures to *Don Giovanni, Così fan tutte, Die Zauberflöte*, and so on.

Current discussions of slow introductions typically suggest two additional, practical functions of such passages. On the one hand, as pointed out by László Somfai, in the eighteenth century they could have a "'noise-killer' effect," calling a bustling audience's attention to the music at hand, particularly within large or spacious rooms.[31] On the other hand, as often in Haydn, they served to set up allegros that began quietly or with off-tonic openings. Orchestral introductions were also explored by other eighteenth-century composers. However important they may have been to the subsequent tradition, Haydn and Mozart were expanding on the work of predecessors.[32]

Any slow introduction to the first movement of a trio, quartet, or quintet—a less familiar practice—must have reinforced the advancing prestige claims of the genre at hand, suggesting that something of special importance was to follow in both the movement and the piece as a whole. The first movement of Haydn's Quartet in D, op. 71 no. 2, prefaces its Allegro with a lyrical, four-measure Adagio, bridging the stasis of the external silence to the suddenly *forte* agitation of the exposition. The fourteen-measure Adagio preceding the Allegro assai in the first movement of Mozart's Quartet in E-flat, K. 171, strikes an initial tone of unanticipated earnestness in its 1773 context. (The introduction also returns to conclude the movement.) Masterly examples of slow introductions from Mozart's later chamber works include the first movements of the Serenade in B-flat for Thirteen Winds, K. 361, the Quartet in C, K. 465 (the celebrated "Dissonance" opening), and the String Quintet in D, K. 593. Beethoven opened his Piano Trio in G, op. 1 no. 2, and both of his op. 5 cello sonatas with substantial, Adagio-tempo introductions.

Slow introductions to first movements of piano sonatas are rare before the 1790s, although one might mention the 29-measure Adagio leading to the Allegro di molto in the first movement of Mozart's Sonata in F for Four Hands, K. 497 (1786). (The composer also appended a full coda to this ambitious movement.) With the 1790s and early 1800s one finds these introductions in an increased scattering of sonatas, including a few by Clementi (such as the Sonatas in G Minor, op. 34, and B Minor, op. 40 no. 2) and Beethoven (Sonatas in F Minor, WoO 47 no. 2; in C Minor, op. 13, "Pathétique," in E-flat, op. 81a, "Lebewohl," and in C Minor, op. 111). Even with such distinguished exemplars the practice remained somewhat exceptional. When it did occur, the implication was probably that of providing an uncommon elevation of aesthetic intention, as if one were producing the pianistic equivalent of a symphony.

Finales of multimovement sonatas before 1800—normally lighter or more playful movements—are almost never prefaced with separate, slow introductions. Within the generic practice most relevant to Haydn, Mozart, and early-middle Beethoven that honor is generically reserved only for the first movement. Consequently, any slow introduction to an eighteenth-century finale would have been regarded as unusual. This is apparently the case in such works as Dittersdorf's Symphony No. 6 in A on Ovid's *Metamorphoses*, "Transformation of the Lycian Peasants into Frogs" (c. 1781–82), in which the finale begins with a mysteriously reflective Adagio that both precedes and interrupts a vigorously contrapuntal, quasi-fugal Vivace, ma moderato (not in sonata form), before the movement dissolves into amphibian croaking at the end; or in Boccherini's Symphony in D Minor, op. 12 no. 4 (G. 506, ca. 1771), nicknamed "La casa del diavolo" ("In the devil's house"; borrowings from Gluck suggest an underlying Don Juan program), in which the same slow introduction precedes both the first movement and the last.

More well-known instances also occur in

---

31. Somfai, "The London Revision of Haydn's Instrumental Style," *Proceedings of the Royal Musical Association* 100 (1973–74), 166, referring especially to Symphonies No. 93 and 104.

32. See Marianne Danckwardt, *Die langsame Einleitung:*

ihre Herkunft und ihr Bau bei Haydn und Mozart, 2 vols. (Tutzing: Hans Schneider, 1977). Cf. A. Peter Brown's review of this book, *Journal of the American Musicological Society* 33 (1980), 200–204.

the late-eighteenth and early-nineteenth centuries. What happens in the astonishing G-minor Adagio before the "false-front" G-major finale of Mozart's String Quintet in G Minor, K. 516 (1787) strikes one as extraordinary, within a piece that has a multimovement logic all its own. Early Beethoven is also relevant: his String Quartet, Op. 18 no. 6 (1798–1800), whose finale features the celebrated "La Malinconia" *Adagio* introduction, comes immediately to mind, as does the last movement of the Symphony No. 1 in C (1800), with its coy, witty introduction. Once intensely serious slow introductions begin to be written for finales later in the nineteenth century (as in Beethoven's Piano Sonata in B-flat, op. 106, "Hammerklavier," his Symphony No. 9 in D Minor, op. 125, and his Quartet in F, Op. 135; in Mendelssohn's Symphony No. 5 in D Minor, op. 107, "Reformation"; in Brahms's Symphony No. 1 in C Minor, op. 68; and in many other works), the effect is generally that of reopening a serious issue initially broached in the first movement: the issue now has to be reconfronted in a "do-or-die" finale.

Characteristic Zones within a Slow
Introduction

While it is difficult to generalize about what can happen in slow introductions, a generically typical introduction has available to it four expressive or functional zones, which usually become accessible in order. By no means do all introductions make use of all four zones. An introduction may omit, elide, or intermix one or more zones for localized expressive purposes. One may also encounter an idiosyncratic introduction in which the zone-concept seems inapplicable or strained as a background interpretive device. The zones, which may be treated very flexibly, are:

1. *Heraldic or annunciatory call to attention.* This is an initial *forte* impulse launching the entire work in a grand or "important" style, claiming and clearing space for what is to follow. It

might be a single phrase or two (often with grandly-robed, "regal" dotted rhythms or *coups d'archet*), a stiffly formal *exordium* (rhetorical formal sign of opening), a fanfare-like gesture (Haydn, Symphony No. 104, "London"), a set of striking, cadence-like gestures (Beethoven, Symphony No. 1), or even a single, imperious chord (Beethoven, Symphony No. 2, *Egmont* Overture). When the initial impulse is compact, it sometimes melts into gentler, zone-2 material, and it may return to relaunch or invade some of the subsequent phrases as well.

2. *Quieter material, often a brief, lyrical melody.* Especially when articulated with a lyrical melody—by no means the invariable case—this zone gives the impression of blocking out a roomy expanse of musical space, thus already predicting the ample breadth of the sonata-to-come and the consequent proportions of the whole. This zone may be occupied by the *piano* aftermath of zone 1, emerging as that which is released by the initial *forte* impulse. Or it may exist on its own, without being preceded by an earlier *forte*. In a major-mode work it sometimes happens that the major collapses here to minor or displays significant borrowings from the parallel minor. If so, the atmosphere typically becomes one of brooding or foreboding, one of "the fall" that must be restored in the subsequent sonata. In more advanced compositions this zone might modulate fleetingly away from the tonic, perhaps temporarily escaping the implications of a reigning minor mode, perhaps framing itself off from its surroundings as a mini-tableau (as in Beethoven's Overtures *Leonore 2* and *3*), or perhaps tonicizing a different key for other expressive reasons. This zone may also initiate a mixture of different "topics," figures, and rhetorical gestures, as suggested by Ratner.[33]

3. *Sequences.* These often give the impression of a "searching"—groping toward the attainment of the structural dominant. Once again, this often involves either a decay to the minor mode or a continuation of an earlier such decay, thereby suggesting considerable anxiety. When such sequences are greatly extended, they can

---

33. Ratner, *Classic Music*, pp. 104–6, provides a much-cited discussion of the introduction to Mozart's "Prague" Symphony along these lines.

have the local effect of a fantasia, as in Mozart's "Prague" Symphony and his Overture to *Don Giovanni*, K. 527, both of which also invoke the darkened, ominous "ombra" ("shadow") topic.[34]

4. *Dominant preparation.* At some point near its end the zone-2 or zone-3 music locks onto a structural dominant (V of I) to begin one or more measures of final dominant prolongation. Occasionally, the V is not prolonged at length but merely attained at the introduction's end. However it is introduced, the last measure (V) ends generically with an expectant *fermata*—a harmonic interruption on the dominant—that separates the introduction from the sonata form that it has prepared. As part of deformational practice this zone can even prepare the "wrong dominant," as, most famously, in Haydn's two late Symphonies in E-flat, Nos. 99 and 103, both of whose final, preparatory introduction-zones set up V of C minor (V/vi), although in No. 99 the "wrong dominant" is "artificially" corrected through the last-moment addition of an extra measure, V^7 of E-flat. But with Haydn—as always—the situation is even more unpredictable. As James Webster has pointed out, the mature Haydn employed a number of "through-compositional" procedures to soften the virtually inbuilt break between an introduction and the sonata form that follows. These included: the use of a "harmonic progression [that] deviates from the customary -V | I- (Symphonies 60, 73, 88, 90, 92, 94, 99, and 103)," in the simplest of cases of which, "the introduction still ends on the dominant, but the allegro begins off the tonic" (Nos. 60, 73, 86, 88, and 94); and, especially in his later symphonies, the appeal to "run-on" introductions, in which the introductory music flows more directly into the sonata form, sometimes even with the suppression of the normal fermata into the exposition, as especially in Nos. 86 and 97 ("No other Haydn introduction is run-on to [the] extent [of Sym-

phony No. 97]."[35] A further "dramatic" development in the ever-transforming concept of the introduction is the idea of bridging over the end of the introduction to the beginning of the sonata proper with a special link, often *accelerando*, giving the impression of a precipitously accumulating energy out of which the sonata is hurled forth like a javelin, as happens in Beethoven's Fourth Symphony, in his *Leonore 1* and *Egmont* Overtures, and in several other works.

Although these four zones and their subtypes provide many of the basic patterns and expressive effects for eighteenth-century introductions, they do not underpin them all. Some introductions might rework individual aspects of individual zones to the exclusion of others. The opening of Mozart's Quartet in C, K. 465, "Dissonance," for example, may be understood as beginning at once with Zone 3—sequential, foreboding, and "searching." The same might be said of an introduction that shares many of the same characteristics: that found at the opening of Beethoven's Quartet in C, op. 59 no. 3.

In addition, as has been widely noted, from the "Paris" Symphonies onward Haydn often experimented with introductions that motivically and harmonically foreshadow musical events and themes of the sonata-to-follow. (As Webster put it, "In general, the later the work, the closer and more pervasive the relations [to the following fast movement]."[36] One classic instance occurs in the introduction to the first movement of his Symphony No. 98 in B-flat, which starts with an Adagio, minor-mode version of the idea that will become the sonata's major-mode P (m. 16) at an Allegro tempo. Similarly, his Piano Trio in C, Hob. XV:21 (1795) begins with a six-bar Adagio pastorale, an idea in 6/8 meter that springs to life at the opening of the ensuing, 6/8 Vivace assai. Introductions that are generative or that serve as sources in other ways for the material of the subsequent sonata will be readdressed below in the section on "expressive

34. On the presence of "ombra" and a discussion of the topic more generally see, e.g., Elaine Sisman, "Genre, Gesture, and Meaning in Mozart's 'Prague' Symphony," in *Mozart Studies 2*, ed. Cliff Eisen (Oxford: Clarendon Press, 1997), pp. 27–84; cf. Ratner, *Classic Music*, pp. 24, 104–6.

35. Webster, *Haydn's "Farewell" Symphony and the Idea of Classical Style*, pp. 162–65.
36. Webster, *Haydn's "Farewell" Symphony and the Idea of Classical Style*, p. 162.

or representational functions." Obviously, they are also found in works by Mozart, Beethoven, and numerous other composers.

Finally, one should observe that some introductions, such as the opening, 22-measure Largo in Haydn's Symphony No. 102 in B-flat, imply a truncated rounded-binary design, AA'B . . . (instead of AA'BA"). The structural dominant and fermata are reached at the end of B. As a result one of the exposition's functions is that of beginning to supply (*in extenso*) the final limb of the rounded binary. This is especially notable when the P-theme is related to the introduction, as is the case here. From a larger perspective this rounded binary structure, begun in the introduction, will not attain its own tonal closure until the sonata form itself also does so—that is, at the moment of the ESC.[37]

Variants and Later Deformations of the "Slow" Introduction

Much less frequently, perhaps deformationally, the broad introduction can also be laid out in a more energetic tempo, as in Rossini's Overture to *Il Signor Bruschino* (1813), where a 38-measure Allegro precedes a Type 1 sonata in the same tempo (into which characteristic portions of the introduction return to fill in the interstices); or in the same composer's Overture to *La gazza ladra* (1817), which begins with a snappy Maestoso marziale to set up the principal Allegro. Even more deformationally, on very rare occasions, the slow-introduction concept is merged with the sonata proper, at least in such a way that it participates in the expositional repeat as well. In the first movement of Mozart's Violin Sonata in C, K. 303, a Type 1 sonata, P and TR of the exposition and recapitulation play out as an Adagio, while S and C shoot forward in an Allegro molto. A similar, though more elliptically compressed (and complex), version of this, with tempos reversed (Vivace, then Adagio espressivo), begins Beethoven's Piano Sonata in E, op.

109, a movement without an expositional repeat. And in the first movement of Beethoven's String Quartet in B-flat, op. 130, the opening (and recurring) Adagio ma non troppo, preparing a contrasting Allegro, is not only repeated with the whole exposition but may also be understood simultaneously as both an introduction—clearly its principal role—and the onset of a deformational P. The first movement of his earlier Piano Sonata in D Minor, op. 31, no. 2 ("Tempest"), had provided a less self-evident forerunner of this procedure.

Associated with the above are *false-start* sonatas, a relatively late development in the genre. In these cases the piece begins with a fast-tempo flourish (often either the P-idea itself or something related to it) only to be called up short, reined back into a more "proper" slow introduction or other slow passage. One's impression is that of a sonata movement rashly eager to plunge forth, only to be stopped, "set back," for the generic formalities. Alternatively, one might regard such a procedure as a vivid animating of the characteristic "call-to-attention" heraldic fanfare or illuminated initial encountered so frequently at the openings of slow introductions—a manic impulse that writes over the standard, usually more majestic gesture. In Beethoven the touchstone case occurs in the *Fidelio* Overture: an abrupt Allegro, mm. 1–4; a reflective Adagio, mm. 5–12; a return of the brief Allegro, now on the subdominant, mm. 13–16; and then a longer slow introduction eventually merging into the Allegro onset of the sonata deformation. Rossini provided some related examples in his overtures, notably in those to *La Scala di Seta* and *Le siège de Corinthe*.[38] The main components of the false-start procedure—impulsively fast and brief but aborted; slow and more properly deliberate; and an ensuing fast sonata form—recur as a virtually normative practice in several of Berlioz's sonata-deformational overtures, such as *Benvenuto Cellini*, *Le carnaval romain*, and *Le corsaire*.

---

37. It is thus not correct to assert, with Webster (*Haydn's "Farewell" Symphony and the Idea of Classical Style*, p. 163), that the Allegro's "first theme (or even the entire first group) is a large-scale 'consequent' to the introduction as a whole."

38. Cf. Rossini's Overture to *Semiramide* (1823), in which the opening Allegro vivace is merely a large crescendo over a tonic pedal and the space of the slow introduction is taken up with an Andantino.

Obviously relatable to this procedure is its reverse: slow introduction; false first start with Allegro P-material, aborted; return to slow introduction; restart or continuation of the Allegro. The impression is of two or more attempts to launch a P-theme, only the last of which succeeds. In turn this suggests either a need to go back to the "reflective" introduction to allow the faster theme to be gestated more sufficiently or a momentary indecision or reluctance to face the task that is to follow. We have already mentioned the opening of Beethoven's String Quartet in B-flat, op. 130, in a slightly different context. That of the Quartet in A minor, op. 132, is in many ways comparable.[39]

Expressive or Representational Functions

In addition to carrying out their standard generic duties, individual introductions took on expressive or representational roles vis à vis the sonata-to-come, as though their implications continued to resonate throughout the rest of the movement. The specific effects varied from piece to piece, although certain families of introduction types were normative by 1800 and the ensuing decades. These supplementary functions were not so much objectively "in the music" (as raw, tangible "facts" to be agreed upon by all commentators) as they were available to imaginative and thoughtful listeners as part of the spirit of interpretation that enveloped the sonata enterprise. The composer invited a circle of listeners to discover or read such implications into the piece. From time to time additional clues (nicknames, titles, identifiable topics) were provided to assist in this process.

By no means was an introduction limited to conveying only one expressive implication. Viewed simultaneously from differing perspectives — not usually a difficult interpretive task — an ambitious introduction could provide several at once. (We take it as axiomatic that in the realm of hermeneutics one should regard most instrumental pieces, usually underdetermined in the specifics of their connotations,

as open to more than one defensible reading. One should not discard such readings as empirically unverifiable: confusing knowledge with interpretation, this strict view would only impoverish the musical experience. Each reading is limited, provisional, metaphorical, an act of conjecture in dialogue with the music as a historically informed, inevitably personalized response.) The listing here of some commonly recognizable functions is intended only as a set of loose categorizations projected back from the present onto a large and varied body of music. The proposed types overlap considerably. In some instances one category can be understood as a special case of another, a subset, or a slight rephrasing of a similar, more general kind of connotation.

Representation. Introductions could take on an imitative or pictorial function either by a generalized implication or by various means supported by a verbal or topical suggestion. Examples include the "sunrise" introduction of Haydn's Symphony No. 6 in D, "Le matin" ("Morning"); the prolepsis (flashforward) of the appearance of the statue of the Commendatore in Mozart's Overture to *Don Giovanni*; and the prolepsis of the imprisoned Florestan in Beethoven's *Leonore* Overtures Nos. 2 and 3. In each case the subsequent sonata form responds in one way or another to the illustration set forth in the introduction. More broadly, this typically suggests:

The World, Condition, or Field of Implications within Which the Subsequent Sonata Form Plays Itself Out. This is clear within overtly or connotatively programmatic introductions and sonatas, such as in all the overtures mentioned in the category above, as well as in Beethoven's Overture to *Egmont* (a world of tyrannical oppression, responded to by heroic actions of resistance), Weber's Overtures to *Der Freischütz* (rustic village life) and *Oberon* (the idealized fairy-world of the forest), and many other works. Mozart's Overture to *Così fan tutte* asks us to imagine its

---

39. The procedure was obviously taken up again toward the end of the nineteenth century in, for example, Franck's Symphony in D Minor. (Cf. the first movements of Mahler's Symphonies Nos. 3 and 7.)

presentation of a skeptical maxim about the instability of human erotic relationships (with an implied text-underlay toward the end, "Così fan tut-te"), then, one presumes, illustrates the maxim with a madcap romp of constantly switched and intermixed rhetorical roles in the materials of the subsequent sonata—whereupon the maxim returns at the end (indeed, returns to accomplish the ESC) as the musical equivalent of "Q. E. D." Mozart's Overture to *The Magic Flute* invites us to interpret the introduction as evoking a sanctified realm of Enlightenment wisdom (and occasionally mysticism), then suggests that the goal of the ensuing sonata process, and the following opera as a whole, is to prove worthy of entering "these sacred halls." In all such cases—even more abstract ones in nonprogrammatic (or less programmatic) works—one might understand the initial condition proposed by the introduction to persist conceptually throughout the sonata as its framing *raison d'être*, that which, in the fiction or game at hand, makes it possible and gives it a purpose for existing at all.

"The Fall"/"Fallen World." Intersecting with the type above, this category presents an initially confident, positive, or serenely pastoral, major-mode world shattered by a sudden shift into the minor-mode negative ("lights-out"), perhaps also with supernatural, *ombra* evocations. It is the overt demonstration of the loss of the major mode that is crucial here. Additionally, the minor mode is not a merely momentary experience within an otherwise major-mode introduction: once it enters it persists for the rest of the introduction. Classic examples include: Mozart's Symphonies No. 34 in C, "Linz," K. 425, and No. 38 in D, K. 504, "Prague"; Beethoven's Symphony No. 2 in D, op. 36; and Weber (once again), Overture to *Der Freischütz* (perhaps the archetypal representation of a "fallen world,"

despoiled, as we learn in the opera, through the demonic intervention of Samiel). However accustomed we may have become to such modal changes within introductions to standard-repertory pieces, many of them were surely originally intended to convey the sense of something catastrophic, and it is worth the effort to reawaken the image of urgency, darkness, and alarm that they present. That major-to-minor prefatory passage suggests that it is the task of the major-mode sonata form that follows to repair the problem, to restore a fully stable world of major. This does not happen at once, with the forward vector of the exposition's major-mode P-idea. It can occur with full presence only at the end of the essential sonata process, at the moment of the ESC. When prefaced by this introduction type, a sonata is portrayed as having significant tonal and modal work to accomplish throughout its trajectory.[40]

The Negative (Minor-Mode) State of Affairs or Situation to Overcome. This is similar to the above category, except that the introduction is entirely in the minor mode. The "fall" into minor—the crisis from which one seeks to emerge—has been set in place before the piece has begun. Once again, there may or may not be representational implications, and once again the task of the subsequent sonata—often in the major mode—is to overturn the situation sketched out in the introduction. Examples from Haydn include the Symphonies No. 98 in B-flat, No. 101 in D, "Clock," and No. 104 in D, "London." Clementi prefaced his Piano Sonata in D, op. 40 no. 3 (1802), with a D-minor Molto Adagio. The starkest of examples (perhaps even involving the subsequent sonata's denial of what precedes it) is provided in the Adagio introduction to the finale to Mozart's String Quintet in G Minor, K. 516.

Before 1800 slow introductions to sonatas

---

40. Cf. the deformational variant of this category found in the first movement of Beethoven's Cello Sonata No. 4 in C, op. 102 no. 1. Here the Andante introduction is sounded entirely in C major, ending emphatically with the tonic chord in that key in m. 27. "The Fall" away from this initial purity, however, happens in a flash with the m. 28 downbeat of the Allegro vivace sonata

form—a sonata that plays itself out in the submediant, A minor. In other words, op. 102 no. 1/i presents a tonic introduction and a completely *off-tonic sonata*. The aim of the entire piece is to work through a multimovement tonal process that will eventually restore the C major so astonishingly lost in the first movement.

in the minor mode were less frequent, though they were not unheard of. In an earlier section we mentioned a handful of early examples from piano sonatas in the 1790s by Clementi and Beethoven. (Is it significant that Haydn's Symphony No. 95 in C Minor was both the only minor-key symphony in the twelve "London" Symphonies and also the only to lack an introduction?) After 1800, and certainly once plunged into more "Romantic" waters, the practice becomes more normative. When the sonata that follows is still in the same minor mode, the self-evident hope of that turbulent, Allegro structure is to use the sonata process as a vehicle to turn the minor mode into major and provide a major-mode ESC in the recapitulation. Should this fail, that hope is dashed, and the tonal and modal problem persists: it may be deferred either into the coda or into subsequent movements—especially a later finale—should they exist. (Chapter 14 discusses this aspect of the psychology of minor-mode sonatas.) The first movement of Beethoven's "Pathétique" Sonata, op. 13, provides a familiar example (one without eventual resolution into the major), as does his F-minor *Egmont* Overture (whose tonic-major cadential resolution occurs only late into the F-major discursive coda).

The Setting of a Tone of High Seriousness or Contemplative Absorption. A more generalized category available in either major or minor, this suggests through its earnestness that what follows is the product of sober and significant thought, as in Haydn's Symphony No. 103 in E-flat, "Drum Roll" (which at the opening gives the impression of quoting the incipit of the "Dies irae"). Here the implication can be purely musical—reflecting on the act of composition itself, music about the making of music. In such cases the introduction may suggest the presence of the composer (either "in reality" or as a staged aesthetic persona), absorbed in thought and about to produce not merely a sonata-movement but a whole multimovement work. Under these lights an introduction can be read as a representation of preparing for and setting about the compositional act—although probably falling short, in most cases (at least in this period), of being necessarily a direct self-representation. More obvious self-representations of precompositional searchings for the proper theme, tone, and style were famously presented by Beethoven at the openings of the finales of his "Hammerklavier" Sonata and Ninth Symphony. Self-referentiality would become a familiar implication in several later nineteenth-century works by other composers, sometimes with a sense of self-questioning with regard to the aesthetic obligation of the post-Beethovenian symphony, sonata, or quartet. A related variant, perhaps worthy of a category in itself, is:

The Ceremonial Gathering or Assemblage of Forces Available for the Sonata Form Proper. The archetypal example is found in Beethoven's Seventh Symphony. Here the introduction accomplishes many tasks, laying out much of the harmonic, registral, and timbral space that will provide the field and forces of the sonata that follows. (See also the category to this effect below.) Of interest within this subcategory is its obvious impression of assembling and setting all of the available material in order—by the end, everything is poised and ready, checked, double-checked, and triple-checked—before the composition is sent off into the sonata form proper. Relatable to this general concept are the highly formalized, largely ceremonial introductions to many of Rossini's overtures. These often include a lyrical, separate melody largely unrelated to the sonata form that is to follow, with the whole introduction-formula giving the impression of using ample time both to give a sense of the glittering prestige of the operatic occasion and to prepare the orchestra and the audience to settle down to undertake the onset of the real Allegro action. One might imagine, for example, that a preliminary, first curtain lifts at the introduction; a second one at the start of the exposition; and a third one—the final one—at the opening of the act.[41]

---

41. Cf. Gossett, "The Overtures of Rossini," esp. pp. 5–7.

The Searching, Foreboding, or "Mysterious" Introduction. This is another variant of the "contemplative absorption" type, typically providing the impression that the ideas of the work—perhaps aspects of tonal assertion itself—are still in a state of unclear formulation. The paradigms are the openings of Mozart's "Dissonance" String Quartet, K. 465 and Beethoven's Quartet in C, op. 59 no. 3. A related and instructive example (though not an introduction to a sonata) is the opening representation of "Chaos" from Haydn's *The Creation.*

The Source-Material for Much of What Follows. In this broad (and common) category with many subtypes the introduction is perceived, retrospectively, as having furnished many of the central ideas for the sonata-to-follow. As such it exists as something of a caldron of motives, a resource or "inkwell" into which the composer's pen dips in the writing of the subsequent piece. Presented as such a broad category, this is an almost-too-obvious introductory function. Many introductions take on this task, which stresses motivic consistency between it and the subsequent sonata, sometimes to the point of inaugurating a process of what Schoenberg would later call "developing variation." An introduction may foreshadow harmonic or tonal regions that will take on an added importance later in the piece; it may anticipate certain features of register, timbre, voice-leading, or other features that will turn up in the sonata; or it may present embryonic versions of melodic contours, themes, or portions thereof that blossom more fully in the ensuing Allegro.

Since demonstrating such relationships has been among the most common staples of analysis for several decades, we need not deal with it at any length here. The procedure is certainly characteristic of many of the introductions to Haydn's twelve "London" Symphonies. (The opening contour of the introduction to Symphony No. 100 in G, "Military," anticipates that of the P-theme, as do those of the Symphonies No. 101 in D, "Clock," and No. 102 in B-flat; the initial intervals of the introduction to Sym-

phony No. 103 in E-flat, "Drumroll," are explicitly refashioned into an importantly situated rapid-thematic module of the later TR⇒FS zone, mm. 74–79; and so on.)[42] These concerns are equally evident in Mozart and Beethoven. Instead of belaboring the obvious, one might turn instead to some notable subtypes:

The Generative Introduction (Producing the P-Theme). Here one might give a nod to those even more explicit situations in which the introduction, or at least the concluding portion of it, spawns, nurtures, or otherwise generates the theme that will be fully formed and launched with the sonata's P-theme. Several of the Haydn examples cited just above would qualify in any broad sense, but sometimes the generative principle seems to be more overtly thematized. Haydn's Symphony No. 98 in B-flat provides a classic example, mentioned earlier, as does the finale to Beethoven's First Symphony, whose brief introduction "constructs" the P-theme, step by step, until it is ready to take flight. Introductions with a final accelerando link (also mentioned earlier in this chapter) into the Allegro—Beethoven's Fourth Symphony, the *Leonore 1* Overture, and others—also usually participate in this general compositional logic. This type of introduction would become especially characteristic of later nineteenth-century works: Schumann's Symphony No. 4 in D Minor, op. 120; Brahms's Symphony No. 1 in C Minor, op. 68; Franck's Symphony in D Minor; and many others.

Direct Statements of Thematic Material to Come in the Interior of the Sonata. Here one is presented with an idea (often, the "slow" version of an idea) that literally—or very nearly—will be re-sounded more actively sometime after the onset of the exposition's TR-space. When the theme in question is P, the introduction might be more properly considered generative of the idea that launches the sonata. Interestingly, the theme in question is sometimes used later as S, as in Cherubini's Overture to *Eliza* (1794); in Beethoven's Overtures *Leonore 2* and *3* (where the incipit of S refers explicitly to the introductory theme — Florestan's imprisonment aria); and in Wagner's Overture to *Rienzi* (where the relevant melody, "Rienzi's Prayer," is deployed as S¹ in the exposition but suppressed in the recapitulation). Similar instances occur in Haydn's Symphony No. 103 in E-flat, "Drumroll," mentioned above, and in Weber's Overture to *Oberon*, where the opening horn call reappears in the sonata as the inauguration of a programmatic, expanded caesura-fill.

Introductory functions such as these persisted and were developed further in later nineteenth-century works. Two offshoots of the trope of the introduction's establishment of the "world" in which the sonata-to-follow plays itself out might be appended here to provide a sense of what was to come much later. Neither of the two subcategories below are characteristic of the decades around 1800. They are typical, though, of the second half of the nineteenth century and beyond, in the world of the symphonic poem, the (quasi-) programmatic symphony, and emerging "nationalistic" composition.

Representation of the "Narrator"—or Perhaps the Raison d'être *or the Animating Force—of the Tale Told in the Sonata.* Something of this effect is present in Mendelssohn, Overture to *A Midsummer Night's Dream* and, perhaps, in Berlioz's *Symphonie fantastique* (the representation of the opium overdose as precondition for the rest of the piece). But the concept reaches a different level in symphonic poems that are about the representation of well-known stories or the telling of tales. One might sense the presence of a represented narrator in several introductory sections of Liszt's symphonic poems (as if setting out to relate the narrative of, say, Tasso). It occurs even more overtly in Tchaikovsky's *Romeo and Juliet* (in which the strumming of the harp even more characteristically calls up images of a bard singing the age-old tale, even while surrounded by the Friar Laurence motive); in Rimsky-Korsakov's *Sheherazade*; and in Strauss's *Till Eulenspiegel.*

The Lyrical-Expressive "Folk-Soul" or "Native Landscape" Out of Which the Sonata Proceeds. This is especially characteristic of nationalistic works of the later nineteenth century. Its larger implication is obvious, standing ideologically for the deep and uncontaminated reservoir of ethnic essence or *Volksgeist*—a quality to be understood as generally untouched by (or otherwise preceding) the present-day court-and-urban cultures of the powerful cities of Western Europe. As such the vector of the motion from introduction to Allegro is in part metaphorically both temporal and historical: "Out of our ancient and 'authentic' reservoir will emerge the following symphony, quartet, or sonata, genres that we intend to engage the urban contemporaneity and cultural prestige of the Western European present. We, too, can now master and appropriate these things." Such introductions are usually folk-like in one way or another, and may even allude to a folk song (as does Gade's Symphony No. 1 in C Minor). Touchstone examples are obvious: Dvořák's Symphony No. 8 in G, op. 88; Tchaikovsky's Symphony No. 2 in C Minor, op. 17; Glazunov's Symphonies No. 2 in F-sharp Minor, op. 16, and No. 4 in E-flat, op. 48; Sibelius's Symphony No. 1 in E Minor, op. 39; and many others.

The Introduction-Coda Frame

One striking deformation of normative practice was the *introduction-coda frame*, in which material from the introduction returns as all or part of the coda. Examples before 1800 are sparse, but they include the first movements of Mozart's String Quartet in E-flat, K. 171 (Adagio—Allegro assai—Adagio), his String Quintet in D, K. 593, Haydn's Symphony No. 103 in E-flat, "Drum Roll" (here the recurrence is more of a deformationally *ad hoc*—and vast—expansion of a C-module with pronounced CRI-effect than a literal coda, since the concluding portion of that last C-module, Allegro con spirito, returns to complete the movement), and Beethoven's "Pathétique" Sonata, op. 13 (whose Grave introduction had also preceded the opening of the development proper). Beethoven revisited the deformation in the first movement of his Piano Trio in E-flat, op. 70 no. 2 (1808).

The framing introduction-coda combination becomes more common in the later decades of the nineteenth century. The first movement of Schubert's "Unfinished" Symphony comes close to producing a perfect example, except that the in-tempo opening idea in question, mm. 1–8 (also occupying the bulk of the development and recurring, expanded, in the coda, mm. 328–68), is probably better regarded as a P⁰ module (discussed in chapter 5); nonetheless the psychology of the gesture is much the same. Even clearer examples may be found in the first movement of Schubert's Symphony No. 9 in C; in Mendelssohn's Overtures to *A Midsummer Night's Dream* and *The Fair Melusine*; in the first movement of Mendelssohn's Symphony No. 3, "Scottish"; in some of Berlioz's overtures, including *Benvenuto Cellini*; in Wagner's Overture to *Tannhäuser*; and in many other works (including such later "nationalistic" pieces as the first movements of Tchaikovsky's Symphony No. 2 and 4, the finale of his Symphony No. 5, and his Overture "1812," in which the massive introduction and coda dwarf the relatively small but vigorous sonata deformation within).

Whenever we find an introduction-coda frame the interior sonata seems subordinated to the outward container.[43] The introduction and coda represent the higher reality, under whose more immediate mode of existence — or under whose embracing auspices — the sonata form proper is laid out as a contingent process, a demonstration of an artifice that unfolds only under the authority of the prior existence of the frame. Metaphors of narrativity are not inevitably implied — the external narrator and the tale told — but in some cases they can spring to mind and appear to be hermeneutically relevant.[44]

The extraordinary conclusion of Mendelssohn's E-major Overture to *A Midsummer Night's Dream* (1826) is instructive with regard to the complications that could arise. The opening four-chord introduction (and subsequent, sustained B♮), mm. 1–7, function as a gateway to the sonata proper, which begins with the E-minor elfin scurrying at m. 8. The introduction recurs as a bridge (mm. 394–403) famously linking the C-sharp-minor end of the development with the E-minor onset of the recapitulation, a procedure also with rotational implications. And it recurs as the overture's final bars, 682–86, providing an introduction-coda frame for the whole. What is curious, though, is that the overture had already been provided with a separate Allegro di molto discursive coda of its own, beginning in m. 620. Moreover, this coda has escaped outside of the "formally presented piece" itself, which Mendelssohn apparently wants us to imagine has been brought to a conventional (coda- or codetta-like) end with the generically emphatic, "curtain-down" chords of, say, mm. 608–20 — as though, once the merely human drama and assorted love-tangles have been sorted out and brought to a close, the attention shifts to the supernatural elves and fairies, who pre-existed the piece and will continue to thrive beyond the confines of whatever the human personages imagine to be their own "story." The broadening-out of the music at the end, and the final chords, suggest the conclusion of a series of multiple coda-sections or programmatic actions, rounded magically at the end by the four chords with which the piece had begun. Mendelssohn's later revisiting of much of this music in the complete incidental music from 1843 — which includes a verbal text from Shakespeare — helps to clarify the expressive intent of all of this.

---

43. The introduction-coda frame was also occasionally applied to works that were not organized as sonatas. See, for instance, Weber's *Invitation to the Dance* (*Aufforderung zum Tanze*), rondo brillant in D-flat, J. 260 (1819, publ. 1821); Beethoven, Bagatelle in E-flat, op. 126 no. 6 (1823–24; here the normative tempi are reversed: an impetuous Presto frame surrounds an Andante amabile e con moto interior); the Larghetto slow movement of Chopin's Piano Concerto No. 2 in F Minor, op. 21; and Mendelssohn's *Lied ohne Worte* in A Major, op. 19b, no. 3 (1829, publ. 1832 — the so-called Jägerlied).

44. The introduction-coda frame has also been mentioned with regard to later repertory in Hepokoski, "Beethoven Reception: The Symphonic Tradition," in Jim Samson, ed., *The Cambridge History of Nineteenth-Century Music* (Cambridge: Cambridge University Press, 2002), p. 451; and treated at greater hermeneutic length in Hepokoski, "Framing Till Eulenspiegel," *19th-Century Music* 30 (2006), forthcoming.

CHAPTER FOURTEEN

Sonata Form in Minor Keys

The Extra Burden of Minor-Mode Sonatas

Virtually all of the guidelines for sonata-form movements in the major mode hold true for those whose initial tonic is minor. Here, too, the sonata process involves structural points common to all sonatas: two-part or continuous expositions; P TR ' S / C zones in two-part expositions; trajectories toward the EEC (exposition) and ESC (recapitulation); the possibility of a dialogue with the rotational principle; and so on. In these respects the morphology of the minor-mode sonata is analogous to that of the major-mode sonata.

There is, however, a crucial difference between them. In addition to articulating the rhetorical shape familiar from a major-mode sonata form, a minor-mode sonata bears an additional burden. This is that of the minor mode itself, generally interpretable within the sonata tradition as a sign of a troubled condition seeking transformation (emancipation) into the parallel major mode. Since many minor-mode sonata structures do attain a major-mode ESC in the recapitulation and do sustain that major mode for the rest of the composition, the sonata process can function as a strategy capable of transforming tonic minor into tonic major. It is true, of course, that some minor-mode sonatas are dominated by the minor throughout or sternly

reaffirm the minor mode at the ESC and beyond. What matters at this level of consideration is not whether the initial tonic minor is converted into a stable tonic major at or around the ESC but rather that minor-mode sonatas, unlike major-mode ones, are uniquely capable of effecting this modal transformation. This is the extra burden under which minor-mode sonatas are placed, regardless of the results of the minor-major musical drama engaged.

The possibility of a tonic-minor-to-tonic-major trajectory (or the represented inability to attain that transformation) is rich in metaphorical implication. If we understand sonata form as a metaphor for an idealized but nonspecific human action (chapter 11), minor-mode sonatas provide the means by which an initially negative state (the minor mode) is acted upon in order to seek to overturn it by means of major-mode assertion at or around the ESC point, even though that quest might be unsuccessful. Minor-mode sonatas contend with the initial presence of the tonic minor—often a turbulent or threatening expressive field—either to overcome it or to be overcome by it. Composers turn to the minor-mode sonata to project an either successful or unsuccessful modal action—attainment or failure—even though all other criteria for the sonata process (such as the production of an adequate ESC) are to be satisfactorily met. From this perspective, minor-mode sonatas present composers with additional opportunities for varied realizations.

Major and Minor as Binary Opposites (Positive and Negative)

Perhaps because they are sometimes based on unexamined assumptions — or perhaps because the subjects are often handled in an overly elementary fashion — even modest claims regarding the affective qualities of the major and minor modes can raise warning flags within the analytical community. Surely it would be incautious to reduce the nuances of the major and minor modes into simplistic descriptions. Major is not consistently collapsible into "happy" nor minor into "sad." Aldwell and Schachter addressed this issue and went on to make a more compelling point:

> Sophisticated musicians often question this association, believing that it is a purely arbitrary one based on nothing except, perhaps, habit. And of course it is true that the emotional character of a piece depends on many factors in combination. Light and even comical pieces — some of Mendelssohn's scherzos, for instance — are in minor. And some very solemn pieces are in major, for example the "Dead March" in Handel's *Saul*. But it is a mistake to ignore the likelihood that choice of mode is one of the factors that determine the character of a piece. And sometimes it may be the most important factor.
>
> For one thing the association of mode and emotion is a very old one. . . . Writing in 1558, Gioseffo Zarlino, the greatest theorist of the late Renaissance, remarks that melodies (and modes) featuring a major 3rd above the central tone sound cheerful and that those with a minor 3rd sound sad. Any cultural tradition that has persisted for so long takes on a certain importance even if it is based on nothing more than custom. That the

great composers of the eighteenth and nineteenth centuries believed in this association is evident to anyone who studies their songs and other music they composed to texts.[1]

Once one takes an interest in the ways in which that mode has been understood or explained over centuries, one may sidestep the vexed question of whether the minor mode is "really" imbued with these expressive implications.[2] We remain content to regard these affective properties as the product of social custom, as cultural matters or tacit agreements within interpretive communities, agreements that were reinforced over many years.

On both historical and experiential grounds, it is absurd to suggest that within the post-1750 style the compositional usage of minor or major was objectively neutral, a matter of little consequence, a creative choice made arbitrarily, in the abstract, "for (unexplained) reasons of contrast," or for merely formalist reasons. On the contrary, this modal dichotomy was one of the basic binary oppositions of tonal music. Daniel Harrison recently explored this issue in a closely argued monograph on the topic, proposing "a renewed dualist theory," particularly with regard to the analysis of chromatic music of the late-nineteenth and early-twentieth centuries. As Harrison put it, in Western tonal practice the major and minor systems "can be [and typically were] organized and developed in two opposed directions, creating sets of dualistically paired tonal concepts"; "the dependence of tonal music and its theory on the contrariety of major and minor is far reaching"; music analysis should recognize them as "a basic duality," "a virtual primitive of tonal music," "a fundamental dualism" that led to dual modal "networks" or "systems" possessing different implications for their associated scales, chords, and tonal relationships.[3] The affective impact of many pas-

---

1. Edward Aldwell and Carl Schachter, *Harmony and Voice Leading*, 2nd ed. (San Diego, New York, etc.: Harcourt Brace Jovanovich, 1989 [1st ed., 1978]), pp. 19–20.

2. Cf. Aldwell and Schachter, *Harmony and Voice-Leading*, p. 26: "Nowadays most musicians would maintain that the foundations for music theory should lie in the works of great composers, not in the laboratories of ac-

ousticians. . . . [On the basis of this we conclude that] in major-minor tonality, the major mode is normally the positive, happy, bright one, and the minor is the negative, sad, dark one. This again points to the greater stability of the major triad."

3. Daniel Harrison, *Harmonic Function in Chromatic Music: A Renewed Dualist Theory and an Account of Its Precedents* (Chicago: University of Chicago Press, 1994);

sages resides in the composer's skillful use of the chiaroscuro shadings made possible through this antithesis, coupled with a manipulation of the musically narrative implications of those shadings. Needless to say, musical paragraphs governed by one of the modes are often mixed with borrowings from the other.

No single emotive description suffices to describe the general sense of major or minor. According to the circumstances, the major mode may underpin expressions of energetic assertion, accomplishment, brightness, joy, stability, contentment, pastoral relaxation, eroticized (or noneroticized) lyricism or "sensibility," confidence, exuberance, majestic splendor, marchlike vigor, radiant wonder, and many other emotional states as well. Similarly, the minor mode may support representations of melancholy, "sweet and tender" sadness,[4] majestic gravity, oppression or threatening circumstances, anxiety, rage, defiance, storminess (*Sturm und Drang*), sorrow, resignation, fatalism, grief, darkness or shadows (as with the *ombra* topos), instability, the unnatural, demonic, antique, or exotic (as with certain tints of *alla turca* music), and so on.

But even these generalized descriptions can be insufficient when coming to terms with the expressive impact of an individual passage—or even an entire movement—in major or minor. Any specific effect is conditioned by the local context in which it appears. The characteristic moods of the minor mode, somewhat more consistent, even in their variedness, may be less problematic in this regard. Within the eighteenth-century style the minor mode is typically a special negative condition operating as a conventionalized exception to the more normatively prevailing major mode. Assessing the character of a passage in the major mode, though, can be more difficult when it appears

"unnaturally" within a psychologically negative or minor-mode context that seems otherwise overwhelming. In such circumstances one should be attuned to the possibility of a chillingly ironized or "false major": the posture of sheer bluff or cruel deception; the pitiable embracing of an illusion or an emotional mirage; the projection of something intensely desired but no longer available; the deep sigh of "if only" amidst a situation of profound loss. Such expressive situations denaturalize the major mode. The major is now framed ironically, "from outside," as a false front not properly accessible in the context supplied by the immediate musical or aesthetic surroundings. One might interpret the much-discussed, seemingly frivolous G-major finale of Mozart's String Quintet in G Minor, K. 516, under these lights. The concept may also apply in varying degrees to major-mode slow movements within minor-mode-dominated pieces. Localized appearances of the denaturalized, even "pathetic" major mode are particularly associated with such psychologically troubled and complex music as that of Schubert (as in the sudden turn toward the "false major" in the final stanza of the first song from *Winterreise*, "Gute Nacht"), Brahms, and Mahler. Considerations along these lines also provide an approach to the classic illustration of the major mode deployed in sorrowful circumstances, "Che farò senza Euridice" from Gluck's *Orfeo ed Euridice*, an example commonly trotted out by critics and philosophers, from Hanslick onward, skeptical of the proposition that certain emotional qualities are properties inherent to the major and minor mode.

Notwithstanding these caveats, on the most general level we refer to major and minor as binary signs of the positive and the negative (light and dark or, colloquially, "lights on" and "lights out"). Eighteenth-century theorists (Christ-

---

quotations from p. 15 ("can be organized"); p. 17 ("the dependence," "a basic duality," and "a virtual primitive"); pp. 22–23 ("a fundamental dualism", "networks," and "systems"). "Saying that a composition is in 'major,' for example, references qualities of scale, of primary chords, of modulatory structures, etc. Yet it also references something larger: a set of relationships that links these items into a system" (p. 23).

4. As mentioned (citing Rameau and other eighteenth-century theorists) in Gretchen A. Wheelock, "*Schwarze Gredel* and the Engendered Minor Mode in Mozart's Operas," in Ruth A. Solie, *Musicology and Difference: Gender and Sexuality in Music Scholarship* (Berkeley: University of California, 1992), p. 207.

mann, Rousseau, Kirnberger) confronted this binary opposition in predictable ways. Summaries of some of these discussions—consistently characterizing the minor mode as depressive, sad, hollow, unsettling, less natural or complete than the major, hesitating, indecisive, and so on—have been provided in studies by Ratner, Steblin, and Wheelock.[5] Ratner's conclusion: "From these comments and others, the rhetorical implications are clear: the minor mode provides less than the major in periodic definition and confirmation of key."[6]

Adding to the mix of implications, in his *Grundregeln zur Tonordnung insgemein* of 1755 Joseph Riepel referred—apparently with humorous intent—to the social (and gendered?) status of the parallel minor of a "master" [*Meyer*] major tonic as the *schwarze Gredel*, or, in Ratner's explanation, "black Margaret—a local nickname for a Swedish queen whose swarthy complexion made her look like a man."[7] In Wheelock's later interpretation "the power of [Riepel's] *schwarze Gredel* is not far to find: unnaturally feminine/masculine, she shares the Master's tonic, and her chromatic mutability is capable of destabilizing his natural domain." Seeking to enlarge "contemporary associations of minor keys with grieving and passive gloom," which she described as "simply limited," Wheelock explored the rich, "deeper ambivalence" of this often "feminized" mode, the

> seemingly disparate constructions of the minor mode [in the eighteenth century]—as weak and passive in affect, but also as powerful and subversive in function. . . . [In Mozart's dramatic works] the minor mode was a vehicle for often menacing forces, the expression of which threatened to exceed the bounds of the 'natural'. . . . For male and

female, comic and serious characters alike, episodes in the minor mode expose the darker side of human passions, memories, and actions. In reaching to universal fears of irrationality and death, the elusive and mutable mode . . . [had] audible powers to destabilize tonal order and to evoke disordered states of human consciousness.[8]

The custom of making interpretive distinctions between the opposites, major and minor, continued throughout the nineteenth century (Hauptmann, Helmholtz, Oettingen, Riemann) and into the twentieth.[9] Expanding upon the earlier tradition—still with an ear turned toward the "scientific" certainty of the overtone series—the two modes were sometimes characterized as the binaries "natural" (following the "law of nature") and "artificial" (not found in nature—and therefore problematic). Such was the basis, for instance, of the extended discussion at the opening of Schenker's *Harmony* (1906): "The minor mode springs from the originality of the artist, whereas the sources, at least, of the major mode flow, so to speak, spontaneously from Nature."[10] Viewed from this perspective, minor-mode sonatas begin under the condition of artifice and, as part of their generic burden, seek an emancipation into a more natural condition, even though that quest might fail within any individual sonata narrative.

Writing in the mid-twentieth century, Theodor W. Adorno captured this condition of major-minor polarity in his discussion of a much-later repertory, that of Mahler's compositions. To be sure, in the passage quoted below Adorno was referring to a late stage in the conceptualization and effectiveness of the minor mode: in fact, he was insisting that the traditional understanding of the minor mode (its generally

---

5. Leonard G. Ratner, *Classic Music*, pp. 50, 55–56; Rita Steblin, *A History of Key Characteristics in the Eighteenth and Early Nineteenth Centuries* (Ann Arbor: UMI Research Press, 1983); Wheelock, "*Schwarze Gredel*," pp. 201–21.

6. Ratner, *Classic Music*, pp. 55–56.

7. Ratner, *Classic Music*, p. 50. Compare these considerations with the remark of Robert Schumann in 1834: "The difference between major and minor must be allowed beforehand. The former is the active, virile principle; the latter, the passive, the feminine." Quoted in *Robert Schumann: On Music and Musicians*, ed. Kon-

rad Wolff, trans. Paul Rosenfeld (New York: Norton, 1946), p. 60.

8. Wheelock, "*Schwarze Gredel*," pp. 203, 205, 219–20.

9. Some of these "dualist" theoretical positions are reviewed in Harrison, *Harmonic Function in Chromatic Music*, pp. 215–322.

10. Heinrich Schenker, *Harmony*, ed. and annotated by Oswald Jonas, trans. Elisabeth Mann Borgese (Chicago: University of Chicago, 1954, rpt. 1980), p. 52. Cf. n. 2.

implied effect within the tradition) had deteriorated and existed primarily as a loss that was exposed in Mahler's anguished music. Still, the distinction between the modes and the interplay within any structure that depends upon its presentation as the affective "divergence" or "deviation" [*Abweichung*] from the more normalized major is stated with uncommon force here. Once again, we do not insist on a unitary or reductive meaning to the minor mode in any period. Nevertheless, Adorno's remark affords an insight into generic issues in minor-mode sonatas written a century or more before Mahler:

> [In Mahler's hands] the long neutralized minor, sedimented as a formal element in the syntax of Western music, only becomes a symbol of mourning when modally awakened by the contrasting major. Its nature is that of divergence; in isolation it no longer produced this effect. As a deviation, the minor defines itself equally as the not integrated, the unassimilated, the not yet established. . . . Minor is the particular [that is, that which strives to be assimilated], major the general [that which assimilates or is taken as the norm]; the Other, the deviant, is, with truth, equated with suffering. In the major-minor relationship, therefore, the expressive content is precipitated in sensuous, musical form. . . . Mahler's minor chords, disavowing the major triads, are masks of coming dissonances.[11]

Expositions in the Minor Mode: EEC in III

The expositions of most minor-mode sonata-form movements in the decades around 1800 move from i to III, the tonicized key of the major mediant. C-minor sonatas go to E-flat major; D-Minor ones to F major, and so on. This move to III is a strong first-level default with regard to key-choice. Proceeding to any other key area for the exposition's part 2 overrides the much more normative choice and suggests a set of uncommonly forceful expressive circumstances. (This observation includes an establishing of the second-level default key, minor v, discussed separately below.) From a Schenkerian perspective, the normative tonal task of the development is to move from this stabilized III to $V_{A^{\flat}}$, (an "active" V functioning as a dominant chord within the principal tonic), which will usually be harmonically interrupted to rebegin the recapitulation on the tonic minor (i). The large-scale motion up to the structural harmonic interruption is still from tonic to dominant (i–III–V), but the dominant is not reached until the end of the development, and the path from i to V is bisected by the third-divider III, attained at the EEC and sustained throughout the rest of the exposition. The III at the close of the exposition is thus only a temporary point of rest, a way station on the path to the more compelling tonal goal, the structural V. The resulting arpeggiation i–III–V outlines the tonic minor triad. (See the section that concludes chapter 7, "Some Schenkerian Implications.")

The customary expressive connotation of the expositional move from i to III in a minor-mode sonata is different from that of the standard move from I to V in a major-mode one. This is due to the negative implications of the movement-governing minor mode. (For the sake of clarity let us confine our discussion to the most common expositional rhetorical type, the two-part exposition. The principle at hand is easily extended to continuous expositions.) In normative major-mode sonatas both parts of the exposition (P TR ' and S / C) are underpinned by major-mode tonalities. These two parts (tonally, I and V) may be modally characterized as *major-major*, or *positive-positive*, {+ +}, even though local stretches of music might show signs of minor-mode mixture (which not infrequently happens within TR — especially at the approach to the MC, or even within portions of S). The psychology of first-level-default minor-mode sonatas is different. Here the two parts of the exposition (i and III — and here by part 1 we generally mean P, since various modal options are possible for TR, as mentioned in chapter 6) are ar-

---

11. Theodor W. Adorno, *Mahler: A Musical Physiognomy*, trans. Edmund Jephcott (Chicago: University of Chicago Press, 1991), p. 26. Orig. published as *Mahler: Eine musikalische Physiognomik* [1971], rpt. in Adorno, *Die musikalischen Monographen* (Frankfurt am Main: Suhrkamp, 1986), pp. 174–75.

rayed as *minor-major*, or *negative-positive*, {– +}, even though moments within the structural zones may include intermixtures with their opposite modes. While the I–V move in a major-mode exposition generates tonal tension as a central expressive effect, the i–III move in the minor-mode exposition produces the impression of temporarily escaping from the troubled minor mode into the major.

The desire to be emancipated from minor into major constitutes the basic narrative paradigm—the extra burden—of minor-mode sonata form. Within this paradigm a minor-mode exposition can offer the promise of modal release by electing to follow the first-level tonal default, proceeding to the mediant major for part 2 and its EEC. A more stable emancipation from the tonic minor, however (a "truer" liberation), can be effected only by a lasting conversion into the *tonic* major. But within the genre that conversion can only occur—if at all—within the recapitulatory space, wherein the modal aspect at and around the ESC will be telling.

This {– +} modal conversion in the exposition is accomplished with the generic knowledge (the shared understanding of the genre within the interpretive community) that, as a nontonic space, the major mode supporting S and C can exist only temporarily. In multi-movement works with expositional repeats the exposition's major III will almost immediately vaporize—and thus be shown to be provisional—by being cast back at the repeat sign (sometimes through an active dominant) to the tonic minor, that is, to the original modal condition, with all that that might imply metaphorically. In addition, within the norms of the genre it is understood that the major III at the end of the exposition will be replaced with other tonalities both in the development-to-come and, most important, in the recapitulation.

How long the initial, negative-minor condition will prevail within part 1, the P and TR zones, varies from piece to piece. In the narratives offered by some compositions the minor-mode conditions of the onset seem intolerable, and the music seeks to leap out of the minor as soon as possible {– +}—generally around the onset of TR, as discussed in chapter 6. Conversely, in a few cases the threat or initial field of the minor mode is represented as so coercive that it seems not to permit the generic modulation at all within part 1, resulting in a i:HC or highly rare i:PAC (or i:IAC) MC, which defers the task of modulation either to a passage of caesura-fill or to the first modules of S. Such is the case with the first movement of Mozart's String Quintet in G Minor, K. 516, which may be compared with Schubert's treatment of the tonic-key authentic cadence MC in the opening movement of the "Unfinished" Symphony, in which the modulatory/modal task is accomplished by caesura-fill.

Regardless of the manifold ways in which it may be accomplished, the point of a typical exposition within a minor-mode sonata is to produce the escape into major and to secure that major mode with the PAC that accomplishes the EEC (and, of course, to secure it even further—or to celebrate its being secured—with C). This is the expressive goal of the exposition, but since the EEC is sounded in III, not in I, the problem of the minor mode is not yet solved. It will be addressed only in the recapitulation, when (hopefully) the parallel moment will produce the ESC in the tonic parallel major, I. In a minor-mode sonata the exposition represents the building of a structure of promise, a structure that, when it reappears in the recapitulation, will manage to do what the exposition could not do: decisively emancipate the tonic minor by converting it into the parallel major. The expressive promise of part 2 of such expositions suggests something like: "This is how the victory/relief/liberation will be secured in the recapitulation-to-come. This is how the sonata narrative will rid itself of the 'imperfect' or 'special-condition' minor mode (although it still has to pass through the development—which may prove to be an arduous process)."

Since the attaining of the major mode is so important an expressive event, any erosion away from that major within the exposition's part 2 (S / C)—predictive of the material-to-come around the recapitulation's ESC—is a significant occurrence within the narrative at hand. Of particular consequence is any deflation of the expected major-mode III to minor-mode iii—a "lights-out" effect or perhaps an unstable, back-and-forth flickering between major and minor—either at the beginning of or toward the end of the S theme (or S/C complex).

In the first movement of Beethoven's "Pathétique" Sonata in C Minor, op. 13, the initial minor-mode conditions (announced at the onset with a non-normative, perhaps funereal slow introduction, Grave) last considerably longer than generically expected. Following a III:HC MC in m. 49 (the actual mode at the MC, whether III or iii, is left uncertain), Beethoven provides us with a prolonged S[0] theme, mm. 51–88 (over the dominant—also discussed in chapter 7) that, taken as a whole, expresses V/iii, E-flat minor. An evaded PAC at m. 89 (avoiding the more concretized EEC-effect in minor) suddenly clarifies the mode into the "natural" or "emancipated" E-flat major (III) for the next module of S, beginning in that m. 89. After a few additional evaded III:PACs the EEC is finally articulated in the major mode, III:PAC, in m. 121. A brief C-theme (the generic *forte* P-based-C, often an indicator of the onset of the closing zone) is elided to this in m. 121. Here this C proves unable to confirm the shift to major mode with its own cadence. Instead (*pathétiquement*), the major-mode EEC-promise runs aground and hurtles back to an expositional repeat with its initial C minor.

The first movement of Beethoven's "Appassionata" Sonata in F Minor, op. 57, adopts a related but different strategy. S emerges confidently in III, A-flat major (m. 36) but soon runs into a harmonic catastrophe involving mixtures with the minor mode, mm. 42–43. This is the point at which the structure of promise—the introduction of the major mode—collapses like a house of cards. What is probably best regarded as an S[C] theme (also mentioned in chapter 9) registers this breakdown in minor-mode iii, A-flat minor (m. 51ff), thus predicting (accurately) a modally devastating recapitulation, which will fatalistically reconstruct the expositional calamity and end (m. 204) in the tonic minor, completing a sonata-tale of stern failure. Whereas in the "Pathétique" the modal quality of part 2 (S / C) had been {– +}, delaying the expected generic production of the emancipatory major mode, the "Appassionata" first movement reverses the procedure into a more harrowing representation of hope extinguished: {+ –}. The "Appassionata" model—marked by a modally decaying S—would recur in later nineteenth-century works (with some additional complications)—for instance, in part 2 of the exposition of the first movement of Brahms's Symphony No. 1 in C Minor, op. 68, which proceeds through E-flat major to close in E-flat minor.[12]

Recapitulations and Codas in Sonatas with Expositions of the i–III Type

During the recapitulation of the i–III type of minor-mode sonata the composer has two options. Earlier mediant-major material may be recapitulated either in the tonic major, thereby preserving the original mode of the exposition's part 2 (S/C) and achieving the minor-major emancipation (one "wins"), or in the tonic minor, thereby altering the mode (and the entire character of the material) and denying the minor-major emancipation (one "loses"). Once the recapitulatory S begins in the tonic major, the local assumption is that the positive outcome is in the offing, and indeed, if S is strictly transposed, a major-mode ESC will happen automatically. Many sonatas project a sense of confidence with the onset of a recapitulatory, major-mode S and are able to glide smoothly into that ESC. Others suggest that the task of sustaining the major mode throughout S will be difficult, perhaps impossible. The first movement of Beethoven's Ninth Symphony provides a trenchant object lesson in the shattering of initial recapitulatory hopes, displaying *en route* an eventually permanent decay of the multimodular S into the minor mode. On the other hand, if the once-major S begins in the minor mode, the expectation is that the entire S/C block is likely

---

12. In the nineteenth century the "Appassionata" model, as characterized above, was not limited to minor-mode works. See also, e.g., the first movement of Brahms's Symphony No. 3 in F Major, op. 90, part 2 of whose exposition decays from A major to A minor.

TABLE 14.1   Modal Options in Major- and Minor-Mode Sonatas

+ = major mode   − = minor mode

The two signs within the braces refer to parts 1 and 2 of a two-part exposition: especially the onset of P and all of S / C.

	Exposition	Recapitulation
1. Major-Mode Sonata I–V	{+ +}	{+ +}
2. Minor-Mode Sonata i–III option with positive recapitulation	{− +}	{− +}
3. Minor-Mode Sonata i–III option with negative recapitulation	{− +}	{− −}
4. Minor-Mode Sonata i–III option with mixtures in part 2: positive outcome within sonata-space	{− [− +]}	{− [− +]}
5. Minor-Mode Sonata i–III option with mixtures in part 2: negative outcome within sonata-space	{− [+ −]}	{− [+ −]}
6. Minor-Mode Sonata i–III option with mixtures only in recapitulatory space: positive outcome	{− +}	{− [− +]}
7. Minor-Mode Sonata i–III option with mixtures only in recapitulatory space: negative outcome	{− +}	{− [+ −]}
8. Minor-Mode Sonata i–v option	{− −}	{− −}

to be minorized throughout (although further modal changes may also occur). Table 14.1 furnishes a fuller review of some of the possibilities.

In the negative, minor-mode case (minorized S, at least at the EEC-point, usually followed by a minorized C), nos. 3, 5, and 7 in table 14.1) the emancipatory paradigm has been unfulfilled, and for this reason we may speak of one type of sonata-process failure. (This is not a compositional shortcoming on the part of the composer. Rather, it indicates that the musical tale told is that of a tragedy, or at least one that ends in failure or sorrow—an inability to overcome the negative or special-effect conditions prevailing at the opening.) To adapt the language of Kerman, such a recapitulation is subject to "minor-mode saturation."[13] A return to the major mode may take place, however, in an emancipatory or redemptive coda. Conversely, a recapitulation that concludes in major may be undercut by a negative, minor-mode coda—darkly pessimistic in its implications—as in the first movements of Beethoven's String Quartet in C Minor, op. 18 no. 4; Piano Concerto No. 3 in C Minor, op. 37; String Quartet in E Minor, op. 59 no. 2; Symphony No. 5 in C Minor, op. 67; String Quartet in F Minor, op. 95—and (to cite a non-Beethovenian example) Schubert's Symphony No. 8 in B Minor, D. 759, "Unfinished."

There is little more powerful or more affecting within minor-mode sonatas of the i–III type than the bleak realization that all of part 2—sounded in major in the exposition—might come back entirely in minor in the recapitulation. To sound all of part 2 in minor is, beat-by-beat, to cancel out the hopes raised in the expo-

---

13. Kerman, "Beethoven's Minority," in *Write All These Down: Essays on Music* (Berkeley: University of California Press, 1994), pp. 217–37 (quotation from p. 222).

Here Kerman was referring not to recapitulations but to minor-mode sonatas that move to the minor dominant in the exposition.

sition: a moving wave of despair passes through this music, inexorably reversing former hopes. It is helpful to remember that part 2 represents the "active" part of the sonata—the part that should secure what the sonata sets out to accomplish. Within the fictional narrative usually presented in a minor-mode sonata, one's hopes are understood to reside in the major-mode part 2 (S and C). To witness these hopes dashed in the recapitulation is one of the most telling things that a composer can show us. This negative vision is the one invariably presented to us by Mozart in his minor-key sonata form movements.[14] Haydn, on the other hand, is usually eager to get to the major mode quickly within these recapitulations—sometimes at the earliest available opportunity. To be sure, there are a few notable cases in which the minor mode persists or even prevails in Haydn, but they are less common. (One instance occurs in the first movement of the Symphony No. 44 in E Minor, "Trauer.")

Beethoven presents us with a more complicated situation with regard to these matters. In a recent study devoted to Beethoven's key relations in minor-mode sonatas, Kerman noted that Beethoven is more inclined to use the i–III exposition type in C minor than he is in other minor keys, and that C-minor works nearly always feature a prominent section of C major somewhere near the end (either in the sonata itself or in the subsequent coda). "The tendency of works in C minor to break into C major is something we take for granted, perhaps, because of the Fifth Symphony. It is still rather remarkable to see this tendency played out on one level or another in every single one of Beethoven's many works in this key. It is doubly remarkable when the other minor-mode works [which are less inclined to share this minor-major concern] are also brought into consideration." "At some point, early on, Beethoven had a . . . vision of troubled C minor ceding to serene C major. The vision haunted him."[15] Kerman ar-

gued throughout for the exceptionalism of C minor within Beethoven's works. There the minor-mode redemption paradigm often grew into the *per aspera ad astra* narrative trajectory (heroic struggles concerned with moves from darkness to light, sickness to health, suffering to redemption) so important also to later nineteenth-century composition.

This is not to say that Beethoven inevitably preferred to bring back S and C in major (or with some sort of expressive major-minor mixture, eventually releasing a minorized S into major or vice-versa). In some i–III compositions of particularly tragic import S comes back entirely, or nearly so, in the tonic minor. These include the first movements of the Piano Sonata in F minor, WoO 47 no. 2 (along with its last movement as well), the Piano Sonata in F Minor, op. 2 no. 1, the String Trio in C Minor, op. 9 no. 3, and the Piano Sonata in C Minor, op. 10 no. 1 (after an initial nontonic feint in IV, F major), and the Piano Sonata in G Minor, op. 49 no. 1. Even bleaker and more minor-mode saturated, however, are the several Beethoven works that have expositions of the i–v type.

Expositions in the Minor Mode: EEC in v (the Minor Dominant)

In the later eighteenth century and extending shortly into the nineteenth, the main alternative to the i–III move in the exposition was one into the minor dominant, i–v: C minor to G minor, D minor to A minor, and so on. During this period this pattern may be regarded as a second-level default with regard to key-choice. It was still a recognized generic option, one with deep roots in the tonal past, but one much less frequently chosen. (Before too long into the nineteenth century it would become an even less standard choice, used only for extraordinarily negative tonal narratives.[16] At least

---

14. Data along these lines are provided in Rey M. Longyear, "Parallel Universes: Mozart's Minor-Mode Reprises," *Mozart-Jahrbuch 1991* (Kassel: Bärenreiter, 1992), pp. 810–15.

15. Kerman, "Beethoven's Minority," pp. 223, 230. Part of the essay traces Beethoven's increasing "clarification" of this vision throughout his works.

16. For an example, see the first movement of Mendelssohn's Symphony No. 3 in A Minor, op. 56, "Scottish," in which the EEC occurs in E minor, m. 181, and is reinforced with an E-minor C-space.

as common by the 1820s and beyond would be a modulation to the major-mode submediant, i–VI, discussed at the end of this chapter.)

In some respects the i–v option mirrors the tonal course of a major-mode sonata, whose exposition conventionally moves from I to V. In both types the development normally detonicizes this dominant and ends on V_A; at this point, a large-scale harmonic interruption occurs, and the recapitulation rebegins on I (or i). The difference between the major-mode exposition and the i–v minor-mode exposition lies in their prevailing modal qualities. While the former are major-mode saturated (and therefore typically more positive in metaphorical implication), the latter are minor-mode saturated.[17]

This less common move to the minor dominant is not merely "just another option." On the contrary, it is a doggedly negative tonal choice. Once we recall the extra burden of minor-key sonatas—their generic will to explore the possibilities of a transformation into the major mode, even though that endeavor might fail—we recognize that the i–v expositional option produces a chillingly dark, fatalistic, punishing, or pessimistic referential layout. In the more common type of minor-mode exposition, i–III, the point was to build a major-mode structure of promise, leading to a major-mode mediant EEC and thus constructing the possibility of a major-mode ESC in the recapitulation-to-come. In the i–III type the major mode offered a space of relief, brightness, or hope within the prevailing tonic minor. In the i–v type no such relief is permitted.[18] Table 14.1, no. 8, summarizes this situation as {− −}. What is being predicted within such an exposition is a tonic-minor ESC, and with it the failure of that sonata to overcome its initial modal conditions. The sonata's

modal "fate" is decreed in advance. All exits are blocked. We still encounter a structure of promise—all expositions seek to forecast the procedures of their recapitulations—but what is promised here is an inescapable recapitulatory negativity. Typically, the remainder of the sonata experience unfolds as something to be endured or struggled against, grimly, determinedly, or stoically. If this is a first movement, subsequent movements either alter or confirm the fate decreed here.

Expositions of this type are rare in Mozart, who nearly always works with the i–III option. A few examples do occur, though, in the early works, such as in the slow movements of the String Quartet in F, K. 168 (exposition keys: F Minor to C minor) and the String Quartet in E-flat, K. 171 (C minor to G minor). Isolated examples may also be found in Haydn, for instance in the first movement of the "Farewell" Symphony, No. 45 in F-sharp Minor (F-sharp to C-sharp minor, discussed more closely below).

The move to the minor v instead of to the more normative major III occurs with more frequency in Beethoven, invariably with a grimly tragic or negative effect. As Kerman pointed out, Beethoven never used this option within multimovement C-minor works, preferring instead the move to III (but see the discussion below of the *Coriolan* Overture). On the other hand, many of his minor-mode works in other keys move to the minor dominant. These include the first movements of: the Violin Sonata in A Minor, op. 23; the Piano Sonata in D Minor, op. 31 no. 2 ("Tempest"); the Violin Sonata in A Minor, op. 47 ("Kreutzer"); and the Piano Sonata in E Minor, op. 90. Beethoven seemed even more likely to employ this option

---

17. The phrase, again, is taken from Kerman. See n. 13.

18. Note, however, the unusual (and rare) deformation of an exposition that moves "illicitly" from a *minor* tonic to a (normatively unavailable) *major* dominant—that is, from i to V. In such a case the major dominant impresses one as a delusion, a denial, a "false major"—pathetically seeking to overturn the negative implications of the initial tonic or to proceed "as if" the initial tonic had been in the major mode, "as if" the governing minor-mode circumstances did not exist. The touchstone

example occurs in the first movement of Schubert's Piano Sonata in A Minor, D. 784, the second part of whose exposition plays out in E major. See also the first movement of Schubert's Quartet in D Minor, D. 810, "Death and the Maiden": here the exposition tracks structurally through F major and A minor (III and v), although the initial, ominous presence of that A minor (cf. mm. 90–99) is reacted to by a substantial passage of "delusionary" A major, mm. 102–12, a stretch of modal denial torn to shreds in mm. 112–14.

in non-C-minor finales, doubtless as negative signs of the "sealing of the fate" of the entire piece. Examples of such finales are: the Piano Sonata in F Minor, op. 2 no. 1; the Violin Sonata in A Minor, op. 23; the Piano Sonata in C-sharp Minor, op. 27 no. 2 ("Moonlight"); the Piano Sonata in D Minor, op. 31 no. 2; the Piano Sonata in F Minor, op. 57 ("Appassionata"); the String Quartet in E Minor, op. 59 no. 2; the String Quartet in F Minor, op. 95; and the String Quartet in A Minor, op. 132. Commented Kerman: "Both of these Beethovenian syndromes—the hankering of C minor for its parallel major, and the tropism of other minor keys toward their minor dominants—are aberrant according to the norms of the Classic period. They are certainly not characteristic of Haydn and Mozart, Count Waldstein's anointed models for the young prodigy."[19]

Minor-mode expositions of the i–v type, therefore, are appropriate only for special-effect negative statements. Moreover, since the far more common first-level-default option is the i–III exposition with its assertion of major mode {−+}, selecting the second-level default i–v option carries with it the connotation of having bypassed (or somehow "lost") the more normative, major-mode option. Composers sometimes demonstrated this by constructing a tonal path that first seeks a move to the positive III, then collapses *en route* or gets derailed at some pivotal moment. The major III is thus depicted as a vision that cannot be realized, leaving open only the minor-v option. Such a strategy actualizes the collapse of modal "hope" within the generic sonata: we literally hear the possibility of the major mode being liquidated. One should be attentive to any suggestions that the more normative III-option is being sought and lost within TR-space.

The *locus classicus* of such a thematization of loss occurs in the first movement of Haydn's

Symphony No. 45 in F-sharp Minor, "Farewell." The famous *Sturm und Drang* opening (perhaps referring wittily, according to Griesinger's famous report of Haydn's underlying program, to the "ardent" frustration of the musicians kept too long at Eszterháza castle, away from their homes and wives in Eisenstadt)[20] proceeds into a continuous exposition that in the vigorous TR at first seems to move (normatively) into III (mm. 21ff, although the new key is not yet secured by means of a PAC—it remains a promise) and thence into an encouraging V^7 of A major in m. 30 (albeit one that is not articulated as an MC). But this promise of A major collapses at once to A minor (iii) in m. 38 with a return of a variant of the plunging *Sturm und Drang* theme. At this point, lacking any preceding MC-effect, the continuous (non-two-part) nature of the exposition declares itself. The supposedly "intended" A major and its presumed comforts are shown as lost, and the exposition storms onward to the only other tonal option, C-sharp minor (v), within which key the EEC is produced shortly before the first ending (m. 65, whose bass C$\sharp$ is then held for eight measures).

Equally instructive is Beethoven's *Coriolan* Overture, op. 62, which is also concerned with quasi-programmatic matters, although commentators have differed on the details of what is being represented. In the exposition the P-theme (doubtless standing for Coriolanus or the "heroic manner" in general) sets out determinedly in C minor. A III:HC MC-deformation (V^6 of III) is planted in m. 50, and two bars of elegant, falling caesura-fill lead to the emergence in m. 52 of a nobly contoured S-theme in the normative E-flat major (III). This E-flat major proves unstable, incapable of producing an EEC in III. Its heroic major-mode promise is turned into something grimmer—something forecasting the ultimate demise of the hero.[21] S's

---

19. Kerman, "Beethoven's Minority," p. 220. Pp. 218–28 provide a table of key relations in Beethoven's minor-mode sonata movements.
20. See the discussion in James Webster, *Haydn's "Farewell" Symphony and the Idea of Classical Style: Through-Composition and Cyclic Integration in His Instrumental Music* (Cambridge: Cambridge University Press, 1991), pp. 1–2, 113–19.

21. Many commentators have repeated Wagner's speculation from 1852 that the loss of E-flat and subsequent rising sequences of the S-theme represents the pleading wife and mother of Coriolanus outside the city gates—S as a representation of the feminine. Notwithstanding the tenacity of this belief no evidence suggests that it is inescapably correct. See ch. 7, n. 31, and its associated text.

once-confident E-flat major is placed through rising sequences—sequences of loss—through F minor (m. 64) and into G minor (m. 72), in which negative key, after several bars of resistance, the EEC is sounded (m. 102). This is followed by a confirming closing zone in G minor (mm. 102–18). In sum, the exposition first presents us with the normative i–III, {−+}, only to demonstrate the extinguishing of major-mode hope through the III–iv–v sequences. The result is an unusual realization of the {−[+ −]} exposition.

Beethoven and Haydn were not alone in this thematizing of the "lost" key in the middle of the exposition. Clementi's Piano Sonata in F-sharp Minor, op. 25 no. 5 (1788–90) displays an engaging adaptation of a trimodular block (TMB) that articulates two different secondary keys. An initial III:HC MC, m. 24, leads to TM[1] ("S") in A major (III). But this A major does not produce an EEC capable of being sustained, although one is claimed provisionally, a III:PAC at m. 40. Instead the music proceeds onward, moving toward C-sharp minor to set up a second "apparent" MC, v:HC (m. 49), a postmedial caesura (PMC) in what we had originally supposed was C-space—a classic strategy of EEC-deferral (see chapter 8). At this point another theme ensues (now to be regarded as TM[3]) in C-sharp minor. It is in this key that the EEC will occur.

(Nineteenth-Century) Expositions in the Minor Mode: EEC in VI

In music from the nineteenth century one encounters the occasional exposition that moves from a minor tonic to the key of the major submediant, i–VI: for example, from D minor to B-flat major. This may be found in the first movements of Beethoven's String Quartet in F Minor, op. 95, his Piano Sonata in C Minor, op. 111, his Symphony No. 9 in D Minor, op. 125, and his String Quartet in A minor, op.

132. One also encounters the i–VI pattern in Schubert, as in the first movements of his (deformational) Symphony No. 4 in C minor, D. 417 ("Tragic"), his Piano Sonata in A Minor, D. 537, and his Symphony No. 8 in B Minor, D. 759 ("Unfinished"). Before long this option became more frequently employed, and it might be argued that by the 1840s it had replaced the i–v option as a second-level default. (By the mid- and late-nineteenth century other "experimental" second-key areas also turn up with some regularity.)

This is not the place to enter into a discussion of the tonal implications of the submediant as the secondary key within a minor-mode sonata. (To some extent it may have been foreshadowed by a few celebrated slow movements in VI within minor-mode multimovement works toward the end of the eighteenth century—such as the E-flat Andantes of two celebrated G-minor Symphonies, Haydn's No. 83 ("Hen") and Mozart's No. 40, K. 550. Chapter 15 mentions additional examples.) It may suffice to point out that Ernst Oster's commentary to Schenker's *Free Composition* suggests that in such cases (including their parallel appearances in major-mode works) "the VI, which ends the exposition, acts as a third-divider within the descending fifth I–IV [which IV often appears near the opening of the development]. . . . [In other cases] the VI probably has to be understood as a neighboring note of the eventual V, and not as a third-divider."[22] Notwithstanding the different tonal "color" and long-range linear implications of VI (as opposed to III), these two nineteenth-century second-key options do share at least one fundamental similarity: they both represent havens or escapes from the minor-mode tonic (havens that keep open the possibility of a major-mode ESC). Both types of exposition, i–III and the later i–VI, may be regarded as examples of the {−+} exposition. Consequently, the remarks above about the typical modal drama carried out in the normative i–III exposition also apply here.

22. Schenker, *Free Composition (Der freie Satz)*, p. 140.

CHAPTER FIFTEEN

The Three- and Four-Movement
Sonata Cycle

The idea of seeking to grasp successive movements as a coherent whole rather than as a string of dissociated contrasts—that is, to understand them as a planned cycle bearing intermovement implications—seems at once self-evident and dauntingly difficult. For some the illusory "naturalness" of the cycle can appear unproblematic through the very familiarity of its patterns. Yet once we start asking questions about it, the notion blurs into uncertainty. Are the movements among differing late-eighteenth-century works interchangeable? What significance might there be in the order in which the movements appear? Does it matter which of them, if any, is in the parallel mode (in F minor, for instance, within an F-major sonata) or in a nontonic key? Why does tempo matter?[1]

One thing that makes such issues resistant to empirical analysis is that the sought-for coherence, or lack of it, is by no means a function only of the raw data provided by the acoustic surface of music—the sounds that one literally hears. This sense of cohesiveness, construed as a web of interrelations, is not to be conceived exclusively as a pre-existing "object" to be discovered through research. Instead, perceiving degrees of multimovement integration also belongs to the realm of interpretation. This aspect will be revisited at the end of this chapter, under "The Role of the Listener."

One's sense of cyclic coherence is assisted by focusing on demonstrable relationships among the movements. Some relevant factors can be dealt with apart from an examination of indi-

---

1. The past few decades have seen a number of historical studies of the late-eighteenth-century sonata cycle in both theory and practice. Fundamental background reading includes the general, sometimes statistical surveys of "the cycle as a whole" in William S. Newman, *The Sonata in the Classic Era* (New York: Norton, 1972), pp. 133–43; the useful, often Beethoven-oriented summaries of Germanic eighteenth- and early-nineteenth-century writers on theories of "unity within diversity" and "the older cycle-theory" in Christoph-Hellmut Mahling, "Zur Frage der 'Einheit' der Symphonie," in *Über Sinfonien: Beiträge zu einer musikalischen Gattung: Festschrift Walter Wiora zum 70. Geburtstag*, ed. Christoph-Hellmut Mahling (Tutzing: Schneider, 1979), pp. 1–40, Wilhelm Seidel, "Schnell–Langsam–Schnell: Zur 'klassischen' Theorie des instrumentalen Zyklus," *Musiktheorie* 1 (1986), 205–16, and Seidel, "Die ältere Zyklustheorie, überdacht im Blick auf Beethovens Werk," in *Beiträge zu Beethovens Kammermusik: Symposion Bonn 1984*, ed. Sieghard Brandenburg and Helmut Loos, Veröffentlichungen des Beethovenhauses in Bonn, Neue Folge, 4, Reihe: Schriften zur Beethovenforschung, 4 (Munich: Henle, 1987), pp. 273–82; and the reflections on this problem with special regard to Haydn in James Webster, *Haydn's "Farewell" Symphony and the Idea of Classical Style*.

vidual content. General features of style and tempo can be perceived as creating abstractly satisfying balances among themselves—fast outer movements (often fast and faster) enclosing different, contrasting movements, for example; or a multimovement work that increases in tempo as one movement gives way to the next. More commonly, this line of discussion turns to those observations that current music theory conventionally teases out from single works: shared motives, keys, themes, harmonies, instrumentation, texture, and the like. One may contend that Mozart's three-movement Piano Sonata in F, K. 332, is self-referentially balanced because the first and last movements share certain form-defining features, inviting the conclusion that the finale reworks procedures that had originally been set into relief at the opening. The finale may be understood as re-presenting them from a different vantage point (as with a sleeve drawn inside-out): both movements overdetermine their P-zones with a series of unusually redundant I:PACs; both initiate TR with an unprepared lurch into the submediant; and both feature post-MC spaces that emphasize a prominent module that has decayed into the minor mode (a later module in the first movement; an initial one in the finale).

Some helpful thinking along these lines is found in James Webster's 1991 study of Haydn's "Farewell" Symphony and related works. Webster identified two musical strategies capable of affecting our perception of long-range, multimovement coherence. Normally the two are found simultaneously and overlap in practice. One was *through-composition*, descriptive of "destabilizing techniques" within early movements that defer resolution to later points, of "dynamic or gestural phenomena (run-on movements, recalls, unresolved instabilities, lack of closure and so forth)." The other was *cyclic integration* or *cyclic organization*, those aspects that contribute toward the multimovement stabilization of the cycle as a whole. By these latter terms Webster did not limit himself only to the resurfacing of earlier themes in later movements (which in any

event rarely happens in this period) but opened the concepts to other "aspects of musical construction and technique (commonalities of material, tonal relations, and the like [among the movements])"—something like the features of K. 332 mentioned above.[2]

The utility of identifying such technical features is self-evident. It is a necessary step in the analysis of all works considered as wholes. Most of this chapter, however, is concerned with a different matter: the coherence provided by the norms of the relevant background genre, against which the individual work throws itself. This involves a look at conventional movement plans, common structural and tonal choices and their implications, movement order, and, toward the end, a broader consideration of what it might entail to grasp a multimovement work as a single entity.

Number of Movements

In his inventories of "the sonata in the classic era" William S. Newman noted that multimovement sonatas in the decades before and around 1800 normally contained two, three, or four movements, with the most common number being three. Within nonorchestral pieces labeled as sonatas (which usually begin with a sonata form)

> there can be no question that by far the largest number . . . are in three movements. . . . In the three-movement cycle, the most frequent order of movements is F(ast)–S(low)–F, or F–M(oderate)–F. . . . Haydn uses a minuet as the middle or final movement in more than half his three-movement sonatas. Mozart uses it only twice, as the middle movement, and Beethoven not at all in his three-movement sonatas. . . . In centers other than Vienna, when the three-movement cycle is not built on the favorite F–S–F or F–M–F plan (as it is so regularly in Germany), it sometimes reverts to the late-Baroque plan of S–F–F. Otherwise, the variety of movement plans [can be] so great that often we shall be able

2. Webster, *Haydn's "Farewell" Symphony and the Idea of Classical Style*, pp. 7–8.

to note only the frequency of the minuet finale, the fondness for rondos and variations, the need for contrast between movements, and perhaps a tendency to step up the meter (or fractional time signature) from one movement to the next."[3]

There appears to have been a correlation between the number of movements in a keyboard sonata (or other nonorchestral work) and the seriousness of the work, at least when the number deviated away from the standard three. Two-movement sonatas were almost certainly viewed as lighter works; four-movement ones (infrequent in the eighteenth century) as more ambitious, particularly toward the end of the century and thereafter. Although several of Haydn's piano sonatas are in two movements, in the eighteenth century the two-movement sonata may have been associated with such Italian keyboard composers as Alberti, Paradisi, Galuppi, and Rutini (hence the term sometimes used for them, "Italian sonata"). "The chief two-movement plans are M−F, F−F, F−rondo, and F−minuet. . . . A slow movement in two-movement sonatas is rather rare."[4] (Needless to say, late-Beethoven two-movement sonatas provide significant exceptions to the earlier norm of lightness.) Four-movement keyboard sonatas are rare before the mid-1790s. Beethoven's frequent expansion of the piano sonata to four movements is doubtless to be understood as an enriching of the genre, which had already seen some three-movement advances in the works of Haydn and Mozart.

In the last three or four decades of the eighteenth century the highest compositional prestige within instrumental genres was claimed by the Austro-Germanic string quartet and symphony. Here one often finds the three-movement plan expanded to four movements. Mozart's quartets illustrate the shift. His "Italian" cycle of six quartets, K. 155−60, contains only three-movement works; his next set, the "Viennese" cycle, K. 168−73, comprises four-movement works, as do the remainder of his quartets. Most of Haydn's quartets are also in four movements. The most typical four-movement plan is F−S−minuet−F. (Instead of either a conventional minuet-finale or a fast-finale after the slow movement, one had both.) Occasionally, the minuet was placed in second-movement position.

There are currently two points of view with regard to the origin of the four-movement symphony. The more standard, as summarized in 1986 by Wolf, is that four-movement symphonies were created "by the insertion of a minuet and trio before the finale," a pattern encountered in some of the Mannheim composers—notably Johann Stamitz—"from approximately the mid-1740s on."[5] In 1991 Webster proposed an alternative interpretation: "The development of the four-movement symphony may have entailed, not so much the insertion of a minuet into the F−S−F pattern, as is usually assumed, as the addition of a finale to the traditional three-movement pattern ending with a minuet."[6] While the three-movement symphony continued to exist, often as an overture-*sinfonia* or a brief, lighter composition, four-movement works became more the norm throughout the eighteenth century, particularly among the master composers. To borrow Sisman's summary, "By 1780, symphonies had long since abandoned the three-movement format that linked them to earlier Italian opera overtures. Haydn wrote no three-movement symphonies after 1765, while Mozart's 'Prague' Symphony, with its famously absent Minuet, remains the exception that proves the rule."[7] On the other hand, concertos—which became a much-elaborated genre with Mozart—were almost invariably three-movement works with their own expanded version of sonata form (Type 5) for the

---

3. Newman, *The Sonata in the Classic Era*, pp. 133, 135.

4. Newman, *The Sonata in the Classic Era*, pp. 134−35.

5. Eugene K. Wolf, "Symphony," *The New Harvard Dictionary of Music*, ed. Don Michael Randel (Cambridge, Mass.: Harvard University Press, 1986), p. 823.

6. Webster, *Haydn's "Farewell" Symphony and the Idea of Classical Style*, p. 183, with references to Karl H. Wörner, *Das Zeitalter der thematischen Prozesse in der Geschichte der Musik* (Regensburg, 1969), chap. 1 "Finalcharakter"; and Bernd Sponheuer, "Haydns Arbeit am Finalproblem," *Archiv für Musikwissenschaft* 34 (1977), 199−224.

7. Sisman, *Mozart: The "Jupiter" Symphony*, p. 7.

first movement, similar adaptations for whatever formal plans undergirded the slow movement and finale, and an overall F−S−F plan. (See chapters 19−22.)

Five- and six-movement works were also possible, especially in such "entertainment" genres as serenades and divertimenti. The loose correlation between a greater number of movements (and their lengths) and the enhanced prestige-claim of the work breaks down when the number of movements exceeds four.[8] This may be a residue of earlier suite practice, and indeed, several of Mozart's such works contain an introductory march, one or more minuets, and so on. To be sure, in Mozart's hands the serenade with more than four movements could take on profound connotations, as in the seven-movement Serenade in B-flat for Thirteen Winds, K. 361, and the five-movement Serenade in E-flat for Eight Winds, K. 375. The unexpected element is the concealed depth in what seems to advertise itself as unpretentious entertainment. (On other occasions Mozart's four-movement serenades took on the serious tone of higher genres, most notably in the Serenade in C Minor for Eight Winds, K. 388, reworked into the String Quintet in C Minor, K. 406. The Serenade in G, K. 525, "Eine Kleine Nachtmusik," is essentially an elegant string symphony with a "lighter" tone throughout.)

What follows is an outline of the norms of the most standard four-movement plan as found in Haydn, Mozart, Beethoven, and their immediate successors. Most of the discussion here has the four-movement symphony and quartet in mind, although its observations generally apply equally well to other ambitious four-movement works. It is also applicable to most three-movement works: concertos, sonatas, and so on: one merely has to set aside the absent movement—most often (though not invariably) the minuet.

First Movement

When the first movement was in a rapid tempo—as was the case most frequently—its structure was obligatory. It was to be cast in "grand binary" structure (Reicha's "la grande coupe binaire"), which we now call sonata form.[9] The opening movement declares the tonic that will govern the whole work. We find here an assertion of the tonic key in its full complexity within a sophisticated structural trajectory aimed at the ESC. The first movement sets the emotional tone for the work, designed to match the social prestige of the occasion or "ceremony" at which it is to be performed. (A symphony could be understood as a marker of the grandeur, formality, or splendor of its own realization as a public event; chamber music as something more intimate, appealing more explicitly to the individual performers or the connoisseur.)

Within a symphony this first-movement structure was to be carried out in the high or elevated style. In J. A. P. Schulz's much-cited words from 1774, the opening movement was to unfold in such a way as to become the initial statement of a work whose task it was to be

the expression of the grand, the festive, and the sublime. Its purpose is to prepare the listeners for an important musical work, or in a chamber concert to summon up all the splendor of instrumental music. . . . The allegros of the best chamber symphonies contain great and bold ideas, free handling of composition, seeming disorder in the melody and harmony, strongly marked rhythms of different kinds, powerful bass melodies and unisons, concerting middle voices, free imitations, often a theme that is handled in the manner of a fugue, sudden transitions and digressions from one key to another . . . strong shadings of the forte and piano, and chiefly of the crescendo. . . . Such an allegro is to the symphony what a Pindaric ode is to poetry. Like the ode, it lifts and stirs the soul of the listener and requires the same spirit, the same sublime power of imagination, and the same aesthetics in order to be happy therein.[10]

---

8. A similar conclusion is drawn in Michael Talbot, *The Finale in Western Instrumental Music* (New York: Oxford University Press, 2001), p. 29.

9. Anton Reicha, *Traité de haute composition musicale* (Paris, 1826), 2:300.

10. From J. A. P. Schulz's article "Symphonie" in Johann Georg Sulzer, *Allgemeine Theorie der schönen Künste* (Leipzig, 1771−74). Cited here is Elaine Sisman's adaptation of Bathia Churgin's translation [Churgin, "The Symphony as Described by J. A. P. Schulz: A Com-

The first movement sounds the tone of importance for the entire composition, which in a symphony is a celebration of instrumental music and its expressive capabilities. This was particularly true of grander symphonies, characterized by broader gestures and increasingly considered to have attained the level of the Pindaric sublime. Sonatas and chamber music made less public claims and unfolded in a more private, elaborate, nuanced, or detailed style. First-movement rhetoric was to be shaped according to the genre of the composition at hand.[11] From another perspective—encompassing also ambitious sonatas and chamber music—this movement, as a demonstration of compositional skill, lays out the aesthetic and expressive levels at which the remainder of the "game" will be played. The first movement sets the terms of understanding for the movements to follow. The flexibility and implied drama within the grand-binary structure are naturally suited to this task. In all likelihood the structure was developed precisely to permit the accomplishment of these things.

Slow Movement

The slow movement presents a space of contrast within the four-movement plan. Especially in major-mode works, the slow movement is often sounded in a nontonic key. When it is, it usually functions as the only escape from the governing tonic of the whole. Other features can add to the impression of the second movement as a foil to its predecessor: its more leisurely contrast to the energy and bustle of the first movement; its more persistent lyricism; its frequent clarity of texture and relative contrapuntal simplicity; its tendency to favor less complex formal structures; and its occasional selection of the minor

mode within an otherwise major-mode work, or vice versa.

This movement is conventionally placed (as a first-level default) in the second-movement position. Exceptions do occur, though. Occasionally a two- or three-movement sonata will begin with a slow movement (as in Haydn's Piano Sonatas in D, Hob. XVI:42; in C, Hob. XVI:48; and in D, Hob. XVI:51; it is rarer to begin a four-movement work with a slow movement, as in Symphony No. 49 in F Minor, "La Passione"). Within four-movement works one might also encounter the slow movement displaced to the third position (a second-level default), following the minuet instead of preceding it. This happens, for example, in seven of the twelve quartets constituting Haydn's op. 20 and op. 33. (Additionally, in op. 33 each of the six "minuet" movements is labeled as either a "scherzando" or a "scherzo.") This slow-movement/minuet exchange of positions can also be found in Haydn's middle symphonies but not in the late ones. Placing the slow movement in the second position of a four-movement scheme is almost invariable in Haydn's symphonies from the mid-1760s onward. A few exceptions may be found, however—for instance, in Nos. 37, 44 ("Trauer"), and 68, in all three of which the minuet is placed second. The same later reluctance to switch the more standard placements of the slow movement and minuet may be found in Mozart's and Haydn's later quartets. Although the practice does not disappear in these works, it is less common.

Unlike the situation with a first movement, the slow movement's form is nonobligatory. One cannot predict what the form will be in advance of hearing it. It can be another sonata-form structure: a Type 3 ("textbook") or, quite often, a Type 1 (without development) sonata. Type 2s ("binary," without a full recapitulation)

mentary and Translation," *Current Musicology* 29 (1980), 7–16], in Sisman, *Mozart: The "Jupiter" Symphony*, pp. 9–10. Cf. Neal Zaslaw's remarks in 1989: "The first movements represent the heroic, frequently with martial character. . . . Later [eighteenth-century symphonic first movements] contain contrasting lyrical ideas. Appropriately, given the origins of the sinfonia in the opera pit, the two sorts of ideas—lyrical and martial—may be

seen as comparable to the persistent themes of opera seria itself: love versus honour." Zaslaw, *Mozart's Symphonies: Context, Performance Practice, Reception* (Oxford: Clarendon Press, 1989), p. 417:

11. See, e.g., Michael Broyles, "The Two Instrumental Styles of Classicism," *Journal of the American Musicological Society* 36 (1983), 220. Cf. Sisman, p. 10.

and Type 4s ("sonata rondos" of varying kinds) also turn up from time to time. The slow movement may also unfold as a ternary ABA', as a simpler rondo structure, or as a theme and variations or a set of alternating variations.[12] On rare occasions, it is appropriate to understand a slow movement in different terms from those provided by the more standard guidelines. Such is the case with the Andante of Beethoven's Fifth Symphony, which is most profitably grasped as an early illustration of rotational form deployed on its own, without significant intersection with other, pre-established formal patterns. (Such an overriding rotational structure foreshadows some of those found in both slow and fast movements in Berlioz, Bruckner, Mahler, Sibelius, and others.)[13]

In his 1774 discussion of the symphony as a genre, J. A. P. Schulz mentioned that "the andante or largo between the first and last allegro has indeed not nearly so fixed a character [as the first movement], but is often of pleasant, or pathetic, or sad expression. Yet it must have a style that is appropriate to the dignity of the symphony."[14] Summarizing Mozart's symphonic slow movements, Neal Zaslaw remarked that "the andantes deal with the pastoral, as the origin of a few of Mozart's in bucolic operatic scenes reveals."[15] More generally, the pastoral or sentimental slow movement resonated with the lighter expression of personal, *galant* sentiment and *cantabile* discourse. Still, it would be misleading to consign more ambitious slow movements only to the realm of conventional sentiment. With the increasing importance given to instrumental music in the later eighteenth century—and especially with its transformation in the hands of Mozart and Beethoven—the slow movement would take on an inward turn. As Margaret Notley noted, the formerly sentimental ideal often gave way to the ideal of emotional depth, one typically associated, especially in Beethoven and afterward, with the Adagio tempo, which was now capable of becoming the expressive centerpiece of an entire work.[16] By the mid-nineteenth century A. B. Marx (and others) would refer to such slow movements in quasi-spiritual terms: the slow movement represented the "sabbath-day rest" of the composition, Marx claimed. Elsewhere, he wrote that in Adagio movements the composer often seems to ask "Who am I?"[17]

Key Choice in Slow Movements:
Major-Mode Sonatas

Among the first things to notice about a slow movement is its choice of key: does it retain the original tonic of the first movement—perhaps with a change of mode—or (as is more common)

---

12. According to Sisman, *Mozart: The "Jupiter" Symphony*, p. 8, Haydn introduced the slow variation movement into the symphony in 1772 with his Symphony No. 47.

13. Cf. Darcy, "Bruckner's Sonata Deformations," *Bruckner Studies*, ed. Timothy L. Jackson and Paul Hawkshaw (Cambridge: Cambridge University Press, 1997), pp. 256–77; Darcy, "Rotational Form, Teleological Genesis, and Fantasy-Projection in the Slow Movement of Mahler's Sixth Symphony," *19th-Century Music* 25 (2001), 49–74; and Hepokoski, "Jean (Christian Julius) Sibelius," in *The New Grove Dictionary of Music and Musicians*, 2nd ed., 23: 319–47. A clear instance of an overriding rotational structure in a rapid movement of Berlioz may be found in the Overture, *Le carnaval romain* (which at best responds awkwardly to "sonata-form" analysis, not the least because it gives the impression of containing a repeated exposition, normally not available in overtures). Elsewhere in Berlioz (the Overtures *Benvenuto Cellini* and *Le corsaire*, the first movements of the *Symphonie fantastique* and *Harold en Italie*) the "circular" rotational principle can be intermixed in provocative ways with "linear" sonata deformational procedures and the process of teleological genesis—successive nurturings of an underlying idea that will eventually be treated to a climactic statement. EEC and ESC attainment (or nonattainment) remain crucially important features of all of these works, as does the sheer sense of Berlioz's purposely frictional, transgressive treatment of sonata norms, often in pursuit, it seems, of a swashbuckling or ego-charged "Romantic" freedom, sometimes tied loosely to an extramusical image.

14. Translation as quoted in Sisman, p. 10.

15. Zaslaw, *Mozart's Symphonies*, p. 417.

16. Notley, "Late Nineteenth-Century Chamber Music and the Cult of the Classical Adagio," *19th-Century Music* 23 (1999), 33–61.

17. Marx, *Ludwig van Beethoven: Leben und Schaffen* (1859), quoted in Ian Bent, ed., *Music Analysis in the Nineteenth Century, vol. 2, Hermeneutic Approaches*, (Cambridge: Cambridge University Press, 1994), p. 215; and Notley, "Late Nineteenth-Century Chamber Music and the Cult of the Classical Adagio," p. 35.

does it shift to a different key? Because the memory of the first movement persists conceptually throughout the remainder of the piece, the key of the slow movement is to be interpreted with regard to at least three factors. The first is its "abstract" relationship to the governing key of the whole piece. The second is the earlier role that the slow-movement key had already played in the first movement: that key arrives in the slow movement with a history. The third is the role that the first-movement key is able to play, albeit secondarily, in the slow movement. All (re)appearances of the large-scale governing tonic within the slow movement are noteworthy as such.

The composer had available several options for the key of the slow movement. If we arrange them in order of frequency, we arrive at a set of default choices. During this period these defaults might be ordered as follows, from most to least common:

1. Subdominant (IV)
2. Dominant (V)
3. Tonic minor (i)
4. Submediant minor (vi)
5. Various types of III or VI (available primarily after 1790)
6. Tonic major (I)
7. Other

Cases 1 and 2: Slow Movement in a Nontonic Major Mode, Subdominant or Dominant. This is a swinging outward to a fifth-related key, one that retains the major mode. The escape into a nontonic *cantabile* or dreamlike elsewhere is particularly clear in slow movements with pastoral or Arcadian connotations or in those speaking the erotic language of love, desire, or seduction. Examples are ubiquitous in the repertory. To give a sense of proportion: in Haydn's major-key symphonies after No. 70, sixteen move to IV for the slow movement; twelve move to V.[18]

The first-level default, the subdominant-key slow movement, lowers the first movement's tension toward the more relaxed IV. Here the opening movement's tonic is to be reapproached only from below, as the dominant of that sub-

dominant. This occurs as a matter of course when we have a subdominant slow movement that is disposed in one of the sonata-form types, in all of which the S- and C-zones will appear in V of that IV. This situation permits the real tonic of the whole work to emerge as temporarily subordinate, locally under the sway of the reigning slow-movement tonic. Any such real-tonic appearances refer both to an earlier condition (the first movement) and to the condition-to-come (the third and fourth movements). But within the slow movement they are "fated" not to last. They exist on a different conceptual plane, bracketed, fragile, ephemeral.

When the composer presents the slow movement in the second-level default key, the dominant, the effect is different. Moves to the dominant are gestures toward increased brightness and tension—the opposite from that produced by the choice of the subdominant. Any dominant-key slow movement aligns itself tonally with the S- and C-zones of the first movement's exposition. (As the exposition's dominant-key zones eventually resolved to the tonic in the recapitulation, so too will the slow movement's prevailing dominant be brought back to the tonic in subsequent movements, although with differing thematic material.) In dominant-key slow movements the original tonic of the first movement is less "automatically" available, since it would have to appear as the subdominant of its own V—a key that need not recur generically in any of the sonata types (although it could certainly be touched upon in the development, recapitulation, or coda). What is more likely is that this dominant key will push upward to its own dominant, rendering its S- and C-zone even more tensely distant from the original first-movement tonic.

Cases 3 and 4: Slow Movement in Tonic or Nontonic Minor Mode (i or vi). In both cases it is the unprepared switch of mode to the minor—the "lights-out" effect—that provides the initial impact: the sudden precipitation of an ominous antitype to the first movement's type. (The pro-

---

18. Moving to the subdominant are Nos. 72, 73, 75, 79, 82, 85, 86, 87, 90, 93, 94, 96, 97, 100, 101, and 104. Moving to the dominant: Nos. 71, 74, 76, 77, 81, 84, 88, 89, 91, 92, 98, and 102.

cedure is also analogous to the conventional *minore* variation in theme-and-variation sets, minor-mode slow movements within major-mode suites, and the like.) We refer to case 3, the presentation of the slow movement in the tonic minor, as the *prison-house effect*, as if one were shackled fast to an immovable tonic. Since the nontonic escape normally occurs, if at all, in the slow movement—and since it is not occurring here—we are led to expect that there will be no relief from this tonic in any of the movements. This sense of *no escape* is redoubled through the collapse of mode into minor. Metaphorically, when we hear the beginning of such a slow movement, the coldest of shadows passes over the tonic; the prison-house door closes and locks.

A few examples spring to mind at once: the groaning, D-minor Largo e mesto in Beethoven's Piano Sonata in D, op. 10 no. 3, the F-minor slow movement (in third-movement position) in his String Quartet in F, op. 59 no. 1, the D-minor Largo assai ed espressivo movement from the Piano Trio in D, op. 70 no. 1, "Ghost," and the relentless, A-minor variation movement in his Symphony No. 7 in A, op. 92. This case-3 option turns up with some frequency from the mid-eighteenth century onward. It is readily found in early Mozart: in the tonic-minor slow movements from the Violin Sonata in F, K. 13; the Piano Concerto "No. 4" in G, K. 41; the Symphony in C, K. 96 (111b); the String Quartets in C, K. 157, and in F, K. 168; the Piano Sonata in F, K. 280; and elsewhere. Examples from Haydn's symphonies include the slow movements of No. 3 in G, No. 4 in D, No. 12 in E, No. 17 in F, No. 19 in D, and others, including No. 63 in C and No. 70 in D—though not the later symphonies, in which the composer preferred nontonic slow movements. Any appearance of the tonic major within these tonic-minor movements can strike us as a poignant flash of hope predestined to be reabsorbed back into the minor—the "if only" mirage of what one cannot have, at least in this movement, as in the A-major "dreamlike" alternative passages in the A-minor slow movement of Beethoven's Seventh Symphony, mm. 102ff, 225ff.

In the case-4 option the minor-mode key chosen is not the tonic but the submediant, vi, which may be heard as a much-prolonged upper neighbor to the dominant of the multimovement work's real tonic. From another perspective, it may seem as though the first-movement tonic has undergone a 5–6 shift with added bass support (C major to A minor, for instance), which also suggests intersections with neo-Riemannian interpretations of chordal transformations. Under any reading the submediant minor is likely to be heard as an antitype to the previously governing key—as the deep-sinking into the gloomy, spectral, grotesque, or funereal underside of the tonic (the relative minor, retaining the key signature of the work's real tonic). A submediant-minor slow movement also carries the potential of producing the original major-mode tonic as its most probable secondary key, the mediant (III). This transient retouching of the first-movement tonic within the local control of the dark submediant can be used to powerful effect—the passing vision of what once was (and may yet be again in subsequent movements).

The most familiar example of this option may be the C-minor funeral march from Beethoven's (E-flat) *Eroica* Symphony. Or it may be the F-sharp minor Andante, rocking back and forth in grief, from Mozart's Piano Concerto No. 23 in A, K. 488. Or perhaps the C-minor Andante più tosto Allegretto of Haydn's Symphony No. 103 in E-flat. However celebrated such movements, there were several precedents for their adoption of the submediant minor. To mention only a few from early and early-middle Mozart: the Symphony No. 1 in E-flat, K. 16; the String Quartet in G, K. 156, the String Quartet in E-flat, K. 171, and the Piano Concerto No. 9 in E-flat, K. 271.

Case 5: Major-Mode Keys a Third Away from the Tonic (III or VI). When such third-related keys begin to crop up in several of Haydn's slow movements in the years around 1790 (they are only very rarely to be found in Mozart's),[19] they are best regarded, at least in those early years, as

---

19. Some unusual examples may be found among Mozart's early serenades. The Serenade in D, K. 185, is a seven-movement work with two slow movements (the second and the fifth). The first of these, an Andante, is

deformations of normative practice (that would later be standardized as lower-level defaults).[20] The option could have been borrowed from the idea of moving from a major key to its relative minor (or vice versa) for the slow movement, although in this adaptation the third-relation typically involved two *major* keys, while the interval between them could be either a major or a minor third. As with all such third-relations, they may be interpreted according to either Schenkerian, linear-contrapuntal principles or neo-Riemannian chordal transformation theory. In most cases the original, first-movement tonic will be unavailable—or will be at least more unlikely to be touched upon—in the new key, which will probably emphasize its own dominant. As a result the sense of slow-movement escape from the tonic is more deeply registered here.

The idea of a slow movement in a major III or VI was not new to Haydn: the practice may have been indebted to eccentric key choices made earlier by C. P. E. Bach. Reviewing the latter's six "Hamburg" String Symphonies, Wq 182/1–6 (H. 657–62, 1773), for example, one finds a G-major First with a highly unsettled, Poco Adagio in E (VI); a B-flat-major Second

with a Poco Adagio in D (III); and an A-major Fourth with a Largo ed innocentemente in F (♮VI).[21] Within Haydn's output some important instances occur in Piano Trios. Examples include Hob. XV:14 in A-flat (1789–90), with an Adagio in E major (enharmonic ♭VI), claimed by David Wyn Jones to be the earliest such example in Haydn's instrumental music;[22] Hob. XV:20 in B-flat (1794), with an Andante cantabile in G (VI); and Hob. XV:29 in E-flat (1795–97), with slow movement, Andante et innocentemente, in B (enharmonic ♭VI). A few late-quartet examples from the 1790s, and one from a symphony, may also be included: the F-sharp-major Largo, Cantabile e mesto (III) from the Quartet in D, op. 76 no. 5; the B-major Fantasia-Adagio (enharmonic ♭VI) from the Quartet in E-flat, op. 76 no. 6; the E-flat Adagio (♭VI) from the Quartet in G, op. 77 no. 1; the D-major Andante (VI) from the Quartet in F, op. 77 no. 2; and the G-major Adagio (III) of the Symphony No. 99 in E-flat.[23] The rash of third-related slow movements spread to early Beethoven almost at once: the E-major Adagio (III) of his Piano Sonata in C, op. 2 no. 3 (1795), and many other examples.

in F (♮III), the second in A (V). Curiously, the third movement, an Allegro, is also in F. The Serenade in D, K. 203, is an eight-movement work with two slow movements (the second and the sixth). The first is in B-flat (♭VI), the second in G (IV). The third movement is a non-tonic minuet in F (with trio in B-flat), and the fourth movement (an Allegro) is in B-flat. Thus the overall key plan is: D–B♭–F–B♭–G–D–D. The F–B♭–F of the third movement minuet and trio reverses the tonal pattern of movements 2–4 taken as a unit. If movements 2–4 are considered as a large expansion of B♭, then the deep-level tonal plan is D–B♭–G–D, enacting a downward arpeggiation to the subdominant.

20. Cf. the discussion in Webster, *Haydn's "Farewell" Symphony and the Idea of Classical Style*, p. 212: "Beginning around 1790, and increasingly thereafter, Haydn employed remote key relations between contiguous movements." Cf. also David Wyn Jones's treatment of Haydn, early Beethoven, and third-related keys for slow movements in H. C. Robbins Landon and David Wyn Jones, *Haydn: His Life and Music* (Bloomington: University of Indiana Press, 1988), pp. 296–97; and Ethan Haimo, "Remote Keys and Multi-movement Unity: Haydn in the 1790s," *The Musical Quarterly* 74 (1990), 242–68.

21. Also related, it seems, is the C-major Third with a much-anguished Adagio centered around E minor (iii), although in this case the main slow-movement key (al-

beit not reflected in the key signature) is in the minor mode. Cf. also the first of his "Kenner und Liebhaber" keyboard sonatas from the first book, Wq 55/i (H. 244, publ. 1779), in C major with a slow movement in E minor.

22. "The Adagio [of 'Trio No. 27 in A-flat' = Hob. XV:14] is notated in E major (really F-flat major to the A-flat of the first movement), the first time in any instrumental genre that Haydn does not choose the opposite mode or a directly related key. Though this colourful choice of key had been presaged in the chain finales of *La fedeltà premiata*, in Haydn's instrumental music it grew naturally out of the extended tonal and harmonic vocabulary of the 1780s, and in this particular Trio from the harmonic adventures of the previous movement. Mediant relationships within and between movements were to fascinate Haydn for the rest of his life, and it was a feature of his style that fired the imagination of the young Beethoven. In Haydn's case it added a new sense of colour and drama to his music that complemented and sometimes interacted with more traditional relationships" (Robbins Landon and Wyn Jones, *Haydn: His Life and Music*, p. 211).

23. Obviously related but more striking (since it sets out from a minor-mode first-movement tonic) is the E-major Largo assai (♮VI) of the Quartet in G Minor ("The Rider"), op. 74 no. 3 (1793).

Case 6: Major Tonic (I). Examples in which all four movements are in the same tonic-major key (perhaps recalling earlier aspects of the major-mode dance suite) may be found, but they are considerably less common than the choices discussed above. Here one is again locked into the tonic throughout—without escape—although there is no "prison-house" collapse to the tonic minor for the slow movement. Instead the whole is unremittingly bright, never swerving from its major-tonic security. In some cases this is a result of placing the slow movement in first-movement position, as in Haydn's Symphonies No. 5 in A, 11 in E-flat, 18 in G, 21 in A, and 22 in E-flat ("Der Philosoph")—along with, for instance, Mozart's Quartet in G, K. 80, and a few other early works. Less frequently, the major-tonic slow movement is placed in an interior position: in Haydn's Symphonies No. 62 in D; in a substantial number of his piano sonatas (which sometimes also feature tonic-minor slow movements);[24] or in Mozart's Serenade in E-Flat for Eight Winds, K. 375 (all five movements of which are in the major tonic).

Case 7: Other. This category encompasses more explicit deformations, which demand to be confronted on an *ad hoc* basis. The obvious touchstone is found in Haydn's Piano Sonata in E-flat, Hob. XVI:52 (1794), whose center is occupied by a much-noted slow movement in E major, an enharmonic ♭II of the original tonic (a key famously prepared by an E-major passage in the first movement). One precedent for this choice occurs in a Symphony in D by C. P. E. Bach, Wq 183/1 (H. 663, composed 1775–76, published 1780), which features a central Largo in E-flat, selected by Tovey for one of his *Essays in Musical Analysis*.[25]

Key Choice in Slow Movements: Minor-Mode Sonatas

Minor-mode sonatas differ from major-mode ones because of the "extra burden" of the minor mode itself: its seeking to be emancipated into the major mode (chapter 14). This aspect of the prevailing minor mode is played out not only within individual sonata movements but also throughout the multimovement sonata. As a result, mode choice within slow movements takes on a heightened importance. The options for key choice are listed below. In this case the ordering does not imply a hierarchy of options, particularly because Nos. 1, 2, and 3 seem almost equally available. (One should also recall that minor-mode works were much less plentiful than major-mode ones at this time.) For most of the period under consideration no. 1 may have been more regularly selected than No. 2 (especially by Haydn), although its frequency seems to decline after 1790. Similarly, No. 3 was a common choice—probably more standard than no. 2—particularly from the 1770s onward.

1. Tonic major (I)
2. Mediant major (III)
3. Submediant major (VI)
4. Tonic minor (i)
5. Other

Case 1: Tonic Major (I). This is a common key choice for the slow movement, particularly in the decades prior to 1790. The usual result is that all of the movements appear in the tonic key, with the slow movement providing the contrast by means of mode only. There is no escape from the tonic, but for at least one move-

---

24. Cf. Newman, *The Sonata in the Classic Era*, p. 138: "Of Haydn's 39 keyboard sonatas with 3 or 4 movements, over 40 per cent have no change either of key or mode in any of the movements." See also Somfai's summary of key organization in *The Keyboard Sonatas of Joseph Haydn*, pp. 205–6: "It is surprising how many of Haydn's mature piano sonatas keep the same tonic for all the movements. . . . [This might] suggest a more archaic taste in key relations between movements than that of Mozart or other contemporaries. A better interpretation might be that Haydn liked a strong cohesion in the overall key structure."

25. Tovey, "Carl Philip Emanuel Bach, 'Symphony in D major,'" *Essays in Musical Analysis*, vol. 6 (London: Oxford University Press, 1939), pp. 8–12—an essay, according to E. Eugene Helm (*Thematic Catalogue of the Works of Carl Philipp Emanuel Bach* [New Haven, Conn.: Yale University Press, 1989], p. 145), "containing hardly a paragraph that is not misinformed." Tovey's interest in the work was doubtless sparked by its slow movement's tonal anticipation of that in Haydn's later piano sonata (a comment that surfaces more than once in his essays).

ment we experience its parallel other. The effect is poignant: following an arduous first movement we encounter a temporary liberation into the emancipatory tonic, a premature brightening of that tonic into the major mode. Often the local impression is that of a dream, a false hope—especially when we are given to expect that we are under the "sentence" of a return to the tonic minor (the work's "true reality") in the minuet/scherzo or the finale. On the other hand, if the finale is to end in the major mode, the slow movement can also suggest a prolepsis of what is to come. These effects are produced regardless of whether the slow movement is in second- or third-movement position. Examples from Haydn include: the Quartets in G Minor, op. 20 no. 3, in F Minor, op. 20 no. 5, in B Minor, Op. 64 no. 2, and in D Minor, op. 76 no. 2 ("Quinten"); the Piano Trios in E Minor, Hob. XV:12, and in F-sharp Minor, Hob. XV:26; and the Symphonies Nos. 44 in E Minor ("Trauer") and 52 in C Minor. A Mozartian illustration is available in the Quartet in D Minor, K. 173. Examples from Beethoven may be found in the Piano Sonata in F Minor, op. 2 no. 1, and the Violin Sonata in A Minor, op. 23.

Case 2: Mediant Major (III). The tonal logic of moving to III for the slow movement requires little comment. This is an obvious choice, combining the desirable escape away from the tonic with the shift into the major mode. Additionally, the move to III for the slow movement activates tonal allusions to what may have been the key of the first movement's S and C in the exposition. Examples from Haydn's quartets are to be found in those in B Minor, op. 33 no. 1, and in F-sharp Minor, op. 50 no. 4; from the symphonies, in No. 45 in F-sharp Minor ("Farewell"), No. 78 in C Minor, and No. 95 in C Minor. Examples from Mozart include the String Quartet in D Minor, K. 421, the Piano Sonata in C Minor, K. 457, the Piano Quartet in G Minor, K. 478, and the Piano

Concerto in C Minor, K. 491. Beethoven selected this option in his Piano Trio in C Minor, op. 1 no. 3.

Case 3: Submediant Major (VI). Like other major-mode options for the slow movement in a minor-mode sonata, the submediant provides a temporary haven from the work's prevailing mode—in this instance a comfortingly cool shadow or short-lived respite (again, "if only") from the tensions that surround it. As was the analogous case in major-mode works, the movement's VI may be understood as a prolonged upper neighbor to an implied dominant (a relationship made especially clear in the link between the slow movement and finale of Beethoven's Piano Concerto No. 5 in E-flat, op. 73, "Emperor") and as a coloristic chordal transformation of the reigning tonic. This option, while striking, was not as unusual at might be initially suspected in the period under consideration. One finds it in the works of *Kleinmeister* (Vanhal's Symphony in G Minor [g2], probably written before 1771)[26] as well as in those of the master composers. From Haydn: the Piano Sonata in C Minor, Hob. XVI:20; the Quartet in D Minor, op. 42; the Piano Trio in D Minor, Hob. XV:23; and the Symphonies No. 39 in G Minor, No. 80 in D Minor, and No. 83 in G Minor ("Hen"). From Mozart: the two G-minor Symphonies, No. 25, K. 183, and No. 40, K. 550; the A-minor Piano Sonata, K. 310; the G-minor String Quintet, K. 516; the D-minor Piano Concerto, K. 466; and several other works. Within Beethoven's works, the Ninth Symphony has many precedents in this regard (the "Pathétique" Sonata, the Fifth Symphony, and several others).

Case 4: Tonic Minor. When the slow movement retains the tonic and mode of the first movement, this normally indicates not only that there is no nontonic "escape" to be experienced in this work but that all three or four movements

---

26. This dating was suggested by Paul Bryan in the Preface to Johann Vanhal, *Six Symphonies: Part 1* (Madison, Wisc.: A–R Editions, 1985), p. ix. Bryan also considered the use of the submediant for the slow movement to be "generally an unusual tonal-level relationship, but one in fact frequently found in G-minor symphonies, such as Mozart's Symphony K. 183 and Haydn's Hob. I:39" (p. x).

will unfold in the same tonic minor. This is an intensely negative statement, suggesting a grief so profound that it cannot be shaken. One finds it only in self-consciously extreme works, such as Haydn's Symphony No. 49 in F Minor, "La passione," and Clementi's Piano Sonata in G Minor, op. 50 no. 3 (published in 1821), "Didone abbandonata."

Case 5: Unusual or Deformational Tonal Choices: v, iv, V, IV, and So On. By analogy with the slow movement in the relative major (which recalls the probable secondary key of the first movement), one might suppose that the other normative secondary key, the minor dominant, might also turn up as the governing tonic of a slow movement. In fact, this is an extremely rare choice. One may find it in Clementi's Piano Sonata in F Minor, op. 13 no. 6, which includes a C-minor middle movement. (Curiously, however, the first movement's exposition had modulated to III, not to v.) Also unusual is a move to the minor subdominant (iv), which may also be found in Clementi's Sonata in F-sharp Minor, op. 25 no. 5, with its B-minor slow movement. One presumes that the subdominant minor is accessed by analogy with the major-mode sonata's predilection for its (major-mode) subdominant—suggesting a forlorn attempt to apply major-mode psychology in an alien, minor-mode landscape.

Such an impression is even more affecting when the slow-movement key is a major key that would be properly available only if the first movement had itself been in major (which is not the case here). In this situation there is an element of self-deception represented ("This is how the second movement *might have been* had the circumstances of the first movement been otherwise"). Classic instances of such "false major" keys taking their bearings from the parallel major of the first-movement tonic may be found in Schubert. When we confront such examples

as his Piano Sonata in A Minor, D. 537 (op. 164 from 1817), with its second movement, Allegretto quasi Andantino, in E major (major V), or his B-minor "Unfinished" Symphony, with its Andante con moto in E major (major IV), the first thing to be noticed is the sheer "impossibility" of their keys: these are key-selection deformations, dreaming off into fantasy-spaces. The usual sense of escape is compounded with a denial of the modal experience of the first movement. If one misses this, one misses everything.[27]

Also relatable to these interpretations are such cases as one finds in Beethoven's Quartet in F Minor, op. 95, "Serioso." Here movements 1, 3, and 4 are in the tonic F minor, while the "slow movement," Allegretto ma non troppo, is in D major. (The scherzo also contains a D-major trio.) D major is not smoothly accessible via F minor, but it would have been available more easily as VI—even as relatively normative practice in this period of Beethoven's output—had the governing key of the whole piece been F major rather than F minor. Reflections along these lines permit one to interpret the latent irony behind deformational key choices.

Minuet/Scherzo

It cannot be the purpose of this book to detail the practices of the normal and deformational minuet (or scherzo) and trio. Here we shall mention only a few things about its often-implicit relation to the first movement and its larger role in the multimovement sonata. A minuet (or later, scherzo) is normally in the tonic key and, especially from the later 1780s onward, most regularly appears after the slow movement. This makes it the third movement of a four-movement plan—its most familiar placement—or sometimes, particularly in earlier or lighter pieces, the last movement of a three-movement plan. From time to time one

---

27. An almost perfect inverse of the Schubert "Unfinished" situation, more properly belonging under major-key sonata deformations, appears in Mendelssohn's Symphony No. 4 in A Major, op. 90, "Italian," with its slow movement in D minor (minor iv). Here the "normal" major-mode IV is negatively inflected, casting a "Romantic" minor-mode shadow over this movement—something that will find resonances later in the work, which will end with an A-minor finale.

finds a minuet instead of a slow movement in a three-movement work; more typically, though, it is the minuet that is absent, producing the common F–S–F pattern. As mentioned earlier, it is also common to find a four-movement work with a minuet in the second-movement position, before the slow movement.

Potential Correspondences with the First Movement

In its normative third-movement position the minuet or scherzo re-establishes a principle of schematic order after the typical "escape" of the slow movement. When the slow movement had been in a nontonic key, the minuet normally restores the tonic. In addition, the minuet/scherzo returns not merely to obligatory structure but to a preformatted array of obligatory binary forms. This produces a virtually invariable pattern, usually consisting of two smaller rounded binaries, one of which, heard twice, encloses (contains) the other. The container is also referred to separately as the "minuet" or the "scherzo"; what is contained is the "trio." The resulting form, minuet/trio/minuet *da capo*, is a compound ternary structure (M–T–M or A–B–A). Minuets or scherzos with two different trios [M–T^1–M–T^2–M] are possible, as in some of Mozart's serenades, but the practice is almost unheard of in higher-prestige, four-movement works. In Beethoven (most famously, perhaps, in Symphonies No. 4 and 7) we sometimes find the same trio being visited twice, S–T–S–T–S, but this is a less frequent pattern to be perceived as an expansion, one with rotational implications.

In short, the first movement's ruling shape ("grand binary") is multiply resuscitated here in a compact succession of smaller binary formats. This is underscored by the minuet's sharing of (or return to) the key of the first movement.[28] The minuet/scherzo represents the return of many of the main principles of the first movement, but on different terms. One should be attentive to any thematic or motivic resemblances that might exist between the minuet and the first movement—as though aspects of the first were re-emerging here as a new, transformed beginning (perhaps with rotational implications on the multimovement level).

A few of Beethoven's scherzos deviate from the customary form. Some of them have more problematized tonal plans than one might expect to find in a comparable late-eighteenth-century movement. On occasion Beethoven cast aside certain traditions altogether. The scherzo sections of the Fifth Symphony—reworking the "Fate" rhythm of the first movement—articulate an *ad hoc*, quasi-triple-rotational form substantially removed from the normative rounded binary structure with repeats. In comparison, the ensuing structure of the trio (though not its content) is more normative.

When Beethoven, and then later composers, began to write scherzos that *as a whole movement* are in dialogue more with sonata form than the usual scherzo-trio form (as in the second movements of Beethoven's Quartet in F, op. 59 no. 1, and Mendelssohn's Symphony No. 3 in A Minor, op. 56, "Scottish"), this may be taken as an extension of the often-implicit principle of regenerating certain features of the first movement. The "entire-scherzo-as-sonata" should not be confused with the situation in which only the *outer* "scherzo" (or "minuet") section (not including the trio) is devised as a multithematic sonata and subjected to a complete repeat in the *da capo*. The still-compact minuet-section of Mozart's Quartet in G, K. 387, famously anticipates this latter condition, as do a number of other extended minuets. A more expanded example may be found in the scherzo of Beethoven's Ninth Symphony. (On the other hand, the Ninth's trio, while hardly orthodox in the eighteenth-century sense, more clearly alludes to the proportions found in the standard rounded binary form.)

---

28. Beethoven sometimes problematized the difficulty of reattaining this tonic. The scherzos of Symphonies Nos. 1 and 3, for example, levitate up to the dominant before solidifying the first "real" tonic of the movement. Similarly, the attaining of the ESC (essential structural closure) in the second half of the minuet (scherzo) section often becomes a highly charged, dramatic effect in Beethoven: not infrequently, the seeming reprises of the "scherzo" theme begin in the "wrong key."

Expressive Connotations: Minuets and Scherzos; Major and Minor Modes

This is normally a movement given over to an enhanced charm and usually also to a stylized dance, rhythm, or mood. In the eighteenth century the minuet movement is the one most saturated with an "obligatory" social connotation. This centers around the social norms of ("old-world") aristocratic society; breeding and elegance; public expression; controlled, ritualized eroticism; formalized containments of the pairing of the sexes; and the like. In Zaslaw's view, "the minuets stand for the courtly side of eighteenth-century life, and an old-fashioned and formal aspect of it at that. The trios, on the other hand, often deal with the antic, thus standing in relation to the minuet as an antimasque to its masque, and providing [an] element of caricature."[29] It is worth observing that within a multimovement work the minuet's call back to tonic-order occurs simultaneously with that movement's underscored assertion of the privileged social norms of the aristocracy.

On the other hand, once the minuet became more of an abstraction in a multimovement work, it took on a life of its own. It became a musical genre subjected to the compositional craft of style-variation, something to be manipulated with wit and skill. Thus arose some subtypes of the minuet: the canonic, fugal, or otherwise "learned" minuet (a display of compositional or contrapuntal ingenuity in the manner of a scholastic game); the stormy or pathetic minor-mode minuet; and so on. Moreover, some late-eighteenth-century symphonic minuets resemble faster and far less aristocratic "German dances."[30] This signified a shift of the genre away from aristocratic connotations toward those of a more universal public. With the increasing delegitimation of aristocratic privilege in the age of modernity, the minuet's more traditionally formal mood would be the most vulnerable convention within a multimovement work. Beethoven would transform it into a "scherzo," which harbors aspects of a critique of the traditional minuet and its social connotations.

Major-mode minuets and scherzos are typically bright, positive statements, often reveling in elegant compositional workmanship. Those in the minor mode are quite another matter. This impression is especially striking when a third movement restores the tonic minor first asserted in the first movement but put aside in a major-mode slow movement: the return of a negative condition that had been temporarily kept at bay. Particularly with nineteenth-century works, the minor mode and its concomitant treatment can result in such special effects as "predatory," "trapped," "nightmarish," or "demonic" scherzos (Beethoven, Schubert—much later, Mahler).[31]

The Nontonic Minuet/Scherzo

It occasionally happens, though initially only as a deformation toward the end of the eighteenth century, that the movement expected to reinstate tonic-key tonal order is displaced into a nontonic key. When this happens we are usually facing one of three possibilities. In the first—within a three-movement work—the minuet as middle movement might have taken on the role of tonal escape from the tonic, as in Mozart's Piano (Clarinet) Trio in E-flat, K. 498, "Kegelstatt" (with Menuetto in B-flat, including a G-minor trio). In the second—consider-

29. Zaslaw, *Mozart's Symphonies*, p. 417.
30. William Malloch, "Toward a 'New' (Old) Minuet," *Opus* 1/5 (1985), 14–21, 52. E.g., from p. 16: "a real whirling dance; heady and athletic, with nothing lumpish about it, it moves like the wind. . . . The new Deutsche carried with it a nice antiroyalty dig. . . . And there is plenty of evidence to indicate that the 'minuets' in the later symphonies of Haydn and Mozart were simply urban German dances in minuet costume, and that these dances were played extremely fast by our standards." Cf. Malloch, "The Minuets of Haydn and Mozart: Goblins or Elephants?" *Early Music* 21 (1993), 437–45, which includes a bibliography of related articles concerning the subsequent controversy over minuet tempos.
31. Cf. Schopenhauer's nineteenth-century reactions to both dance music and minor keys: "The short, intelligible phrases of rapid dance music seem to speak only of ordinary happiness which is easy of attainment. . . . Dance music in the minor key seems to express the failure of the trifling happiness that we ought rather to disdain; it appears to speak of the attainment of a low end with toil and trouble." *The World as Will and Representation*, trans. E. F. J. Payne (New York: Dover, 1966), 1:260–61.

ing now the four-movement work—it may be that the slow movement, in whichever movement-position it might occur, is itself in the tonic. Here the minuet and the slow movement will have exchanged their more normative tonal roles: one finds a tonic slow movement and a nontonic minuet or scherzo, as in Beethoven's A-major Seventh Symphony, whose scherzo is in F, and Schubert's early (and incomplete) Piano Sonata in E, D. 157, with a minuet in B. (In both of these instances the preceding slow movement is in the tonic minor.) With only a few exceptions, within four-movement works this deformation is limited to the nineteenth century.[32] In the third, the slow movement and the minuet are placed in two differing nontonic keys, as in Beethoven's String Quartet in E-flat, op. 74, "Harp," whose four movements are in E-flat, A-flat (slow), C minor (scherzo), and E-flat, and Schubert's Fifth Symphony, D. 485, where the succession is B-flat, E-flat (slow), G minor (minuet), and B-flat. We shall return to this topic in the final section of this chapter in a review of the complete cycle as a whole.

The Key and Character of the Trio

The choice of the key for the trio was not obligatory, but there were some standard options. The most common was to present the trio in the same tonic and mode as the minuet (and as the work as a whole, continuing to reaffirm the renewed authority of that tonic). Within Haydn's symphonies this was the almost invariable symphonic practice from Symphony No. 66 onward. Two late-period exceptions are from the *London* Symphonies: No. 99 in E-flat (trio in C

[VI]); and No. 104 in D, "London" (trio in B-flat [♭VI]).[33] Second, the trio could introduce a modal shift from the minuet's tonic minor to the trio's tonic major, or vice versa.[34] In minor-key works, tonic-major trios forecast the major-mode emancipation that one hopes might be achieved in the finale. Within the limited boundaries of the minuet or scherzo, however, such a major-mode passage is fated to be obliterated by the return to the minor with the *da capo*. (In Mozart's Symphony No. 40 in G Minor, K. 550, the G-major trio dreams of a condition that will never come to pass in the finale; in Beethoven's Fifth and Ninth Symphonies the tonic-major trio foreshadows the major mode to be secured in the finales.) Third, the trio could be centered on a contrasting tonic to that of the minuet (perhaps its subdominant). When this happens, the trio's key may be—although it need not be—that of the slow movement, thereby establishing connections to that movement. This happens occasionally in earlier Haydn, as in the Symphonies No. 35 in B-flat (slow movement and trio in E-flat); No. 38 in C (slow movement and trio in F); and No. 56 in C (slow movement and trio in F).[35]

Structurally, the trio normally mirrors the rounded binary format of the minuet that surrounds it, although the trio is often simpler, even more compact in its phrase structure. The trio is usually more relaxed in mood than is the minuet: it is typically simpler, calmer, more rustic or folk-like. Many variants can be rung on this, but if a trio turns away from its usual character—into something brusque, complex, learned, or frenetic—we are probably dealing with low-level default or a deformation.

---

32. One can find a few examples from the eighteenth century, but typically in such out-of-the-way places as program symphonies, little-known repertory, and the like. For example, the first of Dittersdorf's Symphonies on Ovid's *Metamorphoses* (Symphony No. 1 in C, "The Four Ages of the World," c. 1781) is a four-movement work whose third movement is a "Minuetto con garbo" in A minor. (Its trio is also in A minor.)

33. There are also a few odd instances of this in the middle Haydn symphonies: No. 39 in G Minor (trio in B-flat); No. 43 in E-flat, "Mercury" (trio in C minor); and No. 62 in D (trio in G—the one escape from the tonic, since the slow movement is also in D). As with his choice of keys for slow movements, the "third-

related" key possibility for trios emerges in the 1790s: for instance, in the Quartets, op. 74 no. 1 in C (trio in A) and Op. 74, No. 2 in F (trio in D-flat).

34. As in Haydn Symphonies No. 44, "Trauer" (E minor with E-major trio), No. 46 (B major with B-minor trio), 48, "Maria Theresia" (C major with C-minor trio), 49 "La Passione" (F minor with F-major trio), and No. 65 (A major with A-minor trio).

35. Again, this practice was anything but invariable. None of the contrasting-key trios mentioned in n. 33, as well as those of Symphonies No. 99 and 104 (mentioned in the related text), reinstate the key of their preceding slow movements.

The most celebrated example is the trio in the scherzo of Beethoven's Fifth Symphony, with its imitative, C-major fugato probably representing a panicked "flight" (Latin, *fuga*—punning on the term) from the threat of the C-minor cadence that sets it off.

Deferral of the ESC in Compound Ternary (ABA) Forms

Because the rounded binary structure of the minuet- (or scherzo-) section of this movement, considered apart from the trio, is a miniature version of the "grand binary" or sonata-form structure of the first, the concepts of the EEC and ESC are applicable to it. In the rounded-binary "minuet" the EEC-equivalent would typically occur at the first satisfactory PAC toward the end of the first part, before the first repeat sign. (This PAC may or may not be in the tonic, and an extra phrase or "codetta-like" extension, analogous to an exposition's C-space, might also be appended to it). Similarly, with the second-part return of all or some of this first-part music, the ESC would occur at the parallel point at or near the end of minuet section, before the second repeat sign and just before the trio. (In this case, the ESC-equivalent is marked by an authentic cadence in the tonic.)

During the first, pre-trio statement of the "minuet/scherzo" this ESC-effect should be regarded as only provisional. This is because of our awareness of the genre in which it is participating, which encompasses the entire formal pattern, minuet/trio/minuet *da capo*. (Our foreknowledge of the genre provides the guidelines for understanding any individual exemplar.) Because we know that this first section is not to provide the immediate end to the movement, we may arrive at two conclusions. First, however resolute the minuet section's ESC-effect, it is not strong enough—yet—to suppress the trio and finish off the movement on the spot. And second, because the genre dictates that this initial section is to come back literally (or nearly so) as a *da capo*, we also understand that only

in its second, post-trio statement will this same I:PAC be justifiably regarded as the real ESC of the entire movement. Conceivably, the ESC potential of even this second appearance of the I:PAC might be deferred, if the piece proceeds to either a second trio or another statement of the first one, both of which strategies are ESC-delaying tactics. In these instances the ESC-effect is deferred again to its third statement, which must be regarded as the real ESC: there are no more trio options left within the genre.

Finale

Tonally, the last movement of a multimovement sonata serves as a final grounding or reaffirmation of the tonic key. Like the slow movement, the finale has a nonobligatory structure: it may be laid out in any of a number of formal patterns. Summarizing the standard choices in nonorchestral sonatas over some six or seven decades, Newman surveyed the options as follows:

> The minuet served as the finale in countless [three-movement] pre-Classic and not a few high-Classic sonatas. . . . Along with dance movements [including the polonaise, the march, the gigue, and others], the most frequent finales are the rondeaux and rondos, the sets of brilliant display variations, the incipient or larger-scale 'sonata forms,' about on a par with the first quick movements, and various combinations of these. A relatively small number of fugal finales can be found in sonatas throughout the Classic Era.[36]

Finales of all of these types may be found in the works of Haydn, Mozart, and Beethoven. Still, the choice among them was anything but arbitrary. The main issue at hand was the desired weightiness of the whole piece, to which the finale makes an obviously large contribution. Some finales are extremely light (dance-movement related); others are more substantial, presenting sonata forms (and even the occasional fugue) of various complexities and implications.

---

36. Newman, *The Sonata in the Classic Era*, pp. 161, 164.

Rondo finales occupied the broad middle of this scale. Simpler rondos of alternating themes occupied the lighter side; rondos intermixed with the sonata (sometimes producing Type 4 sonatas of uncommon subtlety) made higher claims.

But even such generalizations need qualification. Seemingly simpler generic choices could be composed on a grand scale or be placed in compositions whose preceding movements were conceived along the most elevated and searching lines, all of which enhanced their own implications. One thinks of the substantial variations concluding Mozart's Quartet in D Minor, K. 421, or Piano Concerto No. 24 in C Minor, K. 491—not to mention those in Beethoven's *Eroica* Symphony. On the other hand, many eighteenth-century sonata-form finales present a lighter, more entertaining tone—suggesting a playful wrap-up to the whole piece, an effervescent display of wit, charm, or skill that, while appropriate to the large-scale trajectory of the whole work, only rarely seemed to bear the same conceptual weight as that offered by the first movement.

Characteristically lighter choices of tempo, meter, and style for the thematic subjects of sonata and rondo finales became second nature among eighteenth-century composers. Zaslaw's generalizations about Mozart's symphonies as a whole are typical: "The finales [like those of many other composers] are generally based on rustic or popular dances: gavottes, *contredanses*, jigs, or quick steps."[37] Finales of this period also often have light, jocular, or humorous connotations. Dance-like, triple-time finales (3/8, 6/8) are particularly common, especially in the mid-eighteenth century, and toward the end of the century (especially in Haydn) finales

sometimes mark the arrival of an expressive world that is more elemental, rustic, direct, or folk-like—more fundamentally "natural" or stable—than was that of the first movement. In general, as Michael Talbot observed in a recent monograph on concluding movements, "Whereas 'long' metres such as 4/4 and 3/4 are characteristic of opening movements, 'short' metres such as 2/2, 2/4, 3/8, and 6/8 belong more to finales."[38] Moreover, finale themes often also give the impression of what Talbot called "regression": a "going back" that "often reaches back beyond previously heard material to strive for something more basic. It is, so to speak, development by stripping down rather than by the more usual process of elaboration."[39]

When the finale was a sonata form (usually a Type 3 or Type 4 sonata; much more rarely a Type 2, as in Haydn's Symphony No. 44 in E Minor, "Trauer," and Mozart's *Eine Kleine Nachtmusik*), it provided a sense of recasting certain features of the first movement. The two tonic-key "bookends" of such a multimovement work invite us to discern a relationship or potential balance between them. This is especially apparent with Type 3 sonata finales, which also restore the usual repeat-sign conventions found the first movement.[40] This concluding return to a reaffirmation of sumptuous balances and architectural symmetries is an important element of many finales.

The Role of the Finale in the Trajectory of the Whole Work

Much scholarly reflection has been applied to the issue of the comparative weights of the first and last movements in eighteenth-century

---

37. Zaslaw, *Mozart's Symphonies*, p. 417.
38. Talbot, *The Finale in Western Instrumental Music*, p. 55, also crediting Wilhelm Seidel with the observation in the latter's "Schnell–Langsam–Schnell" (see n. 1 above).
39. Talbot, *The Finale in Western Instrumental Music*, p. 38. Cf. p. 8: "the stripping down of thematic material into even more basic shapes, a kind of 'reverse' development." The traditional sense of lightness was also typically achieved "by a quicker tempo . . . a shorter metre . . . a simpler texture . . . a more quadratic, or at least more transparent, phrase structure . . . a formal structure in

which simple repetition is preferrred to elaboration or complex development . . . an effusion of virtuosic brilliance . . . [and/or] a humorous or quirky tone" (p. 8).
40. We might mention once again (see chapter 2, n. 12) that even though in 1826 Reicha wrote that some "grand-binary" finales—sonata-form finales—can dispense with the expositional repeat, in practice among the major composers this is rather infrequent, though not nonexistent: see, for example, Haydn's Quartets in F, op. 74 no. 2, and in D Minor, op. 76 no. 2, "Quinten.").

three- and four-movement works. In large part this is because of the early-nineteenth-century shift of weight toward the apotheosis or climactic finale found in Beethoven and subsequent composers—the rise of the "finale symphony."[41] The orthodox view has been that the multimovement work began its historical course in the mid-eighteenth century as something weighted toward its first movement (resulting in a sequence of movements lightening toward a mannered playfulness at its end) and by degrees, and sporadically, ratcheted up the heft of its finale to a position of rough equality with the first movement—say, by the period of later Haydn and Mozart—and, eventually, to that of the high point to which an entire composition ascended.

Although the general outlines of this account are accurate, one should neither minimize the contributions of Beethoven's predecessors nor overlook the substance of many eighteenth-century finales. Webster has mounted a telling argument that the idea of "the finale as a culmination" (the result of a "through-composed effect") was explored at length by Haydn, Mozart, and other composers from the 1760s onward. "The paradigmatic example remains Beethoven's Symphony No. 5. . . . But the features on which such effects depend were by no means unknown during the eighteenth century." The features that Webster had in mind (and proceeded to illustrate in several analyses of Haydn) included "run-on movements," "recalls of earlier movements," "the transformation of minor into major," "prominent and unusual tonal relations," "an impression of incompleteness of unfulfilled potential before the finale," and "a mood of tension or irresolution [in earlier movements]." Not surprisingly, Webster granted a special importance to the emergence

of fugal (or otherwise highly contrapuntal) finales with their "effect of culmination," as in Haydn's Symphony No. 40 in F, in three of the Quartets from op. 20 (no. 2 in C; no. 5 in F Minor; no. 6 in A), and in the Quartet in F-sharp, op. 50 no. 4; and in Mozart's Quartets in F, K. 168, in D Minor, K. 173, and in G, K. 387, and his Symphony No. 41 in C, K. 551, "Jupiter."[42]

Major- and Minor-Mode Finales in Minor-Mode Works

Turning things brighter in the finale, following a minor-mode first movement and minuet/scherzo, is a commonly selected option (and one of Webster's indicators of "the finale as culmination"). Haydn's Symphony No. 95 in C Minor ends with a C-major finale, as does, most famously, Beethoven's Fifth Symphony. Even if the finale to a minor-mode work begins in the tonic minor, it may well end in the major mode, spurred onward by the psychology outlined in chapter 14. But it is also normative to find a finale to a minor-key work that both begins and ends in the minor mode, thus carrying the negative connotations throughout the whole work. This procedure stages the finale as a negative culmination or an expression of unrelieved despair, as often in Mozart. Although Mozart occasionally does write major-mode finales to minor-mode works (most controversially in the G-minor String Quintet, K. 516), his much more frequent practice is to retain the minor mode all the way to the bitter end. To be sure, a small number of his obsessively minor-mode finales are released into the major mode at their conclusions (Piano Concerto in D Minor, K. 466). This turn to major, however, typically occurs in the coda, not in the sonata or sonata-rondo form proper.

41. A brief review of this perennial "motif" within discussions of multimovement works is provided in Talbot, *The Finale in Western Instrumental Music*, pp. 12–15, 170–71.

42. Webster, *Haydn's "Farewell" Symphony and the Idea of Classical Style*, pp. 184–85. Cf. Michael Talbot's threefold categorization of finale types circa 1700–1900 (and beyond) in *The Finale in Western Instrumental Music*. For Talbot, finales may be classified primarily as "relaxant" ("inducing relaxation" [p. 50]; "summative" (weightier,

aiming "to sum up the cycle as a whole," including "a more overt thematic (and hermeneutic) relationship to the earlier movements" [p. 50]; or "valedictory" (characterized by a slow tempo, where the sense of "[psychological] homecoming is pushed back still further—beyond the boundary of the work, in fact" [p. 198]. Talbot (p. 64), apparently *contra* Webster, was more likely to regard eighteenth-century fugal finales as "relaxant" rather than "summative" on the basis of what he regarded as their ironic or parodistic tone.

Is it conceivable to conclude a major-mode work with a minor-mode finale, suggesting an unanticipated reversal of fortune? There are a few (very few) early instances of this, occasionally underpinned with programmatic implications. Some are liberated into the major mode toward the very end. Such is the case with Dittersdorf's Symphony No. 6 in A after Ovid's *Metamorphoses*, "The Transformation of the Lycian Peasants into Frogs" (c. 1781–82), in which the unfortunate metamorphosis is reflected upon in an A-minor finale that turns, at the end, into an A-major, *diminuendo* fade-out. The situation may also be found in Haydn's Quartet in G, op. 76 no. 1, in which the finale's G-minor sonata, Allegro ma non troppo, converts into the major mode for the recapitulation. On the other hand, Boccherini's spectral Symphony in D Minor, op. 12 no. 4 (G. 506, 1771), "La casa del diavolo," is a three-movement work in which a D-minor introduction leads to a D-major sonata form for the first movement,[43] while the finale both begins and ends in D minor. There are also some parallel examples from the nineteenth century. One is Berlioz's *Harold en Italie* (a G-major work with a G-minor finale entitled "Orgie de brigands"—although one ending with a blazing conclusion in G major). Others, more pessimistically, conclude in the minor mode, as in Mendelssohn's Symphony No. 4 in A, op. 90, "Italian" (the finale is the famous saltarello, Presto, a frenzied dance—or better, death-dance—in A minor that persists to the end) and Brahms's Piano Trio No. 1 in B, Op. 8, which in both versions features a B-minor finale that also ends in that key.

The Multimovement Cycle as a Complete Gesture

Apart from their realizations in any specific work, the familiar three- and four-movement patterns can be viewed as generic wholes, satisfying ways of building a musical span over temporal space. In part this is because the movement successions themselves suggest possibilities for aesthetically pleasing inner relationships, self-references, and balances.

The Three-Movement Pattern

In a three-movement cycle, fast–slow–fast (F–S–F), the obvious implication is that of a balanced, arch-like shape with rapid-tempo outer sections and a slower, more lyrical center providing a space of contrast. The first and last movements are consequently thrown into an inevitable correspondence as comparable "bookends"—tempo, length, beginning and ending positions. The relationship between the two movements may be made more palpably present through musical interconnections, including similar structural shapes.

The chiastic (and as such static) A–B–A' implication of the three-movement plan is enriched by the simultaneous overlay of linear concerns. If the finale's tempo is faster than that of the first movement, the effect is that of a passage through an affective, slow center—and sometimes also an "escape" tonality—in order to arrive at an increased exhilaration. The slow movement can be understood a site of transformation: a process to pass through in order to arrive at the heightened spirits of the finale. If that finale is also lighter in tone, style, or structure, more dance-like or nimble, then the linear effect of a multimovement pathway into an enhanced vivacity is underscored further. When the three-movement pattern deploys a minuet or other dance movement as its finale (fast–slow–minuet), the linear aspect takes on a different connotation: now the whole piece stages its progress from a dynamic sonata-form world into one of stylized, *ancien-régime* grace and short-winded *galant* symmetries. In this case the pathway brings us to the affirmation of high-prestige (if slightly empty) aristocratic stabilities.

---

43. This would suggest that the work would more normally be called a Symphony in D *Major*, although its minor-mode finale may have overturned that option.

Multimovement ESC Deferral

Another aspect of linearity within the otherwise "rounded" three-movement plan (A–B–A') —an aspect applicable to all multimovement successions—is our awareness that no first movement can provide large-scale closure on its own. Since we know that other movements are to follow, we are aware that the entire piece is not yet brought fully to rest. Indeed, the tonic secured by the first movement's ESC may be lost or abandoned in the second. In these cases the finale will be obliged to recover the displaced tonic with its own ESC. Consequently, in any multimovement work the first movement's ESC is only a provisional attainment, valid for that movement only. (The same point was made above regarding the first ESC-effect of the "minuet" [pre-trio] section of the minuet movement as a whole.) From the multimovement perspective, early-movement ESCs are continually deferred until they find their resting-point in the ESC of the finale, even if that finale is not structured in one of the sonata types. Only at this point are no further options for additional movements available. As a group, multiple movements imply a broader structural trajectory toward the last movement's ESC. This feature of through-composition is built into the multimovement genre *qua* genre.

The Standard Four-Movement Pattern

All of the generalizations regarding the three-movement pattern and ESC deferral are readily adaptable to the four-movement pattern. The latter also merges aspects of static roundedness (the "bookend" outer movements, often featuring other similarities) with aspects of multimovement linearity. When we consider the most common four-movement pattern (fast–slow–minuet–finale), an additional factor of large-scale, 2 + 2 symmetry can be introduced into the whole. This is suggested in figure 15.1.

In each half of the 2 + 2 format an obligatory (binary-based) structure gives way to a nonobligatory one, although the second pair of movements usually accomplishes this in a lighter tone. Moreover, when the second move-ment is in a nontonic key, one can perceive two complementary tonal arcs: tonic to nontonic (first and second movements) and tonic to tonic (minuet and finale). Even without clear thematic correspondences between the slow movement and the finale, the tonal trajectory of the whole suggests the displacement-correction pattern typical of sonata form in general. Particularly if all of this is reinforced by thematic or other interconnections, there may be broad rotational implications in this complementarity. In any event, the minuet/scherzo often provides a sense of a "return to business" (tonic, faster tempo, binary schemes) after the relative calm of the second movement—the beginning of a broad second half to the whole work. In this respect the finale is relatable to both the first and second movements: with regard to the former, as one of the "bookends"; with regard to the latter, as the second part of a two-movement complementary pair.

Alterations of the Normative Movement- or Key-Order Scheme

Movement-order and key-succession are important factors in the multimovement work. Changing the traditional movement order and key (or simply selecting alternatives) produces differing implications. We shall take up some of the options and relate each of them to the following normal-order diagram:

1. Allegro, tonic → 2. Slow, often nontonic ("escape")

3. Minuet, tonic → 4. Finale, tonic

Tonic Minuet in Second Position. Assuming a nontonic slow movement (which is usually, but not always the case), this produces the following pattern:

1. Allegro, tonic → 2. Minuet (or scherzo), tonic

3. Slow, nontonic → 4. Finale, tonic

Here one of the main features is the persistence of the tonic into the second movement (the more normal place to move away from that key). This results in a heavily weighted tonic-balance in the work's first half. At times the impres-

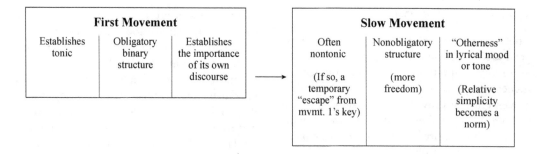

balanced and "resolved" by the complementary gesture:

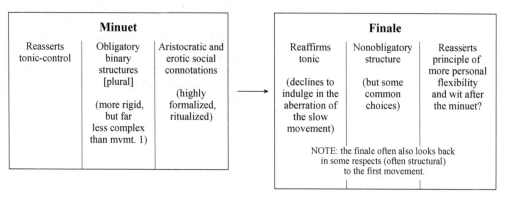

FIGURE 15.1   2 + 2 Symmetries in the Four-Movement Cycle

sion is that the tonic cannot be escaped from, as though it were insistently exerting its authority. In minor-mode works (with a tonic-minor, second-movement minuet or scherzo) this effect can be ominous or menacing. The possibility of an expressive escape from the tonic is consequently deferred to the (slow) third movement, and the burden of resecuring the tonic falls squarely on the shoulders of the finale.

Since this was a common option—a second-level default—in the eighteenth and early-nineteenth centuries, it is anything but deformational. As mentioned earlier, three of Haydn's six quartets from op. 20, feature the minuet/slow-movement switch, No. 1 in E-flat, No. 3 in G Minor, and No. 5 in F Minor—although in two of these, No. 3 and No. 5, the succeeding slow movement is also in the tonic key (the parallel major in both cases)—while in the op. 33 set the first four place the "scherzo" or "scherzando" in the second-movement position. One also finds it in three of Mozart's six

"Haydn" Quartets: those in G, K. 387, in B-flat, K. 458 ("Hunt"), and in A, K. 464, as well as in the Quartet in D, K. 499 ("Hoffmeister"), the String Quintet in G Minor, K. 516, and several other works. The most "colossal" example of this option is found in Beethoven's Ninth Symphony, and it occurs in some of his other works as well, such as the Piano Trio in B-flat, op. 97, "Archduke."

Tonic Slow Movement in (Normal) Second-Movement Position; Nontonic Minuet/Scherzo in (Normal) Third Movement Position. This option is rare—virtually nonexistent—in the eighteenth century. In the nineteenth century it was introduced as a deformation but before long became a lower-level default choice:

1. Allegro, tonic   →   2. Slow, tonic (perhaps with a switch of mode)

3. Scherzo, nontonic   →   4. Finale, tonic

Here the normative movement order is retained with regard to tempo and character, but the escape from the tonic key is assigned—unusually—to the scherzo, in third-movement position. This nontonic aspect can add to the scherzo's flavor of caprice, although it may also suggest a fleeing from a heavy-handed tonic. Since the musical material of scherzos, rhetorically, often reinstates features from the first movement, the connotations of placing the scherzo in a nontonic key are especially subtle. The tonic burden on the first half of the work is heavy, with the corresponding obligation upon the finale to resecure the tonic adequately.

One well-known example occurs in Beethoven's Symphony No. 7 in A, op. 92. In this case the second movement's collapse to A minor is additionally telling (the "prison-house" tonic minor). The third movement is in F major, but the first section of the scherzo—up to the first repeat sign—modulates back to the work's tonic, A major, as if recalling the key in which it "ought" to have been. (The sonority of that A will also pervade the trio [as $\hat{5}$ of D] as a stationary, suspended vision.) Similar logic may be perceived in Brahms's Symphony No. 4 in E Minor, op. 98. Here the Andante moderato is situated in its normal, second-movement position. Spanning outward from an unharmonized E♮ (thus sustaining via linkage the "E"-sonority of the preceding movement), its famous opening four bars suggest that it is about to unfold in C major (with C♮, D♮, F♮, and G♮), in which the E is to serve as $\hat{3}$ of a non-tonic slow movement in VI. (This would be a normative procedure: one need not insist on a "phrygian" reading here.) In the second half of m. 4, however, the potential for C major is rejected. The tonal center of the first movement asserts itself, as though the normative slow-movement pull away from the tonic had not been strong enough, and the movement's key instantly transforms into the tonic major, E major. The "lost" C major is reinstated in the third movement, the nontonic Allegro giocoso.

Minuet/Scherzo and Slow Movement Exchange Positions; Nontonic Minuet and Tonic Slow Movement. Again, this is rare or nonexistent in the eighteenth century, and it is to be regarded as a deformation in the period of Beethoven's works.

1. Allegro, tonic → 2. Scherzo, nontonic

3. Slow, tonic → 4. Finale, tonic
(perhaps with a
switch of mode)

In this case the key-plan of the four movements is normative (tonic/nontonic; tonic/tonic), but the tempos and styles of the two middle movements have switched positions. The second-movement slot retains its tonal role of providing the "escape" key but is occupied by the scherzo instead of the slow movement. In short, the scherzo has usurped the slow movement's tonal role. The third movement restores the tonic, but now with the only remaining movement type available, the slow movement.

One example occurs in Beethoven's Quartet in F, op. 59 no. 1, in which the second-movement scherzo is in B-flat, while the third-movement Adagio molto e mesto is in F minor. In such a situation the slow movement, pushed to third position (and with little hope of escaping to a nontonic key, since that option has already been taken up by the scherzo), is obliged to take on the responsibility of returning to the tonic after its absence in a preceding movement. Considerations of this sort may suggest why in this case Beethoven collapsed this key to the "prison-house" tonic-minor—charging the *thème-russe* finale with the task of restoring F *major*. The opposite situation is found in Mendelssohn's Symphony No. 3 in A Minor, "Scottish." Here we have a minor-mode work with second-movement scherzo in F major, followed by a lyrical slow movement in A major, before A minor is restored in the finale (although an epilogue in A major is subsequently added to this). In this third-movement position, the A-major slow movement seems like a lost dream, a fragile major within an overriding minor-key context, an "if only" effect.

Slow Movement and Scherzo in Normal Order, but Each is in a Different Nontonic Key.

1. Allegro, tonic → 2. Slow, first nontonic key

3. Scherzo, → 4. Finale, Tonic
second nontonic key

This situation is much more a nineteenth-century phenomenon than an eighteenth-century one. It places the burden of restoring the tonic entirely on the finale, while the interior movements, sometimes retaining their normative slow/scherzo order (as in the schema above), each occupy differing nontonic keys. Third-relations among the movements are common, either surrounding the initial tonic key above and below or building one third onto another, resulting in an upward arpeggiation to the dominant or a downward one toward the subdominant. In all instances one is invited to speculate on the central issue at hand: what set of musical or conceptual circumstances permits (or encourages) the scherzo not to return to the tonic?

As mentioned earlier, one example occurs in Beethoven's Quartet in E-flat, op. 74, "Harp," in which the four movements outline a I–IV–vi–I scheme. The practice is more commonly found in Schubert, as in Symphony No. 4 in C Minor, D. 417, "Tragic" (i–VI–III–i), and Symphony No. 5 in B-flat, D. 485 (I–IV–vi–I). And it is especially frequent in Mendelssohn, especially in the chamber music, as in the Octet in E-flat, op. 20 (I–vi–iii–I) and the Quintet No. 1 in A, op. 18 (I–♮VI–iv–I). It is somewhat more common in Mendelssohn to find it coupled with a scherzo displaced to second-movement position. This occurs, for instance, in Mendelssohn's Quartets No. 1 in E-flat, op. 12, and No. 5 in E-flat, op. 44 no. 3, and in the Quintet No. 2 in B-flat, op. 87. In the first the tonal plan is I–iii–V–(vi–I); in the second, I–vi–IV–I; in the third I–vi–iii–I.

The Role of the Listener

It would be short-sighted to presume that locating coherence within a multimovement work is only a matter of being able to locate properties thought to be objectively "in" that work. Coherence is not primarily a property of "the notes themselves." On the contrary, making the piece,

or any portion thereof, into an integrated whole is largely the task—and to a significant extent a creation—of the listener. Any consideration of the "coherence" problem that does not acknowledge this is inadequate. This takes us out of the empirical realm (scientific knowledge) and into that of hermeneutics (interpretation), a different mode of thinking altogether.

Put another way (drawing upon strands of phenomenology, Gestalt psychology, and current studies of cognition), human perception is influenced by a drive to make wholes, coherent shapes and continuities, out of otherwise merely successive, scattered, disparate, or partial information. We seek to fill gaps, to fashion incompleteness into a recognizable totality, to find meaningful patterns in what might otherwise be random—in short, to make the cohesiveness that we crave. Perceptual integration is as much a function of the perceiver as it is of the musical object. This is all the more true when our perception is to operate within a guidelines of a genre system—such as the varying types of sonata form and multimovement construction—that encourages us to find the coherence that is presupposed by the system in the first place. Within the enabling and constraining conditions of any genre system (the "rules of the game") we are not to do this arbitrarily. We perceive (or create) this music's coherence in large part because we are expected to do so.

Several factors can assist us in our willingness to precipitate a multimovement *Gestalt*. While many of the important internal relationships within a piece can be dealt with in standard theoretical terms, many other factors transcend the specificities of the acoustic surface considered alone. These factors include background expectations, relevant presuppositions, prior knowledge of normative procedures, an awareness of extramusical details pertaining to an individual piece, and so on. In some respects these recall the impulses behind Ingarden's descriptions of the "nonsounding" elements of a work of music.[44]

Of these we might single out two. The first

---

44. Roman Ingarden, *The Work of Music and the Problem of Its Identity*, trans. Adam Czerniawski, ed. Jean G. Harrell (Berkeley: University of California Press, 1986), esp. pp. 83–115.

is the imposition of any verbal or visual program onto the work. A program may be supplied by the composer (in varying degrees of concreteness), as with Dittersdorf's Symphonies on Ovid's *Metamorphoses*; it may be inferable from other available evidence (letters, anecdotes, personal communications from the composer, subtitles, nicknames, use of characteristic musical topics, and so on); or it may be a metaphorical narrative of images or emotions (even a poetic idea or a Marxian *Grundidee*) projected onto the acoustic details of the work by either a single listener or a community of listeners. The presumption of a background narrative can trump the purely technical expectations of work-immanent musical coherence. What might otherwise be perceived as a non sequitur or a generically transgressive event tends to be absorbed and interpreted as illustrative of that implicit narrative.

The second is the assumption of a consistent (or consistently implied) field of psychological affects that suffuses the otherwise diverse, multimovement work, bringing the piece's contrasts together as belonging to the same family of feelings. This is the network of "inner relations" among the musical ideas, sometimes presumed to be governed by a "single dominant feeling," that was occasionally mentioned by contemporaries of Haydn, Mozart, or Beethoven.[45] Minor-mode multimovement works, such as Haydn's Symphony No. 44 in E Minor, "Trauer" ("Mourning"), are among the clearest illustrations of this. As an initial premise of listening, one is invited to assume that there must be an interrelatedness among the changeable affects, a kinship among their differences. The listener is encouraged to presuppose that the differing contents of the disparate movements will inhabit the same psychological world. This presupposition is even clearer when that music's original world differs from our own in many of its cultural assumptions, as is the case with music from the "classical" period. Situated in a substantially altered world of thought and feelings, the current listener may "automatically" bracket what he or she hears as circumscribed by the expressive ranges and limits established by the culture of the *galant*, the culture of Enlightenment sensibility, the culture of burgeoning "genius" and *Sturm und Drang*. So long as those conceptual boundaries are not perceived as transgressed, virtually any work may be perceived as internally consistent, even in its variety.

Reflections like these can help us to reframe what was emphasized by Zaslaw in his 1989 study of *Mozart's Symphonies*. Observing the sparse eighteenth-century evidence that would encourage us to look for "unity and high purpose as criteria for symphonies," Zaslaw offered us more modest conclusions: "Most eighteenth-century composers of symphonies . . . appear to have been less interested in . . . philosophical concerns and more in pragmatic estimates of how best to entertain their audiences. For them, the symphony may have worked simply by juxtaposing movements so that changes in tempo and mood from movement to movement—and as the century wore on, increasingly within movements—offered a pleasing variety of aural experiences."[46]

This is the baseline, the bare minimum, of one's experiences with these works. But the experiences of generations with Haydn, Mozart, Beethoven, and others urge us to be alert for more. Three- and four-movement works, especially the most ambitious of them, invite us to wonder about such utterances more deeply, to seek more compelling implications within them. In part this can be done by looking for internal consistencies and cross-references among the movements, by finding evidence (motivic, tonal, linear, or other) that the musical argument is proceeding "logically," perhaps through a process of developing variation, perhaps through strategies of linkage connecting one idea to the next, or perhaps through some other means demonstrable within traditional music theory. Those even more interpretively inclined might go further, with Adorno and others, and assert that traces of cultural processes are inscribed on musical technique itself, which we experience as proceeding through linear time in each individual work. However we regard it,

45. See, e.g., the summary in Webster, *Haydn's "Farewell" Symphony and the Idea of Classical Style*, pp. 179–80.

46. Zaslaw, *Mozart's Symphonies*, p. 416.

a fully text-adequate coherence can be drawn forth only by a thoughtful listener familiar with the norms of the genre at hand.

If we take seriously the expectation that there must be a long-range sense of coherence obtainable from what we hear, we should also foreground our awareness that individual moments of the music do not die away into loss once they have been replaced by the next audible module. They continue to exist in our memory, creating an ongoing string of contexts, the conditions for the existence of what is currently being sounded. From this perspective, listening to a musical work is a process of accumulation over time. In 1976 Wolfgang Iser described such a situation in the reading of a literary text as "the synthesizing process":

> The whole text can never be perceived at any one time.... The 'object' [that is the whole] text can only be imagined by way of different consecutive phases of reading.... The relation between text and reader is therefore quite different from that between object and observer: instead of a subject-object relationship, there is a moving viewpoint which travels along *inside* that which it has to apprehend....
>
> The synthesizing process, however, is not sporadic—it continues throughout every phase of the journey of the wandering viewpoint....
>
> Throughout the reading process there is a continual interplay between [the reader's] modified expectations and transformed memories.... Each sentence correlate contains what one might call a hollow section, which looks forward to the next correlate, and a retrospective section, which answers the expectations of the preceding sentence (now part of the remembered background). Thus every moment of reading is a dialectic of [what Husserl called] protension and retention....

In literary texts, not only is the sequence full of surprising twists and turns, but indeed we *expect* it to be so—even to the extent that if there *is* a continuous flow, we will look for an ulterior motive.[47]

These remarks correspond with what it is like to listen closely to a multimovement work (or any musical work), pondering how it might be put together as a meaningful whole. Entering the acoustic surface of a second movement, we can draw the memory of the first into it: the first movement's ideas and grounding tonality remain present as a tacit backdrop against which the otherwise self-contained processes of the second movement can be read. (This is one reason why appearances of the original tonic within a nontonic movement can be so important—such as that electrifying moment in the fugato-section of the C-minor funeral march of the *Eroica* Symphony, mm. 135–39, when E-flat major, led by *fortissimo* French horns, briefly rises up with incomparable effect, then with a single blow is bludgeoned back into C-minor grief.) Entering the third movement, we can draw the first and second into it; and it is possible to make the first, second, and third movements dwell tacitly in the sounding fourth, which may be understood as a reaction or response to what has preceded it. Throughout all phases of the work, we can trace an ongoing conceptual narrative—a master thread—not so much in what we literally hear as in our reconstructions of the work's ongoing dialogue, moment by moment, with a pre-existing, flexible, and constellated network of generic norms—norms not only for individual zones and individual movements, but for multimovement works as a whole.

---

47. Wolfgang Iser, *The Act of Reading: A Theory of Aesthetic Response* (Baltimore: Johns Hopkins University Press, 1978 [orig. German, *Der Akt des Lesens*, 1976], pp. 108–12.

CHAPTER SIXTEEN

Sonata Types and the Type 1 Sonata

Five Sonata-Form Types

Much energy has been expended in the literature seeking to declare which eighteenth-century structure does and which does not qualify as a sonata form. The label was unknown to the age of Haydn and Mozart. It has been retrojected into music of that period from German-language music-theoretical discourse apparently generated around the years 1824–40.[1] Thus we have narrower definitions (such as James Webster's in the *New Grove Dictionary*, proposing the criterion of the "double return," the return of both the tonic key and main theme at the beginning of the recapitulation)[2] and more expansive definitions (such as Charles Rosen's in *Sonata Forms*, whose plural title, following Tovey, was pointedly chosen). Such terminological questions reflect nothing more (and nothing less) than larger heuristic intentions. Given the history of the term and its self-consciously ahistorical application to eighteenth-century works, what one chooses to call a sonata type or a so-

nata form depends on the interpretive purposes one has in mind for doing so. There is no reality question at stake here.

Once one takes a more sophisticated view of a genre (or a form) not as a concrete thing to be found in the music proper but as regulative idea guiding analytical interpretation, many of the problems associated with this terminological concern become less pressing.[3] What we find as we analyze eighteenth-century instrumental works (along with some kinds of arias and other vocal pieces) are interrelated families of musical processes that are generically appropriate for similar types of compositional situations. In some cases the related processes are functionally interchangeable: one "type" of sonata form can stand in for another. Finales, for instance, are typically cast either as sonatas or sonata-rondos; single-movement overtures may or may not have a development section; what we call Type 2s below are almost as common as Type 3s in the Allegro movements of the symphonies and keyboard sonatas of J. C. Bach; and so on.

---

1. For the dates of the earliest usages of the term, see the opening of ch. 2, especially n. 1.
2. Webster, "Sonata Form," *New Grove Dictionary of Music and Musicians*, 2nd ed., ed. Stanley Sadie and John Tyrrell (London: Macmillan, 2001), 23:688. What Webster sought to disallow as a sonata form proper is

what we call the "Type 2 sonata," which he regarded instead as a "binary variant of sonata form" (see ch. 17) or "expanded binary" form (cf. Webster, "Sonata Form," *New Grove*, p. 690).
3. On the regulative principle concept, see appendix 1, "Some Grounding Principles of Sonata Theory."

We acknowledge this relatedness of family resemblances by housing them all under the idea of differing sonata-form types. All of the types share similar structural principles. These include: a modulatory, expositional layout consisting of functionally differentiated modules; a structure-determining dialogue with the principle of large-scale rotation; and the need for a quasi-symmetrical tonal resolution in the last sonata-space rotation. From this perspective, sonata-form-related structures may be partitioned into five broad categories, five different types. To avoid the sometimes unhelpful connotations of prior terminology, we designate these types only with numbers. In brief (putting aside subtypes and internal complications):

Type 1 sonatas are those that contain only an exposition and a recapitulation, with no link or only a minimal link between them. These have been referred to as "sonatas without development" (or instances of "exposition-recapitulation form," "slow-movement sonata form," or the "sonatina"). Type 1s normally lack internal repeats. Fast-tempo examples of the Type 1 sonata include Mozart's Overture to *The Marriage of Figaro* and most of Rossini's overtures.

Type 2 sonatas are (to use terms that we shall replace in chapter 17) those "binary" (or "binary variant") structures in which what others have called the "recapitulation" begins not with the onset of the primary theme (P) but substantially after that point, most commonly at or around the secondary theme (S). Like Type 1s, they are double-rotational sonatas (two cycles through an extended thematic pattern, the first of which constitutes the exposition), but the treatment of their second rotation differs from that found in Type 1s. In a Type 2 format that rotation begins as a more normatively developmental section in a nontonic key. Type 2s may or may not call for internal repeats: both practices are represented in the literature. Examples of the Type 2 sonata include the first movements of Mozart's Symphony "No. 1" in E-flat, K. 16, "No. 5" in B-flat, K. 22, and Piano Sonata in E-flat, K. 282; and the finale of *Eine Kleine Nachtmusik*, K. 525.

There are many variants of the Type 2 sonata, many different options for realization. In the second rotation, for instance, one may find episodic substitutions for certain expected elements (especially early ones, such as P-based material). Unless one keeps in mind the underlying rotational basis of the structure, along with a memory of prototypical examples, it is easy to misunderstand the architecture of this sonata type. At their conclusions, Type 2 sonatas may also be provided with a post-tonal-resolution (post-second-rotation) coda based on P, which can give rise to the misconstrued impression of a "reversed recapitulation" or a "mirror form" sonata. This issue is discussed more thoroughly in chapter 17.

Type 3 sonatas are the standard "textbook" structures, with expositions, developments, and recapitulations that normally begin with P in the tonic. (At times Type 1s with modestly expanded retransitional links connecting the exposition to the recapitulation become virtually indistinguishable from Type 3s with small development sections. In these instances the categories of Type 1 and Type 3 shade into each other.) Because the Type 3 is the most familiar type of sonata, and because the preceding chapters have dealt with its many possible realizations and deformations, it does not require additional treatment here.

Type 4 sonatas are the differing types of sonata-rondos. Along with that of the Type 3 sonata, the sonata-rondo format was a frequently selected option in many symphony, concerto, chamber-music, and solo-sonata finales, as well as in some slow movements. The rondo theme at the beginning is the opening gesture of an initial rotation laid out as a sonata exposition, usually complete with energy-gaining transition, medial caesura, secondary theme, EEC, and so on. Thus the Type 4 sonata begins with an expositional rotation that traverses the usual P TR ' S / C pattern. Additionally, that rotation's last module normally dissolves into a retransition leading, without expositional repeat, to the next tonic statement of the rondo theme, or P. The expositional rotation is usually balanced by a recapitulatory rotation with the same features. What happens in the substantial space separating the expositional and the recapitulatory rotations can differ from piece to piece (episode? development?). The traditional, seven-part rondo letter-scheme, ABACABA, is inadequate to describe sonata-rondo structures.[4] While the letter-format suggests juxtaposed blocks (which does occur in some rondos), the sonata-rondo proper, the Type 4 sonata, is more strongly in dialogue with the expositional-rhetorical norms that underpin all of the sonata formats. Such distinctions are elaborated in chapter 18.

Type 5 sonatas encompass concerto-sonata adaptations. These are blends between earlier ritornello (or tutti-solo) principles and other sonata types—most commonly the Type 3 sonata. Type 5s are marked by an initial *Anlage* (layout) normally given to the orchestra alone (Ritornello 1 or Rotation 1). The opening orchestral ritornello is almost always stated entirely in the tonic key—or it at least begins and ends with strong, extended thematic statements in that key.[5] A modulatory solo exposition follows, one whose materials should be heard in relation to what had been sounded in the preceding Ritornello 1. Other Type 5 conventions are found in the remainder of the movement: later ritornello/tutti punctuations and cadential confirmations, a solo cadenza near the end, and so on. The definitions of the Type 5 exposition and recapitulation require special care and nuance. These definitions are elaborated in chapters 19–22.

In Mozart's concertos the Type 5 format came to be a laboratory of formal surprise, complexity, and personalized experimentation. It became the most complicated of the sonata types, particularly because of the modular multiplicity and variety that he presented in them, along with his frequently employed thematic-modular substitutions, omissions, or reorderings in all of the rotations after the first one. In Type 5 sonatas, thematic layouts within corresponding rotations can become volatile, provisional constructs. Understanding Type 5s adequately presupposes a thorough grasp of the options and alternative (less normative) procedures available in Sonata Types 1–3.

The numbering for the five sonata-form types may seem arbitrary, but there is a logic behind it. Type 1s are the simplest, most problem-free sonatas. Type 2s are also double-rotational sonatas—the next step in expansiveness and complexity after Type 1s (since they contain a developmental space). By a happy coincidence, Type 2s have often been called "binary" structures (emphasizing "two-ness"); similarly, Type 3s, the most common of the types, are sometimes thought of as containing an emphatic ternary layout.[6] Type 4s are the typical remaining sonata-alternative in nonconcerto instrumental compositions (especially for finales). And Type 5s, capable of becoming the most complex of the structures, are special treatments reserved, at least in purely instrumental practice, for concertos.

The Type 1 Sonata

Sometimes referred to as a sonata form without development, this pattern is the most elementary type of double-rotational sonata. The essence of the Type 1 sonata lies in the minimal retransitional-link (or lack of a link) between the two large-structural blocks: the expositional and recapitulatory rotations. In this type of sonata the second rotation begins immediately or very shortly after the end of the first with the

---

4. Is A always to be confined only to P? Or can it sometimes encompass P + TR? Or is it B that always begins with TR (in which case B extends from TR to the end of S/C)? If so, within B is no distinction to be made between TR and S materials? Or does B begin only with S? For all of its familiarity, the traditional letter-apparatus is too coarse a filter to serve as an adequate description of the sonata-rondo.

5. Exceptions are noted in ch. 20.

6. Our first three types also correspond to the three types of "large-scale configuration" singled out by Eugene K. Wolf in his entry "Sonata Form" in *The New Harvard Dictionary of Music*, ed. Don Michael Randel

(New York: Norton, 1986), p. 766. Wolf did not suggest that these were the only three types of early sonata design. Indeed, the contrary is true: "All these and many other designs existed side by side at approximately mid-century" (p. 766). Still, by singling out only these three, the implication is that they were the clearest and most helpful ones to perceive, even though individual variants abounded. (The quoted passages were unaltered in Wolf's slight revisions to the entry "Sonata Form" in the most recent edition of that reference book, *The Harvard Dictionary of Music*, 4th ed., ed. Don Michael Randel [Cambridge, Mass.: Harvard University Press, 2003], pp. 799–802.)

sounding of P[1] in the original tonic. This immediate rejoining of the tonic and a recapitulatory P[1] is a cardinal feature of the Type 1 sonata.[7] Additionally, the strong first-level default (almost invariable option) for Type 1 sonatas is to dispense with repeats. Normally, neither the expositional rotation nor the recapitulatory rotation is repeated.[8] Perhaps for this reason the Type 1 sonata is particularly suitable for overtures and slow movements. (As a matter of generic principle, all overtures lack repeats,[9] but not all overtures are Type 1 sonatas: they can also be Type 2s or Type 3s.)

Most typically, the second rotation is a close, minimally adjusted replica of the first. The only required adjustment is the transposition needed to produce the recapitulation's tonal resolution. It is not unusual, particularly in a slow movement from a smaller-scale example, to be able to map the second rotation (the recapitulation) bar-for-bar, onto the first (the exposition). Still, this feature is to be understood flexibly. Not uncommonly, one finds alterations here and there, especially in the TR zone, which can show signs of recomposition, especially (but not only) if in the exposition it had led to a V:HC medial caesura. Moreover, as with recapitulations in general, a second rotation will sometimes be compressed, perhaps omitting repetitions of individual modules or even suppressing some modules altogether. Nevertheless, even if we allow for ellipses, expansions, and recompositions, the impression given by the second rotation is that of an immediately undertaken, complementary rotation that balances and resolves the expositional layout. (Expanded Type 1s, a special subset, are treated separately below.)

Lacking both repeat signs and a development, the Type 1 sonata, often a succession of entertaining melodies or contrasting topics, has connotations of lightness, economy, simplicity of elaboration, and relative brevity. This is especially true of fast-movement Type 1s. Slow movements, while still usually renouncing development and complexity, typically favor a broader lyricism or eighteenth-century sentiment. And yet at times the Type 1 slow movement could suggest deeper or darker things in its tone and character. This deepening is related to the general expressive shift in some late-eighteenth-century slow movements from a stylized *galant* sentimentality to more personalized introspection, a move associated with later Mozart and, especially, with Beethoven.

Terminology

A. B. Marx may have been the first to use the term "sonatina" for this format. In his system from the 1840s it was viewed as a way-station on the teleological path to "sonata form."[10] Within music-theory discourse, Marx's term

---

7. Note, however, that the anomalous onset of what amounts to the recapitulatory rotation in the subdominant in the C-minor Andante espressivo ("Abwesenheit" or "L'Absence") of Beethoven's Piano Sonata in E-flat, op. 81a, "Das Lebewohl" ("Les Adieux"), m. 21 (= m. 5 of the exposition!)—in dialogue with the Type 1 sonata with P-based coda—is clearly deformational. In its seemingly aimless, circular loss, it doubtless reflects the underlying program. See also the similar observations regarding op. 81a/ii in ch. 11, n. 21 (and related text), and ch. 12, n. 12.

8. If the simplest Type 1s (no linkage between the expositional and recapitulatory rotations) were provided with a double-set of repeats, we would confront four consecutive statements of the basic modular layout with little or nothing separating them. And yet at times one finds slow movements with both halves repeated and only minimal linkage between the two rotations, perhaps eight or fewer bars of primarily retransitional material. This happens, for example, in a few of Mozart's early works, such as the A-major Andante grazioso (fifth

movement) of the Serenade in D, K. 185, and in some of the early string quartets. In such cases the presence of repeats may suggest the underlying idea of a more developed, Type 3 sonata, even though the developmental space is attenuated. From slightly altered points of view, though, some of these might also be heard as Type 1s with repeats.

9. Only a few rare exceptions crop up in the major literature. See ch. 2, n. 7, which cites in this regard the "Intrada/Prologus" to Mozart's earliest opera, *Apollo et Hyacinthus*, K. 38. There may also be some exceptions to this overture-principle in a few of the earliest Neapolitan opera overtures of the 1730s and 1740s, concerning which Wolf ("Sonata Form," *The New Harvard Dictionary of Music*, p. 766) asserted that "no development section is present, and repeat signs are *nearly always* omitted" (our emphasis: the full quotation is provided later in this chapter). See also the more general discussion of repeats in ch. 2.

10. Marx considered the sonatina to be a sonata form with what he presumed was a subtracted middle part.

seems instantly to have come to mean "sonata form without development." It is with that meaning that the term has survived in both the Austro-Germanic and the English-speaking music-theory world for the past century and a half. The term "sonatina" [*Sonatine*] may be traced through the writings of Marx, Riemann, Schoenberg, Leichtentritt, and so on—and, in the Anglophone tradition, in those of Prout, Goetschius, and others. Among many music theorists today, this is still the term of choice, one reflected in the American textbook on form by Douglass M. Green.[11] The principal dissident in this regard was Heinrich Schenker, who in *Der freie Satz* called the structure "Four-Part Form" $(A_1–B_1 : A_2–B_2)$.[12]

Since the middle of the last century (in the wake of writings by Leonard G. Ratner, Jan LaRue, and others), musicologists have been adamant in avoiding the term "sonatina" because of its historically faulty connotations. The characteristic LaRue argument was that "'sonata form without development' and 'abridged sonata form' suggest incompleteness in a form composers obviously felt could stand on its own; and 'sonatina form' sounds ridiculous when applied to large symphonic movements."[13] In the revision of *Sonata Forms* Charles Rosen objected to the term on similar grounds.[14]

Rosen preferred to call the design "slow-movement form," because it is often found there in the canonic works of the Austro-Germanic tradition. Still, that format also surfaced in rapid first movements (for example, in the first movements of those "early" Neapolitan opera overtures of the 1730s and 1740s—Leo, Jommelli, and so on), and it was very much at home, as mentioned above, in single-movement overtures from the decades around 1800 and slightly beyond: Mozart, *The Marriage of Figaro*; Beethoven, *Prometheus*; almost all of Rossini's overtures (with only a few exceptions, such as that to *La scala di seta*, a Type 3 sonata with an S-based development); and many others. Hence LaRue's initial objection to Rosen: "'Exposition-recap form,' . . . although admittedly multipedalian, at least has the virtue of descriptive accuracy. All the other terms that have been suggested are partly misleading: 'slow-movement' form occurs in many fast movements and by no means all slow movements."[15] So far as it goes, this makes sense. But the term "exposition-recapitulation form" is not widely recognized, particularly among music theorists, and it is identified with a specific and outdated methodology with which we are in little sympathy. Our term, the "Type 1 sonata," is more connotationally neutral.

This view may be consulted in Marx, *Musical Form in the Age of Beethoven: Selected Writings on Theory and Method*, ed. and trans. Scott Burnham (Cambridge: Cambridge University Press, 1997), pp. 82 (a "poorer and lighter" form but one that is "more unified"), 93 (also known as the "small sonata form"), 94. More broadly, Marx understood the "sonatina" as a transitional form between the "fifth rondo form" and the "sonata form" proper. This mode of establishing the form corresponded to his own conceptual derivation of the structure, not to the historical appearance of the form, of which Marx knew little or nothing.

11. Green, *Form in Tonal Music: An Introduction to Analysis*, 2nd ed., p. 230: "From the point of view of musical structure the sonatina form is a sonata form without a development section, its place being taken by a link or transition leading to the recapitulation."

12. Schenker, *Free Composition*, 1:141. "It is most often considered to be a sort of sonata form, in some way altered or mutilated. In actuality, the four-part form is just as independent as the two- or three-part forms. It is found especially in the slow movements of sonatas, chamber works, or symphonies. . . . The unity of this

form, too, is guaranteed only by the fundamental line and the bass arpeggiation. B_1 rests upon V, or is at least moving toward it, whereas B_2 is based on the I."

13. LaRue, rev. of Charles Rosen, *Sonata Forms*, in *Journal of the American Musicological Society* 34 (1981), 563, n. 5.

14. Rosen, *Sonata Forms*, rev. ed., p. 29n. LaRue's own explication of the term—cited as "Exposition-Recap Form"—may be found in *Guidelines for Style Analysis*, 2nd ed. (Warren, Mich.: Harmonie Park Press, 1992), p. 188. Within this discussion La Rue locates the structure in a questionable "evolutionary series" of forms (pp. 187–90). These range from "primitive binary form" [sic] through "polythematic binary" and "large binary with full thematic differentiation" to "early sonata form with incomplete recapitulation after a strongly differentiated exposition and fairly evolved development" [roughly equivalent to what we are calling Type 2 here] and "full sonata form in its most evolved state" [similar to our Type 3].

15. LaRue, review of Rosen, *Journal of the American Musicological Society* 34 (1981), 563, n. 5. The text continues directly with the quotation from LaRue just cited a few lines above.

Historical Origin

The historical sources of the Type 1 design have also been disputed. On the one hand, we have Eugene K. Wolf, following the work of Helmut Hell. Thus Wolf in *The New Harvard Dictionary of Music* (1986), under the entry "Sonata Form":

> The Neapolitan overture mentioned above presents a third large-scale configuration. . . . In most first movements of these [F–S–F] works from the late 1730s on, a full recapitulation enters in the tonic either immediately after the close of the exposition or after a brief retransitional passage. No development section is present, and repeat signs are nearly always omitted (an option in the other types, as well). Historically, this 'exposition-recapitulation' form (Jan LaRue) was derived from tri-ritornello form [as found, for example, in the contemporaneous ripieno concerto] by reduction or elimination of the middle section (see Hell 1971).[16]

Charles Rosen disagreed, perhaps observing that this passage could serve as the basis for a challenge to his contention in the first edition of *Sonata Forms* (1980) that "slow-movement form" was derived primarily from ritornello structures within the eighteenth-century opera aria.[17] Accordingly, in the revised edition from 1988 Rosen added a new paragraph to expand his original argument even further.[18]

We do not take sides in this controversy, and in any event the two positions hardly seem mutually exclusive. What does seem to be the case is that Type 1 sonatas ("exposition-recapitulation" forms) and Type 3 sonatas (full, tripartite sonata forms) appear—at least in their earliest prototypes—to have emerged side-by-side in the 1720s or 1730s. So far as we currently know, neither of them seems to be historically derivable as a variant of the other. Once Types 1 and 3 had appeared as concretized options— by the mid-eighteenth century—it was possible to create a large-scale form poised tantalizingly between the two. Such a structure would be a Type 1 sonata with a modestly expanded link between the rotations ("almost" a development), or, from the opposite point of view, a Type 3 sonata with small, rather insignificant development (so small that it seems virtually to be classifiable as a mere link).[19] Although historically Types 1 and 3 are two different things, in practice, we might find sonata forms that seem suspended between the two possibilities.

How much does it take to expand a serviceable link into a small development? Is it a matter of the number of measures involved, or does it depend on what happens in those measures? This is not always an easy decision.[20] In confronting this problem of classification, the presence or absence of repeat signs might also help us, as might the genre of the composition. Or we might be content to let the conceptual suspen-

---

16. Wolf, "Sonata Form, p. 766 (minimally altered in the same entry in the updated *The Harvard Dictionary of Music*, 4th ed., p. 801, where "the Neapolitan overture" was changed to "the Italian overture"). The entry under "sonatina" (p. 767)—not by Wolf, and defined only as a multimovement sonata, "but on a smaller scale and often less technically demanding"—is not relevant to this discussion. The "sonatina" entry makes no reference to the music-theoretical use of this term to signify a single-movement structure. Wolf's Helmut Hell reference is to *Die neapolitanische Opernsinfonie in der ersten Hälfte des 18. Jahrhunderts* (Tutzing: Schneider, 1971).

17. Rosen, *Sonata Forms*, rev. ed., pp. 28–70, 106–12, 136. An adaptation of Rosen's argument with slightly different terminology could proceed as follows. The first "two parts" of a standard midcentury five-part da capo aria were often organized as what might be called a sonata-without-development, although other possibilities and clever variants—including compressions of the final section, adaptations of Type 2 sonatas, and so

on—also abounded at midcentury. Putting aside such complications, however, one may observe that da capo arias [A–B–A] usually set two stanzas of text (1, 2). The initial and final A section typically presented stanza 1 *twice*: thus A (1, 1) B (2) A (1, 1). The double-presentation of the first stanza, each usually preceded by a ritornello figure, often took the format of a Type 1 sonata: the first stanza modulated to V and confirmed that key; the second rotation of that pattern—and the text—resolved back to I. When the second stanza of the A section began with "P" in the tonic, what was produced in the A section alone was very much like a Type 1 sonata. (In other words, if the aria was a full da capo—with its final A section a literal reprise of the first [as opposed to a shortening thereof]—each aria would present the Type 1 effect twice.)

18. Rosen, *Sonata Forms*, rev. ed., p. 44.

19. See n. 8.

20. Rosen, *Sonata Forms*, rev. ed., pp. 106–12.

sion stand. When the decision one way or the other does not matter for more important issues of hermeneutics, there is no need to make it.

The Type 1 Sonata with P-Based Discursive Coda

When a Type 1 sonata is provided with a substantial, P-based coda in the tonic, it can resemble what in Chapter 18 we call the "Type 1 sonata-rondo mixture." Under such circumstances it can be tempting to consider P to be a rondo theme and the expanded coda as its last appearance. The two structures are close and can easily shade into one another, but the current category may be distinguished from that of the Type 4 sonata-rondo (without development or central episode) in two ways. First, the end of Rotation 2, the recapitulatory rotation, will not have a significant retransition (RT) to set up the last return of P. (This RT is a central feature of rondo forms and sonata-rondo mixtures.) Second, the last appearance of that P-idea may be presented in dissolution or only fragmentarily, as opposed to a more literal appearance of an earmarked rondo theme. The *locus classicus* is the A-flat major Adagio molto of Beethoven's Piano Sonata in C Minor, op. 10 no. 1. Here the exposition (mm. 1–44) is linked by a single bar (V[7], *forte*) to the recapitulation (mm. 46–91). Instead of providing a retransition back to the P idea (in the manner of a sonata-rondo), the final cadence of the recapitulation elides directly with it (m. 91)—a version with an altered continuation. As a result, this movement is best understood as a Type 1 sonata with an extended, P-based coda—one that, like many discursive codas, is divided into sections and also features a final coda-to-the-coda (mm. 102–12).

The Expanded Type 1 Sonata

The pure Type 1 sonata contains no development or extensive elaboration in the second rotation (the recapitulation). Whenever such an elaboration does occur, we may speak of an expanded Type 1 sonata: an expositional rotation followed by an expanded restatement. Such an expansion is typically to be found in the recomposed P–TR zones of the recapitulation, Rotation 2.[21] This expansion/recomposition produces a billowing-out of one section of the referential rotational layout. This may be a relatively small matter, but it can also result in the impression of a more thoroughgoing, implanted "development" section.

Relatively modest in size (but still compositionally intense) expansions of P–TR may be found in some of Mozart's string quartets, as in the slow movements of the Quartets in G, K. 387, and B-flat, K. 589. A slightly larger expansion occurs in the otherwise much-compressed, strikingly non-normative second movement, Allegro molto vivace, of Beethoven's Quartet in C-sharp Minor, op. 131; and expansions emerge even more decisively in the finale of Schubert's String Quintet in C, D. 956, and in many works of Brahms, an early example of which is the first movement of the Piano Quartet in G Minor, op. 25. The expanded Type 1 format, which interpolates a substantial P- or TR-based development shortly into the recapitulation of a Type 1 sonata, has often been considered a typically Brahmsian procedure, and it has been much discussed—using different terminology—in the literature on that composer.[22] Brahms's op. 25/i is extraordinary in employing this format for a first movement; Beethoven's op. 131/ii aside, rapid-tempo expanded Type 1s are much

---

21. A much rarer option in the decades around 1800 was to expand the "tonal resolution" section of the second rotation: its S and C areas. Still, by overriding the norm this could happen. The F-major slow movement of Mozart's String Quartet in C, K. 465 ("Dissonance"), for example, is a Type 1 sonata in which the second rotation (recapitulation) turns out at several important points to be an intensified, expanded restatement of material from the first. Not only is TR expanded, quasi-developmentally, from thirteen to eighteen measures, the S theme is also enlarged from fourteen to twenty-seven measures. This is an extraordinary Type 1 sonata

deformation: a more or less normative rotational layout followed a subsequent, decidedly non-normative problematization and expansion of the initial pattern *en route* to the ESC.

22. Green discusses the structure as an "enlarged sonatina" in *Form in Tonal Music*, 2nd ed., pp. 231–32. See also the discussion, e.g., in John Daverio, "From 'Concertante Rondo' to 'Lyric Sonata': A Commentary on Brahms's Reception of Mozart," *Brahms Studies*, vol. 1, ed. David Brodbeck (Lincoln and London: University of Nebraska Press, 1994), pp. 111–36. Daverio's article (p. 114, 116) provides lists of examples in Mozart and

more commonly found as finales. The finales of Brahms's Symphony No. 1 in C Minor, op. 68, and Symphony No. 3 in F, op. 90, may stand as touchstone examples, while other familiar instances include those of his Piano Quintet in F Minor, op. 34, and Quartet in C Minor, op. 51 no. 1. Brahms's *Tragic Overture*, op. 81, is also laid out as an expanded Type 1 sonata form.

The postexpositional thematic pattern of an expanded Type 1 resembles that of a typical second rotation of a Type 2. The only difference between it and that of a standard Type 2 is the *tonic* relaunching of P in Rotation 2. The second rotation of a Type 2, on the other hand, begins in the key in which the exposition ended or in some other nontonic key. From this perspective the expanded Type 1 pattern mixes certain features of Type 1 (the tonic P-incipit-launch at the outset of Rotation 2) and Type 2 (the developmental billowing-out shortly thereafter). In addition, as is the situation with Type 2s, expanded Type 1 formats rejoin the expositional pattern (they begin to display correspondence measures) at some later, post-P^1 crux-point, usually in TR, though occasionally earlier.[23] In an expanded Type 1 design all of Rotation 2 (unlike the case with the analogous portion of Type 2 sonatas) participates in the psychology of recapitulation because the rotation begins with the P-theme in the tonic. It is a recapitulation, but one with a developmentally expanded P–TR zone.[24]

Because of the possibilities for variants and deformations, all of this can be confusing unless fundamentals are kept in mind. As a rule-of-thumb, if one is encountering a double-rotational sonata in which P^1 is returned to directly after a nonrepeated exposition, one should ask whether P^1 is sounded in the original tonic. If so, the double-rotational sonata belongs to the Type 1 category, even though subsequent deformations and expansions might occur. If not—if P^1 is sounded in anything other than I—then the structure is best considered within the confines of Type 2.

The Type 3 Sonata with Expositional-Repeat Feint: A Related but Differing Structure

We should add one caveat to this discussion of the expanded Type 1 sonata. Because of the immediate restatement of the P-theme in the tonic once the exposition has ended, one might conclude that it would be conceivable for a composer to play momentarily on the idea of an expositional repeat. In the later nineteenth century this possibility may be relevant, for example, to certain types of Brahmsian, blended sonata structures—ones in which, by midcentury, the availability of an expositional repeat was an option, not an obligation. In some instances it might be part of the sonata-game at hand initially to take the immediate return of the P theme in the tonic for an expositional re-

---

Brahms of what he calls the "amplified binary form," as well as an engaging discussion of the issue. We, however, come to somewhat different conclusions and reframe the issue in different ways. (See also our treatment of these and related issues—and Daverio's analyses—in ch. 18.) Cf. the discussion in Robert Pascall, "Some Special Uses of Sonata Form by Brahms," *Soundings*, ed. Arnold Whittall, No. 4 (1974), 58–63; Cf. also, e.g., Walter Frisch, *Brahms: The Four Symphonies* (New York: Schirmer, 1996), p. 61; David Brodbeck, "Medium and Meaning: New Aspects of the Chamber Music," in *The Cambridge Companion to Brahms*, ed. Michael Musgrave (Cambridge: Cambridge University Press, 1999), pp. 98–132 (especially p. 111 and the corresponding p. 297, n. 23).

23. One might suggest further, as with Type 2s, that it might be possible to substitute new material (an episode) into the space normally reserved for developmental elaboration in the expanded Type 1.

24. In this, too, the terminology differs from that which we use for Type 2 sonatas. For Type 2s we no longer speak of a recapitulation at all. As discussed in ch. 17, this is because the term, by definition and historical tradition, carries the connotation of a "full recapitulation." For this reason, in Type 2 formats—which do not begin their second rotations with statements of P in the tonic—we dispense with the term "recapitulation" and identify only a "tonal resolution" beginning around the S-point. The tonal resolution, the statement of the S/C complex in the tonic, occurs in all sonata types. (See ch. 2.) Only in the Type 2 sonata, though, does it emerge in the absence of the normative tonic-key P launching a recapitulation proper. (Occasional exceptions to the tonic-P recaiptulatory launch within Type 3 sonatas are considered in ch. 12.)

peat. This false implication may be part of the piece's logic at this point, even though the rest of the structure might prove to be a more or less normative expanded Type 1.

Here one needs to proceed with caution: confronting the issues at hand requires that one make careful distinctions. First, we should recall that such a repeat is generically inappropriate in the Type 1 ("exposition-recapitulation") design. Hence that repeat-feint reference could be made only in situations in which a listener might expect a sonata form with expositional repeats. This expectation applies neither to overtures (which lack expositional repeats) nor, later, to symphonic poems. At least in principle, however, it might apply to either of the outer movements of a multimovement work.

In late-eighteenth century and early-nineteenth-century Type 3 movements, in which a repeated exposition was strongly normative, this tactic of making a feint toward a generic repeat, then abandoning it, was rare. The classic instance occurs in the first movement of Beethoven's Quartet in F, op. 59 no. 1.[25] The "op. 59 no. 1" variant of the Type 3 sonata consists of the following elements: a nonrepeated exposition; an expositional-repeat feint with a few bars of P in the tonic, soon merging into development; and, later on, a generally full recapitulatory rotation beginning with another statement of P in the tonic. (Later examples include the first movements of Beethoven's Symphony No. 9 in D Minor, op. 125, Brahms's Violin Sonata No. 1 in G, op. 78, and Brahms's Symphony No. 4 in E Minor, op. 98. The opening movement of Mahler's Symphony No. 4 is also in dialogue with this paradigm.) When this occurs in a first movement, the issue of considering the possibility that the tonic-P at the out-

set of Rotation 2 might be the beginning of a recapitulatory rotation does not emerge. These are situations in which Type 1 or expanded Type 1 formats are extremely rare: as such, they do not rise to the level of a significant compositional option for first movements (despite the deformational case of Brahms's op. 25/i). Nor, under these circumstances, should one mistake the "op. 59 no. 1" variant of a Type 3 sonata for a Type 4 design (sonata-rondo): Type 4 sonatas are historically and generically unavailable for first movements.

In a nineteenth-century finale, however, the issue is less clear. The Type 4 format was very much at home here, and the expanded Type 1 was also to become a viable option, especially with Brahms. The local impression of an exposition-repeat feint in a concluding movement, for instance, might also be interpreted under some circumstances as the first return of a rondo theme. Type 4s, that is, can also display a nonrepeated exposition followed immediately (though usually after a clear retransition) by a restatement of P or a portion thereof in the tonic that soon dissolves into development. Still, if the relevant P-theme does not have an obvious "rondo character"[26] or if the movement is not labeled by the composer as a rondo—or if other signals suggest that assigning the finale at this point to the sonata-rondo category is not the most informed choice[27]—the encountering of what seems to be an exposition-repeat feint can be construed along different, non-Type-4 lines. At the point of the feint we should remain open to two other possibilities for interpretation. Deciding between the two will depend on whether or not P returns once again in the tonic to trigger a recapitulatory rotation proper. If it does, the finale's structure is to be understood as

---

25. Two precedents from Mozart and Haydn, the first movements of the former's Serenade in E-flat for Eight Winds, K. 375, and the latter's Piano Sonata in D, Hob. XVI:51, were also mentioned in ch. 2, n. 9.

26. As, for example, in the last movement of Beethoven's Symphony No. 2 in D, op. 36, which, as a finale, is more likely to impress us as a Type 4 sonata.

27. This impression is fortified: (1) if the finale is preceded by a weighty, slow introduction (uncharacteristic of Type 4 movements), or (2) if the tonic-P state-

ment opening Rotation 2 dissolves away rather quickly, before proceeding through very much of its entirety. In the case of Brahms, the contextualizing awareness of other expanded Type 1 finales within his œuvre is obviously also a factor. Chapter 18 outlines the several different signals of Type 4 (sonata-rondo) behavior in finales, which, of course, also feature a tonic-P-led second rotation following a nonrepeated exposition. It also considers the hybrid that we call "the expanded Type 1 sonata-rondo mixture."

the "op. 59 no. 1" variant of the Type 3 sonata. This is what happens in the finale of Brahms's Symphony No. 2 in D, op. 73 (whose design, in other words, is also similar to that of the first movements of Brahms's opp. 78 and 98, mentioned above). But if P does *not* return again in the tonic, and if the other criteria for the structure are met (most importantly, if the ongoing rotational pattern continues to be pursued at the crux-point after the development), the finale is best regarded as an expanded Type 1. As mentioned earlier, examples of such finales include those of Brahms's First and Third Symphonies, along with those of his F-Minor Piano Quartet, op. 34, and String Quartet No. 1 in C Minor, op. 51 no. 1.

CHAPTER SEVENTEEN

The Type 2 Sonata

Both Type 1 and Type 2 sonata forms are double-rotational sonatas: both provide two cycles through the governing layout (P TR' S / C) with little or nothing separating them. The differing characteristics of their second rotations distinguish the Type 1 from the Type 2 format. In a Type 1 sonata ("sonata without development") the second rotation, following a nonrepeated exposition, begins with an intact P sounded *in the tonic*. In other words, it begins and continues as a normative recapitulation. In a Type 2 sonata, however (sometimes thought of as a "binary variant" of a Type 3), the exposition may or may not be repeated, and the second rotation begins as a developmental space; only in its second half—often from S onward—does it take on "recapitulatory" characteristics. As is common within developments in general, Type 2's Rotation 2 normally begins with the first theme (P) sounded either as an explicit thematic reference or in an immediate developmental elaboration but *in a nontonic key*, most often the key in which the exposition had ended. Shortly thereafter, this off-tonic P-reference broadens into more explicit, modulatory developmental activity (often based on P and/or TR-material) that usually drives toward a crux-point and the explicit tracking through correspondence measures at or shortly before S. Continuing (or sometimes beginning) these measures, the sec-

ondary theme (S), along with any closing materials (C), will then be resolved in the tonic, just as they would be in the other sonata types. In all sonata types we refer to this tonic-grounding presentation of the S + C block (part 2 of the rotation) as the *tonal resolution*. S, of course, accomplishes the ESC. Figure 17.1 lays out the most basic scheme, although many variants of it are found in the music of this period.

Inappropriateness of the Term "Recapitulation"

While casually one might suggest that the second rotation of a Type 2 sonata form begins as a development and turns into a recapitulation, such a claim can be misleading. As will be elaborated below, most sonata-form discussions in the eighteenth, nineteenth, and twentieth centuries overlooked the Type 2 option. Within this discourse the term "recapitulation" (German, *Reprise*) was devised to describe the normative situation in the postexpositional spaces of what we call Types 1, 3, 4, and 5 sonatas, namely, that space usually begun by the simultaneous arrival of P and the tonic key and proceeding onward to include S and C. Even while variants and deformations of this practice do crop up, a crucial component of the recapitulation-concept as it emerged historically in the music-theoretical

Internal repeats of each of the rotations are optional: some Type 2 sonata forms call for both rotations to be repeated, while others do not.

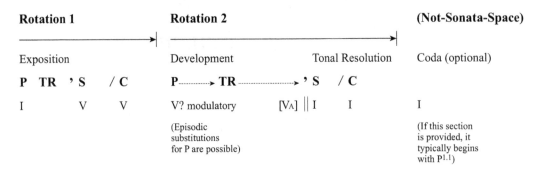

FIGURE 17.1   The Basic Pattern of the Type 2 Sonata

literature was the initiating function of P, that marker that launches what we called in chapters 11 and 12 the recapitulatory rotation. One of P's central functions in all of the sonata-form types is to signal the onset of a structural rotation (exposition, development, recapitulation, or coda). But the same cannot be said of S. On the contrary, S's role—above all in the expositional and recapitulatory rotations—is within an ongoing rotation to proceed from the medial caesura to drive toward and secure the EEC or ESC. Whenever it is also participating in a larger rotation, S never begins a large structural unit but continues one already in progress, one that has been preparing for its arrival. This is a fundamental characteristic of S *qua* S, one that is established in the expositional *Anlage*. (The relatively infrequent S-based development, considered in chapter 10, is a special case. Such an S-initiation would not succeed a pre-established P and/or TR, or their substitutes, earlier in the rotation.)

For this reason, it is inappropriate to claim that the "recapitulation" in a Type 2 sonata "begins with S." Such an assertion, still commonly encountered, is one of several unfortunate consequences arising from the eagerness in the mid-twentieth century to define a sonata only in tonal terms, pushing to the side important considerations of thematic function and arrangement. After all, the reasoning seems to have gone, when the tonic is finally regained and stabilized, that must be the beginning of the "recapitulation," must it not? The answer is

"no." What does begin with the arrival of the tonic-key S—and this is by no means to minimize its structural importance—is the tonal resolution, the second portion of the second rotation. There is no reason to consider this the beginning of a "recapitulation," as if the preceding P–TR material, the first half of the second rotation, setting up the tonal-resolution function of this S, were an insignificant matter. Here the primacy of the rotational principle—obvious enough for those who choose to observe it—trumps traditional, erroneous terminology. Type 2 sonatas do not have recapitulations at all, in the strict sense of the term. Instead, their second rotations have developmental spaces (P–TR or, sometimes, their episodic substitutes) grafted onto tonal resolutions (S–C). This topic will be revisited and expanded later in this chapter, in our treatment of the fallacy of the "reversed recapitulation" (a structure more accurately understood as a Type 2 sonata with a P-based coda).

Because the Type 2 sonata has been underinvestigated or misconstrued in the literature, it bears reflecting on more deliberately here. The only secure way to approach Type 2 sonatas is not to begin with advanced examples of them—Mozart's much-cited Piano Sonata in D, K. 311/i, for instance—but rather to follow a chain of historical examples from a few of Domenico Scarlatti's binary-form sonatas through Mozart and beyond, noting the incremental changes, additions, and deformations that can accrue to the basic schema as one proceeds decade by decade, from composer to composer. Unless one keeps in mind how these accretions and alterations came to enter the Type 2 sonata in the first place, it is easy to slip off the rails and revert to such misjudgments as reversed recapitulations, "mirror forms," and the like.

Historical Considerations

Reconstructing the genealogical lines of "classical" structures is a perennially controversial endeavor. Still, some of the historical antecedents of the full-fledged Type 2 sonata seem clear enough. At least in part, it seems to have affinities with the less fully elaborated, earlier-eighteenth-century binary dance forms, particularly those in which the two structural parts conclude similarly (though in different keys) with rhyming material. The binary sonatas of Domenico Scarlatti are also instructive along these lines. Although one hesitates to generalize over such a varied repertory, typical Scarlatti sonatas (as has been remarked more than once) include at least two main types, disposed in a generous diversity of realizations.[1] The first, less common, is a simpler pattern in which the second part tracks the melodic material presented in the first, while reversing its original tonic/nontonic motion (here represented by superscripts). In the literature this has been described as the pattern $\|: A^1 + B^2 : \|: A^2 + B^1 :\|$, in which B is not typically a theme or even a distinct melodic idea but merely a "clause" or a continuation of A.

A touchstone example may be found in Scarlatti's Sonata in G, K. 2 (example 17.1, one of the *Essercizi* published in 1738 but doubtless composed several years before this). Here a thirty-seven-bar, repeated first part modulating

from I to V ($A^1 + B^2$) is followed by a forty-one-bar, repeated second part beginning in V and moving back to I ($A^2 + B^1$). The second part begins (mm. 38–49) by replicating mm. 1–12 in V (the beginning of the A segment, down a fourth), then diverging slightly from exact correspondence measures—but retaining the model figuration—for modest alterations and a brief extension that regains the G-major tonic. After some twelve freer bars (mm. 50–61 vary mm. 13–20), the strict correspondence measures resume at m. 62, the crux, and persist to the end of the piece (mm. 62–78 = mm. 21–37, in effect the B segment now transposed to the tonic).[2] The last correspondence bar (m. 78 = m. 37) extinguishes the musical process: there is no coda. The double-rotational aspect of such a structure is self-evident, and we may refer to it as a straightforward parallel binary form.

A second, more complex (and more common) type of Scarlatti sonata involved the crystallizing of more distinct thematic ideas throughout and the suppression of a literal return of the A module at the beginning of the second part. Instead of presenting the A idea at that point of "new beginning," as in K. 2, Scarlatti frequently substituted a succession of new, usually modulatory ideas. This new material eventually joined up, at a crux-point, with a pronounced thematic—and harmonically resolving—parallelism, sometimes of substantial length, with the end of the first part. This pattern is usually represented as something along the lines of: $\|: A^1 + B^2 : \|: C + B^1 :\|$.[3] Following the terminology of Douglass M. Green, this may be regarded as a balanced binary structure, a generically available alternative to or variant of the parallel binary, or vice versa.[4] Particularly if one keeps the simpler K. 2 pattern in

---

1. Here we follow, with simplifications, the discussions found in Ralph Kirkpatrick, "The Anatomy of the Scarlatti Sonata," *Domenico Scarlatti* (Princeton, N.J.: Princeton University Press, 1953), pp. 251–79; and Malcolm Boyd, *Domenico Scarlatti—Master of Music* (New York, Schirmer, 1986), pp. 166–78. See also the more recent discussion of Scarlatti's binary forms in W. Dean Sutcliffe, *The Keyboard Sonatas of Domenico Scarlatti and Eighteenth-Century Musical Style* (Cambridge: Cambridge University Press, 2003), pp. 320–75.

2. For a discussion of our slight reinterpretation of Kirkpatrick's term "crux," see ch. 11, n. 11.

3. Sutcliffe, *The Keyboard Sonatas of Domenico Scarlatti*, pp. 320–75 (ch. 7, "Formal Dynamic") takes pains to emphasize the degree of inventiveness that was possible within this format.

4. Green, *Form in Tonal Music: An Introduction to Analysis*, 2nd ed. (New York: Holt, Rinehart, and Winston, 1979), pp. 78–79. The term "parallel binary," so far as we are aware, has not been used before. The term was suggested by the similar formal category, "parallel period."

EXAMPLE 17.1 Scarlatti, Sonata in G, K. 2, mm. 1–78

EXAMPLE 17.1   (continued)

EXAMPLE 17.1   (*continued*)

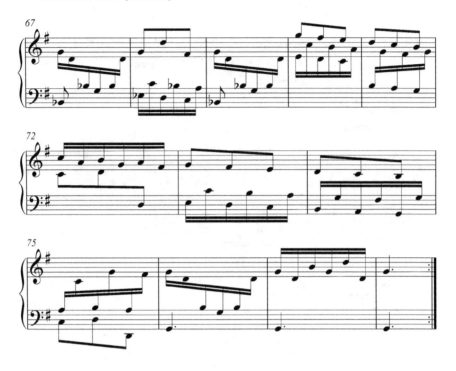

mind, one may regard the double-rotational principle as still operative in this balanced-binary pattern at a conceptual, background level. The often-modulatory C may be interpreted as an episodic stand-in or proxy for the more generically unadventurous A² found in the parallel-binary option. In Sonata Theory terms, C may be heard as writing over A². The degree to which the seemingly discarded A² remains conceptually present in this second rotation, even though it is literally unsounded, remains an open question (one that we would generally answer in the affirmative). In turn, this invites one to consider the degree of rhetorical or motivic distance between Scarlatti's suppressed A² (= A¹) and the acoustically present C, a distance that differs from piece to piece. Such a consideration should be central to our understanding of the inventive fantasy presented at the opening of the second part. One might additionally notice—though it is a thought that is unlikely to come up in Scarlatti sonata analysis considered by itself—that the balanced-binary suppression of A² at the onset of Rotation 2 does not create

any need to restore that lack at the end of the composition. A² never reappears after its initial statement in Rotation 1. This unproblematic point in Scarlatti should be kept in mind when we consider later, more developed models of the Type 2 sonata—in Haydn or Mozart, for example—in which the Rotation-2 absence of P (relatable to A²) has sometimes been adduced as necessitating the later return of that module elsewhere in the piece.

By the late 1730s and 1740s, with the advent of movement structures that more closely foreshadow what we would come to call sonata form, we may find the coexistence of Type 1, Type 2, and Type 3 sonatas as possibilities especially for Allegro-movement construction, although in practice of selection they are not equally weighted. The symphonies of Sammartini, mostly from the early 1740s, favor a Type 3 organization (with a recapitulation beginning with P in the tonic) for their first movements, but it is possible to find Type 2s or Type 2/Type 3 hybrids here and there, as in what Bathia Churgin has edited as his "Symphony No. 3" in D (but which is cited in the later Jenkins-Churgin catalog as No. 14).[5]

Similarly, although overshadowed by more prevalent Type 3 antecedents, Type 2 organization also turns up occasionally in C. P. E. Bach's keyboard sonatas from the early 1740s. It is the formative principle, for instance, in the finale of the first "Prussian" Sonata (in F, H. 24 [W. 48/1]—the first movement is a Type 3 sonata) and in the first movement of the fifth (in C, H. 28 [W. 48/5]), although not in the others. These two movements are instructive with regard to the early history of the Type 2 sonata, providing touchstone examples of the unelaborated, foundational schema for the type. In both, Rotations 1 and 2 are to be repeated. Both begin their second rotations with a statement of P in the dominant (in the manner of a parallel binary), proceed onward to brief passages of modulatory activity while still retaining P or TR material, maintaining the order of materials found in the referential Rotation 1, and rejoin and resolve the expositional material at a crux-point midway through the second rotation. Neither is provided with a coda. As with the Scarlatti examples, the final correspondence-measure bar of the second rotation brings the piece to a close.

Example 17.2 reproduces the finale of C. P. E. Bach's F-major Sonata, H. 24 (W. 48/1), composed in 1740–42. From the perspective of later sonata-form practice, one may regard Rotation 1 (mm. 1–40, repeated) as a continuous exposi-

tion, although one might perceive an embryonic MC-gesture in m. 16 (V:HC). The EEC occurs only at the end of the rotation, m. 40; there is no C. The first four bars of Rotation 2, mm. 41–44, reproduce mm. 1–4 in the dominant but immediately expand outward in sequences, "protodevelopmentally," touching on F (m. 46), B-flat (m. 48), G (m. 50), C again (m. 52), and F again (m. 54), thereupon proceeding to the "embryonic MC" in m. 64, here altered to become a mere tonic arrival on F. The remainder of the rotation consists of correspondence measures resolved into the tonic (mm. 65–88 = mm. 17–40). No additional coda-bars follow. In sum, we find a clear double-rotational pattern and a miniature model for the basic pattern of the Type 2 sonata of succeeding decades. Even if we apply sonata-form terminology to this early, incompletely fledged binary example, there would be no point of recapitulation, only one of tonal resolution (mm. 65–88).

As has been widely noted, what we are calling the Type 2 structure became a common option in mid-eighteenth-century sonata-form compositions. It is readily found among Italian and Italian-influenced composers (such as J. C. Bach), in the works of the Mannheim School (especially in those of Johann Stamitz, who employed this sonata type frequently, although its presence is frequently complicated by modular reordering in the second rotation),[6] and in those of early Mozart, in whose first few symphonies

---

5. "No. 3" in *The Symphonies of G. B. Sammartini*, vol. 1, *The Early Symphonies*, ed. Bathia Churgin (Cambridge, Mass.: Harvard University Press, 1968), pp. 76–82; "No 14" in Newell Jenkins and Bathia Churgin, eds., *Thematic Catalogue of the Works of Giovanni Battista Sammartini: Orchestral and Vocal Music* (Cambridge, Mass.: Harvard University Press, 1976), p. 54. The *Thematic Catalogue*, p. 22, also generalizes about first-movement types. With regard to "No. 3/14": The second part of its opening movement regains the tonic only with material from the middle and end of part 1, not with the head-motive of the movement: in this sense it is in dialogue with "Type 2" organization. There is no "second theme" per se: assuming that one decides to use sonata-form terminology for this movement, this would be an early example of a continuous exposition. Looking more closely at Part 2 (mm. 29–80), one notices that it is structured around not one rotation (the more normative Type 2 procedure) but two. Mm. 29–57 (cadencing in vi) retrack the main elements found in Part 1, as do, more freely, mm. 57–80 (returning to the tonic around m. 62 and rejoining orig-

inal material—now in the tonic—at m. 70). Thus the movement is an instructive overlay of certain aspects of Type 2 sonatas with the option of triple-rotation more normally associated with Type 3s.

6. Eugene K. Wolf, *The Symphonies of Johann Stamitz: A Study in the Formation of the Classic Style* (Utrecht: Bohn, Scheltema & Holkema, 1981), e.g., p. 153 ("As noted already, the typical Stamitz movement disregards the option of full recapitulation in favor of a return to material originally heard after *P* in the exposition. . . . Of the 60 first movements here under consideration, 50 (83%) exclude any significant return of opening material to begin the recapitulation. . . . [Moreover,] a significant proportion of Stamitz's full recapitulations—'full,' we should recall, only in the sense that they return first to *P* rather than to later material—come from his early and middle works, thus confounding any conclusions as to 'proper' evolution"; and p. 279 ("Most of the thirteen middle[-period] first movements with *S* themes make their principal return to those themes, preceded in many cases by the end of *T* ([the transition] employed as a retransition)").

EXAMPLE 17.2 C. P. E. Bach, "Prussian" Sonata in F, H. 24 (W. 48/1), iii, mm. 1–88

EXAMPLE 17.2 *(continued)*

a Type 2 first movement is standard procedure. (Mozart began including Type 3 first movements only with some symphonies from 1768.)[7] The first movements of Mozart's Symphonies "No. 1" in E-flat, K. 16 (1764–65) and "No. 6" in F, K. 43, provide easily consultable instances of the Type 2 sonata form at its least complex. As in the finale of C. P. E. Bach's "Prussian" Sonata in F, H. 24 (W. 48/1; example 17.1)—although now with a clearer two-part expositional organization, with MC and S/C—we find a strictly enforced thematic parallelism between the two rotations and no add-on coda-complications at the end to blur the rhyming endings of Rotations 1 and 2. A third easily available illustration of the Type 2 sonata is the opening movement of Johann Stamitz's Symphony in E-flat (Wolf E♭-4; c. 1750–53).[8] Others include the first movements of J. C. Bach's Symphonies, op. 3 [1765] nos. 4 and 5 (B-flat and F)—and the finale of No. 1 in D, op. 3 no. 1—along with the first movements of his keyboard Sonatas, op. 5 [1766] nos. 1, 3, and 5 (B-flat, G, and E) and op. 17 [ca. 1779], Nos. 1, 3, and 6 (G, E-flat, and B-flat). Generally considered, in the initial movements of J. C. Bach's symphonies and so-

natas (1760s and 1770s), Type 2s and Type 3s appear with roughly equal frequency.[9]

Many other works of Mozart may also be cited here, ones that sometimes add complicating factors that can lead to analytical misinterpretation—such as the suppression of internal repeats, the substitution of different (non-P-based) contents within developmental spaces, and, very commonly, the addition of perhaps-compensatory P-based codas—factors to be dealt with later in this chapter. Among them are the first movements of Symphonies "No. 4" in D, K. 19/i, "No. 5" in B-flat, K. 22/i, and "No. 20" in D, K. 133; the finales of two "unnumbered" symphonies in D, K. 81 and K. 95; the overtures to *Apollo et Hyacinthus*, K. 38 (with added internal repeats) and *Il re pastore*, K. 208; the slow movements of the String Quartet in D, K. 155 and the Flute Quartet in G, K. 285*a*; the opening slow movement of the Piano Sonata in E-flat, K. 282; the complementary first movements of the Violin Sonata in D, K. 306, and the much-discussed and structurally "difficult" Piano Sonata in D, K. 311; and the finale to *Eine kleine Nachtmusik*, K. 525.

One also finds the Type 2 sonata in Haydn—

---

7. The first suggestion of a Type 3 occurs in "No. 7" in D, K. 45/i, which Mozart reworked into the Overture to *La finta semplice*. Here, following a brief, largely episodic development, the composer touched only briefly on the presentation-module basic idea of P on the tonic, m. 56—thus implying the start of a recapitulatory rotation—before subjecting it to an immediate set of sequences on IV and V, all within a much-compressed merger with TR. The Type 3 idea is more clearly in evidence in the first movement of Symphony "No. 8" in D, K. 48, which is usually regarded as the first example of this in his symphonies. See also the discussion of "binary" first-movement form in early Mozart in Zaslaw, *Mozart's Symphonies*, e.g., pp. 33–35 (K. 16), 41 (K. Anh. 223 = 19*a*), 48 (K. 22), 95 (K. Anh. 214 = 45*b*), and 112 (K. 43). Cf. Zaslaw on the form of K. 48/i (p. 121): "The recapitulation gives [the exposition's ideas] again in full (for the first time in his symphonies), and the movement thus provides a lucid demonstration of the apparently paradoxical description [by James Webster in the first edition of the *New Grove Dictionary*] of sonata form as 'a two-part tonal structure, articulated in three main sections.'"

8. A score of this symphony is readily available in Eugene K. Wolf, ed., *The Symphony at Mannheim*, Series C, Vol. 3 of *The Symphony 1720–1840*, ed. Barry S. Brook

(New York: Garland, 1984), pp. 93–122 (first movement, pp. 95–109). The reader might be warned that this work is not the same one as the E-flat Symphony available in the *Norton Anthology of Western Music*, 4th ed., ed. Claude Palisca (New York: Norton, 2001), 2:66–74: that one is Wolf E♭-1, which presents more challenging Type 2 complications, particularly in view of its second-rotation modular reorderings.

9. Slightly more complicated Type 2s in J. C. Bach's works include the first movements of the Symphony in G, op. 3 no. 6 (the complication involves a reinterpretation of "S" material in the second rotation) and the Sonata in C Minor, op. 5 no. 6 (a *Grave* movement; moreover, the second rotation omits the usual reference to P in the second rotation and remains tonally open, preparing the second movement). The remaining fast movements are usually Type 3 sonatas, although a few finales unfold as rondos. The exception is the first movement of the Symphony in D, op. 3 no. 1, which is a hybrid between Types 2 and 3. One might add that five of the six slow movements of the op. 3 symphonies (the exception is No. 3) are in dialogue with the Type 2 principle as double-rotational structures, although in their brevity one might prefer to regard them as relatively undeveloped binaries, not as thematically differentiated sonata forms.

especially in early Haydn—although that composer's penchant for persistent originality and non-normative surprise sometimes renders his works less usable as paradigms for this sonata type. One might mention here only the first movement of "Haydn's" Piano Sonata in A, Hob. XVI:5 (1750s?; the dating and authenticity of the sonata are not solidly established);[10] the first movement of the Piano Sonata in G, Hob. XVI:6; the G-major second movement, Andante, of the Symphony No. 9 in C; the finale to Symphony No. 44 in E minor ("Trauer," which begins with a continuous exposition); and the F-major second movement, Adagio, from the Piano Sonata in C, Hob. XVI:35. A few other examples from Haydn, though ones with additional and sometimes challenging complications, will be cited in due course.[11]

Similar examples from the mid- and late-eighteenth century are easily multiplied. In past decades many have been noted in doctoral dissertations devoted to overviews of the symphonic outputs of individual composers, although the percentage of Type 2s differs from one to another. To select almost at random: of the "64 known symphonies *a* 4 and larger" of Wagenseil (from ca. 1740 to the mid-1770s)

surveyed by John Kucaba in 1968 "only four recapitulations do not begin with the main theme."[12] Margaret G. Grave's 1977 study of first movements in Dittersdorf's symphonies, on the other hand, reports that nine of the thirty-seven early-period symphonies (late 1750s–c. 1773) have as their first movements what we would call Type 2 sonata forms. This is also the case with two of the thirty-seven middle-period works (c. 1773–85); and one of ten from the late period (1788–c. 1793). Most of the remainder are the more typical Type 3s.[13] A wider view of general European practice demonstrates that Type 2s occurred less often than did Type 3s. This was increasingly the case as the decades passed, and it was particularly true after 1770, by which point the Type 2 format was becoming a far less frequently employed choice.[14] As composers grew to favor the perhaps more dramatic Type 3 structures (with full recapitulations), the Type 2 option was pushed to the margins.

Still, within historically significant composition it never disappeared entirely. Type 2s and their variants—including the possibilities of large codas based on P-material—did surface from time to time. With an initial word of caution, insisting that none of the following

---

10. See A. Peter Brown, *Joseph Haydn's Keyboard Music: Sources and Style* (Bloomington: Indiana University Press, 1986), pp. 69, 119. On p. 110 Brown lists XVI:5 as a work of "plausible" authenticity status. On p. 123 Brown proposes a date of circa 1750–55, for this work, labeling it on stylistic grounds as one of the "very earliest," "pre-Esterházy" sonatas. Cf. László Somfai, *The Keyboard Sonatas of Joseph Haydn*, p. 354. Georg Feder's works-list in the "Haydn, (Franz) Joseph" entry in the 2nd ed. [2001] of the *New Grove Dictionary* (11:245) cites the work only as an early "harpsichord" sonata "attributed to Haydn" and provides the Hoboken date (before 1763) along with a more precise estimate, "[?c. 1750–55]."

11. James Webster provided a table of "tonal returns not coordinated with the reprise of the main theme in early Haydn instrumental music"—one that lists fifty-five "early binary movements" from the symphonies, divertimenti, string quartets, string trios, keyboard divertimenti, keyboard trios, and keyboard sonatas—in "Binary Variants of Sonata Form in Early Haydn Instrumental Music," *Joseph Haydn: Bericht über den Internationalen Joseph Haydn Kongress, Wien, Hofburg 5–12 September 1982*, ed. Eva Barura-Skoda (Munich: G. Henle, 1986), pp. 127–35 at 130–32. Many of the movements

cited in the table, though, are not Type 2 sonatas as construed in this chapter. (Some, for instance, are Type 3 deformations of differing kinds.) If one is seeking an inventory of Type 2 sonatas in early Haydn, Webster's list, built around observations generated through a LaRue-based analytical-descriptive practice, should be approached with caution. Cf. our observations on the tables found in Bonds, "Haydn's False Recapitulations and the Perception of Sonata Form in the Eighteenth Century" (ch. 10).

12. John Kucaba, "The Symphonies of Georg Christoph Wagenseil," Diss., Boston University, 1967, pp. 83, 124.

13. Margaret G. Grave, "First-Movement Form as a Measure of Dittersdorf's Symphonic Development," Diss. New York University, 1977, pp. 73–78, 180–81, 276. Grave distinguishes between "sonata form" and "binary structure." Grave's diagramming of Dittersdorf's "binary" procedures support the discussion of Type 2 norms provided below.

14. This was also observed by Eugene Wolf in the "Sonata Form" entry in the *New Harvard Dictionary*, p. 766. A similar point was made in Rosen, *Sonata Forms*, rev. ed., p. 161, in the context of a consideration of "the stylistic revolution of the 1770s."

works should be approached apart from a close awareness of how the Type 2 sonata was transformed and subjected to deformations decade by decade, we may suggest that the roster of Type 2s and their (often strikingly original) variants includes works by Cherubini (Overture to *Médée*, from 1797), Weber (Overture to *Der Beherrscher der Geister*, from 1811, Schubert (a few early quartet movements, such as the first movement of "No. 6" in D, D. 74; additionally, the much-debated C-minor *Quartettsatz*, D. 703, is most fundamentally in dialogue with the Type 2 principle),[15] Spohr (Overture to *Jessonda*, from 1823—here what ought to be its tonal resolution begins in IV), Mendelssohn (slow movement of the Octet in E-flat, op. 20, from 1825), Chopin (first movements of the Piano Sonatas Nos. 2 in B-flat Minor and 3 in B Minor, opp. 35 and 58), Schumann (finale of the Symphony No. 4 in D Minor, op. 120), Wagner (Overture to *Tannhäuser*),[16] Liszt (*Les préludes*), Verdi (Overture to *Luisa Miller*), Brahms (finale of the Quartet in C Minor, op. 51 no. 1; Bruckner (finale of Symphony No. 7), and several others. The list extends to Tchaikovsky and Sibelius (in both cases, the initial movements of their Fourth Symphonies) and even to the extravagantly deformational finale of Mahler's First Symphony, which, while perhaps not a Type 2 strictly considered, is very much staged as being concerned with the Type 2 option as it ponders the structural problem of how to continue and complete a generically normative, symmetrical tonal resolution following the convulsion of

its celebrated mid-movement C-to-D "breakthough" (*Durchbruch*).

Given the Type 3 sonata-form lenses that the analytical tradition has given us to perceive these later works—the wrong lenses, we would argue—it is not surprising that they have provoked so much analytical controversy in the past. Our task here is not to provide discussions of these later works—much less to indulge in glib generalizations about their structures, each of which would call for detailed and nuanced individual argument. For the present, we maintain only that the necessary preliminary work required for an adequate analysis of these works remains largely unaccomplished: confronting the eighteenth-century Type 2 sonata and the manner in which that waning tradition might have been bridged into and reconceptualized within the nineteenth century.

Eighteenth-century "sonata-form" theorists—with the exception of Galeazzi—ignored this sonata type completely. At best a faint glimmer of the idea, within binary-form contexts (not yet "sonata forms"), might be discerned in an early essay from Johann Adolph Scheibe in 1739 (reprinted in his *Critischer Musicus* of 1745), although the remarks there are anything but unambiguous.[17] Later writers, including Portmann (1789), Koch (1793), and Kollmann (1799), among others, were clearer in this regard: they concerned themselves only with what we are calling Type 3 sonatas, overwhelmingly the most common option by the last decade of the century. Only Francesco Galeazzi, in the

---

15. See also the mention of "the older bipartite sonata form" in some early Schubert quartets and in *Quartettsatz* in Martin Chusid, "Schubert's Chamber Music: before and after Beethoven," in *The Cambridge Companion to Schubert*, ed. Christopher H. Gibbs (Cambridge: Cambridge University Press, 1997), pp. 174–92, especially at 175–79).
16. On the final return of P as the onset of coda-space in the *Tannhäuser* Overture, see n. 54.
17. Scheibe, *Critischer Musicus* (Leipzig, 1745); Essay 68, reprint of an essay from Tuesday, December 15, 1739, pp. 623–24. Scheibe discussed two-part (binary) movements of "chamber symphonies" in ways that might initially seem to suggest a rotational, Type 2 organization: "The second section begins again with the principal idea (*Haupterfindung*), and in the working-out (*Ausführung*) of this idea it follows quite precisely the

layout and the thoughts (*nach der Beschaffenheit und nach den Gedanken*) of the first part. One has the freedom, however, to change key more than once in this part and thus in the middle of it to move into other keys or to cadence [*schließen*]. One must ultimately arrange things [*den Zusammenhang*], though, so that we return at last in a lively and unforced manner to the principal key again, in which the second section can end." Only a few sentences later, however, Scheibe seems to revise the "Type 2" implication by remarking that toward the end of the second part, following the usual series of modulatory surprises, "everything must be again united to and linked [*vereinbaret und verknüpft*] with the principal idea (*Haupterfindung*)"—which suggests instead something along the lines of a Type 3 sonata, with its return of the initial theme in the tonic.] We thank John Spitzer for calling Scheibe's remarks to our attention.

second volume of his *Elementi teorico-pratici di musica* of 1796, alluded to the Type 2 option, and then only in passing, as an alternative to Type 3 practice that facilitates the creation of a briefer movement, if desired. If we read Galeazzi literally, the composer's structural decision of how to proceed is made only at the end of the development. Rotational considerations are nowhere to be found (the normative preceding of the tonal-resolution S by P–TR). So far as Galeazzi suggests, perhaps naively, the decision appears to be arbitrary and related only to matters of ultimate length:

> The Reprise [*Ripresa*] succeeds the Modulation [*Modulazione*—our "development"]. However remote the Modulation is from the main key of the composition, it must draw closer little by little, until the Reprise, that is, the first Motive of Part 1 [P] in the proper natural key in which it was originally written, falls in quite naturally and regularly. If the piece is a long one, the true Motive in the principal key [P] is taken up again, as it has been said, but if one does not want to make the composition too long, then it shall be enough to repeat instead the Characteristic Passage [S, *il Passo Caratteristico*] transposed to the same fundamental key. . . . If the second method has been used—that is, the reprise of the Characteristic Passage [only]—then the Modulation shall be ended on the dominant of the key, in order to start then the Characteristic Passage in the main key; and also in this case [as also in the first method] it is good practice to touch upon somewhere, though slightly, the modulation to the subdominant of the key.[18]

Galeazzi apart—an exceptional and isolated case—the more-entrenched theoretical tradition of describing only Type 3s continued with Momigny (1806) and Reicha (1813, 1826) and proceeded into the Beethoven-based Czerny (c. 1837–48), and Marx (1838, 1845), who by this time was referring to it explicitly as "sonata

form." In this process of verbal simplification and reification, continuing into the second half of the nineteenth century, Type 2 formats existed only under the radar of theoretical notice. Since they were overlooked as viable late-eighteenth- and even nineteenth-century options among the most influential theorists, they were also largely absent, one presumes, from discussions of sonata form carried out within the emerging nineteenth-century academic institution of art music: universities, conservatories, critics, commentators, performers, theorists, historians, and so on. The Type 2 tradition was kept alive—in memory and in aggressively original adaptations—primarily as a little-used, alternative sonata practice among composers themselves.

Earlier Musicological Treatments of Type 2 Sonatas: "Binary-Variant" Structures and the Problem of "Reversed Recapitulations"

At first consideration, Type 2 sonatas might strike a modern listener as early, not fully developed, or perhaps compressed sonata forms—steps on the road to the real thing. This seems to have been the opinion of Rudolf von Tobel, in his monumental 1935 survey of classical forms, *Die Formenwelt der klassischen Instrumentalmusik.* For Tobel, who furnished references to many related examples, the form fell generally under the category of the "incomplete recapitulation" (*unvollständige Reprise*), while that of the Type 3 sonata, with both the *Hauptthema* and *Seitenthema* represented (P and S), was "complete" (*vollständig.*)[19] This was also the view of Jens Peter Larsen, who, in a much-read overview from 1956 of Mozart's symphonies, mentioned that the form of the initial movements of such symphonies as K. 16 and K. 19 could be described as "a not fully worked-out sonata form without complete recapitulation."[20] Especially when

18. The translation is that of Bathia Churgin, "Francesco Galeazzi's Description (1796) of Sonata Form," *Journal of the American Musicological Society* 21 (1968), 195–96, which also provides the original Italian.

19. Tobel, *Die Formenwelt der klassischen Instrumentalmusik,* vol. 6 of the Berner Veröffentlichungen zur Musikforschung, ed. Ernst Kurth (Bern and Leipzig:

Paul Haupt, 1935), pp. 148–58. Tobel additionally contributed to the mistaken idea of the reversed recapitulation with his category of *Umstellungen der Reprise,* also laid out on these pages.

20. Larsen, "The Symphonies," in *The Mozart Companion,* ed. H. C. Robbins Landon and Donald Mitchell [1956] (rpt. New York: Norton, 1969), p. 158.

applied to sonatas before 1800, such judgments imply the granting of either a chronological or conceptual priority to full, "ternary" sonata form (our Type 3) that is difficult to justify on historical grounds.

What Tobel, Larsen, and others were noticing is that the Type 2 sonata was more common in the 1740–70 period—that of the early sonata—and that while it did not disappear after that time it turned up much less frequently. This situation may have suggested to them an evolutionary process that came to transform an apparent incompleteness into completeness, that is, either to transform the one type into the other or that elbowed out the lesser form in a seeming survival of the fittest. Nor was such a judgment free from national, cultural, or ideological concerns: in this telling the transformation from the merely partial to the full coincided with the hegemonic rise of Austro-Germanic "great music" and its masters, the mature Haydn, Mozart, and Beethoven.[21] But this seemingly direct line from the one type of sonata form to the other seems not to have been the case—a point also underscored by Wolf in his 1981 study of Stamitz's symphonies.[22] Although Type 3 sonatas—providing a strategy of greater breadth and more emphatic articulation of parts—may have been favored among some composers, the Type 2 alternative coexisted as a viable option standing side-by-side with it, even though it was one less often adopted, especially toward the end of the century. Within midcentury multimovement sonatas, both Type 2s and Type 3s can lay

claim to similar, almost interchangeable functions. Deciding which option to select seems to have been a matter of preference and compositional convention. For this reason, the two types are most helpfully understood—adopting more modern terminology—as equally legitimate sonata procedures. The Type 2 sonata is by no means a "not fully worked-out" structure as opposed to a satisfactorily complete one. Assessed by its own standards, the Type 2 sonata lacks nothing.

Nonetheless, this has been anything but a shared view within past scholarship. At best, musicological conversations surrounding it have dealt primarily with classification, noting its presence and commenting, however briefly, about its different, more compact articulation of the sonata idea. Typically, previous descriptions have centered around the designations "binary," "bipartite," or "binary variant," and writers have differed on the question of whether the word "sonata" should appear in the description. Thus in the literature one comes across both "binary form" and "binary sonata form."[23] In either case, the implication has usually been that the structure falls short of being a true "sonata form" in its own right, a position that—once again (dubiously, in our view)—can be sustained only by taking the full, tripartite sonata as the absolute norm or only "real" sonata form.[24] This assessment was made even more explicit in a mid-1980s overview of "binary variants of sonata form in early Haydn" by James Webster. Here Webster insisted on

---

21. Thus Tobel, *Die Formenwelt*, p. 151—contributing to the German-language musicological discourse of 1935—noted, for instance, that the sonata forms of the Italian composer Francesco Antonio Rosetti are frequently incomplete (*unvollständig*). As opposed to this "as a rule, L[eopold] Mozart brings [the reprise] in completely and therein shows himself to be an Austrian. On the other hand, his great son at first still stayed open to Italian influences, among which the pages of J. C. Bach are also to be numbered." In part this was because in the "preclassical" period as played out in Vienna—as opposed to in Italy—"thematic permeation of the [whole] movement was encouraged, and so the masters did not shrink from the complete recapitulation, which was already the rule by 1750" (p. 150).

22. See n. 6.

23. For another overview of past discussions of this structure, along with some additional citations of related terminology, see Laura Alyson McLamore, "Symphonic

Conventions in London's Concert Rooms, circa 1755–1790," diss. University of California, Los Angeles, 1991, pp. 274–76. McLamore also chronicles the waxing and waning use of this structure among several composers, including Hellendahl, Holzbauer, Beck, and others.

24. In this usage the term "binary" is meant to distinguish this structure from the full "ternary" design of sonata form proper. There are obvious problems involved with this, not the least of which is that in terms of historical origin and harmonic motion—whether defined by Koch or by Schenker—all sonatas (including full Type 3s) are "binary." This is an aspect of ambiguity within the term "binary" that we must acknowledge; still, the general sense intended here is clear enough. This issue has been thoroughly aired in the literature and (thankfully) need not be thrashed out again here. See, e.g., William S. Newman, *The Sonata in the Classic Era*, 2nd ed., pp. 143–47, and Leonard G. Ratner, *Classic Music*, pp. 220–21.

a single critical distinction—that between sonata form and expanded binary form. . . . This distinction is equivalent to the presence or absence, respectively, of the "double return" within the second part of the movement: the simultaneous return to the opening theme and to the tonic which constitutes and defines the beginning of the recapitulation in sonata form. . . . If the hypothesis stated above is correct, the growth of a feeling for the "double return," more than any other single variable, can stand for the rise of sonata form itself.[25]

Webster carried over the same conclusion into his *New Grove* entry on "Sonata Form" in both editions of that work.[26]

However one assesses such an eccentric claim, the precise terminology surrounding the Type 2 sonata form has differed, and it might prove helpful to sample some of it. In *The Sonata in the Classic Era* (1963, rev. 1972) William S. Newman used the term "complementary binary plan" to describe midcentury sonata-like structures that featured an "incomplete [tonic] return" of expositional materials in Part 2.[27] Rey M. Longyear devoted an article to the subject in 1969—one in part responding to separate repertory studies by Newman and by Roger Kamien—and referred to the pattern as the "binary sonata form."[28] In his 1980 *New Grove* article on Mozart Stanley Sadie avoided the term "sonata" when confronted with this structure: rather, the early symphonies of Mozart sometimes "follow the extended binary form preferred by J. C. Bach and many Italians."[29] The revision of the Mozart article in the 2001

second edition of *The New Grove*, by Cliff Eisen and Stanley Sadie, put it somewhat differently. In the early symphonies "the first movements are in expanded binary form, in common time, and have tempo indications of Allegro, Allegro molto or Allegro assai, while the second movements, also in binary form, are in 2/4 time and are marked Andante. . . . The first movement of K16 is an expanded binary form of a type more common among Viennese symphonies."[30] Similarly, in his 1979 study of *The Keyboard Sonatas of Joseph Haydn*, László Somfai noted as a "basic form" the "binary sonata form" ["sometimes called *Scarlatti sonata form*"], which in early Haydn "is articulated with a repeat sign after the first section. The second section starts with the primary theme in the second key. There is no double return, that is, no recapitulation of the first theme in the tonic."[31] The somewhat familiar term, "'Scarlatti' sonata form," also appeared in a brief discussion of the Type 2 design in Ratner's *Classic Music* of 1980.[32]

In Eugene K. Wolf's extensive description and analysis of some of the most prominent midcentury examples of this form in *The Symphonies of Johann Stamitz* (1981) this structure was identified as the "polythematic binary form, by far the most common type in Stamitz's quick movements, [which] frequently features thematic development in the first half of Part 2. In addition, it often accentuates in various ways a coordinated return of both *S* and the tonic key, contributing a tangible sense of recapitulation even though no primary material has recurred."[33] Five years later, in *The New Harvard*

25. Webster, "Binary Variants of Sonata Form in Early Haydn Instrumental Music," p. 127.
26. See our discussion of this "double return" issue also at the beginning of ch. 16, n. 2.
27. Newman, *The Sonata in the Classic Era*, pp. 145–46.
28. R. M. Longyear, "Binary Variants of Early Classic Sonata Form," *Journal of Music Theory* 13 (1969), 162–83. Roger Kamien's preceding work featured a survey of seventy sonatas published between 1742 and 1774, of whose first movements apparently 17 percent were in what Longyear calls "binary sonata form" (our Type 2). (Roger Kamien, "The Opening Sonata-Allegro Movements in a Randomly Selected Sample of Solo Keyboard Sonatas Published in the Years 1742–1774 (Inclusive)," Diss., Princeton University, 1964.)
29. Rpt. in Sadie, *The New Grove Mozart* (New York: Norton, 1983), p. 23.

30. Eisen and Sadie, "[Mozart] (Johann Chrysostom) Wolfgang Amadeus Mozart," *The New Grove Dictionary*, 17:295.
31. Somfai, *The Keyboard Sonatas of Joseph Haydn*, p. 191.
32. Ratner, *Classic Music*, p. 232.
33. Wolf, *The Symphonies of Johann Stamitz*, p. 139. See also n. 6 above. Cf. the slightly different connotation of the term "polythematic binary" in Jan LaRue, *Guidelines for Style Analysis*, 2nd ed. (Warren, Mich.: Harmonie Park Press, 1992), p. 188. LaRue's equivalent description for our Type 2 or Wolf's "polythematic binary form" is "early sonata form with incomplete recapitulation after a strongly differentiated exposition and fairly evolved development, a type commonly used by composers of the Mannheim School" (p. 189).

Dictionary of Music (1986), Wolf once again distinguished this structure from the more common "sonata form with a full recapitulation" (our Type 3): "By contrast, where the tradition was predominantly a binary one, as in the sonatas of Domenico Scarlatti and at Mannheim, the result was a "polythematic binary" or "binary sonata form" of the type outlined earlier, in which the recapitulation begins with the second theme."[34] In his *Sonata Forms* (1980, 1988) Charles Rosen did not take up the subject in any detail, although he did mention the practice of "recapitulation in the older style of the binary dance form, i.e., only of the second group," a form that he judged to have become "reactionary" by the late eighteenth century.[35]

The situation has been further complicated by modern scholarship's concern to distinguish between two related varieties of this "binary" (or Type 2) sonata. In the first the secondary theme (S) and closing theme (C) in Part 2 (our Rotation 2) is not followed by any clear, strong, or sustained allusion to the first theme (P). Here, as a consequence, Rotations 1 and 2 usually contain parallel or rhyming endings. In the second variety this rhyming effect is fully or partially subordinated by the recurrence of significant elements of P in the tonic at the end of the movement after the tonic-sounding of S (and of C as well, if closing material exists within the rotation). This latter possibility, familiar from the Mannheim symphonists, is what Webster again identified and exemplified

in his revised 2001 *New Grove* article as "that variant of rounded binary called 'mirror' form (occasionally described as a sonata form with 'reversed recapitulation'), in which the main theme returns at the end of the movement. . . . Mozart also occasionally used this form in the 1770s (Violin Sonata K306/300*l*)."[36] The term "mirror form" had also appeared in Newman's *Sonata in the Classic Era*: "One is less conscious of a return in the ternary sense when the final section reverses the order of themes, displaying what has been called the M–N–O–N–M or mirror form, as in [the Piano Sonata in D] K.V. 284c/i [K. 311] by Mozart."[37]

This implication of the apparent primacy of a "mirror-like" structure (as opposed, for example, to its arising in some works as, at best, a secondary effect—perhaps even a sonic illusion—generated by some other, more governing principle of organization) and the related notion of the "reversed recapitulation" pose the most significant conceptual problems within the subvarieties of Type 2 structures. We shall take them up as separate topics below. For now, we might only observe that mirror forms and reversed recapitulations have typically been adduced with the implication that they were merely another expressively neutral formal option within mid- and late-eighteenth-century practice.[38] Our view of such structures is different. On both historical and generic grounds we reject the twentieth-century concepts of mirror form and the reversed recapitulation. The

34. Wolf, "Sonata Form," *The New Harvard Dictionary of Music*, p. 766. Other writers have used the term "bipartite sonata form" for this structure. See, e.g., Eva Badura-Skoda, "Introduction," to *Carl Ditters von Dittersdorf (1739–1799): Six Symphonies . . .*, Series B, Vol. 1 of *The Symphony 1720–1840*, ed. Barry S. Brook (New York: Garland, 1985), p. xxxi. Referring to Dittersdorf's Symphony in E-flat (Them. Index E♭3), for instance, Badura-Skoda wrote: "The first movement, Italian in style . . . is again in a bipartite sonata form. . . . The 'development' starts with the main subject, which, on the other hand, is omitted in the rather short recapitulation."

35. Rosen, *Sonata Forms*, rev. ed. (New York: Norton, 1988), p. 144 and 145, in an overview of some keyboard sonatas of Rutini (1757) and Latrobe (1791). Cf. also Rosen's discussions of so-called reversed recapitulations: see n. 38 below.

36. Webster, "Sonata Form," *New Grove*, 2nd ed., 23:691.

37. Newman, *The Sonata in the Classic Era*, 2nd ed., p. 146.

38. As in Rosen, *Sonata Forms*, rev. ed., pp. 97, 286–87, 322–23. Rosen's claims, however, refer occasionally to pieces—such as the first movement of Mozart's Symphony No. 34 in C, K. 338—within which we would contend that that observation is misleading. In recent years, however, extravagant hermeneutic claims—seriously misinformed—have been made on behalf of this formal pattern not merely as "reversed" but as a *"tragic* reversed sonata form" (italics ours). See Timothy L. Jackson, "The Finale of Bruckner's Seventh Symphony and the Tragic Reversed Sonata Form," *Bruckner Studies*, ed. Timothy L. Jackson and Paul Hawkshaw (Cambridge: Cambridge University Press, 1997), pp. 140–208.

works commonly adduced as sonatas displaying these properties (such as the first movements of Mozart's Symphony "No. 5" in B-flat, K. 22, his Symphony "No. 20" in D, K. 133, his Violin Sonata in D, K. 306, or his Piano Sonata in D major, K. 311) are more accurately construed as expansions of Type 2 structures in which the late appearance of P often has the quality either of a coda to the second rotation or of a late, coda-rhetoric interpolation within its closing zone (C).

The Type 2 Sonata as a Constellation of Generic Options

While Type 1 structures are usually straightforward and easily recognizable, Type 2s present us with a wider range of possibilities. There are two reasons for this. First, their second rotations are open to varying treatments—developmental expansions, interpolations, episodic proxies for individual thematic elements, occasional reorderings of thematic modules, and the like. These things can make the underlying Type 2 pattern more challenging to recognize. Second, as mentioned above, the ends of second rotations frequently merge into either brief cadential material or more extended codas (often P-based and describable as "incipient third rotations"). And when the second complication is overlaid on the first, the situation calls for an exceptionally cautious application of historically grounded analytical principles.

Type 2 sonatas may be distinguished from other sonata types by the treatments of their second rotations. In other words, no first rotation (exposition) is by itself capable of predicting the sonata type of the movement at hand. The sonata type becomes clear only once we have passed into postexpositional material, and sometimes (as with the distinction between Type 2 and Type 3 sonatas) we must be well into it before this issue is clarified. Correspondingly, a composer's concern for the larger question of sonata type comes into play only after the final cadence of the exposition. This is the moment when deciding how to proceed becomes a structural and expressive issue. What is needed, therefore, is a laying-out of commonly encoun-

tered options, subvariants, complications, and exceptions within the second rotation of a Type 2 sonata form.

The End of the Exposition and the Beginning of Rotation 2: Two Options

In a Type 2 format the work's sonata-space consists of a double thematic rotation in which the first usually gives way immediately to the second. Only exceptionally will one find a brief transition between the two rotations proper. (One does occur in the finale of Mozart's String Quartet in G, K. 387, in which, after the expositional repeat sign, m. 125, an eighteen-bar transitional-link serves as an entry corridor to the beginning of Rotation 2 in m. 143.) As a general rule, leaving aside the issue of possible repeat signs, the end of the first rotation (the final cadence of the exposition) normally plunged into the rest of the sonata by relaunching $P^{1.1}$ material in a key other than the tonic.

The ways in which Rotation 1 may conclude merit special attention. The most common option (first-level default) was to end the exposition with a strong perfect authentic cadence (V:PAC or, in minor-mode sonatas, III:PAC or v:PAC) reinforced with a final caesura. This caesura could be marked with an explicit rest, as in Mozart's Symphony "No. 1" in E-flat, K. 16, first movement, m. 58; Mozart's Quartet in D, K. 155, second movement, Andante, m. 20; "Haydn's" Piano Sonata in A, Hob. XVI:5, first movement, m. 62; and J. C. Bach's Symphony in B-flat, op. 3 no. 4, first movement, m. 49. Even when a literal rest did not occur, the implicit caesura could be articulated at least with a decisive, closing cadence providing an unambiguous conceptual break from what follows, as happens in the F-major "Prussian" Sonata movement by C. P. E. Bach shown in example 17.2, m. 40, or in J. C. Bach's Sonata in B-flat, op. 5 no. 1, first movement, m. 34. The exposition may or may not be marked with repeat signs.

Alternatively, a composer could override the caesura-reinforced closure of the above procedure and select instead the second-level default for ending the first rotation. This strategy merged the final cadence of a nonrepeated Rotation 1 (either the EEC or the end of C-space,

EXAMPLE 17.3a   Mozart, Symphony "No 5" in B-flat, K. 22, i, mm. 1–9

depending on the circumstances) with the onset of Rotation 2, which was normally a treatment of P, the initial module of the rotational layout. This "run-on" procedure omitted the customary caesura-gap at the end of the exposition by an elision of the exposition's last PAC with the beginning of the developmental space. This final-caesura suppression seems to have been characteristic of middle and late Stamitz[39] (Symphony in E-flat, Wolf Eb-4, first movement, m. 28 = m. 1, now in the dominant) and of certain works of early Mozart. Example 17.3a–b shows the beginning of the exposition of the first movement of Mozart's Symphony "No. 5" in B-flat, K. 22 (beginning with a nine-bar Mozartian-presentational "loop"), along with Rotation 1's final bars (mm. 35–39, a repetition of C-material following an earlier EEC at m. 31) and the onset of the developmental space

(Rotation 2, beginning in m. 39) with P now sounded, normatively, in the dominant (mm. 39–47 = mm. 1–9, now in V).

Once again, a direct elision into the second rotation was available only within sonatas that also suppressed the expositional repeat. This is an important point. Unless the first-level default and less ambiguous exemplars with repeat signs are kept in mind (such as those found in the first movement of Mozart's E-flat symphony, K. 16), one can mistake the onset of a dovetailed, post-expositional Rotation 2—an otherwise normative developmental onset, with a sounding of P in V—for a final element of C that brings back P-material. Such a misreading, which would erroneously include that P within the expositional *Anlage*, immediately distorts the perspective needed to perceive the double-rotational aspect of the Type 2 sonata and leads to a misperception

---

39. The frequency of this "truncated or elided connection" in Stamitz was elaborated in a discussion by Wolf in *The Symphonies of Johann Stamitz*, p. 141. Wolf's surrounding point was that of suggesting that concerto influence—and in particular, ritornello construction—is not the deciding factor in the reappearance of P in this manner at this point. In general, Wolf argued that supposedly "ritornello" influences within Stamitz sym-

phonies seem to be, at best, minimal. This point, too, is a helpful corrective to another common misreading of certain kinds of sonata practice. Broadly considered, the term "ritornello," in any analytical context, is out of place in dealing with any portions of Types 1–4 sonatas. It is properly applicable only to certain sections of Type 5 sonata forms.

EXAMPLE 17.3b Mozart, Symphony "No 5" in B-flat, K. 22, i, mm. 35–47

[Allegro]

of the generic structure of the entire movement. It would also have to assume, mistakenly, that a near-literal restatement of P in the dominant—such as is found in K. 22/i, mm. 39–47—could normatively appear as the concluding element of a series of otherwise contrasting C-modules (perhaps as a C^2 or C^3), something that seems virtually never to be the case. (As pointed out in chapter 9, vigorous P-based C-ideas are more commonly sounded at the opening of C-space, not at its end. Moreover, as example 17.3 suggests, what is often heard in these Type 2 cases is less a potential P-based C than a literal, somewhat extensive restatement of P in V. This, too, would be non-normative within an exposition's C-space and would provide substantial reinforcement for the interpretation of this P as the beginning of Rotation 2, not the end of Rotation 1.) In short, this misreading, in part facilitated by the absence of the "corrective" indications of repeat signs, would misinterpret such a return of P as is found in K. 22/i, m. 39, as still belonging to expositional space.[40] Similarly, if the effect were to be replicated in the tonic at the movement's end, it would be misconstrued as existing in recapitulatory space. In those instances, as in the concluding bars of K. 22/i, mm. 89–98, what is actually occurring is the appearance of a P-based coda—a normative option for codas within all sonata types.

P-Based Openings to the Developmental Space

As discussed in chapter 10, in the eighteenth century the developmental space usually began with a nontonic reference to P, although this reference could be made in various ways. Type 2s are no different from Type 3s in this respect. The most direct of P-references would be a restatement of the opening measures of the rota-

tional pattern, normally describable as $P^{1.1}$, in the key in which the exposition had just ended: in V for a major-key sonata, or in III (less often, v) for a minor-key work. In some major-key instances the opening nontonic restatement of P-material within Type 2s—as was also the case in many Type 3 developments—is immediately restated down a fifth, that is, on the tonic-level, before proceeding to development proper. (The once-common, though inaccurate, term for this much-discussed tonic possibility within developments, "premature reprise," should of course be avoided here, just as it is in Type 3 developments.)[41]

When it occurred, this bar-for-bar, nontonic statement of the opening of P—assuming here the simpler case of a single P-reference, not a sequenced one—typically lasted only a few measures before merging into a freer development, as happens in the Type 2 first movement of J. C. Bach's Symphony in B-flat, op. 3 no. 4, and the finale of Mozart's Symphony "No. 11" in D, K. 84. A second way was to begin the second rotation not with a literal restatement but directly with a nontonic developmental variant of P-material. One example may be found in Mozart's Piano Sonata in E-flat, K. 282, a Type 2 sonata in Adagio tempo, where in m. 16 the original version of P proper is suppressed, and the second rotation begins with a troubled, clouded allusion to P. Still another option—at least within extended P-complexes whose contrasting modules may be identified as $P^{1.1}$, $P^{1.2}$, $P^{1.3}$, and so on—was to begin the second rotation not with $P^{1.1}$ but with one of the later modules. Found in Stamitz and others, this strategy suppressed an initial module (or two), sometimes reserving the right to restore it later as the onset of a coda-rotation.

Our focus here, though, is on the more ge-

---

40. Here a similar matter regarding binary movements lacking an interior repeat sign was brought up by Wolf, *The Symphonies of Johann Stamitz*, p. 141. Wolf cited a passage from Joseph Riepel's *Tonordnung* (1755, pp. 69–70) in which Riepel underscores that the presence or lack of a repeat sign does not alter the basic structure of a binary movement. "Riepel prints a symphonic first movement without repeats, yet at the letter *P* labels the return of the primary theme in the dominant 'Anfang des zweyten Theils' (p. 69). The remainder of the move-

ment shows it to be in an asymmetrical binary form. . . . [Writes Riepel:] 'At *P* I have written *Beginning of the Second Part*; for there could have appeared at that point a major repetition with a :||: sign. But I have noticed that this repetition is used only very rarely these days. It [the repetition] may perhaps show a composer's poverty of ideas.'" Wolf noted additionally that it is Stamitz's middle and late symphonies that are most likely to lack repeat signs, not the earlier ones.

41. Cf. the discussion in ch. 10, n. 14.

nerically normative *P-incipit-launch* option: a literal P[1.1] in V or another nontonic key. (Recall that an initial recurrence of P in the tonic key would trigger the expectation of a Type 1 sonata.) The mere presence of this option by no means marks a sonata as belonging to the Type 2 category, since the more frequent Type 3 sonata-practice also includes this possibility as one of its most common choices. Since by the mid- and late-eighteenth century (and certainly later as well) Type 3s were more commonly encountered than Type 2s, the most reasonable assumption for listeners to have made as this type of postexpositional material proceeded would be that they were in the midst of a Type 3 discourse. Within the implied generic rules of the game, if the postexpositional material continued more or less in rotational order (P–TR), a conceptual conversion into a Type 2 sonata was always possible at or around the S-point. On the other hand, any deviations from rotational order within the initial sections of developmental-space material decreased the clarity and relevance of the rotational principle, and with it, the possibility that the listener would continue to consider the Type 2 option—grounded in the perception of rotational practice—to be still viable. Put another way, nonrotational developments seem, *ipso facto*, to be a sign of canceling the Type 2 option, which is so reliant on the concept of a double-rotational structure. Encountering one would only reinforce the conviction that one is dealing with a Type 3 sonata.

In cases in which the exposition-pattern's P-zone is brief—perhaps only a phrase or two—the recycled theme at the opening of Rotation 2 may be sounded in full and proceed directly into a development of P- or TR-material. In this situation the whole P-theme (and sometimes the incipit of the transition as well) can be cited verbatim—or nearly so—before veering into freer thematic elaboration. This means also that the developmental space can take its initial bearings from a complete or nearly complete restatement of P before proceeding to more recognizably developmental or modulatory textures proper. This is what happens in K. 22/i (example 17.3b). Another illustration may be found in the initial movement of the Symphony in E-flat, K. 16 (this time, with expositional repeats). Sometimes the near-verbatim statement can proceed into a few measure of TR. This situation sometimes arises in the works of J. C. Bach, whose relatively unelaborated sonata structures often feature short P-themes, as happens in the first movement of the Sonata in B-flat, op. 5 no. 1. Here the closed P-theme proper occupies mm. 1–8 (interpretable as a two-loop presentation), eliding its local, concluding PAC-effect into a TR-continuation of the dissolving-continuation variety, mm. 8–14. Rotation 2 begins with a full sounding of P in F major (rhetorically, mm. 35–42 = m. 1–8), and the first five measures of TR (mm. 42–46, with a slight variant in the last sixteenth note of m. 46) are transposed directly from mm. 8–12. At this point the music departs from the expositional pattern to steer into quasi-episodic elaboration, moving through the expected minor keys (G minor and C minor), and so on.

A second-level default for the opening of Rotation 2 was the presentation of P-material—either literal or developmental—shifting away at once from the key in which the exposition had ended. Here the P-grounded music sets out in a key other than V (for major-mode sonatas) or III or v (for minor-mode ones). This option is found in the Type 2 first movement of Mozart's Symphony "No. 6" in F, K. 43, in which the development (m. 50) begins with TR textures (based on P) suddenly presented on an A-chord, which immediately serves as V of D minor (V of vi). So long as the P- or TR-derived material is not sounded in the tonic, which would suggest a Type 1 structure, we may consider the result to be the launching of a normative developmental space, characteristic of both Type 2 and Type 3 sonatas.

Episodic Openings to the Developmental Space

A third-level default within the Type 2 format was to override the normal P-related launch with more or less new, "episodic" material—in effect, to blank it out with differing music that we are invited to understand as standing in structurally for P. This procedure seems to have been less common in the mid-eighteenth century, but it did occur in several works of Mozart. One of the clearest illustrations occurs in the A-major Andante of the Quartet in D, K. 155. Example 17.4a shows the first eight bars of the movement, a single sentence leading to a half cadence that serves as a I:HC MC at the end of m. 8. (Mm. 1–8 constitute a P⇒TR merger with the TR portion, the sentence's continuation, beginning in m. 5.) Example 17.4b provides the beginning of the modestly sized developmental space and ensuing bars (mm. 21–32). Here the normative P proper, the presentation-idea from mm. 1–4, is suppressed for the first eight bars of the postexpositional space, although the sequential (and sentential) mini-"episode" that replaces it is clearly related to P—as if the "silent" four-bar P in generic expectation were pressing into the eight-bar fabric of the episodic substitute, which is efficiently brought to V of the tonic A minor in m. 28. M. 29 is a crux-point: mm. 29–32 recover and retrack the TR materials from the exposition (mm. 29–32 = mm. 5–8, here at the same pitch level), thereby producing the same I:HC MC—which is then followed by the tonal resolution (the original S now in I). Strictly considered, this brief developmental space occupies only mm. 21–28.

What is crucial to recognize here is that a more straightforward Type 2 second rotation would have presented its modular materials in the order, P TR ' S. In this case, beginning "developmentally" in m. 21 and extending past the MC (m. 32) into the tonal resolution through the end of S in m. 44, what we have is the exposition's materials in the order, X TR ' S. Thus the P-alluding, modulatory X (mm. 21–28) substitutes for the more standard statement of P. Apart from this, all of the other elements of the rotation are in place and presented in order. Only the first, P, has been erased or written over by something else. (The procedure and its related interpretive problem recall those of the typical Scarlatti-sonata binary structure, ||: A¹ + B² : ||: C + B¹ :||, discussed above.)

In these cases the background or conceptual double-rotational aspect from m. 21 onward remains implicit, even though a literal restatement of P has been suppressed at the onset of Rotation 2. (A more extended discussion of writing over within developments was presented in chapter 10.) K. 155/ii has one final complication that needs to be addressed here. As if by way of compensation, Mozart converted the end of Rotation 2, m. 44, into an I:IAC, not a I:PAC, and appended six bars of coda at the end—the first four of which restore the "missing" P—finally achieving a I:PAC and articulating a delayed ESC in the final bar, m. 50. The last six bars thus bring back the "lost" P, mm. 1–4, only after the last bar of the second rotation has been sounded. This is a common occurrence in mid- and later-Mozartian Type 2 practice. As the rotational principle makes clear, these six measures are in coda-space (post-tonal-resolution space), not in recapitulatory space. (Returning to P is a sign of beginning a new rotation, not ending one.) We find this especially persuasive when coupled with the awareness that some Type 2s in early Mozart that suppress a literal P at the onset of the developmental space do not restore it at the end, after the completion of the last module of Rotation 2. This situation will be dealt with further below.

Another clear instance of a developmental space beginning with a writing-over of the expected, more literal allusion to P occurs in the first movement of the Violin Sonata in D, K. 306. Here an eight-measure episode, mm. 75–82 (whose bass may have been derived from that of P), is introduced after the expositional repeat sign and is followed immediately in m. 83 by a development of the rotationally "proper" TR material (based motivically on P).[42] In such a clear case (provided that a sufficient number of later elements of Rotation 2 remain intact to render the resultant large-scale pattern recognizable as a rotation—as happens in K. 306) we may speak of a substitution or proxy for a generically expected individual element of the pattern. But if such proxies multiply as Rotation 2 proceeds, it becomes more difficult to perceive the rotational nature of the whole. At

---

42. In this case the suppression of P at the outset of Rotation 2 is compensated for toward the end of the movement, when the head motive of P returns in m.

158 as the onset of a stretch of coda-rhetoric interpolation (CRI).

EXAMPLE 17.4a   Mozart, String Quartet in D, K. 155, ii, mm. 1–8

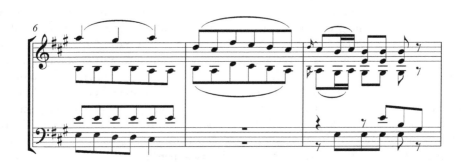

EXAMPLE 17.4b   Mozart, String Quartet in D, K. 155, ii, mm. 21–32

some point, that sense disappears altogether, and it is more difficult to speak convincingly of the presence of a rotation.

S- or C-Based Openings to the Developmental Space: Type 3⇒Type 2 Conversions

Related to this third-level, "P-substitute" default was the overriding of an expected element (such as the P-related launch) with a thematic or motivic element taken from the S or C zones (the markers of rotational endings, not beginnings), which are then immediately treated developmentally. This option probably belongs more to a theory of Type 2 structural deformation than to a theory of standard practice. Such a procedure flouts the notion of rotation, which is conceptually linked with recurrences of a more or less fixed thematic ordering. To begin postexpositional work by developing aspects of

S or C would seem to be a declaration that rotational principles were being abandoned for the development. And abandoned with them, by extension, would be the Type 2 option, which is grounded in these principles.

And yet, once thus audibly "thrown away" as an option, a non-normative Type 2 sonata deformation could apparently be recuperated by simple *fiat*. This appears to be the case in the curiously asymmetrical—and exceptional—first movement of Mozart's Symphony "No. 4" in D, K. 19, whose exposition manages to occupy substantially more than half of the movement. Even stranger, neither P nor TR are heard again after the nonrepeated exposition (mm. 1–46). The development (syncopated upbeat to m. 47) instantly veers into modulatory regions on S-based material (m. 49, for instance, is related to S⁰, m. 21), and no significant P or TR modules are presented at all. Under these nonrotational circumstances, one would assume that the Type 2 option is nowhere in sight—that Mozart is obviously in the midst of a Type 3 sonata with an S-based development, and that a return to a tonic P and a recapitulatory rotation will soon ensue. The surprise, however, is that this development soon leads to a crux-I:HC:MC-effect in m. 59 (= the MC in m. 20) followed not by P but by the tonal resolution only, a slightly recomposed S- and C-space in the tonic. Moreover, the movement provides no compensatory coda to restore the "lost" P. The movement ends in a manner parallel to the end of exposition—with no added coda at all. As will be revisited later, K. 19/i, along with the first movement of the Symphony "No. 6" in F, K. 43, demonstrates that at this time there was still no generic requirement to restore in an appended coda a P that is "missing" in postexpositional space.

One way to grasp the unusual structure of K. 19/i is to suppose that, for reasons of high play, young Mozart presented us impishly with generic signals that would be workable only within Type 3 sonatas (the presentation of a nonrotational development) and then staged the music as impulsively "changing its mind" at the MC-effect and tonic-S-launch point (mm. 59–60). What we had assumed *en route* was a Type 3 sonata is suddenly yanked into Type 2 status. More precisely, this sonata form ends in the manner of a Type 2, with a tonal resolution only (S and C), not a recapitulation beginning with P, even though the literal Type 2 status of the result is not fully realized, since the development proper cannot reasonably be construed as contributing to the first half of an ongoing second rotation. (It would be difficult to make a case that the normative P in the development was being written over *in toto* by S-based modules.)

This example demonstrates the possibility of a conceptual interplay between two different sonata types—a wrenching of expectations as the listener shifts from those of the one model to those of the other. For a composer to invite us to predict the proportions of a Type 3 sonata by means of nonrotational developmental

activity—preparing us for the Type 3 temporal breadth that the rest of the piece is likely to occupy—only to compress that remainder into a Type 2 format (as in K. 19/i) results in a dramatic collapse of anticipated sonata-space, a substantial foreshortening of the expected latter portion of a work. Mozart revisited the "K. 19" conversion-effect (in which a predicted Type 3 shifts into a Type 2) in the much-discussed Piano Sonata in D, K. 311, whose development begins with continued reiterations of the module that had ended the exposition, C^2. An equally "extreme" example from Haydn may be found in the second movement, Presto, of the Symphony No. 21 in A. Here the development is dominated by a treatment of the TR-based S. The subsequent tonal resolution, led into with the related TR-module-crux at m. 66 (= m. 10) is thoroughly overhauled to "omit" this version of that S-module.

Type 3⇒Type 2 conversions are not restricted only to pieces that feature nonrotational developmental spaces, such as those just discussed. Related cases occur where developments that start out as P-based "go past" the P- and TR-zones to refer, however briefly, to a module of S or C. This would render the development, or at least a portion of it, fully rotational. This situation also seems to rule out the expectation of a normative Type 2 continuation, since that option usually reserves the second-rotation S and C for the tonal resolution and its correspondence measures. But if what follows the developmental rotation rejoins the expositional pattern at a post-$P^{1.1}$ idea that is earlier in the rotation than the last one already heard in the development—probably at a TR- or S-module, thus providing only a tonal resolution, not a recapitulation—we would seem once again to have a Type 3⇒Type 2 conversion. This arrangement of events may be found, together with a few additional complications, in the finale of Haydn's Symphony No. 21 in A and in the earlier, D-major slow movement of Symphony No. 14 in A.[43]

The reverse effect could also occur, in which

---

43. As is clear from the discussion, we currently regard all of the above situations as Type 3⇒Type 2 hybrids, in which a seemingly Type 3 development, not a Type

2 one (by definition), leads only to a tonal resolution, not to a full recapitulation. These are instances where the Type 2 tonal resolution is present (a "full recapitula-

Type 2 signals, following a seemingly obvious crux point within Rotation 2 (a Type 2 convention discussed below), disintegrate in favor of a P-based recapitulation. This produces a sense of sudden spatial extension: a predicted Type 2 is made to change its course to convert into a grander, broader Type 3 sonata. Such an effect plays a central role in the first movement of the Symphony No. 38 in D, K. 504, "Prague," in which a mid-developmental joining of TR modules in the tonic (a crux, mm. 177–89-mm. 59–71) initially suggest that the piece will proceed as a Type 2 sonata form, only to see it fall apart at the "first MC" point (m. 189) in order to turn into a Type 3 sonata with recapitulation beginning with P (m. 208). (Even more rarefied are the extremely uncommon instances in which one or more of an exposition's S-materials appear briefly in the tonic—something of a "false tonal resolution"—in what then turns out to be the center of the developmental space of a Type 3 sonata.)[44]

Developmental Activity Proper

Following the P-material-launch (or that of its proxy), we expect to find a freeing of the thematic rhetoric into more recognizable developmental processes. This occurs at the point at which the second rotation's P- or P-TR-material is no longer mappable as correspondence measures onto that of the first's. All of this is similar to the common developmental practice discussed in chapter 10, which need not be repeated here. The length of the development in a Type 2 sonata is not predictable. In some cases it is quite short (as in K. 155/ii, example 17.4b—if that passage may be regarded as developmental at all); in others, particularly later in the century, it is remarkably extended. The composer's choice in this matter bears on the larger question of how much time the sonata is striving to span. Lengthier developments need to be as-

sessed according to the proportions predicted in the exposition.

The strong first-level default is for a Type 2 development to be based on elements of P or TR—that is, on elements from only part 1 of the exposition—in order to preserve the diachronic unfolding of the rotational pattern. The development may also mix materials from P and TR in an unpredictable order, as though one were free to reassemble the part-1 modules within a generalized developmental space that still may be understood as preserving the larger rotational ordering. This emphasis on P or TR modules is usually what one finds in Type 2 sonatas, although relatively new episodes or thematic digressions may also be encountered. Conversely, within this developmental portion of Rotation 2—whether literally developmental or quasi-episodic—one would normally expect no elements of S or C (part 2) to intrude. When they do, we would be dealing with an exceptional procedure (an expressive deformation) that would call for a special explanation. Such an exception occurs in the Type 2 first movement of J. C. Bach's Sonata in G, op. 5 no. 3, into whose development an element of C-texture—identifiable as C^2 from m. 31—is introduced and expanded, mm. 57–62.

Another unusual deformation, already discussed in a different context in chapter 10, may be found in Mozart's three-movement Symphony No. 32 in G, K. 318, the entirety of which articulates a Type 2 sonata. The first movement proceeds into a largely P-based development, which is interrupted by an unrelated slow movement. The finale begins with a retransitional link and preparation for the tonal resolution (not for a full recapitulation)—the sounding of the original S and C in the tonic. As a whole, K. 318 merges the episodic variant of the Type 2 sonata with what has been called the *da capo symphony* or *reprise overture*.

---

tion" is lacking) but the span from the onset of the development through the end of the tonal resolution does not constitute a single, clear rotation. It may also be, however, that these Type 3⇒Type 2 hybrids constitute what others might regard as a separate, "early" sonata type found in some midcentury works. See also the dis-

cussion at the end of this chapter, "Confronting Hard Cases: Flexibility in Sonata-Type Recognition."

44. For a discussion of this atypical situation see Hepokoski, "Beyond the Sonata Principle," pp. 130–39, which also locates an exceptional example in the first movement of Haydn's Quartet in B-flat, op. 64 no. 3.

The Crux

After a span of development, the music will (sometimes almost imperceptibly) lock onto some middle portion of the expositional pattern on a bar-by-bar basis either at the original pitch level or transposed to an appropriate key to lead to or produce the tonal resolution. These correspondence measures are then pursued, for the most part, for the rest of the rotation. As outlined in chapter 11, and adapting the terminology devised by Ralph Kirkpatrick for Scarlatti sonatas, we call this moment the *crux*.[45] Within a Type 2 sonata, by definition, the expositional pattern was never rejoined here at its opening point, $P^{1.1}$.[46] If it were, it would be an example of a Type 3 sonata—with a full recapitulation. In a Type 2 sonata the crux must occur at some later, post-$P^{1.1}$ point in the thematic pattern, a point that also serves to maintain the rotational ordering.

The moment that a development based on P- or TR-modules or on an appropriate episodic proxy (a writing-over) establishes a crux-event on a subsequent module of the rotational pattern is the moment when the Type 2 intentions of the sonata form are declared. This can happen, for example, at $P^{1.2}$, at $TR^{1.1}$, at TR^2, at the MC, or even at the S-point. As we process the moment-to-moment events of the piece, we notice that the crux-event occurs instead of any Type-3-identifying "recapitulatory" tonic arrival of $P^{1.1}$ and thereby declares that we are no longer to expect that arrival at all. As a result, this is the point at which the composer invites us to understand that the Type 3 option (signaled by the appearance of that $P^{1.1}$ return) is being discarded in favor of the more compact, double-rotational alternative of the Type 2 sonata. With the attainment of a Type 2 crux, we are to abandon the expectation of a $P^{1.1}$-launched recapitulation.

Since we have dealt with issues surrounding the crux in chapter 11—differing transposition levels, the possibility of a double crux, and so on—these matters will not be revisited here. In most cases, locating the crux in a Type 2 sonata is unproblematic. It usually occurs near the center of Rotation 2, at or shortly before the medial caesura that opens the path to S and the tonal resolution. In this case, the P and/or TR modules are given over entirely, or nearly so, to development. Still, it is impossible to predict where the crux will be situated. In unusual circumstances and for special expressive purposes, it may occur relatively early in the expositional pattern, with, say, $P^{1.2}$. The *locus classicus* of this occurs in the finale of Mozart's Quartet in G, K. 387, with "early" $P^{1.2}$ crux at m. 175 (= m. 17, now in the subdominant), although this seems to have been an infrequently selected option.[47]

In sonatas whose expositions had featured a I:HC MC, the crux is likely to be sounded in the original tonic, not in IV. To the extent that a prolonged $P^{1.2}$ or TR module is sounded in the tonic (following an "early" crux) and is followed by correspondence measures only slightly adjusted to lead to the proper S-resolution, that whole tonic-based section approaches a Type 3 "recapitulation" (which would normally begin with $P^{1.1}$).[48] In other words, the further back the crux is pushed, the more that the Type 2 sonata begins to take on the attributes of a Type 3. In such situations—"recapitulations" beginning with the second or third module of the P-pattern (an occasionally encountered occurrence in mid-eighteenth century sonata forms)—one might be tempted to speak of a "mixed" sonata type, or a type existing on a continuum somewhere between Types 2 and 3. Additionally, to what extent these considerations might implicate recapitulations that omit P proper to

---

45. Cf. n. 2.

46. See, however, the complications and ambiguities raised in ch. 12 dealing with Type 3 variants: recapitulatory rotations that begin in nontonic keys, especially in those beginning in IV.

47. Perhaps related to it, though, are the cases described in Rosen, *Sonata Forms*, rev. ed., p. 157. Cf. also, e.g., Rosen's discussion of C. P. E. Bach's Sonata in F-sharp minor [1763] on pp. 285–86.

48. Again: the standard alternative for an early tonic-crux would be to sound $P^{1.2}$ in the *subdominant*. Here one needs to recall that within Type 3 sonatas beginning a recapitulation in IV was always an option, albeit not a frequently chosen one. See the relevant discussion in ch. 12, which again brings up the K. 387/iv issue.

begin with (P-based) TR material—a feature of recapitulatory compression—is a vexed question that admits of no easy solution, and we shall not address it here.

The most common Type 2 crux-strategy, however, was less problematic: to rejoin the pattern at a point midway through the transition, perhaps around $TR^{1.2}$ or $TR^{1.3}$. It was also possible to delay the crux until or immediately after the medial caesura. In this case the development presents a recomposition of P–TR and proceeds to the medial caesura in a manner that is not a direct restatement of the corresponding zone of the expositional pattern. When this happens, the crux is usually attained with the tonic onset of S, the launch of the tonal resolution. This occurs, for instance, in J. C. Bach's Sonata in B-flat, op. 5 no. 1, first movement, m. 63 (= m. 15).

In extreme cases—apparently rare—a composer could begin to engage S-material (or its equivalent in a continuous exposition) outside of the tonic, without a sense of tonic-key crux, regaining the crux-effect of correspondence measures only later in the composition, perhaps around the area of the ESC. Here an easily consulted example is the exceptional Type 2 finale of Mozart's Symphony "No. 6" in F, K. 43. Following the repeated, unproblematic exposition (mm. 1–47), the remainder of the finale unfolds as an obvious second rotation. The P-based development, however, leads to the "wrong" MC, on V of D minor (V/vi) at m. 67, whose triplets recall that of the exposition's I:HC MC at m. 16. This is a crux on the wrong tonal level, and the sentential S sounds its presentation modules, $S^{1.1}$, for eight measures on that nontonic D minor, mm. 68–75 (= mm. 17–24). As if registering the "comically tragic" impossibility of the situation, Mozart now interpolates twelve bars wrenching the music into the proper F major (mm. 76–87), and the S-continuation at m. 88 ($S^{1.2}$), finally a tonally proper crux (= m. 25), proceeds with the appropriate correspondence measures in the tonic, to the ESC (m. 95 = m. 32) and beyond, into closing material. A somewhat similar instance of a "wrong-key" crux may be found in the G-major slow movement, Adagio, of Haydn's Symphony No. 24 in D (brief first crux, m. 36 = m. 14 [$S^{1.1}$], only now

in vi, leading a vi:PAC in m. 41, tonally corrected in the next several measures and leading to a second crux, m. 45 = m. 18 [$S^{1.2}$]).

The Tonal Resolution (S+C)

Normatively, at this point the second rotation's tonic-oriented S- and C-material would now retrack, bar-for-bar, the analogous music of Rotation 1, and this is very often the case. As is also true within the other sonata types, this principle of mere transposition and correspondence measures is not inflexible. Slight variants, occasional reorderings of modules, and expansions or compressions were always possible. However these S and C themes might be varied, they still give the effect of being correspondence or referential measures. To this section of tonal resolution is given the task of articulating essential structural closure (the ESC) and, usually, the task of following this with rhetorical, postcadential confirmation.

As elaborated at the beginning of this chapter, in a Type 2 sonata the tonal resolution normally does indeed "recapitulate" (restate and resolve tonally) the S+C portion of the exposition, but it is a conceptual error to think of it as the start of any sort of "recapitulation." Rather, it is the continuation of a rotationally ordered series of events—P TR ' S / C—that had begun in the developmental space. The S-event is an action that occurs midway through the governing rotational pattern at hand. From that perspective there is no sense of large-sectional structural rebeginning at the onset of the tonal resolution. The real structural rebeginning or recycling had already occurred with Rotation 2's P-material launch (or that of its proxy). To posit the existence of a rebeginning or "recapitulation" at this S-point is conceptually to erase the fundamental rhetorical principle guiding the double-rotational structure as a whole—thus missing the expressive and architectural point of the Type 2 sonata.

The "Recapitulation" Question and Tonal Resolutions in Continuous Second Rotations

One reason that it has been tempting to misconstrue the onset of the tonic S as the beginning of a "recapitulation" in Type 2 or "binary" sonata forms is that in any two-part exposition or recapitulation (that is, one with a medial caesura) S articulates a structural relaunch halfway through the rotation. Something does indeed "begin" with S: a highlighted second part of the rotation. But this is not the impression given by sonata forms with continuous expositions—those lacking a medial caesura and an S-theme. As a result, Type 2s with continuous expositions demonstrate even more clearly why positing a supposed "recapitulation" in the center of Rotation 2 is conceptually shaky. If the sonata's second rotation—development plus tonal resolution—is also continuous, it will provide no mid-rotation break and relaunch on which to hang the term "recapitulation." Instead, one will experience only a P-based development, a merger into TR, a point of crux somewhere in the central expansion section, a continuation of all of this with the normative TR⇒FS conversion (chapter 4), and, eventually, a drive to the ESC and whatever C-space might follow. There is no point in the central *Fortspinnung* that might reasonably be isolated as the take-off point of any supposed "recapitulation."

A perfect example of such a movement may be consulted in the Type 2 finale of Haydn's Symphony No. 44 in E Minor, "Trauer," which also contains the characteristic complication of a substantially recomposed latter portion of Rotation 2, along with a P-based coda.[49] But if Type 2 sonata forms with continuous recapitulations such as that in the "Trauer" finale cannot be processed as having a point of "recapitulation" in the center of their second rotations, why should we be eager to grant the existence of such a point in two-part expositions? Rather than trying to devise dodges around this substantial problem, it makes more sense to realize that the term "recapitulation" is inappropriate also at S-points in two-part second rotations.

Type 2 Sonata Forms without Codas

Once Rotation 2 has completed its cycle, the piece may be over. In such cases—the most elementary instances—the sonata has no coda. In this familiar option the end of the piece rhymes with the end of Rotation 1 after a prolonged set of correspondence measures, a situation by no means infrequent in the mid-eighteenth century. The coda-free Type 2 is common, for instance, in the Allegro movements of J. C. Bach, occurring in two of the three Type 2 first movements of the six op. 3 symphonies, neither of which, as it happens, calls for block-repetitions of the rotations—Nos. 5 in F and 6 in G—and in all of the three Type 2 first movements in the six op. 5 Keyboard Sonatas—Nos. 1 in B-flat, 3 in G, and 5 in E. One also finds this simpler procedure in some of the early Mozart symphonies, such as in the first movements of "No. 1" in E-flat, K. 16 (with each rotation repeated), "No. 4" in D, K. 19 (with no repeats indicated),[50] and "No. 6" in F, K. 43 (with each rotation repeated). The basic structure without coda also seems to be the historically earliest kind of Type 2 sonata form, with roots in such pieces as the keyboard sonatas of Domenico Scarlatti and the "Prussian" sonatas of C. P. E. Bach. (See example 17.2 and the surrounding discussion.)

It is this coda-free format for Type 2, the simplest version of the generic norm, that should be kept in mind as one confronts varieties with additions and interpolations. In standard mid-eighteenth-century practice once the end of the second rotation had been reached—the conclusion of the S + C area, the moment parallel to the ending of the first (expositional) rotation—there was no generic obligation to add anything further to the composition. This is the case regardless of whether P or a P-variant had launched Rotation 2 or whether the normative P had been suppressed in favor of a modular

---

49. Another instructive instance occurs in the first movement of Vanhal's Symphony in F [F3, c. 1768–71). In this case, however, the continuous exposition is not of the expansion-section subtype but rather of the "second" or alternative type, that with an early V:PAC followed by repetitions of the cadence. Nonetheless, such a structure poses the same questions to the analyst as does Haydn's "Trauer" finale.

50. In K. 19 the single-chord end of Rotation 1, m. 46—immediately undermined by a syncopated "episode" launching the second rotation—is slightly expanded to a more typical triple hammerstroke at the end of Rotation 2, m. 78

proxy or other non-P idea (as in the coda-less Type 2 first movements of Mozart's K. 19 and K. 43). From the standpoint of midcentury generic practice, at least, there was no widely shared, compelling urge to shore up any "missing" P in the second rotation with a P-based coda. The issue of whether or not a coda is appended to the second rotation (following the tonal resolution) is also a conceptually separate matter both from the issue of internal repetitions and from the manner in which the exposition yields to the onset of Rotation 2, the developmental space.

Type 2 Sonata Forms with P-Based Codas and the "Reversed Recapitulation" Fallacy

From time to time—and increasingly after the 1760s, as a first-level default—major composers chose to append elaborations or coda-extensions of differing sorts and lengths onto the end of Rotation 2. The coda typically extends beyond the final bar of Rotation 2 (and the sonata proper) into postsonata-space. Another option was to provide not a literal coda but a coda rhetoric interpolation (CRI), wedged in before the final module of Rotation 2 proper. (The CRI alternative in general is discussed in chapter 13. It also occupies a space that is not part of the sonata form proper, although by definition it is inserted before the full completion of the tonal resolution.) None of these parageneric additions jeopardized the essential Type 2 structure, but each provided a more emphatic or rounded ending. Sometimes this took the shape merely of a more elaborated final cadence that was scarcely coda-like at all, as in the transformation of the final correspondence measure into two bars found in the first movement of J. C. Bach's Symphony in B-flat, op. 3 no. 4, a movement that is otherwise a straightforward, double-rotational Type 2 sonata.

An unassuming final-cadence enhancement could be expanded by degrees into something more substantial. A significant step in this process may be observed in the finale of Mozart's Symphony "No. 11" in D, K. 84, a brisk,

efficient Allegro in 2/4. At the movement's end we find an appended four bars after the last correspondence measure of the tonal resolution. Those four bars recapture the initial gesture of the finale: a perfunctory march up and down the tonic arpeggio in octaves. (In the exposition, mm. 1–4, this module had functioned as the first half of an eight-bar antecedent.) Here we find perhaps the most modest instance of a P-related coda rather than a mere cadential expansion. Redeploying the P-incipit at this point was no surprise. The principle of rotation suggests that what follows the close of the C-zone should be the reopening of the P-zone and the implied onset of a new cycle. This produces the common situation of a coda that begins as an incipient rotation (in this case, an incipient third rotation). In the K. 84/iii coda, though, the postsonata rotation is cut short after only four bars.

Codas that begin rotationally (with P-material) are common occurrences in all of the sonata types as a first-level default for coda treatment. (See chapter 13.) This is worth underscoring. As Charles Rosen put it, "Ending a symphony or sonata with the first theme *forte* was too common a practice for me to cite examples: if the reader cannot remember any, he can amuse himself by looking—he will find them with ease."[51] It is not reasonable to claim that when such a tonic P-restoration occurs in a Type 3 sonata it is self-evidently a coda, while when it is found in a Type 2 sonata it is to be considered part of a presumed "reversed recapitulation." Recall again that the "reversed-recapitulation" misunderstanding relies on the unfounded premise that a supposed recapitulation had in fact begun at the tonic-S-point. This claim rides roughshod over the actually governing double rotation. References to P in the tonic at the ends of Type 2 sonatas are more accurately understood as codas existing in an extra space beyond the sonata form proper.

As it happens, one may appeal to evidence beyond generic reconstruction to fortify this claim. In the first movement of Mozart's Piano

---

51. Rosen, *Sonata Forms*, rev. ed., p. 97. Rosen's accurate remark is followed, however, by a reinscribing of the classic "reversed recapitulation" fallacy for Type 2 sonatas. See n. 59 below.

Sonata in E-flat, K. 282, an Adagio, each of the two rotations is provided with a repeat sign. Once past the repetition of the second rotation (development and tonal resolution, ending in m. 33) the sonata proper is over, but Mozart appended three extra bars (mm. 34–36) whose initial five beats provide an only slightly varied recapturing of the opening of P in the tonic—a return to an eloquent version of P that had not been heard in that manner since m. 1. Above m. 34 Mozart wrote the word "Coda," thus clarifying how he was thinking of such P-returns.[52] (Supporting evidence along these lines may also be drawn from the arrangement of text-blocks in such vocal works as the Type 2 Quartet from the third act of *Idomeneo*, K. 366.)[53] In the case of K. 282/i it is likely that because of the repeat-sign interventions in the text, few analysts today would suggest that this return of the P-incipit in the tonic is the tail-end of a "reversed recapitulation." Still, as we have seen, the repeat structure of a movement has no necessary relationship with its Type 2 or Type 3 structure. Mozart might just as readily have elected to omit the repeats to provide a briefer Type 2 format. Had he done so—and had he not written "Coda" above m. 34—one might expect that inaccurate analytical observations would have

been made about this movement's "reversed recapitulation."

Needless to say, even a fleeting return to or paraphrase of a version of P that had been unsounded since the repeat of m. 1 can have a poetic effect—the recovery of the original launching-impulse for the sonata process, nothing less than the *Hauptgedanke*. Nevertheless, that is no reason to include the add-on coda-statement of P within sonata-space. (This line of reasoning, it appears, is also defensible within much later, mid- or late-nineteenth-century Type 2 sonatas.)[54] In rejecting the concept of the reversed recapitulation—along with any claims of mirror form as a primary formal construct—we also align ourselves with Wolf's general position in 1981 on this matter with regard to the Allegro movements of Stamitz's symphonies, whose multimodular designs and second-rotation reorderings often render the simplistic notion of a mere thematic reversal indefensible: "There seems little doubt that the idea of mirror [or reversed] recapitulation stems in this instance from the inappropriate application of a dualistic nineteenth-century conception of sonata form, one in which expositions consist 'essentially' of *P* and *S*."[55]

---

52. Our observations here are based on the edition of the sonatas found in the *Neue Mozart Ausgabe*, ed. Wolfgang Plath and Wolfgang Rehm (Kassel: Bärenreiter, 1986), p. 42.

53. In the Quartet from *Idomeneo* the provided text is set—as a first run-through—in the exposition. In parallel fashion, the second rotation—mm. 68–153, encompassing the developmental space and tonal resolution—lays out the complete text for a second time. With the return of the P-incipit in the tonic at the end, following an "undermined" conclusion to the second rotation on a held V[7] chord (m. 153), Idamante returns to the initial textual line of the piece, "Andrò ramingo e solo" (m. 154). This restoration beyond the now-twice-fully-consumed text of the Quartet (as if a new text-rotation were beginning) identifies the motto-incipit as an add-on coda-accretion to the Type 2 format proper.

54. The idea of interpreting a return of P in a Type 2 sonata as a coda evidently persisted in some quarters at least into the middle of the nineteenth century—and perhaps beyond. Liszt's 1849 discussion in the *Journal des débats* of Wagner's *Tannhäuser* identifies the final return of the P-idea in the Overture, the Venusberg music at m. 273, as a coda: "La Coda résume les principaux dessins du début de l'Allégro, et arrive à son plus haut

degré de frénésie, par une descente chromatique sur la pédale de *si*, opérée par la dernière répétition de la phrase corollaire." Rpt. in Liszt, *Lohengrin et Tannhäuser de Richard Wagner* (Paris: Adef-Albatros, 1980), p. 158 (for the identification of the "phrase corollaire," see pp. 156–57). We thank Michael Puri for calling this to our attention in a seminar paper on that overture. On the other hand, cf. Thomas S. Grey's identificaton of this overture as featuring a reversed recapitulation, in "Wagner, the Overture, and the Aesthetics of Musical Form," *19th-Century Music* 12 (1988), 3–22, e.g., the diagram of the overture on p. 15 and the discussion on pp. 16–17.

55. Wolf, *The Symphonies of Johann Stamitz*, pp. 155–56. To this statement Wolf added the following footnoted remark, p. 162, n. 47: "The idea of mirror or reversed recapitulation evidently arose in the early nineteenth century; see Robert Schumann, 'Sinfonie von H. Berlioz,' in his *Gesammelte Schriften*, ed. Martin Kreisig (5th ed., Leipzig, 1914), 1:73, in which Schumann attempts to show that the first movement of the *Symphonie fantastique* is an arch form (A B C D C B A); he specifically compares this scheme with dualistic sonata form." A convenient translation of Schumann's puzzling analysis may be found in Berlioz, *Fantastic Symphony*, ed. Ed-

The P-Based Coda: The Potential for a Secondary "Completion-Effect"?

While we do not accept the concepts of the reversed recapitulation and mirror form, we recognize that a P-based coda can take on an additional set of connotations in a Type 2 sonata, as opposed to its presence in a Type 3 work. In Type 2 formats P-based codas provide us with the potential for perceiving a particularly suitable "completion-effect" that is not typically present in Type 3s. Here one might tread cautiously. On the one hand, the Type 2 sonata, in any historical and generic sense, is not properly viewed as an incomplete structure. It does not require anything beyond itself for completion on its own terms. On the other hand, from the perspective of the Type 3 sonata, which had grown to become the preponderant norm after the 1770s, it could have been interpreted as a format that could be enhanced, made more satisfying, by means of restorative-P-coda supplementation.

Even under these terms, a P-based coda within a Type 2 sonata form should not be considered part of any presumed recapitulation. (This judgment responds to a sonic illusion that stems from a fundamental misunderstanding concerning the role of modular arrangement within sonatas.) Still, the P-based coda in a Type 2 sonata furnishes an unmistakable sense of "wrapping things up" at the end with a highlighted restoration of the piece's main idea, its *Hauptgedanke*, in the tonic. This impression is made all the more telling because of the lack of any preceding Type 3 structure, in which a tonic-key P, unheard since the exposition, would have recurred to launch a bona fide recapitulation.

The important thing is to distinguish between primary structural principles—those governing the sonata form proper—and the potential for secondary effects (or even illusions), however vivid those effects might initially seem to be. In a Type 2 sonata the primary guiding

postulate is the production of a double-rotational format. We are given an expositional layout, usually of the P TR ' S / C type, followed by a second rotation of that *Anlage* starting off with a development based on P and/or TR (or, sometimes, a proxy for the one or the other) and leading to an MC and a tonal resolution of S and C. To this primary structure a tonic-P-based coda may or may not be added, the onset of an incipient, soon aborted third rotation. Since that P-based coda is often thematic, in the sense that, however fleetingly, it recaptures (even celebrates) the supposedly "missing" tonic return of the P-idea—an absence only perceivable by importing the perhaps inapplicable Type 3 perspective—the temptation is to regard that restoration as a fundamental aspect of the Type 2 structure, which it is not.

In most works in which it occurs, the once-presumed "mirror" quality of such a P-coda restoration is also questionable. Here one would have to argue that, in terms of the ordering of broad sonata spaces according to this perspective, we have: (1) an exposition that may be regarded as pre-MC material followed by post-MC material; (2) a developmental space (which from this strained point of view is to be regarded as non-participatory); (3) the return of the post-MC material in the tonic (the tonal resolution) followed by the tonic return of the P-incipit from the exposition's pre-MC material (as coda). This argument would insist that the pattern of material that is most obviously "thematic" (not developmental), the exposition's P (tonic)⇒post-MC (nontonic), seems recaptured and reversed at the movement's end: post-MC (tonic)⇒P (tonic). But the supposed "reversal" (or mirror) as Wolf pointed out, is ultimately grounded in an unacceptably simplistic and outdated view of modular arrangement within rotational layouts. S- and C-spaces are often multimodular in a way that renders claims about simple "mirror effects" naïve, particularly if they are taken as fundamental structural features.

---

ward T. Cone (New York: Norton, 1971), pp. 220–48 ("A Symphony by Berlioz"). The first movement of the *Symphonie fantastique*, however, is no Type 2 sonata. Rather, it is a deformational Type 3 whose recapitulatory rotation begins in the unusual key of V: see our

mention of this piece in ch. 12. Schumann's remark does play into the general fallacy of "reversal," but it remains unclear where the misconstrual of the "reversed recapitulation" within Type 2 format was codified in analytical practice. Cf. our remarks on Tobel, n. 19.

That said, there can be little doubt that the restoration of P-as-coda, one source of the "reversed recapitulation" fallacy, was doubtless viewed by composers, early on, as a particularly attractive option within Type 2 sonata forms. The concluding return of P in the tonic, reanimating the "lost" tonic opening, however briefly, before merging into the final coda-cadences, does fill what might be felt from the Type 3 perspective as a purposeful absence. Not only do P-incipit-based codas in Type 2 sonata forms become more frequent as the century progressed, but composers also increasingly staged them as spotlighted, significant returns.

Within Type 2 sonatas the P-based coda-option became more and more attractive in the last decades of the eighteenth century, to the point where it became a strong first-level default. It was deployed more often than not, especially in Allegro movements. P-based codas are fairly common in Stamitz symphonies, for instance, and within the mature works of Haydn (for whom the Type 2 option was generally less attractive) a classic example may be located, as mentioned above, in the finale of his "Trauer" Symphony, No. 44. For Mozart P-based codas became a strong first-level default in Type 2s soon after his earliest symphonies. Two early instances—amidst several counter-examples without codas—can be found in the first movements of his Symphony "No. 5" in B-flat, K. 22, from 1765 (some thematic material for which is shown in example 17.3) and the unnumbered Symphony in B-flat, K. Anh. 214 (45*b*), perhaps from 1767.[56]

By the early 1770s it had become Mozart's most common practice within Type 2s to provide a P-based coda (or CRI). P returns in the tonic as a genuine, full-blown coda in the first movement of Symphony No. 20 in D, K. 133.[57] P-material codas may also be found in the slow movement of the Quartet in D, K. 155 (cited in example 17.4); in the Overture to *Il re pastore*, K. 208; and in the Piano Sonata in E-flat, K. 282, also discussed above. Similarly, the tonic P-incipit returns as coda rhetoric interpolation (CRI) in the slow movement to the Flute Quartet in G, K. 285*a*; and in the two obviously related first movements that are often cited in this regard, that of the Violin Sonata in D, K. 306, and the Piano Sonata in D, K. 311 (which, we recall, also displays a conversion from Type 3 to Type 2 principles midstream).

A P-incipit-based coda or CRI may therefore be regarded as in some senses compensatory within the Type 2 sonata form.[58] Because the P-incipit had not been sounded in the tonic since the opening of the piece, it was at least pleasing to bring it back in this way in the coda. The restorative effect is even more gratifying if the developmental space—the beginning of Rotation 2—had suppressed a more obvious return of P-material in favor of something freer or more episodic that had written over that P, as in K. 133/i, K. 155/ii, K. 285*a*/i, K. 306/i, and K. 311/i. In these cases one might conclude that what was to be most essentially perceived at the opening of the developmental space was the absence of the more normative P, particularly in a sonata form that was ultimately to be interpreted through Type 2, double-rotational lenses. Such sonatas can give the impression of a P shunted aside in the initial bars of Rotation 2. From that vantage-point, such a developmental opening can seem like a crucially placed rotational blank. One purpose of this could be to

---

56. Here we follow the suggested dating of K. Anh 214 (45b) in Zaslaw, *Mozart's Symphonies*, p. 95.

57. As noted also in Zaslaw, *Mozart's Symphonies*, p. 238, with an allusion to "a kind of mirror form." P's return as coda also "corrects" the deceptive cadence in the original theme (the sentential mm. 3–10) to a PAC in m. 169—literally the first time that this theme is ever brought to authentic-cadence completion. It may be this long-sought resolution to which the full tutti responds with such an ecstatic, *forte* repetition, mm. 170–77 (pure affirmation, with another I:PAC), followed by a "coda to the coda," mm. 177–82, that in part returns to the

final bars of the second rotation in a grand gesture of inclusion. It is also helpful to hear K. 133/i as one of a set of similarly structured works (with crescendo-themes for P) that include Stamitz's Symphony in D, op. 3 no. 2/i, and Mozart's own Symphony "No. 5" in B-flat, K. 22/i.

58. For the concept of compensatory effects or "fulfillments" within codas in general—especially in Beethoven's Type 3 structures—see ch. 13. There (n. 30) we also note Caplin's listing of compensatory functions for codas in his *Classical Form*, pp. 186–91.

keep the more normative P in reserve to be restored in the tonic, and satisfyingly so, in the post-Rotation-2 coda—as Zaslaw proposed was the case with regard to the thematic arrangement of K. 133/i. In terms of the historical tradition, a compensatory return of P in the coda was not originally generically obligatory, even in cases where references to P had been omitted entirely in Rotation 2 (K. 19/i, K. 43/i). It was principally in later years, especially after 1770, that it advanced to become a strong first-level default, while never attaining the status, it seems, of becoming absolutely necessary or a fixed part of the essential form itself.

P-Compensatory Codas in Non-Type 2 Sonatas

Finally, with regard to compensatory codas that restore a fuller tonic sense of P, we might only point out that these are not limited to Type 2 sonatas. It can happen in a Type 3 sonata, for instance, that the moment of recapitulation makes only a perfunctory gesture at P in the tonic—a mere bar or two, as if merely marking an obligatory structural station, before proceeding into recapitulatory recomposition. Here a touchstone example is the first movement of Mozart's Symphony No. 34 in C, K. 338. The exposition's P opens majestically and is quite expansive, mm. 1–20. The exposition is not repeated, and the developmental space begins with a link in m. 112 and is noticeably dominated by episodic (nonrotational) material. Toward the development's end the music grasps onto a prolonged dominant-lock, V of the tonic C, at mm. 148–57, clearly a preparation for the recapitulation. That recapitulation begins at once, with mm. 158–61 reanimating the grand opening of P, mm. 1–4, in the tonic. At this point, though, the music stalls into a slightly varied repetition of the preceding two

bars (mm. 162–63) and promptly fizzles into a compressed and recomposed TR. The effect is that of an original P–TR space subjected here to an unanticipated collapse—producing a lack or "failure" at the onset of the recapitulatory rotation (which is nonetheless recognizable as such). Following that rotation, the initial moments of a more expansive, though still incomplete and recomposed, P return, now as compensatory discursive coda, beginning with an elision at m. 237. Here we get ten bars of the initial theme subjected to ellipses: mm. 237–46 reanimate mm. 1–6 but move directly to the major-minor decay of mm. 11–14 before dissolving into freer coda material, mm. 247–53, with a "coda to the coda" added at mm. 253–64.[59]

Confronting Hard Cases: Flexibility in Sonata-Type Recognition

As categories of analysis, and from our perspective today, Types 1, 2, 3, 4, and 5 formats are heuristic tools, historically defensible ways of construing familiar repertories that make possible an unusually robust processing of what we now call sonata-form movements. The sonata types are not "real" in the normal sense of the word, and we do not seek to reify them or make them rigid here. In the mid- and late-eighteenth century there is no reason to think that they had any concrete and separate existence apart from the structure- and meaning-effects that they made possible—or that they make possible for us today. Instead, they are regulative ideas (in the Kantian sense), reconstructed modes of apprehension that make certain types of perceptual coherence and meaning possible within this and later repertories. (Appendix 1 has more to say on this aspect of Sonata Theory's "Grounding Principles.")

Nor are the five sonata types absolutely in-

---

59. On discursive codas unfolding in two or more stages, the first part of which often accomplishes something more dramatically participatory vis à vis the preceding sonata form and the last part of which is a "coda to the coda," see ch. 13. It was probably the collapsing P at the onset of the recapitulation and the discursiveness of this partially restorative coda that led Charles Rosen to mistake K. 338/i, more than once, for a sonata with "the appearance of a recapitulation in reverse order" [*sic*]—our Type 2 with P-based coda—in *Sonata Forms*, rev. ed., pp. 97 and 286. (Cf. n. 51 above.)

dependent of each other. Here and in other chapters we have suggested potential points of intersection between some of them, occasionally gray areas where the Type 1 sonata with an expanded retransitional link might come to resemble a Type 3 with only a brief developmental space; where Type 3s appear to convert midstream into Type 2s, or the reverse; where some Type 2 norms are mixed with others from Type 3; where the Type 1 sonata with an extended P-based coda can come to resemble one kind of Type 4 sonata; and so on. Blends and overlaps among the sonata types are possible, even if they are not regularly encountered in standard-repertory works. In confronting hard cases, we should be advised not to assume that the point of our analysis is to shoehorn a problematic composition into only one category to the exclusion of another. When hybrids or ambiguities occur—as perceived through the conceptual grids of the five sonata types—we should be prepared to accept them and even to use the resultant structural friction as a potential enhancement of our own analytical work. Explicating the analytical problem is always preferable to pretending to solve it through a decisionistic categorization.

We have devised the sonata types primarily to serve as modes of processing the works of the most historically influential composers in the decades after 1770—Haydn, Mozart, and Beethoven in particular (although our system is also applicable, with only modest adjustments, to most nineteenth-century work as well). As many scholars have noted, mid-eighteenth-century sonata formats and those sometimes found in the lesser masters of the second half of that century often seem less regularized, looser in their architectonic realizations—as though what came to be the various "standard types" of the form had not yet been fully crystallized in the wide-ranging field of compositional practice. In our own work we have tried to bring several of these other composers into the discussion from time to time, even while concentrating on the three most celebrated figures. This second- or third-tier repertory—encompassing thousands of less ambitious and now largely forgotten works—is where, from the perspective of the five sonata types, numerous hard cases are likely to be found. Even here, though, employing the sonata types as tools for analysis can help us to realize just what is and what is not "unusual" in these compositions.

CHAPTER EIGHTEEN

Rondos and the Type 4 Sonata

Type 4 sonatas comprise a variety of sonata-rondo mixtures. The "unmixed" rondo, along with its simpler predecessor, the rondeau, is a structure built primarily by the juxtaposition of discrete sections, each of which is normally marked by memorably tuneful ideas. Its defining feature is the recurrence of a tonic-key refrain (or "rondo theme") separating the appearances of differing or contrasting episodes (or "couplets"), which are often, though by no means always, in nontonic keys.[1] The rondo proper encompasses formats traditionally described by such letter-schemes as ABACA, ABACADA, ABACABA, and the like, within which thematic variations or shortenings of the A-idea, the refrain, are also possible in its later appearances. The "mixed" Type 4 sonata (sonata-rondo) is a rondo that has been shaped to be in dialogue with a Type 1 or Type 3 sonata or, from another perspective, a Type 1 or Type 3 sonata that is also in dialogue with the rondo principle. In standard practice this usually means that the stark AB juxtapositions of the simpler rondo formats (such as ABACABA) are converted into a nonrepeated exposition and—at least in the most standard cases—a generally symmetrical

recapitulation. Each of these is usually arrayed in the customary P TR ' S / C pattern, although a continuous format (AB = P TR⇒FS / C) is also possible, especially in some of Haydn's Type 4 sonata forms. (As will be discussed toward the end of this chapter, Haydn also often treats the recapitulatory spaces of his Type 4s freely, sometimes in asymmetrical or recomposed ways that challenge their expected "recapitulatory" functions. In these cases it is the existence of at least an unequivocal exposition that is to be regarded as the hallmark of the Type 4 sonata.) In other respects the Type 4 recalls the older, more traditional rondo practice, which remained viable as an alternative even after the rise of the sonata-rondo in the early 1770s. This is most notably the case in the near-inevitability of its retransitions (RT) and tonic-key rondo-theme refrains at pre-established locations.

Within multimovement works, especially in pieces from the 1760s and 1770s onward, rondos and sonata-rondos (Type 4s) may be found as a typical option for fast finales and slow movements. As also noted by Malcolm S. Cole, the rondo format was used only "rarely as the first movement (Haydn, Piano Sonata HXVI: 48)."

---

1. Any nontonic appearance of the refrain—qua "refrain"—would be deformational to the norm. See the later discussions of C. P. E. Bach's *Kenner und Liebhaber* rondos and Beethoven's occasional practice of sounding the rondo theme in the "wrong key" near the beginning of the coda rotation.

Moroever, "it had limited use in chamber music and the symphony; it was more freely employed in sonatas and serenades, but only in the concerto was it the almost invariable choice for finales."[2]

Before proceeding to examine the Type 4 mixture, it will be helpful to consider the rondo concept generally and then to look more closely at the unmixed rondeau and rondo formats. As will be seen, the basic idea of the sonata-rondo (Type 4) is not particularly challenging. At one level of inquiry, we need ask only: does the presumed "rondo" begin with a nonrepeated sonata exposition—including a TR-idea following the refrain—or does it not? But such simplicity is deceptive. The real analytical difficulty is that of attaining the ability to navigate through the many variants and overlapping subtypes of rondeaux, rondos, and Type 4s that one finds in the late-eighteenth-century repertory. Once one investigates the details of movements or individual pieces labeled as rondos, one finds that they often differ from each other in such matters as the structure and scope of the refrain and the contrasting sections, the presence or absence of transitions and (especially) retransitions, the presence or absence of developmental and recapitulatory features, and so on.

Definitions

There is no disagreement on the basic principle underpinning the rondo. As Schoenberg put it, "the rondo forms are characterized by the repetition of one or more themes, separated by intervening contrasts."[3] Cole's definition of the rondo in the revised, 2001 *New Grove Dictionary* reproduced his earlier one from the 1980 edition: "One of the most fundamental designs in music, the rondo is a structure consisting of a series of sections, the first of which (the main section or refrain) recurs, normally in the home key, between subsidiary sections (*couplets*, episodes) before returning finally to conclude, or round off, the composition (*ABAC . . . A*)."[4] Essentially the same definition was provided by Douglass M. Green in 1979.[5] And in 1998 William E. Caplin introduced the form in a similar fashion, noting additionally that "in the classical era, however, most rondos can be situated in one of two main categories—the *five-part rondo* (ABACA) and the *sonata-rondo* (ABACABA). Variants of each type create a number of other formal designs (e.g., ABACADA, ABACBA)."[6]

It is not our intention to trace the historical origins and development of this form or the many varieties of its treatment by eighteenth- and nineteenth-century composers.[7] As has been noted, the term "rondo" is sometimes used to designate three different manifestations of the general principle outlined above. Moving from the simplest to the most complex, these are: (1) the *rondeau*; (2) the *rondo*; and (3) the *sonata-rondo* (which we refer to as the Type 4 sonata). These formal categories differ in size, scope, and internal elaboration. Their separateness from one another, while generally clear, is not absolute. The categories blend into one another on a continuum of possibilities. Some of the problem is bound up with unstable terminology from the eighteenth century. "*Rondo*, from the Italian, became the standard term in classic times to cover all versions of this form," while "the

---

2. Cole, "Rondo," *The New Grove Dictionary of Music and Musicians*, 2nd ed., ed. Stanley Sadie (London: Macmillan, 2001), 21:651.

3. Arnold Schoenberg, *Fundamentals of Musical Composition*, ed. Gerald Strang and Leonard Stein (London: Faber and Faber, 1967), p. 190.

4. Cole, "Rondo," p. 649.

5. Green, *Form in Tonal Music: An Introduction to Analysis*, 2nd ed. (New York: Holt, Rinehart, and Winston, 1979), p. 153: "The word 'rondo' is a generic name referring to those compositions that are distinguished by frequent recurrence of a *refrain*. The refrain is normally a self-contained, harmonically 'closed' passage. It begins

the rondo and reappears at least twice. The passages between appearances of the refrain are called *episodes* or *couplets*."

6. Caplin, *Classical Form*, p. 231. As will emerge, we do not define the Type 4 sonata (sonata-rondo) with the familiar ABACABA design—which, more appropriately, describes the seven-part symmetrical rondo. For an exposition and critique of Schenker's view of rondo form, see Joel Galand, "Form, Genre, and Style in the Eighteenth-Century Rondo," *Music Theory Spectrum* 17 (1995), 27–52.

7. See also, e. g., Cole, "Rondo," and Ratner, *Classic Music*, pp. 248–59 ("Couplet Forms").

prescription for a rondeau [the French term] was [more] explicit."[8] Even so, present-day assessments of individual pieces usually fall more or less comfortably into one category or another. Those assessments have different implications for analytical interpretation. For the purposes of analysis and hermeneutic clarity, it is helpful to recognize distinctions among these three rondo formats. Our presentations of the rondeau, rondo, and Type 4 are heuristic constructs or "ideal types"—conceptual formats that are useful in sharpening current analytical precision. In brief overviews we shall define and delimit each of these structures separately.

Before doing so we might underscore a few things. First, while the customary alphabetic labeling (ABACA, and so on) may be useful for the simpler rondeau and the rondo, it proves counterproductive when applied to the elaboration and complexity of the Type 4 sonata. This is also the case with the terms "couplet" or "episode," which last term has been used almost invariably in prior discussions of the sonata-rondo. We use "couplets" for the contrasting sections of the rondeau, but "episodes" for the usually more elaborate ones found in the rondo. In the sonata-rondo we switch instead to the P TR ' S / C labels. To be sure, in the Type 4 sonata P also functions as a refrain—a characteristically "rondo-style" theme recurring in the tonic at predesignated spots. For this reason we usually designate it as the *P-refrain* or P[rf]. But we discard the term "episode" as unhelpful when applied to the expositional and recapitulatory rotations.

It might be useful at the outset to suggest diagrammatically some of the distinctions that we observe among the three types—rondeau, rondo, and sonata-rondo. Once again, the possibilities exist on a continuum, potentially shading into one another. Yet, for the most part, they remain conceptually and heuristically separable, as suggested in table 18.1.

Rondeaux, Rondos, and Rotations: A Preliminary Note

Rondeau, rondo, and sonata-rondo formats are in dialogue with the rotational principle. Each successive appearance of the refrain ("A" in the usual schematic letters appropriate for rondeaux and rondos) begins a new rotation. Each rotation is marked by a similar opening, even though what follows in the remainder can differ from one rotation to the next: AB–AC–AD (if applicable)—and so on, usually concluding either with a single A (a half-rotation) or A + coda (a full coda rotation). In the cases of the symmetrical or tonally resolved formats, two of the rotations will contain similar materials: an initial rotation, "AB" with B in the dominant or other nontonic key, may be recycled toward the end, with B at that point sounded in the tonic. Assuming for the moment a four-rotation procedure, this could produce a rondo format on the order of: AB–AC–AB'–A + coda. A simpler, three-rotation (or two-and-a-half-rotation) structure could be schematized as: AB–AC–A. The rondo refrain is always a beginning, never an ending. It always begins something new.

To construe rondo structures in this way might at first seem unusual, since most analysts have been accustomed to the undivided string of letters found in such textbook formulas as ABACA or ABACAB'A. And yet our rotational divisions find support in the writings of two early-nineteenth-century theorists, Anton Reicha and Carl Czerny. In the second volume of his *Traité de haute composition musicale* (1824–25), Reicha supplemented his somewhat curious discussion of what we refer to as a symmetrical rondo (or perhaps a sonata-rondo proper) with an explanatory diagram that segmented the movement in a way that bolsters a rotational understanding of the form.[9] Reicha's paradigm in this "Coupe du Rondo" diagram, however, was not the ABACAB'A pattern commonly associated with the sonata-rondo but rather a lengthier and non-normative one, ABACADAB' coda

8. Ratner, *Classic Music*, p. 249.
9. Reicha's discussion is summarized in Malcolm Cole, "Sonata-Rondo: The Formulation of a Theoretical Concept," *The Musical Quarterly* 55 (1969), pp. 185–86.

This article is the source for our discussions of Reicha and Czerny on rondos. The original Reicha source, as listed by Cole, is *Traité de haute Composition Musicale* (Paris: 1824–25), 2:301–3.

TABLE 18.1   From Rondeau to Sonata-Rondo: A Continuum of Formal Categories

Rondeau	Rondo	Sonata-rondo (Type 4)	[Sonata]
"Refrain" and "couplets"	"Refrain" and "episodes"	Sonata terminology is preferable: P TR ' S / C	
Alternation of simple melodic structures (period, hybrid, or group of phrases)	Alternation, but of somewhat more complex/expanded structures (esp. binary, rounded binary, sometimes with repeats)	TR-zone follows the initial "refrain" (refrain = P or P[rf])	
Few or no links or retransitions between the sections	More elaborate retransitions as the episodes return to the refrain, but no TR between A and B	First rotation is explicitly structured as the exposition of a sonata, with RT at its end	
Refrain usually returns literally	Returns of refrain are sometimes truncated	A later rotation recapitulates and resolves the expositional rotation	
		May be in dialogue with the Type 1, the expanded Type 1, the Type 3, or the Type 5 sonata	

(with no return of A prior to the coda). Nevertheless, his larger point is clear. He unequivocally divided his theoretical major-mode rondo into four "sections": (1) AB; (2) AC; (3) AD; (4) AB'—followed by the coda. (He also indicated that B was to be in V; C in IV; D in i (tonic minor); and B' in I.)[10]

Similarly, in his *School of Practical Composition* (1849) Czerny first devoted considerable space to a rondo of the ABACA type, which he divided into three principal "periods," each beginning with the refrain: AB–AC–A + coda.

He then went on, however (as noted by Cole), to describe another possibility:

> If this Rondo had been written on a greater scale, a longer and more decided middle subject must have been interwoven, which would then have been repeated in the third principal period (AB'); after which a *fourth principal period* would have followed, which would have formed a more extended and brilliant conclusion, and a longer Coda. Hence, a Rondo, according to its extent, consists of three or four principal periods, and of as many repetitions of the principal subject.[11]

---

10. In his treatment of Reicha on the "sonata-rondo" ("Sonata-Rondo: The Formulation of a Theoretical Concept," pp. 185–86), Cole also pointed out that the theorist's quirky treatment of the form indicated that the fourth section was to be "the longest and the most important," with its B' section "recalling that which is the most salient in the three preceding sections." Cole additionally noted that "all sections are connected by transitions and retransitions" and quoted Reicha's remark that his prolix pattern could "be abridged by suppressing the second section; but in this case it will resemble

too much the ternary style [i.e., sonata form]." If one were to suppress Reicha's Section 2, the result would be AB–AD–AB'–coda, which would indeed bring the form close to either our symmetrical seven-part rondo or our Type 3 sonata-rondo mixture (what we call the Type 4[3] sonata), especially if the coda were based upon, or preceded by a return of, the main idea (A).

11. Quoted in Cole, "Sonata-Rondo: The Formulation of a Theoretical Concept," p. 187. Czerny's discussion of rondos, as cited by Cole, appeared in his *School of Practical Composition, Opus 600* (London, 1849), 1:67–81.

Czerny's rondo of four principal periods (AB–AC–AB'–A + coda) is either the symmetrical seven-part rondo or the Type 3 sonata-rondo mixture proper. The main point, though, is that his segmented layout of the form is congruent with our rotational view of these structures. At least some nineteenth-century theorists recognized the rotational aspect of this form, an insight that was apparently lost in the middle of the nineteenth century, perhaps as a result of A. B. Marx's evolutionary view concerning his five rondo types as progressive steps of the "spirit," striving ultimately to attain the greater cohesiveness and "ternary" symmetry provided by sonata form.[12] However the swerve away from the quasi-rotational views of Reicha and Czerny occurred, its loss was perpetuated during the production of twentieth-century *Formenlehre*, which sometimes, misleadingly, viewed the symmetrical rondo types as large-scale ternary structures.[13]

The Rondeau

As presented by Malcolm S. Cole (whose *New Grove* descriptions of earlier formats we summarize and adapt slightly here), the term "rondeau," suggesting a round or circular motion, has been applied to a body of seventeenth- and early eighteenth-century French compositions characterized by the alternation of a harmonically closed refrain (A) in the tonic key with contrasting *couplets* (B, C, and so on), usually in different keys.[14] The rondeau appeared in a variety of contexts in the decades before 1750: ballet, opera, orchestral music, violin sonatas, and harpsichord pieces.[15] The number of couplets varied from one to as many as eight, but most rondeaux contained two (the usual number in Rameau's harpsichord works), three, or four. Differentiations may therefore be made among the single-couplet rondeau (ABA), the two-couplet rondeau (AB–AC–A), and the multicouplet rondeau or "chain rondeau" (AB–AC–AD– . . . A).

Traditional and Expanded Rondeaux

Especially when confronting pieces from multi-movement works written in the last several decades of the century, one might also make the distinction between the traditional and the expanded rondeau. The traditional rondeau—associated with the simple letter-schemes suitable for works of Couperin and Rameau—is characterized by the straightforward alternation of brief melodic structures. With its short-winded

---

12. Marx's view may be found, e.g., in *Die Lehre von der Muikalischen Komposition*, 2nd ed. (Leipzig: Breitkopf & Hartel, 1848), 3:94–200 and 307–13. A translation of the most relevant material is available in Marx, *Musical Form in the Age of Beethoven: Selected Writings on Theory and Method*, ed. and trans. by Scott Burnham (Cambridge: Cambridge University Press, 1997), pp. 78–82. Marx's *fourth rondo form*, for instance, is basically an ABACAB' structure, similar to the sonata-rondo form. Rather than calling attention to its rotational underpinnings, Marx sought to call attention to its "clearly delineated ternary structure"—that is, the outer relationships between AB and AB' (the two *Hauptsatz-Seitensatz* pairs, the second of which is tonally resolved). (Marx, *Musical Form*, pp. 80–81.) As pointed out in Cole, "Sonata-Rondo: The Formulation of a Theoretical Concept," p. 188, Marx's ("historically inaccurate") point was to suggest that each rondo type showed an increased striving toward the goal of sonata form, with its exposition and symmetrical recapitulation. Thus each rondo type, he argued, developed (in Cole's words) "when composers sensed something lacking in the type immediately preceding." Marx's own way of expressing this

was more florid and bound up with the Germanic philosophies of the time (*Musical Form*, pp. 77–78): "Every form is a restraint, a fetter for the spirit that has come to belong to it. With every succeeding form, the spirit is released into a new perspective. The spirit is free only when it possesses all the forms, as well as the complete power to build them—and, in requisite cases, to build new ones. Every form is an expression of formative reason, which finds its complete justification only in the sum [*Inbegriff*] of all forms."

13. Green, for example (*Form in Tonal Music*, 2nd ed., p. 161), divided one type of symmetrical rondo into three parts, ABA–C–AB'A, thereby obscuring the rotational impulse that underlies this form.

14. On the historical etymology and principle of circularity or roundedness embedded in the term "rondeau" ("rondo"), stretching back to poetic formats of thirteenth and fourteenth centuries, see also Fritz Reckow, "Rondellus/rondeau, rota," in Hans Heinrich Eggebrecht, ed. *Handwörterbuch der musikalischen Terminologie* (Stuttgart: Steiner, n.d.), pp. 1–7.

15. Cole, "Rondo," pp. 649–50.

themes and nonpostponed recurrences of the refrain, the traditional rondeau establishes the base-line of assessment when confronting later adaptations. The refrain is usually a simple period or a similar, comparably concise musical idea. Each couplet is also brief, generally either a period or a group of phrases. Sometimes—especially in earlier examples—the refrain is written out only once, with directions to repeat it after every couplet. Only the briefest of links (if any) leads from the end of a couplet into the return of the refrain.[16] Any couplet may be tonally closed in a single (contrasting) key, or it may be harmonically progressive, modulating from one key to another. As Cole reported, Rameau's two-couplet rondeaux (AB–AC–A) display a fairly uniform key scheme. His major-mode rondeaux typically traverse the keys, I-V—I-vi—I; the minor-mode ones, i-III—i-v—i.[17]

What we call the expanded rondeau, which will be treated further below, builds on and complicates the traditional rondeau principle either by turning some or all of the couplets into a string of small melodic-harmonic forms, thereby postponing the return to the melodically brief A, or by expanding one or more of its sections into a larger format, perhaps a rounded binary structure or something similar—an expansion that nudges the whole piece in the direction of a rondo. For the moment we shall set these issues aside to confine ourselves to the traditional rondeau.

The Two-Couplet Rondeau

The qualification "en rondeau" ("in the form of a rondeau") might be appended to any dance title: "gigue en rondeau," "menuet en rondeau," and the like. J. S. Bach's Fifth English Suite in E Minor (BWV 810) contains a movement entitled "Passepied en Rondeau," which serves as a clear exemplar of the form (and demonstrates that neither the form nor the term was confined to France). This dance movement unfolds as a two-couplet rondeau: AB–AC–A. Each sec-

tion is sixteen bars long. The tonic refrain (A) is a compound period with cadence pattern IAC/PAC. The first couplet (B) is a modulating compound period that begins in G major (III) and leads to a PAC in B minor (v). The second couplet is a compound sentence that begins in A minor (iv) and leads to a PAC in G major (III). The strongest cadences articulate the tonal design i-v—i-III—i, a pattern that reverses the Rameau minor-mode design. Each return of the refrain is written out, and there are no transitions or links between sections. The basic principle is one of simple, sectional juxtaposition.

The Multicouplet Rondeau

Even as Cole noted that the "assimilation [of the rondeau] into the music of other nations and its transformation into the rondo of the Classical period have not been adequately investigated,"[18] it does seems clear that in the early 1770s the young Mozart was writing them, even though he may have labeled a piece or movement in this format as a "rondo" instead of a "rondeau." Neither a simple respelling nor the adoption of the Italian version of a formal term amounts to a transformation of essential formal structure.

Consider the finale, Allegro grazioso, of Mozart's Quartet in B-flat, K. 159, written in 1773. Although marked "rondo," this is a clear four-couplet rondeau (AB–AC–AD–AE–A). The refrain (A) recurs each time in the tonic B-flat, while the four couplets are tonally closed in F (V), G minor (vi), B-flat minor (i), and B-flat major (I), respectively. The overall harmonic plan is thus: I-V—I-vi—I-i—I-I—I. (Here one notices that the first five sections replicate the Rameau major-mode model: I-V—I-vi—I.) The brief refrain (A, mm. 1–8) is most simply regarded as a clipped, eight-bar period with an only slightly altered consequent. On its first two appearances (the second is in mm. 25–32), it is literally repeated, while its third and fourth statements (mm. 49–64, 97–112) are both subjected to written-out, varied repeats. Couplet 1

---

16. While normative, the transitionless rondeau is not without exception. Cole, "Rondo," p. 650, notes that in the later eighteenth century "Leclair . . . was among the first to compose a linking passage to connect a *cou-*

plet with an ensuing return of the refrain (op. 2 no. 4, Aria)."
17. Cole, "Rondo," p. 650.
18. Cole, "Rondo," p. 650.

(B, mm. 9–24), the most "loosely" structured of the four contrasting sections, is a sixteen-bar phrase comprising four different four-bar modules, the last of which drives to a V:PAC. Couplet 2 (C) is a sixteen-bar compound period in the minor submediant. Couplet 3 (D, mm. 65–96) is a thirty-two-bar sectional simple binary that comprises two compound periods, both tonally closed in the tonic minor. Couplet 4 (E, mm. 113–28) is a sixteen-bar compound "hybrid 1" (antecedent + continuation). The form is complicated by the insertion of a coda-rhetoric interpolation (CRI, mm. 129–36) before the final return of the refrain (mm. 137–44), as well as by the addition of a genuine coda following this return (mm. 145–59). This piece may thus be more precisely schematized as: AB–AC–A'D–A'E [CRI]–A + coda.

Several factors place this movement in the category or tradition of the rondeau rather than that of the more elaborated, normative rondo (notwithstanding Mozart's designation of the movement). First, there are no transitions or (especially) retransitions between the sections. Second, the refrain is laid out as a simple eight-bar, two-phrase design. Finally, couplets 1, 2, and 4 are symmetrical sixteen-bar structures, each containing either one or two phrases and only one PAC. Couplet 3 is the only section that contains two periodic structures (16 + 16 bars) and consequently two PACs. Additionally, as we shall see, a distinguishing feature of the classical rondo is the expansion of the contrasting sections, and sometimes the refrain as well, into tonally closed binary forms of either the simple or rounded variety. In the finale of K. 159 only

couplet 3 suggests such an expansion (a sectional simple binary); otherwise, each section is a two-phrase period or hybrid, or (in the case of couplet 1) a single phrase.

The Symmetrical Three-Couplet Rondeau

Two other rondeaux by Mozart are worth examining, especially since these two pieces have been cited as the first two sonata-rondos: the finales of the Quartet in C, K. 157 (1772–73) and the Symphony No. 23 in D, K. 181 (1773).[19] But if we define our subtypes carefully, such a matter-of-fact statement claims too much. Neither movement contains a sufficient number of features to be considered a genuine sonata-rondo (or Type 4 sonata). Indeed, in their structural simplicity they even fall short of being properly classified as normative rondos. Instead, each is a rondeau that has been submitted to one or more additional factors (especially tonal factors) that suggest a conceptual slide in the direction of what would eventually become a full-scale sonata-rondo. Both pieces exemplify a three-couplet rondeau of the AB—AC—AB'—A variety, where couplet 3 (B') is a transposition to the tonic key of the nontonic couplet 1 (B). This procedure can hardly be said to produce a full-scale sonata-rondo, since it lacks the defining feature of the Type 4, that of beginning with a generic expositional rotation that includes a section of TR. At most we might observe that each of these two rondeaux registers the effects of modest sonata urgings. We refer to such a structure as a *symmetrical three-couplet rondeau*—a structure defined by its featuring of

19. Cole, "Rondo," p. 653: "Mozart, in the String Quartet K157 (1772–73), composed the first known sonata-rondo. . . . Haydn adopted it somewhat later (Symphonies nos. 64, 66, and 69 of the 1770s in one view; Symphony no. 77, 1782, in another)." Cf. the earlier remarks of Cole from 1969, "Sonata-Rondo, The Formulation of a Theoretical Concept," p. 182: "In 1924, Wilhelm Fischer ascribed the invention of the sonata-rondo to Haydn. In 1935, Rudolf von Tobel stated decisively: 'The sonata-rondo is created [by Mozart] in 1773, C Major Quartet K. 157, D Major Symphony K. 181.' Tobel's view is the prevailing one today, and my investigations so far tend to confirm his statement." For the original claim and its context in Tobel ("Mit dem Jahre 1773 ist das Sonatenrondo geschaffen: C-Quar-

tett 157, D-Symphonie 181"), see his *Die Formenwelt der klassischen Instrumentalmusik* (Bern and Leipzig: Paul Haupt, 1935), p. 183. Internal structure aside, arguments against the absolute priority of Mozart for the sonata-rondo concept are presented in Stephen C. Fisher, "Further Thoughts on Haydn's Symphonic Rondo Finales," *Haydn Yearbook XVII [1992]*, ed. H. C. Robbins Landon, Otto Biba, I. M. Bruce, and David Wyn Jones (Eisenstadt: Joseph Haydn Stiftung, 1992), pp. 85–107, e.g., at p. 85 ("Haydn's first symphonic sonata-rondo by the usual formulation is the orphan finale Hob. Ia:4, which may well pre-date his first meeting with Mozart," and at p. 106, "The sonata-rondo concept was plainly in the air, though, and Mozart has lost his claim to priority."

a tonal resolution of couplet 1 later in the piece, in the space traditionally allotted to couplet 3. (When we find the same sectional pattern, AB–AC–AB'–A, with B' as a tonic transposition of the nontonic B, in the classical rondo, which typically features more elaborate internal structures than that of the rondeau as well as clear retransitions back to A, we refer to it as a *symmetrical seven-part rondo*, a structure that has still not yet attained Type 4 status.)

Consider first the Presto assai finale of Mozart's Symphony No. 23 in D, K. 181, which may be schematized as AB–AC (RT)–AB'–A + coda, with a tonal scheme of I–V—I-i—I-I—I. The D-major refrain is a sixteen-bar compound period stated by the full orchestra, *forte*; its second and third appearances (mm. 41–56, 81–96) are exact, while its final statement (mm. 121–52) is repeated. During the repeat, mm. 137–52, the antecedent phrase is played *piano* by strings alone, while the consequent phrase is again played *forte* by full orchestra, to which a brief coda is appended (mm. 153–66). Couplet 1 (B, mm. 17–40) shifts to the dominant key with a twenty-four-bar hybrid comprising a presentational-antecedent phrase followed by a repeated and varied continuation phrase. The continuation is first played *forte* by the full orchestra; its varied repetition is sounded *piano* by the strings alone. The B theme is grounded in A major (V). When it recurs as couplet 3 (B', mm. 97–120), the antecedent phrase is rewritten to remain in the tonic key, while the continuation phrase and its repetition are transposed to the tonic and revoiced. Couplet 2 (C, mm. 57–72) is a sixteen-bar period in the tonic minor. An eight-bar dominant preparation (mm. 73–80) ushers in the third appearance of the refrain.

As in the case of the multicouplet rondeau mentioned earlier, K. 159/iii, the relatively elementary structure of the refrain and the couplets, as well as the general lack of retransitions, situate this piece squarely within the tradition of the rondeau, not that of the more elaborate rondo. On this interpretation, the only "rondo tendency" is the extended dominant retransition (mm. 73–80) that prepares the third statement of the refrain, while the only "sonata tendency" is the transposition to the tonic (with slight recomposition) of the dominant-oriented Couplet

1 material. To be sure, if one were to invoke the earlier image of the continuum of formal types (table 18.1), with the "pure" rondeau at one end and the fully-formed sonata-rondo (Type 4 sonata) at the other, these two tendencies in K. 181/iii might push it a small distance along the scale away from the rondeau end. But bluntly to call it one of the first sonata-rondos ever composed is exaggerated.

The same is true of the slightly earlier piece, the Presto finale of Mozart's Quartet in C, K. 157. Here yet another "sonata tendency" might be observed in that the refrain (A, mm. 1–16) is followed by a four-bar transition (TR, mm. 17–20) that modulates to the dominant in preparation for couplet 1 (B). Following the third statement of the refrain, however (mm. 65-80), this transition is eliminated before the tonic transposition of the B material as couplet 3 (B'). Couplet 2 is sounded in the minor tonic (i). The entire formal design is A (TR) B–AC–AB'–A + coda, while the tonal design is I-V—I-i—I-I—I. Both the refrain (A) and couplet 2 (C, mm. 49–64) are sixteen-bar periods, while couplet 1 (B, mm. 21–32) is a sentence with repeated continuation motivated by a deceptive cadence. During couplet 3 (B', mm. 81–100) this sentence is stated twice, the first time without the deceptive cadence and the repetition of the continuation. The formal simplicity of each section and the absence of retransitions urge us not to consider this piece within the category of a rondo proper. The presence of a modulatory transition, though, however slight, does increase the "sonata tendency" evident in the dominant-to-tonic transposition of the B material. We might therefore nudge this movement further along the table 18.1 continuum than we did K. 181/iii. Nevertheless, it is still not a full-scale sonata-rondo. It is specifically to cover such situations that we use the term "symmetrical three-couplet rondeau."

With the consideration of the symmetrical three-couplet rondeau the rotational aspect of rondeau (and rondo) practice becomes more evident. Rather than viewing it as a simple alternation of seven contrasting sections (eight if one includes the optional coda), it may also be heard as a series of four rotations, each of which begins with the tonic refrain:

Rotation 1: A B   Ends V:PAC
Rotation 2: A C   Ends X:PAC
Rotation 3: A B'   Ends I:PAC
Rotation 4: A Coda   Ends I:PAC

As discussed earlier in this chapter, such a rotational reading of this format (which is also transferable to other rondeau and rondo variants) is also consistent with early treatments of this and similar structures by the early theorists, including Reicha and Czerny. We might also observe that in the symmetrical three-couplet rondo the fourth refrain is the only one that follows a rotation that ends with a PAC in the tonic key. In other words, only the final refrain takes place within a tonic that has been fully actualized, made into a concrete reality.[20]

The Expanded Rondeau

The traditional rondeau, including those cited above, alternates a brief refrain (sentence, period, hybrid) with a series of comparably brief, single couplets, in the AB–AC– . . . A pattern. In this directly juxtaposed, back-and-forth melodic practice, the tonic-key A-refrain returns immediately after each short-lived couplet, and transitions between the melodic blocks are nonexistent or rare. The effect is that of a rapid alternation of memorable themes, every other one of which is the A-refrain. If one or more of the couplet sections, however, were to be enlarged to include a series or cluster of two or more characteristic ideas—each of which still maintained the completeness and short-windedness of a typical couplet theme—we could speak of an *expanded rondeau*. The B couplets, for instance (and/or later ones as well), could be expanded into a chain of differing short melodies, B^1, B^2, B^3, and so on, before returning to the A-refrain.[21] This perhaps "playful" scenario, capitalizing on the connotations of lightness and freedom surrounding many rondeaux

and rondos, produces a string of differing but often complementary melodies, each of which on its own might have qualified as a more or less self-sufficient couplet in a traditional rondeau. Especially when this principle is carried out in more than one couplet, the result is an extended chain of differing melodies, one after another, which only occasionally "decide" to return to the A-refrain as a melodic stabilizer for the whole succession.

A touchstone case of the expanded rondeau can be found in the finale, Allegro molto, of Mozart's Serenade in B-flat for Thirteen Winds, K. 361 (which the composer himself marked as a "rondo"). Here we find a series of eight- and sixteen-measure simple structures (sixteen bars for the refrain, eight bars for each contrasting melody), each closed with a PAC in the relevant key and each (excepting the final appearance of the refrain) individually subjected to a literal repeat by means of a notated repeat sign. Thus each melodic unit is set off from what precedes and what follows it. The recurring B-flat-tonic refrain (A, mm. 1–16, a compound period), the multiple short melodies, and the complete absence of transitions mark the movement as belonging to the rondeau (not the rondo) category. In this mushrooming additive structure one should probably regard all of the repeated eight-bar melodies as couplets, forming sets or clusters between the sixteen-bar refrain. On this reading, the movement could be schematized as follows (remembering that each "letter" is heard twice via a literal repeat, except for the final A):

mm. 1	17	25	33	41	57	65	73	81	89	104-46
A	B^1	B^2	B^3	A	C^1	C^2	C^3	C^4	A	Coda
I	I–V	→I	vi	I	IV	ii	→vi	vi→iii	I	I

Looming behind such a structure is the traditional two-couplet rondeau (AB–AC–A), although the latter's normatively single-strain

---

20. On the concept of the ontological status of the tonic within modulatory structures such as sonatas, see the section, "Tonal Potential, Tonic Presence," near the conclusion of chapter 11, along with the section at the end of this chapter, "ESC Issues in Type 4 Sonatas: the Double Perspective."

21. Cf. the description of rondos (and episodes) that may contain multiple "sections," in A. F. C. Kollmann, *An Essay on Practical Musical Composition* (London, 1799), [chapter 1, section 10] (rpt. New York: Da Capo Press, 1973), p. 4.

B and C couplets have now multiplied into a succession of contrasting, self-enclosed tunes. Moreover, in K. 361/vii the otherwise differing couplet-ideas B^3, C^2, C^3, and (possibly) C^4 are interrelated with each other through their shifts to the minor mode and their deployment of the "Turkish" idiom—a favorite topical allusion in many rondeaux, rondos, and Type 4s (mildly evoking a sense of the Near-Eastern "Other," apparently with an "insider," witty intent from an assumed position of implied cultural superiority). In other words, the B and C sectionally additive couplet-strings begin in a "Western"-style major mode (essentially the tonic in B^1-B^2, the subdominant in C^1) only to "turn Turkish" as they proceed—more emphatically so in the C-cluster. The mock-exotic implication is also reinforced by the Serenade's thick-wind timbres, also a component of Turkish janissary music.

Another example is Haydn's famous *Rondo all'Ongarese*, the Presto finale of the Piano Trio in G, Hob. XV:25—like K. 361/vii, expanding the AB–AC–A rondeau format, albeit in different ways and with differing implications. Like K. 361/vii, this piece features closed, "catchy" melodic sections, several repeat signs, and no transitions or retransitions at any point (although there are sometimes patches of connective fill at the joints). Moreover, its B-space comprises an additive series of brief, though unrepeated, melodic forms (B^1, B^2, B^3, B^4). These features would seem to place it in the general category of the expanded rondeau. But in this instance two of its major sections are not mere one-strain tunes but larger structures—binary forms—which slide this expanded-rondeau movement in the direction of a rondo proper. In short, the movement is an expanded rondeau with significant leanings toward becoming a rondo. Moreover, the A-refrain is itself one of these larger units: a sectional rounded binary, a b+a' with internal repeats (the first of which is written out), mm. 1–34; the melody is shortened to aba, without repeats, in later appearances. (Haydn—and others—often prefer a

binary or rounded binary format for A [or P] in a rondo [or Type 4] proper.) Similarly, the C section is a sectional balanced binary, again with internal repeats, whose second part, a sententially designed "bbc–c," features in its immediately reiterated continuation, c, a rhyming cadence with that of the first part, a.

While most closely related to the expanded rondeau in its emphatic, transitionless sectionalism and additive string of related "B" melodies, Haydn's *Rondo all'ongarese* is poised somewhere between that format and the rondo proper. In addition, all sections of this finale remain fixedly in the tonic G (unlike the normative rondeau or rondo), although shifting from time to time to G minor and back again in a clear *maggiore-minore* alternation that is doubtless part of the Hungarian flavor, along with the vigorously folk-like, perhaps Romany topoi of the melody types.[22]

The Rondo

Influence of Earlier Dance-Suite Binary Formats?

One way that the rondo proper may be distinguished from the rondeau is that it expands the latter's relatively simple phrase structures (periods, hybrids, and so on) into more complex forms, usually various types of binary forms. This expansion may have been influenced by the Baroque da capo procedure in suite movements, in which a composer could write, for example, two minuets, entitle them "Menuet I" and "Menuet II," and follow the second with the instruction "Menuet I da capo." This is of course the origin of the Minuet and Trio form within multimovement sonata practice, but in earlier times it was also applied to gavottes, bourrées, passepieds, and so on. The second dance usually employed the same tonic as the first, perhaps with a change of mode, although a contrasting key was a possibility. But the important structural point is that each dance was itself

---

22. Another variant of the expanded rondeau, that found in Mozart's "Polonaise en rondeau," the second movement of the Piano Sonata in D, K. 284, is mentioned in n. 45.

a binary form (complete with double bars and repeats); the result was a *compound ternary form*.

Similarly, the refrain (A) of normative later-eighteenth-century rondos (for example, those in the formats AB–AC–A, AB–AC–AD–A, or AB–AC–AB–A) was often constructed as a rounded binary form (a b+a', with double bars and repeats), perhaps recalling da capo practice. Subsequent statements of the refrain were often truncated, perhaps limited to the a or a' section, or slightly varied. The contrasting sections were usually also structured as binary forms (simple, rounded, balanced, or parallel). In rondos we refer to these more elaborate contrasting sections as "episodes," to distinguish them from the relatively simple couplets of the rondeau.

The Retransition: A Crucial Marker of the Rondo

The episodes of the rondo usually explore contrasting keys and/or modes, much as did the couplets of the normative rondeau. As in the rondeau, these contrasting keys generally enter without preparation. Unlike the rondeau, however, a genuine rondo almost always features more or less elaborate retransitions. A retransition (RT) is a passage that leads from the end of an episode to a dominant preparation that sets up the subsequent reappearance of the tonic refrain. In this way the composer gives the audience an aural signal that the refrain is about to recur ("Get ready, dear listener: here it comes again!"). In a major-mode rondo this can create an effect of playfulness and wit, while in a minor-mode rondo it can suggest a tragic inevitability. In either case the presence or absence of the retransition is often the single factor that distinguishes the rondo (and also the Type 4) from simpler formats to which it might be otherwise closely related.

Refrains of "Rondo Character"; Occasional "False Predictions" and Composers' "Mislabelings"

In rondos in Allegro tempo or faster (encountered in finales), the A-refrain is usually nimble, playful, or "tuneful." There is a characteristic, lighter feel to many of these rondo themes—something popular in flavor, something instantly memorable, a *"contredanse* character."[23] In the *New Grove* "Rondo" entry Cole noted the beginning of an Austro-Germanic "vogue" in the early 1770s "for simple, tuneful rondos of a quite different stamp from the French products." The light or "popular character" of the rondo theme was one of its main features at the time. Notwithstanding a few minor-mode examples, "the typical rondo [of the time] was supposed to be bright and cheerful."[24] Slow-movement rondos, of course, might provide a quite different thematic impression.

Still, with regard especially to fast concluding movements, the experienced listener soon comes to recognize the "rondo character" of such an opening melody. Hearing one at the outset of a finale—particularly when the melody is structured in a rounded-binary or other binary format—invites us to interpret it as a signal predicting that a rondo movement (or a Type 4, which usually begins with a similarly styled "rondo theme") may well ensue. But thoughts along these lines should be approached with caution, and all such predictions should be only provisional. While what follows is indeed often a rondo or a Type 4, such a purposely planted "rondo-theme" impression at the finale's opening can be amusingly deceptive. As has been noted before, in later Haydn and Mozart, along with some earlier Beethoven and Schubert, such "rondo-character" themes—even ones that might display "rondo-like" internal repeat

23. The *contredanse* description is frequently encountered in descriptions of initial rondo themes in the writings of musicologists in the past three decades. See, e.g., Malcolm. S. Cole, "Haydn's Symphonic Rondo Finales: Their Structural and Stylistic Evolution," *Haydn Yearbook XIII 1982*, ed. H. C. Robbins Landon, I. M. Bruce, and David Wyn Jones (Cardiff: University College Cardiff Press, 1983), pp. 113–42 at p. 132; and the several such references in the Cole-Fisher exchange, cited in n.

50. On the *contredanse* as a musical style or topic ("the melodies of contredanses are most often in duple time . . . well articulated, brilliant, and gay . . . [and] quite simple," according to Rousseau in 1768), see Leonard G. Ratner, *Classic Music*, pp. 13–14.
24. Cole, "Rondo," *New Grove Dictionary*, vol. 21, pp. 650–51. Cf. the similar remarks in Ratner, *Classic Music*, p. 249.

signs—sometimes turn out to proceed as Type 3 sonata movements.[25] Occasionally from this and other structural evidence once sometimes gets the impression that some "playful" Type 3 finales, strictly considered, have the rondo character (the rondo "attitude")—or the Type 4 blend—very much on their minds, referencing it in flavor if not in structure. The finale of Haydn's Piano Trio in C, Hob: XV:27, is a perfect example. While at nearly every moment it "sounds like" a rondo-oriented Type 4—even to the point of displaying a closed, rounded-binary P-theme—it is in fact a Type 3 sonata (with an expositional repeat, a crucial Type 3 identifier), written to suggest that it apparently "wishes" it were a genuine sonata-rondo. Similarly witty impressions can be found several other Type 3 finales as well, such as those in Haydn's Symphonies No. 76 in E-flat and No. 77 in B-flat, both containing rounded-binary "rondo-like" themes including written-out internal repetitions. (Needless to say, Type 3 finales with playful, *contredanse*-character P-themes, though ones not additionally constructed in a rounded-binary format, are legion in the repertory.)[26]

On rare occasions, a composer might even explicitly designate an individual piece or movement as a "rondo"—apparently a quite free term at that time—that is in fact, from today's perspective, an unequivocal sonata form. This occurs, famously, in Mozart's Rondo in D, K.

485, which is an unambiguous Type 3 sonata, with a playful opening theme, a P-based S, and a repeated exposition; and in the finale, marked "rondo," of his *Eine kleine Nachtmusik*, K. 525, a Type 2 sonata, with both halves repeated, featuring an "RT"-prepared, P-based TM^3 in V that can sound like an off-tonic rondo-refrain. In both cases it may have been the multiple recurrences of the witty, P-based ideas, along with, perhaps, their general character, that led Mozart to what seems today to have been a mislabeling.[27] A precedent of such a "mislabeling," though without a P-based S, may be found in the finale of C. P. E. Bach's Sonata in F minor (composed in 1774) from the *Kenner und Liebhaber* series, collection 3 sonata no. 3, H. 173 (Wq 57/6/iii, which, curiously, is a Type 1 sonata with highly non-normative internal repeats).

The Five-Part Rondo (AB–AC–A)

The pattern AB–AC–A is a schematic rendering of the normative "five-part rondo" (sometimes called the "short rondo form"). If we also use "RT" for the obligatory retransitions, V_A for an active dominant chord, X and Y for non-tonic keys, and assume the addition of a coda, the most standard version of the form can be diagrammed more precisely as:

---

25. Cf. Hans Keller's remark (*The Great Haydn Quartets: Their Interpretation* [London: Dent, 1986], p. 133) that Haydn, in particular, will sometimes lead us to "expect a form, not in view of his successive structural events, but in view of the sheer character of his themes." Also quoted in W. Dean Sutcliffe, *Haydn: String Quartets, op. 50* (Cambridge: Cambridge University Press, 1992), p. 55, which goes on to note that this strategy, prominent in four of the op. 50 sonata–form finales, "is found in other Haydn genres of the time, such as the finales of Symphony No. 83 of 1785 or Piano Trio No. 27 from about 1789. Just to increase the confusion in the latter instance, Haydn actually marks the movement 'Rondo'!"

26. We thus concur with the similar ideas outlined in Fisher, "Further Thoughts," p. 90. It was the same article, p. 95, that called our attention to the last movements of Symphonies No. 76 and 77: "These are the only finales in the Haydn symphonies to begin with a theme in rounded binary form with written-out repeti-

tions for both strains. After the opening themes, however, sonata procedures predominate."

27. This use of "rondo" must have referred more to the pieces' thematic character and frequent resurfacings of that P-idea than to structure *per se*—our more ordinary sense of "rondo." One might recall additionally that Mozart labeled K. 382, his theme-and-variations replacement movement for the finale of early Piano Concerto "No. 5" in D, K. 175, as a "Rondo." See, e.g., the discussion of K. 382 in John Irving, *Mozart's Piano Concertos* (Aldershot: Ashgate, 2003), pp. 173–75; and Elaine Sisman, *Haydn and the Classical Variation* (Cambridge, Mass.: Harvard University Press, 1993), pp. 40–41. Sisman also noted (p. 41) the term "'rondeau' . . . in the late eighteenth century was sometimes synonymous with 'finale.'" An appended note (n. 98) informs us that "Albrechtsberger copied a Gassmann symphony and labeled the finale 'rondo,' although the movement is actually a set of variations." See also the largely parallel remarks in Galand, "Form, Genre, and Style," p. 37.

A	B	RT	A	C	RT	A	Coda
I	X	$\Rightarrow V_A \parallel$	I	Y	$\Rightarrow V_A \parallel$	I	I

This form typically displays a twice-interrupted harmonic structure. For example, if the two episodes occur in the keys of the submediant and the subdominant respectively, the harmonic structure is: I–vi–V_A $\parallel$ I–IV–V_A $\parallel$ I. Such is the key scheme of the Adagio second movement of Mozart's Piano Sonata in B-flat, K. 570, a clear example of the five-part rondo. Here each section except the coda is structured as a binary form with repeats: the refrain (A) is a sectional rounded binary, episode 1 (B, mm. 13–24) is a continuous rounded binary, while episode 2 (C, mm. 32–39) is a continuous simple binary. Separate and clear retransitions bridge the move from B to A (mm. 25–27) and from C to A (mm. 40–43). The second and third statements of the refrain (mm. 28–31, 44–47) occur in abbreviated form, bringing back only its first (a) section, and in this case the coda (mm. 48–55) restores elements of both episodes, now in the tonic key.[28]

As K. 570/ii suggests, later-eighteenth-century composers sometimes employed the AB–AC–A five-part rondo for the slow movement, where the dance-like character of the rondeau yielded to the slow movement's predilection for lyrical discourse. Most often, the slow movement usually represents a large-scale swinging-away from the tonic key (chapter 15); this is mirrored on a lower level by the rondo's *multiple* swinging-away from, and return to, the tonic. Mozart also used this form for his Rondo in A Minor, K. 511, a stand-alone Andante for piano whose refrain is written in *siciliano* style and whose key scheme is: i–VI–V_A $\parallel$ i–I–V_A $\parallel$ i. Here Mozart employed the opposite mode of the tonic key for Episode 2.

The two five-part rondos cited above suggest that there is no standard pattern of keys for the five-part rondo. Major-mode rondos tend to explore IV, vi, and i as contrasting keys, while minor-mode rondos tend to use III, VI, and I. The dominant major (V) or minor (v) is also a possibility, but composers sometimes avoid it, perhaps because the retransitions emphasize the active dominant. Nor should this discussion be taken to imply that AB–AC–A rondos do not occur in rapid-tempo finales, although at that tempo the format is likely to produce a short movement. One example, however, occurs in Mozart's Piano Sonata in C, K. 545, all of whose movements unfold in smaller proportions. Another is the finale of Haydn's Quartet in B-flat, op. 33 no. 4.

Variants of the Five-Part Rondo
(AB–[…]C–A and AB–AB–A)

In the Allegretto finale of Mozart's Piano Sonata in B-flat, K. 570, we find an invitation to perceive an AB–AC–A format whose expected second appearance of A has been eliminated, thus producing the pattern ABCA, or, more clearly, AB–[...]C–A. The refrain (A, mm. 1–22) is a sectional rounded binary in the tonic key. Episode 1 (B, mm. 23–42) follows directly, without transition, and it is deployed as a continuous rounded binary with internal repeats, also (somewhat exceptionally) in the tonic key. There follows a brief but important two-bar transition, mm. 43–44. Since this is a rondo movement, such a link would normally create the impression of a retransition heralding the return of the refrain. Instead, however, it tilts toward V^7/IV, and triggers a "premature" second episode in E-flat (C, mm. 45–56), also presented as a continuous rounded binary with repeats. Thus one gets the sense that the central refrain has been bypassed. There may be a witty purpose behind this choice. If episode 1, for example, had been deployed in the key of the dominant, then this two-bar RT, introducing a flatted seventh scale-degree (mm. 43–44) would have worked perfectly, leading back to the tonic key and the refrain. But episode 1 was placed in the tonic key, and as a result the otherwise normative RT takes us a fifth lower, to IV. This quick-tip to the "wrong-key" may be what triggers the early episode 2 in IV, creating an ellipsis in the more normal form. Following episode 2, a retransition (mm. 57–62) leads to a

---

28. This episodic allusion is not to be taken as a evidence on behalf of Cone's "sonata principle." See He-

pokoski, "Beyond the Sonata Principle," pp. 112–15, mentioning K. 570/iii on p. 114.

dominant preparation based upon the "b" material of the original refrain. The refrain itself follows, limited to its a' section, and the piece concludes with a coda based primarily upon material from the first episode. The whole may be represented as:

A	B	RT?	[no A!]	C	RT	A' +	coda
I	I	$\Rightarrow$ V/IV		IV	$\Rightarrow V_A \parallel$	I	I

From this piece one may conclude that even in the "pure" rondo, one return of the refrain could be (deformationally) eliminated. The result here is a single interrupted harmonic motion: $I-IV_T-V_A \parallel I$.

Another structure related to the familiar AB–AC–A design is that in which episode 2, instead of providing something new, essentially revisits episode 1, producing an AB–AB'–A format. Three finales from Haydn's op. 33 quartets are in dialogue with this pattern. The first is No. 2 in E-flat: the two nonclosed, *Fortspinnung* B sections, based "developmentally" on A-material, begin at mm. 36 and 107; both dissolve into RT at their ends. The second is No. 3 in C: the two B sections proper (B and B') occupy mm. 23–36 and 93–107, the first moving from A minor to E minor (from vi to its minor dominant), the second from C minor to E-flat major (from i to its major mediant). Both give the impression of providing only the first half of a binary structure: each of their expected "second halves" is wittily (impudently?) displaced by a lengthy, A-based RT, mm. 37–72 and mm. 107–24. The third is No. 6 in D, although its lack of retransitions also suggests an only mildly developed rondeau format. Moreover, both of its B sections are in the tonic minor. Since both A and B material return in decorated ways in their recurrences, the result might also be re-

garded as being a rondo-variation, a format that is additionally in dialogue with the principle of alternating variation.[29] (If the AB sections of a seeming AB–AB'–A pattern were to trace through a recognizable exposition-recapitulation format, we would regard the result as a Type 1 sonata-rondo mixture, a Type 4[1], a design visited further below. That is not the case, however, in these Haydn examples.)

The Seven-Part Rondo or "Chain Rondo" (AB–AC–AD–A)

If a composer adds a third contrasting episode and a fourth statement of the refrain, the result is the AB–AC–AD–A seven-part rondo, a rather rare occurrence in Haydn and Mozart. One example is found in the finale of Mozart's Clarinet Trio in E-flat, K. 498 ("Kegelstatt"), although the initial AB (mm. 1–51) is shaped into a sonata exposition—with a P-based S in V—which never returns symmetrically as a recapitulation. This movement's Type 4 (sonata-like) features are limited to that opening section, following which it proceeds as an unambiguous seven-part rondo with two clearly demarcated, harmonically closed episodes with internal repeats (C, in vi, mm. 67–90; D in IV, mm. 116–53).[30] One piece that Caplin cited as exemplifying this form is the Allegretto finale of Mozart's Piano Trio in G, K. 564.[31] To be sure, this is a possible interpretation of the piece, according to which the three episodes explore the keys of D (V), G minor (i), and C (IV). The D-major material, however, is more properly heard as the b section of a sectional rounded binary, with the preceding and following passages as the a and a' sections respectively. On this reading, the refrain comprises a rounded binary form (a b+a' with

---

29. Sisman, *Haydn and the Classical Variation*, p. 174, described op. 33 no. 6/iv as an "alternating rondo-variation finale." See also p. 72 for her distinction between "rondo-variation" and "variation-rondo," the difference being the assessment of which principle, rondo or variation, is uppermost.

30. As also mentioned below, other examples with a seemingly "extra" episode, such as that in the finale of Mozart's Violin Concerto No. 5 in A, K. 219, are more clearly understandable as Type 4s (sonata-rondos) with

an additional refrain-statement and episode in the developmental space—in this case an extended and unforeseen "Turkish invasion," A minor, into the hypergalant European minuet.

31. *Classical Form*, p. 284, n. 20. Caplin also cited the finale of Beethoven's Quartet in C Minor, op. 18 no. 4. This movement, however, is cast in the AB–AC–AB'–A symmetrical seven-part rondo form, to be discussed in the next section.

the first part subjected to a written-out repeat) rather than a repeated period. Thus the piece reduces to an AB–AC–A five-part rondo.[32]

The Symmetrical Seven-Part Rondo (AB–AC–AB'–A)

From time to time one comes across an AB–AC–AB'–A design, in which episode 3 (B') is a tonic transposition of the off-tonic episode 1 (B). This is the rondo counterpart of the symmetrical three-couplet rondeau (that is, with larger thematic units and employing retransitions). Accordingly, we term it the *symmetrical seven-part rondo*. Most obviously, the tonic transposition of B is analogous to the tonal resolution of a sonata form. It is also frequently the case that a V:PAC or III:PAC concluding episode 1 becomes a I:PAC or i:PAC ending episode 3, thereby suggesting the sonata's EEC/ESC relationship (a feature also common to the symmetrical three-couplet rondeau). Nevertheless, since A and B are merely juxtaposed thematic blocks (since there is no TR after the rondo theme proper), this structure should not be considered a full-scale sonata-rondo (or Type 4 sonata).

An example may be found in the Allegro finale of Beethoven's Quartet in C Minor, op. 18 no. 4. The refrain (A, mm. 1–16) is structured as a continuous rounded binary form with repeats. Episode 1 (B, mm. 17–40) is a sectional rounded binary (with repeats) in A-flat (VI). The C-minor refrain recurs (m. 41) without retransition or dominant preparation, and each of its two parts is now subjected to a written-out varied repeat (as in a "rondo-variation"). Episode 3 (C, mm. 73–86) is a continuous rounded binary (with repeats) in the tonic major (I). Again the C-minor refrain enters with no preparation (m. 87), and this time its part 1 is given a literal repeat, while part 2 is given a varied repeat. A transition (mm. 111–16) leads to a prolonged dominant seventh chord, which prepares for episode 3 (B', mm. 117–36), a transposition to the tonic major (I) of the first part of episode 1, here given a varied and extended repeat. The second part of the binary is bypassed

in favor of a lengthy retransition (mm. 137–62, based upon the refrain theme) that leads to a dramatic dominant preparation. The final return of the C-minor refrain is rendered Prestissimo (mm. 163—and without internal repeats). It is followed by a coda (m. 178) that eventually breaks through to the tonic major (m. 204)—though perhaps surfacing here at the end only as an ironic or negative sign of what the rondo proper had been unable to achieve. The movement may be diagrammed as:

A	B	A	C	A	TR		B'	RT		A + coda
i	VI	i	I	i	$\Rightarrow V_A$ ‖	I		$\Rightarrow V_A$ ‖	i	i—I

Op. 18 no. 4/iv begins without retransitions, and refrains follow episodes immediately, in the manner of the old rondo. This allows Beethoven to set up a provocative dialogue with the principle of harmonic interruption. We normally associate an interruption with a double rebeginning: the music starts over again on the tonic harmony with the original thematic material. In this rondo the second refrain marks a thematic rebeginning without a harmonic interruption; the third refrain does the same. The onset of episode 3 (B') follows an interrupted dominant but does not create a thematic rebeginning. Only at the final refrain (which also follows an interrupted dominant) are harmonic and thematic rebeginnings synchronized, and this structural convergence triggers the sudden breakaway tempo.

The rotational implications of the symmetrical seven-part rondo are similar to those of the symmetrical three-couplet rondeau. The model of a major-mode piece may be shown as follows:

Rotation 1: A B RT	Ends V:PAC, then V_A
Rotation 2: A C RT	Ends X:PAC, then V_A
Rotation 3: A B' RT	Ends I:PAC, then V_A
Rotation 4: A + coda	Ends I:PAC

In a minor-mode piece Rotation 1 would probably end III:PAC or VI:PAC, while Rotation 3 would end either I:PAC or i:PAC.

---

32. This second interpretation is strengthened by the fact that the D-major material is based upon the opening theme. The G-minor and C-major sections, however, also display a kinship to this theme.

Refrain-Material in Nontonic Keys:
The Rondos of C. P. E. Bach

Rondo-refrains (A) nearly always recur in the tonic key: a return to the refrain is also a reaffirmation of the tonic. The most notable late-eighteenth-century exceptions to this norm occur in the idiosyncratic rondos of C. P. E. Bach—especially in thirteen individual clavier rondos published in collections 2–6 of the *Kenner und Liebhaber* series from 1780 to 1786 (mingled with sonatas and fantasias). These rather free compositions often articulate the rondo theme—or at least its incipit—in keys other than the tonic. This gives the impression of a modulatory or free-floating refrain, perhaps recalling earlier ritornello practice. Charles Rosen assessed them as "essentially modulating fantasias."[33] In so doing, they would appear to fall under the implicit censure of the theorist Kollmann, who in 1799 (citing works of Bach) distinguished between "proper" rondos ("in which the first section always returns in the principal key, either in its original form, or varied") and "improper" ones ("in which the subject or first section also appears in keys to which a digression may be made").[34]

C. P. E. Bach's unusual rondos are anomalous, and they are not to be used as paradigms of that form. (As might be expected, they also differ one from another in interesting ways.) By way of example, we might note only that in the first of the thirteen rondos—C major, H. 260, *Kenner und Liebhaber* 2/i—the refrain idea, a simple eight-bar period, recurs several times in the piece, often incompletely, sometimes dis-

solving away from its final cadence, sometimes materializing only as an isolated antecedent or consequent, and sometimes called forth as a hesitant reference to the refrain-incipit only, its first two bars. Apart from several crucially placed C-major tonic appearances—doubtless the structural anchors of the piece—one also hears the idea in G (V, m. 21, consequent), in E minor (iii, m. 54, incipit only, broken off), in F (IV, m. 57, incipit only), in A minor (vi, m. 68, incipit only), in B-flat (♭VII, m. 71, almost complete), and in E (III, m. 107, varied and almost complete). It would be a mistake, however, to assume that each appearance of the rondo idea occupies an equal structural status. Not every "A-theme" statement should be considered a refrain proper. Mm. 21–24, in G—a first, "wrong-key" attempt at a local reprise—are subordinated to their position within the larger, tonic-centered rounded-binary block, adapted and varied as a whole in mm. 1–42. To regard mm. 21–24 as a genuine refrain of comparable structural weight as the one found in m. 1 would miss the point. Moreover, in H. 260 some later nontonic refrain-surfacings seem like impulsive local intrusions (momentary "visits") inside predominantly episodic domains, all within a compositional style in which refrain material and quasi-episodic alternatives interpenetrate and are treated liberally, not in the customarily schematic way that we associate with other rondos. In sum, while refrain-material does appear in several different keys, it is anything but clear that all of the nontonic, often incomplete soundings are "refrains" in any appropriately structural sense.[35]

---

33. Rosen, *Sonata Forms*, 2nd ed., p. 126.

34. A. F. C. Kollmann, *An Essay on Practical Musical Composition*, p. 6 (chapter 1, section 12). Kollmann's attitude, of course, is not necessarily that of censure: he could merely have been registering an irregular practice. See also the discussion in Malcolm S. Cole, "Rondos, Proper and Improper," *Music & Letters* 51 (1970), 388–99; and Fisher, "Further Thoughts," p. 89 n. 14.

35. Cf. the remarks of Ulrich Leisinger in the entry "Rondeau—Rondo" in *Die Musik in Geschichte und Gegenwart*, 2nd ed., ed. Ludwig Finscher, Sachteil, vol. 8, col. 554. According to Leisinger, "With the finale of [C. P. E. Bach's] Clavier Trio of 1775, Wq 90.2, the rondo is found in a new, already nearly ripened form for the first time [in Bach's works]. The principal theme [*Hauptthema*],

an eight-bar period, is heard seven times—in the keys of G, D, B, G, C, E-flat, and G." Leisinger then proceeds to recall Forkel's 1778 "theory of the rondo" (*Musikalisch-kritische Bibliothek*, vol. 2), which somewhat sternly advises composers that any episode should be related to and spring naturally from the rondo theme itself, often in the manner of a paraphrase. As a result, "the frequently read claim that in his rondos C. P. E. Bach made use of the refrain in keys other than the tonic . . . is to be modified, if we assess the situation on the basis of Forkel's theory, since the principal idea [*Hauptgedanke*] can also serve as the foundation for the episodes. There, however, it is not perceived to have the function of a refrain." See also Galand, "Form, Genre, and Style," p. 37.

The Sonata-Rondo (The Type 4 Sonata)

What Qualifies as a Sonata-Rondo?

In the symmetrical three-couplet rondeau and the symmetrical seven-part rondo (both schematized as AB–AC–AB'–A), we noticed the principle of tonal resolution characteristic of the sonata: the transposition to the tonic key (as episode 3 or B') of material that was originally stated in an off-tonic key (as episode 1 or B). This carries with it the implication that a V:PAC (or III:PAC, v:PAC, VI:PAC, and so on) that closes episode 1 will eventually become a I:PAC (or i:PAC) to close episode 3. We also commented upon its rotational implications, along with those of the three-couplet/seven-part pattern (AB–AC–AB'–A-coda), which are particularly telling in the parallels between Rotation 1 and Rotation 3. Both the tonal and rotational aspects of these rondeau and rondo formats display an obvious kinship to the tonal and rhetorical features of sonata form. This suggests that they may be understood as formal hybrids—as mixtures of the rondo (or rondeau) and the sonata. While this is relevant to any analyses of pieces organized by means of these structures, it may also be said that they do not rise fully to the level of the "sonata-rondo" in the strictest sense of the term. For that reason we do not consider them to be sonata-rondos (Type 4 sonata forms).

A piece or movement should not qualify as a (full-scale) sonata-rondo, or Type 4 sonata, unless its first rotation is structured as the exposition of a sonata (P TR ' S / C), and a later rotation either recapitulates this expositional pattern (the strong norm) or recomposes the pattern in what may still be reasonably (and flexibly) considered to be recapitulatory space (as often in the exceptional practice of later Haydn, as will be seen). To consider the matter in broad generalizations: if the material immediately following the closing PAC of the refrain's opening statement is structured as a simple period or hybrid (usually in a contrasting key), the piece is probably a rondeau, particularly if the refrain itself is comparably brief. If it is structured as a more elaborate binary form, the piece is a rondo. But if it begins as a recognizable expositional transition, then we are dealing with a sonata-rondo or Type 4 sonata. That TR typically leads to other features characteristic of sonata expositions. In most cases, it will drive to a medial caesura, followed by a secondary-theme zone with EEC, and perhaps a closing zone as well before initiating a retransition back to the refrain. It is also possible, especially in several of Haydn's Type 4s, for the TR not to produce an MC at all but to carry out a TR⇒FS process producing a continuous exposition with EEC and possible closing zone. Whatever its internal format, the exposition of a standard Type 4 sonata is never repeated. The absence of any repeat sign at this point is often the clearest "early" notational signal that the movement is a Type 4, not a Type 3. Instead of a literal repeat, the exposition, ending with an obvious retransition back to an active dominant, will proceed ahead to the reappearance, full or partial, of the rondo theme.[36]

Especially with full-scale sonata-rondos, the traditional letter designations (A, B, and so forth) become inadequate and should be dispensed with. In dealing with the thematic modules of the Type 4 sonata, it is more accurate to use the terminology of the sonata, not the rondo—with only a few adaptations. In a Type 4 exposition we consider the initial, closed rondo theme not as "A" but as a P-refrain (P^{rf}), a primary theme with "rondo-character," whose simultaneous function also as a rondo refrain remains intact throughout the piece. Following the I:PAC close of P^{rf} we have the customary sonata designators, TR, MC (or TR⇒FS), S (not "B" or "episode 1"), EEC, and C.

Type 4 sonatas usually mix the rondo principle with the Type 3 sonata, but a less common hybrid with the Type 1 design is also possible. Accordingly, we will jettison such traditional terms as "seven-part sonata-rondo" and "five-

---

36. A few exceptions in Haydn's works are noted in the section below on "Haydn's Treatments of Type 4 Finales."

part sonata-rondo" and regard these as *Type 3 sonata-rondo mixtures* (Type 4³—or, more simply, Type 4 without the superscripted numeral) and *Type 1 sonata-rondo mixtures* (Type 4¹). In addition, the Type 1 sonata-rondo is often treated to a special type of expansion, fairly often encountered in Mozart's works, which we call the *expanded Type 1 sonata-rondo mixture* (Type 4¹⁻ᵉˣᵖ). For most analysts, though, the term sonata-rondo immediately conjures up the mixture with the Type 3 sonata—so familiar from many of Beethoven's finales, where many of the clearest examples (sometimes with small variants) are to be found. We shall deal with that format first.

The Standard Type 4 Sonata (The Type 3 Sonata-Rondo Mixture)

This hybrid typically begins with a light, square-cut, and memorable "rondo-style" opening theme, Pʳᶠ, which is almost always harmonically closed. It may be a simple period or sentence, but in larger pieces it is often shaped as a rounded binary or simple binary structure, sometimes with internal repeats. In a Type 4 sonata this "rondo-identifier" Pʳᶠ proceeds directly into TR-space and thence further into the exposition, either at the onset of the next bar following the concluding I:PAC of Pʳᶠ, or sometimes directly elided with that PAC, often with a sudden *forte* affirmation. The nonrepeated expositional rotation concludes with either an RT or a C⇒RT passage that reactivates the tonicized dominant (or, in the case of a minor-mode piece, that leads from the tonicized III or v to an active dominant). The second (developmental-space) rotation begins with a tonic statement of P (full or partial) and then proceeds either to a development of the expositional material or to an episode; this episode may be a closed binary form similar to the typical episode 2 (C) of a symmetrical seven-part rondo. The developmental rotation ends with a retransition and dominant preparation. The third (recapitulatory) rotation also concludes with a retransition and dominant preparation that leads to a fourth tonic statement of all or part of P; this P may or may not be followed by a coda. Hence this for-

mal hybrid always ends with a partial fourth rotation that comprises either P alone or P + coda, and may be referred to as the "coda rotation" ("the rotation that contains the coda").

The normative Type 3 sonata-rondo mixture may be diagrammed as:

Rotation 1: Pʳᶠ TR ' S / C⇒RT   EEC on V:PAC or III:PAC, then Vₐ

Rotation 2: Pʳᶠ development   Ends Vₐ
or episode   RT

Rotation 3: Pʳᶠ TR ' S / C⇒RT   ESC on I:PAC or i:PAC, then Vₐ

Rotation 4: Pʳᶠ + optional coda   Ends I:PAC

This form exists on a continuum somewhere between the "pure" Type 3 sonata and the "pure" symmetrical seven-part rondo. In composing such a hybrid the composer may emphasize either the sonata or the rondo aspect by structuring the post-Pʳᶠ portion of Rotation 2 as either a development or an episode. A Type 4 with a central development tilts more in the direction of the most normative Type 3 proper than does one with a closed, interior episode (although one should also recall that such an episode may also occur within the developmental space of a Type 3 sonata). Here again, however, it is not the presence or absence of a development proper that makes the larger structure a sonata-rondo (or Type 4 sonata) but rather the expositional layout of Rotation 1 and the normatively symmetrical tonal resolution of Rotation 3.

The Allegro grazioso finale of Mozart's Piano Sonata in B-flat, K. 333, provides a clear example of the Type 4³—although, as is common, one that also displays a few unusual features. In this case Pʳᶠ is structured not in a more expansive binary format but only as a repeated parallel period (mm. 1–8) whose *forte* restatement (mm. 9–16) might suggest the orchestral *tutti* repetition commonly heard at this point in some of his concerto finales. This is followed by a modulating sentence with an obvious TR-function (mm. 17–24)—a central marker of a Type 4 sonata (as opposed to a "pure" rondo). This TR leads to a rhetorically weak V:HC medial caesura in m. 24. An S-theme in the dominant follows, a sentence with a varied repetition of its continuation⇒cadential module (upbeat to m. 25–36; the recomposed repetition is motivated by an evaded cadence in m. 32). The secondary theme's V:PAC EEC (m. 36) is elided with a five-bar RT that ends on an active V^7 chord. Thus Rotation 1 follows the P TR ' S / RT pattern. There is no closing zone. What we have heard so far (perhaps with the adjustment of the RT into a more normative C-zone) could equally well have been the exposition of a Type 3 sonata. It is only with the absence of an expositional repeat, the presence of an RT, and the tonic-key return of P^{rf} as the onset of the next rotation that the Type 4 status of this movement becomes clear.

Rotation 2 begins with a literal restatement of the *grazioso* P^{rf} (mm. 41–56), followed by the same presentation module that had initiated TR (upbeat to m. 57). This time the TR-based passage leads via an augmented-sixth chord to the dominant of G minor (V/vi, m. 64). A new theme follows, initiating a central episode. This is an eight-bar sentence (upbeat to m. 65–72) in G minor (vi) that ends on another half cadence in that key (V/vi, m. 72). A brief, chromatic transitional link (mm. 72–75) leads unexpectedly to the key of E-flat (IV) and to the "second stage" of this central episode. (It sometimes happens that interior episodes are subdivided into two or more stages—unseparated by any sounding of P^{rf}—each giving the impression of an individualized "episodic" theme and tonality.) We are now given another new theme beginning in m. 76, a sentence whose attempts to cadence are continually frustrated. As a result, this second stage of the central episode is left harmonically unclosed. Just at the point of its potential closure, though (an explicit cadential formula in E-flat, IV, in m. 89), its completion is starkly undercut by a return of P^{rf}-based material on C minor (m. 90)—entering incisively to block the predicted episodic cadence in IV with a chill and also to initiate a P^{rf}-based retransition, one that also recalls the "false-start" procedure ("wrong-key" attempts to start the recapitulatory rotation) outlined in chapter 12. This RT leads ultimately to a prolonged dominant preparation (mm. 102–10) that incorporates RT-material from the end of Rotation

1—an element that helps to predict the "inevitable" return of P^{rf}. The modulatory aspect of Rotation 1's entire post-P^{rf} material, as well as its harmonic incompleteness, suggests its larger role as that of filling out a developmental space within the Type 4 sonata. Rotation 2 as a whole moves I–vi$_T$–IV$_T$–V$_A$.

Beginning in m. 112, Rotation 3 follows a typical recapitulatory path. P^{rf} returns unchanged, while TR is recomposed (and expanded) in order to close with a I:HC MC (m. 147), one whose rhetorical features are much stronger than those of the relatively unassuming V:HC MC of the exposition. S is transposed to the tonic (upbeat to m. 148), and its repeated continuation is dramatically expanded to make the arrival at the I:PAC ESC especially strong (m. 163). The RT passage from Rotation 1 is also expanded and leads to the most surprising feature of this movement—and certainly to something exceptional within Type 4 norms. This RT, most unusually, leads to a cadential $\frac{6}{4}$ chord sustained by a fermata (m. 170), and Mozart follows it with a fully composed "Cadenza in tempo" (upbeat to m. 171–98) that ends on an active dominant (V^7, m. 198). This cadenza setup and interpolation suggests yet another hybrid feature of this movement—a mixture with at least this element of the Type 5 sonata (concerto first movement), outlined in chapters 19–22. (One might also recall the "concerto-like" *forte* restatement of the initial P^{rf} period at the opening, mm. 9–16. In this case we may say that while Mozart mixed rondo norms here primarily with Type 3 format-structures, at one or two points, and especially toward the end, he alluded in a separate, *ad hoc* way, to Type 5 practice as well.)

Following the non-normative cadenza, Rotation 4, the coda rotation, starts with a single statement of P^{rf} whose consequent phrase is greatly expanded through evaded cadences and subsequent extensions. (Even its "definitive" trill cadence, mm. 212–13, is undermined by $\hat{3}$ in the bass at the downbeat of m. 213.) The "struggling" consequent is followed by a P^{rf}-"fade-out" coda proper (mm. 214–24), which ends, finally, with a conclusive, *forte* cadence.

The finales to several of Beethoven's piano

sonatas also provide instructive examples of the standard Type 4 sonata, though usually—and most typically—with individual quirks that are of special interest. The otherwise paradigmatic Sonata in C, op. 2 no. 3/iv, for instance (with a closed, F-major central episode), is marked by a dramatically "failed" exposition and non-resolving recapitulation (no EEC or ESC in sonata-space; in both spots the repetition of S collapses into minor and proves unable to reca-dence); and by witty, "wrong-key" references (in A major, m. 298, then A minor, m. 302, each halted with tentative pauses of reflection) to P^{rf} at nearly the end of the coda-rotation. The Sonata in E-flat, op. 7/iv (again with closed central episode, here in C minor) introduces the coda-rotation's P^{rf} on the "wrong" tonal level, E-major (a half-step too high), m. 157—as if the tonal processes have momentarily slipped off-track—before correcting the key at m. 161 and subsequently appending a tonic coda proper, m. 166, that also looks back to the central ep-isode. The Sonata in D, op. 10 no. 3/iv—an edgy, nervous movement throughout—provides a disturbingly compressed exposition (with S at m. 17); no EEC; a tonally shifting, rapidly dis-solving central episode that starts in ♭VI (m. 33); a "wrong-key" attempt to restart the recapitula-tory rotation (m. 46, beginning on ♮III), with tonal correction at m. 56; and a radical defor-mation of what one expects to the be recapitula-tory rotation, which, in its fidgety tension, finds itself "unable" to reprise the original S at all, much less in the tonic, and instead strays off into differing tonal areas, failing also in the process to secure an ESC. The Sonata in C Minor, op. 13/iii, is more normative in its overall effect, but its preparation for what must surely be regarded

as S (m. 25) is abrupt and deformational—no effective MC is articulated—and, famously, the movement's final gesture once again features a by-now-typically Beethovenian "wrong-key feint" of the opening bars of P^{rf} in VI, the key of the central episode (and the slow movement), before the aggressive C-minor tonic correction ("no escape!") in the final bars.[37]

In the hands of Haydn, Mozart, Beethoven and others, both the simple rondo and the Type 4 sonata-rondo were invitations to high-formal extravagance and wit—a propensity for struc-tural play congruent with the "popular," often insouciant simplicity of the refrains that pro-pelled them forward. "Surprising" deviations from an implied heuristic norm were part of the game.

The Type 1 Sonata-Rondo Mixture (Type 4¹)

This hybrid, Type 4¹, merges the rondo principle and the Type 1 sonata. As discussed in chapter 16, the Type 1 sonata, lacking a development, is a double-rotational structure—an expositional rotation followed by a recapitulatory rotation. An optional coda begun with P^{rf} may suggest a perhaps partial third rotation. When the Type 1 sonata is blended with the rondo, both the ex-positional and the recapitulatory rotations end with a retransition (or C⇒RT) and dominant preparation for a tonic return of P^{rf}. After the recapitulation is completed, its subsequent RT leads once again to a third tonic statement of P^{rf} —or to a slightly varied allusion to it. This refrain may or may not be followed by a coda proper. Hence this formal hybrid always ends with at least the onset of a third rotation (the coda rotation) that comprises either P^{rf} alone or

37. The final moments of op. 13/iii are discussed, in the context of Edward T. Cone's misleading "sonata principle" claims about them, in Hepokoski, "Beyond the Sonata Principle," *Journal of the American Musicologi-cal Society* 55 (2002), pp. 115–18. Beethoven's penchant for witty, "wrong-key" entrances of P^{rf} does not undo the norm that P^{rf} is to make its reappearances in the tonic. On the contrary, it is precisely on the strength of that norm that the effect of Beethoven's transgres-sions of it relies. Another instance from the period in question, among several, occurs in his C-major Rondo for Piano, op. 51 no. 1. Not unlike the deformational

Type 4 procedure in op. 10 no. 3/iv, this piece provides a "wrong-key" start to what listeners might at first take to be a recapitulatory rotation (P^{rf} in A-flat, m. 76), fol-lowed by a dissolution of that theme and its subsequent correction into the "right key," the tonic (m. 92), and a "failed" recapitulatory remainder that is unable to pro-duce the original S idea at all. Thus while the piece does display an exposition—the most crucial marker of a Type 4 sonata—it does not provide a full recapitula-tion. See also the discussion above of C. P. E. Bach's keyboard rondos with seemingly modulating refrains.

P^{rf} + coda. The Type 1 sonata-rondo mixture may be laid out as follows:

Rotation 1: P^{rf} TR ' S / C⇒RT   EEC on V:PAC or III:PAC,
                                            then V$_A$

Rotation 2: P^{rf} TR ' S / C⇒RT   ESC on I:PAC or i:PAC,
                                            then V$_A$

Rotation 3: P^{rf} (+ coda)   Ends I:PAC

Until we arrive at the end of the second rotation, it may be difficult to distinguish a Type 4^1 from a "pure" Type 1, since many Type 1 expositions also end with an RT or a C⇒RT in order to prepare the recapitulation. In addition, many Type 1 sonatas conclude with a P-based coda. The distinguishing feature of the Type 1 sonata-rondo mixture, Type 4^1, is the extensive retransition that also concludes Rotation 2, as well as the relatively literal restatement of P that follows. Thus the retransition that leads from the recapitulation back into a relatively intact P^{rf} for the beginning of the third refrain-statement and coda rotation is a crucial indicator of this format. (This distinction is also discussed in chapter 16.) The composer may additionally emphasize the rondo aspect of this structure by fashioning P^{rf} as a "refrain-like" rounded binary form with internal repeats. Because most Type 4 sonatas exist on a continuum, situated somewhere between the "pure" sonata and the "pure" rondo, it is occasionally difficult to determine whether the sonata or the rondo elements predominate in a given piece. Sometimes the interplay between the sonata and the rondo conventions forms the expressive core of the piece. Insisting that hard cases must be decided one way or the other might miss the point. The (nonexpanded) Type 4^1 is an infrequently encountered form. The Type 1 with P-as-coda, easily mistaken for the Type 4^1, seems to crop up more often. Generally considered, one should not give the nod to the Type 4^1 category unless two factors are also present: a "rondo-block" structure, or at least character, to the P theme (a convincingly "rondo-like" P^{rf}) and, especially,

the presence of the RT setup for the final appearance of that P^{rf}.

Examples of this Type 1 sonata-rondo mixture may be found in the finale of Mozart's Quartet in E-flat, K. 428, in the slow movement of Piano Sonata in D, K. 311 (though with very short, one-bar RTs), and in the slow movement of his Symphony No. 39 in E-flat, K. 543. In K. 543/ii (Andante con moto) the opening theme (which we eventually realize is P^{rf}) is structured as a 27-bar rounded binary with internal repeats in the tonic key of A-flat. Because the primary-theme zone of a sonata exposition does not normally contain double bars and repeat signs, the listener might well anticipate a more clearly sectional form, perhaps something on the order of a compound ternary or a five part rondo. Following this theme, however, a two-measure link (mm. 28–29) bursts open into a *forte*, nine-bar *Sturm und Drang* TR (m. 30)—the first of many dramatic contrasts in this movement. This TR begins off-tonic in F minor (vi)[38] and leads to a first-level default medial caesura (V:HC, m. 38): at this point, the sonata aspect of the design comes to the fore. The MC is followed by a trimodular S that may also be construed as a sentence. We first hear a triple presentation of the "b" idea from P^{rf} that "holds open" the dominant harmony of the MC, in the manner of an S^0 (or S$^{1.0}$) module (mm. 39–40, 41–42, 43–45), giving the impression, perhaps, that the movement's aesthetic protagonist—marked by his or her own thematic module—is reacting to the storm that was so violently and unexpectedly unleashed in the preceding TR.[39] This is succeeded by the *forte* unleashing of a four-bar continuation (mm. 46–49) featuring fragmentation and a descending fifth sequence; and finally by yet another quieter reaction, *piano*, a five-bar cadential unit (mm. 50–54) that brings about the V:PAC EEC. This cadence at m. 54 elides with the onset of a C⇒RT zone. A seven-bar sentence, at first suggesting an obvious drone-pastoral mood (mm. 54–57, the calm

---

38. TRs that begin with a sudden plunge into vi, typically following a P-theme that overdetermines the tonic, are discussed in chapter 6.

39. An alternative interpretation might regard the bars following the MC-effect as "place-holding" caesura-fill.

On that reading the CF flowers into a set of differing modules, and no S-theme proper is ever fully launched. From this perspective what we have is one type of continuous exposition, "unable" to produce a genuine S.

after the storm?), reinforces the V:PAC with a *forte*, cadential module (mm. 58–60; a spontaneous outpouring of heartfelt gratitude?), which itself elides with a slightly varied repeat of the presentation-drone (m. 60). This time the repeat reactivates the dominant and is converted into a retransition that prepares the recapitulatory rotation.

By this point we may suspect that a Type 4^1 sonata-rondo mixture is in progress. Rotation 2 is launched with a restatement of P^{rf} (m. 68) that eliminates the internal repeats and varies the texture and orchestration. Most important, its final limb, the a' section, is tonally derailed (mm. 91). The theme now seems to crumble away before being able to complete itself, and at m. 96 the music drops instead into a PAC in the unexpected key of C-flat minor (♭iii, enharmonically respelled as B minor.) The expressive impact of this unexpected swerve away from the tonic into such a dark tonal region cannot be overemphasized. This tonally estranged PAC sets off the stormy TR, here recomposed and lengthened, leading to the normative I:HC MC (m. 108). The recapitulation's tonal resolution follows: S, slightly extended, is transposed to the tonic, and the ESC at m. 126 is followed by C⇒RT, which this time first tonicizes (mm. 137–42), then reactivates the dominant. Rotation 3 (m. 144) restates only the first part of P^{rf} (the a section of the rounded binary), greatly expanding the consequent phrase of the original

parallel period, as if to compensate for the tonal disruption in Rotation 2.

The Expanded Type 1 Sonata-Rondo Mixture (Type 4^{1-exp})

It sometimes happens that the second rotation of a Type 4^1 sonata-rondo mixture—the recapitulatory rotation—features the same sort of pronounced internal expansion found in the unmixed Type 1 sonata, turning that structure into the "expanded Type 1" variant (chapter 16). Most commonly, this "billowing-out" occurs during the recomposition of the P–TR zones, that is, in the pre-MC portions of the recapitulation. Recomposing parts of P–TR, of course, is a common feature of sonata practice. In the present sonata-rondo case, though, we are confronting internal expansions that are significant in terms of thematic contrast, key, length, or developmental earnestness. The expanded passage should impress one as either a manifestly separate episode (which would emphasize the rondo-character of the entire hybrid structure) or a genuinely sustained patch of "development" (conversely, underscoring its sonata-character), not merely a momentarily intensified and recomposed P–TR zone. It should strike one as something beyond what one might normatively expect at this point.[40] We indicate this important, expanded variant of the Type 4^1 sonata form—found with some frequency in Mozart's works—as Type 4^{1-exp}.[41]

---

40. In the second movement of Mozart's Symphony No. 39 in E-flat, K. 543, for example, analyzed above, the *Sturm und Drang* transition is expanded from nine to thirteen bars. As a reaction to the preceding tonal lurch, this expansion is certainly noteworthy, but is insufficient to lift the piece out of the category of the "pure" Type 4^1 sonata-rondo. The same is true of the finale (Allegro vivace) of Mozart's Quartet in E-flat, K. 428. Here TR is expanded from twenty-five bars in Rotation 1 to thirty-three bars in Rotation 2. Because this sort of expanded recomposition may also be encountered in the recapitulation of any sonata type, it is insufficient to warrant a consideration of the movement under the norms of a separate category.

41. One might wonder whether the Type 3 sonata-rondo mixture (Type 4^3) may be treated to a similar sort of expansion—that is, whether its third (recapitulatory) rotation may feature an interpolated development or episode. Although rare, instances do exist. One

example is the Allegro finale (marked "rondeau") of Mozart's Piano Sonata in B-flat, K. 281. In this piece, the post-P^{rf} portion of Rotation 2 comprises a continuous simple binary in G minor (vi, mm. 52–67) followed by a brief retransition (mm. 68–70). Rotation 3 begins with a restatement of P^{rf} (m. 72) followed by a sudden inflection toward E-flat (IV) and a new, closed theme in that key (mm. 90–101). A lengthy retransition (mm. 102–23—including an internal reference to P^{rf})—leads to an extended dominant preparation that seems to prepare yet another return of P^{rf}, but instead leads to the delayed tonal resolution (S in the tonic key, m. 124). After the ESC (m. 136), a retransition prepares Rotation 4, which is limited to a final return of P^{rf} (m. 143). (One should not misinterpret this finale as a "nine-part sonata-rondo" that lacks a fourth return of A.) Another example may be found in the finale of Violin Concerto No. 3 in G, K. 216.

For inexperienced analysts the Type $4^{1\text{-}exp}$ sonata contains a number of traps into which it is all too easy to fall. The most tempting analytical missteps, though, are readily avoided if one approaches the structure with a firm grasp of the rotational practice guiding the large-scale events. To illustrate (here we adapt an argument put forth by John Daverio):[42] in one typical scenario, an episodic or developmental "billowing-out" can occur when the tonic return of P^{rf}, launching Rotation 2 and the recapitulation, is followed by either a closed episode or a genuine development (often of P^{rf} or TR material) or by both. This episodic and/or developmental expansion has frequently been mistaken for "Episode 2 (C)" of a seven-part sonata-rondo in which the third statement of the refrain (A) is eliminated. In other words, some analysts have parsed this familiarly Mozartian pattern as ABACB'A, suggesting that it arises as an "incomplete" ABACAB'A design.[43] Once again we see the pitfalls of reducing the Type 4 sonata to a mere string of alphabetic symbols. Type $4^{1\text{-}exp}$, the expanded Type 1 sonata-rondo mixture, may more meaningfully be conceived as a rotational structure:

Rotation 1: P^{rf} TR ' S / C⇒RT	EEC on V:PAC or
	III:PAC, then V_A
Rotation 2: P^{rf} (TR) [development or	ESC on I:PAC or i:PAC,
episode]...TR ' S / C⇒RT	then V_A
Rotation 3: P^{rf} (+ coda)	Ends I:PAC

It is essential to notice that in a Type $4^{1\text{-}exp}$ sonata form the Rotation 2 interpolation, even if it is a new and separate episode, frequently links up at its end with the end of the original TR, now transposed to the tonic key. The Rotation 2 expansion often leads to a crux-point that slips onto correspondence measures in TR-space. This means that it rejoins an ongoing rotation-in-progress, one that had begun

with the second tonic statement of P^{rf} (the onset of Rotation 2). This is readily perceived if one examines the music on either side of the individualized episode or developmental expansion, looking in particular for evidence of the linear, rotational ordering of the modules first presented in the exposition. Disregarding the episode itself (assuming here the most challenging case of a "new," nontonic episode that functions as a self-contained interpolation), the question becomes: is the rotational ordering otherwise preserved throughout? If so—and if the other Type 4 "rondo" signals are also in play (such as the RT functions and the third statement of P^{rf} to launch the coda rotation)—then one is confronting a Type $4^{1\text{-}exp}$ sonata.

The central thing to observe—the main feature that undermines the erroneous ABACB'A view of this form, with its faulty presumption of a missing rondo element—is that the recapitulatory S is often prepared in the same manner (by the same MC) as it had been in the exposition. The Rotation 2 passage of episodic or developmental expansion does not normally bring us to a standard RT that would lead us to expect a tonic return of P^{rf}. On the contrary, the music from the TR-crux-point onward indicates that the next anticipated rotational event will be not P^{rf} but the tonic return of S. Once this is grasped, any sense of a supposedly "missing" P^{rf} disappears. The attentive and informed listener should not expect the return of P^{rf} until after the RT that concludes Rotation 2.[44]

One of the most common places to find this structure is in the rondo-finales of several (though not all) of Mozart's concertos, where an additional feature of "ritornello" or "tutti-solo" contrast is also thrown into the mix. Mozart's concerto adaptations of this and the Type 4^3 structure are discussed toward the end of the present chapter. Both straightforward

---

42. Daverio, "From 'Concertante Rondo' to 'Lyric Sonata': A Commentary on Brahms's Reception of Mozart," *Brahms Studies*, vol. 1, ed. David Brodbeck (Lincoln: University of Nebraska Press, 1994), pp. 115–17.
43. As still in Cole's revised "Rondo" entry in *The New Grove*, 2nd ed., vol. 21, p. 653. See, also, e.g., n. 60 below.

44. Daverio, "From 'Concertante Rondo' to 'Lyric Sonata,'" pp. 115–17, also made this point, taking to task Malcolm Cole and Charles Rosen in the process. The latter had made a bad situation worse by referring to examples of this form as (in Daverio's words) "sonata-rondos with reverse recapitulations." (See Rosen, *Sonata Forms*, rev. ed., pp. 123–32.)

and adapted versions of the Type 4[1-exp] are also found, however, in several finales of some of his non-concerto works: it became a favored format for the mature Mozart sonata-rondo finale. It occurs, for instance, in Piano Sonatas in C, K. 309/iii, in C Minor, K. 457/iii, and in D, K. 576/iii; in the Sonata in D for Two Pianos, K. 448/iii; in the Piano Quartet in G Minor, K. 478/iv; in the String Quintets in C, K. 515/iv, and in G Minor, K. 516/iv; in the Quartet in D, K. 575/iv; and in several other last movements.[45] Particularly in non-Mozartian finales, however (and especially in later works, such as those of Schubert and Brahms), the analyst should take care not to confuse the Type 4[1-exp] with the expanded Type 1 proper, (the nonrondo version of the form, discussed in chapter 16), whatever their apparent similarities. As with the Type 4[1], the rondo-identifiers of Type 4[1-exp] (apart from the "suggestive" rondo-character of the theme) are the presence of the RTs leading back to P[rf], and the sounding of P[rf] as a satisfactory rondo-refrain at the outset of a coda rotation.

If we look at the Type 4[1-exp] Allegretto finale of Mozart's Quartet in D, K. 575, for example, we find a nonrepeated exposition (normally a sonata-rondo signifier) that features a P-based S (m. 32) and a contrasting C (upbeat to m. 59).[46] A retransition follows, mm. 67–71. In Rotation 2, the start of the recapitulation, P[rf] (m. 72) is followed first by a reworked version of TR (m. 91) that leads to a "false MC" on V of F major (♮III of D, m. 104), then by a "wrong-key," F-major statement of the beginning of S (m. 105). This is evidently to be understood as a witty anomaly that needs correction. And that is precisely what happens. Mozart soon leads the music into the point of TR-crux (m. 124 = m. 28, varied) to the "correct" MC on V of D (m. 127 = m. 31, now in the tonic) and follows this, in continu-

ing correspondence measures, by the true tonal resolution (S in the tonic). As expected, the recapitulation is followed by RT (m. 164) leading to a return of P[rf] (cello, m. 182) and an ensuing coda. In this case Rotation 2, the recapitulatory rotation—with its extra, "wrong-key" expansion—might be diagrammed as:

$$P^{rf} \quad TR\ [\text{——}\ (') \ S \text{——}]\ \text{end of TR}\ '\ S\ /\ C\quad RT$$

The interpolation in K. 575/iii is clearly of the developmental type—a feature that tilts the sonata-rondo hybrid more in the direction of its "sonata" elements. By contrast, the interpolation in the recapitulatory rotation of the Molto allegro finale of the Sonata in D for Two Pianos, K. 448, is an obvious subdominant episode surrounded by "referential" TR material on both sides. Rotation 2 begins with a nonrepeated P[rf] in the tonic at m. 139. Its I:PAC (m. 154) leads to a five-bar transitional link based on the exposition's opening TR[1.1]-module (mm. 16–20) but this time tipping toward the subdominant. This triggers the central episode in G major, IV, a closed rounded-binary structure with written-out repeats (mm. 159–206). After the episode's IV:PAC close the music pulls efficiently toward a crux-point that resuscitates modules from the exposition's TR (m. 215 = m. 26), now sounded at the tonic-key pitch level and leading toward the corresponding MC in m. 229 (= m. 40). Considered rotationally, what we have is an ongoing TR-space that is momentarily "stopped" by the interpolated episode (or whose central modules are written over by it). Nonetheless, the rotational implications of the larger P–TR succession could hardly be clearer. K. 448/iii is as a *locus classicus* of the Type 4[1-exp] with an internal-episode expansion in the recapitulatory space.

---

45. The list of Mozartian works in this and Type 4[1] structure provided in Daverio, "From 'Concertante Rondo' to 'Lyric Sonata,'" p. 114, is more complete—although not every movement on this list rises to the category of a Type 4[1-exp]. We regard the Quartet, K. 428/iv, for example, as merely a Type 4[1]; and the *Polonaise en rondeau* slow-movement center of Piano Sonata in D, K. 284, lacks an exposition proper and is hence

not to be regarded as a Type 4[1-exp] sonata-rondo: it is better understood as a merely sectional, less developed "rondeau" forerunner of the Type 4[1] proper.

46. Particularly in his later works, Mozart may have considered the P-basis of S in some of his finales—suggesting recurrence—to be a feature of the "rondo-character" of the whole, though by no means is the P-based S a unique feature of his Type 4 movements.

Before leaving this topic we might provide an indication of how understanding a background heuristic model helps one to grapple with hard cases. The Allegretto grazioso finale of Mozart's Piano Sonata in C, K. 309, is an intricate Type 4$^{1\text{-}exp}$ sonata (which the composer labeled a "rondeau") with extraordinary recapitulatory complications, among which the central subdominant episode is by no means the most provocative. Following the recapitulation's opening, P^{rf} (mm. 93–111), we plunge into a brief passage of S material (S$^{1.4}$, mm. 111–15, based on figures from mm. 58–62—the first of a series of unexpected, "nonrotational" happenings) that serves as a transition to F major (IV). At this point, the composer stitched in a closed episode in F, a repeated parallel period (mm. 116–31). Moving out of the episode, he provided a retransition (mm. 131–42) that prepares for the tonal resolution (S in the tonic, which begins at m. 143). In this case, unusually, the RT passage is *not* based on anything from the exposition's TR—which is suppressed altogether—but rather, from m. 137 onward, on S$^{1.2}$ (!), thus not producing the usual TR-crux-point and ensuing correspondence measures. This is a curious moment. The seeming disorder of the referential modules on either side of the episode does not suggest a rotational pursuit. The implication of a rotational structure (and a Type 4$^{1\text{-}exp}$ design) is revived only with the return to S at m. 143—as if one were grasping at a principle of order to pull together the whole.

Even though we might feel ourselves "safely" arrived at S (where a succession of correspondence measures is the norm), the surprising events continue to unpin our sense of security. The just-heard S$^{1.2}$ is omitted in favor of a third, varied repetition of S$^{1.1}$, for instance (mm. 151–56), and S$^{1.4}$ fails to produce the expected ESC,

dissolving instead into an "early" RT around mm. 178–79. Shortly thereafter, and in advance of the C-modules that would close out the rotation proper, Mozart (prematurely!) brings back P^{rf} (m. 189), as if beginning a coda rotation. Strictly considered, this would be an instance of coda-rhetoric interpolation (CRI, Chapter 13 above)—coda-like behavior, including the suggestion of a rotational restart—wedged into the concluding sections of a recapitulatory rotation before it has completed itself. This is therefore a premature interpolation of Rotation 3 behavior into the still-unfinished Rotation 2, as if P^{rf} were appearing punctually "on schedule," blissfully unaware that no ESC and C-theme had been sounded.[47] With the I:PAC that concludes this P^{rf} (m. 204), a version of the only apparently "missing" S$^{1.2}$ tumbles in (m. 204), eventually setting up a "corrective" return to the recapitulatory rotation and the return of the original C-idea (m. 214), though in a context in which the ESC has yet to be sounded. Within this context of modular dislocation—comparable to the head-spinning confusions of identity and order typical of *opera buffa*, the giddy defiance of sober but artificial convention[48]—C gives way suddenly to S$^{1.4}$ (m. 221), which, this time, does manage to bring the much-abused Rotation 2 to the ESC (m. 236). A coda proper follows, based on TR (the P^{rf} ticket having been spent prematurely as an interpolation into Rotation 2), and a final view of a *piano*, "expiring" P^{rf} incipit drags its way across the finish line in the concluding bars. In sum, the deformational recapitulatory rotation of K. 309/iii, Rotation 2, can be represented as follows (with the bold-printed letters suggesting the rotationally governing features):

P^{rf} *[S$^{1.4}$── (') Episode S$^{1.2}$──] (')* **S$^{1.1}$ S$^{1.3}$ S$^{1.4}$** ⇒ *RT! (')* *[P^{rf}!! S$^{1.2}$!!](')* **C** *[S$^{1.4}$!!]*

---

47. From a different perspective, Rotation 2 (the recapitulatory rotation) and Rotation 3 (the coda rotation) are composed as overlapping at this point.

48. Daverio, "From 'Concertante Rondo' to 'Lyric Sonata,'" p. 120, referred to cases in which "material from the first group is redistributed or 'scattered' throughout the responsive portion of the design," noting that "Mozart's amplified binary movements feature terminal references to the whole of the principal material that

has come before." He also interpreted these "terminal references" as a "summarizing coda." It is uncertain whether Daverio's claim that such scattering is typical of Mozart's Type 4$^{1\text{-}exp}$ sonata-rondo movements can be fully supported. The more important point would be to come to terms with each individual instance from the perspective of rotation theory, standard coda practices, coda-rhetoric interpolation, and so on.

Haydn's Treatments of Type 4 Finales

Haydn adapted the Type 4 sonata with remarkable freedom. In itself this is hardly surprising, since he, more than any other composer of the period, sought a pervasive originality of content and design in his works, as though he were remelting at each compositional moment the crystallizing forms and procedures that had come to be normative, even schematic, in the hands of others into a persistent volatility of instantaneousness, an unpredictable malleability that often eludes a clean capture by the standard, heuristic formal categories. However "simply" Haydn might begin a movement, each of its subsequent moments—once past the initial idea—bursts with an energy of ongoing invention, a spontaneous sense of "generation on the spot" that can skew the compositional pathway into unforeseen, sometimes asymmetrical directions. One of the central paradoxes of Haydn's style is the vast gulf that separates the seeming simplicity of his thematic materials (the "naïve" or "problem-free" manner in which they are often first stated) from the densely complex, dizzyingly vitalistic treatment to which they are almost immediately put.[49] Ultimately, this aspect may point to a foundational incongruity at the heart of the Haydn style—one that drives to the core of his persona as a composer—but it is surely also a feature of high connoisseurship that the composer invited his most adequate listeners to relish.

While Haydn's high-pressure, bar-to-bar originality is a source of delight for attentive listeners, the same quality makes him a difficult composer to use as a frequent source for paradigms on form. The more or less standard formal options used by his contemporaries seem ever-present in Haydn, but more often principally as benchmarks or background concepts that he persistently tweaks, overrides, and alters on the acoustic surface of the music (what one actually hears). While this is certainly true of his Type 3 sonatas—with their often-thoroughly recomposed recapitulatory spaces, for example—it is even more the case with his Type 4, sonata-rondo finales. Here the "rondo-invitation" to high-spirited play in rapid tempos spurred Haydn to compose even more exuberant transformations of the formal options at hand. As has been recognized by all who have attempted the task, those who approach most of these Type 4 finales with only the standard schemata in hand (much less with only the inappropriately reductive letter-scheme, ABACAB'A) will find themselves challenged at nearly every turn, particularly as one gets past the "expositional" portion of the form. The result has been a tangle of musicological definitions and debates about what ought to count as a bona-fide sonata-rondo in Haydn.[50]

In confronting a fast-tempo Haydn finale that is not a variation movement, one might expect to find that its main lines will be dominated by one of three formal options: the Type 3 sonata (the "standard" sonata form also characteristic of his first movements); the rondo (or rondeau); or—with increasing frequency only from the late 1770s onward—the Type 4 sonata (the so-

---

49. On Haydn and our metaphor of the vitalistic musical particle, constantly in pursuit of growth and transformation, see the section of chapter 11 with subtitle, "Recompositions, Reorderings, Interpolations."

50. Readers wishing to familiarize themselves with some of the musicological discussions and conflicting interpretations regarding this uncommonly complicated topic might begin by reviewing some central articles in the exchanges between Malcolm S. Cole and Stephen C. Fisher in the 1970s, 1980s, and 1990s. Both writers presented a wealth of historical and analytical data, seeking to find defensible paths through Haydn's ever-original finales. Their analyses, including a reliance on (schematic-letter) systems that we have abandoned, are sometimes different from ours. See, e.g., Cole, "Haydn's Symphonic Rondo Finales" (n. 23); and his

"Rondos, Proper and Improper" (n. 34). For Fisher, see his "Sonata Procedures in Haydn's Symphonic Rondo Finales of the 1770s," *Haydn Studies: Proceedings of the International Haydn Conference Washington, D.C., 1975*, ed. Jens Peter Larsen, Howard Serwer, and James Webster (New York: Norton, 1981), pp. 481–87; and his "Further Thoughts on Haydn's Symphonic Rondo Finales" (n. 19). In this debate we prefer Fisher over Cole, even though our own approach to these finales differs from his in some central features. Cf. also the extended studies of Bernhard Moosbauer, *Tonart und Form in den Finali der Sinfonien von Joseph Haydn zwischen 1766 und 1774* (Tutzing: Hans Schneider, 1998); and Reiner Leister, *Das Finale in der Sinfonik Joseph Haydns* (Stuttgart: ibidem-Verlag, 1999). Each of these studies leads one to further bibliography on the topic.

nata-rondo mixture). In fact, though, many of Haydn's finales from the 1780s and 1790s are ingenious hybrids among these options.[51] Under such circumstances any simple classification is insufficient. A number of the finales—including several in his most celebrated works—wittily present conflicting generic signals in different portions of their structures, as if musical processes that begin within one category suddenly shift (or "change their mind") to allude to procedures in another. Movements that begin as fairly clear Type 4s can change midstream to take on more telling characteristics of either the rondo proper or the Type 3 sonata. Conversely, even those finales that are most clearly Type 3s often have a strong rondo or Type 4 character. A central aspect of Haydn's game-like approach to the finales was to ride the dividing lines among the different formal options as the movement proceeds, now tilting this way, now that—ultimately to produce individualized and ingenious syntheses among the "purer" (heuristic) options.[52] The task of the analyst is to explicate the connotations of Haydn's compositional choices as they unfold in time, not to provide the end product with a reductive, monodimensional classification.

When considering any Haydn finale from about 1773 onward,[53] one should initially examine the procedures of the first third of the movement, those through its first rotation. If the movement contains a sonata-exposition (two-part or continuous) that includes a notated, full repeat—the most decisive generic marker—that movement is to be regarded as governed primarily by the norms of a Type 3 sonata, whatever other rondo or Type 4 tendencies it might display elsewhere, for instance

in the style of its P-theme.[54] Only two of the finales from the twelve "London Symphonies" have this repeat sign (No. 98 in B-flat and No. 104 in D); as do two of the three quartets from op. 74 (No. 1 in C and No. 3 in G Minor), three of the six quartets from op. 76 (No. 1 in G, No. 3 in C, and No. 6 in E-flat), and both of the quartets from op. 77.

When a sonata-exposition is present (as opposed to the merely sectionalized portions of a "pure," transitionless rondo, as in the finales of the Quartet in B-flat, op. 76 no. 4, and the Symphony No. 96 in D) and an expositional repeat sign is *lacking*, this should be regarded as a signal that the governing principle of the movement is at least initially announced to be that of the Type 4 sonata-rondo. The Type 4 impression is typically reinforced by the light or playful, *contredanse*-character of $P^{rf,}$ along with Haydn's characteristic structuring of it as a binary or rounded-binary structure, often with notated internal repeats. (In Haydn's finales, the presence of such notated repeats within a binary or rounded-binary P^{rf} is invariably a Type 4 signal, although it is one that is sometimes encountered in other composers in works that turn out to be Type 3s.)[55] Another important Type 4 marker is the presence of a retransition (RT) at the end of the nonrepeated exposition along with the subsequent tonic restatement of at least the opening module of P^{rf} as a refrain-identifer. This last signal, however, is sometimes lacking, as will be outlined below. In any event, if all of these signals are in place, the predominantly Type 4 status of the movement is assured, regardless of the potentially unorthodox treatment of what might follow, especially in the space that we anticipate will be occupied by a recomposed recapitulation.

51. As Fisher put it in "Further Thoughts," p. 101, "Haydn is exploring a spectrum of possibilities that does not take into account the conventional [present-day] distinction between the rondo and the sonata-rondo." Also quoted in Cole, "Rondo," *The New Grove*, 2nd ed., p. 653.

52. Cf. Fisher, "Further Thoughts," p. 86: "Haydn is fond of hybrids incorporating elements of one design into movements that have the overall structure of another."

53. Fisher, "Further Thoughts," p. 85: "Haydn actually began experimenting with the combination of sonata

and rondo elements in a symphonic finale no later than 1773."

54. Here again we agree with Fisher, "Further Thoughts," e.g., pp. 95, 96, 97, and 100. Cf. p. 86: "The position of repetition marks is always an important indication of Haydn's thinking."

55. See, e.g., chapter 5 with regard to Type 3 P-themes in binary or rounded-binary formats, a few of which contain internally notated repeats: the finales of Mozart's String Quintet in D, K. 593, and Schubert's Symphony No. 5 in B-flat.

In sum: Haydn's Type 4 movements are to be identified as such primarily by their binary or rounded-binary themes coupled with the presence of a nonrepeated exposition and the immediate tonic return of at least the beginning of P^{rf}.[56] While some version of P^{rf} nearly always does begin what we presume will be a recapitulatory rotation, a convincingly symmetrical recapitulation is not always forthcoming, nor does the concluding rotation (the coda rotation) always begin with a literal return of P^{rf}. To be sure, in several Type 4 finales Haydn additionally provided at least a quasi-symmetrical recapitulation subjected to his usual thorough recomposition. When this happens, the result is that the normative Type 4 practice is at least more clearly perceptible amidst the recapitulatory recastings: in those, for example, of Symphonies No. 94 in G, No. 99 in E-flat, No. 102 in B-flat, and No. 103 in E-flat. In these recapitulatory spaces Haydn revisited a sufficient number of (often substantially recomposed) thematic modules within the tonal resolution portion to provide a general sense of their quasi-symmetrical return. In other instances Haydn merely touched lightly on an individual referential module or two with a much-compressed tonal resolution, as in the finales of Symphonies No. 85 in B-flat (mm. 190–97 = mm. 39–46, "$S^{1.0}$") and No. 88 in G (mm. 195–97 = mm. 66–68, "$S^{1.2}$," varied and given a different continuation).

Some of Haydn's finales, however, begin in the manner of Type 4s—at least through the nonrepeated exposition—but then pursue other options that produce the effect, unfolding through specific events in time, of a thoroughgoing formal hybridity that eludes simple classifications. Among the complicating procedures that one can find in Haydn are the following.

Type 4[1] Variants

The Type 4[1] sonata, like the more standard Type 4[3], follows a nonrepeated exposition with the return of the primary theme, which in this case simultaneously functions as the onset of the recapitulation. Since both forms invite the return of P^{rf} at this point, the potential for the slippage from the one to the other is present, and the only way to distinguish them is to examine what follows in the rest of the movement. (Will there be a recapitulation after the ensuing development or episode, as in the Type 4[3]? Will that full-blown development or episode—if it exists as such at all—be patched into the already begun P–TR space of the recapitulatory rotation, as in the Type 4[1-exp]? Or will the rotation display not so much a developmental or episodic "expansion" as a comprehensive recomposition, as in the Haydnesque variant of the Type 4[1]?) The generically challenging last movement of Symphony No. 95 in C Minor, for instance, is perhaps best regarded as an unusual example of a Type 4[1] sonata among these finales.[57] In this case, within Rotation 2 the TR⇒FS portion of the continuous exposition returns significantly recomposed—fully reconceived—including the breakout of a quasi-episodic "C-minor storm"

---

56. This is also the view of Fisher, *contra* Cole ("Further Thoughts," p. 86).

57. The formal ambiguities called forth in Symphony No. 95/iv are illustrative of Haydn at his most structurally playful. While by no means minimizing the ambiguities, our preferred interpretation regards m. 78, the emphatic resumption of the TR⇒FS fugato first heard at m. 33, as a "celebratory" onset of C-space rather than as the beginning of a brief development. (If it were a development it would be either one of a Type 3 sonata without an expositional repeat and whose exposition was elided directly into the development—virtually unheard of in Haydn's multimovement works—or of a Type 4[3] sonata that suppresses an appearance of P^{rf} at this point, a Type 4 deformation that does sometimes occur in late Haydn, as mentioned in the next paragraph.) The direct elision of the fugato with the triggering authentic cadence at m. 78 is particularly provocative. This is not the way that Haydn's developmental spaces typically begin. On the other hand, such an elision is a characteristic way to launch a closing zone, C. That said, however, this C at m. 78 seems to aspire to certain features of development (the descending fifths) but is soon cut off from that pursuit with the harmonic discharge onto V/vi in mm. 100–5. This suggests that what begins as an apparent C at m. 78 flirts with the idea of development but ultimately turns into a retransition. Thus mm. 78–105 may be regarded as a C⇒RT link that has been uncommonly expanded—under which interpretation the formal category of choice, lacking a clearly separable development, shrinks to a Type 4[1] format. Nonetheless, its witty interplay with the expectations of developmental activity at this point in the structure should not be overlooked.

(m. 152). A variant of P^{rf} returns only to launch the coda rotation at m. 186. Somewhat similarly—though with different details—the finale of Symphony No. 93 in D, with its developmentally enlarged second rotation (recapitulatory rotation, beginning with the opening phrases of P^{rf} at m. 172), seems most at home as a Type 4^{1-exp} sonata-rondo.

Omission of RT and Any Tonic Reference to P^{rf} after the Exposition

Since one of the defining features of the sonata-rondo is the immediate return of the refrain after the exposition, its pointed omission—moving instead immediately into the development—is a strong indicator of Type 3, not Type 4, behavior. Consider, for instance, the Presto finale of the Quartet in F, op. 74 no. 2. This begins with a "rondo-style" rounded-binary theme with internal repeats (mm. 1–34), clearly suggesting a Type 4 to come. The nonrepeated exposition concludes with an emphatic full-stop in m. 104. This final caesura shuts down any potential for the appearance of the expected RT. As a consequence, the music omits the refrain proper to plunge directly into a P^{rf}-based, rotational development that begins at m. 105 with the head-motive P^{rf} treated in imitation, beginning on V and proceeding through a series of modulations. A recast recapitulation (at first compressed, but then recomposed and enlarged triumphantly toward its end) begins with a tonic P^{rf} in m. 146. Unlike what happens in the exposition, this recapitulation does feature an RT at its end (effectively, mm 259–71), one that leads to a brief allusion to the refrain at the beginning of the coda rotation, m. 272. In sum: once past the exposition, this finale behaves like a Type 3 sonata with a P-based coda, all the while sporting a high-spirited, Presto-driven "rondo character" in its themes.

Haydn revisited the procedure of op. 74 no. 2/iv—the Type 4 that strives to become a Type 3 *en route*—in the last movements of two quartets from op. 76: no. 2 in D Minor and no. 5 in D. Op. 76 no. 2 is a clear Type 3 in all features except for two decisive markers of the Type 4: its binary, "rondo-like" P-theme (Vivace assai), with notated internal repeats; and

its nonrepeated exposition. In this instance the large-scale Type 3 impression is heightened by omitting any reference to P^{rf} after the recapitulation. (On the other hand, if we choose to regard this finale as a Type 3 *tout court,* it would be an isolated example in Haydn of a Type 3 whose P-theme contains internal repeats and that does not display an expositional repeat.) In op. 76 no. 5/iv Haydn took the procedure a step further: this time the presto P-theme, while certainly sufficiently *contredanse*-like to serve as a rondo refrain, is not structured in a binary format. Still, the exposition is not repeated (mm. 1–120)—again, something that never happens in Haydn's "pure" Type 3 finales—and the music moves at once into the development at m. 126.

More Radically Recomposed Recapitulatory Spaces

While it was Haydn's general practice to vary and recompose his recapitulatory spaces, in some of these finales the recomposition is so substantial that the concept of "recapitulation" becomes strained. At what point of alteration does an expected "recapitulation" turn into something different—suggesting, perhaps, yet another "episode" of an ongoing rondo, albeit one that might be construed as "standing in" for a more normative recapitulation? In the Vivace finale of Symphony No. 101 in D the Type 4^3 outlines are clear through the developmental rotation (which begins with a variation of P^{rf} in m. 103 and persists through m. 188). The presumed recapitulatory space, however, is completely reconceived as a brilliant fugato based on the P^{rf} head-motive (m. 189), with, at best, only the most passing of potential allusions, if any at all, to figuration originally heard in the later parts of the exposition. This "recapitulation-substitute" section is broadly symmetrical with the exposition in its normative position within the movement, in its P-references, and in its thorough grounding of the tonic, D. But as something that can give the impression of a "new" fugal episode, it is certainly not a normative recapitulation. While Symphony No. 101/iv is an extreme case, radicalized recompositions of the recapitulatory space might also be observed in the last movements of Symphonies No. 97 in C and 100 in G.

The concept of a movement that starts, at least potentially, as a Type 4 (with a sonata-style exposition) but falls short of a full recapitulatory symmetry as it continues is one of the source problems underlying the ongoing debates about the structures of these finales. One way of resolving this problem is to take a more supple, *rotational* approach to these movements. Whatever Haydn's "recapitulatory" alterations to a potential Type 4^3 sonata, the compositional space in question, leading off with P^{rf}, is most emphatically another rotation, one that usually highlights the final solidifying of the tonic key. As pointed out in the discussion of rondo-rotations toward the opening of this chapter, in rondos and Type 4 sonatas each rotation is initiated by P^{rf} but may then spin outward to produce differing continuations or alternatives, which can be quite freely conceived. Thus a Type 4^3 sonata is one with three rotations plus (usually) a final coda rotation. Each of the three rotations begins with P^{rf} and ends with an RT. In order minimally to qualify as a Type 4 sonata-rondo, Rotation 1 must be recognizable as a sonata exposition (nonrepeated), in either a two-part or a continuous format. Rotation 2 often begins with a shortened version of P^{rf} (sometimes only the "a" limb) and proceeds either to an episode or to a development. (Occasionally this central section may consist of two subrotational cycles, with an intervening P^{rf} and further development, as in Symphony No. 94/iv, mm. 104 and 146.) In Haydn's hands Rotation 3, the recapitulatory rotation, is the most variably treated and often the most puzzling. To construe what happens here primarily as another rotation in a process of delineating an ongoing formal freedom—a rotation at least standing in for normative recapitulatory space—goes a long way toward facilitating our approach to these finales.

No Return to P^{rf} as a Literal Refrain after the Recapitulation

It often happens in Haydn's Type 4 variants that the recapitulation does not recycle the music back to the normative appearance of P^{rf} as a recognizable (or unequivocally "thematic") final refrain. In its place, typically in the general vicinity of the expected start of the coda—though sometimes before or after it—may indeed be P^{rf}-references, perhaps variants of the rondo theme's incipit, but not enough of the idea *qua* "melody" to consider it a refrain proper as encountered in more standard Type 4 sonatas. Haydn's Type 4s often suppress the literalness of the last P^{rf}-return in favor of procedures that are better regarded as more typical of a normative Type 3 coda or CRI (which may or may not be P-based). Examples are legion: at the ends of the finales, for instance, of Symphonies No. 93 in D (m. 292), No. 94 in G (m. 234, P-reference in the "wrong-key" E-flat), No. 95 in C Minor (m. 186), No. 97 in C (mm. 291, 313), and many other works. This alteration of more standard practice helps further to produce the effect of blending between the Type 4 and Type 3 formats. As was the case with several of Haydn's adaptations mentioned above, it suggests that the most commonly encountered trajectory of generic interaction in these finales is for them to start out as more or less regular Type 4s but gradually to sift in features more typical of Type 3 practice.

Type 4 Procedures in Mozart's Concerto Finales

Like those of many of his contemporaries—and like Beethoven's—Mozart's concerto finales are almost always sonata-rondos, Type 4 sonatas. The most notable exceptions are those written as variations, most famously in the last movements of Piano Concertos Nos. 17 in G, K. 453, and No. 24 in C Minor, K. 491.[58] Mozart's concerto finales comprise a collection of stunning individuals, not only in expressive tone and content but also in the local details of their designs. While certain broad principles are shared among them, his creative reshapings of the Type 4 concept from piece to piece remain a challenge to anyone who seeks to generalize about them.

---

58. As noted by Joel Galand, "The Large-Scale Formal Role of the Solo Entry Theme in the Eighteenth-Century Concerto," *Journal of Music Theory* 44 (2000), 381–450, n. 25 (pp. 445–46): "The exceptions: the finale of the Concertone for Two Violins in C, K. 190 is a minuet and trio with a written out *da capo*," and the origi-

By the later 1770s and early 1780s Mozart had developed his own customizations of Type 4 practice. These customizations were also in dialogue with the Type 5, ritornello-grounded structures that he was developing concomitantly in the concertos' first movements. As a result, it is difficult to confront Mozart's Type 4 concerto finales without presupposing an awareness of the principles of his Type 5 first movements, the subject of chapters 19–22. This is especially true of the concertos that most listeners and analysts are likely to confront, the seventeen Viennese piano concertos written between 1782 and 1791 ("Nos. 11–27"—No. 12 in A, K. 414, is the earliest of the set) and the Clarinet Concerto in A, K. 622 (1791), although it applies to several others as well. These features proceed beyond features of local texture—beyond the expected dialogical interaction of solo and tutti.

For this reason, in the present discussion of Mozart's concerto Type 4s we are obliged to allude to concepts and terminology that will be laid out in full only in the following four chapters. These include references to such things as ritornello designs and functions, thematic labeling conventions within broad zones (such as R1:\C to designate an apparent closing theme that initially appears within a first orchestral tutti or ritornello), P-theme prefaces, and *sujet-libre* styled transition themes. Readers coming to this discussion from the concerto chapters that follow should have no difficulty in relating these terms to Mozart's Type 4 concerto-finale movements. Readers who have not consulted chapters 19–22 might wish to work through them first, or at least to consult those chapters now and again for more expansive definitions and examples of the new terms here. To be sure, this discussion of the concerto finales could have been placed at the end of the Type 5 discussion. And yet the rondo-logic of these movements makes them more at home in this chapter, even as we are thereby compelled to anticipate things to come in the remainder of this book.

One should also underscore another aspect that deepens the problem at hand. The mature Mozart's concerto-finale Type 4s constitute a second order of hybridization among the sonata types that Sonata Theory proposes heuristically. The non-concerto Type 4 sonata is already a (first-order) hybrid between the rondo and one of three other types of sonatas: the Type 3, the Type 1, and the expanded Type 1. Mozart's concerto finales usually sift in yet another element of hybridization, an intermixing, in varying degrees from piece to piece, with the composer's own idiosyncratic treatment of the Type 5 sonata, itself a mixture between the earlier, ritornello-based concerto and sonata form. One effect of this intermingling of structural associations is the occasional blurring in concerto Type 4s of some traditional functions that are clearer in the "purer" sonata formats—including Type 5 formats.

Despite these complications, it is possible to cut an efficient path through the topic of Mozart's concerto finales by keeping nonconcerto Type 4 designs firmly in mind—those discussed earlier in this chapter—and then looking at the portions of the concerto finales that are most likely to differ from those simpler designs. This entails a glance at each of three main topics: (1) the varieties of Type 4 designs found within Mozart's concerto finales; (2) the texture and structure of the opening refrain (Prf) and its tutti-extensions, if any; (3) the normative addition of a "new solo re-entry theme" starting in the tonic after the full closure of those P-space tutti-extensions. Once these things are clarified, the remaining features of the individual Type 4 movements become more navigable, notwithstanding their *ad hoc* character and localized differences. Our aim here can be only to present an overview of the central issues, along with an explanation of how these matters appear from the perspective of Sonata Theory.

Type 4 Formats in Mozart's Concerto Finales

Mozart's Type 4 concerto finales fall into two broad categories, each of which in any individual case is usually submitted to additional concerto

---

nal finales of Piano Concerto No. 5 in D, K. 175, and Violin Concerto No. 1 in B-flat, K. 207, are differing variants of what we call the Type 5 sonata. In addition, "the finales to the Sinfonia Concertante in E♭, K. 297b (a doubtful work), and the Concertos in G, K. 453 and C Minor, K. 491, are variation sets."

enrichment. The first is the *Type 3 sonata-rondo mixture*, the standard Type 4, or Type 4^3, with a central development or episode—or both—followed by a full recapitulation. The second is the *expanded Type 1 sonata-rondo mixture*, Type $4^{1\text{-exp}}$, in which the recapitulatory rotation begins immediately after the completion of the exposition and subsequent retransition but contains inner developmental or episodic expansions once P^{rf} has been sounded. Following its central expansion, this second rotation, in most cases, will merge back into correspondence measures—the crux—somewhere in the TR-zone (sometimes, though by no means always, at the convenient point of the solo's "new-theme TR opening") before proceeding into the tonal resolution.

One source of concerto enrichment in both formats is the highlighted interplay of solo-tutti dialogue (theme-sharing, back-and-forth responses, yieldings and collaborations), always a pronounced feature of concerto practice, and treated by Mozart in an unpredictable, individualized manner from finale to finale. Others include: the potential expansion of the tonally closed P^{rf} theme proper into a fuller block by means of a series of tutti-extensions, some with codetta functions; the almost invariable beginning of TR proper with a new theme for the soloist alone; the possibility for two- or three-stage central sections, perhaps juxtaposing developmental passages with episodes; the frequent preparation for and execution of a high-display *cadenza*, normally led into by the last retransition (set forth as an emphatic tutti after the completion of the recapitulation), and followed by the last sounding of P^{rf}, which launches the coda-rotation.

Many of Mozart's concerto finales present the Type 4^3 pattern in full. Examples may be found in Piano Concertos No. 10 in E-flat (K. 365, for Two Pianos), 14 in E-flat (K. 449), 15 in B-flat (K. 450), 16 in D (K. 451), 21 in C (K. 467), 22 in E-flat (K. 482), and 25 in C (K. 503). Additionally, some of Mozart's earlier concerto finales display Type 4^3 architectonic formats but with an "extra" episode or expansion at some point after the central episode. One place for such an additional expansion was between the

"normative" central episode and the recapitulation. This occurs in Piano Concerto No. 9 in E-flat, K. 271/iii, which includes a suddenly static, interpolated minuet in A-flat, IV, after the central episode proper and before the recapitulation; and in an earlier work, Violin Concerto No. 5 in A, K. 219/iii, with its extended, A-minor "Turkish" episode, preceded and followed by P^{rf}—which results in nothing less than the unexpected "invasion" of an entire, "extra" rotation before the onset of the recapitulation. Another place to interpolate an "extra" episode was between a statement of the recapitulatory P^{rf} and the onset of the "new theme" TR proper. This may be found in Violin Concerto No. 3 in G, K. 216/iii, and Concerto "No. 7" in F for Three Pianos, K. 242/iii.

Much notice has been taken of Mozart's other concerto-finale format, the Type $4^{1\text{-exp}}$, a double-rotational pattern plus coda-rotation with only three appearances of P^{rf} (beginning the expositional, recapitulatory, and coda rotations), not four as in the Type 4^3 pattern (which also includes an interior developmental rotation followed by a recapitulatory restart with P^{rf}). Following a thorough study of Mozart's concertos, Joel Galand concluded that what we call the Type $4^{1\text{-exp}}$ design "was Mozart's favorite procedure for composing finales that incorporated the ritornello and recapitulation techniques he was using in his concerto first movements, while also exploiting the popular fashion for rondos."[59] Examples may be found in the finales of twelve concertos: the Oboe Concerto in C (K. 314); the Flute and Harp Concerto in C (K. 299); the Sinfonia Concertante in E-flat for Violin and Viola (K. 364): the Clarinet Concerto in A (K. 622); and the finales of numerous piano concertos—Nos. 11 in F (K. 413); 12 in A (K. 414); 13 in C (K. 415, though with significant complications, discussed further below); 18 in B-flat (K. 456); 19 in F (K. 459); 20 in D Minor (K. 466); 23 in A (K. 488); 26 in D (K. 537); and 27 in B-flat (K. 595).

As might be expected, the main confusion regarding this latter structure—as with its non-concerto version—has been the unhelpful application of schematic letters to it, ABACB'A—

---

59. Galand, "The Large-Scale Formal Role," p. 408.

along with the incorrect assumption that the format should be regarded as a seven-part sonata-rondo with a supposedly expected "third A" omitted after C.[60] This misconstruction, which sometimes multiplies the analytical missteps by invoking the erroneous concept of a "reversed recapitulation," has been undermined in the past fifteen years in work by Joel Galand (an indispensable source in this regard, who correctly referred to the Type $4^{1\text{-exp}}$ as one type of "expanded binary" pattern—the "exposition-recapitulation pattern . . . [here also] subjected to the ritornello principle"), by John Daverio (calling it the concerto version of an "amplified binary" pattern, our expanded Type 1), and in earlier portions of this book.[61] Galand's position has been reaffirmed in recent work on Mozart's concerto finales by David Grayson and John Irving. (Irving also provides a succinct overview of Mozart's concerto-finale procedures.)[62]

Prf and the Possibility of Tutti-Extensions ("Ritornello 1")

In a nonconcerto Type 4 rondo, Prf may be a relatively brief theme (a period, sentence, or hybrid) or a slightly more developed structure, such as a simple binary or rounded binary form. Whatever the choice, the self-sufficient Prf— the rondo theme proper—comes to a cadential close, I:PAC, before proceeding onward, in most cases, into one or more P-block extensions confirming that cadence. In Mozart's concerto finales Prf typically (though not always) high-lights participation by the soloist in an engaging interplay with the orchestra. In the third volume (1793) of the *Introductory Essay on Composition*, Koch mentioned that "it is more usual that the solo part performs the rondo theme first, before it is repeated as a ritornello by the orchestra."[63] Apart from the problematic word "ritornello" (which creates more difficulties than it solves in many of these finales), Koch's description is indeed often the case in Mozart's concerto finales. It is typical for the soloist to lead off with the first module of the rondo theme proper, which may then be continued and brought to its conclusion through a back-and-forth dialogue between tutti and solo. But neither this familiar solo-onset nor the common solo-tutti interchange within Prf is invariable. A second-level textural default was to sound the entire P-theme complex, including all of Prf, in the orchestra and to bring in the soloist only at the beginning of—or even slightly into—TR. P-theme complexes sounded entirely by the tutti may be found in the finales of Violin Concerto No. 3 in G, K. 216, mm. 1–40 (in which the orchestral violins are also doubled by the *violino principale*), and Piano Concertos No. 11 in F, K. 413 (mm. 1–32), No. 12 in A, K. 414 (mm. 1–20), No. 14 in E-flat, K. 449 (mm. 1–32), No. 16 in D, K. 451 (with TR also beginning in the orchestra in m. 17, into which the soloist soon merges), and No. 25 in C, K. 503 (mm. 1–32). (No. 21 in C, K. 467/iii, also begins with the orchestra, though the soloist enters to conclude Prf in mm. 21–28.) A less common option is to

---

60. With regard to the concerto, this is implied, for example, in Green, *Form in Tonal Music*, 2nd. ed., pp. 251–52 ("The third refrain of the concerto-rondo is frequently omitted [in Mozart]"); cf. n. 43 above for the same issue in nonconcerto versions of Type $4^{1\text{-exp}}$.

61. Galand, "The Large-Scale Formal Role," p. 408. Galand's most extensive study is "Rondo-Form Problems in Eighteenth- and Nineteenth-Century Instrumental Music, with Reference to the Application of Schenker's Form Theory to Historical Context," Ph. D. diss., Yale University, 1990. The central conclusions are summarized in Galand, "Form, Genre, and Style in the Eighteenth-Century Rondo" (n. 6 above) and "The Large-Scale Formal Role" (n. 58 above). See also Daverio, "From 'Concertante Rondo' to 'Lyric Sonata,'" esp. pp. 113–19, with a list on p. 114 of examples that include concertos.

62. Grayson, *Mozart: Piano Concertos Nos. 20 in D Minor, K. 466, and No. 21 in C Major, K. 467* (Cambridge: Cambridge University Press, 1998), pp. 73–92 (esp. p. 82—on K. 466/iii—following Galand and insisting that it is only "a preconceived (and wrong-headed) notion of the form" that results in the erroneous impression "that something [an A refrain] may seem to have been omitted, suppressed, or bypassed"). Cf. the similar conclusions in Irving, *Mozart's Piano Concertos* (Aldershot: Ashgate, 2003), pp. 73–93 (chapter 5; Movement Forms III: Finales," esp. pp. 77–79).

63. Koch, *Introductory Essay on Composition*, trans. Nancy Kovaleff Baker (New Haven, Conn.: Yale University Press, 1983), p. 172, n. 50. Also cited in Irving, p. 81, who provided examples and variants in Mozart.

have P-space occupied entirely by the soloist (as in Piano Concerto No. 9 in E-flat, K. 271/iii, mm. 1–35).

Even more striking is that one often finds—especially in the Viennese piano concertos—that the rondo theme proper (the initial, I:PAC-closed P^{rf}, in which the soloist is often a participant) is only the first element of a more broadly conceived P-space. The square-cut, "rondo-character" P^{rf} proper is almost always followed by several additional, reinforcing tonic modules, normally played by the orchestra alone as a tutti. Sometimes these tutti-extensions to P^{rf} (P^2, P^3, and so on) are brief—only a codetta module or two. On other occasions the tutti-extensions are much longer. Typically, they close with a rhetorically emphatic flourish in the tonic, I:PAC, followed by a final caesura and re-entry of the soloist with a new theme (the onset of TR-space, TR^1, as we shall propose below). These multimodular extensions can take on roles that recall those found in the opening ritornellos of Mozart's Type 5 sonatas, such as a closing-theme or codetta-like function.[64] This hybridization (of Type 4 and Type 5) presents analytical and conceptual problems that must be confronted head-on, and it appears to have been a Mozartian innovation. As Galand concluded, referring to the more extended instances of this possibility, "Mozart appears to be the first to have developed the initial rondo refrain into a full-fledged ritornello section that occupies almost the same proportions as those found in first movements."[65]

When the tutti-extensions are short, they present few if any difficulties under the more normative Type 4 concept. As modest tutti-codettas within a clearly demarcated P-space, they seem little more than examples of more or less standard (non-concerto) Type 4 P^{rf} formats enriched through the juxtaposition of solo-tutti contrasts. Some of Mozart's earliest concerto

finales contain brief codetta-extensions that are not played exclusively by the tutti, and P-space is concluded with music led by the soloist. This happens in the finales of Violin Concertos No. 4 in D, K. 218 (P^2 and P^3, mm. 19–22, 23–30, then linked with a sudden tutti impulse into a solo-led TR proper) and No. 5 in A, K. 219 (P^2, mm. 17–22); and in those of Piano Concertos No. 7 in F, K. 242 (P^{rf}, a solo-tutti antecedent and consequent, mm. 1–8, 9–16, followed by P^2, solo-led cadential codettas, mm. 17–22) and No. 9 in E-flat, K. 271 (in which the piano solo occupies all of P-space, mm. 1–35, and the tutti that follows at m. 35 is a straightforward TR of the dissolving restatement type). In such cases, the concept of any "ritornello" intervention proper (in the Type 5 sense) is hazy—apart from an appeal to the loose, Kochian sense of a tutti restatement of or brief response to a solo-presented module within an otherwise musically closed P^{rf}.

Most often, however, one finds a closed P^{rf} with solo participation that comes to a I:PAC (with or without the soloist at that point) that is elided with a set of vigorous tutti modules, all in the tonic. Examples are plentiful in the Type 4 finales of Mozart's piano concertos. What varies from one instance to the next are a number of factors. As already mentioned, there is the unpredictable degree to which the soloist will participate in the rondo theme proper, along with the varying ways in which the orchestra can repeat or complete P^{rf}. Also variable are other factors that pertain to the post-P^{rf} tutti-extensions that are appended to it while still occupying an expanded P-space: its breadth and extent; the differing quasi-functional characters of its modules (locally TR-like? S-like? C-like?); and the uses to which these modules will be put (or not put) in the remainder of the movement.

In the finale of Piano Concerto No. 27 in B-flat, K. 595, for instance, Mozart laid out P^{rf}

---

64. Koch's writing from the late-eighteenth and early-nineteenth centuries is of little help with regard to this "ritornello" issue in Mozart's concerto rondos. Cf. Irving on Koch, *Mozart's Piano Concertos*, p. 91.
65. Galand, "The Large-Scale Formal Role," p. 419. Galand did note on the same page, however, that shorter

tutti extensions were not unheard of in the concertos of other composers "that Mozart might have known—principally . . . Viennese and Mannheim composers, and those of the French violin school, [in whose concerto rondos] the rondo refrain may be followed by some perfunctory tutti closing measures."

as a sectional rounded binary, aaba, in which the soloist plays the entire theme except for its second limb (the second a, mm. 9–16), which is given over to an affirmative repetition from the orchestra). P^{rf} is an athletic, sprinting theme in 6/8 that comes to a "first conclusion," I:PAC in m. 39. At this point the piano solo drops away, and the tutti-extensions occupy mm. 40–64. These orchestral extensions consist mostly of P-related material (keeping P^{rf} proper alive and developing in the tutti), expanding P-space further outward. They begin with varied recapturings of material related to the previous cadence ($P^{2.1}$, mm. 40–51, as if backing up for a varied repetition), a decisive cadential module ($P^{2.2}$, m. 51–59, with internal self-repetition), and a quiet closing tag, P^{rf}-related at the end (P^3, mm. 59–64). As is typical, the soloist then re-enters to begin a new theme in the tonic (m. 65), which we shall interpret below as the onset of TR-space. None of the tutti-extensions to P will reappear in the movement until the final statement of the refrain following the cadenza.

The general procedure of the finale of Piano Concerto No. 21 in C, K. 467, is somewhat similar. Here, however, as mentioned earlier, the rounded-binary P^{rf} theme is given over mostly to the orchestra, with the piano sounding only its final limb, the reprise (the last a, mm. 21–28). Its I:PAC at m. 28 elides directly with the *forte*-affirmation tutti-extensions. The solo piano now withdraws, and the orchestral ideas, only modestly extended in this case, are readily construed as vigorous P-codetta modules (with final tag). After the tutti's full stop in m. 57, I:PAC, the solo piano re-enters with a tonic theme new to this movement, launching TR.

Interpretive issues arise, though, when the P-space tutti-extensions are more expansive or contain modules that convey a TR, S, or C flavor, as though the P^{rf} + tonic-key tutti-extensions were being more explicitly composed to take on some of the attributes of a compressed Type 5 Ritornello 1, even though what follows seems to begin TR-space (as we shall argue be-

low). There are several ways that this can occur. One of the most obvious is the presence of a nonelided "C-style" tag at the end of the orchestral extensions—a tag more set off and separately stylized than those found in K. 467/iii and K. 595/iii, mentioned above.[66] The end of the P-space in the finale of Piano Concerto No. 22 in E-flat, K. 482, for instance, seems to cross this line into "C-character." Following an aaba rounded-binary P^{rf} (led mostly by the soloist, with the orchestra delivering only the second limb, mm. 9–16, as would also be the case in K. 595/iii), the tutti-extensions begin with a *forte* P^2, interpretable, as in the above cases, as a P-codetta (mm. 41–51). M. 51 is essentially a filled-in gap, and a nonelided, impudently *buffa* tag now enters, *piano*, as an "extra" $P^{3.1}$, mm. 52–59, followed by a $P^{3.2}$ continuation (mm. 59–67)—precisely the sort of cheeky, "afterthought" theme that would be at home in C-space in Type 5 first movement ritornellos. In addition, a *forte* P^4 follows, mm. 67–71, sounding much like the concluding emphatic flourish of a normative ritornello C-space. (In K. 482/iii most of these "C-character" ideas will be reheard only in the final statement of the refrain, after the cadenza. This is another feature, one of subsequent modular postponement, that recalls Type 5 first-movement practice. Only $P^{3.2}$, placed into a different context, will also resurface earlier, in the recapitulation proper.) Only after this set of tutti-extensions does the piano re-enter in m. 74 with a "new" TR—but one that is obviously reacting to the curious "extra," P^3 by recasting it in a different light, as if picking it up and musing on it.

Another way that more substantial, post-P^{rf} tutti-extensions can take on a local ritornello cast is by following the completed refrain proper, one usually led by the soloist, with the onset of a *forte* orchestral restatement that dissolves into more characteristic, energy-gaining TR activity before proceeding to its tonic cadences. (Such a procedure also recalls Koch's 1793 claim, mentioned above, of having the soloist sound the refrain first, then calling upon the orchestra to

---

66. Cf. Irving, *Mozart's Piano Concertos*, p. 82: "A recurring characteristic of [the orchestral continuations of] Mozart's refrains is the clear segmentation of closing material. . . . In taking such an approach, Mozart was importing a feature more familiar from the ritornello design of his concerto first movements."

repeat it as a "ritornello.")[67] This happens in the last movement of Piano Concerto in D Minor, K. 466. Here the strikingly brief P^{rf} is reduced to a blunt period with expanded consequent, played by the soloist alone, mm. 1–13. The orchestra sounds what begins as a *forte* restatement with the upbeat to m. 14, perhaps at first suggesting the more normative second limb of an aaba rounded-binary theme. Whatever our initial impression, we soon realize that the orchestral entrance instead begins the tutti-extensions. Within only a few bars Mozart steers the orchestra's P^{rf} restatement into developmental activity that evokes the texture of a TR, one leading to a dominant-lock at m. 30, to further dramatic activity in the measures that follow, and finally to ringingly declarative final modules that set the seal on the extended "ritornello" effect with two grim and authoritative PACs in D minor (mm. 59, 62) before the re-entry of the piano with its new theme in m. 63.

Any implicit dialogue with the Type 5 Ritornello 1—one of whose roles is to provide a potential source of secondary and closing ideas to come in the ensuing solo exposition (chapter 20)—is made considerably more provocative when seemingly P-completing materials from the tutti-extensions resurface many bars down the road to occupy S-space, now in the dominant. In such cases the "ritornello role" of the opening P-block is even more suggestive, even to the point of taking on quasi-rotational (or subrotational) connotations. What appears to be a simple P^2 module in the finale of Piano Concerto No. 12 in A, K. 414, for instance—a serpentine, coiling figure, mm. 9–16—slithers its way throughout much of the remainder of

the exposition, first as TR^2 (m. 39, following the "new-theme," solo-entry TR^1 in the tonic, mm. 21–38),[68] then, most surprisingly, as S, in V, mm. 56–80.

The last movement of Piano Concerto No. 13 in C, K. 415, provides another illustration—an elegantly styled, seemingly carefree surface that engages substantial conceptual problems of formal type and structural ambiguity. What we presume, according to the concerto-finale Type 4 norm, is the opening P^{rf}-block, mm. 1–48 (in this case with solo participation only in mm. 1–8), articulates an aabc + codetta structure. Considered by itself, this melodic shape presents no analytical difficulties: $P^{rf\text{-}a}$ (mm. 1–8, 9–16), $P^{rf\text{-}b}$ (mm. 17–30), $P^{rf\text{-}c}$ (mm. 31–44, ending I:PAC), and the nonclosed $P^{rf\text{-}codetta}$ (mm. 44–48). What follows, however, is a non-normative Adagio solo interpolation in C minor, mm. 50–64, with more of an $S1{:}\backslash P^{preface}$ effect than that of a typical solo-entry "new theme."[69] Mozart then follows this unusual passage (which has apparently ground Type 4 "progress" to a halt) with a *restart* of the exposition proper—an extremely atypical event within concerto finales—featuring a restoration of the tonic major for a full restatement of $P^{rf\text{-}a}$ (mm. 65–72) leading to the onset of $P^{rf\text{-}b}$, now expanded and treated as the modulatory portion of the transition (mm. 72–91). $P^{rf\text{-}c}$ now appears intact as S in V, mm. 92–101, and new closing material (C) follows. In this virtually unique case, the opening tutti, mm. 1–48, serves also as an initial rotation in the manner of a Type 5 sonata. One might even argue that K. 415/iii begins as a Type 5 movement (or at least with a Type 5 movement in mind) but converts into a Type 4

---

67. At issue here is the dissolving restatement following the completion of the fully closed P^{rf} rondo theme proper. The orchestral restatement of the initial "a" idea midway through P^{rf} within a binary or rounded-binary context, as in K. 488/iii and K. 595/iii, is a different matter. K. 488/iii, however, is notable in that the soloist does not return in the second portion of the binary P^{rf}. Once the orchestra enters with its *forte* repetition of the initial period, mm. 9–16, it continues to take over the texture completely, supplying the closing cadence for P^{rf} proper (m. 40), and proceeding to plunge into the tutti-extensions as well (mm. 40–61)—thus producing, texturally, an extended "ritornello" (or at least "tutti") effect in mm. 9–61.

68. The sometimes-problematic TR^1 status of such separate, closed themes in the tonic (*sujets libres*) is treated in the following section of this chapter.

69. Cf. the similar $S1{:}\backslash P^{preface}$ strategy in Violin Concerto No. 5 in A, K. 219/i—in that case part of an unequivocal Type 5 sonata, as mentioned also in chapter 21. On such labels as R1:\S, R1:\EEC, R1:\C, and so on, see the discussion in chapter 19. In brief, these labels refer to typical expositional-rhetoric zone or functions within tonic-key Ritornello 1-space in a Type 5 sonata (concerto first movement).

sonata-rondo (of the expanded Type 1 subtype) only with the retransition at the end of the solo exposition. At this point of conversion—or of the full declaration of its truer Type 4 status—it drives home its point by suppressing a crucial marker of the Type 5 sonata, the trill-cadence plunge into an unmistakably formalized Ritornello 2 (chapter 20).

The extraordinary finale of Piano Concerto No. 19 in F, K. 459, is another, more fully developed case along these lines. Once past the continuous binary P^{rf} concluding with the usual I:PAC (aabb, mm. 1–32, in which the piano and the orchestra alternate phrases), the aggressively *forte* tutti-extensions elided at m. 32 (presumably P^2) instantly take on the character of an independent, imitative-contrapuntal TR (or R1:\TR), one that even leads to a I:HC dominant-lock (mm. 62–65) and a I:HC MC at m. 65. Even more astonishingly, what follows (perhaps also understandable as P^3, even though it responds to an MC-effect) has the unmistakable character of a P-based S (mm. 67–98, similar to a Type 5 R1:\S in the tonic). And indeed, Mozart would reuse its presentation modules, mm. 67–74, as the initial idea of the dominant-key S in the remainder of the exposition that follows (mm. 167–74).[70] An R1:\EEC-effect (I:PAC) occurs in the tutti-extensions at m. 98, and what seems to be an R1:\$C^1$ of the characteristic $\hat{8}-\flat\hat{7}-\hat{6}-\natural\hat{7}-\hat{8}$ type follows: two short (P^4) subcycles, mm. 99–106 and 107–114. These are rounded off with a short, emphatic close (P^5) in the manner of an R1:\$C^2$ in mm. 115–19—leading to a full-stop I:PAC and a re-entry of the soloist, as usual, with the new, independent theme that is best regarded as the onset, finally, of TR-space proper (m. 120).[71]

The analytical challenge posed by the initial 119 bars of K. 459/iii (as with several other movements described above) is that from one perspective—that of the movement as a whole, especially as construed with Mozart's other, more typical exemplars of the Type 4 concerto-finale genre in mind—they are to

be understood as filling out a much-broadened P-space, one to be followed by the soloist's re-entry with TR. From another perspective, though, Mozart crafted those 119 bars to sound like a Type 5 Ritornello 1, as if the orchestra's normative tutti-extensions "take off" wittily on their own, vaulting past the more modest duties of normative Type 4 P^{rf}-responses, now with impulsive aspirations of shaping themselves into a bona-fide Type 5 opening tutti (notwithstanding the soloist's participation in P^{rf}). The tutti-extensions appear to wish to change the basic format of the piece *en route* from a Type 4 to a Type 5—and they very nearly succeed, until the piano reappears to restore "Type 4 order" and settle the issue, in this case with its new-theme TR in m. 120. The aftershocks of the orchestra's almost-successful generic coup, however, continue to be felt both with the reappearance of the tutti-extension's $P^{3.1}$ (= quasi-R1:\P-based $S^{1.1}$, mm. 67–74) in the exposition's S proper at m. 167 and with the assertive invasions of P^2 (= quasi-R1:\$TR^{1.1}$) in the C-space display episode, mm. 228–33 and 236–41.

There is thus a hybrid-like double perspective at play in several of the opening sections of Mozart's concerto finales. Whatever the extent of the "Type 5 ritornello impression" at the outset, though, the broader course of the movement is governed by Type 4 norms. Virtually all of the tutti-extensions, no matter how expansive they might be, are in the final analysis to be reckoned as operating inside an expanded P-space, albeit one that might be staged as exhibiting local TR, S, or C behavior. When the quasi-ritornello effect surfaces, it is usually nested as a secondary phenomenon within a stretched-out P-space that seeks to open a dialogue with the principle of the Ritornello 1 within a Type 5 concerto first movement. Since such a movement had begun the concerto—often with a grandly outlined Ritornello 1—the P^{rf} + tutti-extensions of the finale's beginning can provide a balancing complement between the openings of the outer movements.

---

70. M. 167 may also be construed as TM^1, the onset of a trimodular block, if we are willing to interpret the V:PAC at m. 202 not as the EEC but as a V:PAC MC followed by a characteristic, periodic TM^3, mm. 203–

18 (instead, for example, of consigning mm. 203–18 to C-space, which might be the preferable view).

71. Once again, regarding the R1:\ and S1:\ labels, see n. 69.

But the fact remains that, unlike the case in the first movement, the expanded, tonic-key tutti of the finale is to be grasped as a specially stylized filling-out of the exposition's P-space, regardless of its internal contents. Instead of laying down a complete referential rotation (first rotation) for the rest of the movement, as happens in Type 5s (see chapters 19 and 20), it almost always occupies only the opening zone (P) of the actual first rotation, which extends from the beginning of the movement through the end of the exposition proper. What follows the final module of the tutti-extensions, with their emphatic closure in the tonic, I:PAC, is to be regarded as the onset of TR, as will be discussed below. For this reason, and despite the potential for the P^{rf} + tutti-extensions to remind us locally of Type 5 Ritornello 1 activity, there is no need to identify its contents as "R1:\ themes," as we shall do in Type 5s (chapters 19 and 20). The thematic modules of the opening zone may be identified merely with such P-superscripts as P^1 (or P^{rf}), $P^{2.1}$, $P^{2.2}$, and so on, although to suggest the full implications of a module one might wish to note, for instance, such things as "P^2 (= quasi-$TR^{1.1}$)," as we have done in K. 459/iii, m. 32.

The Solo Re-entry in the Tonic (the *Sujet-Libre* TR[1])

A much-noticed idiosyncratic aspect of Mozart's concerto finales is the immediate contrast provided after the tutti close with the *re-entry* of the soloist (or, less often, his or her initial entry, if the soloist had not participated in P), usually with a "new theme" that begins (and sometimes also closes) in the tonic before beginning to modulate to the secondary key of the movement.[72] Particularly after the multiple tonic cadences of the preceding P^{rf} + tutti-extensions (tonal overdetermination), this new theme—marked also by a suddenly contrasting solo texture—can give the impression of still another,

"extra" theme in the tonic, a surplus idea that one does not encounter in nonconcerto Type 4 movements. This means that Mozart's sonata-rondo concerto finales begin with a series of challenging signals to interpret within any simpler Type 4 context. Not only is the concept of a closed refrain problematized with the hybridity and ritornello-like aspect of the tutti-extensions, but the solo re-entry theme seems also like a surplus element that lingers further in the already overdetermined tonic. These features have made analytical descriptions of the concerto finales difficult.

One familiar solution has been to consider the new theme in the solo to be the start of "episode 1" of the sonata rondo. This approach, however, is hobbled by the use of "episodic" terminology within an ongoing sonata exposition. (While the term "episode" and its accompanying schematic letter-formats—A, B, and so on—are workable in simple rondos, they are inappropriate for describing the behavior of Type 4 sonata-rondo expositions and recapitulations.) Green went further than this in the 1960s and 1970s, maintaining that the new solo theme in the tonic began not only "Episode 1" but the movement's exposition as well, in a manner somewhat comparable to the post-Ritornello-1 solo exposition of what we call a Type 5 sonata.[73] One can sympathize with the difficulty of the problem of coming to terms with the opening events of Mozart's Type 4 concerto finales, but this explanation only muddied the waters further. It relegated the complex activity preceding the solo re-entry to a refrain (or ritornello-like) status that stands apart as a separate entity, outside of the sonata form proper. (In part this was an inappropriate transference of a classical problem regarding the sonata-form status of Ritornello 1 in a Type 5 sonata, a problem taken up in chapters 19, 20, and 21.) For Green and several others, the exposition of a Mozartian concerto finale gets underway only when the opening rondo-gestures and their tutti-continuations

---

72. Only in rare cases, such as in the finale of Piano Concerto No. 14 in E-flat, K. 449, does the soloist re-enter with a repetition of P^{rf}—in this case launching a TR of the dissolving restatement type (m. 33) following a P^{rf} that had included no solo participation. No. 16

in D, K. 451/iii, provides another exception to the "new theme" norm. Here the pianist merges (m. 21) into a TR already begun by the orchestra (m. 17).

73. Green, *Form in Tonal Music*, 2nd ed., pp. 251–53.

have been decisively completed. This seems both counterintuitive and unlikely. More to the point, it excludes the *Hauptgedanke* of the movement, the rondo theme proper (P^{rf}), from participation in the exposition, something that does not happen in normative nonconcerto Type 4s.

As we have argued above, however, P^{rf} and its tutti-extensions are most profitably understood as occupying a specially crafted and expanded P-space within the Type 4 sonata form. Since the solo re-entry almost never begins a new rotation (by reverting back to P^{rf}),[74] but instead continues the ongoing rotation with a texturally contrasting new theme that begins in the tonic, it is most reasonable to assume that this solo theme operates as the onset of an independent, thematic TR-space. That TR can begin melodically—and with a new melody—was established in chapter 6. There is no generic reason to disallow TR-status to a "new theme" beginning in the tonic at this point. And indeed, as will be elaborated in chapter 21, "new-theme" TRs are a commonly selected option in the solo expositions of Type 5 concerto first movements. In that format, we call these familiar TR openings (adapting terminology from Saint-Foix) *sujet-libre* ("free-subject") S1:\TRs, or S1:\TRs of the *sujet-libre* type.

The "new theme" solo re-entries in Type 4 concerto finales (TR^1) share a number of defining characteristics also found in the Type 5 *sujet-libre* S1:\TR^1. They are independent themes assigned exclusively to the soloist following some type of full tutti close. They thus represent a handing-over of the action from the orchestra to the soloist. Correspondingly, they provide a sense of initiating a new section with a new melody ("onward!"), or with a new variant of or clear response to something heard earlier. Quite often the *sujet libre* is a complete melody—period, sentence, or hybrid—brought to a close in the tonic, I:PAC, before proceeding onward to a modulation. Examples may be found in the Piano Concertos K. 450/iii, mm. 43–62; K. 459, mm. 120–42; K. 466/iii, mm. 63–73; K. 467/iii, mm. 58–74; K. 488/iii, mm. 62–77; K. 503, mm. 33–48; K. 537, mm.

48–64. When this happens it can easily give the impression—doubtless purposefully—of a brief, separately closed idea (or episode) in the tonic before more normatively transitional material (here considered as TR^2) is allowed to proceed forward: a momentary halting of the forward-vector to permit the soloist a neatly framed, individualized statement on his or her own. On this reading, the fully closed TR^1 would not display overtly transitional behavior. Yet it could still be regarded as occupying the beginning segment of the TR-zone, generically considered.

This "TR" understanding is reinforced when we consider an alternative procedure, one in which the solo re-entry theme in the tonic is not fully closed with a perfect authentic cadence. In these instances, the *sujet libre* modulates away from the tonic before any such formal I:PAC is achieved (even though a I:HC might have been articulated before modulating away from the tonic). It thus replaces a sense of local tonic closure with an opening outward toward more "typical" TR behavior. This occurs in the Violin Concertos K. 216/iii, mm. 41ff, and K. 219/iii, mm. 23ff; in the Piano Concertos K. 456/iii, mm. 58ff, K. 482/iii, mm. 74ff, with an evaded cadence in m. 89, K. 595/iii, mm. 65ff, which begins with what might be regarded as two elided, five-bar presentation modules prolonging the tonic over a tonic pedal and lacking a full-closure PAC at the end of each; and in the Clarinet Concerto, K. 622/iii, mm. 57ff.

The *sujet-libre* TR^1, like its *sujet-libre* S1:\TR^1 counterpart in Type 5 first movements, may either reappear or not reappear elsewhere in the movement. It may happen, though less frequently, that the *sujet-libre* TR^1 is a one-time event, as in the Piano Concertos K. 413/iii, K. 450/iii and 459/iii. More often, though, it does play a role elsewhere—perhaps as something to be revisited or varied in the development or central episode (K. 466/iii, K. 503/iii, K. 537/iii), situated in a similar TR-position in the recapitulation (K. 467/iii) or TR-crux-point within the familiar Type 4^{1-exp} variant (K. 456/iii; K. 488/iii, K. 595/iii),[75] or alluded to briefly or in

---

74. One exception, as noted above, is K. 415/iii, with its expositional restart in m. 65.

75. The return of the *sujet libre* TR^1 in K. 595/iii, m. 208, is complicated further by the fermata-prepared re-

varied fashion after the cadenza, as part of the coda-rotation (K. 414/iii, K. 482/iii).

Interpreting the "new" solo re-entry theme in a Type 4 concerto finale as a TR of the *sujet libre* type familiar from Type 5 first movements is the most persuasive interpretation, one that also brings clarity to the otherwise numerous possibilities for misunderstanding the generic resonances of this theme. To be sure, the re-entry theme might also suggest some allegiances to the S1:\P[preface] possibility within Mozartian Type 5s. That, too, is a "new theme" following an emphatic, cadential tutti close (in the Type 5 case, the close of Ritornello 1). But as will be outlined in chapter 21, a Type 5 S1:\P[preface] leads invariably to an emphatic restatement of R1:\P in the orchestra and the clear start of a new rotation (the solo exposition). In the Type 4 concerto finale, on the other hand, even where motives from the refrain, P[rf], might follow fragmentarily after the sounding of the *sujet-libre* TR (as in K. 466/iii and 467/iii, for instance), nobody could sustain the claim that a new rotation was being launched at that point. On the contrary, the *sujet libre*'s claim to exist fully in TR-space—continuing to pursue an expositional trajectory begun at the movement's opening—seems incontestable. Any P[rf] fragments that persist or reintrude after "new-theme" solo re-entry—either in the orchestra or in the soloists' part itself—mark a shift in strategy from a largely independent transition (the *sujet libre*) to a dependent one with back-references to earlier material.[76]

Finally, it might not be amiss to point out the obvious. Not all of the *sujet-libre* TR solo themes are entirely "new" or fully "independent." As a result of the numerous modular interconnections that Mozart composed into each concerto—contributing mightily to their senses of internal coherence, individuality, and long-range dramatic argument—many of them have obvious resonances with material already heard. In some instances the solo re-entry back-reference could be to something presented in the preceding P[rf] + tutti-extensions, as if the soloist were entering into the discussion by picking up an already sounded idea and adapting it in an individualized way. One of the most obvious of these, already mentioned, is that in Piano Concerto No. 22 in E-flat, K. 482/iii, mm. 74ff, which muses reflectively on the rhythm and contour of the highly stylized, "buffa" or "C-character" theme that had appeared in the tutti-extensions at m. 52.

More provocative are cases in which the *sujet-libre* TR reaches back to resuscitate aspects of provocative material from an earlier movement. Reshaping something heard in the first movement not only pulls that earlier gesture into a finale-context at a crucial structural point, but it also suggests outer-movement relationships—contributions to a quasi-cyclic integrity—that help us conceptually to bind the entire work together as a coherent statement. Classic instances occur in Piano Concertos Nos. 20 in D Minor, K. 466/iii, and No. 21 in C, K. 467/iii. In the former the finale's solo re-entry, m. 63, reaches back to the first movement's plaintive S1:\P[preface], m. 77, helping to establish parallels between the two movements. In the latter the finale's *sujet-libre* TR, starting in m. 58, shoots forth with the same upward-striving rhythm as that found in a famously surprising moment of the first movement, the sudden G-minor solo entry, S1:\TM[1], in m. 109, an idea that had appeared only as a one-time event in that movement.[77] About such possibilities for obvious interconnections in other concertos, however, one cannot generalize, except to reaffirm the general principle that the workings of each of these concertos is to be explored not only generically, in terms of what it shares with other works of its kind, but also individually, in terms of its own patterns of memorability and uniqueness.

---

currence of the head-motive of P[rf] on IV, m. 182. Because of the similarities of its ensuing procedures with those of mm. 131ff (tonic-key P[rf] recapitulation-gesture proper leading into development, in the manner of a Type 4[1-exp]), it is probably best to include mm. 182–207 within the sphere of the developmental space as well, as a second subrotation (though one with the idea of a subdominant recapitulation on its mind).

76. A slightly different view of this is provided in Grayson, *Mozart: Piano Concertos Nos. 20 in D Minor, K. 466, and No. 21 in C Major, K. 467*, p. 79.

77. For more on these interconnections, see again Grayson, *Mozart: Piano Concertos Nos. 20 in D Minor, K. 466, and No. 21 in C Major, K. 467*, pp. 79–80, 88–89. On the S1:\TM[1] status of K. 467/i, m. 109, see chapter 21 below.

ESC Issues in Type 4 Sonatas:
The Double Perspective

If the ESC marks the moment of the attainment of the full reality of the tonic in sonata forms (a fundamental principle of Sonata Theory outlined at the end of chapter 11), what may be said of rondo structures? When rondos are not intermixed with sonata formats, the issue presents little difficulty: the corresponding point of essential structural closure (ESC) must arrive with the concluding I:PAC of the final appearance of the rondo theme—with the I:PAC, that is, that concludes its thematic block. Earlier I:PAC's in prior rondo-theme appearances will have proven to be overridden (or merely provisional), since they proceeded onward to (usually) nontonic episodes.

Sonata-rondo structures, however (Type 4 sonatas), present a more complicated conceptual situation. As hybrid forms they can be viewed from two different perspectives: from that of the sonata and that of the rondo. In some sonata-rondos the "sonata" aspect strongly outweighs that of the rondo in structural (governing) importance. These would include compositions with sonata-like melodic material, thoroughly elaborated exposition- and recapitulation-layouts (including transitions, a medial caesura and

S theme, and so on) and developments. In others the tilt toward the sonata rhetoric is not so pronounced. Whatever the balance between sonata and rondo, the "sonata" aspect will ask for the presence of an ESC at the end of the recapitulation's S theme. And this is precisely how we have been using that term in the preceding pages: in a manner analogous to other sonata types, the ESC may be regarded as occurring normally, in the recapitulatory space. As mentioned in the preceding paragraph, however, a simple rondo's ESC is delayed until the moment of the PAC-closure of its final thematic statement—which in a sonata-rondo occurs after the recapitulation is completed. Thus a sonata-rondo presents us with the possibility of two conflicting ESC claims (figure 18.1).

But a sonata-rondo is something that by definition can be viewed simultaneously from the perspectives of two different structural principles. Viewed through the rondo lens, the final statement of Prf is part of the form: it exists unequivocally within rondo-space and may followed by a coda (outside of rondo-space). Viewed through the sonata lens, through, the final Prf stands outside of sonata-space: it initiates the (possibly lengthy or discursive) coda, a parageneric space within a sonata (chapter 13). In this sense two ESCs might be said to co-exist,

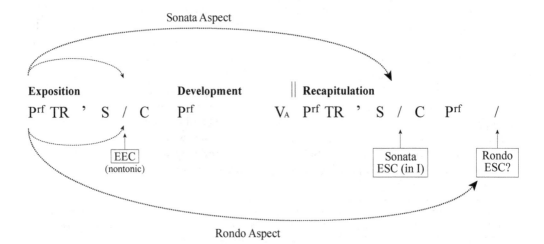

FIGURE 18.1   The Type 4 Sonata: A Doubled ESC?

although depending on the degree of "sonata-ness" of the individual piece (its tilt—or lack of it—in the sonata direction) we might argue that the two ESC moments might not be understood as equally weighted in the overall structure. This formal ambiguity may have important hermeneutic ramifications. Obviously, more sonata-like pieces will favor a heavier weighting of the sonata's ESC-claim; more rondo-like pieces will place their conceptual weight more on the rondo's ESC-claim. Viewed from only the sonata perspective, the final rondo statement is reduced to the post-sonata-space function of a thematic "discursive coda" following the reca-

pitulatory rotation. In that sense, only the final statement of the rondo theme (P^{rf})—following the tonic-securing ESC of the recapitulation—is fully sounded "in" the stable tonic key. All prior statements of P^{rf} (rondo) have been subordinated to other tonal and musical processes that follow it. Here in the coda alone can it exist on its own, in a tonic that has, finally, been fully validated by the preceding musical processes. With its own PAC-closure (the "rondo's" ESC) it completes the tonic-stabilizing process of the movement from the point of view of the rondo. And, of course, its own coda may follow.

CHAPTER NINETEEN

The Type 5 Sonata

Fundamentals

A defining feature of many concerto movements, the Type 5 sonata combines ritornello formats and procedures passed down from earlier eighteenth-century concerto and aria traditions (dramatized tutti-solo alternations) with aspects of sonata form. While this concerto-sonata blend includes a number of identifying features throughout its structure, its most prominent difference from the other sonata types lies in its quasi-introductory opening section, an anticipatory rotation of thematic modules that precedes the onset of the sonata adaptation proper, which may then expand, recast, or otherwise react to those modules in engaging ways. This first section is an initial orchestral *ritornello* of varying length and complexity. Unlike a sonata exposition (which in other respects it often resembles), it usually begins and ends in the tonic, and it often remains in the tonic throughout. This opening, tonic-centered *tutti* is an important "extra" in the Type 5 sonata not found in other sonata types. It sets up and then gives way to a solo entry that normally launches a sonata-form oriented structure, one punctuated and framed by additional, reinforcing orchestral appearances, often, of appropriate portions of the initial ritornello.

Making use of traditions grounded in the history of the genre, this sonata type is not to be derived exclusively from sonata practice (as a variant of it), as was generally supposed some decades ago. On the contrary, the historically separate ritornello formats of earlier concertos, especially around the middle of the eighteenth century, were instead increasingly informed by formal layouts characteristic of the new symphonic writing of the period. (The same may be said of eighteenth-century *opera seria* arias, which at least through the 1770s followed much the same historical path.)[1] All who have dealt with the formal structures of concertos in the period 1730–1820 are aware of the complexi-

---

1. See Martha Feldman, "Staging the Virtuoso: Ritornello Procedure in Mozart, from Aria to Concerto," in *Mozart's Piano Concertos: Text, Context, Interpretation*, ed. Neal Zaslaw (Ann Arbor: University of Michigan Press, 1996), pp. 149–86. In another essay from the same volume James Webster provided an important nuance (in part taking issue with remarks by Charles Rosen): "A serious problem with the aria-concerto hypothesis as applied to Mozart, however, is that the formal similarities entailed affect primarily *seria* arias before 1780, not *buffa* arias, nor the majority of *seria* arias after 1780. As the century progressed, the aria and the concerto increasingly diverged" (Webster, "Are Mozart's Concertos 'Dramatic'? Concerto Ritornellos versus Aria Introductions in the 1780s," *Mozart's Piano Concertos*, p. 109.

ties—and the perils—involved in writing even the most basic things about this topic. If sonatas in general (Types 1–4) present us with challenges of understanding, the concerto-sonata combinations typical of later eighteenth-century concerto first (and sometimes second) movements redouble those challenges, seeding the field of analysis with conceptual and terminological landmines. Merely to select a label for describing certain events or zones ("tutti," "ritornello," "transition," "secondary theme," "exposition," "recapitulation," "episode," "sonata form," and so on) is to wade into a morass of previously established connotations, each of which has been ardently defended and just as ardently opposed, particularly within music-historical scholarship of the last forty years.

The first movements of later-eighteenth-century concertos are almost invariably built around the Type 5 idea. It also shows up in two of Mozart's early concerto finales (Piano Concerto No. 5 in D, K. 175/iii [original finale], and Violin Concerto No. 1 in B-flat, K. 207/iii) and in two interior movements of each of the two Serenades in D, K. 203/ii and iv, and K. 204/ii and iii—a slow movement and a fast movement in each case.[2] Examples of it are also encountered in many concerto slow movements. (An exemplary case is the Adagio of Mozart's Violin Concerto No. 5 in A, K. 219. Additionally, of Mozart's seventeen Viennese piano concertos, from No. 11 in F, K. 413 through No. 27 in B-flat, K. 595—around half are cast in Type 5 formats, sometimes without a developmental space.)[3] Ritornello formats in concerto first and second movements may be in dialogue with Type 1, 2, or 3 sonatas. The Type 5 adaptation of the Type 1 sonata (no developmental space) is found primarily in slow movements: one *locus classicus* is the Andante cantabile of Mozart's Violin Concerto No. 4 in D, K. 218.[4] The infrequent adaptation of the Type 2 sonata ("binary" without a full recapitulation) may be found in the first movement of the same concerto.[5] Most often, especially in first movements, we are dealing with the Type 3 version of the Type 5 sonata. This features a structural merger of the ritornello principle with the "textbook" sonata, including an exposition (without repeat), a developmental space, and a full recapitulation. Ritornello blends with the Type 4 sonata (sonata rondo) are also encountered—in the ingenious finales of Mozart's concertos, for example: an overview of these has been provided toward the end of chapter 18.[6]

To complicate the matter further, the most

---

2. Cf. the exceptional—and anomalous—Type 5-Type 3 hybrid in the Andante from the Serenade in D, K. 185/ii. This is a Type 3 sonata (with repeats!) that features a solo violin and that includes an eleven-bar opening ritornello and a concluding ritornello with interior cadenza.

3. These include the slow movements of: No. 11 in F, K. 413; No. 12 in A, K. 414; No. 13 in C, K. 415; No. 14 in E-flat, K. 449; No. 17 in G, K. 453; No. 19 in F, K. 459; No. 21 in C, K. 467; and No. 25 in C, K. 503. Four of these, K. 414, K. 449, K. 453, and K. 467 are Type 5s in dialogue with Type 3 guidelines—that is, with a developmental space. (K. 449 and 467 also feature unusual tonal plans at various points in their structures. For K. 449 see Hepokoski, "Back and Forth from *Egmont*: Beethoven, Mozart, and the Nonresolving Recapitulation, *19th-Century Music*, 25 (2001–2), 149.) Four others, K. 413, K. 415, K. 459, and K. 503 are Type 5s in dialogue with Type 1 guidelines—that is, without a developmental space. It might be added that the slow movement of No. 16, K. 451, is a Type 5 variant of a rondo: although its initial section does unfold in the manner of a sonata exposition, however, there is no tonal resolution of the presumed S material.

See also the discussion and table in James Webster, "Are Mozart's Concertos 'Dramatic'?," in Zaslaw, ed.,

Mozart's Piano Concertos, pp. 112–14. Using a different set of definitional guidelines, Webster classified the slow movement of K. 467 as being in "concerto/rounded binary" form, while he judged that of K. 449 to be "a more or less unclassifiable ritornello-rondo hybrid." Most recently, John Irving, *Mozart's Piano Concertos* (Aldershot: Ashgate, 2003), pp. 66–69, considered what we regard as Type 5 slow movements to be relatable primarily to vocal music formats, that is, to "ritornello (aria) forms."

4. For other examples see n. 3.

5. Other examples of Type 2 adaptations within Type 5 sonatas include the first movements of J. C. Bach's Keyboard Concerto in F, op. 7 no. 2, Mozart's pastiche Piano Concerto in G, K. 107 no. 2, and the Andante moderato of Mozart's Serenade in D, K. 204/ii. The first movement of the Piano Concerto No. 24 in C Minor, K. 491, also features some Type 2 aspects. Joel Galand, "The Large-Scale Formal Role of the Solo Entry Theme in the Eighteenth-Century Concerto," *Journal of Music Theory* 44 (2000), p. 401, also cites examples from Johann Samuel Schröter's op. 3.

6. Another discussion of these movements was undertaken in "Movement Forms III: Finales" in Irving, *Mozart's Piano Concertos*, pp. 73–92.

impressive examples at hand, some three dozen or more mature concertos by Mozart, present us with his most intricate formal layouts. And each layout is strongly individualized, the result, it appears, of a playful approach to the formal possibilities of concerto form. In Mozart (and others) we typically find unique "solutions" tailored to individual concertos—a differently played chess game each time—even while other broad structural guidelines are held relatively constant. This makes generalizing over this repertory difficult. It may be that the earlier, flexible traditions of the Baroque concerto ritornello movement led to the continuing formal freedom of concerto forms in the last half of the eighteenth century. Even while acknowledging the many elasticities within Types 1–4, it does appear that the Type 5 sonata was given an even freer formal rein, encouraging a "looser" approach to individual realizations of structure.

Often centering around the Mozart concertos, the bibliography on this topic is large. The literature is riddled with differently formatted diagrams of standard and individualized concerto procedures; with contrasting descriptions and interpretations of intricate structural layouts and "standard operating procedures"; and with convoluted numerical or alphabetical (or both)

labeling systems to register the disappearances, reappearances, and rearrangements of the multiple thematic modules juggled about in successive tutti and solo passages. Merely keeping track of what happens to the thematic and textural ideas as the concerto movement proceeds is a complicated business. There is no avoiding such complexity of description. As will be evident in what follows, we, too, shall not be able to avoid it.

Some of the most often-cited writing (Stevens, Davis) has examined the matter historically by compiling relevant discussions of the topic by eighteenth- and early-nineteenth-century commentators and theorists, enriched with synoptic overviews of formal plans of concertos besides those of Mozart (for example, those precedents found in C. H. and J. G. Graun, J. Stamitz, C. P. E. Bach, C. F. Abel, J. C. Bach, and others).[7] Much of the music-historical work has sought to displace ahistorical assumptions embedded in previous habits of concerto description, especially those grounded in nonproblematized sonata-form terminology. Related writings (Leeson and Levin, Küster, Forster, Brück, Webster, Berger, Galand) have provided statistical or analytical overviews of standard practice in Mozart's concertos.[8] Others

7. Jane R. Stevens, "An 18th-Century Description of Concerto First-Movement Form," *Journal of the American Musicological Society* 24 (1971), 85–95; Stevens, "Theme, Harmony, and Texture in Classic-Romantic Descriptions of Concerto First-Movement Form," *Journal of the American Musicological Society* 27 (1974), 25–60; Stevens, "Formal Design in C. P. E. Bach's Harpsichord Concertos," *Studi musicali*, 15 (1986), 257–97; Stevens, "Patterns of Recapitulation in the First Movements of Mozart's Piano Concertos," in *Musical Humanism and Its Legacy: Essays in Honor of Claude V. Palisca*, ed. Nancy Kovaleff Baker and Barbara Russano Hanning (Stuyvesant, N.Y.: Pendragon, 1992), pp. 397–418; and Stevens, "The Importance of C. P. E. Bach for Mozart's Piano Concertos," in *Mozart's Piano Concertos*, ed. Zaslaw, pp. 211–36 (in which Stevens characteristically noted, p. 212, that she has "profound objections (some of which are shared by many others) to this [sonata-form-based sectional] framework," which by 1996 she assumed to be so discredited as to decline to "take time to beat this already rather feeble horse"). Somewhat related in style and intent are: Edwin J. Simon, "Sonata into Concerto: A Study of Mozart's First Seven Concertos," *Acta musicologica* 31 (1959), 170–85; Shelley Davis,

"H. C. Koch, the Classic Concerto, and the Sonata-Form Retransition," *Journal of Musicology* 2 (1983), 45–61; and Davis, "C. P. E. Bach and the Early History of the Recapitulatory Tutti in North Germany," in *C. P. E. Bach Studies*, ed. Stephen L. Clark (Oxford: Clarendon Press, 1988), pp. 65–82. See also the useful surveys by Michael Talbot, "The Instrumental Concerto: Origins to 1750," and Cliff Eisen, "The Classical Period," within the general entry for "Concerto" in *The New Grove Dictionary of Music and Musicians*, 2nd ed., ed. Stanley Sadie and John Tyrrell (London: Macmillan, 2001), 6:242–46 and 246–51.

8. The classic essay in English is Daniel N. Leeson and Robert D. Levin, "On the Authenticity of K. Anh. C 14.01 (297b), a Symphonia Concertante for Four Winds and Orchestra," *Mozart-Jahrbuch 1976/77* (Kassel: Bärenreiter, 1978), pp. 70–96. This was preceded by Levin, "Das Konzert für Klavier und Violine D-Dur KV Anh. 56/315f und das Klarinettenquintett B-Dur, KV Anh. 91/516c: Ein Ergänzungsversuch," *Mozart-Jahrbuch 1968/70* (Salzburg: Internationale Stiftung Mozarteum, 1970), pp. 304–26. See also the three monographs: Konrad Küster, *Formale Aspekte des ersten Allegros in Mozarts Konzerten* (Kassel: Bärenreiter, 1991); Robert

(Charles Rosen) have continued the Toveyan style of commonsense overview coupled with always-provocative aesthetic pronouncement.[9] Still others, seeking to offer syntheses of prior scholarship along with individual interpretations and commentary, provide studies of selected works.[10] Most recently, William E. Caplin has provided a review of Mozart's concerto practice congruent with his own system of *Classical Form* (1998), while John Irving has devoted an entire book to a broad consideration of *Mozart's Piano Concertos* (2003).[11] Perusing the literature on concertos, one soon learns not only that there are no simple ways to track through this topic but also that there are no disciplinarily neutral systems of description.

This and the following three chapters do not present a full account of concerto structure. Our plan is more limited. Keeping our focus on the concertos of Mozart, with a few glances forward to Beethoven, we offer an interpretation of their analytical features from the perspective of Sonata Theory. Our interests foreground three problems, which may not always be kept separate: (1) that of coming to a broad understanding of the large-scale structure and its implications, with an emphasis on the historical residues of tutti-solo alternation as it seeks also to unfold a sonata structure; (2) that of rotational and referential layout (the relationships among the thematic modules of the initial ritornello, the exposition, and the recapitulation); and (3) that of

the EEC and ESC in a Type 5 sonata, concepts central to the other sonata types.

Historical Overview and Initial Questions of Terminology

Like Type 4s, Type 5s are hybrid constructions. One aspect of Type 5 structure looks back to the older Baroque tradition, which exerted demands on the architecture separate from those pressed by sonata form proper. No one should confront the Type 5 sonata without a sufficient historical consciousness of the origin of the concerto and an awareness of earlier formal patterns and their continued claims in the later eighteenth century. For this reason, we need to spend some time summarizing the literature on this topic.

By the early eighteenth century the concerto idea was tied up with the principle of alternating tutti-solo contrasts: the dramatized juxtaposition of a group and an individual (or smaller group) emerging out of that group. From Torelli and Vivaldi onward, this ritornello principle typically involved tonic-centered introductory and closing ritornellos that enclosed an often-modulatory inner series of lightly accompanied, virtuosic solo passages. Each of these was affirmationally punctuated by a briefer, full-orchestra tutti (usually elided with emphatic solo cadences) that usually reanimated selected modules from the initial ritornello.[12]

Forster, *Die Kopfsätze der Klavierkonzerte Mozarts und Beethovens: Gesamtaufbau, Solokadenz und Schlußbildung* (Munich: Fink, 1992); and Marion Brück, *Die langsamen Sätze in Mozarts Klavierkonzerten: Untersuchungen zur Form und zum musikalischen Satz* (Munich: Fink, 1994). Cf. the cumbersome insistence on retaining late-eighteenth-century terminology carried out—then fused with philosophical reflections—in Karol Berger, "The First-Movement Punctuation Form in Mozart's Piano Concertos," in *Mozart's Piano Concertos*, ed. Zaslaw, pp. 239–59. Webster, "Are Mozart's Concertos 'Dramatic'?" in the same volume, pp. 107–37 (see n. 1 above), provides an English-language study and inventory of slow movements. An inventory of various treatments of an individual moment within concerto movements from a music-theoretical point of view is provided in Galand, "The Large-Scale Formal Role," 381–450.

9. Charles Rosen, "The Concerto," in *The Classical Style*, expanded ed. (1997, this section basically unaltered from the 1971 edition), pp. 185–263; "Concerto," in *Sonata Forms*, rev. ed. (1988; orig. 1980), pp. 71–97. Here most relevant backdrop is Tovey's essay from 1903, "The Classical Concerto," *Essays in Musical Analysis*, vol. 3, "Concertos" (London: Oxford University Press, 1936), pp. 3–27, which established some positions with regard to the concerto often reiterated or adapted in English-language musical writing.

10. Recent examples include David Rosen, "The Composer's 'Standard Operating Procedure' as Evidence of Intention: The Case of a Formal Quirk in Mozart's K. 595," *Journal of Musicology* 5 (1987), 79–90; David Grayson, *Mozart: Piano Concertos No. 20 in D minor, K. 466, and No. 21 in C major, K. 467* (Cambridge: Cambridge University Press, 1998); and Leon Plantinga, *Beethoven's Concertos: History, Style, Performance* (New York: Norton, 1999).

11. Caplin, ch. 17, "Concerto Form," in *Classical Form*, pp. 243–51; Irving, *Mozart's Piano Concertos* (see n. 3)

12. As Michael Talbot ("The Instrumental Concerto: Origins to 1750," in the entry "Concerto," *The New*

For the first decades of the "Vivaldian" concerto, the number of tutti and solo passages in any ritornello-based movement was not standardized. Toward the second third of the eighteenth century the concerto gradually came to be informed by aspects of the emerging *galant* style and by the sonata plan used for symphonies and sonatas. In part this was due (as Cliff Eisen put it in the recent *New Grove* entry on the concerto) to "the surprisingly rapid replacement of the concerto by the concert symphony as the dominant orchestral genre in the middle of the 18th century."[13] This slow acclimatizing of the concerto to what we now call sonata form is a complicated matter. The process of *rapprochement* remains a contested topic within musicological research.[14]

Considered generally, we may see the ritornello-solo traditions being bent incrementally in the direction of the symphonic. The figures in the center of this historical process (C. P. E. Bach, C. H. and J. G. Graun, the Mannheim composers, J. C. Bach, and others) furnish examples of this ongoing historical convergence, which is anything but linear: "old fashioned" concertos, without much sonata-form influence, occasionally cropped up as late as the 1770s—such as Josef Mysliveček's violin concertos, which "may have influenced Mozart, who became acquainted with them in Vienna in 1773."[15] The most telling syntheses of traditional ritornello and sonata-form practices occurred in the hands of Mozart, who balanced these complementary force-fields in ever more monumentalized ways.

For some writers over the past decades it has been a point of honor to confront these structures—all the way through Mozart and beyond—primarily in late-eighteenth-century terms, that is, with a suspicion of, if not a contempt for, "modern" sonata-form terminology. Defamiliarizingly "historical" descriptions of these works are readily found in the musicological literature. Their positive effect is to remind us how these concertos might be addressed using only surviving late-eighteenth-century descriptions of form.[16] Still, certainly by the concertos of Mozart—where convergences with the sonata-form ideas found in his other works could hardly be more apparent—such aversions to later, more efficient terminology become excessive and counterproductive. To be sure, we should never marginalize the few eighteenth-century and early-nineteenth-century written views of the concerto that we have—Vogler, Koch, Kollmann, Galeazzi, and so on. Nevertheless, the recent riposte of David Rosen to any methodologically hobbled insistence on limiting ourselves to eighteenth-century, "historical" terminology cannot be improved upon: "Mozart would not have recognized the sonata-form terminology, but we need not make the usual ritual apology for that (or worse, arbitrarily to invent new terminology): I suspect that it would have taken less than ninety seconds to explain it to his satisfaction."[17]

Mozart's concerto-sonata syntheses were continued by Beethoven and others. Eventually, with Mendelssohn especially, the initial ritornello of the Type 5 concerto came to seem

---

Grove Dictionary, 2nd ed., 6: 243) recently summarized one common type of Vivaldian practice from op. 3 (1711) onward, "the ritornello—one or more ideas constituting a refrain played by the full ensemble—is used to establish the opening tonality and subsequently to affirm the various other tonalities reached in the course of the movement; the alternate sections (episodes), scored for the solo instrument with a generally light accompaniment, accomplish the structurally important modulations and supply contrasting themes or figurations."

13. Eisen, "The Classical Period," in "Concerto," *The New Grove Dictionary*, 2nd ed., 6:246.

14. A still-conflicted middle ground is suggested in Eisen's summary ("The Classical Period," 6:246): "Indeed, the nature of the relationship between sinfonia (symphony) and concerto between 1700 and 1750 remains an insufficiently explored area. Unlike the symphony, the concerto did not adopt sonata form but instead continued in the second half of the century to rely on its tried and tested ritornello form, although certain increasingly common features such as the reprise of the material of the first solo towards the end of the movement are evidence of convergence between the two forms. In fact, the division between Baroque and Classical is invisible, structurally speaking, in the concerto."

15. Eisen, "The Classical Period," 6:247.

16. The *ne plus ultra* is Berger's Koch-based "The First-Movement Punctuation Form in Mozart's Concertos." (See n. 8 above.)

17. David Rosen, "'Unexpectedness' and 'Inevitability' in Mozart's Piano Concertos," in *Mozart's Piano Concertos*, ed. Zaslaw, p. 281 n. 2.

redundant, old-fashioned, something that had outworn its original *raison d'être*. With its excision, what had been the favored format for concerto first movements—the Type 5 sonata—collapsed into the Type 3 pattern. At this point the absorption of the concerto idea into sonata form became complete. The history of the concerto in the eighteenth century and beyond, developing alongside the symphony, is that of gradually being attracted to the latter's principles, finding ways of adapting itself to them while retaining important features of its own identity, but eventually (around the fourth decade of the nineteenth century) succumbing rather totally to them. Later concerto reinstatings of the opening ritornello, as in Brahms's concertos, are best regarded as archaizing or retrospective efforts, recalling largely eclipsed traditions of enhanced monumentalization.

Vogler, Koch, and Others:
Six Tutti-Solo Layouts

Vogler's Description (1779) of the Concerto

Because of the persisting imprint of the older Baroque and midcentury traditions in Mozart's concertos—our main concern here—it is helpful to look at the historical state of the genre as that composer may have found it. There is no better place to start than with one of the earliest descriptions of the increasing interaction between the ritornello-movement concerto and sonata form. In 1779, in a now-famous passage from his periodical, *Betrachtungen der Mannheimer Tonschule*, Georg Joseph Vogler provided a simple recipe for producing a concerto:

> Whoever wishes to compose a concerto does well if he first writes [*macht*] an ordinary sonata [*eine gewöhnliche Sonate*]. The first part of it is used for [*giebt*] the first solo, the other part for the second solo. Before the first, after the second [and] be-

tween the first and second parts the instruments execute a prelude, postlude, and interlude [*Vor-, Nach-, und Zwischenspiel*].[18]

Here Vogler addressed the matter in terms of compositional practice. By suggesting that the solo passages were to be composed first, he implied that this *gewöhnliche Sonate* (our Type 3 sonata) was the most essential part of the movement. The ritornellos were afterthoughts, add-ons, mere framing mechanisms for a more telling, often pre-existing structure, though one now shorn of its customary repeats. (Especially since Koch in 1793 shared this view—and since young Mozart seemed to put it into practice a few times—this is a point to which we shall return.) Along the same lines, Vogler also advised that the opening prelude—which he told us almost always began and ended in the tonic[19]—be kept less "beautiful," and by implication shorter, than the first solo (the exposition of the *gewöhnliche Sonate*) in order not to draw attention frivolously from the latter, the principal item of interest.[20]

Vogler was describing a five-part structure. At least preliminarily, we may schematize it (and interpolate the more common term "ritornello," though "tutti" would work as well) as follows:

> *Ritornello 1.* Orchestral prelude; tonic.
> *Solo 1.* Sonata exposition, modulating to and confirming a secondary key.
> *Ritornello 2.* Orchestral interlude, "a short excerpt of the first" ritornello.
> *Solo 2.* Sonata development and recapitulation.
> *Ritornello 3.* Orchestral postlude.

Implicit in such a description, to judge from the musical literature, is that Ritornello 1 is normally the longest of the three and was usually separated from Solo 1 by a I:PAC and clear caesura. On the other hand, Solo 1's and Solo 2's concluding PACs were generally elided with the ritornellos that followed them. In all cases, the

---

18. Vogler, *Betrachtungen der Mannheimer Tonschule*, II, 36. The translation is adapted from Stevens, "Theme, Harmony, and Texture," p. 33.
19. "Only very seldom do those [preludes] occur that conclude on the dominant," *Betrachtungen*, ii, 38, quoted

in Stevens, "Theme, Harmony, and Texture," p. 33 n. 25.
20. Vogler, quoted in Stevens, "Theme, Harmony, and Texture," p. 33 n. 24.

overall sonorous impact of the later ritornello entrances was aptly described well over a century later by Tovey, who in 1903 laid out an essential feature of what he was calling the "concerto principle": "The solo is probably more active, as well as more personal and eloquent, than the orchestra, and can therefore make a brilliant climax if it chooses; but it cannot make its climax very powerful in sound as compared with what the orchestra can obviously do with ease; and so this one missing element may be supplied, and the design rounded off, by bringing in the ritornello forte on the last note of the solo, thus ending the piece."[21]

Koch (1793) and the Two Four-Ritornello Layouts: Subtypes A and B

Vogler's five-part (three-ritornello) plan was only one of several that had sprung up in the mid-eighteenth century, and, if we take Vogler's description literally, it was by no means the most common subtype. Sonata-like procedures could be combined with concerto patterns featuring three, four, or even five ritornello appearances at major structural hinges within the movement—something on the order of ritornello pillars,[22] identifying the movement emphatically as a concerto. These pillars help to precipitate and intensify important structural stations in the form. The most important point is the adaptability of the whole system. Even while today we may extrapolate certain structural paradigms as useful heuristic models, it is wiser to suppose that eighteenth-century composers operated under the assumption that orchestral tuttis, especially the internal ritornel-

los, could be treated freely in individual compositions—via occasional suppressions, displacements, unusual textural treatments, "extra" tutti interjections, and so on.

Adapting the work of Stevens, Davis, and Galand, we identify six heuristic subtypes that, with some flexibility, are commonly found in mid- and late-eighteenth-century Type 5 sonatas. These are laid out, with particular reference to Mozart's works, in table 19.1 as Subtypes A–F.[23] (What may seem to be the unusual numbering of the ritornellos—with some additions and deletions from strict integer sequence—will be explained in due course.)

Of these, the two seven-part (four-ritornello) formats (A and B in the table) are particularly important. Not only are they are the ones most frequently encountered in Mozart's concertos, but one of the two plans, famously—our Subtype A—was also described by Koch in his *Versuch* of 1793—one grounded, he mentioned, in C. P. E. Bach's concerto practice.[24] Koch's explanation provided the basis for much revisionist scholarly work on the concerto toward the end of the twentieth century, and it described the older of the two seven-part plans. As Davis has noted, Koch's *Versuch* model most accurately corresponds to the pattern found especially in many of C. P. E. Bach's earlier concertos—those of the 1730s and 1740s. "Actually, Bach favoured several formal plans; however, the one that Koch described was used with relative consistency by Bach and was also the one most frequently employed in the general repertory bridging the generation between C. P. E. Bach and Mozart."[25] It is particularly characteristic, for instance, of the Mannheim composers and

---

21. Tovey, "The Classical Concerto," pp. 9–10.
22. "Pillars" is taken from James Webster, "Are Mozart's Concertos 'Dramatic?'" in *Mozart's Piano Concertos*, ed. Zaslaw, p. 111: "The later ritornellos are stable pillars, confirming the structural cadences that end each of the major solo sections." As will emerge, Webster and others (including Leeson-Levin and David Rosen) do not consider one of our frequently invoked "pillars," just before or at the onset of the recapitulation (our R3), to be a ritornello.
23. The principal model for the diagrams, on which our differing (and somewhat reordered) versions are based, is in Galand, "The Large-Scale Formal Role of the Solo Entry Theme," pp. 400–401. In table 19.1 we also take

over some of Galand's tabular conventions, which he described on p. 399: "The parenthesized Roman numerals indicate variants not specified by Koch but often encountered in C. P. E. Bach's concertos, which Koch regarded as paradigmatic. For the five other concerto types in the table, only major-mode plans are indicated, and subsidiary keys are designated 'x.'"
24. Two useful introductions to Koch's view of the concerto are Stevens's now-classic "Theme, Harmony, and Texture" (n. 6) and Irving, *Mozart's Piano Concertos*, pp. 1–16 (n. 3)
25. Davis, "C. P. E. Bach and the Early History of the Recapitulatory Tutti," pp. 65, 66.

TABLE 19.1   Six Subtypes of the Eighteenth-Century Type 5 Sonata, with Particular Reference to Mozart's Concertos (Adapted from Galand 2000: 400-401)

Subtype A
Seven-part (four ritornello) format: cf. Koch's 1793 concerto plan.

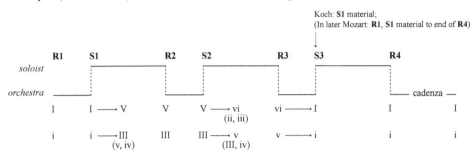

Subtype B
Seven-part (four ritornello) format: variant of Koch 1793: (vestigial?) "Ritornello 3"-effect launches the tonic return (=recapitulation); the most common format in Mozart's mature concertos.

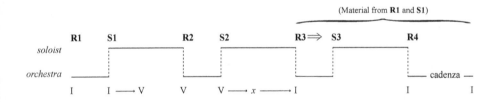

Subtype C
Three-ritornello variant, suppressing or minimizing the potential tutti-effect ("R3" of Subtype B) at the tonic return; cf. Vogler 1779, Koch 1802; Leeson-Levin 1978.

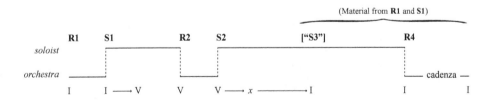

TABLE 19.1   (*continued*)

Subtype D
Nine-part (five-ritornello) format, with an interior ritornello in the developmental space;
"C. P. E. Bach's four-solo plan."

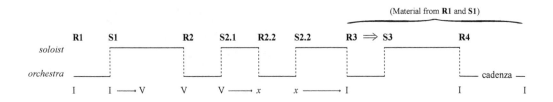

Subtype E
Type 5 adaptation of the Type 2 ("binary") Sonata (in this variant, suppressing a clear
tutti-effect around the area of the tonal resolution).

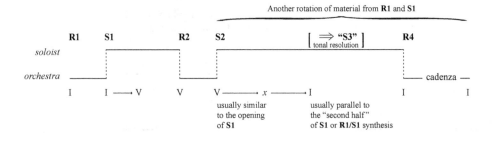

Subtype F
Type 5 adaptation of the Type 1 Sonata (no development, i.e., suppression of S2);
R2 proper may also be suppressed in favor of an "R3"-effect.

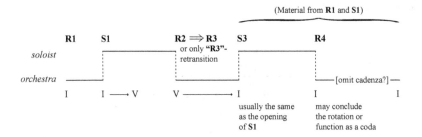

is found in many of J. C. Bach's concertos.[26] This "older" format is also retained in a handful of concerto movements in Mozart. In Koch's description three solos (corresponding roughly to exposition, development, and recapitulation) were set off by four ritornellos:

> The first allegro of the concerto contains three main periods [*Hauptperioden*] performed by the soloist, which are enclosed [*eingeschlossen*] by four subsidiary periods [*Nebenperioden*] performed by the orchestra as ritornellos. In modern concertos, the first ritornello is generally worked out at length. It consists of the principal melodic sections of the plan [*Anlage*] of the allegro, which are brought into a different connection and extended through other means than in the solo of the concerto part. . . .
> Nothing remains to be noted in connection with the three main periods of the solo part, for they have the same external arrangement [*äusserliche Einrichtung*] and the same course of modulation as the three main periods in the first allegro of a symphony. The type of melody, on the other hand, is very similar to that of a sonata. . . .[27]

Koch also furnished brief descriptions of the harmonic structure of each of the ritornellos and the various options at hand. As a result his 1793 seven-part (four-ritornello) format—our Subtype A—is more expansive and detailed than Vogler's. We may summarize Koch's *Versuch* plan as follows:

Ritornello 1. This is a substantial orchestral ritornello "in modern concertos." Although it remains conceptually a subsidiary section, merely a *Nebenperiode*, it does anticipate at least the "principal melodic sections" of the subsequent solo exposition. The opening ritornello is tonic-centered: it may be sounded entirely in the tonic or may contain an interior melody in the dominant (a *cantabile* secondary theme), with or without a formal cadence in that key—although in either case the ritornello will be led back to the tonic for a conclusion.

Solo 1. This is a nonrepeated sonata exposition, modulating to and confirming a secondary key. As the first of the three *Hauptperioden* it has a higher conceptual status than does the opening ritornello. At pivotal cadential or caesura points "the melody of the main part is sometimes interrupted by the orchestra with short passages, which consist either of repeated segments of the principal melody or of phrases which occurred only in the ritornello."

Ritornello 2. Elided with the closing cadence of Solo 1, this shorter ritornello "repeats a few melodic sections which already were contained in the first ritornello and closes likewise with a formal cadence in the fifth."

Solo 2. This is equivalent to a sonata development ("the second main period of the first allegro of the symphony"), though often starting with a new theme and typically closing with a cadence on the minor submediant, the minor mediant, or the minor supertonic.

Ritornello 3. This is a short ritornello of retransition that "modulates back into the main key, in which it closes with a [half cadence]." It may be worth noticing that while Koch mentioned that Ritornellos 2 and 4 are normally based on passages from Ritornello 1, he made no such remark about Ritornello 3.

Solo 3. This is equivalent to a sonata recapitulation ("the third main period of the first allegro of the symphony"). It typically ends, however, with an orchestral passage—which Koch, unlike most modern commentators (as reflected in table 19.1) does not consider a separate ritornello—that leads to a held $^6_4$ chord and fermata, whereupon the soloist performs a cadenza: "At the caesura tone of this period [= the final cadence of the third solo], the ripieno parts usually introduce, by means of a few measures, a fermata on the six-four of the keynote."

26. Davis, "C. P. E. Bach and the Early History of the Recapitulatory Tutti," pp. 70–71.
27. Koch, *Versuch einer Anleitung zur Composition* [1793], 3:333, 336. The translation is that found in Koch, *Introductory Essay*, trans. Nancy Kovaleff Baker, pp. 210, 211.

Ritornello 4. "With the caesura tone of this so-called cadenza, which always ends with a formal cadence, the last ritornello begins. This generally consists of the last melodic sections of the initial ritornello, with which the entire first allegro concludes."[28]

When confronting Mozart's or Beethoven's concertos with Koch's 1793 descriptions in mind, one must provide several nuances and qualifications. The most important thing is to avoid falling into the historicist trap of regarding Koch's outlines as a sufficient guide to the examination of these much more complex works. Koch's simplistic descriptions and Mozart's compositional depth and polish operate on vastly disparate conceptual levels. We concur with John Irving's recent conclusion about this matter: "Reflecting on Koch's detailed assessment of the concerto, one is struck by the gulf between his theory and Mozart's practice."[29]

One technical issue concerns the much-discussed status of the third ritornello (R3), which Koch situated at the end of the development as a passage of retransition. In fact, the compositional treatment of this brief ritornello was variable. At times it does take on this retransitional (sometimes modulatory) role, preparing for a recapitulation begun by the soloist, as in the opening movements of Mozart's first two violin concertos, K. 207 and 211, and those of the Piano Concerto No. 19 in F, K. 459, the Horn Concerto No. 1 in D, K. 412, and the Clarinet Concerto in A, K. 622 (see chapter 22). More often in Mozart's concerto first movements, though, the retransitional function at the end of Solo 2 is provided by the soloist. In this case the third "ritornello"—if we may still regard it as that—is used to provide an opening charge to the recapitulation with a tutti, tonic restatement of the original, Ritornello 1 version of the P-idea, or at least its incipit. In this latter case "Ritornello" 3 has left behind its retransitional function in favor of becoming a point of

ignition for Koch's third *Hauptperiode*, the recapitulation. Normally, the soloist joins in after a few bars, perhaps in a second or third phrase or module: we label this merger with Solo 3 as R3⇒S3. This "recapitulatory tutti" procedure, far and away the norm in Mozart, is presented as Subtype B in table 19.1, the second of the two seven-part (four-ritornello) formats.

The Problematic Status of the Recapitulatory Tutti, R3 (R3⇒S3)

There has been some debate in recent decades about whether the R3 in the Subtype-B case just mentioned—or even in the preceding Subtype-A situation described in Koch's *Versuch*—is a genuine "ritornello" or only a "tutti interjection" marking the juncture between two juxtaposed solo sections, both because of its occasional brevity and because it does not reinforce a cadential close led by the soloist.[30] The frequently encountered tutti-impulse at the onset of the recapitulation, to the extent that it is a ritornello at all, is substantially different in function and effect from R2 and R4, both of which solidify strong perfect authentic cadences at the end of an extended solo passage. What is needed is a sense of the variability of the recapitulatory R3, acknowledging its functional difference from the other ritornellos and its uncertainty with regard to genuine ritornello status.

One factor involved in this question appears to have been the wish to keep the ritornello portions of the form conceptually separate from the three solo sections, within which alone the sonata form is regarded as playing itself out. In part, this decision is based on the descriptions of Vogler, Koch, and other late-eighteenth-century theorists. In recent decades some writers have followed the influential lead of Leeson and Levin, who in 1978 categorized this moment as only the onset of the "recapitulation," which they considered exclusively as the third solo sec-

28. Quotations from Koch, *Introductory Essay*, trans. Baker, pp. 210–12.

29. Irving, *Mozart's Piano Concertos*, p. 12, where the idea is developed further. As is well known, Koch revisited concerto form, now with an awareness of Mozart's concertos, in the *Musikalisches Lexikon* of 1802, but al-

though he changed a few details of his description—to be discussed in the text below—the main points of Irving's assessment still stand. Cf. Irving on the 1802 Koch, *Mozart's Piano Concertos*, p. xv.

30. Cf., e.g., n. 22.

tion, arriving directly after the second without ritornello-intervention, thus steering clear of a confrontation with this spot as a potential ritornello.[31] (Cf. Subtype C in table 19.1.) Similarly, the current tendency in Germanic scholarship is that of not granting ritornello status to this moment. Robert Forster, for instance, has argued that because this "recapitulatory tutti" (*Reprisentutti*), is not really comparable in function to that which orchestrally extends the soloist's final cadences of Solo 1 (exposition) and Solo 3 (recapitulation), it is dominated more by the "recapitulation principle" than by the ritornello principle.[32] (This might involve, however, too narrow a definition of "ritornello." In pursuit of precedents for the recapitulatory "rebeginning" of R3, one might recall the possibility of "da capo" ritornello-effects toward the latter portions of certain Baroque concerto movements, as in the first movements of J. S. Bach's Violin Concerto No. 2 in E, BWV 1042, and the Fourth Brandenburg Concerto, BWV 1049.)[33]

On the other hand, other writers, doubtless with an adaptation of the 1793 Koch in mind, do consider this tutti moment to represent a third ritornello. For Shelley Davis in 1988, it belonged to the "tutti restatement: four-ritornello plan" that he found with some regularity in C. P. E. Bach's and occasionally in J. C. Bach's concertos—a position also discussed (and problematized) with considerable nuance by Jane R. Stevens in 1996.[34] For Karol Berger in 1996, the sometimes-brief tutti impulse at this point in Mozart's concertos represented "the vestigial third tutti"—a useful turn of phrase—which normally begins the "fourth period" (that is, the recapitulation) and is typically joined to the third solo.[35] For the present, granting the complexity of the issue, we shall consider this

quasi-"da capo" impulse to be at least a ritornello-effect, reanimating the opening bars of R1 and having a specialized quasi-ritornello function of calling attention to an important structural moment in the movement—in this case the beginning of the recapitulatory rotation. (We revisit some of these terminological questions in a subsequent section, "More on Terminology: 'Ritornello' or 'Tutti'?")

Tutti-Solo Layouts, Subtypes C–F

It may be this ambiguity surrounding a recapitulatory R3—only a tutti impulse that soon yields to an R3⇒S3 merger in the opening moments of the recapitulation—that led some late-eighteenth-century theorists to appear to agree with Vogler's earlier five-part (three-ritornello, two-solo) plan, which had passed over this possible "third ritornello," and in which the "second solo" comprised both the developmental space and the recapitulation. Such was the case in Francesco Galeazzi's description of the form in 1796 and August Kollmann's in 1799—and even Koch, in his *Musikalisches Lexikon* of 1802, only nine years after the *Versuch* (but now with Mozart's concertos more in mind), omitted any discussion of an orchestral ritornello around the area of the recapitulation.[36] If so, they were providing a different description of our Subtype B in table 19.1. On the other hand, it is heuristically prudent to devise a Subtype C, similar to B but with no ritornello claim at the onset of the recapitulation. This provides a more literal representation of what these writers claimed. Assuming that R3 is not suppressed altogether, as occasionally in J. C. Bach's concertos (for instance, in the first movement of the E-flat Keyboard Concerto, op. 7 no. 5)[37] and (perhaps) in

---

31. Leeson and Levin, "On the Authenticity of K. Anh. C 14.01 (297b)," pp. 90–96; Cf. David Rosen, "The Composer's 'Standard Operating Procedure,'" p. 81, and "'Unexpectedness' and 'Inevitability,'" p. 281, n. 2. Cf. n. 22.
32. Forster, *Die Kopfsätze*, p. 49–50. A similar system of categories is found in Küster, *Formale Aspekte*, p. 7 et seq.
33. Other examples in J. S. Bach: the finale of the Sixth Brandenburg Concerto, BWV 1051, and the first and third movements of the Harpsichord Concerto No. 2 in E, BWV 1053.

34. Davis, "C. P. E. Bach and the Early History of the Recapitulatory Tutti in North Germany," pp. 71–80; Stevens, "The Importance of C. P. E. Bach for Mozart's Piano Concertos," in *Mozart's Piano Concertos*, ed. Zaslaw, pp. 211–36.
35. Berger, "The First-Movement Punctuation Form," in *Mozart's Piano Concertos*, ed. Zaslaw, p. 248.
36. Stevens, "Theme, Harmony, and Texture," pp. 41–43, provides the basic citations from Galeazzi and Koch.
37. Cited by Davis, "H. C. Koch, the Classic Concerto, and the Sonata-Form Retransition," p. 50.

the first movements of Mozart's Violin Concerto No. 5 in A, K. 219, and Piano Concerto No. 13 in C, K. 415,[38] today's analysts might find Subtype C to be helpful in cases in which the R3 effect is unusually abbreviated (demoted to the status of a mere tutti interjection).

We should add a word about our labeling of the Subtype C diagram and subsequent schemes. Since our goal is to confront the concertos of Mozart (as opposed to devising a more encompassing, umbrella theory intended to cover their predecessors and contemporaries as well), we adopt as a heuristic standard the most commonly encountered Type 5 format found in their works. We thus propose a generic backdrop of a seven-part (four-ritornello) framework (Subtypes A and B—the latter is much more frequent in Mozart—in table 19.1), even when all seven parts might not be fully articulated on the acoustic surface of the music. Our labels R1, R2, R3, and R4 are not connotationally neutral designations. They refer to situated functions within the structure.

Our R1 means "the opening tutti," which is also always the longest, most complete ritornello. The R2 function is to follow the solo (or smaller) exposition and precede a developmental space: some writers refer to this with such descriptions as "the "subordinate-key ritornello," or the "medial tutti in the secondary key."[39] Our R3 label, the most flexible of them, refers to that (vestigial) "ritornello" or pronounced

tutti-effect in the area of the recapitulation. R3 normally signifies either a retransitional function, preparing for a solo-launched recapitulation, or a *Reprisentutti*, an orchestral recapturing of the opening sounds of R1 to begin the recapitulatory rotation. Our R4 stands for the ritornello that follows the last solo section, concludes the movement, and is normally divided into two parts surrounding the cadenza, R4[1] and R4[2]. (Some recent writers, most notably Leeson and Levin, have categorized these as two separate tuttis or ritornellos.)[40] If in any given movement the R3-effect is missing (as in the Subtype-C format, table 19.1), we still label the closing ritornello as R4, even though it is literally only the third ritornello heard in that movement. In this case R3 is present only in its absence—something possible only if for practical reasons we take Subtypes A and B as the norm for labeling.

We may deal with the remaining subtypes quickly. Found with some frequency in the mid-eighteenth century (it has been much noted in studies of C. P. E. Bach),[41] Subtype D is a nine-part (five-ritornello) format. It is similar to Subtype B—Mozart's norm—except that from the perspective of Subtype B an "extra" ritornello has been provided to reinforce a central developmental PAC, usually in vi, iii, or ii.[42] The retransition from this mid-developmental ritornello to the *Reprisentutti* (an R3 function) is led by the soloist. Since it is normally situated in

38. Discussions of these works are provided in ch. 22. Davis, "H. C. Koch, the Classic Concerto," pp. 48–49, mentions other examples in J. C. Bach and Johann Samuel Schroeter but also claims that the first movement of Mozart's Violin Concerto No. 4 in D, K. 218, exemplifies Vogler's 1779 and Koch's 1803 format. While R3 is lacking in that Mozart movement, the whole structure is better regarded as a Type 2 adaptation of the Type 5 sonata (Subtype E in table 19.1).

39. Forster, *Die Kopfsätze*, p. 49, "Mitteltutti"; Küster, *Formale Aspekte*, e.g., p. 181, "Mittentutti,'" Caplin, *Classical Form*, p. 248, "subordinate-key ritornello"; Harold S. Powers, "Reading Mozart's Music: Text and Topic, Syntax and Sense," *Current Musicology* 57 (1995), 8, "medial tutti (partial ritornello) in the second key"; and so on.

40. Leeson and Levin ("On the Authenticity of K. Anh. C 14.01 (297b)," p. 96) named these, influentially, as the "ritornello to cadenza" (or precadenza ritornello) and

the "final ritornello." Similar labels are found in David Rosen, "The Composer's 'Standard Operating Procedure,'" and "'Unexpectedness' and 'Inevitability.'" Cf. n. 20 above. For Forster, *Die Kopfsätze*, pp. 50, 55, the remainder of the movement after the third solo section is regarded as a "closing complex" (*Schlußkomplex*), consisting of the "cadenza tutti" (*Kadenztutti*) often lacking a clear or genuine "ritornello" function (thus becoming a merely "secondary tutti"), the solo cadenza itself, and the "closing ritornello" (*Schlußritornell*).

41. E.g., in Davis, "C. P. E. Bach and the Early History of the Recapitulatory Tutti," pp. 67–69; cf Galand, "The Large-Scale Formal Role," p. 402.

42. Stevens, "The Importance of C. P. E. Bach," pp. 214–16, touched on the problematics of such a structure, and, at least initially, regarded some models in C. P. E. Bach as instances of the four-tutti model with a mere tutti interjection at the moment of the "return to the tonic" (the reprise).

the interior of S2, that is, in the developmental space, midway between what is functionally R2 and R3, this "extra" ritornello can be labeled as R2.2 ("another ritornello, sounded after R2 but before the R3-effect"). It would be followed, of course, by S2.2 ("the resumption of S2, now with retransition function"). This solution leads to a more general point: as will emerge in Chapters 21 and 22, brief interior tutti interjections or reinforcements in the exposition and recapitulation, common in many concertos, need not be provided with R-numbers at all.

Subtype E shows the Type 2 ("binary") variant of the Type 5 sonata—the one lacking a full recapitulation.[43] Here the R2 function is normally complete (as is that of R4), and S2 merges directly into the crux and tonal resolution, bypassing any R3 effect. This situation may be described as an S2⇒S3 fusion, although individual circumstances might call for an ad hoc explanation.

Finally, Subtype F illustrates the Type 5 adaptation of the Type 1 idea, something normally found only in slow movements.[44] In this subtype the movement's sonata aspects are limited only to an exposition and a recapitulation: the developmental space is suppressed, replaced by only a brief orchestral retransition (in Mozart, sometimes additionally decorated by the soloist!). In other words, following Solo 1's final cadence, the next ritornello is usually given over primarily (or exclusively) to the retransitional function. In this case, it is the R2 function (the "medial ritornello," preceding the development) that is lacking, and accordingly we label this ritornello as R3. In cases in which the ritornello seems to begin as a genuine extension to Solo 1, then soon to lapse into retransition activity, one could label it as an R2⇒R3 merger.

It is worth repeating that the six ritornello formats are presented here only as heuristic models, not as analytical templates for all concertos. One should expect to find adaptations of these models within individual concertos: later ritornello displacements, suppressions, curtailed allusions, additional tutti or solo interjections, unusual tutti dialogues with the soloist—all

of these things are to be expected within the only modestly constrained aesthetic play of the craft. The goal of the models is only to provide a starting-point for analysis, a lens through which the individual realizations may be perceived.

Overview: Sonata Form, Mozart, and the Seven-Part (Four-Ritornello) Framework

As outlined above, our practice is to consider Subtypes A and B as the most normative in Mozart's works and to use the four ritornello pillars as a standard for labeling: R1, R2, R3, and R4, with S1, S2, and S3 as extended solo sections between them. The question now becomes, how, in Mozart's concrete practice, are these zones placed into a *rapprochement* with sonata form?

First—to consider a position with which we do not concur (at least for Mozart's concertos)—some writers consider it a convenience, if not a historical imperative (interpreting Vogler's and Koch's words strictly), to grant sonata status only to the solo sections. On this understanding, the ritornello pillars stand as separate conceptual entities, cleanly outside of the sonata-unfolding. This position construes R2 as a separate ritornello space that does not participate in the exposition—which is thus reduced to only the "solo exposition" of S1. Similarly, the recapitulation is restricted to only S3; R4 is not interpreted as participating in the sonata process. Such a view has its merits: it is understandable and logically consistent on the basis of the theoretical writings; it is sometimes helpful in coming to terms with earlier concertos by other composers, such as C. P. E. Bach; it acknowledges the (non-sonata-form) historical origins of the ritornello procedure, whose residual traditions are clearly in evidence in the later eighteenth-century and early nineteenth-century concerto; and rather than reducing the concerto-movement structure to only one thing, it emphasizes the provocative interplay between sonata and ritornello form as central features of this hybrid genre. All this is to the good.

But this viewpoint also has its shortcomings, ones that are all the more palpable as we con-

---

43. Examples are provided in n. 5.

44. For examples in Mozart, see n. 3, along with the passage in the text to which it refers.

front Mozart's concerto formats. What it argues is that it is preferable, when considering the "sonata-form" question, to bracket off S1 from everything that precedes and follows it. To be sure, when we do this, we find a sufficient and coherent exposition that exemplifies all of the norms associated with that structural section, those that Sonata Theory describes through its P TR ' S / C system. The problem is that as the Type 5 sonata proceeds in real time, S1 does not stand alone. On the contrary, it emerges in a context. Most importantly, that context emphasizes its sharing of material with the preceding R1, and this sharing is a conspicuous part of S1's essence. With regard to modular material R1 and S1, while not identical, are interdependent. Because this modular interdependence usually also encompasses at least the later portions of R2 (and consequently brings up the concept of governing rotations), it is methodologically inappropriate to isolate S1 from the context within which, in significant part, it derives its meaning.

For the moment, we might anticipate some conclusions that will be buttressed in later sections. While a "bracketed" S1 does indeed furnish a satisfactory exposition, it is also the case, in Mozart's (and Beethoven's) concertos, that if we were place our brackets differently, encompassing both S1 and R2, we would frequently come up with something larger than S1 that also looks like a satisfactory exposition. But some clarification is needed before proceeding further. R2 may arrive at a terminal cadence, in which case its larger function is manifest: it serves as an expositional appendix to the solo exposition (usually invigorating, toward its end, modules from R1 that had not been heard in S1). But in Mozart it can also happen that R2 is rotationally or cadentially incomplete in one way or another, perhaps breaking off before its anticipated final cadence or dissolving into a dominant or other preparation for S2. In the latter cases the impression given is that of a larger expositional appendix or conclusion that is interrupted

en route, or that, instead of closing, converts at its end into a setup for what follows.

Notwithstanding the variability of treatment found in R2, what all of this means is that in a Type 5 sonata by Mozart, one encounters two differing sizes of exposition, depending on which of the two "bracketing" perspectives one is attending to. Neither is "the" (only) exposition, but both are present from different perspectives. In Mozart's concertos, once past the opening ritornello in the tonic, S1 lays out a *solo exposition*, characteristically closing with a trill cadence. On the other hand, S1 and the brief, though emphatic R2 (even when R2 is kept incomplete or otherwise problematized) usually strive to complete a nonrepeated *larger exposition*. Again, from the perspective of the solo alone, the solo exposition, S1, is the governing one of the movement: it presents "everything the soloist wishes to say" along these lines. But from the more inclusive perspective of the orchestral complex within which the soloist is embedded, a broader, more inclusive rotational complex is working itself out (S1 + R2, even if kept nonclosed or incomplete), and it often does so in ways that are in line with the norms of a larger exposition.[45] This double perspective, retaining the interplay and coexistence of two different generic structural fields, is a crucial aspect of Sonata Theory's conception of the Type 5 sonata (in Mozart's hands). We revisit this feature more closely later in this chapter, "Adapting J. C. Bach into K. 107," and in chapter 21.

S2 is normally given over to the modulatory *developmental space*. Harking back to its origins in the Baroque concerto, S2 is frequently more episodic—or given over to new, virtuosic figuration—than it is developmental in any standard sense of the term.[46] In Forster's words, "In contrast to the concepts of exposition and recapitulation (for the first and third solos), the designation of the second solo as a *development* is only really justified in a few cases."[47] Developmental spaces given over to "new" material

---

45. As will be outlined in ch. 21, multimodular R2s often subdivide into a *rotationally inert* first module or two, proceeding directly into a *rotationally participatory* set of modules taken from the end of R1 that had not been sounded in S1. The common functional succession

within R2, inert⇒participatory, may be paralleled in the two halves of R4.

46. Hence the aptness of the term developmental *space*: see the beginning of ch. 10.

47. Forster, *Die Kopfsätze*, p. 49. Cf. Marius Flothuis,

are especially common in Mozart's earlier concertos. Not surprisingly, the principle of development crops up more in the later works, and Beethoven's S2 spaces, as might be expected, are usually more self-consciously developmental.

As discussed above, the brief R3 is variable in function (Subtypes A and B differ in this regard), but in mature Mozart it usually begins the recapitulation (Subtype B). The "double perspective" encountered in the exposition(s) also applies here, as do its caveats. The R3⇒S3 portion constitutes a separate, *solo recapitulation*, referentially analogous to but perhaps differing in some aspects of content from the S1 "solo exposition." The larger complex, R3⇒S3 + R4, constitutes the *larger recapitulation* (which may append a coda at the end). In Type 5s in which S1 had differed substantially from R1 (common in the first movements of Mozart's concertos), the larger recapitulation—and especially its post-MC modules—serves as a synthesis or fusion of the two earlier layouts. When this happens, the larger recapitulation will be more complete than either layout found in the first two rotations. The successive rotations of the whole movement grow in their inclusiveness, culminating in the grand totality provided in the larger recapitulation. One function of the recapitulatory rotation is to serve as the harmonic and rhetorical telos of the ongoing process of modular accumulation.

Following most modern commentators, our R4 differs slightly from Koch's, who restricted it to only that orchestral tutti following the cadenza. But an orchestral tutti also precedes the cadenza (Koch regarded it as a mere orchestral supplement to S3), and today that, too, is usually grouped under the R4 concept. This understanding of R4 always splits it into two parts. What we label as $R4^1$ is the precadenza portion (often rotationally inert, as will be seen) of this two-part ritornello, typically leading to

a preparatory $^6_4$ platform and fermata; $R4^2$ is the postcadenza portion, usually completing the larger recapitulation in a rotationally participatory manner and sometimes adding on a coda at the end. These Ritornello 4 concepts will be more fully explicated both later in this chapter and in chapter 22.

More on Terminology: "Ritornello" or "Tutti"?

To what extent are our R1–4 stations really "ritornellos"? That they are "tuttis" is clear, since their characteristic feature is that of subordinating the soloist to the lead of the orchestra. (The impression will be that the "solo" has either not yet started, as with R1, or has come to a temporary resting-point in its own ideas—even if, as in some performance traditions, the soloist continued playing a subordinate, *basso continuo* role or became reabsorbed back into the tutti.)[48] But are these tuttis also ritornellos? The latter term claims more, both by way of historical resonance with concerto traditions and by the etymological suggestion of the defining feature of a return to material heard earlier (*ritornello:* "little return"). In this sense "ritornello" is a subset of the broader notion of "tutti."

Some recent writers, such as Plantinga in his recent study of *Beethoven's Concertos*, have decided to avoid the connotatively charged term "ritornello" altogether, replacing it with "the more neutral *tutti.*"[49] (Our R1, R2, and so on, are generally equivalent to his T1, T2. . . .) Others, such as Forster, prefer to describe our R1, R2, and R4 with the "neutral covering-concept *tutti*"—as in *Anfangstutti, Mitteltutti,* and *Schlußtutti*—while also admitting that in most cases these moments, and some others, are also ritornello-like in function: "The concept of ritornello is used here only in the literal sense of the word (*ritornare*) to refer to sections that

---

Mozart's Piano Concertos: A Study (Amsterdam/Atlanta: Rodopi, 2001), p. 4: "The development section is the only one reminiscent sometimes of the 'episode' of the baroque concerto; in the early concertos (before 1777) it is neither thematic nor motivic, but freely invented."
48. Grayson opens his summary of differing views as follows: "A variety of evidence suggests that Mozart intended and expected the piano soloist to provide basso

continuo accompaniment during the orchestral ritornellos and perhaps also during the shorter tutti passages within solo sections. . . . Musical evidence also seems to support the use of continuo" (*Mozart: Piano Concertos Nos. 20 and 21,* pp. 104–8, at 104).
49. See, e.g., Leon Plantinga, *Beethoven's Concertos,* p. 17.

would be taken over unaltered from the opening tutti. But ritornellos and ritornello-like sections can also appear inside the solo [portions]. Conversely, a tutti-part need not unconditionally be a ritornello. Instead it can seem to have been built, as it were, on the spot."[50] The presence of such *tutti interjections* within the solo sections complicates the matter. Occasionally they reinvigorate a module, ritornello-like, from the opening R1. (As will be discussed in chapter 21, many of Mozart's concertos feature such a tutti interjection in the vicinity of the P–TR seam within Solo 1.) Others appear in an ad hoc way, part of an ongoing "dramatic dialogue" of "co-operation," "competition," or "confrontation" with the soloist.[51]

While acknowledging the terminological problem, our preference is to retain the familiar term ritornello for the four structural pillars. The passing, ad hoc, or dialogic tuttis we refer to merely as tutti interjections or unnumbered tuttis. In making this choice we hope to underscore the historical roots of the structure (the continued persistence of Baroque norms into the classical concerto) and to suggest that the sections that we designate as ritornello pillars 1–4 are specialized adaptations of older traditions, crafted to mark the most crucial structural hinges of the Type 5 movement.

This terminological question involves two broader issues: what were the words used in the eighteenth century for these sections? and what should be the broader connotations of the current use of the term ritornello? As for the first, eighteenth-century usage was inconsistent. In Scheibe's *Critischer Musicus* (1739) and Quantz's Flute *Versuch* (1752), we find the term *ritornello* (occasionally exchanged with *tutti*, as in Quantz) but with reference to what we would now call the Baroque concerto. In 1779, as we have seen, Vogler called these sections only the prelude, interlude, and postlude. In 1789 Türk mentioned that the opening section was "called the ritornello (tutti)"—so was the final statement at the end—but he used a slightly different term for "interlude" (*Zwischensatz,* not Vogler's *Zwischenspiel*) for interior orchestral statements following the solo sections. In 1793 and 1802 Koch referred explicitly to *ritornellos* for all of these. Galeazzi (1796) and Kollmann (1799) used the term *tutti,* as did Czerny (ca. 1840). It is difficult to generalize from these writers, but one might suppose that the older connotations of the term *ritornello* lingered on, however haphazardly, in some musical circles.

As for the second issue—current understandings of the connotations of the term—we should recall that the tutti sections that we normally label as "ritornellos" in Baroque concertos also serve diverse functions in those pieces. Clearly, an opening ritornello has something of an expository or initiatory function (the beginning of a process), something that in some concerto movements can be recaptured with a "da capo" effect somewhere around the last third of the movement.[52] Interior tuttis most often feature the merger of a modular-return function (the archetypal *ritorno* of something from the opening) with, at least at their outsets, that of a cadence-confirming function. But some later tuttis, for example in some Vivaldi concertos, state material not provided at all in the opening ritornello, and the current term for these passages is also *ritornello.* Well-known instances of "blank" or new-material ritornellos may be found in the first movements of the "Spring" and "Summer" concertos from Vivaldi's *The Four Seasons,* op. 8 nos. 1–2.[53] Such occurrences

---

50. Forster, *Die Kopfsätze,* p. 48.

51. For an extended study of this, see Simon P. Keefe, *Mozart's Piano Concertos: Dramatic Dialogue in the Age of Enlightenment* (Woodbridge, U.K.: Boydell Press, 2001), from which the phrases in quotation marks have been drawn.

52. See, e.g., the J. S. Bach examples cited in n. 33, along with the text to which it refers.

53. In the first movement of the E-major "Spring" concerto, op. 8 no. 1, Ritornello 5 consists of a circle-of-fifths passage moving from C-sharp minor to V of E. Although its rhythm is based on that found in Ritornello 1, the actual modular ("thematic") content of the ritornello differs from that original tutti. The programmatic opening ritornello of the G-minor "Summer" concerto, op. 8 no. 2, represents "exhaustion caused by the heat," even beginning at a slower tempo than much of the rest of the movement. It returns as Ritornello 2, mm. 52–58, but subsequent ritornellos move on to new programmatic material: Ritor-

open the door to the concept of a ritornello with merely a *tutti* function. In short, one needs a broad conception of the several things that the traditional ritornello function could entail, including the possibility of writing over tutti spaces of normative "return" with other, new modules. With a more flexible understanding of the varieties of ritornello spaces in earlier concertos, the apparent controversy involved in selecting the proper terminology for Type 5 sonatas loses some of its urgency.

The Status of Ritornello 1 (R1)

Type 5 sonata movements—especially Mozart's more expansive ones—are normally marked by two important features: their R1 layouts are rhetorically similar to sonata expositions in all ways except tonality (R1 normally does not modulate away from the tonic); and their larger expositions proper (S1 + R2, now including the normative modulation in the center) give the impression of building upon and recasting the materials offered to them by the shorter, often less developed R1s. Such observations raise the issue of conceptual primacy. Which stretch of music, R1 or the following exposition, provides the more central span of interpretive reference, the governing referential layout, according to which everything that happens should be understood as responding? In sonata Types 1–4, the referential layout of materials is obviously the exposition. There the exposition provides the first rotation of ordered modules against which later rotations, partial or full, are to be assessed. But how are we to understand the role of a proto-exposition, the opening ritornello of a Type 5 sonata, which is something of a "first (and usually briefer) rotation" presented before the expositional rotation?

R1 and the Subsequent Exposition: The Question of Conceptual Primacy

In 1779, we recall, Vogler suggested that in creating a concerto movement one could begin by composing an ordinary Type 3 sonata—for example, a piano sonata movement—to which one could then add supplementary orchestral material, encompassing a modest, anticipatory prelude (R1) along with a later interlude and a postlude (our R2 and R4). In passing on such advice Vogler may have had in mind a traditional exercise or rule of thumb given to novice composers.[54] Under this conception R1, since it is subordinated to S1, points forward to the more important exposition that follows it, instead of the other way around. Those wishing to adapt Vogler to the more complex practice of Mozart would conclude that the primary referential layout is the larger solo exposition, S1 + R2, to which R1 is a mere (and thus secondary) anticipation.

Vogler's view of the primacy of the solo exposition was echoed by Koch in 1793, who wrote, as we have seen, that the three solo sections (our S1, S2, S3), considered apart from the four usual ritornellos, produced an acceptable sonata form, one that followed "the same external arrangement and the same course of modulation as the three main periods in the first allegro of the symphony."[55] With regard to their relative importance, Koch considered the concerto movement's S1 (the exposition) as a *Hauptperiode*, a main period, while the initial ritornello is derived as a *Nebenperiode*, a subsidiary period. Moreover, "according to the nature of the task at hand [*der Natur der Sache gemäss*], the first main period of the solo part [within a concerto movement, this is the exposition] is worked out before the ritornello is arranged as the introduction [*Einleitung*] to the execution

---

nello 3, mm. 78–116, is a composite of three images, a new representation of "gentle breezes" and the sudden "north wind," and, finally, a return to the "heat" motive of the first ritornello. The concluding Ritornello 4 is given over only to the "north wind," mm. 155–74. A handy overview of the varieties of ritornello practice in Vivaldi's concertos in general—including such things as "varied ritornellos," "ritornello-variation form," and "progressive ritornello form" (of which the first move-

ment of "Summer" is an example)—is provided in Paul Everett, "Ritornello Forms," Chapter 3 of *Vivaldi: The Four Seasons and Other Concertos, op. 8* (Cambridge: Cambridge University Press, 1996), pp. 26–49.

54. Cf. n. 57. The same may be said of Koch's later view of concerto form. See n. 29 above, along with the remarks in the text to which it refers, and, again, n. 57.

55. Koch, *Introductory Essay*, trans. Baker, p. 211.

[*Vortrage*] of the solo part."[56] This expositional solo period, he insisted, was that which provided the *Anlage*, the plan on which the rest of the work was grounded.[57]

This seems straightforward enough, and especially when initial ritornellos are brief or relatively undeveloped, such comments make perfect sense: opening tuttis may be readily heard as anticipatory prefaces preceding the main structural action of a work. As is always mentioned in this context, in a few instances young Mozart illustrated the advice eventually laid out by Vogler and Koch by producing seven pastiche (or "pasticcio") piano concertos based on pre-existing keyboard sonata movements, to which he added string parts, including the requisite ritornellos. These are Piano Concertos "Nos. 1–4," K. 37, 39, 40, and 41, from 1767, adapted from sonata movements by Raupach, Honauer, Schobert, and Eckard; and the set of three pastiche piano concertos dating probably from 1772, K. 107 nos. 1–3, adapted from J. C. Bach's Keyboard Sonatas, op. 5 nos. 2–4.[58] (We shall return to the Bach adaptations below.) Moreover, as Plantinga pointed out, in the 1790s "Clementi did the same in reverse. His Sonata Op. 33, No. 1 (published in 1794), had had an earlier life as a piano concerto; to change it into a (more saleable) sonata he simply removed all the principal tuttis and transcribed the internal orchestral interjections for piano."[59] All of this argues that from certain points of view opening ritornellos only prepared the way for the "real" formal event to unfold, taking on the role of an extended structural upbeat. As for the expositions, they apparently reacted to nothing that preceded them, content simply to be themselves. Under this interpretive paradigm one could not claim that R1 seeks to become the referential layout for the piece. That status is reserved only for the exposition.

But of course things are not this simple. When R1 broadens in length and diversifies in content, as is the case with most late-eighteenth-century concerto movements that we are likely to encounter, it can strike us as more than a mere introduction. In this situation its inherent introductory role becomes complemented with other functions. In general, the longer the opening tutti, the more the orchestra calls attention to itself as a semi-independent participant in the creative interplay between tutti and solo sections—group and individual. This sense of active, dialogical participation in the larger structure becomes even clearer when R1 is organized (with varying degrees of fullness and clarity) in the manner of a nonmodulating sonata exposition whose themes are destined to be embedded in larger rotations to come. Notwithstanding his assessment of R1 as a *Nebenperiode*, Koch in 1793 was noticing this phenomenon. Again: "In modern concertos, the first ritornello is generally worked out at length. It consists of the principal melodic sections of the plan

56. Koch, *Versuch*, 3:333–34 (footnote ✱✱); trans. adapted from Koch, *Introductory Essay*, trans. Baker, p. 210, n. 85.

57. Koch discusses this feature of the *Anlage* within arias and concertos in *Versuch*, 2:67–69, in which beginning composers are instructed for the sake of economy not to compose a ritornello until the *Anlage* of the first main section—the first solo [section]—is completely constructed. The opening ritornello is "nothing but the introduction [*Einleitung*] to the main thing to be performed [*Hauptvortrage*]" (p. 68). Beginners are also advised to avoid long opening ritornellos to concertos, even though in "modern concertos" these ritornellos are often "very long" (p. 69). Cf. Nancy Kovaleff Baker's similar summary of Koch's view regarding the opening ritornello, *Introductory Essay*, trans. Baker, p. 210, n. 85. For more of Koch's view of the *Anlage* in general—in part borrowed from Sulzer—see Stevens, "An 18th-Century Description of Concerto First-Movement Form," pp. 92–94: "It would appear that [in Koch's description of first-movement form] this *Anlage* corresponds very nearly to what we would call the principal events of the exposition in a symphony movement (pp. 92–93).

58. For the (re)dating of K. 107, see Wolfgang Plath, "Beiträge zur Mozart-Autographie II: Schriftchronologie, 1770–1780," *Mozart-Jahrbuch* 1976/77 (Kassel: Bärenreiter, 1978), pp. 141, 151 ("we say it cautiously: from the second quarter of the year 1772"), and 154. A classic overview of these works (though written before the "new" dating of the pieces) was provided in Edwin J. Simon, "Sonata into Concerto: A Study of Mozart's First Seven Concertos," *Acta musicologica* 31 (1959), 170–85. The most convenient and up-to-date overview of them, is found in Irving, *Mozart's Piano Concertos* ("The "Pasticcio' Concertos, K. 37, 39, 40 and 41; K. 107/i–iii"), pp. 17–25.

59. Plantinga, *Beethoven's Concertos*, p. 14.

[*Anlage*] of the allegro, which are brought into a different connection and extended through other means than in the solo of the concerto part."[60] Koch also recognized that R1 did not normally include every module of S1 and that it could sometimes contain a characteristic idea of its own. And with regard to its proto-expositional structure: "The difference between the form of an initial ritornello and the following first main period of the composition [S1] is principally that it closes in the main key, and not in the most closely related key as does the period."[61] That R1 was coming to resemble a nonmodulating exposition was also clear to Galeazzi in 1796, who wrote that the opening tutti is "conducted in the manner of the first part of the symphony, but with a close in the tonic."[62]

In short, as R1 "grows," along a sliding scale, into a section structured rhetorically (though not tonally) as an exposition, it claims more rights as an active partner in the large-scale Type 5 structure. To the extent that this more extended rotation lays down the most fundamental ideas to be taken up (however altered) in subsequent rotations, it asserts the right to be considered an equally significant—and perhaps the "real"—referential layout of the composition. This claim becomes all the stronger if R1, as is common, concludes with modules not to be heard in S1 (which in this sense falls short of full rotational completion), but which do return in R2 to round off or bring to a grander completion the rotational succession presented in S1. In this case, R1 sets the terms of the opening and closing boundaries of the larger exposition to come. From this perspective, R1 takes on the role of the referential rotation, an *Anlage* or layout that remains conceptually present as a rule

for understanding the unfolding of the larger structure to follow. The larger expositional rotation (S1 + R2) may be understood as an adaptation of (or commentary on) the referential layout provided in R1.

This conception grants a rotationally conceptual priority to R1, although it is at odds with Vogler's and Koch's presentation of the issue. But even if it is true that the larger expositional rotation (S1 + R2) was to be composed first, it is also the case that in the linear time of real performance the expositional rotation follows the R1 rotation. In other words, as it is presented within unfolding time, the larger expositional rotation is heard as a second rotation, recasting or varying the first one. Does it matter whether Mozart composed his concertos along Voglerian or Kochian lines? Probably not. Either way, as a finished work the concerto movement was to be presented to the listener in the linear order, {R1, S1 + R2}, in which S1 + R2 can take on the character of an altered, expanded second rotation following the referential R1. (In fact, the evidence suggests that the mature Mozart did not compose the exposition first. As David Rosen noted in 1996, "If . . . we judge the matter not from Koch's treatise but from Mozart's manuscripts, it seems rather that *his* starting point was the ritornello"—an assessment seconded vigorously in 2003 by John Irving in a clear summary of the issue.)[63]

Conclusion: The Three Structural
Functions of Ritornello 1

In fully developed Type 5s there is a reciprocal or complementary quality between the conceptual priority claims of R1 and S1 + R2. From

---

60. Koch, *Introductory Essay,* trans. Baker, p. 210.

61. Koch, *Introductory Essay,* trans. Baker, pp. 244. Possible differences in thematic content ("sections") between R1 and S1 are mentioned on p. 245.

62. Quoted in Stevens, "Theme, Harmony, and Texture," p. 38.

63. David Rosen, "'Unexpectedness' and 'Inevitability,'" p. 266, which continues: "Consider the autograph of K. 503, where the ritornello and only the first group of the solo exposition seem to have been drafted a few years before Mozart returned to the work and completed it, adding significant new material in the sec-

ond group of the exposition." Rosen's reference here (p. 282) is to Alan Tyson, "The Mozart Fragments in the Mozarteum, Salzburg: A Preliminary Study of Their Chronology and Their Significance," in *Mozart: Studies of the Autograph Scores* (Cambridge, Mass.: Harvard University Press, 1987), pp. 125–61, at 151–52. Irving, *Mozart's Piano Concertos,* p. 10: "Neither does the surviving manuscript evidence support Koch's implication that the solos were composed first of all. . . . In no case is there any physical indication that the solo sections were pre-composed."

Voglerian and Kochian perspectives, the referential layout may be regarded as merely proleptic, preparing for the "real thing" in S1 + R2. This is more clearly the case when R1 is significantly abbreviated, only half-fledged, or markedly underdeveloped as a rhetorical (nonmodulating) expositional array. One recalls Charles Rosen's trenchant remark, "the most important fact about concerto form is that the audience waits for the soloist to enter, and when he stops playing they wait for him to begin again. In so far as the concerto may be said to have a form after 1775, that is the basis of it. This is why the concerto has so strong and so close a relationship to the operatic aria."[64] A different perspective, though, demands recognition as opening ritornellos become longer, more fully outfitted—especially when they are provided with a generous string of post-MC modules. In such cases (as always, along a continuum of assertiveness depending on the abundance of R1's contents), R1 seems to be granted a rotationally conceptual priority, to which S1 + R2, the larger exposition, is already a varied repetition. Considerations resonant with these may have led to James Webster's insistence that "in all of Mozart's concerto first movements, and the majority of the others, the opening tutti is no mere introduction, but a ritornello. The distinction affects size, content, and formal function."[65]

Our view is that both perspectives are correct. Both are held in tension in most Type 5 sonatas—and certainly in Mozart's concertos. From one point of view, an introductory R1 looks forward to the "real" or fuller layout-to-come. From another, the S1 + R2 larger exposition looks backward to and adapts an ordered set of rotational materials that had been presented to it in R1 as material to be shaped into a bona-fide exposition. Although these two differing interpretations coexist in every Type 5 sonata, they are not always weighted equally. Concerto movements with more "complete" opening tuttis, particularly those with expansive successions of modules following the MC-effect, tilt

the balance more toward R1 as the primary referential layout, while never displacing entirely the referential claims of S1 + R2. The opposite is probably the case in less ambitious concerto movements or those with briefer or more perfunctory opening tuttis, which tilt more in the direction of an introductory function. The main thing is to preserve a sense of flexibility in all of this. In a Type 5 sonata the two interpretations not only can but must engage each other in an ongoing tension.

An opening ritornello within a Type 5 sonata harbors at least three structural functions, with degrees of emphasis that can change from work to work, depending on the perceived completeness or rhetorical self-sufficiency of its contents. Analytical descriptions of R1 should seek to perceive an interaction of these different functions, sometimes drawing forth one of them for attention, at times reminding us of the importance of another.

Introductory/Anticipatory Function. Two attributes of R1 underscore this role: its relative brevity (and often "incompleteness") vis à vis the ensuing exposition proper and its general retention of the tonic key throughout. This is the function mentioned by both Vogler and Koch in their later-eighteenth-century descriptions of concerto practice. It is given weight whenever R1 is brief, especially in its post-MC modules, and is built exclusively (or largely) on materials that will also appear in the subsequent S1. In Mozart concertos the balance tips toward the introductory function in some early Type 5 concerto movements, in some of the smaller-proportioned wind-concerto first movements, and in many Type 5 slow movements, in which R1 often provides only an embryonic, not a fully emerged version of the S1 solo exposition to follow.

Expositional-Rhetoric Function. Even many abridged R1s, whose brevity calls attention to their introductory roles, are rhetorically struc-

---

64. Rosen, *The Classical Style,* expanded ed., p. 196, followed by a nuanced description of the essential problems in establishing the proper relationship between extended tutti and the solo exposition.

65. Webster, "Are Mozart's Concertos 'Dramatic'?" in *Mozart's Piano Concertos,* ed. Zaslaw, p. 111.

tured as nonmodulating expositions. This often involves the production of a more energetic, TR-like zone, a rhetorical MC (I:HC), and the introduction of a new module of "secondary-theme" character, though still in (or resolving back to) the tonic. In other cases the layout may be that of a continuous exposition or, as in some early instances and several slow movements, that of a string of modules that "almost" manages to shape itself into a normative rhetorical exposition—a task that will then be successfully accomplished in the more expansive, next rotation. In Mozart's lengthier, mature concertos, and especially in their first movements, the proto-expositional contours of R1 are unmistakable. Regardless of R1's length, its rhetorical-exposition features foreshadow the more complete (and, finally, normative) exposition that is S1 or, more typically, S1 + R2. One role of R1 is to furnish, by means of its interior shaping, an anticipation of the larger sonata trajectory to which the remainder of the movement aspires: the structural goals and increasing completeness and resolution that it will eventually achieve at its end. While this aspect is in a sense preparatory for more complete things to follow, R1's role as a structural signal of a privileged layout-format on its own terms should not be minimized. This aspect of R1 is closely intertwined with its:

Referential-Layout Function. Even half-fledged R1s present a succession of modules whose ordering remains largely constant in the fuller rotations that follow, to the extent that R1's modules appear in them at all. Mozart's later expositions, for instance, often replace some of R1's proposed ideas with new ones and make additional expansions elsewhere. To the extent that R1's ideas are recycled in the exposition, they tend to appear in their original R1 order.[66] In such cases Mozart's more complete recapitulations almost always present all of R1's

modules in order, intercalating them also with S1's new ideas, thereby producing a recapitulatory synthesis. (Any exception to these norms should be regarded as deformational, requiring special hermeneutic treatment.) In this respect, from the perspective of the successive rotational unfolding of the whole movement, R1's nonmodulating proto-exposition also has a referential-layout function.

In addition, R1 normally provides the modules that are to be understood as defining the boundaries of later rotations. Its opening module continues to be the sign of the initiation of a new rotation (although sometimes a complication occurs with an interpolated "new" solo entry in S1, preceding the first module of the rotation proper: see chapter 21). And its final module—when deployed in rotational order in R2 or R4—signals the completion of any later rotation.[67] (It happens with some frequency in Mozart that R2 is not brought to full rotational completion; the recapitulatory rotation, though, ending with R4^2, always is.) Thus we second Stevens's generalization from 1996 and suggest that it now be interpreted also along rotational lines: "The thematic organization of the entire movement . . . is always founded in the material presented in the opening ritornello, which throughout the eighteenth century sets out the initial premises of the piece, the thematic and expressive world within which it will unfold."[68]

Sonata Theory's Thematic Labeling for Type 5 Sonatas

Even through R1 is nonmodulatory (and sometimes brief), its musical modules serve the same zonal rhetorical functions as those in normative, modulating expositions (P, TR, the medial caesura, S, and C). R1 always presents several of the modules to be sounded later in the first solo

---

66. Exceptions, e.g., at the opening of a multimodular R2 or in R4^1, are dealt with in chs. 21 and 22.
67. In Mozart's early concertos the brief, final "flourish" of R1 also often returns "out of order" as an emphatic affirmation of Solo 1's full statement of the P-theme: see ch. 21.

68. Stevens, "The Importance of C. P. E. Bach for Mozart's Piano Concertos," *Mozart's Piano Concertos,* ed. Zaslaw, p. 216.

section, but it also lacks some of them, and it may also feature one or more that will not be taken up in S1, even though they will appear in later sections. In order not to lose track of the modular appearances, one needs a way of designating them and indicating in which section they first appeared. Our system for Type 5s is compatible with the labeling principles devised for Type 1–4 sonatas (subdivisions of P, TR, MC, S, TMB, EEC, C, and so on). As will be elaborated in chapter 20, other systems to monitor the adventures of multiple individual ideas within concertos have been devised, usually based on "neutral" numbers or letters. Ours differs insofar as it also designates the zonal and sonata-structural function of the module at hand.

In Type 5s the task is formidable because of the double-*Anlage* impression typically found in R1 and S1 + R2, which as interdependent rotations share a number of modules, as well as by the intermittent appearances of these musical ideas in later concerto sections. The schematic goal is to provide the maximum amount of information with the most efficient abbreviations. In their most complete descriptions individual modules should be designated by a twofold designation: the first indicates the section in which they first appeared (R1, S1, R2, and so on); the second indicates the zonal or structural function of the module or musical moment (P, TR, EEC, S, C, and the like). The obvious practical problem is that the abbreviation S1 (the broad section, Solo 1) can be confused with S^1 (the first secondary theme, whose label has been established for other sonata types). In our system all Type 5 section designations employ arabic numerals that are not superscripted (S1); as opposed to this, all module designations use superscripts to identify interior elements (S^1, $S^{1.1}$).

In addition, all modular identifiers in Type 5s (only) are double-designations, in the order Section, Zone-Module. The two halves of the label are separated by a colon and a backslash (:\),

loosely adapted from the example of directory path classifications within computer practice.[69] The first half refers to the ritornello or solo section in which the module first appeared. Thus R1:\ means "within section R1" or "within the first ritornello"; S1:\ means "within section S1" or "within the first solo section." The second half of the path label, after colon-backslash, refers to the standard Sonata Theory modular identifier (P, S, C, and so on). The principal value of this system is its ability to distinguish modules that appeared in Ritornello 1 from those that first appeared only in Solo 1. Each module in Ritornello 1 and Solo 1 is therefore identified with a prefix. In order not to multiply labeling complications, R1 modules that reappear within S1 retain their R1:\ prefix. Any module in S1 space that is labeled without this R1:\ prefix—and is labeled with the S1:\ prefix instead—is understood to be a new module introduced within the first solo section. The R1:\ and S1:\ prefixes are also used to identify later appearances of these modules in R2, S2, R3, S3, R4[1], and R4[2]. If a new theme or episode is introduced in the development (the second solo section), it carries the prefix S2:\.

A few examples of sample designations can help to clarify the matter:

R1:\P — "the P-theme introduced within the first ritornello." (When this or any other R1 module appears in later sections, it retains this designation, which identifies the location of its first appearance.)

R1:\P$^{1.2}$ — "the second module of the P-theme (but one still prior to any I:PAC) introduced within the first ritornello."

R1:\TR$^{1.2}$ — "the second module of the transition within the first ritornello."

R1:\MC — "the medial caesura within the first ritornello."

S1:\TR — "a new transition theme within the first solo section." (Were the transition module not new—that is, were it the same as

---

69. Within the computer world the familiar path designation "C:\file," for instance, would mean, "on the C-drive (considered here as the root directory), the subordinate directory called 'file.'" The MS-DOS label structure is: current directory location; colon, back-slash; subordinate directory or individual file location on that larger directory. Our concerto-section and zone-module designation (such as R1:\ for "Ritornello 1," S1:\ for "Solo 1") is motivated by the familiarity of this pattern of abbreviation.

the one in Ritornello 1—it would be designated as R1:\TR. Notice that if one carried out the path-label designations strictly, the most proper label for this latter situation would be S1:\(R1:\TR), which would signify "within the first solo section, the transition module first heard in Ritornello 1." To avoid needless complication, though—since the existence of the section at hand, Solo 1, may be regarded as self-evident—we omit the initial S1:\, obviating the need for the parenthetical complications that would follow. Another option within the first solo section, S1, is for the TR to begin as it had in R1, then to dissolve into new material. This case can be abbreviated as R:\TR $\Rightarrow$ S1:\TR$^{1.2}$ [new].)

S1:\S^1 — "a new initial module launching the secondary-theme zone of the first solo section. (Were this the same secondary theme as the one in Ritornello 1, it would be designated as R1:\S or R1:\S^1. As mentioned directly above, this R1 designation within S1 space, in principle, could be placed in parentheses and preceded in the path label by S1:\. If the S1:\S theme arrives only after something already marked with an R1:\S label, one's designation should be locally crafted to suit the circumstances: perhaps something like S1:\S$^{1.2}$.)

R1:\S^1 = S1:\TM^3 — "the third module of a trimodular block within the first solo section, one that had already been sounded as S^1 in the first ritornello."

Although individual movements provide challenges of labeling, the above guidelines may be adapted flexibly. A larger issue is the question of the meaning of such labels as R1:\S or R1:\EEC. These labels may seem to claim too much or to involve a slippage of basic concepts. Both the S and EEC designations appear to imply that we are insisting that Ritornello 1 is in fact an "exposition." This is problematic, since Ritornello 1 is almost always nonmodulatory. Within the opening ritornello our supposed S and EEC are normally sounded in the tonic. Therefore what is labeled as R1:\EEC is a

I:PAC or i:PAC. But the concept of the EEC depends on its appearance within a subordinate key area: it signals a generically essential cadential close to a modulating exposition. This means that R1:\S is not literally an "S" in the normal sense. Instead, within a structure that is almost, but not quite, an exposition, it is an "S-equivalent" or a "proposal for the S-theme in the next rotation."

On this line of interpretation R1:\EEC (an "EEC-equivalent" or "EEC-proposal") would carry a number of connotations. It suggests such things as: "Were this a full, modulating exposition, this would be the EEC. Here the EEC-effect is carried out only rhetorically, not tonally. Under these circumstances, even while its sense of closure is regarded as only an analogy, R1:\EEC does function as something of a fictive closure-equivalent within R1 space, even while making a suggestion to the next rotation, S1 + R2, regarding one way in which the 'real' EEC could be accomplished." In Mozart's mature Type 5 movements, though not in the case of K. 107 no. 1/i to be examined directly below, R1:\EEC and S1:\EEC are frequently articulated with different preceding S-modules. The "fictive" R1:\EEC is no predictor of the manner in which the S1:\EEC will be sounded. (The issue is even more complicated, since the "double perspective" of Type 5 sonatas—ritornello movement and sonata movement—often leads to the concept of a double-EEC in the new key, S1:\EEC for the solo exposition and R2:\EEC for the larger exposition. This matter will be taken up below and again in chapter 21.)

Basic Concerto Principles: Mozart's Early Pastiche Concertos, K. 107

Mozart's first original piano concerto—in effect, his earliest original work in this genre[70]—was "No. 5" in D, K. 175, from 1773. It would be followed in 1774—restricting ourselves here only to pieces labeled as concertos—by the Bassoon Concerto in B-flat, K. 191; and in 1775

---

70. An earlier original concerto for trumpet, K. 47c (1768), has been lost.

by the five Violin Concertos, K. 207, 211, 216, 218, and 219.[71] As already mentioned, these early concertos had been preceded in the prior half-decade or more by seven concerto-arrangements either from selected pre-existing keyboard sonata movements (four works from 1767, K. 37, 39–41) or from pre-existing complete sonatas (K. 107, nos. 1–3, probably from 1772, transformations of J. C. Bach's keyboard sonatas, op. 5 nos. 2–4 [published in 1766], into concertos accompanied by two solo violins and cello).[72] One of the fascinations of the pastiche concertos is that they demonstrate the compositional "beginner's" exercise that would soon be described by Vogler and later seconded by Koch: to start with a pre-existing "ordinary sonata," self-sufficient on its own terms, and then to add accompaniment and interpolated extra sections in order to turn it into a concerto. Obviously, the suspicion arises that to look carefully at such "simple" works would lead one into some essential features of the concerto-genre that might otherwise be obscured if one confronts only later, more complex and subtle instances of it. This is indeed the case.

The guidelines that we seek may be found in the J. C. Bach arrangements, K. 107. It is helpful to know that of the three first movements of Bach's solo sonatas, two, op. 5 nos. 2 (in D) and 4 (in E-flat), are Type 3 sonatas; the third, op. 5 no. 3 (in G), is a Type 2, providing, in Mozart's hands, an illustration of the less-common Type 5 adaptation of the Type 2 sonata. In all three of these movements young Mozart showed both a certain constancy in his principles of adaptation and a willingness to approach each work as an individual case. With the exception of a measure or two shorn from the ends of the exposition and recapitulation (or tonal resolution in the case of K. 107 no. 2), Bach's music is presented intact in the principal solo sections.[73] In the first movements of nos. 1 and 3 Mozart interpolated music that was

not present in the original sonata into R2, between the original exposition and development. On the other hand, in both of these movements he provided an R3-effect (a retransition back to the solo-led recapitulation, Subtype A of table 19.1) either merely by scoring the final developmental-space module of the original for strings (in no. 1) or by providing an only slightly more florid version of that original module (in no. 3).

In all instances Mozart's R1 is shorter than the S1 "original" and is built rhetorically as a nonmodulating, two-part exposition with medial caesura. The relative brevity of R1 is typically provided by shrinking a multimodular secondary theme of the original exposition (an MMS or TMB) into a single thematic idea or period, which in R1 may then either proceed directly to a cadence or lead to other, very brief ideas. Additionally, in K. 107 Mozart avoided placing "new" themes in the interior of the opening ritornello: almost all of his modules are based on Bach's. The main exceptions occur in nos. 1 and 3, in which he composed a "new" concluding module for R1, one that was then also used to provide the music for R2 and the postcadenza R4[2] in both initial movements. (In no. 3 it additionally appears as an interpolated mid-developmental ritornello in vi, R2.2.) Normally, Mozart was also obliged for harmonic reasons to alter Solo 1's transition (henceforth abbreviated as S1:\TR—see below) to become R1:\TR. And in no. 3 he provided not a literal statement but a varied, smoother version of Solo 1's first two modules (only) of a trimodular block (R1:\S$^{1.1-1.2}$ = S1:\TM$^{1-2}$).

Adapting J. C. Bach into K. 107, no. 1/i: Opening Ritornello and Smaller and Larger Expositions

Let us consider first the opening movement of Mozart's Keyboard Concerto in D, K. 107 no.

---

71. Also to be reckoned in this roster are concerto-like movements found in such works as the violin concertos built into serenades—e.g., the three Serenades in D, K. 185/ii (1773; an unusual Type 5 Sonata within which Mozart included "Type-3-like" repeat signs!), K. 203//ii and iv (1774), and K. 204/ii and iii (1775)—the Concertone in C for Two Violins and Orchestra, K. 190 (1774), and so on.

72. For the dating, see n. 58.
73. The only exception occurs in the third concerto—a mid-development "extra" ritornello (R2.2, within a movement exemplifying Subtype D of table 19.1)—and is discussed below.

1, an arrangement of J. C. Bach's pre-existing Sonata in D, op. 5 no. 2/i. We shall begin by focusing on Bach's original exposition and comparing it with Mozart's adaptation in the R1 and S1 + R2 sections. Once these features are grasped, the remainder of the comparison may be done more efficiently. The exposition of Bach's D-major op. 5 no. 2, first movement (example 19.1), may be understood as follows:

P = mm. 1–9, elided with TR. P is constructed as a reiterated loop (a procedure also found often in Mozart). Each loop is a five-bar compound basic idea, featuring Bach's (and Mozart's) common *forte-piano* alternation and elided with the succeeding module (with m. 5, the reiteration, and with m. 9, TR).

TR = mm. 9–18. This is a TR of the dissolving continuation type. More precisely, it is the subtype that also suggests a breakout from the nonprogressive, circular loop that precedes it, the loop that in effect provided the presentation of a larger sentence. This continuation is itself sentential. Its marchlike basic idea (b.i., mm. 9–10) is treated to a free sequence (mm. 11–12): for later analytical purposes, these four bars may be considered TR$^{1.1}$. This proceeds into a continuation (here considered as a whole as TR$^{1.2}$) that links together an energetic cycling around the tonic (mm. 13–14), a sudden modulatory move (m. 15; notice in this case that $\sharp\hat{1}$ of the original tonic is introduced before $\sharp\hat{4}$), and a dominant lock on V/V (m. 16) driving toward a triple hammer-blow V:HC MC (m. 18).

S = mm. 19–34, now clearly in V, A major. Here we have a multimodular (or trimodular) S, another common feature of J. C. Bach's first movements. S$^{1.1}$ consists of what at first promises to be an antecedent-consequent pair (mm. 19–22, 23–26), although Bach swerves away from the expected V:PAC at its end in order to sound instead a V:HC, which propels the music onward to the next module. S$^{1.2}$ prolongs the dominant of A major (mm. 27–30): the music has slipped into "neutral," as if spinning its gears awaiting a more decisive idea. That idea is the suddenly declarative, *forte* S$^{1.3}$ (mm. 31–34), which sounds an expanded cadential progression (ECP) and produces the EEC at m. 34.

C = mm. 35–42. A grounding A-major tonic pedal begins to sound directly with the EEC (m. 34)—tonic pedals are often heard in C spaces—but the C-idea proper is a four-bar, cadential idea (mm. 35–38) that uses the pedal-effect, *piano*, as a springboard for another expanded cadential progression in V, *forte* (beginning with the I^6 on the upbeat to m. 37). C is repeated in mm. 39–42, although its final measure, concluding the exposition, is fortified to become a triple hammer-blow. (Notice that the hammer-blow idea is used, as is common within the style, to articulate the major points of articulation in the exposition: beginning, MC, and ending.)

Example 19.2 provides a thematic guide through the ritornello (R1) for two violins, cellos, and continuo that young Mozart wrote to precede Bach's original exposition, which was now to occupy S1-space. Table 19.2 illustrates Mozart's layouts for both R1 and S1 + R2. Parallel modules are aligned horizontally. The vertical lines on the left of the Solo 1 column call attention to material in Bach's TR and S that Mozart did not use in R1. Heard in the linear, temporal context of any performance of this concerto movement, they arise as seemingly "new" modules in Solo 1.

While the original exposition (here, S1) comprised forty-two bars, Mozart's R1 occupies only twenty-eight, about 62 percent of the length of Bach's exposition. The first signs of compositional compression occur in Mozart's newly composed R1:\TR$^{1.2}$ (mm. 13–16), which had to be reconceived in order to avoid the modulation toward the V:HC MC of Bach's exposition: six bars of the original become only four here. Most of the shortening, though, occurs in R1's omission of Bach's final two-thirds of secondary-theme space, S$^{1.2}$, S$^{1.3}$, and his repeated C (in the concerto labeled as S1:\S$^{1.2}$, S1:\S$^{1.3}$, and S1:\C), an excision of sixteen bars (the original's mm. 27–42). Mozart did retain the original S$^{1.1}$, but instead of having it steer away from closure in its final bar, as in Bach's exposition, he altered it to close with a I:PAC in m. 24. This marks the end of R1:\S space, accomplishes the R1:\EEC, and does away with the need to import the later S modules into the initial ritornello, which by convention is to be briefer than the exposition that follows it. (Notice also, first, that S$^{1.1}$ produces the EEC-effect

EXAMPLE 19.1   J. C. Bach, Sonata, op. 5 no. 2, i, mm. 1–42 (exposition)

EXAMPLE 19.1 (continued)

EXAMPLE 19.1 (*continued*)

EXAMPLE 19.2 (continued)

TABLE 19.2   Mozart, Piano Concerto in D, K. 107 no. 1, i (Adapted from J. C. Bach, Keyboard Sonata, op. 5 no. 2, i, a Type 3 Sonata)

Ritornello 1

Condensed from the original, especially post-MC, with a different C-module.

R1:\P	mm. 1–5, 5–9: two loops.
R1:\TR$^{1.1}$	mm. 9–13, downbeat: correspondence measures
R1:\TR$^{1.2}$	mm. 13–16, recomposed: shorter than the original by two bars (original's TR$^{1.2}$ compressed, now nonumodulating). Rejoins
R1\MC R1:\S$^{1.1}$	m 16, correspondence with original, but I:HC mm. 17–24: unlike the situation in the original, this period is not undermined but proceeds to a I:PAC in m. 24 (= orig. m. 26). Thus some mild recomposition is required in the last bar. This module produces the R1:\EEC at m. 24.
R1:\C	mm. 24–26, "new" (original to Rit 1): syncoated three-bar cadential module, elided with itself: mm. 26–28: immediate repetition, with a triple hammer-blow as the conclusion.

Solo 1

= J. C. Bach, bar-for-bar, until the last measure of the exposition (whose downbeat elides with Rit 2)

R1:\P	mm. 29–37 = orig. mm. 1–9: two loops.
R1:\TR$^{1.1}$	mm. 37–41, downbeat = orig. mm. 9–13, downbeat.
S1:\TR$^{1.2}$	"new" mm. 41–46 = orig. mm. 13–18: differs from R1:TR$^{1.2}$ (relinquishes march-like topos; two bars longer; modulates to V).
R1:\MC R1:\S$^{1.1}$	m. 46 = orig. m. 18, slightly varied, now a V:HC. mm. 47–54 = orig. mm. 19–26: an undermined parallel period. A straightforward antecedent-consequent pair is denied cadential closure by moving instead to a dominant-lock at m. 54 (= orig. m. 26).
S1:\S$^{1.2}$	"new" mm. 55–58 = orig. mm. 27–30: dominant-lock, the second module of a trimodular S.
S1:\S$^{1.3}$	"new" mm. 59–62 = orig. mm. 31–34: the decisive cadential module, featuring an ECP to the S1:\EEC at m. 62 (= orig. m. 34).
S1:\C	"new" 63–66 = orig. mm. 35–38: a four-bar cadential module.
S1:\C	mm. 67–70 = orig. mm. 39–42: a repetition, but instead of landing directly on the triple hammer-blow (orig. m. 42), that measure elides directly into:

Ritornello 2

Completes rotation in a manner parallel with Ritornello 1.

R1:\C	mm. 70–72: R1's final, syncopated three-bar cadential module, elided with itself: mm. 72–74: immediate repetition, with a triple hammer-blow as the conclusion (cf. orig. m. 42).

only in R1—S1:\S$^{1.3}$ accomplishes the task in Solo 1—and, second, that the stating of only a portion of a multimodular S is a common strategy of opening ritornellos.)

In this R1 Mozart decided not to include the solo exposition's C modules, thereby delaying their first appearance until S1. In compensation he composed a "new" repeated closing idea for R1, a syncopated, three-bar C-module in the tonic, elided with itself (mm. 24–26, 26–28), ending with a triple hammer blow and setting up Bach's original first measure for the onset of S1 (m. 29). Perhaps most important: at the

end of S1, in m. 70 (= m. 42 of the original), Mozart re-employs this "new" R1:\C idea in V to produce R2 as an appended close or extension to Bach's exposition. In order to provide the requisite tutti at the S1–R2 juncture, he suppressed the final bar of Bach's exposition (the triple hammer-blow) and reinforced the originally strong V:PAC at that point with the even stronger, elided return of this "new" (and repeated) R1:\C idea, an additional pair of tonally stable closing ideas, themselves ending with a triple hammer-blow—precisely in the manner of a standard expositional conclusion.

The result was an effect of two expositional expanses, a smaller one extended into a larger one. In an important respect Bach's original exposition, S1, is self-sufficient as a closed space for itself, since it had literally been so in its earlier keyboard-sonata format, which is now only lightly accompanied by strings. Thus from its own perspective—assuming that what precedes and follows it can legitimately be bracketed out—there is no denying that it is a complete solo exposition, precisely in the manner described by Vogler and Koch. But now in its concerto context we should think twice before sidelining R1 and R2 so neatly. For with regard to their modular contents and successions of events R1 and S1 have proven themselves to be interdependent, their fates and roles intertwined with one another. In this context S1 is no longer a purely autonomous statement. Its general course and sense of relative completeness are affected by what happened in R1.

This observation will have important ramifications in more complex concertos. K. 107 no. 1/i shows us the basic point in its purest state, and it is worth the time to reflect on it from different angles. The "bracketed" perspective of viewing S1 alone as the movement's only exposition is insufficient, because S1 is now a conditioned utterance. As a result of the concerto context a larger perspective is in the process of formation. This perspective understands R1 and S1 + R2 as interdependent complexes, both participating in a broader, more compelling rotational logic, as if the larger utterance will not be fully complete, rounded off, until R2 reinvigorates the cadential R1:\C modules as a sign of rotational conclusion. Notwithstanding the original autonomy of S1 in the J. C. Bach sonata, in the concerto this solo exposition is also being treated as only a partial utterance, an important constituent, though only a quasi-independent one, of a larger rotational whole whose most compelling arcs are directed by the orchestra—that is, by the (social) group. From its own ("bracketed") perspective S1 provides an apparently complete *solo exposition*, mm. 29–70, for

the concerto, even while its final bar is elided with the onset of R2, which reinvigorates R1:\C in the dominant. But that string-group R2 extension springs open the "dependent," solo exposition into a more encompassing, larger one, with, in this case, its own conclusion. In doing so R2 reopens the apparent close of the smaller exposition into a broader expanse. This *larger exposition*, encompassing all of mm. 29–74 (S1 + R2), is itself comprehensible as a texturally end-accented exposition in which the orchestra is given the final, emphatic word—one "beyond" the soloist's conception of where its exposition was to end.

Put another way, the larger exposition, S1 + R2, follows the ordered modular succession laid down by R1 but adds new material (and a modulation) to it, thereby expanding the original R1 rotation. This account of the situation adopts the non-Kochian perspective of conceiving S1 + R2 as it really occurs in linear time, in which S1 + R2 is heard in the context of what has already been sounded in R1. From this standpoint, the larger expositional rotation may be understood as the second rotation of the Type 5 sonata, even though the first rotation, R1, is abridged. Apart from the opening ritornello's ordering of the modules that it does present, one function of this R1 is to mark the boundaries of the governing rotational *Anlage*: it proposes what are to be the modular signs of succeeding rotational openings and closes. This fundamental aspect of R1 is also common in later Mozart concertos. S1 may close the solo exposition, but it does not bring an end to the larger expositional rotation, which is continued, and often completed, with R2.[74]

EEC Issues in Type 5 Sonatas:
The "Double Perspective"

An unavoidable complication within this concept of the solo and larger expositions concerns the location (or locations) of the EEC. In the concerto that we have been examining, K. 107 no. 1/i, the issue does not fully arise: R2 is built

---

74. Again, as will be seen in ch. 21, in some later concertos, especially those with a larger and more diversified number of R1 final modules, R2 contains material with this larger-exposition closing function but is stopped short of full rotational completion, which will be attained only in R4.

entirely from a concluding closing-space module originally sounded in R1. Since this was already a C-module in R1 it readily serves C purposes in R2 as well. This means that the EEC of the solo exposition (Bach's original EEC, now the S1:\EEC at m. 62) is also that of the larger exposition, which adds only closing modules to the smaller one.

A differing EEC-situation is found in the third of the J. C. Bach arrangements, the Concerto in E-flat, K. 107 no. 3/i (table 19.3), which in other respects closely mirrors the strategy of the first concerto. As in the first concerto, in K. 107 no. 3/i, a final "new" module in R1 returns in the dominant as R2, concluding the larger exposition after the soloist's formal close. But that last module was originally in S-space (as R1:\S$^{1.3}$), not C-space. In fact, there was no C-space at all in R1. Following the R1:\ MC (m. 16) Mozart had completed the opening ritornello with the succession R1:\S$^{1.1}$ (mm. 17–20), R1:\S$^{1.2}$ (mm. 21–24), and R1:\S$^{1.3}$ (mm. 24–27; S1, the second rotation, begins in m. 28). It is R1:\S$^{1.3}$ that returns in V as R2, the completion of the larger exposition (mm. 68–74—the module is sounded twice here). (R1:\ S$^{1.1}$ and R1:\S$^{1.2}$ appear, varied, as the first two limbs of a TMB in S1; they are succeeded by the "new" S1:\TM^3, producing an unequivocal S1:\ EEC at m. 63, and by S1:\C^1, both of which, of course, were in Bach's original exposition. A final, two-bar module of the original, effectively a C^2 module, was deleted by Mozart in the concerto.) Simply put, in the third concerto (unlike the situation in the first), with the appearance of R2—and several bars after the clear production of the S1:\EEC—we find what appears to be the reopening of what had occupied S-space within R1.

Fundamental to this question is the conviction that once a module has been included within S-space anywhere, it retains the ability to declare itself and its surroundings as S-space in all subsequent post-MC appearances. S-space modules cannot be readily converted into later C-space modules. This is because S-modules have already been marked by the central function of S-space: they are part of the zone whose role it is to bring about the EEC. In effect, each S-module declares that the EEC (or the "real"

EEC) has not yet occurred. Note, however, that the reverse is not true: what we presume are C-modules can become S-modules through the procedure of EEC deferral and the "recovery" or reconstituting of S-space several bars into what we had been presuming was C-space. Several examples of this have been discussed in Chapter 8. The implications for concertos would seem to be that if R1:\S-modules recur in R2, they override the S1:\EEC effect, reopen S-space, and defer the larger-expositional EEC into R2 space (labeled as R2:\EEC, here at m. 74). In other words, they convert what we had once taken to be C-modules in the smaller exposition (S1) into larger-exposition S-modules, continuing past the once-presumed EEC.

But this conclusion is viable only from the perspective of the larger exposition—and from that of the larger rotational process unfolded in the {R1, S1 + R2} succession. It is preferable to conclude something more nuanced, which is a central aspect of our understanding of Type 5 sonatas. Because of the double perspective of Type 5s in general (hybrids of traditional ritornello structures and sonata form), in this sonata type the EEC determination is made from two different standpoints, from that of the solo and the larger exposition. In some instances, as with the first concerto, K. 107 no. 1/i (in which no R1:\S-modules recur in R2), the EEC will occur at the identical spot, and no problematic EEC issues arise. In others, as with the third concerto, K. 107 no. 3/i (in which R2 is built from R1:\S-modules), there are effectively two EECs, one for the solo exposition alone (S1) and one for the larger exposition (S1 + R2), a "later" EEC that overrides and defers the earlier one. In the former case (S1:\EEC), the group and the individual concur about the EEC-point, and the orchestra's role in this matter is merely supportive. In the latter case (R2:\EEC), the group, in R2, trumps the individual's claim to have produced the EEC. There are obvious hermeneutic implications in all of this, but they are focused more clearly when the matter is looked at through the lenses of Sonata Theory. The thorny issue of potentially double-EECs in some concertos will be revisited in chapter 21, in which the main focus is on more elaborate compositions. For the present, we summarize

TABLE 19.3   Mozart, Piano Concerto in E-flat, K. 107 no. 3, i (Adapted from J. C. Bach, Keyboard Sonata, op. 5 no. 4, i, a Type 3 Sonata)

Ritornello 1

Condensed from the original, with "new" TR and "new" closing module.

R1:\P	mm. 1–8, eight bar antecedent ("Hybrid 3"), ends I:HC.
R1:\TR	mm. 9–16, independent TR, an original sentence (TR$^{1.1}$ presentation, with the continuation, TR$^{1.2}$, at m. 13).
R1:\MC	m. 16: I:HC, with same "flourish" as in S1-to-come, although prepared differently, and no fill.
R1\S$^{1.1}$ R1:\S$^{1.2}$	mm. 17–20 (presentation); mm. 21–24 (continuation): A slightly varied recasting of Bach's "original" sentence. The continuation proceeds here to an evaded cadence (m. 24), not to a PAC, and moves to:
R1:\S$^{1.3}$	mm. 24–27, "new" material, original to Rit 1. A syncoated, cadential module, elided with the evaded cadence. A "C-like" flavor, but in S-space because no satisfactory PAC has been produced before it. The final cadence, m. 27, is the R1:\EEC. (Its local figuration is probably based on the last bar of the original's suppressed C^2.)

Solo 1

= J. C. Bach, bar-for-bar, until the last measure of the exposition (whose downbeat elides with Rit 2)

R1:\P	mm. 28–35 = orig. mm. 1–8: eight-bar antecedent ("Hybrid 3"), ends I:HC.
S1:\TR	mm. 36–43 = orig. mm. 9–16: Dissolving consequent to I:HC MC. (This TR will be omitted in the recapitulation.)
S1:\MC	m. 43 = m. 16, I:HC, with brief fill
R1\S$^{1.1}$ and R1:\S$^{1.2}$	mm. 44–47, 48–51 = orig. mm. 17–20, 21–24 (now interpretable "together" as S1:\TM$^{1.1}$): "original" versions of the music varied in R1. An expected V:PAC in m. 51 is subverted into a V:HC, launching the next module:
S1:\TM^2	mm. 52–55 = orig. mm. 25–28: a dominant-lock momentarily "stuck" but leading to a V:HC MC in m. 55. (This S1:\TM^2 will not appear in the recapitulation. There R1:\S$^{1.1}$ and R1:S$^{1.2}$ (= S1:\TM^1) will be brought to a I:PAC and be followed by what is labeled as S1:\TM^3 in the exposition.)
S1:\TM^3	mm. 56–63 = orig. mm. 29–36: a new parallel period producing the S1:\EEC at m. 63 (= orig. m. 36)
S1:\C1	mm. 64–65, 66–68 = orig. mm. 37–38, 39–41; a two-bar cadential module, moving only to a V:IAC, m. 65; repeated, with extension, to a V:PAC in m. 68, elided to R2:

Suppressed by Mozart: C^2 (orig. mm. 41–43), a final cadential reinforcement.

Ritornello 2

Completes rotation in a manner parallel with Ritornello 1.

R1:\S$^{1.3}$	mm. 68–74: Ritornello 1's final, syncopated four-bar cadential module, slightly varied and now looped into self-repetition—to a fully closed V:PAC and final caesura. NB: Produces "new" R2:\EEC at m. 74.

the entire situation by noting that a Type 5 sonata may contain as many as three EEC-effects: one in R1 (a mere effect by analogy), one in S1, and one in the S1 + R2 complex, whenever that R2 contains modules originally claimed as S-material in R1.

The first movements of K. 107 nos. 1 and 3 provide contrasting situations regarding R2 and its effect on the EEC, even while their broader procedures of ritornello adaptation are otherwise similar. A different strategy is found,

though, in the second of Mozart's three Bach arrangements, the Concerto in G, K. 107 no. 2/i, adapted from Bach's Keyboard Sonata in G, op. 5 no. 3/i. As table 19.4 shows, the broad central portion of S1, mm. 31–45 (encompassing S1:\TR and much of the secondary-theme space as well) presents material that was either unheard or not treated in this manner in R1. Here Mozart devised a different R1:\TR (mm. 9–14, with a I:HC MC at m. 14) and filled out the remainder of R1 with material from the end

Table 19.4   Mozart, Piano Concerto in G, K. 107 no. 2, i (Adapted from J. C. Bach, Keyboard Sonata, op. 5 no. 3, i, a Type 2 Sonata)

Ritornello 1

Condensed from the original but ending with the same C-module fragment.

R1:\P$^{1.1}$ & P$^{1.2}$ mm. 1–4, 5–8: sentence.

R1:\P$^{1.2}$ mm. 9–12: "backs up" for a repetition of the continuation only, ending again with a I:PAC in m. 12, elided directly into:

R1:\TR   mm. 12–14: a three-bar extension of the cadence point, landing on a I:HC MC.

R1:\MC   m. 14: slight correspondence with the S1 model, but I:HC and no caesura-fill.

R1:\S   mm. 15–18: extremely brief (only a drive to the cadence), with abrupt arrival at the R1:EEC, m. 18, flush-juxtaposed with:

R1:\C1   mm. 18–20: cadential flourish, flush-juxtaposed with: mm. 20–22: repetition of flourish, extended with a triple hammer-blow as conclusion.

Solo 1

= J. C. Bach, bar-for-bar, until the last two (omitted) bars of the solo exposition.

R1:\P$^{1.1}$ & P$^{1.2}$ mm. 23–26, 27–30 = orig. mm. 1–4, 5–8: sentence.

R1:\P$^{1.1}$, first two bars (= S1:\TR$^{1.1}$)   mm. 31–32 = orig. mm. 9–10: beginning of dissolving-restatement TR, first module of presentation only.

S1:\TR$^{1.2}$ mm. 33–38 = orig. mm. 11–16: altered second module of presentation, plus a differing continuation, mm. 35–39, modulating to V and driving to an MC.

S1:\MC   m. 38 = orig. m 16. V:HC, with caesura fill.

S1:\S^0 mm. 39–43 = orig. mm. 17–21: sentence presentation, now in V, beginning by temporizing over the dominant; S^0-like, though active, energetic.

S1:\S$^{1.1}$ mm. 43–45 = orig. mm. 21–23: the beginning of a sentence continuation; arpeggiated seventh chords; the second module of a trimodular S, elided with:

R1:\S   mm. 45–49 = orig. mm. 23–27: here, the third module of a TMS, with a local S$^{1.2}$ function; a cadential module, with the trill-cadence S1:\EEC at m. 49 = orig. m. 27

R1:\C^1 mm. 49–51 = orig. mm. 27–29: cadential flourish, flush-juxtaposed with: mm. 51–53 = orig. mm. 29–31: repetition, down an octave (no triple hammer-blow), elided at its V:PAC with R2:   *Suppressed by Mozart: C^2 (orig. mm. 31–32), a scalar tag, which does not end with a hammer-blow.*

Ritornello 2

"New" material.

R2:\C^2 mm. 53-55: A new closing module, rhythmically related to R1:\C1; elided to: mm. 55–57: repetition; no triple hammer-blow, but one bar of fill, linking to S3.

of the original trimodular S and the first module of the original C. The perfunctory R1:\S, a short cadential module (mm. 15–18, producing the R1:\EEC at m. 18), was taken from, or would become, S$^{1.2}$ within Solo 1. (The trimodular secondary-theme space in S1—the original sonata movement—may be subdivided as: S^0, S$^{1.1}$, S$^{1.2}$. Recall also that in the first and third concertos Mozart had selected for R1 only the opening modules of Bach's S, omitting the later ones. In this second concerto he did the opposite, choosing only the last module.) Unlike his

procedure in the first and third concertos, Mozart added no "new" modules at the end of R1. This meant that S1 was to conclude as R1 had done, only now in the dominant. Except for the suppression of R1's hammer blow, S1's ending rhymes with that of R1. Most curious, however, is that it elides directly into an R2 of new (previously unheard) cadential-reinforcement material in V.

Beginning R2 with completely new material raises an important issue, especially since the same material would also be used to round off the whole movement at R4² (mm. 108–12, following the cadenza). The contents of R2 are "beyond the expected end" of the rotation, as suggested by the parallel endings of R1 and S1. Yet what is provided in R2 is a recognizable, harmonically stable concluding flourish to a larger exposition. Apart from the originality of its musical material, it is in every other respect parallel to the R2 situation in the first and third concerto arrangements. The only reasonable conclusion is that this "new-material" R2 likewise functions as the close of a larger exposition, even though the final module of R1, in most cases a sign of how the governing rotation is to close, had already been heard at the end of S1. That the new material also reappears in R4² as the last element of the larger recapitulation only bolsters this claim. But how does the presence of these previously unheard modules affect our conception of the governing rotational layout? The situation could be interpreted in two ways. On the one hand, we could understand the new material in R2 finally to provide the "real" rotational conclusion that had been withheld in R1, suggesting that one common second-rotation function, called forth with special clarity in this movement, is sometimes that of becoming more "complete" as a rotation. On the other hand, we could regard this movement's R2 as rotationally neutral, a blank, something of an abstract place-holder filled in with content that differs from what had been presented in R1. Rather than deciding between these alternatives, we might try to sustain them both, at least for the present. As will be discussed in chapter 21, the first portion of more complex, multimodular R2s in later Mozart concertos often have this rotationally inert function, though usually one that gives way to more rotationally participatory material from R1 in its later portions.

Developmental Spaces and Recapitulations in the K. 107 Concertos

These three concerto movements illustrate different kinds of postexpositional spaces. Presumably as "early" works paying homage to older norms, none of them follow the most common format found in Mozart's more mature concertos—the format in which the recapitulation is launched with an R3⇒S3 merger, where a recapitulatory tutti is soon complemented by solo participation (Subtype B of table 19.1). More typically here, what we are labeling as R3 is given a retransitional function preparing a recapitulation that begins as the next solo section, S3 (Subtype A).

The first concerto, K. 107 no. 1/i, is that which most closely approximates Koch's description of the seven-part (four-ritornello) movement, although there are also aspects of the nine-part (five-ritornello) format (Subtype D) lurking in the background. The portion of the developmental space occupied by S2, is identical, bar-for-bar, to all but the last four measures of the Bach original (mm. 75–100 = orig. mm. 43–68). Mozart merely handed over the final four bars of Bach's development to a retransitional tutti for the strings, R3 (mm. 101–04 = orig. mm. 69–72), which sets up the interrupted dominant, V_A of I, on its own terms. An interior complication within S2, though, is a mid-developmental repetition, with tutti reinforcement, of the module that produces the traditional vi:PAC. (In other words, the submediant cadence at mm. 85–88 is repeated as a tutti, with hammer-blow close, at mm. 89–92.) Because this "redundant" repetition had also appeared in the pre-existing sonata (orig. mm. 53–56, 57–60), it is unclear whether its textural reinforcement into a tutti in the concerto is to be reckoned as a separate ritornello. In any event, the smaller recapitulation, S3 (mm. 105–43 = orig. mm. 73–111), also a bar-for-bar replication of Bach's, is launched by the soloist.

While the first concerto makes only a slight nod toward the nine-part (five-ritornello) format—the type with the "extra" ritornello in the middle of the development—the third concerto, K. 107 no. 3/i, tips more decisively in this direction. The essential facts about this development are similar to those of K. 107 no. 1/i, except that the mid-developmental tutti reinforcement of the vi:PAC (mm. 103–06) is a four-bar interpolation not found in Bach's original sonata, and, moreover, one that reinvigorates, now in vi, the R1:\S¹·³ module that had closed both R1 and R2. In these respects, the inserted tutti material takes on the character of a conceptually separate ritornello ("R2.2"), lodged between what we are labeling R2 and R3. As in the first concerto, though, R3 is not a newly composed segment but only a varied, tutti scoring for strings of the last bars of Bach's original development (mm. 113–18 = orig. mm. 79–84)—and, again, the soloist begins the solo recapitulation, which is identical to that of Bach (although once again, as in the exposition, suppressing the final three bars).

The initial movement of the second concerto differs from that of the first and the third insofar as it is a Type 2 ("binary") variant of a Type 5 sonata, taking its guidelines in this matter from the Type 2 format of Bach's sonata, op. 5 no. 3/i. Consequently, there is no full recapitulation triggered with the P-theme in the tonic. Instead, the concerto's "third rotation" (equivalent to the original movement's second rotation, beginning the development with the P-incipit on V), encompasses the developmental space and the tonal resolution, as in a Type 2 sonata. One result of this is a decreased number of passages unambiguously classifiable as ritornellos. Here one might argue that there is no developmental ritornello proper, although the strings are brought in with notable emphasis, *forte*, to reinforce the interior iii:PAC in mm. 80–82 (= orig. mm. 55–57). The merging into the tonal resolution proper—and the crux—is likewise led by the soloist (m. 91 = orig. m 66), without a bona fide preparatory ritornello, although the moment and its general surroundings are thickened with an enhanced string accompaniment. Only what we label as the normatively R1, R2, and R4 stand out as clear ritornellos.

The treatments of R4 in all three concerto movements, extending the smaller recapitulations (those of the Bach original sonatas) into larger ones, are also instructive. As expected, Mozart subdivided each of the three R4s into two portions, pre- and postcadenza, which we designate as $R4^1$ and $R4^2$. $R4^1$ is consistently brief and perfunctory—a matter of three to five bars—whose sole purpose is to set up the $^6_4$ platform for the cadenza. In the first two concertos $R4^1$ is built from "new" material, although it would be more accurate to say that it is filled with generically stock figuration designed to get to the $^6_4$ platform in the most efficient manner possible. One might get the same impression

from the third concerto, although the figuration involved (mm. 149–52) is taken from R1:\TR (from m. 9–12), a module unheard since R1. In each case the important point to extract is that $R4^1$ is rotationally inert—a mere functional tutti-slot capable of being filled in with appropriately vigorous, but rotationally anonymous music.

The "forward gears" of the rotational process are once again clenched into motion only with the onset of $R4^2$, which completes both the larger recapitulation and the movement as a whole. In each of the three concertos $R4^2$ reanimates the music of R2. This means that the larger recapitulation tracks through all of the materials of the larger exposition and adds to them the music of $R4^1$ and the cadenza. (In later Mozart concertos, in which R1 and S1 can diverge more markedly in content, this situation will become more complex: see chapters 20 and 21.) In the first and second concertos of K. 107, all three principal rotations—R1, S1 + R2 (larger exposition), and R3 + S3 (larger recapitulation)—end with the same "rotation-completing" module. In the third concerto (see table 19.2) this is not the case, since Mozart had appended a "new" R2 module to the end the larger exposition, one not sounded in R1. The parallel endings in K. 107 no. 3 are limited only to the larger exposition and recapitulation.

A Summary of Structural Axioms Exemplified by K. 107

Mozart's original concertos, especially from about 1775 onward, would become more varied and intricate than what we have seen in the three concerto arrangements of K. 107, from 1772. Still, the simpler first-movement formats that we find here permit us to draw together a few central points regarding Type 5 sonatas (primarily those of Mozart). All of these points, regarded here as axioms, are drawn from the preceding discussion of the first movements of K. 107. They are repeated in a tabulated form here only as reminders before moving onward. (The fundamentals laid out in the even earlier portions of this chapter are now taken for granted.)

1. R1 is briefer than S1, especially in the extent of its post-MC material; in some respects it is an abridged version of what is to follow.

2. The "abridged" R1 is based on the material of S1 (or vice-versa), although some differences of content are normal. P-spaces—or at least their openings, defining the tone and content of the work (and initiating the rotation)—are normally kept the same in R1 and S1.

3. S1:\S-space is normally multimodular, either an MMS or a TMB; R1 presents only a selection of those modules (usually only the first or the last). Thus S1:\S typically gives the impression of a modular "expansion" of what was heard in R1.

4. R1 may close rhetorically in the manner of S1 or it may present differing modules that can return in the new key as the "rotational" substance of R2, following the soloist's conclusion to S1.

5. Especially toward its end, R1 may present additional secondary or closing modules that do not appear in S1 but return in R2.

6. S1 presents a closed solo exposition with its own S1:\EEC. Nonetheless, in the context of a concerto its modular interdependence with R1 demonstrates that it is not a fully autonomous statement.

7. There is no reason to suppose that the S1:\EEC is deferred until S1's final cadence, leading into R2. In all of the K. 107 concertos the S1:\EEC is followed by C (pre-R2) modules, following the layout of the original Bach models. Nor should we assume that the S1:\EEC ought to be produced, in the new key, by the modules that had articulated the tonic R1:\EEC-effect.

8. All Type 5s potentially have three EEC-events: (1) the "effect," in the tonic, at R1:\EEC; (2) the solo exposition's S1:\EEC; (3) the possibility of the larger exposition's R2:\EEC, trumping that of the solo exposition. Normally, this can happen only when R2 reanimates additional S modules from R1.[75] If R2 brings back only R1:\C mod-

ules, then the larger exposition's EEC is the same as that of the solo one.[76]

9. R2 usually contains some rotationally participatory material taken from the end of R1. The norm in K. 107 (nos. 1 and 3) is to bring this second rotation to a full close with this material, thus rhyming with the end of R1.

10. Alternatively, R2 may be occupied with new (or differing) material, as in K. 107 no. 2. This may be understood either as a new, more complete end to the rotation or as the interpolation of blank or rotationally inert modules. (Nos. 9 and 10 together suggest that R2 may be either rotationally inert or rotationally participatory.)[77]

11. The developmental space (often more episode or figuration than development proper) may or may not contain an R2.2 effect (a mid-development ritornello, Subtype D) to affirm an interior, nontonic cadence.

12. The K. 107 concertos exemplify some broad-structural norms that are less often encountered (though not absent altogether) in more mature Mozart: the selection of Type 5's Subtype A format, with the R3-effect as a retransition into a solo-launched development (thus illustrating what would be Koch's 1793 model); and, in K. 107 no. 2, the choice of the Type 5 adaptation of the Type 2 ("binary") sonata.

13. The principles of solo and larger expositions are replicated in the recapitulatory space. There, R4 extends the solo recapitulation into a larger one.

14. R4 space is subdivided into two halves, precadenza (R4^1) and postcadenza (R4^2). In all three instances in K. 107, R4^1 was rotationally inert (in two cases even consisting of new, "stock" precadenza material). The rotationally participatory gears clenched into forward motion only after the cadenza, with R4^2, which replicated, now in the tonic, the rotational portions of R2 and provided a rhyming close with it.[78]

---

75. It could also happen, in principle, if R2 were to reanimate S-modules already heard in S1, thus reopening the S-space declared by S1.

76. Similarly—to anticipate cases found in later concertos—if R2 brings back only rotationally inert R1:\ pre-MC material (such as the common sounding of R1:\TR$^{1.1}$ at the outset of a multimodular R2), this in itself would not reopen S-space. Whether S-space is reopened in R2 would be clarified only by the rotationally participatory modules that follow. See n. 77.

77. In the later Mozart concertos, multimodular R2s typically begin with a rotationally inert "slot" that can

be filled by a number of different choices (R1:\TR$^{1.1}$ is especially common) followed by a one or more rotationally participatory modules, unheard in S1, taken from the final portions of R1. The participatory modules may or may not bring us to a full-close end to the rotation.

78. As will emerge in ch. 21, the normal sequence of modular functions in R4, rotationally inert⇒rotationally participatory, will often be replicated in longer, multimodular R2s. (Thus a complementarity in this respect can be observed between mature R2s and R4s.)

CHAPTER TWENTY

The Type 5 Sonata

Mozart's Concertos (R1: The Opening Ritornello)

Having laid out the foundations for the enterprise in the preceding chapter, we are now in a position to confront aspects of Type 5 practice as exemplified, especially, in Mozart's concertos. Mozart's adaptations of the Type 5 sonata represent personally customized illustrations of a more generalized framework of background possibilities. Even while his preferences are instructive and provide a basis for investigation outside of the Mozart canon, they should not be elevated into pan-European norms for the decades around 1800. Any study that also included examinations of other composers' concerto practices would introduce other possibilities, other realizations of the more broadly based network of choices. And yet there are reasons to restrict our view here largely to Mozart (even though from time to time we shall allude to related situations in Beethoven). Some of the reasons are practical—considerations of available space within this study. Additionally, though, Mozart's concertos are the richest of their time and probably the most influential for later generations of composers. Many remain entrenched components of the basic repertory today. Considered as a group they provide a sufficiently varied number of pieces—there are around forty of them—to permit the reconstruction of a constellation of flexible norms, one relevant

to any comparable study of the works of other composers.

The next three chapters will deal with Mozart's Type 5 movements zone-by-zone, suggesting norms, options, variants, and interpretive implications. They will focus on concerns peculiar to Sonata Theory: rotational implications in Type 5 sonatas; modular substitutions and rearrangements in post-Ritornello-1 rotations; multiple-EEC and ESC issues; the structure and function of the ritornellos; and so on. This chapter will introduce some of the main issues more generally and then take up the construction of the initial tutti (Ritornello 1 = Rotation 1). Chapter 21 will continue the discussion with an overview of the larger exposition (S1 + R2 = Rotation 2). And chapter 22 will confront the remainder of the Type 5 Allegro movement: development and larger recapitulation. In order not to clutter the text in what will be a closely argued treatment—and to streamline our frequent references to Mozart's many concertos—we shall call upon the most familiar designations for these works, even though, as is well-known, modern scholarship has shown many of them to be flawed. This entails the adoption of the traditional numbers for the piano concertos ("Piano Concerto No. 12 in A," even though this is not literally the twelfth such concerto) and the citation within the text of only the original Köchel number ("K. 414," not "K. 414/385p").[1]

The Paradox of Mozart's Concertos

Complicating all discussions of Mozart's Type 5 procedures is a paradox nearly always present in these works, especially in the mature, more elaborate movements. This is the tension generated by opposing formal-aesthetic tendencies, conceptual forces that pull in two different directions. The expressive core of these concertos resides in the charged gap between these contradictory pulls.

On the one hand, when compared with the relatively trim formats found in his sonatas, chamber music, and symphonies (Types 1–3 sonata movements), Mozart's Type 5s are encumbered by the task of fulfilling certain quasi-archaic (or at least traditional) stations of concerto practice. They are bulkier, clumsier, more unwieldy constructions. In addition to carrying out the zonal requirements also found in other sonata types, in Type 5s one must additionally arrange things to make sure that several extra features are folded in at the right places. These include: the dramatic appearances of (usually) four *ritornello pillars* (some confirmatory, some initiatory or reprise-launching: see chapter 19); occasional *tutti interjections* and *solo-orchestra dialogues* within the solo sections, some of which follow or allude to well-established conventions; the frequent *S-space expansions* in Solo 1 and Solo 3 (often involving TMB procedures, laying out more S-space than that found in Ritornello 1); the appending of a virtuosic *display episode* as the final portion of Solo 1 and Solo 3, a bravura close that by convention ends with a trill cadence igniting the elided confirmations of Ritornellos 2 and 4; the potential (and likelihood) of *replacement themes* in Solo 1 (Rotation 2), plus the *synthesis* of the first and second rotations in the recapitulatory

rotation; and the stiffly ritualized formula of Ritornello 4 (R4[1] driving quickly to an annunciatory $^6_4$ chord sustained by a fermata; solo cadenza with a trill-cadence exit, triggering the R4[2] conclusion).

Consequently, moving from zone to zone in a Mozart concerto-movement gives the impression of passing through a preformatted check-list of concerto-specific tasks that must be accomplished in a certain sequence. Some of this formal "hardening" even extends to the layout of the successive modules in the referential rotations. To facilitate the requisite station-visiting from place to place *en route* to the movement's end, Ritornello 1 (R1) must be assembled in a genre-specific modular way, as a "segmented" succession of discrete ideas of differing dynamics and intensities that will expedite the fulfilling of the "concerto check-list" tasks that follow.[2] (The frequent deployment of a *forte*, vigorous R1:\TR[1.1] or R1:\C[1.1] that will also serve as a workable opening to R2 is only one of these.)

On the other hand, faced with these generic constraints, Mozart took every opportunity to realize them in surprising and inventive ways. One might make an even stronger claim: it might be precisely because he was composing within a more rigid genre (while never resisting it) that Mozart was drawn into making his individual realizations as flexible and unforeseeable as possible. Paradoxically, the more calcified requirements seem to have enabled a more supple response, or at least to have encouraged one by way of a challenge. Surveying Mozart's concertos, one gets the impression that he has individualized as much as can be individualized, that taken together these works provide a treatise on how to refresh even the most rigid of schemes. Mozart exploited the potential for ingeniousness in every standardized zone, turning a genre weighted down with near-obligatory conventions into a continuous source of astonishment. As a result, each work is a world unto itself, with multiple internal interactions and concep-

1. Both old and new K. numbers for all of Mozart's works cited in this book are provided in the index.
2. Cf. Irving, *Mozart's Piano Concertos*, p. 41, who sees the thematic "segmentation of the ritornello" or its

"'modular' handling of . . . thematic material" as one of the "important ways in which the classical concerto built upon [baroque] practices."

tual threads binding together each whole as a unique utterance.

Thus the paradox. Mozart's concertos are simultaneously among the most formulaic of his sonata-based compositions and among the most unpredictable of his works. The two opposing tendencies tug at each other, virtually to the point where their interactions have regularly foiled the attempts of later commentators to generalize about them.[3] This is one reason why so much has been written about these concertos. From one perspective, they seem so formulaically capturable in their broad strokes, which everywhere exude stiffness and postured convention. And yet, from another perspective, in their constant resourcefulness and *ad hoc* feel, these concerto movements place themselves beyond any casual summary description. For each generalization there seems always to be an exception or two, a movement or individual passage whose details slip past the broader claim. Much of the essence of the mature Mozart concerto lies in the gap between these two opposites, in the provocative friction of their contradictory pulls: extreme formulaicism and extreme individuality, coexisting in every movement. It is in this "crease" between the two pulls that responsible commentary must outline its own understandings.

Ritornello 1: The Logic of Modular Succession

In chapter 19 we noted that the opening ritornello has three traditional purposes, whose relative importance can be differently weighted in differing concerto movements: an introductory-anticipa-tory function; an expositional-rhetoric function; and a referential-layout function. Moreover, an R1 can be constructed in varying lengths and degrees of modular plenitude. Ambitious, larger-scale first movements begin with a relatively lengthy orchestral R1 containing a sufficient number of thematic modules to bolster their expositional-rhetoric claims (while still beginning and ending in the tonic key).[4] The R1 modular successions of smaller-scale movements—the first movements of some wind concertos, several Type 5 slow movements—are sometimes much abbreviated or only half-fledged. This sets their potentially proto-expositional role into lower relief, although the depth of that implication (or lack of it) can vary from instance to instance. Thus R1s may be ranked on a continuum with regard to their expanse and complexity, ranging from ones of substantial length, modular variety, and proto-expositional articulation to briefer, compressed ones that seem primarily introductory. Our principal concern here is with the more elaborate R1s, familiar from the first movements of most of Mozart's violin concertos and piano concertos. Most of our discussion will focus on these, although along the way we shall also touch upon R1s constructed on a smaller scale.

Modular Descriptions: Sonata Theory and Some Alternatives (Leeson-Levin, Küster, Stevens)

Most larger-scale R1s, especially in Allegro-tempo first movements, display a modular succession that parallels that of a typical sonata exposition. The main difference is tonal: as a

---

3. Recall also Tovey's throwing-up-of-hands in 1903 ("The Classical Concerto," p. 23) when confronting our inability to predict which of the S-modules from R1 Mozart will also deploy—or replace—in S1: "There is no foreseeing what the solo will select from the ritornello. All that we can be sure of is that nothing will be without its function, and that everything will be unexpected and inevitable."

4. Perhaps needless to say, a large-scale R1 (certainly in Mozart's concertos) almost always begins with the initial module of the proto-expositional rotation (R1:\P), that is, without a preparatory introduction of any kind. Within this context the three enormous chords that Beethoven later called forth as an in-tempo introduc-tion or motto-like R1:\P^0, mm. 1–11, with sustaining fermatas enriched by cadenza-like, *fortissimo* solo arpeggiation, to his Piano Concerto No. 5 in E-flat, op. 73 ("Emperor"), launch the work with an astonishingly impulsive and commanding gesture. The effect is like entering a grand temple through a colonnade of massive pillars (I–IV–V^7 [expanded]–I, elided with R1 proper at m. 11). Somewhat related in opening effect—though not introductory to the rotation proper—is Beethoven's famous surprise of beginning R1:\P with a statement by the soloist alone in the Piano Concerto No. 4 in G, op. 58. Cf., of course, the historically earlier participation of the soloist near the very opening of R1 (mm. 2–4, 5–7) in Mozart's Piano Concerto No. 9 in E-flat, K. 271.

rule, R1 (unlike an exposition proper) begins and ends in the same key. Also possible are local nontonic feints around the R1:\S-point (for example, a transient modulation to V or, in minor-mode concertos, III that is soon "corrected" back to the tonic within R1:\S-space) or the suppression of a clear MC in order to provide a continuous R1 (the nonmodulating analogue of a continuous exposition). These options will be dealt with below. Another aspect of Mozart's opening ritornellos is their insistence on a sharply distinguished "thematic variety" and, in John Irving's recent formulation, a modular "segmentation" that seeks to maximize internal "textural contrast" via a cleverly integrated "fusion of periodicity and counterpoint," and, at least from K. 450 onward, a "liberation of . . . wind writing," that highlights "opposing choruses" of strings and wind.[5]

Because the zonal (modular-textural) inflections of a larger-scale R1 are analogous to the familiar procedures found in Type 1–4 sonata expositions, they are most profitably described with reference to those standard modular functions. This results in the Type 5 designations introduced in chapter 19. In most instances one is confronted with a two-part R1, whose internal zones have the status of R1:\P, R1:\TR (most often an energy-gaining *forte* leading to a I:HC MC), R1:\S (usually in the tonic key and leading, eventually, to an R1:\EEC-effect), and R1:\C (frequently a succession of several C-modules). Since Mozart arranged each R1 to set the stage for the modulatory "exposition" that must follow (the solo exposition, S1, contained within the larger exposition that usually also includes most of R2), and since that subsequent exposition is to be conceptually related to the proto-expositional succession in R1, there is no benefit to be obtained through a merely "neutral" description of the successive modules

in R1—one that labels them only with successive numbers, letters, or a combination thereof. To do so is inappropriately to bracket out from consideration the larger structural purpose and implication of the Ritornello 1 modules within the larger Type 5 structure.

The most well known of the "objective" descriptive systems was proposed in the mid-1970s by Daniel N. Leeson and Robert D. Levin, following an extensive "statistical-structural" inventory of "Mozart's most consistent practices" within forty concertos: ritornello-construction procedures, standard thematic and textural patterns, overall proportions, and so on, many features of which, they concluded, were distinctive to this composer alone.[6] The "Leeson-Levin model," including thematic designations and names for the large structural blocks, has been widely adopted in English-language Mozart scholarship. Leeson and Levin viewed the main "sonata" within a concerto first-movement as being carried out by the solo sections alone, which they referred to as the "solo exposition," the "development," and the "recapitulation." The ritornello blocks were described mostly in terms that did not incorporate them into the central sonata that they encase. Leeson and Levin called our R1 the "opening ritornello" and our R2 the "middle ritornello." They did not grant full ritornello status to our admittedly problematic Ritornello 3 "pillar," which they barely isolated as an event within the "recapitulation." Additionally, they considered our R4[1] and R4[2] to be two separate ritornellos: the "ritornello to cadenza" and the "final ritornello."

Leeson and Levin subdivided of the typical Mozart opening ritornello into seven commonly encountered thematic-textural events. They identified these by Arabic numerals and clustered them into a "primary group" (nos. 1–3) and a "secondary group" (nos. 4–7):

---

5. Irving, *Mozart's Piano Concertos*, pp. 42–44, 41, 97.
6. Leeson and Levin, "On the Authenticity of K. Anh. C. 14.01 (297b), a Symphonia Concertante for Four Winds and Orchestra," *Mozart-Jahrbuch 1976-77* (Kassel: Bärenreiter, 1978), pp. 70–96 (quotations from p. 72). The authors note, p. 96, that Mozart's practice differed "so significantly from the formal scheme of any work by [his] contemporaries—especially in the hierarchical complexity of its various sections—that it pro-

vides a specific and accurate basis for objective comparative analysis"—and, in fact, for suggesting the potential authenticity of concertos whose composer is disputed. "No work in the control repertoire [which included concertos by "Johann Christian Bach, Boccherini, Dittersdorf, Joseph Haydn, Karl Stamitz, Viotti, and Vogler," p. 74] even so much as approximated this elaborate prototype."

1. "The first theme . . . usually piano—or forte followed by piano—is extended to a perfect cadence in the tonic." This "is followed by . . . "
2. "a more active forte passage"
3. "driving to a half-cadence . . . on the dominant."
4. "a more lyric theme . . . piano, that tends to appear again in the solo exposition as the principal theme of the secondary group in concerti up to ca. 1778." "Theme 4 is extended to a perfect cadence in the tonic." Following this, typically appears:
5. "a forte passage . . . that is similar to theme 2 in energy, but has the contrasting purpose of moving the ritornello toward a conclusion." "This first conclusion is often followed by . . ."
6. "a second concluding motive . . . piano and less assertive, which is itself succeeded by . . . "
7. "a brief flourish . . . on the tonic that rounds off the ritornello and immediately precedes the entry of the soloist."[7]

In a stroke, Leeson and Levin had made certain aspects of subsequent concerto description simpler. One could observe, for example, that after the soloist's first entrance and statement of the first theme (within S1), the listener often hears, especially in earlier concertos, "the flourish (7) in the orchestra, confirming the tonality and freeing the soloist to modulate to the dominant key"; new themes within the solo exposition could be given the designations A, B, C, D, and so on (instead of the ritornello themes' numbers 1–7); one could observe that the opening of the "middle ritornello" (our R2) was usually "based upon one of the forte passages of the opening ritornello—2 (more frequently) or 5"; and the like.[8] All this was to the good.

From the standpoint of Sonata Theory, however, what Leeson and Levin had described within R1 was little more than a reduction of a typical modular-textural succession within a "classical" exposition. Thus their theme 2 is our R1:\TR[1.1], the *forte* affirmation that often begins the transition-zone and may lead to further TR-elaborations. Their theme 3 is probably the normal drive to and accomplishment of the I:HC MC. Their theme 4 is our R1:\S[1],

which may require several subsequent modules (including some *forte* ones) to bring about the R1:\EEC. Their theme 5, one presumes, is often our R1:\C[1.1], the characteristic *forte* opening to the closing zone, although in some instances when the I:PAC (R1:\EEC) has not been fully secured, this *forte* is folded—or comes to be folded retroactively—into R1:\S-space. Their *piano* theme 6 is usually a module that we would describe as belonging to R1:\C-space, either as R1:\C[1], C[2], or C[3], depending upon our assessment of the position of the earlier R1:\EEC. Their theme 7 final "flourish" (which, as they acknowledge, is sometimes lacking altogether) is a familiar concluding gesture within R1:\C-space. For the most part, what Leeson and Levin were observing was the diversity of modules within part-two (post-MC) space in a Type 5 sonata, taking special notice of the relative frequency of a *piano*-dynamic R1:\C-theme "afterthought" at the end (or very nearly so) of the R1 rotation. (Having such a multiplicity of contrasting post-MC modules was a useful strategy. It made possible the demonstration of the later rotational implications of the larger exposition and recapitulation, especially, as will be seen, within the final portions of R2 and R4.)

Moreover, Leeson and Levin presented their numbering system in the language and procedures of statistics, claiming a quasi-scientific objectivity. Its explication was set apart from analytical hermeneutics, to which the heart of these concertos more readily responds. Finally, even while acknowledging some intersection with typical expositional practice (with its appeal to primary and secondary "groups"), the Leeson-Levin model invited its readers to exempt R1 and subsequent ritornellos from direct participation in the essential sonata form that followed, the sonata laid out, in their view, only in the solo sections. However familiar the model, it now strikes us as reductive, dated in tone, style, and content.

In 1991 Konrad Küster broadened the Leeson-Levin model in his monograph on "Formal Aspects of the First Allegros in Mozart's Con-

---

7. Leeson and Levin, "On the Authenticity," p. 90. The model is laid out on pp. 90–91 and 96.

8. Leeson and Levin, "On the Authenticity," p. 91.

certos."[9] Küster's more exhaustive description of the *Anfangstutti* (opening tutti, our R1) offered an ordered sequence of potential events from which the opening R1 of each Mozart concerto made a nearly full or only partial selection. Instead of Leeson and Levin's seven themes, Küster identified "fifteen ritornello zones"—a composite collection of the totality of thematic and textural happenings found in all of Mozart's R1s, arranged in sequential order—and labeled them with letters A through P (omitting J). In effect, Küster identified and labeled separately common modular subdivisions within Leeson and Levin's seven. (And again, what the elaborate classification actually describes is the standard expositional construction of the era.) Leeson and Levin's seven themes may be mapped onto Küster's fifteen zones as follows:

1 = A ("beginning of the ritornello with the *Hauptthema*") and B ("continuation of the *Hauptthema*").

2 = C ("*forte* continuation by the whole orchestra").

3 = D ("transition to the dominant" [that is, usually to the active dominant of the original tonic]), E ("confirmation of the transition to the dominant [chord], often over a dominant pedal"), and F (either a brief passage that "returns to the tonic" [our caesura-fill?] or often, in place of this zone F, "a caesura" [our MC]).

4 = G ("*Seitenthema*"), H ("motivically independent consequent [or *Nachsatz*] to the secondary theme;" or a "free, *piano* intermediate module"), and I ("transition to the closing group, [perhaps] a crescendo-module as a transition from the secondary theme to the first *forte* cadence of the closing group," etc.).

5 = K ("*forte* zone; first cadence of the closing group").

6 = L ("*piano* zone; *piano* cadence or *piano* motive-complex in the midst of the cadence-chain of the closing group"). To this Küster adds the possibility of yet another *forte* zone (M) and *piano* zone (N).

7 = O ("*forte* formulation of the ritornello's close"). Küster's final zone, P, is a "*piano* transition to the entrance of the soloist").[10]

Within such a system any first-movement R1 could be described by noting which of the ritornello zones were present and which were not. To illustrate the method, Küster's first example, the opening of the Violin Concerto No. 4 in D, K. 218, contained all of the zones except F [?], H, and P.[11]

The first part of Küster's book takes up the "thematic types" and varied possibilities for each of the fifteen zones, while the later parts outline the appearances of numerous variants and new material found in the subsequent solo and ritornello sections. The book concludes with elaborate tables displaying which lettered zones appear in the sections of all of Mozart's concerto first movements. Küster's work provides a welcome tabular and descriptive inventory of modular successions in the first movements of Mozart's concertos. This advance beyond the Leeson-Levin model offers a resource for further analytical and interpretive work: we draw upon it in what follows. And yet, from the perspective of Sonata Theory, Küster's study has limitations: its music-theoretical basis seems underconsidered; it sometimes strikes one more as a patiently assembled array of statistics and descriptions than a fully developed interpretation; and, as a result, it overlooks several features with which Sonata Theory would be centrally concerned, including the hermeneutic implications of rotation structure, cadential attainment, TMB-situations within S1 and S3, and EEC- and ESC-issues.

Quite the reverse approach to this issue of modular succession within R1 was suggested in 1996 by the musicologist Jane R. Stevens. With a characteristic "historical" eye on C. P. E. Bach (and others) as necessary models for understanding Mozart's concertos, she reduced the number

---

9. Küster, *Formale Aspekte des ersten Allegros in Mozarts Konzerten* (Kassel: Bärenreiter, 1991).

10. Küster, *Formale Aspekte*, pp. 28–29. We have condensed Küster's own descriptions of the lettered zones, which are more elaborate and allow for slightly different possibilities of realization. Kuster himself related his

lettered zones to Leeson and Levin's seven themes on pp. 29–30.

11. Küster, *Formale Aspekte*, pp. 32–34. Since zone F could also be an MC—and since there is an MC present in the example—there seems little need to omit that zone from the example.

of event-zones within an opening ritornello to four, of which only the first, second and fourth, strictly considered, were fundamental: (a) a section that "both provides the main theme of the movement and decisively establishes the tonic key"; (b) "a middle part, usually characterized by unstable harmony and gestures of more rapid movement"; (c) [regarded as an optional addition to the other three zones, one that only occurs "sometimes" in C. P. E. Bach] "a brief respite between the bustling instability of *b* and the cadential drive of *d*," one that is "typically somewhat shorter than the other three"; and (d) " a strongly cadential section."[12] Although Stevens sought to avoid sonata-inflected terminology (to which supposedly anachronistic "framework" she, along with several other music historians of the past decades, registered "profound objections")[13]—her *a, b, c,* and *d* correspond roughly to the broad zones R1:\P, TR, S, and C. The disadvantage of Stevens's minimal-demand model is this: the fewer structural events that one expects to happen in R1 (and the more broadly these event-zones are construed), the easier it is to remain incurious about the precise succession of thematic-rhetorical details. Such a pared-back understanding is inobservant when it comes to Mozart's concerto procedures and their self-evident relationships with other types of sonata practice. A rigid reliance on historical precedent coupled with a scholastic unwillingness to proceed beyond late-eighteenth-century terminology (that of Koch and others) become, in this and parallel analytical descriptions, unnecessarily restrictive.

In sum, there are already in place multiple systems of labeling and identification for the successive modules of an opening ritornello by Mozart. Each system carries methodological baggage along with it—grounding axioms and assumptions that one should keep in mind be-

fore adopting any of them. Obviously, the same is true of the labeling system that we prefer, which we have devised both to remain congruent with our readings of Type 1–4 sonatas and to lead hermeneutically to the sorts of considerations in which we are most interested. What is needed at this point is a closer look at the successive zones within Mozart's R1s.

Ritornello 1: The Individual Zones

The Primary Thematic Zone: R1:\P

In larger-scale R1s within Allegro (first) movements, such as in most of the mature piano concertos, one generally finds a fully extended P-idea (period, sentence, hybrid, or some variant thereof) that comes to a I:PAC close elided with a *forte* R1:\TR. Example 20.1 provides a skeletal outline of the entire opening ritornello of Piano Concerto No. 17 in G, K. 453, a movement that we shall use referentially throughout the following chapters. Here R1:\P occupies mm. 1–16, a compound sentence whose presentation, encompassing mm. 1–4 and 5–8, features an engaging adaptation of the $\hat{8}$–$\flat\hat{7}$–$\hat{6}$–$\natural\hat{7}$–$\hat{8}$ module. The *forte* R1:\TR bursts in at m. 16. Example 20.2, a fuller reduction, shows the opening of Piano Concerto No. 18 in B-flat, K. 456. R1:\P here is a compound period, mm. 1–18, with a sentential antecedent and consequent, the latter expanded at its end, with R1:\TR elided at m. 18. Occasionally an R1:\P idea, including its I:PAC, is restated with reinforced dynamics, with the result that it is the *second* I:PAC, not the first, that closes the R1:\P-zone. Piano Concerto No. 19 in F, K. 459, begins with a simple eight-bar period, *piano*, restated *forte* by the full orchestra in mm. 9–16. The general principle, of course, is that any I:PAC reopened through

12. Stevens, "The Importance of C. P. E. Bach for Mozart's Piano Concertos," in Neal Zaslaw, ed., *Mozart's Piano Concertos: Text, Context, Interpretation* (Ann Arbor: University of Michigan Press, 1996), pp. 216–17.

13. Stevens, "The Importance of C. P. E. Bach," p. 212. In context, her objections may apply most strongly to the simple (and by now long-outdated) consideration of the opening ritornello as an "orchestral exposition" *tout court,* followed by a simple division of the entire

remainder of the concerto, including all ritornellos, into "solo exposition," "development," and "recapitulation." This, at any rate, is the labeling that she placed on her figure 1 (p. 213) and to which she objects on p. 212. Her purpose is to tilt the interpretive balance more toward eighteenth-century written understandings of "ritornello form"—and the examples set by compositional precedents—and away from later conceptions or adaptations of sonata form.

EXAMPLE 20.1   Mozart, Piano Concerto No. 17 in G, K. 453, i,
mm. 1–74

EXAMPLE 20.1 (*continued*)

EXAMPLE 20.1   (*continued*)

EXAMPLE 20.1 *(continued)*

EXAMPLE 20.2   Mozart, Piano Concerto No. 18 in B-flat, K. 456, i,
mm. 1–21

EXAMPLE 20.2   *(continued)*

a nondissolving repetition—including of its cadential module only—normally remains with
the R1:\P-zone.

More compact or smaller-scale opening
ritornellos sometimes reduce the R1:\P-zone
to a mere head motive, a matter of a few thematically stamped bars that proceed efficiently
into an R1:\TR-zone before any such I:PAC
is attained. In these instances we are usually
dealing with P⇒TR mergers, in which a sentence-presentation or some other analogous unit
leads immediately to a dissolving continuation
or succeeding module that in effect takes on an
R1:\TR function. (One may find examples in
the first movements of Violin Concerto No. 1
in B-flat, K. 207; Violin Concerto No. 2 in D,
K. 211; Violin Concerto No. 5 in A, K. 219; and
a few other works.)[14]

Although it is sometimes observed that
Mozart's concertos often begin in a *piano* dynamic—more frequently, at any rate, than do
his symphonies—this impression should be
qualified. While twelve of the seventeen Viennese piano concertos from 1782 onward ("Nos.
11–27") do begin quietly (starting with No. 12
in A, K. 414; the two concertos illustrated in
Examples 20.1 and 20.2, both from 1784, are
typical in this respect), five others do not.[15]
Moreover, as Küster has pointed out, "Up until
his second trip to Paris [1778] Mozart always
began his concertos in a *forte* dynamic, with either a melodic or a pronounced harmonic formula."[16] This would include all of the concertos
up to the Piano Concerto in E-flat, K. 271, from
1777 and the Flute and Oboe Concertos, K. 313
and 314, from 1778.[17] Mozart's *forte* openings

---

14. These include but are not limited to the Flute Concerto in G, K. 313, and the last three of the four Horn
Concertos: No. 2 in E-flat, K. 417; No. 3 in E-flat, K.
447; and No. 4 in E-flat, K. 495.
15. The composition of No. 12 (K. 414/385p) chronologically precedes that of No. 11 in F, K. 413/387a,
and No. 13 in C, K. 415/387b, both from 1782–83.
(The three were published together in 1785 as "op. 4,"
the first of Mozart's Viennese piano concertos. No. 11
in F, in any event, begins not *piano* but with a largely
forte, all'unisono scalar slide, mm. 1–4. Quiet openings
are found in Nos. 12 in A, K. 414; No. 13 in C, K. 415;
No. 15 in B-flat, K. 450; No. 17 in G, K. 453; No. 18 in
B-flat, K. 456; No. 19 in F, K. 459; No. 20 in D minor,

K. 466; No. 21 in C, K. 467; No. 23 in A, K. 488; No.
24 in C minor, K. 491; No. 26 in D, K. 537; and No.
27 in B-flat, K. 595.
16. Küster, *Formale Aspekte*, p. 39 (our translation).
Küster observed that the first concerto movement to
begin *piano* was the fragmentary oboe-concerto movement in F, K. 293. Some of our descriptions below of
thematic types within R1:\P is also indebted to Küster,
pp. 35–40.
17. Note also the retention of the *forte* opening in
the Sinfonia Concertante in E-flat, K. 364, and the
Two-Piano Concerto "No. 10" in E-flat, K. 365, both
from 1779.

were frequently of two types. The first relies on a vigorously driving initial module, sometimes featuring a syncopation on the second beat of the first bar (especially characteristic of the earlier concertos), whose forward vector might be also propelled by a pulsing *Trommelbass* (Bassoon Concerto in B-flat, K. 191; Violin Concerto No. 3 in G, K. 216; Flute Concerto in G, K. 313).[18] The second is the familiar *forte-piano* juxtaposition, featuring a brief, declarative basic idea—often an *all'unisono* module, a triadic arpeggiation or "fanfare," or some other "curtain-raising" effect that announces the prevailing tonality—to which a quieter contrasting idea responds (Violin Concerto No. 4 in D, K. 218 [example 5.9]; Sinfonia Concertante in E-flat, K. 364; Piano Concerto No. 11 in F, K. 413).[19] Occasionally the compressed *forte-piano* juxtaposition creates the familiar effect of initial presentation-"loops," a self-replicating circularity eventually released into a "breakout" continuation or dissolving continuation (Piano Concertos No. 7 in F, K. 242; No. 9 in E-flat, K. 271 [example 5.7], in which the contrasting idea is non-normatively, and famously, supplied as an interjection by the soloist; and No. 22 in E-flat, K. 482).[20]

Many of the most celebrated piano concertos, though, feature quiet openings, frequently ones that burst into a *forte* R1:\TR with an elided I:PAC. As many writers have noted, the choice of a *piano* or *forte* opening creates a preset situation to be revisited at the moment of the solo piano entry, after the conclusion of R1, since the solo exposition (or the second rotation) most often begins with a reiteration of the R1:\P theme, albeit one that might be immediately preceded by an "extra" solo entry of one

sort or another.[21] We shall deal with this issue in a later section.

In several piano concertos, especially those from 1784–5, Mozart favored the idea of a quiet opening in the style of a common-time march, normally with a dotted-eighth/sixteenth figure on the second beat of the first bar. March-like R1:\Ps initiate Nos. 13 in C, K. 415 (a "predecessor" from 1782–83); 16 in D, K. 451 (the only *forte* opening in this group); 17 in G, K. 453 (example 20.1); 18 in B-flat, K. 456 (example 20.2); 19 in F, K. 459; and 21 in C, K. 467 (lacking the dotted-eighth/sixteenth stamp). Other quiet openings feature more lyrical, cantabile melodies: Nos. 12 in A, K. 414; 23 in A, K. 488; and 27 in B-flat, K. 595—as well as the Clarinet Concerto in A, K. 622 from 1791.[22] "Special-effect," ominous *piano* openings launch the two minor-mode piano concertos, Nos. 20 in D minor, K. 466, and 24 in C minor, K. 491.

"Motto" R1:\P as *Idée Fixe* or Later "Wild Card"

Sometimes the initial module or general rhythmic figuration or contour of the *piano* R1:\P opening recurs repeatedly within the movement, spreading out at various locations throughout Type 5 sonata-space. When this happens, the distinctively stamped R1:\P becomes a motto or *idée fixe*. This motto can then function as a wild card, an often rotationally inert card that may be placed onto the sonata-table at any number of later occasions, turning up, so to speak, at nearly every available opportunity. It may be suitable for filling in not only the onset of a P-based C-space but also of insinuating itself into vari-

---

18. Others: Violin Concerto No. 1 in B-flat, K. 207; Oboe Concerto in C, K. 314.

19. See also the Violin Concerto No. 2 in D, K. 211; the Two-Piano Concerto, "No. 10," in E-flat, K. 365; and several others, culminating in the grand-style adaptation opening the Piano Concerto No. 25 in C, K. 503.

20. See the discussion of modular loops in ch. 5.

21. See also the remarks on dynamics in David Grayson, *Mozart: Piano Concertos Nos. 20 and 21* (Cambridge: Cambridge University Press, 1998), p. 31. On the relationship of the opening of R1 to the initial solo entry,

see also, e.g., Küster, *Formale Aspekte*, pp. 39, 84–88; and David Rosen, "'Unexpectedness' and 'Inevitability' in Mozart's Piano Concertos," in Zaslaw, ed., *Mozart's Piano Concertos*, esp. pp. 270–78.

22. Notice within this category the presence of three works in A major. Cf. the *piano*-dynamic, "weak-launch" openings of, e.g., the Symphonies No. 14 in A, K. 114, and No. 29 in A, K. 201. On the other hand, the opening of the Violin Concerto No. 5 in A, K. 219, is set forth with a single, propulsive *forte* chord turning instantly into a *piano*, nervously bustling "rocket" arpeggiation punctuated with sudden *forte* flashes.

ous "soft spots" of the sonata-structure to follow: as medial-caesura fill, as overlay in the concluding display episode of Solo 1, as an internal module within a phrase-chain or multimodular S, as a filler for a rotationally neutral opening portion of R2 space, as a "substitute" element within a recapitulatory transition, and the like. At the same time, the regular resurfacings of the *idée fixe* motto serve as threads binding together a highly varied discourse. The three classic instances of this "wild-card," scattered-recurrence technique—a special and sophisticated effect within the later Mozart concertos—are found in Piano Concertos Nos. 19 in F, K. 459; 21 in C, K. 467; and (with fatalistically negative connotations) 24 in C minor, K. 491. We shall revisit some of them in chapter 21.

The Transition: R1:\TR

In most respects the transition-zone within Ritornello 1 corresponds to characteristic TR behavior and options within Types 1–4 sonatas. Within a two-part R1, its main purpose is to gain energy and drive toward a conventional medial caesura, in most cases a I:HC MC. In smaller-scale Allegro works, as mentioned above, the transition can emerge early on in the context of a P⇒TR merger following only a few declarative bars of P that are not pursued to a fully closed I:PAC. This situation also applies to TR continuations following presentational P-zones, including those structured as double-loops, as in the Piano Concerto No. 9 in E-flat, K. 271 (example 5.7).

Within large-scale Type 5s—including especially most of the Viennese piano concertos—it is most often launched with a strong *forte* affirmation, elided with the I:PAC that concludes R1:\P. This produces a sudden surge of vigor, decisively accepting the offered sonata-contract and propelling the structure onward.

In most of these latter cases—and here is where the "concerto" aspect of this moment most fully applies—the *forte* R1:\TR$^{1.1}$ will be the one used to begin Ritornello 2 and/or Ritornello 4^1 (the precadenza portion of R4). Accordingly, in its energy-level and immediate impact of celebratory *élan*, it is often crafted so that it may also be used as the precipitating head-motive of either or both of those later ritornellos.

Three transition types are most commonly found within Type 5s with a large-scale R1 (one whose primary theme normally ends with an elided I:PAC). As in Type 1–4 sonatas, the TR-type is identified by the module selected for the TR-opening, R1:\TR$^{1.1}$ (see chapter 6). The first, and the most common, is the independent transition, which sets forth a new thematic module. (Piano Concertos Nos. 17 in G, K. 453 [Example 20.1, m. 16], and No. 18 in B-flat, K. 456 [Example 20.2, m. 18] may serve as illustrations. Additional instances abound in the concertos.)[23] The second is the reinforced, varied, and quickly dissolving restatement (Piano Concertos No. 21 in C, K. 467, m. 12; and No. 24 in C Minor, K. 491, m. 13). The third, and least frequent, is the developmental transition or transition that arrives as the motivically related culmination of R1:\P (Piano Concerto No. 20 in D minor, K. 466, m. 16, with the effect of an unnervingly demonic "shock of a thunderclap").[24]

Occasionally one comes across a lower-level default procedure to open R1:\TR-space. Piano Concerto No. 14 in E-flat, K. 449, provides a classic instance of a TR opening with a sudden, stormy shift to vi (C minor, upbeat to m. 17) in response to a tonally overdetermined P-zone (one with obstinately multiple authentic cadences in the tonic).[25] And two of the Viennese piano concertos sound R1:\TR$^{1.1}$ in an uncharacteristically subdued *piano* dynamic, indicating that some other module will have to be used

---

23. E.g., the Two-Piano Concerto "No. 10" in E-flat, K. 365, m. 14; Piano Concertos Nos. 11 in F, K. 413, m. 12; No. 12 in A, K. 414, m. 17; No. 13 in C, K. 415, m. 10; No. 15 in C, K. 415, m. 10; No. 16 in D, K. 451, m. 10; No. 22 in E-flat, K. 482, m. 31 (probably a better choice than the forte in m. 29, which impatiently—and wittily—brings a blandly self-reiterating R1:\P to

a close); No. 23 in A, K. 488, m. 18; No. 25 in C, K. 503, m. 26; No. 26 in D, K. 537, m. 13; and the Clarinet Concerto in A, K. 622, m. 16.

24. Grayson, *Mozart: Piano Concertos Nos. 20 and 21*, p. 32.

25. See the discussion of P-overdetermination in ch. 5.

as the energetic opener of the later R2 and/or R4[1]. One occurs in No. 19 in F, K. 459, m. 17 (nonelided to the preceding I:PAC)—perhaps a staged reaction to the *forte* restatement of R1:\P in mm. 9–16; or perhaps a fleetingly local suggestion of the onset of a b section to a larger, and ultimately not-accomplished aaba' (rounded binary) opening. The other is found No. 27 in B-flat, K. 595, m. 16, which follows an unusual, *forte* R1:\P² flourish-module in mm. 13–16.[26]

R1: Medial Caesura and Caesura-Fill

In most cases R1:\TR eventually produces a dominant-lock and MC, dividing R1 into two parts. Since R1 does not normally modulate, in both major- and minor-mode Type 5s all of this is most often built around an HC in the tonic (although modulatory feints are possible, as will be discussed below). From time to time one comes across a widening of the MC-gap with an expanded caesura-fill (CF) of several measures. Once again, Piano Concerto No. 17 in G, K. 453, provides an illustration (example 20.1).[27] R1:\TR¹·¹ (m. 16, the presentation of a sentence) and TR¹·² (m. 22, the beginning of the continuation) do not modulate but push directly into a dominant-lock, I:HC, in m. 25. The triple hammer-blow effect announcing the

I:HC MC occurs, with a wind-figure of internal decoration, in mm. 29–31 (the downbeat of this last measure is the MC proper). Instead of proceeding directly to R1:\S, we find a continued sounding of the preceding wind-figure, moving downward through scale-steps $\hat{5}$–$\hat{4}$–$\hat{3}$–$\hat{2}$–$\hat{1}$—a classic instance of "juggernaut" caesura-fill, coming to rest, as is common, on scale-step $\hat{1}$ (m. 35) to release the opening of the secondary theme, here R1:\S¹·¹.[28] Other illustrations of an expanded R1:\CF may be found in Piano Concertos No. 16 in D, K. 451, mm. 26–35, No. 18 in B-flat, K. 456, mm. 28–39 (with a sudden "lights-out" chill to minor), No. 22 in E-flat, K. 482, mm. 46–51; and No. 24 in C Minor, K. 491, mm. 35–44 (P-motto-related, and in this case, in part similar to that in K. 482/i, a somewhat uncommon ascending caesura-fill, with R1:\S¹·¹ beginning at m. 44).[29]

Although nearly all R1:\MCs are half cadences in the tonic, we should point out the notably exceptional, locally emphatic V:PAC MC found in Piano Concerto No. 25 in C, K. 503, mm. 48–50 (example 20.3). At least at this moment the music makes a surprising gesture toward a secured modulation to the dominant. Opinions have differed regarding whether we are really "in" or merely "on" the dominant at this point.[30] It is surely relevant to notice, for

---

26. The presence in K. 595 of a second, *differing* P-module within R1 is a non-normative event. In this case the "extra" P² flourish is the kind of gesture that Mozart had used in many earlier concertos at the very *end* of Ritornello 1, one designed to be repeated almost at once as the first *tutti interpolation* within Solo 1 as a characteristic confirmation of the initial I:PAC of the soloist's statement of the primary theme. In K. 595 this confirmational orchestra-flourish is doubtless also related to the brief wind interjections straddling the bar lines at mm. 6 and 10. It appears after P¹ in both Ritornello 1 and Solo 1 (mm. 92–95) but is absent from its normal position at the end of R1. In short, we have a characteristically Solo 1 P-concluding procedure advanced into the equivalent position within R1; or, from another perspective, Mozart has displaced a typically concluding gesture within R1 to become an appendix to the R1:\P-zone. Whatever the interpretation, it is probably in response to this unusual feature that the subsequent R1:\TR¹·¹ falls back to a *piano* dynamic, renouncing the transition's customary opening *forte*.

27. Another example of expanded caesura-fill may be found in the R1 of Piano Concerto No. 26 in D, K. 537,

mm. 32–38 (the last bar, the conclusion of an "apparent" PAC, elides with R1:\S).

28. On "juggernaut" CF, see ch. 3. The procedure in K. 453 is similar to that found in the first movement of Symphony No. 39 in E-flat, K. 543, cited there as the touchstone example.

29. In all such instances the thing to bear in mind is that any CF exists to bridge an otherwise empty space between two standard zones (TR and S). Although at its end the CF often (though not in K. 453) produces the effect of an elided PAC when it joins up with S-space, this authentic cadence is merely local, not structural. It is not to be taken for either a PAC:MC or an EEC. As a general rule, should any CF measures recur in a different position later in the composition, they are to be regarded as similarly incapable of articulating an S1:\EEC or S3:\ESC. Instead, what follows any later revisiting of this CF-PAC will normally be understood to exist within S-space. Realizing this can help to clarify EEC- or ESC-deferral issues later in the composition.

30. Tovey, "The Classical Concerto," p. 18, provided a paragraph of instruction that no real modulation has occurred at this point (we have only "paused on the

EXAMPLE 20.3 Mozart, Piano Concerto No. 25 in C, K. 503, i,
mm. 36–58

[Allegro maestoso]

EXAMPLE 20.3   (continued)

example, the dominant-lock on V of V in mm. 36–40, along with an "attempted gap" at m. 40 in several voices. This might well be taken locally as an initial attempt to offer a V:HC MC. On one line of interpretation, we could maintain that that MC-offer is strenuously declined ("No!") with the three-note upbeat to m. 41, which unleashes a three-bar torrent of "learned-style" contrapuntal activity, descending down the circle of fifths, then sprinting forward cleanly to sound a doubly stated, maximally emphatic V:PAC (mm. 46, 48) followed by aftershocks (mm. 49–50), which themselves reinforce the new MC-effect. From another perspective—simultaneously relevant—it is also possible to hear mm. 41–48 as an unusually aggressive, composed-out version of the sort of "juggernaut" caesura-fill, moving essentially $\hat{5}$–$\hat{4}$–$\hat{3}$–$\hat{2}$–$\hat{1}$, that we just identified in K. 453/i. Under this interpretation the $\hat{5}$–$\hat{4}$–$\hat{3}$–$\hat{2}$–$\hat{1}$ fill apparently becomes so vehement in context that it either shifts the earlier, light MC-offer decisively to m. 50 or stuns the expected, much-quieter R1:\S-theme to the point that it seems hesitant to show its face at the expected spot.

However one decides the matter (both "in" and "on" are integral aspects of this connotatively charged moment), Mozart immediately corrects the planted perceptual problem in the caesura-gap that follows. The G-major chord is reiterated insistently in mm. 48–50, as if the music were either registering its own astonishment at the V:PAC or peremptorily summoning the now-cowed R1:\S-theme. It is thereupon taken as an active dominant, and we proceed directly to the march-like R1:\S[1] in the proper tonic key, at first in C minor, however (mm. 51–58: a fearful or timid entrance? a deflated reaction to the improper MC? a registering of disapproval?), then in C major (the reinflated mm. 59–67, followed, though, by an R1:\S[2] that seems to have those earlier MC-aftershocks still on its mind).

Any interior modulation or near-modulation within a normally tonic-centered R1 is an important event. When one does occur, though, that ephemeral visit to a nontonic key is more typically found around the beginning of R1:\S than, as in K. 503/i, at the end of R1:\TR. (Examples will be provided below.) In other words, such nontonic feints are more characteristic of the second part of R1 (post-MC) than they are of the first. This is an important distinction. K. 503's unusual move into (or onto) V exclusively at the MC point, only to drop it at once for the tonic, suggests a wittily overenthusiastic and premature grabbing after V-as-key in the wrong spot. This is a purposely staged generic "error" (deformation) at the end of the first part of R1, and its consequences ripple forward into the rest of the initial, tonic-grounded tutti.

No R1:\S Produced: The Continuous R1

Not all R1s are divided into two parts with an MC in the center, followed by an S-idea: the continuous R1 is also a possibility. It can happen that no MC-effect is produced at all (Piano Concerto No. 19 in F, K. 459) or that we find a parallel with the second type of continuous exposition in Types 1–4 sonatas (early PAC with successive, varied recapturings of that cadence: Violin Concerto No. 1 in B-flat, K. 207). Of particular interest are the few R1s that sound an MC and begin an expanded caesura-fill (as if an S-theme were imminent) but then allow the CF to spread out at a much greater length than expected. This results in the CF writing over the possibility of a "real" S-theme and accomplishing itself what is likely to be interpreted as the R1:\EEC. The sequence of events is: I:HC MC – much-expanded CF, coming to take on a *Fortspinnung* identity of its own – R1:\EEC and onset of R1:\C. In effect, this is another type of continuous (proto-)exposition, since an S-theme proper is left unsounded. Examples

dominant. . . . [notwithstanding the cadence] it here sounds only like very strong emphasis on the dominant of C"). Plantinga disagreed, *Beethoven's Concertos*, p. 72, and pp. 329–30, n. 10: this passage in the tutti "modulates unequivocally to the dominant" (p. 72) because of "the very long V/V preparation in mm. 36ff" (p. 330,

n. 10). Both writers missed the essential point, namely, this moment's non-normative MC-function—something substantially different from a seeming (and transient) modulation within R1:\S-space, which is a more common ploy within an initial tutti.

may be found in Flute Concerto in G, K. 313 (MC-effect at m. 12, reinforced at m. 14; expanded CF throughout, leading to the R1:\EEC at m. 23) and Piano Concerto No. 13 in C, K. 415 (MC at m. 24; expanded CF at that point, accomplishing the R1:\EEC at m. 36).[31]

The Secondary-Thematic Zone: R1:\S (Tonality)

In terms of its rhetorical shape and purpose, R1:\S is analogous to S in Types 1–4 sonatas. It almost always opens *piano*, usually with a *cantabile* theme; more vigorous S-modules may or may not follow. As opposed to what happens in a normative sonata exposition, however (in which S is to be stated and completed in a nontonic key), R1:\S is almost always stated in the tonic key throughout. More precisely: in Mozart's Type 5s the R1:\EEC always secures the original tonic—declaring R1, considered *in toto*, to be nonmodulatory. And in the large majority of cases R1:\S also begins in the tonic key, following a I:HC MC. Thus one expects as a strong first-level default that R1:\S will remain in the tonic throughout. (This does not exclude the common possibility of a fleeting interior plunge onto a surprising nontonic chord—such as ♭VI—that might even be evanescently tonicized before recollapsing back into functionality within an unequivocal tonic-key center.) The R1:\S-zone of Piano Concerto No. 17 in G, K. 453, mm. 35–57, shown in example 20.1, is normative: it begins and ends in the tonic, G. The G-centricity, of course, is never significantly challenged by the sudden local oscillation around the dominant's upper neighbor, E-flat, ♭VI, in mm. 49–53 (the onset of R1:S$^{1.2}$), a dramatic shift of tonal color

and modular texture initially produced as a deceptive cadence.

The very strength of this norm, its virtual inevitability, throws into vivid relief the few exceptions to it: those instances where R1:\S begins in the nontonic key that would be appropriate were this a sonata exposition rather than Ritornello 1 of a Type 5 sonata. (This procedure is different from that of the seemingly tonicized-V MC-deformation in K. 503/i, example 20.3.) In all cases, this purposeful "S-misstep" is corrected *en route*, and the R1:\S soon restabilizes back to the original tonic. In this situation, up to the point of the tonic correction, R1 resembles the modulatory exposition of the first movement of a symphony (since the soloist has not yet been heard from). The tonal correction is a definitive declaration of the genre at hand: "No! This is not a symphony. This is a concerto!" The nontonic feint and "decision"-aspect of the subsequent correction are mechanisms that draw attention to what this piece *is*—to its very "concerto-ness."

Not counting the K. 503/i variant, there are three celebrated instances of this in Mozart's Viennese Piano Concertos, each with different expressive implications. In Piano Concerto No. 11 in F, K. 413—see example 20.4—a I:HC MC (m. 23) leads to two bars of anacrusis-fill and the beginning of a sentential idea proper, S, that begins in the dominant key, C (m. 26). At the point of the continuation (mm. 30–31) the generic "mistake" is noted: the C-major continuation is aborted ("Wait! This is not a symphony!"), and a corrective modulation is made back to the tonic F. The whole process then backs up and rebegins, only now tracked properly in the tonic: a restatement of the two-bar upbeat fill (mm. 32–33) and the tonally chas-

---

31. The procedure of K. 415, in particular, should be compared to the related but much more problematic situation found in the first movement of Symphony No. 35 in D, K. 385, "Haffner," mm. 48–58. (See ch. 3 on this type of expanded caesura-fill.) In the latter piece we find a local V:IAC at m. 58, which might initially tempt one to suppose that it could serve as a light EEC-effect or EEC-substitute. Moreover, this leads to what certainly seems to be emphatic C-rhetoric (suggesting a P-based C?) at m. 59. Under some interpretations m. 59

might be understood as conventional C-rhetoric jumping in early and, in retrospect (especially after the new "arrival" and subsequent new-C "wind-up"m. 74?), being reconverted into S-space. In any case, the EEC is best regarded as deferred until m. 74, where, in effect, an entirely new C is wittily conjured up to extend the exposition. This effect is probably compensatory in function, in order to avoiding giving the impression of having concluded "too soon."

EXAMPLE 20.4 Mozart, Piano Concerto No. 11 in F, K. 413, i, mm. 22–41

tened sentential S^1-idea (m. 34, with R1:\EEC at m. 41). Mozart carried out the staged generic misstep even further in Piano Concerto No. 14 in E-flat, K. 449, in which an S-idea not only begins in V (B-flat, m. 37) but is actually permitted to continue for some eighteen measures and produce a V:PAC in m. 54. It is apparently too late to back up and restart this theme in the tonic, but Mozart does reinstate that tonic in the subsequent module (mm. 54–62), dutifully detonicizing the dominant on behalf of the concerto-genre actually at hand and eventually proceeding to the appropriately generic R1:\EEC (I:PAC) down the road (m. 84).

Surely the most famous "tonally exceptional" case in Mozart occurs in Piano Concerto No. 20 in D Minor, K. 466 (example 20.5). Following the stormily demonic R1:\P and R1:\TR, which thrashes its way to a i:HC MC in m. 32, R1:\S1 sets out, surprisingly, in F major (III, m. 33), and with a total change of texture, as if seeking refuge from the preceding menace. This F, though, is immediately marked as unstable: in these ominous circumstances—and within the ground rules of this genre—such an R1 escape, we understand, is incapable of being accomplished. After only two bars on a hoped-for F major, the initial module is restated in ascending sequences, though G minor (mm. 35–36) and A minor (mm. 37–38) before being drawn back into the clutches of the tonic D minor and producing a first cadence there (mm. 39–44). (The whole theme is a sentence with a non-normative triply reiterative presentation.)[32] As is well known, Beethoven, too, would make use of the nontonic "feint" in the opening to R1:\S in each of his first three piano concertos. Moroever, if in the Fourth Concerto m. 29 is regarded as the onset of an unstable R1:\S$^{1.1}$, beginning, like the situation in K. 466, with a triple-statement presentation on three tonal levels (only more broadly)—our preferred interpretation—the list should be expanded to include this work as well.

The Secondary-Thematic Zone: R1:\S (R1:\EEC Issues)

The main task of R1:\S is to drive to a satisfactory I:PAC, to be regarded as the R1:\EEC. This may happen within a brief span: R1:\S in Piano Concerto No. 22 in E-flat, K. 482, is a mere eight-bar sentence, mm. 51–58, one of the shortest in the large-scale first movements. More often, R1:\S is longer, and it is frequently multimodular (R1:\S$^{1.1}$, S$^{1.2}$, S$^{1.3}$, and so on, including suddenly *forte* modules). Returning to our larger example 20.1, we may see the situation in the multimodular R1:\S of K. 453/i. Following the expanded caesura-fill, mm. 31–35, R1:\S begins as a *cantabile* sentence ending in a PAC, mm. 35–42. As mentioned earlier, this is elided to a rescored repetition, mm. 42–49, but one that is undercut with a deceptive cadence at the end, m. 49. Experiencing this, we now reconstrue our understanding of the repeated sentence as R1:\S$^{1.1}$. The blustery R1:\S$^{1.2}$, alternating *piano* and *forte* dynamics at its outset, occupies mm. 49–57 and produces the R1:\EEC at m. 57. (R1:\C-space follows, mm. 57–74.)

It can also happen that an S$^{1.1}$ module is immediately repeated as a characteristic "loop," a structural strategy found commonly in Mozart's works. As discussed in chapters 5 and 8, such loops are best understood as a special type of presentation within a larger sentence. Even though an individual loop might (or might not) have a light PAC-effect at its end, that local PAC-effect is not a sign of zonal closure (R1:\EEC), since it occupies only the first part of a broader sentential idea. Such presentation loops are elided with the next module, which functions as a "breakout" continuation, R1:\S$^{1.2}$ (not R1:\S^2), which might sound a different melodic idea. Examples include the initial R1:\S-moments of Sinfonia Concertante in E-flat, K. 364, mm. 38–46 (leading to a contrasting *crescendo* module at m. 46); and Piano Concertos No. 16 in D, K. 451 (mm. 35–43), No. 18 in B-flat, K. 456 (mm. 39–47, with the

---

32. This secondary theme will always begin on a hopeful F in all of its later appearances, including that of the recapitulation (where it appears in m. 288). Thus the opening of this theme is tonally invariant: it is never sounded in D minor.

loop over a sustained, "rustic" tonic pedal), and No. 21 in C, K. 467 (mm. 28–36, provided in example 8.5).

One should be especially alert for other circumstances in which the R1:\EEC can be regarded as deferred past the first S-space PAC or PAC-effect. Situations in which closure is postponed through direct repetition or through $S^{1.1}$-loops normally present few difficulties of interpretation. But things are not always so clear. In some instances, opinions can legitimately differ with regard to the proposing of a best location for the R1:\EEC. Depending on the circumstances, it may be wiser to make out the case for the alternative interpretations than to declare an R1:\EEC with brash confidence: the expressive point of this phase of some R1s might be the uncertainty of just when this sort of closure is attained. More generally, the EEC-effect in Ritornello 1 should be thought of as a more loosely construed expectation, one that admits or even encourages more ambiguity than one expects to find in a normative Type 1–4 sonata exposition. This might be because of the multiple and contrasting modules that usually follow the R1:\MC in large-scale Type 5s. Not only are there often several I:PACs in the second part of R1, but the whole section is usually also unfolded as nonmodulatory and tonic-stable—a prolonged string of "second-part" ideas.

When R1:\S is very brief and lyrical and is followed directly by a second, complementary cantabile theme (instead of proceeding to a first-level-default *forte* R1:\C), it is most hermeneutically reasonable to consider the two themes as R1:\S^1 and S^2. (See the discussion surrounding Piano Concerto No. 9 in E-flat, K. 271, mm. 26–41, example 8.6 of chapter 8.) Another complication is the possibility of *refrain cadences*, that is, the recapturing of a cadential formula or stamp (usually both melodic and harmonic) that suggests the backing-up to and recovery of the PAC of the preceding module, even when

the material leading up to those cadences differs.[33] This seems to be the case in Piano Concerto No. 11 in F, K. 413 (refrain cadences in the tonic at mm. 40–41, 44–45, 52–53 [cf. mm. 50–51], and resulting in R1:\S^1, S^2 [m. 41], and S^3 [m. 45], with the R1:\EEC probably best considered to occur at m. 53.) The potential for refrain cadences can occur at varying degrees of strength: just how much is needed to suggest a clear "recapturing" of an earlier cadence? Interpretations could differ, for example, about the R1:\EEC moment in Piano Concerto No. 20 in D Minor, K. 466.[34]

Another factor surrounding potential R1:\EEC deferrals is Mozart's frequent appending of a nonelided *piano* "afterthought" at or toward the very end of R1. Often this nonelided idea occurs far into what we had been presuming was R1:\C-space. Does the nonelision suggest retrospectively an undoing of the earlier-presumed R1:\EEC and the incorporation into R1:\S-space of that which had preceded the nonelided cadence (in which case R1:\C will now begin with the afterthought)? The issues surrounding this situation in Types 1–4 sonatas have been discussed in chapter 8.[35] In Type 5s, however, the issue is less clear: a concluding *piano*-afterthought C-idea (R1:\C^2? C^3?—corresponding to Leeson and Levin's "theme 6") is a common "special" option within Mozart's mature concertos. As such, it alone need not be taken as automatically indicating an EEC-deferral up to that point. In these circumstances, any consideration of deferral should be bolstered by other evidence as well.

The Secondary-Thematic Zone: R1:\S (Implications for Later Rotations)

The *piano* R1:\S theme (or its opening idea, $S^{1.1}$, if R1:\S is a multimodular zone) normally also appears in the solo exposition's S-space, although there it frequently becomes only one element of

---

33. See ch. 8, "Revitalization of a Portion of S- (or FS-) Material after Stating a New Module."

34. In K. 466/i does the similar bass motion of mm. 42–44, 51–53, and 56–58 suggest the conceptual triggering of a refrain cadence and consequent R1:\EEC deferral to m. 71? Or is the similarity insufficient to

maintain this, in which case the R1:\EEC would be considered to occur at m. 44. Our current preference is to regard m. 44 as the R1:\EEC, although a reasonable case could also be made on behalf of m. 71.

35. "Production of an Additional MC-effect or Nonelided Cadence Shortly into Presumed C-space."

a trimodular block, most often the final element, TM³, where TM¹ is a new theme for the soloist (see chapter 21). Later R1:\S-modules (which can carry such labels as R1:\S¹·², S¹·³, S², and so on) might also appear in Solo 1 (S1), as part of the solo exposition, although it sometimes happens that they are suppressed there, making their next appearance(s) only in R2 and/or R4², to be followed, usually, by R1:\C-modules in the expected order. Put another way, even while S1 interlards, and sometimes replaces, R1's materials with new ideas of its own, to the extent that it does refer intermittently to the R1 succession, it does so in modular order—while retaining the option of tracking them through only part of R1's S-space. Thus Rotation 1's original R1:\EEC might well not be "reached" in S1, even though S1 provides a differing, and suitable, S1:\EEC on its own. When this happens, Rotation 2 (S1 + R2, providing the sense of the larger exposition, as opposed to the S1 solo exposition) will typically be completed, or at least advanced further (almost always to the equivalent of the R1:\EEC-point), in the latter portions of R2. The full rotation, including all R1:\C-material, will always be completed in final, "synthesis" rotation: the R3⇒S3 + R4 complex, or the larger recapitulation.

Most of the rotational implications of this situation have been introduced toward the end of the preceding chapter, in the context of the last of Mozart's concerto arrangements of J. C. Bach, K. 107 no. 3. That discussion will not be repeated here, particularly since it will be revisited also in chapter 21. We might only recall the central principle: modules that were understood as appearing in S-space within R1 will also be considered to recur in S-space in later rotations, even if they reappear only in R2 (thus reopening S-space within the larger exposition, even though S1 will have declared an S1:\EEC within its own spatial limitations) or R4 (reopening S-space within the larger recapitulation, notwithstanding an earlier S3:\ESC). Deciding where to situate the R1:\EEC, therefore, has

significant ramifications for one's interpretation of the relative strength and placement of such later structural points as S1:\EEC, R2:\EEC, S3:\ESC, and R4:\ESC. In turn, this understanding invites one to larger hermeneutic considerations of structural completion or noncompletion at the various points of the Type 5 movement.

The Closing Zone: R1:\C

Once one has decided upon the location of the R1:\EEC, whatever remains within R1, up to its concluding perfect authentic cadence, will occupy R1:\C-space.³⁶ R1:\C zones, especially in the later concertos, are variable in their use of juxtaposed *forte* and *piano* modules. While most R1s come to a reinforced, *forte* close in the tonic (however brief), others end R1 with a sudden *diminuendo* (Piano Concerto No. 24 in C Minor, K. 491, with fatalistic implications) or a brief *piano* module sustained all the way to the end (Piano Concertos No. 11 in F, K. 413; No. 15 in B-flat, K. 450; No. 20 in D Minor, K. 466; No. 27 in B-flat, K. 595).

The beginning of R1:\C can also be handled in different ways. When the cadential material for R1:\S is delivered in a *piano* dynamic and elided with R1:\C, the latter zone often begins with an abrupt and vigorous *forte*. (Occasionally the presence of a strategically placed *forte* module in R1, elided with a PAC, can be helpful evidence on behalf of the preferable location of the R1:\EEC when other factors seem insufficient or non-normative.) In most cases, the *forte* R1:\C is a new theme—in other words, it is not P-based. In part, this may be because the R1:\C¹ idea is the second most common modular choice (after R1:\TR¹·¹) to provide the opening idea for Ritornello 2—thus from the outset of R2 continuing an otherwise "incomplete" larger rotation (see chapter 21). To preserve this possibility and its sense of rotational clarity, it might have been desirable to avoid a sense of P-redundancy at the onset of

---

36. An unusual concluding option may be found in Violin Concerto No. 3 in G, K. 216, which, in effect, comes to a half cadence close in m. 34, then provides

several measures of caesura-fill as a bridge that elides into Solo 1 (m. 38).

R2. Only a few *forte* R1:\C¹ ideas are P-based. These include those of Piano Concertos No. 21 in C, K. 467, m. 64, and No. 24 in C Minor, K. 491, m. 63, both of which are unusually shot through with regular, *idée fixe* recurrences of their P-based mottos.

But the *forte* R1:\C¹ is hardly a necessity. When a discursive R1:\S-space has proceeded through two or more dynamically contrasting modules, it can end with a decisive I:PAC (R1:\EEC), *nonelided* with a *piano* response or "afterthought," often witty, wistful, or ruminative. The presence of a nonelided quiet module at or near the end of R1 is a typical Mozart fingerprint (Leeson and Levin's theme 6), though it, too, is not absolutely required—and is sometimes elided to a concluding *forte* flourish (their theme 7). That this module can serve as R1:\C¹ is evident from such circumstances as those in Piano Concertos No. 17 in G, K. 453, m. 58, with succeeding flourish module, R1:\C², at mm. 69–74 (example 20-1); No. 19 in F, K. 459, m. 62, with its famous effect of *buffa* chuckling, reinforced with two concluding *forte* chords, mm. 70–71; and No. 25 in C, K. 503, m. 82, with similar *forte* strengthening at the end, mm. 89–90. On the other hand, one might also conclude that the nonelided *piano* module is tucked within an already established R1:\C-space. In these situations one will have decided to regard an earlier cadence as the R1:\EEC, following a strict application of the first-PAC guideline. (Even so, once again we admit that such situations offer temptations to make a case that that moment of closure may also be regarded as deferred through the earlier I:PAC up to the point of the nonelided *piano* theme.)[37]

It is quite common to find a concluding *forte* flourish that rounds out R1 with fortified rhetorical punctuation. (In several early concertos—and in some later ones, such as Clarinet Concerto in A, K. 622—this module will be reheard shortly into Solo 1, as a tutti-interpolation confirming gesture marking the end of the P-zone and releasing the sonata process into TR concerns.) Normally R1 is fully closed off from the nonelided S1 that directly follows it. Occasionally one finds an "early" solo entry overlaid onto the final bars of R1, especially if R1 ends *piano*. Such a procedure dramatically shifts the spotlight to the soloist, whose own construction of Rotation 2 is about to dominate the next phase of action. These and other related initial solo entries are dealt with in chapter 21.

Recurrences of R1 Modules in Later Rotations

One expects that every module within R1 will normally appear (or at least be partially represented) in a properly situated location somewhere in the later rotations. To be sure, some modules (R1:\P) will almost always appear in every subsequent rotation (exposition, recapitulation). Other R1 modules, however, may fail to appear in the recrafted Rotation 2 (the larger exposition) but resurface only in the synthesis provided by the final rotation (the larger recapitulation). This can happen when S is completely reconceived in Solo 1, or when Solo 1's S-space does not fully track through all of the R1:\S-modules. If the last few S- or C-modules of R1 do not re-emerge to conclude R2, or if only some of them do (that is, if R2 is rotationally incomplete), the others are likely be withheld until R4—and often until R4², after the cadenza, when all of the previously unsounded concluding modules finally return, in

---

37. Examples include Piano Concertos No. 23 in A, K. 488, m. 63 (probably best heard as a concluding R1:\C²), and No. 27 in B-flat, K. 595, m. 77 (R1:\C³), both perhaps with the sense of a "blessing" over what has preceded it, and Clarinet Concerto in A, K. 622, m. 50 (R1:\C²), with a *forte* flourish in mm. 55–56. Assuming the strict first-PAC guideline, one would observe that K. 488's R1:\C-space had also opened with a sudden, nonelided *piano* drop to the tonic minor ("lights out"), m. 46, and that of K. 595 had opened with still another *piano* possibility—among several others: an elided, crescendo-"loop" *piano* opening of R1:\C¹, m. 39. Still, in each of these three cases one locates the earlier, "literal" R1:\EEC with some uncertainty, realizing that other interpretations are possible.

their proper order, to produce a complete rotation. (In this last case the final R1 modules will never have been heard in a nontonic key.) From time to time one comes across a module in R1 that appears only there—one that is abandoned after R1. This is especially possible within pre-MC modules, for example, an interior module of R1:\TR. Only rarely will an interior R1:\S-module fail to resurface later in the piece. This does happen, though, in Clarinet Concerto in A, K. 622, in which R1:\S2, mm. 31–39, a reinforcement of the preceding theme, is unique to Ritornello 1.[38]

---

38. Cf. Piano Concerto No. 14 in E-flat, K. 449, in which the emphatic R1:\S$^{2.2}$ appears in both Ritornello 1 (mm. 63–70) and Ritornello 2, which it opens (mm. 169–76, in V), but fails to appear at any later point in the movement: it is never recapitulated. Perhaps somewhat similar, strictly considered, is Beethoven's Piano Concerto No. 2, where the first-proposed "wrong-key" R1:\S—the R1:\P$^{1.2}$-based mm. 43–circa 57 (beginning in ♭III)—does reappear in the development, mm. 236–39, but is omitted from the interior of both the exposition and recapitulation, although similar harmonic shifts may be found in each structural space.

CHAPTER TWENTY-ONE

The Type 5 Sonata

Mozart's Concertos (Solo and Larger Expositions: Solo 1 + Ritornello 2)

Chapter 20 outlined aspects of Ritornello 1 (R1) construction in Mozart's concertos, the initial, nonmodulating rotation of the Type 5 Sonata. Especially in large-scale pieces, that initial tutti establishes the movement's prevailing character along with its subsequent interplay of contrasting topical nuances. Even while often retaining a preparatory feel, R1 also determines the rotational sequence of modular events likely to prove decisive for the rest of the movement. The task now is to set forth a "real" sonata exposition that will accomplish an obligatory modulation and secure a nontonic EEC. At the end of R1, the orchestra hands over the beginning of that task to the soloist, who will be spotlighted in most of what follows. For its part, the soloist is expected to respond to what R1 has already made concrete.

This back-referential feature makes a Type 5 exposition different from those in Type 1–4 sonatas. In all of the others, the exposition is autonomous, setting forth the particulars of its *Anlage* (layout) exclusively on its own terms. By contrast, in the Type 5 exposition (normally S1 + R2) the expositional layout is to be un-

derstood not primarily "by itself" but in the relationships of its particulars to the Ritornello 1 precedent. This is a fundamental difference, one that complicates the consideration of every feature of S1 + R2. R1 is the model against which all that ensues is to be understood. It is already what has indelibly happened in the movement's past.

The Soloist Enters: The Interaction Begins

Hermeneutic Issues: Individual and Group

In a Type 5 sonata the initial solo entry is a dramatically charged moment. After the prolonged preparation found in the orchestral R1, the soloist qua individual—from whom the audience has been waiting to hear—steps forth to interact with the modular introduction/proto-exposition/rotation just furnished by the group.[1] Very rarely, the soloist might already have participated with thematic touches—solo interjections[2]—in brief spots of R1, as, famously, near the opening of Piano Concerto No. 9 in E-flat,

---

1. Cf. once again Charles Rosen's remark cited in ch. 19, n. 64 and related text.
2. A word on terminology: we regard any brief solo

insertion within a broader ritornello pillar (R1, R2, [R3], or R4, apart from the standard cadenza)—or, conversely, any orchestral insertion, coinciding with

K. 271, mm. 3–4, 6–7, including upbeats. (In Beethoven we also have the exceptional beginnings of Piano Concertos Nos. 4 and 5.) In these instances, hearing from the soloist "early in the game" could suggest any of a number of things: an initiatory demonstration of the sonic forces from which the rest of the Type 5 sonata will be constructed; a poetic solo-setting of R1 into motion; or a representation of the soloist's impulsive or egoistic impatience to begin a process of self-assertion before the generically appointed moment.

Because the "classical" repertory arose within the social context of a rapidly emerging sense of subjectivity, it has always been enticing when confronting concertos to speculate on the broader significance of the interaction between the individualized soloist and the orchestra, interpretable as the social group that makes the soloist's utterances possible, the group out of which the soloist emerges and with which he or she subsequently engages. In 1793 Koch wrote that while a solo sonata might impress us as "a monologue in passionate tones," in a "well-worked-out concerto" we find instead "a passionate dialogue between the concerto player and the accompanying orchestra," an interchange of feelings, "something similar to the tragedy of the ancients, where the actor expressed his feelings not towards the pit, but to the chorus."[3] Starting up with the initial solo entry, this dialogue can range from various degrees of mutual support and reactive affirmation to more self-assertive or tense exchanges, featuring interruptions, moments of submission before authority, dissolutions of texture, and the like.[4]

To which larger social ends were these solo-group interactions staged? Were Mozart's audiences (and are we today) invited most centrally to identify with the emotional stance of the soloist, thus helping to construct their (our) "modern" sense of subjectivity around the eloquent presence of an individual voice? Or were they (and we) also identifying with the more composite sonic image of the claims of both the individual and the group? That there is an implied discourse between group and individual within each of Mozart's concertos can scarcely be denied. This is also a *social* discourse whose inner tensions have resonances with such things as the rational and ordered basis of Enlightenment thought; the charged interplay of old-world (*ancien-régime*) and newer-world values; the beginnings of the "structural transformation of the public sphere";[5] the rise of the modern conception of the highly personalized, individual artist-as-genius, bolstered by a complementary support group of culturally elite connoisseurs; and, within the concomitantly emerging philosophy of Austro-Germanic Idealism, the ideology of an increasingly "autonomous" art music that was starting to claim inroads into higher expressive truths. All of this is fertile ground for close interpretive work within the concertos, either a sympathetically grounded hermeneutic inquiry or a more skeptical ideology critique—or a provocative combination of the two.[6]

---

the dropping-out of the soloist, into one of the solo blocks—as an interjection, something momentarily inlaid into a broad section governed by a contrasting textural-generic principle. Much of K. 271/i, for instance, is dominated by a "solo-interjection" game, in which the pianist repeatedly intrudes into space normatively given over fully to the orchestra. This happens in R1, R2, R3 (the recapitulation, with the orchestra and piano parts famously switched around), and R4. As will emerge in this chapter, it is also standard practice to include a few orchestral interjections within the S1, S2, or S3 stretches. We describe these as brief "tutti interjections" rather than "ritornello interjections," in order better to distinguish them from the structurally more significant ritornellos, R1, R2, [R3], and R4.)

3. Koch, *Introductory Essay on Composition*, trans. Baker, p. 209. See also the expanded discussion of Koch's ac-

tor-chorus thesis in Irving, *Mozart's Piano Concertos*, pp. 2–6.

4. Cf. ch. 19, n. 51 (the monograph on this topic by Simon P. Keefe).

5. The reference is to Jürgen Habermas, *The Structural Transformation of the Public Sphere*, trans. T. Burger and F. Lawrence (Cambridge, Mass.: MIT Press, 1989); Habermas is also mentioned in this context in Grayson, *Mozart's Piano Concertos Nos. 20 and 21*, pp. 5–6.

6. The relevant literature on this is vast. For a review of some of the positions taken within Mozart's concertos, see, e.g., Joel Galand, "The Large-Scale Formal Role of the Solo Entry Theme in the Eighteenth-Century Concerto," *Journal of Music Theory*, 44 (2000), 381–85, 440–41; and Grayson, *Mozart's Piano Concertos Nos. 20 and 21*, pp. 5–7.

Option 1: Solo Enters with R1:\P Material (Onset of Solo Exposition and Rotation 2)

The initial solo entry after the completion of R1 can be treated in a variety of ways. Within Mozart's concertos the first-level-default procedure—especially in the earlier concertos—is for the orchestral R1 to come to a full close, with final caesura, whereupon the soloist enters (not considering here any non-notated, improvised *Eingang*, or "lead-in")[7] by sounding the opening of the R1:\P theme in the tonic. In this case the soloist's "subjective presence" announces itself by accepting the initial idea of R1. Since R1:\P[1.1] is the normative marker of the onset of a new rotation, this results in a clear articulation of the beginning of the solo exposition and, with it, Rotation 2—in most cases a recasting of Rotation 1, with substitutions, alterations, and expansions.

The soloist, lightly accompanied by the orchestra, may sound the R1:\P theme intact, bar-for-bar, although often with personalized decorations and, occasionally, a more active dialogical participation of the orchestra toward the end (Violin Concerto No. 3 in G, K. 216; Horn Concerto No. 1 in D, K. 412; Piano Concertos No. 8 in C, K. 246; No. 14 in E-flat, K. 449; No. 16 in D, K. 451; No. 18 in B-flat, K. 456; No. 19 in F, K. 459; No. 27 in B-flat, K. 595). Sometimes this Solo 1 restatement is expanded at the end or subjected to a varied repetition of its final module. The extended example 21.1 includes this moment of Piano Concerto No. 17 in G, K. 453, which can be compared with the R1 version of the same theme at the opening of example 20.1. The "added-upbeat" figure in the piano, m. 74, probably recalling the practice of improvised *Eingänge* at this point, bridges the caesura-gap at the end of R1—an exception to beginning directly with the downbeat of the theme itself. Mm. 75–90 present mm. 1–16 of R1:\P, a compound sentence, but m. 90 is kept

open with an IAC, not a PAC. The expansion, mm. 91–94, backs up to sound a decorative repetition of the preceding four bars, this time producing a I:PAC at the end. This cadence (m. 94) is elided to the opening of the "original" transition, R1:\TR[1.1] (m. 94), only now sounded *piano*. Other examples of P-expansions may be found in Piano Concertos No. 12 in A, K. 414; and No. 26 in D, K. 537. In one instance, Piano Concerto No. 23 in A, K. 488, the Solo 1 version of R1:\P, mm. 67–82, is shorter than its R1 version, lacking its earlier two-bar reinforcement of the cadence.

In other cases—particularly in earlier concertos or those with smaller-scale R1s—the model furnished in Rotation 1's R1:\P is brief and may also have been subjected almost at once to an R1:\P⇒TR merger. Solo 1 may begin by tracking through the opening bars of the R1:\P theme only to proceed to an immediate expansion by merging into new material on its own—the first of many soloistic deviations from the R1 model—either early within P-space or perhaps at the original point of the P⇒TR merger. While this procedure is not typical of the piano concertos, instances of it may be seen in Violin Concertos Nos. 1 in B-flat, K. 207; No. 2 in D, K. 211; No. 4 in D, K. 218 (in which the R1:\P-tracking lasts for eight bars, mm. 42–49, before the P-deviations set in); and, in an ingenious variant, at the non-normative onset of the Allegro aperto solo exposition, m. 46, of No. 5 in A, K. 219 (which, exceptionally, is not the soloist's first entrance);[8] and in several other works.

Option 2: Solo Enters with New Material Preceding the Onset of R1:\P: Links, Bridges, and Prefaces ("Rotation 2" Ambiguities)

As has been much discussed in the literature, several of Mozart's concertos call for the soloist to make an initial appearance with a new

---

7. On *Eingänge*, see Grayson, *Mozart's Piano Concertos Nos. 20 and 21*, pp. 101–4, and Irving, *Mozart's Piano Concertos*, pp. 162–64.

8. K. 219 presents a different but relatable situation to those found in the first, second, and fourth violin concertos. Not only is the solo exposition proper, m. 46,

preceded by an interpolated Adagio preface led by the soloist (to be revisited under option 2) but it also features a new theme in the solo violin (in dialogue with option 3) soaring on top of the orchestral replication, mm. 46–54, of the first nine bars of R1:\P.

EXAMPLE 21.1 *(continued)*

EXAMPLE 21.1   (*continued*)

EXAMPLE 21.1 (continued)

EXAMPLE 21.1 (*continued*)

EXAMPLE 21.1   *(continued)*

Example 21.1   (continued)

Example 21.1   (continued)

EXAMPLE 21.1 *(continued)*

507

EXAMPLE 21.1 *(continued)*

EXAMPLE 21.1 (*continued*)

EXAMPLE 21.1   (*continued*)

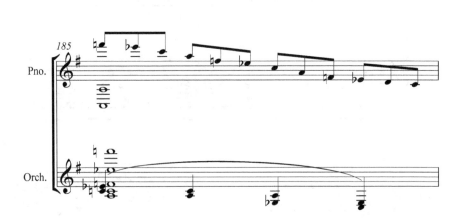

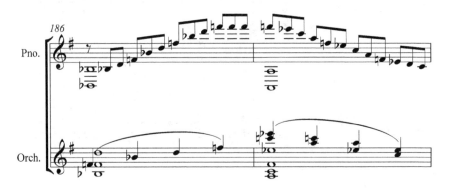

idea of its own, one that had not been presented in R1. This decision may have been associated, however loosely, with the type of main theme presented in R1:\P—that is, with its planned suitability, or lack of it, to be used by the soloist as its first statement after R1.[9] Although the expressive tone and potential sense of self-standing "completeness" of such an apparent interpolation is variable, this is usually not a simple substitution for the R1:\P theme. (The few examples in which it is are dealt with in the subsequent section, "option 3.") Instead, it usually leads to a restatement of R1:\P, the normal sign of a rotational beginning, most often, though not always, in the orchestra.[10] Occasional precedents can be found in a few early concertos by C. P. E. Bach (such as in the first movement of the B minor Harpsichord Concerto, H. 440, from 1753)[11] and others, but in the 1770s and 1780s the practice seems especially characteristic of Mozart.[12] It would also be taken over by Beethoven in several concertos.

Over the years scholars have devised various terms for and interpretations of this often-"extra" module. It has been called a "solo introduction" (Forman), "the flourish," which "provides an introduction to the statement of the first theme of S1" (Green), a "solo entry theme"

(Galand), a "new solo theme at the beginning of the first solo section" that is a "kind of improvisatory-sounding solo entrance" (Stevens), an *Eingang* ("lead-in," found in some earlier German-language writing), *eine motivisch freien Soloeröffnung* (Küster, "a motivically free solo-opening"), an "insert," "a kind of interruption," or an "episode" (Irving), and the like.[13] Caplin's term for several instances of the "entirely new theme" is the "alternative main theme" (as opposed to the "ritornello main theme"), but this can be misleading, since R1:\P, obviously the "main theme" in its own right, usually follows it in one way or another.[14] Our preferred term for the larger, more complete variants of this interpolation is the *preface* (or *S1 preface*). Some of the shorter examples, though, seem not to rise fully to the implications of this term, serving only as brief links or bridges between the end of R1 and the next sounding of R1:\P within Solo 1. As might be expected, the possibilities may be arrayed on a continuum of extremely simple to more complex or expanded semi-autonomous instances. For heuristic purposes it can be helpful to mark characteristic positions on this scale, taking up some of the possibilities in ascending order of length and self-sufficient thematic completeness.

---

9. See, e.g., the hypothesis along these lines proposed in David Rosen, "'Unexpectedness and 'Inevitability,'" pp. 271–74. Cf. also the discussion in Küster, *Formale Aspekte*, pp. 84–88.

10. As Stevens noted ("Theme, Harmony, and Texture," p. 28), Quantz in his 1752 *Versuch* had literally specified, with regard to what we now call the "baroque" ritornello concerto—not yet a Type 5 sonata—that a new opening theme in the solo is normally followed by a restatement of the opening of the original ritornello theme. See Quantz, *Versuch einer Anweisung die Flöte Traversiere zu spielen* (Berlin, 1752), trans. Edward R. Reilly, *On Playing the Flute* (London: Faber and Faber, 1966), pp. 311–12.

11. This work is discussed in conjunction with Mozart's Piano Concerto No. 25 in C, K. 503, in Stevens, "The Importance of C. P. E. Bach," pp. 224–28. Stevens stresses that "the crucial moment for establishing the nature of the tutti-solo relationship is perhaps the solo's entrance at the beginning of the first solo section" [224]. The presence of a new theme here can sometimes "try to establish . . . a striking independence from the tutti" [227].

12. As Joel Galand put it in a recent inventory and analysis of such solo entries ("The Large-Scale Formal

Role," p. 385), "By Mozart's time, it was comparatively rare for the soloist to enter with distinctively new material once past the first ritornello block." Here Galand was also referring to ritornello blocks in ritornello-based sonata-rondo finales.

13. Denis Forman, *Mozart's Concerto Form: The First Movements of the Piano Concertos* (London: Rupert Hart-Davis, 1971), pp. 63–66 (often "a limpid pool of solo piano tone between two noisy bouts of orchestral texture," p. 65); Douglass M. Green, *Form in Tonal Music: An Introduction to Analysis*, 2nd ed. (New York: Holt, Rinehart, and Winston, 1979), p. 247; Galand, "The Large-Scale Formal Role," passim; Stevens, "The Importance of C. P. E. Bach," pp. 226, 236 n. 20, which also mentions David Rosen's (unpublished) term for this in a paper from 1979, "solo insert"; Küster, *Formale Aspekte*, pp. 84–88 (which also discusses and criticizes the common use of the term *Eingang* as misleading, since it also—and more properly—refers to non-notated, improvisatory flourishes); Irving, *Mozart's Piano Concertos*, pp. 11, 44, 50.

14. Caplin, *Classical Form*, p. 245. (As mentioned above, a truly "alternative main theme" would be that outlined in option 3 below.)

Brief Links or Expanded Anacruses. In these cases the soloist does "begin" with R1:\P (often following a full close of R1) but precedes that theme with a brief, energetic upbeat-figure that is not "thematic" in any standard sense. As already described, this occurs in K. 453 (example 21.1), where the soloist's statement of R1:\P (m. 75) is led into by an ascending, decorative anacrusis filling the preceding bar (m. 74). A slightly more expanded, aggressive version of this option may be found in Beethoven's Piano Concerto No. 3: three eruptive C-minor scales, rocketing up three octaves (mm. 111–13), trigger the soloist's *forte* statement of R1:\P in octaves (m. 114).

More Expansive "Nonthematic" Solo-Fill or "Warmup" to S1's R1:\P. Sometimes the added preparatory material, while still nonthematic, is longer than a mere anacrusis—giving the impression of "warming up" to the task via arpeggiated or other stock figuration. A good example may be found in the first movement of Piano Concerto No. 15 in B-flat, K. 450 (example 21.2). Several bars after the R1:\EEC at m. 41, R1:\C² starts to close the initial tutti in m. 53. The expected end of R1 proper is anticipated at the downbeat of m. 60 (note, however, the erosion of bass support at this measure). Meanwhile, the piano has commenced a premature, dovetailed entrance in m. 59 and fills the following eleven bars, mm. 60–70, with running right-hand ("warmup") figuration over a static prolongation of the tonic (here, a one-time event that will not recur in the movement). In effect, this is a quasi-improvisatory, composed-out fermata, sustaining—indeed, overdetermining—the final B-flat tonic of R1. Its light accompaniment from the strings only underscores the sense of expanding that concluding moment.[15] Still, the entrance of the piano is normally an initiating, not a concluding, gesture. From this

perspective, this R1-addendum also has a preparatory role, as though the "sonata clock" has momentarily stopped and is then nudged back into activity with the piano's statement of R1:\P in m. 71 (first heard in m. 1), the literal onset of the solo exposition proper and Rotation 2 of the movement. A dovetailed solo entry of this sort can provide an ingratiating sense of dialogic cooperation between the soloist and the group—the latter providing generic signals of being ready to "hand off" its musical lead to the former, while the former simultaneously acknowledges that it is ready to assume its assigned role in the scripted drama.

A more extravagant and much broadened nonthematic dovetailing may be found in Beethoven's Violin Concerto in D, op. 61. Following the R1:\EEC at m. 77, R1's initially bracing C-material runs into a sudden *diminuendo* (m. 86) and pauses expectantly over a held dominant-seventh (mm. 88ff), as if graciously inviting the soloist to round off R1. The violinist accepts, m. 89—all the while over the stilled dominant-seventh—and through nonthematic figuration expands the V⁷ for some twelve bars (mm. 89–100), before rounding off R1 proper, gently supported by the orchestra, with a I:PAC at m. 101. The expositional rotation then begins, led lyrically by the soloist, at mm. 101–2. This procedure may be compared with the similar, albeit briefer, events in the opening movement of Beethoven's Piano Concerto No. 5 in E-flat, op. 73, mm. 107–11.

Perhaps the cleverest adaptation of the preparatory "warmup" strategy occurs in Mozart's Piano Concerto No. 21 in C, K. 467 (example 21.3). At the point of the much-deferred R1:\EEC, m. 64, the P-based R1:\C rounds out the end of Ritornello 1 with a decisive module, *forte* and march-like, putting an unequivocal lid ("Enough!") on a discursive and errant R1:\S-space.[16] The final I:PAC at m. 68 could

---

15. The effect of tonic overdetermination is in part due to its surplus-grounding function at the close of an R1 totally in the tonic, only to give way to S1 and sixteen more measures of B-flat tonic, mm. 71–86. The immediate lurch to vi, G minor, at S1:\TR, m. 87 (with anacrusis) is a standard TR-strategy within a tonally overdetermined P-zone. See the discussion of "Tonal Under- and Overdetermination" in ch. 5.

16. The EEC deferral procedures in this R1 are extraordinarily sophisticated. The only-apparent I:PAC at m. 36 (echoing that of m. 32) is not sufficient to secure the R1:\EEC because mm. 28–36 are instances of Mozart's characteristic "looping" procedure, discussed at several points earlier in this text. (See the discussion in ch. 8 surrounding example 8.5, the subsection on "Mozartian 'Loops'" in ch. 5, and the R1:\S (R1:\EEC)

EXAMPLE 21.2   Mozart, Piano Concerto No. 15 in B-flat, K. 450, i,
mm. 53–74

EXAMPLE 21.2 *(continued)*

EXAMPLE 21.3   Mozart, Piano Concerto No. 21 in C, K. 467, i,
mm. 64–83

EXAMPLE 21.3   *(continued)*

hardly be more conclusive, and we are to expect an immediate solo-entrance at this point. But instead the orchestra seems to "realize" that the soloist, for whatever reason, is not yet ready to make that appointed entrance. Bridging over the unexpected absence with consummate grace, the orchestra, in the now-prolonged gap between R1 and S1, moves forward at the upbeat to m. 69 with elegant "delaying tactics" in search of the apparently missing (or inattentive?) soloist—or perhaps, as Grayson has suggested, the orchestra seeks to "cajole the [reluctant] soloist into entering."[17] Contact is made in m. 74 (following an augmented-sixth-chord approach to the dominant), and, led back by the supportive "group," the soloist is drawn into

the action, spinning out a clearly preparatory "warmup" elaboration on the dominant, ending on the V^7 in mm. 78–79, held by a fermata—an invitation for an improvised *Eingang*.[18] More or less normal business resumes in m. 80, the beginning of Solo 1, although the opening four bars of the statement of R1:\P are taken over by the orchestra, while the piano (even here still hesitant to participate?) is temporarily stalled on a dominant-trill above.

Brief but "Thematic" Fill. It can happen that the short-lived fill-music preceding the soloist's embrace of R1:\P can take on a thematic contour that, more than mere figuration, presents a fleeting but separate thematic signature. This

---

issues laid out in ch. 20.) As proposed earlier, double-loops of this sort are always to be regarded as incapable of producing a structurally closing cadence on their own. Instead, they lead to a "breakout" that is normatively to be read as the continuation of a special kind of sentence. That breakout occurs at m. 36 (R1:\S[1.2])—a return to the march-like head-motive of R1:\P, which might initially be mistaken for a P-based C (an ambiguity that Mozart probably wished us to register at this point). (In this movement, the head-motive recurs regularly, rushing into any potentially otherwise unoccupied space as an *idée fixe* or "wild card.") This continuation proceeds until the next I:PAC at m. 52. Is this the R1:\EEC? Probably not. Mm. 52–64 are best regarded as R1:\S[2] (and not R1:\C[1]) on the conjoined evidence of three features, no one of which is determinative in

itself: the music drops suddenly to *piano* after a vigorous *forte* close; mm. 54–56 and the expanded variant at mm. 58–64 suggest a return to a shoring-up paraphrase of the cadence at mm. 48–52; and the emphatic, P-based material at m. 64 seems designed to clarify the "real" onset of C-space.

17. Grayson, *Mozart: Piano Concertos Nos. 20 and 21*, p. 48.

18. Grayson, *Mozart's Piano Concertos Nos. 20 and 21*, p. 48: "[This held V^7 is] the point of departure for an *Eingang*, which must be inserted to provide a link to the beginning of the solo exposition. In the autograph score Mozart left space for this *Eingang*—a full page, in fact—but, regrettably, he never filled it in. This blank page remains a tantalizing reminder of our loss."

EXAMPLE 21.4   Mozart, Piano Concerto No. 9 in E-flat, K. 271, i,
mm. 54–67

procedure hovers conceptually between unassuming fill and a genuine, more extended preface. Such is the case in Mozart's Piano Concerto No. 9 in E-flat, K. 271 (example 21.4). The R1:\EEC (best regarded as occurring at m. 41: see example 8.6 and the accompanying discussion) leads to three R1:\C modules, mm. 41–50, 50–54, and 54–59. R1:\C³ brings Ritornello 1 to an end in m. 59, but by this point the soloist has already entered in m. 56 with a characteristic dovetailing trill—calling attention not only to itself but to the imminence of the next expected event in the generic form, the solo exposition. Once released into "empty" post-R1-space, however, the pianist fills the implied caesura-gap with a reflective, new five-measure thematic idea, mm. 59–63 (ending I:IAC), as if it were tempted to drift off elsewhere. The peremptory *forte* return of R1:\P in the orchestra (m. 63) is a stern *rappel à l'ordre*, and the expositional rotation (Rotation 2) begins at this point. The soloist's five-measure drift remains a curious anomaly: it never returns again in the movement.

Closed Entry Theme (Preface) That Is Never Reused Elsewhere in the Movement. When the soloist's new thematic idea is longer than four or five bars it is more likely to be heard as a separate, self-contained utterance—a genuine preface (labeled as S1:\P^pref).[19] Several of Mozart's concertos feature these quasi-*non-sequitur* prefaces, and it is these that have drawn the most commentary from analysts. At their first sounding they can seem like theatrical asides, a sudden stepping-outside of the immediate task at hand, albeit, as Plantinga put it, with "highly distinct profiles that instantly set the soloist apart as a discrete persona. The effect is a little like the beginning of a dramatic scene that introduces a lead character who has not yet been firmly drawn into the central action."[20] Apart from investigating the introductory attitude that any individual preface projects, the analyst will also be on the lookout for whether it remains an isolated occurrence in the movement, unassimilated into the main activity of the sonata proper, or whether the preface also plays a structural role within either the development or recapitulation. Mozart provided examples of all of these.

Our immediate concern is with the isolated-occurrence type of S1:\P^pref, in which the substantial preface-theme is a one-time event, never reused later in the movement. Classic examples are located in Piano Concertos No. 22 in E-flat, K. 482 (mm. 77–94, a compound sentence) and No. 25 in C, K. 503 (mm. 91–112, in part accompanied by the orchestra). In both cases R1 had ended with a quiet afterthought-module (though *forte*-reinforced at the end) and the preface leads to the ensuing R1:\P, a grand *forte* statement, initiated by the orchestra. The much-earlier Violin Concerto No. 5 in A, K. 219, had provided a startling alternative. There the one-time preface had unfolded in a separate tempo, in this case, an arrestingly lyrical Adagio, mm. 40–45 (beginning with a delicious slow-tracking through the $\hat{8}-\flat\hat{7}-\hat{6}-\natural\hat{7}-\hat{8}$ prolongation pattern), following the energetic, *forte* conclusion of R1 (and perhaps foreshadowing aspects of the second-movement Adagio).

What are the rotational implications of such a one-time preface? When considered within the context of the options offered by the more undeveloped precedents mentioned in the paragraphs above, it would seem that they are extra-rotational. As nonparticipants in the rotation, they occupy a widened gap in which the linear elapsing of sonata-time seems momentarily halted. (The gap in question is the normative caesura-gap following R1's final cadence—normally only a few beats long.) In this sense, they are thematically expanded fill-ideas, pushed forward into a suddenly suspended blank space for differing expressive purposes that need to be investigated within each movement. When a preface recurs and becomes more integrated into the remainder of the movement, such a judgment becomes more complicated. Still, in all cases it is helpful to recall that the concept of these solo-piano-entry inserts is grounded in the idea of a temporarily stopped sonata clock. They may be understood as melodically stamped versions

19. As a reminder: the initial S1 label identifies it as a new theme either introduced by the soloist or presented after the close of R1 space. Whether it is to be understood as fully integrated into S1-space proper is a separate question.

20. Plantinga, *Beethoven's Concertos*, p. 73.

of otherwise normative fill options. However one assesses the more complicated cases, to which we now turn, something residual of this fundamental perception remains.

Closed Entry Theme (Preface) That Does Recur Elsewhere in the Movement. A few closed prefaces are more assimilated into the structure of the movement by being revisited at a later point. Since S1 proper is here being preceded by the quasi-aside of S1:\Pᵖʳᵉᶠ, one would suppose that the most logical place to revisit the idea would be at the parallel moment, namely, at the onset of the recapitulation. This was the solution chosen by Mozart in the first movements of two piano concertos early on in the Viennese period. The first is No. 11 in F, K. 413. Following a typically dovetailed overlap-link with the conclusion of R1 (mm. 56–57, beginning with a variant of the final module of R1), the piano slides through another measure of anacrusis to state a ten-bar "new" sentential idea (S1:\Pᵖʳᵉᶠ, mm. 59–68), elided with the orchestra's expected rebeginning of R1:\P at m. 68. Notwithstanding some engaging structural connotations at the end of the development, S2 (which we pass over here), essentially the same thing occurs around the moment of recapitulation: S1:\Pᵖʳᵉᶠ , with anacrusis, at mm. 236–47, elided with the orchestral R1:\P at m. 247). The second, differing in details and local implications, is No. 13 in C, K. 415 (with periodic S1:\Pᵖʳᵉᶠ at mm. 60–67, leading into the orchestrally launched R1:\P exposition; similarly at the recapitulation, mm. 200–7, though the preface proper is preceded by a solo-only quasi-RT prolongation of V).

In these instances the parallel presence of the solo preface at both points, exposition and recapitulation, precipitates an inevitable and surely purposeful ambiguity. Where do the "exposition" and "recapitulation" begin? With S1:\Pᵖʳᵉᶠ or with the subsequent orchestral R1:\P? (Recall once again that the latter module is normatively the signal for the onset of a new rotation.) More advisable than resolving this dilemma with a simplistic declaration is savoring the uncertainty of the situation. The solo preface dwells in a

rotational limbo: in some senses it continues to exist in a spot more normally regarded as structurally blank; in other senses it comes to take on the role of beginning a larger-scale rotation, one marked by a spotlighted solo-launch. Individual interpretations can differ on this point. It would not be incorrect to insist that S1 proper (read: the "solo-expositional-space proper") begins only with the onset of R1:\P, even though that moment is likely to be led by the orchestra. The rotational gears of the movement do seem to engage only here, after several bars of thematic wheel-spinning (or intentional delay?) from the soloist. And yet the recurrence of the preface at both points suggests an overriding of R1:\P's normal rotational-launch function with a nicely styled *obiter dictum* from the soloist. From this perspective one might speak of an enlarged, preface-led exposition or recapitulation. Such a situation implies a separating of two structural functions normally occurring simultaneously. In most cases the entrance of the soloist and the arrival of the R1:\P-relaunch ("exposition") occur at the same time. In this instance they are split apart, and the only way to demonstrate this separation is to provide the soloist with prefatory new material. The ensuing hermeneutic step would be to inquire about potential reasons for this decision: why is the soloist "avoiding" the task of beginning the new rotation with R1:\P?

Mozart's two minor-mode piano concertos present us with another possibility: bringing back S1:\Pᵖʳᵉᶠ not at the recapitulation but as the opening move within the development. In No. 20 in D Minor, K. 466, the soloist's S1:\Pᵖʳᵉᶠ, a sigh-ridden tonic-lament in mm. 77–91, may strike us a delaying tactic, filled with already-weary apprehension ("Must I endure what is surely to follow?"). This preface seems fully aware of the inescapability of being about to be drawn into the onset of the action proper, swept up in the consuming currents of the syncopated, D-minor R1:\P, (orchestra, m. 91)—a generic-ceremonial action whose terrible end seems foreordained from the outset.[21] The preface-lament is elaborated in no fewer

---

21. That m. 91 is R1:\P (as opposed, e.g., to being a version of TR) is clear from its correspondence mea-

sures, mm. 91–98 = mm. 1–8, after which variants ensue that continue as referential measures for several bars

than three subrotations in the S2-development (mm. 192–202, 206–16, 220–30), the first two each being "answered" by the ominous incipit of R1:\P. The recapitulation begins "normally" with R1:\P (m. 254), albeit with an alarming sense of vicious recapture by the tonic D minor, coupled with a terror-stricken awareness of being dragged into the onset of the final ritual-action in this genre, the minor-mode-saturated recapitulatory rotation-to-follow. Were one to consider S1:\Ppref to begin an expositional rotation, in whatever nuanced perspective, then the entire movement, dominated by S1:\Ppref in the development, takes on the flavor of an arcane, sophisticated dialogue with the Type 2 sonata (though surely one's overall impression is that of a true recapitulation beginning at m. 254). Similar issues, with differing local details, emerge in the astonishing No. 24 in C Minor, K. 491: the solo preface first heard in mm. 100–18 returns to begin a partially subrotational S2-development at m. 283, although the fatalistic recapitulation begins with R1:\P at m. 362.[22]

Option 3: Solo Substitutes a New Theme for R1:\P (Onset of Rotation 2 with an S1 "Replacement Theme")

In these instances R1:\P is suppressed at the outset of the solo exposition (S1). Here the entering soloist writes over the normative sign of the beginning of a new rotation with differing materials (though often ones that upon reflection can be traced motivically to parts of R1:\P, as variants). In these cases the soloist is not so much initiating an S1:\Ppref as an S1:\P proper—an alternative way of beginning the expositional rotation—and this will typically occupy all or nearly all of S1:\P-space. Examples from Mozart include the Concertone in C, K. 190 (new S1:\P at m. 45), the Sinfonia Concertante in E-flat, K.

364 (effectively, a new S1:\P at m. 78, launched by the orchestra after a dovetailed, six-bar thematic fill-link in the soloists, mm. 72–77), and the Horn Concerto No. 2 in E-flat, K. 417 (new S1:\P at m. 25, somewhat related to R1:\P¹). Related instances occur in three piano concertos of Beethoven. In each case, even while the ensuing TR is R1:\P-based (as it had also been in the opening ritornello), it remains clear that the solo exposition's P-space proper has been written over with new material. These three are No. 1 in C, op. 15 (new S1:\P at m. 107), No. 2 in B-flat, op. 19 (new S1:\P at m. 90, perhaps related to R1:\P¹·²), and, most inventively, No. 4 in G, op. 58 (piano interrupts the end of R1:\:C in m. 74, initiating a long bridge apparently also writing over the onset of S1; when the tutti returns thematically in m. 89—clearly in S1-space—it does so with R1:\TR, first heard in m. 14).

When R1 and S1 + R2, normally Rotations 1 and 2 in a Type 5 sonata, begin with different (rival?) material, how is the recapitulation to be handled? Each situation is different. The "new" material from the exposition's opening might be dropped altogether (as in Beethoven's Piano Concertos No. 1 and 4—though the latter is very much a special case). It might be situated somewhere else (at the opening of the development in Beethoven's Piano Concerto No. 2, m. 213). Or, appealing perhaps to an earlier tradition, the recapitulation might present both openings, one after another in what amounts to a double-start to the recapitulation, with R1:\P presented before S1:\P, as in Mozart's Concertone in C (mm. 155, 159), Sinfonia Concertante in E-flat (mm. 223, [231,] 237), and Horn Concerto No. 2 in E-flat (mm. 117 [even merging into R1:\TR at m. 121], 126). Chapter 22 treats these and other double-start recapitulations more generally.

(referentially, mm. 99–103 = mm. 9–13). At around this last point we find a P⇒TR merger (a merger into S1:\TR). The situation in the C-minor Concerto, K. 491, is similar but complicated in certain respects: see n. 22. Cf. the remarks from Quantz's 1752 *Versuch*, alluded to in n. 10.

22. Is m. 118 R1:\P or TR? (Cf. n. 21). The *forte* dynamic might suggest a rejoining of the rotation at the

R1:\TR point (cf. the *forte* m. 13). Still, given the precedent of K. 466, it is probably cleanest to suggest that the principal conceptual model underlying the events begun at m. 118 is again that of the P⇒TR merger, in which mm. 118–23 correspond to mm. 1–6. The *forte* TR-scoring overlay (thus suggesting also a correspondence with mm. 13–18) could be regarded as an early feature of the merger.

Implications: How Free Will Rotation 2 Be?

When a soloist begins S1 with a restatement of R1:\P, or even a refashioning of it, that soloist is staged as taking up the materials offered by the orchestra. Individual and group have at least agreed on the same starting point, whatever divergences might follow. Conversely, when the soloist enters with material notably different from that first sounded in R1:\P, this may be taken as either a local assertion of relative independence or decorative flair—a declaration of individual difference vis-à-vis the preceding group utterance, suggesting a potential difficulty of full assimilation down the road—or, at times, as a hesitant reluctance, for whatever reason, to initiate the ensuing rotation himself or herself (implied in the opening movements of Mozart's minor-mode piano concertos, K. 466 and K. 491).

Similar or different starting-points are not absolutely predictive of the congruence of the remainder of the solo exposition with the R1 model. One normally expects some discrepancies and expansions, especially in the TR-approach to the MC and individual spots of post-MC material, but these cannot be predicted in advance. Viewed in this light, one might regard the solo exposition, S1, as an individualized recasting (in a continuing dialogue with the group) of the R1-succession model (Rotation 1). Recognizing each S1-deviation, or nondeviation, is significant for a broader grappling with the structural and expressive implications of the linear succession of the arrayed modules—and ultimately of the piece as a whole.

In sum, S1 (or S1 + R2, normally the larger expositional rotation) may restrict itself largely to working with the materials offered to it in R1 (with the most normative exceptions being the expanded TR and virtually obligatory display episode at the end of S1); it may introduce a few—or several—interpolations or substitutions, especially around S1:\S-space; or it may even (though much more rarely) propose a set of expositional materials that seems largely new. Within mature, large-scale concertos, the extreme points along this continuum might be represented as follows. Toward the one end we find the melodically "conservative" and overwhelmingly R1-based expositions of Mozart's Piano Concerto No. 23 in A, K. 488 and, say, Beethoven's Piano Concertos Nos. 1 and 3 and his Violin Concerto. Toward the other, more radicalized end, we find such expositions as that in the first movement of Mozart's Sinfonia Concertante, K. 364, whose S1 materials are nearly all different from those laid out in R1. Most concertos fall between these extremes, with a modest level of S1-divergences. It is the task of all recapitulations to reconcile or synthesize whatever different "points of view" there may be between R1 and S1, mostly through the process of mutual inclusion in any number of ingenious ways.

Post-P-Theme Option: Orchestral Flourish as Affirmational Tutti Interjection 1 (P-Codetta or Link to a Sujet-Libre Transition)

The close of the P-theme in Solo 1 is usually accomplished by the soloist and leads directly into a brief tutti impulse from the orchestra, as the soloist momentarily drops out. Because this impulse is not one of the four ritornello pillars, it is to be regarded as a *tutti interjection* within S1.[23] In his 1991 study Küster called this the *erste Tuttieinwurf*—the "first tutti interjection"—and noted more than three dozen instances of it in Mozart's concerto movements.[24] One less common type of *Tuttieinwurf*—albeit one familiar

---

23. On the term "interjection," see n. 2.
24. Küster, *Formale Aspekte*, p. 90–92. Küster's *Tuttieinwurf* concept differs from our "tutti interjection" in that for him it also embraces unproblematically the type that initiates an R1:\TR[1.1] transition. Küster identified twenty-four of these tutti interjections as being based on a previously heard R1 module (usually the final module or a module heard toward the end of R1) and

fifteen based on "free-motivic work." German musicologists sometimes also refer to this *erste Tuttieinwurf* as the *'Devisen'-Ritornell* by analogy to the so-called *Devisenarie* in earlier seventeenth- and eighteenth-century *opera-seria* "motto arias," in which a brief head-motive is sounded preliminarily as a false start before the melody is rebegun and then continued. See Küster's criticism of this misleading term on p. 92.

from several of the later piano concertos—is an interjection in texture only: the taking-up of R1:\TR[1.1] as a *forte* affirmation. (We deal with this transition type later in this chapter.) Another standard type is the brief, self-contained orchestral flourish. This type is a more emphatic "interjection," since it not only supplies a sudden *forte* burst of tutti but also wedges in a single module of music that is often extrarotational—as a real, if brief, interpolation. This more frequent type is our immediate concern here.

One normally encounters this orchestral flourish in those cases when the soloist has entered with a version of R1:\P (that is, with the ritornello's "first theme," perhaps decorated or expanded). Elided or flush-juxtaposed with the P-idea's PAC, the *forte* flourish typically occupies only a bar or two, situated in an implied gap between "thematic" P-space proper and the onset of a clearly demarcated TR. In context, this kind of tutti interjection 1 (an "appended-module" S1:\TI[1]) suggests the orchestra's suddenly interpolated commentary—nearly always affirmative—on the implications of the soloist's entrance. Most characteristically, it strengthens the I:PAC of the R1:\P theme with surplus cadential reinforcement, in the manner of an emphatic *P-codetta*. It is usually followed by a short rest and a new push forward, normally led by the soloist, into S1's "new-material" TR-zone. More often than not the vigorous P-codetta material also resuscitates the final or nearly final module of R1, a module at or toward the end of R1:\C-space, creating what Küster has called an endrhyme with the initial tutti.[25]

The Normative Case and Its Hermeneutic Implications: The Nonmodulatory P-Codetta

Since it bears no additional complications or variants, the procedure found in the first movement of the Violin Concerto No. 4 in D, K. 218, may be taken as paradigmatic (example 21.5).

The R1:\EEC at m. 26 ushers in a string of four differing C-modules (the sentential mm. 26–34, followed by mm. 34–38, 38–40, and 40–41), the last two of them mere cadential flourishes, the brief *piano* R1:\C[3] and *forte* C[4]. As is typical, the soloist enters at once in m. 42 with a version of R1:\P, lightly accompanied, and brings its expansion of that theme to a I:PAC close at m. 56. At this point the soloist drops out and the orchestra responds with appended-module Tutti Interjection 1 (mm. 56–57), an endrhyme restatement of R1:\C[4], solidifying the just-attained cadence. Following this, the violinist sets out in m. 58 with a "new" transition-idea, S1:\TR (that is, with a replacement module for the one used as TR in R1), that we shall call the *sujet libre*, to be discussed in a separate section below.

That mm. 56–57 have a concluding, P-codetta function is clear: they round off P-space and reinvoke by end-rhyme the closing-feel of the end of R1. Moreover, in both spots the terminal module leans "inevitably" into a solo-led passage (there P, here TR). In context—surrounded on both sides by heftier orchestral material—the soloist's main-theme entrance (mm. 42–56) can seem tentative, provisional, not yet fully ratified. A metaphorical equivalent of this implied dialogue might be something like, "I'm willing to participate on the terms that you have proposed to me. Shall we continue?" The orchestra responds with pure affirmation, welcoming the soloist into the game with a deal-making musical handshake and opening the gateway to the more forward-vectored TR that immediately follows: "Accepted! Now let's build a sonata. Onward!"

In our paradigmatic K. 218/i the sudden (re)intrusion of R1:\C[4] at mm. 56–57 is an obviously nonrotational gesture. In orthodox rotational practice, C-material does not belong in P-space, only to yield to TR-space. The appended-module type of Tutti Affirmation 1, there-

---

25. Küster, p. 91. Cf. the observation on the practice by Leeson and Levin ("On the Authenticity," p. 91): "The reiteration of the first theme (1) by the soloist is most often followed by the flourish (7) in the orchestra, confirming the tonality and freeing the soloist to mod-

ulate to the dominant key." Note that in these cases S1:\TI[1] could also be designated via an R1 label (e.g., R1:\C[2]). Here we retain the S1 prefix in order to call attention to the generic nature of this tutti interjection, which is not always R1:\C-based.

EXAMPLE 21.5   Mozart, Violin Concerto No. 4 in D, K. 218, i, mm. 38–62

Example 21.5 *(continued)*

fore, does not normally articulate any defining element of the ongoing Rotation 2. R1:\C⁴'s presence is conceptually separate from the larger rotational logic that drives the exposition, the S1 (or S1 + R2) rotation. This is a crucial observation. As already noted in chapter 19, in Mozart's constructions of the Type 5 sonata the larger expositional and recapitulatory rotations are equipped with a few empty slots, free spaces that are *rotationally neutral* and into which nonrotational modules (ones "out of order") may be freely inserted (although a nonrotational insertion is by no means demanded). The most common of these *rotationally inert* slots are this kind of Tutti Affirmation 1 and the opening portions of R2 and R4¹.

The K. 218/i procedure for S1:\TI¹, grounding the attained I:PAC by restating all or most of the concluding gesture of R1, is encountered in many of the first movements of Mozart's concertos. Additional examples may be found in those of the Bassoon Concerto in B-flat, K. 191, mm. 42–44; the Violin Concertos No. 1 in B-flat, K. 207, mm. 30–31 (somewhat varied) and No. 5 in A, K. 219, mm. 60–62; the Oboe Concerto in C, K. 314, mm. 47–50; the Concerto for Two Pianos (No. 10), K. 365, mm. 82–84 (slightly shortened); the Piano Concerto No. 12 in A, K. 414, mm. 82–85; and several others. But it is not always R1 material that is appears in this spot. One variant is to provide an S1:\TI¹ flourish that serves the same purpose of brief tonic-reinforcement as those described above but is entirely new—a "stock" flourish-figure that was not heard in R1, albeit one that would have worked well in that location had it appeared there (Violin Concerto No. 3 in G, K. 216, mm. 48–50).

The P-codetta S1:\TI¹ is much more characteristic of Mozart's concertos—especially the earlier or smaller-scale ones—than of

Beethoven's. Only one of Beethoven's concertos uses this strategy (which by the 1790s may have seemed old-fashioned in its emphatically interpolative stiffness). This is the first movement of the Piano Concerto No. 2 in B-flat, op. 19, mm. 102–6, where S1:\TI¹-space is filled in not with anything from the initial ritornello but with a variant of the formulaic tonic-grounding module, $\hat{8}–\flat\hat{7}–\hat{6}–\natural\hat{7}–\hat{8}$. The TR proper, m. 106, then begins with the solo pianist's stormy variant of R1:\TR¹.

The *Sujet-Libre* Transition Type

The first movement of K. 218, m. 58 (example 21.5) also provides a paradigmatic instance of one of the most common transition types found in Mozart's concertos. This type immediately follows an appended-module S1:\TI¹ or variant thereof with a new idea intended as a fresh impulse, the initial burst of the next (TR) phase of the exposition—a phase now taken over decisively by the soloist. Most commonly, as in K. 218, S1:\TR begins with a tonic-key melodic head-motive and moves into energetic figuration, eventually setting up a medial caesura. (In K. 218/i a nonmodulatory S1:\TR leads to a I:HC MC, m. 65, followed by an aggressive, *forte* caesura-fill. S1:\TR can also be modulatory, producing in major-mode Type 5 sonatas the familiar V:HC MC or, less often—sometimes surprisingly—a V:PAC MC, a sign of a more declarative structural closure.)²⁶ As in Type 1–4 sonatas, the point is to set up the possibility of beginning an S-zone or TMB in the dominant. Because this kind of "new" S1:\TR often begins melodically—a sign of the melodic extravagance found in Mozart's concertos—and because one or more other solo-exposition "new" melodies may soon follow, it is important to be clear about its structural status. (As will

---

26. Examples of the *sujet-libre* S1:\TR carried out at some length and concluded with a decisive V:PAC MC include: the Bassoon Concerto in B-flat, K. 191 (see n. 32); Oboe Concerto in C, K. 314; and the Piano Concertos No. 6 in B-flat, K. 238, No. 10 (two pianos) in E-flat, K. 365, and No. 11 in F, K. 413. The V:PAC MC usually gives way at once to the secondary theme proposed in Ritornello 1, R1:\S, which helps to clar-

ify the transitional status of the preceding section. An exceptional "new" S1:\S-theme (m. 104) follows a V:PAC MC (m. 103) in K. 365. The situation in most of these cases is somewhat similar to S1:\S¹ ideas or TM¹⇒TM² ideas that end with a V:PAC MC and proceed to a recovery of R1:\S as an appended S-extension (or TM³)—a situation discussed below in the treatment of the trimodular block (TMB) in Type 5 movements.

emerge, the rhetorical shape of this kind of TR can be identical to that of a "new" TM^1 ⇒TM^2 portion of a trimodular block, another familiar option in Mozart's solo expositions that has occasioned much uncertainty in the past. This increases the opportunity for analytical misjudgment at these points.)

This TR-type is related to the independent (separately thematized) transition discussed in chapter 6. Still, when one takes all of its characteristics into account, it is a specially customized subtype appropriate to Type 5 Allegro movements. Apart from its being preceded by the (almost) inevitable S1:\TI^1, its central aim is to shift the spotlight to the soloist, who is to accomplish the bulk of the TR with a theme or idea unique to itself, something that will never be played by the orchestra (although the orchestra often accompanies the idea). Assuming that there is no clear P^{pref}—as is usually the case in these situations—this TR-type signals the first moment at which the soloist genuinely strikes out on its own, most often with an idea associated uniquely with that individual. (Linkage-technique variants springing from S1:\TI^1 are noted below.) Consequently, it can be helpful to devise a separate term for this kind of TR.

An engaging suggestion along these lines was made in the 1930s by Georges de Saint-Foix. In his three-volume completion to a massive five-volume, French-language commentary on Mozart's works begun in collaboration with Théodore de Wyzewa early in the twentieth century, Saint-Foix usually designated this new S1:\TR as the *sujet libre* ("free subject," as opposed to the "first" and "second subjects").[27] He apparently regarded such a new theme as *libre* for two reasons. First, it belonged to the soloist as a personalized theme (that is, it had not appeared in R1 and would never be stated anywhere by the orchestra). Second, the theme was sometimes a one-time event, occasionally failing to reappear in the parallel spot—TR—in the recapitulation.[28] (In the early volumes Wyzewa and Saint-Foix had referred to occurrences of this theme as "the subject that belongs to him [the soloist] in his own right" [here referring to m. 58 of K. 218], "the subject reserved for the soloist," or similar words.)[29] Saint-Foix's clearest explanation of the term may be found in his 1936 discussion of the new-theme S1:\TR^1 of Concerto No. 10 (for Two Pianos) in E-flat, K. 365, m. 84—a classic instance of the type: "At this point the first piano sounds the *sujet libre* (that which figures only in the soloist's part). The second piano repeats it, and as is always the case [*sic*] with what we are calling the *sujet libre*, it does not reappear [later in the movement]."[30]

To be sure, Saint-Foix's analyses are often

---

27. Wyzewa and Saint Foix (vols. 1 and 2), Saint-Foix (vols. 3–5), *W.-A. Mozart: Sa vie musicale et son œuvre*, 5 vols. (Paris: Desclée, de Brouwer et Cie., 1912–46). Saint-Foix's term *sujet libre* may be found in 3:36 (K. 314), 66 (Symphonia Concertante for Winds, K. 297b, K. Anh C. 14.01), 147 (K. 365), 320 (K. 413), and 326 (K. 415); 4:23 (K. 449), 27 (K. 450), 31 (K. 451), and 221 (K. 503); and 5:170 (K. 595, "*libre sujet*"). Three of these usages mistakenly refer to what we would identify as S1:\TM^1—those in K. 415, 503, and 595. A fourth usage of the term, in K. 449, is unclear: did Saint-Foix mean S1:\TR or TM^1?

28. The term *sujet libre* was also invoked by Robert D. Levin, "Das Konzert für Klavier und Violine D-Dur KV Anh. 56/315^f und das Klarinettenquintett B-dur, KV Anh. 91/516^c: Ein Ergänzungsversuch"—in English, notwithstanding the title (!)—in *Mozart-Jahrbuch 1968/70* (Salzburg: Zentralinstitut für Mozartforschung der Internationalen Stiftung Mozarteum, 1970), p. 312 (regarding K. 315^f): At the point of the onset of the transition, "we are still in the tonic, and Mozart usually leaves it by means of one of the purest forms of his genius—a theme which St. Foix calls the *sujet libre*—one

which often does not reappear in the recapitulation, but serves as a harmonic catalyst in moving the piece from the tonic to V or V of V, sometimes dwelling on the latter degree at length (or for only a few bars) (e.g., K. 191, 216, 313, 314, 364, 365, 450, 537)."

29. Wyzewa and Saint-Foix, *W.-A. Mozart: Sa vie musicale*, II, 151 ("le sujet réservé au soliste," K. 191); 253 ([le] sujet propre du soliste," K. 216); 256 ("le sujet qui lui appartient en propre," K. 218; ("le soliste entame son sujet propre," K. 219); and so on (II:282, 290).

30. "Puis, le premier piano fait entendre le sujet libre (celui qui figure seulement dans la partie du soliste); le second piano le répète et, comme il en est toujours de ce que nous nommons le *sujet libre*, il ne reparaîtra plus" (Saint-Foix, *W.-A. Mozart: Sa vie musicale*, vol. 3 [1936], p. 147). It is true that in K. 365 this S1:\TR does not reappear in the recapitulation. It is not the case, though, that all themes so designated by Saint-Foix are one-time expositional events. He referred, for instance, to Piano Concertos No. 11 in F, K. 413, m. 82 (3:320) and No. 15 in B-flat, K. 450, m. 87 (4:27) as *sujets libres*, but both do return in the recapitulation's TR-space. (K. 450/i, mm. 216ff, is a variant of mm. 87ff.)

dubious. Some ideas that he identified as *sujets libres* do reappear in the recapitulation; he sometimes labeled as *sujets libres* themes that are more correctly regarded as post-MC TM[1]s; and he is reluctant (though inconsistently so) to label a new-idea S1:\TR[1.1] a *sujet libre* if it begins non-thematically, that is, with figuration or arpeggios.[31] Still, the term may be adapted and made both more general and more precise.

Accordingly, and without embracing Saint-Foix's concomitant implications or analytical axioms, we call any new-idea S1:\TR[1.1] a *sujet libre* and the whole transition a "TR of the *sujet-libre* type." We may summarize this kind of TR—one of three concerto TR-types—as follows. It is an independent, often-melodically-led TR; it always driven by the soloist and follows directly after the close of P, usually after an orchestral P-codetta (an appended-module S1:\TI[1]); rotationally, it replaces the R1:\TR proposed in the opening tutti; it features material consistently associated with the soloist, not the orchestra, often being that soloist's first individualized theme; it provides the sonata-structural sense of a new embarking ("Onward!") into the processes of the movement, frequently soon merging into characteristic TR-activity and setting up an MC; and because it occupies pre-MC space—which never "requires" restatement later in the movement—it may or may not return in the recapitulation's TR zone, whose content is "optional" (R1:\TR or S1:\TR? or a combination?). The *sujet-libre* type of TR normally begins squarely in the tonic. Only rarely will it begin in another key, as happens in the Bassoon Concerto in B-flat, K. 191, m. 45,

which sets off directly in the dominant key, F.[32] There are also a few instances of S1:\TI[1] that shift quickly to the submediant, whereupon the *sujet-libre* TR begins off-tonic, in vi. (They are discussed below, in "The modally shifting or modulating S1:\TI[1].")

Sujet-Libre TR-Variant 1: "Linkage Technique"

In most cases the *sujet libre* is a new musical idea—something fresh springing up after a very different, P-codetta tutti interjection. One not uncommon variant, though, is to have the soloist take its cue from the motivic-work animating the end of S1:\TI[1] and begin to build a transition that leads off with a refashioning of that material (Violin Concerto No. 5 in A, K. 219, m. 62, beat 3; Piano Concerto No. 12 in A, K. 414, m. 86).[33] In these latter cases of "linkage technique" (*Knüpftechnik*), Tutti Interpolation 1 has a double- or pivotal function, both rounding off S1:\P and providing the motivic springboard for S1:\TR-to-come. Conversely, the soloist, eager to display a ready melodic inventiveness, establishes in a stroke an elegant connection to what has just been heard and takes that idea as a motivic seed that flowers in new directions. Saint-Foix tended to disallow these variants as qualifying as *sujets libres*, but we do not.[34] For us the crucial thing is the beginning of TR with a sudden solo-thrust forward (usually following an unmistakable S1:\TI[1])—something relatable to the more common "new-idea" launches at these points. Once the norm is grasped ("a *sujet-libre* TR of the linkage type"), it is not

---

31. For the first two caveats, see nn. 27 and 30. Regarding the third, Saint-Foix presumably did not identify (as would we), the S1:\TR[1.1] of Piano Concerto No. 13 in C, K. 415, m. 78, as a *sujet libre*, because of its non-"thematic" opening, its "série d'arpèges" (3:326)—and compounded the problem by suggesting that what we would call a new S1:\S at m. 93 is both a "second sujet" *and* a "sujet libre." The same reluctance is found in his discussion of Piano Concerto No. 26 in D, K. 537, m. 103, in which he preferred instead only to point to the long stretch of ascending and descending scales (4:318).

32. Adding to the potential for misunderstanding, the Bassoon Concerto's S1:\TR is one of the few that, fol-

lowing an extensive elaboration, drive toward an emphatic V:PAC MC (m. 58) that may easily be mistaken for an early S1:\EEC attempt. The TR-status of mm. 45–58, though, is clear: the section follows directly after the close of P; the V:PAC MC leads directly to a recovery of R1:\S; and in the recapitulation, this *sujet libre* starts off a fifth below the tonic, in IV, E-flat major (m. 112).

33. Cf. the dovetailed effect in Horn Concerto No. 1 in D, K. 412, 29–30,

34. This may be why Saint-Foix did not identify as a *sujet libre* the music found in Piano Concerto No. 13 in A., K. 414, m. 86 (3:323), or Piano Concerto No. 27 in B-flat, K. 595, m. 95 (5:170).

difficult to perceive Mozart's occasional adaptations of it. In Piano Concerto No. 27 in B-flat, K. 595, for instance, S1:\TI¹, mm. 92–95, does not stem from the conclusion of R1 but was a similarly interpolated or non-normative "extra" flourish after the P-theme in R1 (mm. 13–16, an R1:\P²)—a most unusual procedure and one that in this case preserves the rotation. What follows, S1:\TR¹, m. 95, picks up on the tutti interpolation and begins to spin out an S1:\TR from it.

Sujet-Libre TR-Variant 2: S1:\TI¹ Omitted

In this more uncommon situation, no orchestral moment follows the soloist's first I:PAC (normally the close of the R1:\P-theme). The soloist leads directly into a "new-idea" S1:\TR (*sujet libre*) on its own. In these cases one could get the impression that the traditional two- to four-bar S1:\TI¹-gesture (P-codetta or brief link) has simply been omitted. Following this line of interpretation, one might look for anomalies or special situations within the preceding music that might help to contextualize this compositional choice. Examples may be found in the first movements of Piano Concertos No. 14 in E-flat, K. 449 (S1:\TR at m. 104); and No. 21 in C, K. 467 (new lyrical S1:\TR theme at m. 91, which, as with many *sujets libres*, does not return at any point later in the movement; the P^pref situation in K. 467 has already been discussed above).

S1:\TI¹ as Mediator between the P- and TR-Zones

Depending on the circumstances, the normative P-codetta function of the appended-module tutti interjection can also shade into a mediating function. When it is of sufficient length, two or more measures (as in K. 218), its primarily P-codetta function is evident. But when this TI¹ material is briefer—perhaps only a measure in length—it can also provide the impression of a short push into the TR, an active link between the P- and TR-zones. Generally built from new ("stock") figuration, such an orchestral thrust gives the impression of a punchy exclamation-point, as in the fleeting orchestral jolts

in Piano Concertos No. 11 in F, K. 413, mm. 81–82, and No. 13 in C, K. 415, mm. 77–78 (in this case on an active dominant), and in Horn Concerto No. 2 in E-flat, K. 417, mm. 33–34. Such underdeveloped figuration scarcely seems to qualify as a "tutti interjection" proper—much less as an unequivocal P-codetta—and yet its relationship to the appended-module type of S1:\TI¹ is obvious.

Also taking on a role somewhere between pure codetta and pure link are the few standard-length instances in which previously heard material from non-normative locations (that is, not from the end of R1) are called on to fill the TI¹-slot. Most similar to the P-codetta would be instances such as the immediate repetition of S1:\P^{1.2} in Horn Concerto No. 3 in E-flat, K. 447, mm. 37–40. Perhaps less so might be the unusual instances of S1:\TI¹ found in the reinvigoration of the head-motive of R1:\P in Piano Concerto "No. 5" in D, K. 175, mm. 46–48 (a "second try" after a more normative but resolutely "declined" TI in m. 42) and a reaching-back to R1:\S² (or perhaps TM²) in Piano Concerto No. 26 in D, K. 537, mm. 99–103 (cf. mm. 50–54). Each unusual case invites a contextualized interpretation.

The Modally Shifting or Modulatory S1:\TI¹ and *Sujet-Libre* Transitions That Begin Off-Tonic

Another variant involves an expansion of the end of an appended-module S1:\TI¹ in such a way as to set up the ensuing TR in a contrasting mode or key. In the Clarinet Concerto in A, K. 622, Tutti Interjection 1, reinstating the final module of R1:\C, begins in A major in m. 75, but instead of concluding vigorously, it draws back from the task with a sudden *piano* (m. 76) and collapses into A minor with the elided, "lights-out" onset of the *sujet-libre* S1:\TR in m. 78.

More striking are those instances in which Mozart destabilized the tonic-grounding aspect of this type of S1:\TI¹ by having it execute a modulation away from the tonic—most typically, to the submediant minor—then hand over the TR to the soloist in that nontonic and considerably more somber key. In these modulatory instances of Tutti Interjection 1, the musical materials may be based, as expected, on the closing flourish of the preceding R1 (as in the Flute Concerto in G, K. 313, mm. 44–46, modulating to vi, example 21.6), or they could be largely original to that moment (Sinfonia Concertante in E-flat, K. 364, mm. 90–94, modulating to an active dominant of vi). The first movement of the Piano Concerto No. 15 in B-flat, K. 450, provides a quicker jolt at this point, the fleeting interpolation of a new tutti-gesture, mm. 86–87, a sudden twist to vi following a tonally overdetermined S1:\P-zone. And aspects of the TR of Piano Concerto No. 16 in D, K. 451—anything but a pure example of this situation—are in dialogue with this technique but provide additional complications and multiple overridings of stock procedures. Here one first encounters a surprisingly "whispered" orchestral restatement of R1:\TR[1.1] under the continuing soloist (m. 85), followed by a dissolution into what turns out to be a "false" S1:\TR (m. 92, as if setting up an MC). The predicted MC, however, turns out to be undermined (emphatically declined at the moment of its near-arrival) by having the orchestra blurt out the somewhat delayed S1:\TI[1] (mm. 96–98), which includes a sudden lurch to vi (m. 98), initiating a "special" *sujet-libre* TR-extension.[35]

Such modulatory gestures at the opening of S1:\TR might be regarded as deformations of more standard practice—unpredictable high-play with familiar expectations. On the one hand, these situations are analogous to those TRs in Sonata Types 1–4 that begin off-tonic (recalling that since this TR-material is in pre-MC space, it does not claim any need to be "resolved" later in the piece). On the other hand, they also illustrate a characteristic strategy-variant found in Mozart's Type 5 movements: sometimes normative orchestral blocks that we expect to be tonally closed or key-reinforcing either dissolve away before completing themselves (as in some R1s and R2s) or effect an unexpected modulation that, as a tonal "link," merges into the next

section (a strategy that is not uncommon also in the R2 block, normatively reinforcing the solo exposition).

Two Other Solo 1 Transition Types

Mozart's Type 5 Allegro movements select among three broad categories of transition strategies—which, as with TR zones in other kinds of sonatas (chapter 6), gain energy, drive toward an MC (I:HC, V:HC, or the less common V:PAC), and prepare for the onset of the next expositional zone (secondary theme or TMB), which is to begin in the appropriate nontonic key. The first is the *sujet-libre* strategy family (and variants) outlined above, usually following an appended-module S1:\TI[1]. It represents a more traditional, smaller-scale, or "earlier" option for Mozart, one that emphasized sharply contrasting blocks of sonority at this point in S1. Hence it underscored differences of demeanor, posture, and expressive attitude between the group and the newly entered individual. Even as it led off by displaying an initial problem of separation and otherness, it also invited us, by way of implied affirmation, to step forward into a sonata process that could encourage a more intertwined reconciliation as the movement unfolded.

One of the most striking features of the appended-module S1:\TI[1]-gesture was its insistence on interpolating a nonrotational idea into the discourse right off the starting block—interrupting it with an out-of-order (or sometimes merely rotationally inert) module. Perhaps it was this aspect that contributed both to its simpler impression of an juxtaposed contrast between the soloist and the orchestra and to its slightly old-fashioned, less seamlessly "symphonic," flavor. However this might have been understood at the time, Mozart's two alternative strategies of negotiating the P–TR seam within Type 5 Allegro movements refuse to veer off-track into an out-of-order module at this point. Both

---

35. Thus prior to the aborted MC at mm. 96–98 (=S1:\TI[1]) K. 451/i furnishes a typical case (except for the dynamics) of a TR of the dissolving R1:\TR[1.1] type, the second of the three concerto transition types, to be discussed below.

EXAMPLE 21.6   Mozart, Flute Concerto in G, K. 313, i, mm. 27–49

EXAMPLE 21.6 *(continued)*

EXAMPLE 21.6   (*continued*)

transition options are familiar from several of Mozart's later and best-known piano concertos and also from several of Beethoven's concertos as well. We shall take up each in turn.

Alternative 1: Solo 1 Transition as Dissolving R1:\TR[1.1], Usually with Subsequent Expansions

The concluding I:PAC of the solo-led P-theme (often a decorated or expanded R1:\P) may be elided with the same TR-music found in Ritornello 1: R1:\TR[1.1], sounded as a typical *forte* affirmation. In this procedure the progress of the new rotation is not interrupted by an "extra," nonrotational TI. Instead, the thematic materials of R1 are tracked in the proper order, and this expositional Rotation 2 remains governed, at least up to this point, by the pattern set in Rotation 1. To be sure, since the soloist typically drops out at the moment of the I:PAC—at least for a few bars—the orchestral R1:\P moment is another type of formulaic tutti interjection. Nevertheless, its effect is different from the appended-module type. Instead of suggesting a momentary interruption before a solo-guided TR proper, the orchestra pulls the music immediately into the tow of the energetic TR—

and on its original terms (R1:\TR[1.1]). This is an immediate shift forward. The gears clench at once.

The orchestral tutti, though, is almost always short-lived. Within a few bars the soloist merges into the transition and soon begins to control the course of events, steering the music into "free" and usually expanded directions on the way to the MC. In most cases, then, the familiar orchestral R1:\TR[1.1] dissolves into new music. The new, solo-led TR-continuation could be labeled S1:\TR[1.2], suggesting that the original head-motive of TR has now led to a different musical outcome. The situation found in Piano Concerto No. 17 in G, K. 453 (example 21.1) is instructive even as it contains a few *ad hoc* occurrences. At the point of the soloist's first I:PAC the tutti R1:\TR[1.1] is heard in mm. 94–97, albeit at an uncommonly subdued dynamic, *piano*. (It had been sounded *forte* in the model R1-statement, m. 16: see example 20.1.) In this case the re-entering soloist intervenes with a variant of the same music (mm. 97–100), which replicates the second modular loop also heard in R1:TR (compare mm. 19–22). At m. 100 the pianist provides a new breakout continuation (S1:\TR[1.2]) to the preceding presentational loops, pushing in this instance toward a modulation in mm. 102–4, and before too long to the first MC (V:HC) as well.[36] Related instances in Mozart, each with its own idiosyncrasies, may be found in the first movements of Piano Concertos No. 8 in C, K. 246, No. 18 in B-flat, K. 456, No. 19 in F, K. 459, and No. 23 in A, K. 488. This is a procedure also favored by Beethoven, as in the Violin Concerto in D, op. 61, and Piano Concertos No. 1 in C, op. 15, No. 3 in C Minor, op. 37, No. 4 in G, op. 58, and No. 5 in E-flat, op. 73.

The effect of this kind of transition is that of the first genuine "partnership" of the piece. Having just begun TR, the orchestra graciously hands over the remaining control of it to the soloist. For its part, the soloist's intervention now suggests an individualized florification, a self-display within a newly "free space," or a blossoming into lyrical or virtuosic figuration. The events found within this freshly opened space vary from piece to piece. They may refer back to certain R1:\TR moments (as reference points, sometimes prompted by the orchestra) or they may follow a course quite different from the R1-pattern. (As always, one should remember that as pre-MC material this "new" TR music may or may not return in the recapitulation: it is under no structural obligation to do so. K. 453's new S1:TR^{1.2}, for instance, is a one-time event that does not reappear.) The medial caesura may be articulated in a number of ways. The soloist may drop out at the last moment, permitting a new tutti interjection (S1:\TI^2) to articulate the MC with appropriate structural force. Alternatively, the soloist may sound the MC, either alone or reinforced by the orchestra. In some cases a second tutti interjection is called upon to provide a highlighted flash of caesura-fill (K. 453, mm. 109–10, example 21.1; K. 218/i, mm. 65–66).

Alternative 2: Solo 1 Transition as Dissolving P⇒TR Merger

As discussed earlier, when S1:\P-space opens with a preface (S1:\P^{pref}), it is common at the cadence-point for the soloist to drop out and the orchestra to re-enter with the R1:\P-theme, as if starting Rotation 2 proper. Once again, one gets the sense of a brief "tutti-obligation" being fulfilled after an initial solo entrance, but here the circumstances are such that the tutti serves as a rebeginning of the expositional rotation. As with the situation just described, the initial R1:\P-tracking usually dissolves soon after the soloist re-enters and eventually directs the music, sometimes with either a new continuation or differing material altogether (S1:\TR^{1.1}), into clear TR-behavior. Reckoned from the tutti entrance, the music takes on the character of a P⇒TR merger: what begins as an orchestral P-statement slides into TR-activity without an intervening I:PAC. This occurs in Piano Concertos No. 9 in E-flat, K. 271 (R1:\P at m. 63, merger at m. 69);[37] No. 20 in D Minor, K. 466 (R1:\P at m. 91, merger beginning at mm. 99–104, with this last bar as unequivocally new material); No. 22 in E-flat, K. 482 (R1:\P at m. 94, merger at m. 106);[38] No. 24 in C Minor, K. 491 (R1:\P at m. 118—also suggesting aspects of R1:\TR, merger at m. 124); and No. 25 in C, K. 503 (R1:\P at m. 112, full merger c. m. 136).

From the (First) MC to S1:\EEC (S- or TMB-Space)

Regardless of the transition type selected, Solo 1's TR drives toward a I:HC, V:HC, or V:PAC MC—or, in minor-mode Type 5s, toward their analogues. Often articulated with a separate orchestral gesture (Tutti Interjection 2, S1:\TI^2, which may or may not have been borrowed from the original R1:\TR), the MC opens the

---

36. In general, the idea of sounding the presentational modules of a sentence initially heard in R1 but following them with a new continuation—at least temporarily suppressing the original continuation—is a common procedure that may crop up in Mozart at virtually any point within an S1.

37. Measure 69 is a new breakout-continuation to the preceding presentational loops. Cf. nn. 16 and 36.
38. Again, m. 106 is a new breakout-continuation to the preceding compound presentational loops. In this case, it is probably also in dialogue with the *sujet-libre* strategy. Cf. the preceding note.

door onto a new, nontonic zone of sonata activity, one almost invariably started by the soloist. This new zone is normally larger in span than was its predecessor in the R1 model. It thereby gives the impression of a purposeful expansion of that model, opening up into new ideas or decorative variants.

The S1:\EEC: A New Requirement in the Type 5 Sonata

The structural-harmonic purpose of this newly opened space, as with Sonata Types 1–4, is to attain and secure the nontonic point of essential expositional closure within Solo 1, the S1:\EEC. But here the situation is complicated by the existence of a previous model-rotation. Unique to the Type 5 sonata, the solo exposition (Solo 1) is not as free to declare its own uncontested EEC, because the most fundamental aspect of S1 is that its events are heard only in relation to the orchestral model-rotation that preceded it. Most important, R1 had articulated a tonic-key R1:\EEC following its own proposal for S-space. In so doing, it had defined the closing boundary of what is to be considered S-space in the movement's later (and larger) exposition and recapitulation. Simply put, any module that the analyst decides is to be considered within R1's secondary-theme zone (pre-R1:\EEC) remains as "S-space defining" (or occupies S-space) within his or her analytical reading no matter where it might be found later in the movement.[39]

As a result, the moment of Solo 1's essential expositional closure, the S1:\EEC, has not one but two defining features. It is not only the first satisfactory perfect authentic cadence that goes on to differing material (as in Types 1–4) but also the first V:PAC (or III:PAC) that has no

R1:\S-module sounded after it within Solo 1. Any recurrence of any R1:\S-module within the broader post-MC space of Solo 1 is to be understood as existing in S-space, even if it had been preceded by an apparent S1:\EEC-effect (a satisfactory V:PAC that goes on to differing material). To sound any R1:\S-module after a seemingly decisive S1:\EEC reopens that PAC, defers the S1:\EEC to the next satisfactory PAC, and converts what one had initially assumed to be C-space into S-space.

S1:\S-space may take one all the way to the trill-cadence close of Solo 1. In this option the considerably delayed S1:\EEC discharges into the orchestral R2. Here the final portions of S will probably also have merged into a new, climactic, and virtuosic display episode (S1:\DE) —another standard, solo-tailored feature of Type 5s (discussed in a separate section below). Such a DE is also to be considered as playing out within S-space. Alternatively, Solo 1's S1:\EEC may elide with the display episode, now to be regarded as S1:\C-space; or it may trigger a C-idea that merges into DE virtuosity, plunging toward the final trill cadence. Wherever the display episode might be placed—either within or after S-space—in one way or another, the solo exposition, S1, will invariably articulate its own S1:\EEC. (Again, however, if any module from R1:\S appears in Ritornello 2—after the S1:\EEC and perhaps even after an expanse of S1:\C—larger S-space is reopened in that R2. As outlined in chapter 19, a differing R2:\EEC can be provided in the *larger exposition*, the one that continues to be pursued, and is often concluded, in Ritornello 2. When it is, the solo exposition and the larger exposition that contains it will have differing EEC-points, as discussed below in the section on Ritornello 2 procedures.)

---

39. The nuance regarding the analyst's decision is advisable and appropriately timed at this point for at least two reasons. On the one hand, the analyst does not "find" conceptual "objective facts" (such as an EEC) that are there in the music for the taking. On the contrary, he or she makes those "facts" through the act of reading the music through a particular conceptual lens, such as Sonata Theory. On the other hand, as discussed in ch. 20, although some R1:\EECs are unequivocal and obvious (to those using this hermeneutic lens), others are subject to interpretation and reasonable disagreement. In part this is because of the extravagantly multimodular aspect of so many R1:\post-MC spaces that often characterizes Mozart's opening tuttis—an aspect that invites one to speculate about a broader or freer treatment of the standard EEC-deferral strategies (outlined in ch. 8).

The Musical Content of S1:\S-Space

Here the principal issue is the thematic relationship of this "new" S-space (in Rotation 2) to that laid out in R1 (Rotation 1). Mozart treated this matter in ingenious ways, providing each concerto with a different solution—though in hindsight an eminently "logical" one. In a few instances R1's proposed S-material is replaced by new S1:\S-material throughout. Sometimes only some of R1's S-music appears in S1:\S-space, placed into a differing context. While it is possible to fill S1:\S-space with only a single S-idea (either R1:\S or something new), S1's secondary-theme zone is more frequently multimodular and carried on at some length. Most often, it stages a mini-drama of contrasting poses, featuring a freer dialogue and more flexible back-and-forth exchange with the orchestra.[40] Multimodular space of this type can impress one as an extraverted display of thematic assemblage, as if Mozart were seeking to stun his audiences with one astonishing idea after another. Most commonly, Mozart laid out S1:\S-space as a trimodular block (S1:\TMB), with a second MC-effect in the middle, followed by a strongly profiled lyrical theme (most often R1:\S1, whose appearance has been "delayed" to serve as TM[3]). Another option was to extend that space through a series of S-modules, several of which might end with a strong authentic cadence (an S-chain, in which intervening V:PACs are subjected to the kinds of EEC-deferrals suggested in chapter 8).

From this perspective each movement creates an individual world of inner relationships and topical moods that may be profitably approached "from within." And yet, taken as a group the multiple realizations of S1:\S-space are relatable also to each other. This suggests certain families of loosely shared strategies among generically available choices, albeit in ways that are not easy to sort into neatly arrayed taxonomies. For this reason, the following classifications are to be taken neither as rigid prescriptions nor as self-sufficient explanations of Mozart's S-spaces. Instead, they are only groupings of relatable choices, the close details of whose separate realizations must also be assessed within the contexts of the movements at hand. Such categories have the primary function not of explanation but of suggesting S-contextual information to the analyst inquiring into any single movement. (Which other movements present similar things? How common an S1:\S-format, broadly construed, is this particular choice?) It may be convenient to divide these S-solutions into two broad groups: those that include some or all of R1:\S and those whose expositional S-space is entirely new. Within each we shall identify subgroups.

Options in Which All or Some of R1:\S Appears in Solo 1

Mozart adopts this general strategy for most of his Type 5 Allegro movements. It provides an important connection between the second parts of Ritornello 1 and Solo 1, implying that the latter continues to be a free expansion of the former. This option also underscores the introductory function embedded to a greater or lesser degree in all R1s (chapter 19). It is surely the older or more traditional option: we recall that in 1793 the (somewhat outdated) Koch mentioned that R1 was to anticipate the "principal melodic sections" of S1 (which he regarded as the providing the real *Anlage* of the piece).[41] In practice, Mozart's approach to this option was variable.

R1:\S Is Taken Over into S1 without Significant Additions or Substitutions. The simplest solution, although an infrequently encountered one, is to have Solo 1 revisit R1:\S as the entirety of its own S-space, though perhaps with some variants, expansions, contractions, or inner repeti-

---

40. In other words, while pre-MC orchestral moments within Solo 1 are most often relatable to the "generic" Tutti Interjections 1 (appended-module or R1:\TR[1.1]) and 2 (reinforcement of the MC), the solo-group dialogue after the (first) MC is less predictable, more *ad hoc.*

41. Koch, *Introductory Essay,* trans. Baker, pp. 210–12. See the discussion in ch. 19, e.g., nn. 27–29 and the related material in the text.

tions. A touchstone example may be found Piano Concerto No. 23 in A, K. 488.[42]

The Opening Module of R1:\S Also Begins Solo 1 S-space but Is Provided with a Different Continuation. A more common strategy is to compose a Solo 1 S-theme that begins with the head motive of the R1:\S-theme (often the presentation modules of a sentence, $R1:\backslash S^{1.1}$)—thus giving the impression of stating "the same theme"—only to provide it with a new continuation around four or five bars later, which may be labeled $S1:\backslash S^{1.2}$ (sometimes merging into a display-episode expansion). Especially in the early concertos and in some of the wind concertos, Solo 1 S-space is filled completely with $R1:\backslash S^{1.1} + S1:\backslash S^{1.2}$ (Piano Concertos No. 5 in D, K. 175, and No. 6 in B-flat, K. 238; Bassoon Concerto in B-flat, K. 191; Horn Concerto No. 2 in E-flat, K. 417).[43] In such situations the suppressed $R1:\backslash S^{1.2}$ and any succeeding R1:\S-modules may be recovered in either Ritornello 2 or 4, or perhaps in both.

A clever combination of this category and the one before it may be found in Piano Concerto No. 16 in D, K. 451, whose S1:\S-space, viewed broadly, presents all of R1:\S but interpolates a different continuation to the initial $R1:\backslash S^{1.1}$ (the "binary loops," $R1:\backslash S^{1.1}$, mm. 128–36, are now followed by $S1:\backslash S^{1.2}$, m. 136, a sudden switch to the minor mode), leading to a first V:PAC (m. 143). This elides with a resumption of the syncopated original continuation, $R1:\backslash S^{1.2}$ (m. 143 [cf. m. 43], keeping S-space open and including its strenuously *forte* R1 contrapuntal variant at m. 152 [cf. m. 52]), all of which merges into a freer display episode and finally plunges into a trill-cadence S1:\EEC, launching R2 at m. 170.

R1:\S Is Treated as an S²-appendix in Solo 1, Following a New S1:\S¹ That Has Led to a V:PAC. In a very few cases, Mozart outfits Solo 1 S-space with a new theme (or set of themes) that proceeds to a V:PAC that we would normally expect to be an opportune S1:\EEC, giving way at once to C-space. Instead, the "ignored" R1:\S reappears as an afterthought-complement to the soloist's S, an S²-appendix or "reminder" from the orchestra. In this strategy S-space is kept open by the reappearance of S-material from Ritornello 1. While this "add-on R1:\S" is a common feature within "R1/S1-synthesis" recapitulations (in which an expositionally "missing" R1:\S is sometimes tacked onto the end of S3:\S-space as an afterthought-appendix following a clear I:PAC in order to bring back all of the requisite material), it is rarer within expositions. Moreover, expositional instances typically bring with them other analytical challenges as well.

A serviceable example, blended with the above category and featuring the ingenious complications typical of the Viennese piano concertos, occurs in Piano Concerto No. 12 in A, K. 414. Elided to the close of what seems to be a sudden V:HC MC-attempt (upbeat to m. 98), a single, "new" compound sentence spins forth at mm. 98–114, at first prolonging that dominant, then proceeding to a clear V:PAC. The S-status of this sentence is ambiguous, particularly since its elided beginning (on V⁷ of E, no less) continues to hold open the MC dominant (as "fill" or "S⁰"). Yet its sentential shape as a whole and its V:PAC conclusion also suggest a striving to be understood locally as an S1:\S-theme. Immediately thereafter, in m. 115, we find $R1:\backslash S^{1.1}$ begun in the orchestra as a "second" S-theme, but, as is common, the soloist replaces its original continuation module ($R1:\backslash S^{1.2}$, m. 41) by a new

---

42. Cf. the slightly differing but related strategy in the first movement of Piano Concerto No. 11 in F, K. 413, whose later, "free" S-spaces are linked by refrain cadences. Unusually, Horn Concerto No. 3 in E-flat, K. 447, provides a shortened version of R1:\S in Solo 1. R1:\S consists of at least three discrete modules (1.1., 1.2., 1.3, mm. 10, 13, and 19), and Solo 1 concerns itself only with the first two, the last of which merges into

a brief drive to cadence, probably to be regarded also as an underdeveloped display episode. Cf. the relatable but more expansive situation in the Oboe Concerto in C, K. 314 (within Solo 1, $R1:\backslash S^{1.1}$ and $R1:\backslash S^{1.2}$ at mm. 78 and 84, merging into a broader, "new" $S1:\backslash^{1.3}$ as a display episode).

43. Cf. n. 42 (Horn Concerto No. 3, Oboe Concerto).

one (S1:\S$^{2.2}$, m. 123, merging into the display episode).[44] On the other hand, in the much-earlier Concertone in C, K. 191—an extraordinary case—the original R1:\S had reappeared (m. 82) only after Solo 1 had laid out an entirely new trimodular block (TMB) within S-space (mm. 56–81). In Beethoven's works the classic instance of a new-theme S1:\S concluding with a V:PAC and proceeding to an appended R1:\S occurs in Piano Concerto No. 4 in G, op. 58 (compound-sentential S1:\S^1, mm. 119–34, non-normatively begun in the orchestra; multimodular R1:\S, elided in m. 134 [= m. 29] and beginning with a sudden "lights-outs" shift to D minor).[45]

Considered broadly, this "S^2-appendix" procedure shares features of two other formal strategies classified in this chapter. Sometimes distinguishing among them is not easy. The first, discussed earlier, is that of a *sujet-libre* S1:\TR that ends with a V:PAC MC and proceeds into a statement of R1:\S as the opener of S-space.[46] In the present case, by contrast, the "new" S1:\S-theme (unlike a *sujet libre*) seems to respond, however uneasily, to a potential MC-gesture in the orchestra, even though, typically, the theme's potential S-status may be compromised by an uncertain or partially still-transitional role of its opening bars. (In other words, some analysts might prefer to construe it as the second half of a TR following a misfired or declined MC.) The second related strategy is the situation in which R1:\S or its initial portions return only as a TM^3 within a trimodular block,

a TM^3 set up by a second apparent MC that is a V:PAC. This situation, though, is more typical of thematically reordered recapitulations than of expositions.

R1:\S (or R1:\S$^{1.1}$) Serves as TM^3 in a Solo 1 Trimodular Block (TMB). Mozart's most frequent strategy for expanding Solo 1-space is to make use of the trimodular-block procedure. Clear instances of it appear in the S1:\S-space of around seventeen—some two-fifths—of his Type 5 first movements, especially in his later or larger-scale compositions, including many of his most well-known concertos.[47] The TMB option, featuring not one MC-effect but two—the occurrence of apparent double medial caesuras—is an even more central feature of concertos than of other types of sonata movements. (Chapter 8 furnished an introduction to TMB basics.) Because this procedure has not been previously isolated as such, this aspect of the concertos has been a perennial source of misinterpretation in the literature.

Within the trimodular-block strategy, Mozart's most common practice within Solo 1—accounting for twelve instances of the seventeen mentioned above—was to pursue a three-stage process that places R1:\S^1 at the end.[48] First, the initial MC-effect is seized upon with a newly-composed S1:\TM^1, a theme identified with the soloist. Second, this thematic idea usually merges into S1:\TM^2 activity on the way to another MC. (At some point TM^2 usually revives a few measures of R1:\TR's pre-MC features,

---

44. Complicating the matter in K. 414/i further, an originally "second" R1:\S-idea—R1:\S^2, mm. 51–58, an S-appendix within R1—is omitted from the exposition. The recapitulation provides a creative recombination of all of these elements. It will incorporate the beginning of the exposition's "new S1:\S^1 theme" much more clearly into TR-space at m. 224—in effect pushing it leftward, out of S-space and in front of the MC. (S1:\S-modules can apparently lose their S-status in recapitulations by being shifted to a position before an MC.) Recapitulatory S-space will now be defined by enriched versions of the double-theme R1:\S$^{1.1}$ at m. 233 (the version with much of the S1:\S$^{1.2}$ continuation and folding in at the end the cadential gesture from the end of S1:\S^1, mm. 251–52) and R1:\S^2 (m. 253), itself now taking on the burden of merging into the display episode.

45. Cf. the minor-mode TM^2 procedure outlined in n. 49 and its accompanying text.

46. Cf. n. 26 and its related text.

47. Here we include, viewing the matter with flexibility, Piano Concertos, K. 242, 246, 449, 453, 456, 459, 466, 467, 482, 503, 537, and 595; Violin Concertos No. 4 and 5, K. 218 and 219; the Flute and Harp Concerto, K. 299; the Flute Concerto, K. 313; and the Clarinet Concerto, K. 622. Cf. n. 48.

48. Cf. n. 47. Of the seventeen cited there the exceptions are Piano Concertos K. 459, 467, 482, and 503, in which the TMB is new, without a clear citation of R1:\S^1, and K. 466, in which R1:\S becomes S1:\TM^1, not S1:\TM^3.

thereby approaching the now-second MC in a parallel way, all the better to lead to the restoration of R1:\S1, the "next step" provided by the R1 model.) Third, the music proceeds to a recovery of R1:\S or its initial modules as TM³, often led off by the soloist, but occasionally begun by the orchestra (in these cases, presumably, as a launching of "its" theme).

While we have identified twelve instances of this compositional choice in the concertos, there remain substantial internal differences among them. The most important include: the occasional "closing" of TM¹ with a V:PAC; differing selections for the two MC cadences (especially when the second of them is a V:PAC); the sometimes uncertain "S-claims" of S1:\TM¹; and the subsequent continuation of TM³, along with its S1:\EEC treatment, an individual matter in the concertos.

A characteristic occurrence, with the expected *ad hoc* idiosyncrasies, may be found in Piano Concerto No. 17 in G, K. 453 (example 21.1). Ritornello 1 had provided a string of S-modules, of which only the repeated R1:\S¹·¹ (example 20.1, mm. 35–42, 42–49) recurs in the solo exposition, as the final element of a TMB. In Solo 1 a transition of the dissolving R1:\TR type (m. 94, example 21.1) leads to a V:HC MC at m. 108 with two bars of fill, the first a solo decorative reiteration, the second an orchestral link into what follows. Non-normatively, Mozart structured TM¹ as a compound period seeking to close with a V:PAC in m. 126 (antecedent, mm. 110–17 by the soloist alone; consequent, mm. 118–126, begun by the soloist but thematically completed by the orchestra, with piano embellishment). The PAC of local TM¹-closure at m. 126 is the less common feature here—a second- or third-level default, which is also present in the Clarinet Concerto in A, K. 622, m. 115. (Were the first-level default active here, S1:\TM¹ would not come to such a point of closure but instead merge into the S1:\TM² that sets up another MC normally built around a half cadence.)[49]

As if registering the potential smugness of this ("too early?") cadence, the major-mode S1:\TM¹ idea—cheerily periodic in its self-satisfaction, suspecting nothing amiss—finds its cadential moment stalled in circular reiterations (mm. 124–25), then switched off by a chilly turn to the minor mode, m. 126. This is also the elided onset of the reactive S:\TM², a head-spinning slide, albeit a sonorously rich one, down the circle of fifths ("What happened?"), accelerating the rate of its precipitous drop downward in mm. 130–31, until it reaches the spectral Neapolitan chord of D, E♭⁶, in m. 132.[50] This low point—hitting bottom—also marks the onset of a typical "recovery" operation. In m. 132 we find a one-bar chromatic hoist upward to a new dominant lock, V of D minor, at m. 133, which also seizes onto a correspondence-measure crux with R1's m. 29, providing the model for the music that follows. Thus the second Solo 1 MC, again a v:HC MC, m. 135, leads "inevitably" to several bars of caesura-fill of the juggernaut $\hat{5}-\hat{4}-\hat{3}-\hat{2}-\hat{1}$ type, which also part the minor-mode clouds and restore the music to major. The R1 model is then pursued further: R1:\S¹·¹ steps forth at m. 139, led by the soloist, and the anticipated repetition, now guided by the orchestra, occurs at m. 146. This time, however, the theme leads

<hr>

49. For examples, see Violin Concerto No. 5 in A, K. 219 (TM¹ and TM² reduced to a mere sentence, with S1:\TM¹ at m. 74 merging at m. 78 into the very brief, dissolving continuation serving as S1:\TM² (=V:HC MC setup); this second MC occurs in m. 80, and R1:\S is then heard as TM³ at m. 81; and Piano Concerto No 14 in E-flat, K. 449 (again, evoking aspects of a sentential structure: S1:\TM¹ at m. 121 merges into a brief, dissolving-continuational S1:\TM² around m. 129, recapturing at m. 131 the original m. 31 and setting up the second MC, built around V:HC, in m. 135; R1:\S follows as TM³, m. 137). See also the similarly sentential aspects in Piano Concerto No. 8 in C, K. 246, where the continuation, S1:\TM² takes off from an only locally "apparent" IAC, m. 64—not a real point of S1:\TM¹ closure.

50. Cf. the reactive behavior of S1:\TM² in the Clarinet Concerto in A, K. 622. After S1:\TM¹ closes with a V:PAC in m. 115, S1:\TM² drops at once to a more desolate vi of V, C-sharp minor; at the same time the clarinet gloomily explores aspects of its bottom register, mm. 118–19 and 122–23). The subsequent continuational "recovery" and return both to the major mode and to the second MC at m. 127 (here V⁷ of V, with fermata) may be compared with the situation in K. 453. Cf. n. 45 and its accompanying text for a related (but non-TMB) case in Beethoven's Piano Concerto No. 4 in G, op. 58.

directly to a V:PAC at m. 153, the S1:\EEC, elided with the display episode, here unfolding in S1:\C-space. (In R1 the S$^{1.1}$ theme had lead to a deceptive cadence, m. 49, and the onset of R1:\S$^{1.2}$, a surprise-effect that Mozart reserved for the seam between the trill-cadence conclusion of S3 and the onset of R4^1 at m. 319.)

In K. 453 both of the MC-effects articulate the same harmonic function: V:HC (mm. 108–9) and V:HC again (more correctly, v:HC, m. 135). Such cases do not follow the norm of the typical deployment sequence of MC-options outlined in chapter 3, in which each option (I:HC, V:HC, or V:PAC) is available more typically as a once-only event. Here in K. 453 the "backing-up" of S1:\TM^2—its crux-like recovery of the pre-MC measures of the TR model provided in R1 (m. 133 = m. 29)—might suggest an attempt to erase the potential S-implications of S1:\TM^1 or conceptually to unravel some of the S-like effects that it might have had by returning to a "point of rotational-sonata-time before S," as furnished in the R1 model. Put another way, the S1:\TM^2 crux with R1 material might imply a musical "wishing" that S1:\TM^1—which in K. 453 had sounded very much like a "real S theme"—might be retucked back on another level of interpretation into a broader TR-space. All of this stages a purposeful uneasiness with simple formal solutions to an unfolding process of expositional expansion of the R1 model. Part of the internal anxiety and resultant sense of depth being expressed stems from the interactions of the standard formal categories among themselves, making available a multitiered set of formal and hermeneutic implications that the analyst may pursue at any level desired.

Situations in which the second apparent MC is a V:PAC followed by the return of R1:\S as TM^3 would be less problematic in terms of the normative MC-deployment sequence, but while

this is a familiar procedure in "rearranged" recapitulatory TMBs (chapter 22), it is less common in expositions. One instance may be found in Violin Concerto No. 4 in D, K. 218. The first MC (I:HC) at m. 65 is reinforced by one bar of orchestral caesura-fill (S1:\TI^2), and S1:\TM^1 begins with solo figuration at m. 66. This merges into quasi-transitional S1:\TM^2 around m. 73 and eventually proceeds to a decisive V:PAC (the second MC) at m. 86. This bar serves also as a crux-measure with the last bar of R1:\TR (m. 86 = m. 18). At this point the soloist begins TM^3, a recovery of the opening module of R1:\S (m. 87 = m. 19), eventually to lead it, though, in a different direction. Another example occurs in Piano Concerto No. 26 in D, K. 537 (S1:\TM^1 begins at m. 128, merging to a lengthy S1:\TM^2 ending with a trill-cadence V:PAC MC at m. 164; R1:\S^1 is elided with this cadence as an "afterthought" TM^3). The "TM^3 as S^2-appendix" situation is also approximated in the ingenious solution found in Piano Concerto No. 18 in B-flat, K. 456. Here the "V:PAC second MC" in question, m. 128, results from the recovery of a much-expanded caesura-fill from R1 (mm. 117–28 = mm. 28–39). In all such cases the recurrence of R1:\S assures that we are to understand S-space to remain open beyond the first V:PAC. This procedure is similar to that of the non-TMB "S2-as-appendix" and the *sujet-libre* TR that ends with a V:PAC—both discussed earlier.

In every TMB situation the potential S-status of TM^1 rises as an issue. As mentioned above, in K. 453 the new-theme S1:\TM^1 (example 21.1, m. 110) initially strikes us in every way as a viable opening of S1:\S-space. It is led off by the soloist; it is obviously thematic; it begins in the proper key and sustains that key, D major (V); it is preceded by an obvious passage of transition; and it has been unmistakably prepared by a V:HC MC.[51] We recall from the discussion in

---

51. Cf. Saint-Foix's nuances regarding this S1:\TM^1 theme in K. 453, *W.-A. Mozart*, IV, 40: "Properly speaking, this subject is not the second subject of the concerto [i.e., it is not R1:\S] but the second subject belonging to the soloist" ("A proprement parler, ce sujet n'est pas le second sujet du concerto, mais le second sujet appartenant au soliste"). Similarly, S1:\TM^1 in Piano Concertos No. 18 in B-flat, K. 456, and No. 21 in C,

K. 467—to cite only two other examples—are referred to as "le second sujet (réservé au soliste)" and "un second sujet, à lui destiné" (4:52, 87). As mentioned earlier (n. 27), Saint-Foix sometimes also regards an S1:\TM^1 as a *sujet libre* (Piano Concerto No. 25 in C, K. 503, "le sujet libre du soliste, sans accompagnement, en *mi bémol*," 4:221), a potentially confusing usage that we do not follow.

chapter 8, though, that other TM¹s are less clear in this regard. It is just as common, if not more so, for a TM¹ to contain signs that it is not viable as an unambiguous S: a premature thematic entry; an inability to sustain itself; a wrong-key or wrong-mode (minor-mode) entrance; and so on. In such cases, TM² functions as a corrective action setting up the more "real S" at TM³. At the one end of a continuum of possibilities, we may situate cases of S1:\TM¹ that do assert a clear S-status. Moving toward the other end, we encounter instances that tilt more toward the role of MC-declined and a prolongation of TR-space. Recognizing the TMB-strategy is the crucial thing, however, which is why TM-labels, rather than S-labels, are appropriate. Merely to identify something as S1:\TM¹ does not imply that we are simultaneously granting it unequivocal S-status.

Examples of the new-theme S1:\TM¹ that seem capable of being regarded as the first expositional S-theme, in addition to that in K. 453, include those found in Violin Concerto No. 5 in A, K. 219 (m. 74); in Piano Concertos Nos. 8 in C, K. 246 (m. 57), 14 in E-flat, K. 449 (m. 121), No. 18 in B-flat, K. 456 (m. 102), and No. 26 in D, K. 537 (m. 128); and in Clarinet Concerto in A, K. 622 (m. 104). Slightly less assertive as S-space openers—but still to be regarded as such—are the S1:\TM¹s found in Violin Concerto No. 4 in D, K. 218 (mm. 66, more figurational than thematic), and Piano Concerto No. 27 in B-flat, K. 595 (m. 107, opening in the minor dominant, F minor). The unusual "wrong-key" start to S1:\TM¹ in Piano Concerto No. 25 in C, K. 503 (m. 148, on E-flat, ♭III of C)—prematurely to cite a concerto that does not include *any* R1 theme in its TMB (a category dealt with further below)—moves one further down the scale of internal "flaws" that cloud one's certainty regarding an immediately perceptible S-status.

More problematic in this regard—more unstable in their S-claims—are S1:\TM¹s that arrive after only a very brief TR or are elided with the first MC (Piano Concerto No. 7 in F, K. 242, m. 74; Flute and Harp Concerto in C, K. 299, m. 68). Even more so (and once again we include here concertos without a restatement of R1:\S in the solo exposition) are Piano Con-

certos No. 21 in C, K. 467, m. 109, and No. 22 in E-flat, K. 482, m. 128, both of which not only provide us with instances of an S1:\TM¹ elided with the potential MC but also simultaneously collapse to the dominant minor—leaping in rashly ("No!"), as if to keep the MC from becoming fully effective.

R1:\S (or R1:\S¹·¹) Serves as TM¹ in a Solo 1 Trimodular Block (TMB). Although deploying a trimodular block is a common strategy of Mozart within Type 5 Allegro movements, there is only one case in which the composer both retained R1:\S¹·¹ and placed it at the beginning of the TMB (as TM¹, leading to a "new" S1:\TM² and TM³) rather than at its end. This occurs in Piano Concerto No. 20 in D Minor, K. 466, m. 115, following a i:HC MC (V of D minor). This is the wistful, initially modulatory idea that had been prepared similarly and had also begun in F major (III) within R1 (example 20.5). Its similar reappearance as the first module of S-space in Solo 1 doubtless alludes back to its ephemerally "hopeful" role within Ritornello 1 (a brief glimpse at the major mode). In Solo 1 its F major is once again sequenced away from (F major, G minor, A minor), but in this case it is just as quickly recovered with the merger into the S1:\TM² dominant-lock (V of F) at m. 124, leading to a III: HC MC at m. 127. A new, still wistful S1:\TM³ is heard at m. 128. Its repetition by the orchestra at m. 136 accomplishes the S1:\EEC at m. 143, elided with the display episode.

Options in Which R1:\S Does Not Appear in Solo 1

This is a less common strategy, one which Mozart entertained seriously starting around 1779, with the Sinfonia Concertante in E-flat, K. 364, and the Concerto "No. 10" for Two Pianos, K. 365. In such cases the soloist or soloists furnish completely new material within Solo 1 S-space, thereby sidelining the S-idea(s) proposed in Ritornello 1. In turn, these new-material options may be placed into one of two categories: those simpler types that are not laid out as trimodular blocks (as in both K. 364 and 365) and those that are (four of the later piano concertos, K. 459, 467, 482, and 503).

This replacing of important aspects of the R1 model with S1 alternatives may be understood in a variety of ways. If we consider this procedure within the internal processes of the piece, it is difficult to regard it as other than an act of self-assertion on the part of the soloist qua "individual" (or qua "individuals" in the case of K. 364 and 365). It is the soloist who insists on dominating S1:\S-space and bringing about an S1:\EEC prepared exclusively on his or her own terms. On the other hand, it is also true that the orchestra participates throughout S1, usually in a supportive dialogue. This suggests that the relationship between the individual and group is not necessarily hostile. Still another reason why S-substitutions within Solo 1 need not be construed reductively, ideologically shoehorned into only agonistic terms, is that some larger sense of collaboration and synthesis between the S-materials of Rotations 1 and 2 always occurs in the larger recapitulation (S3 + R4). The recapitulatory synthesis more likely suggests a broader cooperation between not only two different musical "personalities" but also two different formal layouts within the first two rotations. From this perspective, the governing demonstration is self-referential, that of the "virtuoso Mozart" enacting a show of his own creative brilliance: the initial production, and then the clever solution, of a wittily heightened compositional problem of recapitulatory resolution, including the generically imposed need for the full accounting of an abundance of initially overproliferating musical modules.

The New S1:\S-space Is Not Elaborated as a TMB. In these cases S1:\S is usually formatted as one of the standard shapes also common to R1:\S: period or sentence. The briefest of them is the simple period found in the Sinfonia Concertante in E-flat, K. 364, mm. 126–33, although this one follows a broad and repeated passage of an extraordinarily expanded caesura-fill (mm. 106–25).[52] Somewhat similar, though less problematic in its MC-setup, is the new S1:\S¹ period in Piano Concerto No. 13 in C, K. 415, mm. 93–108.[53] In the Concerto for Two Pianos (No. 10) in E-flat, K. 365, the new S1:\S that at first promises to be a simple period turns out to be one with an undermined consequent, converted into a second half cadence (mm. 104–11). Mozart then treats the two "expectant" phrases as the presentation modules of a broader sentence, whose (also sentential) continuation spans mm. 112–21. New S1:\S sentences also appear in Piano Concerto No. 15 in B-flat, K. 450, mm. 104–19; and in Horn Concerto No. 1 in D, K. 412, mm. 38–51. In each case the new S1:\S-materials will be combined with R1:\S in the recapitulation. Most solutions to this problem are more subtle that that found in K. 450, in which S1:\S returns intact, sounds a I:PAC, and is followed by the return of R1:\S as an S-appendix.

The most unusual new S1:\S-space that is not a TMB is found in one of Mozart's most astonishing first movements, that of Piano Concerto No. 24 in C Minor, K. 491. Here the larger expressive aim of the movement is to suggest being caught within a destructive whirlpool of a fatalistic C minor. One is assailed throughout by recurring nightmare-visions of the thematic representation of that threat, namely the R1:\P motto or *idée fixe*, which sprouts up in various parts of the form. Following an eerily rising *idée-fixe* caesura-fill (mm. 35–44), R1:\S, a compound sentence in C minor, occupies mm. 44–63 and will recur only in a much-rearranged recapitulation, in the same key. In Solo 1 what we find instead is a broad S-chain, comprising five thematic segments, each thematically different and ending with a III:PAC, but each connected conceptually to its predecessor by an obsessively reiterative cadence-figure at the end—as though each segment were being pulled back compulsively to the "identically" repetitive close. S1:\S¹, a sentence, starts at m. 147 and provides the model for the III:PAC refrain-cadence in mm.

---

52. In this respect, K. 364 may seem to house an S1:\TMB whose TM¹ and TM² (represented by the caesura-fill, and ending with a V:PAC) occupy the first elements of the trimodular block. The expanded caesura-fill here is similar to that found in the Symphony No. 35 in D, K. 385, "Haffner," and the Piano Concerto No. 13 in C, K. 415. On this CF type, see ch. 3.

53. In K. 415 the situation is complicated by an ensuing display episode, possibly an S², in which fragmentary elements from R1's caesura-fill are recycled.

155–56. An expanded repetition follows in the orchestra, though a deceptive (non)resolution of the refrain-cadence leads into an unexpectedly broad and multimodular expansion, mm. 165–200, which seeks to close things off with a differing trill-cadence. At this point the unnerving phrase-chain commences in earnest, each segment concluding with a similar refrain-cadence: S1:\S² (mm. 201–20); S1:\S³ (the "uncanny," E-flat-minor reappearance of the *idée fixe*, like a recurrent fear, mm. 220–41); S1:\S⁴ (starting the display episode, mm. 241–49); and S1:\S⁵ (mm. 249–57, with evaded refrain cadence at m. 257, followed by a short expansion to the final trill-cadence and final III:PAC release onto Ritornello 2 at m. 265).

R1:\S Is Replaced by a New TMB. These are the most extreme and complicated cases, ones in which a possibly multimodular R1:\S theme is suppressed in favor of a TMB-complex of new modules, many of which are strongly thematic.[54] This situation occurs only in four piano concertos: No. 19 in F, K. 459; No. 21 in C, K. 467; No. 22 in E-flat, K. 482; and No. 25 in C, K. 503. (Tovey used the last of these as a model in his much-quoted 1903 treatment of Mozart's creative freedom within "The Classical Concerto").[55] Identifying the TMB within S1 is not difficult, although in each case Mozart took pains to suggest a problematized, fragile S1:\TM¹ moving eventually to a more "real S," S1:\TM³. In K. 459 TM¹ (m. 96) seems to arrive too soon, after only the presentation modules of a R1:\TR-sentence, cut short with a tonicized half cadence at m. 95, a still-active dominant (preceded by its own V⁷), subsequently taken as the first MC. Here S1:\TM¹ might initially be understood as a sentence-continuation still to be conceptualized within a not-fully-closed transition. In K. 467 and 482, as cited earlier, S1:\TM¹ is thrust forward as an alarmed, minor-dominant *forte* intervention, as if seeking to block the effect of the first MC (mm. 109

and 128). In K. 503, also mentioned earlier, S1:\TM¹ sets off in the "wrong key," ♭III.

In these situations the most important thing to realize is the seemingly intractable difficulty set up for the recapitulation-to-come. Given the competing sets of S-space modules in R1 and S1, we have too many ideas in play to be absorbed into any normative recapitulatory space. Most often (K. 459, 467, 482) Mozart's solution involved the suppression of S1:\TM¹ in a substantially rearranged recapitulation: this theme is dropped in order to make room for the inclusion, at some point, of R1:\S. When this happens, S1:\TM¹ remains a one-time-event, occurring only in the exposition, a solution that underscores the fragility—apparently the disposability—of that problematized S1:\TM¹ module, not to be taken for the "real S." The most "ample" solution occurs in K. 503, which brings back all of the thematic R1 and S1 S- and TMB-modules in a massive, five-module (three-MC) complex, with R1:\S¹ as the concluder.

The Display Episode (S1:\DE) and the S1:\EEC

One feature of Solo 1's conclusion was *de rigueur* within large-scale Type 5 Allegro movements. This was the appending of a bravura close, often of substantial length, as the final element of the solo exposition, finishing it off in spectacular fashion. This passage has come to be known as the *display episode* (S1:\DE), and it features the climactic spotlighting of rapid-fire technique on the part of the soloist—brilliant runs, scales, arpeggios, vivid demonstrations of invertible counterpoint, compositional models and intensified variants, and the like—all for the purpose of bringing a heady kinetic energy to the brink and then discharging it via a stylized trill-cadence into the elided Ritornello 2. Its function and effect were described in 1999 by

---

54. An early precedent, as mentioned earlier, is the Concertone in C, K. 190, whose Solo 1 features an "all-new" S1:\TMB that is then followed by the recurrence of R1:\S as an S-appendix.

55. See ch. 19, n. 9.

Plantinga, who also helped to stabilize what we regard as the best English-language term for it: "One more predictable element occurs toward the ends of [Solo 1 and Solo 3]. . . . The closing parts of these solos are regularly given over to ebullient virtuoso solo playing—Hans Engel named these sections 'display episodes' [*Spielepisoden*]. Here, thematic matter yields to brilliant passagework that drives inexorably to the end of the section."[56] A characteristic example, whose beginning is elided with the S1:\EEC, may be found in Piano Concerto No. 17 in G, K. 453, mm. 153–71 (example 21.1).

The terminology is worth reflecting on. As Plantinga also mentioned, in the 1840s Carl Czerny had referred to these intensified conclusions as "brilliant passages, which are indispensable in a concerto," while Denis Forman, in 1970, had written about the "piano climax" that was necessary at this point in piano concertos. In 1978 Leeson and Levin, misleadingly, had referred to such a passage merely as an expositional "coda," while in 1991 Küster called it a relatively free "closing group" (*Schlußgruppe*) with "virtuoso elements," a passage often divisible into discrete sections by means of internal "virtuoso cadences" and possible interludes.[57] Engel's term *Spielepisode*, it seems (literally "play-episode"), was rendered into English as "display episode" in a recent translation of writings by Carl Dahlhaus, who had taken over Engel's term to apply in differing contexts.[58]

However it might have filtered into English, it is a serviceable way of describing these dazzling conclusions to S1. On the one hand, they are often defensible as "episodic" insofar as they graft a specialized concluding passage, customarily not much foreshadowed in R1, to the end of S1. And on the other hand, their function, surely, is that of exhibiting a finally attained lavishness of self-display. Calling attention to the virtuosity of the soloist, now singled out as an isolated feature, they dash toward the finish-line marked by the final trill-cadence (V:PAC) and the onset of the elided Ritornello 2.

The Relationship of the Display Episode to the S1:\EEC

As was pointed out in chapter 19, it is possible heuristically to bracket off the solo exposition, Solo 1, as a self-standing conceptual unit. Within this space alone—not considering anything that might happen in the subsequent R2, which typically extends S1 into a "larger exposition"—one may almost always locate an S1:\EEC, even though the full rotation of R1 materials is not yet complete. The placement of this S1:\EEC is variable. One should assume neither that the display episode always occupies S1:\C-space nor that it always brings about the S1:\EEC with its final trill-cadence. Both situations are possible, and both occur in Mozart's concertos. (It can also happen that a DE might

---

56. Plantinga, *Beethoven's Concertos*, p. 13. Cf. Plantinga, p. 263 for a further description of the display episode as it changed over time. Some of what follows above—including the tracing of the Czerny and Forman terms—is also indebted to Plantinga, pp. 13, 73–74, 314 (n. 9), 330 (n. 12). For one source of the term *Spielepisoden* see Hans Engel, *Die Entwicklung des deutschen Klavierkonzerts von Mozart bis Liszt* (Leipzig: Breitkopf & Härtel, 1927), p. 124. The source cited by Plantinga (p. 314, n. 9) is Engel, *Das Instrumentalkonzert* (Wiesbaden: Breitkopf & Härtel, 1974), 2:2.

57. Plantinga, *Beethoven's Piano Concertos*, pp. 73–74, 314, n. 9; Carl Czerny, *School of Practical Composition, or, Complete Treatise on the Composition of All Kinds of Music*, trans. John Bishop (London, [1848]), p. 160; Denis Forman, *Mozart's Concerto Form: The First Movements of the Piano Concertos*, p. 56; Leeson and Levin, "On the Authenticity of K. Anh. C 14.01 (297b)," p. 91; Küster, *Formale Aspekte*, pp. 119–25.

58. For the English term "display episode," see Dahlhaus, *Ludwig van Beethoven: Approaches to His Music*, trans. Mary Whittall (Oxford: Oxford University Press, 1991), pp. 96–105 ("Models of Sonata Exposition"). Citing Engel's work from 1927, Dahlhaus granted that "the virtuoso 'display episode' was impossible to overlook" in solo concertos, but he proceeded to transfer the term to what he called any "nonthematic continuation of the second subject" within a piano-sonata exposition and pointed at some examples from several of Beethoven's earlier ones. The argument is dubious in the extreme: Dahlhaus was grappling with what we call either the multimodular S or the TMB situation and noticing, e.g., that sometimes one of the modules is transitional or nonthematic in character. Moreover the entire argument is set up in terms of lumbering, untenable formal categories heavy with superannuation.

occupy C-space within the solo exposition but be inlaid into S-space in the rearranged recapitulation.)

The clearest cases, and the most common, are those, as in K. 453/i (example 21.1), in which S1:\S-space comes to a clear S1:\EEC and is elided with a contrasting display episode. Here the suddenly "clicked-on" virtuosity concludes the solo exposition as a self-enclosed interpolation occupying S1:\C-space, even though one might find within it fleeting references to ideas from R1:\C or other, non-S portions of R1. (Recurrences of R1:\S material here would keep open S1:\S-space.) There is no formula for producing a display episode, and Mozart's solutions are increasingly clever from at least K. 453 onward. The general situation, though, occurs in many Piano Concertos: Nos. 5, K. 175; 8, K. 246; 10, K. 365; 13, K. 415; 14, K. 449; 17, K. 453; 19, K. 459; 20, K. 466; and 22, K. 482. From time to time, as in No. 18, K. 456, the soloist's virtuoso figuration has already started toward the end of S1:\S-space (m. 146, with the S1:\EEC at m. 149), creating a dovetailed effect. Other examples may be found in Nos. 15, K. 450, and 25, K. 503.

One alternative is to begin S1:\C-space with a thematic statement of R1:\C$^{1.1}$, which before long merges into the display episode (R1:\C$^{1.1}$⇒ S1:\DE). Identifying such cases is highly interpretive. Much depends on the analyst's prior decision about the location of the R1:\EEC and subsequent R1:\C-space—not always an easy decision. Here we suggest six examples. The first two, smaller-scale works, have much reduced display episodes, if they are to be counted as such at all: the Flute and Harp Concerto, K. 299 (S1:\EEC at m. 107) and the Flute Concerto, K. 313 (S1:\EEC at m. 79). The remaining four are: Piano Concertos Nos. 7, K. 242 (S1:\EEC at m. 101), No. 23, K. 488 (S1:\EEC at m. 114, although the following minor-mode module could also be regarded here, as in R1, as an extension of S-space following an attenuated PAC), and No. 27, K. 595 (S1:\EEC at m. 153); and the Clarinet Concerto, K. 622 (S1:\EEC at m. 134).

The remaining option is to begin the DE within ongoing, and now much-expanded, S-space. Thus it may happen that the thematic S-materials do not bring about a conclusive S1:\EEC. Instead, what one assumes is to be the final S- or TMB-module (perhaps even the varied repetition of that presumed last module) dissolves and merges into the display episode (for example, S1:\TM^3⇒S1:\DE). In another option, one might enter into the display episode assuming that it serves as S1:\C only to find motives or modules of earlier R1:\S-material placed into the accompaniment. When either of these situations occurs, the S1:\EEC is to be regarded as deferred until the final trill-cadence. This kind of solo exposition will contain no C-space, and the S1:\EEC occurs at the downbeat of the elided R2. This is the best solution even when the display episode contains internal PACs and shifts of motivic material: the point of the DE, after all, is that it is a single stretch of "similar" music pointed at the final trill-cadence. Examples may be found in Piano Concertos Nos. 9, K. 271; 11, K. 413 (in which refrain cadences keep S-space alive); 12, K. 414; 16, K. 451; 21, K. 467 (R1:\S$^{1.2}$ [*sic!*] at m. 143⇒S1:\DE), No. 24, K. 491 (again, with persistent refrain cadences); and 26, K. 537 (launching the DE with a V:IAC, a quasi-S-appendix, at m. 193).

The Morphology of Display Episodes

Smaller-scale works and many wind concertos make only perfunctory gestures at the display-episode technique. The Bassoon Concerto, K. 191, and the four horn concertos feature merely a slightly activated conclusion of S1, only minimal or no DE-activity. The violin concertos provide more along these lines, but the most extended examples are to be found in the piano concertos. Display episodes are structured in an *ad hoc* manner, appropriate for the mood and local circumstances of the movement in which they are embedded. Still, a few generalizations about them might be helpful.

Most typically, the longer pianistic display episodes are multisectional, divided into demarcated segments often separated by PACs. One commonly finds a chain of lightly accompanied but soloistically vigorous DE-phrases— stock figuration *in excelsis*—one or more of which might conclude with a provisional (but "not good enough") trill-cadence and be directly elided with another phrase, producing a "nonstop" effect. The effect is one of inexorable accumulation, that of approaching the final trill-cadence through multiple stages, each either leveraging up the floridity of its predecessor or simply adding another element to an ever-proliferating virtuosity. Throughout all of this the orchestra typically plays a merely supportive role, occasionally intervening to spur the action onward toward the trill-cadence, although from time to time in the later concertos Mozart elevated some of the orchestral interventions or overlays into special-effect participation or (usually witty) "side-commentary."

The display episode in K. 453/i (example 21.1) is one of modest size for the later piano concertos and is divided only into a single sentential phrase and its expanded recasting. The model phrase is a standard eight bars long (mm. 153–60, launching S1:\C-space) and features a characteristically nonthematic, exercise-like running-pattern in the right hand. It concludes with a V:PAC at mm. 159–60: a familiar cadence-formula decorated lightly with a trill, albeit one predictive of the grander one to follow at mm. 170–71. The elided second phrase is built on the harmonic scaffolding of the first, but it is now expanded from eight to twelve bars (mm. 160–71). Overlaid onto the presentation modules (mm. 160–63, an oscillation of I, V^7, I, V^7) one finds a *buffa*, *Figaro*-like gesture in the winds ("amusing activity underway")—an example of layered orchestral commentary—that recedes into a more typical subordinate role with the expanded continuational windup to the cadence (m. 164). As for the piano, it changes figuration from "new" arpeggios shared between the hands (mm. 160–63), to rapid ascending-scales (mm. 164–67) soon converting back to arpeggios (m. 168) to the inevitable plunge into the unmistakable signals of full conclusion: the grand cadential $\frac{6}{4}$ of arrival (m. 169), formulaically igniting the final trill (on V^7, m. 170) and PAC-triggering of R2 (m. 171).

The technique of model-statement and expanded recasting, as here, is common in the DEs of the piano concertos (as indeed it is throughout Mozart's nonconcerto expositional zones as well). These sometimes display a high standard of contrapuntal ingenuity, brandishing a masterly display of compositional originality wrested out of seemingly stock materials.[59] Similarly unpredictable—but much to be looked for—is any evidence that rotationally participatory or other motivic materials might be concealed (or even openly expressed) within the soloistic display or its accompaniment. As mentioned earlier, if these materials are identifiable as belonging to R1:\S, then S1:\S-space is being extended into the display episode. On the other hand, the appearance of R1:\C suggestions can both confirm the DE as existing in S1:\C-space and help one to interpret the continued rotational material likely to be found in R2.

Display-Episode Variants: Playing with Signs[60]

That the obligatory display episode is recognizable by its grasping onto stock virtuoso-figuration makes it an ideal playground for the manipulation of those formulas into local surprises and ad hoc adaptations. Mozart's occasional decisions to make the DE rotationally participatory through a partial sharing of R1:\S or C modules illustrate one possibility. Another is the mixing of more thematic orchestral material into some DEs, as with the four-bar *buffa*-commentary in K. 453/i, mentioned above. In another example, Piano Concerto No. 19 in F, K. 459, the first portion of the DE (m. 149) is shot through with sprouting R1:\P "march-motto" references, which amusingly seek to close the first phrase on their own terms (mm. 160–62), though the attempt is wittily undermined by evasion (I^6,

---

59. For a closer discussion of the wide array of differing techniques that Mozart used to produce internal variants in piano-concerto display episodes—imaginative elaborations of standard voice-leading structures, the "swapping around of hands" and textures, the regular patterning of cadences, and so on—see Roman Ivanovitch, "A Practical Theory of Variation," ch. 3 of "The Process of Variation in the Music of Mozart" (Ph.D. diss., Yale University, 2003). In part, the subtitle for the next section, "playing with signs," was suggested by Ivanovitch's citation, in a different context, of V. Kofi Agawu's much-noted *Playing with Signs* (Princeton, N.J.: Princeton University Press, 1991).

60. Cf. the preceding note.

m. 163) and an unexpected "backup" recovery of R1:\TR$^{1.3}$ (taken from m. 32). The sudden withdrawal of the soloist for two tutti interventions in Piano Concerto No. 25 in C, K. 503, mm. 195–98 and 202–4—participatory spurs toward closure—is also countergeneric, as is the interruption of the soloist for the gleamingly lyrical moment for the winds in Piano Concerto No. 27 in B-flat, mm. 164–70.

The most conventional sign of all is the preparation for and execution of the expanded trill-cadence. This is the final, *forte* signature-flourish that wraps up the S1-package and triggers the start of R2. (A similar flourish is expected at the ends of S3 and the cadenza in R4.) As such the onset of a pronounced cadential trill serves as a generic announcement that the soloist is now finishing and Ritornello 2 is being cued to enter on schedule. Mozart's frequent practice of providing "false," insufficient, or undermined "early" trill-cadences within the DE—only to pursue that display-episode section into a varied repetition or new module—has already been remarked upon as one aspect of his strategy of building intensity through the frustration of expectations. One amusing deformation occurs in Piano Concerto No. 13 in C, K. 415, in which the piano delivers a fully executed, obviously "final" trill-cadence (m. 132–33) only to find that the orchestra fails to enter with an elided R2. (Apparently the trill-cadence was sounded an octave too low?) The piano finds itself stranded in silence and is obliged to crank up the DE-engine on its own one more time (using R1:\C^3 material) at m. 133, leading finally to the more effective trill-cadence (in the generically correct octave) at mm. 147–48.

Beethoven, particularly in his middle-period concertos, sought ways of either heightening this trill-cadence moment or submitting it to surprising deformations. In Piano Concerto No. 3 in C Minor, op. 37 (example 21.7), one hears a solo-trill for a full seven bars, mm. 219–25. More to the point, the trill is first broached "early," at the moment that the cadential $^6_4$ of E-flat major is attained (m. 219—normally the trill sounds above a subsequent V^7), at a *piano*

dynamic, and on the "wrong" pitch, $\hat{1}$ (E$\flat_6$) instead of the customary $\hat{2}$ (here, F$_6$). This permits the audible staging of an adjustment in the trill, nudged up chromatically to F$_6$, $\hat{5}$, in mm. 222–23, prompted by the orders of the inlaid R1:\P march head-motive in the winds. The mysteriously subdued *piano* dynamics throughout all of this provide a sense of unnatural quiet, of something powerful being held back in what ought to be a climactic spot. At m. 225 the dam bursts. Suddenly *fortissimo*—the moment of decision— the solo breaks out of its dynamic confinement for a spectacular four-octave plunge downward into the cadence at m. 227, a dramatic gesture well described by Plantinga as one of the "highly distinctive dive-bomber-like cadences ending the three big solo sections of the first movement."[61] What follows is R2 at m. 227, here a major-mode restatement of R1:\C^3 (from m. 98), preserving the ongoing sense of expositional rotation, since that module had not been sounded in S1.

The idea of a quietly prolonged trill at this moment, changing pitches and leading finally to a decisive concluding gesture, resurfaced in Beethoven's Violin Concerto in D, op. 61 (mm. 205–24, with the added twist of a deceptive cadence into Ritornello 2, m. 224). An extraordinary variant of it would appear, more deformationally, in Piano Concerto No. 4 in G, op. 58 (example 21.8), in which a notable trill (here a double-trill) is first attained in m. 166, *forte*— as expected—but within four bars is choked down to a *diminuendo* fading-away for a rapt high-register *piano* restatement, *dolce e con espressione*, of R1:\S$^{1.3}$. Thus the soloist, at first plunging efficiently toward Ritornello 2, undergoes a change of mind, seeking now to stop linear time, reluctant to bring such beauty to an end and wishing to back up for one more statement of R1:\S$^{1.3}$ in a wondrous recovery ("Wait! Did you hear that theme? Did you realize what it meant?"). Eager to press forward—notice also the crescendo-pressure in mm. 172–73—the impatient orchestra, uncued by a trill (!), cuts the reverie short after four bars with R2, rushing in at m. 174, mid-phrase, to complete on

---

61. Plantinga, *Beethoven's Concertos*, p. 156.

EXAMPLE 21.7   Beethoven, Piano Concerto No. 3 in C Minor, op. 37, i, mm. 217–31

EXAMPLE 21.7   *(continued)*

its own terms what the soloist was unwilling to end. The result is an R2 that is not articulated as a separate, post-solo-expositional block. Instead, the solo exposition does not close at all but moves directly into a larger-expositional R2 completion. This may also be understood as a structural ellipsis at the moment of the shift, one occasioned by the soloist's stalling on R1:\S[1.3].[62]

*Ritornello 2 and Its Role in the
Larger Exposition*

Whatever its divergences from the modular layout provided in R1, the solo exposition provides a complementary commentary on or reaction to that earlier succession. As it does so, S1 also traces its way through a rotation (Rotation 2) that should be compared, moment to moment, with R1's layout, the model to which it responds. Here one finds as a virtually invariable norm that S1 stops short of executing a full rotation. (The relevant concept of fullness was established in R1, bordered by recognizable beginning- and ending-modules.) S1's display episode and final trill-cadence, signaling the end of the solo exposition, bring us rotationally only to a point that is short of the real conclusion laid down by the Rotation 1 model.[63] Passages

corresponding to R1's concluding modules have not yet been attained.

From a textural point of view, as Tovey underscored in 1903, one goal of R2, beyond marking an arrival-point in the form and moving us onward to the next phase,[64] is to provide an enhancement of the merely "brilliant" cadential conclusion of S1—as if this display of the "powerful in sound" had been built up to by the display episode and triggered by the trill-cadence.[65] R2 provides the unmistakable impression of an ardently supportive orchestral celebration of the final V:PAC simultaneously achieved by the soloist. Because of the near-invariability of this affirmational *éclat* ("Yes!"), the relatively infrequent instances in which the beginning of R2 instead undermines the soloist's PAC with a deceptive cadence, either sternly or amusingly ("No!")—usually onto ♭VI—are worth noting: in Viotti's once-famous Violin Concerto No. 22 in A Minor, for example, or in Beethoven's Triple Concerto in C, op. 56 (m. 225) and his Violin Concerto in D, op. 61 (m. 224).

And yet beyond cadential affirmation it is also a task of Ritornello 2 to seek to complete the still-ongoing Rotation 2 by supplying some or all of the missing modules from the end of R1. It may do this either beginning directly at the start of R2 (for example, with an R1:\C module not reached in S1) or only after the interpolation

---

62. One might add, for the sake of completeness, that the Fourth Concerto's successor, No. 5 in E-flat, op. 73, provides a monumentalized display-episode drive toward the end of S1 but replaces the expected trill-cadence with a spectacular contrary-motion flourish in the piano, flaring outward toward both extremes of the piano's register (mm. 225–27).

63. K. 107 no. 2, discussed in ch. 19, is a rare and odd exception.

64. Rosen's characterization of R2 as essentially a transition, *Sonata Forms*, rev. ed., p. 85, is potentially misleading.

65. Tovey, "The Classical Concerto," pp. 9–10. Cf. ch. 19, n. 21 and related text.

EXAMPLE 21.8 Beethoven, Piano Concerto No. 4 in G, op. 58, i, mm. 164–82

Example 21.8 *(continued)*

EXAMPLE 21.8   *(continued)*

of a suitably energetic but rotationally neutral initial module or two (often R1:\TR¹·¹)—options to be discussed below. By doing so, as also demonstrated in chapter 19, it reopens the semi-autonomous solo exposition into a larger exposition that measures itself against the R1 model. Whatever the strategy employed here, at some point R2, as one of its central features, will continue the rotation that had been left incomplete by S1. (This is one reason why Irving's recent characterization of the second tutti as the "tutti 'codetta'" is misleading.)[66]

In this task R2 may provide a revisiting of all of the relevant final R1-modules, bringing R2 to a rhyming close with R1 (only now in V or III, not in I). This is the least problematic case, presumably the traditional default-choice, and it occurs with some frequency in Mozart,

either concluded with an emphatic final caesura or elided or flush-juxtaposed with the onset of S2 (Piano Concertos K. 175, 238, 242, 414, 415, 450, 456, 466, 482, 491, and 537). On the other hand, R2 might begin to provide that revisiting but then fall short of making it all the way to the full rotation's end, perhaps dissolving away from completion in a modulatory link to S2 (the developmental space); perhaps being interrupted or shattered apart before reaching the end; or perhaps simply omitting the final cadential or "*piano*-afterthought" module that is characteristic of many R1 endings. The larger-expositional Rotation 2 (S1 + R2) may be judged to be either complete or incomplete, depending on these circumstances. One should also be aware that the larger-recapitulatory rotation-to-come (normally R3⇒S3 + R4) will always be com-

66. Irving, *Mozart's Piano Concertos*, e.g., pp. 19–20, 45–47.

plete, bringing back at the end any concluding modules that might have been missing from the end of R2 (and thus suppressed since the end of R1). In these cases the "unfinished" larger exposition, Rotation 2, can be understood to aspire to a completeness that it does not attain in fact. Only the larger recapitulatory synthesis, with its drive toward a full inclusion and resolution, will manage to put together a full rotation of both R1 and S1 elements. Under these circumstances the larger recapitulation, as a whole, may be heard as the *telos* of the ongoing rotational strivings.

The R2:\EEC

If the missing but "next-in-line" modules that R2 now supplies were ones that were originally located in R1:\C-space (R1:\C^1, R1:\C^2, and so on), then the previously attained S1:\EEC in Solo 1 continues to stand as the EEC of Rotation 2, the larger exposition. If any of R2's modules, however, come from R1:\S-space— things that had been replaced by differing music in S1—then we consider S-space to have been reopened in R2.[67] The effect is as if R2 backs up to recapture its original manner of producing the R1:\EEC-prototype, now claiming its right to accomplish this in R2 as well, beyond what had happened in Solo 1. A typical example can be found in the first movement of Piano Concerto No. 8 in C, K. 246. Here S1:\S-space had sounded R1:\S$^{1.1}$ as the presentational onset of a sentential S1:\TM^3 (mm. 73–76) but had suppressed the expected R1:\S$^{1.2}$, a frequent ploy in Mozart, in favor of a differing continuation (mm. 77–81, producing the S1:\EEC at m. 81). Elided with the DE's trill-cadence, R2 jumps in at once with the missing S1:\S$^{1.2}$ at m. 91, which produces its own V:PAC at m. 97, closing off that newly revived S-space.[68] This is an EEC-effect pertaining to the larger exposition, overriding that of the earlier S1:\EEC. We refer to such a moment as the R2:\EEC.

Depending on whether R1:\S modules are recovered within it, R2 may or may not contain an R2:\EEC point. If it does, it provides a "second" EEC operative from the perspective of the larger exposition, while the S1:\EEC remains in play only secondarily. If it does not, it "accepts" the S1:\EEC provided in the solo exposition. In either case the hermeneutic implications regarding an implied individual-group interaction are self-evident and should be folded into any larger consideration of the movement in question. It is also possible, though rare, for an R2 to reopen S-space with the inclusion of a "missing" R1:\S module but then to be unable to proceed to a V:PAC that would close off that space. Any such reopened S-space that lacks an R2:\EEC is to be considered within the category (chapter 8) of a failed [larger] exposition, even though its solo exposition had produced the expected S1:\EEC. Such a situation occurs, for instance, in Piano Concerto No. 16 in D, K. 451, in which the repetition within R2 of what we regard as R1:\S$^{1.4}$, m. 185, dissolves into the developmental space, S2, before producing another V:PAC.[69] More common than such R1:\S dissolutions within R2-space, however, are R1:\C dissolutions, which leave any attained R2:\EEC intact, although subsequently problematized.

Option 1: R2 Begins with a Rotationally Inert Space before Shifting into Rotationally Participatory Modules (R1:\TR$^{1.1}$ and Other Openings)

This alternative is the one most frequently encountered in Mozart's concertos. Here the rotationally participatory modules do not begin at the outset, although they do appear several bars later. One presumption would be that in style or tone these later modules, perhaps more continuational or codetta-like, could not serve as effective R2-igniters. Since their appearance is delayed, the ongoing rotation is temporarily suspended, while the orchestra sounds an appropriately spring-loaded, *forte* outburst to launch

---

67. A larger account of the logic behind this was provided in the K. 107 analyses at the end of ch. 19.
68. Unusually, a "new C" afterthought-tag, not heard in R1, follows this to conclude R2, mm. 97–99.

69. Cf. the more analytically challenging situation in Piano Concerto No. 14 in E-flat, K. 449.

R2 in proper style. This type of R2 subdivides into two portions. The first is a rotationally inert or neutral space that in principle could be filled in with anything, although the material most often interpolated here is the assertive initial module of R1:\TR, devised in advance within Ritornello 1 to take on this role. This merges, sometimes mid-phrase, into the second portion, a rotationally participatory section, a recovery of R1:\S- or C-modules, which may or may not bring Rotation 2 to a full completion.[70] When confronting this kind of R2, one needs to pose some basic questions. Is the rotationally inert module that begins Ritornello 2 the standard one, R1:\TR$^{1.1}$, or is it something else? Where is the precise point at which it shifts into rotational R1:\S- or C-material? How is this merger accomplished? What R1:\S- or C-material is it? And is the remainder of the rotation parallel or nonparallel with the ending of R1?

That this use of R1:\TR$^{1.1}$—or other alternatives—contravenes the expectations of normal rotational succession ("out of order") is not an interpretive problem. One should neither regard its appearance at the opening of R2 as puzzling or random nor suppose that it challenges the larger theory of rotations in any fundamental way. Instead, one comes to realize that we are confronting specialized modular behavior within the Type 5 sonata. In some of its realizations the Type 5 sonata is outfitted with a few structural slots—a zone of expanded caesura-fill, perhaps, or the opening sections of R2, R4^1 and R4^2—that may be filled in with music that carries no immediate rotational implications. Within the Ritornello 2 option under consideration here, the first portion of R2 is to be construed as a free zone or blank whose contents need not be held up to the scrutiny of rotational expectations. Its main purpose would seem to be textural, along the lines of what Tovey called "the concerto principle"—that of engineering things in order to display with self-evident de-

light "the antithesis between one and many," of making "the best effect expressible by opposed and unequal masses of instruments or voices" through the climactic vitality of its local, emphatic onset along with, we might add, some implication of a command to drive the music forward to the next stage.[71]

Although Mozart usually mixes complications into each of his R2s, a sense of the normative may be gotten, paradoxically, from an expressively extraordinary first movement, that of the Piano Concerto No. 20 in D Minor, K. 466 (example 21.9). As is customary, Ritornello 2, in F major, elides with the final trill-cadence of the display episode (m. 174): a dovetailed triplet-upbeat in the bass gives the elision an extra push. Mm. 174–84 revisit most of R1:\TR —which in this case had not appeared in the solo exposition—turning its originally "demonic" minor-mode model (mm. 16–26) into a still-turbulent major (though notice the "grinding" minor-mode mixture in mm. 179–80). At the downbeat of m. 185 the music splices to a cadential figure that had been typical of the end of what we regard as R1:\C$^{1.3}$: mm. 185–86 (compare with mm. 64–65, 69–71). Since some of the preceding display episode had been based on R1:\C$^{1.1}$ (m. 153 = m. 44), this R1:\C$^{1.3}$ module is one of the next modules in line: shifting into even part of it at m. 185 changes what had been rotationally inert in R2 into something rotationally participatory. The correspondence measures are now pursued further, bar-for-bar. Mm. 186–92 provide a major-mode version of R1's last module, the final "afterthought" R1:\C^2 (originally in minor, mm. 71–77), a close to R2 that is rotationally complete and rhymes with the ending of R1. (In this case, the correspondence bars continue beyond R2, as the developmental-space S2 opens with a redeployment of the S1:\P^{pref}, m. 192.)

A more complicated situation—arguably more "typical" in its idiosyncrasy—may be

---

70. Irving, *Mozart's Piano Concertos*, p. 46, sensed the general pattern but was unable to make much of it: "The choice of material [for the second tutti] is impossible to categorise exactly, although there is a tendency to 'telescope' phrases from near the beginning and near the end of the first tutti."

71. Tovey, "The Classical Concerto," pp. 6–7. Our view would make something less of the notions of "antithesis" and "opposition"—or at least to downplay their potentially hostile implications, since, one presumes, cooperation and staged interplay of differences are also expressive options.

EXAMPLE 21.9 Mozart, Piano Concerto No. 20 in D Minor, K. 466, i, mm. 171–95

EXAMPLE 21.9   *(continued)*

found the first movement of Piano Concerto No. 17 in G, K. 453 (Example 21.1). Here the *forte* R2 rushes in at m. 171 with the standard R1:\TR[1.1] module, which had first been heard at m. 16 (example 20.1). But in this piece, unlike the situation in K. 466, R1:\TR[1.1] had also been used to begin Solo 1's transition-space, in m. 94, albeit damped down to a quieter, *piano* dynamic. Thus its role as the lead-module of R2 is not only "out of rotational order" (a TR-module should not succeed the S-modules of Solo 1) but is also redundant within the rotation—something that may or may not happen, depending on the S1 transition type. Both aspects argue on behalf of the rotationally inert conceptual status of this opening portion of R2.

In K. 453, R2 is unusually fragmentary and compressed. The normative R1:\TR[1.1] is tracked for a mere three bars (mm. 171–73 = mm. 16–18, now in V). A two-bar new link (mm. 174–75) is then written in to join with the final measures of the rotationally participatory R1:\S[1.2] (mm. 176–77 = mm. 55–56). This simultaneously reopens the S-space left behind in the solo exposition, and a new moment of larger expo-

sitional closure, the R2:\EEC, is attained at m. 178 (mirroring the R1:\EEC at m. 57). At this point Mozart's more normative practice, as in K. 466/i, would be to elide directly into the next available module, here R1:\C[1], the first module of R1:\C-space (a TR-based module heard in mm. 58–69). Instead, at m. 178 he omitted R1:\C[1] and skipped forward, via an ellipsis, into the R1:\C[2] module (mm. 178–81 = mm. 69–72). Notwithstanding the absent R1:\C[1], R1:\C[2] still preserves the sense of progress through the rotation. But not for long: this idea is cut short in m. 181. Rotationally the larger exposition is broken off here, two bars short of a conclusion that would rhyme with the end of R1. Substituting for that *forte* conclusion (mm. 73–74, which will be restored only in R4[2]) is a *piano* cadential figure at m. 182, meeker and more submissive (whose rhythm recalls that of mm. 13–14 and the characteristic imprint of the sighing syncopation in R1:\S, mm. 36, 38, 43, 45, and so on). But it, too, is undermined with a deceptive cadence onto ♭VI of V, B-flat major, at m. 184, the start of S2 and the developmental space.[72]

Retracing its essential features once again: K.

---

72. This deceptive cadence, of course, was anticipated by the similar one at R1:\S[1.2], m. 49—which will return

only once more, as the surprising, deceptive-cadence onset of R4[1] at m. 319.

453's larger exposition is provided with a new R2:\EEC (m. 178), although Rotation 2 as a whole is left unclosed, lacking a final authentic cadence. R2 also divides into the usual two sections, a rotationally inert initial three measures bringing back R1:\TR$^{1.1}$ and a rotationally participatory section beginning with material from R1:\S$^{1.2}$ at m. 176. In this case the two sections are connected with a free two-measure link, mm. 174–75. (It is more common to shift from the first to the second section directly, without a newly composed link.) Most surprising is the additional ellipsis to an only partially realized R1:\C^2 at mm. 178–81. Beyond registering the mere details, though, one should also attend to their larger expressive effect. The impression given by this much-foreshortened R2 is that what starts out to be a normative succession shatters into modular shards shortly before or around the moment of the R2:\EEC. We are presented with a sudden crack-up, a musical wreckage in which only angular and edgy scraps are still audible. The undermining of the final cadence at m. 184 only adds to this effect of a ritornello-space of unanticipated troubles. What is more often a space of pure affirmation finds itself in near-disarray halfway through.

While each case invites individual attention, instances of a two-section R2 beginning with an inert R1:\TR$^{1.1}$ and shifting into a rotationally participatory R1:\S- or C-module abound in the first movements of Mozart's concertos. In this category may be cited the Concertone, K. 190; the Bassoon Concerto, K. 191; the Violin Concerto No. 3, K. 216; the Flute and Harp Concerto, K. 299; and the Piano Concertos, K. 238, 450, 451, 453, 456, 466, 467, 488, and 537. Obviously related is the situation in Piano Concerto No. 24 in C Minor, K. 491, whose R2 begins with a varied version of R1:\TR$^{1.2}$ (compare m. 265 with m. 16). Beethoven's Violin Concerto, op. 61, contains an R1:\TR-based opening to R2, while his Triple Concerto, op. 56, provides an interesting variant, that of beginning R2 with the transition material first heard in Solo 1, S1:\TR$^{1.1}$. (As mentioned earlier, both opp. 56 and 61 also feature a deceptive-cadence opening.)

Once the larger concept of an R2 beginning with a rotationally blank or neutral space is grasped—it is an important feature of Mozart's concerto practice—it is easy to imagine that that space might be filled in with things other than the most standard choice, a reactivation of R1:\TR$^{1.1}$. Here is a review of two other options.

R2 Begins with Altogether New Material. If one of the central concerns of the blank-space opening of R2 is to provide a sense of *forte* cadential affirmation, then it could be filled in with stock figuration new to that moment—a generic interpolation—even though in some cases one might here and there identify mild correspondences with certain motives earlier in the movement. In some early concertos the new-material opening continues all the way to the end of R2, in which case there is no shift to rotationally participatory modules and R2 is occupied by essentially new figuration throughout. This happens in the second of Mozart's J. C. Bach adaptations, K. 107 no. 2 (chapter 19), and in Violin Concerto No. 1, K. 207. More often, the rotationally inert stock figuration does give way to modules that pursue the larger-expositional rotation further, R1:\S- or C-modules. Examples occur in Violin Concerto No. 2, K. 211 (here the opening of R2, m. 53, may be derived from the fleeting caesura-fill triplets of m. 30); Piano Concerto No. 7, K. 242; and the Sinfonia Concertante, K. 364. As always, Rotation 2 may or may not be presented as complete.

R2 Begins with an R1:\P Module. This is a potentially problematic choice, since R1:\P is usually taken to mark the onset of a new rotation. Yet in Mozart's concertos—at least in the Allegro movements—this concept is normatively alien to R2-space, which is nearly always concerned with providing a larger extension to the exposition.[73]

---

73. Occurrences of P-based R2 openings in Mozart's slow movements can sometimes suggest a different rotational interpretation. In the B-flat-major Andantino of Piano Concerto No. 14 in E-flat, K. 449, the R1:\P opening of Ritornello 2, m. 52, does begin a new, developmental rotation, albeit one that begins in the "wrong key" (A-flat, ♭VII!) as a result of a tonally curious twist at the end of the preceding solo exposition.

In situations in which this "P-opening" eventually shifts into a more rotationally participatory module, from R1:\S or R1:\C, it seems clear—again, at least in Mozart—that the initial R1:\P is to be understood as rotationally inert, functioning as a head-motive wild card (chapter 20) interpolated at this point. The *locus classicus* is found in the Flute Concerto in G, K. 313, whose R2 begins with an R1:\P variant (m. 91)—even touching on R1:\TR[1] at m. 97 (= m. 9)—that shifts to a recovery of R1:\C[2] in the concluding mm. 100–3 (= mm. 27–30, slightly altered). Related situations occur in the first movements of Piano Concertos No. 5, K. 175 (R2 begins with R1:\P[1.2]), No. 13, K. 415, and No. 19, K. 459.[74] The K. 415 case is telling: the R2 version of the R1:\P[1.1] is much intensified—quite different from the *piano* version heard at the movement's beginning—which suggests that what might be evoked here is a "hypothetical" P-based R1:\TR (the more standard option) that never existed in Ritornello 1. And in K. 459, R2 is saturated throughout with wildcard R1:\P-material, with no shift to rotationally participatory modules.

Option 2: R2 Begins with an R1:\C Module Unsounded in S1

Unlike option 1, this strategy, along with option 3 below, opens R2 with rotationally participatory material. Thus it does not begin with a rotationally inert space, the key feature of option 1. While option 2 is not the most frequent course of action selected in Mozart's concertos—option 1 is the more common choice—beginning R2 with an energetic, *forte* R1:\C module does result in the analytically simplest situation, since it provides no R2:\EEC complications and in virtually all cases resumes the modular progress of the rotation that had been temporarily suspended with the S1 display episode. Its back-reference to the rotational model provided in R1 is unmistakable, and Mozart normally has the remainder of R2 proceed in order, moving onward to any additional R1:\C-modules that are waiting in line, whether or not the rotation is brought to a full completion. The R1:\C[1] opening may be found in Violin Concerto No. 5 in A, K. 218, and Piano Concertos No. 9 in E-flat, K. 271, No. 12 in A, K. 414, No. 22 in E-flat, K. 482—and in Beethoven's Piano Concerto No. 2 in B-flat, op. 19. An R1:\C[2] opening occurs in Mozart's Violin Concerto No. 4 in D, K. 218, and Piano Concerto No. 27 in B-flat, K. 595.

Option 3: R2 Begins with an R1:\S Module Unsounded in S1

This third-level-default option also begins R2 in a rotationally participatory way. Since S1:\S-space had already moved past (and bypassed) this module in the solo exposition—perhaps even moving into S1:\C-space—reinstating it here in R2 has two structural effects: it gives the impression of backing up to recapture an earlier sense of S-space; and by doing so it reopens the S1:\EEC, promising a new, R2:\EEC down the road. The most commonly encountered R2-opening of this type begins with R1:\S[1.2], which is often the continuation of an R1-sentence that had been replaced by a different continuation somewhere in Solo 1. An R2 that begins in this way usually does not contain a sudden ellipsis or shift to later R1:\C-modules (the standard practice of option 1). Instead, it is more often led to new material or simply extended throughout all of R2—which, again, may be rotationally incomplete, omitting some R1:\C-modules. Examples of the R1:\S[1.2] opening occur in Piano Concertos No. 8, K. 246, and No. 10 for Two Pianos, K. 365. An R1:\S[1.3] opening is found in the Oboe Concerto, K. 314. Also to be noted are Piano Con-

---

(See the brief discussion of this unusual movement in Hepokoski, "Back and Forth from *Egmont*," p. 149.) And in the Andante of Piano Concerto No. 17 in G, K. 453, the brief R2 also begins the developmental space with a statement of the "invocational" R1:\P alone, mm. 64–68.

74. Also related are the fourth movement of the Ser-

enade in D, K. 203, and the third movement of the Serenade in D, K. 204. But these present anomalous situations. In both, R2 outlines a succession of modules that could be considered a separate rotation. K. 204/iii is especially noteworthy, since it revisits, with only small variants, all of R1, now in the dominant.

certos No. 11, K. 413 (whose R2 begins with what we regard as R1:\S³, not an R1:\C-module), and No. 14, K. 449 (beginning with R1:\S²·²).

Option 4: Alternative or Quasi-Deformational R2 Spaces

This category is provided to cover individual-ized or *ad hoc* choices that are decidedly unusual. For all of Mozart's separately crafted treatments of R2-space, few of them are not treatable as varied realizations of options 1–3. It is perhaps only to call attention to something genuinely unique that one might wish to suggest its in-clusion within the catch-all option 4. A few R2 deformations in Mozart are less concerned with thematic-modular selection than they are with unexpected solo-group interaction, as in the non-normative solo participation in Piano Concerto No. 9 in E-flat, K. 271, mm. 135–47. Others are more clearly thematic. One such case might be Horn Concerto No. 1 in D, K. 412, in which a normal conclusion to R2 (m. 61) does not yield to the soloist at once but appends its own start to the next rotation by sounding R1:\P (m. 62) as a modulatory link to the de-velopment proper. Another is found in the R2 of the Piano Concerto No. 23 in A, K. 488 (in-terestingly, the one with the most straightfor-ward solo exposition vis-à-vis the R1 model). This begins with the standard R1:\TR¹·¹ open-ing (m. 137) but breaks that off to conclude with a new, lyrical theme(!), suddenly wistful and leading only to a tentative, V:IAC conclu-sion (mm. 143–48), an unanticipated idea that will intrude repeatedly into the S2 development and be included in the recapitulation as well. Yet another occurs in Piano Concerto No. 25 in C, K. 503, in which the initial R1:\TR¹·¹ (m. 214) shifts not to the usual post-MC mod-ule but only to another transition module, R1:TR¹·³, at the upbeat to m. 219, with the result that the previously deformational R1:\V:PAC MC from m. 50 now recurs, at the same pitch level, as the conclusion of R2 (m. 228).

Some Beethovenian R2-spaces are also curi-ous enough, by Mozart's standards, to consider

in this category. Both Piano Concertos Nos. 1 and 3 reverse the procedure outlined in option 1. They begin, that is, with a rotationally active module (R1:\S¹·² in No. 1; R1:\C³ in No. 3) and conclude with a wrenching shift to a re-capturing of rotationally inert pre-MC material from R1:\TR. The effect of this is to outfit R2 with a close that rhymes with the R1:\MC, not with, as is more customary, the end of R1. In No. 1 the MC-music is reshaped to produce a convincing authentic cadence in V, not a half cadence, as in R1. No. 3's R2, however, repli-cates the half-cadence effect of R1, only now in v, G minor (m. 249—the R1:\C³-module had modulated from E-flat to V of G minor): thus R2 does not close with an authentic cadence. (A few of Mozart's R2s also end with a preparatory half cadence, as will be noted below, but except for the already mentioned situation in K. 503, they do not replicate the R1:\MC-effect.)

Perhaps the most extraordinary R2s in Beethoven are those that are expanded into vast canvases, spreading out mightily throughout a much lengthier space than anything found in Mozart's concertos. The breadth of R2 in his Violin Concerto, op. 61, is astonishing in this regard. After beginning with R1:\TR-material (m. 224), it proceeds to review at length yet one more time (redundantly) almost all of R1:\S (239–63). It then splices onto a C-major recap-turing of the music that had led to the R1:\EEC (mm. 264–72), followed by a replication of R1's C-space conclusion (mm. 272–c. 299), which dissolves away, as had R1, into a restatement of the solo's expanded initial entry—thus begin-ning S1, the development, in a manner parallel to that of S1. Viewed as a whole, particularly with regard to its sense of expanse, the Violin Con-certo's R2 seems to provide a separately interpo-lated rotation into the first movement, albeit one that begins with a TR-module.⁷⁵ A somewhat similar R2 strategy is found in Piano Concerto No. 5 in E-flat, op. 73, although Beethoven did not lay it out as a fully separate rotation. Instead, Ritornello 2 backs up to recover an exten-sive stretch of R1:\S-material (mm. 227–66), only some of which had been recast in S1.

---

75. Again, for a much smaller precedent, one begin-ning with R1:\P, see the third movement of Mozart's

Serenade in D, K. 204 (cited in n. 74). One can imagine a similar claim being made about any R2 that begins

Alternative Tracks for the End of R2: Modulations, Half Cadences

The first-level tonal default for R2 is to remain in and ground the secondary key attained in Solo 1: V or III. Similarly, it usually ends with the orchestra sealing things off with a perfect authentic cadence in that key, even though it may remain rotationally incomplete, sometimes omitting a final R1-module or two. In such situations the border between R2 and S2 is clearly marked, and R2 is confined only to its normative function of concluding the larger exposition. But Mozart deviates fairly often from this explicit clarity, and he does so in a variety of ways. One of the simplest is to deny access to the final PAC, perhaps through a deceptive cadence at the R2–S2 seam (Violin Concerto No. 5, K. 219, m. 118; Piano Concerto No. 17 in G, K. 453, m. 184 [example 21.1]) or perhaps through such things as a sudden and startling breaking-off of R2 (Piano Concerto No. 27, K. 595, m. 190; cf. again K. 453, m. 181, example 21.1). Another is to provide an effect of R2-dissolution into S2, as the soloist enters to pick up or continue aspects of the final module of R2 (Violin Concerto No. 4, K. 218, m. 115, Piano Concertos No. 8, K. 246, m. 99, No. 14, K. 449, m. 182, and No. 16, K. 451, m. 187, and several others). This device is similar to the "linkage-technique" opening of S2, in which the soloist begins by picking up the last module sounded by the orchestra (chapter 22).

Instead of remaining tonally stable, a few of Mozart's R2s modulate to a different key toward their end, preparing the ground for the next entrance of the soloist at S2. Such modulatory R2-endings take on the role of a bridge or entry-zone into the developmental space proper, a space that normally begins with S2. When this happens, R2 begins as the expected conclu-

sion of the larger exposition but destabilizes to merge into a preparatory or quasi-developmental function. Confronting such mergers, it is often difficult to isolate a point at which the "development" clearly begins. A well-known case in point occurs in the first movement of Piano Concerto No. 21 in C, K. 467 (example 21.10). Here R2 occupies mm. 194–222. It begins with the "wild-card" motive that sprouts throughout much of the movement, perhaps best labeled here as a varied R1:\TR$^{1.1}$ (m. 194 = m. 12). The expected splice to rotationally participatory modules occurs at m. 205, now tracking R1:\S^2 (m. 205 = m. 52). This module begins its expected repetition with the V:PAC in m. 209 (= m. 56), but instead of proceeding to another perfect authentic cadence and subsequent tonal closure, as in the R1 model, the music deviates away from expectation at m. 215 (cf. m. 62) in order to modulate from G major to V of E minor, with a new dominant-lock at m. 219 coasting gently into an ad hoc caesura-like preparatory effect, iii:HC (vi:HC of V), at m. 222. (This quasi-MC gesture does not replicate any preceding MC in the movement.) The soloist now enters with the upbeat to m. 223, initiating the developmental space with a new thematic episode in E minor, one that recalls not only the triplet figure and sentential structure of R1:\P but also the R1:\P^{pref} of the preceding concerto, K. 466, perhaps establishing a hidden or expressive relationship between these two complementary but very different works.[76]

In K. 467 the modulatory R2 moves toward a caesura-like half cadence in the new key, a strategy anticipated years earlier in the Concertone in C, K. 190, in which R2, mm. 118–33, is wrenched from the normative G major to a suddenly interrupted vii^{o7} of A minor at the end. Other modulatory R2s provide a PAC in the

---

with a pre-MC module, such as R1:\TR$^{1.1}$, and shifts to a concluding set of post-MC modules, R1:\S$^{1.2}$, R1:\C, etc.—option 1 above. (Cf., again, Irving's concept of a "telescoped" second tutti, n. 70 above.) Taken out of context, these R2s might seem to fulfill the literal demands of a rotation. The crucial difference, though, is this: in virtually all such cases the concluding post-MC modules do not resuscitate ones that had already been heard in S1, as is the situation in Beethoven's Violin

Concerto. In the more common cases, it is clear that the opening R1:\TR$^{1.1}$ is indeed rotationally inert, not to be taken for the potential onset of any new rotation. The Violin Concerto differs in this regard, and that difference is also complemented by R2's unusual length.

76. Cf. the remarks along this line in Grayson, *Mozart: Piano Concertos Nos. 20 in D Minor, K. 466, and No 21 in C Major, K. 467,* pp. 52–53.

EXAMPLE 21.10   Mozart, Piano Concerto No. 21 in C, K. 467, i, mm. 193–229

Example 21.10 (*continued*)

EXAMPLE 21.10   *(continued)*

new key, elided with the onset of S2. Examples may be found in the Sinfonia Concertante in E-flat, K. 364, mm. 158–74 (B-flat major to a PAC in G minor), Piano Concerto No. 19 in F, K. 459, mm. 189–211 (C major to a PAC in A minor) and Horn Concerto No. 3 in E-flat, K. 447, mm. 69–85 (B-flat major to a PAC in D-flat major). More generally, this last procedure is close to that in which Mozart appends a brief orchestral link—sometimes a modula-tory one—to the developmental space proper (Violin Concerto No. 3, K. 216, mm. 103–05; Flute and Harp Concerto, K. 299, mm. 130–33; Horn Concerto No. 4, K. 495, mm. 94–97). In all such cases, the point is to provide an expressive connection or merger with the S2 onset of the developmental space. Negotiating that seam within all Type 5s is an important feature, and it will be revisited in the following chapter.

CHAPTER TWENTY-TWO

The Type 5 Sonata

Mozart's Concertos (Development and Recapitulation: From Solo 2 through Ritornello 4)

The central conceptual problems associated with Mozart's Type 5 realizations are those that must be confronted in the double layouts of R1 and S1 + R2 (chapters 19–21). Once the initial expositional hurdles are cleared, one's approach to the remainder of the movement becomes more manageable. In part this is because the standard procedures of development and recapitulation, treated in chapters 10–12, remain in force within the first movements of concertos. Nevertheless, these movements do favor certain developmental patterns over others, and the recapitulatory syntheses of the materials presented in R1 and S1 + R2, along with the special treatments of R3 and R4, are matters unique to Type 5s. (Before proceeding, one might recall that not all Type 5s contain developmental spaces. As mentioned in chapter 19, some slow-movement Type 5s are in dialogue with the Type 1 sonata format, that lacking a development. Similarly, a few of Mozart's Type 5 movements are adaptations of the double-rotational, Type 2 format, which, properly considered, does not feature a recapitulation—one leading off with R1:\P1—but rather a tonal resolution beginning several bars into the second rotation.)[1]

The Developmental Space: S2 or S2 + "R3"

Modular Content: Frequency of "Episodic" Developments

The tonal layouts of Solo 2 are those characteristic of development sections in general: circle-of-fifth or other discursive progressions, exploration of minor modes (especially vi or iii), dominant-locks toward the end, and so on. The discussion in chapter 10 need not be repeated here. In general, Mozart's solo-dominated Type 5 developments tend to be more "free" or episodic than those in Type 2 or Type 3 sonatas. Type 5s often pursue material only loosely related to expositional material, if related at all, although several of them do take up an idea or two that had been sounded in Rotations 1 and 2.[2] In nearly all such cases one can find some connection to earlier music: a characteristic rhythm or a small feature of figuration. The closed C-minor solo episode launching S2 in Horn Concerto No. 4 in E-flat, K. 495, for instance, mm. 97–112, grows out of a horn rhythm heard in S1:\P1.1, mm. 45–46. Still, the impression of starting out with something fresh remains.

---

1. See ch. 19, nn. 3 and 5 and the accompanying text. Referred to here are those formats designated as Subtypes E (Type 2 adaptation) and F (Type 1 adaptation) in table 19.1. Cf. also the discussion in ch. 19 of K. 107 no. 2/i.

2. Also noted in Irving, *Mozart's Piano Concertos*, p. 48.

When a Type 5 developmental space is mainly episodic, this aspect typically announces itself at the outset by having the soloist plunge into essentially new material either at once or after only a brief link, sometimes veering immediately into a minor mode. While this soloistic material might be primarily figurational, as in Piano Concerto No. 19 in F, K. 459, m. 211 (beginning aggressively with a new excursus in A minor, although the orchestra soon reiterates pointed, march-like reminders of R1:\P in the background), it is more often declarative, lyrical, or otherwise melodically memorable, although it may include passages of virtuosic figuration as well. At times the melodic profiles of such episodes are crafted to suggest their roles as (in Küster's words) "development themes" (*Durch-führungsthemen*) with a "self-standing" character, even though they may also serve as momentary, modular vehicles for tonally shifting sequences that begin almost at once.[3] One might imagine a continuum ranging from figurational episodes (as in K. 459) to melodic episodes. At the melodic end of the scale are such emphatically *cantabile* openings as the C-minor episode in the Horn Concerto No. 4, K. 495, mentioned above, and the two similarly ruminative beginnings shown in example 22.1, those from Piano Concertos No. 12 in A, K. 414, upbeat to mm. 153–68 (a full, tonally closed compound period in E major), and No. 21 in C, K. 467, upbeat to measures 223–29 (a sentence in E minor, subjected to a varied, dissolving repetition at m. 231). The *cantabile* S2-opening in Piano Concerto No. 20 in D Minor, K. 466, upbeat to m. 193, is also relatable to these last two, although here the music is a major-mode recycling of S1:\P^{pref} from m. 78 (as also occurs in No. 24 in C Minor, K. 491).

Modular Content: Linkage Technique

Not infrequently, Mozart began an S2 by having the soloist seize upon the final figure of R2 (sometimes even interrupting it), reiterate it as a germinal idea, and lead it into new modular directions. (As mentioned in chapter 21, the same linkage technique also characterizes the openings of several *sujet-libre* S1:\TRs.) One instance occurs in Piano Concerto No. 26 in D, K. 537 (example 22.2). Following the R2:\EEC in m. 230, the final portions of R2 play out as correspondence measures to the end of R1, only now in the dominant, A major (mm. 230–36 = mm. 74–80, R1:\C^1+C^2), although the final, two-beat octave drop from m. 80 is suppressed in m. 236. Cutting it short is the impulsively *forte* solo entrance on the second beat of m. 236, the onset of S2. With a sudden "lights-out" shift to A minor, the soloist picks up the R1:\C^2 cadential figure and leads it through three stormy bars, followed by a contrasting, more lyrical cadential module reinforcing that A minor (mm. 239–42). In this case the tutti-solo pattern of mm. 234–42, including material from both the end of R2 and the beginning of S2, serves as a model for an altered and dissolving repetition. R1:\C^2 returns insistently in the orchestra in A minor (mm. 242–44), now as a typical early tutti interjection within S2, prolonging a momentary (and characteristic) tug-of-war, tussling with the soloist's alteration of the idea. This time the soloist grasps the same figure but shifts at once to F major, bringing it to an IAC in m. 251, which releases a set of rising, central sequences underpinned by the same R1:\C^2 figure. At this point the texture shifts to one typical of the developmental spaces of these concertos: rapid, nonthematic figuration in the solo, lightly accompanied by the orchestra, which sounds a supportive motivic or rhythmic figure—a texture also recalling possibilities within display episodes.[4] (A similar texture is exemplified at the beginning of S2 in K. 453: see example 21.1, mm. 184–87; cf. the figurational beginning of S2 in K. 459, mm. 211ff.)

In K. 537 the opening portion of S2 is dominated by the R1:\C^2 figure, treated as a temporary though earnest obsession. This sort of developmental-work is more typical of the later

---

3. Küster, *Formale Aspekte*, p. 128, who also observed that the episodic Solo 2 was a possibility mentioned by Koch.

4. Irving, *Mozart's Piano Concertos*, p. 49, also commented on this and cited several examples.

EXAMPLE 22.1a   Mozart, Piano Concerto No. 12 in A, K. 414, i,
mm. 153–68

EXAMPLE 22.1a   *(continued)*

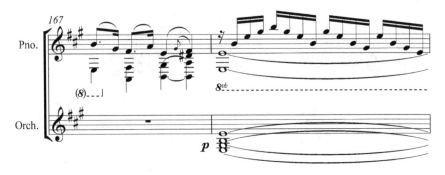

EXAMPLE 22.1b   Mozart, Piano Concerto No. 21 in C, K. 467, i,
mm. 223–29

concertos than the earlier ones, which tend to be more episodic. One might compare K. 537, though, with a few developments that are similarly obsessive, sometimes even more so, in their treatments of individual figures. In Piano Concerto No. 14 in E-flat, K. 449, much of S2 (mm. 182ff) features another tutti-solo, modulatory

tug-of-war centered on a trilled and twisted, growling R1:\S³ figure (from mm. 76–79)—here with four tutti interjections in the first part of S2. The development of Piano Concerto No. 23 in A, K. 488 (mm. 149ff), is preoccupied—again with nervous tutti interjections—with the new theme introduced at the end of R2, in the

EXAMPLE 22.2 Mozart, Piano Concerto No. 26 in D, K. 537, i,
mm. 230–57

EXAMPLE 22.2   (*continued*)

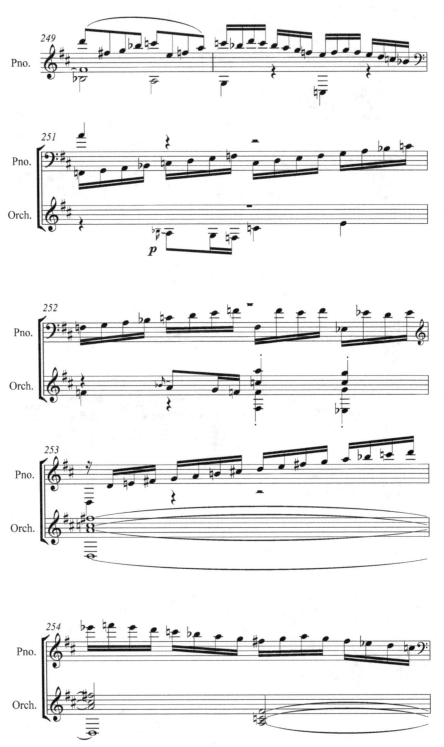

EXAMPLE 22.2   (continued)

second half of m. 143.[5] And following its un-usual R2 close, rhyming with the R1:\MC (m. 228 = m. 50), the developmental space of Piano Concerto No. 25 in C, K. 503, is fixated on the "lost" R1:\S theme (from m. 51). Recalling that that theme had been replaced in the solo exposition with an altogether new TMB raises the potential within Type 5s for a "compensatory development" or section thereof, one that touches on materials from R1 that were suppressed in S1, as if those ideas were now registering that loss and claiming their due.[6]

Rotational Developments

While many concerto developments are chiefly episodic or extend a figure from the end of R2 into S2, a few others return to variants of R1:\P at or near the opening of S2. By doing so, they adopt the more standard procedure found in Type 2 and Type 3 sonatas, thereby suggesting the onset of a developmental rotation. This is more characteristic of later concertos than of earlier ones. Although not infrequent in other types of sonatas, fully rotational developments are virtually nonexistent in Mozart's Type 5s. (As laid out in chapter 11, fully rotational developments focus near the opening on a selected module or two of pre-MC material, P or TR, and shift their attention at some point to one or more post-MC modules, S or C.) They do occasionally appear in Beethoven's more self-consciously "symphonic" concertos, though, as in his Piano Concertos No. 2 in B-flat, op. 19 (S1:\P at m. 213 [cf. m. 90]; R1:\S, which had not appeared in S1, at m. 232 [cf. m. 43]), and No. 5 in E-flat, op. 73 (minor-mode R1:\P at m. 280; R1:\S[1.6] at the upbeat to m. 334 [cf. m. 98]).

More common in Mozart—and also occur-ring in some of Beethoven's concertos—are half-rotational S2s. In these developmental spaces, those references to R1 or S1, however fleeting, are restricted only to P and/or (less often) TR. An exemplary half-rotation is found in his Piano Concerto No. 9 in E-flat, K. 271. Although S2 begins with a solo statement of the "out-of-order" R1:\TR[1.1] (m. 148 = m. 7), the rotational procedures proper are reset by another stern *rappel à l'ordre* from the tutti (m. 156; cf. m. 1), a corrective effect also encountered near the beginning of S1 (cf. m. 63). Transition materials re-emerge with a switch to the R1:\TR[1.3] module in m. 182 (= m. 14). The Clarinet Concerto in A, K. 622, furnishes another example of an S2 that includes the P–TR succession. Here the lengthy developmental space begins with a sentential reference to the incipit of R1:\P (mm. 172, 176), now led into different material, and gives way to a new, somewhat similar section built around a substantial resounding of S1:\TR[1.2] (upbeat to m. 201—cf. m. 86). Related instances of a P-based, half-rotational development include Piano Concertos No. 24 in C Minor, K. 491 (beginning with a return to S1:\P[pref], m. 283, followed by a central sequential action-zone based on R1:\P and triggered by the tutti, m. 302), and No. 27 in B-flat, K. 595 (beginning, famously, with R1:\P in the remote key of B minor, m. 191).

Occasionally one encounters multiple subrotations within a portion of the developmental space, usually P-based. The *locus classicus*, also considered in chapter 21, occurs with three subrotations each begun with S1:\P[pref] in Mozart's Piano Concerto No. 20 in D Minor, K. 466. Another double-set of R1:\P-cycles may be found in Horn Concerto No. 1 in D, K. 412. The opening melody is sounded first—wittily and non-normatively by the orchestra—as a

---

5. The soloist's initial S2-entry of passagework, mm. 149–56, is a figurational variant of the new idea. The orchestral winds respond repeatedly, however, with modulatory interruptions based on the original incipit of the new theme.

6. Cf. Piano Concerto No. 21 in C, K. 467, some of whose minor-mode orchestral figuration (mm. 231, 233), as Grayson has pointed out (*Mozart: Piano Concertos Nos. 20 and 21*, p. 52), might suggest a similarly

"lost" R1:\S (a major-mode "horn-call") from Ritornello 1 (m. 28, 32), "showing that even this most jubilant of themes has the potential for sorrow." Similarly, the orchestral accompaniment of the opening of S2 in No. 17 in G, K. 453—example 21.1, mm. 184ff—suggests a much-transformed evocation of R1:\S[1.2] (m. 49), missing from the solo exposition, an evocation underscored by the deceptive-cadence entry.

"developmental" R2 extension, m. 62. This is obviously the beginning of a new rotation, still in the dominant, although the music soon decays onto V of B minor, mm. 69–72. The soloist enters at the upbeat to m. 73 to assist in a modulation to G major, the key of the subdominant. The second subrotation begins in that key at m. 78: the initial module (only) of R1:\P is restated by the tutti, a whole step lower than its previous statement in m. 62.

Overall Shape: Event Zones

Despite the relative freedom of modular content in Mozart's Type 5 Allegro movements, most of them pass through phases familiar from the developments of other late-eighteenth-century sonatas. These were outlined at the end of chapter 10 as an (optional) *link* (here, from R2); an *entry or preparation zone* (in concertos often involving some initial tutti-solo interplay); a *central action or set of actions* (here, almost always a modestly sized central block of sequences with a display of rapid passagework from the soloist); and an *exit or retransition* in order to prepare for the recapitulation. Only rarely will a concerto development by Mozart expand to include other phases. (Beethoven's concerto developments are often lengthier, more complex.)

This observation may be buttressed with an appeal to Konrad Küster's 1991 statistical study of Mozart's Allegro concerto movements. After examining 45 developments, he concluded that, far from being the free "fantasy" that some had claimed (Girdlestone, Forman), Mozart usually led his concerto developments through four zones of activity.[7] The first was a customary "opening zone" (*Eröffnungsbereich*), often divided into separate, short subsections. These often featured a virtuosic or *Durchführungsthema* module that was either repeated with variants or treated to initial modulatory sequences, sometimes with tutti interjections.[8]

The potential second event, which Küster located in twenty-three of the forty-five cases, he called the "'middle' of the development" ("*Mitte" der Durchführung*).[9] This refers to an interior point where the initial activity (customarily sequences or varied modular repetition) stabilizes, however briefly, usually into an HC or a PAC, often in vi or iii, that prepares the onset of the next section. ("The [initial] modulatory process comes to a standstill for a moment," or, at a minimum, the motivic-work undergoes an "incisive change.")[10] Küster's third developmental section is a broad, churning sweep of tonally shifting musical space that he called the "central sequence-zone" (*zentraler Sequenzbereich*). It is

---

7. The argument is laid out in Küster, *Formale Aspekte*, pp. 126–50, with the results conveniently summarized in his table 3, pp. 262–63.

8. Küster's table 3, *Formale Aspekte*, pp. 262–63, registered that only the Oboe Concerto, K. 314, and Horn Concerto No. 1, K. 412, lacked such an *Eröffnungsbereich*. In Küster's view, the former begins with section 3, the "central sequence-zone"; the latter with section 2, the "'middle' of the development."

9. Some examples that he cited, sometimes puzzlingly, from the piano concertos (*Formale Aspekte*, pp. 262–63) are: K. 413 (m. 197), K. 414 (m. 168), K. 415 (m. 176), K. 453 (m. 200), K. 482 (m. 222), K. 488 (m. 165), K. 491 (m. 318), K. 537 (m. 248), K. 595 (m. 207). Lacking such a "middle," according to Küster, are K. 271, 365, 449, 450, 451, 459, 466, 467, and 503.

10. Küster, *Formale Aspekte*, p. 135. The concept of the "middle" is apparently quite flexible, both in potential length and in compositional significance. In his paradigm case, the Bassoon Concerto, K. 191, mm. 88–89 (discussed as an example in *Formale Aspekte*, pp. 135–36), the "middle" extends for only a few beats, a mere vi:HC, leading at once into the ensuing sequence-block

beginning at m. 89. By contrast, the developmental "middle" of Piano Concerto No. 17, K. 453, beginning with m. 200—the point at which the sequences begin to dissolve—is taken up largely with a prolonged dominant-lock on V of vi (mm. 203–7), merging with a central, modulatory tutti interjection (207–11, leading away from V of vi toward IV for the next developmental zone, that of sequences). On rare occasions, the "middle" can be a central, largely tonally stable episode, like the G-minor episode in Piano Concerto No. 6 in B-flat, K. 238, mm. 109–20. In other cases Küster's concept of "middle" is open to challenge, particularly in those where its presumed appearance is only fleeting, merely marks the point of a sectional shift of activity, or is more logically integrated into a different formal process. For example (p. 263), he listed m. 176 of Piano Concerto No. 13 in C, K. 415, as the "middle" of the development, while m. 177 begins the next section, the "central sequence-zone." Yet m. 176 is the bar that begins this subsection, since at this point it reintroduces R1:\P in A minor. In other words, m. 177 is better regarded as the second bar of the module that starts in m. 176.

generally equivalent to our "central action," and in this case it is also similar to Caplin's positing of a developmental, sequential "core."[11] This is a standard strategy found in almost all of Mozart's concerto developments: on Küster's tally, it appears in all but three of the forty-five examined concerto movements.[12] The procedure is familiar to anyone acquainted with even a few of these movements: laying down a brief, initial model-statement—often with broadly scalar or arpeggiated passagework in the solo—and rolling it repeatedly through more or less standard sequential formulas (circle-of-fifth or other harmonic motions) with a strong sense of shifting to a "large-stride" hypermeter. As expected, the sequence formula is normally shut down in stages, by subjecting it to familiar procedures of liquidation and merger into the final section of the development.

This last section is the retransition (Küster's *Rückleitung*). Its role in preparing for the recapitulatory rotation is identical to that in Types 1–4 sonatas (chapter 10). As expected, this zone most often steers into a structural-dominant lock, of variable length, at the end. That dominant-lock almost always occurs on an active V of the tonic, which is then subjected to a harmonic interruption that prompts the immediate start of the recapitulatory rotation as the next structural event. Bridging the end of the one with the beginning of the other through a connective of caesura-fill is always an option, although a less commonly chosen one. One finds solo-fill at this moment, for instance, in Piano Concerto No. 14 in E-flat, K. 449, mm. 228–34; orchestra-fill in No. 18, K. 456, mm. 229–32. Related to the orchestra-fill moments are those in which the soloist continues its non-thematic, "static" figuration over V while the

orchestra provides the gravitationally sliding, linear motion toward the tonic and moment of recapitulation, as in Piano Concertos No. 21 in C, K. 467 (mm. 268–74), and No. 22 in E-flat, K. 482 (mm. 259–64). On a few occasions, parallel with options of RT-practice in other sonata types, the most prominent lock occurs instead on V/vi, followed by a passage of fill that leads back to the tonic at the point of recapitulation. Variants of this option are found in Horn Concertos Nos. 2 in E-flat, K. 417, and No. 3 in E-flat, K. 447; and in Piano Concertos Nos. 12 in A, K. 414, No. 19 in F, K. 459 (Example 22.4), and No. 27 in B-flat, K. 595.

While RT often features a more activated orchestral backdrop intensifying the structural moment, it is not usually a tutti passage. In most cases the soloist continues to play throughout RT, then drops out for the moment of recapitulation, which is begun by the orchestra. The orchestral tutti that begins most of Mozart's Type 5 recapitulations in a quasi-"symphonic" manner is what we designate as Ritornello 3, one of the structural pillars of the generic architecture. (This is the format designated as Subtype B in chapter 19, table 19.1—the most common subtype in Mozart and Beethoven.) In a few works (especially in some violin and wind concertos) Mozart switched this pattern around, giving the RT or expanded-fill role to an orchestral tutti, without soloist, and calling upon the soloist to re-enter to take the lead at the onset of the recapitulation. As many have noted, even though this latter, presumably older format (Subtype A in table 19.1) is more consistent with the concerto formula elaborated by Koch in 1793, it renders the ritornello status of this RT ("Ritornello 3?") more questionable. We revisit this less common option below.

---

11. For Caplin (and before him, Ratz) on the "core"—defined primarily by central sequential activity (Küster's *Eröffnungsbereich* would thus resemble Caplin's "pre-core")—see his *Classical Form*, pp. 141–55. Ratz, Caplin, and Küster provide similar schemes for phases of a development, and the schemes work well for Type 5 developmental spaces in Mozart. See also, though, our caveats regarding the application of this concept generally to all Type 2 and 3 developments, toward the end of ch. 10.

12. The three are the Concertone in C, K. 190; the fourth movement, a Type 5 Allegro, of the Serenade in

D, K. 203; and the first movement of Piano Concerto No. 6 in B-flat, K. 238. Küster, *Formale Aspekte*, p. 262–63, locates the onsets of the "central sequence-zone" as follows: in the violin concertos, K. 207/i (m. 86), K. 211 (m. 71), K. 216 (m. 122), K. 218 (m. 126), K. 219 (m. 127); in the major piano concertos, K. 271 (m. 162), K. 365 (m. 159), K. 413 (m. 205), K. 414 (m. 180), K. 415 (m. 177), K. 449 (m. 205), K. 450 (m. 166), K. 451 (m. 201), K. 453 (m. 211), K. 456 (m. 201), K. 459 (m. 219), K. 466 (m. 230), K. 467 (m. 237), K. 482 (m. 226), K. 488 (m. 170), K. 491 (m. 330), K. 503 (m. 262), K. 537 (m. 251), and K. 595 (m. 209).

Tutti Interjections

The number of tutti interjections in the development—brief outbursts or responses from the orchestra alone—is variable. When they do occur, they are more likely to appear early on, in the entry zone, creating a back-and-forth exchange with the soloist and helping to stamp the opening character of that particular S2. In these cases the tutti texture, so pronounced in R2, is staged as having more to say or as being reluctant to recede into the background, even as the soloist begins its own journey into S2. It is common to find one or two tutti interjections inlaid into the opening passages of S2, but at times one might find as many as four (as in Piano Concerto in E-flat, K. 449, mm. 188–90, 192–94, 196–98, 200–2—a nervously charged dialogue). Mid-developmental tutti interjections typically highlight or respond to a point of arrival: an authentic cadence or half cadence (with a quasi-caesura-effect) or perhaps a passage of modulatory fill between discrete sections. One should also be prepared to find the occasional idiosyncratic or isolated case. In K. 503 an unusually extended, thirteen-bar tutti interjection repeats in A minor (mm. 241–48) the "lost" R1:\S theme just sounded in E minor by the piano (mm. 231–38), then rearticulates stuttering, quasi-MC and modulatory fill-figures (mm. 249–53) that had begun the development proper (mm. 227–31).

A few concerto developments are riddled with tutti interjections more or less throughout: five developmental TIs appear in Piano Concertos No. 9 in E-flat, K. 271, and the "obsessive" No. 23 in A, K. 488; six are found in No. 24 in C Minor, K. 491, extending well into the central sequence-block. On the other hand, some concertos do without any. In these instances the soloist spins out an uninterrupted course throughout the development, much of which is accompanied by an orchestral backdrop, sometimes also containing thematic material. Examples may be found in Piano Concertos No. 12 in A, K. 414, No. 15 in B-flat, K. 450, No. 18

in B-flat, K. 456, No. 19 in F, K. 459, and No. 21 in C, K. 467.

The Retransitional "Ritornello 3" Option Proceeding to a Solo-Led Recapitulation

Most of the interior tuttis found in the developments of Mozart's Type 5 movements are best understood as interjections. They are *ad hoc* events within S2, not structural pillars in the generic architecture of the movement. In about twenty percent of the concerto first movements, however—eight or nine, depending on one's criteria for inclusion (four of the five violin concertos, three wind concertos, and one or two piano concertos)—and in one concerto finale (K. 207/iii), we encounter a different implication in the final moments of the developmental space and the opening of the recapitulation. In this second-level-default situation, a solo-led recapitulation (the reverse of the norm described above, an orchestra-launched reprise) is prepared by several bars of RT-tutti from which the soloist has dropped out. The tutti may occupy all or most of the RT; it may extend a pre-existing dominant-lock already secured by the soloist; or it may serve only as expanded and harmonized caesura-fill, leading from the interrupted dominant proper to the downbeat of the recapitulation, often with the local effect of a I:PAC at the end.[13] In almost all of these cases (the exception is the caesura-fill tutti) the developmental space extends beyond the close of S2. This is not what happens in the normative format. There the soloist continues to play throughout the development's final zone, the retransition.

While some of these RT-tuttis seem more like interjections than something generically structural, in their historical resonances they suggest a dialogue, however transitory, with the residues of an older formal norm. When followed by solo-led recapitulations, such retransition-tuttis (or even brief, CF-tuttis), in varying degrees of strength, appeal to an alternative possibility for R3 treatment, one that comes closer to conforming with Koch's 1793 *Versuch*

---

13. An extraordinarily strong I:PAC—much more decisive, it seems, than that normally associated with mere caesura-fill—occurs at this spot in the first movement

of Beethoven's Piano Concerto No. 4 in G, op. 58, mm. 251–53.

prescription for adding ritornellos to precomposed, Type 3 sonata movements. As outlined in chapter 19 (where this procedure was classified as Type 5 structural Subtype A), Koch called for the modulatory second solo to end with a cadence on vi, iii, or ii, and it was to be followed by an interposed third ritornello, without soloist, that "modulates back into the main key, in which it closes with a [half cadence]," while the ensuing third solo was to start with what we today call the recapitulation.[14]

Koch apparently regarded this strategy as one of refashioning a traditional concerto ritornello (or tutti) to adapt to the norms of an important hinge-point in sonata-form practice. It was now to serve as a retransition, even when (as occurs often) it did not literally recycle material heard in R1. In such instances one recalls (as proposed in chapter 19) that it is best to understand the ritornello concept broadly, rather than haggling over terminology and etymologies. Within Type 5s what we designate as a structural ritornello pillar may have a cadence-confirming function (as in R2 and R4), a reinitiating or *da capo* function (as does the more normal R3-gesture that usually begins the recapitulation), or, as in the "R3" option under consideration here, a retransitional or even CF-fill function in the final moments before a solo-led recapitulation. Even so, under some paradigms of description the ritornello status of some of these development-ending retransitions is weak, particularly when they are brief or reduced to mere fill. Again, the idea of a "vestigial third tutti" ("R3" in quotation marks) can be called upon to provide a useful nuance.[15]

When "R3" both occupies several bars and executes standard RT-functions, the passage is easier to perceive as a structural ritornello. In Mozart's concertos, near-classic Kochian "R3" patterns within the Type 5 sonata—moving from the region of vi back to the tonic—may be found in both the first movement and the finale of Violin Concerto No. 1 in B-flat, K.

207. In the first movement (example 22.3), the last soloistic statement in the development is a "one-more-time" repetition of a G-minor cadential figure, mm. 96–99, undermined at the end with a deceptive cadence onto VI, E-flat, at mm. 99 (the only point that deviates from Koch's prescription). At this point the *violino principale* abandons its solo role to rejoin the tutti for a nine-bar "R3" gesture, leading from the initial E-flat, through a set of *unisono* descents, to an active V of the tonic, B-flat, articulated as a caesura with *Nachschlag* (m. 107). In the following bar, m. 108, the soloist begins the recapitulation as it had the exposition, with R1:\P (cf. m. 25). In this case all of the "R3" music is essentially new, stock material previously unsounded in the movement, always an option within such an RT. As for the K. 207 finale, it provides an even more lucid instance of an "R3" retransitional tutti, moving through some twenty-four bars from a tonicized vi at its opening to V of the governing tonic at its end (mm. 201–24, based on R1:\TR throughout and also concluding with a parallel, MC-replicating caesura-gap).

Similarly clear and extended (hence also paradigmatic) RT-"R3s" may be found in the first movements of Horn Concertos No. 1 in D, K. 412 and No. 4 in E-flat, K. 495, and in Clarinet Concerto in A, K. 622. In K. 412 the last developmental entrance of the horn occurs in mm. 82–85, an E-minor sounding of R1:\P. Mm. 86–97 interpolate a vigorous tutti, elaborating a dominant-lock, V of D, throughout, with m. 97 as a bar of descending caesura-fill in parallel sixths, elided with the solo-led recapitulation at m. 98. In K. 495 we have what is best regarded as a seven-bar "R3" proper (mm. 132–38)—intensifying the dominant, V of E-flat, already locked into by the soloist a few bars earlier (m. 128). M. 138 begins a passage of caesura-fill (mostly descending parallel-thirds) into the final bars of which the soloist joins with an anticipatory anacrusis doubling the orchestral fill (mm.

---

14. See ch. 19, nn. 25–26 (Davis, "C. P. E. Bach and the Early History of the Recapitulatory Tutti"), and n. 34 (which also cites Stevens, "The Importance of C. P. E. Bach for Mozart's Piano Concertos"). See also the essay cited in ch. 19, n. 7: Stevens, "Patterns of Recapitula-

tion in the First Movements of Mozart's Piano Concertos."

15. The term is Karol Berger's: see ch. 19, n. 35 and the text to which it refers.

EXAMPLE 22.3 Mozart, Violin Concerto No. 1 in B-flat, K. 207, i, mm. 96–114

[Allegro Moderato]

EXAMPLE 22.3   *(continued)*

140–41), and the full shift to the soloist occurs at the downbeat of the recapitulation, m. 142. K. 622 contains Mozart's most extended retransitional "R3." Incorporating both a free opening passage, then some R1:\TR-modules, this expands outward for no fewer than twenty-two bars, mm. 227–48, modulating from the soloist's concluding vi:PAC (m. 227) to an active V of the tonic A. It is followed by three more bars of fill—this time led off by the solo clarinet (m. 248)—which elides in its fourth bar with the onset of the solo-led recapitulation, m. 251.

When the retransitional "R3" is reduced to four bars or fewer or occupies only the non-structural role of caesura-fill, its ritornello-pillar claims shrink, and one must be content to appeal to the merely vestigial status of the gesture within the context of more elaborated examples. In Violin Concerto No. 2 in D, K. 211, "R3" proper is reduced to three "new-material" bars of V:HC caesura-articulation (m. 79 to the downbeat of m. 82), with m. 82 as an extra bar of orchestral fill in parallel-thirds and

sixths bridging into the recapitulation at m. 83. The situation is similar in Violin Concerto No. 5 in A, K. 219, where "R3," resuscitating the R1:\MC-music (cf. mm. 16–19), occupies only three bars and one beat (mm. 139–42), while the two bars of succeeding fill are supplied by the violin soloist, anticipating its launch of the recapitulation at m. 144.[16]

In Violin Concerto No. 3 in G, K. 216, "R3" consists only of a four-bar wind-up and descent (mm. 152–55) into the solo-led recapitulation (m. 156). This passage is best regarded not as RT proper but as a more fully harmonized stretch of "stock-material" caesura-fill that extends the final I:HC caesura of the development, which had been dramatically articulated (probably including an improvisatory moment filling out a notated fermata) by the solo violin. The situation is not dissimilar in Piano Concerto No. 11 in C, K. 413 (mm. 233–36), although the fill-music there elegantly recovers R1:\C—the graceful last gesture of Ritornello 1 (mm. 54–57)—and dovetails neatly, as it had earlier, into S1:\Ppref. A

---

16. In K. 219/i, note that if the "R3" measures were regarded as only an *ad hoc* tutti interjection recovering the R1:\MC figure, then this movement would exemplify our Subtype C on table 19.1. It is only to the extent that one regards it as a vestigial reference to a retransitional "R3"—as laid out in Koch's 1793 *Versuch* plan (our preferred interpretation)—that we may observe its rudimentary dialogue with second-level-default, Subtype

A features. (Subtype C, in which there is no gesture toward any "R3" either before or at the moment of the recapitulation, is exemplified in Piano Concerto No. 13 in C, K. 415/i—presuming that one agrees to consider the recapitulation as beginning with the S1:\Ppref (m. 200) rather than with the tutti-led R1:\P-theme a few bars later.)

particularly clever stretch of "R3"-fill occurs in Piano Concerto No. 19 in F, K. 459, mm. 241–47 (example 22.4). The solo piano concludes its developmental appearance (literally, its expanse of S2) with a seven-bar, unaccompanied dominant lock over A, V/vi (mm. 235–41). M. 241 marks the point of the final caesura of the development, and the "R3" tutti that picks up at this point—a rapidly alternating wind-string dialogue on the *idée-fixe* dotted-rhythm—serves as fully harmonized, modulatory fill back to F major and the solo-led recapitulation at m. 247. Its status as fill, rather than RT, is confirmed by the "apparent" I:PAC at m. 247, a characteristic feature of expanded CF. (The multiple ways to understand the familiar harmonic motion at this point, V/vi–I, were treated in chapter 10, "The Development," under "Tonal Layout.")

The Solo Recapitulation: S3, R3 + S3, or R3⇒S3

Solo and Larger Recapitulations

Just as one may conceptually bracket off a solo exposition (S1 only), one may isolate a *solo recapitulation*, which extends from the texturally variable onset of the recapitulatory rotation through the final trill-cadence elided with R4. Like S1, with which it has much in common, the solo recapitulation is dominated by the soloist, although in most instances it is led off with a brief burst of tutti energy (an R3 gesture or "recapitulatory tutti") before the soloist joins in.[17] In those instances, of course, the term "solo recapitulation" is not literally accurate as a description of the entire space, since its initially defining moment is not solo-led. Nevertheless, we adopt the term both for the sake of simplicity and for its analogous role to the solo exposition, S1.[18] As demonstrated in chapters 19 and 21, the

solo exposition does not normally account for the entire exposition. The distinction must be made between it and the larger exposition, almost always S1 + R2. (This S1 + R2 succession may not be complete, when measured against the *Anlage* provided in the initial ritornello. It might break off prematurely or dissolve into an S2-merger before the final modules of the conceptual rotation are attained.) So, too, the solo recapitulation is extended into a *larger recapitulation* with the addition of the R4 block. Among other things, R4 will complete the rotational succession by presenting materials that had not been sounded in that solo recapitulation. Thus the solo recapitulation, pursuing its own delimited purposes, is a subset of the larger recapitulation. This double-focus is a result of the hybrid nature of the Type 5 sonata, and it complicates all considerations of the recapitulation within these movements.

The Recapitulation as Rotation 1– Rotation 2 Synthesis

The harmonic aim of both the solo and the larger recapitulation is that of tonal resolution. The post-MC material of S1 + R2, sounded there in the dominant or, in minor-mode concertos, in the major mediant, is to be revisited here in the tonic. Beyond this, and beyond its self-evident supplying of the obligatory sense of proportional symmetry to the musical architecture, the larger recapitulation has at least two other tasks to fulfill. One is that of rotational completion, mentioned in the section above. The other is the related task of Rotation 1 and Rotation 2 synthesis (or reconciliation), some of which may occur within a refashioned solo recapitulation.[19] Caplin's summary provides a quick explanation of the basic idea: it often happens that "the [solo] recapitulation is organized differently from either of the earlier 'ex-

---

17. The term "recapitulatory tutti" is also found, e.g., in Irving, *Mozart's Piano Concertos*, p. 51.

18. Thus a workable definition of the solo recapitulation is "within a Type 5 sonata, that recapitulatory space, predominantly featuring solo activity, which precedes R4 and which is complementary to that space established by the solo exposition, S1."

19. The idea of a recapitulatory "synthesis," as opposed to a mere "combination" or "recombination" is not new to us: see, e.g., Küster, *Formale Aspekte*, p. 151; and Caplin, *Classical Form*, p. 249. See also the concept of the concerto recapitulation as the "fusion of orchestral and solo expositions" in Rosen, *Sonata Forms*, rev. ed., p. 96, an idea attributed to Tovey. According to Rosen—apparently

EXAMPLE 22.4   Mozart, Piano Concerto No. 19 in F, K. 459, i, mm.235–50

[Allegro]

positions' [in this context, our R1 and S1 only]. In particular, the recapitulation is likely to reintroduce ideas from the opening ritornello that were not used in the solo exposition and that find no place in the subsequent subordinate-key ritornello [R2] or development section."[20] But once one considers the matter outside of the inadequate conceptual boxes provided by Vogler, Koch, and other early theorists—according to whom ritornellos were to be grasped as subordinated extras, not as part of any essential sonata structure, which took place only in the solo sections—one realizes that the situation in Mozart (and Beethoven) is more complicated. Again, this is because in these Type 5s the concepts of exposition and recapitulation are more accurately regarded as double-concepts (solo and larger exposition, solo and larger recapitulation), all portions of which are to be understood most fundamentally in their relationships to a pre-existing R1 model. This multiplication of opportunities for interior cross-referencing opens possibilities for different realizations of recapitulatory synthesis. All of them, however, are normally governed by the larger concept of successive linear ordering—the rotational principle.

As indicated also in chapter 21, the contents of nonmodulatory Rotation 1 (the opening, proto-expositional ritornello, R1) typically differ, in varying degrees, from those of the solo exposition (S1) and hence also from those of modulatory Rotation 2 proper, the larger exposition (S1 + R2). Not only is Rotation 2 longer, more expanded, and provided with additional material, but S1 + R2 may also suppress or provide substitutions for music proposed in R1, thus tracking an alternative course through now-modulatory expositional space. When this occurs, most of the changes from the R1 model will usually be found within the solo exposition (S1), and R2 may not restore all of that which S1 had omitted. In turn, this suggests

that the "missing" R1 modules—especially any R1:\post-MC modules, which are more compelling in this regard—are to be reintegrated into the larger recapitulatory rotation, either slotted conveniently into the solo recapitulation or recovered only in the appended R4, the section that extends the solo recapitulation into the larger one.

Under these circumstances, one is faced with a tonal situation unique to Type 5 sonatas. Since all of R1:\post-MC space (unlike S1:\post-MC space) is conceptually organized around the tonic, and since any expositionally "missing" modules from it will normally be restored in the tonic in the larger recapitulation, those restored modules will never have been sounded in a nontonic key. As such, they do not play a role in the task of tonal resolution. In all appearances they remain tonic-centered. Their recapitulation is exclusively rhetorical or linear. Any such recovered R1 modules are rotationally participatory, but they do not contribute to the tonal processes of the sonata—at least as those processes are to be construed in Types 1–4 sonatas. And yet one still perceives the pull of rhetorical custom in all of this. Any module that had appeared in R1:\S- or C-space—even though it had been sounded there in the tonic—still maintains a rhetorical claim to be slotted into an analogous spot in the tonic-grounded larger recapitulation.

Varying Relationships of the Solo Recapitulation to S1

Viewed broadly, the recapitulatory-synthesis question involves the modular events that occur in R2 and R4, those blocks that extend the solo exposition and recapitulations into the larger ones. Nevertheless, for both heuristic and historical reasons one may begin to approach some of these issues by bracketing off only the more contained solo exposition and solo recapitulation and inquiring into the extent to which the

with Wagenseil's and J. C. Bach's keyboard concertos in mind (the context for his remark)—"this principle begins to act long before Mozart." Cf. Tovey, "The Classical Concerto," in *Essays in Musical Analysis*, 3:23, n. 1, considering primarily Mozart's most mature and complex works (K. 503/i is Tovey's exemplar): "The re-

capitulation in the tonic is a recapitulation of the opening tutti as well as of the first solo. It does not omit the features peculiar to the solo, but it adds to them those features of the ritornello which the solo had not at first adopted."

20. Caplin, *Classical Form*, p. 249.

latter's materials are modeled on those of the former. From this perspective, one might at least initially consider Mozart's solo recapitulations with regard to their modular congruence with or deviation from the corresponding solo exposition.[21]

The simplest procedure was to compose a solo recapitulation that tracks through only the modules laid out in S1, as though the S1 rhetorical pattern were the only direct source from which the solo recapitulation was to draw its materials. (To be sure, despite the many correspondence measures between the two, one can expect some deviations, such as a recomposed TR, a more vigorous extension before the final trill-cadence, and the like. But the modular ideas will still be only those found also in S1.) This was apparently a generic default or conceptual starting-point that we find in some of Mozart's earliest concertos (and occasionally in some of his later ones as well). In Violin Concerto No. 3 in G, K. 218—an extreme instance of this—the solo recapitulation consists entirely of correspondence or referential measures, bar-for-bar, with the solo exposition, even through the adjusted recapitulatory S1:\TR. More typically, we find one or two compositional variants in the solo recapitulation, even though all of the ideas included are referential to S1—incorporating no previously omitted R1 material. Early examples include two first movements that also feature "double-start" recapitulations (see below): Piano Concerto No. 5 in D, K. 175 (expansion of *sujet-libre* S1:\TR, mm. 170–73; unexpected reordering of S-modules, with S1:\S$^{1.3}$, m. 188, now preceding S1:\S$^{1.2}$, m. 195); and Bassoon Concerto in B-flat, K. 191 (with a much-expanded *sujet-libre* S1:\TR, mm. 112–37).

Confronting such relatively simple solo recapitulations, the obvious impulse is to conclude that, indeed, the real sonata activity is unfolding in the solo sections only, à la Vogler and Koch, or that "the tutti and solo each retain an independent role, that is, each has a chance to 'recapitulate' its most important gestures."[22] But S1 was never fully autonomous ("independent") in the first place. Notwithstanding any materials that it will have substituted or introduced on its own, much of S1 will still have been built from R1 modules. More to the point, it is central to the experience of any S1 that it not be understood as independent but rather that it be heard in relation to the model just heard, however fragmentarily, in R1. In addition, beyond the conceptually bracketed confines of the solo exposition, the R2-extension (producing the sense of a larger exposition), normally restores one or more R1 modules that were either replaced in S1 (R1:\TR$^{1.1}$, R1:\S$^{1.2}$, and R1:\C are typical candidates for this) or may have not been rotationally attained (if the solo exposition stops before sounding all of the R1:\C ideas). In this sense any larger exposition, whether rotationally complete or not, is already something of a newly proposed synthesis (a freshly minted combination) of ritornello ideas and solo ideas. This would also be true of even the simplest of larger recapitulations, especially those that reinstate R1-material lacking or unattained in the larger exposition.

The idea of a recapitulatory synthesis is easier to grasp, though, if there are at least some passages of the solo recapitulation that both differ from the solo exposition and that also reinstate at least one expositionally suppressed R1-module. Even in some of Mozart's earliest concertos, it is possible to find small—almost insignificant—recapitulatory deviations from the practice of strict S1 modular-tracking described above. Here and there we can find a

---

21. Küster, *Formale Aspekte*, p. 151, identified this, e.g., as a central concern of Robert Forster, in "Zur Funktion von Anfangsritornell und Reprise in den Kopfsätzen einiger Klavierkonzerte Mozarts," *Mozart-Jahrbuch 1986* (Kassel: Bärenreiter, 1987), pp. 74–89. Küster, p. 166, also informs us that "as a rule, Mozart's concerto recapitulations are longer than the earlier solo exposition. In thirteen of the forty-three movements examined, the reverse relationship occurs (K. 218, 299, 314,

365, 451, 453, 467, 482, 491, 503, 537, 595, and 622). The degree of shortening varies between two (K. 314 and 595) and fifty-four bars (K. 491). . . . Only in five movements does the recapitulation compare referentially to the exposition without any change in the effective length: K. 216, 219, 246, 313, and 415."

22. This is the conclusion (in part in reference to K. 175/i) in Stevens, "Patterns of Recapitulation," p. 411.

fleeting R1-interpolation or two, as if Mozart were beginning to gesture toward the idea of a more thoroughgoing Rotation 1-Rotation 2 recapitulatory synthesis. Violin Concerto No. 5 in A, K. 219, furnishes an example of this at its most embryonic stage. The solo recapitulation retraces the pattern of the solo exposition except for one difference. Within its P-zone we find—at least from the perspective of the S1 layout—four "new" measures of R1:\P-material interpolated at m. 152, beat 3. More precisely: m. 152, the ninth bar of S1:\P (a variant of R1:\P), continues its expected course as a correspondence measure with m. 54, but is interrupted for four measures until it is permitted to resume with purely solo-identified material on the third beat of m. 156 (= that of m. 54). In between one finds wedged a segment of R1:\P (= m. 9, beat 3 to m. 13, beat 1) that had not been heard since R1, but which is also a logical, R1-based continuation of the material presented up to this point.[23]

While the recapitulatory alterations in K. 219 represent an only modest step, it is easy to understand the compositional desire to incorporate more trenchant interventions of purposely "lost" R1 material into solo recapitulations. Such restorations contribute more strongly to a recrafted, recapitulatory synthesis, one in which R1 and S1 differences are reconciled in the solo recapitulation as an important part of the larger project of R1-module recovery undertaken in the larger recapitulation, which includes the R4 block. Mozart pursued this interest in his more mature concertos, many of whose solo recapitulations, as a consequence, differ remarkably from their corresponding solo expositions. These situations are especially compelling—and structurally requisite—in those concerto movements whose R1:\S is discarded in S1 in favor of new S-material: most or all of the original R1:\S idea will normally be restored in an S-synthesis within the solo recapitulation's S-space. While each individualized Type 5 recapitulation demands examination on its own terms, extreme instances of the rethinking and rearrangement of solo-recapitulatory space may be found in Piano Concertos No. 21 in C, K. 467, and No. 24 in C Minor, K. 491.

Solo-Led (S3) Openings

One convention found in several of Mozart's earliest Type 5s was to have the soloist, not the tutti, begin the recapitulation in a manner parallel with how it had begun S1. The result is a solo recapitulation occupied entirely by S3. This procedure is especially associated with the violin concertos (1775), which provide paradigms in the first movements of Nos. 1–3 and No. 5—and in the finale of No. 1, K. 207.[24] A few later concerto first movements also adapt this formula, usually in more sophisticated ways: Piano Concerto No. 19 in F, K. 459; Horn Concertos No. 1 in D, K. 412, and No. 4 in E-flat, K. 495; and Clarinet Concerto in A, K. 622.[25] In these last cases Mozart revisits an older, now less common norm in order to integrate it into more complex musical thought. This kind of solo recapitulation is the type most closely relatable to the prescriptions of Vogler and Koch, both of whom described a format in which the recapitulatory space was launched by the solo, not by a renewed tutti-charge, as is more common in Mozart's concertos. In most of the situations in Mozart, the solo-led recapitulation is preceded by a tutti passage of variable length—the retransitional "R3" tutti dealt with earlier in this chapter. That discussion, which also provides illustrations from K. 207 and K. 459 (examples 22.3 and 22.4), need not be replicated here.

Two additional first movements are also in

---

23. Since S1:\P is a variant of R1:\P—featuring only a new melodic overlay—the tracking followed from the onset of the recapitulation through this seeming interpolation, mm. 144–56, is that which also corresponds to mm. 1–13.

24. No. 4 in D, K. 218, is similar but is a Type 2 variant of the Type 5 sonata (the corresponding passage is a solo-led S1:\TR in m. 146). As such, the term "recapitulation" is problematic in this case.

25. Piano Concerto No. 9 in E-flat, K. 271, which also begins its recapitulation with a short statement from the soloist (m. 196, reversing the procedure found at the opening of R1), is a special case, an *ad hoc* situation, that falls outside the norms of the present category. In K. 271/i unpredictable and transgressive tutti and solo entries are recurring aspects of the piece's wit.

dialogue with this "older" norm but add a new twist. Instead of leading off the recapitulation with the traditional R1:\P, the soloist revisits the S1:\P-preface that it had sounded at the point of its initial entry. These are Piano Concertos Nos. 11 in F, K. 413 (upbeat to m. 236), and No. 13 in C, K. 415 (m. 200, which presents the added anomaly of lacking even a vestigial "R3" retransition before the onset of the solo preface, making it the unique example in Mozart of Type 5 Subtype C, table 19.1.) In both cases the S1:\P^{pref} is followed by a statement of R1:\P by the tutti—normally the signal for the recapitulation proper. As such, the issue becomes one of where the recapitulatory rotation is considered to have begun. This problem is already addressed in chapter 21, in the discussion of expositions beginning with an S1:\P^{pref} module.

Double-Start Openings (R3 + S3)

Some of Mozart's Type 5 recapitulations feature a decisive tutti beginning (the incipit or interjection, R1:\P$^{1.1}$, reanimating the opening of the piece) that serves—like an illuminated initial—to mark the structural moment of recapitulation but that then gives way, usually within four or five bars, to a second, solo-led beginning that replicates the opening of S1. From one perspective, these double-start openings (R3 + S3) are similar to the solo-led ones treated above, except that the "R3" tutti is no longer a retransition (or brief fill) at the end of the development but has been shifted to a place of increased prominence, becoming a declarative, tonic orchestral-charge—a true structural pillar—that begins the recapitulatory rotation with an emphatic push. From another, the R1 "group"-persona takes an initially commanding charge of the recapitulation, then yields graciously to the soloist for an S1-based rebeginning.

This is another recapitulation strategy associated especially with Mozart's earliest concertos, even, though, as with the solo-led openings, some more advanced adaptations of it occur in a few later concertos. Two subtypes are worth distinguishing: those in which the soloist had begun S1 with a reiteration of R1:\P$^{1.1}$; and those in which the soloist had suppressed R1:\P$^{1.1}$ in order to substitute a new idea associated exclusively with itself, S1:\P. Three early examples of the first type are found in the first movement of Piano Concerto No. 5 in D, K. 175 (m. 143, orchestra; restart at m. 146, soloist); in the finale of the same concerto (m. 156, orchestra; restart at m. 162, soloist); and in the first movement of Bassoon Concerto in B-flat, K. 191 (m. 98, orchestra; restart at m. 102, soloist—example 22.5a).[26] A more developed example occurs in the opening movement of Horn Concerto No. 3, K. 447, in which the first recapitulatory start in the orchestra, m. 112, is extended beyond a mere incipit-gesture to proceed as far as R1:\TR and R1:\MC before yielding to the second, horn-led recapitulatory beginning at m. 121.

The second subtype, with differing material for each recapitulatory start (R1:\P$^{1.1}$ and S1:\P) may also be found in two early works: in the Concertone in C, K. 190 (m. 155, orchestra; restart at m. 159, soloists—example 22.5b) and in the fourth movement of the Serenade in D, K. 203 (m. 99, m. 103). Mozart reworked this more extravagant subtype in the first movement of the Sinfonia Concertante in E-flat, K. 364 (m. 223 is the moment of the first start; m. 237 is that of the second, even though it is also launched by the orchestra, as had also happened in S1),[27]

---

26. A variant is provided in the A-major third movement, Allegro, of the Serenade in D, K. 204. The opening theme of R1 is a sentence that begins with a binary-loop presentation. The looped R1:\P$^{1.1}$ appears at mm. 1–5 and 5–9, elided with the breakout-continuation at m. 9, R1:\P$^{1.2}$. S1 opens similarly (m. 23), only with the soloist providing a decorative variant of the R1:\P$^{1.1}$ loop-idea. In the recapitulation the first loop is given to the orchestral model, R1:\P (m. 119), the second to its solo variant (m. 123).

27. In K. 364 most of the complications at the moment of recapitulation are predicated on the non-normative events that had begun the solo exposition, where a dovetailed early entrance of the soloists had led to an unusual, orchestra-launched S1. The double-start recapitulation begins unmistakably in the orchestra with R1:\P (m. 223 = m. 1). After six bars this music splices to the *end* of R1, for R1:\C (m. 229 = m. 70), presumably in order to replicate the dovetailed "first-entrance" effect of the soloists (m. 231 = m. 72). This leads inexorably to the second recapitulatory start at m. 237, two orchestral bars that had also begun the solo exposition at m. 78.

EXAMPLE 22.5a Mozart, Bassoon Concerto in B-flat, K. 191, i, mm. 95–105

EXAMPLE 22.5b   Mozart, Concertone in C, K. 190, mm. 152–62

and in that of Horn Concerto No. 2 in E-flat, K. 417 (m. 117, orchestra; m. 126, soloist).

R3⇒S3 Merger Openings

In this procedure the solo recapitulation begins with a decisive tutti pillar replicating the beginning of opening ritornello theme, R1:\P, but usually within a few bars the soloist re-enters to assist with or to take over its continuation. This strategy avoids the redundancy of the double-start recapitulation, with which it is conceptually related.[28] Here, instead of a backup and restart, an initial R3 texture soon merges into an S3 one. This is the most common option for the middle and later Mozart concertos, from Piano Concerto No. 6 in B-flat, K. 238 (1776), onward. In its many variants and realizations, it soon became the first-level-default option, especially in the piano concertos.

As already indicated, this R3⇒S3 merger has been noted and discussed in the literature, with much debate about whether the R3 opening portion should qualify as a real ritornello or as merely a tutti interjection. We regard it as a ritornello pillar, R3, for reasons already laid out in chapter 19 (the structural reprise or *da capo* function of this kind of ritornello), reasons that are not dependent on the number of bars for which the soloist is absent from the onset of the recapitulation—usually the central topic around which this debate has focused. Obviously, the longer the tutti, the more stable the R3 impression and the sense of unfolding a reanimation of the opening of R1.

It is unusual for the recapitulatory tutti (R3) to be sustained without the soloist for more than eight bars.[29] The longest R3s, frequently cited in this regard, are those found in Piano Concertos No. 21 in C, K. 467 (a non-normative twenty-three bars, mm. 274–96, extending well into R1:\TR [m. 285] and the onset of a surprising, new *idée fixe* interpolation on IV [m. 295]), No. 27 in B-flat, K. 595 (fifteen bars, mm. 242–56), and No. 17 in G, K. 453 (ten bars with extended upbeat, mm. 227–36). At the other extreme, the shortest are those in which the soloist enters

within a bar or two of the onset of R3, beginning to participate at once in the now-joint and fully shared project of recapitulation. Examples may be found in Piano Concertos No. 6 in B-flat, K. 238 (mm. 131, 133), No. 15 in B-flat, K. 450 (mm. 197, 199, initiating an opening recapitulatory dialogue), and No. 16 in D, K. 451 (m. 219, 220, with nonthematic, affirmative scalar flourishes in the solo).

Once the decision has been made to merge the soloist into a recapitulation begun with an R3 gesture, this may be accomplished in any number of ways. It is unproductive to try to categorize them. Some solo entrances are non-thematic, providing a decorative overlay to the thematic material still continuing in the orchestra (a sustained trill, with upbeat, in Piano Concerto No. 18 in B-flat, K. 456, m. 240; scalar passagework in Piano Concerto No. 22 in E-flat, K. 482, m. 272). Others participate in a decorative or agitated doubling of the melody (Piano Concerto No. 20 in D Minor, K. 466, m. 262) or a brief back-and-forth dialogue with the tutti (K. 450, mentioned above). Still others enter by taking over the melodic lead of the P-idea, thereby completing the theme begun by the orchestra. The soloist provides the complementary consequent to an orchestral antecedent, for instance, in Piano Concertos No. 12 in A, K. 414 (m. 204), and No. 23 in A, K. 488 (m. 206). In No. 25 in C, K. 503, m. 298, the soloist provides the complementary reiteration of a broad sentence-presentation module. In other cases the piano enters into the thematic current mid-phrase, at more unpredictable moments (Concerto for Two Pianos in E-flat, K. 365, m. 209, reiterating the opening *unisono* flourish in the orchestra with a modal shift; Piano Concerto No. 17 in G, K. 453, m. 237, midway through the sentence-continuation; No. 21 in C, K. 467, m. 297, suddenly picking up on the freshly interpolated wild-card, *idée-fixe* march that had just intervened in the orchestra, m. 295; No. 24 in C minor, m. 368, replicating one of its early entries in the exposition [= m. 124]).

---

28. See also the similar conclusion in Grayson, *Mozart's Piano Concertos Nos. 20 and 21*, p. 27.

29. Irving, *Mozart's Piano Concertos*, p. 50, regarded this as more or less the norm.

The Solo Recapitulatory Transition

In purely harmonic terms, recapitulatory transitions in Type 5 sonatas follow the same norms as those in other types. In order to prepare for the recurrence of the S-theme(s) now in the tonic, these TRs conclude with either a I:HC or a I:PAC MC (the expositional option, V:HC, is no longer available), and they often effect a move toward the subdominant that might occur either at a sudden shift-point or through a more gradual modulation. Because this topic has been dealt with earlier (chapter 11), the only matters that need to be touched upon here concern whatever issues might be unique to Type 5s. Those issues center around modular content—particularly the degree to which this TR might reintroduce modules from R1 as part of a process of recapitulatory synthesis.

Young Mozart's norm was to base the recapitulatory TR on S1:\TR materials, without any "new" infiltration from R1:\TR.[30] In these concertos S1:\TR was often a solo-led *sujet-libre* transition that, following a brief tutti interjection, served as a substitute for R1:\TR$^{1.1}$. That *sujet libre* also led off the recapitulatory TR, at times starting in the original key (Piano Concerto No. 5 in D, K. 175, m. 161), at times shifted at once onto the subdominant (Bassoon Concerto in B-flat, K. 191, m. 112; Violin Concerto No. 1 in B-flat, K. 207, m. 115). When these S1:\TR-modeled recapitulatory transitions began in the tonic, they usually led to a passage of mild precrux alterations almost at once (as in K. 175/i), a practice much later restored in Piano Concerto No. 27 in B-flat, K. 595 (linkage-technique *sujet-libre* S1:\TR$^{1.1}$ at m. 256 [= m. 95], precrux alterations at m. 260; full crux with TI^2, m. 266 [= m. 104], producing an MC at the same pitch-level as that of the exposition, I:HC, at m. 268). On rare occasions no alterations were made to the recapitulatory TR, which was therefore identical, bar-for-bar, with the expositional TR, leading to the same I:HC MC, as in Violin Concerto No. 5 in A, K. 219. (The next bar, S1:\TM^1, is then shifted

into the tonic, down a fifth from its appearance in the exposition.)

As Mozart's career developed, he explored ways of treating the recapitulatory TR more imaginatively. One approach was to subject the traditional S1:\TR-modeled recapitulatory transition to a significant shortening (typically following an expansion of P and the suppression of the first tutti interjection) through the surprising decision to omit its most memorable module, the head-motive *sujet-libre* TR$^{1.1}$. In these cases, S1:\TR$^{1.1}$ became a one-time event, not heard again after the exposition. We find this solution in the Oboe Concerto in C, K. 314 (expositional *sujet libre* at m. 50; cf. its omission ca. m. 133 [= m. 61]),[31] and in the Concerto for Two Pianos in E-flat, K. 365 (*sujet libre* at m. 84; cf. its omission c. m. 225, a crux with S1:\TR$^{1.2}$ [= m. 96]), and Piano Concertos No. 16 in D, K. 451 (*sujet libre* at m. 98; cf. c. m. 235), and No. 26 in D, K. 537 (*sujet libre* at m. 103; cf. the radical P–TR telescoping perceptible at the crux, mm. 305–6 [= mm. 121–22]).

Another set of solutions entailed the replacing of certain S1:\TR modules with ones from R1:\TR—basing the recapitulatory TR more on the one in the initial ritornello than on the replacement for it found in the exposition. Any such resubstitution of R1:\TR modules deviated markedly from the more traditional practice of composing an S1:\TR-modeled recapitulatory transition. These strategies emerged especially in Mozart's Viennese piano concertos from 1784 to 1785. Within the concept a number of solutions were possible. One of the earliest, a "both-and" or "double-start" procedure, appears in No. 15 in B-flat, K. 450. In the exposition we had heard, at the end of P, a brief, modulatory TI^1 (mm. 86–87), elided with a *sujet-libre* S1:\TR beginning in G minor (m. 87). In the recapitulation, the original TI^1 is absent, and the music plunges instead into a tonic-key recovery of R1:\TR$^{1.1}$ in m. 210 (= m. 14)—a module that had also been used to begin R2 in V (m. 137). After four bars the continuation of R1:\TR$^{1.1}$ destabilizes and is broken off (mm.

---

30. Cf. the discussion of the recapitulatory TR in Küster, *Formale Aspekte*, pp. 154–59.

31. As if by way of compensation, K. 314's recapitulatory TR also includes five newly interpolated bars, mm. 137–41 (cf. the figuration in R1:\P$^{1.2}$, mm. 44–45).

214–15) with a modulation toward C minor (ii), whereupon the exposition's *sujet libre* recurs, with some variants, on C minor in m. 216 (cf. m. 87). The recovery of the original R1:\TR[1.1] module at m. 210—a move toward Rotation 1-Rotation 2 synthesis—serves as a longer replacement for the exposition's modulatory TI[1].

From K. 450 onward Mozart's solutions become more inventive. He now began to explore the idea of a recapitulatory TR that leaned more toward that of the initial ritornello. Each solution is idiosyncratic and requires exploration on its own terms. In one of the most complicated of these, No. 21 in C, K. 467, he replaced the original *sujet libre* (m. 91) with a return to the *forte* R1:\TR[1.1] (m. 285 = m. 12), continuing for some ten bars. In this case even stranger things follow: an unexpected interpolation of the wild-card *idée-fixe* march (in its R1:\S[1.2] version) in the subdominant, m. 295 (= m. 36) and a merger into S1:\TM[2] (!) at m. 304 (cf. m. 121), setting up a I:HC MC with expanded fill (mm. 307–12) and leading to a completely reordered TMB beginning with S1:\TM[3] (m. 313).[32] Somewhat related is the situation in No. 22 in E-flat, K. 482. Here what had been the "new" breakout-continuation from S1 (m. 106, a passage probably also with the *sujet-libre* procedure in mind) is replaced by the return of R1:\TR[1.1] (mm. 31, 294),[33] following a broad P-space that had resubstituted the lengthy R1:\P music for its Solo 1 version. No. 20 in D Minor, K. 466, avoids the briefer P⇒TR merger in

the solo exposition with a full restoration of the iron-willed, negative R1:\TR (m. 269), only the MC conclusion of which had been replicated in the expositional transition.

In the expositions of other Viennese piano concertos (such as No. 17 in G, K. 453, and No. 18 in B-flat, K. 456) Mozart pursued the differing, more "symphonic" strategy of beginning the S1 transition with R1:\TR[1.1] before dissolving into a differing solo continuation, whose modules we normally label as S1:\TR[1.2], S1:\TR[1.3], and so on. In these cases he usually retained the R1:\TR[1.1] opening for the recapitulatory transition but replaced the soloist's original continuation with a restoration of that of R1:\TR. K. 453's R1:\TR restoration is complete and assigned to the tutti throughout (mm. 242–57 = mm. 16–31, though with the solo piano supplying the caesura-fill in mm. 257–60). Thus, as Irving noted, in K. 453 "virtually all of the first solo transition is discarded."[34] In the similar K. 456 the restoration proceeds as far as R1:\TR[1.2] (mm. 255–58 = mm. 24–27), after which two bars of solo-fill (mm. 258–59 = mm. 101–2) lead directly to the recapitulation of S1:\TM[1] (m. 260 = m. 103). (The remainder of R1:\TR —its much-expanded, minor-mode-ridden caesura-fill—is cleverly tucked, as in the exposition, into S1:\TM[2]: m. 274 = m. 117 = m. 28.)

In all such cases from the later works, the crucial analytical point is to perceive the varying degrees to which the more traditional practice—retaining the modular materials of the S1

---

32. The concepts of wild cards and *idées fixes*, along with that of their functions—a crucial aspect of this movement, the touchstone example of them—are elaborated in ch. 20. For another view of the unique interpolation of the march figure in IV, see Grayson, *Mozart's Piano Concertos Nos. 20 and 21*, p. 54. Also to be noted is the unusual feature of moving what had been in S-space earlier into recapitulatory TR-space—shifting it leftward, to a position before the MC. A similar occurrence may be found in Piano Concerto No. 12 in A, K. 414, in which what may be construed as an S1:\S[0] module (from m. 98) is more clearly in TR-space in the recapitulation, m. 224. Mozart apparently considered such a move to neutralize the S-aspects of these modules, in effect deactivating them as S-material. As such it represents the exception to what we have regarded as the general principle that what was initially sounded within

S-space will continue to define itself and its surroundings as S-material regardless of where it appears. Accordingly this principle holds only for S-material that appears after the MC, that is, within the tonally active, structural-cadence-attaining portions of the recapitulation.

33. Our recapitulatory measure-numbering of K. 482/i follows that of the current critical edition, which restores two measures following m. 281 that are lacking in some other editions. See K. 482/i in *Neue Ausgabe sämtlicher Werke*, Serie V, Werkgruppe 15, vol. 6, ed. Hans Engel and Horst Heussner (Kassel: Bärenreiter, 1961), pp. xv–xvi, 206. Thus what had appeared as m. 282 in some editions is now m. 284, and two-bar numbering discrepancies persist for the rest of the movement.

34. Irving, *Mozart's Piano Concertos*, p. 53.

transition—is overridden by the urge to reinsert alternative R1 ideas into the musical discourse. Such recapitulatory syntheses display creative interactions, stage a negotiated play of forces, between the group and the individual, the dual claims of R1 and S1. Especially in the mature works, once such interactions have begun in the recapitulatory P- and TR-spaces, they are likely to continue throughout the remainder of the recapitulation.

Solo Recapitulatory S- and C-Space (S3:\ESC)

Following the first MC, the solo recapitulation proceeds into the zones of *tonal resolution*, revisiting in the tonic ideas associated previously with S- and (when it had existed) C-material. As in the solo exposition, this complementary post-MC block will normally end with a display episode finished off with an emphatic trill-cadence plunging into the next ritornello pillar, here R4. Solo recapitulatory S-space persists as long as it includes modules associated with either R1:\ or S1:\S-space. It ends only when a satisfactory perfect authentic cadence is sounded—proceeding onward to differing material—and S-modules are definitively abandoned for the remainder of the solo recapitulation. The tonic-key S3:\ESC-point is usually the recapitulatory equivalent of the nontonic S1:\EEC, but in rearranged or otherwise altered recapitulations the two points may not be parallel. The S3:\ESC may be articulated only with the final trill-cadence (in which case there will be no S3:\C-space; the display episode will be part of S-space) or it may occur earlier (in which case the display episode will have been played in C-space, perhaps even after the reappearance of a separate C-theme).

As with other portions of solo-recapitulatory space, the background default option—a generically offered template—was to revisit the post-MC materials from S1, bar-for-bar (or very nearly so), now transposing them to the tonic with only small adjustments in register, melodic line, or scoring. The obvious benefit of this solution was one much valued in the late-eighteenth century: the attaining of a gratifying, "classical" symmetry between the most structurally important portions of the solo exposition and recapitulation. Its chief drawback, at least from the perspective of later compositional practice, was the largely mechanical aspect of the mere transposition. While this procedure is not invariable in Mozart's earliest concertos, it occurs often enough in them to suggest that any deviations from it, including those in several of the more complex later concertos, are to be perceived as overridings of that norm for local purposes that invite individual investigation. Our first concern, then—option 1—is that more generically formulaic type of solo recapitulation that does not reinstate R1-materials that had been "missing" in the solo exposition.

Option 1: No Restoration of R1:\Post-MC Material Suppressed in the Larger Exposition

One may find the simplest solution, bar-for-bar correspondences with the solo exposition, in Violin Concerto No. 3 in G, K. 216, and in Flute Concerto in G, K. 313. More typically, the solo recapitulation will tweak a solo-expositional moment or two, lengthening or shortening it slightly. Thus in the Concertone in C, K. 190, Mozart interpolated a "new" two-bar tutti interjection—yet another "false R4-effect" within C-space—into the ongoing correspondence measures at mm. 223–24, while in the Bassoon Concerto in B-flat, K. 191, the recapitulatory equivalent of the exposition's mm. 69–70, the final drive to the trill-cadence, is intensified and stretched to four bars, mm. 148–51.[35] The procedure found in K. 191, an expansion only at the end, is found also in Violin Concerto No. 5 in A, K. 219, and in Piano Concerto No. 6 in B-flat, K. 238.

The operative principle in both K. 191 and K. 238 is that of keeping the emphatically melodic materials intact and expanding or altering

35. In K. 191 notice also the switching of the parts in the sounding of R1:\S. In the exposition the theme had been carried by the orchestra, upbeat to m. 60; in the recapitulation it is played by the soloist, upbeat to m. 139.

things only at the nonthematic display episode. This principle may be found in several of the Viennese piano concertos, such as Nos. 11 in F, K. 413 (display-episode expansion at mm. 341–51; cf. mm. 160–63), No. 13 in C, K. 415 (one added measure in the display episode, m. 281), No. 14 in E-flat, K. 449 (expanded and partially recomposed portion of the display episode, mm. 309–18; cf. mm. 162–67), and No. 20 in D Minor, K. 466 (recomposed first portion of the display episode, mm. 318–30; further expansions in mm. 333–38 [cf. mm. 156–59]; and a recomposed and lengthened final portion, mm. 343–56 [cf. mm. 164–74]). It also occurs in Horn Concerto No. 3 in E-flat, K. 447, although here one also finds a substantially recomposed $S1:\backslash S^{1.3}$ (m. 147 [cf. m. 59]) merging into a much-lengthened and reconceived display episode.[36] Two instances in which the expositional display episode is altered by being made shorter rather than longer occur in Piano Concertos No. 17 in G, K. 453 (mm. 315–16 provide a compressed recomposition of mm. 164–68), and No. 27 in B-flat, K. 595 (mm. 323–24 telescope mm. 161–63; another bar is omitted between mm. 332 and 333).

Occasionally, one finds more idiosyncratic changes within option-1 solo recapitulations. In the first movement of Mozart's earliest original piano concerto, No. 5 in D, K. 175, the exposition's S-modules ($R1:\backslash S^0$, $R1:\backslash S^{1.1}$, $S1:\backslash S^{1.2}$, $S1:\backslash S^{1.3}$, in mm. 66, 68, 72, and 76) appear in a different order in the recapitulation as part of a whirligig reassembling of fast-paced materials ($R1:\backslash S^0$, $R1:\backslash S^{1.1}$, $S1:\backslash S^{1.3}$, and $S1:\backslash S^{1.2}$ in mm. 183, 185, 188, and 195). Additionally, in K. 175/i, one could make the case that the original $S1:\backslash C$, m. 83, is folded into recapitulatory S-space at m. 199, since it now functions as the continuation of a "new" sentence begun with the presentational $S1:\backslash S^{1.2}$ at m. 195. In the finale of Violin Concerto No. 1 in B-flat, K. 207, whose solo exposition had provided a new S, bypassing the one proposed in R1, Mozart shifted the $R1:\backslash S$ that had reappeared only in R2-space (mm.

151–63 [cf. mm. 33–45]) into the solo recapitulation as an S-appendix, slightly varied, at mm. 315–35, now accomplishing the $S3:\backslash ESC$ and leading to a new display episode.[37]

Four comparable situations involving the displacement of $R1:\backslash S$-materials from R2 into the end of the solo recapitulation crop up in the first movements of Violin Concerto No. 2 in D, K. 211, and Piano Concertos No. 16 in D, K. 451, No. 18 in B-flat, K. 456, and No. 23 in A, K. 488. In the solo recapitulation of K. 211 we find two additional bars of $R1:\backslash S^{1.3}$, mm. 109–10 (= mm. 13–14), which in the exposition had been placed into R2 (mm. 56–57). In K. 451 the newly imported materials (heard in R2 at mm. 179–91) consist of a march variant of $R1:\backslash S^{1.3}$ (mm. 280–83 [cf. mm. 57–60]) and a much-expanded $R1:\backslash S^{1.4}$ (mm. 283–307, including a merger into recomposed display episode; [cf. mm. 60–68]). In K. 456 the final, fanfare module of the S-theme of Ritornello 1, $R1:\backslash S^{1.4}$, mm. 61–67, is omitted in the solo exposition (in which $R1:\backslash S^{1.1-1.3}$ serves as an extended TM^3, mm. 128–49) but does resurface in a shortened version in Ritornello 2 to effect the $R2:\backslash EEC$, mm. 185–89. In the solo recapitulation, whose post-MC-space is otherwise parallel to S1, an "extra" $R1:\backslash S^{1.4}$ fanfare, mm. 331–35, is interpolated cheekily at the end of the display episode, thereby converting what we had presumed to be C-space (as in the solo exposition) into S-space. $R1:\backslash S^{1.4}$ also reappears once again in $R4^2$ (mm. 355–61), producing the $R4^2:\backslash ESC$ that overrides the $S3:\backslash ESC$ at m. 337 (S3's concluding trill-cadence).

The situation in K. 488 is more unusual—a masterstroke of imagination. As mentioned earlier, this movement's opening sections present a poised, purposely unadventurous reliance on symmetry and balance: no new modular ideas except the display episode are introduced in S1. After an sudden interruption in the middle of R2 (m. 142: "Stop! I have something else to say!") comes the unexpected feature of this movement. Into that interruption-gap Mozart

---

36. Cf. the recomposed $S1:\backslash S^{1.2}$ in the Second Horn Concerto, K. 417, mm. 155–63.

37. This procedure is related to that in option 2, which typically restores $R1:\backslash S$ material into solo-recapitula-

tory space. The difference is that the $R1:\backslash S$-material missing in the solo exposition had been sounded in the larger exposition, within R2.

introduced a radical change of topic, a wistful new *piano* theme (m. 143, beat 3) blossoming up out of nowhere—like a cherished after-thought-idea, a special gift, that had not been thought of within R1. This previously unheard theme not only dominates the ensuing development but is interpolated into the solo recapitulation's C-space, mm. 261–75, where it is treated wondrously, as a precious gem.

Option 2: Restoration of R1:\Post-MC Material Suppressed in the Larger Exposition

By the early and mid-1780s Mozart's understanding of the structural and expressive possibilities within the Type 5 sonata had been much deepened. In around a dozen concerto first movements, nearly all of them strongly individualized piano concertos from the center of his Vienna period—especially from No. 15 in B-flat, K. 450 (1784), onward—one finds a more complex handling of the solo recapitulation. This centered around the recrafting of S- or C-space in such a way as to restore one or more R1:\S-modules that had been omitted in the larger exposition—in other words, modules that had not been heard since R1. We regard such procedures as exercising a set of "option 2" realizations. Most importantly, they fortified the role of the post-MC portion of the solo recapitulation (as opposed to the R4-block of the larger recapitulation) in the task of providing a recapitulatory synthesis of Rotation 1 (R1) and Rotation 2 (S1 + R2). Such an opportunity arose in any Type 5 structure in which the larger exposition had failed to include an R1:\post-MC module. Moreover, any expositional omissions of all of R1:\S or of at least its head-motive, R1:\S$^{1.1}$, would have been especially noticeable. This means that what one does not hear in the larger exposition is as central to

our understanding of it as what one does hear. Whatever the internal plenitude of such an S1 + R2, in its post-MC differences from R1 it also registered a lack, an absence, something that would have to be restored in the larger recapitulatory rotation. Our option 2 addresses those instances in which significant aspects of that restoration were placed into post-MC positions in the solo recapitulation. (Restorations made after the solo recapitulation—that is, within R4, concluding the larger recapitulation—are dealt with separately below.)

We find anticipations of this practice in two of Mozart's earlier, Salzburg concertos, although in each early case the restored module is not one from the crucial R1:\S-space. The earlier occurs in Violin Concerto No. 4 in D, K. 218 (1774), where a previously missing R1:\C$^{1.2}$ module, mm. 177 (beat 3)–181 (= mm. 30–34), originally the continuation of a sentence), is spliced into the end of TM^2, part of a trimodular block that is otherwise fully parallel with that of the exposition. The second is that found in Piano Concerto No. 9 in E-flat, K. 271. Here the solo recapitulatory display episode, still in S-space, includes an interpolated restoration, introduced by the orchestra, of an "out-of-order" R1:\TR$^{1.1}$ (mm. 251–58), the module that had previously been heard only as the break-out-continuation (P⇒TR merger, mm. 7–11) of the R1:\P$^{1.1}$ binary loops at the opening of the piece (see example 5.7). In this instance the tutti interpolation at m. 251 suggests the witty interjection of a premature, "false R4," even in the absence of the characteristic trill-cadence in the solo part.

Solo recapitulations that restore a module from R1:\S first appear with that of the Sinfonia Concertante in E-flat, K. 364 (1779; example 22.6).[38] Here the "lost" R1:\S$^{1.1}$, originally a binary-loop presentation module of a sentence

---

38. Cf. also the restoration of a "lost" R1:\S$^{1.1}$ on the tonic, but more accurately expressing the active dominant, near the end of the developmental space of the Concerto for Two Pianos (No. 10), in E-flat, K. 365/i, mm. 187–99 (cf. mm. 30–42). This moment functions primarily as an expanded caesura-fill—a prolonged moment of static suspension. It appears also to suggest a fleeting dialogue with the Type 2 variant of the Type 5 sonata, as if that idea were momentarily crossing Mo-

zart's mind before being rejected as a viable option at m. 199, with the sudden deflation to E-flat minor. The solo recapitulation of this movement also shows other "experimental" anomalies, including a second quasi-redundant appearance of R1:\P$^{1.1}$ at the opening of S3:\C-space, m. 253 (from m. 5, following R1:\P$^{1.0}$ at m. 1)—perhaps compensating for its earlier minor-mode collapse at m. 209.

EXAMPLE 22.6 Mozart, Sinfonia Concertante in E-flat, K. 364, i,
mm. 285–302

[Allegro maestoso]

Example 22.6   (continued)

EXAMPLE 22.6   *(continued)*

(mm. 38–46), reappears as TM^3 in a newly fashioned trimodular block. In the solo exposition S1:\S, a replacement for the secondary theme proposed in R1, had been brief, a mere eight-bar period (mm. 126–33). In the solo recapitulation S1:\S returns, now in the tonic (m. 285) and with the order of its solo parts reversed, but its earlier, concluding PAC (m. 133, the S1:\EEC) is now reshaped into a half cadence and second MC-effect (mm. 291–92, a brief S3:\TM^2 merely articulating the caesura). At this point Mozart interpolated the expositionally absent R1:\S$^{1.1}$ loops, mm. 293–301 ("Don't forget me!"), which at m. 301 rejoin measures that are referential to the exposition's display episode (cf. m. 133), now functioning as the breakout-continuation of the presentational loops. The recomposition also defers the expected S3:\ESC. While in the solo exposition the display episode had occupied C-space (m. 133), it is now drawn into a much-expanded, though largely nonthematic S-space. The S3:\ESC is attained only with the concluding trill-cadence at m. 328, elided with R4.

Three years later Mozart, now in Vienna, employed a similar solution in Piano Concerto No. 12 in A, K. 414. This time he expanded the end the S-sentence found in the solo exposition (mm. 115–22, 123–31, R1:\S$^{1.1}$+S1:\S$^{2.2}$)[39] and brought it to an unequivocal PAC close in the tonic (mm. 233–52). Following this, he reinstated the "forgotten" R1:\S^2 as an S-appendix (upbeat tom. 253 [cf. upbeat to m. 51, where it had also served as an R1:\S-appendix]) and within a few bars merged it into the display episode (ca. mm. 261–64). The S-appendix status of the restored R1:\S is even clearer in No. 15 in B-flat, K. 450 (1784). Here R1:\S, a balanced sentential period, is suppressed in the expositional Rotation 2 but is plugged back into the sonata in the solo recapitulation (mm. 249–64 [= mm. 26–41]), nonelided after a full restatement of the "alternative" S1:\S, mm. 233–48, ending with an emphatic I:PAC.

From this point onward Mozart became even more fully committed to overriding the earlier norm of keeping his solo recapitulations largely parallel with the corresponding solo expositions. Anticipated especially by the recapitulatory procedures of K. 364 and K. 414, K. 450 marks the point at which Mozart was determined to make the relationships among R1, the solo and larger expositions, and the solo and larger recapitulations more complex. Often central to this enhanced richness was the production of one or more thematic R1:\S-module absences within the solo and larger expositions—conceptual blanks that demanded refilling later in the movement—and then reinstating the sidelined material at unanticipated moments within the solo recapitulation, or perhaps even deferring the reappearances of that material until R4 (as

---

39. Many portions of K. 414/i present problems of classification. (Cf. n. 32.) If in its exposition m. 98 is regarded as the start of S1:\S (perhaps S1:\S^0 on V^7 of V), then that portion of the secondary theme comes to a close with the V:PAC in m. 114. M. 115 then starts a second S-sentence, one whose presentation recaptures R1:\S$^{1.1}$. Its continuation at m. 122, however, is new to Solo 1: hence the S1:\S$^{2.2}$ label.

in K. 453, revisited at the end of this chapter). By K. 450 this practice had become Mozart's norm rather than the exception. It was now a personally customized first-level default that emphasized the solo and larger recapitulations as spaces of unpredictable synthesis, reassembling and fusing the disparate materials of Ritornello 1 and the larger exposition. Whenever Mozart did return to the earlier, simpler norm of keeping the solo exposition and solo recapitulation essentially parallel, as in Piano Concerto No. 27 in B-flat, K. 595, or the Clarinet Concerto in A, K. 622, he produced the effect of a smooth, uncorrupted balance of parts, a classical equipoise existing "transcendently" beyond any forces that might introduce unwelcome elements of disequilibrium.

Even as they beguiled listeners with one astonishing idea after another, the first movements of Mozart's concertos had now become stunningly complex. Notwithstanding all of its inbuilt archaic rigidities, the Type 5 sonata—with its added requirement of assessing all of the sonata-spaces in relation not only to each other but also to the proto-expositional model provided in R1—had been transformed into a field of abundant structural possibilities, the *ne plus ultra* demonstration of ingenious sonata-organizational technique. Mozart's synthesis-solutions were now so individualized that the only way to do justice to them is to examine each of them separately and in detail, a task beyond the scope of this chapter.

The solo recapitulation of Piano Concerto No. 19 in F, K. 459, for instance, is so intricate as virtually to defy a quick description. The restored R1-module at issue here—beginning as a set of melodically descending thirds—recurs as a "surprise" interpolation, mm. 341–47, wedged into the display episode. But that passage is not really an R1:\S-module, since K. 459 is the only piano concerto to contain not a two-part but a continuous proto-exposition in R1. Thus the restored module is extracted from the latter part of the central portion (that is, of TR⇒FS) of R1, mm. 43–49. Shortly after this, the recapitulatory display episode features a large expansion from the solo expositional model. An original seven bars (mm. 181–87) are inflated to twenty-two (mm. 356–77), many of which

are preoccupied with the further multiplication of the ever-proliferating, *idée-fixe* march motive that dominates much of this movement. Shifting our attention now to the music prior to the recapitulatory display episode, we notice also that the solo exposition's TMB (whose constituent parts had begun in mm. 96, 103, and 131) is shorn of its TM¹ module—mm. 96–102, which, as a consequence, never recurs anywhere else in the movement. This means that much of the exposition's *idée-fixe*-grounded TM², for the most part an expanded caesura-fill ending with the usual PAC, now appears in recapitulatory TR-space. As a result, the exposition's S1:\TM³ (mm. 131–49) is restated as the beginning of the solo recapitulation's S-space (mm. 298–316). From the perspective of the movement's overall proportions, the recapitulation's "shortened" thematic-S-space is compensated by the R1 interpolation and later expansion within the display episode.

When interpolating a thematically marked but expositionally absent R1:\S-module into the solo recapitulation, Mozart's nearly invariable practice was to restore it at or very near the end of the reconfigured S-block. The recapitulatory pattern thus provided was typically that of first sounding whatever S1:\S- or TMB modules that he chose to include (from time to time, the ever-"fragile" S1:\TM¹ was dropped out entirely, which sometimes had the effect of pushing whatever remained of the original S1:\TM² into recapitulatory TR-space), then appending the R1-module as the concluding *thematic* gesture of the S-block (even though in some instances S-space continues with a largely nonthematic display episode.) The missing R1:\S-module returns at the end both as a clever restoration of something that one might have assumed was long lost ("Remember this?") and as a large-scale wraparound gesture, in which the R1 model rotation's S-space is demonstrated as being ultimately decisive in the rotational proceedings: all of the thematically tagged S1:\S-substitutions are to be construed as having emerged conceptually within R1:\S's apparently expandable interior. Such is the case in Piano Concerto No. 21 in C, K. 467. In this ingenious solo recapitulation, S1:\TM¹ is banished altogether (cf. its expositional appearance on G minor, m. 109), and the newly recrafted TMB-space proceeds in the order, S1:\TM³ (m. 313, hence now functioning in the role of TM¹), *idée-fixe* march merging into a slightly varied recurrence of the display episode, all of which serves as a new and expanded TM² (m. 328, originally sounded at m. 143 as what is best construed as an S-appendix to S1:\TM³), and—finally—the restoration of R1:\S, begun by the orchestra, at m. 351.

No. 24 in C Minor, K. 491, presents a similar but even more dizzyingly complicated situation. The solo exposition's S-block had omitted R1:\S (first heard in mm. 44–63, preceded by orchestral caesura-fill, mm. 35–44) in favor of a disturbingly lengthy, seemingly unstoppable S-phrase-chain in III, E-flat major, with multiple refrain PACs (mm. 147–265). (As discussed in chapter 21, these may be labeled as S1:\S¹ through the largely nonthematic conclusion of the display-episode S1:\S⁵.) In the solo recapitulation—apart from several other alterations of local detail—S1:\S³ and S1:\S⁴ do not reappear at all, and S⁵ is only briefly alluded to at the end of the display episode (mm. 469–73 = mm. 261–65). The opening two, "thematic" S1:\S-modules are retained as central players—now wearily in the tonic, C minor—but they are sounded in reverse order (mm. 391, 410), as the first two parts of a strained TMB. They are followed—again, finally—by the C-minor reinstating of R1:\S (m. 444 [cf. m.44], preceded by several bars of its own R1:\CF (m. 435 [cf. m. 35]). K. 491's many substitutions, reorderings, and asymmetries among Ritornello 1, the solo exposition, and the solo recapitulation, were doubtless intended to convey a nightmarish irrationality coursing through this obsessive, mi-nor-mode movement. The "classical" principle of an ordered tidiness is constantly undermined by the psychological disturbance represented by the movement's opening *idée fixe*.

Mozart's general "option 2" principle that the expositionally missing R1:\S-module is to be brought in as the last thematic S-module of the solo recapitulation was most clearly abandoned in Piano Concerto No. 22 in E-flat, K. 482.[40] Here, uniquely, it is shifted to the first S-position. As in K. 467, Solo 1 had sidelined R1:\S in order to present an all-new TMB, thus providing an extended maximal contrast with the secondary theme proposed in Ritornello 1. Such a procedure yields an overabundance or excess of S-material to confront in the solo recapitulation. Mozart's solution was to rewrite the transition in such a way as to restore much of R1:\TR and CF, thus permitting him to omit the first two modules of S1:\S-space: S1:\TM¹ (sounded in m. 128, an aggressive and surprising gesture on B-flat minor; cf. the S1:\TM¹ in K. 467) and the transitional S1:\TM² (c. m. 139) and second MC (m. 149). All of that was now replaced with a gratifying restoration of R1:\S (m. 314), ending with a I:PAC elided to the original S1:\TM³ as an S-appendix (m. 330 [cf. m. 152]).

Finally, in two extraordinary first movements from 1786 and 1788, those of No. 25 in C, K. 503, and No. 26 in D, K. 537—his creative imagination now running at full tilt—Mozart produced a solo-recapitulatory synthesis by means not of a mere trimodular block (with the standard two MC-effects) but rather of a virtually unprecedented five-module block containing three MC-effects. The simpler of the two, K. 503, first brings back in the solo recapitula-

---

40. Depending on one's interpretation of the piece, another exception might be found in the solo recapitulation of a smaller-scale work, Horn Concerto No. 1 in D, K. 412 (1791). Most unusually, recapitulatory S-space begins with a brief, interpolated module, mm. 114–17, that had been heard nowhere before in the movement—a scale-and-arpeggio signal-figure idiomatic for the solo horn. This elides to S1:\S¹·¹, the presentation of a sentence, in mm. 117–20 (= mm. 38–41). At this point Mozart restored R1:\S and its repetition, mm. 121–24, 125–28, now serving as the sentence's continuation. A two-bar tutti interjection follows, mm. 129–30, perhaps related to R1:\C (cf., e.g., mm. 20–21), and the soloist initiates a largely new display episode, mm. 131–37, which might, however, recall aspects of the solo-expositional continuation, S1:\S¹·² and S1:\S¹·³ (mm. 42–46, 47–51). If that is the preferred reading of this passage, the missing R1 module would have been interpolated into the middle of material taken or adapted from S1:\S-space. On the other hand, if the display episode is regarded as essentially figurational, nonthematic, then R1:\S would have been reinstated as the last self-evidently thematic moment of recapitulatory S-space.

tion the all-new S1:\TMB from the solo exposition. (In other words, in this concerto, unlike the case in K. 467, 482, and a few others, the original S1:\TM¹ is not suppressed. Provocatively, though, it still begins in the "wrong key," E-flat major, m. 326, as it had done in m. 148. The nontonic aspect of this module is doubtless relevant to the decision to produce a five-module block.) Instead of closing S1:\TM³ (m. 345 [cf. m. 170]) with a PAC, the composer altered the ending of its repetition to set up a third MC at m. 364. Thus invited, the major-mode version of the march-like R1:\S finally strides in at the end, cheerily and dutifully bringing this thematic parade to a congenial close (m. 365). The situation in K. 537 is complicated by the existence of an amusing, three-element S-chain in Ritornello 1: R1:\S¹ (m. 38), S² (m. 50), and S³ (m. 59). Of these, only R1:\S¹ appears in the exposition, serving as the head-motive of TM³ (m. 164). The same TMB returns in the solo recapitulation, but, as in K. 503, its TM³ veers away from closure to produce a third MC (m. 383), permitting the restoration of the insouciant R1:\S³ (upbeat to m. 384).

Ritornello 4 and the Conclusion of the Larger Recapitulation

Even as the final trill-cadence of S3 closes the solo recapitulation, the larger recapitulation continues with the onset of the fourth and last ritornello pillar, R4. As with R2, normally the model against which the R4 events should be interpreted, Ritornello 4 may begin either with rotationally inert or rotationally participatory modules. However it begins, R4 always completes the recapitulatory rotation by bringing back the concluding modules of R1—modules that were not included in the solo recapitulation and that may or may not have been attained in R2, the (often incomplete) end of the expositional rotation. A primary task of R4, beyond that of framing its central event, the non-notated and implicitly improvised cadenza,[41] is to pick up any remaining loose ends of the com-

position—to restore any R1 modules (especially R1:\post-MC modules) that had not been heard since the opening ritornello. Many of the first movements of Mozart's concertos feature one or more such reinstatements at the end. This means that some of the most memorable, thematic modules of these movements, quite often their tag-conclusions, occur only in R1 and R4, and only in the tonic.

R4¹ and R4² Subdivisions

In almost all cases, Ritornello 4 is subdivided into two parts: an orchestral R4¹, pressing efficiently toward the formulaic, grand $^6_4$ chord, pinned into stasis with a fermata, that opens the path to a solo cadenza; and an orchestral R4², elided with the soloist's last trill-cadence and completing whatever leftover modular-rotational business remains to be addressed. (In the piano concertos K. 271 and 491 the soloist, exceptionally, returns in R4². In K. 595 it intervenes in what initially seems to announce itself as R4¹, the passage beginning at m. 335, elided with the normative trill-cadence.) Only three of Mozart's concerto first movements lack a cadenza within R4. Consequently, these instances do not subdivide into the normative R4¹ and R4². All come from Vienna-period wind concertos, and two of them emerged in the last year of Mozart's life: Horn Concerto No. 2 in E-flat, K. 417 (1783), Horn Concerto "No. 1" in D (1791), K. 412, and the Clarinet Concerto in A, K. 622 (1791). Similarly, Beethoven's Piano Concerto No. 5 in E-flat, op. 73, may be said to lack a cadenza proper in its R4, although the formulaically held $^6_4$ platform (m. 496) is still present, splitting the section into R4¹ and R4², and it is followed by an intensifying passage for solo piano, one that the composer famously marked, however, "non si fa una Cadenza, ma s'attacca subito il seguente." This cadenza-like "non-cadenza" almost immediately softens into a revisiting of the minor-mode beginning of R1:\S¹·¹ (m. 508; [cf. m. 41]), and it is soon joined by the orchestra sounding the theme's major-mode "correction" (m. 516) and flowing,

---

41. We also possess, of course, numerous separately notated cadenzas written by Mozart, Beethoven, and oth-

ers. See below on "the cadenza" as treated generally in Sonata Theory.

with the soloist, into a vast review of prior sonata material.

In Mozart's works, once the final rotational module is attained in R4²—with the sounding of the last module laid out in R1—the movement usually comes to a close. The end of R4² typically rhymes with the end of R1 (on infrequent occasions with an additional bar or two of emphasis), unless, for whatever reason, R1 had been left unclosed by merging into the solo exposition, as in Violin Concerto No. 3 in G, K. 216, and the Sinfonia Concertante in E-flat, K. 364. Along with the Flute and Harp Concerto in C, K. 299 (the addition of mm. 262–65, R1:\P-based), however, eight of Mozart's piano concertos append an extension or coda (or CRI equivalent) after the end of the recapitulatory rotation: No. 9 in E-flat, K. 271 (mm. 302–07, extension of a restored R1:\C³ figure, including the non-normative return of the soloist, as also in R4¹),[42] No. 15 in B-flat, K. 450 (mm. 305–08, another extension to a final C-module, though here more normatively, without soloist), No. 17 in G, K. 453 (mm. 344–49, coda-return of an earlier, jocular MC-fill idea), No. 20 in D Minor, K. 466 (390–97, ominously quiet, minor-mode R1:\P-figuration), No. 21 in C, K. 467 (mm. 414–17, *piano*-dynamic echoes of the *idée fixe*, probably heard here as rebounding echoes of the preceding, restored R1:\C), No. 22 in E-flat, K. 482 (mm. 380–83, *forte* reinforcement of the preceding *piano* cadence), No. 23 in A, K. 488 (mm. 310–14, again a *forte* reinforcement of an otherwise *piano* close), and No. 24 in C Minor, K. 491.

The last of these, K. 491, is the most extraordinary. No notated cadenza by Mozart survives for this movement, and the autograph is unique in not showing any indication of a final trill-cadence emerging out of an improvised one. However it is to have been prepared, R4² starts with two sweeping bars of C-minor

anacrusis (mm. 487–88), a bar of fill, and a restoring of an extended passage from R1:\C, unheard since the initial ritornello (from R1:\C¹·², mm. 490–97 [cf. mm. 80–87]; R1:\C¹·³, mm. 498–501 [= mm. 88–91]; and all of R1:\C², mm. 501–09 [= mm. 91–99, the end of R1]). At the point of the final structural cadence ending the recapitulatory rotation, m. 509, Mozart appended a fifteen-bar passage that he marked explicitly as the "Coda." Here, perhaps recalling the unusual solution in K. 271, Mozart unexpectedly brings back the soloist, mm. 509–23, who participates in a spectral, *sotto-voce* fade-out with rippling, *legato* arpeggios coursing through a final visiting of R1:\P, *idée-fixe* shivers. This final passage is likely to have been the model for the parallel coda with soloist, in the first movement of Beethoven's Piano Concerto No. 3 in C Minor, op. 37, mm. 417–43.[43] In this case Beethoven's piano-enhanced coda substitutes entirely for the more traditional R4². Non-normatively, Beethoven choked back the cadenza's final trill-cadence to a *piano/pianissimo* dynamic at the start of the "R4²-position" coda and undermined its resolution through the substitution of a V⁷/iv chord (m. 417). This is the start of a broad, fatalistic crescendo to the end of the movement, at first pushed forward ominously by the *idée-fixe* march-motive in the timpani (mm. 417–18, 419–20, and so on) and reacted to with "K. 491-style arpeggio-shivers" in the piano. As might be expected, Beethoven broadened the concept of retaining the soloist throughout all of the postcadenza space in his later concertos.

R2 Material within Parts of R4: Three Options

In Mozart's concertos, the R4¹ and R4² subdivisions, each with its own generic task, virtually mandate that R4 will normally be longer

---

42. In K. 271 the repeated reappearances of the soloist in R4¹, R4², and the coda—all tutti spaces that are almost invariably occupied by the orchestra alone—provide a good example of an R4 textural deformation. In this instance these recurrences play into the established textural "game" that pervades that movement, in which the soloist and orchestra exchange expected positions with amusing regularity, especially in moments that in-

volve the abrupt, recurring R1:\P¹·¹ loops. Cf. the discussion of K. 491 below.

43. See the similar conclusion in Plantinga, *Beethoven's Concertos*, p. 158, 165–66. Extended, solo-reinforced R4²s and/or codas would also recur prominently in Beethoven's Violin Concerto and in his Fourth and Fifth Piano Concertos.

and incorporate more modular material than did R2. The modular content of these subdivisions is flexible: indeed, Robert Forster has recently devoted the larger part of a full monograph to cataloguing Mozart's many realizations of R4^1, the cadenza, and R4^2.[44] In almost all cases, significant parts of R4 revisit and tonally resolve the music of R2, a factor of structural importance with regard to the rotationally participatory modules. R2 is normally the most immediate model—an underlying basis—to be expanded upon in the R4^1–R4^2 complex. Movements in which neither R4^1 nor R4^2 correspond to R2 are rare. Even when both largely differ from R2, one or the other (usually R4^2) will include a brief, anchoring module near the end to solidify the R2 connection. This can occur in pieces in which R2's rotationally participatory modules are minimized or prematurely cut short. One such instance found in Piano Concerto No. 17 in G, K. 453, in which only Ritornello 2's interrupted attempt to sound an R1:\C^2 module, mm. 178–81, returns—and is concluded—in a portion of R4^2, mm. 340–43. The remainder of R4^1 and R4^2 is taken up with the tonic restoration of modules unheard since R1. A similar situation occurs in No. 13 in C, K. 415, while in the Concertone in C, K. 190, it had been only R4^1 that touches on material from R2.

Just where the now-tonicized R2 material will be relocated varies from concerto to concerto. Generally considered, there were three available options. Arranged in order of frequency, these are: R2 material returns primarily in R4^2; R2 material is divided between R4^1 and R4^2; or R2 material reappears only in R4^1. We shall take up each of these in turn.

Option 1. Most commonly, Mozart outfitted R4^1 with differing material—another module that is usually, though not always, rotationally inert—and brought back the R2-referential music, nearly always fully intact, after the cadenza, in R4^2. R4^2 begins in the manner of R2 in four violin concertos, K. 207, 216, 218, and 219; in the Flute and Harp Concerto, K. 299; in the Oboe Concerto, K. 314, in Horn Concerto No. 4, K. 495; and in the piano concertos K. 175, 238, 242, 246, 365, 413, 414, and 595. In a slight variant, the first module of R2 may be suppressed in order to start R4^2 with its second, as in K. 449 (m. 330, with R1:\S^3, music from m. 70) and K. 450 (m. 295, with R1:\C$^{1.2}$, from m. 45). Additionally, three other piano concertos begin R4^2 with a differing module but proceed at the end to R2 material, which thereby seems embedded within it: K. 415, 453, and 491. Of all of these R4^{2}s, ten provide the familiar additional concluding modules, beyond the R2-model proper, a restoration of "lost" modules or measures from the end of R1 that allow them to complete the rotation in a manner parallel to the model Rotation 1: K. 218, 219, 246, 299, 365, 413, 449, 453, 495, and 595.

Within this most frequently deployed, first option, it is also possible for the *ad hoc*, precadenza R4^1 to reinstate one or more expositionally suppressed R1 modules on its own. When it does, it most often restores an otherwise abandoned R1:\TR module (not necessarily R1:\TR$^{1.1}$), which is always rotationally inert in this position. A classic instance occurs in the brief R4^1 of Violin Concerto No. 5, K. 219, m. 216–19, which brings back the "lost" pre-MC module from R1 (mm. 16–17); its R4^2, like its R2, begins with R1:\C (m. 220). Other R1:\TR-material restorations in R4^1 are found in the piano concertos K. 175, 365, 413, 415, and 449 (m. 320, with its sudden jolt to vi, as in R1:\TR$^{1.1}$, m. 16). When such an R4^1 begins with now-restored R1:\S-material, it is both rotationally participatory and reopens the solo recapitulation's S3:\ESC. This happens in two piano concertos, K. 414 (m. 283, R1:\S$^{1.2}$ [cf. m. 41]) and K. 453 (m. 319, R1:\S$^{1.2}$ [cf. m. 49], ushered in with an unanticipated deceptive cadence undermining the soloist's final trill-cadence). Another possibility is to reinstate "missing," rotationally participatory R1:\C modules at the opening of R4^2, as happens in the piano concertos K. 246, 450, and 491.

---

44. Forster, *Die Kopfsätze der Klavierkonzerte Mozarts und Beethovens: Gesamtaufbau, Solokadenz und Schlußbildung* (Munich: Fink, 1992).

Still another was to interpolate essentially new, "stock" material into $R4^1$—merely serviceable tutti-activity that gets one efficiently to the fermata-pinned $^6_4$ platform, as in Violin Concertos Nos. 1 and 3, K. 207 and 211 (in which the new material soon merges with $R1:\backslash TR^{1.1}$). While this "free" alternative seems more suitable to the early, more purely "generic" concertos, it does reappear in Horn Concerto No. 4, K. 495. In three instances Mozart filled $R4^1$ not with material that was lacking in the solo exposition, but with $R1:\backslash P^{1.1}$ material that had not reappeared in R2. This produced the effect of a spliced-in "false start" to a new rotation that never materializes: in the Concerto for Three Pianos (No. 7), K. 242 (m. 245); in the Flute and Harp Concerto, K. 299 (m. 243); and in the Oboe Concerto, K. 314 (m. 174, an $R1:\backslash P$ variant).[45]

Option 2. If Mozart most frequently introduced the earlier R2 material into $R4^2$ space, as described above, his next most common choice was to split the R2 music between $R4^1$ and $R4^2$. This strategy demonstrates the concept of Ritornello 4 as a single formal entity, despite its cadenza-separated subdivisions (which are now bound together in their sharing of R2 ideas). In this procedure $R4^1$ usually begins with the same module as R2, only now in the tonic. As outlined in chapter 21, this module may be either rotationally inert (as with the commonly encountered, "out-of-order" $R1:\backslash TR^{1.1}$ module) or rotationally participatory (for example, a later $R1:\backslash S$ or C module). Sounding it again at the opening of $R4^1$ recaptures the same tutti affirmation that had reinforced the soloist's trill-cadence at the end of S1. Normally, R2's first module will now be pushed without delay toward $R4^1$'s obligatory, held $^6_4$ platform and sub-

sequent cadenza, and all or most of the remainder of R2 will resume in $R4^2$ after the cadenza, interpolating or adding additional modules as desired, especially when needed to complete the rotation left unfinished in R2. Mozart's earliest approach to this double-span procedure is found in the Bassoon Concerto, K. 191, although that first movement is atypical in that it also presents a reshuffling of the relevant modules in order to keep the opening of $R4^2$ parallel with that of R2.[46] More normative examples, with the R2 opening-module being placed into $R4^1$ and the subsequent modules into $R4^2$, occur in Violin Concerto No. 2, K. 211; in the Flute Concerto, K. 313; in the Third Horn Concerto, K. 447; and in two piano concertos, K. 271 and 482. In Piano Concerto No. 26, K. 537, the procedure is similar, but $R4^1$ omits the first module of R2 in order to begin with the second (m. 409, $R:\backslash TR^{1.2}$ [cf. m. 21], while $R4^2$ completes the succession (m. 416, $R1:\backslash C^1$, C^2). And in three piano concertos, K. 456, 466, and 467, $R4^1$ is normative, beginning with the initial module of R2, while the remainder of R2, and any subsequent modules required to produce the full rotation, appear only after $R4^2$ has begun with differing material. In K. 456, $R4^2$ starts by backing up to revisit a redundant $R1:\backslash S^{1.2}$ and $S^{1.3}$ (mm. 349, 352, already heard in the solo recapitulation, mm. 293, 299); in K. 466 and 467, it begins with the restoration of one or more modules unheard since R1—less expansive presentations of the R1 version of $R1:\backslash C^1$ and of $R1:\backslash C^2$ in K. 466 (mm. 366 and 375 [cf. mm. 44 and 58]);[47] $R1:\backslash S^{1.3}$ in K. 467 (m. 397 [cf. m. 44]).

Option 3. The remaining possibility was to include R2 material only (and often incompletely) in $R4^1$, leaving $R4^2$ free to restore pre-

---

45. These cases are to be distinguished from those in which R2 had begun with $R1:\backslash P^{1.1}$ or the $R1:\backslash P$-motto, an effect replicated also in the R2-material-launched $R4^1$, as in the Flute Concerto, K. 313, and Piano Concerto No. 19, K. 459—both mentioned in this regard in ch. 21.

46. In K. 191 the R2 succession is: $R1:\backslash TR$ (mm. 71–73, rotationally inert) and $R1:\backslash C^1$ (mm. 73–80, rotationally participatory). $R4^1$ begins, exceptionally, with the second of these, $R1:\backslash C^1$ (mm. 152–60). Follow-

ing the cadenza, we first hear $R1:\backslash TR$ (mm. 161–63), quickly spliced to two modules completing the rotation, unheard since R1: the restorations of $R1:\backslash S^{1.2}$ (mm. 163–68, thus producing the $R4:\backslash ESC$ at m. 168) and $R1:\backslash C^2$ (mm. 168–70).

47. In K. 491 the S1 and S3 display episodes had also touched on recast versions of $R1:\backslash C^1$, as in mm. 153 and 330. In this sense the $R1:\backslash C^1$ idea is not literally "restored" in $R4^2$. What is brought back is its characteristically R1 version.

viously "lost" material from R1. This third option was appropriate in cases either where the larger exposition had differed remarkably from the opening ritornello or where R2 had broken off before the final module(s) of the complete rotation. Thus the final touches of the larger-recapitulatory synthesis can come to occupy the whole of R4², or very nearly so, and are not delayed to its final bars only, as in some instances of the other R4 strategies. While an early approach to this option may be found in the Concertone, K. 190 (although R4² here restores nothing, merely bringing back R1:\P for six bars in the manner of a coda), Mozart was most interested in exploring this solution in four piano concertos from 1784 to 1786: K. 451, 459, 488, and 503. K. 488 differs from the other three. Its R4² begins not with "missing" material but with the return of the fuller, less decorative, R1 version of the otherwise redundant R1:\C¹·² module (= R1, m. 56), also heard in a variant in the solo recapitulation, m. 254. The "lost" module restored is the one that follows, R1:\C², mm. 307–10, serving here, as in R1, like a "final blessing" of the whole.

The Cadenza

From some perspectives the cadenza may be regarded as the central presentational event of R4. Its appearance could hardly be more dramatically staged: R4¹ exists largely to set it up; R4² responds to it, as if all of the requisite soloistic business has now been finished; and in it, the orchestra recedes completely in order to permit the soloist, the concerto's central focus of attention, to stand forth on his or her own terms, spotlighted and released into a relative freedom. It was fundamentally an improvisatory event, even though Mozart did notate several

now-celebrated cadenzas for many of his concerto movements—often more than one for an individual movement—most likely, it seems, for the use or instruction of others.[48]

Three points regarding the late-eighteenth-century cadenza are of interest to our concerns here. First, this space of improvisatory freedom was a near-obligatory feature and climactic event of the Type 5 sonata. Unlike the other types, this one contained a built-in generic moment, an expandable zone of performative freedom, in which the typical "group" constraints of sonata practice were shown to be temporarily lifted. (That the suspension of sonata activity is allowed only temporarily, and as the soloist's "last word" in the movement, is doubtless hermeneutically significant.) Second, the contents of the cadenza, virtually by definition, were to vary from one performance to another, in large part to exemplify that provisional freedom. And third, with the fermata-pause at the end of R4¹—along with its formulaic suspension of harmonic motion on the cadential $^6_4$ chord, resolved only with the V⁷–I trill-cadence that finishes off the cadenza—the sonata clock stops, only to resume once the cadenza is finished.

In Mozart's concertos the cadenza is best grasped as an idiosyncratic, solo-performative event operating outside of the structural processes of sonata form proper. It was a specialized bubble interpolated into the broader Type 5 structure, a substructural parenthesis that simultaneously, and paradoxically, was temporarily to hold at bay the forward motion of the larger formal demands. The silence of the now-stilled orchestra only highlights this aspect, as does the virtuosic flair with which the cadenza was to be improvised and delivered, widening the structural gap with each successive module that it presents. The fundamental structural processes

---

48. Cf. also n. 41. Overviews of many of the issues surrounding cadenzas may be found in Irving, *Mozart's Piano Concertos*, pp. 152–62, Grayson, *Mozart: Piano Concertos Nos. 20 and 21*, pp. 101–4, and Plantinga, *Beethoven's Concertos* (where the written cadenzas for each of these works are discussed individually). More details about Mozart's cadenzas are available in Eva and Paul Badura-Skoda, *Interpreting Mozart on the Keyboard*, trans. Leo Black (New York and London: Barrie & Rockliffe, 1962); Paul Badura-Skoda, *Kadenzen, Eingänge und*

Auszierungen zu Klavierkonzerten von Wolfgang Amadeus Mozart (Kassel: Bärenreiter, 1967); Philip Whitmore, *Unpremeditated Art: The Cadenza in the Classical Keyboard Concerto* (Oxford: Clarendon Press, 1991); Christoph Wolff, "Zur Chronologie der Klavierkonzert-Kadenzen Mozarts," *Mozart-Jahrbuch 1978-79*, 235–46; and Wolff, "Cadenzas and Styles of Improvisation in Mozart's Piano Concertos," in R. Larry Todd and Peter Williams, eds., *Perspectives on Mozart Performance* (Cambridge: Cambridge University Press, 1991), pp. 228–38.

of Type 5 sonata form were unaffected by the variable contents of this separable cadenza-moment interpolated into one of its interstices, a "musical moment" that is expandable in "real" clock-time. And yet, because the production of this solo-filled gap is one of the Type 5's generic obligations, one might wish to pursue some of its potential implications.

While it might seem strained to interpret the content of an improvisatory and variable "moment," it is also clear that Mozart's notated cadenzas, especially those written for the piano concertos from K. 271 onward, typically include passages that recover, or reflect upon, some of the melodic material of the movement proper, sometimes in a manner that can seem "tightly structured."[49] That the notated cadenzas normally display an "opening-middle-closing" pattern of organization, as noted by Eva and Paul Badura-Skoda, far from being surprising, is precisely what we would expect.[50] Nor is it surprising that some of Mozart's surviving piano cadenzas, like many of his *sujet-libre* S1:\TRs and Solo 2 developmental spaces, begin with the linkage-technique of taking up material that had just been stated in the orchestra (as in his cadenzas for K. 415, 449, 450, 451, and 456), while others begin—as with developmental spaces—in either a purely virtuosic or explicitly thematic way.

More interesting are the potential rotational implications of the modular content within those cadenzas that reconfigure previously heard material. Cadenzas that cite or rework only one previously heard theme generally evade these issues, although they might be heard as making a half-rotational gesture.[51] Of the two surviving cadenzas for K. 414, for instance, one presents a variant of R1:\P only in its center, m. 12, while the other, much briefer, begins with a reference

to R1:\S^2 (an S-appendix first heard in R1, upbeat to m. 51; this module had been "lost" in the solo exposition but restored in the solo recapitulation, upbeat to m. 253). A handful of Mozart's other surviving cadenzas are more fully rotational in that at various points they embed citations of two or more modules, in order, with at least one from each side of the MC-divide.[52] These include cadenzas written for K. 271 (R1:\TR$^{1.1}$ [from m. 14] + R1:\S2 [from m. 34]); K. 453 (variants of R1:\P + R1:\S [from m. 35] + the last half of the S1:\TM^1 antecedent [from m. 114]); K. 456 (a linkage-technique, nonrotational R1:\TR$^{1.2}$ [originally from mm. 24–27] leads to R1:\P + R1:\S$^{1.3}$ [from m. 54] + R1:\S$^{1.2}$ [from m. 47], these last two "out of order"); and K. 459 (the *idée-fixe* motto, based on R1:\P, + S1:\TM^3 [from the variant at m. 139]). Beethoven also seems to have preferred extended cadenzas with rotational implications.

Do such rotational flickerings within what appear to be otherwise improvisatorily "arbitrary" modular selections carry hermeneutic connotations? One might propose that even within this structural parenthesis, while the rest of the composition is put on hold, the linear current of the modular successions provided in R1 and S1 + R2 continues to exert its influence. Or it might be that some cadenzas are written to take on the role of "freely" reflecting "from outside" on previously heard material— thus providing a moment in which the sonata becomes self-reflexive, pondering some of the modules from which the "real" structure has been built. In so doing, a rotational cadenza provides an ordered, if abbreviated, revisiting of the concept of rotation itself, one of sonata form's most essential principles—thereby interpolating a telescoped, "last-glance," nonstructural rota-

---

49. Additional summary-descriptions are provided Irving, *Mozart's Piano Concertos*, pp. 153 and 159.

50. Eva and Paul Badura-Skoda, *Interpreting Mozart on the Keyboard*, pp. 215–16. Cf. Paul Badura-Skoda, *Kadenzen, Eingänge*. See also the summary of this strategy in Irving, *Mozart's Piano Concertos*, pp. 160–61.

51. The exception among the surviving cadenzas for the later concertos would appear to be that for K. 488—as it happens, the only cadenza that Mozart actually wrote

into his autograph score—which opens with a reference to a moment in the development (mm. 158, 162), not to any R1 or expositional module proper. (See the summary of this " 'beginning—middle—end' strategy" in Irving, *Mozart's Piano Concertos*, p. 160, and pp. 169–70, n. 85.)

52. The appearance of "secondary material" in the interior of cadenzas is also noted in Irving, *Mozart's Piano Concertos*, p. 161.

tion-within-a-rotation. Still, one might be advised from forwarding such speculations without the proper caveats: the cadenza, after all, remains a structurally free space. Moreover, in at least one case from the end of Mozart's career, the surviving cadenza seems, if anything, counterrotational, citing no fewer than four modules in reverse rotational order. This happens in the cadenza for K. 595, in which the succession is: R1:\C [from m. 39] + R1:\TR$^{1.1}$ [from m. 16] + an interior module of R1:\P (cf. mm. 5–6, although the reference may be to its version in the development, mm. 194–96) + R1:\P proper [cf. m. 1]).

From time to time one encounters discussions of such cadenzas as "developmental" or as "secondary developments," particularly if their interiors deviate momentarily onto nontonic areas.[53] As was the case in altered or expanded recapitulatory transitions (see chapter 11), this terminology is unhelpful, since the "development" or "developmental space" is a zone-specific term within sonatas. To be sure, the attraction of such a description is clear: there is no doubt that such cadenzas can sometimes bring into play a differing style of *thematische Arbeit* (thematic work). Still, there is little or any essentially structural sonata work that is implied in this procedure, however much individual modules might be improvisatorily reshaped.

A larger question would be whether it is possible for a cadenza to restore or compensate for otherwise "lost" or understated material from the sonata proper, thereby providing a balance or completion lacking in the rest of the movement. Here one would have to posit the composition of an absence or incompleteness into the sonata proper, which could then be addressed as a conceptual topic in the cadenza-improvisation. Remote as such a possibility might seem, there is at least one case in Mozart where it seems to have happened. In Piano Concerto No. 14 in E-flat, K. 449, a prominent dotted-rhythm figure, R1:\S$^{2.2}$ (m. 63), returns as the opening

module of R2 (m. 169) but is thereafter dropped from the rest of the composition. Thus it does not figure in the larger recapitulation and is never resolved back into the tonic. Mozart's surviving cadenza for the movement restores the missing module prominently, and in the tonic, in m. 15—reminding his listeners of what the recapitulation had "forgotten."

Finally, we might open the issue of what it could mean for a cadenza to end with a trill-cadence that recaptures the one that had ended S3 not too long before. It is a principle of Sonata Theory that an apparent ESC can be regarded as deferred if its most essential cadence-defining particle is revisited as a refrain cadence concluding a later, differing module. One might therefore ask, in cases where the S3:\ESC has been articulated at the downbeat of R4^1, whether the return of the same trill-cadence at the end of the cadenza implies that the S3:\ESC has been shifted to that point—thus passing over the new-zone implications of R4^1 or at least creating a cadence-structural interlock between R4^1 and the cadenza. This interpretation would grant a genuinely structural potential to the otherwise "arbitrary" cadenza: that of trumping the end of some S3s by producing the "real" S3:\ESC. Rather than deciding the issue one way or the other, it is preferable to explicate the ambiguity, which is inextricable from this moment of the Type 5 sonata. From another perspective, one might wonder whether the explicit return of the trill-cadence could also be understood as implying a "backing-up" of the composition to the concluding S3-point, erasing whatever structural work might have been accomplished in R4^1. This underscores the generic fragility of the R4^1 position, which under this interpretation is conceptually marginalized through such a backup maneuver. Obviously relevant in such a reading would be whether R4^1 had been rotationally inert, rotationally participatory, or perhaps both.

---

53. Cf. Irving, *Mozart's Piano Concertos*, pp. 161 and 169, n. 83.

Some Grounding Principles of Sonata Theory

The Intellectual Backdrop

Sonata Theory aims to facilitate issues of musical and cultural meaning. We regard the multiple meaning-systems present within musical compositions as conceptually divisible into these two tracks, which are often treated singly or separately. Toward the end of bringing them together—or at least much closer—the theory seeks in its vectored language and terminology to ensure that its analytical observations are connotationally rich with interpretive implications. In part it does this by considering each observation against the backdrop of a proposed system concerning "how sonatas work." *Elements of Sonata Theory* provides the music-analytical outlines of that backdrop, along with glimpses of what lies ahead in more advanced work.

Sonata Theory is a method attentive to the details of individual compositions, but it is also more than that. If at first Sonata Theory seems almost exclusively formalistic in its concerns, this is because obtaining an adequate background in analysis is the *sine qua non* of the larger system in which we are interested. Music analysis is a first stage that cannot be dispensed with. In any discussion of music, insufficient or defective analysis undermines the legitimacy of broader interpretive claims and calls the commentator's competence into question; cultural readings of individual works unsupported by adequate music analysis are all too easily produced and ring hollow. Conversely, even though analysis, with all of its technical terminology and lumber-room mechanisms, looms large at the initial stage of one's inquiry, that first stage is no end in itself. Rather, all analysis should be directed toward the larger goal of a hermeneutic understanding of music as a communicative system, a cultural discourse implicated in issues of humanness, worldview, and ideology, widely construed—the second stage of the process. Once one is sufficiently comfortable with the analytical system, the two stages proceed simultaneously.

Sonata Theory is grounded in a blend of many strains of later-twentieth-century thought. Seeking maximal flexibility, it is methodologically pluralistic, a hybrid between the rigorous precision of current English-language analytical practice and several registers of the broad-gauge interpretation and imaginative sweep encountered in much continental thought of the past century (thought often pursued also in recent Anglophone writing in the humanities). In this respect Sonata Theory brings together aspects of traditional music-disciplinary work—especially some of the newer developments in recent music theory and musicology—with bolder interpretive considerations often sidelined in former decades as extra-disciplinary. Most prominently, these latter include: *genre theory* (work by Mikhail Bakhtin, E. H. Gombrich, Alistair Fowler, Tzvetan Todorov, Hans Robert Jauss, Adena Rosmarin, Fredric Jameson, Thomas O. Beebee, Margaret Cohen, and others); certain features of *phenomenology* (aspects of Edmund Husserl, Martin Heidegger, Roman Ingarden, and others—Sartre, Merleau-Ponty—on one's perception and processing of the artwork); the explorations of *hermeneutics* by Hans-Georg Gadamer and that method's immediate successors; and *reader-response theory* (particularly the issues raised by the Constance school, including Wolfgang Iser and, once again, Hans Robert Jauss). As the occasion demands—though admittedly not much in the more explicitly "music-theoretical" *Elements* itself—we are also prepared to fold into our interpretations ideas suggested by a number of prominent *sociological theories* (Pierre Bourdieu on the field of cultural production, Anthony Giddens on structuration, Niklas Luhmann on modern social differentiation and art as an autopoietic system, Jürgen Habermas on modernism and the public sphere). And we remain open to personal intermixtures or accents from critical theory. These include theories of *cultural materialism* and the *theory of ideology and institutions*—for instance, those of Raymond Williams, Theodor W. Adorno, Fredric Jameson, Peter and Christa Bürger, or Terry Eagleton—as well as a broad array of *postmodernist-poststructuralist concerns* including work by Roland Barthes, Michel Foucault, Jacques Derrida, Jean Baudrillard, Slavoj Žižek, and others. The wellsprings and potential resonances of the theory are many. To reconstruct and defend them in any metatheoretical detail would produce a different book altogether.[1]

Sonata Theory may also be described as the *style* of analysis and hermeneutics resulting from the flexibility provided by that particular blend. One of its convictions is that in order to arrive at an adequate sense of meaning within a work, we must reconstruct a sufficiently detailed generic and cultural backdrop against which such individual works sought to play themselves out. Genre theory, flexibly construed, is not necessarily the *primus inter pares* of the extra-disciplinary sources of the Sonata Theory blend, but because of the vastness of detail that it encourages as an initial step, it is something that one bumps up against immediately and frequently. A substantial part of the *Elements* stems from it.

Genre theory is a complex and contested constellation of interests. It comprises many things at once: theories of how genres may be said to exist at all; speculations on the way that they are formed and how and for which social purposes they are sustained; studies of the ramifications of the proposal that individual works can exemplify, illustrate, or contend with the genres; more current reinterpretations of genres as social contracts, social relations, or Bourdieuian "position-takings" (*prises de position*) in a contested cultural field;[2] and so on. In addition, many would argue—as would we—that genres are hermeneutic tools: rules-of-thumb or regu-

---

1. There are those, we realize, who would view the intermixing of such disparate intellectual paths (which we would characterize as the strategic tacking from one set of influences to another) to be a dubious enterprise. Nevertheless, we agree with Carl Dahlhaus's observation—originally formulated in response to East-West Germanic methodological challenges of the 1960s and 1970s (*Foundations of Music History*, trans. J. B. Robinson [Cambridge: Cambridge University Press, 1983], e.g., pp. 24, 116, 122)—that the only other available alternative today, a dogmatic or arbitrary adherence to one system or one set of interests alone, is not only less attractive but also indicts itself, especially now in the twenty-first century, as naively reductive and outdated. The analyst must be free to use whatever tools will assist him or her to address the questions at hand. There are many questions to ask of a piece of music—analytical, social, cultural, ideological, and so on—none of which should be regarded as illegitimate. Different questions require different sets of tools in pursuit of answers. (See proposition 9.)

2. On genres as social contracts see, e.g., Fredric Jameson, *The Political Unconscious: Narrative as a Socially Symbolic Act* (Ithaca, N.Y.: Cornell University Press, 1981), p. 104, and Jameson, "Beyond the Cave: Demystifying the Ideology of Modernism," in *The Ideologies of Theory: Essays, 1971–1986* (Minneapolis: University of Minnesota Press, 1988), 2:115–32, esp. p. 116. For a recent endorsement of Jameson's view coupled with an interpretation of genres as cultural *prises de position*, see Margaret Cohen, *The Sentimental Education of the Novel* (Princeton, N.J.: Princeton University Press, 1999), pp. 16–26.

lative principles (in the Kantian sense) to guide interpretation. (For the Kantian aspect, see Proposition No. 3 below.) From this perspective, choosing a genre to serve as an interpretive lens predetermines the patterns of what one is likely to find in the individual object under scrutiny.

"Texts Always Take Place on the Level of Their Reader's Abilities"

Rather than presenting a philosophical/literary-critical argument to buttress each point of the Sonata Theory blend, it might be more helpful at this stage merely to present some of the convictions and conclusions that helped to generate the theory throughout the 1990s and early 2000s.[3] These are provided in the following set of propositions, albeit in a compressed and under-argued format: to take even the first steps toward a sufficient documentation would be cumbersome in the extreme. Instead, we hope that, taken together, the collection of proposals might serve to suggest a style of thought that is characteristic of the theory when it shifts into a self-reflective mode.

1. A piece of music may be said to exist on many conceptual levels. (The mode of existence of a work of art is a perennial issue in philosophy.) For the purposes of structural analysis it exists most substantially in the ongoing dialogue that it may be understood to pursue with its stated or implied genre—a dialogue that may be recreated (more accurately, proposed as

a reading) in the mind of the informed listener.[4] It exists less substantially in the manuscript score or printed notation; much less in the fleeting representations of any individual performance or diachronic set of performances. The essential character of this dialogue is not self-evident on the music's acoustic surface alone (its literal sounds). Therefore the central task of analysis is to reanimate this implicit dialogue in a way that is historically and musically sensitive.

2. Toward that end, an intellectually responsible, culturally aware reading should seek to reconstruct the historical norms and variable options of the relevant genre. Absent a master-set of detailed instructions known to have been carried out by composers, this must be done inductively, leading to constantly tested-and-retested conclusions (a procedure similar to that of formulating scientific hypotheses, consistently open to amendment and revision)[5] that emerge from the study of the works of the more influential composers of the period. To be sure, original theoretical writings—Koch, Galeazzi, Reicha, and so on—are to be taken into account, but as massively reductive generalizations they ultimately prove to be of secondary importance. A more robust quality of information is to be gained by the close study of actual musical practice. One goes directly to the musical sources to learn what the masters do in real composition.

3. The genre thus reconstructed is to be regarded as an implicit and necessary backdrop that functions heuristically. In other words, it exists not literally but rather as something like a (Kantian) regulative principle,[6] a rule for in-

---

3. The section title quotes Wolfgang Iser's paraphrase of a remark made by Jean-Paul Sartre. See proposition 11 and n. 13.

4. Cf. the remarks of Wolfgang Iser concerning the role of the "implied reader" within literary texts: "No matter who or what he may be, the real reader is always offered a particular role to play, and it is this role that constitutes the concept of the implied reader. . . . The text must . . . *bring about* a standpoint from which the reader will be able to view things that would never have come into focus as long as his own habitual dispositions were determining his orientation, and what is more, this standpoint must be able to accommodate all kinds of different readers. How, then, can it evolve from the

structure of the text?" Iser, *The Act of Reading: A Theory of Aesthetic Response* (Baltimore: Johns Hopkins, 1978 [orig. German, 1976], pp. 34–35.

5. These hypotheses should be stated as "falsifiable propositions," open to and inviting "intersubjective criticism," in Karl Popper's sense. See, e.g., Popper, "The Problem of Demarcation" [1974] in *Popper Selections*, ed. David Miller (Princeton, N.J.: Princeton University Press, 1985), pp. 118–30.

6. In Kant, *Critique of Pure Reason*, trans. J. M. D. Meiklejohn (London: Dent[Everyman], 1934), pp. 305, 388–89 (from book II, "Transcendental Dialectic," ch. 2, section 8; and ch. 3, "The Ideal of Pure Reason," section 7), the philosopher distinguished a "regulative"

terpretation that enables and constrains the production and subsequent reading of compositionally placed musical events. Sonata form—the topic of this book—is one such regulative principle. The genre-system is the decoder of an otherwise unintelligible or free-floating musical message. For such reasons the most substantial existence of a piece of music (No. 1) may be called forth only by an act of hermeneutics—a conceptual concretization of the work—on the part of the informed listener/analyst. Once the composition is out of the composer's hands, it is the listener/analyst who creates or reawakens the substantial work of art. This concretization can also impact the performance of that work.

4. As we construe them, musical genres (such as "sonata form" or "the multimovement sonata") are to be distinguished from mere forms insofar as they also carry an implicit social or ideological content.[7] A schematic form becomes a genre when we also attend to its social and cultural ramifications—among which is its decisive position-taking on a contested social field of cultural production. Musical genres are usually not the conceptual products of isolated individuals. Instead, they are socially constituted and reinforced, the results of hundreds of choices made by numerous pivotal individuals over a span of time and ratified by communities of listeners to suit their own purposes. Musical genres inevitably implicate communities of listeners.[8] For this reason genres contain social and ideological connotations that may also be teased out—or proposed—by means of hermeneutic inquiry.[9] Genres transform over time and differ from place to place. They are not static entities. Rather, they are elaborate constellations of norms and traditions. Generic forces are fluid, systems-in-motion.

5. Thus a genre is not an autonomous, separate organism existing apart from society. Instead, a genre (such as the network of conceptual forces that we call sonata form) is an agreed-upon set of guidelines devised and used by producers and receivers in a given time and place in order to permit certain kinds of meaning to happen. Genres exist only insofar as production and reception communities agree to act as if they really did exist, as sets of rules, assumptions, or expectations. In that sense a genre system resembles a game. In order to play that game as opposed to a different one (in the former case, to approach the originally desired sorts of meaning), one has to be willing to ac-

principle from a "constitutive" principle: only the latter, he believed, existed in reality. Thus adapting from Kant's first *Critique*: "[The regulative principle] is a principle of reason, which, as a *rule*, dictates how we ought to proceed in our empirical [inquiry], but is unable to *anticipate* or indicate prior to the empirical [inquiry] what is given in the [analytical] object itself. . . . [It] is valid only as a rule. . . . It cannot tell us *what the object is*, but only *how the empirical* [inquiry] *is to be proceeded with* in order to attain to the complete conception of the object." Or: "The [regulative] idea is properly a heuristic, and not an ostensive conception; it does not give us any information respecting the constitution of an object, it merely indicates how, under the guidance of the idea, we ought to *investigate* the constitution and the relations of objects in the world of experience. . . . [Regulative ideas] cannot, therefore, be admitted to be real in themselves; they can only possess a comparative reality. . . . They are to be regarded not as actual things, but as in some measure analogous to them."

7. This point was also proposed in Hepokoski, "Genre and Content in Mid-Century Verdi: 'Addio, del passato' (*La traviata*, Act III)," *Cambridge Opera Journal* 1 (1989), 249–76.

8. Once again to invoke Jameson (n. 2), "genre is itself a social institution, something like a social contract in which we agree to respect certain rules about the appropriate use of the piece of language [or music] in question" ("Beyond the Cave," p. 116).

9. Ideology, in this sense, is not a "thing," no simple listing of commonly shared ideas; it is perhaps closer to Gramsci's much-cited concept of "hegemony," perhaps as elaborated by Raymond Williams. Another treatment of such a position may be found in Thomas O. Beebee, *The Ideology of Genre: A Comparative Study of Generic Instability* (University Park: University of Pennsylvania Press, 1994), pp. 18–19: "Ideology is no longer something that can be represented or paraphrased. Instead, it becomes something like a magnetic field that arranges a chaotic mass of iron filings into intriguing, ordered curves on a piece of paper. Ideology itself is usually invisible. . . . It is only in the deformations and contradictions of writing and thinking that we can recognize ideology; genre is one of those observable deformations. . . . As a form of ideology, genre is also never fully identical with itself, nor are texts fully identical with their genres. Furthermore, if genre is a form of ideology, then the struggle against or deviation from genre are ideological struggles. . . . The generic classification of a text determines its meaning(s) and exposes its ideology."

cept the regulative and constitutive rules. Moreover, participants within the game can come to modify or influence some of the appropriated rules, gradually and over time, through individual choices and interactions with the system. Whenever such devised agreements (even if tacit) were widely shared in the past (or even assumed to have been shared in most of their essentials), genre study is open to historical inquiry. We may also study their diachronic transformations, and we may speak, however loosely, of genres as having arisen, flourished, or declined.[10]

6. When a composer creates an individual work in dialogue with a genre, many compositional decisions are pre-given socially by that genre. Beethoven was by no means the only composer of the *Eroica*: he cannot lay exclusive claim to the totality of the work's implications. Many of the compositional features of that piece are more accurately regarded as dramatized affirmations of (or dialogues with) pre-existing, culturally produced norms that were external to Beethoven: the very concept of the "symphony"; expectations regarding standard designs, lengths, tonal norms, sonata-form conventions, and orchestral practice; the inbuilt awareness of probable occasions for performance; the presence of the existing symphonic tradition and well-known remembered works; and so on. Because the tacit societal aspects inscribed within a genre-constellation were also given and accepted as self-evident, they cannot be made subject to an act of personal intentionality. No composer composes the generic aspects of his or her composition. Those aspects are socially predetermined (although the composer may arrange pre-existing genre-blocks into individual patterns).[11] Thus in any composition there are at least two voices: the composer's voice and the genre's voice. (To complicate matters further, the genre's voice is itself a pluralistic site of social tensions.) There is no reason to assume that what the composer seeks to say and what the genre seeks to say will be in concord.

7. In any hermeneutic study of a work it is crucial to distinguish between genres and individual exemplars of genres (individual compositions). This leads at once to the possibility of making a distinction between cultural critique and aesthetics and affirming the need for both perspectives. On the one hand, the potential sociohistorical content of a musical artifact resides most purely in its genre, not in any individual exemplar of it. Genres are social sites of discourse. For an interpreter to decenter a work into a social text is, in part, to override its claim to individuality in order to dissolve the utterance back into a concern for the social embeddedness of its genre. One important aspect of Beethoven's *Eroica*, in other words—an aspect that is social, cultural, and ideological—is its affirmative participation in the game of "symphony-ness," a game of cultural prestige socially devised in the pursuit of specifically advantageous social positions. On the other hand, the potential within a given reception community to discern differing degrees of aesthetic content resides most purely in the particularities of the exemplar.[12] By a sense of aesthetic presence, we

---

10. The term "transformation" is used here to sidestep the more loaded (and usually much misunderstood) term "evolution," with its organic and natural-selection implications. (Cf. "transform" instead of "evolve" in no. 4.)

11. Cf. the famous remarks of Roland Barthes (which in hindsight may be best regarded as a performative exaggeration on Barthes's part, even as the remarks continue to serve as a challenging corrective on more commonly held views): "[The text is] a multi-dimensional space in which a variety of writings, none of them original, blend and clash. The text is a tissue of quotations drawn from the innumerable centres of culture. . . . [The author's] only power is to mix writings, to counter the ones with the others, in such a way as never to rest on any one of them. Did he wish to *express himself*, he ought at least to know that the inner 'thing' he thinks to 'translate' is itself only a ready-formed dictionary, its words only explainable through other words, and so on indefinitely." ("The Death of the Author" [1968], in *Image Music Text*, trans. Stephen Heath [New York: Noonday, 1977], p. 146.)

12. There are no ontological claims here: these contents are not objectively "in" the piece, except to the extent that communities agree—socially—to believe in their existence. In this proposal we are not sketching out a rigid dichotomy in which *only* genre is cultural and *only* the individual utterance is aesthetic. Rather, we are referring to general tendencies, and there is much ambiguity, overlap, and interplay between them. The seeming separation here of the aesthetic and the cultural is principally to furnish a conceptual clarity at this stage of the discussion.

mean the invitation to experience the thing aesthetically—to "delight" in [*delectare*] an individual object's "made-ness" [*poiesis*], or through sustained attention to call forth, savor, or become self-absorbed in the being and details of that made-ness. At this point the object is considered to exist primarily—though not necessarily exclusively—for aesthetic contemplation. From this perspective, other aspects of potential meaning or connotation within the object are not sidelined altogether but are rendered secondary to the immediate purpose at hand. The reader or listener chooses to isolate the specific qualities and distinctions of the individual exemplar, considered in dialogue with the background genre that regulates the class of objects to which it belongs.

8. Reinforcing No. 7: Because of their participation in genres and differing patterns of reception, musical works are both ideological and aesthetic. Any claim that wishes methodologically to invalidate either side by trumping the one with the other is incomplete and misguided. The either/or issue commonly insisted upon by partisans is a false dualism. One need not decide which side is correct. Both are, since the answer depends entirely on the kinds of questions one finds interesting and wishes to pose regarding the work. A sufficient awareness of the nature of both the genre and the exemplar—both the preponderantly social and the potentially aesthetic—is necessary to produce an adequate discussion of any composition. On this side of the new challenges in the humanities, one-sided discussions—from either faction of the partisan divide—are likely to seem inadequate, simplistic, or reductive. There is no returning to simpler times and simpler methodologies.

9. More generally, musical works should not be supposed to contain only one correct meaning (what the piece "really" means) to be uncovered, in the manner of a lost object or thing, by the analyst. Instead, they house multiple, sometimes conflicting strata of meaning(s) to be drawn forth through differing readings (which include current performances). Works are therefore fields of expressive possibility that harbor differing, potential configurations of meaning, configurations that may be concretized only in their awakenings (constructions) by

individual or group listeners. Obtaining the impression of a meaning depends on the effectiveness of the hermeneutic genre that one uses to process the work—and hermeneutic genres are legion. A work will generally seem to provide an answer to any question posed of it. While in the abstract there may be no "wrong questions," the abstract claim can be misleading—or inappropriately comforting. Shallow questions call forth shallow answers. Some questions are more informed, more text-adequate, more historically relevant, and more appropriate than others. The questions that we ask of a musical work depend on our own interests in doing so. Where one situates oneself in asking the questions is important: we do not ask questions "from nowhere." The perspectives from which these questions may be asked seem endless. Realizing the complexity of the issues at hand invites each of us to interrogate—and possibly to modify—the hidden interests of our own subject-positions as we devise our own sets of questions to pursue.

10. One should be cautious in reconstructing the internal anatomy and details of the formal aspects of musical genres. The characteristic error is to reconstruct these things too sparsely or too stiffly. Far from being rigidly prescriptive, genres, properly construed, provide for a flexible set of options at any given point in the realization of any individual exemplar. (This is certainly true of sonata form.) In practice, some generic options were more frequently favored than others. Within any "zone" of the genre there were hierarchies of choices, hierarchies of norms that we may consider to have been arranged into first-level defaults (the most common options, the standard choices pre-made by the genre unless they were overridden), second-level defaults, and so on. (As suggested whimsically in ch. 1, the compositional situation is analogous to a selection of preranked formatting choices arrayed on "wizard" help feature within a computer program.) Genres are preformatted along lines of social preference, although the favored choices may be (and are) altered with time. Reconstructing the genre involves recreating the specifics of this flexible set of weighted default-choices for each interior zone.

11. At any point in producing the individual composition, a composer may realize with

personally crafted music the preformatted suggestions of the various default options provided to him or her by the genre (elegantly or dramatically realizing, for example, the first-level, second-level, or third-level formatting default). On the other hand, if desired, the composer may strain any of the preformatted options to produce, in extreme cases, a deformation of the originally provided generic suggestion. Or the composer may override all of the default options entirely, thus refusing to follow any of the options that were socially provided (that were likely to have been provided, that is, in the hypothetical "wizard" help feature in the computer analogy suggested above)—presumably in order to provide a strong, surprising, or individualized effect. This, too, is a deformation of the genre. (On the term "deformation," see appendix 2.)

12. It is also possible that in any compositional zone a composer could choose to suppress a strongly expected or normative event within the genre. In these cases—which are by no means as infrequent as one might suppose—it is the absence of a certain occurrence, norm, or process that is the important factor. (The norm can be written over by other material or options on the acoustic surface of the music.) Thus any thoroughgoing analytical system should have a procedure to come to terms with the presence of absence—with what is clearly implied but does not literally happen (blocked or unattained goals, ellipses of supposedly obligatory events, non-normative articulations of certain zones overriding a now-silenced norm, and so on). Many current music-theoretical approaches to form were designed to deal only with what is printed on the page. But what occurs notationally—or does not occur—can make sense or create an impression only within a backdrop-field charged with generic expectation: the larger conceptual field of implication and normative practices within which the acoustically heard music asks to be construed. The notation on the page is not self-sufficient in the production of any adequate interpretation of the music. While several other theories of large-scale form seek to account only for what happens in an individual piece or passage, Sonata Theory intertwines this with a concern to observe also what does not happen or what is kept from happening. This is a necessary consequence of understanding individual works dialogically—as dialogues with existing genres (No. 1).

13. The preceding propositions may be reinforced with a quotation from Wolfgang Iser (1976) about "blanks and minus functions" that we endorse. This is a differing articulation of a general concept central to our theory.

> If we say that an unfulfilled function can become a background, we are presupposing familiarity with literary [for us, musical] texts. As Sartre has rightly pointed out, texts always take place on the level of their reader's abilities. Now if a literary text does not fulfill its traditionally expected functions, but instead uses its technique to transform expected functions into "minus functions"—which is the deliberate omission of a generic technique [as Lotman has argued]—in order to invoke their nonfulfillment in the conscious mind of the reader, anyone who is not familiar with these traditional functions will automatically miss the communicatory intention of this technique widely applied in modern literature. He will experience a sense of disorientation and may react accordingly, thus involuntarily revealing the expectations to which he appears to be irrevocably committed. But the more familiar the reader is with the functions that are now being "nonfulfilled," the more definite will be his expectations, and so the more responsive will he be to their frustration.[13]

---

13. Iser, *The Act of Reading*, pp. 207–8. Iser's Sartrean reference—undocumented in *The Act of Reading*—alludes to that author's set of 1947 essays, *What is Literature?*, especially to the section, "Why Write?" There Sartre had written: "Thus, for the reader, all is to do and all is already done; the work exists only at the exact level of his capacities; while he reads and creates, he knows that he can always go further in his reading, can always create more profoundly, and thus the work seems to him as inexhaustible and opaque as things." ('*What is Literature?' and Other Essays*, trans. anon. [Cambridge, Mass.: Harvard University Press, 1988], p. 54. Cf. the original text from its first publication as a complete book, *Qu'est-ce que la littérature* [Paris: Gallimard, 1948], p. 58: "Ainsi, pour le lecteur, tout est à faire et tout est déjà fait; l'œuvre n'existe qu'au niveau exact de ses capacités.")

14. When individual occurrences happen within a piece that are extrageneric or contravene the generic norms, this in itself does not alter or change the genre within which it is participating. That genre continues to exist as a background rule for interpretation. In order to be considered a sonata, a work does not have to fulfill a certain number of tonal, melodic, or structural criteria before being admitted under that classification. Instead, to call a work a sonata is to conclude that, on the basis of the evidence at hand, it does indeed invite us (in any number of ways) to use our generic conception of a sonata as the regulative principle of interpretation by which to understand its events. (As a corollary, there would have to be a sufficient set of reasons within the work—sonic signals, movement-or-work titles, positional placements within multimovement constructions, and so on—to justify why we would be tempted to consider it as a sonata at all. Obviously, many pieces in different genres would not even begin to extend this invitation.) What literally happens on the piece's acoustic surface may or may not be normative for sonatas, but those events are not the ultimately determining factors in defining what a sonata is. If the deviations in any given work are extreme, we may be better off, however, referring to it instead as a sonata deformation—as an unusual, perhaps *ad hoc* structure still dependent on sonata norms for interpretation.

15. Master composers typically create "customized" versions of the socially produced genre for their own use. Such customizations involve the arraying of characteristic choices that they prefer to make as part of their own individualized styles. (This is analogous to the setting-up of personalized formatting options, involving selective modifications of what is pregiven.) Haydn's customization—his sense of his own standard practice—was different from Mozart's. Broad, idiosyncratic patterns of customization are in dialogue with the larger, more generalized generic norms (with the normal or preformatted style generally obtained by all). When one finds a seemingly unusual effect in Haydn, for example, one might ask: is the effect only part of Haydn's customized deformation of standard practice? (is it a norm for Haydn, though not for Mozart or J. C. Bach?); or is the effect a deformation even of his customization?; to what degree? and so on.

16. In any adequate genre-based analysis, the goal must not be merely to identify patterns and to assign labels to them. To be sure, a background taxonomy of labels is necessary to cover the basic set of possibilities within a genre: such labels provide a shorthand way of talking about these things. But any analysis that stops after the mere labeling is no analysis at all. Under no circumstances should an analysis seek to normalize unusual occurrences and anomalies: one should acquire a healthy distrust of all systems and catch-phrases that work in this direction. Rather, in confronting potentially ambiguous situations—and sonatas are filled with them—the proper goal of analysis is to explicate the ambiguities, to reawaken the strains and uncertainties within the text, not to suppress them or filter them out. Moreover, analyses that seek a facile closure of explanation are invariably short-sighted. Unless a musical text is problematized—or brought to a deeper level of questioning and inquiry, where lurking and troublesome questions still remain (or are finally glimpsed at a more proper level)—then that analysis is inadequate. The goal of analysis must never be to explain away the difficulties of a musical work but rather to call forth a work's problems, tensions, and larger implications.

Terminology

"Rotation" and "Deformation"

Rotation

Although they differ in their degrees of subtlety and strictness, sonata movements are engaged in a dialogue with a more basic architectural principle of large-scale recurrence that we call *rotation*. Rotational structures are those that extend through musical space by recycling one or more times—with appropriate alterations and adjustments—a referential thematic pattern established as an ordered succession at the piece's outset. In each case the implication is that once we have arrived at the end of the thematic pattern, the next step will bring us back to its opening, or to a variant thereof, in order to initiate another (often modified) move through the configuration. The end leads into the next beginning. This produces the impression of circularity or cycling in all formal types that we regard as rotational. One metaphorical image that might be invoked here is that of a clock-hand sweeping through multiple hours, with the face of the clock representing the successive stages of the thematic pattern. 11:59:59 leads inevitably to 12:00:00 (= 0:00:00) and another round through the cycle. Similarly, the regeneration of day upon day, calendar year upon calendar year, suggests how strongly this perception of circular recurrence has been impressed upon our experience.

Another, perhaps more sophisticated, metaphor is that of tracking a large spiral through two or more cycles. No set of events that unfolds in nonrecoverable, ever-elapsing time can exist in a condition of complete identity to any similar set that has preceded it. An essential feature of all such constructions is the tension generated between the blank linearity of non-repeatable time and the quasi-ceremonial circularity of any repeatable events or structures that are inlaid into it. Rotational procedures are grounded in a dialectic of persistent loss (the permanent death of each instant as it lapses into the next) and the impulse to seek a temporal "return to the origin," a cyclical renewal and rebeginning. And indeed, quite apart from the issue of merely inhabiting a different temporal space, successive rotations in music are often subjected to telling variation: portions of them may dwell longer on individual modules of the original musical arrangement; they may omit some of the ordered modules along the way; or they may be shortened, truncated, telescoped, expanded, developed, decorated, or altered with *ad hoc* internal substitutions or episodic interpolations. Not infrequently these varied multiple recyclings build cumulatively toward a longer-range goal. In addition, within any individual rotation an internal, smaller-pattern cycling can give the impression of a local subrotation. These include such things as thematic-block restatements, the altered recurrences of larger sequential blocks or zones, and the like.

The rotational idea is an archetypal principle of musical structure: a referential model followed by (usually varied) recyclings or restatements. It underpins a generous diversity of forms that may be distinguished from one another on more surface-oriented levels: theme and variations; strophic songs; strophic variation; rondos (chapter 18); different types of ostinato-grounded works; and the like.[1] Any form that emphasizes return and rebeginning is in dialogue with the rotational principle.[2] One of the defining features of a sonata is the particular way in which it textures and shapes the underlying rotational idea. In a sonata-form composition the referential pattern laid down at the beginning is typically much longer and more internally differentiated than that found in the smaller strophic or variation forms. Here the relevant pattern is the exposition, the musical configuration provided, in a two-part exposition, by P TR ' S / C, including the subdivisions of each zone, if any. Discussions of the rotational implications of the remainder of the sonata movement—in each of the five sonata types—are omnipresent in the *Elements*.

Within a sonata, tonality is irrelevant to the task of identifying the rotational principle. The central thing is an implied or actualized ordered sweep through a temporal sequence of thematic modules, along with the assumption that the most "natural" or expected continuation of the layout's last module will be to lead to a relaunching of the initial module of the next, thus producing the characteristic spiral or circular effect. Rotation is what we call a rhetorical principle rather than a tonal one: it is governed by the expectation of a temporal presentation-sequence of thematic-modular elements, not by harmonic procedures, even though, on another plane of analysis, those harmonic features have their own structures to articulate.

The underlying principle of recycling or restatement has also been widely noticed by others. In *Sonata Forms*, for instance, Charles Rosen pointed out the relevant feature particularly with regard to what we would call triple-rotational Type 3 sonatas: "The need for a balanced symmetry always remained essential to any conception of sonata in all its forms. (Many

---

1. Our additional discussions of the rotational principle—especially as applied to music from later decades—may be found in the following: Hepokoski, *Sibelius: Symphony No. 5* (Cambridge: Cambridge University Press, 1993), pp. 23–26, 58–84; Darcy, "The Metaphysics of Annihilation: Wagner, Schopenhauer, and the Ending of the Ring," *Music Theory Spectrum*, 16 (1994), 1–40 (see esp. pp. 10ff); Hepokoski, "The Essence of Sibelius: Creation Myths and Rotational Cycles in *Luonnotar*," *The Sibelius Companion*, ed. Glenda Dawn Goss (Westport, Conn.: Greenwood, 1996), pp. 121–46; Darcy, "Bruckner's Sonata Deformations," *Bruckner Studies*, ed. Timothy L. Jackson and Paul Hawkshaw (Cambridge: Cambridge University Press, 1997), pp. 256–77; Hepokoski, "Rotations, Sketches, and [Sibelius's] Sixth Symphony," *Sibelius Studies*, ed. Timothy L. Jackson and Veijo Murtomäki (Cambridge: Cambridge University Press, 2001), pp. 322–51; Darcy, "Rotational Form, Teleological Genesis, and Fantasy-Projection in the Slow Movement of Mahler's Sixth Symphony, *19th-Century Music* 24 (2001), 49–74; Hepokoski, "Beethoven Reception: The Symphonic Tradition," in Jim Samson, ed., *The Cambridge History of Nineteenth-Century Music* (Cambridge: Cambridge University Press, 2002), pp. 424–59; and Hepokoski, "Structure, Implication, and the End of Suor Angelica," *Studi pucciniani* 3 (2004), 241–64.

2. Baroque ritornello structures, for instance, suggest a set of varied refrain-like recurrences—the first ritornello (or tutti) often first sounded as a patterned "beginning"—that spin off into freer, diverse episodes for the remainder of each rotation. (Or, conversely, once into the piece we could also construe the rotations as comprising freer, episodic beginnings—the "solo" passages—each of which is concluded by a refrain-like reference to the ritornello or a portion thereof.) Extending such ideas to varied strophic songs with refrains and to rondos is an easy matter. Similarly, da capo (large-formatted ABA's) or other emphatically ternary structures could be interpreted as two "external" rotations of a musical pattern, separated by a contrasting interpolation in the middle. Extending the metaphor further, one might wonder whether we should entertain the possibility that the contrasting central section of such forms might even be understood as a substitution for an unsounded middle rotation: an erasing or writing over a rotation that is potentially conceptually present but rendered tacit by the events sounded on the acoustic surface. However we might seek to assess these "ternary" considerations and interpretive possibilities, they are relevant to the ways in which we choose to understand the developmental spaces of sonata forms.

development sections reveal this, as they take up the complete thematic pattern of the exposition, and develop each theme in turn.)"[3] So much is obvious. But even while endorsing such prior statements, Sonata Theory distinguishes itself from them in three ways. First, we conceive the restatement-symmetry postulate as wedded to the notion of circularity (as opposed to mere carriage-return repetition.) Second, we treat the idea more flexibly. We include into the general concept of circular repetition the related idea of substantially altered restatements, such as developmental half-rotations, truncated rotations, rotations with episodic substitutes "writing over" some of the expected individual elements, rotations with newly included interpolations, internal digressions from the governing rotational thread, occasional reorderings of the modules, and the like. In general, the rotational character of the whole sonata movement is underscored whenever a development section begins with a treatment of the primary theme (P) or whenever a coda is added that is based on P-theme material—regardless of what follows that material. (Interpreting "freer" thematic patterns that only begin rotationally is a challenge called forth by the theory.) Third, because the rotational idea was so important as an underlying assumption in the historical formation of the genre of sonata form (and because it persisted so palpably in so many later sonatas, extending through the nineteenth century and beyond), Sonata Theory urges the elevation of the rotational principle to become a foundational axiom of interpretation that in one way or another is implicated in every sonata, even when it is apparently absent or deeply obscured in developments. To be sure, literally nonrotational developments are an option within the style—though they are not as common as might be supposed—and we hope that we are not misread as encouraging the interpretational forcing of any such development

along Procrustean-rotational lines. For such developments the main hermeneutic problem might be to wonder whether (and to what degree) what is actually presented on the music's acoustic surface as a nonrotational event is to be grasped as blanking-out or writing over a more normatively rotational option. The question remains open: Is the rotational norm for developments sufficiently powerful to suggest its tacit presence (perhaps as "a choice not made") even in cases when it is replaced by something else?

Devising a term for a previously unlabeled but generally recognizable practice is not easy. We use "rotation" in the familiar sense provided in definition 2a of the *Oxford English Dictionary*: "the fact of coming round again in succession; a recurring series or period."[4] This meaning of the word is virtually identical with two of the OED definitions of "cycle": "a recurrent round or course (of successive events, phenomena, etc.); a regular order or succession in which things recur; a round or series which returns upon itself" [definition 3]; or "a round, course, or period through which anything runs in order to its completion; a single complete period or series of successive events, etc." [definition 4]. In the abstract, then, another term for rotational form would be *cyclical form* or *cyclic organization*. The problem here is that that term already means something different not merely in formal analysis but also in analytical work applied directly to sonata-based structures. It refers to a compositional strategy in which important or motto themes or motives from an initial movement return, however transformed, in later movements.[5] "Rotation" and "rotational form" do not have these prior (and in this situation, misleading) connotations. This is not to say that "rotation" is unused for other purposes in music theory. The term has a specific meaning in the analysis of serial practice and ordered musical sets—as well as in the techniques of cer-

---

3. Rosen, *Sonata Forms*, p. 157.
4. *The Compact Edition of the Oxford English Dictionary* [1971]. Definition 1 of "rotation," not surprisingly, invokes the presence of an axis, which is less unproblematically applicable to our use of the term in Sonata Theory: "The action of moving round a centre, or of turning round (and round) on an axis; also, the action of producing a motion of this kind." Closer again to our

application of "rotation" is definition 2b: "Regular and recurring succession in office, duties, etc., of a number of persons. Freq. In phr. *by* or *in rotation.*"
5. See, e.g., the discussions of cyclic integration, cyclic organization, and cyclic form—with nuanced definitions—in Webster, *Haydn's "Farewell" Symphony,* pp. 7–9, 179–82, 246–47, 250–51, 252, 254–57, 258–59, 262–67, 280–300, 308–13, 318–20, and 327–34.

tain kinds of minimalist patterns that are subsequently subjected to an organized reordering. (It can refer, for example, to the shifting of the last element of a succession to become the first—a single operation that is itself usually considered a "rotation," although, properly considered, the full rotation would not have occurred until all of the elements in play have gone through one cycle of these reorderings.) These other usages of "rotation," though, refer to different repertories and different kinds of discussions from the one in question here. Confusion among these uses of "rotation" seems unlikely.

What other substitutions might there be for "rotation"? "Strophic form" carries verbal and poetic-textual connotations not appropriate here. "Theme and variations" suggests irrelevant generic connotations and traditions of a different kind. "Varied repetitions" or "varied restatements"—when used apart from the rotational concept as the guiding backdrop—seem bland, unimaginatively divorced from the implied circularity of the procedure. Robert P. Morgan's recent treatment of what he called "circular form" displaying successive "cycles" and "cyclic renewal" (for example, in the *Tristan* Prelude) closely approximates our use of "rotation," although the methodology and interests at stake in that description differ from our own.[6] Of the available terms, we have come to favor "rotation," although by no means do we seek to banish parallel descriptions from our own work: we sometimes also refer to our rotations as cycles, varied repetitions, or varied restatements, as the occasion suggests. In referring to the larger structure and musical process, however, the term "rotational form" is to be preferred.

Deformation

Sonata Theory views compositions as individualized dialogues with an intricate system of norms and standard options. We seek to illuminate the expressive, dramatic, and contextual meanings of single compositions, in part by inquiring how the compositional choices presented in the individual work confirm, extend, or override those options as we move from phrase to phrase. The desired goal is to be able to read the moment-to-moment action of a piece through the lenses of (reconstructed) generic expectation and flexible generic possibility.

We use the term "deformation" to mean the stretching of a normative procedure to its maximally expected limits or even beyond them—or the overriding of that norm altogether in order to produce a calculated expressive effect. It is precisely the strain, the distortion of the norm (elegantly? beautifully? wittily? cleverly? stormily? despairingly? shockingly?) for which the composer strives at the deformational moment. The expressive or narrative point lies in the tension between the limits of a competent listener's field of generic expectations and what is made to occur—or not occur—in actual sound at that moment. Within any individual exemplar (such as a single musical composition) operating under the shaping influence of a community-shared genre-system, any exceptional occurrence along these lines calls attention to itself as a strong expressive effect. As such it marks an important event of the composition at hand. A deformation may occur either locally, producing a momentary or short-range effect, or broadly, over the large-scale architecture of a piece of music as a whole.

Connotations of "Deformation": Paradoxes of the "Normative" and "Non-Normative"; the Need for Nuance

Since the concept of deformation is a central feature of Sonata Theory, we have tried to be careful in selecting and applying that term. While we do intend "deformation" to imply a strain and distortion of the norm—the composer's application of uncommon creative force toward the production of a singular aesthetic effect— we do not use this term in its looser, more colloquial sense, one that can connote a negative assessment of aesthetic defectiveness, imperfec-

6. Morgan, "Circular Form in the *Tristan* Prelude," *Journal of the American Musicological Society* 53 (2000), 69–103.

tion, or ugliness. Here our definitions must be explicit. Within our system, "deformation" is a technical term referring to a striking way of stretching or overriding a norm. As a technical term it is intended to carry no judgmentally negative connotation, as in some popular usages of the word.[7] We understand that other scholars, for other purposes, may have used the term to suggest some of these negative connotations.[8] But that is not our intention. We are suggesting neither that a sonata deformation is an unattractive structure (as opposed to any supposedly more attractive or socially preferable norm) nor that it is the result of a misguided execution on the part of the composer. Nor, more locally, are we implying that the deformation of a medial caesura, for example, results in something that is aesthetically negative.[9] To avoid encouraging such connotations in our own writing, we steer clear of the verb "to deform" along with (especially) the related word "deformed" (let alone "deformity"!) to describe the effect of a deformation. Instead of a "deformed recapitulation" we prefer to write of a "recapitulation subjected to a deformation."[10] The abstract noun "defor-

mation" is cooler, more detached—hopefully, more connotationally "technical." It marks only our noticing (and often relishing) of a remarkably unusual compositional choice; it is not judgmental.

Nevertheless, we also recognize that however carefully one might insist upon one's intentions to provide only a "technical" definition of any term, words have connotational, lateral slippages and past histories that can escape our control. And it may still be that some readers, for whatever purposes, might mistakenly read into it only unintended implications of the negative or the critical. For such readers—and for any readers curious about a more expanded treatment of our view of the term and its connotations—we pause here to examine the matter (and related issues) with more patience and nuance. This initially entails a backing-up to some fundamental aspects of how we understand sonata form.

As indicated in chapter 1, our view of sonata form is essentially *dialogic*, not conformational. It is not the task of a sonata merely to "conform" to a pre-existing template. On the

---

7. *The Compact Edition of the Oxford English Dictionary* [1971] provides three definitions for the word "deformation." The first two have negative implications that do not reflect how we are using the term: (1) "The action (or result) of deforming or marring the form or beauty of; disfigurement, defacement"; (2) "Alteration of form for the worse; *esp.* in controversial use, the opposite of *reformation*. . . . An altered form of a word in which its proper form is for some purpose perverted [as *God* to '*od*]." Instead, our adoption of the term is analogous to the third, more technical (and nonjudgmental) definition: (3) "*Physics*. Alteration of form or shape; relative displacement of the parts of a body or surface without breach of continuity; an altered form of."
8. As perhaps in Renato Poggioli, *The Theory of the Avant-Garde,* trans. Gerald Fitzgerald (Cambridge: Harvard University Press, 1968), esp. pp. 176–79, in which Poggioli refers, among other things, to the effects of "neoprimitivist deformation," "ritual and allegrorical deformation," "stylistic deformation," and "avant-garde deformation" ("shocking" or nonrealistic representations) in early twentieth-century modernist art.—Picasso, Braque, and others. Poggioli initially played up the negative connotations of these things in the language of their critics ("the principle of dehumanization," etc.) but soon turned to something of an *apologia*: "Avant-garde deformation . . . also becomes a tradition and a stylistic convention.")

9. Complementarily—to suggest a clarifying *reductio ad absurdum*—no serious scholar could maintain, within an analytical situation, that merely recognizing a familiar compositional choice as a "norm" or as "normative" inevitably connotes a tacit personal approval or moral endorsement of that norm. On the contrary (of course), it is merely an acknowledgment of standard operating procedure within the quasi-formulaic genre under observation (as in, e.g., "in tonal practice the norm has been to resolve dissonant sevenths downward"), an awareness of what usually occurs, for whatever historical reasons, under certain circumstances and traditions of musical manufacturing.
10. *OED,* "Deformed," first definition: "marred in appearance; disfigured, defaced." Under the entry "deformed" there is no technical or neutral use that would be applicable to its potential relevance to the field of physics (see n. 7, definition 3 above—closer to our usage of "deformation"). Nonetheless, the term "to deform" is encountered in scientific writing, as in the *New Encyclopedia Brittanica: Micropedia* (1994) entry, "Deformation and Flow," cited in the text above. Still, its absence from the *OED* helps to confirm our sense that "deformed" has stronger negative connotations, a situation that we do not believe is true for "deformation."

contrary, a sonata is a musical utterance that is set into dialogue with generic options that are themselves taken socially to be sonata-defining (establishing the guidelines for composition and reception under the categories of the genre). In this dialogic process the flash-point "now" of the unfolding structure moves progressively through various action-spaces. Within a sonata, what we regard as an action-space—a flexible concept—can be quite small (P, TR, MC, S, C), rather broad (exposition, development, recapitulation, coda), or very broad indeed (single movement, multimovement plan). The dialogue inherent in any sonata form may include the occasional stretching or overriding of the options on offer from the genre. These decisions bring those moments into the realm of what we call deformation. But how can we characterize more carefully what it is that is being subjected to a deformation?

Each action-space of the sonata is generically present to make possible an ongoing dialogue of compositional decisions with a background constellation of standard or traditional options (norms). This is nothing less than what it means to work within a genre—any genre—one that furnishes an ongoing horizon of expectations for the receiver. All genres (indeed, all familiar actions) involve systems of norms and guidelines, typical and expected procedures. In the case of music these are grounded in increments of elapsing time. We are inescapably involved with the results of laying down compositional decision after decision, module after module, in time, presumably with a larger purpose or grander coherence in view all the while. The result is a *temporal* process of ongoing dialogue—successive modular decisions that invite us to understand them, one by one (and then conceptually joined together in groups or clusters), according to the guidelines of a backdrop of a set of implied norms for the genre, which the reception community is assumed to share. Since the basic, *initial* process here is temporal, the fundamental concept is that of a process, not

a "thing," a self-realizing *verb*, unspooling itself in time, not a static noun.

Nonetheless, once a compositional (modular) decision has been made (via notation or performance in the case of a sonata), it is now part of the piece's history, fixed in place, unalterable. This is because chronological time is irreversible on the work's acoustic surface: one cannot take back in reality what has already been sounded.[11] From this perspective, the already sounded is converted into fixed units of modular space. In chapter 2 we compared the process of composition to that of constructing a sonic bridge over ever larger stretches of otherwise empty time or to the laying-down of "one appropriately stylized musical tile after another"—in which each tile, more fundamentally, was also described as a "space of action." In this way decisions regarding the filling of offered spans of time lay out realized *spaces*, which in turn are analogous to conceptual spaces. The result is an individualized "shape": an array of modules that has produced a fixed musical idea in time. The "shape" produced is metaphorically analogous to a "shaped" vessel or container: one can perceive the musical result sculpturally, in terms of how it realizes melodic pattern, meter, tempo, articulation, dynamics, timbre, density, drive-to-cadence, and the like. One might regard music as sculpted time, as a temporal sculpture in sound.

All genres of music presuppose genre-defining guidelines for the production of typical or more or less standardized "shapes" (modular arrays in each of the available action-zones). In the case of sonata form, with all of its complexities and possibilities, these guidelines are manifold and varied. Within the sonata we have not merely one or two but numerous standard procedures available, which in turn means that the expected contours or "energy-shapes" of any individual work are supple in their realizations. (There is no single standard "shape" for expositions, for instance, nor for its internal zones, P, TR, S, and C, although in a more general sense one is invited to recognize any individ-

---

11. As pointed out elsewhere in this book, however, in music the fictive artifice of "psychological" time (suggesting the possibility of backing up, recapturing, de-

nying, repeating, re-experiencing, and so on) is typically counterpointed against the inescapable "reality" of chronological time.

ual exemplar of the possibilities when one hears it.)

Under these circumstances, it is compositionally possible—and was even doubtless encouraged—to submit such generically received, standardized "energy-shapes" to significant strain, stretching, and overriding. The term *deformation* refers to such situations. Musical deformations are purposeful distortions of the standardized "action- or texture-shapes" on offer to the composer from the ordered complex of pre-existing generic expectations and traditional procedures. Structural deformations are the results of applications of compositional tension and force to produce a surprising, tension-provoking, or engaging result. More to the point, on both the production and reception side of things, as part of the compositional "game" it was *expected* ("normative") that, within the then-current boundaries of taste and decorum, a composer would apply conceptual force here and there to strain or alter what is otherwise a bland or neutral set of conventional options and procedures—mere starting-points for the mature and experienced artist. As has been observed over the decades by virtually all commentators on the sonata repertory, applying such forces and purposeful generic "misshapings" is just what can give a composition personality, memorability, appeal, interest, expressive power.

This is a crucial point. Deformations are compositional surprises, engaging forays into the unanticipated. But the paradox of art is that the nature of the game at hand also and always includes the idea that we are to expect the unexpected. If deviations from the merely expected never happen within an individual work, that is no sign of aesthetic health or integrity.[12] On the contrary, if expressively charged stretchings or transgressions of standardized shapes and procedures are not present at all, the work is more likely to be sidelined by historical consensus as unimaginative, composition-by-the-numbers, a boiler-plate product. This means that in the case of sonata form—and certainly in the hands of classical masters—it was perfectly "normative" to intersperse into the individual work instances of the "non-normative" or the rivetingly deformational. Within the artifice of art the concept of the "non-normative" or "nonconforming" is housed under a broader concept of what one is generically prepared to accept as standard procedure. Simply put, what is "non-normative" on one level of understanding becomes "normative" under a wider span of consideration.[13]

In this more expansive sense, instances of aesthetic deformation are indications of normality within strong works of art. It is both historically inaccurate and simple-minded to understand deformations as *ipso facto* violating a fundamental premise of the genre at hand or introducing illicitly foreign, unpleasant, or moralistically tainted elements of the "abnormal" or "disfigured" into an originally idyllic, positive model. Indeed, the reverse is true. Deformation, strain, and conceptual distortion were standard strategies within the sonata game, which was played increasingly under the auspices of a growing demand for originality and apparent "depth" of the compositional idea. (What would have been aesthetically "abnormal," if not amateurish, would be to shy away from all signs of them altogether.)

Within the sonata structures of the period in question "progressive" connoisseurs have typically taken such thematic or structural deformations—in Johann Stamitz, C. P. E. Bach, Haydn, Mozart, Beethoven, and so on—as signs of creative vigor, not of any debilitating negative. The distortions and localized reshapings of these composers have historically been assessed as positive features, marks of original-

---

12. Nor, of course, do health and integrity (compositional "excellence" or community "legitimacy") lie only in the deformational moments. The central thing is the clever interplay—the dialogue—between a work's adherence to and departures from conventional expectation. Both have their roles to play, and the genre *qua* genre has things that it (socially) "wants to say" through the vagaries of the individual work. See appendix 1.

13. See also the final subsection of chapter 15, "The Role of the Listener," especially n. 47, which references Wolfgang Iser (*The Act of Reading*, p. 112) on the role of the reader in expecting the unexpected within the plots of novels.

ity and personal voice. With the exception of a few grumbling caveats from waning sectors of "old-world" traditionalists circa 1780–1820, they have not been regarded as off-putting disfigurements or "disabilities" to be contrasted with some tacitly posited concept of the supposedly "normal" or "well formed" of how exemplars of the genre "ought" to proceed.[14] Such a viewpoint—which would see in structural deformations and innovative procedures only implications of the exceeding of proper or socially acceptable limits, only transgressions of good taste—is historically associated principally with social and aesthetic conservatives wielding their eroding claims of authority to cling to the way things once were (or were imagined to be). Nonetheless, what becomes clear, especially as one moves further into the nineteenth century, is that a primarily technical local strategy within an individual piece—what we are calling a structural deformation (*Witz* and originality in various degrees of strength)—could be seized upon by both proponents and opponents of any "new" or "developing" art form as evidence of either, on the one hand, a brilliant display of breathtaking creativity or, on the other, a lapse of compositional judgment from a composer of questionable taste or talent.[15]

For all of these reasons one should not call attention to only the potentially negative slippages of the word "deformation" or conflate them inappropriately with concepts of deformity or disability. Such a one-sided view, in historical terms, promotes the blinkered views of aesthetic and social reactionaries. Moreover, it misses the complexity of what the term, with all of its purposely implied connotations of strain and distortion, seeks to convey. Above all, such an interpretation bypasses the crucial distinction, central to the philosophy of art for centuries, between life and art. As Aristotle noted in the *Poetics* with regard to the effects of staged tragedy, what would displease us in life—terrors and sorrows, violence and tears, brutal and unhappy outcomes—can be profoundly moving in the displaced realm of art. We often savor and applaud in art what we do not in life. Judgments that we might make in life-situations are not properly transferable to the world of distanced artifice, to the world of artificiality that is the most basic presupposition of the art-situation. Similarly, terminology that can carry negative connotations when applied to assessments in life can carry neutral or positive ones when applied to the very different situation of art. Potential negatives in life can be reversed into positives in the reception-worlds of their metamorphosed analogues within art. It may be for reasons along these lines that musical distortions or intentional "misshapings" of a generically received action- and texture-space within music ("deformations") have so often been hailed as attributes of genius and originality—indicators of aesthetic seriousness and pleasure. Our term "deformation," with its charged edginess and flavor of aesthetic risk, seeks to convey this richer, more complex world of connotation.

---

14. This claim has been made recently, and mistakenly attributed to us as a latent implication within the terms "norm" and "deformation," by Joseph N. Straus, "Normalizing the Abnormal: Disability in Music and Music Theory," *Journal of the American Musicological Society* 59 (2006), forthcoming. In our view the arbitrary and exclusive binaries driving Straus's argument—the categories that he offered his readers were limited to only "well formed" vs. "deformed" and "normal" vs. "abnormal" —are false choices, too narrowly drawn to engage the complexities of the topics at hand.

15. This obviously touches on the historical-reception issues surrounding certain later, more "extreme" or flamboyant rhetorical- or structural-deformational procedures—those found in Schubert, Berlioz, Cho-

pin, Schumann, Liszt, Wagner, Tchaikovsky, Strauss, Mahler, and so on. To be sure, each of these composers had their legions of champions. On the other hand, in varying degrees, some of the works of these composers came to be placed under a quasi-moralistic suspicion by conservative, masculinist, or aggressively nationalist (sometimes racialist) critics as deviant, dilettantish, socially undesirable, decadent, or degenerate. As strategies within an aesthetic genre, structural-deformational strategies may be "morally neutral" in themselves, but history has also shown us—often much to our consternation—that they may also be seized upon and denounced by cultural critics for their own cultural purposes.

Precedents in the Use of the Term

Strictly considered, the term "deformation" is not new with us, although prior to our use of it, it has not been much applied to musical works. We have adapted it primarily from leading traditions of twentieth-century literary criticism (Russian formalism, narrative theory, genre theory, reader-response theory) but also, metaphorically, from its usages in physics and mechanics. Within the latter fields the term is emphatically technical. *The New Encyclopedia Britannica: Micropedia*, 15th ed., vol. 3 (Chicago, 1994), for instance, contains an entry under "Deformation and Flow," one that even uses the verb "to deform" neutrally:

> In physics, [deformation refers to the] alteration in shape or size of a body under the influence of mechanical forces. Flow is a change in deformation that continues as long as the force is applied. . . . Under normal conditions . . . solids deform when they are subjected to forces. Most solids initially deform elastically; that is to say, they return to their original shape when the load is removed. . . . Eventually, plastic flow will come to an end: deformation will ultimately tend to concentrate in one area, which will break. This ability of ductile materials to flow plastically under load is fundamental to their usefulness in engineering.

Here "deformation" is descriptive of a certain state of a solid object—a change of shape, a departure from its original, normal, or customary state resulting from the application of force.[16] No judgment is made that the deformation in question (say, the bending of a steel bar, which might be a desirable end) is a negative disfigurement or the result of a marring of the way that the object in question ought really to be. If, metaphorically, we wish to imagine the genre of sonata form (or any portion thereof, such as a medial caesura or an EEC) as a solid object— such things are at least solid concepts governed by norms—the application of force that would subject it to distortion or reshaping would be the creative will of the composer.[17] The act of composition, producing something in dialogue with norms as they are socially received, could be understood as producing a "flow" in certain portions of those norms—perhaps a straining, a stretching, an expansion, or a bulging-out; perhaps the omission of an important procedure; perhaps the substitution of an unexpected event for an expected one. In the case of musical norms the composer does not alter the genre itself through such deformations. Existing outside the composition proper, the genre is that which provides the guidelines for understanding what occurs inside the individual piece.

Within the humanities the notion of expressive alterations applied to a conventional model (in our case, a highly complex one) is familiar. Here one encounters the term "deformation" with some regularity, often as a technical term without a judgmentally negative connotation. In its individual appearances the term has significant, sometimes broad intersections with our use of it. Those appearances help to illuminate the history behind our selection of the term. But in the literature those intersections are not always total. It is also true that "deformation" has sometimes been used to describe effects (or to address issues) that are different from those that we have in mind in Sonata Theory. It can be helpful to remind ourselves of these usages.

Some derive from the early-twentieth-century tradition of Russian formalism and refer especially to the "enstrangement" or "defamiliarization" of ordinary language within poetry—a concern that extends to the very definition of art itself.

> The basic concepts of formalism—"transrational language," "deautomatization," "deformation," "deliberately difficult form" . . . and others—are merely negations corresponding to various indices

---

16. Cf. n. 7, definition 3.

17. If the scientific metaphor were applied strictly to musical composition, every creative shaping of the generic norms, however minimal, would be considered a deformation. Such a metaphor could be sustained, but we prefer to use the term "deformation" to refer primarily to *extreme* strainings of the norms, or to their abandonment altogether—a situation sometimes similar to the "breaking of plastic flow" in physics. One reason for this is that aesthetic norms are flexible concepts, remaining essentially "themselves" even while permitting much variation in their realizations.

of practical, communicative language. (Mikhail Bakhtin, 1928 [critical of Russian formalism])[18]

Dynamic form is not generated by means of combination or merger (the often-used concept of "correspondence"), but by means of interaction, and, consequently, the pushing forward of one group of factors at the expense of another. In so doing, the advanced factor deforms the subordinate ones. The sensation of form is always the sensation of the flow (and, consequently, of the alteration) of correlation between the subordinating, constructive factor and the subordinated factors. . . . Art lives by means of this interaction and struggle. Without this sensation of subordination and deformation of all factors by the one factor playing the constructive role, there is no fact of art." (Yuri Tynianov, 1924)[19]

Or, as explained in an overview of such thought by two more recent writers (and extended here to include the idea of narrative, which brings us close to Sonata Theory concerns):

The many Formalist studies in this tradition [plot studies, narratology] describe how narratives are "made" by "deforming" everyday narrative much as poetry is "made" by deforming everyday language. They developed an arsenal of techniques and concepts that are by now familiar: *fabula, siuzhet,* repetition, parallelism, morphology, substitution, motivation, and baring the device. (Gary Saul Morson and Caryl Emerson, 1990)[20]

In the 1920s Roman Jakobson applied the term "deformation" to the larger issue of the validity of anti- or nonrealistic representation. His argument on behalf of the "deformation" of "artistic norms" also comes close to serving as a clearer precedent for the (perhaps more limited) way in which we use the term:

But the perception of those of a more conservative persuasion continues to be determined by the old canons; they will accordingly interpret any deformation of these canons by a new movement as a rejection of the principle of verisimilitude, as a deviation from realism. . . . [Thus in the "realism" debate one needs to consider the basic issue:] *The tendency to deform given artistic norms conceived as an approximation of reality. . . .* [Some anti-realists may take as an artistic principle:] *I rebel against a given artistic code and view its deformation as a more accurate rendition of reality . . .* [while critics may argue:] *I am conservative and view the deformation of the artistic code, to which I subscribe, as a distortion of reality. . . .* The conservative, of course, fails to recognize the self-sufficient value of deformation. (Roman Jakobson, 1921)[21]

A similar position vis-à-vis the "art" question has been taken in reader-response criticism, for instance, in the work of Wolfgang Iser (taking off, here, from a related idea that he wishes to adapt and improve upon, E. H. Gombrich's well-known principle of "schema and correction").[22] In this case Iser's remarks, both in their content and in their general tone, are close indeed—virtually identical—to the concepts that underpin our sense of deformation:

Thus [in Gombrich's view] the act of representation is seen as a continual process of modifying traditional schemata, the correction of which provides an ever more "suitable" representation of the world. . . . What is important for our purposes, however, is the fact that the correction violates a norm of expectation contained within the picture itself. In this way, the act of representation creates its own conditions of reception. . . . [The observer of a work of visual art] is guided by the correction to the extent that he will try

---

18. P. N. Medvedev/M. M. Bakhtin, *The Formal Method in Literary Scholarship: A Critical Introduction to Sociological Poetics* [1928], trans. Albert J. Wehrle (Baltimore: Johns Hopkins University Press, 1978), p. 87. Cf. pp. 89, 97.
19. Tynianov, *The Problem of Verse Language* [orig. 1924], ed. and trans. Michael Sosa and Brent Harvey (Ann Arbor, Mich.: Ardis, 1981), p. 33.
20. Morson and Emerson, *Mikhail Bakhtin: Creation of a Prosaics* (Stanford: Stanford University Press, 1990), p. 19.

21. Jakobson, "On Realism in Art" [orig. 1921] in *Readings in Russian Poetics: Formalist and Structuralist Views*, ed. Ladislav Matejka and Krystyna Pomorska (Ann Arbor: Michigan Slavic Publications, 1978), pp. 41, 43.
22. E.g., in Gombrich, *Art and Illusion: A Study of Pictorial Representation* (Oxford: Phaidon, 1960; 5th ed. 1977); and *The Image and the Eye* (Ithaca, N.Y.: Cornell University Press, 1982).

to discover the motive behind the change in the schema.

It is in this sense that the concepts of schema and correction have a heuristic value as regards the strategies of literary texts. . . . Herein lies the particular function of the literary schemata ["the repertoire of social norms and literary conventions"]—in themselves they are elements of the text, and yet they are neither aspect nor part of the aesthetic object. The aesthetic object signalizes its presence through the deformations of the schemata, and the reader, in recognizing these deformations, is stimulated into giving the aesthetic object its shape. . . . It is here that the strategies play their part, in laying down the lines along which the imagination is to run. (Iser, 1976)[23]

Also close to our use of the term is a passage from Paul Ricoeur.

Innovation remains a form of behavior governed by rules. The labor of imagination is not born from nothing. It is bound in one way or another to the tradition's paradigms. But the range of solutions of vast. It is deployed between the two poles of servile application and calculated deviation, passing through every degree of "rule-governed deformation" . . . .

What is more, this deviation may come into play on every level, in relation to the types, the genres, even to the formal principle of concordant discordance. The first type of deviation ["types"], it would seem, is constitutive of every individual work. Each work stands apart from every other work. . . . Rule-governed deformation constitutes the axis around which the various changes of paradigm through application are arranged. It is this variety of applications that confers a history on the productive imagination and that, in counterpoint to sedimentation, makes a narrative tradition possible. (Ricoeur, 1983)[24]

Sonata Theory, too, is concerned with "rule-governed deformation," and, with Iser, we affirm that the text's "reader"—in our case the listener to the composition, the analyst, the interpreter—needs to be familiar both with sonata norms and with the standard principles and strategies of their deformation. As for the term "deformation," it has both a solid and an honorable history within several disparate fields in the twentieth century. For us, no substitute for it ("transformation"? "alteration"? "variant"?) carries as historically rich—or, more importantly, as proper—a connotation.

---

23. Iser, *The Act of Reading: A Theory of Aesthetic Response* [orig. 1976] (Baltimore: Johns Hopkins University Press, 1978), pp. 91–92.

24. Ricoeur, *Time and Narrative* [orig. 1983], trans. Kathleen McLaughlin and David Pellauer (Chicago: University of Chicago Press, 1984), 1:69–70.

Bibliography

Adorno, Theodor W. *Beethoven: The Philosophy of the Music*, ed. Rolf Tiedemann; trans. Edmund Jephcott. Stanford: Stanford University Press, 1998.

———. *Mahler: A Musical Physiognomy*, trans. Edmund Jephcott. Chicago: University of Chicago Press, 1991.

Adrian, Jack. "The Function of the Apparent Tonic at the Beginning of Development Sections." *Intégral* 5 (1991): 1-53.

Agawu, V. Kofi. *Playing with Signs: A Semiotic Interpretation of Classic Music*. Princeton, N.J.: Princeton University Press, 1991.

Aldwell, Edward and Carl Schachter. *Harmony and Voice Leading*. 2nd ed. New York: Harcourt Brace Jovanovich, 1989.

———. "The Ternary-Sonata Form." *Journal of Music Theory* 34 (1991): 57–80.

Anson-Cartwright, Mark. "Chromatic Features of E♭-Major Works of the Classical Period." *Music Theory Spectrum* 22 (2000): 177–204.

Badura-Skoda, Eva and Paul. *Interpreting Mozart on the Keyboard*, trans. Leo Black. New York and London: Barrie & Rockliffe, 1962.

Badura-Skoda, Paul. *Kadenzen, Eingänge und Auszierungen zu Klavierkonzerten von Wolfgang Amadeus Mozart*. Kassel: Bärenreiter, 1967.

Barford, Philip T. "The Sonata-Principle: A Study of Musical Thought in the Eighteenth Century." *The Music Review* 13 (1952): 255–63.

Beach, David. "A Recurring Pattern in Mozart's Music." *Journal of Music Theory* 27 (1983): 1–29.

———. "Schenker's Theories: A Pedagogical View" In *Aspects of Schenkerian Theory*, ed. Beach, 1–38. New Haven, Conn.: Yale University Press, 1983.

———. "Schubert's Experiments with Sonata Form: Formal-Tonal Design versus Underlying Structure." *Music Theory Spectrum* 15 (1993): 1–18.

Bent, Ian, with William Drabkin. *Analysis*. The Norton/Grove Handbooks in Music. New York: Norton, 1987.

Berger, Karol. "The First-Movement Punctuation Form in Mozart's Piano Concertos." In *Mozart's Piano Concertos: Text, Context, Interpretation*, ed. Neal Zaslaw, 239–59. Ann Arbor: University of Michigan Press, 1996.

———. "Toward a History of Hearing: The Classic Concerto, A Sample Case." In *Convention in Eighteenth- and Nineteenth-Century Music: Essays in honor of Leonard G. Ratner*, ed. Wye J. Allanbrook, Janet M. Levy, and William Mahrt, 405–29. Stuyvesant, N.Y.: Pendragon, 1992.

Bonds, Mark Evan. "Haydn's False Recapitulations and the Perception of Sonata Form in the Eighteenth Century." Ph.D. diss., Harvard University, 1988.

———. "The Paradox of Musical Form." In *Wordless Rhetoric: Musical Form and the Metaphor of the Oration*, 13–52. Cambridge, Mass.: Harvard University Press, 1991.

Brown, A. Peter. *Joseph Haydn's Keyboard Music: Sources and Style*. Bloomington: Indiana University Press, 1986.

———. Review of Danckwardt, *Die langsame Einlei-*

tung: ihre Herkunft und ihr Bau bei Haydn und Mozart. Journal of the American Musicological Society 33 (1980): 200–4.

Broyles Michael. "Organic Form and the Binary Repeat." *The Musical Quarterly* 66 (1980): 339–60.

———. "The Two Instrumental Styles of Classicism." *Journal of the American Musicological Society* 36 (1983): 210–42.

Boyd, Malcolm. *Domenico Scarlatti: Master of Music.* New York: Schirmer, 1986.

Brodbeck, David. "Medium and Meaning: New Aspects of the Chamber Music." In *The Cambridge Companion to Brahms*, ed. Michael Musgrave, 98–132. Cambridge: Cambridge University Press, 1999.

Brown, A. Peter. *Joseph Haydn's Keyboard Music: Sources and Style.* Bloomington: Indiana University Press, 1986.

Brück, Marion. *Die langsamen Sätze in Mozarts Klavierkonzerten: Untersuchungen zur Form und zum musikalischen Satz.* Munich: Fink, 1994.

Burnett, Henry and Shaugn O'Donnell. "Linear Ordering of the Chromatic Aggregate in Classical Symphonic Music." *Music Theory Spectrum* 18 (1996): 22–50.

Burnham, Scott. "A.B. Marx and the Gendering of Sonata Form." In *Music Theory in the Age of Romanticism*, ed. Ian Bent, 163–86. Cambridge: Cambridge University Press, 1996.

———. *Beethoven Hero.* Princeton, N.J.: Princeton University Press, 1995.

Bushler, David. "Harmonic Structure in Mozart's Sonata-Form Developments." *Mozart-Jahrbuch 1984/85*, 15–24. Kassel: Bärenreiter, 1986.

Cadwallader, Allen and David Gagné. *Analysis of Tonal Music: A Schenkerian Approach.* New York: Oxford University Press, 1998.

Caplin, William E. "The Classical Cadence: Conceptions and Misconceptions." *Journal of the American Musicological Society* 57 (2004): 51–117.

———. *Classical Form: A Theory of Formal Functions for the Instrumental Music of Haydn, Mozart, and Beethoven.* New York: Oxford University Press, 1998.

———. "The 'Expanded Cadential Progression': A Category for the Analysis of Classical Form." *Journal of Musicological Research* 7 (1987): 215–57.

———. "Hybrid Themes: Toward a Refinement in the Classification of Classical Theme Types." *Beethoven Forum* 3 (1994): 151–65.

———. "Structural Expansion in Beethoven's Symphonic Forms." In *Beethoven's Compositional Process*, ed. William Kinderman, 27–54. Lincoln: University of Nebraska Press, 1991.

Cavett-Dunsby, Esther. "Mozart's Codas." *Music Analysis* 7 (1988): 31–51.

———. "Mozart's 'Haydn' Quartets: Composing Up and Down without Rules." *Journal of the Royal Musical Association* 113 (1988): 57–80.

Churgin Bathia. "Francesco Galeazzi's Description (1796) of Sonata Form." *Journal of the American Musicological Society* 21 (1968): 181–99.

———. "Harmonic and Tonal Instability in the Second Key Area of Classic Sonata Form." In *Convention in Eighteenth- and Nineteenth-Century Music: Essays in Honor of Leonard G. Ratner*, ed. Wye J. Allanbrook, Janet M. Levy, and William P. Mahrt, 23–57. Stuyvesant, N.Y.: Pendragon, 1992.

———. "The Symphony as Described by J. A. P. Schulz: A Commentary and Translation." *Current Musicology* 29 (1980): 7–16.

Chusid, Martin. "Schubert's Chamber Music: Before and after Beethoven." In *The Cambridge Companion to Schubert*, ed. Christopher H. Gibbs, 174–92. Cambridge: Cambridge University Press, 1997.

Cohn, Richard L. "As Wonderful as Star Clusters: Instruments for Gazing at Tonality in Schubert." *19th-Century Music* 22 (1999): 213–32.

———. "Maximally Smooth Cycles, Hexatonic Systems, and the Analysis of Late-Romantic Progressions." *Music Analysis* 15 (1996): 9–40.

Cole, Malcolm S. "Czerny's Illustrated Description of the Rondo or Finale." *The Music Review* 36 (1975): 5–16.

———. "Haydn's Symphonic Rondo Finales: Their Structural and Stylistic Evolution." *Haydn Yearbook XIII 1982*, ed. H. C. Robbins Landon, I. M. Bruce, and David Wyn Jones, 113–42. Cardiff: University College Cardiff Press, 1983.

———. "Sonata-Rondo: The Formulation of a Theoretical Concept in the 18th and 19th Centuries." *The Musical Quarterly* 55 (1969): 180–92.

———. "Rondo." *The New Grove Dictionary of Music and Musicians.* 2nd edition, ed. Stanley Sadie and John Tyrell, 21: 649–56. London: Macmillan, 2001.

———. "Rondos, Proper and Improper." *Music & Letters* 51 (1970): 388–99.

Cone, Edward T. *Musical Form and Musical Performance.* New York: Norton, 1968.

Czerny, Carl. *School of Practical Composition*, trans. John Bishop. 3 vols, ca. 1848. Reprint, New York: Da Capo, 1979.

Dahlhaus, Carl. *Ludwig van Beethoven: Approaches to His Music*, trans. Mary Whittall. Oxford: Clarendon Press, 1991.

———. *Nineteenth-Century Music*, trans. J. Bradford

Robinson. Berkeley: University of California Press, 1989.

Danckwardt, Marianne. *Die langsame Einleitung: ihre Herkunft und ihr Bau bei Haydn und Mozart.* 2 vols. Tutzing: Hans Schneider, 1977.

Darcy, Warren. "Bruckner's Sonata Deformations." In *Bruckner Studies,* ed. Timothy L. Jackson and Paul Hawkshaw, 256–77. Cambridge: Cambridge University Press, 1997.

———. "The Metaphysics of Annihilation: Wagner, Schopenhauer, and the Ending of the Ring." *Music Theory Spectrum,* 16 (1994): 1–40.

———. Review of William E. Caplin, *Classical Form. Music Theory Spectrum* 22 (2000): 122–25.

———. "Rotational Form, Teleological Genesis, and Fantasy-Projection in the Slow Movement of Mahler's Sixth Symphony." *19th-Century Music* 25 (2001): 49–74.

Daverio, John. "From 'Concertante Rondo' to 'Lyric Sonata': A Commentary on Brahms's Reception of Mozart." In *Brahms Studies,* vol. 1, ed. David Brodbeck, 111–36. Lincoln and London: University of Nebraska Press, 1994.

Davis, Shelley. "C. P. E. Bach and the Early History of the Recapitulatory Tutti in North Germany." In *C. P. E. Bach Studies,* ed. Stephen L. Clark, 65–82. Oxford: Clarendon Press, 1988.

———. "H. C. Koch, the Classic Concerto, and the Sonata-Form Retransition." *Journal of Musicology* 2 (1983): 45–61.

Drabkin, William. "Beethoven's Understanding of 'Sonata Form': The Evidence of the Sketchbooks" In *Beethoven's Compositional Process,* ed. William Kinderman, 14–19. Lincoln: University of Nebraska Press, 1991.

Dunsby, Jonathan. "The Formal Repeat." *Journal of the Royal Musical Association* 112/2 (1987): 196–207.

Einstein, Alfred. *Mozart: His Character, His Work.* Oxford: Oxford University Press, 1945.

Eisen, Cliff. "The Classical Period" (subsection of "Concerto"). *The New Grove Dictionary of Music and Musicians.* 2nd ed., ed. Stanley Sadie and John Tyrell, 6: 246–51. London: Macmillan, 2001.

Engel, Hans. *Die Entwicklung des deutschen Klavierkonzerts von Mozart bis Liszt.* Leipzig: Breitkopf & Härtel, 1927.

———. *Das Instrumentalkonzert.* Wiesbaden: Breitkopf & Härtel, 1974.

Everett, Paul. "*Vivaldi: The Four Seasons and Other Concertos, op. 8.* Cambridge: Cambridge University Press, 1996.

Feldman, Martha. "Staging the Virtuoso: Ritornello Procedure in Mozart, from Aria to Concerto." In

Mozart's Piano Concertos: Text, Context, Interpretation, ed. Neal Zaslaw, 149–86. Ann Arbor: University of Michigan Press, 1996.

Fillion, Michelle. "Sonata Exposition Procedures in Haydn's Keyboard Sonatas." In *Haydn Studies. Proceedings of the International Haydn Congress, Washington, D.C., 1975,* ed. Jens Peter Larsen, Howard Serwer, and James Webster, 475–81. New York: Norton, 1981.

Fisher, Stephen C. "Further Thoughts on Haydn's Symphonic Rondo Finales." *Haydn Yearbook XVII [1992],* ed. H. C. Robbins Landon, Otto Biba, I. M. Bruce, and David Wyn Jones, 85–107. Eisenstadt: Joseph Haydn Stiftung, 1992.

———. "Haydn's Overtures and Their Adaptations as Concert Orchestral Works." Ph.D. diss., University of Pennsylvania, 1985.

———. "Sonata Procedures in Haydn's Symphonic Rondo Finales of the 1770s." In *Haydn Studies: Proceedings of the International Haydn Conference Washington, D.C., 1975,* ed. Jens Peter Larsen, Howard Serwer, and James Webster, 481–87. New York and London: Norton, 1981.

Flothuis, Marius. *Mozart's Piano Concertos: A Study.* Amsterdam/Atlanta: Rodopi, 2001.

Forman, Denis. *Mozart's Concerto Form: The First Movements of the Piano Concertos.* London: Rupert Hart-Davis, 1971.

Forster, Robert. *Die Kopfsätze der Klavierkonzerte Mozarts und Beethovens: Gesamtaufbau, Solokadenz und Schlußbildung.* Munich: Fink, 1992.

———. "Zur Funktion von Anfangsritornell und Reprise in den Kopfsätzen einiger Klavierkonzerte Mozarts." *Mozart-Jahrbuch 1986,* 74–89. Kassel: Bärenreiter, 1987.

Gagné, David. "The Compositional Use of Register in Three Piano Sonatas by Mozart." In *Trends in Schenkerian Research,* ed. Allen Cadwallader, 23–39. New York: Schirmer Books, 1990.

Galand, Joel. "Form, Genre, and Style in the Eighteenth-Century Rondo." *Music Theory Spectrum* 17 (1995): 27–52.

———. "The Large-Scale Formal Role of the Solo Entry Theme in the Eighteenth-Century Concerto." *Journal of Music Theory* 44 (2000): 381–450.

———. "Rondo-Form Problems in Eighteenth- and Nineteenth-Century Instrumental Music, with Reference to the Application of Schenker's Form Theory to Historical Context." Ph.D. diss., Yale University, 1990.

Galeazzi, Francesco. *Elementi teorico-pratici di musica.* Vol. 2. Rome: Puccinelli, 1796.

Gossett, Philip. "The Overtures of Rossini." *19th-Century Music* 3 (1979): 3–31.

Gratzer, Wolfgang. "Mozart, oder? Der Unisono-Beginn in Streichquartetten der Wiener Klassik: Fragment zu einer Poetik des musikalischen Anfangs." *Mozart-Jahrbuch 1991*, 641–49. Kassel: Bärenreiter, 1992.

Grave, Margaret G. "First-Movement Form as a Measure of Dittersdorf's Symphonic Development." Ph.D. diss. New York University, 1977.

Grayson, David. *Mozart: Piano Concertos No. 20 in D Minor, K. 466, and No. 21 in C Major, K. 467.* Cambridge: Cambridge University Press, 1999.

Green Douglass M. *Form in Tonal Music: An Introduction to Analysis.* 2nd ed. New York: Holt, Rinehart, and Winston, 1979.

Grey, Thomas S. "Wagner, the Overture, and the Aesthetics of Musical Form." *19th-Century Music* 12 (1988): 3–22.

Haimo, Ethan. "Haydn's Altered Reprise." *Journal of Music Theory* 32 (1988): 335–51.

———. *Haydn's Symphonic Forms: Essays in Compositional Logic.* Oxford: Clarendon Press, 1995.

———. "Remote Keys and Multi-movement Unity: Haydn in the 1790s." *The Musical Quarterly* 74 (1990): 242–68.

Harrison, Daniel. *Harmonic Function in Chromatic Music: A Renewed Dualist Theory and an Account of Its Precedents.* Chicago: University of Chicago Press, 1994.

Hell, Helmut. *Die Neapolitanische Opernsinfonie in der ersten Hälfte des 18. Jahrhunderts.* Tutzing: Schneider, 1971.

Hepokoski, James. "Back and Forth from *Egmont*: Beethoven, Mozart, and the Nonresolving Recapitulation." *19th-Century Music* 25 (2002): 127–53.

———. "Beethoven Reception: The Symphonic Tradition." In *The Cambridge History of Nineteenth-Century Music*, ed. Jim Samson, 424–59. Cambridge: Cambridge University Press, 2002.

———. "Beyond the Sonata Principle." *Journal of the American Musicological Society*, 55 (2002): 91–154.

———. "The Essence of Sibelius: Creation Myths and Rotational Cycles in *Luonnotar*." In *The Sibelius Companion*, ed. Glenda Dawn Goss, 121–46. Westport, Conn.: Greenwood, 1996.

———. "Framing Till Eulenspiegel." *19th-Century Music* 30 (2006): forthcoming.

———. "Masculine/Feminine." *The Musical Times* 135 (August 1994): 494–99.

———. "*Ottocento* Opera as Cultural Drama: Generic Mixtures in *Il trovatore*." In *Verdi's Middle Period 1849–1859: Source Studies, Analysis, and Performance Practice*, ed. Martin Chusid, 147–96. Chicago: University of Chicago Press, 1997.

———. "Rotations, Sketches, and [Sibelius's] Sixth Symphony." In *Sibelius Studies*, ed. Timothy L. Jackson and Veijo Murtomäki, 322–51. Cambridge: Cambridge University Press, 2001.

———. *Sibelius: Symphony No. 5.* Cambridge: Cambridge University Press, 1993.

———. "Structure, Implication, and the End of Suor Angelica." *Studi pucciniani* 3 (2004): 241–64.

Hepokoski, James, and Warren Darcy. "The Medial Caesura and its Role in the Eighteenth-Century Sonata Exposition." *Music Theory Spectrum* 19 (1997): 115–54.

Hill, George R. "The Concert Symphonies of Florian Leopold Gassmann." Ph.D. diss., New York University, 1975.

———. "Introduction" to *Florian Leopold Gassmann, 1729–1774: Seven Symphonies*, in *The Symphony 1720–1840*, ed. Barry S. Brook, Series B, 10:xiii–xxiii. New York: Garland, 1981.

Hinrichsen, Hans-Joachim. "Sonatenform, Sonatenhauptsatzform," In *Handwörterbuch der musikalischen Terminologie*, ed. Hans Heinrich Eggebrecht, 1–20. Stuttgart: Steiner, c. 1972ff.

Hoyt, Peter A. "The Concept of *développement* in the Early Nineteenth Century." In *Music Theory in the Age of Romanticism*, ed. Ian Bent, 141–62. Cambridge: Cambridge University Press, 1996.

———. "Haydn's 'False Recapitulations,' Late Eighteenth-Century Theory, and Modern Paradigms of Sonata Form." Unpublished paper.

———. Review of Bonds, *Wordless Rhetoric: Musical Form and the Metaphor of the Oration. Journal of Music Theory* 38 (1994): 123–43.

Hyer, Brian. "Reimag(in)ing Riemann. *Journal of Music Theory* 39 (1995): 101–38.

———. "Tonal Intuitions in *Tristan und Isolde*." Ph.D. diss., Yale University, 1989.

Irving, John. *Mozart's Piano Concertos.* Aldershot: Ashgate, 2003.

———. *Mozart's Piano Sonatas: Contexts, Sources, Style.* Cambridge: Cambridge University Press, 1997.

———. *Mozart: The "Haydn" Quartets.* Cambridge: Cambridge University Press, 1998.

Ivanovitch, Roman. "The Process of Variation in the Music of Mozart." Ph.D. diss. Yale University, 2003.

Jackson, Timothy L. "The Finale of Bruckner's Seventh Symphony and the Tragic Reversed Sonata Form." In *Bruckner Studies*, ed. Timothy L. Jackson and Paul Hawkshaw, 140–208. Cambridge: Cambridge University Press, 1997.

Kamien, Roger. "The Opening Sonata-Allegro Movements in a Randomly Selected Sample of Solo Keyboard Sonatas Published in the Years

1742–1774 (Inclusive)." Ph.D. diss., Princeton University, 1964.

Keefe, Simon P. *Mozart's Piano Concertos: Dramatic Dialogue in the Age of Enlightenment.* Woodbridge, U.K.: Boydell Press, 2001.

Keller, Hans. "The Chamber Music." In *The Mozart Companion*, ed. H. C. Robbins Landon and Donald Mitchell, 90–137. New York: Norton, 1956.

———. *The Great Haydn Quartets: Their Interpretation.* London: Dent, 1986.

Kerman, Joseph. *The Beethoven Quartets.* New York: Norton, 1966.

———. "Beethoven's Minority." In Kerman, *Write All These Down: Essays on Music*, 217–37. Berkeley: University of California Press, 1994.

———. "Notes on Beethoven's Codas." In *Beethoven Studies 3*, ed. Alan Tyson, 141–59. Cambridge: Cambridge University Press, 1982.

———. "Tovey's Beethoven." In Kerman, *Write All These Down: Essays on Music*, 155–72. Berkeley and Los Angeles: University of California Press, 1994.

Kinderman, William. *Artaria 195: Beethoven's Sketchbook for the Missa solemnis and the Piano Sonata in E Major, Opus 109.* Urbana: University of Illinois Press, 2003.

———. *Beethoven.* Berkeley: University of California Press, 1995.

Kirkpatrick, Ralph. *Domenico Scarlatti.* Princeton, N.J.: Princeton University Press, 1953.

Kollmann, Augustus Frederic Christopher. *An Essay on Practical Musical Composition, according to the Nature of That Science and the Principles of the Greatest Musical Authors.* London: Kollmann, 1799. Reprint, New York: Da Capo Press, 1973.

Koch, Heinrich Christoph. *Introductory Essay on Composition: The Mechanical Rules of Melody, Sections 3 and 4*, trans. Nancy Kovaleff Baker. New Haven, Conn.: Yale University Press, 1983.

———. *Versuch einer Anleitung zur Composition* [Leipzig: Adam Friedrich Böhme, 1793]. Reprint, Hildesheim: Georg Olms, 1969.

Kramer, Lawrence. "The Strange Case of Beethoven's *Coriolan*: Romantic Aesthetics, Modern Subjectivity, and the Cult of Shakespeare." *The Musical Quarterly* 79 (1995): 265–80.

Kucaba, John. "The Symphonies of Georg Christoph Wagenseil." Ph.D diss., Boston University, 1967.

Küster, Konrad. *Formale Aspekte des ersten Allegros in Mozarts Konzerten.* Kassel: Bärenreiter, 1991.

Landon, H. C. Robbins, and David Wyn Jones. *Haydn: His Life and Music.* Bloomington: University of Indiana Press, 1988.

Larsen, Jens Peter. "Sonata Form Problems." In Larsen, *Handel, Haydn, and the Viennese Classical*

Style, trans. Ulrich Krämer, 269–79. Ann Arbor: UMI Research Press, 1988. First published as "Sonatenform-Probleme," in *Festschrift Friedrich Blume zum 70 Geburtstag*, ed. Anna Amalie Abert and Wilhelm Pfannkuch, 221–30. Kassel: Barenreiter, 1963.

———. "The Symphonies." In *The Mozart Companion*, ed. H. C. Robbins Landon and Donald Mitchell [1956], 156–99. Reprint, New York: Norton, 1969.

LaRue, Jan. *Guidelines for Style Analysis.* 2nd ed. Warren, Mich.: Harmonie Park, 1992.

———. Review of Charles Rosen, *Sonata Forms* (1st ed., 1980). *Journal of the American Musicological Society* 34 (1981): 557–66.

LaRue, Jan and Eugene K. Wolf. "Symphony. I. 18th Century." *The New Grove Dictionary of Music and Musicians.* 2nd ed., ed. Stanley Sadie and John Tyrell, 24:812–33. London: Macmillan, 2001.

Leeson, Daniel N., and Robert D. Levin, "On the Authenticity of K.Anh C.14.01 (279b), a Symphonia Concertante for Four Winds and Orchestra." *Mozart-Jahrbuch 1976/77*, 70–96. Kassel: Bärenreiter, 1978.

Leichtentritt, Hugo. *Musical Form.* Cambridge, Mass.: Harvard University Press, 1951.

Leister, Reiner. *Das Finale in der Sinfonik Joseph Haydns.* Stuttgart: *ibidem*-Verlag, 1999.

Levin, Robert D. "Das Konzert für Klavier und Violine D-Dur KV Anh. 56/315f und das Klarinettenquintett B-Dur, KV Anh. 91/516c: Ein Ergänzungsversuch." *Mozart-Jahrbuch 1968/70*, 304–26. Salzburg: Internationale Stiftung Mozarteum. 1970.

Levy, Janet M. "Gesture, Form, and Syntax in Haydn's Music." In *Haydn Studies: Proceedings of the International Haydn Conference, Washington, D.C., 1975*, ed. Jens Peter Larsen, Howard Serwer, and James Webster, 355–62. New York: Norton, 1981.

———. "Texture as a Sign in Classic and Early Romantic Music." *Journal of the American Musicological Society* 35 (1982): 482–531.

Lockwood, Lewis. "*Eroica* Perspectives: Strategy and Design in the First Movement." In Lockwood, *Beethoven: Studies in the Creative Process*, 118–33. Cambridge, Mass.: Harvard University Press, 1992.

Longyear, Rey M. "Binary Variants of Early Classic Sonata Form." *Journal of Music Theory* 13 (1969): 162–83.

———. "Parallel Universes: Mozart's Minor-Mode Reprises." *Mozart-Jahrbuch 1991*, 810–15. Kassel: Bärenreiter, 1992.

Longyear, Rey M., and Kate R. Covington. "Sources

of the Three-Key Exposition." *Journal of Musicology* 6 (1988): 448–70.

McLamore, Laura Alyson. "Symphonic Conventions in London's Concert Rooms, circa 1755–1790." Ph.D. diss., University of California, Los Angeles, 1991.

Mahling, Christoph-Hellmut. "Zur Frage der 'Einheit' der Symphonie." In *Über Sinfonien: Beiträge zu einer musikalischen Gattung: Festschrift Walter Wiora zum 70. Geburtstag*, ed. Christoph-Hellmut Mahling, 1–40. Tutzing: Schneider, 1979.

Malloch, William. "The Minuets of Haydn and Mozart: Goblins or Elephants?" *Early Music* 21 (1993): 437–45.

———. "Toward a 'New' (Old) Minuet." *Opus* 1/5 (1985): 14–21, 52.

Marston, Nicholas. "The Recapitulation Transition in Mozart's Music," *Mozart-Jahrbuch 1991*, 793–809. Kassel: Bärenreiter, 1992.

Marx, Adolph Bernhard. *Die Lehre von der musikalischen Komposition, praktisch-theoretisch*. Vols. 2 and 3, 1st eds. Leipzig, 1838 and 1845.

———. *Die Lehre von der musikalischen Komposition, praktisch theoretisch*. 4th ed. Leipzig: Breitkopf und Härtel, 1868

———. *Ludwig van Beethoven: Leben und Schaffen*. Berlin: Janke, 1859.

———. *Musical Form in the Age of Beethoven: Selected Writings on Theory and Method*, ed. and trans. Scott Burnham. Cambridge: Cambridge University Press, 1997.

Mellers, Wilfrid. *The Sonata Principle (from c. 1750)*. Fair Lawn, N.J.: Essential Books, 1957.

Momigny, Jérôme-Joseph de. *Cours complet d'harmonie et de composition*. 3 vols. Paris: Momigny, 1803–6).

Moosbauer, Bernhard. *Tonart und Form in den Finali der Sinfonien von Joseph Haydn zwischen 1766 und 1774*. Tutzing: Hans Schneider, 1998.

Morgan, Robert P. "Coda as Culmination: The First Movement of the 'Eroica' Symphony." In *Music Theory and the Exploration of the Past*, ed. Christopher Hatch and David W. Bernstein, 357–76. Chicago: University of Chicago Press, 1993.

Moyer, Birgitte. "Concepts of Musical Form in the Nineteenth Century with Special Reference to A.B. Marx and Sonata Form." Ph.D. diss., Stanford University, 1969.

Newman, William S. *The Sonata in the Classic Era*. Revised ed. New York: Norton, 1972.

Notley, Margaret. "Late Nineteenth-Century Chamber Music and the Cult of the Classical Adagio." *19th-Century Music* 23 (1999): 33–61.

Palm, Albert. "Mozarts Streichquartett D-moll, KV 421, in der Interpretation Momignys." *Mozart-Jahrbuch 1962/63*, 256–79. Salzburg: Zentralinstitut für Mozartforschung der Internationalen Stiftung Mozarteum, 1964.

Pascall, Robert. "Some Special Uses of Sonata Form by Brahms." In *Soundings*, ed. Arnold Whittall, No. 4 (1974): 58–63.

Plantinga, Leon. *Beethoven's Concertos: History, Style, Performance*. New York: Norton, 1999.

———. *Clementi: His Life and Music*. London: Oxford University Press, 1977.

Plath, Wolfgang. "Beiträge zur Mozart-Autographie II: Schriftchronologie, 1770–1780," *Mozart-Jahrbuch 1976/77*, 131–73. Kassel: Bärenreiter, 1978.

Powers, Harold. "Reading Mozart's Music: Text and Topic, Syntax and Sense." *Current Musicology* 57 (1995): 5–44.

Ratner, Leonard G. *Classic Music: Expression, Form, and Style*. New York: Schirmer, 1980.

———. "Harmonic Aspects of Classic Form." *Journal of the American Musicological Society* 11 (1949): 159–68.

Ratz, Erwin. *Einführung in die musikalische Formenlehre: Über Formprinzipien in den Inventionen und Fugen J. S. Bachs und ihre Bedeutung für die Kompositionstechnik Beethovens*. 3rd ed., enl. Vienna: Universal, 1973.

Reicha, Anton. *Traité de haute composition musicale*. Vol. 2. Paris, 1826.

Réti, Rudolph. *The Thematic Process in Music*. New York: Macmillan, 1951.

Ritzel, Fred. *Die Entwicklung der 'Sonatenform' im musiktheoretischen Schrifttum des 18. and 19. Jahrhunderts*. Wiesbaden: Breitkopf & Härtel, 1968.

Rosen, Charles. *The Classical Style: Haydn, Mozart, Beethoven*. Revised ed. New York: Norton, 1997.

———. *The Romantic Generation*. Cambridge, Mass.: Harvard University Press, 1995.

———. "Schubert's Inflections of Classical Form." In *The Cambridge Companion to Schubert*, ed. Christopher H. Gibbs, 72–98. Cambridge: Cambridge University Press, 1997.

———. *Sonata Forms*. Rev. ed. New York: Norton, 1988.

Rosen, David. "The Composer's 'Standard Operating Procedure' as Evidence of Intention: The Case of a Formal Quirk in Mozart's K. 595." *Journal of Musicology* 5 (1987): 79–90.

———. "'Unexpectedness' and 'Inevitability' in Mozart's Piano Concertos." In *Mozart's Piano Concertos: Text, Context, Interpretation*, ed. Neal Zaslaw, 261–84. Ann Arbor: University of Michigan Press, 1996.

Rothstein, William. *Phrase Rhythm in Tonal Music*. New York: Schirmer, 1989.

Schenker, Heinrich. *Free Composition*, ed. and trans. Ernst Oster. New York: Longman, 1979. First published as *Der Freie Satz* (Vienna, 1935).

———. *Harmony*, ed. and annotated by Oswald Jonas; trans. Elisabeth Mann Borgese. Chicago: University of Chicago, 1954, rpt. 1980.

Schoenberg, Arnold. *Fundamentals of Musical Composition*, ed. Gerald Strang and Leonard Stein. London: Faber & Faber, 1967.

Schmalfeldt, Janet. "Cadential Processes: The Evaded Cadence and the 'One More Time' Technique." *Journal of Musicological Research* 12 (1992): 1–51.

———. "Towards a Reconciliation of Schenkerian Concepts with Traditional and Recent Theories of Form." *Music Analysis* 10 (1991): 233–87.

Schmalzriedt, Siegfried. "Durchführen, Durchführung" [1979]. In *Handwörterbuch der musikalischen Terminologie*, ed. Hans Heinrich Eggebrecht, 1–16. Stuttgart: Steiner, c. 1972ff.

———. "Reprise/ripresa (nach 1600) [1981]" In *Handwörterbuch der musikalischen Terminologie*, ed. Hans Heinrich Eggebrecht, 1–16. Stuttgart: Steiner, c. 1972ff.

Schmitz, Arnold. *Beethoven's 'Zwei Prinzipe.'* Berlin and Bonn, 1927.

Schoenberg, Arnold. *Fundamentals of Musical Composition*, ed. Gerald Strang and Leonard Stein. London: Faber & Faber, 1967.

Schulenberg, David. *The Instrumental Music of Carl Philipp Emanuel Bach*. Ann Arbor: UMI Research Press, 1984.

Seidel, Wilhelm. "Die ältere Zyklustheorie, überdacht im Blick auf Beethovens Werk. " In *Beiträge zu Beethovens Kammermusik: Symposion Bonn 1984*, ed. Sieghard Brandenburg and Helmut Loos. Veröffentlichungen des Beethovenhauses in Bonn, Neue Folge, 4, Reihe: Schriften zur Beethovenforschung, 4, 273–82. Munich: Henle, 1987.

———. "Schnell—Langsam—Schnell: Zur 'klassischen' Theorie des instrumentalen Zyklus." *Musiktheorie* 1 (1986): 205–16.

Seiffert, Wolf-Dieter. *Mozarts frühe Streichquartette*. Munich: Fink, 1992.

Simon, Edwin J. "Sonata into Concerto: A Study of Mozart's First Seven Concertos." *Acta musicologica* 31 (1959): 170–85.

Sisman, Elaine R. "Brahms's Slow Movements: Reinventing the 'Closed' Forms." In *Brahms Studies: Analytical and Historical Perspectives*, ed. George L. Bozarth, 79–103. Oxford: Clarendon Press, 1990.

———. "C. P. E. Bach, Beethoven, and the Labyrinth of Melancholy." Unpublished paper delivered at the American Musicological Society, Toronto, November 2, 2000.

———. "Genre, Gesture, and Meaning in Mozart's 'Prague' Symphony." In *Mozart Studies 2*, ed. Cliff Eisen, 27–84. Oxford: Clarendon Press, 1997.

———. *Haydn and the Classical Variation*. Cambridge, Mass.: Harvard University Press, 1993.

———. *Mozart: The "Jupiter" Symphony*. Cambridge: Cambridge University Press, 1993.

Snyder, John L. "Schenker and the First Movement of Mozart's Sonata, K. 545: An Uninterrupted Sonata-Form Movement?" *Theory and Practice* 16 (1991): 51–78.

Somfai, László. "The London Revision of Haydn's Instrumental Style." *Proceedings of the Royal Musical Association* 100 (1973–74): 159–74.

———. *The Keyboard Sonatas of Joseph Haydn: Instruments and Performance Practice, Genres and Styles*, trans. Somfai and Charlotte Greenspan. Chicago: University of Chicago Press, 1995.

Spies, Claudio. "'Form' and the *Tragic Overture*: An Adjuration." In *Brahms Studies: Analytical and Historical Perspectives*, ed. George S. Bozarth, 391–98. Oxford: Clarendon, 1990.

Stevens, Jane R. "An 18th-Century Description of Concerto First-Movement Form." *Journal of the American Musicological Society* 24 (1971): 85–95.

———. "Formal Design in C. P. E. Bach's Harpsichord Concertos." *Studi musicali*, 15 (1986): 257–97.

———. "The Importance of C. P. E. Bach for Mozart's Piano Concertos." In *Mozart's Piano Concertos: Text, Context, Interpretation*, ed. Neal Zaslaw, 211–36. Ann Arbor: University of Michigan Press, 1996.

———. "Patterns of Recapitulation in the First Movements of Mozart's Piano Concertos." In *Musical Humanism and Its Legacy: Essays in Honor of Claude V. Palisca*, ed. Nancy Kovaleff Baker and Barbara Russano Hanning, 397–418. Stuyvesant, N.Y.: Pendragon, 1992.

———. "Theme, Harmony, and Texture in Classic-Romantic Descriptions of Concerto First-Movement Form." *Journal of the American Musicological Society* 27 (1974): 25–60.

Steinberg, Michael. "The Late Quartets." In *The Beethoven Quartet Companion*, ed. Robert Winter and Robert Martin, 215–82. Berkeley: University of California Press, 1994.

Straus, Joseph N. "Normalizing the Abnormal: Disability in Music and Music Theory." *Journal of the American Musicological Society* 59 (2006): forthcoming.

Strunk, Oliver. "Haydn's Divertimenti for Baryton, Viola, and Bass." *The Musical Quarterly* 18 (1932): 216–51. Reprint, Strunk, *Essays on Music in the Western World*, 126–70. New York: Norton, 1974.

Sutcliffe, W. Dean. *The Keyboard Sonatas of Domenico Scarlatti and Eighteenth-Century Musical Style.* Cambridge: Cambridge University Press, 2003.

———. *Haydn: String Quartets, op. 50.* Cambridge: Cambridge University Press, 1992.

———. Review of Charles Rosen, *The Classical Style* (rev. ed.). *Music & Letters* 79 (1998): 601–4.

Talbot, Michael. *The Finale in Western Instrumental Music.* New York: Oxford University Press, 2001.

———. "The Instrumental Concerto: Origins to 1750" (subsection of "Concerto"). *The New Grove Dictionary of Music and Musicians.* 2nd ed., ed. Stanley Sadie and John Tyrell, 6:242–46. London: Macmillan, 2001.

Tobel, Rudolf von. *Die Formenwelt der klassischen Instrumentalmusik.* Bern and Leipzig: Paul Haupt, 1935.

Tovey, Donald Francis. "Brahms's Chamber Music. *The Main Stream of Music and Other Essays,* 220–70. Oxford: Oxford University Press, 1949.

———. *A Companion to Beethoven's Pianoforte Sonatas.* London: Royal Schools of Music, 1931.

———. *Essays in Musical Analysis.* 7 vols. London: Oxford University Press, 1935–39. Partially reprinted in *Symphonies and Other Orchestral Works.* Oxford: Oxford University Press, 1989.

———. "Haydn's Chamber Music." *The Main Stream of Music and Other Essays,* 1–64.

———. "Musical Form and Matter." *The Main Stream of Music and Other Essays,* 160–82. Oxford: Oxford University Press, 1949.

———. "Some Aspects of Beethoven's Art Forms." *The Main Stream of Music and Other Essays,* 271–97. Oxford: Oxford University Press, 1949.

———. "Sonata Forms." *Musical Articles from the Encyclopaedia Britannica,* 208–32. London: Oxford University Press, 1944. Reissued (1956) under the title *The Forms of Music.*

Tyson, Alan. "The Mozart Fragments in the Mozarteum, Salzburg: A Preliminary Study of Their Chronology and Their Significance." In Tyson. *Mozart: Studies of the Autograph Scores,* 125–61. Cambridge, Mass.: Harvard University Press, 1987.

Wallace, Robin. "Background and Expression in the First Movement of Beethoven's op. 132." *The Journal of Musicology,* 7 (1989): 3–20.

Webster, James. "The Analysis of Mozart's Arias." In *Mozart Studies,* ed. Cliff Eisen, 101–99. New York: Oxford University Press, 1991.

———. "Are Mozart's Concertos 'Dramatic'? Concerto Ritornellos versus Aria Introductions in the 1780s." In *Mozart's Piano Concertos: Text, Context,*

Interpretation, ed. Neal Zaslaw, 107–37. Ann Arbor: University of Michigan Press, 1996.

———. "Binary Variants of Sonata Form in Early Haydn Instrumental Music." In *Joseph Haydn: Bericht über den Internationalen Joseph Haydn Kongress, Wien, Hofburg 5–12 September 1982,* ed. Eva Barura-Skoda, 127–35. Munich: G. Henle, 1986.

———. "The General and the Particular in Brahms's Later Sonata Forms." In *Brahms Studies: Analytical and Historical Perspectives,* ed. George S. Bozarth, 49–78. Oxford: Clarendon, 1990.

———. *Haydn's "Farewell" Symphony and the Idea of Classical Style: Through-Composition and Cyclic Integration in His Instrumental Music.* Cambridge: Cambridge University Press, 1991.

———. "Schubert's Sonata Form and Brahms' First Maturity." *19th-Century Music* 2 (1978): 18–35 and 3 (1979), 52–71.

———. "Sonata Form." *The New Grove Dictionary of Music and Musicians.* 2nd ed., ed. Stanley Sadie and John Tyrell, 23:687–701. London: Macmillan, 2001.

Wheelock, Gretchen A. *Haydn's Ingenious Jesting with Art: Contexts of Musical Wit and Humor.* New York: Schirmer, 1992.

———. "*Schwarze Gredel* and the Engendered Minor Mode in Mozart's Operas." In *Musicology and Difference: Gender and Sexuality in Music Scholarship,* ed. Ruth A. Solie, 201–21. Berkeley: University of California Press, 1992.

Whitmore, Philip. *Unpremeditated Art: The Cadenza in the Classical Keyboard Concerto.* Oxford: Clarendon Press, 1991.

Will, Richard. *The Characteristic Symphony in the Age of Haydn and Beethoven.* Cambridge: Cambridge University Press, 2002.

Winter, Robert S. "The Bifocal Close and the Evolution of the Viennese Classical Style." *Journal of the American Musicological Society* 42 (1989): 275–337.

Wolf, Eugene K. "The Recapitulations in Haydn's London Symphonies." *The Musical Quarterly* 52 (1966): 71–89.

———. "Sonata Form." In *The New Harvard Dictionary of Music,* ed. Don Michael Randel, 764–67. Cambridge, Mass.: Harvard University Press, 1986.

———. "Symphony," *The New Harvard Dictionary of Music,* ed. Don Michael Randel, 822–27. Cambridge, Mass.: Harvard University Press, 1986.

———. *The Symphonies of Johann Stamitz: A Study in the Formation of the Classic Style.* Utrecht: Bohn, Scheltema & Holkema, 1981.

Wolff, Christoph. "Cadenzas and Styles of Improvisation in Mozart's Piano Concertos." In *Perspectives on Mozart Performance*, ed. R. Larry Todd and Peter Williams, 228–38. Cambridge: Cambridge University Press, 1991.

———. "Zur Chronologie der Klavierkonzert-Kadenzen Mozarts." *Mozart-Jahrbuch 1978–79*, 235–46. Kassel: Bärenreiter, 1979.

Wyzewa, Théodore de, and Georges de Saint Foix. *W.-A Mozart: Sa vie musicale et son œuvre*. 5 vols. Paris: Desclée, de Brouwer et Cie., 1912–46.

Zaslaw, Neal, ed. *Mozart's Piano Concertos: Text, Context, Interpretation*. Ann Arbor: University of Michigan Press, 1996.

———. *Mozart's Symphonies: Context, Performance Practice, Reception*. Oxford: Oxford University Press, 1989.

Index of Names

These references identify appearances of names within the text as well as expanded discussions of those persons in footnotes. Brief footnote-citation appearances are not listed. For individual composers listed here, see also the Index of Works: this index of names cites only references that are not linked in the text to specific compositions. For individual issues and subsections of sonata form listed below, see also the Index of Concepts.

Index of Works

Index of Concepts

This index does not locate every occurrence of the entries listed below. (Several of the terms recur regularly throughout the book.) Instead, it is a guide to their initial or central discussions, along with selected other appearances. Definitional and other key passages are indicated in italics.

8–♭7̂–^6–♮7̂–8̂ pattern. *See under* closing zone (C); primary-theme zone (P); transition (TR)

action-space (action-zone), *9*, 16, 18, 19, *23–24*, 180, 250, 616–18
aesthetic presence, 607–08
Anlage. See exposition, *Anlage* (referential layout, model rotation), role as; Type 5 sonata, Ritornello 1 (R1), *Anlage* (referential layout), role as
anti-recapitulation. *See under* recapitulation
aria formats, 343, 348
da capo, 198, 203, *348 n. 17*
Mozart, 249 n. 26
Type 5 sonata, similarity to, 430

bait-and-switch tactic (in continuous expositions), *54–60*
binary form. *See also* Type 2 sonata ("binary")
balanced, 355, 358
lyric, 111

parallel, 355 (including n. 4), 359
rounded, 108–11, 330, 397–99
sonata form, "binary" aspect of, 16, 19, *147–49*, 366 n. 24

cadence
attenuated. *See under* cadence, perfect authentic
deceptive (DC), *xxv*
definitions, controversies over, 24 n. 1–2, 28 n. 6, *66–67 n. 5*, 106
evaded. *See under* cadence, perfect authentic
expanded cadential progression (ECP), 63, *121 n. 7, 131*
half (HC), *xxv*, 19, *24 (including n. 2)*
dominant-arrival effect (MC), 24
energetic prolongation via dominant-lock (MC), 24, *31 (including n. 11)*
half-cadence effect, 24, 25
medial caesura ("built around" an HC), *24–27, 31*
"tonicized," 30–31 n. 9
imperfect authentic (IAC), *xxv*
opening gesture of P, 66–68

perfect authentic (PAC), *xxv*, 17 (fig. 2.1), 18, *66–67 n. 5*
attenuated, *170*, 215 n. 20
evaded, *169–70*, 215 n. 20
medial caesura, serving as, 27–29
reopening (undoing closure-effect), 60, 123–24, *151–63*
refrain (method of EEC deferral), *158–59*, 492
trill, 176 n. 6, 470, 534, *546–48*, 596, 602
cadential span. *See under* phrase
cadenza. *See under* Type 5 sonata, Ritornello 4 (R4)
caesura, 12, 34
development, end of, *197–98*, 217
fill. *See* caesura-fill (CF)
final, 12
medial (MC), *xxv*, 12, 17 (fig. 2.1), 18, *23–50* (fig. 3.1), 117
blocked, 44, *47–48*, 49, 116, 132 n. 18
compensatory, 58
declined, 27, *45–47*, 48, 53, 175, 176
defaults, harmonic, in major, *25–29*

649

CPSIA information can be obtained
at www.ICGtesting.com
Printed in the USA
BVHW061946060122
624975BV00002B/3